D0144940

Paul Lauter
Trinity College
General Editor

Richard Yarborough
University of California at Los Angeles
Associate General Editor

Juan Bruce-Novoa
University of California at Irvine

Jackson Bryer
University of Maryland

Elaine Hedges
Towson State University

Anne Goodwyn Jones
University of Florida

Amy Ling
University of Wisconsin—Madison

Daniel F. Littlefield, Jr.
University of Arkansas at Little Rock

Wendy Martin
The Claremont Graduate School

Charles Molesworth
Queens College, City University of New York

Carla Mulford
Pennsylvania State University

Raymund Paredes
University of California at Los Angeles

Linda Wagner-Martin
University of North Carolina, Chapel Hill

Andrew O. Wiget
New Mexico State University

Instructor's Guide
for
The Heath Anthology of American Literature
Second Edition

Paul Lauter
General Editor

Edited by
John Alberti
Northern Kentucky University

D. C. Heath and Company
Lexington, Massachusetts   Toronto

Address editorial correspondence to:
D. C. Heath and Company
125 Spring Street
Lexington, MA 02173

Published simultaneously in Canada.

Printed in the United States of America.

International Standard Book Number: 0-669-32974-6

10 9 8 7 6 5 4 3 2 1

Contents

75 Tales of Incorporation, Resistance, and Reconquest in New Spain

Eighteenth Century 79

83 Tradition and Change in Anglo-America

98 Enlightenment Voices, Revolutionary Visions

116 Contested Boundaries, National Visions: Writings on "Race," Identity, and "Nation"

160 Missionary Voices of the Southwest

Early Nineteenth Century: 1800–1865   167

173 Myths, Tales, and Legends

189 Humor of the Old Southwest

191 Explorations of an "American" Self

413 Issues and Visions in Post–Civil War America

435 New Explorations of an "American" Self

Modern Period: 1910–1945   449

455 Toward the Modern Age

496 Alienation and Literary Experimentation

558 The New Negro Renaissance

597 Issues and Visions in Modern America

Contemporary Period: 1945 to the Present   653

Teaching the American Literatures: An Electronic Conference

Randy Bass, Georgetown University
Moderator and List Manager

Teaching the American Literatures (T-AMLIT) is a moderated, electronic conference and discussion list devoted to critical and pedagogical issues related to teaching the new and expanded American literatures. **T-AMLIT** promotes dialogue on all aspects of teaching and studying the literatures of the United States. Structured as an electronic conference, **T-AMLIT** features special topics and sessions on specific problems and literary traditions, and serves as an information clearinghouse for both print and electronic resources related to the American literatures.

Subscription Information

To subscribe to **T-AMLIT**

1. send mail to either of the following addresses:

    LISTSERV@BITNIC.BITNET (Bitnet Address)
    or
    LISTSERV@BITNIC.EDUCOM.EDU (Internet Address)

2. leave the "Subject" line blank
3. type the message

    subscribe T-AMLIT [your name]

T-AMLIT is sponsored by **D. C. Heath**; host computer space and technical support are kindly provided by **EDUCOM**.

To the Instructor

To those of you familiar with the first edition of *The Heath Anthology of American Literature*, you will find the basic format of this instructor's guide to be the same: the contributing editors have written teaching suggestions to accompany the texts in *The Heath Anthology*. As with the first edition, the entries in the instructor's guide are organized into the following categories:

Classroom Issues and Strategies

Major Themes, Historical Perspectives, and Personal Issues

Significant Form, Style, or Artistic Conventions

Original Audience

Comparisons, Contrasts, Connections

Questions for Reading and Discussion/Approaches to Writing

Bibliography

New entries appear for the material added to the second edition, and many contributors from the first edition have used feedback from instructors to revise their entries for the second edition. In particular, the section "Comparison, Contrasts, Connections" has been revised to include discussion of other entries in the anthology.

The most significant additions to this edition of the instructor's guide are the discussions of pedagogical theory found in the various pedagogical introductions as well as in the afterword, "Classroom Issues in Teaching a New Canon," by general editor Paul Lauter. This new material recognizes that revising the canon of American literature and developing multicultural curricula, of which *The Heath Anthology* is a part, represent not just a rethinking of what texts to include on a syllabus, or the simple replacement of one group of privileged texts with another, but a fundamental re-examination of the purposes and practices of literary study as a whole and of American literature in particular. While we wish to preserve the diversity of pedagogical approaches found in the various contributors' entries in the first edition of the instructor's guide, we feel it is useful and necessary to include material that provides a theoretical context for these approaches, material that addresses general strategies for class planning and the teaching of texts that cover a wide range of cultural perspectives, artistic forms, and rhetorical situations.

Overall, the pedagogical introductions are based on three main pedagogical assumptions: 1) the reading experience of students should be the focus of class discussion and analysis; 2) classification systems—whether formations of historical periods, cultural movements, or canons of literary value—influence and shape those reading experiences in crucial ways; and 3) the production, reception, and interpretation of texts is an active process of cultural negotiation, opposition, assimilation, and transformation, a process that is centered on the reading experiences of the students.

This process-oriented approach, stressing the importance of social context in understanding the form and structure of particular acts of writing and reading, should sound familiar to composition teachers and theorists who remind students that in order to figure out what and how to write, a writer needs to ask why and to whom she is writing. Borrowing a term from composition studies, then, we might describe the pedagogical focus of this guide as the study of cultural rhetoric: the analysis of literary texts as complex and purposeful transactions between speaking/writing/reading subjects and the culture that both constitutes those subjects and acts as medium and object of that transaction.[1] In Jane Tompkins' words,

> instead of seeing . . . novels as mere entertainment, or as works of art interpretable apart from their context . . . I see them as doing a certain kind of cultural work within a specific historical situation. . . . I see their plots and characters as providing society with a means of thinking about itself, defining certain aspects of a social reality which the authors and their readers shared, dramatizing its conflicts, and recommending solutions. (200)

The central pedagogical aim of this approach is to encourage students to consider themselves as just such speaking/writing/reading subjects and to see themselves as active participants in the process of cultural definition and transformation through their interpretation of and response to the texts in this anthology as well as through their participation in the institutionalized study of culture—in other words, to see the literature class itself as a kind of cultural work.

In operation, the cultural rhetoric approach is more inductive than deductive, more centrifugal than centripetal. It takes as its pedagogical starting point the variety of American cultural expression and readers' equally varied responses to those expressions, rather than beginning with predetermined criteria about what "American Literature" is and seeing how well particular texts do or don't fit these criteria. Providing a definition of "The American Renaissance" or "Transcendentalism"

---

[1]The term "transaction" is borrowed from Louise Rosenblatt's reader-response model of literature pedagogy.

before approaching the literature of the 1840s and 1850s does give students a means of organizing and understanding that literature, but it also limits both the meaning and scope of the works being considered by moving the focus of the class from the creative activity of reading to the acquisition and preservation of those definitions.

By warning against relying too heavily on reductive historical formulas, however, I am not endorsing a Romantic—or New Critical—belief that we can abandon all such preconceptions and classification systems in order to embrace "the text itself " in some kind of ahistorical purity. Indeed, generalization and classification are central to the learning process, as new information can only be assimilated in terms of preexisting ways of knowing and thinking. In any case, even if instructors somehow could prevent "contaminating" the students' first experience of a text by avoiding generalizations about historical periods or intellectual trends, students will always bring with them just such large scale conceptions, generalizations, myths, and beliefs about American cultural history. While "American Renaissance" may only resonate with a small group of students, terms like "slavery," "abolition," "the Civil War," "Manifest Destiny," and "the North and the South" will call forth a wide range of associations, assumptions, and generalizations. These assumptions do not merely influence the reading experience; they are intrinsic to it, and the rhetorical approach to literary study recognizes that it is just as important for students to think about why and how they came to hold these assumptions as it is to question the historical validity of these assumptions.

In other words, the cultural rhetoric approach in particular and multicultural pedagogy in general, is not about replacing "false consciousness" with "true consciousness," or an old-fashioned and rigid classification system with an updated but equally rigid classification system. Instead, the focus on literature as an active strategic cultural process recognizes the pedagogical importance of what Paul Lauter refers to in his afterword as "starting points"—the basic frameworks and assumptions readers bring to texts and instructors bring to the class in the form of syllabus design and teaching practices. As a result, many of the pedagogical introductions suggest that study of the texts in this anthology should begin by exploring the assumptions, biases, and historical consciousnesses that students—and instructors—bring to a class. The point of these exercises is not to undertake the impossible task of freeing students from the influence of classification systems (particularly theories of interpretation or versions of cultural development) but to study how different assumptions, mind-sets, and beliefs affect the reading experience, where these assumptions come from, and, perhaps most important to any rhetorical approach, what and whose interests they serve.

This concern with, as Lauter puts it, "knowledge . . . not as a precious object but as an intellectual construction, situated in a particular historical moment, and erected with a specific cultural space," implies that a strategic maneuvering for social power, influence, and authority is intrinsic to literary activity, including the reception and discussion of that activity in the classroom. If teaching the new canon means foregrounding discussions about the workings of cultural authority and power, that discussion must also include the classroom and institutional context of instruction as well, in order for students to become aware of and reflect critically upon the part they play in arguments about cultural identity and values.

As Paul Lauter's afterword also points out, the teaching approaches outlined in this instructor's guide do not require completely abandoning the pedagogical techniques many of us experienced as students and now use in our classes. If anything, a cultural rhetoric approach demands an ever-closer "close reading," but a close reading that includes the cultural context of the reading experience; a close reading that indeed problematizes the boundary between text and context in order to get at the strategic questions of the kinds of cultural work engaged in by the creators of the texts in the anthology, the students in the classroom, and the teacher in the class.

Works Cited

Rosenblatt, Louise. *The Reader, the Text, the Poem: The Transactional Theory of the Literary Work*. Carbondale and Edwardsville: Southern Illinois University Press, 1978.

Tompkins, Jane. *Sensational Designs: The Cultural Work of American Fiction: 1790–1860*. New York: Oxford University Press, 1985.

As with the first edition of the instructor's guide, thanks are due to the contributing editors who prepared materials not only for the anthology but for this instructor's guide as well.

Finally, I'd like to thank Paul Lauter and Paul Smith for the opportunity to work on this project; Lois Rudnick and Randy Bass for their suggestions regarding the second edition of the instructor's guide; and Shira Eisenman and Martha Wetherill at D. C. Heath for their support, skill, and patience. Most of all, I give special thanks to my wife Kristin and my daughter Martha for their wisdom, love, and tolerance.

John Alberti
Northern Kentucky University

Colonial Period
to 1700

In many ways, "Cultures in Contact" can serve as a pedagogical model for the entire anthology. The phrase points not only to the diversity of cultural experiences represented in the selections of *The Heath Anthology,* but also to the key moment of cultural contact in any literature class: the reader's experience with the text. Cultural contacts—whether the historical encounters that generated many of these texts, the juxtaposition of texts on a syllabus, or the act of reading—take many forms. Many of us are probably most familiar with the assimilation model, involving the absorption of one culture by another: the culture of the conquered by that of the conquerors; the culture of immigrants by the dominant culture; of slaves by the enslavers. A similar pedagogical model holds that education is likewise a process of assimilation or absorption, an essentially one-way street of information flowing from teacher to students. But cultural contact—including that form of contact we call pedagogy—is of course much more complicated than that, for even the most relentless attempt at cultural domination involves a complex process of cultural resistance, negotiation, and transformation, as various groups of people attempt to dominate, coexist, or simply survive. The same complexity is true of the classroom, where effective pedagogy recognizes not only the need for students and teachers to work together in the process of cultural exploration but also the inevitability of conflict and the necessity for negotiation, debate, and compromise. Whether we acknowledge it or not, the classroom experience represents personal change, development, and transformation for all the members of the class, both teachers and students.

Native American Oral Literatures

The texts in this section can be viewed from the perspective of first contacts—not just the historical contact between the indigenous peoples of the Americas and European explorers and colonists in the fifteenth and sixteenth centuries, but for many students, their own first contact with Native American cultures.

In the classroom, the idea of "first contact" can become a point of departure for analysis and discussion, as students examine their own reading experiences as examples of cultures in contact. Those aspects of the texts that students may find difficult or strange can lead to discussions of how culture shapes our understanding of the terms "strange" and "familiar," the "same" and the "other," along with attitudes toward oral cultures. As a result, the examination of the students' reading experiences of Native American literatures always involves as much analysis of the cultural perspective of the readers as of the texts involved.

Views from the Imperial Frontier

The texts in this section give students the opportunity to look at how various European writers made sense of, explained, and justified the results of their encounters with Native American cultures; and to re-examine the various cultural myths of "discovery," "exploration," and "colonization" that students bring to class. To what extent, for example, does the Columbus of his journals match the Columbus of history books, movies, and even cartoons? Students can use their experiences reading Native American texts to discuss questions of what the Europeans could and could not see in indigenous cultures (for example, the belief expressed in Columbus's journals that the natives he met had no religion), of what they found "strange," of how they fit native peoples into their own stories about a "new world" of "noble savages" and "blood-thirsty heathens."

The diversity of texts in this section also allows for the consideration of the diversity of European responses, from Columbus's cultural blindness and assumption of superiority to Samuel Purchas's legalistic justification of colonization, to Cabeza de Vaca's growing awareness (as a captive) of the complexity of Indian life and the tragic consequences of European conquest.

Voices from the Anglo-American's "New" World

This section again allows the class to examine some powerful cultural myths: the arrival of the Pilgrims and the English colonial experience. The selections included here underline the complexity and diversity of that experience: from the views of colonial leaders like William Bradford and John Winthrop to those of the indentured servant Richard Frethorne; from colonists concerned with building a "new Jerusalem" to those intent on creating a "new" England; from men and women; from the perspectives of poets, diarists, government officials, ministers, and housewives. The wide variety of styles, forms, and rhetorical situations allows for discussions about the social construction of our literary expectations—what we expect a poem or a journal to be. An examination of what seems "timeless" or "dated" in terms of style and theme can lead to an understanding of the contingency of our own cultural tastes.

In addition "captivity narratives," as exemplified by Mary Rowlandson's famous seventeenth-century best-seller, provide a useful analytical model for considering the question of cultural contact. The physical captivity that is experienced and then shaped into narrative by Rowlandson (or John Williams or Cabeza de Vaca) marks the beginning of an important genre in the literature of the Americas, a genre dealing with what Gloria Anzaldúa calls the "borderlands"—the marginal area where culture meets culture, a place of transformation, of impermanence, of both possibility and danger. As a teaching strategy, this idea of "captivity" can be extended to a variety of cultural borderlands, whether between native and European cultures (Rowlandson, Cabeza de Vaca), between English Protestants and French Catholics (Williams), or later between Africans and Europeans (Olaudah Equiano), slaves and masters (Frederick Douglass).

Tales of Incorporation, Resistance, and Reconquest in New Spain

Finally, not only do the texts from the Spanish colonies offer a contrast to the traditional Anglocentric model of colonial history, but the Hopi story of the Pueblo revolt also gives an example of history from the "other"—or perhaps another—side. The Virgin of Guadalupe serves as a fitting conclusion to these first sections of "cultures in contact" by returning us to the tricky question of "assimilation," of how the forcible entrance of Catholicism into native cultures resulted not in the erasure of native religious traditions but in the creation of a hybrid used by both conquered and conquerors in a continuing process of negotiation and resistance. Such a complicated cultural revolution prepares students for a consideration of the "age of revolution" in the eighteenth century.

Native American Oral Literatures

Contributing Editor: Andrew Wiget

Classroom Issues

Teachers face a number of difficulties in bringing before their students something as unfamiliar as Native American oral literatures. The problems will vary, of course, from situation to situation. Jeanne Holland's article in the Bibliography on page 13 outlines some of the difficulties she faced in using the first edition of this anthology, some of which we have tried to remedy in this second edition, others of which I addressed in a recent issue of *The Heath Anthology of American Literature Newsletter* (see Bibliography).

In the absence of real knowledge about other cultures or other periods in time, most students tend to project their own sense of appropriate human behavior onto all other peoples and call it "universal human nature." The principal problem teachers will have, not only with their students but with their own experience, is the recognition that people in other cultures understand the world and human behavior in significantly different ways. This means, in literary terms, that we may not be able to apprehend the motivation of characters nor the significance of their actions without supplying a good deal of cultural information. To address this problem instructors should avail themselves of the notes that are supplied with the texts, perhaps even going over this material explicitly in class, coupled with the additional information provided in the headnotes and the introductions. There are also a number of resources readily available that an instructor can consult. Wiget's *Native American Literature* and Ruoff's *American Indian Literatures* constitute a very valuable core of essential reference works. Instructors should also consult the Smithsonian's new, multivolume *Handbook of North American Indians,* for its many articles on the history and culture of specific tribes and its extensive bibliographies, and Murray (1990) for a thorough discussion of how the dynamics of the translation/transcription situation shape the text we read.

Many students will come to class with assumptions about how American Indians lived, their historical relations with the United States, and their contemporary situation. Many of these stereotypes—that Indians were in perfect harmony with nature; that they were communalists and shared everything; that they did not believe in any form of individualism; and most frighteningly, that there are no more real Indians today—will need to be addressed in class as a preface to the discussion of any kind of Native American literature. Concerning stereotypes, I find it best to begin any discussion of Native American literature with an exploration of what students in fact think they know about Native Americans, and I provide some basic background in terms of the population of Native Americans as of the 1990 census, cultural information about modes of living and adaptation to particular environments, and historical information. I also make it a point to emphasize that every society has evolved a useful and fitting adaptation to its environment. That adaptation is called *culture.* Culture is a system of beliefs and values through which a group of people structure their experience of the world. By working with this definition of culture, which is very close to the way current criticism understands the impact of ideology upon literature, we can begin to pluralize our notion of the world and understand that other peoples can organize their experience in different ways, and dramatize their experience of the world through different symbolic forms. If time is available, I would highly recommend that the class view "Winds of Change," a PBS documentary that dramatizes the adaptability of contemporary Indian cultures, and goes a long way toward restoring the visible presence of Indian diversity.

Many forms of Native American literature also employ different kinds of artistic devices that are unfamiliar or even antithetical to conventional Anglo-American notions of aesthetic response, such as acute brevity, much repetition, or cataloging. None of these literary conventions appeal to the experience of contemporary readers. To address this problem, I illustrate how cultural conventions that students assume as essential characteristics of literary experience, in fact, have changed over time. This is very easy to do. A classic example is to point out how conventional notions of what constitutes good poetry have changed significantly from the Renaissance through the early nineteenth century and up to the present day, and that we recognize contemporary poetry as being marked by the absence of some features that used to be valued as significant in poetry. This will show the changeableness of literary forms and undermine the students' assumptions that the way things look today is the basis for all judgments about what constitutes good art. I might also indicate the important influences of American Indian literature on American literature, and that some of these Native forms and conventions and themes were borrowed by Anglo-American writers from Cooper through the Imagists and up to the present.

Classroom Strategies

Anthologies present the possibility of successfully developing several teaching strategies. There is enough material in both volumes of the anthology, for instance, to develop a semester-long course just on American Indian literatures. Most teachers, however, will be teaching American Indian traditions in the context of other American literatures. I will suggest three basic strategies.

I think the most important teaching strategy for Native American literature is to single out one text for extensive in-class treatment and to embed it richly in its cultural and historical context. Work through a text with constant reference to notes. Also offer startling images for the class's contemplation, inviting them to reflect upon a range of possible meanings, before suggesting how this imagery or symbol might have meaning in its original cultural context. It's also very helpful to use films, because they provide visual connections to the cultural environment. For the Zuni material, I particularly recommend for a general southwestern Native American world view, "Hopi: Songs of the Fourth World," a film by Pat Ferreiro.

A second strategy uses culturally related materials, or even materials from the same tribe, and teaches them back to back, mixing the genres, in order to let the context that you develop for one enrich the other. There is enough Iroquoian and Zuni material here, for example, to do just that. An especially good unit would include showing the film, teaching the Zuni "Talk Concerning the First Beginning," contrasting it with Genesis, then moving on to teach "Sayatasha's Night Chant" under the Native American Oral Poetry section. This way the cultural context that you have built up (by understanding fundamental symbols like corn and rain and how they emerge from the people's experience with the land) can serve more than one work.

A third strategy I have used successfully involves what I have called elsewhere "reading against the grain." Many Native American texts invite comparison with canonical texts from the Euro-American literatures. I always teach the Zuni creation story with readings from the Bible. Genesis 1 through 11 offers two versions of the creation of the world and a flood story, as well as opportunities to discuss social order in chapters 4, 5, and 10. Genesis 27, which gives the story of Jacob and Esau, provides a biblical trickster figure in the person of Jacob. And finally the book of Judges, with its stories of Samson and Gideon, provides good examples of culture heroes, as do other classics such as the *Aeneid,* the *Odyssey,* and the various national epics. These classical works are also good counterparts to the Navajo story of Changing Woman's children, the hero twins, who are also on a quest to transform the world by ridding it of monsters, which, like Grendel or the Cyclops, are readily understood as projections of our fears and anxieties, as well as interesting narrative agents. The Yuchi story of "The Creation of the Whites" and Handsome Lake's version of "How America Was Discovered," together with the Hopi version of the Pueblo Revolt, are powerful antidotes to the European mythopoeticizing of the invasion of North America. This is a point I emphasize in my article on "Origin Stories," which reads the Zuni emergence story against Villagrá's epic poem on the history of New Mexico and Bradford's *Of Plymouth Plantation,* both of which are excerpted in Volume 1 of this anthology. Finally, the Iroquoian description of the confederacy is usefully compared with colonial political documents that envision various social orders, including the Declaration of Independence, the Constitution, and the Federalist papers.

Native American Oral Narrative

Contributing Editor: Andrew Wiget

Major Themes, Historical Perspectives, and Personal Issues

Some very important themes evolve from this literature. Native American views of the world as represented in these mythologies contrast strongly with Euro-American perspectives. Recognizing this is absolutely essential for later discussion of the differences between Anglo-Americans and Native Americans over questions of land, social organization, religion, and so on. In other words, if one can identify these fundamental differences through the literature very early on, then later it becomes easier to explain the differences in outlook between Native American peoples and Anglo-American peoples that often lead to tragic consequences.

If culture is a system of beliefs and values by which people organize their experience of the world, then it follows that forms of expressive culture such as these myths should embody the basic beliefs and values of the people who create them. These beliefs and values can be roughly organized in three areas: (1) beliefs about the nature of the physical world; (2) beliefs about social order and appropriate behavior; and (3) beliefs about human nature and the problem of good and evil.

The Zuni "Talk Concerning the First Beginning" speaks directly to the nature of the physical world. If we look closely at the Zuni "Talk," the story imagines the earth as hollow, with people coming out from deep within the womb of the earth. The earth is mother and feminine and people are created not just of the stuff of the earth, but also from the earth. They are born into a particular place and into a particular environment. In the course of this long history, imagined as a search for the center (a point of balance and perfection), they undergo significant changes in their physical appearance, in their social behavior, in their social organization and in their sense of themselves. By the time they have arrived at Zuni, which they call the center of the world, they have become pretty much like their present selves. It is especially important to follow the notes here with this selection and with the Navajo selection. Both of these stories talk about transformations in the physical world. The world is populated by beings who are also persons like humans; all of the world is animated, and there are different nations of beings who can communicate with each other, who are intelligent and volitional creatures.

Both the Zuni story and the Iroquoian story of the origins of the confederacy also talk about how society should be organized, about the importance of kinship and families, about how society divides its many functions in order to provide for healing, for food, for decision making, and so on. The Iroquoian confederacy was a model of Federalism for the drafters of the Constitution, who were much impressed by the way in which the confederacy managed to preserve the autonomy of its individual member tribes while being able to manage effective concerted actions, as the colonists to their dismay too often found out. The Navajo story of Changing Woman and the Lakota story of White Buffalo Calf Pipe Woman are important illustrations not only of the role of women as culture heroes, but also of every people's necessity to evolve structures such as the Pipe Ceremony or the Navajo healing rituals to restore and maintain order in the world.

The Raven and Hare narratives are stories about a Trickster figure. Tricksters are the opposite of culture heroes. Culture heroes exist in mythology to dramatize prototypical events and behaviors; they show us how to do what is right and how we became the people who we are. Tricksters, on the other hand, provide for disorder and change; they enable us to see the seemy underside of life and remind us that culture, finally, is artificial, that there is no necessary reason why things must be the way they are. If there is sufficient motivation to change things, Trickster provides for the possibility of such change, most often by showing us the danger of believing too sincerely that this arbitrary arrangement we call culture is the way things really are. When Raven cures the girl, for instance, he does so to gain her sexual favors, and in so doing calls into question the not-always-warranted trust that people place in healing figures like doctors. The Bungling Host story, widespread throughout Native America, humorously illustrates the perils of overreaching the limits of one's identity while trying to ingratiate one's self.

Significant Form, Style, or Artistic Conventions

Perhaps the most important thing that needs to be done is to challenge students' notions of myth. When students hear the word "myth," they succumb to the popular belief that mythology is necessarily something that is false. This is a good place to start a discussion about truth, inviting students to consider that there are other kinds of truth besides scientific truth (which is what gave a bad name to mythology in the first place). Consider this definition of myth: "The dramatic representation of culturally important truths in narrative form." Such a definition highlights the fact that myths represent or dramatize shared visions of the world for the people who hold them. Myths articulate the fundamental truths about the shape of the universe and the nature of humanity.

It is also important to look at important issues of form such as repetition. Repetition strikes many students as boring. Repetition, however, is an aesthetic device that can be used to create expectation. Consider the number three and how several aspects of our Euro-American experience are organized in terms of three: the start of a race ("on your mark, get set, go"); three sizes (small, medium, and large); the three colors of a traffic signal; and of course, three little pigs. These are all commonplace examples, so commonplace, in fact, that initially most students don't think much of them. But there is no reason why we should begin things by counting to three. We could count to four or five or seven, as respectively the Zunis, the Chinooks, and the Hebrews did. In other words, these repetitions have an aesthetic function: they create a sense of expectation, and when one arrives at the full number of repetitions, a sense of completeness, satisfaction, and fulfillment.

Original Audience

The question of audience is crucial for Native American literature, in that the original audience for the literature understands the world through its own experience much differently than most of our students do. As a result, it's important to reconstruct as much of that cultural and historical context as possible for students, especially when it has a direct bearing upon the literature. So, for instance, students need to know in discussing Zuni material that the Zunis, Hopis, and Navajos are agricultural people and that corn and moccasins figure prominently as symbols of life. Rain, moisture, and human beings are imagined in terms of corn, and life is understood as an organic process that resembles a plant growing from a seed in the ground, being raised up, harvested, and so forth. Historically it's important to realize too that visions of one's community and its history differ from culture to culture. So, for instance, the Hopi story of the Pueblo revolt imagines the revolt as a response to a life-threatening drought that is caused by the suppression of the native religion by the Franciscan priest. This way of understanding history is very different from the way most of our students understand history today. Its very notion of cause and effect, involving as it does supernatural means, is much more closely related to a vision of history shared by Christian reconstructionists, seventeenth-century Puritans, and ancient Hebrews.

At the same time, students should be cautioned about the presumption that somehow we can enter entirely into another cultural vision, whether it be that of the Lakota during the Ghost Dance period of the 1880s or the Puritan Separatists three centuries earlier. This is not only a matter of translation and transcription. As both Murray and Clifford point out, what is sometimes blithely called "the need to understand" or "the search for knowledge" is not a neutral quest, but one determined in great measure by the often unarticulated aims and attitudes of the dominant society that structures fields of inquiry and creates the need for certain kinds of information. Although most contemporary students often assume that all differences can be overcome, the facticity of difference will remain.

Questions for Reading and Discussion/ Approaches to Writing

1. The number of works addressed in this section is so great and the material so varied that particular questions would not be useful. A good lead-in to all of these works, however, would focus on motivation of characters or significance of action. I would want students to identify some action in the narrative that puzzles them, and would encourage them to try to explain the role of this action in the narrative and what might motivate it. They will not necessarily be successful at answering that question, but the activity of trying to answer that question will compel them to seek for meaning ultimately in some kind of cultural context. There is, in other words, a certain kind of appropriate aesthetic frustration here, which should not necessarily be discouraged, because it prepares the student to let go of the notion that human behavior is everywhere intelligible in universal terms.

2. I usually have students write comparative papers. I ask them to identify a theme: for example, the relationship between human beings and animals, attitudes toward death, the role of women, or other similar topics, and to write comparatively using Native American texts and a Euro-American text that they find to be comparable.

Bibliography

Babcock-Abrahams, Barbara. " 'A Tolerated Margin of Mess': The Trickster and His Tales Reconsidered." *Journal of the Folklore Institute 9* (1975): 147–86.

Fenton, William. "This Island, the World on Turtle's Back." *Journal of American Folklore 75* (1962): 283–300.

Geertz, Clifford. "Religion as a Cultural System." In *The Interpretation of Cultures.* New York: Basic Books, 1973.

Holland, Jeanne. "Teaching Native American Literature from *The Heath Anthology of American Literature.*" *CEA Critic 55* (1993): 1–21.

Krupat, Arnold. *Ethnocriticism: Ethnography, History, Literature.* Berkeley: University of California Press, 1992.

Murray, David. *Forked Tongues: Speech, Writing, and Representation in North American Indian Texts.* Bloomington: Indiana University Press, 1990.

Radin, Paul. *The Trickster.* New York: Schocken, 1972.

Reichard, Gladys. "Literary Types and the Dissemination of Myths." *Journal of American Folklore 34* (1914): 269–307.

Ruoff, A. LaVonne Brown. *American Indian Literatures: An Introduction, Bibliographic Review, and Selected Bibliography.* New York: MLA, 1990.

Sturtevant, William, ed. *Handbook of North American Indians,* 15 vols. Washington, D.C.: Smithsonian Institution Press.

Swann, Brian, ed. *Smoothing the Ground: Essays on Native American Oral Literature.* Berkeley: University of California Press, 1987.

—— and Arnold Krupat, eds. *Recovering the Word: Essays on Native American Literature.* Berkeley: University of California Press, 1987.

Toelken, J. Barre. "The 'Pretty Language' of Yellowman: Genre, Mode, and Texture in Navajo Coyote Narratives." *Genre 2* (1969): 21–235.

Wheeler-Voegelin, Erminie and R. W. Moore. "The Emergence Myth in Native America." *Indiana University Publications in Folklore 9* (1957): 66–91.

Wiget, Andrew. "Oral Narrative." In *Native American Literature.* Boston: Twayne, 1985. Chapter 1.

——. "Reading Against the Grain: Origin Stories and American Literary History." *American Literary History 2* (1991): 209–31.

——. "A Talk Concerning First Beginnings: Teaching Native American Oral Literatures." *The Heath Anthology of American Literature Newsletter* IX (Spring 1993): 4–7.

——. "Telling the Tale: A Performance Analysis of a Hopi Coyote Story." In *Recovering the Word: Essays on the Native American Literature,* edited by Brian Swann and Arnold Krupat, 297–336.

Native American Oral Poetry

Contributing Editor: Andrew Wiget

Classroom Strategies

The Inuit and Aztec poetry requires the introduction of cultural background in order to understand some of its themes and imagery, but it is much more accessible than "Sayatasha's Night Chant." Because it is expressive of individual emotional states, it is much closer to the Western lyric poetry tradition, and therefore more readily apprehended by students than the long Zuni chant. "Sayatasha's Night Chant," on the other hand, is very difficult for students for a number of reasons, which, if properly addressed, make it a rich aesthetic experience.

First of all, it is absolutely essential to refer students to the notes that supply important, culture-specific, contextual information that is necessary for understanding the poems. This is less urgent in the more accessible poetry of the Aztecs and the Inuit, but it is required for the other very brief song texts and especially for "Sayatasha's Night Chant," which I think will pose the most problems for students. One can enrich the cultural context of the "Chant" by teaching it in conjunction with the Zuni "Talk Concerning the First Beginning." This origin story establishes some of the fundamental symbols that are expressive of the Zuni world view and some of the fundamental themes, so that if the students read "Sayatasha's Night Chant" following the emergence story, they can carry forward some of the cultural information acquired from reading the origin story to support their reading of "Sayatasha's Night Chant."

Major Themes, Historical Perspectives, and Personal Issues

The Inuit and Aztec poetry is relatively accessible to students, who recognize in it some fundamental human emotions that have literary expression in Euro-American traditions as well. The Inuit poetry is remarkable for its juxtaposition of human beings against the natural world. Nature is viewed as an enormous arena that dwarfs human beings, who are continually struggling to secure their existence. Much of the Inuit view of nature corresponds rather well to the notions of the Romantic sublime. This is a Nature that the Inuit face with a combination of awe, terror, and humility, as reflected in the Copper Eskimo "Song" and Uvavnuk's "Moved." On the other hand, the "Improvised Greeting" suggests that in the presence of such an overwhelming Nature, which isolated people, the experience of social contact was a cause for tremendous joy. And yet, as the "Widow's Song" suggests, alienation from one's community left one isolated and trapped in one's self. (Inuit poetry can be very reflective.) Orpingalik's song speaks to a loss of competence and power experienced in one's old age that undermines the sense of accomplishment and identity. A good poem to read to workaholics, whose identity usually rests in their work!

Aztecs, it seems, are familiar to everyone. Their popular reputation rests on a series of images—the offering of human hearts to the sun, cruel and violent warfare, a powerful militaristic empire—many of which were true. Thus it comes as a surprise, having set up this cultural and historical context, to discover a poetry whose central theme is the fragility of life, the transience of beauty, and the elusiveness of truth. At the height of their power, the Aztecs experienced life, beauty, and truth as inexorably slipping away. They expressed this theme in their poetry through three images or vehicles, the most important of which are images associated with flowers. Flowers in their fragile beauty represented for the Aztecs the very essence of life. In the poem "Like Flowers Continually Perishing," the poet imagines that we are like flowers slowly dying in the midst of and despite our beauty. Flowers throughout literature are symbols of fragility as well as great beauty. A second cluster of images has to do with feathers. Feathers in Aztec culture represented things of great value and preciousness because many of them had to be imported from the jungles of Central America. They were also objects of great delicacy, and, like flowers, became symbols of the fragility, beauty, and preciousness of life. The third and most important image was poetry itself. Aztecs wrote poetry to achieve immortality. Because they experienced life as transient, they looked to create an ideal world through the images articulated in their poetry. In this they felt they were imitating their principal deity, Omeoteotl, the creator of the universe, also called the Lord of the Close and the Near. Omeoteotl achieved immortality through creativity, and the Aztec poets sought to do the same.

"Sayatasha's Night Chant" is more accessible to students if one can view it as a quest, in which a human being, representing the Zuni people, is sent on a journey from the village to the Zuni "heaven," Kothluwalawa. The purpose of this journey is to obtain the seeds and power needed to regenerate life for a new year. "Sayatasha's Night Chant" is a poem recited in the context of a world renewal ritual. In narrative form, it describes how a man has been appointed in the beginning of the poem (line 106) to represent the Zuni people. His mission, which takes the better part of a year to accomplish, is undertaken because the world is in need of renewal (line 67). His appointment takes place in January, and throughout the next nine or ten months this person is busy visiting many shrines at Zuni to plant prayer sticks (physical representations of the basic elements of life in this world) as offerings to the deities (lines 120–33). Later, forty-nine days before the Shalako ceremony in early December, the man who will impersonate Sayatasha is formally invested with the symbols and the costume of his role (see notes 8 and 9). Now having been transformed into a being who represents the spirit world of the rain-bringing ancestors, the Sayatasha impersonator returns to the village bearing the seeds of new life. Before he reaches the village, however, he visits twenty-nine separate springs around Zuni, each of which represent the different places where the Zuni people stopped on their way to the Center of the World, the village of Zuni. In reenacting this migration, the Sayatasha impersonator recovers the force, energy, and potency of that first creation to reenergize life in the village. The poem ends as the Sayatasha impersonator, on the eighth night of Shalako, confers upon the entire village the blessings of life and fertility that he had been sent to gain for them.

Significant Form, Style, or Artistic Conventions

Students need some initial help in understanding the meaning of prevalent images, like flowers in Aztec poetry. They might also need assistance in seeing some potent juxtapositions that occur in the Inuit poetry. For example, the despairing woman in the "Widow's Song" holds an amulet (a token of religious faith) in her hands while she stares angrily at the northern lights that taunt her with their beauty and promise.

In the case of "Sayatasha's Night Chant," there is much ritual language, and students will need help in working through the characters and understanding the ritual actions that are a key to the poem. Ritual poetry is very formulaic and repetitive. Students are frequently frustrated by repetition and aggravated by the apparent lack of spontaneity and the stiltedness of the language. Point out to them that in serious religious settings, spontaneity is not valued, not only in Zuni settings but also in ritual contexts throughout the world, including Euro-American cultures. It's also good to develop in them some understanding of the key symbols, like water and corn as symbols of life. Water, in particular, is something that they ought to be able to relate to. Notes 1, 3, and 8 should help students understand ritual poetry.

All of these songs were sung in different ways, which affects the way in which they were experienced. The "Night Chant" is just that, a narrative chant in which the words are uttered on a sustained tone with a falling tone at the end of each line. The short songs were sung to more complex melodies, sometimes by the individual alone, sometimes with an audience chorus response. Short songs were often repeated many times in order to deepen the emotional experience stimulated by the song.

Original Audience

I make it a point to try to reconstruct the cultural context of the poems' origins in order to recover for the students the aesthetic force that these poems must have had for their original listeners. I remind them of the terrible and frightening confrontation that human beings have with the physical environment in the Arctic and how people cling to each other under such circumstances. Understanding the relationship between the physical and the social worlds in Inuit life is a necessary precondition for understanding the poetry. The same thing is true of the Aztecs. One juxtaposes the poetry against the cultural and historical context from which it emerged.

In all cases, I also stress the unique context in which these songs were first performed. The Eskimo, for instance, had song festivals in which these very intense and private songs were sung in public. The Inuit, in other words, had created a socially sanctioned forum for the expression of one's most private joys and griefs. This suggests a new way of thinking about the function of poetry and the relationship between an individual and his social context. Among the Aztecs, poetry was composed principally by the nobility, most of whom had also earned great fame and success as warriors. It is effective to point out to students that the poetry most sensitive to the fragile beauty of life was created by the noble warrior class. In terms of the Zuni poem, it is useful to remind students that ritual poetry is recited publicly in the context of a variety of significant and meaningful religious actions, and that these actions are as much a part of the total experience as the recitation of the poetry. Consider also Jane Green's "Divorce Dance Song" as a kind of publication. The notion that poetry is coupled with action and so comes closer to approximating the condition of drama than any other Western form is initially unfamiliar to students. They may need some help in realizing that poetry, even in the Western tradition, emerged from the recitation of hymns in dramatic settings in ancient Israel and Greece.

Comparisons, Contrasts, Connections

The Aztec and Inuit poetry compares well in theme and form to British and American Romantic lyric poetry. Certainly the Aztec poetry compares well with Western poetry in the elegiac tradition. The Inuit and Aztec poems also offer opportunities for comparing and contrasting the role of poetry as a vehicle for self-expression and for the creation of individual identity, another important Romantic theme. One can contrast "Sayatasha's Night Chant," in which the individual identity of the speaker of the poem is totally submerged in his ritual role or persona, with the Inuit and Aztec poetry where the "I" reflects the personal identity of the poet/subject. "Sayatasha's Night Chant" can also be effectively contrasted with British and American poetry whose subject is the power of Nature. Reading "Sayatasha's Night Chant" against Bryant's "Thanatopsis," Emerson's "Nature," or Thoreau's *Walden* will lead students to consider Native American views of Nature as something very different from the Anglo-American Romantic understanding of Nature. Such contrasts are especially instructive because they enable students to understand why Native Americans and Anglo-Americans might hold different attitudes toward the land and activities involving the natural world.

Discussion Strategies

Begin the discussion of Eskimo and Aztec poetry by inviting students to consider, in the case of the Eskimo, the physical environment in which the Inuit people live and the need for powerful social bonds in the face of the overwhelming power and intimidating scale of the natural world of the Arctic. By the same token, begin the discussion of Aztec poetry with a presentation of the scale and scope of the Aztec military, political, economic, and social achievements. In both cases the poetry stands against this powerful cultural context and effectively discloses its key themes sometimes by contrast to one's expectations (as in the case of the Aztecs) and sometimes by conforming to one's expectations (as in the case of Inuit poetry). With "Sayatasha's Night Chant," I usually begin by insisting that most cultures have rituals, such as first fruit feasts (like our Thanksgiving) or foundational feasts (like our Fourth of July or New Year's), which are designed to commemorate the forces of life and order that structure and animate our world. I talk about the role of ritual in people's lives, and I disassociate ritual from its popular definition of something routine. This discussion of ritual and the role of the sacred in culture is an enormously valuable preface to approaching this particular poem.

Questions for Reading and Discussion/ Approaches to Writing

1. I would draw students' attention in the Eskimo poetry to the place of human beings in the physical universe and the relationship of the individual to society; and in the Aztec poetry, to the images of flowers and to the function of poetry. In "Sayatasha's Night Chant," I would focus on important images such as cornmeal and invite students to make connections between symbols that they discover in "Sayatasha's Night Chant" and their antecedents in the Zuni origin myth, "Talk Concerning the First Beginning."
2. Aside from obvious thematic papers focused around topics such as nature, death, ritual, and so on, I would invite students to write on broader topics such as the role of poetry in these societies and to compare how poetry functions in them with how it has functioned in the Western tradition.

Bibliography

Bunzel, Ruth. "Zuni Ritual Poetry." *47th Annual Report of the Bureau of American Ethnology* (1930): 611–835.

Finnegan, Ruth. *Oral Poetry: Its Nature, Significance and Social Context.* Cambridge: Cambridge University Press, 1977.

Geertz, Clifford. "Religion as a Cultural System." In *The Interpretation of Cultures.* New York: Basic Books, 1973.

Leon-Portilla, Miguel. *Pre-Columbian Literatures of Mexico.* Norman: University of Oklahoma Press, 1969.

Lowenstein, Tom, trans. "Introduction." *Eskimo Poems From Canada and Greenland.* Pittsburgh: University of Pittsburgh Press, 1973.

Wiget, Andrew. "Aztec Lyrics: Poetry in a World of Continually Perishing Flowers." *Latin American Indian Literatures* 4 (1980): 1–11.

——. "Oratory and Oral Poetry." In *Native American Literature*. Boston: Twayne, 1985.

——. "Sayatasha's Night Chant: A Literary Textual Analysis of a Zuni Ritual Poem." *American Indian Culture and Research Journal* 4 (1980): 99–140.

Cultures in Contact: Voices from the Imperial Frontier

"Creation of the Whites" (Yuchi)

See also the Instructor's Guide material on Native American Oral Literatures (p. 5) for more information.

Christopher Columbus (1451–1506)
Alvar Nuñez Cabeza de Vaca (1490?–1556?)
A Gentleman of Elvas (fl. 1537–1557)
René Goulaine de Laudonnière (fl. 1562–1582)
Pedro Menéndez de Avilés (1519–1574)
Fray Marcos de Niza (1495?–1542)
Pedro de Casteñeda (1510?–1570?)
Gaspar Pérez de Villagrá (1555–1620)
Samuel de Champlain (1570?–1635)

Contributing Editors: Juan Bruce-Novoa and Carla Mulford

Classroom Issues and Strategies

Students' lack of general historical knowledge is compounded by the usual disinformation they learn in U.S. history as taught in this country. To address this problem, I give the students a list of historical facts as they probably have learned them (i.e., dates of Jamestown, Plymouth, etc.), and we discuss this traditional way of teaching U.S. history. I sometimes ask them to draw a map representing U.S. history in movement. Then I give them a second list with the Spanish and French settlements included and discuss how this new context changes the way we conceive of U.S. history. Next I take time to explain the European backgrounds of the fifteenth and sixteenth centuries in which Spain, the first national state, was a dominant power and England a marginal and even second-rate power. Third, I emphasize the economic reality of colonization. Students must understand that none of the Europeans viewed the Native Americans as equals. The destruction of the Acoma people is just the start of a long U.S. tradition of subjugating conquered peoples and should not be read as a Spanish aberration. The Cabeza de Vaca experience is unique in that it prefigures not only captivity literature but also migrant literature of the nineteenth and twentieth centuries: he and his comrades had to assimilate and acculturate to survive, working at whatever job they could get among a majority culture that did not necessarily need or want them around.

Students often ask why these texts are important and how they relate to more conventional U.S. literature. You might suggest that they entertain a change in their traditional concept of the U.S. as an English-based country, considering the paradigm of a land that from the start was in contention by forces of several language groups and distinct origins. Students should be taught that this situation is still the same, in spite of the assumption that English won out. The forces present in this period are still contending for a place in U.S. territory. Perhaps the oldest tradition in the U.S. is the struggle among different groups for the recognition of the right to participate fully in making the future of this land.

Major Themes, Historical Perspectives, and Personal Issues

The headnotes specify two major themes: the newness of the experience and the need to relate it in European terms. Columbus initiated the dialogue between American reality and the European codes of signification.

Another theme would be the strategies utilized to convince powerful readers of the benefits of the New World. Again, Columbus marks the beginning. These authors are constantly selling the unknown to potential investors and visitors. Here begins the tradition of hawking new property developments beyond the urban blight of the reader's familiar surroundings.

Cabeza de Vaca introduces the familiar theme of wandering the back roads of the country—a sixteenth-century Kerouac. It is the theme of finding oneself through the difficult pilgrimage into the wilderness—a Carlos Castaneda *avant la lettre.* Cabeza de Vaca is transformed through suffering, perseverance, and the ability to acculturate.

The Laudonnière and Avilés texts introduce inter-European rivalries as a major theme of American culture. Competition over territory resulted in violent encounters. The encounters with the Native American population were equally violent, introducing the theme of the subjugation of the native peoples, who would rather retain their own way of life. The arrogant assumption that one's own system is naturally superior to the native's way is again an indisputable characteristic of U.S. history.

Another theme is the sincerity of religious motivation, in spite of the contradicting evidence of economic ambitions. This conflict between philanthropic ideals and exploitative motivation still underlies U.S. foreign policy.

Significant Form, Style, or Artistic Conventions

First, the form of much of this material is the epistolary chronicle: a subjective report on the events without the limitations of supposedly objective historical science. It is a personal account like a memoir, but it is also a letter to a powerful reader, not the general public. It has no literary pretensions, but the circumstances demanded rhetorical skill.

Second, the period is one of transition from the Middle Ages to the Renaissance, so there will be mixtures of characteristics from the two, the Medieval chronicle alongside the Renaissance epic of Villagrá.

Style is also hybrid. While most of these authors were educated well above the average commoner of the period, most of them were not trained in letters. Thus their writing is mostly unpretentious and direct. Again, Villagrá is an exception.

Most of these texts record personal experiences in the New World and thus have a ring of realism and direct contact with the earth and people.

Original Audience

The audience then was specifically the powerful leaders. One can compare U.S. military reports on Vietnam or propaganda films on World War II like *Victory at Sea* to get a sense of nationalistic justification.

Comparisons, Contrasts, Connections

There are plenty of writers in this section to compare and contrast. I would also recommend comparisons with Virginia and New England writers to get a sense of the newness encountered, the use of divine right to justify the project, and the determination to hold and civilize what is seen as wilderness.

Questions for Reading and Discussion/
Approaches to Writing

1. Ask students to review what they learned about this period in previous classes: who, what, where, when, why. Have them formulate a brief summary of the period according to this training. Have them compare it to the list of places and events you gave them at first and then to consider what the second list implies.
2. General assignments: Write about how this information changes their view of U.S. history. Write on the imagery used by the authors to characterize the New World.
3. Consider the role of violence in the colonization of the Americas.

Specific possibilities: On Cabeza de Vaca: Compare his experience with Robinson Crusoe's. On Villagrá: Compare his version with the Native American one in the anthology selections.

Bibliography

See headnotes for references.

Cultures in Contact: Voices from the Anglo-Americans' "New" World

Handsome Lake (Seneca)

Please consult the headnote in the text as well as the Instructor's Guide material on Native American Oral Literatures (p. 5) for complete information.

John Smith (1580–1631)

Contributing Editor: Amy Winans

Major Themes, Historical Perspectives, and Personal Issues

Since the time of their writing, Smith's works have evoked wildly divergent responses from readers: Smith has been viewed both as a self-aggrandizing and inaccurate historian and as the savior of the Virginia colony and friend to Native Americans. For example, one historian, Karen Ordahl Kupperman, has suggested that Smith's writing was most self-consciously literary—and therefore most historically suspect—in those passages that recount his interchanges with Powhatan. Interestingly, she and others also contend that Smith offered his readers a fairly reliable ethnographic account of Native American life. Students might usefully examine the process of Smith's self-fashioning that has evoked this variety of responses. Such an examination could also provide the basis for a discussion of the opposition between the New England and Virginian models of colonization, as well as strategies of self-representation.

Comparisons, Contrasts, Connections

Smith's individualized portrait of Powhatan is unique among early writers who often referred to Native Americans in much more generic terms, typically invoking a Manichean allegory. Still, these selections can usefully be compared to the selections from Roger Williams, Thomas Morton, and William Bradford. Consider, for example, the differences between Smith's account of Powhatan and Bradford's accounts of Samoset, Squanto, and the Pequot War. As background for this discussion, review differences between the Jamestown settlement and the Massachusetts settlements.

Smith should also be examined in the context of the other Jamestown writers included in the anthology: Richard Frethorne and Edward Wingfield.

Bibliography

Greene, Jack P. *Pursuits of Happiness: The Social Development of Early Modern British Colonies and the Formation of American Culture.* Chapel Hill: University of North Carolina Press, 1988. See chapter one for a useful comparative social history of Virginia and New England.

Consult Hayes's annotated bibliography included in the headnote for additional sources.

Edward Maria Wingfield (1560?–1613?)

Contributing Editor: Liahna Babener

Classroom Issues and Strategies

Surprisingly, despite its centrality in the colonization of America, there is also very little particular data and few firsthand accounts of the Jamestown enterprise. A comparison with other eyewitness accounts (cf. John Smith, Frethorne letter in the anthology) helps clarify and balance Wingfield's point of view. Presentation of background on the settlement history of Jamestown is also useful, as is a review of the political, religious, and social issues that shaped colonization experiences in various regions of America, particularly New England, the Middle Colonies, and the South.

Students are most interested in the problems of maintaining discipline, managing provisions, and fostering cooperation. They like to explore the contrasts between settlements undergirded by strong religious ideology and those driven by economic ambitions (often reluctantly concluding that the former are more "successful" if also more regimented communities). Students also debate whether Wingfield is too timorous, whether he pads his case, and whether he manipulates their sympathies.

Major Themes, Historical Perspectives, and Personal Issues

1. The problem of leadership and political authority in early colonial government. Class, economic, and political conflicts among constituencies of colonists. The impact of these issues on the evolution of colonial democracy. Relations between New World and mother country.

2. Wingfield's personal strengths and failings as a colonial administrator. The conflicts between the drive toward anarchy and the pressure for authoritarian government, where Wingfield is poised precariously between the two.
3. Conditions of life at Jamestown, including class stresses, daily life and its deprivations, illness and calamity, the absence of women, etc.
4. Can we begin to discern an image of America (as a culture in its own right, as distinct from its English occupants) in this document?
5. In what ways does the Jamestown experience as Wingfield tells it reflect the fact that it was an all-male society?

Significant Form, Style, or Artistic Conventions

We may view this document as a political treatise, apologia, manifesto, historical chronicle, and memoir. A consideration of the conventions of each genre and a comparison with other examples of each from the colonial period is illuminating. We may use it to discern the ethos of a male English gentleman, and explore the collision between his world view and the realities of life in Virginia under the devastating stresses of colonization.

Original Audience

Because the document is a self-defense, it is useful to determine whom Wingfield meant to address, and how his particular argument might appeal to his implicit audience. Would investors in the Virginia Company respond differently from fellow colonists? Would upper-class readers respond differently from the working class? Which groups might be alienated by his self-portrait and vision of leadership?

Comparisons, Contrasts, Connections

Compare express accounts of the Jamestown settlement and issues of colonial governance by John Smith (*A True Relation of Occurrences and Accidents in Virginia*, 1608, and *General History of Va.*, 1624), George Percy (*A True Relation of . . . Moments Which Happened in Va.*, 1608), and Richard Frethorne ("Letters to His Parents"). Other documents that explore the pressures facing colonial executives and the crises of colonization and community include Bradford's *Of Plymouth Plantation* and Morton's *The New English Canaan*. Especially suitable for its parallel case of deposed leadership and its differing vision of government is John Winthrop's "Speech to the General Court" included in his *Journal*. What differences between religiously and economically motivated settlements can be seen?

Questions for Reading and Discussion/ Approaches to Writing

1. (a) Discern the underlying world view of Wingfield, taking into account his background as an upper-middle-class male Englishman and perhaps a Catholic.
   (b) Identify his various strategies of self-justification. Are you sympathetic? Why or why not? Do you think his audience is won over? Explain.
   (c) Which issues seem more imperative: political struggles over power or economic struggles for provisions? What about military concerns about the colony's safety from Indians?
2. (a) Compare Wingfield's style of leadership to Bradford's, Morton's, Winthrop's, John Smith's.
   (b) Recreate a vivid picture of daily life at Jamestown.
   (c) How might the situation have been different if women had been present in the colony from the outset? If Wingfield had been an artisan or worker?
   (d) What were the particular obstacles to effective governance at Jamestown?

Bibliography

There is surprisingly little particularized history of Jamestown. Wingfield appears as a footnote or brief entry in most textbooks or historical accounts of the Jamestown colony. In John C. Miller's chapter "The Founding of Virginia" in *This New Man, The American: The Beginnings of the American People* (1974) there is a substantive and articulate account of the colony's story. Richard Morton's treatment of the same material in the first two chapters of Vol. 1 of *Colonial Virginia* (1960) is also useful and very detailed, though, again, does not contain much express material on Wingfield. I had hoped to find a feminist reconsideration of the Jamestown experience to address the problems of a gender-imbalanced society, but found no sustained inquiry on that issue.

Richard Frethorne (fl. 1623)

Contributing Editor: Liahna Babener

Classroom Issues and Strategies

Virtually no historical data about Frethorne is available, so placing him in the context of the Jamestown colony is a bit difficult, since he settled near—rather than in—that assemblage.

In the absence of corroborating information, the writer's candor about his own experience is convincing. He used vivid details to describe his discontent, deprivation, and discomfort. The small specifics of daily life (quantities and kinds of food, items of clothing, catalogs of implements) and the data of survival and death (lists of deceased colonists, trade and barter statistics, numerical estimates of enemy Indians and their military strength, itemized accounts of provisions, and rations records) lend credibility to Frethorne's dilemma and enable students to empathize with his distress.

Students respond to reading Frethorne with questions like these:

What happened to Frethorne?

Did he remain in the New World, return home, or die?

Did he receive provisions from his parents?

Why is there no other historical record of his life or his fate?

Why was there so much rancor over provisions, and why couldn't the English authorities address the scarcity?

Major Themes, Historical Perspectives, and Personal Issues

I invite students to imaginatively recreate, through the detail in the text, the world Frethorne inhabited, gleaning his world view as a white, Christian, European (English), and presumably working-class man. What assumptions does he make about the mission of settlement, the character of the New World, the nature of the native peoples, the relationships between colonists? What does he expect in terms of comfort and satisfaction? What class attitudes does he reveal? Compare his implicit vision of the New World with the region he actually encounters. What religious, social, political, ethical beliefs does he bring to his account, and how do they shape his view of his experience? What can be inferred about the constraints upon indentured servants—and the lives they led—from Frethorne's record?

Significant Form, Style, or Artistic Conventions

1. Consider the "letter" as a literary genre, exploring issues of format, voice, reliability and self-consciousness of speaker, assumed audience, etc.
2. Discuss the letter as a social history document as well as a personal record and literary construct.
3. Discuss the strategies of persuasion and justification employed by the speaker. How does he win over his parents' support and pity through rhetorical tactics as well as emotional expression?
4. Consider the literary precedents and background of biblical allusion related to Frethorne's letter.

Comparisons, Contrasts, Connections

1. Use other letters and firsthand accounts from colonists in the New World: cf. letter from "Pond," a young Massachusetts settler, to his parents in Suffolk, England (repr. in Demos, John, ed., *Remarkable Providences, 1600–1760*. New York: George Braziller, 1972, p. 73).
2. Use Pond to compare New England and Jamestown experiences.
3. Use chronicles by Bradford, Smith, Wingfield—recording both personal and communal life in the colonies—to discover the diversity of such experiences, the impact of his background and ethos upon Frethorne's viewpoint in these letters. Use women's accounts to identify gender issues.
4. Use Calvinist pieces to contrast the relatively secular focus of Frethorne's chronicle.

Questions for Reading and Discussion/
Approaches to Writing

1. (a) Invite students to itemize the basic assumptions (world view components) that Frethorne brings to his experience—these then become the basis for class discussion (as we discern them from evidence in the document).
   (b) Ask students to try to determine what aspects of Frethorne's appeal have been calculated to move his parents to aid him. How does he use persuasive and manipulative techniques (or does he?) to affect them?

2. (a) Write out responses to (a) and (b) above.
   (b) Using other primary sources, imaginatively recreate the world of Jamestown by inventing your own letter or diary entry or newspaper story or other fabricated "document" that conveys a vivid sense of colonial life.
   (c) Write an imagined reply from Frethorne's parents.

Bibliography

There is no secondary source material on Richard Frethorne, so one must reconstruct his world to know him.

Edited anthologies of primary source documents (cf. Demos) that diversify the voices of recollection have been the most useful for doing so. Social histories of the colonial period and feminist reconstructions of the age and enterprise of settlement and of the authorial process have done the most to alert me to the matrix of issues one should explore when using a memoir or other personal document.

Thomas Morton (1579?–1647?)

Contributing Editor: Kenneth Alan Hovey

Original Audience

Most students have some knowledge of Puritans and their role in the settlement of New England, but very few are familiar with pioneering Cavaliers like Morton. His values, therefore, and their relation to the more familiar swashbuckling Cavaliers of Europe need to be carefully explained. According to his own self-description, Morton was the university educated son of a soldier, devoted to the British crown and old English ways, and a staunch supporter of the Church of England, its liturgy, and its holy days.

His portrait of the Indians is an attempt to show how, despite their uncivilized state, they share many values with the traditional Englishmen whom he takes to be his audience. The Indians' personal modesty, hospitality to strangers, respect for authority, and even religious views mirror those of England, and their contentment surpasses that of the English because of their greater closeness to nature. They are swashbucklers without the trappings of Europe, indulging in pleasures because they are natural and upholding authority because it allows indulgence.

By contrast, the Pilgrims appear to be ill-educated rabble-rousers who despise all tradition and authority. Devoid even of common humanity, they serve their own self-glorifying appetites and deny the bounty that nature has left open to all.

Questions for Reading and Discussion/ Approaches to Writing

Morton is best read beside Bradford to bring out the full contrast between their views of Cavaliers, Indians, and Pilgrims. Morton also provides an interesting contrast in style to Bradford. Both works are highly rhetorical, but where Bradford uses his rhetoric to magnify God and humbly to minimize his poor persecuted people, Morton uses his to satirize those same people and to flaunt the superiority of his own wit and learning. All students should be able to pick out the clear cases of Morton's fictionalizing, especially in the account of Standish's response to Morton's escape, and some may see how he uses *Don Quixote* and medieval romance to shape his own mock-romance.

The contrast between Morton and Bradford can serve not only to establish the relative credibility of the two authors and the nature of their rhetoric, but to raise important moral questions about the whole colonial endeavor, especially with respect to the Indians. Were the Pilgrims, for instance, inhumane in denying the Indians firearms? Did Morton display true humanity in encouraging the Indians, male and female, to party with him and his men? To what extent could both groups be called hypocritical? Did British culture corrupt natural Indian ways or did Indian ways corrupt in different ways both the industrious Pilgrims and the pleasure-loving Cavaliers? Can the meeting of two such different cultures ever bring out the best in both, especially when each is itself divided into tribes or factions? Such questions rise naturally from much of colonial literature but perhaps most glaringly from Morton's work.

John Winthrop (1588–1649)

Contributing Editor: Nicholas D. Rombes, Jr.

Classroom Issues and Strategies

The sweeping nature of the journal encompasses social, political, economic, and "daily survival" issues. Thus, it might be wise to focus on an area, or areas, at least to begin with. When looking at cultural or historical implications, consult supplemental information. That is, although Winthrop's writings illuminate his biases and assumptions, they "shape" the history of the period as well as record it.

Students are generally shocked by the rigidity of Winthrop's view of the world. Their shock may be addressed by consulting outside sources (e.g., on the Hutchinson affair) and making them aware of Winthrop's assumptions concerning power, patriarchy, etc., as well as the position and voice of women in the Puritan community. However, it might be wise to note, as well, how our twentieth-century notions of what is fair and unfair can sometimes impose themselves upon the cultural environment Winthrop was operating within. Winthrop and the Puritans should be approached not only as philosophical, political, and religious figures, but also as real people who struggled daily against nature, hunger, and disease.

Students are often curious about the distinctions between the Covenant of Works, the Covenant of Grace, and the Elect. You might explore the notion of community and social structures and the role of the individual in these structures, or you could discuss the Bible as a typological model for the Puritans, as well as Puritan conceptions of original depravity, limited atonement, grace, and predestination.

Major Themes, Historical Perspectives, and Personal Issues

Certainly, based on the selections in this anthology, it would be fruitful to focus on the Hutchinson controversy and its implications for the Puritan oligarchy. Examine the early Puritans' conception of liberty and its inextricable connections with their obligation to God. Likewise, the notion of a "city upon a hill" and the Puritans' link between America and the "new Israel" is important. You could discuss as well the providential interpretation of events and the nature of hierarchy in the Puritan community.

Significant Form, Style, or Artistic Conventions

Winthrop had training as a lawyer; the style and form of *A Modell of Christian Charity* reflects this. Likewise, the entire self-reflexive nature of the Journal lends itself to examination: Who was Winthrop's audience? Where does the Journal belong in the convention of the personal narrative or spiritual autobiography? What was his purpose for writing?

Original Audience

Recent examinations of *A Modell of Christian Charity* suggest that the sermon was not only intended for those who would soon be settling in America, but also for those who were growing weary (and by implication becoming disruptive) during the long voyage aboard the *Arbella*. In what ways was Winthrop's audience (especially in the Journal) himself?

Comparisons, Contrasts, Connections

Perhaps compare Winthrop's sermons with those of Jonathan Edwards (who was writing a century later). Note how the style changed, as did the emphasis on religious experience (the experience becomes more sensory and less restrained). Compare Winthrop's vision of God's grace with Roger Williams's vision.

Questions for Reading and Discussion/
Approaches to Writing

1. (a) What motivated the Puritans to flee England?
   (b) Did the Puritans have a "blueprint" for organizing their new communities, or did the social structure evolve slowly?
   (c) From what type of social, cultural, religious, and economic background did Winthrop emerge?
2. (a) Examine Winthrop's 1645 speech in which he responds to charges that he exceeded his authority as governor. Is this speech a fruition (or expression) of the Puritan ambiguity between the value of religion and the value of individual liberty?
   (b) How did the Hutchinson controversy potentially threaten the Puritan oligarchy?

(c) Explore the "spiritual autobiography" and its characteristics. What philosophical purposes did it serve? What pragmatic purposes?

(d) In *Modell*, have students trace image patterns Winthrop uses, i.e., allusions to Biblical passages, discursive form of sermon, etc.

Bibliography

Dunn, Richard S. "John Winthrop Writes his Journal." *William and Mary Quarterly* 41 (1984): 185–212.

Miller, Perry. *Errand into the Wilderness*. Cambridge: Harvard University Press, 1956. (Essays)

Morgan, Edmund S. "John Winthrop's 'Modell of Christian Charity' in a Wider Context." *The Huntington Library Quarterly* 50 (Winter 1987): 145–51.

Rutman, Darrett B. *Winthrop's Boston: A Portrait of a Puritan Town, 1630–1649*. Chapel Hill: University of North Carolina Press, 1965. (Look especially at Chapter I, "A City upon a Hill"; Chapter III, "The Emergence of Town Government"; and Chapter VI, "Diversity and Division."

William Bradford (1590–1657)

Contributing Editor: Phillip Gould

Classroom Issues and Strategies

Bradford's history at once perpetuates and demystifies the mythic status that mainstream American culture has bestowed upon the "Pilgrims" of New England. This might be a useful place to start: the ways in which Bradford's narrative mythologizes first-generation heroism, and yet exposes the all-too-human squabbling, selfishness, and greed of the Plymouth settlers.

The tension between Bradford's desire to construct a place for Plymouth in a divine historical plan, and his eventual, implicit recognition of the diminution of Plymouth's status, lends itself to discussion of the nature of history-writing in general. This tension, which involves

Bradford's painful negotiation of correctly reading providential design, shows students how the supposedly objective genre of "history," like all forms of narrative, is a construction of prevailing ideologies.

As in Winthrop's *Journal, Of Plymouth Plantation*'s account of the quotidian realities of a frontier society dismantles the quasi-Victorian stereotypes that students bring to the concept of the "Puritan" (or, in this case, the Separatist). As a text composed, for all intents and purposes, on the frontier, students might consider how this historical reality also shapes Bradford's treatment of Amerindians.

The issue of Bradford's composition of his history may raise issues about the coherence of the text. Do students see distinctive subjects, thematic motifs, or narrative tones in each of the two parts?

Major Themes, Historical Perspectives, and Personal Issues

The concept of community pervades the entire text of Bradford. The history demonstrates the problematic maintenance of the national covenant—the community's collective dedication to live by the purity of God's ordinances—as a parallel to the covenant of grace, by which each individual "saint" was redeemed (through Christ) by belief itself. Ironically enough, the logical extension of a "covenanted" people was a communitarian enterprise that at first simulated a kind of socialism, one which soon proved to be untenable. In Bradford's account of this minor crisis lies (as in a well crafted novel) a foreshadowing of the eventual dispersal and fragmentation that later beset the colony. In this context, *Of Plymouth Plantation* recounts both the internal (material greed, "wickedness") and external (Thomas Morton, the Pequod—so far as Bradford perceives them) threats that constantly besieged the community.

The relationship between sacred and secular history, if theologically reconcilable, poses another thematic tension in the text. Bradford's insistence upon the "special providences" of God (those reserved for the elect in times of crisis) exists in counterpoise with the detailed catalogues of human negotiations, contrivances, and machinations that describe daily life in England and America.

Some scholars believe that Bradford's wife committed suicide while awaiting disembarkment from the *Mayflower*. This personal tragedy, along with the cycles of disappointment and success that Bradford underwent, and the constant struggle to maintain the communitarian ideal, all raise the issue of his narrative tone. The text modulates tenors of resolve, sadness, and humility.

Significant Form, Style, or Artistic Conventions

Of Plymouth Plantation exemplifies, perhaps as well as any colonial New England text, the aesthetic virtues of the "plain style." The simplicity of its syntactic rhythms and the concreteness of its imagery and tropes demonstrate the rhetorical power of understatement. The plain style theoretically reflected the need to erase the self (which Bradford also achieves in referring to himself as "the governor") in the very act of creation, by having one's words stylistically approach the biblical Word of God. Bradford's history, however, shows students how the theological rigors of Puritan thought nonetheless allowed for distinctive "voices" to emerge, in this case, Bradford's uniquely compassionate, humble, and sometimes embittered one.

The issue of Puritan typology—which read the Old Testament not only as a prefiguring of the New Testament, but of contemporary history as well—is also somewhat problematic in Bradford's history. The correlation, in other words, between the Old Testament Hebrews and the Plymouth "saints" is not a stable one. For example, when Bradford alludes to Mount Pisgah in chapter IX, he, in effect, suggests a distinction between the Israelites' Promised Land and the wild terrors of New England.

Original Audience

The private nature of Bradford's history and its delayed publication in the nineteenth century complicate the issue of the text's reception. A close reading, however, suggests that Bradford appeared to have envisioned multiple audiences for the text. As certain scholars have noted, the narrative seems to be addressed to lukewarm Anglicans at home, the remaining Scrooby Congregation, members of the larger Massachusetts Bay colony, and, perhaps most visibly, to members of the second generation who had strayed from the founders' original vision.

Moreover, students might be reminded that, despite its delayed publication, the manuscript significantly influenced a number of later New England historians such as Nathaniel Morton, Cotton Mather, and Thomas Prince.

Comparisons, Contrasts, Connections

Although the latter sections of Winthrop's *Journals* were written retrospectively, *Of Plymouth Plantation* provides a useful distinction between a retrospective narrative and an ongoing chronicle of historical events.

Bradford's relatively austere prose style, as well as his problematic moments in interpreting providence—and thus the meaning of New England—contrasts strikingly with the productions of Cotton Mather. These distinctions help to prevent students' tendencies to see "Puritanism" as a monolith. There are parallels, however, between Bradford's mythologizing of first-generation founders like Brewster and John Robinson and the kind of biography Cotton Mather conducts in the *Magnalia*.

Bradford's history is an early instance of themes prevalent in American immigration and frontier literatures. The cycles of struggle, survival, and declension characterize, for example, a much later writer—such as Willa Cather, who was far removed from Puritan New England. The instability of community in these genres make for a line of thematic continuity between Bradford and writers of frontier romance such as Catharine Maria Sedgwick and James Fenimore Cooper.

Bibliography

Cressy, David. *Coming Over: Migration and Communication Between England and New England in the Seventeenth Century*. Cambridge: Cambridge University Press, 1987.

Daly, Robert. "William Bradford's Vision of History." *American Literature* 44 (1973): 557–69.

Howard, Alan B. "Art and History in Bradford's *Of Plymouth Plantation*." *William and Mary Quarterly*, 3rd ser., 28 (1971): 237–66.

Levin, David. "William Bradford: The Value of Puritan Historiography." *Major Writers of Early American Literature*, ed. Everett Emerson, 11–31. Madison: University of Wisconsin Press, 1972.

Wenska, Walter P. "Bradford's Two Histories." *Early American Literature* 8 (1978): 151–64.

Roger Williams (1603?–1683)

Contributing Editor: Raymond F. Dolle

Classroom Issues and Strategies

Williams was a controversialist who used his Cambridge training in medieval disputation to compose prolix, rhetorical, erudite arguments, supported with biblical and classical allusions and quotations. This style and complex syntax (often rambling, gnarled, and incomplete) is difficult for today's undergraduate to follow. The problem is often compounded by Williams's Puritan theology, formal subject matter, and didactic religious purpose.

The selections in this anthology avoid much of Williams's most opaque prose, such as that in his most frequently anthologized tract, *The Bloody Tenent*. These selections exemplify the logic and structure of Williams's thought, and so allow us to appreciate the radical vision and hear the distinctive voice of America's most famous religious dissenter despite our problems with his language. Once students understand that Williams represents an early expression of the American ideals of religious toleration, equal rights, and individual freedom, they are usually willing to make the effort to read his writings.

Students admire Williams's rebellion against authority and his argument for individual liberty of conscience. Although they may not understand his religious beliefs, they respect his courage and determination to stand up for what he believed.

The satire of so-called "Christians" and "civilization" never fails to amuse students, many of whom see themselves as virtuous pagans. They should be encouraged to speculate on what Williams would think about modern America.

Parallels between the Indians' religious beliefs and Christian concepts often surprise students and stimulate discussion of the nature of religion.

Williams's apparent toleration of personal religious differences often confuses students because it seems to contradict his radical and extreme Puritanism. Students must be reminded that his acceptance into his colony of such sects as the Quakers does not mean he thought that their beliefs were acceptable. Rather, he believed that the free search for Truth and the liberty to argue one's beliefs would lead the elect to God.

Major Themes, Historical Perspectives, and Personal Issues

In order to understand the conflict between Williams and the Puritan leaders that led to his banishment, we need to understand the three extreme positions he expounded:

1. Civil magistrates should have no jurisdiction over religious matters, and Christian churches should be absolutely divorced from worldly concerns (i.e., separation of church and state)—a position destructive to the prevailing theocracy of Massachusetts Bay and Plymouth. The elect had to be free to seek God as they believed right. His letter "To the Town of Providence" refutes the *reductio ad absurdum* charge that this position leads ultimately to political anarchy if individuals can claim liberty of conscience to refuse civil obedience.

2. The Puritans should all become Separatists because the Church of England was associated too closely with political authority—a position that jeopardized the charter and the relative freedom it granted.

3. The Massachusetts Bay Company charter should be invalidated since Christian kings have no right to dispose of Indian lands—a position again based on separation of spiritual and material prerogatives. Williams was a friend of the Narragansett Indians, a defender of their legal property rights, and an admirer of their natural virtue. He devoted much of his life to understanding their language and culture so that he could teach them about Christ. An "implicit dialogue" intended to bridge cultures for their mutual benefit, *A Key* exploits the paradoxical contrast between barbaric civility and English degeneracy. The savages had to be Christianized, but this colonizing process often had tragic effects. The importance of bringing knowledge of Christ to the Indians, despite this dilemma, created one of the central conflicts in Williams's life.

The banishment of Williams from the colony reflects basic conflicts and concerns in the patriarchal Puritan society of colonial New England. The community leaders felt an urgent need to maintain authority and orthodoxy in order to preserve the "city on a hill" they had founded. Any challenge to their authority undermined the Puritan mission and threatened the New Canaan they had built with such suffering. Of course, the zeal and pure devotion needed to continue the efforts of the founding fathers were too much to ask of most colonists, so consequently their congregational social structure began to fracture almost before it was established. Not only did secular attractions, worldly concerns, and

material opportunities distract immigrants, but also the strict requirements for church membership denied many full status in the community. Like Anne Hutchinson, Williams advocated attractive individualistic
principles that threatened the prevailing system, and he was banished
from Christ's kingdom in America in an attempt to hold the community
of saints together.

Significant Form, Style, or Artistic Conventions

One of the most appealing rhetorical devices in these selections is
Williams's use of analogy, metaphors, and emblems. The introduction to
A Key (in fact, the title itself) invites attention to such figurative language, as in the proverb, "A little key may open a box, where lies a
bunch of keys." The meaning and implications of such statements are
fruitful points for class discussion. Other good examples are the ship
metaphor in the letter to Providence and the emblematic poems at the
end of the chapters in *A Key*.

Throughout *A Key*, especially in the General Observations, the
satiric contrast between true natural virtue and false Christianity creates
a tension that invigorates the text and makes it a unique example of the
promotional tract tradition.

The catechism in the vocabulary lists is worth attention.

Original Audience

Although Williams usually wrote with particular readers in mind, his
themes and subjects have universal relevance and can still reward readers today.

Williams tells us that he intended *A Key* "specially for my friends
residing in those parts." In other words, he wants to instruct fellow missionaries and traders how to interact with his other friends, the Indians.
He is determined to dispel the stereotypes and false conceptions of them
as subhuman savages current in the early colonies. Images of the Indians
in writings from Williams's contemporaries and earlier explorers should
provide students with a clear sense of the audience, their assumptions,
and their needs. Williams has much to say still about interracial understanding, respect, and harmony. Moreover, his observations are still
keen insights into human nature.

The audience for the letter to Providence is again quite specific,
with a particular misconception and need. Williams writes to settle a
controversy over freedom of conscience and civil obedience. Again, this
controversy is still alive, and we can consider Williams's statement in

light of the writings on the subject by such men as Thoreau and Martin Luther King.

Comparisons, Contrasts, Connections

Williams's descriptions of the Indians can be compared to descriptions in many other texts, ranging from the orthodox Puritan attitudes toward the satanic savages, as in Mary Rowlandson's captivity narrative, to eighteenth- and nineteenth-century Romantic tributes to the Noble Savage.

Similarly, Williams is often seen as a forerunner of Jefferson and Jackson, but we must remember that he did not advocate liberty as an end in itself for political reasons, but rather as a means to seek God.

Questions for Reading and Discussion/ Approaches to Writing

1. (a) What can we infer about Williams's intentions from the fact that he chose to compose *A Key into the Language of America* as an "implicit dialogue" rather than as a dictionary?
   (b) Characterize the persona of the first-person narrator in *A Key*. What kind of person does Williams present himself as?
   (c) How is Williams's book like a key?
   (d) How do the various sections of each chapter in *A Key* relate to one another and to the whole work?
   (e) What lessons can a Christian learn from the Indians?
   (f) Why might Williams once have objected to Europe and the rest of the West being referred to as "Christendom"?
   (g) In what ways was a colony in the New World like a ship at sea?
   (h) What did Williams gain from his treaty with the Indians besides legal ownership of some land?
2. An anthology as innovative as *The Heath Anthology* calls for innovative pedagogy and assignments. Here are some alternatives to the traditional junior-level LITCRIT papers:
   (a) Personal Response Paper: Ask the students to compare one or more of Williams's observations to their own experiences and observations.
   (b) Creative Response Paper: Ask the students to write a letter back to Williams by a spokesman for the town of Providence refuting Williams's argument and defending the right to act as one believes one's religious beliefs demand.

(c) Creative Research Paper: Assign supplemental readings from Winslow's biography of Williams (or other sources) related to his trial and banishment. Then ask the students to compose a transcript of the trial proceedings.

Bibliography

In addition to the books listed at the end of the headnote in *The Heath Anthology*, many useful articles on Williams are available. Here are some of the most recent:

Brotherston, Gordon. "A Controversial Guide to the Language of America, 1643." In *Literature and Power in the Seventeenth Century*, edited by Francis Barker, et al. 84–100. University of Essex, 1981.

Felker, Christopher D. "Roger Williams's Uses of Legal Discourse: Testing Authority in Early New England." *New England Quarterly* 63 (1990): 624–48.

Guggisberg, Hans R. "Religious Freedom and the History of the Christian World in Roger Williams' Thought." *Early American Literature* 12, no. 1 (Spring 1977): 36–48.

LaFantasie, Glenn W. "Roger Williams: The Inner and Outer Man." *Canadian Review of American Studies* 16 (1985): 375–94.

Peace, Nancy E. "Roger Williams—A Historiographical Essay." *Rhode Island History* 35 (1976): 103–13.

Teunissen, John J. and Evelyn J. Hinz. "Anti-Colonial Satire in Roger Williams' *A Key into the Language of America*." *Ariel: A Review of International English Literature* 7, no. 3 (1976): 5–26.

——. "Roger Williams, Thomas More, and the Narragansett Utopia." *Early American Literature* 11, no. 3 (Winter 1976–1977): 281–95.

Other sources published prior to 1974 can be located by using Wallace Coyle's *Roger Williams: A Reference Guide* (Boston: G. K. Hall, 1977).

Anne Bradstreet (1612?–1672)

Contributing Author: Pattie Cowell

Classroom Issues and Strategies

There are many ways to approach Bradstreet: as a "first" (given that she is the first North American to publish a book of poems), as a Puritan, as a woman. I've found an interplay of all three approaches useful for piquing student interest. Those who are skeptical of my feminist readings may be caught by historical and cultural perspectives. Those who think they want nothing to do with Puritanism may be intrigued by Bradstreet's more personal writings.

Beginning students are generally unfamiliar with the historical and theological contexts in which she wrote. Many close off their reading of Bradstreet and other Puritan writers because they disapprove of what they think they know about Puritan theology. Brief background materials make that context more accessible and less narrowly theological.

Again for reasons of accessibility, I usually begin with the more personal poems from the second edition. The poignancy of Bradstreet's elegies, the simplicity of her love poems, the stark reality of her poem on childbirth, the wit of "The Author to Her Book"—all travel across the centuries with relative ease, even for less skilled readers. When these immediately readable poems are placed in the context of women's lives in the seventeenth century and in the North American colonies, most students find a point of entry.

Major Themes, Historical Perspectives, and Personal Issues

Thematically, Bradstreet's body of work is both extensive and varied. Teachers will find much that can be linked with other materials in a given course. Bradstreet wrote on culture and nature, on spirituality and theology, on the tension between faith and doubt, on family, on death, on history. I like to suggest the range of her subject matter for students and then concentrate on a single thematic thread (though the thread I choose varies with my interests of the moment). It is a strategy that helps students follow their own interests of the moment at the same time that it allows us (by close reading) to see the skills Bradstreet had developed. "Contemplations" is a fine poem for tracing both thematic threads and poetic technique, though its length and complexity present problems for beginning students. "The Prologue" is more manageable in a single class session, short enough to allow multiple readings to develop but complex enough to tantalize. Many of the other short personal pieces—well represented in *The Heath Anthology* selections—work effectively with this approach too.

The remarkable nature of Bradstreet's accomplishment is highlighted when students learn the historical conditions women poets struggled with. Women who wrote stepped outside their appropriate sphere, and those who published their work frequently faced social censure. The Reverend Thomas Parker, a minister in Newbury, Massachusetts, gives a succinct statement of cultural attitudes in an open letter to his sister, Elizabeth Avery, in England: "Your printing of a book, beyond the custom of your sex, doth rankly smell" (1650). Compounding this social pressure, many women faced crushing workloads and struggled with lack of leisure for writing. Others suffered from unequal access to education. Some internalized the sense of intellectual inferiority offered to them from nearly every authoritative voice.

Bradstreet's personal situation gave her the means to cope with some of these obstacles. Before she came to North America, she received an extensive education; she had access as a child to private tutors and the Earl of Lincoln's large library. She was part of an influential, well-to-do family that encouraged her writing and circulated it in manuscript with pride. Her brother-in-law, John Woodbridge, took the manuscript collection to London for publication. Such private support did much to counteract the possibility of public disapproval.

Significant Form, Style, or Artistic Conventions

Bradstreet's attention to form and technique is usefully studied in the context of two quite different aesthetics, both of which influence her: Puritanism's so-called "plain style" (marked by didactic intent, artful simplicity, accessibility, and an absence of rhetorical ornamentation) and seventeenth-century versions of classicism (which stressed poetry as imitation, exalted the genres of tragedy and epic, and worked toward unity of action, place, and time).

Original Audience

Discussions of seventeenth-century English and New English audiences allow room for fruitful digressions on colonial literacy, manuscript culture, print culture, publishing, and book distribution. I frequently challenge beginning students to develop a description of Bradstreet's original readers by exercising their historical imaginations. Those who haven't read much history keep running into the barriers I set for them, but the exercise is useful nonetheless. They begin to "see" the circumstances of literate and literary culture in an environment that is sparsely populated, with only a fledgling publishing and book distribution establishment, without libraries, with books as relatively expensive luxuries.

Having imagined how Bradstreet's poems might have fared with her original audience, I ask students to compare themselves with those readers. How well do her themes and strategies travel across time? What elements seem to connect to contemporary concerns? What fails to relate? Why?

Comparisons, Contrasts, Connections

Bradstreet can usefully be read in relation to

- other Puritan writers, especially the poet Edward Taylor.
- contemporary British women writers, such as Katherine Philips.
- the Mexican nun Sor Juana Ines de la Cruz (Bradstreet's contemporary, also heralded as "the tenth muse").
- Phillis Wheatley. Because Wheatley wrote more than a century later, from a Black perspective and in a neoclassical tradition, she provides points of sharp contrast. But on certain themes (humility, the importance of spirituality), their voices merge.

Bibliography

Caldwell, Patricia. "Why Our First Poet Was a Woman: Bradstreet and the Birth of an American Poetic Voice." *Prospects* 13 (1988): 1–35.

Cowell, Pattie and Ann Stanford, eds. *Critical Essays on Anne Bradstreet.* Boston: G. K. Hall, 1983.

Eberwein, Jane Donahue. " 'No Ret'ric We Expect': Argumentation in Bradstreet's 'The Prologue.' " In *Critical Essays on Anne Bradstreet,* edited by Pattie Cowell and Ann Stanford, 218–25. Boston: G. K. Hall, 1983.

Kopacz, Paula. " 'Men can doe best, and women know it well': Anne Bradstreet and Feminist Aesthetics." *Kentucky Philological Review* 2 (1987): 21–29.

Richardson, Robert D., Jr. "The Puritan Poetry of Anne Bradstreet." In *Critical Essays on Anne Bradstreet,* edited by Pattie Cowell and Ann Stanford, 101–15. Boston: G. K. Hall, 1983.

Schweitzer, Ivy. "Anne Bradstreet Wrestles with the Renaissance." *Early American Literature* 23 (1988): 291–312.

Stanford, Ann. "Anne Bradstreet: Dogmatist and Rebel." In *Critical Essays on Anne Bradstreet,* edited by Pattie Cowell and Ann Stanford, 76–88. Boston: G. K. Hall, 1983.

White, Elizabeth Wade. "The Tenth Muse—A Tercentenary Appraisal of Anne Bradstreet." In *Critical Essays on Anne Bradstreet,* edited by Pattie Cowell and Ann Stanford, 55–75. Boston: G. K. Hall, 1983.

Michael Wigglesworth (1631–1705)

Contributing Editor: Jeffrey A. Hammond

Classroom Issues and Strategies

Students usually find *The Day of Doom* both accessible and puzzling. Although the poem is easy to follow, they are baffled by its popularity in early New England. Their confusion provides an excellent entry into the question of why most Puritans wrote and read poetry. Getting students to see that reading pleasure has meant very different things at different times is an important result of studying Wigglesworth's best-seller. This in turn will help students see that *their* reading expectations and responses also exist within a cultural, historical, and ideological moment. A related classroom issue is the degree to which Puritan popular art reveals the dominant values of early New England culture. *The Day of Doom* might help students consider the degree and manner in which various forms of popular art fulfill a similar function today.

Major Themes, Historical Perspectives, and Personal Issues

Students might be asked to consider the poem in light of the Puritan sense of historical mission, Puritan views of the self in relation to redemptive frameworks, the sense of community fostered by the poem, and the relation of Wigglesworth's themes to the Restoration in England. Students should also consider the situational or performative dimension of a poem that was written for the widest possible readership and often read aloud in families.

Significant Form, Style, or Artistic Conventions

Like all Puritan popular artists, Wigglesworth designed his poem to provide much the same aesthetic "pleasure" as a sermon. Once we recognize this, the central question becomes his effectiveness in trying to instill repentance in his readers. A good place to start is characterization. Not surprisingly, students are usually appalled by the harshness of Wigglesworth's Christ. But the portrayal makes sense within the religious ideology voiced by the poem: Christ appears here in the role of doomsday Judge, a role in which mercy was theologically inappropriate. Puritans insisted that to the rude and headstrong, Christ would be every bit as uncompromising as he seems in the poem, especially at doomsday, when the opportunity to repent and believe had passed. The harsh Christ *in* the poem was designed to push receptive readers toward the merciful Christ who existed *outside the poem,* the Advocate who still offered them a chance to repent. In addition, Wigglesworth's portrayal of the debating sinners would have produced contrition within readers who recognized echoes of their own worst thoughts in the poem.

Original Audience

Wigglesworth's choice of ballad meter is an important reflection of his sense of audience. Illness prompted him to preach through poetry, and his sing-song meter reflects a highly democratic definition of his readership. Many readers of the poem were actually "hearers" of it, for whom the poem offered a systematic treatment of theology that was easy to follow. The poem was used for many years as a verse catechism; there were reportedly people still alive during the American Revolution who had memorized it as children.

Comparisons, Contrasts, Connections

In terms of purpose, language, readership, and effect, the poem may be profitably compared and contrasted with the equally "public" Bay Psalm Book and Puritan sermons, with the more personal lyrics of Taylor and Bradstreet, with the poems in "A Selection of Seventeenth-Century Poetry," and even with Milton's more allusive treatment of similar themes.

Questions for Reading and Discussion/Approaches to Writing

1. Why does Wigglesworth stick so close to the Bible, in some cases offering virtual paraphrases of his biblical sources?
2. How does the poem embody dichotomistic structures reflected in the Puritan view of the Old and New Testaments, the Law and the Gospel, and the Covenant of Works and the Covenant of Grace?
3. What does the poem suggest about how texts were used in Puritan culture?
4. In what ways does the poem link the private framework of personal salvation with the communal mission of the Puritans in New England?
5. How does Wigglesworth connect eschatology (the redemptive future) with psychology (the reader's current response)?
6. How does the poem—in both form and content—reflect Wigglesworth's conception of audience?

Bibliography

Bosco, Ronald A. "Introduction," *The Poems of Michael Wigglesworth*, edited by Ronald A. Bosco, ix–xliii. University Press of America, 1989.

Crowder, Richard. " 'The Day of Doom' as Chronomorph." *Journal of Popular Culture* 9 (1976): 948–59.

Daly, Robert. *God's Altar: The World and the Flesh in Puritan Poetry*. University of California Press, 1978.

Hammond, Jeffrey A. *Sinful Self, Saintly Self: The Puritan Experience of Poetry*. University of Georgia Press, 1993.

Pope, Alan H. "Petrus Ramus and Michael Wigglesworth: The Logic of Poetic Structure." In *Puritan Poets and Poetics: Seventeenth-Century American Poetry in Theory and Practice*, edited by Peter White. Pennsylvania State University Press, 1985.

The Bay Psalm Book (1640)

The New England Primer (1683?)

Contributing Editor: Jean Ferguson Carr

Classroom Issues and Strategies

Readers may assume that both of these texts are simply functional transmissions of doctrine and discipline, representing a narrow and dogmatic religious culture of merely antiquarian interest. Readers should be encouraged to question their prejudgments both about Puritan culture and about religious/educational texts, particularly texts that have many parts, that are written not by a single author but by a group representing broader cultural interests and values. They need to see these texts as an emergent culture's effort to formulate values that can be taught and maintained.

For example, in reading the psalms, it is useful to compare the *Bay Psalm Book* version with those of the King James translation or others, noting the choices made and the interpretation those choices represent. Also, in reading the primer, consider what those lessons suggest about not only what the culture authorized teachers to enforce, but what the culture feared or had difficulty controlling.

Students are often unnerved by the old-style spelling, but with a little practice they can read the material smoothly. Once they are comfortable with these external issues, they are often surprised and impressed by the frankness with which such topics as death, sin, and governmental punishment are treated.

Major Themes, Historical Perspectives, and Personal Issues

The psalm book reflects a concern about making worship contemporary, particular to their time and place and special circumstances as pilgrims to a new land. The book's design and production stress the belief that faith must be attended to on a daily basis by each individual. The small books, written in English and in contemporary verse forms, could be carried into the home and the place of work, their lessons repeated to ward off the dangers and temptations of life in a "wilderness." The primer recognizes the difficulties of remaining faithful and obedient, and it values learning as a way to preserve from one generation to another "that part, /which shall never decay," the cultural and religious values of the community which cannot be silenced by the state or death.

Significant Form, Style, or Artistic Conventions

John Cotton's preface is a fascinating document about translation, advocating use of the vernacular and defending "modern" poetry. The psalms are "contested" versions, retranslated to mark a cultural and religious difference from those versions widely used in Europe and England, as well as to distinguish the Massachusetts Bay Colony Puritans from the Plymouth Pilgrims, who used the Sternhold-Hopkins Psalter of 1562.

Original Audience

The psalm book, written and printed by the Puritans of Massachusetts Bay Colony in 1640, was designed to allow a whole congregation to sing psalms together in church and at home. Neither Cotton's essay nor the poems have been attended to by modern critics: the psalter has been generally treated as a simple "text" of antiquarian interest only. The primer was the chief educational text of the New England colonies for over a hundred years, from its first printing in 1683.

Comparisons, Contrasts, Connections

Melville's call for American readers to "boldly contemn all imitation, though it comes to us graceful and fragrant as the morning; and foster all originality, though, at first, it be crabbed and ugly as our own pine knots" ("Hawthorne and his Mosses," 1850) suggests how the psalms and Cotton's preface might usefully be reread. The *Bay Psalm Book* can be compared with the literary credos of Emerson and Whitman, which prefer originality over literary polish or imitative technical perfection. The primer could be used to frame discussions about attitudes toward learning and childhood, toward the propagation of cultural values through books. It serves as a useful anthology of cultural concerns to compare with such later textbooks as McGuffey's *Eclectic Readers* or Webster's *American Speller*.

Questions for Reading and Discussion/
Approaches to Writing

1. (a) Compare two versions of a psalm (perhaps King James, Isaac Watts, Bay Psalm, or a modern version). What do the changes suggest about what is valued by the translator? What do they suggest about how the translator understands the difficulties or possibilities of faith?

   (b) What does John Cotton's preface propose as the important considerations for poetry and religious song? What established values is he thus opposing?

   (c) What seem to be the daily conditions of life for the readers of the primer, as exemplified in the lessons' details? What did they have to fear or to overcome?

   (d) How does the primer envision the relationship of parent to child? Of state to citizen? Of God to person?

   (e) How do the lessons demark proper social relations? How do they suggest the community's ability to contain crime or misbehavior?

   (f) How does the primer propose to shape (control?) speech and writing?

2. (a) Compare the claims about poetry and national literature in Cotton's preface to one of the following texts: Emerson's "The Poet," Whitman's "Preface" to *Leaves of Grass*, Rebecca Harding Davis's *Life in the Iron Mills*, Melville's "Hawthorne and his Mosses."

   (b) Discuss how *The New England Primer* represents both the importance and difficulty of learning cultural values and behavior.

   (c) Compare *The New England Primer* as a cultural artifact with a contemporary textbook for children. What seem to be the fears each text guards against? What does each text presuppose about childhood and children? How do they represent the relationship of school to children, of parents to children? What do they propose as the proper subjects for children?

Bibliography

Eames, W., ed. *The Bay Psalm Book* (Facsimile), 1903.

Ford, Paul, ed. *The New England Primer* (Facsimile and introduction, pp. 1–53). New York: Teachers College Press, 1962.

Nietz, John. *Old Textbooks*. Pittsburgh: University of Pittsburgh Press, 1961.

Watters, David H. " 'I Spoke as a Child': Authority, Metaphor, and *The New England Primer*." *Early American Literature* 20: 193–213.

Mary White Rowlandson (1637?–1711)

Contributing Editor: Paula Uruburu

Classroom Issues and Strategies

The narrative is best approached from several perspectives, including literary (what makes it a work of literature?); historical (where does fact mix with fiction?); and psychological (what factors may be affecting Rowlandson's interpretation of her experience?).

Students respond well to the personal diary-like quality of the narrative and the trials Rowlandson undergoes. Although most side with her, some also recognize the hardships the Indians have experienced at the hands of the colonists.

Major Themes, Historical Perspectives, and Personal Issues

It is important for the students to get the straight historical facts about King Phillip's War, during which Rowlandson was taken captive. This allows them to see both sides of the issues that caused the "war" and to better understand the Indians' plight as well as Rowlandson's reaction to her eleven-week captivity.

Significant Form, Style, or Artistic Conventions

Discussion of the Indian captivity narrative as a genre is essential. Also, a background on Puritan sermons and their reliance upon the Word in the Bible is important since the movement/structure of the narrative juxtaposes real events with biblical comparisons or equivalents.

Original Audience

We discuss how the Puritans would have responded to the narrative and why Rowlandson wrote it. I ask students for their own reaction (with whom does their sympathy lie—the settlers or the Indians?). We then look at Benjamin Franklin's essay "Some Remarks Concerning the Savages of North America" for an ironic comparison/contrast and then discuss the changes in perception from his time until now.

Feminist perspective: In what ways does this narrative lend itself to a greater understanding of the woman's place in Puritan history? How does being a woman affect Rowlandson's point of view?

Comparisons, Contrasts, Connections

Using Bradstreet's poetry (especially "Some Verses Upon the Burning of our House") and Winthrop's sermon, give two different views of the details and effects of covenant theology on ordinary people's lives and how they were expected to respond to traumatic or trying events and circumstances.

Questions for Reading and Discussion/
Approaches to Writing

1. How does the *Narrative* demonstrate Puritan theology and thinking at work?
2. In what ways does Rowlandson use her experience to reaffirm Puritan beliefs? How does she view herself and her fellow Christians? How does she see the Indians? What do her dehumanizing descriptions of the Indians accomplish?
3. Are there any instances where she seems to waver in her faith?
4. Why does Rowlandson distrust the "praying Indians"?
5. How does she use the Bible and varied scriptural allusions in her analysis of her captivity and restoration?
6. Does her world view change at all during her eleven weeks of captivity? Why or why not?
7. How does the *Narrative* combine/demonstrate/refute what William Bradford in *Of Plymouth Plantation* and John Winthrop in *A Modell of Christian Charity* had to say about the Puritan's mission in the New World?

After addressing any number of the above questions, aimed at a basic analysis of the *Narrative*, an instructor can then continue with a discussion of the possible motives Rowlandson had for writing it. This

aspect appeals to students who are most interested in trying to understand the human being behind the prose.

1. Compare and contrast the Indian captivity narrative with the slave
   narrative genre. What elements and conventions do they share?
   How do they differ?
2. Explain how Rowlandson's narrative reinforces her world view.
   Where (if at all) does her covenant theology fail her or seem
   insufficient to explain actions and events?

Bibliography

Primary Sources

Van Der Beets, Richard. *Held Captive By the Indians: Selected Narratives
1642–1836*. Knoxville: University of Tennessee Press, 1973.

Secondary Sources

Burke, Charles. *Puritans at Bay*. New York: Exposition Press, 1967.

Drimmer, Frederick, ed. *Captured By the Indians*. New York: Dover, 1961.
A collection of fifteen firsthand accounts from 1750–1870.

Slotkin, Richard and James Folsom. *So Dreadful a Judgment*. Connecticut:
Wesleyan University Press, 1978. Puritan responses to King
Phillip's War.

Edward Taylor (1642?–1729)

Contributing Editor: Karen E. Rowe

Classroom Issues and Strategies

Students may recoil from Taylor's overly didactic, seemingly aesthetically rough or unpolished poetry, in part because he seems too preoccupied with issues of sin and salvation, which they find alien. The fundamental need is to familiarize students with basic Puritan concepts,
biblical sources and allusions, and the meditative tradition. This background allows students and teachers to move beyond the easy post-
Romantic definition of the poetry as "lyric," which locks the class into a
quick survey of only the occasional poems. Taylor may also seem both

too easy ("doesn't he tell it all?") and too complicated, because of arcane word choices, the curious compounding of images, and the plethora of biblical images.

The organization of selections in *The Heath Anthology* permits one for the first time to trace Taylor's chronological development as a poet and also emphasizes a more personalized Taylor. By clustering the *Meditations* and engaging students in playing with the multiple meanings of curious words, the poetry comes alive as an intricate orchestration of recurrent themes and interconnected images. The point is to capture Taylor's imaginative flexibility as much as his tortured angst, while at the same time seeing it all as part of an overriding concern with personal preparation for heaven and with how Taylor as poet can best serve God—and in what language.

Students respond initially to the personal anguish and graphic degradations to which Taylor submits himself, yet they are also quick to recognize the pattern of self-abasement followed by Christ's intervention and re-elevation of humankind. Through class discussion, they revise their thinking about both the seeming lack of sophistication in Taylor's poetry and the dismissal of Puritan poets.

Major Themes, Historical Perspectives, and Personal Issues

Major, but different, themes and historical issues emerge from each selection. Metrical paraphrases of Psalms were acceptable "hymns" for Protestants, as reflected in the Massachusetts *Bay Psalm Book*, although Taylor models his poems on the earlier Sternhold-Hopkins Psalter. Important themes include Taylor's adoption of David as his model for the poet; the concept of poetry as an act/offering of ritual praise; distinctions between the godly (righteous) and ungodly; God's power as Creator and Lawgiver; the righteous man as the Lord's servant; Christ as a Rock and Redeemer; and God's voice as that which speaks truly, and which man's voice merely echoes. As Thomas Davis suggests, by "providing a means of fashioning his own experience in the framework of biblical and historical precedent, the paraphrases invited the poet to make poetry a central concern in his life," and with the emergence of an "authentic note of his own voice" point directly to the *Preparatory Meditations*.

Probably completed in 1680, *Gods Determinations* usefully introduces students to Taylor's major dilemmas as preacher and individual saint— how to ascertain *and* sustain the belief in one's place among God's Elect and what admissions standards to uphold for Church membership. In its historical context, *Gods Determinations* reflects Taylor's local need to found a frontier Church for the true Elect (1679). His battles were against both the wilderness and Indians without and Satan within. This mini-sequence from among the total of thirty-five poems allows one to talk about the difficult progress from conversion to justification and sanctification in two ways. A narrative reading opens with the magnificent evocation of God's creation, then the "Souls Groan" for salvation and "Christs Reply" as a lover or mother to a lost child counseling the soul to "Repent thy Sin" and accept Christ's purifying grace, followed by Satan's renewed attempts at casting doubt, and the final triumphant entry into "Church Fellowship rightly attended," whether on earth or in heaven. Hence, the poem becomes a narrative of a spiritual journey. Taylor's position is as narrator and as voice of the saint.

One can read the poems as a "debate," emphasizing various oppositions, between God and fallen man, the unworthy Elect soul and grace-giving Christ, the doubting soul and Satan the tempter, between Christ and Satan, hence between lowly earthly things and God's grandeur, being outside the covenant community of Elect saints and being within (the coach), between doubt and assurance, sin and salvation. The poems also anticipate later allegorical renderings of Christ's marital relationships with the Church and individual soul in terms of the Dove and the Bride, set off against images of Satan as a mongrel cur and his deceptive seductions, hence a battle between loving faith/grace and distorting reason.

The Occasional Poems, which include eight numbered poems, were probably begun in the early 1680s, just as Taylor had completed *Gods Determinations* and was initiating the second version of the Psalm paraphrases and the early *Preparatory Meditations*. Because these poems are the most "lyrical," they are more accessible to modern students. But what motivates Taylor is a desire to meditate upon natural "occurants" in order to extract allegorical or spiritual meanings.

Taylor's fondness for extended metaphors is apparent in "Upon a Spider Catching a Fly" and his famous "Huswifery." The latter leads to discussion of Taylor's frequent use of spinning and weaving terms, frequently in relationship to poetic language or the need for the "Wedden garment" of righteousness that robes mankind for the Lord's Supper and union with Christ. "Upon Wedlock, & Death of Children" reveals Taylor at his most personal and usefully links with other poems from *Edward Taylor's Minor Poetry*, which trace his domestic relationship with Elizabeth Fitch from his courtship (1674) to her death (1689).

"A Valediction to all the World preparatory for Death" permits comparisons among different versions, showing Taylor's substantial revision of late poems even during a time of severe illness. Although only two of the total eight canticles are included in *The Heath Anthology*, they nevertheless display Taylor in the process of shedding worldliness, particularly all things that appeal to the senses and sensualities of the flesh. His "farewell" to the world, the flesh, and the devil is renunciatory and poignant, a meditation on "vanity of vanities, all is vanity" (Ecclesiastes 12:6–8) that evokes the very fondness for created nature that he appears to abjure.

"A Fig for thee Oh! Death" expresses Taylor's defiance of death, and it is a *memento mori* meditation that should be placed side by side with his later Canticles poems, in which he envisions the beauties of heaven. His anticipation of the final judgment and reunion of body and soul gives rise to an ecstatic affirmation of faith in the divine promise of eternal life.

As a complete sequence, the poems selected here, together with those from the *Preparatory Meditations*, trace Taylor's preoccupations over a lifetime:

- from the early focus on creation to the later renunciation of earthly vanities
- from his earliest attempt to map the soul's conflicts with Satan to his later celebration of Church fellowship, the Lord's Supper, and Christ as the divine host
- from his domestic espousal to his spiritual union with Christ as the eternal Bridegroom
- from his questioning of poetic status to his desire to be another David or Solomon, singing hymns for all eternity
- from his entrance into the minister's life to his death—the end of a long preparation recorded in a virtual poetic autobiography

Significant Form, Style, or Artistic Conventions

Taylor's verse experiments range from the common meter of the Psalm paraphrases to the varied stanza and metrical forms in *Gods Determinations* and the Occasional Poems, and finally to the heroic couplets of "A Valediction to all the World preparatory for Death" and "A Fig for thee Oh! Death." Variety also appears in Taylor's choice of forms, including the Psalm paraphrases, a debate or narrative sequence of lyrics in *Gods Determinations*, elegies, love poems, a valediction and reflection on worldly vanities, and *memento mori*—all of which were commonplace among his English predecessors, such as John Donne, George Herbert, and Henry Vaughan. For a more in-depth study of form, students might be urged to read and compare Taylor's elegies on public figures with those on personal losses, such as "Upon Wedlock, & Death of Children" and "A Funerall Poem upon . . . Mrs. Elizabeth Taylor," all in *Edward Taylor's Minor Poetry*.

Taylor's form and style seem too predictable, because of the unchanging six-line, iambic pentameter, ababcc stanza of the *Preparatory Meditations*. Discussion should relate his use of a disciplined, even caged and controlled, verse form to his concept of poetry as ritualistic praise, as a rational framework within which to explore (and contain) irrational impulses of the rebellious soul, as a stimulus to imaginative imagistic variations, and as a habitual exercise of spiritual preparation. These poems are meditative self-examinations, illustrating the Puritan requirement to prepare the heart and soul before entering the Church or partaking of (and administering) the Lord's Supper. They also mediate between Taylor's composition and delivery of his Sacrament sermon.

Taylor's imagistic variations in the *Preparatory Meditations* permit one to teach him in different combinations and ways. Structurally, the poems reflect differing manipulations of image patterns, such as the focus on a single metaphor ("Prologue," 1.6, 1.8, 2.50); figural images and interpretations (1.8, 2.1, 2.26, 2.50, 2.60B); allegorical panoramas of salvation history (1.8, 2.50); associational tumblings of images (2.26, 2.43, 2.60B, 2.115); magnifications and diminutions ("Prologue," 2.43); and allegorical love poems that anatomize the Bridegroom's and Spouse's beauties (2.115).

Thematically, poems cluster around recurrent ideas, such as Christ's nature and life (1.8, 2.43, 2.60B, 2.115); man's nature and estate (1.6, 1.8, 2.1, 2.26, 2.50); Old Testament types (persons, events, ceremonies) that foreshadow New Testament fulfillments in Christ (2.1, 2.26, 2.50); the Lord's Supper as sacramental feast (1.8, 2.60B); the marriage of Christ to his Bride, signifying the Church and individual soul (2.115); and the necessity of poetic praise ("Prologue," 2.43). As a study of Puritan preparation and aesthetics, the meditations also reveal the motivating cause in Taylor's need to celebrate the Lord's Supper with a cleansed soul, robed in the wedding garment of righteousness for the feast (2.26, 2.60B, 2.115), and in poetry's function as spiritual purging and preparation ("Prologue," 2.43).

Chronologically, the *Meditations* move from the first series' dichotomy between mankind (a "Crumb," yet imprinted with the divine "Image, and Inscription") and the perfect Christ of the Incarnation ("Heavens Sugar Cake"). In keeping with a reorientation in Taylor's preaching, the second series begins anew with the Old Testament typology (2.1, 2.26). He then shifts to a Christological New Testament focus (2.43, 2.50) in poems corresponding to the *Christographia* sermons, then to Meditations on the Lord's Supper (2.60B, 2.102–111), and finally the

Canticles (2.115), Taylor's most sensual love poems, which anticipate the heavenly union beyond death (as also in the "Valediction").

Finally, the poems can be organized to reflect the context and progress of mankind's existence, beginning with the magnificent creation in the "Preface" to *Gods Determinations* and the providential schema mapped out in Meditation 2.50, shifting to man's fallen nature (2.1, 2.26) yet divine aspiration (1.6), the necessity of Christ's intervention through the incarnation (1.8, 2.1), shedding of blood (2.60B), and His eternal Godhead (2.43), and concluding with the anticipations of the espousal between Elect souls and Christ (2.115) and of the heavenly feast, which the Lord's Supper spiritually commemorates and foreshadows (1.8, 2.60B, "Valediction").

Original Audience

Taylor never published his poetry, although he carefully transcribed many poems in the manuscript "Poetical Works." A consideration of audience must, therefore, take account of the fact that the elegies and perhaps *Gods Determinations* were written in a more public mode, but that the majority of his Occasional Poems, the *Preparatory Meditations*, and the later "Valediction" and "A Fig for thee Oh! Death" are intensely personal, written it would seem for an audience of God or Christ alone, or as meditative self-examinations of Taylor's soul. As readers, we eavesdrop on Taylor, but we are not easily invited into the poems, except insofar as we identify with the Elect soul in its struggles or with Taylor as a representative pilgrim in his journey toward salvation.

Comparisons, Contrasts, Connections

Fruitful comparisons can be drawn both intratextually and extratextually. For the *Preparatory Meditations*, corresponding sermons are extant from *Upon the Types of the Old Testament* (Meditations 2.1, 2.26, 2.60B) and from the *Christographia* (Meditations 2.43, 2.50). Edward Taylor's *Treatise Concerning the Lord's Supper*, notably Sermon 4, yields excellent excerpts on the need to prepare for the Lord's Supper and the wearing of the "wedden garment" for the feast. Because Taylor habitually clusters poems on the same biblical text, providing students, for example, with all three Meditations (1.8–10) on John 6: 51, 55, "I am the Living Bread" and "My Blood is Drink indeed," contextualizes a reading of the selected Meditation 1.8 and of the Lord's Supper. Similarly, a short typological series, such as 2.58–61, permits a study of Taylor's fascination with the Exodus of Israel from Egypt as well as with the various types that foreshadow man's spiritual journey to salvation under the

New Testament, as well as a more specific contextualizing of Meditation 2.60B on the "Rock of Horeb." Meditations 2.102–111 combine a theological defense with a festal celebration of the Lord's Supper, and the Canticles series that opens with Meditation 2.115 yields many examples of Taylor's interpretation of sensual imagery.

Comparisons with George Herbert's *The Temple*, particularly poems on the types, with John Donne's sonnets on the Ascension, death, and Christ as Spouse, and of 2.24 and 2.50 with contemporary Christmas poems on the Incarnation by Herbert Southweld, and Milton enable students to identify different poetic styles and place Taylor in a broader seventeenth-century meditative tradition.

One might also compare Anne Bradstreet's "The Prologue" and "Author to her Book" with Taylor's meditations on poetic craft in "Were but my Muse an Huswife Good," the "Prologue" to the *Preparatory Meditations,* and Meditation 2.43. Bradstreet's "Vanity of all Worldly Things" and "The Flesh and the Spirit" complement Taylor's "Valediction," and her poems "In Reference to Her Children 23 June 1659" and "Before the Birth of One of her Children" work in tandem with Taylor's "Upon Wedlock, & Death of Children," as do Bradstreet's several elegies on various grandchildren ("In Memory of my Dear Grandchild Elizabeth Bradstreet" and "On my Dear Grandchild Simon Bradstreet"). Selections from the prose meditations of Bradstreet also provide an intriguing counterpoint to Taylor's poetic meditations.

Presentational and Strategic Approaches

It proves particularly helpful to provide students with background information about key Puritan concepts, some of which are detailed in the headnote for Edward Taylor's selections. Many of these should also be discussed in relationship to other Puritan texts. But one can also prepare handouts on areas such as the concept of typology by listing Taylor's sermons and poems on the types (see *Saint and Singer*); a diagram of Israel's tabernacle and temple, its furnishings, the role of the High Priest, and the significant ceremonies; excerpts from a good Bible dictionary on major biblical figures or events; or predistributed excerpts from key biblical passages related to a poem's imagery. Visual arts only approximate the verbal, but Vaughan's emblem of the stony heart from *Silex Scintillans* for "The Ebb & Flow" or Renaissance paintings of death's heads ("A Fig"), worldly vanities and the heavenly Paradise ("Valediction"), Christ, and the Lord's Supper instructively guide textual analysis. A diagram labeling parts of the spinning wheel and spinning process illustrate Taylor's love of using weaving, looms, and webs as metaphors for poetry and the construction of the self in "Huswifery."

Comparing metaphysical with typological conceits stimulates discussion about poetic technique (e.g., Meditations 2.50 on Old Testament types and New Testament fulfillments and 2.60B on Christ as the Rock of Horeb). Finally, reading poems aloud in class captures the surprisingly personal voice and intensity of many poems.

Questions for Reading and Discussion/ Approaches to Writing

1. Specific questions can be generated easily for most poems, but it helps students (not only with Taylor but also with the study of other Puritan literature) to ask them to research key terms, using Donald Stanford's glossary, a well-annotated Bible with a concordance, such as the New Scofield Reference edition, Johnson's *The Poetical Works of Edward Taylor*, or the *Milton Encyclopedia*. Terms might include Elect/election, covenant, baptism, Lord's Supper, preparation, law, grace, typology, providential history, apostasy, marriage, the Dove, the Rock, first fruits, offerings/sacrifices, Adam and Eve, the Garden of Eden, the Fall, Passover, the Exodus, Christ's incarnation, the crucifixion and resurrection, the Bride and Bridegroom, New Jerusalem, and the Second Coming. One can assign students to look up the Bible verses mentioned in the footnotes or to read selections from Genesis, Exodus, Psalms, Canticles, the Gospels, Hebrews, and Revelation. Because of Taylor's playfulness with different meanings of a single image, students might be asked to look up in the *Oxford English Dictionary* the complete history of "fillet," "squitchen," "screw" and "pins," "knot," "kenning," "huswifery," "cocks," or "escutcheon" (one word each, perhaps). They might research the construction of the spinning wheel, thumbscrews and rack, tenon and mortise carpentry, the tabernacle and temple, a mint, and an alembic. Such preparation frequently alerts students to Taylor's multiple strands of imagery, his tricky, punning, even humorous use of language, and the variety of areas from which he draws images and metaphors (architecture, horticulture, heraldry, carpentry, clothing, bookbinding, warfare, alchemy, music, classical mythology, history, printing, domestic chores).
2. Obvious paper assignments involve interpretive readings of poems not otherwise studied in class. Advanced students can be encouraged to compare Genesis as the principal creation story with Taylor's rendering in Psalm 19, the "Preface" to *Gods Determinations*, Meditation 2.50, and his "Valediction to all the World preparatory

for Death." Analysis of different strands of imagery that cut across several poems allows students to see Taylor's recurrent methods and themes, as in the water, blood, and wine associated with Christ and the Lord's Supper. Similar assignments might be made around the concepts of the feast, marriage, the garden, reciprocal relationships (master and servant, Bridegroom/Beloved and Bride/Spouse, God and the elect), or around broad areas of imagery, such as purification by fire, water, and blood ("Christ's Reply," "The Ebb and Flow," 2.1, 2.26, 2.60B) and writing/imprinting ("Prologue," 1.6, 2.43, 2.50, "Valediction").

3. Creative writing assignments also immerse students in the complexities of Taylor's artistry, while challenging them to write poetry that captures his fundamental theological concepts and the Puritan vision of mankind's history and life in relationship to Christ. Students can be asked to compose a paraphrase (or a musical hymn) of a Psalm; to choose a biblical verse (perhaps one of Taylor's own), a dominant image, or Old Testament type, and create a preparatory meditation imitative of Taylor's metrical form and imagistic techniques; to write a lyric on a natural "occurant" or domestic event; to imagine a valediction or *memento mori* poem reflecting the vanity of this world and joys of the heavenly paradise; to use Canticles as a model for a love poem either written to Elizabeth Fitch, Taylor's wife, or as a celebration of the anticipated nuptials between Taylor and Christ as Bride and Bridegroom; or to generate a debate (in allegorical form perhaps) between Christ and Satan over man's soul. Students may also choose to create two poems on the same subject, but reflecting the different style and poetic forms preferred by Anne Bradstreet and Edward Taylor.

Teaching Issues and Interpretation

Placing Taylor in the context of other Puritan literature becomes illuminating in two ways because it responds to the question of what is poetry supposed to be and do. First, Taylor's work shows how the Puritan emphasis on spiritual examination of the individual soul can take the form of meditative and autobiographical poetry. Poetry for Taylor is both an immediate preparation for his ministerial administering of the Lord's Supper *and* a lifelong preparation for eternal life. Students often stumble with Taylor's poetry because they do not understand how intensely Taylor renounces this world in favor of a spiritual life within and a heavenly life yet to come. But they can identify with the human psychology of doubt, fear, loss, and a need for some form of consoling grace, comfort, or higher being to give meaning to the innately corrupt heart.

Second, because Taylor is the most prolific poet of America's first two hundred years (the anomaly of a "poet in the wilderness"), his meditations open up the question of a supposed Puritan disdain for poetry. Taylor's own puzzling over the proper uses of poetic language appears in "Were but my Muse an Huswife Good," the "Prologue" to the *Preparatory Meditations*, Meditation 2.43, and "A Valediction to all the World." By setting Taylor in a seventeenth-century tradition of paraphrases of Psalms, Job, and Canticles and, thus, the sanctioned acceptance of biblical poetry, and of a respect for *Sola Scriptura* as the model of language to be imitated, students can begin to appreciate the roots of an American tradition of poetry. The association of Taylor with David and Solomon as biblical models of poets becomes a useful end point for discussion because it points to Taylor's hope for his role in heaven, validates poetry as a medium of spiritual expression acceptable to God, sets the standards for "a transcendent style," and defines poetry as a ritual (meditative) offering of praise and worship.

Bibliography

Selections from the *Preparatory Meditations* and *Gods Determinations* have been published by permission of Donald E. Stanford, ed. *The Poems of Edward Taylor* (New Haven: Yale University Press, 1960) and the "Psalm Paraphrases," "Occasional Poems," "A Valediction . . .," and "A Fig for thee Oh! Death" by permission of Thomas M. and Virginia L. Davis, eds. *Edward Taylor's Minor Poetry* (Boston: Twayne, 1981).

Aside from sources already mentioned in the headnote's bibliography and the footnotes, the introductions to Taylor's published works by Donald Stanford, Norman Grabo, Thomas and Virginia Davis, and Charles Mignon always prove helpful. The most succinct biographical sketch is Donald Stanford's "Edward Taylor" in the *Dictionary of Literary Biography*. Key chapters on Taylor are found in Sacvan Bercovitch's *Typology and Early American Literature*, Albert Gelpi's *The Tenth Muse*, Barbara Lewalski's *Protestant Poetics and the Seventeenth-Century Religious Lyric*, Mason Lowance's *The Language of Canaan*, Earl Miner's *Literary Uses of Typology*, Peter White's *Puritan Poets and Poetics*, Ivy Schweitzer's *The Work of Self-Representation*, and Jeffrey Hammond's *Sinful Self, Saintly Self*.

Samuel Sewall (1652–1730)

Contributing Editor: Carla Mulford

Classroom Issues and Strategies

Most students have trouble placing the reading of a diary within the context of traditional literary study. Students find Sewall's apparent preoccupation with merchant ships' arrivals, the costs of nutmeats and madeira, the problems of dress and so forth a little disarming, for they are used to finding meaning in texts according to standards (e.g., images, metaphors) artificially set up.

To address this issue, I stress two main points—one about aesthetics, the other about culture. Sewall's diary offers us a direct glimpse into the life of a private Puritan. Unlike the diaries of Winthrop, Edwards, Bradstreet, and other early writers, Sewall's diary was probably written for his eyes alone, not to be passed around among friends and family members. The diary offers us signs of real change, in both ideology and culture. Thus, the notations about practical affairs become signs of culture *and* signs of Sewall's life-preoccupations. Fruitful discussion often arises when I ask students to compare Sewall's seeming preoccupation with material goods with their own preoccupation about name-brand clothes and cars and videotaped weddings. He works particularly well with a middle-class student body.

Students are likely to find the pamphlet *The Selling of Joseph* remarkably conservative in its approach to the issue of slavery. They will seek for openly aggressive statements about the negative moral implications of holding people in bondage. What they will find in the pamphlet, on the other hand, will be exacting biblical exegesis that points to the perceived God-given injunction against holding slaves. Students will want to discuss not only the issue of slave-holding in New England (some tend erroneously to think, given what they've heard about the Civil War, that New Englanders never held slaves, that only southerners held slaves) but the potential usefulness (or lack of usefulness) of Sewall's constant reference to biblical texts to create a sense both of "expert testimony" and of historical necessity for these New Canaanites.

Major Themes, Historical Perspectives, and Personal Issues

I have successfully used the Sewell selections as a sign of a culture in transition, noting with students the seeming shift in Sewell's interests from spiritual to secular issues. (In a broader sense, from Christianity to capitalism, some students like to add.) I usually treat the fact that Sewall—very humanly—seems to have wanted to enter the church in order to get his first child baptized. I usually talk about the Salem witch trials and discuss Sewall's retraction of his behavior during the trials, along with his writing of the first Puritan anti-slaveholding tract, *The Selling of Joseph*.

In addition to the interests which Sewall's diary suggests about early eighteenth-century culture, his many writings that arose from his public positions address specific concerns about the rights of Native Americans and of African-Americans brought as slaves to the colonies. When Sewall felt concerns about Native Americans, he expressed them in council and sometimes circulated his speeches in manuscript so that others outside council would be clear about his positions on key issues. If we consider his diary as only a record of events and material things peculiarly of interest to Samuel Sewall, we cannot begin to assess the importance of the social issues of racial equality and liberty in Sewall's life, as evidenced by even the briefest of diary entries, like this one for June 22, 1716: "I essay'd June, 22, to prevent Indians and Negroes being Rated with Horses and Hogs; but could not prevail." Sewall's pamphlet, *The Selling of Joseph*, is perhaps the most public but certainly not the only sign of Sewall's concerns about the inhumanity of his townspeople.

Significant Form, Style, or Artistic Conventions

Sewall's diary seems to have been private. Thus, we don't find the form of spiritual autobiography that we find in Winthrop's "Christian Experience" or in Edwards's diary of the early 1720s. Yet Sewall's diary provides a wonderful glimpse into the concerns both secular and spiritual of a man whose life was well known and very public in his own day.

Students will want to discuss the constant citation, in *The Selling of Joseph*, of biblical texts. It might be useful to have them discuss Sewall's writing style here in light of the style Cotton Mather, Sewall's contemporary, uses in the *Magnalia Christi Americana* and also in light of another important anti-slavery tract by John Woolman, *Some Considerations on the Keeping of Negroes*.

Comparisons, Contrasts, Connections

Contrast the diary with Winthrop's "Christian Experience" (as spiritual autobiography) and with Winthrop's journal. The first contrast will show the differences between public and private documentation of spiritual questioning; the second, the differences between public history and private meditation.

Contrast the diary with Taylor's *Preparatory Meditations*.

With regard to its more secular impulses, compare and contrast the diary with Sarah Kemble Knight's journal and with Franklin's autobiography.

The Selling of Joseph should be compared and contrasted, as suggested above, with the writings of both Cotton Mather and John Woolman. In terms of biblical citation, students might wish to explore the *kinds* of texts Sewall cites as expert biblical testimony in support of his position against slave-holding. Are these the same kinds of texts referenced in Mary Rowlandson's captivity narrative? Is Sewall signalling a similar kind of spiritual urgency as evident in the Rowlandson narrative?

Compare the notions of liberty held by John Winthrop (as shown in the journal entry of his speech before the General Court, 1645), by Samson Occom (as implied in his sermon on the execution of Moses Paul), and by Lemuel Haynes (in the two selections in the anthology).

Questions for Reading and Discussion/ Approaches to Writing

1. Sophisticated students note that Sewall has for the most part internalized the religious value system after which he strove so heartily early on, so that he is moved to act upon his dealings in the witch trials (and make the retraction) and his attitudes about slavery (and write the anti-slavery pamphlet, *The Selling of Joseph*), rather than simply to be obsessive about these issues privately.

2. Fruitful class and written discussion occurs when students compare and contrast Sewall with other anti-slavery writers, such as John Woolman and Benjamin Franklin, and with the racism of his contemporaries, John Saffin and Cotton Mather.

3. Both Sewall and Cotton Mather wrote about the Salem witch trials, yet their ultimate assessments of this situation were remarkably different. Students might be encouraged to work independently on a project that would compare the records of the two men in light of this question: Was Sewall's behavior in keeping with his authorship of *The Selling of Joseph* and to what extent was his work humane and enlightened?

4. Students might wish to compare and contrast, in independent work, Sewall's incidental journal comments about Indians and blacks with those offered by Sarah Kemble Knight and William Byrd, persons roughly his contemporaries.

Cotton Mather (1663-1728)

Contributing Editors: Kenneth Alan Hovey and Joseph Fichtelberg

Classroom Issues and Strategies

The challenge in teaching Mather is to humanize him without sacrificing the complexity that makes him so fascinating. One solution might be to stress his burdens as an eminent figure in a demanding family, at a time of radical change.

Students might identify with Mather's strenuous attempts to live up to his perfectionist father, Increase Mather, who in his prime dominated the Bay's intellectual life. Cotton's protracted stuttering suggests how fierce the struggle sometimes was; and there often seems to be a contest in his life between optimistic self-assertion and an equally potent despair. Prodigious works like the *Magnalia Christi Americana* show Mather responding to cultural shocks in the same way he confronted personal ones—by attempting to insert them in ever larger and more glorious contexts. Instructors may then explore the tools with which he does so. both the typological figures that convey Mather's optimism and the ambiguities and contradictions that confess his despair.

Major Themes, Historical Perspectives, and Personal Issues

As New England became ever more secular and commercial, Mather strove, both ideologically and personally, to adapt to the change. A guardian of tradition, he was nevertheless an avid naturalist; a member of the Royal Society; a leader in the revolt against Edmund Andros; and, through his interest in evangelical piety, a religious progressive. His numerous biographies assert the continued vigor of New England's millennial role, in elaborate figures linking the colony with both ancient Israel and the Apocalypse. Underlying his interest in witchcraft, for example, is the conviction that such troubles would mount as the last days approached; and his portrait of John Eliot suggests an American Moses redeeming the lost remnant of Israel. Yet Mather's writing often reveals as well the tensions in his hard-won position. His marking off of witches, Native Americans, and the disorderly suggests not only a constant need to police his ideology, but also an acknowledgment of its increasingly rapid erosion.

Significant Form, Style, or Artistic Conventions

Mather's distinguishing literary characteristic is the degree to which he merges history and autobiography. Certain elements of Mather's approach to church history, for example, can be found in the numerous models he used, among them William Bradford. But whereas Bradford's *Of Plymouth Plantation* is narrated in the modest, self-effacing manner one associates with Puritans saints, Mather constantly intervenes, forcing his own voice upon the reader. Such obtrusiveness makes sense if one realizes that Mather's real interest lies not only in conveying the facts of men's lives but also in turning lives into instructive "examples"— examples that allow him, in turn, to extend his own sense of errand. In this regard, it may be useful to compare Mather's self-presentation with that of Mary Rowlandson, whose wilderness ordeal also spoke to New England's providential fortunes.

Mather's treatment of cultural "others" also bears notice. His treatment of Native Americans, for example, has neither the sympathy of William Byrd's nor the sharp-eyed detail of Rowlandson's portraits. What it does, rather, is expose the ideological uses to which Mather put Natives, as figures in New England's cosmic drama.

Finally, Mather has been profitably compared with much later figures such as Henry Adams, whose cultural inheritance left them unprepared for change.

Questions for Reading and Discussion/ Approaches to Writing

1. Compare the rather dry court records of *Wonders of the Invisible World* to Mather's account of the Goodwin children in Book VI of the *Magnalia*. What kinds of concerns does Mather bring to these more personal encounters?
2. Compare Mather's benevolent projects in *Bonifacius* with those described in Franklin's *Autobiography*. What impulses unite the two endeavors? How are they different?

3. Sample other sections of the *Magnalia*. If Mather intends for New England, whether it *"Live* any where else or no," to *"Live* in [his] *History,"* what kinds of materials does he choose to preserve it, and how successful is his project?

Bibliography

Johnson, Parker. "Humiliation Followed by Deliverance: Metaphor and Plot in Cotton Mather's *Magnalia." Early American Literature* 15 (1980/81): 237–46.

Kibbey, Ann. "Mutations of the Supernatural: Witchcraft, Remarkable Providences, and the Power of Puritan Men." *American Quarterly* 34:2 (1982): 125–48.

Levin, David. *Cotton Mather: The Young Life of the Lord's Remembrancer 1663–1703.* Cambridge: Harvard University Press, 1978.

Lovelace, Richard. *The American Pietism of Cotton Mather: Origins of American Evangelicalism.* Grand Rapids: Christian University Press, 1979.

Lowance, Mason. *The Language of Canaan: Metaphor and Symbol in New England from the Puritans to the Transcendentalists.* Cambridge: Harvard University Press, 1980.

John Williams (1664–1729)

Contributing Editor: Rosalie Murphy Baum

Classroom Issues and Strategies

The popularity of the captivity narrative during the Puritan period is being repeated today among students who vicariously enjoy the narrators' experiences and realize the effect such narratives have had on popular frontier and Wild West adventure stories. To many students already familiar with Mary Rowlandson's 1682 *Narrative*, John Williams's 1707 narrative is especially welcome—not simply because it offers a male version of captivity, but also because it describes captivity both by the Indians (for eight weeks) and by the French (for two years). The primary difficulty students have in reading the narrative lies in their lack of knowledge of the French and Indian War and of the differences between Roman Catholicism and Puritanism.

Background information about the relationship between the French and English in North America can eliminate this difficulty and give students a more accurate idea of colonial history. To be stressed first is the fact that the hostilities between the French and the English in North America began as early as 1613 and that the period between 1613 and the Peace of Paris in 1763 was one in which some six extended conflicts, or "wars," resulted in captives, usually women and children, being taken from New England to Canada.

Students also need to be reminded of the theological and ritualistic differences that distinguished the Puritans from the Established Church of England. Roman Catholicism represented a structure and theology even more pernicious to Puritans than the structure and theology of the Church of England. In such a context, Williams's strong reaction to the Indians taking him "to a popish country" (Québec) and to the efforts of the French Jesuits to convert him to Roman Catholicism becomes clear.

Major Themes, Historical Perspectives, and Personal Issues

The Redeemed Captive is, then, an excellent work to dramatize for students what the French and Indian Wars were about and to clarify the antagonism between Catholics and Puritans during this period. It is also a form of the jeremiad more readable and interesting to modern students than most of the Puritan sermons, histories, or personal narratives.

In addition, it illustrates "the significant mythic experience of the early white-Indian relationship" (Louise K. Barnett, *The Ignoble Savage*) and the "Puritan myth of 'America,' " "the first coherent myth-literature developed in America for American audiences" (Richard Slotkin, *Regeneration Through Violence*). Students can see in both Williams's and Rowlandson's narratives the way in which such accounts typically open with an Indian raid in which white settlers are brutally massacred and then proceed to describe the inhuman hardships Indians inflict upon their captives. The concept of the Indian is that of satanic beast. No attempt is made in these narratives to indicate that the Indian aggression is a part of the hostilities of decades and may have been provoked or equaled by white aggression. Little note is made of the decency or kindnesses of the Indians: such good fortune as the captive may experience is never attributed to the customs or virtue of the Indians but to God. Living conditions that are everyday parts of the Indian life or result from the normal state of travel at that time are regarded by captives as horrendous personal injuries being deliberately and cruelly inflicted upon them by the Indians. Clearly no cognizance is taken of the inherent difficulties that arise when two such disparate cultures come together under conditions of warfare.

Significant Form, Style, or Artistic Conventions

Of particular interest to many students will be the subject of the captivity narrative as a genre particularly American in its subject matter years before American writers—like Freneau, Bryant, Irving, Cooper, Hawthorne, and James—became concerned about the question of an inherently *American* literature. This genre was clearly, in its early stages, a religious statement, emphasizing redemptive suffering, with the captivity being either a test that God had set for his people or a punishment to guide them from their evil ways. Williams's narrative was such an excellent example of the type that Sunday School versions appeared as late as the 1830s and 1840s (e.g., Titus Strong's *The Deerfield Captive: an Indian Story, being a Narrative of Facts for the Instruction of the Young*).

Original Audience

Students should be reminded too, of course, that Williams is writing for a Puritan audience. Thus, for a people familiar with the jeremiad, he emphasizes God's wrath against his people for their shortcomings, but also rejoices in God's mercy and goodness toward his people. (See Sacvan Bercovitch, *The American Jeremiad*, for a study of the negative and positive sides of the jeremiad.) He assumes the satanic nature of the Indians, particularly fearsome creatures by which God tests his people or punishes them. And he stresses the diabolical nature of the Jesuits, who, in their zeal to convert him to Roman Catholicism, make him attend a Latin Mass, urge him to pray to the Virgin Mary, and try to force him to kiss a crucifix.

Questions for Reading and Discussion/ Approaches to Writing

For their writing assignments, some students may wish to read other captivity narratives either to compare narratives of redemptive suffering or to trace the changes in the genre emerging during the propaganda and fictionalized thriller stages. Wilcomb E. Washburn's *Narratives of North American Indian Captivities* offers facsimile reprints of 311 such nar-

ratives dating from the late seventeenth century to the late nineteenth
century.

But even without such additional reading, the possibilities for
essays based upon Williams's narrative are considerable. Students may
wish to discuss Williams's *The Redeemed Captive* as a jeremiad, comparing
it to jeremiads they have read in other genres. They may wish to examine Williams's narrative techniques, especially with a view to the
contribution the genre has made to the horror story or thriller. Students
interested in women's studies or feminist criticism may wish to consider
conceptual and stylistic differences between the narratives of Rowlandson and Williams. Students interested in Indian studies can compare attitudes toward the Indians in Williams and other authors studied (e.g., in
Bradford, Roger Williams, Cotton Mather, Rowlandson, or, moving into
a later period, Franklin, Freneau, Bryant, Cooper, Melville). Students
familiar with Joseph Campbell's *The Hero With a Thousand Faces* can consider the archetypal nature of *The Redeemed Captive*, perhaps in the light
of other works they have read.

Bibliography

Of particular value as background reading for teaching *The Redeemed
Captive* is Wilcomb E. Washburn's "Introduction" to *Narratives of North
American Indian Captivity: A Selective Bibliography* (1983), xi–lvv, and
Edward W. Clark's "Introduction" to *The Redeemed Captive* by John
Williams (1976), 1–25.

A Selection of Seventeenth-Century Poetry

Contributing Editor: Jeffrey A. Hammond

Classroom Issues and Strategies

While students are pleasantly surprised at the diversity of poets and
poetic themes in early America, they are often disappointed with the
poems themselves. This disappointment is a good starting point for discussion, since it highlights the differences between seventeenth- and
twentieth-century expectations and responses regarding poetry. When
students articulate what disappoints them about much of the verse—the
generalized speakers, the religious themes, the artificial language, the
high level of allusion—they begin to understand that art and its cultural

functions are subject to historical change. Good questions to begin discussion of particular poems in this selection include: Why was the poem written? What reading response does the text seem to foster? What is the relationship between the poem and the values of the culture that produced it? What view of poetic language does the poem seem to demonstrate?

Major Themes, Historical Perspectives, and Personal Issues

These poems also become more interesting for students when they are asked to identify the blend (or opposition) of Old World and New World features—formal as well as thematic—within the texts. Another issue concerns the expected functions of verse in the seventeenth century. Once students realize that poets were more interested in voicing communal values, commemorating important events, and seeking coherence in their world than in expressing "original" ideas, the poems begin to make better sense. Students may not agree with the literary conventions they encounter, but they will gain a better contextual understanding of them. This in turn may help them see that modern reading expectations also exist in a particular historical and cultural framework.

Significant Form, Style, or Artistic Conventions

For most students these poems are quite difficult. The syntax is sometimes cramped into a rigid meter (Johnson and Alsop), the allusions often seem remote and excessive (Saffin), the speakers seem remote and impersonal, and, for many, the poem's ideology seems trite or alien (Goodhue). A discussion of "metaphysical" wit often helps students understand—if not enjoy—the seemingly strained effects in many of the poems. The Renaissance view of poetry as a frankly artificial discourse is also helpful. The poet is usually not trying to replicate "natural" speech in texts that were written, in one sense or another, for the ages.

Original Audience

The selections here reflect a wide range of intended readers. Students might try to determine the nature of those readers (their social class, education, reading expectations) as a means of humanizing the texts. This will also underscore the contrasts between the literary culture that these poems embody and the students' own literary culture, including its microcosm in the English classroom.

Comparisons, Contrasts, Connections

Students familiar with the English cavaliers and metaphysical poets will bring a great deal to the discussion of these poems, especially in matters of form and style. It is also useful to compare the poems with other treatments of similar themes: Saffin with Shakespeare's sonnets, French with later slave narratives, Steere with later Romantic depictions of nature, Goodhue with Bradstreet, Alsop with promotional tracts and Ebenezer Cook, Johnson and Hayden with Milton's *Lycidas*. In addition, any of the poems could be profitably compared with works by Bradstreet, Wigglesworth, or Taylor.

Questions for Reading and Discussion/ Approaches to Writing

1. What do the poems suggest about the cultural functions of poetry in the seventeenth century?
2. What do they suggest about the relation between individual identity and culture or ideology?
3. What do they suggest about seventeenth-century distinctions between "poetic" discourse and everyday speech?
4. What implied readership is suggested in their diction and allusions?
5. In what sense(s), thematic or formal, are the poems "American"?
6. In what sense(s), thematic or formal, are the poems "British"?
7. What expressions of the cultural diversity characteristic of a later America seem already present in these poems?
8. Do thematic or formal differences emerge in the work of the female and male poets collected here?

Bibliography

Cowell, Pattie. "Introduction" and headnotes, *Women Poets in Pre-Revolutionary America*, 1981.

Meserole, Harrison T. "Introduction" and headnotes, *American Poetry of the Seventeenth Century*, 1985.

Scheick, William J. "The Poetry of Colonial America." In *Columbia Literary History of the United States*, edited by Emory Elliott. New York: Columbia University Press, 1988.

—— and Joella Doggett. *Seventeenth-Century American Poetry: A Reference Guide*, 1977.

—— and Catherine Rainwater. "Seventeenth-Century American Poetry: A Reference Guide Updated." *Resources for American Literary Study* 10 (1980): 121–45.

Silverman, Kenneth. "Introduction" and headnotes, *Colonial American Poetry*. New York: Hafner Press, 1968.

White, Peter, ed. *Puritan Poets and Poetics: Seventeenth-Century American Poetry in Theory and Practice*. University Park: Pennsylvania State University Press, 1985.

Tales of Incorporation, Resistance, and Reconquest in New Spain

History of the Miraculous Apparition of the Virgin
of Guadalupe in 1531
Don Antonio de Otermín (fl. 1680)
The Coming of the Spanish and the Pueblo Revolt (Hopi)
Don Diego de Vargas (?–1704)

Contributing Editor: Juan Bruce-Novoa

Classroom Issues and Strategies

The central issue raised by these selections revolve around the opposing forces of colonialism and native resistance to it. In my experience students tend to side with the Native Americans against the Spanish, focusing on the Hopi text and its act of direct and simple rejection through violence. The protests against the Columbus quintcentennial celebrations provided added impetus to this anti-Spanish sentiment, ironically especially among the U.S. Latino population. A discussion of the legal and moral rights of conquest should not be avoided, but care should be taken to avoid focusing solely on the Spanish. Certainly by the seventeenth century the other major powers in the Americas, the English and the French, were dealing with similar resistance in very similar ways. No European colonial power willingly gave up possession of American territory to its native inhabitants; the U.S. government followed suit in later centuries.

The appropriateness of a Mexican religious legend in an anthology of U.S. literature may be questioned. Justification lies in the pervasiveness of the story everywhere Mexicans have settled in the United States. The hybrid character of the figure suggests an alternate image of American identity, that of the cultural and biological fusion of Old and New World peoples.

Major Themes, Historical Perspectives, and Personal Issues

Two contradictory themes dialogue throughout this section: the Native American's determination to defend their culture to the death and the colonizer's determination to hold conquered territory with equal zeal. Both feel bound by their cultural codes of behavior to resist the efforts of the other and neither seems willing to compromise. The Virgin of Guadalupe, however, represents a possible point of confluence in hybridism. Her tale raises the theme of miscegenation, one which has been treated very differently in Latin America and the United States.

Students lack the historical training to contextualize these tales. The headnotes, as well as references to studies of the period, provide a good introduction. It is most important to keep in mind that these texts reflect the ongoing efforts of the Spanish empire to perpetuate itself by maintaining order and control over its territory and inhabitants.

Significant Form, Style, or Artistic Conventions

The differences in the formal character of these texts reflect the conflicting issues mentioned above. While the Spanish official used the written word, with the full authority of a document within a legalistic political order, the anonymous Hopi resistance text began as oral tales and preserves a kinship with folklore and clandestine communications. The Guadalupe text is, like the image of the Virgin herself, a hybrid of elite and popular styles. The governmental texts obey the conventions of bureaucratic communiques, employing the rhetoric of political justification that appeals to hegemonic regulations; the other texts counter through an appeal to a sense of common justice for the oppressed at the margins of that same order.

Original Audience

Again, the Spanish governors addressed themselves to those few powerful officials in the chain of command whose task it was to judge their conduct and recommend action by the crown. Their texts were never meant for distribution to readers other than those versed in the formalities and legalities of the colonial situation. There was no room for flights of literary fancy among these bureaucrats, yet it is exactly this cut-and-dried style that conveys to us now the harsh realities of the colonial system; its highly organized and controlled character as contrasted with the relatively loose structure of the English colonies.

The Guadalupe text was intended for the Native Americans of central Mexico; a proselytizing text for people of non-European cultures, it was originally published in Náhuatl and thus not directed at a Spanish readership. However, one must consider that the great majority of Native Americans could not read in any language, so the text could have well been intended for trained clerics to use in evangelizing.

The Hopi text was originally an oral story repeated by and for members of this and other tribes. It is still found among the oral tradition tales in the Southwest.

Comparisons, Contrasts, Connections

The Otermín and Vargas texts can be read with Villagrá's account of the resistance at Acoma a century earlier; stylistic differences arise from the roles the authors played within the imperial system. Villagrá chronicled his experience in the epic verse common to his time, free to fictionalize the events and characters, while Otermín and Vargas wrote in the governmental form that they were expected to use to report facts without embellishments.

Students can read Thomas Morton's account of the massacre of the Wessaguscus by the Plymouth colonists. Also, they could consider the difference between the positive image of miscegenation in the Virgin of Guadalupe and the negative image of that possibility in Rowlandson's captivity.

Questions for Reading and Discussion/
Approaches to Writing

1. Ask students to consider the moral and political issues addressed in the selections in a contemporary setting. The particular locality and region in which your institution is located should fit the purpose, since it is difficult to find any place in the United States that did not experience a similar frontier situation at some point. Have them ponder what it would mean for them and their families to be forced to relinquish their property and return to their ancestors'

homeland. What would they expect of their elected official, the court, the police, and the military?

2. Have students think of the Virgin of Guadalupe metaphorically as a figure of cultural confluence designed to ameliorate conflict among ethnic and racial groups. Ask them to consider if such figures could be useful now in the United States and if they have existed in our history. Is the model of hybridism (cultural and racial) viable in the United States?

Bibliography

Consult headnotes for references.

Eighteenth Century

The title of the middle section, "Contested Boundaries," emphasizes the cultural conflicts that marked the eighteenth century and counters both political myths of national unity in the revolutionary cause and intellectual myths of serene Enlightenment rationalism. It is the sense of contestation, of various individuals and groups relying on a myriad of rhetorical strategies in order to take advantage of revolutionary opportunities to control their own destinies or to create models of consensus to consolidate power, that can provide a pedagogical focus for the classroom.

Tradition and Change in Anglo-America
Enlightenment Voices, Revolutionary Visions

The selections in the first two sections highlight arguments within the Anglo-American community. In their diversity of forms and the variety of motives behind them, they challenge the supposed homogeneity of that community and indeed require the class to reconsider what we mean by "community." The "Patriot and Loyalist Songs and Ballads" will perhaps most obviously challenge the common belief that Anglo-Americans were of one mind about the revolution, but texts by women writers, by members of different religious communities, and by members of different social classes will show that whatever Thomas Jefferson may claim about the "truths" he articulates in the Declaration of Independence, they are anything but "self-evident." Indeed, by placing the so-called "Founding Fathers" in their cultural context, we can read a text like the "Declaration" not simply as an enumeration of timeless truths, but as an argument designed to achieve specific and complex political and social ends. Such a view in the classroom provides a sense of the very real stakes involved in "literary" questions of form, style, and structure.

Contested Boundaries, National Visions: Writings
on "Race," Identity, and "Nation"

Among those political and social ends referred to above were not only the fomenting of revolution, but also the channeling and containment of revolutionary energies through the construction of myths of national unity, purpose, and identity. The selections in "Contested Boundaries, National Visions" show students that if the debate was heated *within* Anglo-America, this divided community was only one of many with important interests involved in the progress and outcome of this debate.

Again, as with the texts in the first two sections, class discussion here can focus on the dynamics of the rhetorical situation each writer or group of writers faced in composing and distributing their texts. Now, however, those rhetorical situations become even more complicated, as writers negotiate among cultures and appeal to diverse, even contradictory interests. This is particularly true of black writers like Olaudah Equiano and Phillis Wheatley, whose own identities are caught between the worlds of slaves and slave-owners, Africans and Europeans, Christians and "pagans." By discussing the daunting array of prejudices, political beliefs, and social conventions confronting these slave and ex-slave writers even before they picked up a pen, circumstances that made even the proclaiming of the most pious verities a radical act simply because of who was proclaiming them, students can better see and discuss these texts as the carefully constructed, daring performances they are. The same considerations apply to texts by Native American writers like Hendrick Aupaumut and Samson Occom, or even to the best-selling novels by Susanna Haswell Rowson and Hannah Webster Foster, who wrote novels about the proper relations between the genders for a largely female audience in a male-dominated publishing world. Given such a rich rhetorical context, a discussion of the Federalist/Anti-Federalist papers can look not only at the care with which certain political issues are discussed in those texts, but at the range of political, social, and cultural issues not even brought up for discussion.

Missionary Voices of the Southwest

Many students, particularly but not exclusively outside of the West and Southwest, are surprised to learn of the scope and activity of the Spanish colonies in the eighteenth century. While the entries here can't possibly supply the gap in historical consciousness many in the U.S. have about Latino history, these entries can lend perspective to U.S. history by providing a larger context for a consideration of the American revolution. The report by Fray Carlos José Delgado, for example, gives students another, non-English argument about the purpose of colonization and the proper relations between Europeans and the indigenous population, while Fray Francisco Palou's biography of Junípero Serra shows another process of mythmaking involving a different "Founding Father." For students who have never done so, considering "American" cultural history from the perspective of the Spanish colonial experience raises important questions for discussion about the meaning of center and margins, of frontier and wilderness, and about the traditional view of American history as a movement west from the east coast. For students already familiar with or raised with this perspective, such a discussion not only provides a validation of that perspective, but also allows these students to assume a role of authority and centrality in the classroom.

Tradition and Change
in Anglo-America

Sarah Kemble Knight (1666–1727)

Contributing Editor: Kathryn Zabelle Derounian-Stodola

Classroom Issues and Strategies

This journal is one of the most teachable colonial documents at the undergraduate level. While it is a close contemporary of such Puritan prose classics as Robert Calef's *More Wonders of the Invisible World* (1700), Cotton Mather's *Magnalia* (1701), and John Williams's *The Redeemed Captive* (1707), it differs from them in tone, content, and style. Students respond positively to Knight's humorous portrait of herself and her surroundings. Through this document—and others—a teacher can counterbalance the still all-too-common stereotype of Puritans as dour, somber, unsmiling, and morbidly pious.

Major Themes, Historical Perspectives,
and Personal Issues

Themes

1. The position of women—especially women writers—in late seventeenth- and early eighteenth-century New England.

    In theory, Puritans used the typological significance of Eve's creation from Adam's rib as a way to stress women's dependence, domesticity, and intrinsic inferiority. Ninety-nine percent of women married at least once in Puritan New England, and a wife's major purpose was to serve God and her husband. Sermons, for example, frequently stressed the ideal woman's qualities of modesty, piety, humility, patience, charity, and so on. But in practice, of course, women were often far from ideal, and in a frontier society they sometimes had to take on men's work. Thus there is evidence that women became printers, stationers, writers, and innkeepers, for example—usually on the death of their father or husband. Sarah Kemble Knight is a case in point, and students might be asked to find textual evidence of Knight's business skills.

2. Views of the frontier/wilderness at this time.
3. Sociological issues like views of blacks, Indians, and other settlers in different colonies.

Significant Form, Style, or Artistic Conventions

Discuss the genres of diary, journal, and autobiography and also explain how this journal fits the fictional genre of the picaresque. Compare the popular, colloquial quality of this work with more academic works to understand what the ordinary Puritan citizen might think/read vs. what the well-educated, but few, members of the intelligentsia might think/ read. Such a discussion inevitably involves other colonial works in these genres and helps students understand generic interrelationships. The diary (Sewall's is a prime example) focuses on externals; is unrevised, immediate, and fragmentary; may extend for many years; and usually has no audience in mind except the writer him- or herself. A journal, however (Knight's, for instance), focuses more on internal matters; may be slightly revised; may be written shortly after the fact; may extend over a shorter time period, sometimes to deal with a specific event like a courtship or a journey; should appear relatively coherent; and is probably written with a restricted audience in mind. The autobiography (and the sub-genre the spiritual autobiography) is often considered the most "literary" of the three related genres because it is more carefully structured and composed.

Original Audience

This work was not written with publication in mind, and indeed although written during 1704–1705 was not published until 1825. Like the work of other women writers and amateur authors, this might have been circulated among family and friends by the author, but it did not have a wider readership until it was actually published.

Comparisons, Contrasts, Connections

Compare with other women writers of the time: Anne Bradstreet and Mary Rowlandson, for example. Such comparisons do not reveal a direct influence or sense of tradition among women writers; rather, each person and her work must be considered separately. Contrast with journals of male contemporaries (other travel journals, for example).

Questions for Reading and Discussion

1. Look at Knight as heroine/protagonist of her story/journal.
2. Look carefully at how the wilderness is presented.
3. Look at exactly what she chooses to record in this journal.
4. Notice the lack of religious themes.

Bibliography

I attached a reading list to the headnote. Please see the suggested readings there.

William Byrd II (1674–1744)

Contributing Editor: Kenneth Alan Hovey

Major Themes, Historical Perspectives, and Personal Issues

William Byrd will come as a delightful surprise to students who come to colonial literature with an expectation of unrelieved Puritanism. As a Cavalier author, he picks up where Morton left off, only in Virginia one hundred years later. Much of his charm as a writer derives from the high polish he gives to even his most minor pieces, chiefly by the use of irony. This irony makes his writing constantly entertaining, but its real import is often elusive. Amid all the understatements and overstatements, the sarcasm and the wry humor, it is difficult to find a passage where Byrd does not have his tongue in his cheek or where he simply conveys his views in a straightforward manner.

In his letters he compares colonial America to early biblical times, both those of Eden before the fall and those of the promised land of Canaan under the patriarchs. The comparison is clearly overstated and leaves one doubting whether Byrd doesn't really prefer the fleshpots of Egypt and the fallen world of England. Furthermore, while America lacks the refined vices of England, its national blessings of ease and fertility lead to the crude sins of idleness and overindulgence, further encouraged by the importation of slaves and rum. Yet Byrd clearly glories in his own truly biblical mastership over bondmen and his moderate appreciation of alcohol, and he boasts of his own sexual potency under the guise of blaming American women for breeding like rabbits.

The entertainment provided by the contrasting highs and lows of the very personal *Secret History* is joined to a serious purpose in the contrasting panegyric and satire provided in the impersonal public *History of the Dividing Line*. But as in Byrd's letters, irony undermines virtually all moments of pure praise or blame. The New England Puritans are placed above the Virginians for their industry, but blamed for their fanatical religion. The North Carolinians are placed below the Virginians for their religious indifference and the idleness of their men, yet admired for their fertility and freedom. Indian males are lazier and female Indians dirtier than North Carolinians, but Indian natural religion is better than Carolinian indifference, and Indian wives more innocent and faithful than white. Thus each group is ultimately viewed in a remarkably balanced though highly judgmental way, with neither civilized nor natural man monopolizing all good. Even nature itself, largely epitomized in both histories in the bear, is portrayed equivocally as the source of both good and evil to man, as reproduction and potential death. Byrd's confrontation with the bear, at least in his imagination, is the last of a whole series of events in both letters and histories in which British civilization is forced to confront American nature. By remaining at an always ironic critical distance, Byrd remarkably judges and accommodates both.

Jonathan Edwards (1703–1758)

Contributing Editor: Carol M. Bensick

Assuming that most users of *The Heath Anthology* will be instructors of the American Literature survey course, and that most survey courses using Volume 1 will not overlap its terminus, the teacher of these selections will probably have a week on Edwards. By the time you reach Edwards the students will be accustomed to reading nonfiction "as literature." Of the five texts selected, each may generate its own form of resistance.

The Edward selections can be assessed in terms of their entertainment value and intelligibility. "Resolutions" is highly intelligible. On the other hand, the readability of lists is comparatively low. Your job with "Resolutions" is primarily to demonstrate that it is *uncharacteristic*. When students read the "Personal Narrative," you can point to the moment in the chronology of his movement from anxious lack of conversion to the relief of conversion from which "Resolutions" comes. Note, in particular, the flat condemnation in the "Personal Narrative" of active seeking and the self-manipulation exhibited in "Resolutions." Encourage students to admit that "Resolutions" is either monotonous and dreary or

annoyingly arrogant, then remind them of adolescent diaries and journals they may have kept. In general, ask them to think of the piece as
capturing one phase of the life of a frontier country boy not yet settled
into family or career. Indeed, you might encourage them to admire
Edwards (for being asked to write "A Faithful Narrative," having it published in England, being asked to take "Sinners" on the road, having it
published, and of course going on to become an internationally famous
and admired philosopher of permanent repute) for how well he came
out of the mood of the "Resolutions."

The two "Narratives" probably will be found the most entertaining. Start with "A Faithful Narrative," the simpler and more direct of the
two. A brief description of the work itself and an explanation of the occasion for its composition (noting that Benjamin Colman is a minister of a
rival branch of post-Puritanism, one skeptical of evangelicalism) is
enough to permit the students to follow the story with interest on their
own. Inevitably, the "Personal Narrative," a more private piece of writing, is harder for a student reader to follow. There are some options,
however. Having taught "A Faithful Narrative," the instructor can portray Edwards as spurred by the events chronicled in that text, including
his own part in hearing the validity of the would-be new church members' narratives to try to recall his own exemplary experience, hoping to
guide himself thereby in the assessment of the applicants' testimonies
and to stimulate empathy with what they are undergoing. Here the
teacher might draw a parallel with Edward Taylor's "Preparatory Meditations," in which a pastor similarly performs on himself the same activity he intends to perform publicly on his congregation—namely, evangelical preaching—in order to produce the same effect of activated piety.
Such activities might be compared with the self-analysis conducted in
modern days by classical Freudian psychotherapists, or with the imagin-
able activities of scientists who perform physical experiments on themselves (particularly William James's experimentation with nitrous oxide).

With "Sinners," the requirement for the intelligibility that is the
prerequisite for enjoyment is conversance with the Bible. Looking up
the individual citations is more likely to distract and antagonize the bib-
lically illiterate, and I suggest advising the students to skip or skim the
citations and attempt to read the sermon "for the story." Beginning with
the title, the teacher can ask the following questions: who is the protagonist with whom the reader identifies? (the sinner); who, from his point of
view, is the antagonist? (God); what is the situation? (God is holding you
up, but any minute now, God will drop you into hell). With this much
established, the teacher could challenge the students to make these
abstractions real to themselves. The idea would be to get them to see
that Edwards is interpreting the natural fact of the occurrence of sudden

deaths as a providential sign, which he then goes on to use as an argument to motivate a certain class of the individuals in the audience to adopt a certain behavior.

The class should understand that in "Sinners," a minister is trying to get new members to join his particular sect's churches. The teacher might invoke a parallel with a salesman; what Edwards is selling is church membership. They should be able to see from "A Faithful Narrative" that the "terror" ceases with the cessation of God's "anger." Once inside the church, the convert will enjoy good times. (Here the teacher might suggest a comparison with Taylor's "Gods Determinations.") By the end of the class, students minimally ought to be able to tell you that this sermon will only be scary to a subgroup of the audience and that the members of that subgroup have it (as far as the sermon lets on) entirely within their own power to exempt themselves from the terror.

The instructor should remind students of how long young Edwards himself went before conversion; how scared he was at the threat of sudden death in his fit of illness; and how delighted he was to get onto God's right side. Students should understand that Edwards's God is not always angry and not angry at everyone, and that such fits of anger have a cause. Under original sin, you can explain, no single human being deserves being spared from hell; Christ has purchased that an unknown parcel of humans nevertheless shall enjoy just this reprieve; all they have to do is join the churches; and a group of individuals are actually hesitating to take advantage of this limited-time-only, never-to-be-repeated offer! What's a God to do? (The teacher ought to refer back to Wigglesworth's "God's Controversy" here.)

"The Spider Letter," like "A Faithful Narrative," will become intelligible as soon as the instructor explains that Edwards's father, Timothy, a Harvard graduate and minister interested in the intellectual world, encouraged his teenaged son to send his observations as an amateur entomologist to Paul Dudley, a friend who was a member of the prestigious British scientific organization, the Royal Society. Timothy hoped that Dudley would get Jonathan's letter published in the Society's *Transactions*, which would have been comparable to a youth publishing an article today in the *Smithsonian, National Geographic,* or at least *Scientific Monthly*. Mention that in an earlier generation, Cotton Mather had opened the pages of the *Transactions* to American authors, and that in general there was a strong connection in New England (as in England) between Puritanism and both experimental and theoretical natural science. Encourage the students to think about how different Edwards's life might have been if he had had his first publication in the field of science, before becoming a minister or undergoing his final conversion.

Among texts for possible comparison with "The Spider Letter," one might be Hawthorne's "The Birthmark," for its portrayal of a scientist just slightly younger than Edwards who is involved in the Royal Society. In general, "Insects in American Literature" is a surprisingly fruitful topic for Edwards. For example, students can observe a range of treatments from the theological (Taylor's "Spider Catching a Fly") to the moral (Franklin's "Ephemera," Freneau's "Caty-Did") to the natural or natural-supernatural (Emerson's "Humble-Bee," Dickinson's "Bees are Black"). In contrast with all these, Edwards's approach shows a high proportion of the scientific virtues of literalism, factuality, empiricism, and clinical detachment. In turn, this suggests that contrary to the conventional wisdom, Edwards and Benjamin Franklin have much in common.

Finally, one would like the students to surmount, as definitely as possible, certain historical solecisms and biographical stereotypes that older anthologies have long inculcated. Whatever they think, the students should be embarrassed to be caught ever again saying that Edwards is "a Puritan" (have them compute how long after the *Mayflower* Edwards was born); gloomy (have them tally up the forms of the words "pleasure," "sweet," "joy," "delight" in "A Personal Narrative"); or sadistic. On the latter point, referring back to "Sinners," you can show them that the path of cruelty for Edwards, who has the power to admit you to the fellowship of salvation, would have been to leave you in your unconverted state till you suddenly dropped dead.

Elizabeth Ashbridge (1713–1755)

Contributing Editor: Liahna Babener

Classroom Issues and Strategies

Most students are unfamiliar with the doctrinal differences between the Anglican and Quaker faiths, upon which Ashbridge's *Account* hinges. They tend to be uncomfortable with early Quaker preaching practices, doctrinal assumptions, and social customs. This discomfort sometimes alienates students or prevents them from empathizing with Ashbridge's dilemma. Such anxieties, however, are almost always overcome by the power and poignancy of the text itself.

Providing background about religious and doctrinal tensions in the Great Awakening and gender patterns in colonial America is crucial, and the adoption of a feminist strategy of reading is particularly important.

Comparing other accounts of those who have been impelled by spiritual conviction to act against convention and law is illuminating, as is reading personal narratives of women of the period who use the autobiographical text as a private means of self-vindication in a patriarchal culture.

Students enjoy discussing whether Ashbridge is heroic or perverse. They often identify with her independent spirit and even her proto-feminist rebellion, but lament her increasingly dour tone and her failed marriage. Some wonder whether she gave up too much for conscience's sake. Some students see the husband as abusive or imperious but cannot help sympathizing with his distress over losing a mirthful wife. Students also wonder if Quakers courted their social estrangement, contributing to their own victimization, and ask whether Quakers should be blamed or censured for their martyrdom.

Major Themes, Historical Perspectives, and Personal Issues

1. The expressly female dilemma of having to choose between conscience and husband, as well as the social stresses upon a woman who defies traditional and prescribed sex roles, threatening the stability of the patriarchal order.
2. The doctrinal and social conflicts between Anglicans and Quakers in early America; more broadly, the pressures from a predominantly Anglican, increasingly secularized culture to tame or compartmentalize religious fervor.
3. Ways in which women autobiographers use personal narrative for self-vindicating purposes, or for private rebellion against patriarchal norms.
4. The degree to which autobiography may be read as factual truth as opposed to an invention or reconstruction of reality; the reliability of the personal narrator as witness to and interpreter of events; the fictional elements of the genre.
5. Making a living (as a woman) in colonial America.
6. Marriage, husbands' prerogatives, men's and women's ways of coping with marital estrangement.
7. The nature of religious conviction; Quaker doctrine, patterns of worship, and social customs.

Significant Form, Style, or Artistic Conventions

Study the document as an example of the genre of spiritual autobiography, of personal narrative, of female and feminist assertion, of social history, of eighteenth-century rationalism, and at the same time of revivalist ardor. Explore to what degree the document is confessional and to what degree it may be understood as contrivance or fiction. How is the author "inventing" herself as she writes? How does she turn her experience into a didactic instrument for the edification of her readers?

Original Audience

Social, historical, religious, and political contexts are primary issues. The composition and publication history of the text—penned just before Ashbridge's death—are also illuminating, especially considering that no version of the document in Ashbridge's own hand survives, and scholars are not in consensus about which extant version of the autobiography may be considered authoritative or closest to the original. Consider the Great Awakening audience who may have read this account of religious conversion. Does the document create a sense of feminine solidarity? Can one theorize about the kind of audience to whom Ashbridge directed the *Account*?

Comparisons, Contrasts, Connections

Compare other Great Awakening spiritual autobiographies, such as Jonathan Edwards's "Personal Narrative." Puritan introspective literature and conversion stories, particularly by women, are instructive (such as those by Elizabeth Mixer and Elizabeth White); chronicles of Quaker experience or persecution in colonial America (such as Jane Hoskin's Quaker autobiography or Hawthorne's tale, "The Gentle Boy") are revealing. Diaries, journals, and letters of early American women documenting romantic, religious, and social experiences (compare Sarah Kemble Knight, Jarena Lee, Sarah Osborne, Abigail Adams, and so forth) are useful. Franklin's more cunning and more secular *Autobiography* makes an apt parallel.

Questions for Reading and Discussion/ Approaches to Writing

1. (a) Characterize Ashbridge's spiritual struggles and marital dilemmas. Does she resolve the former at the expense of the latter?

   (b) In what ways do you empathize with Ashbridge in her conflict with her husband? Why or why not? How might you act differently from either or both of them in this situation?

    (c) Does the community treat Ashbridge fairly following her conversion?

    (d) What implicit moral and spiritual advice does the piece contain?

2. How does Ashbridge structure the narrative and construct herself as a character in her own story to win sympathy and intellectual support from readers? Is she successful?

3. (a) Write a counterpart narrative (or defense) from the husband's point of view.

    (b) Write an Anglican's critique of or commentary upon Ashbridge's behavior.

    (c) Invent an imaginative dialogue between Ashbridge and Jonathan Edwards (or any of the following) concerning religious or gender issues: Anne Hutchinson, Mary Rowlandson, Anne Bradstreet, Samuel Sewall, Sarah Kemble Knight Benjamin Franklin, Abigail Adams, and so forth.

Bibliography

Two recent studies have provided important new information on Elizabeth Ashbridge. The most significant published source is Daniel Shea's new edition of Ashbridge's *Some Account of the Fore Part of the Life of Elizabeth Ashbridge*, available with his detailed introduction and textual notes, in *Journeys in New Worlds: Early American Narratives*, edited by William L. Andrews et. al. (Madison: University of Wisconsin Press, 1990), from which this excerpt is drawn. Christine Levenduski's dissertation, "Elizabeth Ashbridge's 'Remarkable Experiences': Creating the Self in a Quaker Personal Narrative" (University of Minnesota, 1989), is an invaluable book-length discussion of the text and its author. Carol Edkins's "Quest for Community: Spiritual Autobiographies of Eighteenth-Century Quaker and Puritan Women in America" in *Women's Autobiography: Essays in Criticism*, edited by Estelle C. Jelinek (Bloomington: Indiana University Press, 1980), pp. 39–52, also discusses Ashbridge substantively. Shea and Levenduski contain useful bibliographies of further materials providing background to Ashbridge's life and narrative.

John Woolman (1720–1772)

Contributing Editor: James A. Levernier

Classroom Issues and Strategies

Students often have a difficult time reading eighteenth-century nonfiction prose. The issues it reveals seem dated and unexciting to them. A writer like Woolman comes across as a moral "antique" to students who would much prefer to skip over the entire period and move on to Melville, Hawthorne, and Poe in the next century.

I try to point out to students that Woolman is, in many ways, very contemporary. He almost single-handedly defied many of the conventional views of his day and was willing to stand up and take the heat for the things that he believed in. I also point out that the principles that Woolman uses to deal with the evils he perceives in society are by no means dated. Many of the issues he brings up still exist today but in different, more subtle, forms, and it is our responsibility to deal with those issues. Social injustices, bigotry, and poverty are, unfortunately, still very much with us today. Woolman offers us an example and guidance in such matters.

Students are often quite interested in Quakers and their culture. Most of them have heard something about Quakers, but they don't really understand them. They are usually quite moved by the conviction behind Woolman's writings and can identify with it. They want to know if he was typical of Quaker thinking and why they haven't been taught more about the effect of Quaker ideas on American culture.

Major Themes, Historical Perspectives, and Personal Issues

Woolman writes about many themes that should be emphasized:

1. Slavery as a historical issue.
2. Racism and prejudice as issues that are still very much alive today.
3. The responsibility of the individual for social injustices.
4. The need for conviction and passion in our moral and social lives.
5. The potential of any one person for bringing about true reform.

Significant Form, Style, or Artistic Conventions

In discussing Woolman, one needs to discuss the practice of keeping journals among Quakers and early Americans generally. Why did Quakers keep journals? Why did they publish them? An analysis of Woolman's simple and direct style is very useful to seeing the "art" in the *Journal*, since his style of writing very effectively underscores and enhances the power of his convictions. I also draw connections between journals written by Quakers and journals written by Puritans to the north. Quaker journals have an inner peace that Puritan journals often lack.

Original Audience

Woolman wrote the *Journal* and his *Plea for the Poor* for future generations. He certainly knew that the *Journal* at least would not be published in his lifetime. There is a rhetorical strategy behind the *Journal* that revisions within the work reveal. Clearly, Woolman wanted us to see the effects of the workings of the "Inner Light" in his own life so that we could perhaps begin to cultivate with equal effect the "Inner Light" he felt was within each of us. *Considerations* (I and II) were more immediate in their audience concerns; they are persuasive tracts, meant to bring about immediate action through a direct appeal to the consciences of those who read them.

Comparisons, Contrasts, Connections

Woolman can be tied to nineteenth-century American autobiographers, especially Henry David Thoreau and Henry Adams. The Quaker influence can also be connected to John Greenleaf Whittier, Emerson, and Whitman. The connections between the Quaker "Inner Light" and the type of transcendentalism expressed in Emerson's works, particularly in *Nature*, should be emphasized. Woolman also should be compared and contrasted to the journal writers and autobiographers of seventeenth- and eighteenth-century New England. John Winthrop, for instance, kept a journal for far different reasons and with far different results than did Woolman.

Questions for Reading and Discussion/ Approaches to Writing

1. (a) Would Woolman feel that his life and ministry made a difference to the world of today?

(b) How would he feel about today's world? About social injustice in third world countries? About our response as individuals and as Americans to poverty and social injustice in other lands?
2. Comparison/contrast papers are very useful ways to develop insights into Woolman. He can be compared, for example, to Bradford, to Emerson, to Adams, and to Whitman. Sometimes I ask students to envision three or more writers together in a room today discussing an issue. What would each writer say about the issue? Feminism, for example, or the atomic bomb. This device often helps students to enter the writer's world and better understand the imaginative process.

A Selection of Eighteenth-Century Poetry

Contributing Editors: Pattie Cowell and Carla Mulford

Classroom Issues and Strategies

Beginning students struggle with these materials, partly because they arise from a time and aesthetic unfamiliar to them and partly because poetry as a genre seems more difficult to many of them. I find it most effective to try two contradictory strategies simultaneously: I ask students to stretch their historical imaginations with a bit of time-travel ("Dr. Who" comes to mind), and I try to highlight the ways in which the themes and concerns of these poets are still with us.

Though the time-travel is more fun at first for me than for the students, most of them get the idea soon enough. I take them back to a time when there was no United States, when poetry was the primary literary genre (and changes were in store), when midwives outnumbered physicians, when western Pennsylvania seemed like the outer edge of white civilization, when manuscript culture flourished alongside a fledgling printing industry, when individualism was not a cultural value (or even a part of the English language), when periodicals were a new phenomenon, when literacy rates were changing dramatically. The more concrete the context becomes, the more accessible the poetry. Some of this can be structured around a fairly accessible piece—Turell's "Lines on Childbirth," for example—if we try to reassemble as much as one can of Turell's world as we read: her literary aesthetic, her educational opportunities, health care, family life, and so forth.

Finding issues relevant to contemporary concerns in these poems is deceptively easy. While it is important not to construct eighteenth-century poets in our own image, they wrote about many of the things that concern us still: the stresses of war, the joys and struggles of family life, health and its absence, nature and human nature, travels, gender roles, religion, race and racism, the human comedy.

Major Themes, Historical Perspectives, and Personal Issues

The eighteenth-century poets represented here concern themselves with issues of class, race, and gender. Ebenezer Cook's "Sot-weed Factor," for example, is a freewheeling satire that takes class consciousness as a given for commenting on the conditions of life in colonial Maryland. Much of the humor derives from the pitiful way colonial subjects—farmers, yeomen, business people, laborers—measure up to their English counterparts. Sarah Morton's "The African Chief" is a prominent example of colonial concern over slavery. The anonymous "Lady's Complaint" attacks gender-based inequalities. And many other examples in this selection touch these issues as well.

From a historical perspective, eighteenth-century poets struggled with the cultural devaluation of poetry as a genre. As prose became more popular and socially influential, poetry lost much of its audience. Poets wrote implicit defenses of poetry, perhaps as counterweights to the shared cultural assumptions that produced de Tocqueville's (later) disparaging comment: "I readily admit that the Americans have no poets; I cannot allow that they have no poetic ideas." Thus poetry itself becomes an important theme.

In addition, the perennial question of geography may be significant here. Is this poetry English or American? Is the tradition that produced it a continuation of Old World traditions or evidence of New World exceptionalism? Or both? Poets continued to invent the New World, and in the later part of the century, the New Republic. What shape did these inventions take? How did they change over time? How did expectations clash with reality? How did authority mediate experience?

Significant Form, Style, or Artistic Conventions

The selections here vary tremendously in form, but students will find a background in neoclassical aesthetics useful for most of them.

Original Audience

The original audience for eighteenth-century American poetry depended on the vehicle for distribution. Of course it was restricted to the literate, making it a mostly white audience. But beyond that given, audiences would vary. Periodical poetry would have wide regional circulation, especially in urban areas. Books and chapbooks might circulate in both England and the colonies. Manuscript verse would circulate largely among family and friends of the writer, perhaps in a club or salon setting, groups more frequently found among well-to-do readers.

Comparisons, Contrasts, Connections

Comparisons with contemporary English poets can be instructive. Geographical or regional contrasts among the colonial selections illustrate the lack of a national voice until very late in the century.

Bibliography

Cowell, Pattie. *Women Poets in Pre-Revolutionary America*. Troy, NY: Whitston, 1981. Entries grouped by individual poets, so access to relevant material is relatively easy.

Davis, Richard Beale. *Intellectual Life in the Colonial South*, Vol. III. Knoxville: University of Tennessee Press, 1978. On William Dawson.

Individual entries in *American Writers Before 1800*, edited by James A. Levernier and Douglas R. Wilmes. Westport, Conn.: Greenwood, 1983.

Lemay, J. A. Leo. "Ebenezer Cooke." In *Men of Letters in Colonial Maryland*. Knoxville: University of Tennessee Press, 1972: 77–110.

——. "Richard Lewis and Augustan American Poetry." *PMLA* 83 (March 1968): 80–101.

Silverman, Kenneth, ed. *Colonial American Poetry*. New York: Hafner, 1976. Anthology.

Watts, Emily Stipes. *The Poetry of American Women from 1632 to 1945*. Austin: University of Texas Press, 1977: 9–61.

Enlightenment Voices, Revolutionary Visions

Benjamin Franklin (1706–1790)

Contributing Editor: David M. Larson

Classroom Issues and Strategies

The primary problem involved in teaching Benjamin Franklin in an American literature course is persuading students to view Franklin as a writer. The myth surrounding Franklin and the fact that he writes in genres many students view as informational rather than literary keep students from viewing Franklin's works as literature. In order to persuade students to treat Franklin as a writer, it is useful to demonstrate through literary analysis that issues of personae, organization, irony, style, and so forth are as applicable to writing that deals with factual information as they are to poetry, fiction, or drama. In teaching the *Autobiography*, instructors should keep in mind that it is helpful to have students approach it as though it were a picaresque novel; they can then bring to bear upon the work the techniques that they have developed for analyzing fiction.

Students usually respond to and are rather disturbed by the protean quality of Franklin's personality and the variety of his achievements. They want the "real" Franklin to stand up and make himself known, and they want to know how he accomplished so much.

Major Themes, Historical Perspectives, and Personal Issues

Franklin's contribution to the creation of an American national identity is perhaps the most important theme that needs to be emphasized. In connection with this, the students can discuss his role in the shift of the American consciousness from an otherworldly to a this-worldly viewpoint. Franklin's abandonment of Puritanism in favor of enlightenment rationalism reflects a central shift in American society in the eighteenth century. In addition, his works reflect the growing awareness of America as a country with values and interests distinct from those of England—a movement which, of course, finds its climax in the Revolution. Franklin's participation in the growing confidence of the eighteenth century that humanity could, through personal effort and social reform, analyze and deal with social problems reveals the optimism and self-confidence of his age, as do his scientific achievements. His belief that theory should be tested primarily by experience, not logic, also reflects his era's belief that reason should be tested pragmatically. Perhaps most important, in the *Autobiography* Franklin creates not only the classic story of the self-made man but also attempts to recreate himself and his career as the archetypal American success story. Since such varied writers as Herman Melville (*Israel Potter,* "Bartleby, the Scrivener," and *Benito Cereno*), Mark Twain, Thoreau (the "Economy" chapter of *Walden*), William Dean Howells (*The Rise of Silas Lapham*), and F. Scott Fitzgerald (*The Great Gatsby*) respond to the myth Franklin creates, the *Autobiography* can be used as a basis for examining the question of what it means to be an American and what the dominant American values are. Given the current debate over multiculturalism, a discussion of Franklin's career as statesman and writer as an attempt to create a unified American identity—and thus to suppress the multicultural elements in the emerging nation—should prove provocative. When placed in context with the works of Crèvecoeur and Jefferson, Franklin's writings should help students understand why, in the later eighteenth century, the shedding of ethnic and religious tradition and the embracing in their place of a national identity based on shared ideas are seen by many progressive intellectuals as ways to free the individual from the constricting hand of the repressive past.

Significant Form, Style, or Artistic Conventions

Franklin must be viewed as an eighteenth-century writer. The eighteenth century's didacticism, its refusal to limit literature to *belles lettres,* its ideal of the *philosophe* or universal genius, and its emphasis on the rhetoric of persuasion all need emphasis. In this connection, students need to become familiar with the use of personae in eighteenth-century writing, with both straightforward and satiric means of rhetorical persuasion, and with the ideal of the middle style in English prose. In addition, students studying Franklin need to become familiar with the conventions of political and other persuasive writing, with those of scientific writing, with those of the letter, and, especially, with the conventions of satire and autobiography in the period. Since for most students the eighteenth century is foreign territory and since the study of eighteenth-century writers has been neglected in American literature, students need to learn the ways in which the ideals and practice of literature in Franklin's age differ from the Romantic and post-Romantic works with which many of them are more familiar.

Original Audience

Since almost all of Franklin's writing is occasional, prompted by a specific situation and written for a particular audience, a consideration of situation and audience is crucial for understanding his work. Each of the satires, for example, is designed for a particular audience and situation. Also, *Poor Richard's Almanac* can only be appreciated when it is viewed as a popular publication for a group of non-literary farmers and mechanics. In contrast, Franklin's French *bagatelles* are written for a very sophisticated audience who would savor their complex personae and ambiguously ironic tone. The *Autobiography* is designed not merely for Franklin's contemporaries but for posterity as well. Consequently, one of the most interesting features of the study of Franklin as a writer is an examination of the ways in which he adapts his style, tone, organization, and personae to a variety of audiences and situations.

Comparisons, Contrasts, Connections

Franklin can usefully be compared to a host of different writers. The traditional comparison between Franklin and his Puritan predecessors remains useful. For example, while Puritan spiritual autobiographies emphasize their authors' dependence upon God for grace and salvation and their inability to achieve virtue without grace, Franklin's *Autobiography* focuses on his own efforts to learn what is virtuous in this world and to put his discoveries to use in his life. Franklin retains the Puritan concern for self-improvement but removes its otherworldly orientation. Similarly, Cotton Mather's and Franklin's views of the importance of benevolence can usefully be compared and contrasted. And Edwards's thought, with its attempt to understand this world in the light of Puritan assumptions about God and His divine scheme for humanity, can be contrasted with Franklin's, which focuses on this world, largely ignores the next, and sees morality and experience as more important than faith. Franklin's works also can be compared to those of the great eighteenth-century English prose writers. In his preference for reasonableness, common sense, and experience over emotion or speculation, Franklin shows his indebtedness to the English writers of the early eighteenth century and to the new scientific spirit promoted by the Royal Society. Franklin's style owes much to the example of Defoe, Addison, and Steele; his satiric practice—especially his mastery of the creation of diverse personae and, at times, his use of irony—reflects his familiarity with Swift's satire, even though Franklin's effects are very different. And Franklin's ideas, persuasive methods, assumptions, and empirical bent can be compared to and contrasted with those of his great British contemporary and pamphlet opponent, Samuel Johnson. Also, Franklin's achievements in such diverse fields as science, literature, politics, and diplomacy can be compared to the achievements of the eighteenth-century philosophes, such as Voltaire, Rousseau, and Diderot, with whom he was classed in his own age. Finally, examine Franklin's stylistic and persuasive methods and his intellectual assumptions in relation to his younger contemporary, Thomas Jefferson.

It is useful at some point to discuss the ways in which contemporary assumptions about literature differ from those of Franklin and affect our response to his works and the reasons Franklin has not traditionally been given the same degree of attention in American literature courses that such figures as Swift and Johnson have in British literature courses. Such topics can lead to a discussion of the formation of canon.

Questions for Reading and Discussion/ Approaches to Writing

The study questions that help students before they read Franklin depend entirely on the works that have been read previously. Since students in a historical survey of American literature usually approach Franklin after reading heavily in Puritan literature, ask questions that force students to confront the similarities and the differences between Franklin and his Puritan predecessors. If most students have had a British literature survey, ask questions that encourage them to pinpoint some of the similarities and differences between Franklin and such eighteenth-century writers as Swift, Defoe, and Samuel Johnson.

With Franklin, topics can be historical (focusing on Franklin's contribution to any number of events or ideas), comparative (comparing Franklin's works to those of American, British, or European writers), cultural (focusing on Franklin's pertinence to American culture at any stage past the eighteenth century), or narrowly literary (focusing on any number of facets of Franklin's artistry as a writer). The success of the topic depends largely on the extent to which it ties in with the approach taken by the teacher of the course.

Bibliography

The headnote contains a list of useful books. In addition, the following works might be helpful.

References

Buxbaum, Melvin. *Benjamin Franklin: 1721–1983: A Reference Guide*, 2 vols. Boston: G. K. Hall, 1983, 1988.

Lemay, J. A. Leo. *The Canon of Benjamin Franklin, 1722–1776: New Attributions and Reconsiderations*. Newark: University of Delaware Press, 1986.

Other Secondary Material

Buxbaum, Melvin. *Critical Essays on Benjamin Franklin*. Boston: G. K. Hall, 1987.

Larson, David M. "Benevolent Persuasion: The Art of Benjamin Franklin's Philanthropic Papers." *The Pennsylvania Magazine of History and Biography* 110 (April 1986): 195–215.

Lemay, J. A. Leo. "Benjamin Franklin." In *Major Writers of Early American Literature*, edited by Everett Emerson. Madison: University of Wisconsin Press.

Levin, David. "The *Autobiography* of Benjamin Franklin: Puritan Experimenter in Life and Art." *Yale Review* 53 (December 1963): 258–75.

Lynen, John F. "Benjamin Franklin and the Choice of a Single Point of View." In *The American Puritan Imagination: Essays in Revaluation*, edited by Sacvan Bercovitch. London: Cambridge University Press, 1974.

Sayre, Robert F. *The Examined Self: Benjamin Franklin, Henry Adams, Henry James*. Princeton: Princeton University Press, 1964.

Wright, Esmond. *Benjamin Franklin: His Life as He Wrote It*. Cambridge: Harvard University Press, 1990.

John Leacock (1729–1802)

Contributing Editor: Carla Mulford

Major Themes, Historical Perspectives, and Personal Issues

Although the writings of John Leacock seem to have been as popular as those of, say, Francis Hopkinson, and although parts of Leacock's biblical parodic satire *The First Book of the American Chronicles of the Times* were as widely reprinted in newspapers as the Federalist Papers, they have largely been lost to American literary historians. Their loss from American literary history probably results from the efforts of nineteenth-century historians to find continuity in the very discontinuous early American culture. If the founding American ideology was taken by our nineteenth-century historians (like the New Englander Moses Coit Tyler) to be a distinctively Puritan ideology, then those historians sought to create an American past—amid the instability of late nineteenth-century American society—that was coherent and continuously Puritan. Indeed, except for the writings of Benjamin Franklin (which found their own odd historical-interpretive path), the writings from the Middle Atlantic states and especially Philadelphia—that is, the largest trade and industrial area for the fifty mid-century years of the eighteenth century—along with writings from the South were for the most part noticed for their "quaintness" only, if noticed at all.

Other reasons, too, might be adduced for the loss to American literary history of the genre—anthologized here for the first time—of biblical parodic satire, despite its popularity in the colonies. Its loss probably results in large measure from the parodic form itself, which brought a possibility for double-voicing that could direct satire not only at England but *at other colonies*. Nineteenth-century literary historians tended not to discuss the inter-colonial contention rife during the Federal period, and they tended to blur the problems texts like Leacock's satire—and even the Federalist Papers—addressed.

Perhaps, too, readers in the past felt uncomfortable with biblical imitation that was not fully and clearly reverential toward the Bible. In addition, the fact that *The First Book of the American Chronicles of the Times* imitated (or parodied) the Bible could have caused dislike among "romantic" readers, who argued that parody was the enemy of inspirational, original (romantic) creations. Its parodic form and its political intent no doubt contributed to the neglect in the American literary past of the *American Chronicles*, one of the most humorous pieces of early American literature.

The selections here from Leacock's biblical parodic satire and from his play allude to Puritan self-justification in terms of a necessary indigenous right to have riches and freedom, a right provided both by God (given as a New Canaan) and by the Indians (given as a representative, native republicanism). Precisely because of the form of the text as biblical parodic satire, *The First Book of the American Chronicles of the Times* at once celebrates and calls into question the Puritan sense of a hegemonic destiny. This is not to say that the satire is anti-"American." The satire is clearly anti-British in support of the American cause of freedom. But the satire questions, as well, the American attitude about military glory, which seems (within the context of this complicated satire) not far different from British (and especially Puritan, as represented by Oliver Cromwell) military vainglory.

Leacock's writings reproduced here would fit well in a syllabus that calls for students to read and discuss writings and issues of Native Americans, Puritans, and/or Philadelphians and to treat questions of genre in early American literature.

Bibliography

For further discussion of John Leacock and his writings, see "John Leacock" in *Dictionary of Literary Biography: Volume 31, American Colonial Writers, 1735–1781*, edited by Emory Elliott (Detroit: Gale, for Bruccoli-Clark, 1984), and *Philadelphia: Three Centuries of American Art* (Philadelphia: Philadelphia Museum of Art, 1976), in addition to the following titles:

Dallett, Francis James, Jr. "John Leacock and *The Fall of British Tyranny*." *Pennsylvania Magazine of History and Biography* 78 (1954): 456–75.

Mulford, Carla. *John Leacock's The First Book of the American Chronicles of the Times, 1774–1775*. Newark: University of Delaware Press, 1987.

Mulford [Micklus]. "John Leacock's *A New Song, On the Repeal of the Stamp Act*." *Early American Literature* 15 (1980): 188–93.

——. *The Fall of British Tyranny. Trumpets Sounding: Propaganda Plays of the American Revolution*, edited by Norman Philbrick. New York: Benjamin Blom, 1976.

J. Hector St. John de Crèvecoeur (1735–1813)

Contributing Editor: Doreen Alvarez Saar

Classroom Issues and Strategies

Letters is a very accessible text; the greatest difficulty in teaching it is establishing the cultural context—the political rhetoric of the Revolution—which makes structural sense of the whole.

Generally, students read the text as the simple story of a farmer and as "truth" rather than as fiction. The teaching challenge is to get students to see how political ideas structure the text. One way into the text is to have the students read Letter II and count the references, both direct and indirect, to the way society should be organized. In the opening section of the letter, James compares his situation to the state of other farmers in other nations. Later in Letter II, note how the supposedly neutral descriptions of animals are used to talk about the conduct of humans in society.

Students are generally intrigued by the idea that members of the colonies were actually against the Revolution.

Major Themes, Historical Perspectives, and Personal Issues

In the course of *Letters*, through the character of James, Crèvecoeur describes for his reader how social principles laid out by the new American society operate in the life of an individual American. There are many interesting themes that can be pointed out in the text: the nature of the American character—the work ethic, the responsibility of the individual, anti-intellectualism; the farmer as a prototype of the American character; the treatment of slaves; the view of new immigrants and their ethnicity; literary resonances such as the escape from civilization in Letter XII and stereotypical American characters. One theme that is frequently overlooked is James's desire not to participate in the Revolution. Students believe that all colonists accepted the righteousness of the Revolutionary cause. A discussion of James's feelings helps students recognize the constancy of division in society and is useful for later discussions of the social and literary reactions to the Civil War and the Vietnam War.

Significant Form, Style, or Artistic Conventions

Eighteenth-century Americans did not share our modern idea that politics and art must be kept separate. Thus, some forms of eighteenth-century writing do not conform to common notions about genres and form. For an interesting discussion of the social form of the American novel, see Jane Tompkins's discussion of Charles Brockden Brown's novels in *Sensational Designs*. Further, the form of *Letters* is related to other less common genres like the philosophical travel book, which was often epistolary in form (Montesquieu's *Persian Letters* is a good example).

Original Audience

When students read *Letters*, they find its substance very familiar because much of this material has become part of the mythology of America. Students need to be reminded that *Letters* was one of the first works describing the character of the average American. Also, its American readers were a society of colonials who had just overturned centuries of tradition and were attempting to define themselves as something new, in order to distinguish themselves from those who were exactly like them but born under monarchical governments in Europe. European readers were trying to make sense of this "new man."

Comparisons, Contrasts, Connections

Letters is a good literary expression of the political principles in the Declaration of Independence and Paine's *Common Sense*. It is very useful to read *Letters* in tandem with Book II of Timothy Dwight's *Greenfield Hill*, which is another imaginative creation of the "ideal" average American.

Bibliography

For a quick introduction to the political rhetoric of the period, instructors might read: pp. 82–86 in *A Cultural History of the American Revolution* by Kenneth Silverman (excerpted in *Early American Literature*, edited by Michael Gilmore); Chapters 1 and 2 of Gordon S. Wood's *The Creation of the American Republic;* and Doreen Alvarez Saar's "Crèvecoeur's 'Thoughts on Slavery': Letters from an American Farmer and the Rhetoric of Whig Thought" in *Early American Literature* (Fall 1987): 192–203.

Thomas Paine (1737–1809)

Contributing Editor: Martin Roth

Major Themes, Historical Perspectives, and Personal Issues

From the perspective of contemporary feminism, Paine displays a mixture of insight and blindness. In his "Occasional Letter to the Female Sex," he is sensitive to the oppression of women. In fact, he acknowledges it to be universal, and he links it somehow with their being adored by men—as if the adoration were the other side of their oppression. On the other hand, he seems to believe that women can properly be identified with their beauty—"when they are not beloved they are nothing"—and motherhood (their only "call" on men). And the tag from Otway suggests that men and women are totally opposite species, contrasting as brutes and angels.

Nature and Reason are not abstract principles for Paine. They are not categories through which it is useful to think about things, but dynamic principles that Paine almost literally sees at work in the world. Reason in *Common Sense* is masculine, a most concrete actor pleading with us to separate from England or forbidding us to have faith in our enemies. Nature is feminine; "she" weeps, and she is unforgiving as part of her deepest nature. Should these agencies be regarded as philosophical principles? As deities? Are they coherent characters? Can they be identified by collecting all their behaviors and their metaphoric qualifications?

How do we think about Paine as an author, a writing "I"? One of his works is presented as having been written by an embodied principle of "common sense," and another piece, *The Age of Reason*, a work on the general truth of religion, opens in an extremely private, confessional mode. But he writes in this way to prove that he could have no private motives for misleading others. What kind of stakes are being waged by writing a work on religious truth just before you die? Is there any distinction for Paine between the private and the public I, the private and the public life? Notice how many statements fold back upon the self: "it is necessary to the happiness of man that he be mentally faithful to himself" and "my own mind is my own church."

Paine evokes the splendor of the visible world to close a unit opened by the notion of a privileged book, a "revealed" book, a Bible.

How are the book and the world opposed to each other? One of these ways is as writing and speech; although, actually, the world transcends the distinction between writing and speech: it "speaketh a universal language" which "every man can read." Could Paine's distrust and rejection of the Bible be applied to those other "revealed" and "privileged" pieces of writing, literary "masterpieces"? Much of Paine can be read as an attack on the book, a motif that connects him with Mark Twain at the end of the next century.

In *The Rights of Man*, Paine assumes that the right to engage in revolution is inalienable. How does he understand this? Can time and complexity alter this characteristic of the nature of things? What is a government for Paine? The metaphors that he uses should again remind us of Twain, images of stealth and deceit, images of theatricality used for purposes of fraud.

Family is crucial here, too, as Paine examines the absurdity of hereditary aristocracy. In this as in almost everything he does, the later writer that Paine most evokes is Mark Twain, here the Mark Twain of *A Connecticut Yankee* and *The American Claimant*. Among the resemblances to Twain that should not be overlooked is a vein of extremely cunning black humor in much of *The Age of Reason*.

John Adams (1735–1826)
Abigail Adams (1744–1818)

Contributing Editors: Albert Furtwangler and Frank Shuffelton

Classroom Issues and Strategies

The formality and elevated decorum of John Adams's language challenge many students, but the opening anecdotes and the witty exchanges between John and Abigail encourage readers to see the personalities behind the mannered language. John Adams (and to a lesser extent Abigail as well) is also somewhat difficult because he has been mythicized as a Founding Father, a figure of national piety who no longer commands a ready allegiance. Additionally, the interests of the Adams in politics and morality do not strike all students as "literature." On the other hand, the questions raised in this material about the political relationships between men and women and by the exchange between Adams and Jefferson over the meaning and impact of "talent" continue to be crucial in our own time. The formal language, the learned references, if brought into play in discussions about the contemporary power of the issues debated by the Adamses and their friends, can set limits on the tendency toward "presentism," and the urge to only see the significance of the past in terms of present meanings. The Adamses talk about questions we care about, but their language, their style, remind us that they did not necessarily see these questions as we do.

Major Themes, Historical Perspectives, and Personal Issues

Major themes in the writing of the Adamses and their friends relate to the discourse of republicanism that dominated the political and social thinking of enlightened people in the eighteenth century. Adams and many others of his time feared the corruption that he thought inevitably followed upon the increasing sophistication of a developing civilization. His letter to his friend Mercy Otis Warren offers a synopsis of this attitude, including the fear of social laxity that will unleash self-indulgent passion, the unnatural tastes fostered by a burgeoning commercial society, and the disruption by faction of the social harmony needed to sustain a republic. Abigail's desire to return to her farm, stated at the end of her journal entry on her return from Europe, links this republican attitude with the pastoralism found in the work of writers like Crèvecoeur, Jefferson, and James Fenimore Cooper, perhaps even with Huckleberry Finn's famous "lighting out."

Abigail Adams's prodding of her husband to "Remember the Ladies" has become a classic benchmark of an emerging feminism, but she is surely no feminist. Nonetheless, she figures as a splendid example of that new sort of woman that Linda Kerber has referred to as the "republican mother" (*Women of the Republic*, 1980). Women like Adams and Mercy Otis Warren took a direct interest in the outcome of the American Revolution, and they spoke their thoughts in private and public, opening the way, perhaps, for more forthright arguments on the behalf of women, such as those by Judith Sargeant Murray and, in a later period, Margaret Fuller.

After the ratification of the Constitution and the creation of the federal government, Adams feared anarchic excesses, encouraged by the French Revolution, among the ill-educated and easily misled populace. Jefferson and the leaders of the emerging Republican party castigated Adams and the Federalists as "monocrats" who wished to seat political power in the hands of a few men of property and family. Adams's belief in a government of laws, however, as well as his suspicion of power that was exerted only by privileged groups earned him the distrust of

Hamilton and the more extreme Federalists. The controversies among these people were not merely over a share of political power, but over the much more crucial question of whether the nation could continue to exist as such. The genuine fear of disorder and social collapse that motivated Adams appears in a different guise in the fiction of Charles Brockden Brown. Jefferson's comments regarding his trust of the good sense of the common people reveal an attitude different from that of Adams, but even he, especially at the end of his life, expressed his fear for the survival of the American experiment. In the correspondence with Jefferson, however, Adams seems rather to have enjoyed playing the cynical foil to his friend's optimism.

Significant Form, Style, or Artistic Conventions

All of the Adams material included here are drawn from the personal, private genres of the journal and letters. They were intended to be read by trusted family and friends, but they were also expected to be shared among a circle of such readers. Jefferson expected that Abigail Adams would read his letters to John, and similarly John Adams would have expected Mercy Otis Warren to have shared her letter with her husband, James, a political leader in Massachusetts. Such correspondence was one aspect of the eighteenth-century republic of letters, the public sphere of discussion about social, political, and learned questions that occurred independently of the narrow limits of the family as well as of the overview of the state. Considered in this way, the letters between John and Abigail, for instance, are both the intimate exchange of husband and wife and the communication between a constituent and her delegate to the revolutionary Congress of 1776.

Comparisons, Contrasts, Connections

These selections make a lively contrast to the impersonal rationality of the Federalist essays or the Declaration of Independence. The journal selections can be used in the context of earlier and later traditions of journal-keeping in New England and are interesting for their moral introspection and regulation as well as for their attention to the way human beings live in the world. They take an interesting position between Winthrop, Sewall, Sarah Kemble Knight, and Emerson and Thoreau. Similarly, Adams's concern for a virtuous republic can be framed against Winthrop's discussion of the city on a hill and Thoreau's "Resistance to Civil Government."

Bibliography

Adams's grandson, Charles Francis Adams, edited his *Works* (1850–56) in ten volumes, still a useful source for those who wish to read more. Albert Furtwangler discusses Adams's newspaper debate with a loyalist in *American Silhouettes* (1987); this book also contains a discussion of Adams and Jefferson. Peter Shaw's *The Character of John Adams* (1976) is a significant discussion, as is Joseph J. Ellis, *Passionate Sage: John Adams and America's Original Intentions* (1993). Edith Gelles, *Portia: The World of Abigail Adams* (1992), is particularly illuminating on the role of letters in Abigail Adams's life.

Thomas Jefferson (1743–1826)

Contributing Editor: Frank Shuffelton

Classroom Issues and Strategies

Jefferson does not write in traditionally conceived literary genres, i.e., fiction, poetry, etc., but his best writing is in the form of public addresses, letters, and a political and scientific account of his home state. One can persuade students to see the cultural significance of these forms and then lead them to see the artful construction of image and idea to move readers and to recognize that the texts work (perform) as literature.

Students are particularly interested in discussing the notion of equality, and most people in general want to talk about Sally Hemings. The contradiction between Jefferson's egalitarianism and his racism (real or apparent) also provokes discussion.

Major Themes, Historical Perspectives, and Personal Issues

For Jefferson, the values of political and moral equality, the scientific interest in variety and complexity in nature and culture, and a kind of skepticism, a doubt that absolute truth can be unequivocally attained in any generation, put him in the line of Ralph Waldo Emerson and William James. At the same time, the fact that he seems to represent the voiceless and the marginal as a political leader even while his own interests and social position put him among the white male elite of his time points to certain tensions in his positions, of which he was not himself always aware.

Significant Form, Style, or Artistic Conventions

Jefferson published only one full-length book, his *Notes on the State of Virginia*, but the Declaration of Independence and his letters are also significant literary achievements. The Declaration matters because of its significance for our national culture, the letters because of their frequent power to express Jefferson's public ideals and commitments, the importance of the many ideas and issues that fall under his consideration, and the clarity of his consideration. We should remember that Jefferson's sense of the historical moment conditioned practically everything he wrote.

Original Audience

The distinction between private audience, as for personal letters, and public audience, as for the Declaration, is interesting to pursue because Jefferson blurred them in interesting ways. Some of his letters were published, usually against his will but not without his recognition that personal letters could always become public, and yet he was somewhat reluctant to publish *Notes on the State of Virginia*.

Comparisons, Contrasts, Connections

Comparisons are effective; for example, the Declaration to Puritan sermons, *Notes on the State of Virginia* to Crèvecoeur's *Letters* or to Bartram's *Travels*. It is also helpful to get students to think about the importance of history and politics as central matrices for eighteenth-century thought, the move toward science and natural history as the nineteenth century approached, and the different ways we in the late twentieth century have for ordering our knowledge of the world.

The Declaration is a kind of jeremiad in Sacvan Bercovitch's sense of the term, which involves an ironically affirmative catalog of catastrophes, an admission of sins to cast them out. *Notes on the State of Virginia*, Crèvecoeur's *Letters*, and Bartram's *Travels* can be seen as different ways of defining the American landscape, as well as the place of America.

Bibliography

Useful essays on a variety of topics appear in *Thomas Jefferson: A Reference Biography*, ed. Merrill D. Peterson (New York: Scribner's, 1986). See also its bibliographical essay.

Cunningham, Noble E, Jr. *In Pursuit of Reason: The Life of Thomas Jefferson*. Baton Rouge: LSU Press, 1987. A convenient one-volume biography.

Miller, John C. *The Wolf By the Ears: Thomas Jefferson and Slavery*. New York: Free Press, 1977. A thorough and balanced view of Jefferson's changing views on race and slavery.

Onuf, Peter, ed. *Jeffersonian Legacies*. Charlottesville: University Press of Virginia, 1993. Informed essays by younger scholars on most aspects of Jefferson's life and thought. Particularly interesting is Lucia Stanton's essay on the slave community at Monticello.

Peterson, Merrill. *Thomas Jefferson: A Reference Biography*. New York: Scribner's, 1986. Contains authoritative essays on Jefferson's interests and the issues in which he found himself involved. Has a useful bibliographical essay.

Patriot and Loyalist Songs and Ballads

Contributing Editor: Rosalie Murphy Baum

Classroom Issues and Strategies

Most students enjoy Patriot songs and ballads but approach Loyalist works with shyness and curiosity. Their studies in elementary, middle, and high school have led them to think of the Revolutionary War as a completely justified and glorious chapter in American history; they tend not to be aware of the Loyalist (Tory) view of the conflict. At the same time, however, their consciousness of recent American history and international events (e.g., the Vietnam War, the Iran-Iraqi conflict, the Israeli-Palestinian struggles) have made them increasingly aware of the complexity of historical events and of the need to understand both sides of issues. The fact that the songs and ballads reflect and articulate two conflicting *American* views about a momentous period can be of great interest to students once they overcome their qualms about literature that questions or criticizes national decisions and actions.

Major Themes, Historical Perspectives, and Personal Issues

Reading the Patriot and Loyalist songs and ballads provides a glimpse of the popular sentiments being expressed in newspapers, periodicals, ballad-sheets, and broadsides during the Revolutionary period. The selections in the text represent various forms: the song and the ballad, the selection addressed to the public at large and the selection addressed to the child, the work expressing the Patriot or Loyalist position and the work commemorating the life of a particular hero. The usual themes of the Patriot and the Loyalist writers are summarized in the introduction to the selections.

A good glossary of literary terms can offer students information about the usual form and conventions of the song and ballad. Students should anticipate uneven work in popular songs and ballads, written in haste and for immediate practical purposes. At the same time, however, they may wish to examine what in these works accounted for their great popularity during the period and their survival through the years. Of particular interest might be an imaginative reconstruction of the response of both Patriot and Loyalist to either a Patriot or a Loyalist song.

Probably the most important facts students need to consider before reading Patriot and Loyalist songs and ballads are (a) at the time of the Revolutionary War, the Loyalists were Americans just as much as were the Patriots (Rebels or Whigs); (b) the Loyalist group included some of the leading figures in the country at the time (e.g., Chief Justice William Allen, the Rev. Mather Byles, Samuel Curwen, Joseph Galloway, Governor Thomas Hutchinson, the Rev. Jonathan Odell, Chief Justice Peter Oliver, the Rev. Samuel Seabury, Attorney General Jonathan Sewall), figures whom students tend not to recognize because of the usual emphasis in the classroom upon only Patriot figures; (c) whatever knowledge the students have of Loyalists probably comes from the remarks and writings of Patriots and thus is heavily slanted. The classroom emphasis on Patriot leaders and Patriot arguments, of course, distorts the political complexion of the time and does not help the student to appreciate the complex issues and emotional turmoil of a period in which it is believed that about one-third of the people were Patriots, one-third Loyalists, and one-third neutrals, with Loyalists being especially strong in Delaware, Maryland, New Jersey, New York, and Pennsylvania.

Comparisons, Contrasts, Connections

The sentiments of these works, both Patriot and Loyalist, can be compared very successfully with the ideas expressed by prose writers like John Adams, Benjamin Franklin, Thomas Jefferson, and Thomas Paine, Patriots who are frequently anthologized. Students, however, may also be interested in reading a few of the Loyalist prose writers, such as the Rev. Samuel Seabury ("A View of the Controversy Between Great Britain and Her Colonies") and Joseph Galloway ("Plan of a Proposed Union Between Great Britain and the Colonies" or "A Candid Examination of the Mutual Claims of Great Britain and the Colonies"). Students interested in popular culture may wish to pursue the difficult question of what characteristics distinguish popular literature, like these songs and ballads, from serious literature, like the poems of William Cullen Bryant, Walt Whitman, or Emily Dickinson. There could be considerable controversy about where the poetry of Philip Freneau should fit in such a comparison.

Approaches to Writing

Some students may simply wish to report on additional Patriot and Loyalist songs and ballads and can consult Frank Moore's *Songs and Ballads of the American Revolution* (1855, 1964) for the most complete collection. Other students may wish to consider the degree to which the Revolutionary War was very much a civil war. They might compare such a struggle to the conflict between the disparate cultures of the whites and Indians reflected in Puritan literature, or draw parallels between the civil conflict in America and similar hostilities in countries throughout the world today.

Bibliography

Two kinds of information can be particularly useful for students or instructors in studying the Patriot and Loyalist songs and ballads. The introductions to *Prose and Poetry of the Revolution* (1925, 1969), edited by Frederick C. Prescott and John H. Nelson, and to *The World Turned Upside Down* (1975), edited by James H. Pickering, give excellent, brief overviews of the period and of the literature.

William H. Nelson's *The American Tory* (1961) offers an excellent discussion of Loyalist views.

Wallace Brown's *The King's Friends* (1965) attempts to identify who the Loyalists were and to determine their motives for remaining loyal to the king.

Contested Boundaries, National Visions: Writings on "Race," Identity, and "Nation"

Jupiter Hammon (1711–1806?)

Contributing Editors: William H. Robinson and Phillip M. Richards

Classroom Issues and Strategies

African-American literature emerges at an auspicious time in the settlement of North America. The number of blacks entering the colonies increased markedly at the middle of the eighteenth century. Settled blacks in the New World may have acquired a new self-consciousness as they encountered large numbers of newly arrived Africans. Their consciousness as a separate group was defined by laws restricting racial intermarriage, by racist portrayals in the press, and by their increased involvement in the evangelical religion that emerged in the aftermath of the Great Awakening.

Jupiter Hammon, whose life roughly covers the span of the eighteenth century, was in an excellent position to see these trends. His writing reflects his efforts to evangelize his black brethren at a time when most African-Americans were not Christians. He is a traditional Calvinist. He is aware of Africa and the experience of the middle passage. Not surprisingly, his use of traditional evangelical rhetoric is deeply suggestive of the political implications that this discourse might have in the work of future writers.

Students should be aware that we read Hammon as we might read any American Calvinist writing in the last half of the eighteenth century. We look for the rhetoric that underlies his evangelical strategies; we try to establish the speaker's relationship to his white and black audiences; and we assess the way in which the religious language of his discourse begins to acquire a political resonance, particularly in its use of words such as "king," "nation," "salvation," and "victory."

Major Themes, Historical Perspectives, and Personal Issues

Psalms is the most quoted biblical book in the poem addressed to Phillis Wheatley. Why would Psalms be such an important book to a black preacher-poet such as Hammon? What importance do you think the broad sweep of Old Testament history might have had to Hammon? What importance did this history have to evangelicals and political revolutionaries in late eighteenth-century New England? At what points do you think that Hammon and his white evangelical peers' understanding of scripture might have diverged?

What poem by Phillis Wheatley has Hammon obviously read? Why do you think that he seized upon this verse in his own longer poem? What stance does the speaker of this poem assume toward his ostensible reader, Wheatley? Does this stance resemble the speaker's stance in Hammon's other work?

Significant Form, Style, or Artistic Convention

Examine the formal impact of the literary structure of the Psalms on Hammon's poems. What literary influence do hymn stanza form and sermon form have on his writing? In what social context do hymns and sermons occur? Why would Hammon be attempting to evoke that context in his writing?

Comparisons, Contrasts, Connections

In what way does the rhetoric of Christian salvation, both personal and national, imply a historical construct? Compare Hammon's and Wheatley's use of that construct. Why would such a construct be important to early American black writers?

Think of other early American writers who treat the subject of salvation in radically different ways. Would Jonathan Edwards and Benjamin Franklin respond to Hammon in the same ways? How would the two white writers differ, if they differed at all?

Questions for Reading and Discussion/ Approaches to Writing

Describe the way in which Christian thought and rhetoric structured Hammon's racial consciousness. Why is it significant that America's first black writers are Puritans? In what sense could a shared religious belief be important for racial relations in the late eighteenth and early nineteenth century?

Samson Occom (Mohegan) (1723–1792)

Contributing Editor: A. LaVonne Brown Ruoff

Classroom Issues and Strategies

"A Short Narrative of My Life" (dated September 17, 1768) is one of the earliest life histories written by an American Indian. Shortly after he returned from England in the spring of 1768, Occom began his "Short, Plain, and Honest Account of my Self" in order to refute false reports that he was a Mohawk, that Wheelock received large sums for his support, and that he had been converted just before the English tour in order to become a special exhibit (Blodgett 27). An important topic both in his narrative and sermon, as well as in the selection from Apess and Copway, is religious conversion. Students, who generally cannot understand why Indians became devout Christian converts, need to know that for Indians and for slaves, Christianity offered the possibility of being regarded by whites as equals under God. Indian authors, like slave narrators, frequently contrasted whites' professed Christianity with their mistreatment of minorities. Students also need to understand that until at least the late nineteenth century, most Indian education was conducted under the auspices of religious organizations. In the twentieth century, many reservation schools were still run by churches; even the Indian schools controlled by the government had a strong religious orientation.

Occom's narrative offers the opportunity to follow the stages of his movement from traditional Mohegan life to conversion and acculturation, his methods of teaching his Indian students and conducting church services, and resentment of being paid far less than white preachers because he was Indian.

In discussing "A Sermon Preached by Samson Occom," students should be given information about the structure and general content of execution sermons. All this is included in the text headnote and in the following section.

There are a number of issues that can help them see the significance of this sermon. I have had good discussions of why execution sermons were so popular during this period. I often relate these sermons and the confessions they contain to modern-day confessional talk shows.

Another issue is the delicate political task Occom faced in addressing both a white and Indian audience. See the discussion of style below.

Major Themes, Historical Perspectives, and Personal Issues

1. Identify the Mohegans as a tribe and give some sense of their background. A member of the Algonkian language family, the Mohegans originally were the northernmost branch of the Pequots, the fiercest of the New England tribes. During the 1637 war with the English, the Pequots were massacred near what is now Stonington, Connecticut. Led by their chief Uncas, the Mohegans, who sided with the English in the war, joined in the massacre. After the war, they remained at peace with the English but resumed hostilities with their old enemies, the Narragansetts. For a brief period, the Mohegans, then numbering 2,000, greatly expanded their territory. However, this had shrunk drastically by the end of the seventeenth century. English settlers, who regarded the nomadic Mohegans as idle thieves, issued orders to remove them from the towns. Uncas and his sons further decreased Mohegan territory by making large land transfers to the whites. By the end of the century, the Mohegans were no longer independent. The first successful attempt to gather them into Indian villages was made in 1717. Eight years later, the Mohegans numbered only 351 and were split into two opposing camps, located one-half mile apart on the west side of the Mohegan river between New London and Norwich, Connecticut.

2. "A Short Narrative of My Life"—Issues for discussion include the status of New England Indians in 1768, the relationship of the document to the spiritual confessions so popular in this period, and Occom's concept of self as expressed in his narrative.

3. "A Sermon Preached by Samson Occom"—
   a. Why were execution sermons so popular in this period? (See below.)

b. Structure and general content of the execution sermons.
All this is included in the text headnote and in the following section.

Significant Form, Style, or Artistic Conventions

In "A Short Narrative of My Life," which was not written for publication, Occom uses a much more conversational style than he does in "A Sermon." Why?

The latter is a typical example of the popular genre of the execution sermon. The first publication in New England to combine the offender's "True Confession" with the "Dying Warning" was Increase Mather's *The Wicked mans Portion* [sic] (1675). His *A Sermon Occasioned by the Execution of a Man found Guilty of Murder* [sic] (1686) expanded the literary form by including the murderer's complete confession as allegedly taken down in shorthand. The 1687 second edition added a discourse between the prisoner and minister, designed to introduce realism. Lawrence Towner argues that the genre demonstrated that New Englanders committed crimes and were led to contrition. Because the listeners to the sermons and readers of the "True Confessions" and "Dying Warnings" were at worst minor sinners, it was necessary to trace the criminal's career back to its origins and to generalize about the nature of crime. As criminals increasingly became outsiders (blacks, Indians, Irishmen, or foreign pirates), the tone of the True Confessions and Dying Warnings changed from moral suasion to titillation. So popular became the genre that in 1773, the year after the publication of Occom's sermon, eleven separate publications dealing with the condemned prisoner Levi Ames were printed. Wayne C. Minnick suggests that the authors of execution sermons ranked among the "best educated, most influential men of their society" (78).

A particularly important issue is the rhetorical strategies Occom uses to appeal to the church fathers, a generally white audience, Moses Paul, and Indian listeners. Having students pick out the phrases and comments that Occom makes to each person or group will help them see how skillful he was. Students need to realize what a politically delicate position Occom was in—he needed to educate his white audience without alienating them and to balance his presentations to the three groups that constituted the total audience. Another point to discuss is how Occom presents himself in the sermon.

Original Audience

It is important to get students to understand the religious milieu of the period, which responded to execution sermons as a form of spiritual confession. This can be compared with the confessions of contemporary born-again fundamentalists. The sermon was sometimes delivered in church on the Sunday or Thursday before the execution, but most frequently just before the time appointed for the hanging. Audiences numbered between 550 and 850.

Comparisons, Contrasts, Connections

"A Short Narrative"—The descriptions of Indian life can be compared with those by George Copway. Comparisons can also be made to the accounts of Indians in the "Literature of Discovery and Exploration" section, the accounts of Indian relations in selections by John Smith and Thomas Morton, and the descriptions of Indian life in the captivity narratives of Mary Rowlandson and John Williams.

Increase and Cotton Mather and Jonathan Edwards—the structure and general themes of their execution and other sermons—can be compared. These preachers emphasized dramatic conversion, which Edwards described as a three-stage process: (1) Fear, anxiety, and distress at one's sinfulness; (2) absolute dependence on the "sovereign mercy of God in Jesus Christ"; and (3) relief from distress under conviction of sin and joy at being accepted by God (Goen 14). This process, reflected in Occom's sermon, became the norm in the Great Awakening and in subsequent revivalism. Evangelists also used emotional extravagance in their sermons.

Questions for Reading and Discussion/ Approaches to Writing

"A Sermon"—Call attention to the structure and the concept of redemption through confession of sin. I do not assign a paper on this work. If I did, two possible topics would be Occom's use of distinct rhetorical strategies to appeal to the various groups in his audience and to Moses Paul; and the extent to which Occom follows the standard structure and basic content for such sermons (see text headnote).

Bibliography

Conkey, Laura E., Ethel Bolissevain, and Ives Goddard. "Indians of Southern New England and Long Island: Late Period." In *The*

Northeast, edited by Bruce G. Trigger, 177–89. *Handbook of North American Indians,* vol. 15. Washington, D.C.: Smithsonian, 1978. Valuable introduction to these tribes.

Goen, C. C. *Revivalism and Separatism in New England, 1740–1800: Strict Congregationalists and Separate Baptists in the Great Awakening.* New Haven: Yale University Press, 1962.

Heimert, Alan. *Religion and the American Mind: From the Great Awakening to the Revolution.* Cambridge: Harvard University Press, 1966.

Jennings, Francis. *The Invasion of America: Indians, Colonialism, and the Cant of Conquest.* New York: Norton, 1976. Standard work on the subject, with lengthy bibliography.

Minnick, Wayne C. "The New England Execution Sermon, 1639–1800." *Speech Monographs* 35 (1968): 77–89.

Salwen, Bert. "Indians of Southern New England and Long Island: Early Period." In *The Northeast,* edited by Bruce G. Trigger, 160–76. *Handbook of North American Indians,* vol. 15. Washington, D.C.: Smithsonian, 1978. Informative introduction to these tribes.

Sturtevant, William C., ed. *Handbook of North American Indians,* vol. 15. Washington, D.C.: Smithsonian, 1978.

Towner, Lawrence L. "True Confessions and Dying Warnings in Colonial New England." In *Sibley's Heir. A Volume in Memory of Clifford Kenyon Shipton,* 523–39. Boston: Colonial Society of Massachusetts and University Press of Virginia, 1982. The articles on the execution sermon by Minnick and Towner are especially good.

Trigger, Bruce G., ed. *The Northeast,* vol. 15. *Handbook of North American Indians,* edited by William C. Sturtevant. Washington, D.C.: Smithsonian, 1978.

Washburn, Wilcomb E. "Seventeenth-Century Indian Wars." In *The Northeast,* edited by Bruce G. Trigger, 89–100. *Handbook of North American Indians,* vol. 15. Washington, D.C.: Smithsonian, 1978. Good overview of these wars.

Prince Hall (1735?–1807)

Contributing Editor: William H. Robinson

Classroom Issues and Strategies

I have encountered no insurmountable problems in teaching Hall except to point out to students the differences (which may well have been "diplomatic") between Hall's almost illiterate manuscripts that were designed to be published and several of his other more acceptably normal manuscripts.

Although Hall wrote and published correspondence and wrote and co-signed almost a dozen petitions, I include him among examples of early American oratory.

Frequently asked student questions: In the two known Masonic "charges" that Hall published (1792 and 1797), where did he find the courage to be so outspoken? Could he find a presumably white Boston printer to publish the pieces?

Major Themes, Historical Perspectives, and Personal Issues

Hall was concerned with many aspects of racial uplift for black America and wrote about them all.

Significant Form, Style, or Artistic Conventions

As noted above, in class I note how Hall's nearly illiterate petitions, requiring an editor's "corrective" attention, may have been deliberately deferential. Hall was aware that not many white printers or publishers would readily publish manuscripts written by obviously literate blacks.

Original Audience

I point out the real differences in tone and general deference between Hall's petitions designed for white Boston legislators and other prominent whites, and the tone and racial outspokenness in his "charges," formal annual addresses to his fellow black Masons.

Comparisons, Contrasts, Connections

Although no black writer contemporary with Hall was so widely concerned with racial uplift, his work might be compared with Phillis Wheatley's letters, which are also concerned with black uplift and even "proper" Bostonian antislavery protest.

Questions for Reading and Discussion/ Approaches to Writing

I have asked students to compare the differences in tone and understanding of biblical injunctions between Jupiter Hammon and Prince Hall.

Bibliography

Crawford, Charles. *Prince Hall and His Followers*. New York: The Crisis, 1914, 33.

Kaplan, Sidney. *The Black Presence in the Era of the American Revolution*. Washington, D.C.: Smithsonian, 1973, 181–92.

Walker, Joseph. *Black Squares and Compass*. Richmond, Va.: Macon, 1979, *passim*.

Olaudah Equiano (1745–1797)

Contributing Editor: Angelo Costanzo

Classroom Issues and Strategies

I use Equiano as an introduction to American slave narrative literature and demonstrate the important influence of autobiographical form and style on the whole range of African-American literature up to the present day, including its impact on such writers as Richard Wright, Ralph Ellison, Alice Walker, and Toni Morrison.

Students are particularly interested in the way the whites conducted the slave trade in Africa by using the Africans themselves to kidnap their enemies and sell them into slavery. Equiano was sold this way. Also their interest is aroused by Equiano's fascinating descriptions of

Africa as a self-sufficient culture and society before the incursions of the whites. Students are moved by the graphic scenes of slavery, the Middle Passage experience described by Equiano, and his persistent desire for freedom. Most of all, they enjoy reading the first-person account of a well-educated and resourceful slave whose life story is filled with remarkable adventures and great achievements.

Since students have no prior knowledge of Equiano's life and work, I give background information on the history and sociology of the eighteenth-century slave trade, placing in this context Equiano's life story—his kidnapping, Middle Passage journey, slavery in the Western world, education, religion, and seafaring adventures. I also describe his abolitionist efforts in Great Britain, and I say something about his use of neoclassical prose in the autobiography.

Major Themes, Historical Perspectives, and Personal Issues

The students need to know about the slave trade and the condition of slavery on the Caribbean islands. As for the literary aspect of Equiano's work, the students should be instructed about the genre of spiritual autobiography, its structure, methods, and styles. In particular, information should be given on how spiritual autobiography was used in the formation of the new genre of slave narrative literature, mainly the three-part structure of slavery, escape, and freedom that corresponds to the spiritual autobiography's three parts that describe the life of sin, conversion, and spiritual rebirth.

Equiano's great autobiography illustrates influences from several popular schools of personal writing current in the eighteenth-century Western world. Among these are the spiritual autobiographical writings of St. Augustine and John Bunyan, the descriptive travel literary works of Daniel Defoe and Jonathan Swift, and the secular stories that display a hardworking youth's rise from rags-to-riches in the commercial world. The latter pattern can be seen quite well in Benjamin Franklin's *Autobiography*, a work that shares some interesting parallels with Equiano's narrative. Equiano, like Franklin, is an enterprising young man rising up in life and playing numerous roles that help to develop his character in a free world of possibility. Both Equiano and Franklin use self-ironic humor to depict their adventures, and frequently they see themselves acting the role of the picaro figure—a stratagem used many times for survival purposes.

Another eighteenth-century mode of writing observed in Equiano's work is the primitivistic style that is related to the noble savage ideal.

Equiano was aware of this type of writing, especially in the books on Africa by Anthony Benezet, the Quaker antislavery writer; when Equiano recalled his early days in Africa, he relied heavily on his reading in the primitivistic literature. However, Equiano's autobiography is remarkable in the account he gives of his African days because his re-creation is a mix of primitivistic idealism and realistic detail, in which he never expresses shame or inferiority regarding his African heritage. Africa is an edenic place whose inhabitants follow their own cultural traditions, religious practices, and pastoral pursuits. But although Africa is a happy childhood land for Equiano, he is not blind to the evil events that lately have befallen his people.

The Europeans have entered to plunder, enslave, and introduce the despicable inventions of modern technological warfare. Equiano himself is a victim of that situation when he is kidnapped and sold into slavery. His early experiences in the American colonies are recreated with a sense of awe and wonder as the young picaro slave observes the Western world's marvels. He is saved from a life of plantation slavery, but his seafaring service gives him the opportunity to witness firsthand the brutal practices of slavery in several areas of the world. Equiano's life story is a journey of education in which he goes from innocence in edenic Africa to the cruel experience of slavery in the West.

Significant Form, Style, or Artistic Conventions

I always discuss Equiano's work in conjunction with the whole genre of spiritual autobiography. I show how Equiano adapted the autobiographical form to the new slave narrative. I also explain the primitivistic elements in his work and say something about the eighteenth-century neoclassical style of writing.

In accordance with the pattern of spiritual autobiography, Equiano's narrative follows the three-part structure of spiritual and physical enslavement, conversion and escape from slavery, and subsequent rebirth in a life of spiritual and physical freedom. Not until he gains his physical liberty is Equiano able to build his character along personal, religious, and humanitarian lines of development. This is the reason he places his manumission paper in the center of his narrative and records his jubilation on attaining his freedom. From that point on in the autobiography, Equiano uses a confident, exuberant, and crusading tone and style as he relates his immersion in the honorable aspects of Western society while he denounces the West's inhumane practices of slavery.

Original Audience

I emphasize the fact that Equiano's reading audience was mostly composed of American and European abolitionists. His immediate purpose was to influence the British political leaders who were debating the slave trade issue in Parliament in the late 1780s. However, Equiano's work was read and discussed by numerous religious and humanitarian readers on both sides of the Atlantic. His work went through nineteen editions and was translated into several languages. It appeared in print well into the middle of the nineteenth century, and its influence on the whole range of slave narrative literature was strong.

Comparisons, Contrasts, Connections

The best comparison is with Frederick Douglass's *Narrative* (1845), which follows the three-part pattern of spiritual and slave autobiographical work. Douglass's work depicts the same search for identity involving the attainment of manhood, education, especially the ability to read, and the securing of physical and spiritual liberations. Other connections concentrating on the spiritual conversion account in Chapter 10 of Equiano's work may be made with the *Narrative of the Captivity and Restauration of Mrs. Mary Rowlandson* and Jonathan Edwards's *Personal Narrative*.

Questions for Reading and Discussion/ Approaches to Writing

1. Questions may deal with definitions of primitivism, form of autobiography (spiritual and secular), history of slave trade and slavery, and eighteenth-century writing styles.
2. (a) Why does Equiano stress that the Africans are "a nation of dancers, musicians, and poets"?
   (b) Chapter 1 contains a mix of borrowed information and personal recollections by Equiano on traditions, familial practices, and religious observances of the Africans. Do you find this technique assists Equiano's aim to erase Western readers' misconceptions about Africa?
3. (a) Describe the primitivistic elements in Equiano's description of his stay in Tinmah.
   (b) What kind of picture does Equiano paint of his African slave experiences as opposed to his later encounters with slavery in the Western world?
   (c) What signs of European influence does Equiano observe during his slave journey to the coast?

(d) Discuss the reversal situation of the cannibalistic theme demonstrated by Equiano's initial meeting with the white slave traders on the African coast.

(e) What are some of the white world's magical arts Equiano observes with a sense of awe and wonder?

(f) Equiano's account of the talking book is a commonly described experience in early slave works. What significant traits of the young enslaved person does the story reveal?

4. How does Equiano's conversion account compare with the spiritual narratives by Jonathan Edwards and Mary Rowlandson?

Bibliography

Andrews, William L. *To Tell a Free Story: The First Century of Afro-American Autobiography, 1760–1865.* Urbana: University of Illinois Press, 1986. (See especially Chapter 2.)

Costanzo, Angelo. *Surprizing Narrative: Olaudah Equiano and the Beginnings of Black Autobiography.* Westport, Conn.: Greenwood Press, 1987. (See especially Chapter 4.)

Davis, Charles T. and Henry Louis Gates Jr., eds. *The Slave's Narrative.* New York: Oxford University Press, 1985. (See Paul Edwards's essay, "Three West African Writers of the 1780's.")

Much of my research and writing has centered on Equiano. As a result, a great deal of the information required for an understanding and appreciation of Olaudah Equiano's great work can be found in my book.

Judith Sargent Murray (1751–1820)

Contributing Editor: Amy M. Yerkes

Classroom Issues and Strategies

The central issue that emerges in a first reading of Murray's writings is the apparent contradiction between her conservative Federalist agenda and her more liberal platform for feminist reform. Murray maintained that society must be based on a strict adherence to order—political, social, family, and personal order—while promoting a change of women's place within that order. This hierarchical Federalist platform is also in conflict with Murray's Universalist religious beliefs, which argue for each individual's ability to establish a direct link with God. By placing her writings within their historical framework, however, some of this tension can be resolved.

An awareness of the central debates of the early Republic—debates on the structure and role of government, on the role of women in the new Republic, on the proper education for the new citizenry—will allow students to appreciate why Murray's responses to these debates were so complex. Reading the selections from The Federalist and Anti-Federalist Papers, as well as the writings of John Adams, Thomas Paine, and Thomas Jefferson (all included in the anthology) will help students to understand the historical framework for Murray's work.

Major Themes, Historical Perspectives, and Personal Issues

In addition to those themes just outlined, Murray was engaged in a struggle to define and create a truly "American" literature. Students might therefore examine her choice of subject matter in the essays, her epilogue to Tyler's play *The Contrast,* and her novel *The Story of Margaretta.* While the latter work has not been included in the anthology, it is available both on microfilm in the Evans series and in Nina Baym's new edition of *The Gleaner* (Union College Press, 1992). Murray's novel continues her exploration of the role and education of women in the new nation.

Murray was also engaged in a reevaluation of history and subscribed to the belief that history was fundamentally progressive. By her own commitment to bettering the education of women and by reevaluating past women's history, Murray hoped to usher in a "new era in female history."

As with many of her contemporaries, Murray drew heavily from the Enlightenment philosophy of such writers as John Locke and Jean-Jacques Rousseau. Her emphasis on reason as the central governing principle of human beings and her educational beliefs might be fruitfully compared to those of her European predecessors.

Significant Form, Style, or Artistic Conventions

Murray's most successful literary work is her *Gleaner* essay series; while the topics of these essays are progressive, the form is rather conventional, following such famous prototypes as the essays of Addison and Steele. The development of Murray's persona, Mr. Vigillius, however, is more innovative; his interaction with the audience, his reporting style, and his personality allow for interesting discussion.

Other considerations of interest are those of poetic style, and her voice as an essayist. While students may find Murray's poetry and essays stylistically constrained, she herself insisted that she was primarily interested in developing a new content for American literature rather than establishing new literary forms.

Original Audience

Since much of Murray's work was originally printed in journals, any consideration of audience should address the readers of these periodicals and the serial nature of the presentation. Furthermore, she was appealing to a very diverse audience: readers who would adhere to her conservative Federalist agenda as well as those liberals who were interested in women's issues. Certainly this wide audience consideration brings with it beliefs about how to appeal to "male" versus "female" readers (as defined in the late eighteenth century). The ways in which Murray was trying to subvert the traditional assumptions that linked masculinity with reason and femininity with passion (the less desirable of the two traits) would allow for an interesting consideration of audience.

Comparisons, Contrasts, Connections

Murray's writings beg comparison with many of her better-known contemporaries, and it is astonishing to realize that she preceded many of these contemporaries in addressing certain issues. For example, her essay *On the Equality of the Sexes* offers an argument very similar to that found in Mary Wollstonecraft's *A Vindication of the Rights of Woman*. Discussion might also focus on a comparison between Murray's feminist essays and those of her nineteenth-century American counterparts Sarah M. Grimké and Elizabeth Cady Stanton.

Fruitful comparisons can be made between *The Story of Margaretta* and contemporary sentimental novels such as Hannah Webster Foster's *The Coquette* and Susannah Rowson's *Charlotte Temple*. Murray's two plays (included in her 1798 collected edition of *The Gleaner*) exhibit an interest in rendering the American experience—an interest shared by her contemporary Royall Tyler, whose play, *The Contrast*, also appears in the anthology.

Questions for Reading and Discussion/ Approaches to Writing

1. Of particular interest in Murray's essays on the equality and education of women are the strategies she adopts to prove this equality. Students might be asked to analyze these strategies and to speculate on why she adopted them, given the time when Murray was writing and her Federalist/Universalist beliefs.

2. Students could explore Murray's guidelines for developing and promoting American literature (in this case drama) by focusing on the prologues and epilogues she wrote for well-known American plays.

Note: The questions mentioned above would also serve as helpful writing assignments and research paper topics.

Bibliography

The only biography of Murray is entitled *Constantia: A Study of the Life and Works of Judith Sargent Murray, 1751–1820,* by Vena Bernadette Field (Orono, Maine: University Press, 1931).

A brief but helpful critical evaluation of Murray's essay series is by Bruce Granger in *American Essay Serials from Franklin to Irving,* Chapter VIII (1978). See also the references to Murray in *Liberty's Daughters: The Revolutionary Experience of American Women 1750–1800* (Mary Beth Norton, 1980), and *Revolution and the Word: The Rise of the Novel in America* (Cathy Davidson, 1986).

Pattie Cowell offers an insightful overview of Murray's poems in *Women Poets in Revolutionary America 1650–1775* (1981).

Finally, Nina Baym's introduction to *The Gleaner* (Union College Press, 1992) is of great interest.

Philip Freneau (1752–1832)

Contributing Editor: David S. Shields

Classroom Issues and Strategies

Some of Philip Freneau's poems require an explanation of the changing political context of the 1770s through 1790s so that their arguments may be understood. Freneau's religious poetry, with its striking absence of scriptural allusion and Christian doctrine, may prove rather alien to students of traditional Christian background.

Discriminations between the beliefs of Patriots and Loyalists, Whigs and Tories, must be supplied for the poems of the 1770s. Discussion of the split of the American revolutionaries into Federalist and Jeffersonian factions during the 1790s is also helpful. "To Sir Toby" is an excellent poem with which to examine the legal justifications of slavery employed during the late 1700s.

I find that early American political cartoons provide a useful way of introducing students to the context of Freneau's politics. (Michel Wynn Jones's *The Cartoon History of the American Revolution* is a good source.) Sometimes I get a reproduction of one of the newspapers in which a Freneau poem first appeared to show how closely his worldview was tied to the journalism of the era.

Major Themes, Historical Perspectives, and Personal Issues

Freneau was a radical advocate of political democracy. As the chief literary spokesman for the Jeffersonian program, he is an original expositor of certain powerful American political myths: of universal liberty, of the reasonability of the common man, of the superior morality of the life of the farmer to that of the commercial enterpriser. These myths still inform political discourse.

As a nature poet, Freneau presents little difficulty to the student, for his arguments are simple and his language straightforward.

Significant Form, Style, or Artistic Conventions

Freneau cultivated a variety of styles, most of which were suited to the newspaper readership of common Americans he envisioned as his audience. As a political poet, he employed the usual neoclassical devices of parody, burlesque, and mock confession in his satires; in his political admonitions he practiced "Whig sentimentalism" in his anti-slavery verse and the "progress piece" in his historical ruminations. In general, Freneau was an eighteenth-century neoclassicist in his political verse. His nature studies and theological speculations, however, looked forward to Romanticism, particularly in its representation of a natural world suffused with divine vitality.

Original Audience

Revolutionary and post-revolutionary Americans were immersed in political rhetoric. The common reader knew a surprising amount of political theory. An interesting exercise is to isolate the imagery in the poems connected with various political systems—monarchy, aristocracy, republicanism, democracy—and construct the mental picture that Freneau projected for his readers.

Comparisons, Contrasts, Connections

Freneau's nature poems work well with those of William Cullen Bryant. The closest analogue to his political poetry is found in Francis Hopkinson (not frequently anthologized) and Joel Barlow.

Questions for Reading and Discussion/ Approaches to Writing

1. I do not usually guide a student's reading of the text with questions. I do, however, usually suggest that a student pay particular attention to the adjectives Freneau employs.
2. I will take a poem from a Federalist Connecticut wit (Richard Alsop, Timothy Dwight, or Lemuel Hopkins) and ask the students to contrast the ideals of government, citizenship, and policy found in it with those expressed in a political poem by Freneau.

Timothy Dwight (1752–1817)

Contributing Editor: Carla Mulford

Classroom Issues and Strategies

An absence of space in the anthology prevented offering the more typical view of Timothy Dwight as a reactionary conservative in the Federalist era rather than as an "enlightened" albeit conservative citizen of the new Republic. Fuller contextualization of Dwight might assist students in their coming to terms with the complexity of the era called the Enlightenment. They might find interesting the fact that Dwight took part in, even as he prepared for the ministry, the writing of *The Anarchiad*, a collaborative and satiric foray against social and political attitudes prevalent during the early years of the new United States. They might also find *The Anarchiad* an interesting counterpoint—if it *is* indeed a counterpoint, and this is something that students might wish to examine—to Dwight's outburst, *The Triumph of Infidelity*, aimed at French rationalist philosophers of the middle and late eighteenth century.

The Dwight presented in the anthology is the same Timothy Dwight, but the representation given here cannot by any means present the whole canon of the writings, just as the long Georgic poem, *Greenfield Hill*, cannot necessarily be said to be fully representative of this complex man and poet. Nonetheless, this selection will enable a teacher to consider several aspects of poetry—such as, most importantly, the Augustan mode and its social implications—along with several of the conflicts of the era of "Enlightenment" so as to present to students a fuller dimension of Enlightenment culture than that usually considered.

Major Themes, Historical Perspectives, and Personal Issues

Themes that this selection suggests include the millennialism of Puritan culture and its cultural descendant, Congregationalism; the poetic (and bourgeois) attempt to find a way to model or represent a civic culture that the populace could only pretend to imitate; the motif, promulgated by whites, of the necessary, even if sorrowful, vanishing of Indians in advance of a growing and more "civic" white population.

By approaching the selection in these three ways, students can begin to see that their easy assumptions about Puritanism (that it somehow "stopped" when "Enlightenment" began), about poetics (that these poems are boring in their supposed harmonious repetitiveness), and about Indian culture (for white students, especially, that it vanished) are fully called into question. By examining the complicated poetics and socio-poetics of this era called the Enlightenment, students can begin to understand the residual effects of this era evident in our own. Trying to get students to phrase this, on their own, is one of my key teaching challenges with these materials.

Significant Form, Style, or Artistic Conventions

This selection shows extremely well the Augustan notion that civic humanism can be modelled in poetry. In terms of poetics, students interested in poetry might be asked to examine the poetic lines for regularity in meter, harmony (or cacophony) in diction, and the sound-and-sense effects of Augustan poetry. They might be encouraged, too, to compare the poetics of the selection with the poetics employed in the selections of seventeenth- and eighteenth-century poems in the anthology, as well as with those of Dwight's contemporaries, Joel Barlow, Philip Freneau, Judith Sargent Murray, and Phillis Wheatley.

Comparisons, Contrasts, Connections

Students might be asked to examine Dwight's social attitudes in light of the writings by Prince Hall, Samson Occom, Hendrick Aupaumut, Benjamin Franklin, and Joel Barlow. They also might find suitable materials for comparison and contrast in the William Byrd, Sarah Kemble Knight, and Mary Rowlandson selections.

A useful exploration of religious culture would result from a comparative treatment of the millennialism of, say, Winthrop, Bradford, or even Edwards, with that of Dwight, and then an examination of Dwight as opposed to, say, Emerson or Thoreau. Contrastively, students might like to explore the rhetoric of Christian humanism as evident in Angelina Grimké and in Timothy Dwight.

Questions for Reading and Discussion/ Approaches to Writing

1. How are Dwight's poetics different from or similar to the poetics of seventeenth-century and other eighteenth-century writers?
2. Are there similarities between Dwight's position on Indians and the positions held by Benjamin Franklin and Samson Occom?
3. Is there a connection between Dwight's "city on a hill" (i.e., Greenfield Hill) and Winthrop's vision of that city, as expressed at the end of his lay sermon, "A Modell of Christian Charity"?
4. How does Dwight's implication about "vanishing" Native Americans get played out in the nineteenth century?

Bibliography

A variety of titles are listed below. They should assist the teacher interested in examining the complexities of both Dwight and his era, as suggested in the material above:

Berk, Stephen E. *Calvinism Versus Democracy: Timothy Dwight and the Origins of American Evangelical Orthodoxy.* Hamden, Conn.: Archon Books, 1974.

Bloch, Ruth. *Visionary Republic: Millennial Themes in American Thought, 1756–1800*. Cambridge, England: Cambridge University Press, 1985.

Dippie, Brian W. *The Vanishing American: White Attitudes and U.S. Indian Policy*. Lawrence: University Press of Kansas, 1982.

Dowling, William C. *Poetry and Ideology in Revolutionary Connecticut*. Athens: University of Georgia Press, 1990.

Elliott, Emory. *Revolutionary Writers: Literature and Authority in the New Republic, 1725–1810*. New York: Oxford University Press, 1982.

Howard, Leon. *The Connecticut Wits*. Chicago: University of Chicago Press, 1943.

McTaggart, William J. and William K. Bottorff, eds. *The Major Poems of Timothy Dwight*. Gainesville, Fla.: Scholars' Facsimiles and Reprints, 1969.

Silliman, Benjamin. *A Sketch of the Life and Character of President Dwight*. New Haven: Maltby, Goldsmith, 1817.

Silverman, Kenneth. *Timothy Dwight*. New York: Twayne, 1969.

Tichi, Cecilia. *New World, New Earth: Environmental Reform in American Literature from the Puritans through Whitman*. New Haven: Yale University Press, 1979.

Phillis Wheatley (1753–1784)

Contributing Editor: William H. Robinson

Classroom Issues and Strategies

One of the difficulties in teaching Wheatley comes in trying to illustrate that she certainly was much more racially aware, and anti-slavery, in her letters (which were intended to be private) than in her more widely known verses (written for a general white public).

I show how, in spite of her fame and the special indulgence of the Wheatley family who owned her, Phillis was necessarily aware of her blackness; for example, in racially segregated church pews, in the widespread menial work (street sweeping and the like) that blacks were forced to do, and in the general lack of educational facilities for Boston blacks.

Students (and even scholars) are sometimes wary of the authenticity of Phillis Wheatley's poetic abilities and, accordingly, ask germane questions. Such students and scholars are disabused of their doubts when confronted with copies of extant manuscripts of verses and letters written when Phillis was known to have not been in the company of whites.

Major Themes, Historical Perspectives, and Personal Issues

It is important to note that Phillis was very much aware of herself as a *rara avis*, who worked hard to show that, given the training and opportunity, blacks could write verse as well as any comparably educated and advantaged Bostonian.

Significant Form, Style, or Artistic Conventions

Familiar with rhetorical devices of classical prosody (especially as practiced by the English masters, Alexander Pope, John Milton, and so on), Phillis preferred a predominant usage of the Neoclassical couplet, which, on occasion, constrained her seemingly natural tendencies toward Romanticism.

Original Audience

Most of her verse was written for prominent white figures of her day— e.g., General Washington, several prominent Boston divines—but in several of her elegies and her "Nature pieces" she wrote some lines that have continuing value to audiences of today. Her work was published largely at the behest of the whites for whom she wrote.

Comparisons, Contrasts, Connections

No other colonial black versifier wrote with Phillis's obviously superior sophistication, and comparison of her work with that of black contemporaries is usually done at the expense of the other writers.

Questions for Reading and Discussion/ Approaches to Writing

I have asked students to examine Phillis's verse and letters for instances of her acquired Boston gentility and of her racial awareness and of herself as "the Colonial Boston poet laureate."

Bibliography

Mason, Julian. *Poems of Phillis Wheatley, Revised and Enlarged*. Chapel Hill: University of North Carolina, 1989, 1–39.

Robinson, William H. *Critical Essays on Phillis Wheatley*. Boston: G. K. Hall, 1982, passim.

——. *Phillis Wheatley and Her Writings*. New York and London: Garland, 1984, 3–69, 87–126.

Lemuel Haynes (1753–1833)

Contributing Editor: Phillip M. Richards

Classroom Issues and Strategies

Lemuel Haynes represents the most complicated African-American response to the strands of evangelical culture and Revolutionary politics of the late eighteenth century and the early nineteenth century. In many respects his work should be read in the context of theological writers such as Jonathan Edwards and political thinkers such as Thomas Jefferson. If America was, at this time, defining itself as a Christian Republican nation, then how did such a definition affect a figure such as Haynes?

Haynes, like Equiano, is a committed Calvinist. He firmly rejects theological innovations, such as Universalism, that were part of the liberalization of Protestant thought in the nineteenth century. What might such a radical Calvinism mean in the hands of a black thinker in the late eighteenth century? How might Revolutionary conceptions of liberty in the period have been informed by Calvinist notions of spiritual liberty?

Haynes's political writing significantly comes before his longer theological efforts. His tract on Revolutionary politics was written before his entrance into the ministry. How might the political ideologies of the Revolution have affected Haynes's later development as a minister?

Major Themes, Historical Perspectives, and Personal Issues

We tend to think of the late eighteenth century as an age of politicization and secularization embodied in a figure such as Benjamin Franklin. Religion and theological formulations, however, remained very important for literate blacks such as Phillis Wheatley, Jupiter Hammon, and Haynes. Why is this so? What does their intensely religious emphasis mean for these writers' larger relationship with an emerging American culture?

Significant Form, Style, or Artistic Conventions

Discuss the importance of the sermon form to Haynes. What was the social, political, and even economic function of the sermon during the Great Awakening and Revolutionary periods? How does Haynes draw upon these functions in his own work?

Original Audience

For whom is Haynes's work written? How do his discourse, his language, his themes, and his ideas reflect his chosen audience? What advantages does the sermon form give to a black addressing this audience?

Comparisons, Contrasts, Connections

Haynes grew up in a literary context similar to Wheatley's and Hammon's. Haynes's literary development was shaped by the presence of evangelical groups, patrons, revivalist religion, and Revolutionary politics. All of these themes inscribe themselves on his writing. One might compare Haynes's consciousness of the conditions of his work with that of Wheatley or Hammon.

Bibliography

The best introduction to Haynes is *Black Preacher to White America: The Collected Writings of Lemuel Haynes, 1774–1883*, edited by Richard Newman. Brooklyn: Carlson Publishing, 1990.

Joel Barlow (1754–1812)

Contributing Editor: Carla Mulford

Major Themes, Historical Perspectives, and Personal Issues

The writings of Joel Barlow were early anthologized among those of his Connecticut contemporaries of 1785–87, when Barlow and David Humphreys, John Trumbull, Timothy Dwight, and a few others engaged in collaborative writing projects and called themselves the Connecticut or Hartford wits. In the first half of the twentieth century, scholars tended to follow the lead of nineteenth-century literary historians and continued to rank Barlow among his conservative contemporaries. Leon Howard's groundbreaking *The Connecticut Wits* (1943) confirmed Barlow's association with this group, and Howard's influence has continued within the scholarly community. Cecelia Tichi's more timely *New World, New Earth: Environmental Reform in American Literature from the Puritans through Whitman* (1979) continues the Howard interpretation, but clearly within a different context. The interpretation is promulgated in literary and biographical handbooks: the recent commentator cited in the head-note to the Barlow readings, for instance, is Jeffrey Walker, in the Barlow entry in *American Writers Before 1800*, eds. James A. Levemier and Douglas R. Wilmes. As a corrective to these assessments of Barlow, scholars should consult the work, cited below, of Arner, Lemay, Mulford, and Richardson.

Original Audience

Central to the reinterpretation of Barlow's writings is an understanding of the audience to which Barlow was addressing his writings. Barlow seems to have believed, in his early years, that patrons of the arts could be found in America. As a poet seeking patrons in the eastern portion of the new nation—from New Hampshire to Georgia—Barlow would predictably have bespoken the traditional Christian assumptions about God, home, and country, assuming them to be his readers' beliefs. But given his own reading of Henry Home, Lord Kames, dissenting minister Dr. Richard Price, and historian William Robertson, Barlow most likely personally espoused a conception of the progress of morals not necessarily Judeo-Christian in orientation—despite his Revolutionary War chaplaincy. His potentially deistic interests, in fact, seem to have entered even the rather conservative (in terms of religion) poem, *The Vision of Columbus* (see the Christensen citation below). Given the context of Barlow's writing during his earliest years, then, there seems little reason to continue the assumption that he necessarily held the beliefs he propagandized. His interests and his readings continued, through his life, to be philosophical, republican, scientific, and propagandist.

Bibliography

The standard biography of Barlow remains the critical biography by James Woodress, *A Yankee's Odyssey: The Life of Joel Barlow* (Philadelphia: Lippincott, 1958).

The standard critical references have been those by Howard and Tichi.

For a reassessment of Barlow's work, see:

Arner, Robert. "The Smooth and Emblematic Song: Joel Barlow's *The Hasty Pudding.*" *Early American Literature*, 7 (1972): 76–91.

Lemay, J. A. Leo. "The Contexts and Themes of 'The Hasty Pudding.' " *Early American Literature* 17 (1982): 3–23.

Mulford, Carla. "Radicalism in Joel Barlow's *The Conspiracy of Kings* (1792)." In *Deism, Masonry, and the Enlightenment: Essays Honoring Alfred Owen Aldridge.* Newark: University of Delaware Press, 1987, 137–57.

Richardson, Robert O. "The Enlightenment View of Myth and Joel Barlow's Vision of Columbus." *Early American Literature* 13 (1978): 34–44.

See also Merton A. Christensen, "Deism in Joel Barlow's Early Work: Heterodox Passages in *The Vision of Columbus*," *American Literature* 27 (1956): 509–29.

For an assessment of Barlow's poetry in light of English poetry, see William C. Dowling, *Poetry and Ideology in Revolutionary Connecticut.* Athens: University of Georgia Press, 1990, passim.

Royall Tyler (1757–1826)

Contributing Editor: Carla Mulford

Classroom Issues and Strategies

Students have trouble reading dramatic works, whether they are written by Shakespeare or O'Neill. But they especially have trouble with Tyler's "The Contrast," which they think wooden, stilted, and clumsy. They sometimes even take the central character—and the hero—as a stiff Steve Martin-like buffoon. There's much to do here.

I spend half a class talking about the values of the culture in which this play was produced and saw overnight success. I tell them especially about the belief, held by the elite culture, that morality could be reified, that is, could find actual material manifestation in language and action. This conception that high culture, if demonstrated fully and well, would produce in the masses a liking for high culture and a desire to emulate high culture fascinates them because it seems to them unbelievably naive. Then I have pointed out to them that this attitude seems to have dominated the Reagan and Bush White House. They don't always agree—and we use the play as a kind of test case.

Major Themes, Historical Perspectives, and Personal Issues

Tyler picked up on the key high culture themes—frugality, industry, sobriety—spoken most fully by Crèvecoeur and Franklin but by other writers of the revolutionary era as well. These themes are in the play, and the students can readily identify them in the contrasts Tyler sets up for dramatic effect. Students also find the discussions about dress and behavior very intriguing, and they sometimes like to discuss the culture's attitudes about "manly" behavior. In this aspect of "manliness," the play compares well with Thomas Paine's implications about "manliness" in *Common Sense.*

For students who like to do biographical reading, the fact that Tyler was himself involved in quelling the Shays's disturbance has proved interesting. For those who prefer source study, it's useful to note Tyler's reliance upon Sheridan's *School for Scandal.* Feminist students sometimes like to explore Tyler's marriage situation.

Significant Form, Style, or Artistic Conventions

As its title suggests, contrast is the defining principle behind the play. The central contrast is one between Europeanized foppishness, a result of luxury, and American forthrightness, a result of sobriety and industry; "manly" virtues. Manly and Maria, the two characters who wed at the end of the play, represent the new American virtues, while Dimple, Charlotte, and Laetitia represent the degrading decadence of European values.

Students like to note the other contrasts within the play, from discussions about hooped dresses to types of reading material to the behavior of servants. Jonathan is considered the "type" of primitive American goodness, an unknowing bumpkin who has lived outside citified life.

Comparisons, Contrasts, Connections

For similar themes, see Crèvecoeur, Franklin, and Paine.

For similar themes and generic contrasts, see Hannah Webster Foster and Susanna Rowson. The women characters here are particularly useful matter for class discussion.

Questions for Reading and Discussion/ Approaches to Writing

1. Given the Puritans' proscription of dramatic presentation, what might have been the cultural changes that allowed finally for the flourishing of drama in America?
2. Students who like biographical inquiry might find it useful to pursue the Shays's Rebellion issue.

Students who enjoy source study like to write on the comparisons and contrasts between Richard Brinsley Sheridan's *School for Scandal* and Tyler's play. Interesting analyses of the contrasts in the play have arisen from their papers.

Some students may want to consider the extent to which the prologue and epilogue reflect the play's content. In this vein, see Judith Sargent Murray's writing on the play in the anthology entry for Murray.

Bibliography

For biographical matters, see the following:

Tanselle, G. Thomas. *Royall Tyler*. Cambridge: Harvard University Press, 1967.

For matters of interpretation, see the following excellent articles:

Pressman, Richard S. "Class Positioning and Shays's Rebellion: Resolving Contradictions in *The Contrast*." *Early American Literature* 21 (1986): 87–102.

Siebert, Donald T. "Royall Tyler's 'Bold Example': *The Contrast* and the English Comedy of Manners." *Early American Literature* 13 (1980): 3–11.

Stein, Roger B. "Royall Tyler and the Question of Our Speech." *New England Quarterly* 38 (1965): 454–74.

Hendrick Aupaumut (Mahican) (?–1830)

Contributing Editor: Daniel F. Littlefield, Jr.

Classroom Issues and Strategies

Some students may be concerned about the deviations from "standards" in matters of syntax and grammar, so you might ask them to examine these deviations in such writers as Madam Knight. Have them consider the Southwestern humorists of the nineteenth century, for example, as models of the ways writers play on the deviations for literary effect. Suggest to students that Aupaumut's style may be seen as an example of "authentic" English dialect of an American Indian. Have them compare the Fus Fixico letter by Alexander Posey in Volume 2 for a literary use of an Indian's English dialect.

Students are amazed at how little the questions of race/political power, race/social bias, and race/fear have changed in two hundred years. And expect to hear this question: "Could Indians actually write back then?"

Major Themes, Historical Perspectives, and Personal Issues

1. Indian identity, racial self-consciousness. (Aupaumut is painfully aware that he is an Indian writing about Indians. He is also aware of his odd position in defending the U.S. when the Indians have ample reason to doubt it. Note the *I–they* posture he takes.)
2. Ethnic identity in the emerging new nation.
3. Indian-white relations, colonial period to period of Indian removal.

Significant Form, Style, or Artistic Conventions

Have the students investigate the narrative's structure.

Original Audience

An Indian, having visited tribes in the old Northwest, is making recommendations concerning the posture the U.S. should take toward those tribes. His report indicates that he advised the tribes how they should act. Also, the piece is a defense of himself against accusations that he betrayed his trust. While his audience was mainly public policy makers, the piece speaks with pointed relevance today about the American Indians' (reasonable) distrust of federal policy makers. (Some things have not changed in the past two hundred years.)

Comparisons, Contrasts, Connections

The "assimilated" Indian, since the "Praying Indians" of the Puritan period, has been in an anomalous position. Aupaumut is caught between the expectations of two societies. Compare this position with that of Copway, Apess, and Boudinot. For texts related to the Indians' distrust of the Europeans, see relevant sections of Smith, Bradford (more relevant to Aupaumut), Franklin, the Pueblo Revolt texts, and Delgado.

Bibliography

Ronda, Jeanne and James P. Ronda. " 'As They Were Faithful': Chief Hendrick Aupaumut and the Struggle for Stockbridge Survival, 1757–1830." *American Indian Culture and Research Journal* 3.3 (1979): 43–55.

Hannah Webster Foster (1758–1840)

Contributing Editor: Lucy M. Freibert

Classroom Issues and Strategies

Teaching Hannah Foster's *The Coquette* raises four issues: (1) the lack of name recognition of both author and work, (2) the questioning of quality, as the work has previously been excluded from the canon, (3) twentieth-century prejudice against didacticism associated with the "sentimental" tradition to which the seduction novel belongs, and (4) the effort required on the student's part to extract the plot from the epistolary structure.

Strategies for dealing with these issues include the following: (1) The lack of recognition may be explained by pointing out that in the latter part of the nineteenth century, publishers, influenced by academics and critics, discontinued the publication of works by women, who had been extremely popular in the earlier part of the century. (2) The high quality of *The Coquette* stems from the careful use of voice to create distinctive characters and from the depth of social analysis of sex roles, customs, manners, and conventions underlying the content of the letters. (3) Foster eliminated didacticism and sharpened her work through astute handling of characterization and voice. Eliza, assertive, speaks with unique rhythm, tone, vocabulary, and intensity. Her voice, echoing Mrs. Richman's, bespeaks the security that Eliza desires, could she have it on her own terms. (4) Small group discussions enable students to clarify questions about the plot structure.

The issue students bring up most frequently is the dependence of men in these novels on the money they would acquire by marriage to women of means. The question asked by both male and female students is: Why didn't Sanford expect to have a regular job? A question frequently asked by young men is: Why didn't Eliza want to marry? Young women want to know: Why didn't Eliza get herself a job? These questions are asked by people from middle- and lower-middle-class families. Students in other economic circumstances might have very different queries.

Major Themes, Historical Perspectives, and Personal Issues

Teaching Hannah Foster's *The Coquette* (1797) within the context of the National Period offers students opportunities to acquire historical, cultural, and literary insights. As Walter P. Wenska, Jr., points out in *"The Coquette and the American Dream of Freedom" (Early American Literature* 12.3 [Winter 1977–78]: 243–55), *The Coquette* raises "the question of freedom, its meaning and its limits, in a new land newly dedicated to births of new freedoms," a theme treated subsequently by many American writers. Wenska sees Eliza Wharton as a rebel who seeks a freedom not typically allotted to her sex, and he shows how she consistently rejects the advice of friends who encourage her to settle into the "modest freedom" of marriage.

Like Wenska, Cathy N. Davidson in *Revolution and the Word: The Rise of the Novel in America* (New York: Oxford University Press, 1986) recognizes *The Coquette* as much more than "simply an allegory of seduction." Davidson reads it as "less a story of the wages of sin than a study of the wages of marriage" and as "a dialogical discourse in which the reader was also invited to participate if only vicariously." Davidson's analysis of *The Coquette* is indispensable reading for anyone who would teach the novel seriously, as are Carroll Smith-Rosenberg's "Domesticating 'Virtue': Coquettes and Revolutionaries in Young America" (*Literature and the Body*. Baltimore: The Johns Hopkins University Press, 1988) and Kristie Hamilton's "An Assault on the Will: Republican Virtue and the City in Hannah Webster Foster's *The Coquette*" (*Early American Literature* 14, 1989). Two other works that offer valuable historical and cultural insights are Mary Beth Norton's *Liberty's Daughters: The Revolutionary Experience of American Women, 1750–1800* (Boston: Little, Brown, 1980) and Linda K. Kerber's *Women of the Republic: Intellect and Ideology in Revolutionary America* (Chapel Hill: University of North Carolina Press, 1980).

Significant Form, Style, or Artistic Conventions

The American novel had its origin in the seduction novel appropriated from the British sentimental tradition of Samuel Richardson and his followers. To make the sensational story of the "ruin" of an innocent girl palatable to readers steeped in Puritan thought, early novelists emphasized the factual and educative nature of their works. Alexander Cowie in *The Rise of the American Novel* (1948) says that didacticism was, in fact, a *"sine qua non* of the early novel."

Although the novel as genre had come into its own by the time Foster wrote *The Coquette*, authors continued to claim basis in fact in order to justify the publication of risqué materials. The Preceptress in Foster's *The Boarding School* explains the prevailing objections: " 'Novels, are the favorite and the most dangerous kind of reading, now adopted by the generality of young ladies. . . . Their romantic pictures of love, beauty, and magnificence, fill the imagination with ideas which lead to impure desires, a vanity of exterior charms, and a fondness for show and dissipation, by no means consistent with that simplicity, modesty, and chastity, which should be the constant inmates of the female breast. . . .' "

While voicing opposition to the novel in general, Foster and other novelists characterized the reading of their own works, which were "founded on fact," as warnings, to keep young women from peril. As Lucy Sumner's last letter in *The Coquette* (LXIII) states: "From the melancholy story of Eliza Wharton, let the American fair learn to reject with disdain every insinuation derogatory to their true dignity and honor." In *The Boarding School*, a former student justifies reading Samuel Richardson's novels by claiming "so multifarious are his excellencies, that his faults appear but specks, which serve as foils to display his beauties to better advantage."

Original Audience

A very effective way of handling student inquiries as to who read *The Coquette* is to read to the class a passage from Elias Nason's biography of Susanna Rowson. Writing in 1870, Nason describes the readership of Rowson's best-selling novel, *Charlotte Temple*, with which *The Coquette* competed during the National Period, as follows:

> It has stolen its way alike into the study of the divine and into the workshop of the mechanic, into the parlor of the accomplished lady and the bed-chamber of her waiting maid, into the log-hut on the extreme border of modern civilization and into the forecastle of the whale ship on the lonely ocean. It has been read by the grey bearded professor after his "divine Plato"; by the beardless clerk after balancing his accounts at night, by the traveler waiting for the next conveyance at the village inn; by the school girl stealthfully in her seat at school.

Insofar as this description applies to *Charlotte Temple*, it likely applies to *The Coquette*.

It is much too early to say whether current interest in novels like *The Coquette* will be lasting or whether the novelty of discovering these earlier writers will wear off. It is exciting to the current generation of students that these books are now available.

Comparisons, Contrasts, Connections

Novels that invite comparison and contrast with *The Coquette* are William Hill Brown's *The Power of Sympathy* (1789) and Susanna Rowson's *Charlotte Temple* (1794), with which it competed for favor through the early decades of the nineteenth century. Frank L. Mott discusses the popularity of these novels in *Golden Multitudes: The Story of Best Sellers in the United States* (New York: Macmillan, 1947).

All three works treat the seduction theme and claim to be based on fact. The British title of *Charlotte Temple* was *Charlotte, A Tale of Truth* (1791); the seduction possibly involved Colonel John Montrésor, a cousin of the author (Richard D. Birdsall, "Susanna Haswell Rowson," *Notable American Women* 3 [Cambridge: Harvard University Press, 1971]). *The Power of Sympathy* drew on the seduction of Frances Theodora Apthorp by her sister's husband, Perez Morton (William S. Kable, "Editor's Introduction," *The Power of Sympathy* [Columbus: Ohio State University Press, 1969]); and *The Coquette*, on the seduction of Elizabeth Whitman of Hartford, Connecticut, by a person of disputed identity (Aaron Burr and Pierrepont Edwards, son of Jonathan Edwards, being among the "accused"). Extensive, yet inconclusive, discussion of the Elizabeth Whitman story appears in Jane E. Locke's "Historical Preface" to the 1855 edition of *The Coquette* (Boston: William P. Fetridge and Company, 1855), Caroline Dall's *The Romance of the Association: or, One Last Glimpse of Charlotte Temple and Eliza Wharton* (Cambridge: Press of John Wilson and Son, 1875), and Charles Knowles Bolton's *The Elizabeth Whitman Mystery* (Peabody, Mass.: Peabody Historical Society, 1912).

Significant differences separate *The Coquette* from *The Power of Sympathy* and *Charlotte Temple*. Characters in *Charlotte Temple* follow relatively stock patterns. Only the villainous Mademoiselle La Rue and Belcour display individuality. Charlotte, generally passive, succumbs easily to La Rue's temptations and threats, Montraville's persuasion, and Belcour's deceit. The characters in Brown's novel have interesting potential. Harriot, for example, displays strong powers of observation, and Ophelia speaks forcefully. But they employ the same voice as Rowson's narrator—the voice and style of the sentimental novel.

Questions for Reading and Discussion/ Approaches to Writing

1. Students should be asked to consult the *Oxford English Dictionary* for the meanings of *coquette* and *rake*, paying special attention to the changes in meaning through time. They might also be asked to investigate the concept of *dowry*, noting what brought about the end of the practice of providing a dowry. Ask them to find out whether the epistolary form is used in novels today.

2. Paper topics may include the following:

   argumentative—Eliza Wharton and Peter Sanford are/are not equally responsible for Eliza's death, or Eliza Wharton's fall was entirely her own fault.

   analytic—a character study of Eliza Wharton using her letters alone, or a character study using only the letters of others.

   research paper—compare *The Coquette* to a British epistolary seduction novel, focusing particularly on social issues.

   research paper (nonliterary)—a study of property rights of men and women in eighteenth-century America.

Bibliography

Helpful sources have been provided above. Both students and teachers might find quick access to the beginnings of the American novel in the introduction, didactic, melodrama, and satire/humor sections of *Hidden Hands: An Anthology of American Women Writers, 1790-1870*, edited by Lucy M. Freibert and Barbara A. White (New Brunswick, N.J.: Rutgers University Press, 1985).

Susanna Haswell Rowson (1762–1824)

Contributing Editor: Laraine Fergenson

Classroom Issues and Strategies

The best approach to Rowson's moralizing and her melodramatic language is to ask students to consider the author's audience and her purpose in writing. As Susanna Rowson saw it, she was arming young women for survival in a perilous world inhabited by seducers, hypocrites, and false friends. The society that forms the background of the novel was dominated by a rigid moral code, and violations of it were dealt with very harshly. Keeping in mind that Rowson intended to reach "the young and thoughtless of the fair sex" (see the "Preface" to *Charlotte Temple*), and, if possible, to protect these vulnerable young women from the pain of social rejection, the modern reader can better understand the author's emphatic moralism and melodramatic language.

The instructor can initiate a discussion of Rowson's notion of sisterhood, which is adumbrated in this selection. Although in other writings, Rowson warns unmarried girls about associating with women of damaged reputations (lest their own suffer,) in *Charlotte Temple* she clearly approves of Mrs. Beauchamp's kindly regard toward Charlotte, whom she later befriends. It is significant that Mrs. Beauchamp is herself safely married, but she is obviously a foil to La Rue, who, established as Mrs. Crayton, shows detestable hypocrisy in shunning Charlotte as a fallen woman. Rowson's idea that women should take care of each other and not join in heaping insults upon a betrayed sister is similar to ideas in the writings of Margaret Fuller in the following generation.

Another issue to discuss in the classroom is the influence of Mademoiselle La Rue and Belcour in Charlotte's seduction. It is clear that in the "Conflict of Love and Duty," the defeat of the latter is due almost as much to La Rue's manipulations as to Charlotte's feelings for Montraville. Charlotte makes her fateful decision to elope after both La Rue and Belcour have "seconded the entreaties of Montraville," and later, when Charlotte regrets her decision, it is La Rue who pressures her into going to meet with Montraville, knowing that the self-delusive Charlotte will not be able to keep her resolve to bid him good-bye and return to the school. Since peer pressure of all sorts is an issue with which modern students are familiar, it might interest them to discuss its application to an eighteenth-century novel.

Major Themes, Historical Perspectives, and Personal Issues

The theme of seduction and betrayal that dominates *Charlotte Temple* is easily recognizable to modern students. They may see it as rooted in the traditional view of woman as a helpless victim, who must have the support of either her parents or a lawful husband. Ellen Brandt discusses the novel's "Clarissa theme," derived from the works of Samuel Richardson, to whom Rowson was indebted. Inevitably, the young woman who abandons the wisdom of her parents for the false promises of a lover is doomed to an early death. An instructor might wish to bring into the discussion the following famous song from Oliver Goldsmith's *The Vicar of Wakefield* (1766):

> When lovely woman stoops to folly,
> And finds too late that men betray,
> What charm can sooth her melancholy,
> What art can wash her guilt away?
>
> The only art her guilt to cover,
> To hide her shame from every eye,
> To give repentance to her lover,
> And wring his bosom—is to die.

Students may want to discuss other works that contain elements of or variations on this theme, such as Theodore Dreiser's *An American Tragedy* (see below).

Rowson's place in American literary history is an intriguing topic. Despite the formidable reputation she enjoyed in the Federalist period, her importance as the first best-selling American author, and the enduring popularity of *Charlotte Temple,* by the middle of the twentieth century Rowson was virtually ignored in anthologies of American literature. Ellen Brandt says she became "a 'forgotten' woman in the archives of our cultural history." A discussion of possible reasons for Rowson's eclipse is a good way to begin or conclude the class work on this author.

The historical background of *Charlotte Temple* and the importance of Rowson as a major literary figure during the nation's infancy should be emphasized. In the preface to her insightful work on Rowson, Patricia Parker states the following:

> Rowson lived during a crucial period in our nation's history, as it turned from provincial colony to preindustrial nation. She herself strongly identified with the political objectives of the new republic and came to consider herself American despite her British birth, as she lived most of her life in this country. Her writings reflect an increasing concern with freedom and democratic principles, both politically and sexually. To study her song lyrics and theatrical compositions during the 1790s is to understand the popular taste of the American public who were trying to decide how to live with their newly acquired independence.
>
> (Preface *i*)

Some of Rowson's song lyrics have been excerpted in the works of Parker and Brandt, and an interesting discussion might grow from reading them to the class. Further, Rowson's role in the early American theater and her association with the prominent theater company of Thomas Wignell could be explored.

The American Revolution had a great impact on Rowson's life and work. She was one of the first writers to use it as the background for a novel. Montraville and Belcour are both British soldiers being sent to America to fight against the rebels. Charlotte, wondering about La Rue's desertion of Belcour, reflects that she thought only true love had made La Rue follow her man to the "seat of war." Montraville, seducing Charlotte, says: "I thought that you would for my sake have braved the dangers of the ocean, that you would by your affection and smiles, have softened the hardships of war."

Significant Form, Style, or Artistic Conventions

Plot, Characterization, and Structure of *Charlotte Temple*

An instructor presenting selections of *Charlotte Temple* would do well to read the entire novel in order to appreciate fully its structure and the sophistication of its characterization. By explaining the motivations of the characters at length, Rowson makes their actions believable and, in doing so, invalidates the charge that she was merely a writer of melodrama. Her portrayal of Charlotte is masterful. The girl's naive and ingenuous character is rendered convincingly. Rowson details the progress of her seduction with sympathy and keen psychological insight.

Rowson devotes considerable space in this short novel to describing Charlotte's parents, and with good effect. Lucy Eldridge (later Temple) and her father had been driven to a debtor's prison by the machinations of an unscrupulous man with designs on Lucy. Her refusal to submit to the kind of arrangement Charlotte enters with Montraville brings disaster upon the household, but the Eldridges and Temple never doubt that she has done the right thing. It is thus doubly poignant that Lucy's daughter, Charlotte, should yield as she does. It is ironic and also perfectly understandable that a couple so idealistic, so perfectly loving, and so trusting could produce a child as dangerously naive as their Charlotte.

Montraville, too, is carefully drawn. Although he plays an evil role in the story, he, like Clyde Griffiths in *An American Tragedy*, is no villain. Attracted to Charlotte and unable to resist seducing her, though he knows that her lack of fortune will make marriage impossible, he abandons her because he believes the lies of his deceitful friend Belcour, and because he cannot resist the charms of Julia Franklin, his new love, who is conveniently wealthy and therefore a good marriage prospect. Although Montraville causes great harm to Charlotte, he, like her, is not so much evil as weak, and he suffers intense pangs of conscience—and eventually an early death—for what he has done. By making Montraville a sympathetic human being instead of a stock figure of evil, Rowson lends plausibility to her story, and she accomplishes her goal, which is to show that yes, such things can really happen—even to the most well-meaning people.

Original Audience

Charlotte Temple was originally published in England, but when Rowson saw it republished in America, she was no doubt aware that its subtitle was particularly appropriate to her American audience. Influenced by their Puritan heritage, the hardworking inhabitants of a new and growing country might look askance at reading novels, but might be more receptive to "a Tale of Truth," only disguised by a "slight veil of fiction" and written to preserve the "happiness of that sex whose morals and conduct have so powerful an influence on mankind in general."

The most striking point about the audience of this book is that it was quite clearly intended to be female. In her "Preface" Rowson explicitly states that she is writing to "the fair sex," specifically to the "young and thoughtless" among them, and in the asides in which she comments on the story, she addresses her readers as "my dear girls." On one aside, interestingly, Rowson addresses herself specifically to the "sober matron" who might be reading the book before she trusts it "to the eye of a darling daughter." But even though she may depart from her view of the audience as exclusively young, it is apparent that this is a book written by a woman for other women, and throughout the nineteenth century and into the twentieth, the book's readership was largely female, a point that was not lost upon its detractors. For example, *Charlotte Temple* was described disparagingly by Carl Van Doren as appealing to an audience of "housemaids and shopgirls" (*The American Novel*, 1921). A class discussion might center on the reasons for the book's appeal to such an audience. Instructors might raise the issue of the vulnerability of women of lower socioeconomic status and hence their identification with Charlotte.

Comparisons, Contrasts, Connections

As noted earlier, Rowson has often been compared to Samuel Richardson, the British author of *Pamela, or Virtue Rewarded* (1740) and *Clarissa, or, the History of a Young Lady* (1747–48). The similarities between Rowson and Richardson are obvious, both in theme and style. Richardson is known for the epistolary form, and in *Charlotte Temple*, letters (often ones that do not get delivered) play an important role. Another comparison mentioned earlier is with Oliver Goldsmith's *The Vicar of Wakefield* (1766), a novel dealing with seduction and the economic oppression of a family by a rake with designs on a virtuous daughter—a situation strikingly similar to one of Rowson's subplots, the story of Charlotte's parents.

An interesting comparison to a twentieth-century American novel is, as noted, to Theodore Dreiser's *An American Tragedy* (1925). The plots have many similarities: in both novels a self-indulgent young man of little personal wealth, but with wealthy connections, seduces a poor girl and then falls in love with another woman, who offers not only superior attractiveness, but money as well. In both stories, the young man, seeing the first girl as an obstacle to his material and romantic happiness with the second, regrets his rashness in seducing the first, who is pregnant and dependent on him. In both novels the seduced women die. Montraville does not plot to kill his mistress, as Clyde plans to and in effect does kill Roberta, but Charlotte dies as a result of her lover's neglect.

Both Dreiser and Rowson depict, to quote Charlotte, "a very bad world"—but their analyses differ. Rowson's solution to the evil is not to change that world, but to help develop in women the strength, wisdom, and common sense they will need to deal with it as it is. Where Dreiser sees Roberta and Clyde as victims of social and economic inequality, Rowson sees Charlotte and Montraville as victims of individual failings. Whereas Dreiser's novel is a sweeping indictment of the class system in supposedly egalitarian America, Rowson's is an indictment of personal evil and weakness.

Questions for Reading and Discussion/ Approaches to Writing

1. Look up information about Rowson's life and show how her biography and the historical period in which the novel is set influence the work.
2. Prepare a critical evaluation of the novel. Consider the author's development of the characters, the plotting of the novel, and the novel's impact on the reader.
3. Write a paper comparing and contrasting *Charlotte Temple* and *An American Tragedy*. (This assignment might be suitable for a term paper or special individual project.)

Bibliography

Brandt, Ellen B. *Susanna Haswell Rowson, America's First Best-Selling Novelist*. Chicago: Serba Press, 1975.

Davidson, Cathy N. Introduction. *Charlotte Temple*. New York: Oxford University Press, 1986.

——. *Revolution and the Word: The Rise of the Novel in America*. New York: Oxford University Press, 1986.

Parker, Patricia. *Susanna Rowson*. Boston: Twayne, 1986.

Rourke, Constance. *The Roots of American Culture*. New York: Harcourt, Brace & Co., 1942.

Vail, Robert. "Susanna Haswell Rowson, the Author of Charlotte Temple: A Bibliographical Study." *American Antiquarian Society Proceedings*. n.s. v. 42 (1933): 47–160.

Charles Brockden Brown (1771–1810)

Contributing Editor: Carla Mulford

Classroom Issues and Strategies

Undergraduates find Brown peculiar when compared to other writers of the era, and they tend to say, "He reminds me of Poe," without realizing that Poe wrote a generation after C. B. Brown. They are unused to first-person narratives of Brown's order if they have been in a chronologically-arranged survey course. They have been used to first-person narratives that explore particular models of behavior, like the spiritual autobiography. Brown, writing in the absence of particular religious ideologies or political agendas, puzzles them. Some students like him immensely; others find him obtuse and irrational.

I play upon students' surprise at Brown's narrative, and I stress that *if* Brown's narratives seem irrational, then perhaps that was part of Brown's point, that life itself is unpredictable according to rational plans. I show them that at the time when most writers were attempting to find ways to model the Federalist political agenda, Brown was questioning the assumptions of the model—that life could be organized like a coherent machine and that people could be taught "moral" behavior. If students can't quite see it this way, then I talk with them about various means by which authors more familiar to them (Poe, Conrad, Hawthorne) have represented the unconscious and seemingly irrational behavior.

Major Themes, Historical Perspectives, and Personal Issues

If students want to explore Brown's life, they find ample interesting material in his letters about authorship. Most biographies on Brown—there are a few readily available—quote from letters.

Significant Form, Style, or Artistic Conventions

Two key issues are raised by Brown's writing:

Brown's first-person narratives differ from those most students will be accustomed to from earlier writers. Brown's narrators, like Althorpe, the narrator of this story, are often unreliable. Students are intrigued by the exploration of psychology that Brown offers them. (They have been trained to think such complexity available only in twentieth-century authors, or in Poe.)

Second, because of the first-person narrative form, the intense psychological issues Brown renders often take on a motif of "the double." In this narrative, young Althorpe, the narrator, has his double in both the unnamed man to whom Constantia Davis is engaged and in the anticipated intruder, Nick Handyside. This is a minor sample of Brown's often-central motif of the double. (See *Wieland, Edgar Huntly*.)

Comparisons, Contrasts, Connections

We talk about the Federalist audience that would have liked Foster and Rowson, in order to put Brown's work in a relief of "conscious" narrative. This enables students to see just how extraordinary Brown's narrative attempts were.

We then, later on (in covering Poe and Hawthorne), discuss the extent to which later authors used some of Brown's interests and techniques. Hawthorne considered Brown one of the best American writers, and he regretted Brown's inability to find an appreciative audience.

Many students then like to make comparisons between Brown and recent authors.

Questions for Reading and Discussion/ Approaches to Writing

Students have written fruitful papers on doubles in Brown; Brown's implied attack against the "rational" Federalist agenda of his day; Brown's relationship to Poe and Hawthorne.

Bibliography

There are many, many studies on Brown. Recent articles have played upon the issues of family and disintegration. Teachers should pursue those articles that might interest them, after reading discussions of books and articles in the entries (well-indexed) in each annual volume of *American Literary Scholarship*.

Federalist and Anti-Federalist Contentions

Contributing Editor: Nicholas D. Rombes

Classroom Issues and Strategies

Students generally respond with more enthusiasm to the Federalist/Anti-Federalist debate once they realize that the issues raised by the debate were very real. It often helps, initially, to have students think of "current event" issues of contention today, such as the "pro-life"/"pro-choice" abortion debates. This helps students to see that debates over the Constitution were not merely abstract exercises in rhetorical showmanship, but real debates about issues that mattered.

Students also seem to identify with one of the three "voices" of *The Federalist Papers*, as well. Some students, for instance, wish that Jay had contributed more essays, finding his voice more democratic and populist than Hamilton's or Madison's. This can lead to fruitful discussions about the rhetorical strategies employed by all three authors as well as the audience they were addressing.

Major Themes, Historical Perspectives, and Personal Issues

Many students assume that once the Revolutionary War was over, the country was solidified and unified. Therefore, it is helpful to review certain key issues such as states' rights, fear of a standing army, and fear of factions. Anti-Federalists argued again and again that a national government was merely a prelude to the establishment of an aristocratic class. Indeed, many Anti-Federalists drew upon the rhetoric of the Revolution to argue against a strong national government.

The Federalist conception of human nature as essentially selfish and depraved is also important to note, since Federalists relied on such conceptions to justify their call for a mildly interventionist national government. Students are often shocked to learn that the word "democracy" was not held in high regard as it is today, and are interested in the distinctions between democracy, monarchy, and republicanism.

For years, many scholars have contended that the Federalists were basically conservative upper-class supporters of the status quo, and that the Anti-Federalists were more "populist." Scholars such as Herbert J. Storing have recently suggested, however, that, if anything, Anti-Federalists were more conservative than their Federalist counterparts, as evidenced in the fact that many Anti-Federalists feared the very idea of change and experimentation that would result from the new form of government proposed by the Federalists.

It is also helpful to introduce students to some of the basic ideas of writers such as Hobbes, Locke, and Montesquieu, all of whose writings influenced the Constitution to varying degrees.

Significant Form, Style, or Artistic Conventions

Students are interested in the different "voices" of Hamilton, Madison, and Jay. Note also how the authors of *The Federalist Papers* allude to classical regimes and civilizations not only to help their arguments but also to show their learning. Finally, note how many of the letters begin with references to "objections" to the proposed Constitution—instructors may want to use this to show that these debates were very real.

Original Audience

The Federalist Papers originally appeared as a series of essays in New York newspapers between October and August 1787. Based on the language and tone of the essays, ask students to try to construct an audience for them: would this audience be literate? educated? What economic class might constitute the majority of the audience? What race? Gender?

Questions for Reading and Discussion

1. Ask students to perform a rhetorical analysis of *The Federalist Papers,* paying special attention to how the authors construct their arguments (logos), how they bolster their authority and credibility (ethos), and how they use the beliefs, fears, and assumptions of their audience (pathos) to help their arguments.
2. Ask students to try to reconstruct the Federalist conception of the relationship between "the people" and government. From where does authority ultimately derive? If students have spent time studying the Puritans, ask them to consider the ultimate source of authority in Puritan writings as compared to Federalist and Anti-Federalist writings. Has the source of authority shifted from God to humans and civic institutions?
3. Ask students to read carefully Federalist No. 54. How does Madison handle the topic of slavery? Have students summarize his arguments.

Bibliography

Carey, George W. *The Federalist: Design for a Constitutional Republic,* 1989.

Epstein, David F. *The Political Theory of The Federalist,* 1984.

Furtwangler, Albert. *The Authority of Publius: A Reading of the Federalist Papers,* 1984.

Main, Jackson Turner. *The Anti-Federalists: Critics of the Constitution, 1781–1788,* 1961.

Missionary Voices of the Southwest

Fray Carlos José Delgado (1677–post-1750)

Contributing Editor: Carla Mulford

Classroom Issues and Strategies

Delgado's report provides teachers a wonderful opportunity to show students several aspects of colonization: the frequency and necessity of reports not just on civil affairs but on ecclesiastical ones; the ability of some colonists (in this instance, some of the missionaries in New Spain) to have empathy for Native peoples; the extent to which missionaries followed what they understood as Christ's injunctions to walk simply and stalwartly with love for all peoples; insight into the suffering and confusion that Native peoples must have felt between their imposed ties (both civil and spiritual) to the Spanish Crown.

Many students might want to see this text stereotypically as another example of the cruel Spanish colonizers exploiting the Native peoples. It is perhaps best to let that stereotype get aired early in class discussion so that the class can move on to a more thorough discussion of the problems of colonization when it would seem as if there was no turning away from it.

Major Themes, Historical Perspectives, and Personal Issues

Taking the four concepts identified above as a guide, teachers might formulate a class and lead class discussion on these themes. First, it should be emphasized that this text is merely one example of thousands of texts—in the form of letters, reports, diaries, and logs—common to colonization, not just of the Americas but of, for example, Africa and the Middle East. Indeed, even the journal-histories of the English colonies—most notably those written by William Bradford (*Of Plymouth Plantation*) and John Winthrop (his voluminous diaries) but even the diary of Samuel Sewall much later on—attest to the issues and problems of colonization in territory unfamiliar both geophysically and interpersonally. The text is merely one paradigmatic example, it should be noted, of the experience of many national groups that have taken over territories held natively by others.

Next, to counterbalance the stereotypical assumptions that have accrued about Spanish colonization, teachers should emphasize the empathy with which the report is constructed. Delgado was himself a Spanish "colonizer," who was interested in what he considered the souls of the colonized. This empathy is clearly a function of what must have been real spiritual belief on the part of Fray Carlos José Delgado but it also is a mark of the "true Christian" motif common in the writings of devout missionaries (the third point made in the opening paragraph above). This motif takes different forms in different cultures—the "Christianity" of John Eliot among the Indians takes a different form from that of Delgado, just as that of French Catholic (and Protestant) missionaries might differ from this text and from John Eliot's. Nonetheless, clear marks of "true Christian" practice are available in the text: Delgado's emphasis upon his own humility, his acceptance of the paternal relation of Spain to New Spain, his discussion of events in terms of "persecution" both of missionaries and Indians, his compassion for the hunger, physical suffering, and personal degradation (especially of women) the Natives experience. In all of these areas, Delgado walks like Christ, serving as a living model of Christ and Christian teachings.

Finally, the report provides remarkable evidence of the treatment Native peoples received at the hands of the Spanish colonizers. Reports like this document abuses the Indian peoples experienced even as they show the extent to which Indians even acquiescent to colonization faced clearly mixed signals from and conflicting loyalties to their oppressors. Surely the conflictedness of the situation complicates students' easy assumptions, voiced (at the outset) in more than one of my classes, that the "Indians should somehow have banded together." Against whom, I ask, and to what end, given the fact that there were always more Spanish people arriving in the land.

Significant Form, Style, or Artistic Conventions

In light of classroom discussion about the motif of the "true Christian" as it becomes apparent in this text, students could be asked to discuss the different ways in which this motif is manifest in biography (as in Palou's hagiography of Serra and Mather's biographies of, say, Bradford, Winthrop, and Eliot), autobiography (Winthrop's diary, Roger Williams's letters, Elizabeth Ashbridge's narrative, John Woolman's journal), reports (this text), and narratives (such as the captivity narratives of Mary Rowlandson or John Williams).

Original Audience

Students might misunderstand Delgado's religious and political position within the colony and, though highlighting his empathy for Native peoples, think him a "traitor" or "tattletale" of the Spanish colonizing effort. Such students will need to be assured that missionaries were often at odds with civil leaders because missionaries were charged with the defense of the converted peoples, a defense accountable not only to the Spanish Crown and ultimately the Pope but also, for the devout, to God. In addition, the converts were assigned to the mission as workers within a familial—but ultimately economic—unit that was, in theory, supposed to function in a cooperative manner and thus teach its members to integrate themselves as equals within the larger paternal system. Civil officials, however, wanted to exploit labor at less than market value, and to do so they sought ways to circumvent the protective organization of the mission. The only voice of opposition—that is, a voice that could receive official hearing, for surely the Indians protested their abuses—came from the missionaries, who had recourse to a separate line of communication to centralized powers.

How this particular report was received is difficult to determine. As Ramón Gutiérrez has commented, "Church-state relations had been rather calm during the first half of the eighteenth century. But in 1761, the scabs were torn off what were now old wounds" (*When Jesus Came, the Corn Mothers Went Away: Marriage, Sexuality, and Power in New Mexico, 1500–1846* [Stanford: Stanford University Press, 1991], p. 306). Civil officials, who wanted the Franciscans removed so that they could claim full control of Native Americans, avowed that the friars were remiss in their duties; missionaries claimed, to the contrary, that the majority of friars were Christian models of virtue.

The complicated rhetorical situation that both missionaries and civil authorities faced—with authorities so far away and mail passage so irregular—no doubt compromised their situations, and probably left hard feelings on both sides, not to mention the conflict that must have been experienced by Native Americans. What is clear is that by the end of the eighteenth century, the pueblos of New Mexico evolved quite independently of each other (Gutiérrez, p. 309), thus suggesting that civil authorities succeeded in breaking down the missionary aim of having an abiding and faithful populace separated merely geographically but not spiritually.

Comparisons, Contrasts, Connections

This text can be usefully compared to Roger Williams's accounts of Native Americans and his experiences of conflict with Puritan authorities. In terms of a comparison of its motifs, see the section, "Significant Form, Style, or Artistic Conventions" above.

To make the text seem more "contemporary," if students have problems with its accessibility, teachers might compare it to the kind of investigative report common today in the news media. As different newspapers and news stations seem to operate as checks and balances in news reportage, some more "conservative" and favoring certain agendas and others more "liberal" and favoring other agendas, just so the differing reports sent back to Spain betrayed the biases of the reporters. Perhaps most telling about this text, its most teachable feature, is that "history" is not "pure," that texts like this that seem like mere dry and dusty documents are clearly "literary" in their rhetorical methods and evident goals to persuade.

Francisco Palou (1723–1789)

Contributing Editor: Juan Bruce-Novoa

Classroom Issues and Strategies

Students may think that the text is an anachronism, coming late in history. While the East Coast is in the midst of its independence struggle, Serra and Palou are still founding missions. Students have been taught to think of Spain as finished internationally after the Great Armada.

The eighteenth century was one of expansion and renewed vitality for Spain. Its missionaries and soldiers were moving on all fronts, founding new cities in Texas and northern New Mexico, moving into the Mississippi and Ohio valleys, solidifying their position in the Caribbean basin, and spreading north along the Pacific Coast to counter the southern movement of the Russians from Alaska. Missionaries were the Spanish equivalent of frontiersmen, but they prove how much better organized the Spanish expansion system was. Also, students should be told that the treaty between France and England in 1763 acknowledged Spain's traditional claim to the Mississippi Valley, which was disputed by the French.

Students often question the purpose of the missionary project. It has become fashionable to denounce Serra as an exploiter of Native Americans, so instructors may find it necessary to prepare for a discussion of the moral issues involved in the activities of Christian missionaries anywhere in the world. More useful, however, is to turn the discussion toward a consideration of how models are always ideologically based and serve the purpose of social indoctrination.

Major Themes, Historical Perspectives, and Personal Issues

Consider the following: the theme of personal sacrifice and determination in the face of great odds; the theme of the traditional moving of borders farther into the territory of the non-Christian that comes from Spain's reconquest of their own territory from the Moors (700–1492).

There is also the literary motif of creating models of cultural behavior in texts that will be used to teach the young.

Significant Form, Style, or Artistic Conventions

The form is biography. Students should consider the task of depicting the life of another, the choices made to emphasize certain traits, the strategies used to convince the reader of the author's objectivity and reliability.

There is also the similarity to the writing on the lives of the saints. Students might consider which virtues are held up for imitation in different settings and times.

Original Audience

Readers then were much closer to the ideals expressed by Palou probably coming from the novices of religious orders. They were much more willing to believe in the values reflected in the life of Serra. Now there is little sense of divine mission in life nor of the virtue of extreme sacrifice for the common good. Students must be urged to comprehend the energy of societies in expansion.

Comparisons, Contrasts, Connections

Compare this to Cotton Mather, as the headnote mentions. Both writers attempt to create models for new generations who have forgotten their founding fathers. One could also pick a favorite section from John F. Kennedy's portraits of courage to compare with Serra.

Questions for Reading and Discussion/ Approaches to Writing

Pose the question of role models in society in different periods. Ask students to consider where the models come from and what purpose they fulfill. How do they differ then and now? They can be asked to write an essay about someone they would want to be the role model for their generation.

Early Nineteenth Century
1800–1865

Myths, Tales, and Legends

These two sections continue the exploration of the creation of myths of national and personal identity that followed the emergence of the political entity known as the United States. Whereas the depth and specificity of scholarly knowledge that any given set of students will have about U.S. history is unpredictable and inconsistent, students will bring to class mythic or legendary senses of those cultural constructs called "America" and "American history." Pedagogy can begin with an examination of this historical consciousness on the part of the students—the "myths, tales, and legends" students bring with them into the class.

The selections in this first section can thus be read in terms of both historical connections with our various contemporary historical imaginations and also their performative dimension as rhetoric intended to shape and create a specific sense of the past. Class can begin by asking what expectations and assumptions are created in a reader by the words "myth," "tale," and "legend." What are the differences between the collectively produced legends and tales of an oral tradition (The "Tales From the Hispanic Southwest," the Native American stories retold by Schoolcraft, or the texts found in the section on Native American oral narratives) and the individualized performances of Washington Irving, Edgar Allan Poe, James Fenimore Cooper, and Catharine Maria Sedgwick? What are the strategies behind deliberately creating a "legend"? These texts also demonstrate how the creators of legends competed and debated with one another over questions of national purpose, whether in Irving's deflation of self-aggrandizing, Eurocentric historians (*A History of New York*) or Cooper's (*The Pioneers*) and Sedgwick's (*Hope Leslie*) alternative versions of the conflict between pioneers and Indians.

Explorations of an "American" Self

This section changes the focus on mythmaking from the national to the personal level. The word "exploration" suggests the rhetorical dimension of these textual performances, as each writer strives to find or create consensus among a diverse national audience in order to construct a sense of personal identity at once collective and individual. From this perspective, Emerson's creation and invocation of an "aboriginal Self" in "Self-Reliance" can be seen as alternative rather than definitive, as one of many claims to articulate a national sense of mission based on the construction of a particular "American" identity. While Emerson brought to his performances an access to cultural authority based on his race, gender, and class status, other writers—Frederick Douglass, Harriet Jacobs, Margaret Fuller, and George Copway—had to work hard simply to establish a right to speak because of these same social factors. The class can highlight the stakes involved in the debate over national identity by asking questions about purpose, audience, and strategy: what was each writer trying to achieve; who did each seem to be talking to; and why did each think the strategy he or she used would work? Such an approach helps focus critical attention on not just how an American identity might be constructed, but for what ends. These questions can also apply to contemporary constructions of the "American Self" and they look forward to the section on "New Explorations of an 'American' Self" in Volume 2 of *The Heath Anthology*.

Issues and Visions in Pre–Civil War America

Most anthologies of literature published over the last fifty years have relied on criteria derived from traditional New Critical models of literary analysis. Those models valued what was taken to be the inherent formal complexity of individual texts, a complexity seen as separate and separable from the historical and cultural circumstances of the production of the text. As a result, many pedagogical arguments over the canon have centered on whether certain texts were "complicated" enough to sustain extended classroom discussion or analysis and thus merit inclusion in an anthology or a course syllabus. The implication was that some texts were somehow self-evident in their meaning and intent, and therefore "simple," while other, seemingly more complicated texts, demanded and therefore deserved close scrutiny; for example, what can you say about a novel as supposedly straightforward and uncomplicated as *Uncle Tom's Cabin*? But the ambiguous, self-referential *Benito Cereno* provides plenty of material for class discussion.

As many instructors will testify, however, classroom experience often tells a different story, where few if any nineteenth-century texts, no matter how supposedly "simple" or "straightforward," are experienced as self-evident by first-time readers in the class. There are at least two other pedagogical problems stemming from an emphasis on "formal complexity" as well: the circularity of the argument—very often definitions of formal complexity were based on the same texts they were supposed to define—and, even more important to literary studies, such a critical model failed to account for a large number of texts considered significant by nineteenth-century readers, and thus prevented a richer understanding of cultural history.

The "Issues and Visions" approach to grouping texts addresses these concerns in the classroom by recognizing that literary and linguistic complexity resides not apart from but within the historical and cultural context of a text. Such an approach emphasizes texts as rhetorical performances, performances as complex as the rhetorical demands and contingencies to which they respond: A Christian Indian appealing to a dominant culture audience responsible for both his religious faith and the subjugation of his people (Elias Boudinot); a Northern single mother writing satirical denunciations of male dominance for a popular press dominated by male editors and publishers (Fanny Fern); an ex-slave demanding both racial justice and gender equality before an audience of white women (Sojourner Truth). The title alone of Angelina Grimké's "Appeal to the Christian Women of the South" suggests the complexity of the rhetorical situation she faced (and hence makes a good starting place for class discussion), balancing issues of gender, race, religion, region, and class in arguing for the abolition of slavery.

By challenging the notion of "background" material, the interrelationship of text and context in this rhetorical approach has important pedagogical implications for the question of how much historical information students need to understand any text, whether its author is Ralph Waldo Emerson or Sojourner Truth; Abraham Lincoln or Mariano Guadalupe Vallejo. Students can be encouraged to explore the historical context *through* the text by raising questions of rhetorical strategy. Beginning with the ideas and assumptions about slavery and abolition, the struggle for women's rights, the Indian experience, or the history of the West that students bring with them, the class can then explore how a particular text confirms, resists, or otherwise complicates those ideas and assumptions. Exploring the students' reading experiences of the texts can lead to questions about why writers use a certain vocabulary, set of references, or set of rhetorical strategies, and these questions in turn involve thinking about who the contemporary audience(s) for that text were and what expectations and values they held. Elaine Sargent Apthorp's teaching guide for John Greenleaf Whittier contains excellent examples of assignments designed to focus students' attention on the complexity of Whittier's performance as a public poet dedicated to political activism.

The Flowering of Narrative

The pedagogical introduction to the "Issues and Visions" section suggests that students should be encouraged to regard texts not as static set pieces but as complex rhetorical performances embedded in cultural debates over race, gender, political legitimacy, and economics. While this "cultural rhetoric" approach seems especially suited for the consideration of "noncanonical" material that doesn't fit neatly into the traditional genre categories of poetry, drama, and fiction (for example, newspaper columns, personal letters, memoirs, political speeches), it represents not a special technique to use with "unusual" materials, but a means of seeing all texts—and all acts of reading—as performative. Instead of regarding the textual performances in the sections on narrative and poetry as standing apart from earlier, less "literary" selections, instructors can use a cultural rhetoric approach to raise questions about the differences in motive, impact, and strategy in such works on race and slavery as Frederick Douglass's autobiography, Harriet Beecher Stowe's openly polemical novel *Uncle Tom's Cabin*, and Herman Melville's elusive *Benito Cereno*. The class might, for example, analyze Nathaniel Hawthorne's narrative choice of Puritan New England as the site of the drama of cultural authority and gender politics in *The Scarlet Letter* in the light of the arguments regarding the political and social status of women in the nineteenth century raised by Margaret Fuller and Elizabeth Cady Stanton.

Depending on the background and training of individual instructors, the names found in "The Flowering of Narrative" will represent a mix of the intensely familiar with the radically new, the canonical with the noncanonical. This mix will also be true for some students; for others, however, "familiarity" may indicate little more than name recognition and carry few if any implications of "greatness" or "classic" status. For the instructor unsure of how to approach the new, and for the students to whom almost every nineteenth-century text is strange and remote, the first step may be the question of the canon itself, and specifically an expansion of the question Judith Fetterley reports her students asking in regard to Caroline Kirkland: Why haven't we heard of these writers before? (For other writers the question would be the reverse: Why *have* we heard so much about them?) As the class reads through these selections, they can classify or reclassify the writers in terms of technique, subject matter, or audience appeal. Such discussions can provide the foreground for considerations of how canons have been constructed historically (it can often be illuminating to look at copies of tables of contents from anthologies from the nineteenth century to the present).

The Emergence of American Poetic Voices

If many students come into class with the assumption that "poetry" is necessarily distant and obscure, the section on "Songs and Ballads" can lead to discussions both about definitions of poetry and where these definitions come from. This in turn can involve discussions about the different kinds of cultural work poems do, from self-expression to the ritual building of a sense of communal solidarity, from self-examination to social protest. Equally important is the inclusion of song lyrics, for they remind students that not only is poetry still an active part of contemporary cultural life in general, but part of many students' lives in particular.

If the texts in the "Issues and Visions" sections provide cultural context for these poems, then the inclusion of poetry and fiction in the "Issues and Visions" sections themselves gives students practice in discussing questions of genre and style from different perspectives: How would we read Whitman differently, for example, if he were included in the section on abolitionist literature? If Whittier were included with Bryant and Longfellow (as he often is) rather than with William Lloyd Garrison and David Walker? If Emily Dickinson or Lydia Howard Huntley Sigourney were included in the section on "The Woman Question"? These exercises in classification and reclassification can also work within this section: many anthologies and syllabi have grouped Whitman and Dickinson as opposed to Longfellow and Bryant. What other possibilities are there, and what do they reveal? And again, such questions lead back to a consideration of the processes and purposes of canon formation.

Myths, Tales, and Legends

Jane Johnston Schoolcraft (Ojibwa) (1800–1841)

Contributing Editor: James W. Parins

Classroom Issues and Strategies

Establishing a framework for discussion helps in teaching Schoolcraft. The instructor needs to address the prehistoric nature of the original oral tales and aspects of the oral tradition itself, and, in addition, explain how the tales were enhanced stylistically and rhetorically once they were written down. The dual audiences (of the original tales and the written versions) need to be addressed as well.

As a helpful teaching strategy, draw parallels with other oral tales, for example, Njal's *Saga*, *Beowulf*, and the *Iliad*. All these existed first in the oral tradition and were later written down. All included super- or preternatural elements.

Students usually have questions on the differences in social values between the American Indian and "mainstream" cultures.

Major Themes, Historical Perspectives, and Personal Issues

Of particular importance are creation myths or stories that explain how things came to be.

Significant Form, Style, or Artistic Conventions

Students can compare the author with others writing in the "standard" style of the time, Hawthorne and Irving, for example, particularly in their self-conscious use of terms like "legend."

Original Audience

Teachers need to address the preliterate society for which the tales were originally composed as well as the non-Indian audience Schoolcraft was writing for. Points to be made include the following: The style was embellished for the non-Indian audience; students should be directed to find examples. Schoolcraft's Romantic style differs from some other narratives, including slave narratives.

Comparisons, Contrasts, Connections

Oral texts from other traditions can be compared and contrasted. Cusick's work is especially helpful for comparison within the American Indian context.

Tales from the Hispanic Southwest

Contributing Editor: Genaro M. Padilla

Classroom Issues and Strategies

Students may need to be reminded that these tales are usually performed orally. So, instructors should help students recreate the oral tradition out of which they emerge. I often read these tales aloud and try to actually reconstruct the performative features of the tale.

Major Themes, Historical Perspectives, and Personal Issues

See headnote.

Significant Form, Style, or Artistic Conventions

Again, the cultural value attached to oral tradition and collective audience should be borne in mind.

Original Audience

The best/ideal audience is youngsters who are still shaping their social and ethical beliefs.

Comparisons, Contrasts, Connections

Other folk tale types should be useful, especially those sustained by other immigrant groups—Italians, Greeks, etc.

Questions for Reading and Discussion/ Approaches to Writing

1. (a) What are our common ideas about death? Why do we avoid discussing death?
   (b) How do stories entertain us into ethical behavior?
2. (a) Students might compare these tales with others they have heard or read.
   (b) They might consider the "usefulness" of the moral tales in a largely secular world.

Washington Irving (1783–1859)

Contributing Editor: William Hedges

Classroom Issues and Strategies

Students generally know the two short stories ("Rip" and "Sleepy Hollow"). With the selections from *History*, it is wise to avoid tipping off students in advance to Irving's attitude toward the treatment of Native Americans by European-Americans; see if they can penetrate through the technically sophisticated irony to Irving's scathing condemnation; some may be tempted to read the passage as approving the harsh treatment. (Note that, strictly speaking, the passage is concerned with Latin America, not America as a whole. But students can be asked whether it has relevance to North American policies relating to Indians.)

Emphasize Irving's humor before getting too serious. Give students a chance to talk about what they find entertaining in the selections and why. Also, try comparing responses of male and female students to "Rip Van Winkle." How sympathetic are each to Rip? Look at the story as the first in a long line of texts by male American writers in which a male protagonist forsakes civilized community life for the wilderness (or the sea) on a quest of sorts and perhaps joins forces with a male companion(s). Consider the psychological or cultural significance of such narratives, as well as the role of and attitude toward women they portray.

Major Themes, Historical Perspectives, and Personal Issues

History: racism, its guises and rationalizations; what it means to be truly civilized—or savage.

"Rip Van Winkle": loss (and discovery?) of identity; a challenge to American values, the work ethic. Does Rip himself represent anything positive? George III vs. George Washington (is the story anti-republican?); is the story sexist?

"Sleepy Hollow": artificiality vs. naturalness; Puritan-Yankee intellectual pretentiousness, hypocrisy, greed, and commercialism as threats to an American dream of rural abundance and simple contentedness; the uses of imagination.

Significant Form, Style, or Artistic Conventions

With the *History* selection, questions of burlesque irony, the reliability of the narrator: Is Irving's persona, the peculiar Diedrich Knickerbocker, a party to the irony? Is he being deliberately ironic himself (saying just the opposite of what he believes about treatment of Native Americans), or does he seem duped by the defenses of brutal mistreatment that he offers? Does it matter which? Could it be either one—or both? Is the reader being played with?

The two stories were written ten years after the *Knickerbocker History*. *The Sketch Book*, from which the two stories come, is generally taken to be the beginning of Irving's transformation into a romantic writer of sorts. What romantic elements can be seen in "Rip" and "Sleepy Hollow"?

These two stories are also, arguably, the beginning of a new genre, the short story. If so, what makes these narratives short stories as opposed to earlier kinds of tales?

Original Audience

Relate Irving's commercial success beginning with *The Sketch Book* to the burgeoning of American popular culture in the early nineteenth century. Discuss *The Sketch Book* as context of "Rip" and "Sleepy Hollow" and the huge vogue for "sketch" books, literary annuals, and gift books that follows.

Comparisons, Contrasts, Connections

Compare the selection from *History* with Franklin's Swiftian satires, "The Sale of the Hessians," "An Edict by the King of Prussia"—or Swift's "A Modest Proposal" itself.

Compare and contrast the rural felicity of the inhabitants of Sleepy Hollow with Crèvecoeur's idealization of American rural life in the *American Farmer* or Jefferson's famous agrarian pronouncements in query XIX of *Notes on Virginia*.

What distinguishes Irving as a short story writer from Hawthorne or Poe?

Questions for Reading and Discussion/ Approaches to Writing

1. The humor of the *Knickerbocker History*—have students read sections of it.

2. Political satire and opinion in the *History*—consider specifically the anti-Jeffersonianism of the section on Governor Kieft. Prepare a personal interpretation of one of the two stories.
3. Papers on varying or contrasting approaches to "Rip" or "Sleepy Hollow," consulting some of the interpretations listed in the bibliography. Discuss the humor in either story.

Bibliography

Fetterly, Judith. Chapter on "Rip Van Winkle" in *The Resisting Reader* (1978). A feminist interpretation.

Hedges, William L. Article on the *History* in Stanley Brodwin, ed., *The Old and New World Romanticism of Washington Irving* (1986). *Knickerbocker*'s politics and Irving's disorienting humor.

Hoffman, Daniel. Chapter on "Sleepy Hollow" in *Form and Fable In American Fiction* (1961). Folkloristic interpretation, Native American humor.

Martin, Terence. "Rip, Ichabod, and the American Imagination." *American Literature* 31 (1959): 137–49.

Ringe, Donald A. "New York and New England: Irving's Criticism of American Society." *American Literature* 21 (1967): 455–67. Irving's pro-Dutch, anti-Yankee posture.

Roth, Martin. Chapters on *Knickerbocker* and on the two stories, in *Comedy in America: The Lost World of Washington Irving*. Very original criticism, mythic and cultural.

Seelye, John. "Root and Branch: Washington Irving and American Humor." In *Nineteenth-Century Fiction* 38 (1984): 415–25. Very solid, well-balanced approach.

Young, Philip. "Fallen from Time: The Mythic Rip Van Winkle." *Kenyon Review* 22 (1960): 547–73. Jungian, the motif of the long sleep in world literature.

Zlogar, Richard J. "Accessories that Covertly Explain: Irving's Use of Dutch Genre Painting in 'Rip Van Winkle.'" *American Literature* 54 (1982): 44–62. Argues story is critical of Rip.

James Fenimore Cooper (1789–1851)

Contributing Editor: Geoffrey Rans

Classroom Issues and Strategies

I have found it better not to insist on Cooper's formal powers at the outset, nor even on his obvious importance as an innovator and initiator in American fiction. Rather, it is effective to invite the students to discuss the substantive issues that arise in a reading of Cooper. Their importance and typicality in the American literary experience remain alive to students in various historical transformations, and Cooper presents them in unresolved and problematic formations.

While the passages selected in *The Heath Anthology* raise obvious and important issues—of empire, of political theory, of nature versus civilization, law, conservation, religion, race, family, American history—one Leather-Stocking novel should be studied in its entirety. Depending on where the instructor places most emphasis, *The Pioneers*, *The Last of the Mohicans*, and *The Deerslayer* are the most accessible. In any case, any study of even the selected passages requires some "story-telling" by the instructor.

The discussion of *The Pioneers* or other novels can become, as well, a discussion of the competing claims on the student's attention to form and content: whether form is always possible or desirable; whether the unresolved issues in history are in any sense "resolved" in works of art; how the desire for narrative or didactic closure competes with the recognition of an incomplete and problematic history and political theory. Approach questions of empire, race, progress, civilization, family, law, and power, and lead back from them to the literary issues.

Major Themes, Historical Perspectives, and Personal Issues

1. Historical myth and ideology. How do they differ? How do they interact?
2. Nature/civilization
3. Law
4. Power and property
5. The land
6. Violence

7. Race
8. Gender and family
9. Cooper's contradictory impulses: see Parrington (10)
10. Hope/disappointment

Significant Form, Style, or Artistic Conventions

1. Didacticism, resolved and unresolved
2. Romance—the Scott tradition: see Orlans (10)
3. Myth
4. Romanticism
5. Conventions of description and dialogue, epic and romantic
6. Epic
7. For advanced students: the question of the order of composition, and the literary effect on the reader of anachronism

Original Audience

I stress how the issues that were urgent to Cooper and his readers (they are evident in the novels, but see also Parrington) are alive today. Some attention should be given to the demand for a national literature, and the expectations of the American Romance (see Orlans).

Indispensable reading for this period is Nina Baym's *Novelists, Readers and Reviewers* (Ithaca: Cornell University Press, 1984).

Comparisons, Contrasts, Connections

Here are some pursuable issues:

1. Crèvecoeur: slavery, Indians, the agrarian ideology and its betrayal.
2. Relate to other writings on the encounter of white and red—see Smith, Winthrop, Williams, Crèvecoeur, Franklin, Jefferson.
3. Stowe—on race, slavery, Christianity and its betrayal, didacticism—Twain, Frederick Douglass.
4. The nonfiction writers of the Revolution and the New Republic: Jefferson, the Federalists.
5. Faulkner: race, history. Carolyn Porter's chapters on Faulkner (see 10) might seem relevant to Cooper to some instructors.
6. Catharine Sedgwick's *Hope Leslie*.

Questions for Reading and Discussion/
Approaches to Writing

1. Before starting Cooper, an assembly of the issues raised in the course about form, the canon, and the literature of Colonial, Revolutionary, and New Republican times should be given by the instructor.
2. I have found the following areas particularly fruitful for student essays on Cooper:
   (a) Confusion, contradiction, and resolution
   (b) Myth versus reality
   (c) Race
   (d) Law and justice
   (e) Power in all its forms: class, race, military, political, and property

Bibliography

The chapters on Cooper in the following books (subtitles omitted):

Bewley, Marius. *The Eccentric Design*. New York: Columbia University Press, 1961.

Fisher, Philip. *Hard Facts*. New York: Oxford University Press, 1985.

Marx, Leo. *The Machine in the Garden*. New York: Oxford University Press, 1964.

Orlans, G. Harrison. "The Romance Ferment after *Waverly*." *American Literature* 3 (1932): 408–31.

Parrington, Vernon L. *Main Currents in American Thought*. Vol. 2. New York: Harcourt Brace, 1927.

Porter, Carolyn. *Seeing and Being*. Middletown: Wesleyan University Press, 1981. The chapters on Faulkner.

Rans, Geoffrey. "Inaudible Man: The Indian in the Theory and Practice of White Fiction." *Canadian Review of American Studies* VII (1977): 104–15.

Smith, Henry Nash. *Virgin Land*. New York: Vintage, 1950.

Tompkins, Jane. "Indians: Textualism, Morality, and the Problem of History." *Critical Inquiry* 13 (1986): 101–19.

——. *Sensational Designs*. New York: Oxford University Press, 1985.

Catharine Maria Sedgwick (1789–1867)

Contributing Editors: Barbara A. Bardes and Suzanne Gossett

Classroom Issues and Strategies

There may be some difficulty in helping students compare early nineteenth-century attitudes toward Indians, who are here referred to as savages, to Sedgwick's treatment of Native Americans, which is so different from that of her contemporaries. Be sure students know the legend of Pocahontas. The tradition of sympathy for Native American culture should be traced back to the period of Spanish arrival and to the literature of the early Puritan colonies. The selections from Cabeza de Vaca and Roger Williams are helpful in this context. It may also be useful to discuss conflicting attitudes toward the primitive: as dangerous savage and as nature's noble soul. The capture of Faith Leslie (and her eventual marriage to Oneco) should be compared to Mary Rowlandson's "Narrative of the Captivity and Restauration. . . ." Mention that according to legend, one of Sedgwick's female ancestors experienced a similar abduction.

Students need to understand Sedgwick's complex attitude toward the early Puritan colonies, which combines patriotism with objections to Puritan oppressiveness. At this point they will need some biographical and historical background, first on Sedgwick and then on the Puritans. They may be referred to the writings of John Winthrop, who appears in the novel. It is also important to note the place of women in the early American republic as teachers of the political culture yet subordinate within the home. Emphasize that Sedgwick occupied an unusual position as an important woman writer, and discuss why she shows so much sympathy for those without power in the society. Some thought should be given to the "ventriloquization" of Native American culture as a way for Sedgwick to express questions about women's culture.

Major Themes, Historical Perspectives, and Personal Issues

1. Sedgwick's picture of solidarity between women (Hope and Magawisca).
2. Sedgwick's sympathy for the Indians who are being destroyed by the English settlers. The Indian massacre repeats an English one;

students can be asked to read the "Speech of Chief Seattle" and to compare its rhetoric to the speech of Mononotto in the first selection from *Hope Leslie*. Sedgwick's sympathy is also shown in the discussion of the marriage of Faith Leslie to an Indian.

3. The political significance of Hope and Magawisca's defiance of the Puritan magistrates: the way in which both Indians and women are excluded from the political system. The emphasis throughout on the political and personal need for liberty and independence. Contrast Magawisca's defiance of the English with the historical Pocahontas's marriage to an Englishman. Discuss the conflicting ideas of natural law and patriarchal law that underly Magawisca's and Winthrop's positions.

4. The place of the family in the political order and the place of women within the family. The family is seen as the primary unit in politics and each family is represented by its male adult members. The interests of wives and children (who have no public voice in political decisions) are represented by the men.

5. "To my dying mother thou didst promise kindness to her children. In her name I demand of thee death or liberty." If time permits, discuss the nineteenth century "cult of the mother" and its manifestations in this novel.

Significant Form, Style, or Artistic Conventions

Sedgwick is important for her participation in the creation of a national literature. Both the extensive descriptions of nature and the subject matter of the novel are specifically American. *Hope Leslie* shows formal development from earlier American women's novels, though it includes, characteristically, a heroine who is to some extent deprived of parental support and creates her own success before marriage. It avoids, however, the "seduced and abandoned" plot found in *The Coquette and Charlotte Temple*, as well as excessive sentiment. Sedgwick allows her heroine to defy female norms conventional both in life and literature. She also deploys the power of public oratory within a novelistic context, and has more "public" scenes than would be expected in a "woman's" novel.

Original Audience

The blend of historical fact and adventure made *Hope Leslie* acceptable reading for young women. The novel was very popular, partly because it fit into a tradition that was established by Sir Walter Scott.

Comparisons, Contrasts, Connections

The novel should be compared with *The Last of the Mohicans*, published one year earlier. Sedgwick even refers to Cooper's novel in the text. But she countenances marriage between an Indian and a white woman, and she shows sympathy for the motives of the Indian attack on the white settlers. In addition, Sedgwick does not make women merely the means of alliance between men, but she puts them at the center of her novel, rather than on the margins.

Questions for Reading and Discussion/ Approaches to Writing

1. (a) Compare the representation of the Indian massacre in *Hope Leslie* with the massacre that occurs in *The Last of the Mohicans*.
   (b) Consider how Sedgwick equates her two heroines, Magawisca and Hope Leslie. In what ways is the scene at the mothers' graves a defining moment in the relationship of the two women?
   (c) What is the basis for Magawisca's refusal of Puritan authority? Is it defensible?
2. (a) Consider the political implications of the parallel judgment scenes in *Hope Leslie*, when Everell is "tried" by the Indians and Magawisca is tried by the Puritans. Do Governor Winthrop and Mononotto operate out of the same principles?
   (b) Compare Cooper's and Sedgwick's attitudes toward relations between the Indians and the white settlers.
   (c) Compare the sympathy for the Indians' vanishing culture in *Hope Leslie* with the narrator's sympathy for undisturbed village life in Washington Irving's "The Legend of Sleepy Hollow." What forces might motivate these two writers to come up with similar attitudes toward vanishing American cultures?
3. Consider Sedgwick's female characters in this novel: In what ways do they fit female stereotypes of the early nineteenth century, and in what ways do they express Sedgwick's own vision of women in the republic?

Edgar Allan Poe (1809–1849)

Contributing Editor: William Goldhurst

Classroom Issues and Strategies

Students confuse Poe's narrator with the author, so that in stories involving drug addiction and murders, students often say "Poe this" and "Poe that" when they mean the narrator of the tale. Poe's reputation for alcohol abuse, drug abuse, poverty, and bizarre personal habits—all exaggerated—often comes up in classroom discussion and should be relegated to the irrelevant. Students ask: "Was he an alcoholic?" "Was he a drug addict?" "Was he insane?" I quickly try to divert attention from such gossip to the themes of Jacksonian America, asking them to ponder the nature and value of Poe's vision.

I have a slide lecture, largely biographical, which always is well received. Lacking such materials, I would recommend a line-by-line reading of the major poems, with explanations as you go along. Particularly "The Raven" and "Ulalume" are understandable by this method. I would also prepare students for effects late in "Ligeia," then have them read aloud the last few pages of this tale. I always prepare the class for the Poe segment with a quick review of President Andrew Jackson's policies and what is meant by "Jacksonian Democracy." I believe this to be essential for a study of Poe.

Major Themes, Historical Perspectives, and Personal Issues

Stress Poe's affinities with mainstream America. He was culturally informed, rather than isolated, reclusive, and warped. I have spent years studying his ties to Jacksonian popular culture. It is unrealistic to ask all teachers to be informed to this extent; but the point should be made, and repeatedly.

Significant Form, Style, or Artistic Conventions

Poe's fictional architecture is unparalleled. Stories such as "The Purloined Letter" and "Ligeia" have definite form and symmetry. On another level, while most critics align Poe with the Gothic tradition, I emphasize his links with the sentimental writers of his time and earlier.

The "cycle" form practiced by many painters of his time is reflected in poems such as "The Raven."

Original Audience

It is important to establish the fact that death literature was common in Poe's day, owing to the high mortality rate among the young and middle-class citizens. In some ways Poe participated in the "consolation" movement of this time, by which he attempted to comfort the bereaved.

Comparisons, Contrasts, Connections

Poe compares with James Fenimore Cooper, Washington Irving, Charles Brockden Brown, Wm. Gilmore Simms, Donald G. Mitchell—in fact, he relates in revealing ways to most of his contemporaries.

Questions for Reading and Discussion/ Approaches to Writing

1. I always ask students to express their concept of Poe the man and Poe the author before we begin our studies. Later, I hope they have changed their image from the stereotype to something closer to reality. I also ask the students to mention more recent figures who compare to Poe. If they say Stephen King, I argue the point. I try to introduce them to Rod Serling and Alfred Hitchcock.
2. Explain the steps involved in the "Initiation Ritual," and then ask the students to trace the initiation pattern in Poe stories. It works out very well for all concerned.

Bibliography

Editions of Poe

The standard edition is the *Collected Works of Edgar Allan Poe*, edited by T. O. Mabbott et. al., 3 vols. Cambridge: Harvard University Press, 1969. Volume 1 of this edition is the best edition of Poe's poems.

Poe's critical and aesthetic works are collected in *Edgar Allan Poe: Essays and Reviews*. New York: Library of America, 1984.

Imaginary Voyages contains texts and elaborate notes for Poe's *Hans Pfaall*, *Pym*, and *Julius Rodman*, edited by Burton Pollin. Boston: Twayne, 1981. "Eureka" is included in the Penguin Edition of *The Science Fiction of Edgar Allan Poe*, edited by Harold Beaver.

The best student edition is *The Short Fiction of Edgar Allan Poe*, edited by Stuart Levine and Susan Levine. Urbana: University of Illinois, 1976, 1990.

Biographies

Of Primary Importance: "Annals" in T. O. Mabbott's Vol. 1 of the *Collected Works of Edgar Allan Poe*. A year-by-year summary of Poe's activities, reliably documented.

The Poe Log, edited by Dwight Thomas and David Jackson. Boston: G. K. Hall, 1987. The most complete documentary of Poe's professional and personal history.

Edgar Allan Poe: A Critical Biography by Arthur Hobson Quinn. Appleton Century, 1941, reissued New York: Cooper Square, 1969. Still the best Poe biography by a conscientious scholar.

Poe's letters have been brilliantly collected and edited in two volumes: *The Letters of Edgar Allan Poe*, 2 vols., edited by John Ward Ostrum. New York: Gordian Press, 1966.

Two recent biographies contain some of the old patronizing and sensational features of nineteenth-century commentary and should be approached very skeptically:

Edgar Allan Poe: Mournful and Never-ending Remembrance by Kenneth Silverman. New York: HarperCollins, 1991.

Edgar Allan Poe: His Life and Legacy by Jeffrey Meyers. New York: Scribner's, 1992.

Criticism

Reviews and essays about Poe during his lifetime are collected in *Edgar Allan Poe: The Critical Heritage*, edited by I. M. Walker. London: Routledge and Kegan Paul, 1986.

More recent criticism is collected in *The Recognition of Edgar Allan Poe*, edited by Eric Carlson. Ann Arbor: University of Michigan Press, 1966.

Poe Studies: Dark Romanticism, a periodical published at Washington State University in Pullman, Washington, publishes up-to-the-moment bibliographies listing critical articles on varied aspects of Poe.

An important supplement to the usual study of Poe's relationship to native culture is Patrick Quinn's *The French Face of Edgar Allan Poe*. Carbondale: Southern Illinois University Press, 1954.

Much attention has been given recent psychoanalytic and deconstructive Poe criticism. Central arguments in these areas are collected in *The Purloined Poe,* edited John Muller and William Richardson. Baltimore: Johns Hopkins University Press, 1988.

Concentrated criticism of Poe's one novel is collected in *Poe's Pym: Critical Explorations,* edited by Richard Kopley. Durham: Duke University Press, 1992.

Myths and Reality: Thy Mysterious Mr. Poe, edited by Benjamin Franklin Fisher IV. The Edgar Allan Poe Society of Baltimore, 1987. Contains thoughtful essays on the tales and the life.

The Rationale of Deception by David Ketterer. Baton Rouge: LSU Press, 1979. Contains some insightful commentary on the tales.

Poe's Fiction: Romantic Irony in the Gothic Tales by G. R. Thompson. Madison: University of Wisconsin Press, 1973. Reads most of Poe's effects as humorous satires or hoaxes.

A delightful review of Poe correspondence, clippings, and early criticism is found in *John Henry Ingram's Poe Collection at the University of Virginia,* edited by John Carl Miller at Charlottesville, 1960.

Bibliography

The standard bibliography, but active only to 1967, is *Edgar Allan Poe: A Bibliography of Criticism,* edited by J. Lasley Dameron and Irby Cauthen, Jr. Charlottesville: University Press of Virginia, 1974. As mentioned earlier, recent criticism is regularly listed in *Poe Studies: Dark Romanticism.*

HUMOR OF THE OLD SOUTHWEST

Davy Crockett (1786–1836)
Mike Fink (1770?–1823?)
Augustus Baldwin Longstreet (1790–1870)
George Washington Harris (1814–1869)

Contributing Editor: Anne G. Jones

Classroom Issues and Strategies

The most crucial problem is getting them read at all. These writers are typically included in anthologies but excluded in syllabi—*vide* the syllabi in *Reconstructing American Literature*. Secondly, the dialect and spelling are forbidding. And finally, this work comes with its set of literary critical stereotypes: it has been a favorite of many of the more conservative literary historians, who tend to see it mainly as grist for Twain and Faulkner mills. Finding new ways to think about the material could be a problem.

Thinking about these writings in the light of gender, race, and class makes them accessible and interesting to students. Indeed, the selections have been chosen with gender issues especially in mind. Having students prepare to read them aloud as a performance should help make the dialect more accessible. And suggesting innovative pairings—with Marietta Holley, with rap lyrics, with "Legend of Sleepy Hollow," for example—should enliven the reading further.

Major Themes, Historical Perspectives, and Personal Issues

The construction of gender on the frontier seems a major project of this writing. The texts can be analyzed closely to see how they construct both manhood and womanhood, and how those constructions differ from mainstream American engendering of the period. The strong and sexual woman in particular appears anomalous; these texts both present and demonstrate some ambivalence about such figures. Class issues are crucial too, particularly in the relation between the voices in the texts: the controlling, omniscient, standard English voice and the disruptive, "carnival" voice in the "Dedicatory" set up the most familiar opposition, one that takes various forms in the selections.

Significant Form, Style, or Artistic Conventions

Much of this material is transcribed from or inspired by anonymous oral sources. And if students have performed selections, the question of the relation between oral and written texts can be foregrounded. The use of language in these selections is a second major stylistic concern; the vigor and power of this writing are attractive, and invite students to look closely at specific linguistic strategies—metaphors and similes, concrete versus abstract diction, etc. And the stories by Harris and Longstreet offer two ways of rendering plot, the one loose and almost episodic, and the other tightly controlled.

Original Audience

The audience for this work most likely consisted of educated white men, "gentlemen of some means with a leisurely interest in masculine pursuits," as Cohen and Dillingham put it. They were likely, too, to be Southerners and pro-slavery Whigs. The audience's relation to the texts, then, was at least a step removed from the primary characters; these tales and stories seem to enable identification with the "masculinity" of the Crocketts and Finks and even Suts, and at the same time allow an "educated distance" from that identification. What happens now, when the audience has vastly changed? How many different ways can these texts be read? How does audience determine a text's meaning?

Comparisons, Contrasts, Connections

Washington Irving ("Legend" inspired much Southwest humor); Hannah Foster and Susanna Rowson (see Cohen and Dillingham: gender issues); Harriet Jacobs and Frederick Douglass (struggle with voices); Marietta Holley (women's versus men's humor); Mark Twain and William Faulkner (do they revise the tradition? how? what do they retain?).

Questions for Reading and Discussion/ Approaches to Writing

1. (a) Do the women in these selections surprise you? Think about how and why. To what uses is this "strong woman" put in

the selections? What do you think has happened to this figure of woman? Does she survive anywhere in our literature?

(b) What can you say about the structure of each selection?

(c) How many voices can you hear in these selections?

(d) What type of manhood is constructed in these pieces? How does "The Death of Mike Fink" fit in?

(e) What does Sut want from the quilting party? Why does he do what he does?

2. (a) Consider "Mrs. Yardley's Quilting Party" in the light of Elaine Hedges's book on quilting, *Hearts and Hands*.

(b) Consider some implications of the various types of narration.

(c) How do language and subject converge in the "Dedicatory" and another text of your choice?

(d) How is the "strong woman" used in these selections?

Bibliography

Cohen, Hennig and William B. Dillingham, eds. *Humor of the Old Southwest*. Athens: University of Georgia Press, 1975, xiii–xxviii. The introduction is useful for information, but also as a representative of a particular critical position on the material. The remarks on gender are particularly provocative.

Curry, Jane. "The Ring-Tailed Roarers Rarely Sang Soprano." *Frontiers* II: 3 (Fall 1977): 129–40.

Explorations of an "American" Self

George Copway (Kah-ge-ga-gah-bowh; Ojibwa) (1818–1869)

Contributing Editor: A. LaVonne Brown Ruoff

Classroom Issues and Strategies

Students need information about the Ojibwas as a group. They also need to understand the relationship between Copway's autobiography, the Indian Removal Bill, and the attempts to move the Ojibwa out of

Minnesota. They need as well an understanding of how Native American autobiography differs from that of non-Indians. See discussion below.

Students respond much more enthusiastically to Copway's description of traditional life than to his references to Christianity. (For Indians' attitudes toward conversion to Christianity, see the comments on Occom and Apess.)

Major Themes, Historical Perspectives, and Personal Issues

The Ojibwa or Chippewa are numerically the largest tribe in the United States and Canada. A member of the Algonkian language family, they are spread out around the western Northern Great Lakes region, extending from the northern shore of Lake Huron as far west as Montana, southward well into Wisconsin and Minnesota, and northward to Lake Manitoba. In early historic times, the Ojibwa lived in numerous, widely scattered, small, autonomous bands.

Families hunted individually during the winter but gathered together as groups during the summer. Thus, the term "tribe" is appropriate in terms of a common language and culture but not in terms of an overall political authority. In the seventeenth century, they were mainly located in present-day Ontario. Their hereditary enemies were the Hurons and Iroquois on the east and the Fox and Sioux on the west.

Copway's autobiography, his plan for a separate state for Indians, and his history of the Ojibwas were undoubtedly responses to efforts of the Lake Superior Ojibwa to resist removal from 1847 through 1849. In 1850 President Zachary Taylor authorized immediate and complete removal of the Ojibwas from the lands ceded in 1842 (Kobel 174–82).

One important issue is the fact that Copway presents himself as a "noble-but-literate and Christianized" savage, an example of what Indians can become if whites educate and Christianize, rather than eradicate, them. By describing the achievements of his father and ancestors, he emphasizes the nobility of his lineage and thus legitimizes his narrative. (Emphasizing one's heritage was a technique also used by slave narrators.) Related to this is the issue of his difficult task of creating audience sympathy for the Ojibwa people and their beliefs while showing the necessity of Christianizing Indians.

Another issue is the techniques he uses to describe the Ojibwas and their traditions to convince readers that Indians were human. Copway emphasizes the basic humanity and generosity of the Ojibwas toward one another, values that non-Indian Christians would recognize as similar to their own. He also humanizes his people by citing examples of how his parents cared for and loved their children. These examples counteract the stereotype of the bloodthirsty Indian ever ready to violate a fair maiden or dash out the brains of an innocent baby, depictions all-too-common in the captivity narratives popular well into the 1830s.

Significant Form, Style, or Artistic Conventions

Copway's *Life, Letters and Speeches* is the first book-length autobiography written by an Indian who was raised in a traditional Native American family. The pattern of including oral tradition, history, and personal experience is one that characterizes most later Indian autobiographies. This mixed form, which differs from the more linear, personal confession or life history of non-Indian autobiographies, was congenial to Indian narrators accustomed to viewing their lives within the history of their tribe or band, clan, and family.

Copway uses a romantic style designed to appeal to the popular taste of the period. His emotional appeals and oratorical style capture his audience's attention. He also uses literary allusions to demonstrate his literacy—the reference to viewing his life "like the mariner on the wide ocean" making "his way amidst surging seas" is undoubtedly meant to remind his audiences of Byron's *Childe Harold's Pilgrimage*. The lines of poetry, probably written by his wife, Elizabeth Howell, also add to this image of Copway as an educated and accomplished man. His romantic tone and language, like that of Robert Burns and other authors before him, allow Copway to cast himself in the image of a person of humble beginnings who has become a writer. Giving students some understanding of the backgrounds of English and American Romantic attitudes toward idealizing humble life and using representatives of the lower class as the subject of literature, particularly in the late eighteenth century, will help students understand why Copway creates himself as he does.

Original Audience

Copway's primary audience was non-Indian. A powerful platform speaker dressed in full Ojibwa regalia, he aroused considerable public enthusiasm for his lectures on traditional Indian life during his tour of the eastern United States and later during his tour of Great Britain, where the second edition of his autobiography was published.

Comparisons, Contrasts, Connections

Copway's description of traditional Ojibwa life and mores can be compared to those incorporated into the stories by Jane Schoolcraft (Ojibwa). The selection can also be compared to Occom's "Short Narrative of My Life." The issues Copway raises with regard to Indian-white relations can be compared with those raised by Occom and Apess. Copway's description of Ojibwa world views and his stress on the importance of oral traditions can be compared to those expressed in the selections of Native American oral narratives and poetry.

Questions for Reading and Discussion/ Approaches to Writing

An important question for both reading and writing is how Copway presents or creates himself to show the Indians' essential humanity and their potential for being assimilated into the dominant culture. Discuss Indian world views and the importance of oral traditions as reflected in Copway's autobiography and selections from Native American oral literature. An additional topic would be Copway's use of Romantic language and tone. Students might compare his style with that of other early nineteenth-century American writers. Students might also compare Copway's description of Native American people and their lives with captivity narratives by John Williams and Mary Rowlandson.

Bibliography

Boatman, John. *My Elders Taught Me: Aspects of Western Great Lakes American Indian Philosophy.* Lanham: University Press of America, 1992.

Densmore, Frances. *Chippewa Customs. Bulletin of the Bureau of American Ethnology*, No. 86. Washington, D.C., 1929. Minneapolis: Ross and Haines, 1976. Essential work.

Landes, Ruth. *Ojibway Religion and the Midewiwin.* Madison: University of Wisconsin Press, 1968. Basic work on the subject.

The Northeast. Ed. Bruce G. Trigger. Vol. 15. *Handbook of North American Indians.* Ed. William C. Sturtevant. Washington, D.C.: Smithsonian, 1978.

Ritzenthaler, Robert E. "Southeastern Ojibwa." In *The Northeast*, edited by Bruce G. Trigger. 743–59.

Robers, E. S. "Southwestern Chippewa." In *The Northeast*, edited by Bruce G. Trigger. 760–71.

Tanner, Helen Hornbeck. *The Ojibwas: A Critical Bibliography*. Bloomington: Indiana University Press, 1976.

Vizenor, Gerald (Ojibwa). *The People Named the Chippewa. Narrative Histories*. Minneapolis: University of Minnesota Press, 1984.

Warren, William Whipple (Ojibwa). *History of the Ojibways, Based on Traditions and Oral Statements*. Collections of the Minnesota Historical Soc., 5 (1885). Rpt. Intro. by W. Roger Buffalohead. Minneapolis: Ross and Haines, 1957; Minneapolis: Minnesota Hist. Soc., 1984.

Ralph Waldo Emerson (1803–1882)

Contributing Editor: Jean Ferguson Carr

Classroom Issues and Strategies

Given the difficulty students often have with Emerson's style and allusions, it seems very important to address Emerson not as the proponent of a unified philosophy or movement (e.g., Transcendentalism or Romanticism), but as a writer concerned with his audience and his peers, and constructing himself as an American scholar/poet/seer. This might lead to, for example, focusing on what specific definitions or categories Emerson faces (categories such as what is "literary" and what is "poetic," what authorizes a scholar as "learned"). And it leads to paying attention to how Emerson characterizes his audience or reading public, how he addresses their difficulties and expectations, and how he represents his "times." Working from Emerson's journals can be extremely useful in this context; students can see a writer proposing and reflecting and revising his own articulations. Emerson's vocabulary and references can be investigated not simply as a given style, but as material being tested, often being critiqued as it is being used. His method of writing can be investigated as a self-reflective experimentation, in which Emerson proposes situations or claims, explores their implications, and often returns to restate or resituate the issue.

It can be particularly useful to have students read some of Emerson's college journals, which show his uncertainty about how to become an "American scholar" or "poet." The journals, like "The American

Scholar," show Emerson teaching himself how to read differently from the ways advocated by past cultures and educational institutions. They show him sorting through the conflicting array of resources and texts available to a young man in his circumstances and times.

Students can also situate Emerson in a range of cultural relationships by using Kenneth W. Cameron's fascinating source books that reprint contemporary materials, such as *Emerson Among His Contemporaries* (Hartford: Transcendental Books, 1967), or *Ralph Waldo Emerson's Reading* (Hartford: Transcendental Books, 1962), or *Emerson the Essayist* (Raleigh: Thistle Press, 1945).

Major Themes, Historical Perspectives, and Personal Issues

Emerson's concern with proposing the active power of language—both spoken and written—in constructing an emergent culture that will be different from the cultures of Europe is a central interest. His attention to what it means to make something "new," and his concern about the influence of the past, of books and monuments, mark him as an important figure in the production of a "national" literature. Emerson's investigation of reading as creative action, his efforts to examine the authority and effects of religious and educational institutions, help frame discussions about literature and education for subsequent generations. As a member of the Boston cultural and religious elite of the early nineteenth century, Emerson reflects both the immersion in and allegiance to English culture and the struggles of that American generation to become something more than a patronized younger cousin. Emerson's tumultuous personal life—his resignation from the ministry, the deaths of his young wife, son, and brothers, his own ill health—tested his persistence and seemingly unflappable energy and make his advocacy of "practical power" not an abstract or distanced issue.

Significant Form, Style, or Artistic Conventions

Emerson challenges and investigates formal traditions of philosophic and religious writing, insisting on the interpenetration of the ideal and the real, of the spiritual and material. His speculations about self-reliance move between cultural critique and personal experience, as he uses his own life as a "book" in which to test his assumptions and proposals. The essays often propose countercultural positions, some of which are spoken by imaginary bards or oracles, delivered in the form of fables or extended metaphors. Emerson's essays enact the dramatic exchanges in such arguments, suggesting the authority and limitations of what is spoken in the world as "a notion," as what "practical men" hold, or as what a "bard" might suggest. Emerson's journals show him rethinking the uses of a commonplace book, examining his own past thoughts and reactions as "evidence" of cultural changes and problems. Emerson argues for a "new" mode of poetry, one that emulates the "awful thunder" of the ancient bards rather than the measured lines of cultured verse.

Original Audience

Many of Emerson's essays were initially delivered as lectures, both in Boston and on his lecture tours around the country. His book *Nature*, the volumes of *Essays*, and his poems were reprinted both in Boston and in England. Several of his essays ("Love," "Friendship," "Illusions") were bound in attractive small editions and marketed as "gift books." His poems and excerpts from his essays were often reprinted in literary collections and school anthologies of the nineteenth century. Emerson represents the audiences for his work in challenging ways, often imagining them as sleeping or resistant, as needing to be awakened and encouraged. He discusses their preoccupation with business and labor, with practical politics and economy; their grief over the death of a child. He uses local and natural images familiar to the New Englanders at the same time he introduces his American audiences to names and references from a wide intellectual range (from Persian poets to sixth-century Welsh bards to Arabic medical texts to contemporary engineering reports). He has been a figure of considerable importance in modern American literary criticism and rhetoric (his discussions about language and speech, in particular), in American philosophy (influencing William James, Dewey, and more recently William Gass), and in discussions about education and literacy.

Comparisons, Contrasts, Connections

Emerson has been particularly significant as a "founding father," a literary figure that younger writers both emulated and had to challenge, that American critics and readers have used to mark the formation of a national literature. He is usually aligned with the group of writers living in or near Concord, Massachusetts, and with the Boston educational and literary elite (for example, Bronson Alcott, Nathaniel Hawthorne, Margaret Fuller, Henry David Thoreau). He also is usefully connected with English writers such as Carlyle, Wordsworth, and Arnold. Whitman proclaimed a link with Emerson (and capitalized on Emerson's letter greeting *Leaves of Grass*); Melville proclaimed an opposition to Emerson (and represented him in his satire *The Confidence-Man*). It is useful to consider Emerson's effect on younger writers and to consider how he is used (e.g., by such writers as T. S. Eliot) to represent the authority of the literary establishment and the values of the "past."

The following women writers make intriguing comments about Emerson in their efforts to establish their own positions: Elizabeth Stuart Phelps, Louisa May Alcott, Rebecca Harding Davis, Lucy Larcom (also the delightful mention of reading Emerson in Kate Chopin's *The Awakening*). Many writers "quote" Emersonian positions or claims, both to suggest an alliance and to test Emerson's authority (see, for example, Douglass's concern about "self-reliance" in his *Narrative*, Hawthorne's portrait of the young reformer Holgrave in *The House of Seven Gables* or of the reformers in *The Blithedale Romance*, Davis's challenging portrait of the artist in "Life in the Iron Mills").

Questions for Reading and Discussion/ Approaches to Writing

1. (a) How does Emerson characterize his age? How does he characterize its relation to the past?
   (b) What does Emerson see as the realm or purpose of art? What notions of art or poetry is he critiquing?
   (c) How does Emerson represent himself as a reader? What does he claim as the values and risks of reading? What does he propose as a useful way of reading?
2. (a) Emerson's writings are full of bold claims, of passages that read like self-confident epigrams ("Life only avails, not the having lived"; "Power ceases in the instant of repose"; "What I must do is all that concerns me, not what the people think"; "Travelling is a fool's paradise"). Yet such claims are not as self-evident as they may appear when lifted out of context as quotations. Often they are asserted to be challenged, or tested, or opposed. Often they propose a position that Emerson struggled hard to maintain in his own practice, about which he had considerable doubts or resistance. Select one such claim and discuss what work Emerson had to do to examine its implications and complexities.
   (b) Emerson's essays are deliberately provocative—they push, urge, outrage, or jolt readers to react. What kinds of critiques of his age is Emerson attempting? And how? And with what

sense of his audience's resistance? How do these function as self-critiques as well?

(c) Test one of Emerson's problematic questions or assertions against the particular practice of Emerson, or of another writer (e.g., Whitman, Hawthorne in *The Blithedale Romance*, Rebecca Harding Davis, Frederick Douglass). Examine how the issue or claim gets questioned or challenged, how it holds up under the pressure of experience. (Some examples of passages to consider: "The world of any moment is the merest appearance"; "The poet turns the world to glass, and shows us all things in their right series and procession"; "Every mind is a new classification.")

Bibliography

Buell, Lawrence. "Ralph Waldo Emerson." In *The American Renaissance in New England*, edited by Joel Myerson, vol. 1 of *Dictionary of Literary Biography*, 48–60. Detroit: Gale Research Co., 1978.

Levin, David, ed. *Emerson: Prophecy, Metamorphosis, and Influence*. Papers of the English Institute. New York: Columbia University Press, 1975.

Matthiessen, F. O. *American Renaissance: Art and Expression in the Age of Emerson and Whitman*. New York: Oxford University Press, 1941.

Myerson, Joel, ed. *Emerson Centenary Essays*. Carbondale: Southern Illinois University Press, 1982.

Packer, Barbara. "Uriel's Cloud: Emerson's Rhetoric." In *Emerson's Fall*. New York: Continuum Press, 1982: 1–21.

Porte, Joel, ed. *Emerson: Prospect and Retrospect*. Cambridge: Harvard University Press, 1982.

Sealts, Merton M., Jr., and Alfred R. Ferguson, eds. *Emerson's "Nature"—Origin, Growth, Meaning*, 2nd ed. Carbondale: Southern Illinois University Press, 1979.

Yoder, Ralph A. "Toward the 'Titmouse Dimension': The Development of Emerson's Poetic Style." *PMLA* 87 (March 1972): 255–70.

Sarah Margaret Fuller (1810–1850)

Contributing Editor: Joel Myerson

Classroom Issues and Strategies

Students have problems with Fuller's organization of her material and with nineteenth-century prose style in general. The best exercise I have found is for them to rewrite Fuller's work in their own words. My most successful exercises involve rewriting parts of *Woman in the Nineteenth Century*. Students are amazed at the roles given to women in the nineteenth century and wonder how these women endured what was expected of them.

I ask students to reorganize the argument of Fuller's work as they think best makes its points. This process forces them to grapple with her ideas as they attempt to recast them.

Major Themes, Historical Perspectives, and Personal Issues

Transcendentalism, women's rights, critical theory, gender roles, profession of authorship, all are important themes in Fuller's writing.

Original Audience

I give a background lecture on the legal and social history of women during the period so students can see what existing institutions and laws Fuller was arguing against.

Comparisons, Contrasts, Connections

Woman in the Nineteenth Century: Emerson's "Self-Reliance" and Thoreau's *Walden* for the emphasis on individual thought in the face of a society that demands conformity; Lydia Maria Child's novels for depictions of gender roles; Sarah Grimké's *Letters on the Equality of the Sexes*. *Summer on the Lakes*: Emerson's "The American Scholar" for a discussion of literary and cultural nationalism.

Questions for Reading and Discussion/ Approaches to Writing

The topics I've received the best responses to are:

1. Compare "Self-Reliance" or *Walden* to *Woman in the Nineteenth Century* as regards the responsibilities of the individual within a conformist society.
2. Discuss whether Zenobia in Hawthorne's *The Blithedale Romance* is a portrayal of Fuller, as some critics suggest.
3. Compare or contrast Fuller's ideas on critical theory to Poe's.
4. Compare Fuller's solution to the assignment of gender roles to Kate Chopin's in *The Awakening* or Theodore Dreiser's in *Sister Carrie*.

Bibliography

Read Robert N. Hudspeth's chapter on Fuller in *The Transcendentalists: A Review of Research and Criticism*, ed. Joel Myerson (NY: MLA, 1984) and see Myerson's bibliographies of writings by and about Fuller; also read in Hudspeth's ongoing edition of Fuller's letters.

Frederick Douglass (1818–1895)

Contributing Editor: James A. Miller

Classroom Issues and Strategies

Readers tend to read Douglass's *Narrative* sympathetically but casually. Although they readily grasp Douglass's critiques of slavery in broad and general terms, they tend to be less attentive to *how* the narrative is structured, to Douglass's choices of language and incident, and to the ideological/aesthetic underpinnings of these choices.

I find it useful to locate Douglass historically within the context of his relationship to the Garrisonian wing of the abolitionist movement. This requires students to pay more attention to the prefatory material by Wendell Phillips and William Lloyd Garrison than they normally do. I also try to focus their attention on the rhetoric and narrative point of view that Douglass establishes in the first chapter of his *Narrative*.

Questions students often ask include the following:

- How does Frederick Douglass escape?
- How does he learn to write so well?
- Is Douglass "typical" or "exceptional"?
- Why does Anna Murray appear so suddenly at the end of the narrative?
- Where is she earlier?
- What happens to Douglass after the narrative ends?

Major Themes, Historical Perspectives, and Personal Issues

Paying careful attention to the unfolding of Douglass's consciousness within the context of slavery draws attention to the intersection of personal and historical issues in the *Narrative*. The movement from slavery to "freedom" is obviously important, as is the particular means by which Douglass achieves his freedom—the role literacy plays in his struggle.

Significant Form, Style, or Artistic Conventions

Douglass's command of the formal principles of oratory and rhetoric should be emphasized, as well as his use of the conventions of both sentimental literature and the rhetoric and symbolism of evangelical Christianity. In short, it is important to note how Douglass appropriated the dominant literary styles of mid-nineteenth-century American life to articulate his claims on behalf of African-American humanity.

Original Audience

Through a careful examination of Douglass's rhetorical appeals, we try to imagine and re-create Douglass's mid-nineteenth-century audience. We try to contrast that audience to the various audiences, black and white, that constitute the reading public in the late twentieth century.

Comparisons, Contrasts, Connections

Jacobs's *Incidents in the Life of a Slave Girl*—for a contrasting view of slavery through a woman's eyes and experiences. Thoreau's *Walden*—for a view from one of Douglass's contemporaries. Franklin's *Autobiography*—for another prototype of American autobiography.

Questions for Reading and Discussion/ Approaches to Writing

1. What is the function of the prefatory material? Why does Douglass add an appendix?
2. What is the relationship of literacy to Douglass's quest for freedom? Of violence?
3. What idea of God animates Douglass?
4. How does Douglass attempt to engage the sympathies of his audience?

Bibliography

Gibson, Donald B. "Christianity and Individualism: (Re-)Creation in Frederick Douglass's Representation of Self." *African American Review* 26 (Winter 1992): 591–603.

Kibbey, Ann. "Language in Slavery: Frederick Douglass' *Narrative*." *Prospects: An Annual of American Cultural Studies* 8 (1985): 163–82.

O'Meally, Robert G. "Frederick Douglass's 1845 *Narrative:* The Text Was Meant To Be Preached." In *Afro-American Literature: the Reconstruction of Instruction*, edited by Robert B. Stepto and Dexter Fisher. New York: Modern Language Association, 1978.

Sekora, John. "Comprehending Slavery: Language and Personal History in Douglass' Narrative of 1845." *College Language Association Journal* 29 (1985): 157–70.

Smith, Stephanie A. "Heart Attack: Frederick Douglass's Strategic Sentimentality." *Criticism* 34 (Spring 1992): 193–216.

Stepto, Robert B. "Narration, Authentication and Authorial Control in Frederick Douglass' *Narrative* of 1845." In *Afro-American Literature: the Reconstruction of Instruction*, edited by Robert B. Stepto and Dexter Fisher. New York: Modern Language Association, 1978.

Stone, Albert C. "Identity and Art in Frederick Douglass' *Narrative*." *College Language Association Journal* 17 (1973): 192–213.

Sundquist, Eric J. "Slavery, Revolution and the American Renaissance." In *The American Renaissance Reconsidered*, edited by W. B. Michaels and Donald E. Pease. Baltimore: Johns Hopkins University Press, 1985.

Harriet Ann Jacobs (1813–1897)

Contributing Editor: Jean Fagan Yellin

Classroom Issues and Strategies

Primary problems that arise in teaching Jacobs include:

1. The question of authorship: Could a woman who had been held in slavery have written such a literary book?
2. The question of her expressions of conflict about her sexual experiences.
3. The question of veracity: How could she have stayed hidden all those years?

To address these questions, point to Jacobs's life: She learned to read at six years. She spent her seven years in hiding sewing and reading (doubtless reading the Bible, but also reading some newspapers, according to her account). And in 1849, at Rochester, she spent ten months working in the Anti-Slavery Reading Room, reading her way through the abolitionists' library.

Discuss sexual roles assigned white women and black women in nineteenth-century America: free white women were told that they must adhere to the "cult of domesticity" and were rewarded for piety, purity, domesticity, and obedience. Black slave women were (like male slaves) denied literacy and the possibility of reading the Bible; as Jacobs points out, in North Carolina after the Nat Turner rebellion, slaves were forbidden to meet together in their own churches. Their only chance at "piety" was to attend the church of their masters. They were denied "purity"—if by "purity" is meant sex only within marriage—because they were denied legal marriage. The "Notes" to the standard edition of *Incidents* read: "The entire system worked against the protection of slave women from sexual assault and violence, as Jacobs asserts. The rape of a slave was not a crime but a trespass upon her master's property" (fn 2, p. 265). Denied marriage to a man who might own a home and denied the right to hold property and own her own home, the female slave was, of course, denied "domesticity." Her "obedience," however, was insisted upon: not obedience to her father, husband, or brother, but obedience to her owner. Slave women were excluded from patriarchal definitions of true womanhood; the white patriarchy instead formally defined them as producers and as reproducers of a new generation of slaves, and, informally, as sexual objects. Jacobs is writing her narrative within a society that insists that white women conform to one set of sexual practices and that black women conform to a completely contradictory set. Her awareness of this contradiction enables her to present a powerful critique; but it does not exclude her from being sensitive to a sexual ideology that condemns her.

Concerning the accuracy of this autobiography, refer to the exhaustive identification of people, places, and events in the standard edition. Concerning the period in hiding, point out that the date of Jacobs's escape has been documented by her master's "wanted" ad of June, 1835, and the date of her Philadelphia arrival has been documented by June, 1842 correspondence; both are reproduced in the standard edition. Discuss the history of Anne Frank—and of others who hid for long periods to avoid persecution (e.g., men "dodging" the draft during World War II and the Vietnam War, etc.).

Major Themes, Historical Perspectives, and Personal Issues

Themes: The struggle for freedom; the centrality of the family and the attempt to achieve security for the family; the individual and communal efforts to achieve these goals; the relationships among women (among generations of black women; between black slave women and slaveholding white women, between black slave women and non-slaveholding white women); the problem of white racism; the problem of the institution of chattel slavery; the issue of woman's appropriate response to chattel slavery and to tyranny: Should she passively accept victimization? Should she fight against it? How should she struggle—within the "domestic sphere" (where the patriarchy assigned women) or within both the domestic and the "public sphere" (which the patriarchy assigned to men)? How can a woman tell her story if she is not a "heroine" who has lived a "blameless" life? How can a woman create her own identity? What about the limits of literary genre? What about the limits imposed on women's discussion of their sexual experiences?

Historical Issues: These involve both the antebellum struggle against white racism and against slavery, and the struggle against sexism. Jacobs's story raises questions about the institution of chattel slavery; patriarchal control of free women in the antebellum period; the struggle against slavery (black abolitionists, white abolitionists, within the white community, within the free black community, within the slave community); the historic struggle against white racism (in the antebellum North); the historic effort of the anti-slavery feminists, among the Garrisonian abolitionists, who attempted to enter the public sphere and to debate issues of racism and slavery (women like Sarah and Angelina Grimké, like Amy Post, who suggested to Jacobs that she write her life story, and like Lydia Maria Child, who edited it); the Nat Turner revolt; the 1850 Fugitive Slave Law; the publication of *Uncle Tom's Cabin*; the firing on Fort Sumter.

Personal Issues: The narrator constructs a self who narrates the book. This narrator expresses conflict over some of her history, especially her sexual history (see above). She is rejected by her grandmother, then later accepted (but perhaps not fully); near the end of her book, she wins her daughter's full acceptance. All of this speaks to the importance of intergenerational connections among the women in this book. Near the conclusion, the narrator expresses her deep distress at having her freedom bought by her employer, a woman who is her friend: she feels that she has been robbed of her "victory," that in being purchased she has violated the purity of her freedom struggle. Writing the book, she gains that victory by asserting control over her own life.

Significant Form, Style, or Artistic Conventions

Incidents appears to be influenced by (1) the novel of seduction and (2) the slave narrative. It presents a powerful, original transformation of the conventions of both of these genres. What is new here is that—in contrast to the type of the seduction novel—the female protagonist asserts her responsibility for her sexual behavior, instead of presenting herself as a powerless victim. This is a new kind of "fallen woman," who problematizes the whole concept of "fallen womanhood." In contrast to the type of the slave narrative, *Incidents* presents not a single male figure struggling for his freedom against an entire repressive society, but a female figure struggling for freedom for her children and herself with the aid of both her family and of much of a black community united in opposition to the white slavocracy. Even from within that slavocracy, some women assert their sisterhood to help. The language in *Incidents* suggests both the seduction novel and the slave narrative. The passages concerning Brent's sexual history are written in elevated language and are full of evasions and silences; the passages concerning her struggle for freedom are written in simpler English and are direct and to the point—or they are hortatory, in the style of Garrisonian abolitionism.

Original Audience

I have touched on this above, in discussing history. Jacobs's Linda Brent writes that she is trying to move the women of the North to act against slavery: these, I take it, were free white women who were not (yet) committed to abolitionism and who were not (yet) engaged in debate in the "public sphere." In class, we talk about the ways in which Jacobs's Linda Brent addresses her audience in Chapter 10, and the ways in which, as a writer reflecting on her long-ago girlhood, she makes mature judgments about her life.

Comparisons, Contrasts, Connections

Incidents can fruitfully be compared/contrasted with the classic male slave narrative, Frederick Douglass's 1845 *Narrative*. It can also be read in connection with *Uncle Tom's Cabin*, *The Scarlet Letter*, and with "women's" fiction, much of which ostensibly centers on a woman's sexual choices and possibilities, and on women's intergenerational relationships.

Questions for Reading and Discussion/ Approaches to Writing

Study questions: Find a troubling passage. What is troubling? Why? What does this suggest? Why do you think that *Incidents* was believed the production of a white woman, not of a former slave? Why do you think that *Incidents* was thought to be a novel, not an autobiography?

Bibliography

The letters appended to the Harvard University Press edition, and the Introduction to that edition, should prove useful. In addition, the secondary works cited in the text headnote should prove of interest and of help.

Issues and Visions
in Pre–Civil War America

INDIAN VOICES

William Apess (Pequot) (1798–?)

Contributing Editor: A. LaVonne Brown Ruoff

Classroom Issues and Strategies

Apess was a powerful orator and the first American Indian protest writer. At a time when whites presumed Indians were dying out or being moved west of the Mississippi, Apess attacks whites' treatment of Indians using forceful language and rhetorical skill. He contrasts the abject degradation of Indians with their natural ingenuity.

The instructor should address attitudes toward the Indians and explain problems faced by Indians in the early nineteenth century. Consider presenting historical material on what had happened to East Coast Indians. The Pequot history (Apess's tribe) is briefly outlined in the section of the headnote on teaching strategy.

Students often ask why Indians turned to Christianity and used it as an appeal to their white audiences. See comments on the Occom selections.

Major Themes, Historical Perspectives,
and Personal Issues

1. Indian–white relations—especially the impact of the Indian Removal Bill. Apess is clearly reacting to the whites' attitudes reflected in the bill to remove Indians from east of the Mississippi River and to the stereotypes of Indians present in Indian captivity narratives.
2. Emphasis by American Indian authors and slave narrators on achieving equality through Christianity.

Significant Form, Style, or Artistic Conventions

1. Use of persuasive, oratorical style and appeal to emotions of audience. Note how Apess compares non-Indians' professed Christianity with their unchristian treatment of Indians and blacks.
2. Use of a series of rhetorical questions to his audience about what Indians have suffered.
3. Use of biblical quotations to support position.

Original Audience

1. Religious orientation of audience, which would have expected appeals to biblical authority.
2. Prejudice toward Indians of early-nineteenth-century audiences.

Comparisons, Contrasts, Connections

Compare with speeches by Indians, Copway's autobiography—sections on worth of Indian and picture of Indian family life, which buttress Apess's arguments for treating Indians as human beings.

Compare with slave narratives, which also argue for essential humanity of people of all races.

Questions for Reading and Discussion/ Approaches to Writing

1. (a) Relationship between publication of this document and debate over passage of Indian Removal Bill. Also relationship to miscegenation bill in Massachusetts passed around this time.
2. (a) Compare/contrast the oratorical styles used by Apess and Douglass and their treatment of Indian-white relations.
   (b) Compare and contrast the oratorical style used by Apess and American Indian orators such as Logan and Seattle.
   (c) Discuss Apess's and the slave narrators' criticisms of the treatment of Indians and slaves by white Christians.
   (d) Discuss the influence of Christianity and its concept of the essential equality of all men under God as expressed by Apess and Copway and by slave narrators such as Douglass.

Bibliography

Listed in headnotes. Best general article on Apess is O'Connell's. Mine deals with Apess's autobiography. On the context, the articles in *The Northeast* are excellent.

John Wannuaucon Quinney (Mahican) (1797–1855)

Contributing Editor: Daniel F. Littlefield, Jr.

Classroom Issues and Strategies

By the time students get to Quinney, they should be familiar with the broad social issues of the period involving non-white peoples: slavery and emancipation, American imperialism in the Hispanic Southwest, and Indian removal and genocide. Quinney's speech can be placed thematically into this broad context. It can also be presented as a text reflecting the culmination of a long historical process of genocide and cultural discontinuity, beginning with Columbus or Bradford.

Major Themes, Historical Perspectives, and Personal Issues

Major themes include cultural decline, assimilation, genocide, racism, Manifest Destiny, "progress," oral versus written history, Christianity and native culture.

Significant Form, Style, or Artistic Conventions

In most ways the speech reflects the oratorical styles of the day, but the reader might find it fruitful to analyze the ways in which Quinney applies his comments to his specific audience, draws on their knowledge of American history, and makes emotional appeals for justice.

Comparisons, Contrasts, Connections

The central issue in Quinney's speech is the displacement of the Mahican people throughout American history. Texts that touch on that displacement in earlier periods—Bradford's or Rowlandson's and other King

Philip's War texts, for example—can provide background to show how Quinney arrived at the views of history he expressed in 1854.

To demonstrate how other Indians looked at Quinney's themes of genocide, cultural destruction, assimilation, and removal, students can analyze the works of other Indian writers of the same period: Apess, Boudinot, and Ridge. For earlier generations, they should look at the works of Occom and Aupaumut.

Questions for Reading and Discussion/ Approaches to Writing

Besides the ideas suggested above, the student might choose a writer from the next or a subsequent generation—Standing Bear, for example—to reach conclusions concerning the effects of removal as a final solution to the "Indian Problem" or to determine whether the justice that Quinney appealed for was gained by Indians. In other words, to what extent do later Indian writers play on the same themes as Quinney?

If such broad questions do not appeal to students, something as specific as the way Jonathan Edwards viewed the Stockbridges (Mahicans) might be fruitful to explore.

Elias Boudinot (Cherokee) (c. 1802–1839)

Contributing Editor: James W. Parins

Classroom Issues and Strategies

Boudinot seeks to and succeeds in breaking the stereotype of the Indian established by Irving's "Traits of Indian Character" and other writing that established the Indian as uneducated and shiftless.

Two major issues that interest students are cultural discontinuity and the position of minorities in American culture.

Major Themes, Historical Perspectives, and Personal Issues

Major themes include the perceptions of minorities by the dominant society, the role of the government in protecting the minorities against the majority, and the social responsibilities of the majority toward minorities.

Significant Form, Style, or Artistic Conventions

In many ways, Boudinot is using "standard" methods of persuasive discourse in use at the time. Students should examine his oratorical and rhetorical devices including diction and structure.

Original Audience

It is important to stress that Boudinot was trying to persuade his white audience to take a particular course of action.

Comparisons, Contrasts, Connections

Boudinot was writing in the oratorical mode used by mainstream writers at the time. Compare with works by Emerson, Frederick Douglass, and Chief Seattle.

Questions for Reading and Discussion/ Approaches to Writing

Students should explore the historical situation in which the address was written, should do comparative studies, and should examine rhetorical and oratorical devices.

Bibliography

See any history of the Cherokees.

John Rollin Ridge (Cherokee) (1827–1867)

Contributing Editor: James W. Parins

Classroom Issues and Strategies

The question of assimilation of a minority figure into white society should be raised. The historical context needs to be firmly established and the implication of assimilation should be addressed, especially as it relates to the loss of culture. The introduction should be consulted carefully as it will help in this regard.

Major Themes, Historical Perspectives, and Personal Issues

The major themes include Ridge's views on progress and how it comes about, the tensions between the dominant society and minorities, and the Romantic aspects of his poetry.

Significant Form, Style, or Artistic Conventions

In his poetry, Ridge follows many of the Romantic conventions common in American and British literature of the period. His prose reflects a vigorous editorial style that spilled over from his journalism into his other prose literary efforts.

Original Audience

Ridge was writing for a white, educated audience. His work is relevant now in terms of the majority-minority relations and is valuable in a historical context.

Comparisons, Contrasts, Connections

Any of the contemporary poets can be fruitfully compared. Contemporary prose writers include Mark Twain, Joaquin Miller, and Bret Hart.

Questions for Reading and Discussion/ Approaches to Writing

Topics include the Romantic elements in his work, the idea of progress in nineteenth-century society, and his attitudes toward the American Indians. The latter subject is interesting because of Ridge's ambiguity toward this topic.

Bibliography

No shorter comprehensive studies exist. Refer to the introduction, as it was written with this in mind.

THE LITERATURE OF SLAVERY AND ABOLITION

David Walker (1785–1830)

Contributing Editor: Paul Lauter

Classroom Issues and Strategies

The first problem with teaching this author is the militance of Walker's *Appeal*. Some students (especially whites) are troubled by the vehemence with which he attacks whites. *They*, after all, don't defend slavery, so why should *all* whites be condemned? Some (especially students of color) prefer not to get into open discussion where their sympathies with Walker's views will necessarily emerge. Some also don't like his criticism of his fellow blacks. Some of the material added to this selection suggests that Walker viewed at least some whites as potential allies and was concerned not to alienate all white people, but to win them over to his view.

A second problem is the rhetoric of the *Appeal*. It uses techniques drawn from sermons (note especially the biblical references) and from the political platforms of the day. Most students are unfamiliar with religious or political rhetoric of our time, much less that of 150 years ago.

One way of beginning to address these problems is to ask students whether they think Georgia officials were "correct" in putting a price on Walker's head and in trying to get his *Appeal* banned from the mails. This can be put in the form of "trying" the text, with arguments for prosecution and defense, etc. Is Walker guilty of sedition, of trying to foment insurrection?

Another approach can be to use a more recent expression of black militance, e.g., Stokely Carmichael on black power: "When you talk of black power, you talk of building a movement that will smash everything Western civilization has created." How do students feel about that? Would Walker approve? Sometimes an effective way to begin class discussion is by reading aloud brief *anonymous* student responses.

Major Themes, Historical Perspectives, and Personal Issues

It's critical for students to understand the difference between "colonization" schemes for ending slavery (which would gradually send blacks back to Africa) and Walker's commitment to immediate and unconditional emancipation.

If they have read earlier (eighteenth-century) expressions of black protest (e.g., Prince Hall, Gustavas Vassa), it's important and useful to see how Walker departs from these in tone, as well as in audience and purpose.

Ultimately, the question is what does Walker want to happen? Blacks to unite, to kill or be killed, if it comes to that?

Significant Form, Style, or Artistic Conventions

To some extent the rhetorical questions, the multiple exclamation points, the quoting of biblical passages, the heated terminology are features of the period. It can be useful to ask students to rewrite a paragraph using the comparable rhetorical devices of our day. Or, vice versa, to use Walker's style to deal with a current political issue like the level of unemployment and homelessness among blacks.

Original Audience

This is a central issue: The *Appeal* is clearly directed to black people, Walker's "brethren." But since most black slaves were not literate, doesn't that blunt the impact? Or were there ways around that problem?

Why isn't Walker writing to whites, since they seem to have a monopoly of power? Or is he, really? Does he seem to be speaking to two differing audiences, even while seeming to address one?

Comparisons, Contrasts, Connections

The Walker text is placed with a number of others concerned with the issue of slavery in order to facilitate such comparisons. While some share the religious rhetoric (e.g., Grimké), others the disdain of colonization (e.g., Garrison), others the appeal to black pride (e.g., Garnet), others the valorization of a black revolutionary (e.g., Higginson), all differently compose such elements. What links (values, style) and separates them?

Questions for Reading and Discussion/ Approaches to Writing

1. How does Walker's outlook on slavery (on whites, on blacks) differ from X (X being any one of a number of previous writers— Franklin, Jefferson, Vassa, Wheatley)?

Why would the government of Georgia put a price on Walker's head?

2. I like the idea of asking students to try adapting Walker's style (and that of other writers in this section) to contemporary events. It helps get them "inside" the rhetoric.

Bibliography

There are not many sources to consult; the best of these are already cited in the primary and secondary bibliographies in the text.

William Lloyd Garrison (1805–1879)

Contributing Editor: Paul Lauter

Classroom Issues and Strategies

Students often don't see why Garrison seemed so outrageous to his contemporaries. Of course slavery was wrong; of course it had to be abolished. There seems to be a contradiction between the intensity of his rhetoric and the self-evident rightness (to us) of his views.

He may also strike them as obnoxious—self-righteous, self-important, arrogant. That's a useful reaction, when one gets it. Even more than Thoreau, who students "know" is important, Garrison may be seen (and be presented in history texts) as a fringy radical. He tends to focus questions of effectiveness, or historical significance, and of "radicalism" generally.

It can be useful to ask whether Garrison is an "extremist" and, if so, whether that's good or bad. (Some may recollect Barry Goldwater on the subject of "extremism.") Garrison was committed to nonviolence; but wasn't his rhetoric extremely violent? Are his principles contradicted by his prose?

Particularly effective presentational strategies include asking these questions:

• Would you like to work with/for Garrison? Explain your reasons.
• What would Garrison write about X (an event expressing prejudice/discrimination on campus or in the community)?

Students often ask the following questions:

- Why was Garrison important? *Was* he important?
- Why was he involved in so many reforms?
- Didn't his many commitments dilute his impact?
- Wasn't he just a nay-sayer, opposed to everything conventional?

Major Themes, Historical Perspectives, and Personal Issues

Students are not generally familiar with the difference between colonization as an approach to ending slavery and Garrison's doctrine of immediate and unconditional emancipation.

They are even less familiar with the implications of evangelical Christianity, as interpreted by people like Garrison. They have seldom been exposed to concepts like "perfectionism," "nonresistance," "millennialism." The period introduction sketches such issues.

It can be important to link Garrison's commitment to abolitionism with his commitments to women's rights, temperance, pacifism. If students can see how these were connected for Garrison and others, they will have a significant hold on antebellum evangelical thinking.

The issue raised by Tolstoi (see headnote) is also significant: What human interactions are, or are not, coercive? How is political activity, like voting, coercive? What alternatives are there? Tolstoi's comments also foreground the issue of human rationality, and they suggest the importance of Garrison's thought and practice to nineteenth-century reformers.

Significant Form, Style, or Artistic Conventions

Students can find it interesting to analyze a typical passage of Garrisonian rhetoric—e.g., "I am aware, that many object to the severity of my language. . . . Tell a man whose house is on fire, to give a moderate alarm. . . ." One finds in that paragraph the whole range of his rhetorical techniques.

How does he compare with an Old Testament prophet like Jeremiah?

Original Audience

Since the work included in the text is the lead editorial for the *Liberator*, the question of audience (or audiences) is crucial. In the passage noted above, Garrison is arguing *against* a set of unstated positions—those who claim to be "moderates," the apathetic. Indeed, throughout the editorial, he addresses a whole range of people, most of whom—when one looks closely—he assumes disagree with him. In a way, the editorial can be used to construct the variety of opposed viewpoints, and if students can do that, they may also be able to discuss why Garrison takes his opponents on in just the ways he does.

Comparisons, Contrasts, Connections

The Garrison text is placed with a number of others concerned with the issue of slavery in order to facilitate such comparisons. While some share the passionate rhetoric (e.g., Walker), others the disdain of colonization, others the sense of commitment and the view that people can achieve change (e.g., Grimké), all differently compose such elements. What links (values, style) and separates them?

He is particularly interesting in comparison with Grimké and Thoreau on the issue of civil disobedience, which doesn't come to the surface in this editorial, but is implicit in it. In particular, Garrison does focus on the idea that "What I have to do is to see, at any rate, that I do not lend myself to the wrong which I condemn" (to quote Thoreau). His emphasis on satisfying his own conscience is important, but is that a sufficient criterion for action? Is this editorial what Thoreau means by "clogging with your whole weight"?

Questions for Reading and Discussion/ Approaches to Writing

1. (a) What is Garrison arguing against?
   (b) How has he changed his own position regarding the abolition of slavery?
   (c) Is it sufficient to "satisfy" one's own conscience? What does that mean?
2. (a) One can easily find quotations suggesting that Garrison was an ineffective windbag. How do students respond to such accusations?
   (b) Do you think his approach would be effective today regarding racism in American society?
   (c) Are Garrison's objectives and his style at war with one another?

Bibliography

The four volumes edited by Garrison's children, *William Lloyd Garrison, 1805–1879; the Story of His Life Told by His Children,* provide a rich source not only of Garrison's writing but of the contexts in which he wrote. They are especially useful for any students interested in doing papers on any aspect of Garrison's life or work.

Lydia Maria Child (1802–1880)

Contributing Editor: Jean Fagan Yellin

Classroom Issues and Strategies

To some, Child's writings appear all too commonplace, not radically different from writings that twentieth-century readers associate with ladylike nineteenth-century writers. Yet Child is radical, although it is sometimes difficult for today's students to understand this. They often ask about her relationship to the feminist movement.

She wrote about the most controversial issues of her time, and she published her writings in the public sphere—in the political arena which, in her generation, was restricted to men. Today's readers need to read Child carefully to think about what she is saying, not merely to be lulled by how she is saying it. Then they need to think about the tensions between her conventional forms and her highly unconventional content.

Focus on problematic passages. What do you do with the first sentence of her Preface to the *Appeal*? It reads like the beginning of a novel—like a private, emotional appeal to readers, not like an appeal to their intellects and not like a public political appeal. Yet it is public and it is political. How does Child's narrator present herself? How does she define her audience? What are the consequences of this strategy for today's reader? What do you think were the consequences of this strategy for the reader in Child's day?

Major Themes, Historical Perspectives, and Personal Issues

Major themes: Chattel slavery and white racism; women's rights; life in the cities; problems of class in America; social change and "Progress."

Historical and personal issues: Garrisonian abolitionism; the movement for women's rights; the development of the Transcendental critique of American society; women's role in American journalism; the discovery of urban poverty in America; the invention of the Tragic Mulatto in American fiction.

Significant Form, Style, or Artistic Conventions

Child characteristically uses a conventional style and appears to be writing from a posture relegated to women novelists and to commonsense male news analysts. But she is saying things that are quite different from other nineteenth-century American writers of fiction *in re*: attitudes about race and gender, just as she is saying things that are quite different from other nineteenth-century American journalists *in re*: attitudes about class and race, and slavery and women's rights. Look at her language and her syntax. Then try to locate the places in her text where she does not say the expected, but instead says the unexpected.

Original Audience

With Child, this seems easy because—as her style suggests—she appears to be appealing to the common man and the common woman; she is not writing for a "special" audience of "advanced thinkers."

Comparisons, Contrasts, Connections

Perhaps it would be interesting to contrast Child's newspaper rhetoric with that of Garrison—or even to contrast her *Appeal* with Angelina Grimké's *Appeal* and with Sarah Grimké's *Letters* in terms of language and syntax and logic—and of course in terms of audience. Like Jacobs and the Grimkés, Child is an American woman who condemns chattel slavery and white racism and attempts to assert women's rights. In what ways does she approach these issues differently from Jacobs and the Grimkés? And it would be interesting to read Child in relation to Emerson and Thoreau, who, like Child, were developing critiques of American capitalist culture. In what ways is Child's critique similar to Emerson's? To Thoreau's? In what ways is it different? Furthermore, it would be interesting to read Child's fiction in relation to American mythologists. Irving and Cooper presented types of Dutch America and of the West. What mythic types does Child present?

Questions for Reading and Discussion/ Approaches to Writing

I try to stress the exceptional: Why was Child's membership in the Boston Atheneum revoked when she published the *Appeal*? What is so terribly outrageous about this book? Why might she have omitted Letter 33 from the edition of *Letters*? How could this letter have affected the sale of the book? It is hard, today, to see Child as a threat. Why did she appear a threat in her own time? Why doesn't she appear a threat today?

John Greenleaf Whittier (1807–1892)

Contributing Editor: Elaine Sargent Apthorp

Classroom Issues and Strategies

Students may be put off by various features of the poetry, such as: the regularity of meter (which can impress the twentieth-century ear as tedious—generally we don't "hear" ballads well anymore unless they are set to music); conventional phrasing and alliteration; place-names in "Massachusetts to Virginia"; effect of stereotyping from a clumsy effort to render black dialect in "At Port Royal."

I think we can take clues from such responses and turn the questions around, asking why, in what context, and for what audience such poetry would be successful. Consider reasons why one might want to give his verses such regular meter, such round and musically comfortable phrasing; consider the message of the verses, the political protest the poet is making—and the mass action he is trying to stimulate through his poetry. This could lead to a discussion of topical poetry, the poetry of political agitation/protest, as a genre—and of Whittier's work as a contribution to that tradition.

Some activities that can bring this home to the students include (1) having students commit a few stanzas to memory and give a dramatic recitation of them to the class (when one has fallen out of one's chair shouting defiantly, "No fetters on the Bay State! No slave upon our land!" one knows in one's own body why declamatory poetry is composed as it is), and (2) comparing samples of topical poetry and song by other authors (e.g., poetry of the Harlem Renaissance; the evolutions of "John Brown's Body," "The Battle Hymn of the Republic," and "Solidarity Forever"; union ballads ["The Internationale"] and protest songs of the Great Depression [Woody Guthrie's "Deportees," for example], and contemporary popular songs of protest, like Michael Jackson's recording of "Man in the Mirror," Bruce Hornsby's "The Way It Is," etc.).

One can use the same general strategy in discussing other thorny elements in the students' experience of the poetry, i.e., asking why a person working from Whittier's assumptions and toward his objectives would choose to compose as he did. What might the effect of all those place-names be on an audience of folk who came from all of those places? How do we respond to a song that mentions our home town? Which praises it for producing us? Which associates us, as representatives of our town, with other towns and their worthy representatives? Assuming that the poet did not mean to convey disrespect to the speakers of the dialect he sought to represent in "At Port Royal," we could ask why he would try to represent the dialect of the enslaved. (Even without recourse to evidence of Whittier's views on African-Americans, this is easy enough to demonstrate: summon up some Paul Lawrence Dunbar or Robert Burns or Mark Twain and consider briefly the difficulties writers face in trying to represent on paper the elements of speech that are uniquely oral—inflexion, accent, etc.)

When you talk in class about these poems as instruments in abolition agitation, students may want to know how blacks responded to Whittier's poetry (Frederick Douglass applauded Whittier as "the slave's poet"); whether Whittier read aloud to audiences; whether readers committed the poetry to memory and passed it on to others (including nonliterate others) by recitation.

Major Themes, Historical Perspectives, and Personal Issues

Naturally one would have to speak about the abolition movement, as these poems were written to express and to further that cause.

Specific to understanding Whittier as an abolitionist, it would be good to point out that the first abolition society was founded by Quakers (a few words about John Woolman and about the Quaker beliefs that led so many of them to labor against slavery—inward light, reverence for all souls, etc.).

Specific to understanding some of the appeals Whittier makes in "Massachusetts to Virginia," one should remind the student of the Revolutionary and democratic heritage of Massachusetts—the state's role in the Revolutionary War, its founding by religious dissenters, its tradition of the town meeting, and so forth.

Significant Form, Style, or Artistic Conventions

Aside from the issue of topical poetry, it would be appropriate to talk a little bit about the "fireside poetry" that was popular throughout the century in the United States—the characteristics of poetry of sentiment, the kind of audience to which it appealed, and the expectations of that audience. In a way this was the most democratic poetry the nation has produced, in that it was both effectively popular and written expressly to appeal to and communicate with a wide audience. To speak of it as popular rather than elite culture might be useful if one is scrupulous to define these as terms indicating the work's objectives and function rather than its aesthetic "quality" or absolute "value." The artists worked from different assumptions about the function of poetry than those that informed the modernist and postmodern poets of the twentieth century. The audience for poetry in America was as literate as primary education in "blab" schools and drilling in recitation from McGuffey's readers could make it. Good poetry was something you could memorize and recite for pleasure when the book was not in hand, and it was something that stimulated your emotions in the act of reading/reciting, recalling to a harried and overworked people the things they did not see much in their day's labor and the values and feelings an increasingly commercial and competitive society obscured.

Original Audience

It would also be useful to point out that the audience Whittier sought to cultivate were northern whites who had no firsthand experience of conditions in slave states, whose attitude toward blacks was typically shaped more by what they had been told than by personal encounters with black Americans, free or slave. To get such an audience to commit itself to agitation on behalf of American blacks—when that entailed conflict with southern whites, and might imperil free white labor in the North (if masses of freed blacks migrated to northern cities to compete for wage-labor)—was a task and a half. He would have to draw his audience to this banner by identifying his cause with that audience's deepest beliefs and values (such as their Christian faith, their concern for their families and for the sanctity of the family bond, their democratic principles and reverence for the rights of man, their Revolutionary heritage, etc.).

Comparisons, Contrasts, Connections

These poems work well in tandem with other topical/protest poetry and song and/or with another abolition piece. One could compare the effects of Whittier's poetry with the effects of a speech or essay by Frederick Douglass, Wendell Phillips, Henry Highland Garnet, Theodore Weld, the Grimké sisters, William Lloyd Garrison, etc.

Questions for Reading and Discussion/ Approaches to Writing

1. I would alert the class in advance to the function these poems were designed to fulfill, i.e., to stir northern listeners and readers—many of them white—to outrage on behalf of slaves and to action defying slave-holding states. How do you get an audience to care for people who are not related to them, not outwardly "like" them (skin color, dialect, experiences, etc.), nor a source of profit by association or alliance? How do you persuade strangers to risk life, prosperity, and the cooperation of other powerful Americans whose products they depend upon, to liberate what Southerners defined as property—perhaps violating the Constitution in doing so?

   It might be fruitful to ask that they compare Whittier's topical/ protest poetry to the work of a poet like Dickinson—asking that they bracket for the moment questions of which they prefer to read and why, in order to focus instead on the different relationship established between poet and audience. How does Dickinson seem to perceive her calling/duty as a poet? How does Whittier perceive his calling/duty as a poet? To what extent does Dickinson challenge/disrupt the expectations and the shared assumptions of her culture? For what purpose? Toward what effect? Does Whittier engage in this or not? Why (given his objectives)?

2. This is a very challenging assignment, but it really stimulates an appreciation of Whittier's achievement and is a hands-on intro-duction to topical poetry—to the effort to employ the aesthetic as a tool for persuasion and political action.

   Have students compose a short poem designed (1) to awaken audience to concern for an issue or for the plight of a neglected, abused, disenfranchised, or otherwise suffering group, and (2) to stimulate assent in the broadest possible audience—agitating as many as possible while offending as few as possible. Then have the students report on the experience: What problems did they have in composing? How did they opt to solve those problems? Why did they choose the approach and the language they chose? Compare their solutions to Whittier's. At stake would be the quality of the students' analyses of their own creative processes, not so much the instructor's or class's opinion of the poem's effectiveness (though such reader response might form part of the "material" the students would consider as they analyzed and evaluated the task of composing this kind of poetry).

Bibliography

Instructors in search of materials on the poet may start with Karl Keller's bibliographical essay on Whittier studies in *Fifteen American Authors Before 1900* (Robert Rees, editor. Madison: University of Wisconsin Press, 1984) which can direct instructors to studies that explore a variety of questions about the poet's life and work.

Two studies I have found useful for their emphasis on Whittier as abolitionist poet/political activist are: (1) Albert Mordell's *Quaker Militant, John Greenleaf Whittier* (Boston: Houghton Mifflin, 1933) and (2) Edward Charles Wagenknecht's *John Greenleaf Whittier: A Portrait in Paradox* (New York: Oxford University Press, 1967). In Wagenknecht I would refer the reader to the chapters "A Side to Face the World With" and "Power and Love."

John Pickard's introduction to Whittier, *John Greenleaf Whittier: An Introduction and Interpretation* (New York: Barnes and Noble, 1961) provides a good tight chapter on Whittier's abolition activities (ch. 3).

Angelina Grimké Weld (1805–1879)
Sarah Moore Grimké (1792–1873)

Contributing Editor: Jean Fagan Yellin

Classroom Issues and Strategies

Angelina Grimké's *Appeal to the Christian Women of the South* is filled with biblical quotations and allusions; it is written as an evangelical appeal, as the appeal of a Christian woman to other Christian women to act to end chattel slavery. Not only is the language that of evangelical abolitionism, but the logic is as tightly constructed as a Christian sermon. In short, it is difficult to read. In like manner, the language in Sarah M. Grimké's *Letters on the Equality* is Latinate, stiff, and formal. Her language, too, makes slow going for the modern reader.

Try teaching Angelina Grimké's *Appeal to the Christian Women of the South* as a religious argument. The informing notion here is that slavery is sin, and that immediate abolition of slavery means immediate abolition of sin, perhaps immediate salvation. Grimké's tactic is to legitimize—using biblical references—the unprecedented involvement of American women in the public controversy over chattel slavery. She is arguing that slavery is sin and must be ended immediately; and she is arguing that women not only can end it, but that they are duty-bound as Christians to do so.

Read Angelina Grimké's *Letters to Catharine Beecher* as a completely different version of the same argument. Where *Appeal* was couched in religious rhetoric and theological argument, *Letters* is written from a political perspective. It is useful to compare/contrast these, to see Grimké moving, both intellectually and formally, toward a secular stance and toward a straightforward assertion of women's political rights.

Consider the following approach with Sarah Grimké's *Letters on the Equality of the Sexes and the Condition of Woman, Addressed to Mary S. Parker, President of the Boston Female Anti-Slavery Society*: Help students discover that the title suggests the letter's central ideas: first concerning the equality of the sexes, which, Grimké argues, was created by God, and second concerning the condition of woman, which, she argues, is oppressive and which was imposed not by God but by man. The full title concludes with the phrase *Addressed to Mary S. Parker, President of the Boston Female Anti-Slavery Society*. This points toward Grimké's suggestion that the way to rectify the current sinful situation is by women uniting, organizing, and acting, as in the Boston FASS under the leadership of Parker. The title spells out the argument of the *Letters*; it is basically a theological argument for women's rights.

Major Themes, Historical Perspectives, and Personal Issues

In a letter she had impulsively written to the abolitionist William Lloyd Garrison, Angelina Grimké had aligned herself with the abolitionists. Garrison published the letter without her consent, and she was condemned by her meeting (she had become a Quaker [Orthodox]) and even by her sister, her main emotional support. She stuck by her guns. However, although she refused to recant, she was for a time unable to decide what action she should next take. Writing the *Appeal to the Christian Women of the South* was the first public abolitionist document that Angelina Grimké wrote *as* a public document, to be printed with her name on it. Here she commits herself, as a southern woman of the slave-holding class, to abolitionism—and to an investigation of women's activism in the anti-slavery cause.

A. E. Grimké wrote the *Letters to Catharine Beecher* for the weekly press during the summer of 1837, while she was traveling and lecturing as an "agent" of the American Anti-Slavery Society. She wrote them to answer Catharine Beecher's attack on her lecturing that had been published as *An Essay on Slavery and Abolitionism, with Reference to the Duty of American Females, Addressed to A. E. Grimké*. Beecher, a leading educator, developed the notion of the moral superiority of females and, asserting the importance of the home, argued that women should oppose slavery within the domestic circle but should not enter the public political sphere—as Angelina Grimké was doing. In her *Letters*, Angelina Grimké defends her almost unprecedented behavior by arguing for women's political rights. The *Letters* should also be read in relation to the abolitionists' petitions—to local, state, and national legislative bodies—to end slavery and to outlaw various racist practices. These petitions were circulated by men and, as Grimké urges here, by women as well. Historians have traced the later petition campaigns of the feminists to these anti-slavery petition campaigns.

In *Letters*, Sarah Grimké raises a whole range of feminist issues—the value of housework, wage differentials between men and women, women's education, fashion, and the demand that women be allowed to preach. (She was bitter that she had not been permitted to do so.) Furthermore, she discusses the special oppression of black women and of women held in slavery.

Significant Form, Style, or Artistic Conventions

Angelina Grimké's *Letters* should be read and contrasted with her *Appeal*, then with other writings by nineteenth-century feminists, both black and white.

Similarly, Sarah Grimké's *Letters* should be read and contrasted with pre-1848 feminists like Margaret Fuller, then with Stanton, et. al. This text marks a beginning. American feminist discourse emerges from this root.

Original Audience

Angelina Grimké's *Appeal*: Audience is stated as the Christian women of the South; by this Grimké means the free white women—many of them slave-holders, as she herself had been—who profess Christianity. It is worthwhile examining the ways in which she defines these women, and exploring the similarities and differences between her approach to them and the patriarchal definition of true womanhood generally endorsed at the time. The patriarchy was projecting "true womanhood" as piety, purity, domesticity, and obedience. Angelina Grimké urges her readers to break the law if the law is immoral—to be obedient not to fathers, husbands, and human laws, but to a Higher Law that condemns slavery. And she urges them to act not only within the "domestic sphere" allocated to women, but also within the "public sphere" that was exclusively male territory.

Angelina Grimké's *Letters*: Written directly to Catharine Beecher, these were published weekly in the abolitionist press, then compiled into a pamphlet that became an abolitionist staple and stands as an early expression of the notions that would inform the feminist movement in 1848.

Sarah Grimké's *Letters on the Equality*, like Angelina's *Letters to Catharine Beecher*, were published in the weekly press, then collected and published as a pamphlet.

Comparisons, Contrasts, Connections

Compare Angelina Grimké's *Appeal* with Lydia Maria Child's *Appeal in Favor of that Class of Americans Called Africans*. Compare both with African-American anti-slavery writings by Walker, Garnet, Truth, Harper, Jacobs, Douglass, and Brown. As suggested above, Angelina Grimké's *Appeal* and her *Letters to Catharine Beecher* present an interesting comparison. Both might be read in connection with the writings on women by Fuller, Child, Stanton, and Fern, as well as in connection with the responses to chattel slavery by white women like the southerner Chesnutt and northerners like Child and Stowe, as well as by African-American women like Truth, Jacobs, and Harper.

Sarah Grimké's *Letters* should be read in relation to the writings of other nineteenth-century feminists like Stanton and in relation to anti-feminist polemics, as well as in relation to depictions of women in nineteenth-century literature by writers such as Hawthorne, Stowe, Cary, and Stoddard.

Questions for Reading and Discussion/ Approaches to Writing

Direct students' attention to the epigraph to Angelina Grimké's *Appeal*. Why Queen Esther? In what ways do Grimké's *Letters* differ from her *Appeal*? How is the argument different? How is the style different? What are the consequences of these differences? In what ways do Sarah Grimké's *Letters* differ from her sister's writings? Why did the later feminists designate Sarah Grimké's *Letters on the Equality* an important precursor?

Bibliography

See the primary and secondary works listed in headnote.

Henry Highland Garnet (1815–1882)

Contributing Editor: Allison Heisch

Classroom Issues and Strategies

Ideas that seem radical in one era often become common sense in another and thus may appear obvious to the point of being uninteresting. Furthermore, out of its historical context, Garnet's "Address to the Slaves of the United States" may be hard for students to distinguish from other, more moderate abolitionist appeals.

Garnet's diction is primarily that of a highly literate nineteenth-century black man who has had a white education in theology. Students will understand what he's saying, but unless they can *hear* his voice they'll have trouble feeling what he means.

To teach Garnet effectively, his work should be presented in the context of the wider (and, of course, two-sided) debate on abolition. Second, it's important to pay attention to the form of this address and to its actual audience: Garnet is speaking before the National Negro Convention (1843). Is he speaking to that audience or is he trying to communicate with American slaves? The former, obviously. Ideally, some of this should be read aloud.

Despite his radicalism, Garnet fits comfortably into a tradition of "learned" nineteenth-century religious/political orators. As such, Garnet is a fine representative of the abolitionists who made the argument against slavery in part by demonstrating their intellectual equality with whites. But there is another strain of American abolitionists—perhaps best represented by Sojourner Truth—who made the same argument on personal and emotional grounds, and whose appeal belongs to another great American tradition, one that is in some sense almost anti-intellectual in its emphasis on the value of common sense and folk wisdom. Particularly since those two traditions are alive and well in contemporary America, it is useful to place them side by side.

Major Themes, Historical Perspectives, and Personal Issues

It may be useful to point out that Garnet's appeal failed (by a single vote) to be adopted by the Convention. Why might this have happened? Garnet's speech is steeped in Christianity, but he seems to advocate violence in the name of Christianity. When is the use of force legitimate? Useful? How is his position different from those taken by contemporaries such as Frederick Douglass? Garnet's audience is implicitly exclusively male; how can one be so opposed to slavery and yet so unconcerned about women's rights?

Significant Form, Style, or Artistic Conventions

Although this speech was eventually printed (1865), it was obviously written for oral delivery. Nevertheless, Garnet's pretext is that he is writing a letter; could his pretended audience of slaves have actually received such a letter? Certainly not. What is the rhetorical purpose of pretending to address one audience while actually addressing another? Could Garnet's "Address" be regarded as a sermon? If so, can a sermon also be a call to arms? It is useful to approach the "Address" as a piece of argumentation, to see how Garnet makes his case, and to show how it builds itself through repetition (e.g., the repeated address to "Brethren") and through the chronological deployment of names of famous men and famous deeds to his conclusion, which is a call for armed resistance.

Original Audience

The simplest way to evoke a discussion of audience is to ask a set of fairly obvious questions: What is the stated audience? What is the "real" audience? How large an audience would that have been in the 1840s?

Comparisons, Contrasts, Connections

First, and most obvious, Garnet can be contrasted with Martin Luther King to discuss theories of resistance and passive resistance. (Consider especially the "Letter from Birmingham Jail" with its "real" and "implied" audiences.) It is also useful to have students read the "Address" against Lincoln's Gettysburg Address or the Second Inaugural (to compare form and content). Garnet may be read against David Walker (to show similarities and differences, the evolution of the radical position) and against Frederick Douglass (to discuss styles of persuasion).

Questions for Reading and Discussion/ Approaches to Writing

Questions *before* reading: Who or what is Garnet's real audience? Why does he pretend to be writing a letter?

Bibliography

Bremer, William. "Henry Highland Garnet." In *Blacks in White America Before 1865*, edited by Robert Haynes. New York, 1972.

Quarles, Benjamin. *Black Abolitionists*. New York, 1969.

Schor, Joel. *Henry Highland Garnet*. Westport, Conn.: Greenwood, 1977.

Wendell Phillips (1811–1884)

Contributing Editor: Allison Heisch

Classroom Issues and Strategies

Students tend not to know enough history (or, for that matter, geography) to understand the setting for *Toussaint L'Ouverture*. In addition, Phillips's view of race and racial difference will strike some students as condescending: He sets out to "prove" that Toussaint is "okay" and seems to imply that his sterling example proves that some blacks are "okay" too. This is not the sort of argumentation that we like nowadays, for we've understood this as tokenism.

A quick history/geography lesson here (including Napoleon and the French Revolution) is in order. Also, review the attitudes toward race generally taken in this period. I've given background reading in Stephen J. Gould's *The Mismeasure of Man* as a way of grounding that discussion. It is equally useful to pair Phillips with a figure such as Louis Agassiz to show what style of thought the "scientific" view of race could produce. Yet, students can and do understand that styles of argument get dated very readily, and this can be demonstrated for them with various NAACP sorts of examples.

Students often ask, "Is this a true story?" (Answer: Sort of.)

Major Themes, Historical Perspectives, and Personal Issues

Phillips's emphasis on the dignity of the individual. The idea of the hero (and the rather self-conscious way he develops it—that is, in his emphasis on Toussaint's "pure blood," and his deliberate contrast of Toussaint with Napoleon). It's useful to show Toussaint as Phillips's version of "the noble savage" (an eighteenth-century British idea still current in nineteenth-century America).

As the headnote points out, the immediate occasion of Phillips's speech was the issue of whether blacks should serve in the military. Since the issue of military service—that is, of women and homosexuals in the military—has been a vexed one in the recent past, it may be useful to point to this historical context for the speech and to the relationship between its rhetoric and content and its functions in its time. This may also raise the question of the symbolic significance of military prowess in general.

Significant Form, Style, or Artistic Conventions

This piece needs to be placed in the broader context of circuit-speaking and in the specific context of abolitionist public speaking. It should also be located in the debate over slavery.

Original Audience

Phillips's assumptions about his audience are very clear: There is little doubt that he addresses an audience of white folks with the plain intent of persuading them to adopt his position, or at least to give it a fair hearing. Students may very well say that Phillips *has* no contemporary audience, and that is probably true. It's useful, however, to point out that long after Phillips's death black students memorized this piece and recited it on occasions such as school graduations. Thus, while the people who first heard this piece were certainly very much like Phillips, his second (and more enduring) audience was an audience of black people—largely students—who probably knew and cared nothing about Phillips, but embraced Toussaint L'Ouverture as their hero. That phenomenon—the half-life of polemic—is very interesting.

Comparisons, Contrasts, Connections

It is useful (and easy) to present Phillips with other white abolitionists (such as Garrison and Thoreau) or to read Phillips against black orators

(F. Douglass, H. H. Garnet, David Walker). Another tack is to put him in a wider spectrum of white anti-slavery writing: Read him with John Greenleaf Whittier or even Harriet Beecher Stowe. One approach to take is to compare his oratorical style with that of Garnet or Douglass. Another is to show the breadth of anti-slavery writing, particularly with reference to the particular genres involved. If the students don't notice this, it's important to point out that this is an anti-slavery piece by implication: Phillips does not address the subject directly.

Questions for Reading and Discussion/ Approaches to Writing

1. I like to have students identify the intended audience for me: How do they know to whom Phillips is speaking?
2. From Phillips's vantage, what are the traits of this ideal black hero? (Part of the point here is to get them to understand Phillips's emphasis on Toussaint's appreciation for white people and to see what kinds of fears he implicitly addresses.)
3. In what ways is this effective (or ineffective) as a piece of argumentation?
4. Is this piece propaganda? And, if so, what *is* propaganda? What are the differences (in terms of content and specifics) between Phillips's argument and one that might be made in a contemporary civil rights speech?
5. A good topic for getting at the heart of the matter (a very good paper topic) is a comparison of Toussaint L'Ouverture and Uncle Tom.

Bibliography

Bartlett, Irving. *Wendell Phillips, Brahmin Radical*. Boston: Greenwood, 1973.

Bode, Carl. *The American Lyceum: Town Meetings of the Mind*. New York: S. Illinois University Press, 1968.

Korngold, Ralph. *Two Friends of Man: The Story of William Lloyd Garrison and Wendell Phillips and Their Relationship with Abraham Lincoln*. Boston, 1950.

Stewart, James Brewer. *Wendell Phillips, Liberty's Hero*. Baton Rouge and London: Louisiana State University Press, 1986.

Thomas Wentworth Higginson (1823–1911)

Contributing Editor: Paul Lauter

Classroom Issues and Strategies

It's almost impossible for students to connect the apostle of Nat Turner with the "mentor" of Emily Dickinson; a Christian minister; a colonel of a black Civil War regiment; an active feminist; an important nineteenth-century editor. All these roles were filled by Thomas Wentworth Higginson, yet only the first two aspects are represented by the texts. So the real issue is whether or not he is significant. And if he is, why?

If students know Higginson at all, they will probably know him as the man who, in putting Dickinson poems into print, disgracefully smoothed them out, changing her words, her punctuation, even her meanings. Why read such a fellow? Why in the world did Dickinson write to him?

At the same time, he doesn't smooth out Nat Turner. Yet, like any historical writer, he "constructs" Nat Turner in a particular way. The nature of that "construction" is not easy to define.

Sometimes it's useful to begin from an example of what Higginson (and Todd) did to a Dickinson poem. Their choices say something about Dickinson, about nineteenth-century sensibilities, and—with Higginson's and Dickinson's letters—about their unique relationship. The revised Dickinson also raises the question of why one might want to include Higginson in this anthology.

At one point in the 1960s, students had heard about William Styron's "Confessions" of Nat Turner. It may still be useful to bring up some of the summary accounts in magazines like *Newsweek* of Styron's version and the controversy that surrounded it. Higginson's picture is, of course, quite different, yet both can be understood, among other ways, as serving certain historical needs in their audience.

Major Themes, Historical Perspectives, and Personal Issues

Is there any unity at all to Higginson's life as minister, military man, activist, writer, editor, mentor? More than most, Higginson's extraordinarily varied career expresses a nineteenth-century commitment by a well-to-do white man to racial, gender, and class equality—in politics, in social relations, and in culture. His sensitivity—and his limitations—say a great deal about the power as well as the constraints upon that kind of progressive politics, and about the forms of culture it inspired. To see why Dickinson sought him out and yet would not be limited by him reveals a great deal about the cultural revolution her writing represents, as well as about the strengths of what Higginson can be taken to illustrate.

The essay on Nat Turner also is very useful in relation to the other abolitionist writers, especially Walker and Garrison. Though Nat Turner's rebellion came after Walker's *Appeal* and the beginning of *The Liberator*, there are ways in which it was taken, literally and symbolically (as Higginson implies), as an outgrowth of such writings.

Significant Form, Style, or Artistic Conventions

Higginson commands a fine and varied prose style, and it can be very rewarding for students to examine certain of his paragraphs—like the initial one on the files of the Richmond newspaper, the early one on the participants in the rebellion, the one on the lives of slaves not being "individualized," and the final one of the essay.

Original Audience

The essay and the letter can be usefully compared on this ground. They are not very distant in time, yet quite distinctly conceived because of audience.

The essay was written before the Civil War began, yet was published only after. What does that say about the limits of "acceptable" discourse? What does the essay imply about the readership of the *Atlantic*, where it was published?

Comparisons, Contrasts, Connections

Higginson's construction of Nat Turner can usefully be compared with Phillips's portrait of Toussaint, with Frederick Douglass's self-portrait (as well as with his picture of Madison Washington), and with the black characters of Melville's "Benito Cereno." All these texts involve the issue of the "heroic slave"—what constitutes "heroism" in a slave. Underlying that is the issue of what constitutes "humanity," since for many Americans, black people were not fully human.

Questions for Reading and Discussion/ Approaches to Writing

How does Higginson account for Nat Turner's motivations, actions?

Why did the essay on Nat Turner remain unpublished until after the Civil War began?

Why, given Higginson's letter about Emily Dickinson and her letters to him, did she wish to write to him?

What does Higginson's relationship to Dickinson (and the way he helped publish her poems) tell you about the kind of culture he represents?

What are the predominant features in Higginson's portrait of Nat Turner? What are the alternative views of Nat Turner between which he is choosing? Is Higginson's Nat Turner a hero or a terrorist?

Bibliography

Henry Irving Tragle's *The Southampton Slave Revolt of 1831* and Herbert Aptheker's *Nat Turner's Slave Rebellion* contain useful brief materials on Nat Turner, including the text of his "confessions," as compiled by Thomas Gray. The view of Nat Turner in that and other texts usefully contrasts with Higginson's.

If one is interested in the problem of how writers construct historical accounts (an issue quite relevant to Melville's "Benito Cereno," for example), such materials provide a useful case in point.

Caroline Lee Hentz (1800–1856)

Contributing Editor: Anne Jones

Classroom Issues and Strategies

Most students will find it easy to dismiss the arguments, the rhetoric, and the writing in this tendentious chapter. What can make things initially more interesting is a careful analysis of the tactics Hentz is so obviously—or maybe not so obviously—using on her readers. What's the point of the setting, in a small village, on a Saturday night? What is she appealing to with her description of the landlord as an "Indian" looking man? What about those "delineators of the sable character" (1904)? The dying young woman's function can't be missed; but what about the

Northern gentleman who accompanies Moreland as he carries her bundle?

Analysis of certain passages invites at least some debate, opening the issues beyond the question of slavery and encouraging students to make argumentative distinctions. What about Grimby's self-contradictory claims (a free country where all must conform, a loss of distinction that means loss of difference); does Hentz have a viable point here? And what about the domestic care versus public welfare point? Are these issues necessarily tied to a defense of slavery?

It could be useful, too, to have students rewrite the story from the point of view of another character. Is Albert having private thoughts of a different sort? Could a sentence like "I wish I may find everybody as well off as I am" (1905) be interpreted as double-voiced discourse? What is motivating the landlord? How does the young woman feel about the men's charity? What do such imaginative efforts show us when we look again at Hentz's point of view strategies?

These discussions raise the question of how we can understand—instead of demonize—people who actively supported slavery, who unashamedly proclaimed black racial inferiority, and who believed, like Moreland, in a clearly hierarchical, authoritarian society. Or *should* we try to understand such positions? Students may discover in thinking about Hentz that their opposition to slavery and racism has never really been thought through. This chapter will give them the chance to do that.

I might start with Bertram Wyatt-Brown's words from *Southern Honor*: "It is hard for us to believe that Southerners ever meant what they said of themselves. How could they so glibly reconcile slaveholding with pretensions to virtue? . . . [Yet] apart from a few lonely dissenters, Southern whites believed (*as most people do* [emphasis added]) that they conducted their lives by the highest ethical standards" (3). What standards does Hentz invoke? Which do you accept? Which do you reject, and why?

Major Themes, Historical Perspectives, and Personal Issues

These are fairly self-evident, I think, particularly when read in the context of abolitionist writing in the anthology. The chapter may be unsettling to students who come to pro-slavery writing with moral certainties in place. Reading pro-slavery arguments together with abolitionist arguments, however, can help them clarify their own positions not only on slavery but also on how to think about the problems of poverty and racism that, unlike slavery, remain unresolved today. I have found students to be very responsive to the early chapters in Lillian Smith's *Killers of the Dream* (New York: 1962), where she eloquently dramatizes the complexity and personal pain of ideological conflict for children and young people, in this case white southern girls who are torn between family and personal values. Faulkner's "Barn Burning" can be read in similar ways.

Significant Form, Style, or Artistic Conventions

Clearly Hentz is working within conventions—clichés—of writing that she feels will work rhetorically to persuade and soften her readers. Students might find it fun to identify what they see as clichéd language, predictable plotting (what do you suppose will happen to that not-dead twenty-year-old whose memory preoccupies Moreland?). Could there be canny reasons for such lack of originality?

Original Audience

Try asking students who they think the intended audience is. They will probably guess white Northerners. How did they know this? This will take them back to the experience of reading the text to see how the words worked on them. Note, for instance, that Hentz carefully explains "Mars." and the relationship of insult to class (in Southern honor, one could not be insulted by—hence one did not respond to—an inferior). These details suggest she is not preaching to the choir. Are there audiences she would not address? If not, why not? Try asking students to rewrite this for a contemporary audience, with contemporary cultural issues in mind. Or ask them to debate the issue of slavery orally (pro and con). If they resist, ask them to discuss their resistance. If they do not resist, ask them to discuss their lack of resistance.

Comparisons, Contrasts, Connections

First compare Fitzhugh's very male-focused defense of slavery with Caroline Hentz's. Is hers markedly "womanly"? From comparing these texts, what can we learn about the nineteenth-century cultural gender differences that each author assumes and exploits? Is Fitzhugh turning for support to nineteenth-century women's culture when he argues (1914) for the superiority of "domestic" slavery over slavery to capital? Is Hentz doing the same when she compares the public institutions of the North to domestic ones in the South? Next compare these writers' arguments with abolitionists' arguments. How do abolitionists deal with

Southern claims about the "hireling's" misery and the slave's relative comfort? About the variety of treatment slaves received? About the emotional relations with slaves? Slave narratives make an excellent comparison also; see Harriet Jacobs, in particular.

George Fitzhugh (1804–1881)

Contributing Editor: Anne Jones

Classroom Issues and Strategies

The most pressing issue will most likely be simple incredulity on the part of students. Not only does Fitzhugh defend a system (slavery) whose evil is a modern given, but he believes abolition "will soon be considered a mad infatuation," England will return to slave-holding, and southern thought will lead the western world.

An interesting starting point then could be the question of tone. Is this guy serious? How can we be sure that sentences like "This, of itself, would put the South at the lead of modern civilization" or "How fortunate for the South that she has this inferior race" are not dripping with sarcasm? Is irony contextual? In what context do these seem ironic statements?

Of course, they are perfectly "straight" in the context of Fitzhugh's essay and audience, which raises the more profound question for the class to deliberate: How can we understand (if, indeed, we should try to understand) and not criticize people who supported slavery and who adhered to the notion of black racial inferiority? Fitzhugh's essay from *Southern Thought* may help students discover that their opposition to slavery and racism has never really been understood.

Start with Bertram Wyatt-Brown's words from *Southern Honor*: "It is hard for us to believe that Southerners ever meant what they said of themselves. How could they so glibly reconcile slaveholding with pretensions to virtue? . . . [Yet] apart from a few lonely dissenters, Southern whites believed (*as most people do* [emphasis added]) that they conducted their lives by the highest ethical standards" (3). What standards does Fitzhugh invoke? Which do you accept? Which do you reject, and why?

Major Themes, Historical Perspectives, and Personal Issues

The vexed relation to socialism evident in Fitzhugh's text might come as a surprise. A connection between socialism and southern thought is evident again in the modern period (see Volume 2), when the Southern Agrarians find themselves sympathetic, like Fitzhugh, to this "other" critique of industrial capitalism and bourgeois individualism. How does Fitzhugh separate his views from those of socialists?

Fitzhugh clearly has an ideological project in mind here; he even locates the most practical venues for indoctrinating the South (and next, the world!) in "Southern Thought." What do students think about such a project? How different is it from contemporary advertising and marketing strategies? More advanced students might compare it to Gramsci's notions of counter-hegemonic discourse to be developed by organic intellectuals.

Fitzhugh's racism which he separates so carefully from his defense of slavery as an institution, is of course egregious. It should, however, be understood (which is not to say condoned) in the context of widespread contemporary beliefs in scientific racism. See, for instance, "Race" by Kwame Appiah in Frank Lentricchia and Thomas McLaughlin, eds. *Critical Terms for Literary Study* (1990). Can we separate his argument for enslavement of blacks from his argument for black difference? What are some modern arguments for black difference and separation? How do they differ from Fitzhugh's? Are they legitimate? Why or why not?

Such questions may be unsettling to students who come to pro-slavery writing with moral certainties in place. Reading pro-slavery arguments together with abolitionist arguments, however, can help them clarify their own positions not only on slavery but also on how to think about the problems of poverty and racism that, unlike slavery, remain unresolved today. I have found students to be very responsive to the early chapters in Lillian Smith's *Killers of the Dream* (1962), where she eloquently dramatizes the complexity and personal pain of ideological conflict for children and young people, in this case white southern girls who are torn between family and personal values. Faulkner's "Barn Burning" can be read in similar ways.

Significant Form, Style, or Artistic Conventions

Fitzhugh's allusions (for example, to abolitionists by name and to European history) may be obscure. Try assigning one name/reference to each student for a collective information pool.

Original Audience

Try asking students who they think the intended audience is. They will probably guess other literate white Southerners, and they will be right (like much pro-slavery argument, it appeared in a southern publication). But how did they know this? This will take them back to the experience of reading the text to see how the words worked on them. How might Fitzhugh have addressed another audience—the British middle class, free/enslaved southern blacks, for instance? Are there audiences he would not address? If not, why not? Try asking students to rewrite this for a contemporary audience, or to debate the issue of slavery orally (pro and con). If they resist, ask them to discuss their resistance. If they do not resist, ask them to discuss their lack of resistance.

Comparisons, Contrasts, Connections

First, compare Fitzhugh's very male-focused defense with Caroline Hentz's defense of slavery. Is hers markedly "womanly"? From comparing these texts, what can we learn about the nineteenth-century cultural gender differences that each author assumes and exploits? Is Fitzhugh turning for support to nineteenth-century women's culture when he argues (1914) for the superiority of "domestic" slavery over slavery to capital? Next, compare these writers' arguments with abolitionists' arguments. A particularly interesting comparison would be with Angelina Grimké, who in "Appeal to the Christian Women of the South" wrote to a similar audience and thus constructed her rhetoric based on presumably similar understandings of what might work with Southerners. How do abolitionists deal with southern claims about "slavery to capital"?

Mary Boykin Chesnut (1823–1886)

Contributing Editor: Minrose C. Gwin

Classroom Issues and Strategies

It is important to consider Mary Chesnut and her work in context. Chesnut is well known for her criticism of slavery and patriarchy. Yet she is also very much a member of the wealthy planter class in her views on race. In addition, this is a massive work—close to 900 pages. It is, therefore, difficult to find "representative" sections that capture the breadth and sweep of the work as a whole.

In teaching Chesnut consider these strategies:

1. Provide historical context with attention to the intersections of race, class, and gender in southern culture. Consider especially the position of white women in a patriarchal slave society. Students also need to understand the rise and fall of the Confederacy.
2. Require students to read and report on diverse sections of the work.

Students often ask questions related to Chesnut's "feminism" and her attitude toward race. For example, why does she blame African-American women for being sexual victims of white men? How implicated is she in the patriarchal order?

Major Themes, Historical Perspectives, and Personal Issues

1. This is an important *social* history of the Civil War era in the South.
2. At the same time, it is interesting both as a woman's autobiography—a *personal* history of struggle and hardship—and as a remarkable story of the trauma experienced by both white and black women in the Civil War South.

Significant Form, Style, or Artistic Conventions

This autobiography is a combination of a journal written on the spot and reminiscences of the Civil War period. (See *The Private Mary Chesnut* for the former.) There is, therefore, a fascinating *combination* of the personal and the public in Woodward's edition.

Original Audience

Hundreds of war reminiscences were published in the forty to fifty years after the Civil War. Poorly edited versions, both called *A Diary from Dixie*, were published in 1905 and 1949. Installments of the first edition were published in *The Saturday Evening Post*. Readers then were more interested in the actual events of the war years so vividly portrayed by Chestnut.

Comparisons, Contrasts, Connections

I would suggest a contrast/comparison to an African-American woman's slave narrative, perhaps Harriet Ann Jacobs's *Incidents in the Life of a Slave Girl*, which also decries white men's sexual misuse of female slaves—from the point of view of the victim. (Also see *Uncle Tom's Cabin* for similar themes.)

Questions for Reading and Discussion/ Approaches to Writing

1. (a) Describe how Chesnut created this massive volume.
   (b) Describe the life of an upper-class white woman in the Old South.
   (c) Describe the editorial history of this volume.
2. (a) Compare to slave narrative, abolitionist or pro-slavery fiction, realistic or plantation fiction, or modern woman's autobiography.
   (b) Discuss Chesnut's relationships and attitudes toward: black women, her own husband and father-in-law, female friends (e.g., Varina Davis), or her own slaves.
   (c) Describe how fictional techniques bring life to the diary format.

Bibliography

Fox-Genovese, Elizabeth. *Within the Plantation Household: Black and White Women of the Old South.* University of North Carolina Press, 1988.

Gwin, Minrose. *Black and White Women of the Old South: The Peculiar Sisterhood in American Literature.* University of Tennessee Press, 1985. Chapter 2.

Jones, Anne Goodwyn. "Southern Literary Women, and Chronicles of Southern Life." In *Sex, Race, and the Role of Women in the South,* edited by Joanne V. Hawks and Sheila L. Skemp. University Press of Mississippi, 1983.

Junker, Clara. "Writing Herstory: Mary Chesnut's Civil War." *Southern Studies* 26 (1987): 18–27.

Muhlenfeld, Elisabeth. *Mary Boykin Chesnut: A Biography.* Louisiana State University Press, 1981.

Woodward, C. Vann. *Mary Chesnut's Civil War*. Yale University Press, 1981. Introduction.

—— and Elisabeth Muhlenfeld. *The Private Mary Chesnut*. Oxford University Press, 1985. Introduction.

Abraham Lincoln (1809–1865)

Contributing Editor: Elaine Sargent Apthorp

Classroom Issues and Strategies

Lincoln's words are familiar to students, who have received those words, or the echo of them, by a hundred indirect sources, and who sometimes conflate the Gettysburg Address with the Pledge of Allegiance—and not by accident. (Similarly, the man himself has been rendered unreal by his status as a culture hero and icon; part of the reconstruction process entails restoring personhood to this historical figure—reconstructing his statesmanship and character by describing the context in which he grew and worked, the forces he had to contend with as a politician and as President, etc.) A problem is how to make the words live in their original context—so that by stripping them temporarily of their canonization in the store of U.S. holy scriptures, we can see why they were so appropriated—what it was about these words that moved Americans in the aftermath of the war. And what about Lincoln's construction of these statements has made them so emblematic of cultural ideals we still cherish (however vague their application)?

To give the meanings back to the words, we need to (1) restore vividly the historical context in which these speeches were composed and to which they were addressed, and (2) read slowly and explicate together as we go. What precedents and values is he calling to his listeners' minds? What does he ask them to focus on? What doesn't he choose to talk about, refer to, or insinuate?

Major Themes, Historical Perspectives, and Personal Issues

I've tried to canvass these in the headnote. It's important that the students know, for example, that the battle of Gettysburg was in many respects the turning point in the Civil War. It was the farthest advance the Confederate forces were to make. In addition, it was the bloodiest and most costly battle (in sheer number of lives lost on both sides) in what was a devastatingly bloody war (over 600,000 battle casualties over four years, with another million and more dead from disease via infected wounds, malnutrition, inadequate medical attention).

Students should know something of how Lincoln was perceived in the North and South during his presidency, the polarized forces with which he had to contend even among the nonseceding members of the Union, his concern for maintaining the loyalty of slave-holding border states and holding out hope for reunion with the Confederate states, in tension with the pressure he felt from the radical Republicans who urged the emancipation of slaves by executive proclamation, and so forth. This kind of information helps us to interpret both of the Lincoln documents in our selection.

Significant Form, Style, or Artistic Conventions

Again, see the headnote on style—biblical allusions and cadence, lawyer's cutting and distinguishing, simplified syntax and diction. In a discussion of oratory as it was practiced in this period, point out ways in which Lincoln participated in and departed from the practice of oratory that was considered eloquent in that day (e.g., Edward Everett who preceded Lincoln on the podium at Gettysburg).

Original Audience

1. The audience could tolerate, and indeed expected, long, florid, syntactically complex speeches. They were, at the same time, both more literate and more aural than we are (we're more visual, attending to images rather than words or sounds).
2. The audience were Christians. War had bitterly divided North from South; politicians debated while many people experienced death at rebel or Yankee hands. Lincoln had to consider how to appease the vindictive rage/triumph/urge-to-plunder of the conquering Union supporters while establishing foundation for political and economic reconstruction and rebuilding. He had to rally maximum support (reminding North and South of their common faith; characterizing the war as a war for the Union's democratic survival, not as a war to free slaves or alter the economic order of society—using Union and Constitution, obscuring states' rights).

3. Consider our own time, and our longing for the rock of humane statesmanship that Lincoln has represented in the popular mind. Consider the motives behind his canonization after assassination, when he had been so unpopular while alive in office. Consider the uses Lincoln has been put to, by politicians, etc. Consider the evolutions in public perception of Nixon, Kennedy, etc.

Comparisons, Contrasts, Connections

1. A bit of Everett's speech at Gettysburg for comparison with Lincoln's little Gettysburg Address.
2. Samples of biblical prose for comparison with Lincoln's.
3. Elements of debates with Stephen Douglas in 1858, again for comparison.
4. Dr. Martin Luther King's "Letter from Birmingham Jail," "I Have a Dream," etc., to discover the uses of Lincoln for other politically active people/groups.

Bibliography

Studies on Lincoln's life and career exist in flourishing and staggering abundance, and most of them examine the language of his speeches and other public and private documents to help develop their interpretations of Lincoln's character, attitudes, and policies as they evolved.

Steven B. Oates's *With Malice Toward None* offers what is finally a sympathetic and admiring account of Lincoln, but it is tempered and qualified by a scrupulous confrontation with inconvenient evidence and careful consideration of the poles of controversy in Lincoln studies between which he means to place his own interpretation.

There are also a number of essays that explore Lincoln's writings as works of literature, which trace one or more of the several strands of law, rural imagery, backwoods humor, Shakespeare, and the Bible, which inform Lincoln's rhetoric. Entire books have been devoted to establishing the historical contexts in which Lincoln developed the Gettysburg Address or the Emancipation Proclamation, but for the instructor on the go nothing beats Jacques Barzun's *Lincoln the Literary Genius* (Evanston, Illinois: Evanston Publishing Co., 1960). It's short but covers much ground and offers perceptive close analysis of Lincoln's rhetorical techniques and style—both identifying these elements and suggesting their effects and implications.

One more recent study that employs analysis of Lincoln's speeches is Charles B. Strozier's psychoanalytic study of Lincoln, *Lincoln's Quest for Union: Public and Private Meanings* (Urbana and Chicago: University of

Illinois Press, 1987; Basic Books, 1982), chapters 6–9 but especially chapter 7, "The Domestication of Political Rhetoric."

LITERATURE AND THE "WOMAN QUESTION"

Sarah Moore Grimké (1792–1873)

See material under "Angelina Grimké Weld" and "Sarah Moore Grimké" earlier in this guide.

Elizabeth Cady Stanton (1815–1902)

Contributing Editor: Judith Wellman

Classroom Issues and Strategies

Stanton's autobiography reads well, in a fresh, personal, and modern style. Students do, however, benefit from some introduction to the Seneca Falls Declaration of Sentiments.

I usually ask students to analyze the Declaration of Sentiments in two ways:

1. How is it like/unlike the Declaration of Independence? It is almost identical to the Declaration of Independence in the preamble, except for the assertion that "all men and women are created equal." It is also divided into three main parts, as is the Declaration of Independence. Instead of grievances against King George, however, the Declaration of Sentiments lists grievances of women against the patriarchal establishment. Supposedly, the women tried to use the same number of items in 1848 as the Second Continental Congress incorporated in 1776, but the 1848 document actually contains one or two fewer.

2. How many grievances of 1848 are still issues for feminists today? Asking students to list them or to compare them with the issues raised at the 1977 Houston convention, ending the International Women's Year, works well.

3. Professors might ask students to imagine they were present at the Seneca Falls convention. Would they have signed this document? Why or why not?
4. Students might also imagine they were Elizabeth Cady Stanton in 1848. What was her state of mind? Does this document reflect her personal life or only her political ideals?
5. Ask students (individually or in groups) to select the one or two grievances from 1848 that they would consider important issues today and to defend their choices in writing or in class discussion. Or ask them to choose one or two contemporary issues that did not appear in the Declaration of Sentiments and to consider why they are important today but were not stated publicly then.
6. Students are often amazed that women were citizens without citizenship rights. They are also amazed at how many issues from 1848 are still unresolved. They have no trouble agreeing that "all men and women are created equal" but they do not always agree on what that means.

   They ask about how well this Declaration was received (widely reported, mixed reception), and they are curious about the relationship between Elizabeth and Henry (difficult even for scholars to figure out).

Major Themes, Historical Perspectives, and Personal Issues

1. What was the political and legal position of women in the early Republic? Were women, for example, citizens? What did citizenship mean for women?
2. What alternative vision did the women and men who signed the Seneca Falls Declaration of Sentiments propose for women?
3. To what extent did the Declaration of Sentiments reflect issues in Stanton's personal life, as well as in her political ideals?

Significant Form, Style, or Artistic Conventions

Contrast between the Declaration of Sentiments, with its attempt to reflect revolutionary writing and therefore revolutionary, egalitarian ideals, and Stanton's own account of her life, designed to emphasize her own experiences, which results in a more direct and personal style.

Original Audience

Professors might emphasize the universal character of the Declaration of Sentiments. It was not designed to appeal to some Americans only but to all Americans.

Comparisons, Contrasts, Connections

Comparisons with the Declaration of Independence and with the report from the Houston convention are both useful.

Bibliography

Flexner, Eleanor. *Century of Struggle*. Rev. ed. Cambridge: Harvard University Press, 1979. Chapter 5.

Griffith, Elisabeth. *In Her Own Right: The Life of Elizabeth Cady Stanton*. New York: Oxford University Press, 1984. Chapter 4.

Melder, Keith. *Beginnings of Sisterhood: The American Women's Rights Movement, 1800-1850*. New York: Schocken Books, 1977. Chapters 8 and 10.

Stanton, E. C. "Address Delivered at Seneca Falls," July 19, 1848. In *Elizabeth Cady Stanton, Susan B. Anthony: Correspondence, Writings, Speeches*, edited by Ellen Carol DuBois, 27–35. New York: Schocken, 1981.

Fanny Fern (Sara Willis Parton) (1811–1872)

Contributing Editor: Barbara A. White

Classroom Issues and Strategies

I have found Fern most accessible to students when presented as primarily a humorist and satirist, rather than a "sentimentalist," and a journalist rather than a novelist. However, I try to avoid setting her up as an exception, as Nathaniel Hawthorne did, a writer "better" than the typical "scribbling woman." Ann Douglas Wood sets Fern apart for her refusal to disguise her literary ambition and conform to prevailing rationales for women writing, and Joyce W. Warren tries to rescue her from classification as a sentimentalist instead of a satirist; Warren includes no "sentimental" pieces in her selection from Fern's work. One might argue, however, that Fern should be recognized as the author of "Thanksgiving Story" as well as "Critics," and that while she was more outspoken than most of her sister authors, she also resembles them in many ways.

Major Themes, Historical Perspectives, and Personal Issues

The rights of women and the problems and status of female authors are obvious Fern themes. I believe it is also important to emphasize Fern's treatment of class, since she is unusual for her time in portraying domestic servants and factory workers as well as middle-class women.

Students have been responsive to approaching Fern through the issue of names and their symbolism. When I was in graduate school studying nineteenth-century American literature, female writers other than Emily Dickinson were mentioned only to be ridiculed as having three names. To use more than two names, like Harriet Beecher Stowe, or two initials, like E. D. E. N. Southworth, was to be *ipso facto* a poor writer, and it was just as bad to adopt an alliterative pseudonym like Grace Greenwood or Millie Mayfield. I don't recall the professors ever referring to Grata Payson Sara Willis Eldredge Farrington Parton, "Fanny Fern."

The "Grata Payson" was supplied by the writer's father, who named her after the mother of a minister he admired; the rest of the family objected to "Grata," and in the first of a series of symbolic name changes, she became "Sara," discarding the influence of the father and his orthodox religion. Later in life Fern explained her pen name as inspired by happy childhood memories of her mother picking sweet fern leaves. In a further repudiation of patriarchal tradition Fern, although she is often referred to in literary histories as Sara Parton, did not use that name; she preferred her pseudonym, extending it to her personal life and becoming "Fanny" even to family and friends.

Ann Douglas Wood (see headnote) views the *nom de plume* "Fanny Fern" as an emblem of Fern's "artistic schizophrenia." She points out that "Fern" is a woodsy, flowery name typical of "sentimental" writers, while "Fanny" suggests the rebel (Fern, who was given the nickname "Sal Volatile" at the Beecher school, once remarked, "I never saw a 'Fanny' yet that wasn't as mischievous as Satan"). Wood, noting the two different types of sketches Fern wrote, concludes that she possessed "two selves, two voices, one strident and aggressive, the other conventional and sentimental." Mary Kelley, in *Private Woman, Public Stage* (Oxford, 1984), also stresses Fern's "dual identity" in arguing the thesis that female authors of the nineteenth century experienced a split between their private selves and public identities. (Teachers who plan to assign *Ruth Hall* should also see Linda Huf's comments on this issue in her chapter on the novel in *A Portrait of the Artist as a Young Woman* [Ungar, 1983].)

Although the "split personality" approach interests students and helps illuminate the cultural context in which women wrote, it can be overdone. Early in her career Fern was obviously searching for a voice, trying out the more conventional approach in pieces like "Thanksgiving Story" and expressing herself more daringly in "Soliloquy of a House-maid." But it could be argued that once she established herself, she successfully united the Fanny and the Fern in her writing—and in her life shed the identity given her by men and became the person she herself created. In any case, it is typical of Fern, who possessed the unusual ability to mock herself, to create a final irony by making fun of her pen name. She advised budding authors in search of a pseudonym to "bear in mind that nothing goes down, now-a-days, but *alliteration*. For instance, Delia Daisy, Fanny Foxglove, Harriet Honeysuckle, Lily Laburnum. . . ."

Significant Form, Style, or Artistic Conventions

Fern's writing is especially useful for getting students to think about style and tone, and the discussion can be related both to the split personality issue raised above and the question of literary worth. Although some students have considered Fern's style human and spontaneous, probably accounting in large measure for her popularity, others have criticized it as too loud ("noisy," "braying"). They tend to view the italics, capital letters, and exclamation points with suspicion ("unprofessional," "feminine," "schoolgirl"). One student claimed that a writer who employs expressions like "Heigho!" and "H-u-m-p-h!" cannot be "taken seriously." He could not explain why, any more than most students (or critics) have been able to explain very successfully what "sentimental" means and why it's bad to be so.

Original Audience

The question of literary value can easily be related to that of audience. Fern's "Thanksgiving Story" lends itself to discussion of these issues. The question of whether "Thanksgiving Story" is "worse" than the other selections by Fern and how so, can be used to provoke discussion of the standards by which literature is judged (and who does the judging) and of the differences between nineteenth- and twentieth-century readers.

Comparisons, Contrasts, Connections

Fern's work can easily be compared and contrasted with that of just about any woman of her time. She can also be paired with male writers, such as Walt Whitman (*Fern Leaves* and *Leaves of Grass*) and Ik Marvel (Donald Grant Mitchell), the essayist, who gained fame at about the same time as Fern. Or she can be treated along with other nineteenth-century humorists.

If Fern's relationship with Walt Whitman is to be emphasized, see J. F. McDermott, "Whitman and the Partons" (*American Literature* 29 [Nov. 1957] 316–19) and William White, "Fanny Fern to Walt Whitman: An Unpublished Letter" (*American Book Collector* 11 [May 1961] 8–9). In "Fern Leaves and Leaves of Grass" (*New York Times Book Review*, April 22, 1945) it is suggested that Whitman imitated *Fern Leaves* in choosing both his title and his binding, particularly the floral designs on the cover. Fern's review of *Leaves of Grass* is reprinted in Warren, pp. 274–77.

In a course that includes Harriet Jacobs's *Incidents in the Life of a Slave Girl* (1861), students will enjoy knowing that the "Mr. Bruce" for whom Jacobs works as a nursemaid was N. P. Willis, Fern's brother; Fern satirizes her social-climbing brother in "Apollo Hyacinth." Jacobs kept her writing of *Incidents* secret from Willis, she wrote her friend Amy Post, because "Mr. W is too proslavery he would tell me that it was very wrong and that I was trying to do harm or perhaps he was sorry for me to undertake it while I was in his family" (*Incidents*, ed. Jean Fagan Yellin, 1987, p. 232). Harriet Jacobs and Fanny Fern were friendly; for an account of their relationship, see Joyce W. Warren, *Fanny Fern* (see headnote).

Questions for Reading and Discussion/ Approaches to Writing

1. I prefer to have students read her without any initial intervention.
2. For the intrepid—have students try to imitate Fern's style. This demonstrates that it's not "natural," i.e., easy, but you may not be forgiven for this assignment. It is also illuminating to compare the original version of "Soliloquy of a Housemaid" (in Warren) and the collected version in this anthology—so that students can see how Fern revised her seemingly slapdash work.

Bibliography

Joyce W. Warren's *Fanny Fern: An Independent Woman* (1992) has become the standard biography. An overview of Fern's writings is available in Nancy A. Walker's *Fanny Fern* (Twayne, 1993).

Sojourner Truth (1797–1883)

Contributing Editor: Allison Heisch

Classroom Issues and Strategies

One reason why Sojourner Truth has not appeared in conventional American literature anthologies until now is that the texts are stenographic transcriptions of spontaneous speeches. Thus, even the orthography is "made-up." Students may tend to dismiss this as nonliterature. Also, the interior structure of the speeches does not follow expected expository modes (i.e., there's no "beginning," "middle," and "end"), so they are vulnerable to rigidly "logical" analysis.

Sojourner Truth offers a wonderful opportunity to raise large questions: What is literature? And what is American literature? Are speeches literature? Is it literature if you don't write it down yourself? What is the purpose of literature? It is useful to set these speeches for the students in the context of anti-slavery meetings, to describe where and how they were held, and also who participated. Students may have difficulty with these texts; old-fashioned close reading in class will help.

I like to talk about "unpopular ideas": Sojourner Truth has several of these! It is also useful to place her in the tradition of oral literature.

Responses to Truth vary widely, depending on the class. Some students may make the argument that she is hostile to men. Generally discussion goes in the direction of contemporary issues involving women.

Major Themes, Historical Perspectives, and Personal Issues

Why did racial equality take precedence over equality of the sexes? How can we explain the conflict between racial and gender equality? What is the difference between Sojourner Truth's argument and the contemporary argument for "comparable worth"?

Significant Form, Style, or Artistic Conventions

Ordinarily, we are able to separate a writer from her work. In this case, we have not only oral presentation, but also a style of presentation in which the speaker presents herself as the major character in the work. In some sense, therefore, she is the subject of her work. To what literary and quasi-literary categories could you assign these speeches (fiction, autobiography, prophecy)? How do they "violate" traditional genre boundaries? Where does oratory end and drama begin? These speeches provide a splendid opportunity to demonstrate to what extent our literary categories are a construct, one that not only defines and makes rules, but one that also excludes.

Original Audience

Because Sojourner Truth's speeches were transcribed and preserved by her admirers, it is by no means clear how her original audiences really responded. We have the laudatory side only. Just the same, it is apparent that to many of her contemporary listeners, she was a figure of mythic proportion. To get at the issue of audience, it's useful, first, to have the students identify the issues of continuing importance that she raises. Second, it is helpful to show them a contemporary parallel (such as Barbara Jordan's "We the People" speech) as a means of generating discussion.

Comparisons, Contrasts, Connections

Frederick Douglass ("What to the Slave Is the Fourth of July?") and Henry Highland Garnet ("An Address to the Slaves of the United States") show the tendency of abolitionist literature to regard slavery as a phenomenon affecting black men and, coincidentally, to consider the abuse of black women largely as an affront to their husbands and fathers. Truth's views can usefully be contrasted with those of some writers, black and white, who believed that women could best exercise power by influencing their husbands.

Questions for Reading and Discussion/ Approaches to Writing

1. What issues does Sojourner Truth raise that you consider to be of contemporary importance?
2. Compare the positions on civil rights taken by Frederick Douglass and Sojourner Truth.

Bibliography

Lerner, Gerda. "While the water is stirring I will step into the pool." *Black Women in White America: A Documentary History*. New York: 1973.

Stanton, Elizabeth Cady, et. al. "Sojourner Truth." *History of Woman's Suffrage*, 3 vols., 1881–1886. New York: 1970.

Frances Ellen Watkins Harper (1825–1911)

Contributing Editor: Elizabeth Ammons

Classroom Issues and Strategies

Two primary issues in teaching Harper are: (1) the high-culture aesthetic in which students have been trained makes it hard for them to appreciate Harper and find ways to talk about her; (2) most students' ignorance of nineteenth-century African-American history deprives them of a strong and meaningful historical context in which to locate Harper's work.

To address the first issue, I ask students to think about the questions and methods of analysis that they may bring to the study of literature in the classroom. What do we look for in "good" literature? Their answers are many but usually involve the following: It should be "interesting" and deal with "important" ideas, themes, topics. It should be intellectually challenging. The style should be sophisticated—by which they mean economical, restrained, and learned without being pretentious. It should need analysis—i.e., have many hidden points and many "levels" of meaning that readers (students) do not see until they get to class. Then we talk about these criteria: "Interesting" and "important" by whose standards? Theirs? *All* of theirs? Whose, then? *Why* is intellectually hard literature judged better than "easy" literature? Why is lean, restrained, educated style "better" than fullsome, emotional, colloquial, or vernacular style (except for keeping professors employed)?

The point here is to talk about the aesthetic students have been taught in school to value and to ask these questions: Where does it come from? Whose interests does it serve (in terms of class, race, ethnic group, and gender—both now and in the past)? What values does it reflect,

morally and spiritually (intellect is superior to feelings, transmitting tradition is a primary goal of high-culture literature, etc.)? Thinking about
our own aesthetic assumptions and expectations in these ways proves a
good way of getting us to see that what we probably accept unquestion-
ingly as "good art" (whether we "like" such art or not) is just one definition of "good art." We can now ask: What aesthetic is Harper writing out
of? Is hers the aesthetic we have just described, and is she simply not
very good at it, or—at best—only half-way good at it? Or is she speaking
and writing out of a different aesthetic—perhaps a mix of what we are
familiar with plus other things that many or all of us are not familiar
with?

   To address the second problem, the historical ignorance that can
hamper students' understanding of Harper, one useful strategy is to
assign a few short reports for students to present in class. The topics will
depend on what selections by Harper one is teaching, and what
resources are available, but might include such things as racist stereotypes of black people in newspaper cartoons in the nineteenth century;
women's resources against wife-abuse in the nineteenth century; the
formation of the WCTU (Women's Christian Temperance Union); the
division between white feminists and black people created by the fight
for the Fifteenth Amendment; the founding of the National Association
of Colored Women. Such reports can give a sense of the intense climate
of controversy out of which Harper wrote and can involve the students
in the process of creating a historical context for Harper. Also, having
students prepare these reports in pairs or small groups is a good way of
spreading the work around, counteracting problems of nervousness
about making presentations, and having them work corporately rather
than individually—which is particularly appropriate for Harper.

   Harper, like many other nineteenth-century writers, wrote to be
heard, not just read. Therefore, a good strategy is to have students prepare some of her work outside of class to deliver in class.

Major Themes, Historical Perspectives, and Personal Issues

Two major themes I emphasize in Harper are, first, her commitment
not to individual psychology, ethics, development, and fulfillment but to
the *group*. Harper, like Emerson, is ever the teacher and preacher, but
the philosophy that she comes out of and lives is not, like his,
individualistic—not focused on the self or Self. It is group-centered. I
think that this is one of the most important points to make about
Harper. Therefore I ask my students to think about this question: Is the

classic dominant-culture American schoolroom theme of the Individual vs. Society relevant to Harper? If so, where and how? If not (and often it is not), what question(s) about America does Harper place at the center? If we use her, a black woman, as "the American"—that is, if we follow her lead and place her at the center rather than at the margin—what does "America" mean? What dominant theme(s) define Harper's America?

Second, I emphasize that Harper is a political writer and a propagandist. Art and politics are not alienated for her but inseparably dependent: art is not above politics; it is the tool of politics. I ask the class to think about our customary high-culture disdain for art in the "service" of politics, our disdain for art as propaganda. Why do we have that disdain? What art is not political?

Significant Form, Style, or Artistic Conventions

Often Harper writes and speaks in popular forms. I ask the class to identify the forms and think about how they work. The sermon, the political stump-speech, melodrama, the ballad, African-American story-telling, and vernacular verse are among the forms Harper draws on. How do these forms work? What devices do they rely on (e.g., accessibility rather than abstruseness; repetition of the familiar; audience response/ recall/participation; deliberate emotion-stirring, etc.)? We talk about the appropriateness of these characteristics of form, style, and artistry to Harper's mission of reaching and affecting large numbers of people, including people not often written for or about with respect by white writers.

Original Audience

The question of Harper's current audience inevitably comes up in the discussion of aesthetics. Because we have been taught not to value the kind of literature she created or to know much about or take seriously the issues she addressed (group justice as opposed to individual development; wife abuse and alcoholism in the nineteenth century; voter fraud and corruption; lynching; divisions between black feminists and white feminists; employment barriers to middle-class blacks in the nineteenth century; black women as the definers of women's issues), most of us have not been exposed to Frances Ellen Harper. Clearly this will continue to change as the authority for identifying what is good, valuable, and important expands to include people traditionally excluded from the profession of professor (white women, people of color). Or will it? I ask how many students in the class plan to be teachers and scholars.

In her own time Harper was very popular and widely acclaimed, especially among black people. She was the best-known black poet between Phillis Wheatley and Paul Laurence Dunbar. "The Two Offers" is probably the first short story published in the U.S. by any black author. For many years *Iola Leroy* was considered the first novel written by a black American woman. Harper's public speaking was uniformly praised as brilliant. In light of the gap between Harper's reputation in her own day and the widespread ignorance about her today, audience as a social construct—as something that doesn't just "happen" but is constructed by identifiable social forces (economics; the composition of the teaching profession in terms of race, gender, and class)—and the issue of why we teach the authors we teach are central to discussion of Harper.

Comparisons, Contrasts, Connections

Many other writers compare well with Harper, but especially other black women writers in the anthology: Harriet Jacobs, Sojourner Truth, Alice Dunbar-Nelson, and Pauline Hopkins. Comparing these writers can give a glimpse of the range of black women writers' work in the nineteenth century, which was broad. It is very important to teach more than one or two black women writers before 1900 and to make comparisons. Otherwise there is a tendency to generalize one author's work and point of view into "the black woman's" perspective, of which there was not one but were many. That point—the existence of great difference and variety as well as common ground—should be stressed.

Questions for Reading and Discussion/ Approaches to Writing

1. Preparing an oral delivery, as suggested above, is an excellent way to get "inside" a work. Also a good exercise is to ask the class to choose one piece and extrapolate from it the aesthetic principles governing it. Before class they should try to arrive at a statement of what a particular poem or speech or piece of fiction does—the effect it is designed to have on the reader/listener—and how it accomplishes that end. Then have them form small groups and work together to make up and write down "A Brief Writer's Guide for Young Writers by Frances Ellen Watkins Harper" to discuss in class.
2. A good assignment for Harper is to ask students to think about her as a black woman writer. What did each of these three terms mean to her? How do the three terms clash? How do they cooperate?

Bibliography

Useful discussion can be found in Elizabeth Ammons, *Conflicting Stories: American Women Writers at the Turn into the Twentieth Century* (1991); Hazel V. Carby, *Reconstructing Womanhood: The Emergence of the Afro-American Woman Novelist* (1987); and Claudia Tate, *Domestic Allegories of Political Desire* (1992).

VOICES FROM THE SOUTHWEST

Juan Nepomuceno Seguin (1806–1890)

Contributing Editor: Genaro Padilla

Major Themes, Historical Perspectives, and Personal Issues

Students should have some background information on American settlement in Texas in the early 1830s and events leading up to the battle of the Alamo (1836) as well as the gradual increase of tension leading to the U. S.–Mexican War in Texas.

Seguin was born in San Antonio into a prominent Texas Mexican (*tejano*) family which had close ties with Stephen F. Austin, the leader of the first American settlers in Texas. Seguin rose to power rapidly in San Antonio, being elected *alcalde* at age eighteen. When events in Texas veered toward revolution in 1835, he sided with the Anglo separatists and organized a company of *tejano* volunteers.

The section of Seguin's *Personal Memoirs* printed here reveals an aspect of the Texas War for Independence little known among American readers: the invaluable participation of *tejanos* alongside the more celebrated figures of Sam Houston, Jim Bowie, and Davy Crockett. Like their American brothers-in-arms, the *tejanos* despised "the tyrannical government of Santa Anna" and yearned for representative and responsive government. In a clear and unadorned style, Seguin recounts the "efficiency and gallantry" of his *tejano* troops as they rode from San Antonio to San Jacinto.

After performing heroically at San Jacinto, the battle that assured Texas independence, Seguin returned to San Antonio to resume his political career. An ardent supporter of the Republic of Texas, he served in its Senate from 1838 to 1840, at which time he was elected mayor of San Antonio. He was the last Mexican-American to occupy that office until the 1980s.

Seguin's tenure as mayor was disastrous, largely because the growing Anglo population, with its intense and long-standing resentment of Mexicans, would not trust nor defer to a *tejano*. By 1842, the *tejanos* of San Antonio were moving away in the face of continuous intimidation and violence from Anglos. After a series of death threats, Seguin relocated his family in Mexico, the country against which he had taken up arms only six years before.

In Mexico, Seguin was coerced into military service and found himself in combat against American troops in the Mexican War of 1846-48. After the war, Seguin returned to Texas, by now homesick and thoroughly disillusioned. He lived there quietly until 1867 when, for reasons not altogether clear, he crossed the Rio Grande one last time, remaining in Mexico until his death.

(Biography and historical information contributed by Raymund Paredes.)

Bibliography

See material on Mariano Guadalupe Vallejo, immediately following.

Mariano Guadalupe Vallejo (1808–1890)

Contributing Editor: Genaro Padilla

Classroom Issues and Strategies

Students' lack of historical knowledge about the U.S.-Mexican War (1846–48), especially events in California, can be a problem. Some historical background needs to be given; Vallejo should be read as a colonized subject. His historical personal narrative gives the Mexican version of events.

Students often wonder why Vallejo seems politically contradictory. They ask whether he wrote other material and are curious about his social position.

Major Themes, Historical Perspectives, and Personal Issues

Vallejo's sense of betrayal comprises an important and intriguing theme. From the selection one can surmise that he actually favored American annexation of California, but was summarily imprisoned by a group of Americans he refers to as "thieves."

Like Seguin, Mariano Vallejo was born into a prominent family, in his case in Monterey, California. Vallejo early decided to pursue a career in both politics and the military and by age twenty-one had been elected to the territorial legislature and had distinguished himself in various campaigns against the Indians. Again like Seguin, Vallejo supported the American presence in his region, hoping that the *yanquis* would bring both prosperity and stability. Accordingly, Vallejo became one of the most prominent *California* supporters of the American annexation of California.

The movement toward American control of California accelerated with the Bear Flag Revolt of 1846. Vallejo was inexplicably taken prisoner by the troops of John C. Frémont and held for two months, an experience that should have raised doubt in Vallejo's mind about his pro-American sympathies. But Vallejo persisted in his allegiance and eventually served in the state's first senate. In the early 1850s he filed for validation of his Mexican land-grants, only to lose much of his property in a ruling by the United States Supreme Court. By the 1860s his fortune and influence had declined considerably, and a wiser Vallejo sat down to compose a "true history" of his territory, free of myths and lies. After a series of mishaps and distractions, he completed his five-volume chronicle and donated it to H. H. Bancroft, the celebrated California historian. Vallejo lived quietly thereafter, tending to the 280 acres of land he had left of his once-vast empire. Like Seguin, he looked back on his support of American expansion with great bitterness.

In "Six Dollars an Ounce," Vallejo writes of an economic revolution that changed California as decisively as San Jacinto changed the course of Texas history. He recounts how the Gold Rush of 1849 threw California into a frenzy. Previously reasonable men gave up respectable trades and careers to pursue the yellow metal. As Vallejo tells it, the Gold Rush unleashed the meanest of human qualities—distrust, avarice, and violence among them—and accelerated the destruction of traditional *California* culture. In the Americanization of California, Vallejo notes that he witnessed change but not progress.

(Biographical and historical information contributed by Raymund Paredes.)

Significant Form, Style, or Artistic Conventions

The Vallejo selection should be thought of as autobiographical historiography.

Original Audience

It was written as a revisionist version of historical events that Vallejo wished Americans would hear.

Comparisons, Contrasts, Connections

Comparison might be made with Native American orations on tribal displacement, uncertainty, subjugation.

Questions for Reading and Discussion/ Approaches to Writing

1. What is the standard version of the Bear Flag Revolt in California in 1846?
2. How does the Vallejo version humanize the Mexican populace?

Bibliography

Padilla, Genaro M. "The Recovery of Chicano Nineteenth-Century Autobiography." *American Quarterly* 40, no. 3 (Sept. 1981).

Pitt, Leonard. *The Decline of the Californios*. Los Angeles: University of California, 1969. A good background history of events during the period.

A CONCORD INDIVIDUALIST

Henry David Thoreau (1817–1862)

Contributing Editor: Wendell P. Glick

Classroom Issues and Strategies

In my experience, an understanding of Thoreau rarely follows the initial exposure to his writings. The appreciation of the profundity and subtlety of his thought comes only after serious study, and only a few of the most committed students are willing to expend the necessary effort. Many, upon first reading him, will conclude: that he was a churlish, negative, antisocial malcontent; or that he advocated that all of us should reject society and go live in the woods; or that each person has complete license to do as he/she pleases, without consideration for the rights of others; or that he is unconscionably doctrinaire. His difficult, allusive prose, moreover, requires too much effort. All such judgments are at best simplistic and at worst, wrong.

If an instructor is to succeed with Thoreau, strategies to meet these responses will need to be devised. The best, in my opinion, is to spend the time explicating to students key sentences and paragraphs in class and responding to questions. Above all, students must be given a knowledge of the premises of Romanticism that constitute Thoreau's world view.

Major Themes, Historical Perspectives, and Personal Issues

What are Thoreau's premises, the hypotheses from which he reasons? Even the most recalcitrant young reader should be willing to acknowledge that the question of most concern to Thoreau is a fundamental one: "How, since life is short and one's years are numbered, can one live most abundantly?" In other words, what values should one live by? "Where I Lived, and What I Lived For," from *Walden*, was Thoreau's personal answer, but he insists that he has no wish to prescribe for "strong natures" who have formulated their own value systems. All persons should live "deliberately," having separated the ends of life from the means, he argued; and the instructor should aid students to identify those ends. Accepting without examination current social norms, most persons give no thought, Thoreau charged, to the question of the values by which they live.

Thoreau's absorption with physical nature will be apparent to all students. Stressing the linkage of all living things, he was one of the first American ecologists. But the instructor should point out that for Thoreau nature was not an end in itself but a metaphor for ethical and spiritual truth. A walk in the woods therefore was a search for spiritual enlightenment, not merely a sensory pleasure. One should look "through" nature, as Thoreau phrased it, not merely "at" her. Honest seekers would find the same truths. Belief in the existence of a Moral Law had had by Thoreau's day a venerable history. Jefferson, for example, opened the Declaration of Independence with an appeal to the "self-evident" truths of the Moral Law. Thoreau's political allegiance was first to the Moral Law, and second to the Constitution, which condoned black slavery.

In his letters to H. G. O. Blake, Thoreau spells out his personal philosophy.

Significant Form, Style, or Artistic Conventions

Thoreau's angle of vision is patently that of American Romanticism, deeply influenced by the insights of Kant and Coleridge and Carlyle. But Thoreau's style differs markedly from that of Emerson, whose natural expression is through abstraction. Thoreau presents experience through concrete images; he "thinks in images," as Francis Matthiessen once observed, and employs many of the resources of poetry to give strength and compressed energy to his prose. Widely read himself, he is very allusive, particularly to classical literature, and is one of America's most inveterate punsters.

Original Audience

The recognition that Thoreau was one of America's greatest writers, like the recognition of Melville and Poe, has been a twentieth-century phenomenon. Emerson recognized Thoreau's importance when the younger man died in 1862, detailing both the dimensions of his genius and his personal eccentricities in an extended obituary. James Russell Lowell, shortly after Thoreau's death, accused him of having been a "skulker" who neglected his social responsibilities. But a few nineteenth-century friends like H. G. O. Blake, William Ellery Channing, and Emerson kept Thoreau's reputation alive until Norman Foerster, F. O. Matthiessen, and an expanded group of later twentieth-century critics became convinced of the qualities of mind and art that have elevated Thoreau into the first rank of American prose writers. *The Recognition of Henry David Thoreau* (Michigan, 1969) traces the vicissitudes of Thoreau's reputation from the publication of his first book, *A Week on the Concord and Merrimack Rivers* (1849) to his present eminence in the literary canon.

Comparisons, Contrasts, Connections

Walden is *sui generis* though there are contemporary writers, e.g., Wendell Berry and E. B. White, who have clearly been influenced by this book in both style and thought. N. C. Wyeth, the American painter, confessed to being "an enthusiastic student of Thoreau." Of major twentieth-century writers, Robert Frost has probably been most indebted to Thoreau. Martin Luther King's philosophy of passive resistance to the state is clearly borrowed from Thoreau's "Resistance to Civil Government." Some Thoreau scholars have discerned Thoreau's influence in Yeats, Tolstoy, and Gandhi.

Questions for Reading and Discussion/ Approaches to Writing

Though Thoreau's life was short, it was fully lived. Conscientiously, he recorded his thoughts in a journal that extends to many volumes over more than twenty years. Consequently, he has something to say about many of the issues that concerned people in his own time, and that still concern us today. I have found it profitable to ask students to write papers taking issue with him on some position he has argued, making certain that they fully understand what his position is. Thoreau is an economist, political theorist, philosopher, literary critic, poet, sociologist, naturalist, ecologist, botanist, surveyor, pencil maker, teacher, writer— even jack of manual trades, so that whatever a student's primary interest may be, the probability is that Thoreau had something to say about it.

The issues of bigotry and racism that so concerned Thoreau will always provide topics for student papers.

Bibliography

Research now extant on Thoreau would fill a fair-sized library. Particularly useful in getting a sense of its scope and variety is *The New Thoreau Handbook*, ed. Walter Harding and Michael Meyer (New York, 1980). This should be supplemented with the section on Thoreau in the annually published *American Literary Scholarship* (Duke), and the running bibliography in the *Thoreau Society Quarterly*. Very useful also are the many articles on Thoreau in the annual *Studies in the American Renaissance*, ed. Joel Myerson. Collections of critical essays on Thoreau have been edited by Sherman Paul, John Hicks, Wendell Glick, and Joel Myerson. The standard biography is still *The Days of Henry Thoreau* by Walter Harding (New York, 1965).

The Flowering of Narrative

Nathaniel Hawthorne (1804–1864)

Contributing Editor: Rita K. Gollin

Classroom Issues and Strategies

Some students find Hawthorne too gloomy, too dense, and too complex. And few understand Puritan beliefs about self, sin, America's moral mission, and so forth, as they evolved into the antithetical beliefs of transcendentalism.

To address these problems, try approaching Hawthorne as a riddler and wry joker who challenged all authority including his own. Students enjoy recognizing Hawthorne's self-mockery and his various forms of ironic self-presentation. Though self-mockery is most overt in Hawthorne's letters and prefaces (the introduction to "Rappaccini's Daughter" and "The Custom-House," for example), students can quickly discern the skepticism underlying Hawthorne's uses of laughter, his assessments of America's Puritan past, and his anatomization of his major characters. Introduce recurrent patterns of character, theme, image, and so forth, then invite students to identify variations on those patterns within Hawthorne's works.

Comment on Hawthorne's attempts to mediate between Puritan beliefs and Emerson's, then encourage students to locate how each of his fictions incorporates, accepts, or rejects particular beliefs. Alert them to Hawthorne's assumptions about what human wholeness and happiness require—including the interrelationship of the mind, heart, spirit, will, imagination, and accommodation (though not indulgence) of bodily needs.

One useful strategy is to ask students what a story is "about," then what it is also "about." They soon realize that the story is accessible even after a first reading, but also that informed attention expands its meaning.

Current debates about relative versus absolute literary value provide a useful context for discussing Hawthorne's reputation. Briefly sketch how criteria for judgment have changed over time (for example, after publication of *The Scarlet Letter,* after Hawthorne's death, during the centenary celebrations of his birth, during the heyday of New Criticism, and so forth), and provide some comments about current critical approaches to Hawthorne (such as comments by feminists and new historicists). Then invite discussion of why Hawthorne has been considered a major writer from the 1830s to the present.

Major Themes, Historical Perspectives, and Personal Issues

Hawthorne's major themes and thematic patterns include self-trust versus accommodation to authority; conventional versus unconventional gender roles; obsessiveness versus open-mindedness; hypocrisy versus candor; presumed guilt or innocence; forms of nurturance and destructiveness; the penalties of isolation; crimes against the human heart; patriarchal power; belief in fate or free will; belief in progress (including scientific, technological, social, and political progress) as opposed to nostalgia for the past; the truths available to the mind during dream and reverie; and the impossibility of earthly perfection.

Historical issues include marketplace facts—for example, where Hawthorne's short stories first appeared (unsigned and low-paid), which stories he chose to collect in *Twice-told Tales* and in later anthologies, why James T. Fields persuaded Hawthorne to complete *The Scarlet Letter* as a novel and why he prefaced it with "The Custom-House." Related issues include how each book was advertised, how well it sold, how much money Hawthorne earned for it, and how it was reviewed. Students should also know something about the whys and wherefores of Hawthorne's career options during and after college, of his undertaking literary hackwork and children's books, of his interlude at Brook Farm, of his appointments to the Boston Custom House, the Salem Custom House, and the Liverpool consulate, and of his efforts to win reinstatement at the Salem Custom House. Additional historical issues include Puritan versus Whig ideas about the self and the historical past; the political practices and social climate of Jacksonian democracy; and genteel assumptions about women's roles. Still other historical issues concern the particular place and period in which Hawthorne set each story.

Personal issues include the various ways Hawthorne's family history and specific events in his life informed his writings—most obviously the introduction to "Rappaccini's Daughter," "The Custom-House," and his letters and journals. Students can easily recognize how "Young Goodman Brown" and "The Custom-House" incorporate facts about his Puritan ancestors, and they are interested in asking such questions as whether the concern with female purity in "Rappaccini's Daughter" and "The Birth-mark" may reflect Hawthorne's anxieties in the aftermath of his marriage, and how Hawthorne's anxieties about his role as an artist are expressed in "The Birth-mark" and *The Scarlet Letter*. Students might also speculate about how Hawthorne's experiences of intimacy and deprivation in the aftermath of his father's death inform his fiction (for example, Robin's nostalgia for a home that excludes him). Other personal issues that interest students include Hawthorne's relationship to the Mannings's mercantile values, his antipathy to Salem, his experiences at Bowdoin College (including his nonconformity and his friendships with Briege, Pierce, and Longfellow), his lifelong strivings to develop his talents and support himself by his pen (during his self-defined "twelve lonely years," during his political appointments, and so forth), his secret engagement, and his identity as doting but fallible husband and father.

Significant Form, Style, or Artistic Conventions

1. Sketch versus tale and short story.
2. Romance versus novel.
3. Characters: recurrent "types" and interrelationships; authorial intrusion or objective display; heroism, villainy, and what Hawthorne seems to condemn, admire, or sadly accept.
4. Image clusters and patterns (for example, dark versus light, natural versus unnatural, sunshine and firelight versus moonlight and reflections, labyrinths).
5. Subjective vision (including fantasies, reveries, dreams, and narrator's questions about objective "reality.")
6. Narrative antecedents, including biblical parable, Spenserian romance, allegory (Dante, Bunyan, and others), Gothic horror tales, sentimental love stories, old wives' tales, fairy tales, and so on.
7. Reworking of notebook entries into fiction, and the relationship between earlier works and later ones.
8. Hawthorne's open-ended endings.

9. The relation of prefaces and expository introductions to Hawthorne's plots.

Original Audience

For the tales and sketches: students should know something about the gift books and periodicals that published Hawthorne's early work (including the practice of anonymous publication, payment, and other material published in a volume where Hawthorne appeared), and reasons for Hawthorne's difficulty in publishing a collection.

For the collections: Hawthorne's 1837 letter to Longfellow; Hawthorne's selections and sequence for a particular volume; his publishers; reviews and advertisements.

For the novels: Hawthorne's aims as expressed in letters, journals, and prefaces and through his narrators; marketing, sales, and reviews; James T. Fields as publisher, editor, banker, and friend—and securer of English copyrights.

Comparisons, Contrasts, Connections

- Irving: Use of America's past including folktales, popular myths, picturesque and sublime settings
- Poe: Use of Gothic settings, themes, and characters; interest in dreams and other threshold states, and in sensitive individuals' propensities to madness
- Melville: Plumbing of the dark depths of the human mind, antipathy to authority, celebration of individual striving and sympathetic nurturing
- Emerson: Celebration of striving toward self-fulfillment, criticism of hereditary privilege, egalitarian vision
- Stowe and the "damned mob of scribbling women": Celebration of women's capacities for dignity and heroism, religious piety
- James: Sensitive hero/narrator; psychological scrutiny; unresolved questions
- Conrad: Journeys to the heart of darkness; parallel of outer and inner experience
- Jewett: Minute attention to nature and to unheroic characters
- Welty: Comic irony, ambivalence, anti-authoritarianism, densely detailed landscapes
- Flannery O'Connor, Updike, Borges: Queries into the mystifying complexities of human behavior, dark comedy

Questions for Reading and Discussion/ Approaches to Writing

Provide some information about books that helped shape Hawthorne's imagination (including historical and scientific writings and the popular literature of his day). Students can better appreciate "Rappaccini's Daughter" after learning about Hawthorne's uses of Milton, Spenser, Dante, and the Bible, his variations on the courtship plot in popular magazines, and his skepticism about contemporary scientific experiments (as well as scientific controversy in Renaissance Padua).

Students enjoy connecting particular works with subsequent ones— most obviously, tracing connections of "Mrs. Hutchinson," "Young Goodman Brown," "My Kinsman, Major Molineux," "The Minister's Black Veil," Hawthorne's letters to Fields, and *The Scarlet Letter*.

"Cultural" questions that students enjoy addressing include attitudes toward art in general and fiction in particular in nineteenth-century America. (Here they need definitions of such terms as picturesque and sublime.)

Formal questions that students can ask of each story include a comparison of the first and last views of a particular character; Hawthorne's ambivalent treatment of women, writers, and artists, but also father figures; the questions the narrator raises but leaves unanswered; Hawthorne's use of "preternatural ambiguity"—offering alternative naturalistic explanations for what seems to be supernatural; exposition versus dramatized scene; parallels between inner and outer landscapes; and a story's formal design (symmetries, contrasts, repetitions, suspense, and climax, and so forth.)

Bibliography

In addition to the secondary works mentioned in the anthology, I would recommend recent books on Hawthorne and his period by Nina Baym, Michael Davitt Bell, Sacvan Bercovitch, Gillian Brown, Laurence Buell, and Philip Fisher, but also books written decades ago by Richard Harter Fogle, Roy R. Male, Leo Marx, and F. O. Matthiessen.

Caroline Kirkland (1801–1864)

Contributing Editor: Judith Fetterley

Classroom Issues and Strategies

Most of the students I have taught love Caroline Kirkland. They find her eminently contemporary. Her prose style is accessible, she is funny, and she deals with a subject familiar to nearly all Americans—the frontier. Some students are put off by her middle-class bias and perspective; they find her attitudes toward the locals patronizing and they object to the fact that (unlike Jewett) Kirkland provides very little space for the stories of any of these people as told by themselves.

Kirkland's letters sound like they were written yesterday to the students reading the letter. One obvious way of breaking open the text and inviting discussion is to ask students to pick one of her "natives" and have them write what they imagine that person would say about their new neighbor, Caroline Kirkland, if they wrote a letter to one of their friends who has moved farther west.

Students often wonder why they have never heard of Kirkland before. They want to know what else she wrote. They wonder why she is so concerned with issue of manners and ask what happened when she published her book.

Major Themes, Historical Perspectives, and Personal Issues

Kirkland is accessible in part because she is writing about a subject that has been made central to the study of American culture—the frontier, the movement west of white settlers. Kirkland is important because she is dealing with this phenomenon from the point of view of the woman who was required, often not of her own will, to follow the man to his new home. She writes specifically of the cost to women of the male model of "upward mobility"—the pattern of constantly moving on under the guise of improving one's position. This theory of "improvement" of course takes no account of the woman's position, which is usually worsened as a result. Thus the most important feature of Kirkland for the survey course is the fact that she inserts the woman's perspective into this male cultural pattern. Kirkland's work thus provides the context for discussing the commitment of the mid-century women writers to values of home, domesticity, etc.

Kirkland is equally important as an example of a relatively early American woman writer who successfully established a voice. The instructor should be familiar with Kirkland's essay "Literary Women," collected in *A Book for the Home Circle* (1853), and included in the forthcoming volume of Kirkland's work from the Rutgers Press American Women Writers series. Kirkland was well aware of the prejudices against women writers and of the strictures governing what they were and were not supposed to write. Her decision to lace her text with literary references may in part have stemmed from her desire to define herself clearly as a literary woman and to defy the strictures and the stereotypes. In a context where there was so much harassment of women writers, her voice is remarkably clear and confident. She writes with a sense of authority and conviction that is not modulated through any other agency. She writes because she likes to write, not because she is trying to save the world or support her children. She is a rare example of an early American woman writer who wrote carefully and published only what she felt was well written.

Significant Form, Style, or Artistic Conventions

First, Kirkland defines herself as a realist. Since American literary history has been based, until very recently, on a study of the works of male American writers, the governing generalization insists that realism in American literature is a post–Civil War phenomenon. However, American women writers were experimenting with realism in the decades before the Civil War and Caroline Kirkland was among the first, the most explicit, and the most articulate. Clearly defining herself against the romantic views of the West provided by contemporary male writers, Kirkland claims to write the truth about Michigan, which means that she intends to include the difficulties that face women who try to put together three meals a day in the wilderness, the state of the Michigan roads with their enormous pot holes, and the general slovenliness of the "natives." So certainly any discussion of Kirkland needs to address her conception of realism and the general contours of American literary history that emerge from including women writers in the map of the territory.

Second, Kirkland identifies herself as participating in a tradition set by women writers. She ends her preface to *A New Home* with a reference to "Miss Mitford's charming sketches of village life" and with a "humble curtsey." It is important to explore the degree to which Kirkland establishes throughout her text her connection to a tradition of women writers presenting a woman's point of view. As is clear from the preface, Kirkland embraces an iconography that clearly identifies her as a woman writer (men don't curtsey) and she wishes to remind her readers that they are reading a work written by a woman. In the process of so doing, she is also attempting to explore the nature of a woman's aesthetics. Implicitly, and on occasion explicitly, she is asking, what kind of book does a woman write, given the nature of woman's experience and perspective?

One can also raise here the question of genre—to what extent is Kirkland's voice, her authority, tied to her use of a relatively unconvention-ridden genre, namely the letter home? Is she freed to do her best because she is not trying to be a great writer but is trying only to write interesting letters to the folks back home? Students might be encouraged to look into the use of the letter as a form for published writing by both men and women in the nineteenth century.

Original Audience

As I have said earlier, Kirkland is useful for raising the larger question of the relation of the nineteenth-century American women writers to their audience. Nineteenth-century white middle-class American male writers had problems establishing an audience, a sense of who they were writing to. A new view could and should question these assumptions. Hawthorne's preface to *The Scarlet Letter*, the chapter on the Custom-House, can serve perhaps as a paradigm for the male situation. Here Hawthorne reveals his fear that he is speaking to no one except himself. Kirkland, on the other hand, has a very clear sense of the "you" at the other end of her letter. One can certainly raise with students the question as to why it is that Kirkland might have such a clear sense of audience. To what degree does it have to do with the world she describes women as inhabiting—a world in which loved ones are left behind, a world in which the letter (and think of the implications of this fact—here we look forward to *The Color Purple*) was left in the hands of women, a world in which there was a clear sense of community and of someone who would want to know what was happening to their daughters who had gone west?

It seems fairly obvious that Kirkland assumed her readers would be of the same social class as herself. Whether or not she assumed her readers would be primarily women is a more complex question. My own sense of Kirkland leads me to believe that she assumed a readership made up of men as well as women, that she was not of that group of women writers who were writing essentially to women even though they knew and hoped that men might read their books and thus overhear their conversation. But I also think Kirkland took her women readers seriously and wrote at least in part to educate them.

Comparisons, Contrasts, Connections

I have already suggested many points of comparison. I will just reiterate them here. Kirkland can be compared with many male writers in terms of her presentation of the frontier and the experience of westward and "upward" mobility. She can also be compared with many male writers in terms of her attitudes toward and handling of the issue of class. A writer like Hawthorne is so completely class-bound that class is never even an issue in his work. In many of the classes I have taught on Kirkland, I have been able to use students' anger at Kirkland's classism to raise the issue of class prejudice in writers like Hawthorne. Many students have come to realize that writers like Hawthorne protect themselves, albeit unconsciously, against charges of classism by simply never raising class as an issue. Kirkland is at least aware that American society is profoundly affected by the issue of class. Kirkland can also be compared to male writers in terms of the question of audience, as discussed above.

Kirkland can be fruitfully compared with other nineteenth-century American women writers in terms of the issue of voice. Students can compare the authority with which Kirkland speaks to the less secure voice of certain other women writers. She can also be compared with other women writers in terms of her commitment to realism and in terms of her commitment to presenting the woman's story.

Bibliography

I refer the instructor to the discussion of Kirkland in Annette Kolodny's *The Land Before Her* and in my own *Provisions*.

There is also a Twayne series book on Kirkland that is useful for an overview but does not provide much in the way of criticism and would not be of much use in the classroom.

The Rutgers Press American Women Writers series has a volume of Kirkland under contract and the introduction to that volume should be very useful.

Harriet Beecher Stowe (1811–1896)

Contributing Editor: Jane Tompkins

Classroom Issues and Strategies

The primary problems you are likely to encounter in teaching Stowe are (1) the assumption that she is not a first-rate author because she has only recently been recognized and has traditionally been classed as a "sentimental" author, whose works are of historical interest only; (2) by current standards, Stowe's portrayal of black people in *Uncle Tom's Cabin* is racist; and (3) a lack of understanding of the cultural context within which Stowe was working.

In dealing with the first problem, you need to discuss the way masterpieces have been selected and evaluated. Talk about the socioeconomic and gender categories that most literary critics, professors, and publishers have belonged to in this country until recently, explaining how class and gender bias have led to the selection of works by white male authors.

The second problem calls for an explanation of cultural assumptions about race, which would emphasize the way—historically— scientific beliefs about race have changed in this country between the seventeenth century and our day. For her time, Stowe was fairly enlightened, although her writing perpetuates stereotypes that have since been completely discredited.

The third problem requires that the instructor fill the class in on the main tenets of evangelical Protestantism and the cult of domesticity, which were central to Stowe's outlook on life and to her work. Beliefs about the purpose of human life (salvation), the true nature of reality (i.e., that it is spiritual), the true nature of power (that it ultimately resides in Christian love), and in the power of sanctity, prayer, good deeds, and Christian nurture would be crucial here.

One useful device is to have different groups of students (three or four in each group) read some of the classic works of American criticism—e.g., F. O. Matthiessen, Richard Chase, R. W. B. Lewis, D. H. Lawrence—and then report to the class why the assumptions that underlie these works made it impossible for their authors to include Stowe or other women authors in their considerations. The purpose is to demonstrate how critical bias determines from the start what work will be thought important and valuable and which will be completely ignored or set at a discount. (The groups meet with me to plan their presentation to the class beforehand. Usually I encourage them to use an imaginative format—e.g., talk show, debate, allegorical dramatization.)

Students love to talk about Augustine St. Clair and to speculate whether Uncle Tom or George Harris is the real hero of *Uncle Tom's Cabin*.

Major Themes, Historical Perspectives, and Personal Issues

Two of the historical issues that are important have already been referred to: evangelical Christianity, and the cult of domesticity. To this should be added the abolitionist crusade in the 1850s, the furor over the passage of the Fugitive Slave Law, and the change in the temper of the country after the Civil War—a turn from moral to social reform, and from romanticism to realism in literature—which accounts for the change in the temper and tone of Stowe's writing in this period.

Significant Form, Style, or Artistic Conventions

The biblical overtones of much of Stowe's prose, the emotionalism of her rhetoric, her addresses to the reader, and the highly oratorical nature of her prose need to be discussed in relation to the predominance of sermons and religious writing in the 1850s and of the view of language which held that words should appeal to the feelings and make ideas accessible to as wide a range of people as possible. In other words, the ideology of Stowe's style is evangelical and democratic, rather than elitist and aestheticizing, aiming for clarity and force over formal innovation.

It should be stressed that Stowe was a brilliant writer of dialogue, one of the masters of American realism before realism became the dominant literary mode; she also had a powerful grasp of literary character. (It is no accident that three of the characters in *Uncle Tom's Cabin* have become bywords in American culture—little Eva, Uncle Tom, and Simon Legree). Stowe also exploited the philosophical possibilities of the novel as a genre, discussing and dramatizing in fictional form complex theological, moral, and political issues of her day.

Original Audience

The astounding popularity of Stowe's first novel is worth noting—she was probably the best-known American of her time throughout the world. *Uncle Tom's Cabin* appealed to people regardless of social class, although it was unpopular in the South, after its initial reception there (which was favorable in some quarters) and was met with only a qualified enthusiasm by black readers in the North. Changes in beliefs about race, gender, religion, and literary value have made *Uncle Tom's Cabin* somewhat less universally appealing today, though it still retains its power to move readers in a way that very few works of the period do.

Comparisons, Contrasts, Connections

Stowe can be usefully compared to Emerson, whose vision of ideal existence, as put forward in essays like "Self-Reliance" and "The American Scholar" is sharply at odds with hers. Emerson's emphasis on individual integrity and self-cultivation, envisioning a time when "man will deal with man as sovereign state with sovereign state" contrasts with Stowe's ideal of a community of co-workers, bound together by Christian love, mutual sympathy, and a common purpose (for instance, the Quaker kitchen scene in *Uncle Tom's Cabin*, and the circle of women around Miss Prissy in *The Minister's Wooing*).

Hawthorne is another author whom it is interesting to compare with Stowe: His view of slavery was diametrically opposed to Stowe's— he condoned it—and his approach to writing, as well as to life in general, is skeptical where hers is believing; self-doubting where hers is self-trusting; detached and withdrawn where hers is active and participatory.

Questions for Reading and Discussion/ Approaches to Writing

1. Topics for discussion
   Discussion questions should depend on the interest of the instructor. But I would encourage people to use Stowe's work as an opportunity to discuss the issue of canon formation: What makes a literary work "good"? Can ideas of what is good change over time? Why in our own century was Stowe ignored in favor of writers like Hawthorne and Melville? Another approach might foreground students' emotional responses to Stowe's writing (it's helpful to ask students to write first about how they felt and use that as a basis for discussion). Some questions to ask: What's the role of emotion in understanding a work of literature? Is Stowe's writing too emotional?

2. Some students might want to compare Stowe to other authors, especially Hawthorne and Emerson. Others might want to think about the text in a more personal way, perhaps looking at issues of race in *Uncle Tom's Cabin* as a starting point for considering their own experience of race, or asking what contemporary issues they find comparable in importance to the issue of slavery in Stowe's day.

Herman Melville (1819–1891)

Contributing Editor: Carolyn L. Karcher

Classroom Issues and Strategies

The primary problems I have encountered in teaching Melville are the difficulty of the language and the complexity of the narrative point of view. This is particularly true of "Benito Cereno," but *Billy Budd* and "The Paradise of Bachelors and the Tartarus of Maids" also present problems for students unaccustomed to allusive and circuitous language and a complex narrative stance. Students usually find "Bartleby" and "The Encantadas" much more accessible. "Hawthorne and His Mosses" is daunting to students because of its allusiveness. It also needs to be set in the context of debate over how nineteenth-century American writers should go about producing an authentic national literature.

Each of the Melville selections demands a somewhat different strategy. What works best for me is not to teach Melville's writings together in a separate unit, but to group individual Melville pieces with texts by other authors on similar themes. For example, "Hawthorne and His Mosses" would make most sense to students in a unit on debates over literary nationalism and aesthetic theory, which could include Emerson's "The American Scholar," Poe's "The Philosophy of Composition" and review of Hawthorne's *Twice-Told Tales*, Fuller's "A Short Essay on Critics," and Whitman's 1855 Preface to *Leaves of Grass* and *Democratic Vistas*. A unit on the Transcendentalists (Emerson, Thoreau, and Fuller) can be used to introduce such themes as individualism versus social responsibility (Emerson's "Self-Reliance" and Thoreau's "Resistance to Civil Government"); alienation and the critique of industrial capitalism (Thoreau's *Walden*); the critique of patriarchy and marriage as an institution, the parallels between the oppression of women and the enslavement of blacks, and the deconstruction of "true womanhood" and "woman's sphere" as ideological concepts (Fuller's *Woman in the Nineteenth Century*). In a follow-up unit of fiction illustrating these themes, "Bartleby" and "Billy Budd" would fit nicely with the Thoreau selections, while "The Paradise of Bachelors and the Tartarus of Maids" and the Hunilla sketch from "The Encantadas" would work well after Fuller, along with Elizabeth Stoddard's "Lemorne *Versus* Huell," Alice Cary's "Uncle Christopher's," and Caroline Kirkland's *A New Home*. In my own current syllabus, I introduce the issue of women's rights by teaching Sarah Grimké's *Letters on the Equality of the Sexes, and the Condition of Woman* (#8), selections from Fuller's *Woman in the Nineteenth Century*, Stanton's "Declaration of Sentiments," Fanny Fern's "Hints to Young Wives," "Soliloquy of a Housemaid," and "Working-Girls of New York," and Sojourner Truth's "A'n't I a Woman?" I then devote several sessions to varieties of narrative and representations of women, in which I group "The Paradise of Bachelors and the Tartarus of Maids" and the Hunilla sketch together with Poe's "Ligeia" and "The Oval Portrait," Hawthorne's "The Birth-mark" and "Rappaccini's Daughter," Kirkland's *A New Home*, Cary's "Uncle Christopher's," and Stoddard's "Lemorne *Versus* Huell." "Benito Cereno" obviously cries out to be assigned with other texts on slavery. Any of the following would work well: David Walker's *Appeal*, Henry Highland Garnet's 1843 "Address to the Slaves of the U.S.A.," Thomas Wentworth Higginson's "Nat Turner's Insurrection," Wendell Phillips's "Toussaint L'Ouverture," Douglass's *Narrative*, Jacobs's *Incidents in the Life of a Slave Girl*, Lydia Maria Child's "Slavery's Pleasant Homes," and selections from her *Appeal*, and Stowe's *Uncle Tom's Cabin*. Olaudah Equiano's *Interesting Narrative* also helps illuminate "Benito Cereno," though it is probably best to teach it with eighteenth-century selections.

I generally try not to overwhelm students with long analyses of style and point of view, but some brief treatment of these matters is indispensable, especially in the case of "Benito Cereno." I often begin by reading key passages aloud to the students and having them analyze the tone of Melville's rhetoric. When they actually hear the tone, they can usually pick up the undercurrent of satire in "The Paradise of Bachelors," the smug insensitivity of Bartleby's employer, and the sense that both Delano and the reader are being subtly mocked.

The question of tone leads easily into the issues of narrative point of view and audience. It is, of course, essential for students to realize that Bartleby's story is narrated by his boss and that "Benito Cereno," though in the third person, is narrated primarily from Delano's point of view, except for the Deposition, which represents Benito Cereno's point of view. After establishing these facts, I ask the students to consider why

Melville did not choose instead to narrate his stories from the viewpoints of Bartleby, Babo, and the factory operatives in "Tartarus of Maids."

It is extremely effective to emphasize the continuing applicability of Melville's insights to our own times. Some of the issues his fiction raises are more relevant than ever. Many students (and their parents) work at jobs as meaningless and dead-end as Bartleby's and identify strongly with him. One student described the law copyists as "living xerox machines." Other students have drawn parallels between Bartleby and the homeless. The disparities between rich and poor are even more glaring now than at the time Melville wrote "The Paradise of Bachelors and the Tartarus of Maids" and the phenomenon called the "feminization of poverty" adds another relevant twist to those disparities. In the 1960s "Benito Cereno" evoked Malcolm X and the Black Panthers. Today it evokes the struggle in South Africa. *Billy Budd* was perhaps never more relevant than during the Reagan-Bush era, with its wholesale glorification of militarism and its rollback of democratic rights in the name of national security.

The most persistent questions my students raise are why Melville chose to address issues of such vital importance through literary strategies so oblique and circuitous, and whether these strategies were at all effective in subverting his readers' ideological assumptions, let alone transforming their political consciousness.

Major Themes, Historical Perspectives, and Personal Issues

A major source of Melville's continuing power is the prescient insight he displays into the central problems of our culture: alienation; violence against women and the repression of the "feminine in man" that usually accompanies it; the widening gap between a decadent ruling class and the workers it immiserates; racism and an ever-more-brutal assault against the world's peoples of color; an unbridled militarism that threatens our very existence while demanding that we resign our civil liberties and human rights in the name of national security. Thus the most effective way of teaching Melville is to encourage students to draw contemporary lessons from the historical predicaments he dramatizes so compellingly.

Each story, of course, centers around a different theme. In teaching "Bartleby" and "The Paradise of Bachelors and the Tartarus of Maids," I emphasize Melville's critique of capitalism and the alienation it produces. "The Communist Manifesto" and Marx's essays "Estranged Labor," "The Meaning of Human Requirements," and "The Power of

Money in Bourgeois Society," from *The Economic and Philosophic Manuscripts of 1844* are extraordinarily relevant to these two stories and illuminate them in startling ways. However, I find it preferable to let Marx indirectly inform the approach one takes to the stories, rather than to get sidetracked into a discussion of Marx. A secondary theme in "Bartleby" is the Christian ethic of Matthew 25, which Melville counterpoises against the capitalist ethic of Wall Street (see Bibliography for useful articles on this subject).

"The Paradise of Bachelors and the Tartarus of Maids" naturally invites a feminist as well as a Marxist approach. Margaret Fuller's *Woman in the Nineteenth Century,* Sarah Grimké's *Letters on the Equality of the Sexes, and the Condition of Woman,* and Lydia Maria Child's *Letters from New York* #50 (Women's Rights) provide a ready-made framework for a feminist analysis of that story. The Hunilla sketch in "The Encantadas" likewise shows that Melville's sympathy for women as victims of patriarchy extended to classes of women invisible to most of his peers, and here, too, Fuller is very relevant. Though "Benito Cereno" and *Billy Budd* do not focus on women, a feminist approach can enrich the students' understanding of key episodes and subthemes.

In "Benito Cereno," for example, Delano's racist stereotypes not only prevent him from recognizing that slave revolt has occurred on board the *San Dominick,* but distort his perception of the African women's role in that revolt. Just as Babo protects his fellow rebels from discovery by catering to Delano's stereotypes about blacks as faithful slaves, so the African woman Delano ogles does so by catering to his stereotypes about African women as sexual objects and primitive children of nature. By reading between the lines of the Deposition from a feminist perspective, we see that the African women have probably been sexually victimized by both their master and Don Benito and that they have played an active role in the revolt. Melville's references to the "inflaming" songs and dances they sing while their men are fighting indicate his probable familiarity with such sources as Equiano's narrative, which speaks of African women's participation in warfare.

Similarly in *Billy Budd,* Melville connects his critique of militarism and the dehumanization it generates with a critique of Western culture's polarization of masculine and feminine. The feminine imagery Melville uses to describe Billy suggests that he represents what Vere later calls the "feminine in man," instructing his drumhead court that "she must be ruled out" of their deliberations. It also suggests that one of the roots of Claggart's and Vere's homosexual attraction to Billy is his embodiment of the "feminine in man" that they have repressed in themselves and must continue to repress by killing Billy. Here again, Margaret Fuller's analysis of the ways in which patriarchy victimizes men as well as women is relevant.

"Benito Cereno" obviously needs above all to be set in the contexts of the antebellum slavery controversy and of the prior historical events to which the story refers (summarized in the footnotes): the Spanish Inquisition; the introduction of African slavery into the Americas under Charles V; the African slave trade and its relationship to the activities of sixteenth- and seventeenth-century English buccaneers; the Santo Domingo slave uprising of 1797–1804; the slave revolt on board the Spanish ship *Tryal* that the real Captain Delano had helped suppress; and the uncannily similar slave revolt that occurred on board the Spanish slave-trading schooner *Amistad* in 1839 (for useful articles on these aspects of the story, see the Bibliography below). As mentioned under "Classroom Issues and Strategies" above, the easiest means of teaching "Benito Cereno" in historical context is to assign it in conjunction with other texts on slavery.

Billy Budd reverberates with implications for the nuclear age and its strategy of Mutually Assured Destruction (MAD). Readers of the 1990s will also find Melville's exploration of Vere's and Claggart's repressed homosexuality highly pertinent to current debates over ending the ban against gays in the military. Teachers should not be afraid to exploit the story's contemporary relevance, but they should also set the story in its twin historical contexts—1797, the date of the action, and 1886–91, the period of composition. See H. Bruce Franklin's "From Empire to Empire," cited below, for an invaluable discussion of these historical contexts.

I have tried to provide biographical facts germane to the stories in the introduction and notes. Teachers might point out, however, that "Bartleby" draws on Melville's experiences of working as a clerk for a brief period and also reflects attitudes he must have associated with his brother Allan, a lawyer; that Elizabeth Shaw Melville's debilitating pregnancies, as well as an actual visit to a paper mill, helped generate the feminist insights Melville displays in "The Paradise of Bachelors and the Tartarus of Maids"; that Judge Lemuel Shaw's conservative views on slavery and controversial role as the first northern judge to send a fugitive slave back to his master may explain the circuitous form Melville adopts in "Benito Cereno"; and that the suicide of Melville's son Malcolm in 1867 may have some bearing on *Billy Budd*.

Significant Form, Style, or Artistic Conventions

The traditional grouping of Melville with Hawthorne and Poe obscures not only the social vision, but the concept of art differentiating Melville from such canonical figures. Unlike them, Melville persistently rejects "the symmetry of form attainable in pure fiction," holding instead to the principle that "Truth uncompromisingly told will always have its ragged edges." Teachers should point out the way in which Melville deliberately subverts formalist conventions in "Benito Cereno" and *Billy Budd* by appending the Deposition and the three chapters of sequel that force readers to determine the truth for themselves. It might also be useful to point out that the concept of art Melville articulates at the end of *Billy Budd* directly opposes Vere's doctrine of "measured forms" (see Edgar A. Dryden, cited below). In contextualizing Melville with writers like Olaudah Equiano, David Walker, Henry Highland Garnet, Thomas Wentworth Higginson, Frederick Douglass, Lydia Maria Child, Margaret Fuller, Alice Cary, Fanny Fern, Harriet Beecher Stowe, among others, teachers might suggest comparisons between their aesthetic of "Art for Truth's Sake" (as Elizabeth Stuart Phelps called it) and Melville's concept of literature as "the great Art of Telling the Truth" (delineated in his review "Hawthorne and His Mosses"). Although Melville's short fiction is much less accessible and more oblique than the protest writings of these other authors, it is important to remember that four out of his first five books were autobiographical accounts of his life as a sailor—a genre not very different from the slave narrative. All five are filled with explicit and passionate social protest, culminating in *White-Jacket*'s powerful appeal for the abolition of flogging in the navy, another parallel with the slave narrative.

Stylistically, I like to emphasize Melville's use of irony and grim humor. If one adopts Babo's point of view in reading "Benito Cereno," one is struck again and again by the humor of the story. The shaving scene is one of the best examples, and I like to go over it at length, beginning with the way in which Babo responds to Don Benito's slip of the tongue about Cape Horn by suggesting that Don Benito and Delano continue the conversation while he shaves his master.

"Bartleby," too, presents many examples of Melville's incisive irony and grim humor. See, for instance, the scene in which Bartleby announces that he will "do no more writing" and asks the narrator, "Do you not see the reason for yourself?"—to which the narrator, who does not see, responds by postulating that Bartleby's vision has become "temporarily impaired."

Original Audience

I generally let the subject of audience come up spontaneously, which it nearly always does. The students often infer—correctly—that Melville was writing for an audience linked by sympathies of class and race to the lawyer in "Bartleby," the bachelors in "Paradise," and Captain Delano in "Benito Cereno." I then talk a little about Melville's social milieu and the readership of *Harper's* and *Putnam's*. (The latter was moderately anti-slavery, and distinctly more progressive than *Harper's*, which Lydia Maria Child characterized as pro-slavery; nevertheless, its readers shared the attitudes Delano exemplifies.)

The question of audience is related to the literary strategy Melville adopted. In discussing Melville's rhetoric and the discomfort it provokes in a reader who has an obscure sense of being made fun of, we speculate about whether Melville hoped to jolt readers into thinking about the implications of their attitudes.

Comparisons, Contrasts, Connections

See suggestions above under "Classroom Issues and Strategies." Bartleby has often been seen by critics as a Thoreau-like figure in his passive resistance, but Thoreau's perspective on industrialization, capitalism, and alienation actually contrasts with Melville's, which is closer to Marx's.

Although instructors who have previously paired "Paradise and Tartarus" with Rebecca Harding Davis's "Life in the Iron-Mills" will miss the latter (now in Volume 2 of *The Heath Anthology*), they will find that Alice Cary's "Uncle Christopher's" also makes an interesting pairing. In different ways, both stories reveal the world of the patriarchs to be as sterile and perverted as the world of the patriarchs' victims. Both "Uncle Christopher's" and "Tartarus" are pervaded by images of freezing cold and make metaphorical use of an icy landscape. The seven girls winding seven skeins of blue yarn and knitting seven blue stockings in Cary's story recall the "blank-looking" factory girls "blankly folding blank paper" in Melville's; in both cases the women are silent and only the noise of their work is heard. While Melville's story comments on how women factory operatives are deprived of a home life and turned into machines, Cary's story shows how the home itself is turned into a factory, whose "boss" is not an "old bachelor" but the patriarchal father.

The Hunilla sketch can fruitfully be compared with both Harriet Jacobs's *Incidents in the Life of a Slave Girl* and Lydia Maria Child's "Slavery's Pleasant Homes." All three portray women who struggle to keep their dignity in the face of rape or sexual harassment, and all three raise the issue of how to narrate a woman's experience of sexual violation without demeaning her, catering to prurient curiosity, or collaborating in her silencing.

The reasons for grouping "Benito Cereno" with other works about slavery are obvious, but teachers can help students make specific connections between the slaves on board the *San Dominick* and Douglass's battle with Covey, between the African women among them and Equiano's reminiscences of women's participation in battle, between the *San Dominick's* "true character" as a slave ship and Equiano's description of the slave ship that transported him across the Atlantic, between Melville's use of the Deposition (and of the three appended chapters in *Billy Budd*) and Child's use of newspaper accounts at the end of "Slavery's Pleasant Homes."

At the same time, one can contrast Melville's rhetorical strategy with the more direct strategy of appeal for the reader's sympathy that other anti-slavery writers adopt. One can further contrast the male and female writers' perspectives on slavery. For Melville and Douglass, the slave's attempt to reclaim his "manhood" by fighting back and risking his life for freedom is central, while the female slave's attempt to defend her children and to resist the violation of her humanity through rape is peripheral. For Stowe and Jacobs the reverse is true; Child balances the two perspectives in "Slavery's Pleasant Homes."

Billy Budd invites comparison with Thoreau's essay on civil disobedience, which casts an ironic light on the arguments Vere uses to have Billy sentenced to hanging. If teachers decide to group *Billy Budd* with the writings on slavery, rather than with those on industrialism and the oppression of women, they can underscore the parallels Melville suggests between the condition of sailors and that of slaves (a theme he develops at great length in *White-Jacket*). The Black Handsome Sailor who appears in the opening pages of *Billy Budd* and incarnates the ideal of the Handsome Sailor more perfectly than Billy also provides a strong, positive counter-image of blacks, offsetting the seemingly negative stereotypes presented in "Benito Cereno." Formally as well, the two stories have much in common and invite comparison with "Slavery's Pleasant Homes."

Questions for Reading and Discussion/ Approaches to Writing

I do not like to use study questions because I find them too directive. I prefer to train students to become attentive readers through more indirect strategies. My principal strategy (borrowed from H. Bruce Franklin) is to give students a quiz requiring them to analyze several key passages in the text, prior to class discussion. (The lawyer's description of the place he assigns Bartleby in his office would be a good choice. So would the passage about the "odd instance" Delano observes of "the African love of bright colors and fine shows.")

I can, however, supply some questions I regularly ask in the course of class discussion.

Questions for class discussion of "Bartleby":

1. What does the subtitle of "Bartleby" suggest? What is the significance of Wall Street and the walls in the story?
2. What is the significance of the information that the narrator provides about himself and his employees at the beginning of the story? How does it prepare us to understand Bartleby and the narrator's attitude toward him?
3. Why does Melville tell the story from the point of view of the employer rather than of the office staff or of Bartleby himself? What effect does this narrative strategy have on the reader?
4. How reliable is the narrator? Are there any indications that he might be obtuse or unreliable? Give examples.
5. What incident unleashes Bartleby's passive resistance? What escalates it at each point?
6. What assumptions govern the question that the narrator asks Bartleby: "What earthly right have you to stay here? Do you pay any rent? Do you pay my taxes? Or is this property yours?"
7. What ethic does Melville implicitly oppose to the ethic of Wall Street? (This question leads into a discussion of the New Testament echoes running through the story.)
8. Why does the narrator conclude that Bartleby "was the victim of an innate and incurable disorder"? How does it affect our responses to the story if we accept this conclusion?
9. What is the significance of the postscript the narrator appends to the story? What psychological (or ideological) purpose does it serve for the narrator? What symbolic purpose does it serve for Melville?
10. How much has the encounter with Bartleby changed the narrator by the end of the story? Is the narrator "saved"?

Questions for class discussion of the "Hunilla" sketch:

1. How would you compare Hunilla to the other women characters we have encountered? (Such a question can invite students to compare Melville's portrayal of Hunilla with Hawthorne's portrayals of Georgiana or Beatrice Rappaccini; interesting comparisons can also be drawn with Poe's Ligeia or the heroine of "The Oval Portrait," or with Linda Brent in *Incidents in the Life of a Slave Girl* or Rosa in Child's "Slavery's Pleasant Homes.")
2. What is the effect of the way in which Melville describes the scene of Felipe and Trujill's drowning? Does it distance us from Hunilla? Or does it force us to replicate her experience?

3. What do you think are the "two unnamed events which befell Hunilla on this isle"? Why does Melville refuse to narrate them? What effects does Melville's narrative technique have on us as readers?

4. What does Melville mean when he offers this justification for his refusal to name the sufferings Hunilla has undergone: "In nature, as in law, it may be libellous to speak some truths"?

5. At various points in the text, Melville invites an emotional response to Hunilla's story. Can you identify passages in which the narrator expresses his own feelings about Hunilla, describes the sailors' emotional reactions to her, or appeals to the reader's emotions? How does Melville seem to want the reader to respond?

6. Hunilla's story, Melville suggests, can lend itself to opposing views of human nature, depending on which aspects one chooses to emphasize. What are the possible conclusions about human nature that one could draw from her story? What conclusions does Melville seem to want readers to draw?

7. In characterizing Hunilla, a "Chola, or half-breed Indian woman" of Spanish-Indian ancestry, Melville seems aware of certain stereotypes about women of color, Indians, and Spaniards. What are some of these stereotypes? To what extent does Melville either play into or play against them?

Questions for class discussion of "Paradise and Tartarus":

1. What contrast does the opening of "Paradise" draw between the Bachelors' haven and the outside world? How does Melville develop the implications of the opening passage in the rest of the sketch?

2. How might the fate of the medieval Knights Templars be relevant to the nineteenth-century Templars?

3. Read out loud the paragraphs about the survival of Templars in modern London and ask: What effect does this imagery have? What attitude does it create toward the Templars?

4. Read out loud the description of the Templars' banquet and ask: What is the significance of this imagery? What associations does it suggest to you? (The teacher might amplify the discussion by pointing out the parody of Plato's *Symposium* suggested by dubbing the field-marshall/waiter "Socrates.") What bearing does this description have on the second sketch of the pair?

5. What role does the narrator play in each of the two sketches? How would we situate him vis-à-vis the bachelors of the first sketch and the factory owner and workers of the second sketch?

6. What business takes the narrator to the paper mill? What might his "seedsman's business" symbolize?

7. Why does Melville link these two sketches as a pair? What devices does he use to cement the links? What connections does he invite readers to make between the bachelors and the maids, between Temple Bar and the New England paper factory? How is the contrast between the bachelors of the first sketch and maids of the second sketch continued within the second sketch?

8. Read out loud the passage describing the landscape of Devil's Dungeon and ask what its imagery suggests.

9. What is the significance of the imagery Melville uses to describe the factory? (Read aloud passages drawing the students' attention to the girls' dehumanization and the machine's preemption of their reproductive functions.)

10. What is Melville critiquing in this pair of sketches? Why does he link the economic to the sexual, production to reproduction?

11. Depending on the order in which assignments are made, teachers can also ask questions about:
    —the continuities linking "Bartleby" with "Paradise and Tartarus."
    —the differences between Melville's portrayals of Hunilla and of the factory girls in "Tartarus."
    —the similarities and differences between Melville's and Alice Cary's critiques of patriarchy.
    —the similarities and differences between the perspectives that Melville and Fanny Fern offer on working women.
    —the insights that emerge from reading "Paradise and Tartarus" in the light of Sarah Grimké's *Letters on the Equality of the Sexes*, Lydia Maria Child's "Letter from New York" #50 on Women's Rights, and Margaret Fuller's *Woman in the Nineteenth Century*.

Questions for class discussion of "Benito Cereno":

1. Through whose eyes do we view the events in the story? Where in the text does Melville shift into Delano's point of view? Whose point of view does the Deposition represent? (N.B. I have found again and again that students confuse third-person narrative with omniscient point of view and a character's subjective point of view with first-person narrative. Unless instructors take special care, students will end up referring to Delano as the narrator in their papers and exams.)

2. Why doesn't Melville choose to write the story from Babo's point of view? What might his purpose be in confining us to Delano's and later Benito Cereno's point of view? What limitations does this narrative strategy impose on us as readers?

3. How reliable are Delano's perceptions of reality? What tendencies in particular make him an unreliable interpreter of the behavior he sees manifested on board the *San Dominick*? (Draw the students' attention to the racial assumptions embedded in his perceptions of the oakum-pickers and hatchet-polishers; in his endorsement of the "contrast in dress, denoting their relative positions," that distinguishes Don Benito from Babo; in his ogling of a naked African woman and his failure to realize the terrible irony of the possibility that she might be one of "the very women Mungo Park saw in Africa, and gave such a noble account of"; in his belief that the blacks are "too stupid" to be staging a masquerade and that no white would be "so far a renegade as to apostatize from his very species almost, by leaguing in against it with negroes"; in his ludicrous misinterpretation of Babo's intent in using the flag of Spain as a bib. Obviously there will not be time to discuss all these passages, but one or two should be singled out for discussion.)

4. The best example of how Delano's racism keeps him from recognizing that the blacks have staged a revolt is the episode in which he sees Babo use the flag of Spain as a bib for Don Benito, but misinterprets it as an "odd instance of the African love of bright colors and fine shows." How does that episode originate? (Draw the students' attention to Don Benito's slip of the tongue and Babo's quick invention of the shave as a ruse to prevent further inopportune slips. Use an analysis of the episode to show how brilliantly Babo manipulates Delano's prejudices.)

5. What attitude toward slavery does Delano exhibit? How does his attitude differ from Benito Cereno's? (Point out passages showing Delano's envy of Don Benito, even as he feels the Yankee's superiority to the decadent slave-holding aristocrat; most crucial is Delano's insistence on pursuing and capturing the *San Dominick* with its cargo of slaves "worth more than a thousand doubloons.")

6. Most of the confusion in interpreting "Benito Cereno" arises from the latter part of the story. It is easy to see that Delano's view of blacks as stupid is wrong, but does Melville present Benito Cereno's view of blacks as a corrective to stereotype, or merely as another stereotype? Does the Deposition represent the "truth"?

7. How does the language of the Deposition differ from the language Melville uses elsewhere in the text? What makes us take it for the "truth"?

8. What is Benito Cereno's interpretation of events, as opposed to Delano's initial interpretation? How does he explain the slaves' revolt?

9. Does the Deposition indirectly provide any alternative explanations of why the blacks may have revolted? What does it tell us about the blacks' actual aims? How do they try to achieve those aims? (If necessary, point out the hints that the slave women have been sexually abused by Aranda and Cereno; also consider the conversation between Cereno and Babo during the revolt, when Babo asks Cereno to transport the blacks back to Senegal and promises that they will abide by the rationing of water and food necessary to effect such a long voyage.)

10. Does Melville provide any clues to an interpretation of the story that transcends the racist stereotypes of Delano and Cereno? (Point out the allusions to the ancient African civilizations of Egypt and Nubia; the allusion to Ezekiel's Valley of Dry Bones; the symbolism of the *San Dominick*'s "shield-like stern-piece" and the way in which the identities of the masked figures get reversed at the end of the story.)

11. What is the narrative point of view of the few pages following the Deposition? How do you interpret the dialogue between the two captains? Does it indicate that either Delano or Cereno has undergone any change in consciousness or achieved a new understanding of slavery as a result of his ordeal?

12. What seems to be the message of the scene with which the story ends? What do you think Melville was trying to convey through the story? How does the story continue to be relevant or prophetic?

13. How would you compare "Benito Cereno" to: David Walker's *Appeal*? Henry Highland Garnet's 1843 "Address to the Slaves of the U.S.A."? Thomas Wentworth Higginson's "Nat Turner's Insurrection"? Wendell Phillips's "Toussaint L'Ouverture"? Douglass's *Narrative*? Lydia Maria Child's "Slavery's Pleasant Homes"? Stowe's *Uncle Tom's Cabin* (or any other assigned readings on slavery)?

Questions for class discussion of *Billy Budd*:

1. Why does Melville begin the story with a description of the Handsome Sailor? What does this figure seem to represent? What is the significance of the fact that the first example Melville cites of the Handsome Sailor is "a native African of the unadulterate blood of Ham"? What characteristics does Billy share with the Black Handsome Sailor? What is the purpose of the analogies Melville suggests between the "barbarians" of pre-Christian Europe, Africa, and the South Seas? In what respects does Billy fail to conform fully to the Handsome Sailor archetype?

2. What are the historical contexts of the story? What is the purpose of the historical background Melville supplies on the Nore and

Spithead mutinies? (Note that the story takes place only a few years after the American War of Independence against Britain and that it begins with an impressment, recalling the frequent impressment of American sailors by the British—one of the grievances that led to the War of 1812. See H. Bruce Franklin's "From Empire to Empire" for a full discussion of the story's historical contexts.)

3. What is the significance of Billy's being impressed from the *Rights-of-Man* to the *Bellipotent*?

4. What relationship does Melville set up between Billy, Claggart, and Vere? What qualities does each represent? Why are Claggart and Vere attracted to Billy? In what ways is he a threat to them?

5. How do you interpret Melville's definition of "Natural Depravity"? To whom does it most obviously apply in the story? To whom else might it also apply? (A number of critics have pointed out the applicability of the passage to Vere as well as Claggart.)

6. How does the tragedy occur? How might it have been avoided?

7. How does Melville invite the reader to judge Vere's behavior and decision to hang Billy? What passages, dialogues, and scenes must we take into account?

8. What tactics and arguments does Vere use to sway his officers? What are the political consequences (in real life as well as in the story) of accepting Vere's arguments? Do you see any contradictions in Vere's arguments, or do you find them rational and persuasive? Is Melville's description of "Natural Depravity" at all relevant to an evaluation of Vere's conduct at the trial ("Toward the accomplishment of an aim which in wantonness of atrocity would seem to partake of the insane, he will direct a cool judgment sagacious and sound")?

9. How do you interpret the many biblical allusions in the story? In what ways do they redefine or amplify the meaning of the story? What relationship(s) do you see between the religious and political interpretations the story invites? How does Melville characterize the role of the chaplain?

10. After the hanging, Vere forestalls possible disturbances by ordering the drums to muster the men to quarters earlier than usual. He then justifies his action by explaining how he views art and the purpose it serves: " 'With mankind . . . forms, measured forms, are everything; and that is the import couched in the story of Orpheus spellbinding the wild denizens of the wood.' " Does Melville endorse this concept of art in *Billy Budd*? How does the form of the story jibe (or conflict) with Vere's ideal of "measured forms"? How does the glorification of the Handsome Sailor, and the imagery

used to describe him, jibe (or conflict) with Vere's view of "the wild denizens of the wood"?

11. What is the effect of the three sequels Melville appends to the story? What further light do they shed on Vere and on the political interests governing his decision? To whom does the story give the last word?

12. Depending on the order of assignments, teachers can invite students to draw connections between:
   —the status of slaves, sailors, and factory workers.
   —the legal arguments Vere uses in his role as prosecuting attorney at Billy's trial, and the portrayal of lawyers and the law in "Bartleby" and "Paradise and Tartarus."
   —Thoreau's essay on civil disobedience and Vere's defense of martial law and the Articles of War.
   —Vere's insistence that "the heart, sometimes the feminine in man, be ruled out" and Fuller's critique of the rigid sexual stereotypes that patriarchal ideology imposes on men and women.

Questions for class discussion of "Hawthorne and His Mosses":

1. How would you compare "Hawthorne and His Mosses" with Emerson's "The American Scholar," Fuller's "A Short Essay on Critics," Poe's "The Philosophy of Composition" and review of Hawthorne's *Twice-Told Tales*, and Whitman's 1855 Preface of *Leaves of Grass*? How would you compare Poe's and Melville's responses to Hawthorne's fiction?

2. To what extent (or in what ways) do you find this essay helpful for understanding Hawthorne's fiction?

3. To what extent (or in what ways) do you find it helpful for illuminating Melville's own artistic aims and practices?

4. Of the Hawthorne stories Melville praises, which ones continue to be highly regarded today? Does Melville omit mention of any stories in *Mosses from an Old Manse* that regularly appear in present-day anthologies? What do you make of the differences in aesthetic taste or judgment that this might suggest?

5. What does Melville value most in Hawthorne's fiction? What does he mean by "blackness"?

6. Why does Melville argue against idolizing Shakespeare? How would you sum up his opinion of Shakespeare?

7. What are the implications of Melville's view that Americans should give their own authors "priority of appreciation" before acknowledging the great writers of other lands? How might this view apply to other nations or groups attempting to create a literary tradition of their own?

8. What do you make of Melville's list of the significant American writers among his contemporaries? Which ones are still considered major American writers? Whom does Melville omit from his list?

9. Why does Melville disparage Irving? What does he reveal in the process about his own literary aims and values?

Since I group readings together, I also try to formulate paper topics that involve comparisons and contrasts of several readings. Most of the following topics are thematic. Instructors who would prefer formalist topics that focus exclusively on Melville's stories might adapt some from the questions for class discussion listed above.

Choose two or three works from the following list, and compare and contrast their literary styles, narrative techniques, and handling of point of view: Hawthorne's "The Birth-mark" or "Rappaccini's Daughter"; Poe's "Ligeia" or another Poe story of your choice; Kirkland's *A New Home—Who'll Follow?*; Cary's "Uncle Christopher's"; Stoddard's "Lemorne *Versus* Huell"; Melville's "Bartleby" or "The Paradise of Bachelors and the Tartarus of Maids" or "Benito Cereno" or *Billy Budd*.

Compare and contrast the aesthetic theories and views of literary nationalism reflected in several of the following: Emerson's "The American Scholar," Fuller's "A Short Essay on Critics," Poe's "The Philosophy of Composition" or his review of Hawthorne's *Twice-Told Tales*, Melville's "Hawthorne and His Mosses," and Whitman's Preface to the 1855 edition of *Leaves of Grass* or *Democratic Vistas*.

Choose some issue explored in the assigned readings and compare and contrast several works that provide different perspectives on it:

1. Use Thoreau's discussion of alienation in *Walden* as a framework for analyzing "Bartleby." In the process, compare and contrast the two authors' political perspectives.

2. Use Thoreau's "Resistance to Civil Government" as a framework for analyzing Bartleby's interaction with his employer. You may wish to consider the forms of "resistance" the other office workers engage in as well.

3. Use Thoreau's "Resistance to Civil Government" as a framework for analyzing *Billy Budd* and the issues it raises.

4. Compare and contrast Thoreau's and Melville's critiques of industrialism and capitalism in *Walden* and "The Paradise of Bachelors and the Tartarus of Maids."

5. Compare and contrast the ways in which Jacobs's *Incidents in the Life of a Slave Girl*, Child's "Slavery's Pleasant Homes," and Melville's Hunilla sketch handle the problem of depicting rape and sexual harassment in a culture that views discussion of such subjects as indecent and that stereotypes women of color as lascivious. If you

wish, you may include (or substitute for the Hunilla sketch) a discussion of the slave women in "Benito Cereno."

6. Compare and contrast Melville's "The Paradise of Bachelors and the Tartarus of Maids" and Cary's "Uncle Christopher's," focusing on some of the following points: the perspectives each provides on the effects of patriarchal (and/or capitalist) ideology; the causes to which each story attributes the dehumanization and sterility it depicts; the kinds of contrasts each story sets up between oppressor and oppressed; the narrative point of view; the role of landscape and setting; the use of symbolism and metaphor.

7. Apply Sarah Grimké's, Lydia Maria Child's, and/or Margaret Fuller's analysis of "the woman question" to one or more of the following:
   —Hawthorne's "The Birth-mark" and/or "Rappaccini's Daughter"
   —Poe's "The Oval Portrait" and/or "Ligeia"
   —Melville's "The Paradise of Bachelors and the Tartarus of Maids" and/or the Hunilla sketch
   —Elizabeth Stoddard's "Lemorne *Versus* Huell"
   —Caroline Kirkland's *A New Home—Who'll Follow?*
   —Alice Cary's "Uncle Christopher's"
   —Harriet Jacobs's *Incidents in the Life of a Slave Girl*
   —Lydia Maria Child's "Slavery's Pleasant Homes"
   —Emily Dickinson's poems (selections of your choice)

8. Compare and contrast the perspectives that Child's "Slavery's Pleasant Homes" and Melville's "Benito Cereno" provide on slavery. You may wish to consider the different literary techniques each story uses (including narrative point of view), the purposes these techniques serve, and the audience(s) to which each is addressed.

9. Apply one or more of the following works to an analysis of Melville's "Benito Cereno":
   —David Walker's *Appeal*
   —Douglass's *Narrative*
   —Henry Highland Garnet's "Address to the Slaves of the U.S.A."
   —Wendell Phillips's "Toussaint L'Ouverture"
   —Thomas Wentworth Higginson's "Nat Turner's Insurrection"

Choose some aspect of slavery explored in the assigned readings, and compare and contrast the perspectives these various works provide on it.

1. The issue of slave resistance and rebellion (can include violent and nonviolent, individual and collective resistance).

2. The issue of Higher Law versus the law of the land.

3. The contrast between the masters' and the slaves' viewpoints and values (e.g., Douglass and Jacobs and their fellow slaves versus their masters; Uncle Tom, Chloe, Cassy, etc., versus the Shelbys, St. Clares, and Legree; Babo versus Cereno and Delano).

4. Religion and slavery, or religion and militarism (can include the indictment of the church's hypocrisy, the use of the Bible to support or condemn slavery, the theme of apocalyptic judgment, the use of typology and religious rhetoric and symbolism).

5. Comparative analysis of the rhetorical techniques, purposes, and intended audiences of three writers among those assigned, or of the metaphors each writer uses to describe slavery and structure his/her narrative.

6. The use of irony in the anti-slavery argument (can analyze the different types of irony found in slave songs, Douglass's and Jacobs's narratives, Child's anti-slavery writings, *Uncle Tom's Cabin*, and "Benito Cereno").

7. The image of Africa and the portrayal of the slave trade in Equiano's narrative and "Benito Cereno."

8. Double meanings and the theme of appearance versus reality in any of the assigned readings.

9. The theme "Slavery proved as injurious to her as it did to me" (a quotation from Douglass's *Narrative* as applied to the individuals who people the assigned works, or to the North and the South, blacks and whites, oppressed and oppressing classes, the American nation in general).

10. The picture of slave life and the slave community that emerges from any three of the assigned works (preferably three representing different racial, regional, or gender perspectives).

11. The theme "Slavery is terrible for men, but it is far more terrible for women," as dramatized in several of the assigned readings.

Bibliography

Ideally, acquaintance with *Typee, Redburn*, and *White-Jacket* would be extremely helpful for teaching the stories in the anthology from the perspective suggested here. The introduction and notes to the selections quote liberally from these three works, however, and several of the critics cited below summarize their bearing on *Billy Budd*.

For a broader intellectual context, teachers who have time to read "The Communist Manifesto" and perhaps Marx's essays "Estranged Labor," "The Meaning of Human Requirements," and "The Power of Money in Bourgeois Society," from *The Economic and Philosophic Manuscripts of 1844* will find them extremely relevant to both "The

Paradise of Bachelors and the Tartarus of Maids" and "Bartleby." In particular, Marx discusses workers' reduction to commodities, their enslavement to machines, and their resulting alienation.

For a complete bibliography, covering all of Melville's short fiction except *Billy Budd* and including overviews of the stories' reception, see Lea Bertani Vozar Newman's *A Reader's Guide to the Short Stories of Herman Melville* (Boston: Hall, 1986). Forthcoming will also be the second volume of Brian Higgins's *Herman Melville: An Annotated Bibliography* (Boston: Hall), covering all Melville criticism published since 1930. For an excellent reconstruction of the stories' chronology, circumstances of composition and publication, and contemporary reception, see Merton M. Sealts's Historical Note in the Northwestern-Newberry edition of *The Piazza Tales and Other Prose Pieces, 1839–1860* (Evanston and Chicago: 1987, 457–533). The volume also reprints the chapter of Delano's *Narrative* that Melville used as a source.

For a biographical study that situates Melville and his family in the context of contemporary politics, see Michael Paul Rogin, *Subversive Genealogy: The Politics and Art of Herman Melville* (New York: Knopf, 1983), especially Chapters 6 and 9.

For challenges to the stereotype of Melville as a writer indifferent or hostile to women, see Kristin Herzog's chapter on Melville in *Women, Ethics, and Exotics: Images of Power in Mid-Nineteenth-Century American Fiction* (Knoxville: University of Tennessee Press, 1983), as well as the essays in the February 1986 issue of *Melville Society Extracts*.

Listed below are the critical studies I have found most useful for illuminating the Melville selections in this anthology, and for developing approaches toward teaching them.

For books containing relevant discussions of more than one story, see Rogin, cited above; Marvin Fisher, *Going Under: Melville's Short Fiction and the American 1850s* (Baton Rouge: Louisiana State University Press, 1977), especially the chapters on "Bartleby" and "The Paradise of Bachelors and the Tartarus of Maids"; and H. Bruce Franklin's chapter on Melville in *The Victim as Criminal and Artist: Literature from the American Prison* (New York: Oxford University Press, 1978), as well as his earlier sections on "Bartleby" in *The Wake of the Gods: Melville's Mythology* (Stanford: Stanford University Press, 1963); Joyce Sparer Adler, *War in Melville's Imagination* (New York: New York University Press, 1981), especially the chapter on *Billy Budd*; and Robert K. Martin, *Hero, Captain, and Stranger: Male Friendship, Social Critique, and Literary Form in the Sea Novels of Herman Melville* (Chapel Hill: University of North Carolina Press, 1986), especially the chapter on *Billy Budd* and pp. 105–106 on "The Paradise of Bachelors."

On "Bartleby," in addition to the books cited above see Stephen Zelnick, "Melville's Bartleby, The Scrivener: A Study in History, Ideology, and Literature," *Marxist Perspectives* 2 (Winter 1979/80): 74–92; and Donald M. Fiene, "Bartleby the Christ," in Raymona E. Hull, ed., *Studies in the Minor and Later Works of Melville* (Hartford: Transcendental Books, 1970): 18–23.

On the Hunilla sketch, see Robert Sattelmeyer and James Barbour, "The Sources and Genesis of Melville's 'Norfolk Isle and the Chola Widow,'" *American Literature* 50 (November 1978): 398–417.

On "The Paradise of Bachelors and the Tartarus of Maids," in addition to the books cited above see Beryl Rowland, "Melville's Bachelors and Maids: Interpretation Through Symbol and Metaphor," *American Literature* 41 (November 1969): 389–405.

Two books situate Melville in the slavery controversy: Carolyn L. Karcher, *Shadow over the Promised Land: Slavery, Race, and Violence in Melville's America* (Louisiana State University Press, 1980), especially chapters 1 and 5; and Rogin, *Subversive Genealogy*, cited above. Robert E. Burkholder's splendid collection, *Critical Essays on Herman Melville's "Benito Cereno"* (G. K. Hall and Macmillan, 1992), includes a number of recent articles, along with some earlier criticism of the story. All the essays are illuminating, but see especially Brook Thomas's "The Legal Fictions of Herman Melville and Lemuel Shaw," Sandra A. Zagarell's "Reenvisioning America," Eric J. Sundquist's "*Benito Cereno* and New World Slavery," Sterling Stuckey's " 'Follow Your Leader': The Theme of Cannibalism in Melville's *Benito Cereno*," Carolyn L. Karcher's "The Riddle of the Sphinx: Melville's 'Benito Cereno' and the *Amistad* Case," and H. Bruce Franklin's "Past, Present, and Future Seemed One." On the relevance of the Spanish Inquisition to "Benito Cereno," see John Bernstein, " 'Benito Cereno' and the Spanish Inquisition," *Nineteenth-Century Fiction*, 16 (March 1962): 345–50. For black perspectives on the story's dramatization of slavery and racism, see Charles E. Nnolim, *Melville's "Benito Cereno": A Study in Meaning of Name Symbolism* (New York: New Voices, 1974); Gloria Horsley-Meacham, "Bull of the Nile: Symbol, History, and Racial Myth in 'Benito Cereno,' " *New England Quarterly*, 64 (June 1991): 225–42; and Joshua Leslie and Sterling Stuckey, "The Death of Benito Cereno: A Reading of Herman Melville on Slavery," *Journal of Negro History*, 67 (December 1982): 287–301. The latter argues convincingly that Melville shows an understanding of African culture based on reading Mungo Park. See also the essays by Horsley-Meacham and Stuckey in Burkholder, ed.

Study of *Billy Budd* should begin with the indispensable notes provided by Harrison Hayford and Merton M. Sealts in their 1962 edition (University of Chicago Press). Besides pointing out innumerable parallels between *Billy Budd* and Melville's other works, of which *White-Jacket* and *Israel Potter* are the most relevant, Hayford and Sealts sum up previous criticism. Among recent critics, Milton R. Stern formulates the most persuasive version of the pro-Vere interpretation in his 1975 Bobbs-Merrill edition of the story. Offering the strongest rebuttals and the most satisfying readings of the story are Adler (cited above) and H. Bruce Franklin, "From Empire to Empire: *Billy Budd, Sailor*," in A. Robert Lee, ed., *Herman Melville: Reassessments* (London: Vision, 1984). Containing pertinent historical information, despite a strained thesis, is Stanton Garner, "Fraud and Fact in Herman Melville's *Billy Budd*," *San Jose Studies* 4 (May 1978): 82–105. Edgar A. Dryden, *Melville's Thematics of Form: The Great Art of Telling the Truth* (Baltimore: Johns Hopkins University Press, 1968) 209–16, analyzes the way in which the form of *Billy Budd* subverts Vere's doctrine of "measured form."

William Wells Brown (1815–1884)

Contributing Editor: Arlene Elder

Classroom Issues and Strategies

It would be extremely useful to recount briefly Brown's own history and to emphasize that he was self-taught after his escape from slavery and, therefore, influenced strongly both by his reading and by the popular ideas current during his time, for instance, common concepts of male and female beauty. Reading the class a short historical description of a slave auction and some commentary about the sale of persons of mixed blood, since even one drop of "Negro blood" marked one legally as black, hence appropriately enslaved, would also provide a context for the chapters from *Clotelle*.

One might provoke a lively discussion by quoting some of the negative comments on writers like Brown present in "The myth of a 'negro literature' " by LeRoi Jones (Amiri Baraka) in *Home Social Essays* (New York: William Morrow, 1966) or Addison Gayle, Jr.'s, designation of Brown as "the conscious or unconscious propagator of assimilationism" (*The Way of the New World, The Black Novel in America*, 11. New York: Anchor, 1976). Any denigration of functional or committed art by critics with New Critical persuasions should provoke thought about the novel's place in the black canon as well as raise current theoretical issues about the political role of art and the artist.

Students are interested in the verification of the sale of "white" slaves: the historical basis for Clotelle as the alleged daughter of Thomas Jefferson; questions of nineteenth-century popular characterization as a source for Brown's handling of his protagonists; the whole genre of the slave narrative; and theoretical issues such as art versus propaganda.

Major Themes, Historical Perspectives, and Personal Issues

1. Brown's own personal experience as an aide to a slave trader.
2. The sexual exploitation of both female slaves and white wives by slave owners. Harriet Jacobs's *Incidents in the Life of a Slave Girl* provides an actual situation of sexual exploitation. Since selections from *Incidents* appear in *The Heath Anthology*, it might be useful to teach *Clotelle* in conjunction with this slave narrative.
3. The historical role of Christianity as both an advocate of slavery and, for the slaves, a source of escapism from their situation.
4. The presence of rebellious slaves who refused to accept their dehumanization.

Significant Form, Style, or Artistic Conventions

One needs to place *Clotelle* within the dual contexts of the black literary traditions of slave narrative and folk orature and the mainstream genre of popular nineteenth-century drama and fiction. This dual influence accounts for what appears to be the incongruous description of Jerome, for instance, who could be seen, in his manly rebellion against an unfair beating as a fictional Frederick Douglass but also is described in a totally unrealistic way both to appeal to racist standards of beauty and to correspond to images of heroes in popular white novels.

Original Audience

Of equal influence on Brown's composition of *Clotelle* are his two very different audiences, the white middle class and the black "talented-tenth," with very different, sometimes conflicting, expectations, histories, aesthetics, education, and incomes, to whom Brown and other nineteenth-century black novelists had to appeal. Interestingly, there is still no homogeneous audience for black writing, *Clotelle* included, because American society is still not equal. Therefore, it should not surprise an instructor if the selections arouse extremely different responses from various class members.

Comparisons, Contrasts, Connections

Brown's intertwined aesthetic and political complexities are echoed not only in the writing by other nineteenth-century African-American novelists but also in the work of all ethnic American writers, especially those of the present day, for whom issues of constituency and audience are extremely complicated. It is for this reason that *Clotelle* is extremely useful to demonstrate not only common subjects and themes with the slave narratives but, just as interesting, the influence of society upon artistic choices and the paradoxical position of the ethnic artist vis-à-vis African- and Euro-American literary heritages and his or her mixed constituency.

Questions for Reading and Discussion/ Approaches to Writing

1. Chapter II:
   (a) How is the idea as well as the historical reality of slaves being treated as dehumanized property expressed in Brown's language and imagery?
   (b) How does the auction process reveal the complete dichotomy between the interests of the slaves and those of their traders and owners?
   (c) What is the intended effect of Brown's description of Isabella on the auction block?
   (d) Why does Brown link the image of the auction block with that of the church spires in this chapter?
2. Chapter X:
   (a) What is the symbolic/thematic effect of Brown's description of Isabella's garden?
   (b) What does this chapter reveal about the sexual exploitation of both female slaves and the wives of the white masters? What contradiction does it suggest about the possibly comforting concept of a "good master"?
   (c) Have we been given enough information to explain Linwood's behavior? How do we account for Isabella's continued kindness toward him?
3. Chapter XI:
   (a) Why doesn't Linwood accept Isabella's offer to release him from his promise to her?
   (b) Do you think a nineteenth-century reader might react differently from a modern one to the unbelievability of Linwood's mutterings in his sleep? If so, why?
   (c) What is the function of religion for Isabella?

4. Chapter XVIII:
   (a) How do you explain Brown's incongruous physical description of Jerome?
   (b) Who are George Combe and Fowler, and why are they alluded to here?
   (c) What do the allusions to certain well-known lovers reveal about Brown's reading?
5. (a) Comparison with details of slave life, especially female concubinage found in Harriet A. Jacobs, *Life of a Slave Girl, Written by Herself* (Cambridge: Harvard University Press, 1987).
   (b) Discussion of Isabella and Clotelle as representatives of the popular "tragic octoroon" stereotype.
   (c) Comparison of *Clotelle* with another nineteenth-century African-American novel about a female slave and her liberation, Frances E. W. Harper's *Iola Leroy* (Philadelphia, 1892).
   (d) Discussion of Jerome as a "counterstereotype" intended to refute negative popular images of blacks. A look at Frederick Douglass's *Narrative of the Life of Frederick Douglass* (Boston, 1845) as well as Thomas Dixon, Jr.'s, *The Clansman* (1902) would provide polar contexts for this subject.

Bibliography

Dearborn, Mary. *Pochahantas' Daughters: Gender and Ethnicity in American Culture.*

Gates, Henry Louis, Jr. *"Race," Writing and Difference.*

Kinney, James. *Amalgamation: Race, Sex, and Rhetoric in the Nineteenth-Century American Novel.*

Takaki, Ronald T. *Violence in the Black Imagination.* (Especially Part III on Brown and *Clotelle*).

Alice Cary (1820–1871)

Contributing Editor: Judith Fetterley

Classroom Issues and Strategies

Students are turned off by what they perceive as her didacticism, the morals attached to the ends of the stories. They also have trouble with what they perceive as her Christian dogma or perspective. And occasionally they perceive her stories as sentimental.

These problems are endemic to the reading of texts by nineteenth-century American women writers. They are useful and interesting problems to encounter in the classroom because they raise quite clearly the issue of aesthetic value and how the context for determining what is good art changes over time. The instructor needs to be aware of how contemporary critics have addressed this issue. The single best book for the teacher to have and use is Jane Tompkins's *Sensational Designs*. The instructor might wish to assign the last chapter of this book, "But Is It Any Good?" to the class, since this chapter raises directly the questions most of them have about nineteenth-century women's texts.

Compared to other nineteenth-century American women writers, Cary is minimally didactic, Christian, or "sentimental." So, in teaching her, my approach consists of comparing her work with that of writers who are much more didactic, Christian, and "sentimental" and asking how it is that she avoids these patterns. What fictional techniques has she developed to tell the story she has to tell without in fact resorting to didacticism, etc.? This usually leads into a discussion of the form of the short fictional piece, and more specifically into a discussion of regionalism. (See the forthcoming *Norton Anthology of American Women Regional Writers*, edited by Fetterley and Pryse.)

Students respond to the issue of story-telling—how women tell stories and the relation between their telling of stories and their context of domestic work. They are also interested in the issue of landscape—how Cary manages to create a mood through her description of the landscape and how she manages to convey the open-ended nature of her stories. Their lack of plot in the conventional sense is worthy of discussion as is the fact that Cary tells stories about women's lives and experience from the point of view of a female narrator.

Major Themes, Historical Perspectives, and Personal Issues

It is important to emphasize that Cary was essentially a self-made writer. She had little formal education, little support from family or extended personal contacts; yet she made herself into a poet whose name was known throughout the country. Her decision to move to New York in 1850 represented an extraordinary act of self-assertion for a woman at the time. She determined that she needed to get out of the "provinces" in order to have the literary career she wished and she did it. She set up a household in New York that included two of her sisters and she supported this household by her own work. She is an example of the way in which nineteenth-century American women writers were able to set up supportive networks that were based on connections with other women. She is an example of a nineteenth-century American woman writer who was genuinely financially independent of men. She ran her house, earned the money for it, and handled her money herself.

In terms of literary themes, it is important to emphasize the fact that Cary began to write seriously about her Ohio neighborhood after she left it for New York. She saw herself as trying to present a realistic picture of this neighborhood and to create a place in literature for the region, but she was able to do this only after she had left it for New York.

Significant Form, Style, or Artistic Conventions

It is important to point out that Cary thought of herself primarily as a poet. Her reputation during her lifetime and thereafter was based on her poetry. The conventions that governed poetry by women in the nineteenth century by and large produced a body of poetry that is not of interest to the late twentieth-century reader. The novel was also a highly determined form. Women were expected to write certain kinds of novels, to produce "women's fiction" with the appropriately feminine perspective and set of values. The short fictional sketch, however, was a relatively undetermined territory. It was not taken as seriously as were the novel and poetry and no theory existed as to what kind of fictional sketch a woman should or should not write in order to demonstrate that she was in fact a woman. As a result, in writing her Clovernook sketches Cary was on her own, so to speak. She was able to write organically, to let the shape of the fiction emerge from the nature of the story she wished to tell. As a result, her short fiction holds interest for the contemporary reader; it seems fresh, new, not written to fulfill convention or previously determined script, but deriving from some deep personal place that produces a uniquely marked and signed prose. Thus any discussion of Alice Cary needs to address the role that the form of the fictional sketch plays in creating fiction that interests us. In other words, the issue of form is central to the discussion of Alice Cary. Specific features of this form include: the freedom this form gives to focus on character and setting as opposed to plot; the lack of closure in many of Cary's sketches; the intermingling of realism and surrealism. For a fuller discussion of these and other issues relative to the form of the sketch in relation to Alice Cary, I refer the instructor to my "Introduction" to the Rutgers Press edition of the short fiction of Alice Cary, *Clovernook Sketches and Other Stories*.

It is also important to discuss the issue of realism in relation to Cary. Since American literary history, until very recently, has been based on a study of male writers, the predominant view is that realism began in America after the Civil War. However, women writers were experimenting with realism in the decades before the Civil War. Cary's "Preface" to the first volume of Clovernook sketches, published in 1852, lays out her theory of realism and the instructor should be familiar with it. She sees herself as participating in the effort to write about American subjects and she sees herself as doing something "new" in choosing to write about these subjects as "they really are." In making this choice she is in effect following the lead of writers like Caroline Kirkland and participating in the development of realism as a mode suited to the needs and interests of women writers in the nineteenth century. Alice Cary thus provides the instructor with the opportunity to at once raise the issue of the bias in literary history and the issue of the development of realism as an American mode.

Original Audience

As I have indicated above, Cary's primary audience during her lifetime was for her poetry. Her short fiction was not a big popular success and was not reprinted. But the nineteenth century, as I said before, did not take the genre of short fiction as seriously as it did that of poetry and the novel. So in a way this does not tell us much about how well her short fiction was received by her readers. Her short fiction, much of which was initially published in periodicals, may well have been as popular as that of any other contemporary writer, male or female. The point is that the genre itself was not as popular. Interestingly enough, however, Cary's greatest critical successes came from her short fiction. Once again, though, this may simply indicate that the genre itself was not taken very seriously.

Comparisons, Contrasts, Connections

Cary can be fruitfully compared with a number of different writers in a number of different contexts. She can be compared with writers like Poe and Hawthorne in her use of fiction as dream work and projection. She creates the same kind of uncanny, eerie, dreamlike atmosphere that they do. She can also be compared with them in terms of her use of the first-person narrator and the complexities of that narrator's relation to the story she tells and the characters she creates. She can also be compared with them in terms of her use of setting.

She can be compared with nineteenth-century women writers like Caroline Kirkland for her use of realism and for her commitment to telling the woman's side of the story. She can also be compared with other nineteenth-century women writers for her ability to avoid some of their didacticism, Christian moralizing, and "sentimentality."

She can be most interestingly compared to Emily Dickinson in her ability to place herself and her imagination at the center of her work. Very few nineteenth-century American women writers were able to overcome the dicta that required of women self-effacement in literature as in life. Dickinson overcame it by virtue of not publishing. Cary overcame it through her use of the nonconventional form of short fiction. Her work is remarkable for the sustained development of first-person narration. Her collections of Clovernook sketches are as much about the narrator as they are about anything else. She creates a remarkable I/eye for her work.

Bibliography

I refer the instructor to the discussion of Alice Cary in *Provisions* and to the "Introduction" to the Rutgers Press volume of Cary's short fiction, *Clovernook Sketches and Other Stories*. Also to Annette Kolodny, *The Land Before Her*.

Elizabeth Stoddard (1823–1902)

Contributing Editors: Sybil Weir and Sandra A. Zagarell

Classroom Issues and Strategies

Stoddard's terse narrative style, the limitation of point of view to the in-direct, ironic woman narrator, and the oblique portrayal of the major act on which the plot turns may make it difficult for students to follow "Lemorne *Versus* Huell." Also, students unfamiliar with conventions of gothic fiction and mid-century history may miss much of the social commentary. It may therefore be useful to ask students to review the plot. It may also be useful to give background on sentimental fiction's featuring of courtship plots and frequent endorsement of female self-sacrifice and male paternalism (as in *The Wide, Wide World*) so that students get a sense of Stoddard's critique of such conventions.

Major Themes, Historical Perspectives, and Personal Issues

Although Stoddard's major subjects, like those of many antebellum women writers, include her protagonists' urges towards selfhood and the sociocultural conventions that thwart or channel those urges, she is at once far more ironic about conventions—including literary conventions—and far more sympathetic to women's personal ambition, her own as well as her protagonists', than a Susan Warner or a Maria Cummins. In "Lemorne" she calls attention to the limitations that gender and class impose on her protagonist and to the limitations of the feminine strategies of irony and passive aggressiveness with which Margaret both adapts to and resists her circumstances. She also emphasizes romantic love as a convention that facilitates the bartering of women and portrays marriage and family as institutionalizing the possession of women who are without power. These aspects of "Lemorne" exhibit the intense critique of bourgeois Victorian American gender arrangements to be found in much of Stoddard's fiction. At the same time, "Lemorne" is unquestioning of other dimensions of antebellum America. It uses slavery and the Fugitive Slave Law as vehicles to suggest the need for more liberal circumstances for white women while remaining silent about the circumstances of the enslaved population of the United States. In converting slavery to a metaphor for the condition of white women,

Stoddard participates in a construction of white femininity that relies on a racially polarized society and is prevalent throughout the nineteenth century and well into the twentieth—as Hazel Carby demonstrates in *Reconstructing Womanhood.*

Significant Form, Style, or Artistic Conventions

Primary questions have to do with Stoddard's use of the literary traditions of her day—traditions of sentimental fiction and gothic romance. She undercuts the standard courtship plot with her ironizing of the hero as rescuer, yet sustains a degree of erotic intensity rare in fiction by antebellum women writers and much influenced by Charlotte and Emily Brontë, whom she esteemed highly. I'd also emphasize Stoddard's interweaving of the Fugitive Slave motif and references to European literature, and her satirization of Newport society.

I would also stress Stoddard's humor and her importance "as an experimenter in narrative method. She anticipates modern fiction in using a severely limited mode with minimal narrative clues" (Buell and Zagarell, "Biographical and Critical Introduction," p. xxiii).

Original Audience

"Lemorne *Versus* Huell" was first published in *Harper's New Monthly Magazine,* suggesting that Stoddard's fiction was directed to a middle-class, educated audience. In fact, neither her short fiction nor her novels were ever popular or recognized beyond a small circle of intellectuals and writers. Presumably, the audience of her own day was put off by her elliptical style and by her often satiric questioning of prevalent assumptions about female virtue, self-abnegation, and religious piety, as they may also have been by what James Russell Lowell termed her "coarseness."

Comparisons, Contrasts, Connections

I would compare Stoddard's fiction with that of Stowe, Alcott, and Spofford. For example, in what ways does her characterization depart from Stowe's emphasis on religious piety or Alcott's affirmation of family and domestic feminism? How do her use of an unusual situation and her intensity compare with those of Spofford? How, and under what circumstances, do all four writers emphasize their heroines' self-reliance (or the perils of self-abnegation)? Other appropriate comparisons and contrasts have to do with point of view (emphasizing Stoddard's rather unusual use of first-person narration) and with gender commentary. An interesting comparison can be made with the journalistic essays of Fanny Fern, which also take up the marriage contract, the condition of women, and women's work, though in a very different mode, and which also use humor, though of a much broader kind.

Questions for Reading and Discussion/ Approaches to Writing

1. What is the effect of the first-person narrative?
2. In what ways is distance from the narrator achieved?
3. What do you make of the ending? Is it unexpected? How does it affect your assessment of Margaret's passivity? Of her marriage?

Harriet E. Wilson (c. 1808–1870)

Contributing Editor: Marilyn Richardson

Classroom Issues and Strategies

Some discussion of the reality of free blacks, both in the North and in the South, is useful, along with some background on the abolitionist movement and its literature.

Major Themes, Historical Perspectives, and Personal Issues

While anti-slavery writers agreed about the urgent need to abolish slavery, there was considerable difference of opinion on the role emancipated blacks might be expected/allowed to play in American society. This book points the finger at the so-called liberal North where, even during the height of the abolitionist period, profound issues of caste and class, as well as overt racism, prefigure struggles to come during Reconstruction and up to the present day.

To date, there is only one edition of *Our Nig* readily available. Gates, as editor, has provided an extensive discussion of these issues in his introductory essay.

Bibliography

Andrews, *Sisters of the Spirit*, Richardson, *Maria W. Stewart*, Harper, *Iola Leroy*, Jacobs, *Incidents in the Life of a Slave Girl*, all give excellent insight into black women's nineteenth-century experience, North and South. Three excellent anthologies, Lerner, *Black Women in White America*, Loewenbert and Bogin, *Black Women in 19th Century American Life*, and Sterling, *We Are Your Sisters*, all provide background information that could be useful with this text.

A new article by Barbara A. White "'Our Nig' and the She-Devil: New Information about Harriet Wilson and the 'Bellmont Family'" (*American Literature* 65 [March 1993]: 19–52) clearly demonstrates the autobiographical basis of *Our Nig* and also may provide students with a splendid model of historical research applied to the interpretation of a text.

The Emergence of American Poetic Voices

Songs and Ballads

Contributing Editor: Paul Lauter

Classroom Issues and Strategies

Students immediately ask, "Is it literature?" The songs raise all of the issues about "popular culture," including their "quality" as literary texts, their changeableness from version to version, their audience, their relationship to music. Can they be, should they be, studied in a literature classroom rather than in a music classroom?

It is useful to play versions of the songs and ballads—especially the spirituals. Surprisingly few students have ever actually heard such a song, and they often find them powerful. But this can be overdone— after all, the musical vocabulary is, on the whole, even more remote from student culture than are the texts. A less inhibited or more skilled instructor may wish to involve students in the singing; indeed, some may be able to lead a class, and that experience can pay off significantly when one gets to the question of audience.

It can be important to confront directly the question of what constitutes the domain of "literature." Who decides what is included there? And on what basis? If these texts are, as some are, extraordinarily simple, does that remove them from what we think of as significant literature? Are questions of audience and function involved? What are—and have been—the functions of such songs? Who sings them, and when, and why? Are these significant literary questions?

Another issue best confronted directly is the question of the mutability of such songs. Is it a good thing or a bad thing that people change them?

Major Themes, Historical Perspectives, and Personal Issues

Obviously, the spirituals draw deeply on the Bible, especially the Old Testament. Many are built on a fundamental analogy between black slaves and the Hebrews. They can also be read ethnographically, for they express a good deal about the character and functions of religion and other forms of culture in the slave period.

Both the songs of black and white communities interestingly focus on everyday experiences of work, courting, religion (as well as on eschatological visions).

Significant Form, Style, or Artistic Conventions

The headnote points to a number of formal features, like refrains and repetitions, qualities of language, characteristic patterns of imagery, the ways in which songs are taken up, reframed, renewed. It can be useful to discuss how these songs are similar to and different from more "formal" poetry and also from one another.

Original Audience

The most interesting issue may be how, in the origins of such songs, the distinction between creator/singer and audience did not, on the whole, exist. The end of the Introduction to the period considers that issue. Raising this problem allows a class to explore the difference between culture as a commodity produced by persons other than oneself, and culture as an integral part of human life, serving a variety of functions, including discharging grief, inspiring hope, and offering opportunities, in the *singing*, for physical and psychological expression. The song, Bernice Reagon has pointed out, is only the vehicle or perhaps excuse for the singing.

Comparisons, Contrasts, Connections

This unit is designed to allow, indeed, encourage, comparisons between varieties of poetic texts from very different cultures.

Questions for Reading and Discussion/ Approaches to Writing

1. (a) How are these songs similar to/different from more formal kinds of poetry?
   (b) What patterns of imagery, features of language, do you notice?
   (c) What are the structural features common to some or all of these songs?
2. (a) Make up an additional verse to . . . . (Useful since it helps students see the formal features of a text, and also to overcome their wariness of "poetry.")
   (b) Should such songs (or other forms of popular culture) be taught in literature courses?

Bibliography

The first chapter of Lawrence Levine's *Black Culture and Black Consciousness* offers important insights about the functions and structure of spirituals.

William Cullen Bryant (1794–1878)

Contributing Editor: Allison Heisch

Classroom Issues and Strategies

Most of the Bryant selections in the anthology are ruminative poems about the nature of life and the nature of nature. Some students really like this sort of thing, but substantial numbers are allergic to it.

The most effective strategy I have found is to provide visual back-up in the form of a Hudson River School slide show. A fancy version would parallel English Romantic poets (especially Gray, Cowper, and Wordsworth) and painters (e.g., Constable and Turner).

Bryant is a fine example of a writer who was not only popular but famous in his day. He can be used to open a discussion of the social and historical implications of such popularity (why it comes and why it goes), the essentially political character of anthologies (yes, even this one), and the idea of "fame" in connection with contemporary poets and poetry.

For students (and they are many) who do not naturally respond to Bryant, the questions generally run to "Why are we reading this?" Or, more decorously, "Why was he so popular?" Yet, they do respond to him as an example of how the American high culture invented itself. In an altogether different vein, the personal philosophy expressed in "Thanatopsis" has some enduring appeal.

Major Themes, Historical Perspectives, and Personal Issues

Bryant is very useful as a means of demonstrating the imitative mode through which New Englanders of an intellectual bent sought to establish an acceptable American literary voice. This is easily demonstrated by pairing his poems with comparable English productions. He can also be linked to the Transcendentalists—though with great caution, since much more is going on.

Significant Form, Style, or Artistic Conventions

Again, he should be shown in connection with his English models. It's useful to point out the self-conscious regularity of these poems both in connection with their particularly derivative subject matter and in contrast with the form and subjects of those contemporary poems and songs (well represented in this anthology) that were not informed by the dominant English literary culture.

Original Audience

I have usually talked about Bryant's audience in connection with the expansion of publishing in nineteenth-century America—especially magazines and newspapers. Ordinarily, students have no idea what a nineteenth-century newspaper would have looked like or contained. They never expect them to contain poetry. To demonstrate the probably contemporary audience, I have found it useful to collect and read commercially-produced greeting cards.

Comparisons, Contrasts, Connections

Freneau's "The House of Night" may be read with "Thanatopsis" to demonstrate both the imitation of dominant English poetic forms and transatlantic lag-time in creating them for American audiences. Obviously, Bryant may be read with Emerson and Thoreau as a pre- or proto-Transcendentalist. It is interesting to contrast Bryant's earnest view of nature with Emily Dickinson's ironic one. Bryant's poem on Abraham Lincoln against Whitman's ("When Lilacs Last . . . Bloom'd") makes a memorable contrast between Anglophile American poetry and poetry with a genuine American accent.

Questions for Reading and Discussion/ Approaches to Writing

1. (a) Based upon what you can glean from these poems, what sort of religious and philosophical outlook does this writer have?
    (b) Compare the view of nature in poems such as "To a Waterfowl" and "The Yellow Violet" with that in "The Prairies."
2. Bryant's "Thanatopsis" is often read as a proto-Transcendentalist poem; yet it was discovered and rushed to publication by Bryant's father, who by all accounts was a Calvinist. Some options:
    (a) Provide a Calvinist "reading" of "Thanatopsis."
    (b) Locate, compare, and explain potentially "Transcendental" and "Calvinist" elements in the poem.
    (c) Argue that it's one or the other (very artificial, but effective).

Bibliography

Brown, Charles H. *William Cullen Bryant*. Scribner, 1971.

Lydia Howard Huntley Sigourney (1791–1865)

Contributing Editor: Sandra A. Zagarell

Classroom Issues and Strategies

Among the biggest hurdles contemporary readers face when encountering much antebellum poetry is this poetry's appeal to a general readership and its conventionality. I'd begin by discussing the often sentimental and religious character of antebellum public poetry and its accessibility, in form and content, to a broad readership. I'd invite students to think about the cultural functions of such poetry as well as the personal effects it could have had on readers who lived in a society in which mortality rates were high, personal hardships frequent, and social inequities strong. I'd also point out the great antebellum popularity of religious literature and stress similarities between some of Sigourney's poetry and religious meditative essays or tracts. If students are familiar with hymns, they might compare voice, emotions, and language in some of the poems to those in hymns. Finally, I'd encourage students to recognize the social critiques embedded in much of Sigourney's writing—of gender constraints and patriarchy ("The Suttee," "To a Shred of Linen," "The Father"), of the genocide of Native Americans ("The Indian's Welcome to the Pilgrim Fathers," "Indian Names"), of war ("The Needle, Pen, and Sword").

Major Themes, Historical Perspectives, and Personal Issues

Sigourney was an educator, an historian, and a devout Christian, and much of her work was, in Nina Baym's phrase, "activist and interventionist." She capitalized on her role as a writer for the general public, producing writing that was often moral and didactic. Her work approached public subjects like social cohesion, social responsibility, nature, and history and encouraged readers' emotional responses to these subjects. Many of her poems, such as "The Suttee" and "The Indian's Welcome to the Pilgrim Fathers," cultivate her readers' sympathy with people from other nations or cultures; often, as in these poems, they also seek to mobilize readers' sympathies on behalf of social betterment (the condition of [all] women in "The Suttee," the nation's treatment of Native Americans in "The Indian's Welcome to the Pilgrim Fathers").

Even in many of her elegies she evokes the experience of death and loss common to all of her readers: "Death of an Infant" is an excellent example.

Significant Form, Style, or Artistic Conventions

Sigourney was a prolific and varied writer. I would draw attention to the adroitness with which her work exhibits the stylistic versatility of public verse. Among the forms her poems take are the ode, the nonsubjective lyric, elegy, and narrative and descriptive verse. She wrote in a variety of meters and verse patterns. Her poetry is situated in a sentimental tradition that contrasts with the Romantic one more familiar to, and more highly valued by, readers in the academy. The striking absence of the subjective consciousness of an organizing persona is a feature I would stress. As Annie Finch has observed, Sigourney's poetry gives religious, moral, and emotional truths what seems an independent or nonpersonal voice, or appears to represent nature or natural states without a mediating subjectivity.

I would also emphasize the poetry's focus on sentiments that are communally accepted (or should be, in Sigourney's eyes), and the ways in which it solicits readers' sense of connection with the subjects represented. Her poems often generalize a highly emotional situation in an objective mode that retains emotional coloration, as in "Death of an Infant," or describes natural phenomena in profoundly felt religious terms, as in "Niagara." She also uses the nonsubjective descriptive poem to represent the history or circumstances of members of racial or national groups different from those of her readers in order to invoke readers' sympathies, and frequently portrays constraints within gender with great feeling. Thus, without direct authorial comment, "The Father" dramatizes the extraordinary possessiveness of the lawyer-father and the dehumanizing inability to feel, and to grieve, to which the individualistic masculinity he embraces condemns him. The tears he finally sheds convert him to a selfless ethos, and arguably a communal one, which is similar to that of many of the poems. The implicit critique of antebellum masculinity in "The Father" also compares significantly with the much more direct exposé of patriarchy in a foreign country in "The Suttee."

I also call attention to the wit Sigourney's poems can display: "To a Shred of Linen" elicits an earlier agrarian New England while reflecting wryly on continuing societal ambivalence about women's creativity in a sphere other than the domestic.

Original Audience

Sigourney was antebellum America's most popular woman poet. She wrote for a northern (and, increasingly, a western) general readership. She published her work in newspapers and religious magazines, in anthologies and annuals, and in book form. She wrote using a variety of popular forms, including educational books, histories, and advice manuals as well as poetry, sketches, and autobiography. Her work helped create a community of readers in antebellum America, and much of it can be read as a conscious contribution to the establishment of America as a cohesive, humane, and Christian nation.

Comparisons, Contrasts, Connections

Many connections suggest themselves. The egolessness of Sigourney's highly public poetry can be contrasted interestingly with the subjectivity of Dickinson's very private poetry, just as Sigourney's conventionality contrasts with Dickinson's unconventionality. Similarities between the two can also be explored—their concerns with nature, with religion, and with women's circumstances—as can the use to which both put religious verse forms. Sigourney's work can also be compared fruitfully with that of contemporary male public poets. For instance, the presence of a perceiving persona in the poems of Bryant and the absence of such a persona in hers illuminates the permissible stances of male and female poets, while the use to which each puts these conventions can also be discussed. Additionally, the sympathy she elicits for Native Americans contrasts interestingly with the perspective of his "The Prairies," whereas a comparison of the relative reticence of the religious sentiment of her "Niagara" with the more consistent religious didacticism of his "To a Waterfowl" can show that gendered poetic stances did not absolutely determine the tone or approach writers took.

"The Father" can be taught very successfully with Poe's "Ligeia." Both are gothic short stories, written in the first person, that involve a man's possessive, and obsessive, love for a woman. Poe's stress on psychology contrasts nicely with Sigourney's emphasis on gender.

Questions for Reading and Discussion/ Approaches to Writing

1. How do we read these poems? What reading strategies are effective? (Such strategies might include exploring the trajectory of students' emotional responses to particular poems, discussing the ways in which certain poems elicit connections to students' personal ex-

perience, talking about the religious sentiment or the urge toward "humanitarian" connection, which some students may find compelling and others offensive.)

2. What is the effect of the generalized emotion, not tied to a particular speaker or persona, in many of the poems? Does it increase the poems' accessibility? Contribute to their didacticism?

3. How does "The Father" dramatize the self-serving nature of the narrator's fatherhood without overtly commenting on it? (Consider the effects of features such as the prominent "I," the sentence structure, the absence of characters' names, the kinds of analogies the narrator makes.) Why does his friends' concern allow him to cry? What sorts of changes does this expression of grief precipitate in him?

Henry Wadsworth Longfellow (1807–1882)

Contributing Editor: Allison Heisch

Classroom Issues and Strategies

If students have encountered Longfellow before taking a college course, the poems they know are not in this anthology: *Evangeline, The Song of Hiawatha, The Courtship of Miles Standish*. The Longfellow of this anthology is our late twentieth-century "revisionist" Longfellow, and except in poems such as "A Psalm of Life," he is almost unrecognizable as a writer who might have written those famous poems. If students have not actually read Longfellow, but merely heard of him (the typical case), they want to know why he's so famous.

Longfellow *is* accessible, and the fact is that in almost any class there will be students who adore "A Psalm of Life" and students who cannot stand it. Such a division, of course, presents the teacher with an ideal point of departure.

Although Longfellow is now very unfashionable, he is nevertheless an excellent vehicle for teaching about poetry either to the unlimited or the turned-off. Oddly enough, students in general respond to the story of his life almost more readily than to his poetry. That, therefore, is a good place to begin. They often ask about his fame. Some respond very positively to his sentimentalism, which can be tricky.

Major Themes, Historical Perspectives, and Personal Issues

Longfellow's themes in the poems in this collection are nearly indistinguishable from those of his contemporaries in England. It's useful to show him, therefore, as an example of the branch of American literature that created itself in admiring imitation of English literature. He is also that rare thing, a genuine celebrity of a poet, whose fame has subsided and whose stature has shrunk accordingly. Many of the poems we now admire most are from his later years, and conform better to modern taste than the poems for which he was famous in his lifetime. Thus, he can be used as a good example of the ways in which changing literary tastes alter literary reputations.

Significant Form, Style, or Artistic Conventions

Longfellow's poems are not only accessible in their meaning, but they are also highly regular in their form. It is very simple to teach metrics with Longfellow because he provides easy and memorable examples of so many metrical schemes. These can be presented in connection with Longfellow's personal history, for he is of course an academic poet, and as such a poet writing often self-consciously from a learned perspective. Thus, nothing with him seems wholly spontaneous or accidental.

Original Audience

Two points are easy and convenient where audience is concerned: First, the fact that Longfellow was in his time as popular as a rock singer might be in ours. Second, the fact that while he was writing for an audience descended from transplanted Englishmen, he was nevertheless trying to create for them an American poetry crafted from "native" materials, thereby making chauvinist myth. Admittedly, it's hard to get to that point from the selections in the present anthology, but since "The Jewish Cemetery at Newport" was originally part of *The Courtship of Miles Standish*, a way *can* be found.

Comparisons, Contrasts, Connections

There are many directions to travel here: First, locate Longfellow in New England with Emerson and the Transcendentalists; second, locate him as a (necessary?) predecessor to Whitman, and then compare their views of America; third, set his view of life and nature against that of native poets.

Questions for Reading and Discussion/ Approaches to Writing

1. (a) To whom is he writing? What is his message?
   (b) Translate "A Psalm of Life" *literally* and say whether you agree or disagree.
   (c) What are Longfellow's favorite words?
2. How has Longfellow changed or maintained his essential view of life between "A Psalm of Life" and "Aftermath"?

Bibliography

Because his poetry is more impressive taken together than individually analyzed, Longfellow has commanded whole books more often than single articles.

Wagenknecht, Edward. *Henry Wadsworth Longfellow*. New York: Ungar, 1986.

Walt Whitman (1819–1892)

Contributing Editor: Betsy Eikkila

Classroom Issues and Strategies

I use the 1855 versions of "Song of Myself" and "The Sleepers" because I think these poems represent Whitman at his unrevised best. I begin with a biographical introduction, stressing Whitman's active engagement as radical Democrat and party journalist in the major political conflicts of pre–Civil War America. The inscription poem "One's-Self I Sing" and his vision of the poet balanced between pride and sympathy in the 1855 Preface serve as a good introduction to "Song of Myself." I usually begin by asking the students to talk about Whitman's free verse technique. What ordering devices does he use in the opening lines to achieve his poetic design: these include repetition, biblical parallelism, rhythmic recurrence, assonance, and consonance.

Section 15 is a good illustration of the ways Whitman's catalog technique serves as a democratizing device, inscribing the pattern of many and one. By basing his verse in the single, end-stopped line at the same time that he fuses this line—through various linking devices—with the larger structure of the whole, Whitman weaves an overall pattern of unity in diversity. This pattern of many and one—the *e pluribus unum* that was the revolutionary seal of the American republic—is the overarching figure of *Leaves of Grass*.

I present "Song of Myself" as a drama of democratic identity in which the poet seeks to balance and reconcile major conflicts in the body politic of America: the conflict between "separate person" and "en masse," individualism and equality, liberty and union, the South and the North, the farm and the city, labor and capital, black and white, female and male, religion and science. One can discuss any of the individual sections of the poem in relation to this conflict. Moments of particular conflict and crisis occur in sections 28 and 38. I ask the students to discuss the specific nature of the crisis in each of these sections. Both involve a loss of balance.

In section 28, the protagonist loses bodily balance as he is swept away by an erotic, masturbatory urge. Ask the students to think about why a masturbation fantasy occurs in a poem about democracy. Ask them to think about why the masturbatory fit is represented in the language of political insurrection. These questions lead to interesting observations about the relation between political power and power over the body. Masturbation is, in effect, the political ground on which Whitman tests the theory of democracy. Within the democratic economy of his poem, the turbulence of the body, like the turbulence of the masses, is part of a natural regenerative order.

If section 28 involves a loss of bodily balance, section 38 involves a loss of self in empathetic identification with others. In discussing the crisis in section 38, ask the students what Whitman means by the lines: "I find myself on the verge of a usual mistake." This will usually lead back to the end of section 3, where the poet begins identifying with scenes of suffering, carnage, and death. Some of these scenes are linked with the nation's history: the hounded slave, the Texas war, the American Revolution. The poet appears to be on the verge of losing faith in the divine potency of the individual and the regenerative pattern of the whole. He resolves the crisis by remembering the divinity of Christ as a living power existing within rather than outside of every individual.

The resolution of this crisis leads to the emergence of the divinely empowered poet who presides over the final passages of the poem, declaring his ultimate faith in the "form, union, plan" of the universe. Here you might want to discuss the relation between this poetic affirmation of democratic faith and union and the fact of an American Union that was in the throes of dissolution.

Since Whitman's poetic development corresponds with stages in his own and the nation's history, a chronological presentation works well in the classroom. After discussing "Song of Myself," you might want to discuss other 1855 poems such as "The Sleepers" and "There Was a Child Went Forth." "The Sleepers," which was toned down in later versions, represents in both its form and its content the half-formed, erotically charged, and anxiety-ridden fantasies of the dream state. The poem anticipates Freud's "unconscious" and the literary experiments of the surrealists. But the poem is revolutionary not only in its psychosexual dimension. The poet also descends into a kind of political unconscious of the nation, dredging up images of regeneration through violence associated with Washington and the battle for American independence, the slave as black Lucifer, and the Indian squaw.

If you have time to do later work by Whitman, the 1860 poems might be grouped together since they correspond with a period of both personal and national crisis. This crisis is most effectively represented in "As I Ebb'd with the Ocean of Life"; within the context of *Leaves of Grass*, "Out of the Cradle Endlessly Rocking" appears to respond to this crisis. Ask the students to comment on the differences between the "amative" poems of *Children of Adam* and the "adhesive" poems of *Calamus*. This will lead to a discussion of Whitman's sexual politics.

Women students have particularly strong and mixed reactions to "A Woman Waits for Me": they are attracted by Whitman's celebration of an erotically charged female body, yet are repelled by the fact that she seems rhetorically prone. The students will usually note that Whitman's poems to men seem more immediate and personal than the poems of *Children of Adam*. "In Paths Untrodden" reflects Whitman's split at this time between the public culture of democracy and his desire to tell secrets, to "come out" poetically by naming his hitherto unspeakable passion for men. You might want to remind the students that the term "homosexual" did not yet exist, and thus Whitman was breaking the path toward a language of male love. His invention is particularly evident in "When I Heard at the Close of the Day," where the power and tenderness of his feelings for his lover are linked with the rhythms of a completely natural order. The "confessional" note in the poems anticipates the later work of Allen Ginsberg, Robert Lowell, and Sylvia Plath. Ask the students to reflect on why it was the poems of *Children of Adam* and not *Calamus* that most shocked the literary establishment. It was really not until Allen Ginsberg wrote his comic tribute to Whitman, "In a Supermarket in California," that Whitman, the homosexual poet, came fully out of the closet—at least in America.

I usually begin discussion of the war poems by asking how the experience of fratricidal war might affect Whitman as the poet of national union. This will lead to reflections on the tragedy of the Civil War. The poems of *Drum-Taps*—which proceed from militant exultation, to the actual experience of war, to demobilization and reconciliation—might be read as an attempt to place the butchery of the war within a poetic and ultimately regenerative design. Ask the students to compare Whitman's war poems with his earlier poems. They are at once more formally controlled and more realistic—stylistic changes that are linked with the war context. "A March in the Ranks Hard-Prest, and the Road Unknown" and "The Artilleryman's Vision" are proto-modern poems in which the individual appears as an actor in a drama of history he no longer understands nor controls. Whitman's ambivalence about black emancipation is evident in "Ethiopia Saluting the Colors." "Vigil Strange I Kept on the Field One Night" and "As I Lay with My Head in Your Lap Camerado" are particularly effective in suggesting the ways the wartime context of male bonding and comradeship gave Whitman a legitimate language and social frame within which to express his love for men.

In discussing Whitman's famous elegy on the death of President Lincoln, it is interesting to begin by asking what remains unsaid in the poem. For one thing, Lincoln is never named as the subject within the context of the poem; his death becomes representative of all the war dead. By placing Lincoln's death within a timeless regenerative order of nature, Whitman's "Lilacs" also "covers over" the fact of Lincoln's unnatural and violent assassination. Although the vision of battle in section 15 is often passed over in critical considerations of the poem, this bloody sight of "battle-corpses" and the "debris" of war is, I believe, the unspeakable honor and real subject of the poem.

Democratic Vistas (1871) might be read either as an introduction to or a conclusion to the study of Whitman. In the essay, he struggles with the central tensions and paradoxes of American, New World experience. These conflicts intensify and are more urgently addressed in the post-Civil War period as the unleashed force of market capitalism and the dynamic of modem civilization appear to spin out of control. "Who bridles Leviathan?" Whitman asks in *Democratic Vistas*. It is a fitting question with which to conclude the study of Whitman and to begin the study of the modern world.

Emily Dickinson (1830–1886)

Contributing Editors: Peggy McIntosh and Ellen Louise Hart

Classroom Issues and Strategies

Students may have problems with the appearance of the poems—with the fact that they are without titles; that they are often short and compact, compressed; that the dash is so often used in the place of traditional punctuation. Some students will be put off by the grammatical elisions and ellipses, and some by the fact that the poems often do not quickly display a central, controlling metaphor or an easily identifiable narrative theme. Students who are already intimidated by poetry may find the poems difficult and unyielding. Some, however, may find Dickinson's brevity and conciseness startling and enjoyable. Those who have false notions that everything in poetry means or symbolizes something else, and that the reader must crack the code and come up with a "solution" to each poem's meaning, will be frustrated by Dickinson or will read the poems with atrocious insensitivity. Dickinson's work requires intense concentration, imagination, and unusually high tolerance for ambiguity.

Some students may want to dismiss Dickinson as an "old maid" or as a woman who "missed out on life" by not marrying. One student asked, "Why didn't she just move to Boston and get a job?" Students want to know about Dickinson's life and loves, her personal relationships with both men and women; they are curious about why she chose not to publish; they are interested in her religious/spiritual life, her faith, and her belief in immortality. They want to know what the dilemmas of her life were, as they manifested themselves in her writing: What her psychic states were, what tormented her, what she mourned, what drove her close to madness, why she was fascinated with death and dying. Addressing these questions allows the opportunity to discuss the oversimplifying and stereotyping that result from ignorance of social history as well as insistence on heterosexism.

Students should be prepared for the poems by being encouraged to speculate. An instructor can invite students to explore each poem as an experiment, and to ease into the poetry, understanding that Dickinson was a poet who truly "questioned authority" and whose work defies authoritative readings. All of her difficulties as listed above can be seen as connected with her radically original imagination.

Students can be directed toward approaching these poems with "lexicon" in hand, as Dickinson wrote them. Here is the perfect opportunity for an exercise with the OED. Students can be asked to make a list as they read of words that begin to seem to them particularly Dickinsonian; "Circumference," for example. They can also list characteristic phrases or images. The selection of poems can be parceled out in certain groupings in which linked images, emotions, or descriptions of natural phenomena are easily recognizable.

Students can be assigned to write journals in which they record their first impressions and discoveries, as well as later commentary on poems and further stages of interpretation. Asking people to read poems out loud will help them to learn to hear the poet's voice and to tune their ears to her rhymes, rhythms, and syntax. Above all, the instructor should not pretend assurance about Dickinson's meanings and intentions.

It works well to have students make a selection of poems on a theme or image cluster, and then work in groups with the selected poems, afterwards presenting their readings. Such group work can create flexibility while giving students confidence in their own perceptions.

Another presentation that is very useful is the kind of demonstration Susan Howe gives and which some other teachers now use. Make a copy of a Thomas Johnson version of a poem and then make a typed transcription of the same poem using Franklin's *Manuscript Books*. This can lead to interesting discussions of editing questions involved with Dickinson: how to represent the line breaks and the punctuation; how to render these unpublished poems in print.

Major Themes, Historical Perspectives, and Personal Issues

Students need to know something about Dickinson's life, her schooling, religious upbringing and subsequent rebellion, her family members, and the close friends who became the audience for her poems. (Much of this is outlined in the headnote.) They will be helped by having some historical sense of women and men in nineteenth-century New England. They need information on women's habits of reading and writing, on friendships among women, religious revivalism, and life in a small college town like Amherst. Awareness of class, class consciousness, and social customs for families like the Dickinsons and their circle of friends will help prevent questions like the one cited above on why Dickinson didn't just move and "go for it" in a city. Students should be discouraged from discussing the poems as "feminine" or as demonstrating "the woman's point of view."

A discussion of homophobia is necessary. Here the headnote should be helpful. The love poems are not exclusively heterosexual. Students should be encouraged to examine the erotics of this poetry without being limited to conventional notions of gender. Dickinson uses a variety of voices in these poems, writing as a child (often a boy), a wife-to-be, a woman rejected, and as a voice of authority which we often associate with maleness. These voices or roles or "poses," as they are sometimes called, need to be identified and examined. Here are the multiplicities of self. Do we need to reconcile these voices? What happens when we don't? Students may reflect on or write about multiplicities of experience, perspective, and voice in themselves.

Significant Form, Style, or Artistic Conventions

Information should be provided about other American and British writers publishing at this time, those whom Dickinson read, those especially popular at the time but not as well known, as well as those still recognized: Emerson, Longfellow, Stowe, Helen Hunt Jackson, Elizabeth Barrett Browning, George Eliot, Dickens.

Dickinson's poetry is very dissimilar to poetry being published at the same time. Attention needs to be drawn to this fact and to the originality, the intentional and consistent innovativeness, of her style. Questions of style can also lead to observations concerning the thin line between poetry and prose in Dickinson's letters, and about the complex and integral relationships between the two genres throughout her writing. Students can be invited to read letters as poems and to read poems as letters, exploring the ways in which Dickinson's work challenges traditional notions of the boundaries of genre.

Students need to know about the publishing and editing history of the poems, to understand how Dickinson worked—collecting poems into packets, identifying words for revision, sending poems to various recipients, and apparently avoiding publication during her lifetime. There is also the question of the editing: What did a given poem look like when early editors published it, and when Thomas Johnson published the same poem in the variorum edition? Students should be made familiar with Thomas Johnson's variorum as well as R. W. Franklin's *Manuscript Books of Emily Dickinson*. What did the variorum edition of the poems bring to Dickinson scholarship? What was available before? What has R. W. Franklin's publication of the manuscript books meant? And what about Susan Howe's argument that Dickinson's original line breaks must be honored? Some students may wish to take up the question of how to represent in type Dickinson's marks of punctuation.

For two poems in our selection we include in footnotes all the "variants," or alternate word choices Dickinson noted for each poem. Using Franklin's *Manuscript Books,* students can observe in detail the

326 • *The Heath Anthology of American Literature*

poet's system for marking possible changes and listing variants. Furthermore, study of the facsimiles in the Franklin edition will give students an opportunity to observe the artistic conventions in Dickinson's
manuscripts—lineation and punctuation as well as her handwriting, or
calligraphy, and her use of space between letters, words, and at the end
of a line. Investigation of the manuscripts will give students the opportunity to discuss what has been lost in her visual art in the print transcriptions of the poems. In addition, reading the poems in the
manuscript volumes encourages students to test out the theories of some
critics that these volumes are artistic units with narrative and thematic
cohesion.

It is important to point out that the number that appears at the
head of each poem in our selection is not a part of the space of the
poem, and that these numbers were never used by the poet. They were
established by Thomas Johnson in his attempt to arrange the complete
poems chronologically. Since so few of Dickinson's manuscripts can be
dated, the Johnson numbers are most often speculative. Their standard
use has been as a system of reference, and as convenient as this system
may be, a less artificial way of referring to a poem is to use the first line.

Original Audience

Students should look at Franklin (or photocopies of pages from
Franklin) to see how the "packets" or "fascicles" looked. Reading poems
sent in letters or with letters is a way of considering audiences, both
Dickinson's immediate audience and her writing for posterity. The variorum edition identifies poems sent in letters; the three volumes of *Letters*
list many enclosed poems.

Comparisons, Contrasts, Connections

Dickinson can be read with her contemporaries, the American and
British writers of her time. She may also be read in the context of
twentieth-century New England writers, Robert Frost and Robert Lowell, for example, or with current New England women writers, May Sar-
ton and Maxine Kumin, for example. A regional sense is a strong thread
in Dickinson's writing. She may be read in the context of experiments in
modernism, in relation to e. e. cummings, for example. Dickinson also
fits within a continuum of American women poets from Anne Bradstreet
and Phillis Wheatley through Amy Lowell, Gertrude Stein, Edna St. Vincent Millay, H.D., Marianne Moore, Sylvia Plath, Anne Sexton, Adrienne
Rich, Audre Lorde, and Judy Grahn. (This, of course, is only one selec-

tion, which represents many of the best-known American writers. There
are other such lists.)

Questions for Reading and Discussion/
Approaches to Writing

Cumbersome term papers "arguing" a single thesis on Dickinson are
usually quite out of tune with her own multifaceted sensibility and intelligence. Reading a poem as a statement of a creed, i.e., as a "proof" that
Dickinson believed this or that, is usually fatal to common sense. We
suggest that the following 15 writing assignments on Dickinson will suit
a variety of students with a variety of learning styles.

1. All her life, Emily Dickinson seems to have felt she was encum-
   bered by structures that did not fit her, whether structures of religion, belief, value, language, thought, manners, or institutions. If
   you share her feeling, give some examples of her sense of the
   problem and then some examples of your own sense of it, in your
   life.

2. 1862, a year in which Dickinson wrote more than 300 poems,
   seems to have been a year of great emotional intensity for her.
   Drawing on poems from 1862 given in this anthology, trace some
   recurrent themes or designs in the poems of that year.

3. Kathleen Raine has written: "For the poet when he begins to write
   there is no poem, in the sense of a construction of words; and the
   concentration of the mind is upon something else, that precedes
   words, and by which the words, as they are written, must constantly
   be checked and rectified."

   If this quotation rings true for you, choose one or more poems
   and discuss the "something else" and the process by which Dickinson apparently revised toward it, using Johnson's three-volume
   edition, which shows all known revisions.

4. You are Emily Dickinson. An acquaintance who does not know you
   very well has just suggested that the time you spend alone must feel
   somewhat empty. Write a fragment of a letter or a poem in which
   you respond as you think she might.

5. Many of Dickinson's poems are not so much about ideas or themes,
   as about the process of seeing or coming to see, or guess, or know.
   Trace the *elements of process* in one or more poems; then imitate the
   sense of process in a passage of poetry or prose of your own.

6. What do you appreciate about Emily Dickinson, and what do you
   think she hoped readers would appreciate about her?

7. Read Jay Leyda's collection of documents about Emily Dickinson's year of college in *The Years and Hours of Emily Dickinson,* and read Dickinson's letters from her year away. Compare your own college experience with hers. Considering both the pressures on you and the pleasures you experience, how do you differ from or resemble her?

8. Dickinson's poems have both authority and obliqueness, as suggested in her line "Tell all the Truth but tell it slant." Discuss examples of Dickinson's techniques of slantwise style and some of their effects on you as reader.

9. Reading Dickinson is a personal matter, and readers' perceptions of her change continually. On each of three different days, begin an essay entitled "On Reading Emily Dickinson." Do not work for consistency, but rather for a fresh account of your perception on each day.

10. For many English and American poets, moments of "seeing" accurately have often been moments of affirmation. For Dickinson, they were often moments of pain. Discuss any aspects of the poems on pain that interest you, shedding light, if possible, on her words "A nearness to Tremendousness/An Agony Procures. . . ."

11. Richard Wilbur wrote:

    "At some point Emily Dickinson sent her whole Calvinist vocabulary into exile, telling it not to come back until it would subserve her own sense of things. . . . Of course, that is not a true story, but it is a way of saying what I find most remarkable in Emily Dickinson. She inherited a great and overbearing vocabulary which, had she used it submissively, would have forced her to express an established theology and psychology. But she would not let that vocabulary write her poems for her."

    Analyze some of the religious poems that seem to you unorthodox or surprising, and write a short piece of your own, in poetry or prose, in which you use the vocabulary of a religious tradition in an unusual way that "subserves your own sense of things."

12. Write four alternative first paragraphs to a paper entitled "Emily Dickinson."

13. Imagine a conversation between Emily Dickinson and any one of the other women writers read for this course. What might they have to talk about? Add a third woman (perhaps yourself) to the conversation if you like. Draw on all the sources of evidence that you have.

14. Dickinson used traditional hymn meter, but her poems are not like traditional hymns. Choose the words to any hymn you know, and

rewrite them until they sound as much like Dickinson as possible. You may virtually have to abandon the original hymn.

15. Emily Dickinson's first editors thought they were doing her a favor by changing certain words, repunctuating her poetry, and standardizing the line breaks. Using the three-volume Johnson edition and the Franklin manuscript books, judge for yourself, in the case of two or three poems in which changes were made.

Bibliography

See the bibliography in the Emily Dickinson headnote in *The Heath Anthology*. The following list should be helpful as well.

Cameron, Sharon. *Choosing Not Choosing: Dickinson's Fascicles*. Chicago: University of Chicago Press, 1992.

Howe, Susan. "Women and Their Effect in the Distance." In *Ironwood* 28, "Dickinson/Spicer: A Special Issue," vol. 4, no. 2 (Fall 1986): 58–91.

Juhasz, Suzanne, Cristanne Miller, and Martha Nell Smith. *Comic Power in Emily Dickinson*. Austin: University of Texas Press, 1993.

Leyda, Jay. *The Years and Hours of Emily Dickinson*. 2 vols. New Haven: Yale University Press, 1960.

McNeil, Helen. *Emily Dickinson*. New York: Virago/Pantheon Pioneers, 1986. This is a short, readable critical biography of Dickinson that is informed by the theories of feminism as well as deconstruction. This text talks of Dickinson in current critical language. As a biography, it is more convenient for the teacher with little time than sifting through Sewall's book. McNeil uses Sewall's research for the text, so it is very helpful. We recommend a run through the entire text of 181 pages; in a pinch the introduction and the first two chapters, "Dickinson and Knowledge" and "Dickinson and Difference," provide a starting place.

St. Armand, Barton Levi. *Emily Dickinson and Her Culture*. Cambridge: Cambridge University Press, 1984.

Late Nineteenth Century
1865–1910

The Development of Women's Narratives
Regional Voices, National Voices

The conjunction/contradiction of the terms "regional" and "national," along with the focus on gender indicated by *women's* narrative, both suggest a turn away from a deductive approach to literary categorization and analysis based on assumptions concerning what is universal or central about the human—and more specifically the national—experience and a move toward an inductive approach that recognizes the value of regarding the specificity of cultural context in understanding how a text works. Rather than *a priori* assuming certain texts or cultural experiences to be marginal because they foreground issues of region and gender, and thereby assert the centrality of other texts supposedly free of such "ancillary" considerations, we can instead expand the possibilities for classroom discussion and pedagogical practice by regarding all human experience and cultural expression as profoundly "regional," as intimately concerned with questions of region and gender, as well as race, social class, and other crucial processes of social definition. To group together, either in the anthology or on a syllabus, Henry James and Charles Chesnutt, African-American folktales, and *Adventures of Huckleberry Finn,* is not to argue for the "equivalency" of these texts according to some external standard of literary evaluation, but to invite a consideration and comparison of their regionalness—the unique cultural contexts of their productions—as well as the dialogue, debate, and competition going on among them. Instead of using a set methodology for the reading of all texts, the conjunction of the texts in these sections asks students and teachers to consider how different texts signal different audience expectations, how they indicate or counter-indicate a desired audience, how they speak to a variety of audiences and audience expectations at once, how "regions," whether regions of gender or geography, race or class communicate with each other.

If we regard all texts as regional, from the perspective of pedagogy the primary region for class investigation is the classroom itself, where the particularity and "regionality" of each student's response to the literature occurs. As a preparation for a discussion of terms like "central" and "regional," "major" and "minor," "representative" and "marginal," students can explore their own responses to see what they find familiar and foreign in these texts. Here again the inductive approach works well, for while such reactions will obviously vary from student to student and from class to class, they provide us with a region-specific context for the consideration of the reception history of these works. Following

Judith Fetterley's lead in *The Resisting Reader,* not only women in the class can explore the traditional experience of reading texts that assume the centrality of male experience, but all students can consider the difference represented by texts that assume the definitiveness and centrality of female experience—the texts in the section on women's narrative and Kate Chopin, Grace King, and Alice Dunbar-Nelson in the section on regional literature. Similarly, students from outside the Northeast can discuss what it's like reading texts that take the geography, climate, and culture of New England as a norm, or that figure the West as someplace wild, exotic, and mysterious. Clearly, this approach allows for a variety of cultural configurations and can be adapted to the specific demographics of the individual classroom.

Late nineteenth-century women's narratives, because they were long dismissed as merely "regionalist" writing, are in many ways now central to this regional approach to pedagogy. In her essay on "Regionalism and Woman's Culture," Marjorie Pryse suggests that the women writers traditionally classified as "regionalists" (writers such as Mary Wilkins Freeman and Sarah Orne Jewett) used the idea of region rhetorically as a means of demonstrating that supposedly universal terms like "mother," "home," "black," and "white" are in fact socially constructed, while at the same time negotiating a cultural space to make such demonstrations. These texts thus raise the question of how to get to center stage from the margins. Such a question functions both as a means of interpreting a story like the chapter entitled "The Actress" from Louisa May Alcott's novel *Work* and a way of understanding Alcott's position as a writer. Such a manipulation of center and margin can be applied equally to Paul Laurence Dunbar or Charles Chesnutt, who write of the African-American experience in the language of formal European literary traditions (Henry Louis Gates, Jr.'s work on the African-American cultural tradition of "signifyin(g)"—of both appropriating and ironically transforming forms and values from the dominant culture as part of an originally African rhetorical tradition—is especially applicable here as well as suggestive of rhetorical strategies used by any marginalized group), and to Samuel Clemens, who uses dialect and satire to write about a middle-class white world he both despised and aspired to.

Works Cited

Fetterley, Judith. *The Resisting Reader: A Feminist Approach to American Fiction.* Bloomington: Indiana University Press, 1978.

Gates, Henry Louis, Jr. *The Signifying Monkey: A Theory of African-American Literary Criticism.* New York: Oxford University Press, 1988.

Pryse, Marjorie. " 'Distilling Essences': Regionalism and 'Women's Culture.' " *American Literary Realism* 25 (1993): 1–15.

The Development of Women's Narratives

Julia A. J. Foote (1823–1900)

Contributing Editor: William L. Andrews

Classroom Issues and Strategies

Julia Foote's intensely religious view of life often contrasts with the secularism of today's students. Students often wonder whether she was self-deceived in thinking herself authorized by the Holy Spirit to assert her will over those of the general mass of people in her church. It is important, therefore, to emphasize the relationship of Foote's religious world view to her feminism. She supports her feminism by citing biblical precedent.

Major Themes, Historical Perspectives, and Personal Issues

Major themes include Foote's search for her authentic self and the black woman's search for power and voice in male-dominated religious institutions.

Significant Form, Style, or Artistic Conventions

How does Foote turn a straightforward narrative of her life into an argument for Christianity, feminism, and holiness?

Original Audience

I stress to the students that Foote is addressing someone in particular—ask them how they can identify who this is.

Comparisons, Contrasts, Connections

Interesting comparisons can be made with slave narrators like Frederick Douglass, since Foote and Douglass are both concerned with affirming their sense of a spirit within that owes its allegiance only to transcendent ideals.

Bibliography

Andrews, William L., ed. *Sisters of the Spirit: Three Black Women's Autobiographies of the Nineteenth Century*. Bloomington: Indiana University Press, 1986. Discusses and annotates Foote's entire autobiography.

Rebecca Harding Davis (1831–1910)

Contributing Editor: Judith Roman-Royer

Classroom Issues and Strategies

Problems in teaching Davis include: dialect, allusions, confusing dialogue, hard-to-identify speakers, vague frame story, religious solution, and the juxtaposition of sentimental language with religiosity and realism. To address these problems consider the following:

1. Explain the dialect (see the footnotes).
2. Try to ignore the allusions; most are not important to the heart of meaning.
3. The names of characters, their jobs, the speakers, and their roles need to be clarified.

   Kirby, son of Kirby the mill owner—He is aware of the problems of the workers but sees them as insoluble; he takes the attitude of Pontius Pilate.

   Dr. May, a town physician—He is idealistic, sympathetic to the workers, but naive about reality and thus unintentionally cruel to Hugh.

"Captain"—The reporter for the city paper.

Mitchell, Kirby's intellectual brother-in-law, visitor to the South—He is cold, cynically socialistic.

4. Discuss the frame story. Careful readers will find inconsistencies in the frame narratives that explain the narrator's perspective. Early in the story, the narrator "happens" to be in the house, apparently a visitor, but at the end of the story, the house and statue of the korl woman seem to belong to her. The story of the Wolfe family is said to be set thirty years in the past, so how did the narrator come to know it in such intimate detail? One of my students suggested that the narrator may be Janey, who has somehow risen above her environment and become a writer, a solution that is provocative but unsubstantiated by the text.

5. Show how Davis is ambiguous about religious solution. She espouses it, but her realistic picture of the problem is so vivid that it seems impossible to the reader that just Quaker kindness will solve the problems.

6. The swing between romanticism and realism is at the heart of this author.

Some students find this work depressing, but some like it. They can be asked to compare the situation of the poor today, especially the homeless and uneducated and today's immigrants. Students can also be interested in a discussion of religion's role in comforting and/or silencing the poor.

Major Themes, Historical Perspectives, and Personal Issues

"Life in the Iron-Mills" is an accessible text that can be assigned and discussed in a single class meeting. Many students reject the "naturalistic" view inherent in the story that the characters could do little to help themselves. Contemporary students, educated to believe in the Alger myth, are eager to protest that Hugh could have lifted himself out of his poverty or moved to the city to become an artist.

Perhaps a greater problem may be students' unwillingness to see the feminist subtext of the story discovered by Tillie Olsen. The story deals quite openly with the life of an iron-worker; how, then, do we find in it the story of a thwarted "spinster" fiction writer? To make this reading credible, students will need to know something of Davis's life story (see headnote); the position of unmarried women in society (their dependence on their families, the lack of socially acceptable ways for a woman to earn a living, and the impossibility of living alone); and the incredible isolation of writers who lived anywhere in America outside of Boston and perhaps New York at this period. In the context of a traditional American literature survey, Davis's frustration could be related to that of writers like Cooper and Irving and the sense of the U.S. as an artistic wilderness that prevailed early in the century.

Significant Form, Style, or Artistic Conventions

As far as style, many would have found the work oppressively realistic and unpleasant. The Hawthornes used words like "gloomy" and even "mouldy" to describe Davis's writing.

Original Audience

The work was written for an upper-middle-class and upper-class audience, the readers of the *Atlantic,* who were the elite of the country at the time. Many had familiarity with languages and the literary allusions in the work as well as intimate knowledge of the New Testament. Most were "liberal" Christians and although some were social reformers, virtually all believed the individual Christian had a responsibility to people like Hugh and Deb. The audience was highly receptive to Davis's message.

The difference in the audience now is that college students come from a broader spectrum of society. This has two effects: First, some of them may have worked in factories or come from blue-collar families and have experience closer to that of Hugh and Deb; second, the language of the text is apt to be more difficult for them. The excess of punctuation is an impediment. The sentimental exclamations probably differ little from some kinds of contemporary popular literature that students may have encountered.

Comparisons, Contrasts, Connections

Davis can be compared to

1. Hawthorne, who had an influence on Davis, especially *House of the Seven Gables*; American Romantic literature.
2. Dickens—sentimental realism.
3. Popular literature of today.
4. Novels of social criticism, such as *Uncle Tom's Cabin*; even later muckraking novels, such as *The Jungle*.

Questions for Reading and Discussion/ Approaches to Writing

1. What is the purpose of the rhetorical questions posed by the author/narrator at various points in the story? Do they refer simply to the prospect of salvation for a man convicted of stealing, or do they imply the naturalistic view that Hugh's theft is excused by his unfortunate environment and heredity? Some students may recognize what is probably religious rhetoric in the questions: perhaps the teacher can simply encourage students to seek additional possibilities.

2. They could write a paper discussing the story as a transitional work between Romanticism and realism, using traits outlined in Richard Chase's *American Novel and Its Tradition.*

Bibliography

Tillie Olsen's essay in the Feminist Press edition is probably the most accessible place to go for additional information. It is highly personal but helpful.

Louisa May Alcott (1832–1888)

Contributing Editor: Elizabeth Keyser

Classroom Issues and Strategies

"Actress," the third chapter of Louisa May Alcott's novel *Work,* provides an ideal introduction to the author, for throughout her career Alcott was concerned with woman as actress—both on and off stage. Students, however, may be perplexed as to why Christie equates acting first with rebellion, then with the loss of her womanliness. Thus they need to understand that professional acting in Alcott's day placed women beyond the pale of respectable society. Even as amateur theatricals were becoming a staple of Victorian parlor entertainment, the exposure of women to public view was still thought to compromise their innocence, purity, and, in a word, virtue. But Alcott's contemporaries may also have believed that the element of duplicity involved in acting was incompatible with their ideal of woman as simple, artless, without guile. This disjunction between woman and actress is suggested by the title of a recently reprinted Alcott sensation story, "LaJeune: or, Actress and Woman" (one of four stories with actress heroines in *Freaks of Genius*). The male narrator mistrusts the brilliant actress "LaJeune," but though he proves her vaunted youth a fraud, he finds it perpetrated for the sake of her invalid husband, not, as he suspected, for her opium-eating or gambling habit. Like "LaJeune," Alcott's actress stories imply that a woman can preserve her integrity while pursuing a public career but that a patriarchal society forces women to become actresses in their private lives. Thus, Judith Fetterley has recently observed of Jean Muir, the professional actress turned governess in Alcott's best-known sensation story, "Behind a Mask," that in order to analyze the needs of every person in the house, Muir must be supremely conscious. Ironically, therefore, the innocence, simplicity, even stupidity imputed to her is in fact incompatible with her role (6).

Some of Alcott's heroines, like Christie Devon, Jean Muir, and La-Jeune, are professional actresses, but the heroines of other authors, such as Jane Austen, Charlotte Brontë, and Edith Wharton, appear only in amateur theatricals or *tableaux vivants*. Sylvia Yule, the heroine of Alcott's first novel, *Moods*, enacts scenes from Shakespeare for male friends (as Christie later does in *Work*) and, like Jo March in *Little Women*, revels in male roles, giving vent to feelings she cannot otherwise express. Similarly, Gladys, the angelic heroine of Alcott's full-length sensation novel, *A Modern Mephistopheles*, suggests the complexity of women's nature, its intellectual and emotional range, by playing the villainous Vivien from Tennyson's *Idylls of the King*. But even entirely off-stage Alcott's heroines strike poses and assume disguises, play roles and contrive scenes. They position themselves against becoming backdrops, then feign ignorance of a man's approach; they arrange their hair so as to conceal their facial expressions; they take opium so as to appear more radiant; they take still more so as to appear passionless. They affect to cry and then pretend to attempt in vain to conceal the tears. The pervasiveness of stagecraft in Alcott's fiction—the extent to which her heroines don masks and play roles—has led some critics to suspect the author of a similar duplicity. Fetterley and others see Alcott's persona as Aunt Jo, the author of *Little Women* and its sequels, as a kind of mask. Angela Estes and Kathleen Lant read *Little Women* as a melodrama in which the author whisks Jo from the stage and replaces her with Beth, confident that her readers will not detect the masquerade. Rena Sanderson and others argue that Alcott, in having the hero of *A Modern Mephistopheles* confess to having passed off another's works as his own, confesses to her own literary hoax.

The male narrator of Alcott's story "A Double Tragedy" asserts that "an actor learns to live a double life." So, too, according to Alcott's fiction, do women—and women authors. In the selection "Actress," Christie comes to grief when, as an actress, she steps from the frame in which she impersonates another actress, who in turn impersonates a portrait of herself. Thus Alcott, by having Christie play Peg Woffington in Charles Reade's *Masks and Faces,* signifies the entrapment of women in multiple roles and the difficulty of escaping them without injury.

Major Themes, Historical Perspectives, and Personal Issues

In "Actress" we find that the professional actress acquires a measure of power and independence, but that the theater in many ways mirrors larger society. The chapter opens with Christie "resolving not to be a slave to anybody." And by becoming "Queen of the Amazons," she seems to have escaped that subservient condition. Further, in becoming an actress, Christie continues to declare her independence to Uncle Enos. At the thought of his disapproval "a delicious sense of freedom pervaded her soul, and the old defiant spirit seemed to rise up within her." Yet to obtain her role, Christie must first subject herself to dehumanizing scrutiny. In fact, her manager's examination reminds us of the slave market scenes in *Uncle Tom's Cabin.* And her Amazon troupe is described as "a most forlorn band of warriors . . . afraid to speak, lest they should infringe some rule." Far from being true Amazons, capable of terrorizing their male enemies, the show girls cower in terror of male authority. Christie recovers some of her enthusiasm on opening night, but the narrator tells us that her warlike trappings are "poor counterfeit." Even the "grand tableau," in which the martial queen stands triumphantly over the princess she has rescued, seems not so much a reversal of as a variation on the familiar male script. Yet at the end of the chapter, Christie effects a genuine rescue, thereby anticipating her role later in *Work* as what Estes and Lant have called the "Feminist Redeemer" or "Female Christ."

Significant Form, Style, or Artistic Conventions

While a number of critics have recognized the importance of the drama in Alcott's life and art, not all of them view her use of it as consistently subversive. As early as 1943 Madeleine Stern, in "Louisa Alcott, Trouper," provided an account of Alcott's youthful dramatic activities and perceived that both her sensation and her autobiographical fiction were indebted to them. Since then Sharon O'Brien and Karen Halttunen (among others) have discussed Alcott's adolescent melodramas:

O'Brien sees them foreshadowing Alcott's inability to reconcile "the energetic, assertive self represented by her tomboy period with an adult female identity"(365); Halttunen views them as subverting her father's use of allegorical drama "to control every aspect of self-expression" (237–38).

Comparisons, Contrasts, Connections

Alcott's use of theatricals can be fruitfully compared to that of Jane Austen in *Mansfield Park*, Charlotte Brontë in *Jane Eyre* and *Villette*, and Edith Wharton in *House of Mirth*. Interesting comparisons might also be drawn between Christie's experience as a professional actress and that of Dreiser's Carrie.

Christie as an artist can also be compared to Elizabeth Stuart Phelps's Avis. While Christie does not have Avis's strong sense of vocation, she eventually finds "a never-failing excitement in her attempts to reach the standard of perfection she had set up for herself." Just as Avis feels torn between the conflicting demands of her art and family, so Christie feels torn between the gratification she derives from individual achievement and the qualities that would enable her to subordinate her own needs to another's. Finally, Christie's sense of sisterly solidarity, to which she finally sacrifices her career, links her with the female characters and communities created by Sarah Orne Jewett and Mary E. Wilkins Freeman.

Bibliography

Alcott, Louisa May. "Behind a Mask." In *Alternative Alcott*, edited by Elaine Showalter, 383–441. American Women Writers Series. New Brunswick: Rutgers University Press, 1988.

——. "A Double Tragedy. An Actor's Story." In *The Double Life: Newly Discovered Thrillers of Louisa May Alcott*, edited by Madeleine B. Stern, Joel Myerson, and Daniel Shealy. Boston: Little, Brown, 1988.

——. *Freaks of Genius: Unknown Thrillers of Louisa May Alcott*, edited by Daniel Shealy, Madeleine B. Stern, and Joel Myerson. New York: Greenwood, 1991.

——. *Work: A Story of Experience*. "Introduction" by Sarah Elbert. New York: Schocken, 1977.

Auerbach, Nina. "Afterword." In *Little Women*. New York: Bantam, 1983.

Bedell, Jeanne F. "A Necessary Mask: The Sensation Fiction of Louisa May Alcott." *Missouri Philological Association Publications* 5 (1980): 8–14.

Estes, Angela M. and Kathleen Margaret Lant. "The Feminist Redeemer: Louisa May Alcott's Creation of the Female Christ in *Work*." *Christianity and Literature* 40 (1991): 223–53.

——. "Dismembering the Text: The Horror of Louisa May Alcott's *Little Women*." *Children's Literature* 17 (1989): 98–123.

Fetterley, Judith. "Impersonating 'Little Women': The Radicalism of Alcott's *Behind a Mask*." *Women's Studies* 10 (1983): 1–14.

Halttunen, Karen. "The Domestic Drama of Louisa May Alcott." *Feminist Studies* 10 (1984): 232–54.

Harris, Susan K. "Narrative Control and Thematic Radicalism in *Work* and *The Silent Partner*." In *19th-Century American Women's Novels: Interpretive Strategies*, 173–96. Cambridge: Cambridge University Press, 1990.

Keyser, Elizabeth Lennox. "'The Most Beautiful Things in All the World'? Families in *Little Women*." In *Stories and Society: Children's Literature in its Social Context*, edited by Dennis Butts, 50–64. London: Macmillan, 1992.

Langland, Elizabeth. "Female Stories of Experience: Alcott's *Little Women* in Light of *Work*." *The Voyage In: Fiction of Female Development*, edited by Elizabeth Abel, Marianne Hirsch, and Elizabeth Langland, 112–27. Hanover, N.H.: University Press of New England, 1983.

Murphy, Ann B. "The Borders of Ethical, Erotic, and Artistic Possibilities in *Little Women*." *Signs* 15 (1990): 562–85.

O'Brien, Sharon. "Tomboyism and Adolescent Conflict: Three Nineteenth-Century Case Studies." In *Women's Being, Women's Place: Female Identity and Vocation in American History*, Boston: G. K. Hall, 1979: 351–72.

Sanderson, Rena. "*A Modern Mephistopheles:* Louisa May Alcott's Exorcism of Patriarchy." *American Transcendental Quarterly* 5 (1991): 41–55.

Yellin, Jean Fagan. "From *Success* to *Experience:* Louisa May Alcott's *Work*." *Massachusetts Review* 21 (1980): 527–39.

Harriet Prescott Spofford (1835–1921)

Contributing Editor: Thelma J. Shinn

Classroom Issues and Strategies

Students need to develop an appreciation for "domestic imagery"—symbols and images drawn from female experience but used to represent universal values. In addition, they also should become aware of the transitional elements from romance to realism evident in the writings of Spofford and her contemporaries.

To address these issues, show contemporary appreciation of Spofford in better known authors (such as Dickinson and Whittier). Help students discern the *patterns* of imagery so that they do not dismiss individual images as "popular" or "sentimental." Point out the metaphorical implications of the setting which, while realistic (with its historical roots in Spofford's family), is also part of the romantic tradition.

Major Themes, Historical Perspectives, and Personal Issues

Major themes include:

> The Female Artist
> Humanity as Animal versus Spirit
> Music/Art as Communication
> Romance versus Realism (particularly in defining naturalism)
> The Forest in American Literature
> Importance of Popular Culture (well-known songs)
> Preservation of Family History (true incident)

By basing "Circumstance" on an incident in the life of her maternal great-grandmother, Spofford shifts time and place to enter Hawthorne's "neutral territory, . . . where the Actual and the Imaginary may meet." While Hawthorne turns back two centuries to the suggestion of a historical event in *The Scarlet Letter*, however, Spofford chooses a closer time and a specific personal/historical moment. In doing so, she reflects the female consciousness that personal events—events recorded orally and handed down from mother to daughter—define human history perhaps more accurately than official records. In these records she finds a circumstance that can embody female and human experience in finite and infinite terms.

Although *circumstance* refers to essential and environmental conditions in which we find ourselves, the singular form specifically refers, according to *Webster's New Collegiate Dictionary*, to "a piece of evidence that indicates the probability or improbability of an event." While the existence of God cannot be proved, Spofford can present a "circumstance" that indicates for her its probability. And so she has in this story. The religious theme is all the more powerful because it is couched in the "Actual" and discovered by a woman not given to the "Imaginary." Spofford reveals Hawthorne's "neutral territory" to be the world in which we live, and it is in her journey through this world that the narrator must find evidence of the omnipresence of God.

Significant Form, Style, or Artistic Conventions

Spofford anticipates the styles and themes of the realists, even of the naturalists who will surround her later writing career. Already in this 1860 story, her narrator must abandon her romantic notions of nature ("If all the silent powers of the forest did not conspire to help her!") and face that "the dark, hollow night rose indifferently over her." At the same time, she has recognized the naturalistic corollary to nature's indifference in humanity's animal antecedents. Impending death by a "living lump of appetites" forces her to acknowledge the self-loathing as the beast "known by the strength of our lower natures let loose." The primitive cannibalism of humanity seems to be reflected in her fear of becoming a part of the beast again: "the base, cursed thing howls with us forever through the forest." Such pessimistic reflections indeed bring misery, as they will to later writers. "The Open Boat" finds Stephen Crane's correspondent (also reflecting a true incident in Crane's own life) similarly trapped in nature and discovering its indifference to him.

Original Audience

Consider the following:

1. The time period during which the story was written and the New England setting.
2. The fact that the story was first published in a periodical.
3. The Puritan background of Spofford's contemporary audience.
4. The familiarity of the audience with the popular music mentioned.

Comparisons, Contrasts, Connections

Useful comparisons may be made with the following works:

Emily Dickinson, "Twas like a maelstrom . . ."
Nathaniel Hawthorne, "Young Goodman Brown"
Stephen Crane, "The Open Boat"
Henry James, "The Beast in the Jungle"

Questions for Reading and Discussion/
Approaches to Writing

1. What songs do *you* know that she might be singing in each category? Where did you learn these songs? From whom?
2. (a) Find parallels in your experience to the story, its themes and particulars (consider sharing family stories).
   (b) Examine the roots of a genre (e.g., oral roots of fiction).
   (c) Interpret one art through another (art and music here).
   (d) Also try traditional thematic and stylistic approaches and comparisons to other stories.

Bibliography

Fetterley, Judith. *Provisions*. Bloomington: Indiana University Press, 1985.

Halbeisen, Elizabeth K. *Harriet Prescott Spofford: A Romantic Survival*. Philadelphia: University of Pennsylvania Press, 1935.

Elizabeth Stuart Phelps (1844–1911)

Contributing Editor: Carol Farley Kessler

Classroom Issues and Strategies

While it may be difficult for a few of the male students to enter the viewpoint of the heroine of *The Story of Avis,* many students—especially women—find this a profoundly rewarding novel to read.

I acknowledge to a class that Phelps's style sometimes causes a problem. I explain that she was an anxious person, that in *Avis* she was tackling taboo subjects—such as the view that marriage is not good for women, and that women are as creative as men. I ask students to note other taboo viewpoints that arise. Then I ask them to consider how they write when they are afraid of how people may react to their ideas. Phelps's writing is sometimes precious, overwritten—the tactic of a worried person. I also point out that sometimes contorted language occurs with personally difficult or socially controversial subjects; students need to consider the possible emotional significance of the text for its author. The problems of style can inform us.

Women respond strongly, positively to this realistic novel depicting women's three-role status (mother-wife-person), which they recognize as unresolved in the 1990s as in the 1870s. Men may be less aware of the potential for overwork entailed in this three-role status; however, some will be sons of single or divorced mothers, hence more aware of the dilemma of women's unpaid, often invisible labor. They, rather than the instructor, may be guided to provide explanations to less-aware men. Also women (and some men) need the conscious support of an instructor to feel safe enough to respond with emotional honesty to male (and some female) classmates who don't understand the issues Phelps tackles.

Perry Miller Adato's thirty-minute film on "Mary Cassatt" (1844–1926), a Philadelphia artist who worked in Paris, provides an overview of the status of the nineteenth-century creative woman.

Erica Jong's essay, "The Artist as Housewife: The Housewife as Artist," in *Ms.* (October 1972), reprinted in *The First Ms. Reader* (New York: Warner, 1973, pp. 111–22), demonstrates surprisingly little contrast between 1877 and 1972.

The marriage/career conflict engages students' attention, as does the general contemporary relevance of the concerns of Phelps's novel. They wonder, especially the women, why these problems continue to exist. They wonder how to solve them. They take the issues addressed by the novel very personally.

Major Themes, Historical Perspectives, and Personal Issues

An overview of these matters is Kessler's Introduction to *The Story of Avis* (New Brunswick, N.J.: Rutgers, 1986, pp. xiii–xxvi, plus notes).

Themes include role conflict and overload for women, conditions needed for creativity, the reality of unhappy marriages for women, freedom with singleness and constraint with marriage, possibilities emerging from atypical choices.

Historical issues: The novel attacks the socialization of women to be "true women" (Phelps's essay, in the Rutgers reprint of *Avis*, elucidates the role construct of true womanhood—to be compassionate, cheerful, submissive, selfless); it espouses women's movement beliefs in women's right to meaningful work and emotional support.

Personal issues: Avis seems to be an ideal composite of Phelps, her mother, and female relatives (see "A Literary Legacy" in *Frontiers* 5 [Fall 1980] 28–33). The longest publication gap in Phelps's career occurs between *The Silent Partner*, 1871, and *The Story of Avis*, 1877: consider Tillie Olsen's view that "censorship silences" (see her *Silences* [New York: Delta, 1979], p. 9). In a 1903 letter to Harriet Prescott Spofford, Phelps wrote, "The married are hampered in what they can say. I remember that when I wrote *Avis* I said 'were I married, I could not write this book' " (*Avis*, Introduction, p. xxxi). See also chapters 3 and 7 from *The Silent Partner* on the silencing of women in marriage.

Significant Form, Style, or Artistic Conventions

Form/Convention: A feminized version of the Grail legend, hence a romantic quest, though this is not particularly evident in the two excerpted chapters; Bildungsroman/Künstlerroman—the growth and development of the protagonist/artist; American literary realism, contemporaneous with Henry James and William Dean Howells; also New England regionalism.

Style: Emotionally loaded, highly allusive and imagistic. "Avis" equals Latin for bird; the caged bird, according to Ellen Moers in *Literary Women*, 1976, pp. 245–51, is characteristic of women's writing; ironic social commentary; occasional Christian sentiment.

Aesthetics: Art for truth's sake—"art implies truthful and conscientious study of life as it is," notes Phelps in her autobiography (*Chapters from a Life*, 1896, p. 261); "life *is* moral responsibility," essential to beauty, she believes; didactic function of literature. She assumed the seriousness of her mission as author.

Original Audience

One reviewer found the book unacceptable, especially for young female readers; on the other hand, feminist Lucy Stone was sure it was destined for "a permanent place in English literature." Currently its return to availability was noted favorably (*Legacy* 2 [Spring 1985]: 18). Student reports on standard reference articles—AWW, 1982; DAB, 1936; NAW, 1971—provide a challenge as each presents a very different viewpoint on Phelps, resulting from differing audiences and historical contexts.

Comparisons, Contrasts, Connections

Henry James's early Künstlerroman, *Roderick Hudson*, 1875, in which the artist is overcome by a disappointment in love and commits suicide; Louisa May Alcott, "Diana & Persis" (written in 1879; in *Alternative Alcott*, 1988, edited by Elaine Showalter), in which two friends discover that maybe marriage and art can mix; Charlotte Perkins Stetson Gilman, "The Yellow Wallpaper," 1892 (*The Heath Anthology*, Volume 2), and *Endure: The Diaries of Charles Walter Stetson, 1881–88* (edited by Mary A. Hill, Temple University Press 1985), which reveal spousal control of a woman's creative energies; Kate Chopin, *The Awakening*, 1899, in which a woman resists an eventless married life and strikes for independence; Edith Wharton's short stories collected as *The Muses's Tragedy and Other Stories, 1890s–1910s* (edited by Candace Waid, Signet, 1990), or the novelette *The Touchstone*, 1900 (edited by Cynthia Griffin Wolff, Harper-Perennial 1991), in which women's aesthetic capacities appear ironically twisted; Willa Cather, *The Song of the Lark*, 1915, a novel depicting the origins and development of artistic genius. Avis has a stronger character than James's Roderick Hudson, but has less optimism than Alcott's Persis, less impatience and rebelliousness than Chopin's Edna Pontellier, less firm commitment to her art than Cather's Thea Kronborg.

Of the many possible multi-ethnic comparisons, consider the Asian-American short story by Hisaye Yamamoto, "Seventeen Syllables," 1949 (*The Heath Anthology*, Volume 2), a devastating instance of lost creative freedom, and the final chapter from Maxine Hong Kingston's *The Woman Warrior*, "A Song for a Barbarian Reed Pipe," 1976, a vision of empowerment; African-American experience in Lorraine Hansberry's play *To Be Young, Gifted, and Black*, 1969, a searching examination of the impact of race upon creativity; in Alice Walker's story "Everyday Use," 1973, concerning the inheriting and using of art; and in Rita Dove's novel *Through the Ivory Gate*, 1992, an upbeat example of creativity blending education, mime, and music.

Questions for Reading and Discussion/ Approaches to Writing

1. (a) Discuss the conflict between caring and creativity that Avis experiences. How does Phelps plot this?
   (b) Delineate how marriage figures in the plot pattern of entrapment and escape.
   (c) What ideas about relationships between women and men presented in the novel are still historically unrealized?

    (d) At the end of the novel, Phelps argues that making a woman will take three generations. How, in the chapters read, does she provide support for this hypothesis?

2. (a) Keep a reading journal of responses to the daily assignments, with notations of specific (i.e., page, paragraph, word) support for generalizations noted.

    (b) In-class paragraphs written during the first fifteen minutes providing detailed support for an opinion about the novel, on topics assigned for later class discussion.

    (c) Individual reports relating supplementary articles or other literary selections to the *Avis* chapters.

Bibliography

Legacy: A Journal of Nineteenth-Century American Women Writers provides critical articles about authors of Phelps's era.

Recent reprints of Phelps's best novels—*The Story of Avis*, *The Silent Partner* (about a mill town social worker), *Doctor Zay* (about a homeopathic physician)—contain useful introductions or afterwords.

In addition, *Woman in Sexist Society* (ed. Vivian Gornick and Barbara K. Moran, NAL, 1972) contains three relevant articles: Jessie Bernard, "The Paradox of the Happy Marriage," 145–62; Linda Nochlin, "Why Are There No Great Women Artists?" 480–510; and Margaret Adams, "The Compassion Trap," 555–75.

Finally, see Susan K. Harris, *Nineteenth-Century American Women's Novels: Interpretive Strategies*. Cambridge: Cambridge University Press, 1990.

Sarah Orne Jewett (1849–1909)

Contributing Editor: Elizabeth Ammons

Classroom Issues and Strategies

I've encountered some problems teaching Jewett's *Country of the Pointed Firs* because at first it seems dull to students, but they love "A White Heron" (hereafter WH) and I'm confident that they will also respond enthusiastically to "The Foreigner" (hereafter F), though I have not taught it. (There is, by the way, a film of WH that many people find excellent.)

Students often don't like the ending of WH (the author's intrusion) and are baffled by it; they wonder about Sylvia's mother—what's Jewett saying about her?—and about why the girl's grandmother sides with the man. Also they wonder why the bird is male.

Major Themes, Historical Perspectives, and Personal Issues

Both of these stories are characteristic of Jewett, not only in focusing on women but also in focusing on women-centered or women-dominated space, geographic and psychic. The existence and meaning of such space is probably the most basic theme in Jewett.

Female-defined space is celebrated in F, which shows the boundaries of such space transcending the physical world and also national and ethnic barriers. The bonds between women find expression in and are grounded in the acts of mutual nurture, healing, story-telling, shelter, feeding, touching, and transmission of wisdom denigrated in the dominant culture as witchcraft. Female-defined reality is threatened but then reaffirmed, at least for the present, in WH, in which the intrusion of a man from the city into the grandmother/cow/girl-controlled rural space upsets the daily harmony, and potentially the life-balance itself, of nature.

Historically these stories explore the strength and depth of female bonding at a time when same-sex relationships between women in western culture were being redefined by sexologists such as Freud and Havelock Ellis as pathological and deviant. Jewett recognizes in WH the threat posed to same-sex female bonding by the allure of heterosexuality in the person of the hunter, who is sexy and deals in violence and death: if Sylvia falls for him, she will be participating, symbolically, in her own death (the killing and stuffing of the heron). In F, written later, Jewett sets against a stormy background a story affirming women's love, despite divisions of region, nationality, and culture.

Sororal, filial, maternal, erotic: bonds between women in Jewett's work no doubt reflect her own feelings and those of women close to her. While she numbered men among her friends and associates, her closest, most intimate friends were women. Debate about whether to call Jewett a lesbian writer exists because the term was not one Jewett would have used; our highly sexualized twentieth-century view of same-sex romantic and erotic attachment may very well not be a historically accurate way to describe Jewett's world, fictive or biographical. So labels need to be carefully thought about. Whatever terminology is used, though, the central, deep, recurrent theme in Jewett's work is love between women.

Significant Form, Style, or Artistic Conventions

F uses many features of the traditional western ghost story to tell a love story. The storm, the cat, the ghost—the tale is deliberately encoded with ghost-story trappings, yet is in the end not scary but healing. The story is formally interesting to think about therefore as a transformation of something Poe or Hawthorne might do into a narrative that instead of scaring or depressing, succors. A kind of serious fierce maternalization of masculine form? Certainly WH plays with masculine form, reproducing in its structure the build to a high climax (literally the tippy-top of a tree) that both traditional, white, western dramatic structure (exposition/conflict/complication/climax/resolution) and, it can be argued, male-dominated heterosexual relations inscribe. Then at the end of WH Jewett disrupts and undoes this tight, linear pattern with a flossy, chatty final paragraph so exaggeratedly "feminine" in character as to call attention to itself. One question often asked by students is: Why does the narrative voice switch like this in the end? One answer is that, just as Sylvia's decision thwarts the hunter, the narrative switch at the end deliberately deconstructs the traditional inherited masculine narrative pattern of climax-oriented fiction grounded in aggression and conflict that has preceded.

Original Audience

Jewett was widely read and admired in the late nineteenth century, but until recently she has been dismissed in the academy as minor, regional, slight. Her recent revival reflects in large part the increasing numbers and strength of women in the profession of professor and scholar. Not of interest (threatening?) to a predominantly white, male, heterosexual group of critics and scholars, Jewett is now finding an increasingly large audience as women gain power within the system of higher education. That is, Jewett is the beneficiary of a new group of people being able to define what is "interesting" and "important." Thus Jewett, when we ponder the question of audience, vividly raises highly political issues: Who defines what is "good" and worth studying? How do the politics of gender and sexual orientation shape the politics of the classroom, without their ever even being acknowledged? What writers and kinds of writers are currently being excluded or denigrated because of the composition of the profession of professor?

Comparisons, Contrasts, Connections

Jewett is often compared quite productively with Mary Wilkins Freeman, a fellow New England writer. Jewett admired Harriet Beecher Stowe's New England writing and therefore is fruitfully thought of in conjunction with Stowe. Willa Cather was encouraged by Jewett to write full time and, particularly on the topic of women's relationships with each other, Cather's work is very interesting to compare and contrast with Jewett's. As a regionalist—a writer engaged in trying to capture in detail and with great accuracy and sensitivity life as it was experienced in a particular region, rather than attempting to fill in a huge and more diffuse canvas, Jewett compares illuminatingly with other regionalists, especially across regions: Kate Chopin and Alice Dunbar-Nelson focusing on New Orleans, Hamlin Garland picturing the northern Midwest, Abraham Cahan on the Lower East Side in New York.

Questions for Reading and Discussion/ Approaches to Writing

1. F: Who is the foreigner? Is this story racist?
   WH: Who/what does the heron symbolize? Why is the cow in the story? Why does it matter that Sylvia is nine years old?
2. These two stories together and individually lend themselves well to traditional kinds of textual analysis of symbols, imagery, characterization, authorial point of view, and so forth: for example, animal imagery and symbolism in either or both; nature as a character in either or both; comparing the portraits of old women in the two stories.

Bibliography

Two sources for essays are: *Critical Essays on Sarah Orne Jewett* (Boston: G. K. Hall, 1984) and *The Colby Library Quarterly: Special Issue on Jewett* (March 1986). WH and F are discussed from various points of view in a number of excellent essays in these two volumes. An important book-length study is Marilyn Sanders Mobley's *Folk Roots and Mythic Wings in Sarah Orne Jewett and Toni Morrison* (1991).

Mary E. Wilkins Freeman (1852–1930)

Contributing Editor: Leah Blatt Glasser

Classroom Issues and Strategies

The best strategy in approaching Mary Wilkins Freeman's work is to provide a full context in terms of both her life and period and to select particularly paradoxical passages for class discussion. It is especially enlightening to discuss the endings of her stories, which often disappoint students or trouble them. Have students consider possible revisions of these endings and then discuss why Freeman might have chosen to conclude as she did.

Students may wish to consider the title of "The Revolt of 'Mother' " and its implications. What is the nature of Sarah's "revolt"? Why does Freeman put "mother" in quotation marks? Students may be interested to know that Freeman's father, Warren Wilkins, gave up his plan of building the house Eleanor, Freeman's mother, had hoped for. Instead, the family moved in 1877 into the home in which Eleanor was to serve as hired housekeeper. Freeman's mother was thus "deprived of the very things which made a woman proud, her own kitchen, furniture, family china; and she had lost the one place in which it was acceptable for her to be powerful: her home" (Clark 177).

Another interesting comment is this one, made by Freeman in the *Saturday Evening Post*, published December 8, 1917 (long after the publication of the story). In the following excerpt, Freeman disparages her story for its lack of realism:

> In the first place all fiction ought to be true and "The Revolt of 'Mother' " is not true. . . . There never was in New England a woman like Mother. If there had been she certainly would have lacked the nerve. She would also have lacked the imagination. New England women of that period coincided with their husbands in thinking that the sources of wealth should be better housed than the consumers.

"A Church Mouse" provides a good example of Freeman's duality. Ask students to study the tone and quality of Hetty's early expressions of determination with her final plea to the community. Focus also on passages that depict the role of work in Hetty's life. The sunflower quilt, for example, plays an important part in the story as it serves the function of both dividing Hetty from the other churchgoers and celebrating her capacity as an artist. Hetty's battle to establish her right to live alone and to do the work she loves may be compared with aspects of Freeman's life.

It can also be useful to draw comparisons between Hetty's strategy and other forms of nonviolent direct action, as proposed by writers like Sarah Grimké, William Lloyd Garrison, Henry David Thoreau, and Martin Luther King, Jr. Students will often perceive that, whatever one believes about nonviolence as a "way of life," it can be a useful strategy to help mobilize an otherwise indifferent or even hostile community on behalf of the cause of the weak.

As the story progresses, students may notice that the action moves from an individual plea to a collective demand. Moreover, Freeman achieves what Hetty does; she rebels, but she does so safely and she is heard—her story is published in *Harper's Bazaar*, a woman's magazine that would reach a similar audience composed largely of women. As indicated above, Hetty's position in the church behind the sunflower quilt she has made in church suggests a context for Freeman's feelings about the role of work in her life.

Freeman wrote "Old Woman Magoun" during her unhappy marriage to Dr. Charles Freeman. It is one of the few short stories written during this period in which she managed to maintain her mastery. It is interesting to consider Freeman's experience of marriage in relation to the fears she invests in Old Woman Magoun of losing the young Lily to men like Nelson Barry and Jim Willis. In a letter to a newly-married friend, Harriet Randolph Hyatt Mayor, she had written, "I shall find the old you. It will never be lost. I know how you feel . . . I am to be married myself before long. . . . If *you* don't see the old *me*, I shall run *until I find her*" (Kendrick 205). Unfortunately, Freeman was forced to part with the "old me" until her husband's alcoholism and abusive behavior finally ended in his being committed to the New Jersey State Hospital and her separation from him.

Students may wish to consider the nature of Old Woman Magoun's extreme actions. A close study of the scene in which she allows Lily to eat the poisoned berries will yield a lively class discussion. Reward for being recognized as a writer caused Freeman to say "I felt my wings spring from my shoulders, capable of flight." In this scene, she has Old Woman Magoun give wings, in a sense, to her grandchild for a flight that will not bring her "home" as Mary Wilkins Freeman's "wings" successfully did.

Major Themes, Historical Perspectives, and Personal Issues

The major themes of Freeman's work illuminate aspects of her life. Mary Wilkins Freeman's words to describe the feeling of receiving her first acceptance and check for a short story provide an interesting context: "I felt my wings spring from my shoulders, capable of flight, and I flew home" (*New York Times*, April 1926). Her statement characterizes the dilemma this remarkable turn-of-the-century New England writer faced, the paradox that she expressed in almost all of her work. Feeling "capable of flight" because of the power of her capacity as a writer, Freeman nevertheless could only fly "home." Most striking in her life and work is the haunting echo of two inner voices: a voice that cries out for rebellious flight, another voice that clings to the safety of home. The heroines of Freeman's short stories, even they rebel, struggle with this conflict. Students may compare the heroines of "A Church Mouse," "The Revolt of 'Mother,' "and "Old Woman Magoun," listening for the ways in which Freeman invests the women with power and yet simultaneously limits their power, bringing their rebellious "flights" to what Freeman considered "home"—the realities of nineteenth-century New England.

It is important to explore her depiction of relationships between women, her focus on the role of work in women's lives, the way in which she explores the psychology of rebellion as characters rebel, submit, or face the consequences of their rebellion. Of particular interest in offering a biographical context is the intensity of Freeman's relationship with Mary Wales, with whom she lived for twenty-five years. Her stories reflect a great understanding of female friendships.

Significant Form, Style, or Artistic Conventions

Freeman has often been categorized as a local colorist, a New England writer of the post–Civil War period whose primary talent lay in depicting the peculiarities of her region. This view has tended to minimize her work. Certainly she does offer a vivid sense of life in New England. Most significant, however, is the way in which she moves beyond region to offer a focus on the psychology of women's conflicts at the turn of the century. Her use of dialect may be compared with Mark Twain's as she manages to bring us the voices she knew with fine precision.

Original Audience

This is an interesting question. Freeman published in magazines for young women (*Harper's* primarily) and her audience consisted largely of women readers. She was influenced at times by her editors' demands for "gentility" in accordance with their sense of the codes of female behavior at the turn of the century. Consequently, Freeman's endings often couch rebellious content in acceptable, domestic scenes of female submission. The shift in Hetty's behavior in "A Church Mouse" is interesting in this context, as is the reunion of Sarah and her husband in "The Revolt of 'Mother.'"

Comparisons, Contrasts, Connections

It is fruitful to compare Freeman with male peers such as Mark Twain, Henry James, and William Dean Howells. Her capacity for psychological portrait compares well with James, and many of her heroines may be compared with the heroines in James's short fiction. She did participate in a project with James, a collaborative novel, entitled *The Whole Family: A Novel by Twelve Authors* (Harper & Brothers, 1908). Her chapter in this novel should be compared with the chapter by James, particularly on the themes of rebellion and repression. Both writers held a fascination with patterns of repression and rebellion, although Freeman's focus was almost entirely upon women in this light. Twain's use of dialogue may also be explored in relation to Freeman's. Finally, she should be compared with other American women writers at the turn of the century (particularly Sarah Orne Jewett, Edith Wharton, Willa Cather).

Questions for Reading and Discussion/ Approaches to Writing

1. (a) Study the role of work in each story in relation to the development of Freeman's heroines.
   (b) Analyze the conclusions of "A Church Mouse" and "The Revolt of 'Mother.'" What seems paradoxical or unexpected? How do these conclusions relate to earlier stages of revolt in each story?
   (c) Note the image of wings in "Old Woman Magoun" and consider possible contexts. What does the final scene suggest?
   (d) Note references to madness in each story. What might Freeman be suggesting in each case?
2. Students enjoy focusing on the development of Freeman's heroines, their contradictions and strengths. Consider a paper on the attitudes toward women the story suggests and its influence on the heroine's actions. Ask students to study a particular scene or set of images (Sarah Penn's work in her house: "She was an artist";

Hetty's quilt in "A Church Mouse." Does Freeman's work suggest anything about her sense of the artist?) Study the death scene in "Old Woman Magoun." What do you make of the language of the old woman as she eases the child into death?

Bibliography

A useful and brief discussion of Freeman's life and work can be found in *Legacy: A Journal of Nineteenth Century American Women Writers*, Volume 4, Spring 1987 ("Profile: Mary E. Wilkins Freeman" by Leah B. Glasser).

Useful biographical material can also be gleaned from *The Infant Sphinx: Collected Letters of Mary E. Wilkins Freeman*, intelligently edited and introduced by Brent L. Kendrick. Her letters, though cautious and unrevealing on the surface, hint at the intensity of her relationship with her childhood friend Mary Wales. Freeman lived with Wales for over twenty years, and it is likely that much of her focus on friendships between women was drawn from this relationship. The difficulties of her marriage are also apparent in many of her letters written during that trying period of her life. The numerous letters she wrote to her editors reveal Freeman's seriousness about her career.

The two existing biographies on Freeman are useful, although somewhat outdated: Foster's *Mary E. Wilkins Freeman* and Westbrook's *Mary Wilkins Freeman*.

Interpretive studies of her work can be found in Clark's Afterword to *The Revolt of Mother and Other Stories*, Marjorie Pryse's Introduction and Afterword to *Selected Stories of Mary E. Wilkins Freeman*, and Leah Glasser's essays "Discovering Mary E. Wilkins Freeman" in *Between Women* and "The Stranger in the Mirror" in *The Massachusetts Review* (Summer 1984).

For a good sampling of Freeman's short stories through the successive phases of her career, see *Selected Stories of Mary E. Wilkins Freeman* (New York: Norton, 1983).

Freeman's novels are not as strong as her short stories; the novel most representative of her talent is *Pembroke* (1894).

The Shoulders of Atlas (1908), *Madelon* (1896), and *By the Light of the Soul* are fascinating examples of Freeman's duality as protagonists are continuously caught between rebellion and submission.

Students may find it interesting to compare the chapters written by Mary Wilkins Freeman and Henry James, her contemporary, in the collaborative novel entitled *The Whole Family: A Novel by Twelve Authors* (New York: Harper & Brothers, 1908).

Pauline Elizabeth Hopkins (1859–1930)

Contributing Editor: Jane Campbell

Classroom Issues and Strategies

The problems I have encountered include the students' unfamiliarity with racial issues and African-American history. Students may find Hopkins's diction and style ponderous and alienating. Taken out of context, these two chapters can be baffling. I have found it helpful to introduce Hopkins by putting her into context and fleshing out the headnotes to explore social, historical, and racial particulars during the two periods she fictionalizes in *Contending Forces*. I emphasize her stylistic similarities to other writers of her day and point out that she is writing a romance that bears comparison not only to work by other African-American and white writers of her time but to contemporary "romance/novels," as they are called today. I review the plot and intentions of *Contending Forces*, as described in the headnote. Many of the issues Hopkins explores can be made accessible by pointing out their prevalence today. Racism, whites' objectification of African-American women, and color prejudice are still very much alive.

I recommend peer interaction in teaching Hopkins. Students might work in small groups or pairs to raise questions about barriers to understanding the excerpts from *Contending Forces*. I suspect male students, by and large, will need coaxing to identify with the excerpts. Such problems as students raise may then be tackled by the class as a whole.

Journal writing may work, as well, to give students an opportunity to consider how Hopkins's novel does or does not seem relevant to our times or to their lives. Journals can also lead to fruitful comparisons with other works read so far in the course.

White students may be shocked or surprised by historical particulars and contemporary examples of racism, Klan activities, discrimination, and rape and sexual harassment of black women, but they also express gratitude about learning of these issues. Students of color, while painfully cognizant of such issues, may be open to sharing their experiences or citing specific examples of racism in their community or on campus.

Major Themes, Historical Perspectives, and Personal Issues

I emphasize lynching and Klan activities and stress that the Klan is still active all over the United States. I discuss the convergence of racism and sexism, interracial blood lines, voting disenfranchisement, job discrimination against blacks, and color prejudice. I also stress Hopkins's emphasis on feminist issues such as the rape of African-American women during slavery by their masters and the ongoing attitudes toward black women as sexually available. Positive feminist themes such as female bonding and empowerment and women's collective political action also emerge from *Contending Forces*.

Significant Form, Style, or Artistic Conventions

It is essential that students grasp the obstacles facing an African-American woman of Hopkins's day. Her ability to transcend cultural, racial, and gender barriers in order to write fiction is extraordinary.

Fitting Hopkins into the tradition of African-American writers should involve discussion of cultural/literary conventions of the time. The tragic mulatto, a character appearing in many works by both black and white writers during the nineteenth and early twentieth centuries, can lead to some interesting discussion, especially in light of why mulattoes appeared so often in African-American fiction, and how the device of the tragic mulatto simultaneously encouraged racial equality and underlined color prejudice.

It might be helpful to note Hopkins's emphasis on the pleasures of homemaking, love, and motherhood—usually derided as "the cult of domesticity" by male critics—deriving from her reliance on the literary romance. Sappho's depiction as a ravishingly beautiful, extraordinarily talented, strong heroine who overcomes numerous obstacles and serves as a model for her audience also reveals Hopkins's allegiance to the conventions of the romance.

Original Audience

Hopkins was writing to a mixed audience of African-Americans and whites. Her use of romance conventions demonstrates that many of her readers were women, and that she was interweaving politics and entertainment, thus raising the consciousness of a large audience. Her reliance on precise diction and cultural/literary allusions is clearly intended to remind her audience that many African-Americans are intelligent, educated, and cultured.

Comparisons, Contrasts, Connections

If any students have read contemporary African-American novels, such as Maya Angelou's *I Know Why the Caged Bird Sings* or Alice Walker's *The Color Purple*, they will discover parallels. Romances such as *Charlotte Temple* or *Uncle Tom's Cabin* might link Hopkins with white authors of her time concerned with similar issues and using the same literary mode to present them.

Questions for Reading and Discussion/ Approaches to Writing

1. Explore how "Ma Smith's Lodging-House—Concluded" delineates educated from uneducated characters. Why do you suppose such distinctions were important to Hopkins's novel? How do you react to the use of black English, or black dialect, as it is sometimes called? Is it a realistic device, or does it demean the speaker?

2. What did you learn from "The Sewing Circle" about African-Americans during Hopkins's day? What does Hopkins teach her audience about American history?

3. Could a novel similar to *Contending Forces* be written today? Explore what differences you might expect.

4. Might there be other African-American writers of Hopkins's time whose work has been lost, writers we have not yet rediscovered? Why might their works have been lost?

5. How do you account for the resurgence of interest in early African-American women writers?

Bibliography

Campbell, Jane. *Mythic Black Fiction: The Transformation of History.* Knoxville: University of Tennessee Press, 1986.

Carby, Hazel. *Reconstructing Womanhood: The Emergence of the Afro-American Woman Novelist.* New York: Oxford University Press, 1987.

Shockley, Ann Allen. *Afro-American Women Writers, 1746–1933: An Anthology and Critical Guide.* Boston: G. K. Hall, 1988.

Regional Voices, National Voices

African-American Folktales

Contributing Editor: Susan L. Blake

Classroom Issues and Strategies

Some of the questions about these folktales I would anticipate from students are: The tales are so simple—are they really art? If they didn't actually contribute to the abolition of slavery, how are they subversive? Both African-American students and others may be made uncomfortable by stereotypical characterizations and dialect. What's the point of perpetuating images of slavery today? Answering these questions is not easy; I've tried to address them in the material below.

Major Themes, Historical Perspectives, and Personal Issues

Folktales interpret the experience of tellers and audience. While motifs endure from century to century and culture to culture, details and emphases vary with group experience and individual talent. Indeed, the art of the tale is to adapt the traditional motif to particular circumstances. Most African-American tales are about power relations, but as power relations are contextual, so are interpretations of the tales. Students familiar with slavery and willing to take metaphoric leaps will be able to read the John and Old Marster tales and the animal stories as critiques of slavery and, more generally, a racist society. But it is important, too, to think of the range of meanings the tales might hold for tellers and listeners in various social positions at various historical moments.

The ongoing conflict between John and Old Marster dramatizes the contradiction between humanity and slavery. The John tales turn on the paradox that John is a man and yet a slave, Old Marster's colleague/confidant and yet his chattel. John keeps trying to close the gap between his status and that of Old Marster. When he succeeds—in, for example, claiming a right to the chickens he's raised—he in effect achieves freedom, an interpretation John Blackamore makes explicit at the end of "Old Boss Wants into Heaven." Even when John fails or appears foolish, the tale still skewers slavery by its use of metaphor. In "Ole Massa and

John Who Wanted to Go to Heaven," for example, Ole Massa's imper-
sonation of the Lord represents, and ridicules, the slave master's assumption of godlike control over the slave's life—and death. There is little evidence, however, that these tales were told during slavery, and the
slave-master relationship they depict, between two individual men, for
all its metaphoric power, is narrow and relatively genial. Another way to
think of the tales would be as an interpretation of race relations under
"freedom" as slavery.

Unlike the John tales, the animal tales, which were told during
slavery, do not distinguish neatly between unjust and justified antagonists. They can, however, be seen as a pointed refutation of the romantic
myth of the old plantation that developed in the 1830s and may be most
popularly represented in *Gone with the Wind*. On the plantation of myth,
status is based on virtue, and human relations are governed by honor,
pride, justice, and benevolence. In the recognizably human society of the
animal tales, status is based on power, honor is absent, pride is a liability,
justice is anything you can get away with, and benevolence is stupidity.
Animal characters provide not only camouflage for social criticism but
the essential metaphor of society as jungle.

The two conjure tales collected by Zora Neale Hurston, in which
the rivals for the power represented by conjure are not master and slave
but male and female, provide an interesting counterpoint to the John
tales and animal stories. These tales draw attention to the absence of
women in the other tales and raise a host of questions: Are they about
gender conflict? Is there a specifically woman's point of view missing
from the body of African-American tales? Is it significant that these tales
were collected and published by one of the few female folktale collectors? Would these tales be read the same way in the 1930s and the
1990s?

Significant Form, Style, or Artistic Conventions

Folktales might be said to have three audiences, all of them in some
sense "original": The people who hear and help create the oral tales;
folklorists who persuade story-tellers to perform their tales for publication; and readers of the published collections. It can be difficult for students to grasp that the tales were not "written" by a single "author" but
are the product of a historically and politically mediated collaboration.
Some of the stylistic features of the tales are conventional—the reproduction of animal sounds in dialogue, for example, and the retort that
concludes the tales of John "stealing" Old Marster's livestock. At the
same time, the tales bear the stamp of an individual performer's style
and emphasis—E. L. Smith tells a snappy tale, John Blackamore a highly

developed one; Mrs. Josie Jordan's "Malitis" concludes with a comment on slavery, J. D. Suggs's "Who Ate Up the Butter?" with a comment on the present. The tales also show the fingerprints of the collectors: the introductions to the two tales of the Flying Africans from *Drums and Shadows*, the distanced narration of Zora Neale Hurston's two conjure tales, the gratuitous misspellings ("lide" for "lied," "rode" for "road") in W. A. Eddins's "How Sandy Got His Meat." It would be useful for students to look for evidence of both the performers and the collectors in the published texts. For example, what are the characteristics of John Blackamore's or J. D. Suggs's style? Which tales seem most nearly quoted from the performer, which most edited by the collector, and why? What can you tell from the texts about the collectors' attitudes toward the tellers or the interaction between collectors and tellers? How might the conditions of collecting—the historical moment, the collectors' race (Hurston is black, the other collectors represented here are white), and the recording technology—affect the collecting event and the published text?

Comparisons, Contrasts, Connections

Comparison between any of the tales and a European, African, or other American variant (Dorson, *American Negro Folktales*, provides comparative references) highlights both the political analysis and the art of the African-American tale. Comparison between the told-for-true story "Malitis" and any of the food-stealing stories in the John cycle reveals the conventions of folk fiction. Comparisons might also be drawn with contemporary African-American humor, rap lyrics, the tales of the southwestern humor tradition, and the fiction of Langston Hughes, whose Simple stories update the John tales, and Toni Morrison, whose *Song of Solomon* is based on the tale of the flying Africans. A comparison between Zora Neale Hurston's fiction and the folktales she published might illuminate her strategies in folktale editing as well as fiction.

Questions for Reading and Discussion/ Approaches to Writing

Topics for discussion, in addition to those suggested above, include the following: The function of violence in the animal stories, John as loser and fool, the way retorts work, kinds of racial experience not reflected in the tales, narrative strategies of indirection, whether and in what contexts the stories could be considered subversive.

The repetition of plot elements in a number of short texts makes folktales good subjects for analytic papers. Students might also write their own folktales following a traditional pattern. The terms of a creative assignment, which might be worked out by the class in discussion, should be quite specific so writing their own tale helps students see the structure, implications, and limitations of the traditional form. Such an assignment might be the following: Write a John tale in which John transgresses against slavery in some way not represented in the tales we've read (learns to read, dances with the Old Marster's daughter), or the slave is not John but Johnetta, or the two protagonists are not slave and master but representatives of some other relationship of unequal power (student-teacher, worker-boss). In any case, establish at the beginning that the dominant character trusts and depends on the subordinate and conclude the tale with a retort that undermines the principle of the unequal power relationship that has been transgressed.

Samuel Langhorne Clemens (Mark Twain) (1835–1910)

Contributing Editor: Everett Emerson

Classroom Issues and Strategies

The question might be asked, "Why is it that Mark Twain's writings and personality are so appealing?" I share my affection for the author with my students. I note that Mark Twain's readers enjoy *Huckleberry Finn* more if they know some Shakespeare and something about the French Revolution. Both of these loomed large in the author's consciousness when he wrote his masterpiece.

Mark Twain began his career as a humorist. In both *Huckleberry Finn* and all of his other better pieces, an important aspect of his work is the speaker's presentation of himself. What connection does this interest in the speaker or teller have to Mark Twain's humor?

Students are interested but edgy when I raise the question of the word "nigger" in the book. They ought to know that the term was used not long ago by many blacks as well as unsympathetic whites. But the appearance of the word in the book, despite the historical accuracy of the use of the term, needs careful consideration.

Major Themes, Historical Perspectives, and Personal Issues

I think it important to see how the shorter works by Mark Twain in the anthology shed light on *Huckleberry Finn*. I also suggest that the book (*Huckleberry Finn*) be read as the education of a racist, and that the limits of the education that Huck receives be recognized. Huck loses *some* of his prejudiced attitudes toward one particular black. Huck is free and easy with Jim because he regards Jim as his inferior. He records no regret when it appears that Jim has perished in the riverboat accident.

Consider the characteristics of Jimmy's speech (some of which are mentioned in the Mark Twain headnote) in "Sociable Jimmy." In her forthcoming book, Shelley Fisher Fishkin argues that there are close connections between the speech patterns of Jimmy and Huck. Students might be encouraged to compile a list that later could be compared to a similar list of Huck's speech patterns.

It seems that only one scholar has ever been interested enough in "Sociable Jimmy" to see that it is reprinted. It appears along with other mostly unknown or little known pieces in the handsome book *Mark Twain Speaks for Himself*, edited by Paul Fatout (West Lafayette: Purdue University Press, 1978). The attention the piece is getting stems wholly from Fishkin's idea that it is an important antecedent to *Huckleberry Finn*. Is it of enough value that it should be included in an anthology such as *The Heath Anthology*? Should it be "canonized"?

Significant Form, Style, or Artistic Conventions

Mark Twain was always attempting to escape from the established standard of literary propriety, as the Notice posted at the beginning of *Huckleberry Finn* shows. Why was he attempting to escape? Was he successful?

Original Audience

I remind my students that though the setting is the antebellum South, the book was written after Emancipation; it ought to be recognized that the book is not so much an anti-slavery novel as is *Uncle Tom's Cabin*. But the mind-set that put property values ahead of human values made slavery possible and did not disappear after the Civil War.

Comparisons, Contrasts, Connections

I invite comparison with John Milton and James Joyce. I invite a consideration of Mark Twain's availability to readers. I suggest that one might ask if this availability has any unfortunate consequences.

Questions for Reading and Discussion/ Approaches to Writing

1. What is the role of Tom Sawyer in *Huckleberry Finn*? If you have read *The Adventures of Tom Sawyer*, what is the difference between Tom in the earlier book and in *Huckleberry Finn*?
2. What aspects of *Huckleberry Finn* are as vital today as they were one hundred years ago? What in the book helps you understand an earlier era in American history, different from our own?

Bibliography

Robinson, Forrest G. *In Bad Faith: The Dynamics of Deception in Mark Twain's America*. 1986, 1–2, 111–22.

George Washington Cable (1844–1925)

Contributing Editor: James Robert Payne

Classroom Issues and Strategies

Students need to have some knowledge of southern American history as distinct from the historical emphasis on the Northeast that generally prevails in American history and literature courses. They should have a sense of the historical pluralism of southern American society, understanding that it includes American Indians, blacks, Hispanic Americans, exploited poor whites, as well as the conservative white elite, which tends to be the object of most attention. Cable's perception of multicultural southern America is central to his fiction.

Students need to be reminded that not all southerners supported slavery before the Civil War nor did all support segregation after the Civil War. For example, George Washington Cable, a middle-class white native of Louisiana, actively supported civil rights through his writings and through ordinary political work.

To break up tendencies to stereotype the South, students may be reminded that many southern cities voted against secession from the Union before the Civil War, and the voting was by white males only. Cable's fiction is expressive of pluralism in southern life and values.

With specific reference to "Jean-ah Poquelin": Discuss how Cable is interested in pairing and contrasting two types of male character, the "strong" Jean Marie Poquelin and his "gentle" half-brother, Jacques. Consider and discuss how in "Jean-ah Poquelin" Cable critically compares and dramatizes conflicts between colonial French-American and Anglo-American values. Note how scenes of mob violence in "Jean-ah Poquelin" prefigure violence in later periods in the South.

Major Themes, Historical Perspectives, and Personal Issues

1. A central theme of Cable's fiction is the impact of the complex history of the American South on modern southern life. In his sense of the profound influence of history on the present, Cable anticipates the later master southern fictionist, William Faulkner.

2. An issue that might be regarded as more personal concerns Cable's relation to New Orleans Creoles (in New Orleans, people of French or Spanish ancestry who preserved elements of their European culture). Creoles felt that their fellow New Orleanian betrayed them by what they saw as Cable's excessively biting satire and critique of the Creole community in his fiction.

Significant Form, Style, or Artistic Conventions

Cable needs to be taught as a southern American realist author (at least insofar as his early, most vital fiction is concerned) who combines tendencies of critical realism (in his critique of southern social injustice and hypocrisy) and local color realism (in his evocation of old New Orleans and plantation Louisiana in all their exoticism).

Yet unlike the work of his fellow realists of the North, such as William Dean Howells and Henry James, Cable's greatest works, *Old Creole Days*, *The Grandissimes*, and *Madame Delphine*, are historical "period" fictions.

Original Audience

In Cable's day, many southerners objected to what they saw as his unjust and disloyal criticism of southern social injustice. More specifically, some of Cable's New Orleans Creole readers expressed offense at what they regarded as Cable's sharp satire (amounting to caricature, as they saw it) on the Creole community. Cable found his readership by publishing his fiction in *Scribner's Monthly*. It was a readership much like that of his fellow authors William Dean Howells and Henry James, essentially middle class, "genteel," and mostly outside the South. Cable's audience today admires his work as giving the best depiction of old New Orleans and of Louisiana as well.

Comparisons, Contrasts, Connections

1. *Mark Twain*—The greatest of all southern writers of Cable's day, Mark Twain, is comparable to Cable in certain important ways. Both were essentially liberal southerners whose writings effectively criticized problems in southern life. Both Mark Twain and Cable also convey their love and understanding of their region through their endeavors to convey its varied dialects, complex social relationships, and dramatic history.
2. *Kate Chopin*—Cable shares with his fellow Louisiana writer Kate Chopin a strong interest in the Louisiana French-American community and the tensions between the French and Anglo communities, as well as a concern for the situation of women in the South of their day.

Questions for Reading and Discussion/
Approaches to Writing

1. (a) Consider and discuss how mob violence as represented in the *charivari* scene in "Jean-ah Poquelin" prefigures lynch mob and other violence in the South of Cable's day and in later periods.
   (b) Consider how the critical realist Cable undercuts romantic myths of the "noble aristocracy" of the "Old South."
2. (a) In an essay, discuss the significance of Cable's method of representing American language in relation to his themes. Hint: Remember that American language does not always mean English. Consider his representation of communication in French and, depending on which of Cable's works are being studied, other languages.

    (b) Consider residual romantic tendencies in the fiction of the southern realist George Washington Cable.

    (c) In an essay, discuss and demonstrate—with specific references to passages of Cable's fiction—how Cable undercuts ethnic stereotyping in his work.

Bibliography

Butcher, Philip. *George W. Cable*. New York: Twayne, 1962. Short, highly readable, solid book-length study of Cable and his work.

Clark, William Bedford. "Cable and the Theme of Miscegenation in *Old Creole Days* and *The Grandissimes*." *Mississippi Quarterly* 30 (Fall 1977): 597–609.

Eaton, Richard Bozman. "George W. Cable and the Historical Romance." *Southern Literary Journal* 8 (Fall 1975): 84–94.

Fulweiler, Howard W. "Of Time and the River: 'Ancestral Nonsense' vs. Inherited Guilt in Cable's 'Belles Demoiselles Plantation.' " *Midcontinent American Studies Journal* 7 (Fall 1966): 53–59.

Hubbell, Jay B. *The South In American Literature: 1607–1900*. Durham, N.C.: Duke University Press, 1954. Section on Cable.

Payne, James Robert. "George Washington Cable's 'My Politics': Context and Revision of a Southern Memoir." In *Multicultural Autobiography: American Lives*, edited by James Robert Payne, 94–113. Knoxville: University of Tennessee Press, 1992.

Petry, Alice Hall. *A Genius in His Way: The Art of Cable's Old Creole Days*. Rutherford, N.J.: Fairleigh Dickinson University Press, 1988. Short, readable, stimulating new study of Cable's best short fiction.

——. "Universal and Particular: The Local-Color Phenomenon Reconsidered." *American Literary Realism: 1870–1910* 12 (Spring 1979): 111–26.

Pugh, Griffith T. "George Washington Cable." *Mississippi Quarterly* 20 (Spring 1967): 69–76.

Turner, Arlin, ed. *Critical Essays on George W. Cable*. Boston: G. K. Hall, 1980.

——. *George W. Cable: A Biography*. Baton Rouge: Louisiana State University Press, 1966. The best single source on Cable by far.

Grace King (1852–1932)

Contributing Editor: Anne Jones

Classroom Issues and Strategies

This small jewel of a story should be accessible and immediately interesting to most student audiences, since it represents its issues so starkly, and since those issues (cultural repression and its internalization, the awakening of desire and identity, the loss and discovery of parents, the impact of religion, racism, and gender, for example) are concerns of many undergraduates. Happily, "The Little Convent Girl" also provides the opportunity for some remarkable conjunctions of teaching strategies: Its taut, understated, suggestive style invites careful close readings, its allusions and issues invite intertextual and contextual readings, and the political questions it raises, concerning the intersections of race and gender, invite readings through contemporary theory, such as Judith Butler's essay on Nella Larsen's *Passing* (in *Bodies That Matter*: New York, 1993).

Students might be drawn into these discussions through the highlighting of key words, images, and phrases (see below, "Significant Form"), historical allusions (see below, "Major Themes"), or intertextual connections (see below, "Comparisons"). Or, for something a bit different, they might "enter" the story by focusing not on text but on the white space that intrudes into it immediately after the first utterance of the word "Colored!" What happens in the month between that utterance and the girl's death—in the white space? If students are invited to invent and compare their own narratives to fill in this absence, many of the story's central ambiguities may surface as well.

Major Themes, Historical Perspectives, and Personal Issues

Grace King has frequently been seen as a woman of letters whose major projects, both literary and personal, had to do with defending the conservative South. It is certainly possible to read "The Little Convent Girl" in such a vein, as the story of the terrible consequences of miscegenation, for example: after all, her parents' cross-racial relationship ends in the girl's death. But the story's position on race is complicated by its connection with gender. Blackness—from the bodies of laborers to the

curl of the girl's hair—represents a vitality and desire whose "management" becomes a repeated question in the story; the fact that the girl's
vitality and desire are "managed" by a repressive churched femininity
suggests an alliance between racial and sexual problematics frequently
thought to be more characteristic of northern than southern discourses.
Cincinnati was, of course, a major center for slaves seeking freedom.
The story appeared in 1893, three years before Plessy *v.* Ferguson
authorized segregation, and in the thick of the proliferation of Jim Crow
laws and practices in the South. King even uses the phrase "Jim Crow"—
but how? In what ways does the story comment on its historical context?

Significant Form, Style, or Artistic Conventions

This story seems to be looking toward modernism, with its understatement, its absences, its unobtrusive symbolism, and its economy of language. "Unpacking" passages can be a fruitful enterprise. The first
paragraph, for example, suggests several continuing themes: the question of the significance of "good-bys," the connection between the girl's
passivity and the bolted door, and the journey down river, away from the
historical site of freedom for slaves. Other image patterns worth tracing
with care include mouths and lips; sound and noise; needlework; pleasure and constraint (*ad libitum* literally means "at pleasure"); the doubled
rivers and mothers; and of course whiteness and darkness.

The point of view from which the story is narrated is critical, for it
never allows readers to "enter" the girl's thoughts and—since she
doesn't speak—keeps her subjectivity opaque. How precisely can we describe the point of view? And how does the narration achieve its power?

Original Audience

"The Little Convent Girl" appeared in Grace King's collection *Balcony
Stories* (New York: Century, 1893) and in *Century Magazine*, XLVI
(August 1893), 547–51. In both forms it reached a wide national audi-
ence of men and women who were most likely white and middle class.
Balcony Stories remained in print a remarkably long time; new editions
were published in 1914 and 1925.

Comparisons, Contrasts, Connections

Robert Bush suggests comparing "The Little Convent Girl" as a "mixed
blood" story to Sherwood Bonner's "A Volcanic Interlude" and George
W. Cable's "'Tite Poulette" and "Madame Delphine." One might add
Kate Chopin's "Désirée's Baby" and Charles Chesnutt's "The Wife of

His Youth" to that list, among others. Mark Twain's *Adventures of Huckleberry Finn* tells a very different story of a slow boat down the Mississippi and a problematic arrival, but one whose differences might help to highlight the conjunctions between race and gender that seem so crucial to King. Kate Chopin's sketch "Emancipation" plays on some of the same liberation keys; *The Awakening* introduces what King's story avoids, female desire expressed as explicit sexuality, but its thematics of mothering and its relation to female desire (Adele Ratignolle's "mothering" of Edna on the beach, for instance, and its effects on Edna's voice) are worthy of comparison. Frances E. W. Harper treats "passing" from the point of view of the woman who "knows" she is black, in *Iola Leroy*; and Anna Julia Cooper, in *A Voice from the South*, in a sense gives speech to the silent convent girl. The life of an octoroon woman in New Orleans is imagined by Quentin Compson and his roommate in *Absalom, Absalom!* by William Faulkner.

Joel Chandler Harris (1848–1908)

Contributing Editor: George Friedman

Classroom Issues and Strategies

Get ready to meet some resistance to Harris, particularly to the Tar-Baby story, because the dialect is initially so daunting. It might be useful to tell students (particularly those from north of the Potomac River) that the dialect becomes easier to read as the story progresses; if you have the time at the end of the class preceding the Harris assignment, you might want to go over some of the more common words such as "sezee," "kaze," "gwine." I have on occasion been asked (by students who never saw "Song of the South") just what a Tar-Baby looked like; I use the analogy of a snowman.

As for "Free Joe," I find it useful to ask students to look for signs that this story was the creation of a *white* man. Your most perceptive students will have no trouble zeroing in on such lines as "The slaves laughed loudly day to day, but Free Joe rarely laughed. The slaves sang at their work and danced at their frolics, but no one ever heard Free Joe sing or saw him dance." Students should also notice and question Harris's assertion that no slave could possibly envy Joe's freedom.

In many instances, discussion of these lines generates a lively debate over the nature of slavery and harshness of life on an antebellum plantation. That slaves sang in the course of their daily labor is not to be denied, but it is useful to point out the lyrics of these songs, particularly the more religious ones, with their strong emphasis on the book of Exodus and eventual emancipation.

Students should also be encouraged to debate Harris's principal message in "Free Joe," and in particular the overall impression he wants to convey of Joe himself. Is it fair to dismiss Joe as an "Uncle Tom," passively taking whatever meanness that Spite Calderwood doles out? Students who characterize him as such will be challenged by others, who will point out that in the world of central Georgia in the middle of the nineteenth century, there wasn't much Joe could do to resist Calderwood. Nonetheless, other students will say, he doesn't seem to need to suppress rage, because he doesn't seem to feel any rage to begin with. A related question then arises: Is Harris's principal point in this story that no one should have such boundless power over the life of someone else, or is he saying that an African-American is unable to function without a white guardian? Let your class discuss this at some length, but don't expect a consensus.

Major Themes, Historical Perspectives, and Personal Issues

As the preceding section suggests, "Free Joe" opens up a host of questions about the nature of slavery in the antebellum South and the extent to which a "Free Negro" was really free. You might want to tell your students that historical accounts of Southern slavery have varied drastically in their characterizations of it, with some historians likening plantations to "vocational training schools" and others declaring Southern slavery the cruellest in western history, principally because it did not face organized opposition from the church and masters were rarely encouraged, by the clergy or anyone else, to emancipate their slaves or even to think of them as human beings.

It is useful to point out that Harris's treatment of slavery is much closer to the first of these two characterizations, and to put both "Free Joe" and the Tar-Baby story in the context of an age that sentimentalized the antebellum South—to point out that in story after story in the closing decades of the nineteenth century, the antebellum South was depicted as a land where races lived in harmony and both master and mistress considered their slaves part of the family, as did the slaves themselves. Point out that this idealized version of the antebellum South survived well into this century and reached its apogee in *Gone with the Wind*.

Original Audience

Harris's original audience, particularly for the Uncle Remus stories, was heavily northern. The stories originally appeared in his Atlanta *Constitution*, but they were quickly syndicated, and appeared in many northern newspapers. He also put out an *Uncle Remus Magazine* at the turn of the century and it had a brisk sale nationwide. Letters to Harris, reprinted by his daughter Julia, suggest that some of his most admiring readers considered themselves sincere champions of the rights of African-Americans.

It is very important to stress that at the turn of the century there were a great many writers and politicians eager to roll back the thirteenth, fourteenth, and fifteenth amendments, and that these people railed against African-Americans in extremely shrill and vicious terms, to very wide and very gullible audiences. It might be useful to quote from Thomas Dixon's *The Leopard's Spots*, which sold over 1,000,000 copies in 1902, or read from Senator "Pitchfork Ben" Tillman's (a Democrat from South Carolina) famous speech on the floor of the Senate in defense of lynching. Harris's condescension toward African-Americans might look a bit less defamatory when placed alongside such savage and widely accepted views of the race.

Comparisons, Contrasts, Connections

In addition to the comparisons and contrasts cited above, Charles W. Chesnutt's Uncle Julius stories offer the most logical point of contrast— to both the Uncle Remus stories and "Free Joe." It is useful to point out that Uncle Remus's only apparent motive in telling his stories is to entertain a little white boy, whereas Chesnutt's Uncle Julius is a far craftier character; he always has an underlying motive rooted in his own self-interest. Regardless of the Chesnutt story you use, it will depict the institution of slavery itself in terms far more bleak than what is found in Harris's stories—no one sings in Chesnutt's stories and no one frolics, either.

Other African-American writers of the age suggest themselves: certainly Dunbar's poem, "We Wear the Mask" could be cited, since the mask Dunbar describes in this poem appears to have fooled Harris himself. Booker T. Washington's own memories of slavery would form a useful comparison, as would the more critical observations of W.E.B. Du Bois, in "The Sorrow Songs."

Questions for Reading and Discussion/ Approaches to Writing

I've already suggested the most fruitful questions: for the Tar-Baby story, you might ask why these stories would have held so much appeal for the slaves themselves. See if your students can discern for themselves the connections between the weak but wily rabbit and the slave; and strong but oafish fox or bear and the master.

For "Free Joe," ask them to look for signs that the work was written by a white man, and see how many pick up on Harris's emphasis on the slaves' singing and dancing, and his certainty that no slave would ever envy Joe's freedom.

One final point for discussion in "Free Joe" would be Harris's attitude toward poor whites, as represented by the Staleys. For one whose origins were themselves so humble, Harris seemed to have very little sympathy for poor whites; the Staleys are insensitive and superstitious. They nevertheless open the only doors in the story for Joe; does Harris want us to think of them in a positive light?

Bibliography

For "Free Joe," try R. Bruce Bickley, *Joel Chandler Harris* (1987), pp. 113–16, and Catherine Starke, *Black Portraiture in American Fiction* (1971), pp. 53–54.

Just about everything written about the Tar-Baby Story concentrates on Harris's use of dialect. The best of such studies is probably Lee Pederson's "Language in the Uncle Remus Tales," *Modern Philology* 82 (1985): 292–98.

A useful took for Harris is *The Atlanta Historical Journal*, 30 (1986–87): iii–iv. The entire issue is devoted to articles on the man and his work.

Charles Waddell Chesnutt (1858–1932)

Contributing Editor: William L. Andrews

Classroom Issues and Strategies

Classroom issues include: How critical or satirical of blacks is Chesnutt in his portrayal of them? Does he treat them with sympathy, even when they behave foolishly? Is Chesnutt's satire biting and distant or self-involving and tolerant?

There's rarely one source of authority in a Chesnutt story. Different points of view compete for authority. Get the students to identify the different points of view and play them against each other.

Stress that Chesnutt's conjure stories were written in such a way as not to identify their author as an African-American. How effective is Chesnutt in this effort?

Students want to know what Chesnutt's social purposes were in writing his conjure stories. How could stories about slavery have any bearing on the situation of blacks and on race relations at the turn of the century—when Chesnutt wrote—and today?

Major Themes, Historical Perspectives, and Personal Issues

Major themes include the following: Chesnutt's attitude toward the Old South; the myth of the plantation and the happy darkey, the mixed-blood (monster or natural and even an evolutionary improvement); and miscegenation as a natural process, not something to be shocked by.

Significant Form, Style, or Artistic Conventions

Chesnutt wrote during the era of literary realism. What is his relationship to realism, its standards, its themes, its ideas about appropriateness of subject matter and tone?

Original Audience

I stress that Chesnutt wrote for genteel magazine readers much less critical and aware of their racism than we. How does he both appeal to and gently undermine that audience's assumptions?

Comparisons, Contrasts, Connections

Chesnutt wrote to counter the stories of Thomas Nelson Page and Joel Chandler Harris. Chesnutt might also be compared to Paul Laurence Dunbar and Frederick Douglass as depicters of blacks on the plantation before the Civil War.

Bibliography

Read the chapter on the dialect fiction in William L. Andrews, *The Literary Career of Charles W. Chesnutt* (Baton Rouge: LSU Press, 1980).

Paul Laurence Dunbar (1872–1906)

Contributing Editors: Elaine Hedges and Richard Yarborough

Classroom Issues and Strategies

Although Paul Laurence Dunbar also produced novels, short stories, and a large number of poems written in conventional English, he is best known for his adoption in verse of what was presented as the language (or "dialect") of the black southern folk. Indeed, he has been viewed by some commentators as an artist who used negative stereotypes of his own people to satisfy a white audience, and there are still those who suggest that his work lacks substance.

In his lifetime, however, Dunbar was generally considered a glowing symbol of African-American literary artistry and an apt representative of his race, and a close reading of his poetry reveals him to be far more than an unimaginative purveyor of antiblack images. In addition, few modern readers are aware of the essays on American race relations and other contemporaneous issues that Dunbar published at the height of his popularity. It is perhaps no wonder that from shortly after his death through the mid-twentieth century, his name was associated with numerous respected institutions in the African-American community. Practically gone now are the various Paul Laurence Dunbar Literary Societies that flourished throughout the country, but the schools and housing projects bearing his name still exist in many cities.

In order for students to appreciate the enduring literary achievement represented by Dunbar's best work, they should be given some sense of the daunting obstacles arrayed against black authors at that time and, accordingly, of the complex constraints placed upon them by white editors and readers alike. To put it another way, students should be encouraged to consider not just *what* Dunbar wrote but *why* he wrote as he did.

Significant Form, Style, or Artistic Conventions

One cannot overemphasize the fact that Dunbar lived during a period when the access allowed blacks to major white publications was extremely limited. Although there were a number of important African-American periodicals in existence as well, for the ambitious black author eager to make his or her mark on the mainstream literary landscape, magazines such as *Century* and the *Atlantic Monthly* constituted the height of success. All too often, however, editors of these and similar periodicals expected African-American writers dealing with black material to follow the conventions of what has been termed the Plantation Tradition, which dominated the literary representation of black life and culture in the late nineteenth century. When coupled with the popularity of dialect verse of all kinds at the time, these conventions (perhaps best embodied in the fiction of Joel Chandler Harris and Thomas Nelson Page) exerted tremendous pressure upon aspiring African-American authors. As a result, one should urge students not to search Dunbar's work for outright protest and direct rejection of the dominant racial stereotypes of the day but rather to attend to the subtle use of irony and the often veiled allusions to the dilemmas of race that mark much of his writing.

It is also important to recall that Dunbar wrote at a time when American poetry was in a state of transition. Authors such as Henry Wadsworth Longfellow and James Whitcomb Riley were seen as "true" poets, and such sentimental pieces as Eugene Field's "Little Boy Blue" and Will Carleton's "Over the Hills to the Poorhouse" were celebrated as the epitome of poetic genius. Although Emily Dickinson had died in 1886, her work was virtually unknown until the 1930s; and scant serious attention was paid to Ralph Waldo Emerson's poetic theory or Walt Whitman's free verse innovations. The invigorating literary experiments of the modernist period were still several years off.

The state of American poetry at the turn of the century explains, to some extent, the diverse, occasionally conflicting formal strains in Dunbar's work. If, on the one hand, his dialect poems reflect his adoption of stylistic strategies of both James Whitcomb Riley and also the Plantation Tradition writers, on the other hand, he modelled his conventional English poetry after the popular sentimental magazine verse of his day. Ultimately, neither approach was conducive to a realistic rendering of either the psychology or the vernacular expressions of African-Americans. (One should also keep in mind that Dunbar was born and raised in the post–Civil War North and thus had little firsthand knowledge of southern life generally and none of slavery.)

Original Audience

Dunbar was read widely in both the black and the white communities, with the extraordinary sales of his books making him one of the most successful American writers of his time, regardless of race. Some attention should be given in the classroom to the possible consequences for Dunbar's art of this dual audience, especially given that most white readers were not just unaware of the complexities of African-American life and culture but possessed of attitudes toward blacks shaped primarily by the racist images disseminated in the popular press, on the minstrel stage, and by post-Reconstruction southern politicians.

Comparisons, Contrasts, Connections

Despite the creative and personal tensions that plagued his tragically brief career, Dunbar was, without question, the single most influential African-American poet before Langston Hughes, even if many of the writers of the generation that followed his rejected aspects of his work. Extremely useful comparisons can and should be drawn between Dunbar's poetry and that of the New Negro Renaissance.

Questions for Reading and Discussion/ Approaches to Writing

For "Mr. Cornelius Johnson, Office-Seeker":

1. What did the Reconstruction Amendments to the U.S. Constitution (1865–70) accomplish? What did they fail to do?
2. Given the method of character presentation, do you—as the reader—sympathize with Cornelius Johnson? Do you find any weaknesses in him that might tend to explain his predicament?

For Dunbar's poetry:

1. By "scanning" Dunbar's poetry, does a reader learn anything about Dunbar's poetic technique?
2. Analyze Dunbar's representation of black southern life in "When Malindy Sings" and "An Ante-Bellum Sermon." In particular, consider the tactics he utilizes in attempting to undermine the stereotypes that his characterizations appear on the surface to endorse. How successful are these tactics? Examine the role of religion and the use of irony in both poems.

3. From your knowledge of Frederick Douglass, does Dunbar's poem entitled "Frederick Douglass" transmit important information about the nineteenth-century leader?

Bibliography

Gayle, Addison, Jr. *Oak and Ivy: A Biography of Paul Laurence Dunbar.* Garden City: Anchor/Doubleday, 1971.

Martin, Jay, ed. *A Singer in the Dawn: Reinterpretations of Paul Laurence Dunbar.* New York: Dodd, Mead, 1975.

Revell, Peter. *Paul Laurence Dunbar.* Boston: Twayne, 1979.

Alexander Lawrence Posey (Creek) (1873–1908)

Contributing Editor: Daniel F. Littlefield, Jr.

Classroom Issues and Strategies

Students should have no problems with the "Ode" but may have difficulties with the dialect in the Hotgun poem and the Fus Fixico letter.

Present these matters in the same way one would present them in relation to other dialect writers of the period: e.g., Clemens, Cable, Harris, Chesnutt, Dunbar, Chopin. Present the "Ode" as one would the lesser lyrics of a Bryant or a Longfellow, for instance.

Students are interested in the question of Indian-U.S. relations, not only in Posey's time but before and after. They are also curious about the "Americanization" of Indians like Posey (e.g., his romantic lyrics, his classical education, etc.). This issue leads ultimately to questions of assimilation and cultural discontinuity.

Major Themes, Historical Perspectives, and Personal Issues

1. Passing of the Indian (that foolish concept of the "vanishing American"). The interesting point is that Posey, and many other Indian writers, bought the idea to some extent.
2. Romanticizing the "great" man, whether he is Sequoyah or Yadeka Harjo. (Why would an Indian choose these as great men?)

3. "Progress" as it translated into materialism; the learned "need" for material things versus the desire for a "simpler," culture-centered society; uncertainty in time of culture change.
4. Indian humor—most students are surprised to find that Indians have any.

Significant Form, Style, or Artistic Conventions

Discuss with the students the same questions that apply to any lyrical poetry, to any dialect poetry, and to any dialect prose, especially Joel Chandler Harris and the professional dialect humorists, the "Phunny Phellows" of the late nineteenth century. Posey's dialect fits squarely into the local color movement. If we can have Harte in the West, Cable and Chopin in Louisiana, Garland in the Midwest, Harris in Georgia, why not Posey in the Indian Territory?

Original Audience

Posey published most of his poems in Indian Territory newspapers and magazines. He wrote for a western audience. Posey, like many Indians at the turn of the century, witnessed a great attrition in Indian culture as the U.S. pushed a policy of assimilation. He attempted to document the passing of Indian folk heroes, great and small. Recent American Indian writing deals in large measure with attempts at rediscovering what has been lost. Writers like Posey anticipate the themes of many contemporary American Indian or Chinese or Japanese or Chicano writers.

Bibliography

The most complete treatment of Posey's life is Daniel F. Littlefield, Jr.'s *Alex Posey: Creek Poet, Journalist, and Humorist.* Lincoln: University of Nebraska, 1992.

John Milton Oskison (Cherokee) (1874–1947)

Contributing Editor: Daniel F. Littlefield, Jr.

Classroom Issues and Strategies

Students are interested in American society's insistence that Indians conform to the expectations of Anglo-dominated society versus the social exclusion of blacks of the same period.

Major Themes, Historical Perspectives, and Personal Issues

1. Imposition of one's ideology upon another
2. Cultural roots of personal world views
3. Racial-cultural biases, stereotyping
4. Religous ideology's role in destroying cultures
5. Religous zeal and the devaluing of cultures

Significant Form, Style, or Artistic Conventions

The story should be dealt with in the context of the short story form. It relates to the local color writing of the late nineteenth and early twentieth century.

Original Audience

The piece was written for a popular audience during a period when federal policy aimed to move the Indian into mainstream American society, to eliminate cultural differences, to make the Indian, as it were, a red white person. In retrospect, present-day readers see the failure of such policies. But on another level, the story has something to say to the reader who is concerned about the imposition of one's ideology upon the unwilling, whether that ideology is religious, social, or political.

Comparisons, Contrasts, Connections

The same issues raised by works of Posey ("Fus Fixico's Letter"), Eastman ("The Great Mystery"), and Bonnin are raised by Oskison's Story. The Indians' anti-assimilationist response is recorded in "Ghost Dance

Songs." In its harsh tone and didacticism, the story can be compared with some of Chesnutt's or those of other black writers of the period. After the student has read his story, Bonnin's "Why I Am a Pagan" is a good chaser.

Alice Dunbar-Nelson (1875–1935)

Contributing Editor: Akasha (Gloria) Hull

Classroom Issues and Strategies

The state of African-American literature when these two stories were published (1899–1900) was the transition period between post-slavery Reconstruction and the flowering of black literature in the nineteen-teens (1915 into the Harlem Renaissance)—before Booker T. Washington's *Up From Slavery* (1901) and W.E.B. Du Bois's *The Souls of Black Folk* (1903) had articulated the terms of a racial debate that highlighted the difference between old and new ways of conceptualizing and presenting (politically and artistically) black American culture. There was continuing richness in folk literature, but it still did not represent an extensive scribal tradition. Two black men-of-letters had achieved national recognition—Paul Laurence Dunbar for his dialect poetry (which, despite its original genius, still used familiar minstrel and plantation motifs) and Charles Chesnutt, author of *The Conjure Woman* and *The Wife of His Youth* (1899), stories that featured a tale-telling trickster figure and the "color line," respectively. Clearly, Dunbar-Nelson is helping to define a nascent modern tradition, and doing so in ways that avoided limitations and stereotypes but also skirted race.

One must remember, too, the context of nineteenth-century popular fiction with its penchant for narrative modes and devices we now eschew—romance, melodrama, moralizing, etc. Of particular relevance is the flourishing of the local color tradition, in which women writers excelled. The South and Louisiana had its representatives, and Dunbar-Nelson wrote and was read in the light of George Washington Cable and Kate Chopin. In an early letter to her, Paul Laurence Dunbar said:

> Your determination to contest Cable for his laurels is a
> commendable one. Why shouldn't you tell those pretty
> Creole stories as well as he? You have the force, the fire

and the artistic touch that is so delicate and yet so strong.

Do you know that New Orleans—in fact all of Louisiana—seems to me to be a kind of romance land. . . . No wonder you have Grace King and Geo. W. Cable, no wonder you will have Alice R.[uth] M.[oore] [Dunbar-Nelson's maiden name]

Major Themes, Historical Perspectives, and Personal Issues

Race and racism within the U.S. is a contextual given. One of the specific results/manifestations that is relevant is *intra*-racial color prejudice, especially the prejudice against darker-skinned black people and the hierarchy of color. These contexts relate to Auguste in "Pearl." So does the phenomenon of "passing" (usually economically motivated). Dunbar-Nelson herself casually passed on occasion—to see a theatrical performance, to have a swim at a bathing spa, to travel comfortably.

Auguste does so in a much more serious and sustained way for, in the eyes of the Irish politicians, his free black grandfather makes him just as much a "nigger" as Frank and the others.

The ambiguous racial status of the Louisiana Creoles is an even further refinement on the race/racism theme. Their admixture of French-Spanish-Indian-black-white blood, their often free status, their closed/distinct society/culture, etc., set them apart. Readers did not (do not?) tend to see these Creole characters as black/African-Americans, but as some kind of non-white exotics.

Significant Form, Style, or Artistic Conventions

Race and the African-American writer. There has always been feeling and discussion on the black writer's proper role/stance with regard to her/his racial roots and the use of this material. This has been complicated by the pseudo-argument of whether one wants to be a "black writer" or a "writer" (recall the shibboleth of being "universal").

Original Audience

Answering questions like this was also affected by questions of audience and readership, since the authors had to write for predominantly white or mixed audiences. Furthermore, whites controlled the mass markets. Black newspapers and journals furnished independent outlets, but these were comparatively few and small. Clearly, Dunbar-Nelson was writing for a larger, mostly white readership. She had also learned from experience that this audience did not accept controversial treatments of blacks or black-white relations.

Comparisons, Contrasts, Connections

Dunbar-Nelson has usually been taught—if at all—as a very minor female poet of the Harlem Renaissance, partly because of that period's notoriety and also because only a few of her poems have been available. Literary historians knew/know of her "Creole stories," but they have not been easy to access. It radically alters our view of her to see that poetry was the least significant genre for her and short fiction the most important. After *Violets* and *St. Rocque*, she wrote two other collections that were never published (though a few individual stories were): *Women and Men*, more nature and original Creole and non-Creole materials, and *The Annals of 'Steenth Street*, tales of Irish tenement youth set in New York City. She also wrote various other types of stories until she died.

Bibliography

Possible further reading: Two other Dunbar-Nelson stories: "The Goodness of St. Rocque," which typifies, perhaps, her mode in these works, and "The Stones of the Village," an even more overt and tragic handling of race, passing, and the black Creole; plus "Brass Ankles Speaks," an autobiographical essay about growing up in New Orleans as a "light nigger," which Dunbar-Nelson wrote pseudonymously toward the end of her life.

Secondary criticism: The biographical-literary chapter devoted to Dunbar-Nelson in Gloria T. Hull, *Color, Sex, and Poetry: Three Women Writers of the Harlem Renaissance* (Bloomington: Indiana University Press, 1987), and the Introduction to *The Works of Alice Dunbar-Nelson*.

William Dean Howells (1837–1920)

Contributing Editor: John W. Crowley

Classroom Issues and Strategies

Students are usually unfamiliar with Howells and his central position in nineteenth-century American literature. If they have heard of him at all, they are likely to have picked up the (still) prevailing stereotype: that Howells was a genteel prude whose realism could not possibly be of any interest to contemporary readers. Another problem is that students are not often sensitive to quiet irony in what they read; they are not prepared to hear the subtle nuances in Howells's narrative voice—or to read between the lines in his treatment of sexuality, which he handled with Victorian decorum but did *not* avoid as a subject.

It is useful to tell students about the history of Howells's literary reputation: his contemporary fame, his fall from grace during the 1920s, his currently anomalous position in the canon. Students are usually pleasantly surprised by Howells, in part because his prose is not "difficult" (like James's) and because they find more complexity than they had expected. It is best to start, perhaps, with the "Editor's Easy Chair" selection, which introduces students to his characteristic tone and prepares them to recognize his use of the dramatic method in the fiction: the apparent (but only apparent) narrative detachment, the embodiment of themes in the characters' dialogue and interactions.

I have sometimes introduced Howells by reading from the famous account of the Whittier Birthday Dinner in 1877, as reported in *My Mark Twain*. The narrative is very engaging and amusing; it catches students' attention. It is also revealing of Howells's "inbetweenness" in the literary culture of his time and of the collision of East and West, decorum and humor. Howells often seems remote from the world of current students. They may wish to know why they are reading him at all—a question that can usher in a discussion of canon formation.

Major Themes, Historical Perspectives, and Personal Issues

The personal theme I would emphasize—because it is not well recognized—is Howells's neuroticism: his history of psychological perturbation and its bearing on his sensitivity to undercurrents of motive in his characters. I would also stress his role as the "Dean" of American letters as indicative of the changing means of literary production in the late nineteenth century. It is also important that Howells's career spanned virtually the entirety of American literature up to his time: from the romantics to the forerunners of modernism.

Significant Form, Style, or Artistic Conventions

Obviously, the key issue for Howells is literary realism: what it means, how it came to develop in America. Since realism has become something of a whipping boy for poststructuralist theory, it makes sense to use Howells to examine the enabling ideological assumptions of realism. There is in Howells, however, especially in his later work, a strong debt to Hawthorne and the American romance. This side of his work is not well known.

Original Audience

Howells was acutely aware of the female dominance of the audience for fiction in the period. He clearly imagined that he was writing for women primarily and believed further that he had a moral responsibility not to offend the sensibilities of young women readers. Insofar as the current audience for literature has been "masculinized" by modernism, Howells's work may sound out of key in the same way that much women's fiction from the period does. In this sense, Howells is best understood as a "woman's" writer.

Comparisons, Contrasts, Connections

Howells makes a nice contrast to almost any American fiction writer of the period because his work assimilated so many of its literary discourses. One conventional way of placing Howells is to put him between James and Twain, his closest literary friends—or to compare him to the generation of his literary sons (Crane, Dreiser, Norris, etc.). A fresher approach would be to pair him with women writers, many of whom he helped to establish. In this regard, "Editha" is a useful text.

Questions for Reading and Discussion/
Approaches to Writing

Although the general approach to teaching literature—and my own approach—seems to have become broader and more theoretical, I still find that students do not know how to read closely enough; they don't understand basic literary codes. With realism, it is especially important to stress the role of reader inference, and I tend to assign topics that focus closely on workably small bits of text.

Bibliography

For a general orientation to recent Howells criticism, I know nothing better than my own omnibus surveys, published as "Howells in the Seventies" and "Howells in the Eighties" in *ESQ:A Journal of the American Renaissance* (1979, 1986–87). See also the recent Howells issue of *American Literary Realism* (1988), which contains several articles and a bibliography keyed to individual Howells texts.

The standard biographies are still Edwin H. Cady, *The Road to Realism/The Realist at War*, and Kenneth S. Lynn, *William Dean Howells*.

Henry James (1843–1916)

Contributing Editor: Alfred Habegger

Classroom Issues and Strategies

In "The Beast in the Jungle," James's late style will be a problem. In "Daisy Miller," students may well miss the important social nuances of the language used by the characters and the narrator. Most of us take for granted certain usages—"ever so many," "it seems as if," "I guess," "quaint"—that are indications of the Millers' lack of cultivation. Also, there are some genteelisms in their speech—Mrs. Miller's "the principal ones." Then there's the narrator's somewhat inflated diction—"imbibed," "much disposed towards."

Distribute ahead of time a short list of usages, divided according to categories, and ask the students to add some usages from their own reading of "Daisy Miller."

Another problem that should be mentioned is point of view. Tell the students ahead of time that both "Daisy" and "Beast" use the same technical device of restricting the reader's perspective to what one character sees and knows. Ask them to decide what character this is. Give examples, find exceptions where the narrator speaks out.

"Daisy Miller": Some students inevitably despise Daisy for her occasional social crudity and inexperience. A good tactic to deal with this attitude is to emphasize such matters right at the start, trusting to other students to feel that they must speak up and defend Daisy's naturalness and boldness. I also recommend getting the obvious fact that the Millers represent vulgar new money out in the open from the start; otherwise, some rather slow reader will triumphantly announce this fact later on in order to simplify the heroine's character.

Students will appreciate some facts about Rome. The story takes place before the floor of the Colosseum was excavated and before the cause of malaria was discovered. The 1883 Baedeker guide reminded tourists of the traditional danger of malaria: "In summer when the fever-laden *aria cattive* [bad air] prevails, all the inhabitants who can afford it make a point of leaving the city." Some students will have no experience of Giovanelli's type—the public dandy and lounger.

Students consistently enjoy analyzing and judging (with great ferocity) the various characters. I am often surprised at the harsh judgments passed on Daisy's flirtatiousness and game playing.

"Beast": Few students respond well to "Beast," partly because of the aridity of the lives portrayed. The students may want to know why the story is so long, why it delays the revelation of Marcher's emptiness.

Major Themes, Historical Perspectives, and Personal Issues

In "Beast" I like to stress Marcher's eerie hollowness, the fact that he isn't quite alive and doesn't know it (until the end). In "Daisy Miller" students will probably need a detailed explanation of the Colosseum scene, where Winterbourne finally makes up his mind about Daisy, not only deciding that she isn't respectable but showing her by his behavior that he scorns her as beyond the pale. He learns the truth about her (and his own feelings for her) too late, of course—just like Marcher.

Significant Form, Style, or Artistic Conventions

"Daisy Miller" may be presented as a classic instance of nineteenth-century realism in presenting "a study" of a modern character-type. Simultaneously, since the story follows Winterbourne's point of view, James's subject becomes a double one and also concerns the male character's process of vision and understanding. In this sense, the story is about Winterbourne's "studying."

In "Beast" the emphasis on the man's process of vision becomes even more salient. The lack of objective detail points to modernism.

Original Audience

For "Beast," students need to be told that the two characters are late nineteenth-century or early twentieth-century English, and that Weatherend is an upper-class country house frequented by weekend guests.

In "Daisy Miller" students will need help in grasping the leisure-class European social code: the importance of restraint, public decorum, the drawing of lines. When Daisy looks at Winterbourne and boasts of having had "a great deal of gentleman's society," she doesn't know (though Winterbourne and James do) that she is coming on precisely as a courtesan would.

Comparisons, Contrasts, Connections

Many valuable comparisons can be drawn between "Daisy Miller" and "The Beast in the Jungle." Both stories tell of an aborted romance in which the man distances himself emotionally until it is too late. This fundamental similarity can help bring out the real differences between the works, especially the fact that "Daisy Miller" supplies a good deal of pictorial background and social realism, while "Beast" focuses far more intensively on Marcher's state of mind and perceptions. "Beast" may also profitably be compared with Eliot's "Prufrock."

Questions for Reading and Discussion/ Approaches to Writing

1. Ask students to pay attention to those situations in "Daisy Miller" where one character tries to gauge or classify another. They may notice that Winterbourne's social judgment is much shakier than at first appears. Not only does he misread Daisy (in the Colosseum) but he is wrong in pronouncing Giovanelli "not a gentleman." Giovanelli turns out to be a respectable lawyer.
2. I like to ask students to compare and contrast the scene in the Colosseum where Winterbourne decides Daisy is a reprobate and laughs in her face to the scene in *Huckleberry Finn* where Huck decides to go to hell out of friendship with Jim. One character gives way to a rigid social exclusion, the other defies it.

Bibliography

The preface that James wrote for "Daisy Miller" in the New York edition is illuminating but must be used with care. The preface was written about thirty years after the story, and James's attitudes had changed somewhat. Now he was much more uneasy about the vulgarity of speech and manners of American women, and he decided he had been too easy on the Daisy Miller type. Hence he labeled this story "pure poetry"—a way of calling it romance rather than realism.

Two helpful and somewhat contrasting studies: Wayne Booth's discussion of "Daisy Miller" in *The Rhetoric of Fiction* and Louise K. Barnett, "Jamesian Feminism: Women in 'Daisy Miller,' " *Studies in Short Fiction* 16, no. 4 (Fall 1979): 281–87.

It's difficult to know whether Daisy Miller is a historically accurate type. Upper-class single women did not apparently go out alone in the evening in New York of the 1870s, but they did not require a duenna when accompanied by a man.

Kate Chopin (1851–1904)

Contributing Editor: Peggy Skaggs

Classroom Issues and Strategies

Chopin's irony is too subtle for some students, who may see her female characters as cold, unloving, unfeeling women. They have difficulty understanding that the protagonists in, say, "A Respectable Woman" and "The Story of an Hour" really do love their husbands, although in the one case the wife seems sure to commit adultery and in the other the wife exults in her freedom when she believes that her husband has died in an accident. The same students almost surely will judge Calixta (but probably not Alcée) in "The Storm." Students almost always respond to Chopin's treatment of the relationship between men and women. Often the male students intensely dislike such characters as Mrs. Mallard and Mrs. Baroda. Often, also, they judge the mother in "A Pair of Silk Stockings" to be uncaring about her children and frivolous in spending her little windfall. In other words, students today still hold many of the notions about women that inspired Chopin's best irony and satire.

Class discussions usually help a great deal to clear up such misunderstandings. These discussions are based on a very close reading of the text, calling attention to the myriad small clues Chopin always provided but readers do not always observe. "The Storm," being a sequel to "At the Cadian Ball," becomes much clearer in characterization and theme when students understand the groundwork that was laid in the earlier work. Indeed, without such explanation, "The Storm" hardly makes sense to many students.

Since Chopin wrote everything she produced during the last decade of the nineteenth century but was too advanced in her thinking to be accepted until the last quarter of the twentieth century, she offers a fine vehicle for exploring the intellectual and aesthetic tides of American thinking and American literature. In important ways, she summarizes the nineteenth century with her fine mixture of romanticism, realism, and naturalism. But in other ways, she predicts the latter part of the twentieth century with her feminism and existentialism. I like to close one century and begin the next with her works.

Major Themes, Historical Perspectives, and Personal Issues

Chopin's feminism certainly is a major theme, but an instructor must be careful not to overstate it. Chopin seems to have believed that men and women alike have great difficulty reconciling their need to live as discrete individuals with their need to live in close relationship with a mate; these conflicting needs lie at the center of her work.

Significant Form, Style, or Artistic Conventions

Since Chopin's works contain clear elements of romanticism, transcendentalism, realism, naturalism, existentialism, and feminism, her stories can help students understand these literary modes and the directions in which American literature has developed during the last century and a half. Chopin's style offers opportunities to point out the virtues of conciseness; strong, clear imagery; symbolism; understatement; humor; and irony.

Original Audience

I discuss the intellectual background against which Chopin was writing in the 1890s. I share with the students some of the vitriolic reviews received by *The Awakening* in 1899. I trace the history of Chopin's literary reputation from the time the critics buried her in 1899 until a Norwegian, Per Seyersted, resurrected her work in 1969.

Comparisons, Contrasts, Connections

Chopin admired Maupassant's stories enormously, and she translated a number of them into English. Many writers have noted his strong influence, especially apparent in the sharp, ironic conclusions Chopin favored in many stories ("The Story of an Hour" and "Désirée's Baby," for example). The influence of Hawthorne, Whitman, and Henry James has been noted by various critics, also.

Questions for Reading and Discussion/ Approaches to Writing

1. I try to get students to look for irony, simply because so many of them are prone to miss it in Chopin's work.
2. Writing a character study of Mrs. Mallard in "The Story of an Hour" sometimes helps a student to accept that she can be both grief stricken and relieved that her husband is dead.

    A similar assignment focused on the protagonist in "A Respectable Woman" occasionally forces a student to admit that Mrs. Baroda tries valiantly to resist her temptation.

    If the class has read Whitman, I often have them write an essay about how the two authors use lilacs as a symbol or how they both emphasize the importance of both body and spirit.

Bibliography

Particularly useful is *Approaches to Teaching Chopin's "The Awakening,"* edited by Bernard Koloski (New York: MLA, 1988). The backgrounds, biographical information, discussion of critical studies, bibliography, and aids to teaching all contain information useful for teaching Chopin's short stories as well as the novel.

Mary E. Papke's chapter, "Chopin's Stories of Awakening," discusses "The Story of an Hour" and "A Pair of Silk Stockings."

In *Kate Chopin* (Boston: Twayne Publishers, 1985), I discuss each of the stories in this anthology as well as everything else Chopin wrote.

Thomas Bonner, Jr., in *The Kate Chopin Companion, with Chopin's Translations from French Fiction,* Westport: Greenwood Press, 1988, has made Chopin's translations of Maupassant's stories easily available for the first time—a very important resource in understanding Chopin's own stories.

And Emily Toth's *Kate Chopin,* New York: William Morrow and Company, 1990, gives us for the first time a comprehensive biography filled with previously unknown or simply rumored details about Chopin's life.

Ambrose Bierce (1842–1914?)

Contributing Editor: Cathy N. Davidson

Classroom Issues and Strategies

Two primary issues present themselves in teaching "Chickamauga." First the details are grotesque. The procession of bloody, dying men and the macabre humor of the small child mounting one as he would a pony (or his father's slaves "playing horsey") often disturbs students very much. This, of course, is exactly Bierce's intention. Second, the ending seems like a gratuitous trick. Is it necessary that the child be deaf and dumb? Realistically, this is necessary since the child does not hear the great battle—we are told so explicitly. But it's also important symbolically: the temptation to war is so great in male culture that even this small child learns it, even though there is so much he does not understand.

To address these issues, first I read some conventional war accounts and war stories—or even the lyrics to war songs. I then read aloud the most grotesque parts of Bierce. I next ask my students which is, in its consequence, the more violent. We then discuss protest literature and Bierce's disgust that several prominent generals of the Civil War were rewriting the incomparably brutal history of that war. Second, we go through the story isolating how the child learns, what he knows and doesn't. The picture book lesson at the beginning makes the point that a child is already learning values at the earliest age, prelinguistically. These are *powerful* messages, calls to violence.

Try reading some definitions from the *Devil's Dictionary*. "*War*, n. A by-product of the arts of peace. War loves to come like a thief in the night; professions of eternal amity provide the night." "*Peace*, n. In international affairs, a period of cheating between two periods of fighting."

I usually give a full biographical lecture on Bierce because he was such a character and such a successful muckraker. Students are always fascinated by his disappearance—no skeleton was ever found. (Several expeditions were mounted and, since he was over 6 feet tall and had a full head of pure white hair, the rumors of his every move were rampant: but there has never been confirmation of his death.) Brigid Brophy insists he did not die but merely came back again when the world was more ready for his wild, stylistic experiments. According to Brophy, he now writes under the nom de plume of "Jorge Luis Borges." (Actually, since Borges died recently, I suppose that must mean Bierce finally did, too.)

Major Themes, Historical Perspectives, and Personal Issues

War, the tendency toward violence, the idea that we fear what we do not know but perhaps should most fear what we know (i.e., ourselves, our fellow humans, those people we love who nonetheless perpetuate the values of violence). The child sees nothing wrong with war until it literally comes home—the burned house, the dead and probably raped body of the mother. Note, too, the rampant animal imagery throughout the story. Early critics called it an "allegory" and it is.

Significant Form, Style, or Artistic Conventions

Unlike most so-called naturalists, Bierce blamed humans, not Fate, for determining the course of human existence. However, he was a naturalist in his use of macabre and even lurid details that force the reader to see the full implications of war. Stylistically, he brilliantly mimics the actions of the boy (as well as his perceptions, devoid of sound and often sense, since, as a small child, he lacks the experience to know what is harmful, what not: bears are cute in the picture books, so is war) and of the dying soldiers. The famous passage of the ground in motion and the creek relies on repetition to heighten the sense of relentless violence. Allegory is another important genre to discuss and elucidate here.

Original Audience

I always discuss the memoirs of the Civil War veterans as well as the beginning of America's full-fledged attempt at imperialism in Latin America, the Spanish-American War. Bierce, in his other capacity as a journalist, vociferously denounced the war that William Randolph Hearst bragged he started (saying people buy newspapers during wars). Bierce was fired from that job but went on to other newspapers where he was equally adamant in his opposition to the war. He died (or rather disappeared) sometime in 1914, over 70 years old, when he went to Mexico to see Pancho Villa firsthand. Carlos Fuentes's *The Old Gringo* is a retelling of Bierce's journey into Mexico where peasants still insist Bierce wanders the Sierra Madres.

Comparisons, Contrasts, Connections

Stephen Crane learned his craft from Bierce. Hemingway later borrowed some of his techniques. Bierce is highly regarded by postmodernists such as Fuentes as well as Jorge Luis Borges and Julio Cortázar. He is said to be similar to Guy de Maupassant or O. Henry. But while both of those authors use trick endings, most of Bierce's "tricks" have some larger metaphysical purpose.

Questions for Reading and Discussion/ Approaches to Writing

1. I let students be surprised by the ending and horrified by the language. I try not to give anything away before they get to the story.
2. I sometimes have them do historical research on the Spanish-American War.

Bibliography

I have a long section on "Chickamauga" in my *Experimental Fictions of Ambrose Bierce*.

Hamlin Garland (1860–1940)

Contributing Editor: James Robert Payne

Classroom Issues and Strategies

Discussion and explanation of Garland's populist values and political activities definitely enhance an appreciation of his fiction, as does some consideration, however brief, of his interest in Henry George's economic theories. Relate the populist movement of late nineteenth-century America to present-day grievances and problems of American farmers. More generally, compare social and political tensions between southern, midwestern, and western American regions on the one hand, and the northeastern region on the other in Garland's day and today.

Garland's profound empathy for the life situation of the rural and small-town midwestern farm woman requires discussion and may be productively studied in relation to Garland's biography. If feasible (depending on student interest), compare Garland's "single-tax" notions (derived from Henry George, 1839–97) with present-day tax reform schemes. What would be the social impact of such schemes, then and now?

Students express interest in Garland's representation of the impact on rural society of national economic policies and laws. They are also interested in comparing the role of women in rural America as given in Garland's writings with what they perceive as the role of women in rural areas today. Students will also compare the impact of land speculators and monopoly industries on society today with the impact of such forces as represented in Garland's writings.

Major Themes, Historical Perspectives, and Personal Issues

1. Central to much of Garland's best fiction and autobiography is an attempt to contrast actual conditions of American farm families with nineteenth-century (and earlier) idealizations of farm life.
2. As we see in his story "Up the Coulé" and elsewhere, Garland was very interested in the drama inherent in relations between farm families and their urbanized children.
3. Garland's theme of white America's injustice to Indians, apparent in his novel *The Captain of the Gray-Horse Troop* and his collection the *Book of the American Indian*, is very important though neglected in teaching and writing about Garland.

Significant Form, Style, or Artistic Conventions

1. If the instructor is interested in such conventions as "realism" and "naturalism," Garland may be taught as a transitional figure between the relatively genteel realism of William Dean Howells and the harsher naturalism we associate with Stephen Crane (as in *Maggie*, 1893) and Theodore Dreiser (as in *Sister Carrie*, 1900).
2. Consider represented speech in Garland's fiction, including suggestions of German language, as we see in "Up the Coulé," as indicative of Garland's efforts toward realism.

Original Audience

Although Garland's early fiction, such as that collected in *Main-Travelled Roads* (which includes "Up the Coulé"), shocked many with its frank portrayal of the harshness of actual farm life, as Garland perceived that life, by the end of his career, particularly through such works as *A Son of the Middle Border*, Garland was a recognized, even beloved, chronicler of the opening up and settlement of the American Midwest and West. In Garland's day, many rural midwesterners read *A Son of the Middle Border* as their region's analogue to Benjamin Franklin's *Autobiography*. Readers today value Garland's work as giving a most authentic dramatization of post–Civil War midwestern rural life.

Comparisons, Contrasts, Connections

Emile Zola (1840–1902)—French naturalist author who endeavored to convey an accurate picture of the poor and marginalized of France in his day. Compare and contrast with Garland's drama of the harsh life on nineteenth-century American farms.

Willa Cather (1873–1947)—Compare Cather's presentation of rural midwestern life to Garland's. Is the picture that Cather gives us more balanced, varied, and perhaps more positive than Garland's generally bleak views?

John Steinbeck (1902–1947)—With particular reference to Steinbeck's *The Grapes of Wrath* (1939), compare unrest of farmers in 1930s (Steinbeck) to that in the late nineteenth century (Garland).

Questions for Reading and Discussion/ Approaches to Writing

1. Items that follow refer specifically to Garland's story "Up the Coulé":
   (a) As you read, recall a time when you returned to your parental home after a considerable period of absence during which you achieved, perhaps, a new sophistication. Compare your experience, feelings, and family tension to family tensions and feelings represented in "Up the Coulé."
   (b) Compare Garland's portrayal of farm life to your experience of farm life.
2. Discuss Garland's fiction against the background of the populist movement of late-nineteenth-century America.

(a) Research Garland's autobiographies, especially *A Son of the Middle Border* and *A Daughter of the Middle Border* and trace autobiographical tendencies in Garland's fiction.

(b) Research Henry George's "single-tax" theories (see George's *Progress and Poverty*, 1879) and compare George's ideas and themes with ideas implicit in Garland's *Main-Travelled Roads* stories.

(c) Compare and contrast themes and values of Garland's *A Son of the Middle Border* to Franklin's *Autobiography*.

Bibliography

Ahnebrink, Lars. *The Beginnings of Naturalism in American Fiction*. Cambridge: Harvard University Press, 1950, 63–89. European influences on Garland.

Bledsoe, Thomas. "Introduction." In *Main-Travelled Roads*. New York: Rinehart, 1954.

Folsom, James K. *The American Western Novel*. New Haven: College and University Press, 1966, 149–55, 180–84. On Garland's writings about Indians.

Gish, Robert. *Hamlin Garland: The Far West*. Boise State University Western Writers Series, No. 24. Boise: Boise State University, 1976.

McCullough, Joseph B. *Hamlin Garland*. Boston: Twayne, 1978. Short, readable, solid introductory book.

Pizer, Donald. "Hamlin Garland's *A Son of the Middle Border*: Autobiography as Art." In *Essays in American and English Literature Presented to B. R. McElderry, Jr.*, edited by Max L. Schultz, 76–107. Athens: Ohio University Press, 1967.

——. *Hamlin Garland's Early Work and Career*. Berkeley: University of California Press, 1960. Best treatment of Garland's most vital years as fictionist.

——. "Herbert Spencer and the Genesis of Hamlin Garland's Critical System." *Tulane Studies in English* 7 (1957): 153–68.

Taylor, Walter F. *The Economic Novel in America*. Chapel Hill: University of North Carolina Press, 1942, 148–83. On Garland's social and economic views.

Walcutt, Charles C. *American Literary Naturalism, A Divided Stream*. Minneapolis: University of Minnesota Press, 1956, 53–63.

Frank Norris (1807–1902)

Contributing Editor: Joseph R. McElrath, Jr.

Classroom Issues and Strategies

As in Stephen Crane's overtly *avant-garde* works, Frank Norris's writings frequently seek to unsettle or disorient the "average" reader. The Norris canon includes some of the most conventional turn-of-the-century short stories possible in the realm of genteel fiction. More experimental fictions such as *"Fantaisie Printanière,"* however, are conceived in radically different ways. *"Fantaisie"* is, from one point of view, clearly designed as a droll tale for a sophisticated, "elite" readership seeing itself as having risen above the ethos of *petit bourgeois* morality and jaded to Dickensian melodrama eliciting sympathy for the "lower classes." The Olympian perspective on the antics of the vulgar characters represented here (and in the first half of *McTeague,* 1899) is adopted and maintained by the patrician Norris—his sense of humor resembling that of Stephen Crane, especially in the conclusion of *Maggie* where Mrs. Johnson's lugubrious response to her daughter's death is rendered tongue-in-cheek.

At the same time, decadent delight in an artifice featuring two women who take pride in their husbands' refined skills in wife-beating is not an experience accessible to more zealously humane and moral readers of late Victorian or modern society. In effect, Norris, like his male characters McTeague and Ryer, is deliberately abusive—toward these readers who, like their Victorian-era predecessors, maintain a high regard for the dignity of individuals of both sexes and cannot countenance so light-hearted a reaction on the part of Norris to the brutal behaviors described in detail and without censure here.

The instructor will want to describe and invite discussion of decadence and the decadent sensibility inferable from this 1897 story; this, in turn, should be related to the general breakdown or questioning of traditional western values that is a hallmark of the emergence of the post-Victorian, naturalistic, and modern sensibilities. Also to be discussed— undoubtedly with considerably more ease—is the moral perspective that the story is designed to test and, predictably, outrage. Clarification of the moral perspectives for the students who react negatively will perhaps be aided by a simple question: Is there any moment in the story where there is a genuinely successful comic development? If not, why not? If so, does one reconceive the risible moment upon later reflection? Those students who found the tale truly comic should also be encouraged to speak: how can so inarguably "tragic" a situation in real life be viewed in "comic" terms in literature?

Major Themes, Historical Perspectives, and Personal Issues

Norris was writing at a time when, because of Darwin's influence and the advent of the naturalistic sensibility, human beings' animalistic characteristics—vestigial and active—were receiving much attention. A contemporary of Freud, Norris was also developing his major themes when the refinements made available by civilization were being considered by many as relatively superficial, veneer-like traits; speculations abounded at the turn of the century regarding a brute-like "second self" within the individual, as in Robert Louis Stevenson's *The Strange Case of Dr. Jekyll and Mr. Hyde* (1886). Norris does not posit the existence of Freud's id, but like Jack London he does focus in *McTeague* and elsewhere on the emergence of the "brute" within. In *"Fantaisie"* the characters do not experience an "atavistic lapse" to a more primitive evolutionary state. They immediately stand forth as unredeemed primitives of the lower socioeconomic order, indicating Norris's opinion of human nature in its crudest condition, exacerbated by alcohol. Another fixed notion of the late nineteenth century relevant to the female characterizations in *"Fantaisie"* as well as in *McTeague* is that female love-behavior is characteristically expressed in active submission or dynamic passivity while males are typically more aggressive and dominating; the sado-masochistic relationships featured in the story thus have their roots in a popular assumption about a natural difference between males and females.

Significant Form, Style, or Artistic Conventions

With the title he chose, Norris duplicitously specifies a literary form that he quickly turns inside out for the sake of a sensational effect. The title invites the reader to expect a conventional indulgence in a revery related to carefree springtime frolic, traditionally occurring in a pastoral setting and embellished by imagery related to rejuvenation, delight in lovemaking, and joyful procreation. Norris instead establishes in a frolicsome tone a squalid and malodorous urban setting, in which the sterility of the childless couples replaces fecundity, the apparently pathological dependence of the masochistic wives upon their sadistic husbands stands forth instead of wholesome love, and violence rather than "thrice times happy" lovemaking is the constant.

The response of the student readers to this horrendous account of suffering rendered in a waggish, tongue-in-cheek style may prove complex. The majority will, of course, be initially perplexed, resisting the conclusion that Norris is actually making light of so serious a social problem as wife-abuse, and expecting a finale in which Norris returns the reader to a more morally or socially acceptable perspective. When this "dark" fantasy ends without a readjustment of its amoral point of view, Norris will very likely be judged by many as an irresponsible commentator who, at twenty-seven years of age, is behaving like an especially immature artist and perhaps encouraging his readers to assume a like point of view on wife-beating. Three points should be considered, though, after the worth of such an observation is acknowledged. First, Norris was inclined toward parody, and he is deliberately employing the conventions of a pastoral fantasy in a parodic manner. Second, it should be noted—for better or worse—that Norris's tone is a consistently amoral one: The narrative voice is one that has, in effect, declared a moral holiday. The tale is, after all, a fantasy and not to be confused with a realistic depiction. Third, the story is not didactic, though some readers may infer that Norris is suggesting the "naturalness" of what is depicted as occurring in San Francisco. Note, however, that the tale implies the extraordinariness of the Ryers and McTeagues.

Original Audience

This story was not written for a national readership or for a mass-circulation popular magazine. It was published only once during Norris's lifetime, in the weekly San Francisco magazine, *The Wave.* Its readership was upper middle class; the weekly's tone was "smart," up-to-date, and decidedly patrician; several of its writers were markedly iconoclastic, associated with the local decadent magazine, *The Lark,* and a bohemian group, *Les Jeunes.* Editor John O'Hara Cosgrave allowed Norris to take liberties unthinkable in most respectable American magazines of the time, and Norris capitalized upon this, especially in 1897, by producing fiction in which various cultural taboos were stylishly violated with impunity. The novel *Vandover and the Brute* is another measure of how Norris pushed the limits of what was then acceptable in the publishing world; written in the 1890s, it could not be published until 1914 when tolerance for the "immoral" in sexually-focused fiction had expanded.

Comparisons, Contrasts, Connections

The amorality and insensitivity to the plight of the underclass in this story are signs of a mass rejection of Victorian values among American writers through the next generation. The narrator's point of view stands in marked contrast to, for example, Rebecca Harding Davis's compassionate and didactic tone in *Life in the Iron-Mills* (1861). Norris's distancing of himself from his characters and their peculiarities is characteristic of post-Victorian contemporaries such as Stephen Crane and Ambrose Bierce; like Bierce in "Chickamauga" (1889), Norris sometimes gives the impression of one insensitively toying with ungainly specimens of humanity for the sake of shocking the reader. Like his French mentor, Émile Zola, Norris did not hesitate to find "suffering humanity" comic as well as tragic; see chapter 3 of Zola's *L'Assommoir* (1877) for a model of the kind of "dark comedy" that Norris cultivated.

Significant contrasts will be seen within Norris's canon, for Norris frequently reveals compassion for humanity at large, thus disclosing a very different side of his personality than *"Fantaisie"* does. *The Octopus* (1901) and "A Deal in Wheat" (1902), for example, feature sympathetic portrayals of the downtrodden; and *McTeague* offers in its second half a markedly more empathetic handling of the horrors of wife-abuse.

Questions for Reading and Discussion/ Approaches to Writing

1. How and why does Norris seek to shock his conventional readers? Or, what kind of reader does Norris imagine as finding this story pleasantly comical throughout?
2. How does Norris invert the conventions of pastoral literature? Or, to what degree is Norris a parodic author?
3. Is a comic tone ever appropriate for subject matters such as wife-beating?
4. With what gender-based popular assumptions is Norris working when characterizing the submissive wives and the violently aggressive husbands?
5. What are the attitudes toward social class and "race" (the alcoholic Irish figure) inscribed in this text? How is Norris's status as an upper-middle-class Anglo-American male relevant at a time when the "immigrant problem" was a matter of national debate?
6. Compare Norris's descriptions of sadism in *Moran of the Lady Letty* (1899) and sadomasochism in *McTeague* with those in this story. Contrast the ideal portrait of male-female relationships in *Blix* (1899) with the representations of the marriages in *"Fantaisie."*
7. How does *"Fantaisie"* stand as a spin-off tale derived from Norris's then unpublished *McTeague*?

8. How much was known about the extent of the wife-abuse problem in the United States in 1897? Do national circulation magazines and San Francisco newspapers reveal significant interest in the problem? Do women writers such as Charlotte Perkins Gilman and Frances Willard offer a perspective different from Norris's?

Bibliography

See the secondary works listed in the headnote, particularly William B. Dillingham's *Frank Norris: Instinct and Art* regarding Norris's sometimes condescending attitudes toward his "lowly" characters. In *Frank Norris Revisited,* Joseph R. McElrath, Jr., gives close attention to Norris's attempts at fashioning sensational fictions designed to violate Victorian decorum and traditional moral values.

Stephen Crane (1871–1900)

Contributing Editor: Donald Vanouse

Classroom Issues and Strategies

Stephen Crane's works present sudden shifts in tone and point of view, and frequently the works end without establishing either certainty about characters or resolution of thematic issues. Crane's imagery is vivid, but the works seldom provide final interpretations (e.g., the empty bucket in "A Mystery of Heroism"). These qualities contribute to Crane's multilayered irony.

The instructor should attempt to shift the focus from *resolving* issues of plot or character (e.g., "Is Collins a hero?") to showing the students that Crane seems to encourage the reader to *enrich* and *re-evaluate* ideas about patterns of action and thought. Crane asks questions rather than providing answers.

Consider using the poems to introduce some of his major themes. Crane seems to have valued them quite highly as expressions of his sense of the world. In like manner, the pace and drama of "A Mystery of Heroism" and "The Bride Comes to Yellow Sky" make them easier as doorways to Crane than the more stately and ambitious reflectiveness of "The Open Boat."

Like other scholars, students in class often are concerned with Crane's attitude toward God. It is useful—if complex—to invite them to look at "God Lay Dead in Heaven," "A Man Said to the Universe," "Do Not Weep, Maiden, For War Is Kind," "Chant You Loud of Punishments," and "When a People Reach the Top of a Hill." These poems, along with the "prayer" in "The Open Boat" indicate the *variety* of religious experience in Crane.

Major Themes, Historical Perspectives, and Personal Issues

Crane writes about extreme experiences that are confronted by ordinary people. His characters are not larger-than-life, but they touch the mysterious edges of their capacities for perception, action, and understanding.

In his themes and styles, Crane is an avant-garde writer.

The New York City sketch, "A Detail," was reprinted in 1898 with "The Open Boat," and the two works express parallel naturalistic themes. In both, individuals are shown to struggle for communication while being buffeted by tumultuous forces.

Significant Form, Style, or Artistic Conventions

Crane's works reflect many of the major artistic concerns at the end of the nineteenth century, especially naturalism, impressionism, and symbolism.

His works insist that we live in a universe of vast and indifferent natural forces, not in a world of divine providence or a certain moral order. "A Man Said to the Universe" is useful in identifying this aspect of Crane. But Crane's vivid and explosive prose styles distinguish his works from those by many other writers who are labeled naturalists.

Many readers (including Hamlin Garland and Joseph Conrad, who were personal friends of Crane) have used the term impressionist to describe Crane's vivid renderings of moments of visual beauty and uncertainty. Even Crane's "discontinuous" rendering of action has been identified as impressionist.

In "The Open Boat," Crane has been seen as a symbolist. Perhaps it is most appropriate to see the story as a skeptical balancing of concern with vast archetypes with an equal concern with psychology of perception: personal and cultural symbol grids.

Original Audience

Crane had a popular audience as well as a cultivated, literary audience during his lifetime.

Crane was a "star" journalist, and he published many of his best fictional works in the popular press. Nonetheless his comment that a newspaper is a "collection of half-injustices" indicates his skepticism about that medium of communication.

Comparisons, Contrasts, Connections

Crane's relationship to naturalism links him to such writers as Frank Norris, Theodore Dreiser, and John Dos Passos.

Crane's brief free-verse poems invite comparison with those of Emily Dickinson (Howells read them to him), and with a number of twentieth-century poets, particularly those influenced by imagism (Carl Sandburg, Amy Lowell, Ezra Pound, William Carlos Williams, for example). In brevity and in the authors' desire to escape conventional poetic rhetoric, these poems are comparable to Crane's. There are, of course, some vast differences in subject.

Questions for Reading and Discussion/
Approaches to Writing

1. Why does Crane use the term "Mystery" in the title of his war story? What is the mystery? Or do you find more than one?
2. In "The Bride," Crane seems interested in the role of women. Does the story show a shift of power from male violence?
3. In "The Open Boat," Crane seems very interested in what the correspondent learns. What does he learn about nature? Or about seeing nature? Or his relationship to other human beings?
4. How useful is "A Man Said to the Universe" in understanding the correspondent's experience?
5. "There Was a Man with Tongue of Wood" and "Chant You Loud of Punishments" are poems about poetry. What do these poems say about Crane's ambition or purpose as a poet?

    Crane's vivid prose makes him particularly valuable in developing student skills in discussing literary style.

    Also, his spare and startling structures (especially "endings") provide useful occasions for assignments on literary structure.

    Crane's relationship to naturalism provokes questions about individual freedom and responsibility.

Bibliography

Ralph Ellison's essay in *Shadow and Act* (1964), first published as the introduction to *The Red Badge of Courage and Four Great Stories by Stephen Crane*, New York: Dell, 1960, brings fresh insight to the issue of Crane's value to American culture.

David Halliburton's "The Farther Shore: Poems," in *The Color of the Sky: A Study of Stephen Crane*, Cambridge: Cambridge University Press, 1989, provides a valuable examination of Crane's decisions in metrics and prosody.

Lee Clark Mitchell's "The Spectacle of Courage in Crane's *The Red Badge of Courage*," in *Determined Fictions: American Literary Naturalism*, New York: Columbia University Press, 1989, links Crane to other naturalists and argues that Crane's styles subvert certainties about human character.

Jack London (1876–1916)

Contributing Editor: Joan D. Hedrick

Classroom Issues and Strategies

I explore the way in which the class divisions of society, demarcated by "The Slot," create divisions in an individual's consciousness. This will open up a way to discuss "South of the Slot," particularly if students have themselves experienced a self divided between two (or more) cultures. I have found that foreign students and working-class students have very strong, positive responses to London's stories of the hazards of cultural mobility.

Major Themes, Historical Perspectives, and Personal Issues

The double is a familiar theme in American literature, but London gives it a new twist by exploring it in class as well as psychological terms. London's politics were shaped in the 1890s by the depression, labor disputes, and the Socialist Labor Party. During the same period he also determined that he would become a writer, motivated in part by his fear of slipping into the underclass, which he called "the Social Pit." London struggled to reconcile his radical, working-class identity with that of his middle-class, literary self. His satirical portrait of Freddie Drummond distances him from a self he might have become.

Significant Form, Style, or Artistic Conventions

In general, naturalism is the literary movement that provides the best context for Jack London. Naturalism has been understood as a dialectic between free will and determinism (Charles Child Walcutt, *American Literary Naturalism, A Divided Stream* [Minneapolis: University of Minnesota Press, 1956]), but it is probably most intelligible through social history. The appeal of naturalistic tales is often escape. The urban problems of unemployment, labor wars, and poverty are left behind for a spare scenario in which an individual can be tested. A stock naturalistic device involves taking an "overcivilized" man from the upper classes into a primitive environment where he must live by muscle and wit. Frank Norris uses this device in *Moran of the Lady Letty*, as does London in *The Sea-Wolf*. *The Call of the Wild* also fits this pattern, although here the hero is a dog. Buck, a dog of northern ancestry who has been raised in southern California, is kidnapped and taken to Alaska where he must adapt to snow and the rule of the club.

In another common naturalistic pattern, the hero who stays in the city either becomes an ineffectual dandy or degenerates into a lower-class brute. Frank Norris's *Vandover and the Brute*, set in San Francisco, traces the downward arc of Vandover's career from a Harvard education through the urban horrors of drink, dissipation, and aimless drifting to his ultimate reward: he literally becomes a primitive brute when he falls victim to lycanthropy and finds himself barking like a wolf. London treats these materials more realistically, yet employs the same pattern whereby the city is associated with degeneration and the open country with rebirth. Both *Burning Daylight* and *The Valley of the Moon* contrast the vitality of the heroes in the country to the dissipation and bad luck they encounter in the city. "South of the Slot" departs from this pattern by portraying the city as the setting for a working-class victory.

Original Audience

London's goal was to write radical stories and publish them in mainstream, middle-class journals. "South of the Slot" was published in 1909 in *The Saturday Evening Post*, George Lorimer's highly successful magazine for upwardly aspiring self-made Americans.

Comparisons, Contrasts, Connections

As a story about a double, "South of the Slot" may be compared to Poe's "William Wilson" or to Hawthorne's stories of allegorically paired characters, such as Arthur Dimmesdale and Roger Chillingworth in *The Scarlett Letter*. Treated as a story of social types, it may also be compared to Stowe's portraits of class, race, and regional types in *Uncle Tom's Cabin*.

Questions for Reading and Discussion/ Approaches to Writing

I begin discussions of London by putting up on the board a paired series of contrasts between working-class and middle-class stereotypes. In "South of the Slot" this contrast is embodied in Big Bill Totts and Freddie Drummond. Then I ask, where do these notions come from? Why is the lower class associated with, for example, muscle and a free expression of sexuality? What are the psychosocial implications of this division of human characteristics along class lines?

Bibliography

The best work on London's stories is in James McClintock's *White Logic: Jack London's Short Stories*. Grand Rapids, Michigan: Wolf House Books, 1975.

For a biographical context for London's writing, see Joan D. Hedrick, *Solitary Comrade: Jack London and His Work*. Chapel Hill: University of North Carolina Press, 1982. Chapters 1–2, pp. 3–47.

Issues and Visions in Post–Civil War America

The "Issues and Visions" section in Volume 1 defined four initial contexts for the study of literary texts as rhetorical performances: "Indian Voices"; "The Literature of Slavery and Abolition"; "Literature and the 'Woman Question' "; and "Voices from the Southwest." One initial point of departure for classes using either one or both volumes of *The Heath Anthology* is the question of what difference the Civil War makes, both in general historical terms and in relation to these particular issues. Many institutions still structure their survey classes in American Literature using 1865 as the dividing line between old and new, the past and the modern, and this division reflects and reinforces widespread, if often conflicting and loosely defined, beliefs about the Civil War as the seminal event in American history. Again, the versions of this general historical sense that students bring to class can create the context for the reading and discussion of these post–Civil War texts, beginning with considerations of how different interpretations and representations of the Civil War serve different social, political, and cultural purposes. (The recent PBS documentary series, with its aestheticized presentation, the attendant controversy over its romanticizing of the Confederate military and political leadership, and its current status as fund-raising cash cow can be one starting point.)

While texts dealing specifically with issues of race, the struggles of African-Americans in post–Civil War America, and myths about Reconstruction are found in the section on "Regional Voices, National Voices," the texts in this section focus more on the evolution of the women's movement and the efforts of both Native American and Latino cultures to survive the continuing expansion of the U.S. empire. Again, the idea of cultural rhetoric can serve as a pedagogical entry into these texts by asking how these writers positioned themselves amidst various and often conflicting cultural identities related to gender, ethnicity, social class, religion, and region.

The question of empire—political, economic, and cultural—is particularly important to the historical study of post–Civil War America and can provide entry to these texts as well. Henry Adams's famous, and now canonical, use of the image of the Virgin and the dynamo to signify the cultural difference of modernity can be paired with Upton Sinclair's metaphor of "the jungle," along with his harrowing depictions of the meat-packing industry, as contrasting, yet not necessarily contradictory, visions of the impact of the expanding capitalist economy. In both cases, asking students to consider the perspectives from which these accounts are written (that of a member of one of America's elite families versus that of a crusading socialist journalist) can lead to discussions that integrate issues of political philosophy, rhetorical purpose, audience, tone, diction, and structure.

For example, Adams's scholarly allusions and ornate prose style, which are often alienating for students, can be studied as strategies meant to register with different members of the reading public in specific ways, so that questions about the difficulty of his style can lead to questions both about the audience he wants to reach and the audience he doesn't, and about why a writer would deliberately aim for a narrow readership while making claims for the universality of his analysis. The students can then examine where they feel they stand in relation to Adams's intended audience. The same questions, of course, can be posed in relation to Sinclair. In his case, the strategy is to reach a wide readership and incite moral outrage. Such questions of audience and rhetorical purpose lead to questions of canonicity, questions of which styles and strategies come to be considered "literary," which styles merely instrumental. Seeing and reading Adams in terms of his particular cultural and social position extends this discussion of canonicity to considerations involving the supposed universality of certain texts and the equally supposed limited appeal of others. Why, for example, has the skillfully rendered mid-life crisis of an upper-class New England intellectual been seen as universal in significance while the carefully constructed portrayal of the social practices leading to the nervous breakdown of a middle-class woman (Charlotte Perkins Gilman's "The Yellow Wall-Paper") has until recently been ignored or thought of as interesting only to a limited group of readers? Just as important, why have attitudes changed regarding "The Yellow Wall-Paper"? The purpose of such questions is not to insist that students adhere to a new version of the canon or simply to discredit an older version, but to understand that all considerations of literary merit and cultural significance take place in the context of changing social and cultural values and as part of ongoing debates about those values, debates that include college students as both observers and participants.

New Explorations of an "American" Self

While earlier in American history, writers like Benjamin Franklin, Hector St. John de Crèvecoeur, Ralph Waldo Emerson, and Frederick Douglass can be seen to have engaged in a highly self-conscious process of creating models for a national identity, the texts in this section can be read as attempts to assimilate, negotiate, and restructure established myths of national identity. Students can prepare for reading these texts by exploring their own received versions of these myths and by discussing various myths of immigration and assimilation, including the implications, desirability, and undesirability of the "melting pot" and other metaphors.

Beyond this examination of cultural mythology, the class can ground their discussions by compiling their own individual and family immigration histories. This project can include oral histories and research into various immigrant experiences. These immigration histories, along with the texts in this section, can then be approached in terms of how they do or don't fit into stereotypical models of the American self and the immigrant experience; more specifically, students can discuss the strategies these writers—as well as students and their ancestors—used in confronting these models. Rather than simply reacting to a cultural situation, these texts attempt in various ways to alter and revise that situation. How did the large influx of Russian and Eastern European Jewish immigrants, for example, adapt to and transform the American cultural landscape? Finally, Gertrude Bonnin's text continues the tradition among Native American writers of turning the immigrant myth inside out by addressing the question of how members of indigenous cultures deal with the experience of finding themselves strangers in their own land.

Issues and Visions in Post-Civil War America

Standing Bear (Ponca) (1829–1908)

Contributing Editor: Daniel F. Littlefield, Jr.

Classroom Issues and Strategies

It is difficult to provide a historical framework for Standing Bear, though this can be overcome by acquainting students with the modes, conventions, and protocol of Indian oratory, getting them to understand the word as a spoken record of a nonliterate culture. It might be useful to place the dispossession of the Poncas of lands that were traditionally theirs alongside the economic aspirations of immigrants to America and the excesses of the Gilded Age as evidenced in the literature. Teachers who feel hesitant here can make some literary connections by looking at Helen Hunt Jackson's *A Century of Dishonor*.

Major Themes, Historical Perspectives, and Personal Issues

Three major themes are an understanding of those who were victimized by national goals of Manifest Destiny; the rights of those outside constitutional protection; and the dehumanization of people in the march of nineteenth-century progress.

Significant Form, Style, or Artistic Conventions

Introduce the modes, conventions, and protocol of Indian oratory.

Comparisons, Contrasts, Connections

Concerning the theme of destruction of Indian cultures in the late nineteenth century, Indian writers like Posey, Eastman, Bonnin, and Oskison offer useful points of comparison. The position of the Indians as non-white peoples in America might be usefully compared and contrasted to the position of other such groups, like the African-Americans.

Bibliography

See primary and secondary works listed with the text headnote.

Ghost Dance Songs

Please refer to the headnote in the text for complete information.

Charles Alexander Eastman (Sioux) (1858–1939)

Contributing Editor: Daniel F. Littlefield, Jr.

Classroom Issues and Strategies

Students need to know what the Ghost Dance movement was, its importance to the Indians, and reasons why U.S. officials viewed it as something that had to be suppressed. James Mooney's *The Ghost-Dance Religion and Wounded Knee* is a good starting point. They also are curious about the status of an assimilated Indian like Eastman. Supply background on these issues. It is also helpful to deal with Eastman's work in the same manner as you would an autobiographical narrative written by any other author of the same period.

Major Themes, Historical Perspectives, and Personal Issues

Discuss cultural ignorance, social discontinuity, national goals versus cultural integrity, cultural assimilation, the narrator as an "in-between" person, the creation of national symbols (Wounded Knee as symbol in the Sioux Nation and for American Indians in general in this century).

Significant Form, Style, or Artistic Conventions

Attention can be focused profitably on the form of the autobiographical narrative, touching on such matters as narrative control, style, self-revelation, etc.

Comparisons, Contrasts, Connections

Compare the autobiographical works of other Indians, such as Gertrude Bonnin, John Joseph Mathews, and Thomas Whitecloud, as well as any other autobiographical works, especially by writers who belong to other racial or cultural minorities. Compare "The Great Mystery" and Bonnin's "Why I Am a Pagan."

Bibliography

The list of primary and secondary works in the headnote is comprehensive.

Marietta Holley (pseud. "Josiah Allen's Wife") (1836–1926)

Contributing Editor: Kate H. Winter

Classroom Issues and Strategies

It is helpful to read the early part of the chapter aloud so student readers can catch the rhythm of the language and see the humor in the odd spellings. Equally helpful is Jane Curry's recorded rendering of Samantha's voice in the tape cassette that accompanies *Samantha Rastles the Woman Question*.

Have students list the unfamiliar language usages and colloquialisms they encounter in their college community. Discuss what is amusing and/or revealing about these, what values are implicit in their use, and their use as a means of establishing community. Students often want to know whether Holley's audience found it difficult to read dialect and whether they took pleasure in it.

Ask students to examine the Declaration of Independence before reading the Holley selection. A journal or freewriting assignment could follow in which students respond to what they understand to be the values implicit in that document. Or you might ask students to rewrite the Declaration of Independence in their vernacular.

Students often have difficulty understanding how women might feel religiously disenfranchised, so we do some quick exercises demonstrating the power of exclusion—for example, not allowing anyone with blue eyes to speak in class for a set period. In addition we discuss briefly the patriarchal structure of Christian religious practice and its impact.

Major Themes, Historical Perspectives, and Personal Issues

Much of the book is taken up with Samantha's descriptions of how the local church women are refurbishing and maintaining the church counterpointed with her disagreements over Josiah's wrong-headed interpretations of Scripture. Samantha uses feminist arguments to explain away or circumvent the difficulties in biblical texts that excluded women: There may have been an error in translation; or the context within which the Scriptures were written rendered the literal meaning irrelevant to modern times; or the writer (St. Paul, for example) was just one man giving his personal opinion. The chapter included here extends the disagreement to interpreting the Declaration of Independence, thereby linking religious with legislative hypocrisy.

The language issues inherent in this text also provide an excellent opportunity to have students look at sexism in language, the significance of dialect (which students are apt to be familiar with from their own usages), and the standardization of English. Most classes can address questions about the ability of language to exclude or include privileged groups.

Through Samantha, Holley tackled the prevailing ideas of what gifts, responsibilities, and rights "Nater" and law had given women and men.

Significant Form, Style, or Artistic Conventions

In addition to showing the faults in the logic of the brethren, Holley was attempting to reproduce phonetically the patois of upstate New Yorkers. Holley captures the style and character of much upstate New York fiction as does Philander Deming, whose Adirondack stories are gems of local color writing, and Irving Bacheller, whose novels of New York's North Country preserve an era and place long since lost.

Holley's audience often thought her spellings were the result of her being an uneducated country woman; only more sophisticated readers recognized that she, like Twain, adopted a persona for the distance it provided between audience and writer and the comic effect of the naive commentator. Vernacular humor often opposed the assumptions of gentility. It would be useful to ask which aspects of genteel society are being attacked. How does her humor seem to reinforce stereotypes? How does it subvert them?

As the headnote indicates, Holley's work blends several American literary traditions, including the verbal play of the male literary comedians. She also turned humorist Ann Stephens's vernacular humor and Frances Witcher's humorous modes to her own ends. Her style includes the elements of anticlimax, misquoted Scripture, decorative spelling, puns, malapropisms, comic similes, mixed metaphors, extravagant images, language reversals, and proverbs and maxims. She handles these techniques with the same flair and assurance that the male writers who dominated the tradition did. Furthermore, there is the comic irony of her saying one thing, doing another, and having Josiah deny the reality or validity of both. While the literary and social value of the satiric humor of the male writers in the tradition has rarely been debated, Holley's place in the canon of American humor—because of her subject matter—has been small and narrow.

Original Audience

In addition to the work described above, I sketch for students the political background. In 1888, the National Methodist Conference (the "Brethren" of the title) had refused to seat four duly elected women delegates. Holley's response to the outrage was this book, which is dedicated to "All women, who work trying to bring into dark lives the brightness and hope of a better country." The author's intimate friend within the church hierarchy, Bishop John Newman, and his wife, provided her with most of the background material and arguments that informed the debates. At the back of the first edition, the publishers append six of the speeches delivered in deliberation at the conference. Students may wish to contrast the rhetoric in them with Samantha's.

Comparisons, Contrasts, Connections

Two other texts included in this collection make useful corollary reading for this chapter. In Mary Wilkins Freeman's "A Church Mouse," we see the local colorist's use of dialect and dialogue that also marks Holley's work and a similar struggle between patriarchal habit and the newly feminized Christianity of the late nineteenth century. The conflict that Freeman depicts is underlaid by the bedrock of prejudice that Josiah represents in Holley's work. Students may want to consider what assumptions about gender differences form the basis for Josiah's and the townspeople's arguments. Holley's fiction is particularly subversive because of Samantha's willingness to work at the role of country wife while she chips away at the granite convictions about male superiority that her husband Josiah clings to. A look into Charlotte Perkins Gilman's *Herland*, especially chapter 10 on religion, also provides parallel material for discussion.

Questions for Reading and Discussion/ Approaches to Writing

I attempt to give writing tasks that invite the students to connect their own experience with what is in the text so that they begin to "own" the ideas and feelings. For example: have students write imitations of a short piece—even a paragraph—to approximate stylistic features; have them rewrite a piece in their own words to help them see the importance of the language community in shaping a text; ask them to transform a text by rewriting it in another genre—perhaps a news story, poem, dialogue, letter, etc. With any of these methods, the students get a glimpse of the decisions informing the author's choice of language and genre and contribute to their understanding of the creative process in a cultural context.

Anna Julia Cooper (1858?–1964)

Contributing Editor: Richard Yarborough

Classroom Issues and Strategies

It is essential that, at some point, Anna Julia Cooper's *A Voice from the South* be situated historically if students are to get a clear sense of what was at stake for Cooper in writing this book and of why she wrote as she did. Nonetheless, one effective approach to opening a discussion of the anthologized selections from *Voice* can be to encourage students to link Cooper's arguments and observations regarding race and gender with those put forward by commentators today. For example, her stance on women's rights locates her in a tradition that leads quite directly to contemporary feminist ideas with which many students will be familiar, even if only indirectly.

Cooper's prose style itself might present difficulty for some students, given the leisurely pace of her writing and her use of irony and indirection. Yet she can also be fiercely forthright in her condemnation of racism and quite emotionally expressive in her outrage at unjust treatment. One important tactic then, in teaching these selections, is to counsel patience on the part of the students and to emphasize at the outset the tension between Cooper's tightly-controlled prose and the anger fueling her arguments.

Major Themes, Historical Perspectives, and Personal Issues

In developing a sense of the historical context of Cooper's work, students need to appreciate the diverse obstacles against which Cooper and others like her labored in making their voices heard. First, she was writing at a time of extraordinarily virulent racism, when blacks of all classes were being physically assaulted, socially segregated, characterized in the scientific and popular literature as immoral and a threat to political stability, and, in the case of the men, disenfranchised throughout the South. (The harsh treatment in the late nineteenth century of other racial and ethnic groups, such as American Indians, is relevant here as well.) Instead of giving way to despair, however, Cooper and others dedicated themselves to improving the condition of blacks not just through community action but also through appealing to whites in the hope of having them recognize the injustices to which blacks—especially the middle-class blacks—were subjected. In addition, Cooper confronted as assertively as did any of her peers a second set of barriers, these placed in her way by many black men who, like their white fellows, held a conception of women's role that did not allow for the range of professional, scholarly, and political possibilities claimed by Cooper as her birthright.

Perhaps the thematic keystone in Cooper's writing is her conviction that the African-American woman's unique perspectives ideally suited her to serve as the moral leader in a society that betrayed so blatantly the democratic and Christian values that it claimed to embody. In the essay "Woman Versus the Indian," Cooper focuses particularly on the hypocrisy of white members of the Women's Movement—especially, in the South—whose prejudice prevented them from accepting blacks as their equals. In condemning racism among white feminists and also sexist attitudes within the African-American community, Cooper foreshadows the work of contemporary black feminists who stress the uniquely "intersectional" nature of black women's experiences, which fall outside of paradigms drawn exclusively from analyses of white women or black men.

Cooper's conception of the social role of bourgeois black women reveals the continuing potency in her day of the nineteenth-century concept of "true womanhood." That is, informing Cooper's position is the assumption that middle-class women can and should bear responsibility for the moral condition of society. Within the bourgeois African-American women's community in the late nineteenth century, commitment to this ideal found its practical manifestation in educational efforts, the black women's club movement, and religious and secular organizations of social uplift.

At a personal level, *A Voice from the South* reflects not just Cooper's own firm belief in education and rational discourse as effective ways to combat racial prejudice but also her desire to present her narrative persona as representative. In drawing upon her own experiences and those of other blacks in dramatizing the condition of the middle-class African-American woman, she seeks to speak quite self-consciously on behalf of *all* black women as a group. This tactic links her with a wide range of African-American writers throughout U.S. history.

Significant Form, Style, or Artistic Conventions

As an excellent example of Cooper's prose, "Woman Versus the Indian" amply rewards close stylistic analysis. At times formal, at times conversational, this essay reflects the various narrative strategies that Cooper adopts in the effort to sway readers of her time who were likely ill-disposed to take her side. In particular, one should pay close attention to the way in which Cooper opens the piece, to her strategically deployed asides, to her diverse figures of speech, and, above all, to her use of irony—one of the most commonly wielded weapons in the nineteenth-century black author's rhetorical arsenal. Finally, given that this essay was designed to be argumentative, to forward as aggressively as possible a particular position in the difficult, ongoing debate over the status of blacks in U.S. society, its logical construction merits examination as well.

Comparisons, Contrasts, Connections

Fruitful comparisons and contrasts can be made between Cooper's writing and that of other turn-of-the-century African-American authors. One important figure with whom Cooper, with her diverse interests and extraordinary intellectual abilities, might be constructively considered is

W.E.B. Du Bois. Both of these ambitious and highly trained scholars felt driven to turn their energies not just to education and uplift but also to direct engagement with the most pressing political questions of the day. In structure, tone, and even intent, Cooper's *A Voice from the South* and Du Bois's *The Souls of Black Folk* share some striking similarities. Broadening the range of useful connections, one might also discuss Cooper in the context of other female activists and social critics—from Margaret Fuller, Harriet Jacobs, Lydia Maria Child, Sarah Grimké, and Harriet Beecher Stowe through Frances Ellen Watkins Harper, Charlotte Perkins Gilman, and Pauline E. Hopkins.

Questions for Reading and Discussion/ Approaches to Writing

One place to begin a discussion of Cooper's work is the title of the anthologized essay. Why does she call this piece "Woman Versus the Indian"? How does the conflict to which this phrase apparently alludes relate to Cooper's examination of the status of African-American women at the end of the nineteenth century? Can one, in fact, determine her attitude toward the American Indian here? Another critical issue raised in Cooper's writing is that of class. Are there indications in the selections that her target audience may be primarily bourgeois readers? And does she seem to be addressing primarily bourgeois women? What is the role of class in Cooper's definition of women's role in effecting social change?

Students might also be asked to speculate on the contemporary efficacy of Cooper's arguments as a way to identify her goals in writing "Woman Versus the Indian," to come to grips with what exactly she wants her readers to do about the situation that she decries. This approach, in turn, can provide the opportunity for the class to consider not just what Cooper is contending in the essay but *how* she makes those contentions. As in the case of, for example, Du Bois's essay "Of Mr. Booker T. Washington and Others" (anthologized in *The Heath Anthology*), the logical construction of "Woman Versus the Indian" is quite carefully crafted.

Bibliography

Despite the attention paid over the past decade or so to the work of nineteenth-century black women writers, the body of scholarship specifically on Anna Julia Cooper remains small. In addition to the books listed in the headnote to the Cooper selections, the following titles provide valuable background information: Carby, Hazel. *Reconstructing Womanhood:*

The Emergence of the Afro-American Woman Novelist, 1987. Christian, Barbara. *Black Women Novelists: The Development of a Tradition, 1892–1976.* Westport, CT: Greenwood Publishing, 1980. Collins, Patricia Hill. *Black Feminist Thought: Knowledge, Consciousness, and the Politics of Empowerment.* New York: Unwin Hyman, 1990. Crenshaw, Kimberle. "Demarginalizing the Intersection of Race and Gender." In *Feminist Legal Theory: Readings in Law and Gender,* edited by Katherine T. Bartlett and Rosanne Kennedy. San Diego: Westview Publishing Company, 1991. Davis, Angela. *Women, Race and Class,* 1981. Giddings, Paula. *When and Where I Enter . . .: The Impact of Black Women on Race and Sex in America.* New York: Morrow, 1984.

Charlotte Perkins Gilman (1860–1935)

Contributing Editor: Elaine Hedges

Classroom Issues and Strategies

Students respond well to "The Yellow Wall-Paper." They like the story and don't have serious difficulty understanding it, and they enjoy discussing the meanings of the wallpaper. They may, however, oversimplify the story, reading the ending either as the heroine's victory over her circumstances, or her defeat. Have students choose and defend one or the other of these positions for a classroom debate (with the aim of showing that there is no easy resolution). Students might also want to debate (attack or defend) the role of the husband in the story.

Background information on medical treatment of women, and specifically white, middle-class women, in the nineteenth century, especially Dr. S. Weir Mitchell's "rest cure" (mentioned in the headnote) is useful.

Naive students sometimes wonder why the woman in the story can't just leave; they need to understand the situation of white, middle-class married women in the nineteenth century: The censure against divorce, and their limited opportunities in the paid labor force.

"Turned," like "The Yellow Wall-Paper," deals with the situation of women inside marriage, but it offers a wife who takes matters into her own hands and recreates her life. The two stories can thus be profitably compared and contrasted. Significant differences, of course, include the greater freedom (she is childless) and professional training (she can support herself) of the wife, Mrs. Marroner, in "Turned." Gilman, in her major sociological work, *Women and Economics,* argued that only economic independence would release women from their subordination within marriage, and Mrs. Marroner is an example of this thesis. One might note the changes in her attitude toward Gerta, from a class-biased one to one of female bonding. "Turned" is also noteworthy as a frank treatment of an issue—an employer's sexual abuse of a female domestic—that wasn't openly discussed in fiction at the time.

Major Themes, Historical Perspectives, and Personal Issues

Consider both stories as critiques of male power, including sexual power, and of marriage. Students can be asked how relevant these critiques are today: whether similar or comparable situations still exist.

Significant Form, Style, or Artistic Conventions

In "The Yellow Wall-Paper," less sophisticated students may identify the narrator with Gilman, since the story is based on an episode in her life. Discussion of the literary convention of the first-person point of view and of differences between an author and her persona are useful. The dramatic immediacy of the first-person point of view (versus the use of the third person in "Turned") can be demonstrated.

Although Gilman's intention in both stories was didactic (she wrote "The Yellow Wall-Paper," she said, to warn readers against Dr. Mitchell's treatment), discussions of form and style can suggest how a text can transcend its author's intention or any narrow didactic purpose. In what ways is "Turned" more clearly didactic than "The Yellow Wall-Paper"?

"The Yellow Wall-Paper" is, of course, highly appropriate for a discussion of symbolism: how it emerges and operates within a text. Students enjoy discussing the symbolism of the wallpaper and of the room to which the narrator is confined.

Original Audience

I discuss Gilman's difficulty in getting "The Yellow Wall-Paper" published, and ask students to consider why it might have disturbed her contemporaries. (It was rejected by the editor of the *Atlantic Monthly* on the grounds that it would make readers too miserable.) Gilman received letters of praise for the story from readers who read it as an accurate clinical description of incipient madness. It seems not to have been read as it is read today, as a critique of marriage and of medical treatment of women.

Readers in Gilman's time would have been familiar with Poe's stories. Might "The Yellow Wall-Paper" have been perceived as similar to a Poe story? In what significant ways is it different from Poe's stories?

"Turned" is one of about two hundred short stories Gilman wrote and published in her magazine, *The Forerunner*. They were intended to dramatize the ideas she expounded in her nonfiction about women's roles and status in society, and to suggest reforms. *The Forerunner* never had a circulation of more than a thousand copies. Today, however, more and more of these stories by Gilman are being reprinted. For others, see Barbara H. Solomon, editor, *HERLAND and Selected Short Stories of Charlotte Perkins Gilman*, Penguin USA, 1992.

Comparisons, Contrasts, Connections

In the same section of the anthology, other texts dealing with marriage and with male-female power relations include: Elizabeth Stuart Phelps's, some of Kate Chopin's, and Mary Wilkins Freeman's. One could also contrast the Gilman pieces with the comic/satiric treatment of husband-wife relations in Marietta Holley.

Two of Emily Dickinson's poems provide useful contexts for "The Yellow Wall-Paper": "Much madness is divinest sense" and "She rose to his requirement."

Bibliography

Elaine Hedges, "Afterword," *The Yellow Wallpaper*, Feminist Press, 1973, has an analysis of the story and a brief biography of Gilman.

Catherine Golden, ed., *The Captive Imagination: A Casebook on "The Yellow Wallpaper,"* Feminist Press, 1991, reprints a good selection of both nineteenth-century materials relevant to the story and contemporary critical treatments of it.

Ann Lane, ed., *The Charlotte Perkins Gilman Reader*, Pantheon, 1980, includes a selection of Gilman's stories and excerpts from her longer fictions, including the utopia, *Herland*.

José Martí (1853–1895)

Contributing Editor: Enrique Sacerio-Garí

Classroom Issues and Strategies

Students face a difficult task as they read Martí within an *American* anthology. Even as part of a diverse group, with some knowledge of the role of the United States in Latin America and an awareness of issues of identity in our hardly homogeneous society, your strategy must recognize the exciting difficulties of reconciling differences in Martí's text as well as in your own classroom. What is *your* America?, I would ask the students. A good day may bring many voices that speak about communities, regions, neighborhoods, nations, ethnicity, race, and class. Are we empowered or disempowered by our most intimate America? In "Our America," does Martí empower a nation, a people, a whole continent, with his voice? The obstacles to integrating the different views may then be discussed, leading (perhaps) to Martí's call for understanding by means of direct knowledge and respect of others and by self-esteem through self-knowledge. Stylistic issues of images and themes that surface and resurface (see below) could be related to the sociopolitical experiences of nations and groups.

Major Themes, Historical Perspectives, and Personal Issues

A discussion of Martí's emphasis on the racial composition of America, and his vision aligned with the indigenous groups, should contrast civilization and barbarism, false erudition and direct knowledge, imported colonizer culture and indigenous culture. Here, one could ask where the indigenous groups are now and how Martí's treatment of transcultural and transracial issues contrasts with current views. Another important topic is the psychology of the colonial situation, which could reconsider the polemics between Mannoni and Fanon. Martí's text could help promote thoughts on the hybrid nature of Latin America, where the metaphors of Ariel and Caliban are reconciled as an empowered *mestizo* culture.

As you explore our America as distinct realities, you could probe the class as to basic knowledge of geography and history of various regions and the culture of different Native American peoples. Considering the historical background offered in the introduction to "Our America," you might ask the class to research topics such as: the name *America,* Pan-Americanism in the late nineteenth century and free trade in the late twentieth century, writing in exile, immigrant voices in New York journals, ethnic and racial issues then and now, and how to "do the right thing." An interesting comparison could be made with Jacob Riis (1849–1914), another famous New York City nocturnal walker, who immigrated from Denmark in 1870. As a reporter and photographer for the *New York Tribune,* he conducted a crusade against the dire conditions of the slums around "the Bend" of Mulberry Street. He was a close friend and biographer of Theodore Roosevelt.

Significant Form, Style, or Artistic Conventions

Read the first two paragraphs in class. A thorough discussion of this passage should be sufficient to acquaint the students with Martí's *modernista* style, which he initiated in Latin America. If further work with *modernista* poetics is desired, exposure to the ideals of Parnassian poets and the musicality of symbolist writers should be considered. This close reading will facilitate intratextual understanding of subsequent elaborations as, for example, "[l]et the world be grafted onto our republics, but the trunk must be our own." An examination of resurgent images associated with greed, war, ignorance, and violence, contrasted with an informed resistance and knowledgeable (natural) defenses, may lead to a good discussion of how a reader produces meaning within Martí's text. Footnotes 4, 9, and 14 to Martí's essay offer suggestions on reading other passages.

Comparisons, Contrasts, Connections

Of significance to an American poet in New York in the latter half of the nineteenth century was Ralph Waldo Emerson and Walt Whitman. In one of the notebooks he left with his literary executor, Martí describes a future project, "My Book: *The Rebel Poets,*" in which he planned to study Walt Whitman. Indeed, a backward glance over Martí's works reveals many references to Whitman, including a historic essay "El poeta Walt Whitman," published in Mexico and Argentina in 1887. In a necrological note, published in Caracas in 1882, Martí describes Emerson as "a man who found himself alive, shook from his shoulders and his eyes all the mantles and all the blindfolds that past times place over men, and lived face to face with nature, as if all earth was his home . . ." With candor, "flooded with his immediate age," as Whitman advised American poets of all nations, Martí wrote poetry and prose distilled from his experiences as a human, political, transcultural being. Martí strove to remove all the layers of the unexamined, taxing culture of Europe as false erudition, and demanded that Americans stand face to face with *nature,* that is, the hybrid *cultures* significant of our real lands. By knowing each other's poets, mythologies, and noblest expectations, without reverting to hatred and racism, Martí expected the new Americans to rise.

Most significant to new American readers would be an acquaintance with the works of Latin American poets who follow Martí and Whitman. You might consider using Nicaraguan poet Rubén Darío's "To Roosevelt," written after the United States invasion of Panama, or "The Heights of Macchu Picchu" by Chile's Pablo Neruda. Martí's own *Simple Verses* could be suggested as part of your supplemental readings.

Corridos

Contributing Editor: Raymund Paredes

Major Themes, Historical Perspectives, and Personal Issues

In this group of *corridos,* it's important to note that American cowboy culture derives largely from Mexican culture: the *corrido* "Kiansis I" lauds the superiority of Mexican cowboys over their Anglo counterparts. The point is that Mexican-Americans have resented the appropriation of their culture without due recognition. "Gregorio Cortez" and "Jacinto Treviño" are epic ballads that deal with Mexican/Mexican-American responses to "American" injustice and bigotry. They are also of great interest because they make no distinction between a Mexican citizen and resident like Treviño and a resident of the United States like Cortez. Both are simply "mexicanos" who fight for their community's rights and dignity.

Corridos not only treat epic historical issues like cultural conflict along the south Texas border but focus on more intimate matters that reflect and preserve traditional family values. "El Hijo Desobediente," one of the best-known and best-loved of *corridos,* emphasizes the need for sons to respect their fathers. In this ballad, the son Felipe is agitated to the point of threatening his father, an action that seals his tragic fate.

A final point about *corridos* to be made here is that this musical tradition is still vigorous and still exists primarily in Spanish. "Recordando al Presidente" fondly recalls John F. Kennedy, whose Catholicism endeared him to "mexicanos" and other Latinos. The "Corrido de César Chávez," of still more recent origin, recounts the victory of Chávez and the United Farm Workers over grape growers as a result of a brilliantly executed boycott.

Finley Peter Dunne (1867–1936)

Contributing Editor: Charles Fanning

Classroom Issues and Strategies

There are two kinds of pieces here: vignettes of daily life and national commentary. Discuss the aims of each kind, and Dunne's ways of achieving them. The vignettes are like short stories; the commentaries are closer to the traditional newspaper column.

The issue of dialectical writing should be raised. What are the risks entailed? What are the benefits?

Major Themes, Historical Perspectives, and Personal Issues

Immigrant/ethnic voices in the 1890s. Consider Dunne as presenting "Irish-American" perspectives: Ireland as a colonized country, the perspective on imperialism, reactions against American Anglophilia. The rise to respectability in the new world of Irish immigrants.

Dunne switched gears in 1900, moving to New York and national commentary, leaving the community-based Chicago perspective behind. What did he gain and what did he lose by this shift?

Significant Form, Style, or Artistic Conventions

Consider the limits of the weekly newspaper column. How did Dunne work within them and expand the possibilities? Look again at the issue of dialectical writing, and what the quality of these pieces tells us about the level of literacy (very high) assumed in the newspaper audience from the 1890s to World War I.

Original Audience

Newspaper readers, at first in Chicago, and then all across the country in the syndicated post-1900 pieces were Dunne's original audience. In fact, he was the most famous columnist in America from 1900 to 1914. Why was this so?

Comparisons, Contrasts, Connections

Useful comparisons can be made with contemporary columnists familiar to the college-age audience, such as Mike Royko, Russell Baker, Dave Barry, Art Buchwald.

Compare also the ethnic perspective of other writers of the eighteen-nineties and subsequently. Dunne's pieces add the Irish-American voice to this chorus.

Compare other nineteenth-century humorists, from Mark Twain to the lesser figures—Artemus Ward, Petroleum V. Nasby, James Russell Lowell in the "Big'low Papers." A comparable twentieth-century figure to Mr. Dooley is Harlem's Jesse B. Semple, or "Simple," the creation of Langston Hughes.

Questions for Reading and Discussion/ Approaches to Writing

Students may try their hands at writing a short, short story with some of the punch of Dunne's best work, such as "The Wanderers," or writing a column of commentary on national policy comparable to "Immigration," which again in our time is a big issue. Such an exercise should illustrate the genius of the original pieces, which looks so effortless upon first reading.

Bibliography

The most accessible paperback collection of Dunne's Chicago pieces is Charles Fanning, ed. *Mr. Dooley and the Chicago Irish: The Autobiography of a Nineteenth-Century Ethnic Group.* Washington: Catholic University of America Press, 1987. The most accessible paperback collection of Dunne's national pieces is Robert Hutchinson, ed. *Mr. Dooley on Ivrything and Ivrybody.* New York: Dover Press. A recent assessment of Dunne can be found in J. C. Furnas, "The True American Sage." *American Scholar* 60 (Autumn 1991): 570–74.

Upton Sinclair (1878–1968)

Contributing Editor: James C. Wilson

Classroom Issues and Strategies

Students generally respond to Sinclair's portrait of the unsanitary conditions in the meat-packing industry. They tend to be interested in the history of *The Jungle*—how it was written, the federal legislation that was passed because of the public reaction to it, etc. The most difficult problem in teaching *The Jungle* is how to approach a text in which literary qualities are subordinated to political purpose. *The Jungle* does not lend itself to the kinds of literary discussions that most of us are accustomed to. Its literary shortcomings are obvious.

One way to begin discussing *The Jungle* would be to approach it as a political novel. Work with your students to define the genre of the political novel. Compare *The Jungle* to other political novels the students might have read. Discuss the criteria by which we evaluate—or should evaluate—a political novel. Should our criteria include social and/or political considerations? (It might be useful here to draw a parallel between a political novel and a postmodern novel, for example, in which ideas overshadow the other ingredients of the fiction.)

Major Themes, Historical Perspectives, and Personal Issues

Any discussion of *The Jungle* should mention the unsanitary conditions in the Chicago meat-packing industry at the turn of the century and the federal legislation that Congress passed as a result of the national furor that Sinclair's muckraking novel created. However, it is equally important to emphasize that *The Jungle* was—and is—primarily an indictment of wage slavery. Sinclair's purpose in writing the novel was to document the inhumane treatment of working men and women in industrial capitalism and to argue that socialism provided the only solution to the problem.

Significant Form, Style, or Artistic Conventions

Questions of style and form often seem irrelevant to *The Jungle*. However, it is possible to discuss the primitive, at times brutal, prose of the novel as an appropriate vehicle to convey the quality of human life that Sinclair found in the stockyards of Chicago: working men and women reduced to the level of the dumb beasts they were butchering on the killing fields.

Comparisons, Contrasts, Connections

The Jungle should be considered in the context of three separate but related literary movements in America. First, the novel comes out of the muckraking era. The Muckrakers—so named by Theodore Roosevelt because they, like the Man with the Muckrake in *Pilgrim's Progress*, looked down at the filth and ignored the celestial crown—exposed and attempted to correct graft and corruption in both government and business. The most famous of the Muckrakers, in addition to Sinclair, were Lincoln Steffens and Ida Tarbell, whose major works, *The Shame of the Cities* and *History of the Standard Oil Company* respectively, appeared in 1901.

The Jungle also has its roots in American naturalism, with its first twenty-one chapters conforming, in both form and content, to the typical naturalistic novel of that period. For example, both style and psychological complexity are subordinated to the necessary machinations of the plot—the inevitable movement toward chaos and disintegration. Jurgis and his family, like the heroines of Stephen Crane's *Maggie*, Frank Norris's *McTeague*, and Theodore Dreiser's *Sister Carrie*, are victims of hereditary, environmental, social, and economic forces beyond their control—forces that shape their lives in an impersonal, mechanistic way.

Of course, what distinguishes *The Jungle* from these other examples of American naturalism is the turn toward socialism in the last four chapters, which allows Sinclair to end his novel on an optimistic note. The fact that Sinclair was a socialist, and that he used his writing as a vehicle to express his socialism, identifies him with the group of radical writers and artists that was centered in Greenwich Village (where the radical socialist magazine *The Masses* was published) and that included Floyd Dell, Randolph Bourne, Lincoln Steffens, Max Eastman, and John Reed. Sinclair, like these other socialist writers of the Progressive Era, understood that journalism and fiction could be used as political tools. Sinclair's critique of American capitalism has much in common with his fellow socialists in the pre–World War I period.

Questions for Reading and Discussion/ Approaches to Writing

1. (a) Discuss *The Jungle* as an indictment of wage slavery and compare it to other works of literature that attack antebellum slavery (e.g., Harriet Beecher Stowe's *Uncle Tom's Cabin*).

   (b) Discuss Sinclair's portrait of industrial capitalism in *The Jungle*. Look at the connection between the meat-packing industry and the other institutions represented in the novel. Look at the function of money and the false sense of security it promises. Look at Jurgis's response to hardship: "I will work harder."

   (c) Discuss Sinclair's portrait of European immigrants in *The Jungle*. Discuss his portrait of the American city at the beginning of the twentieth century and compare it to other treatments of the American city in similar novels.

2. (a) Examine one or more of the major works of other American writers referred to as Muckrakers (especially Lincoln Steffens's *The Shame of the Cities* and Ida Tarbell's *History of the Standard Oil Company*). Compare these works to *The Jungle*. What common values and assumptions do all of these works share?

   (b) Explore Sinclair's connection with the radical writers who wrote for *The Masses* (1911–17). Read Sinclair's novel *King Coal* (1917) and compare its treatment of the Colorado mine wars of 1913–14 with Max Eastman's in "Class War in Colorado" (*The Masses*, June 1914) and John Reed's treatment of the famous Patterson, New Jersey, textile strike in "War in Patterson" (*The Masses*, June 1913).

   (c) Examine Sinclair's theory of literature in *Mammonart* (1925) and an early essay entitled "Our Bourgeoisie Literature— The Reason and the Remedy," published in the October 8, 1904, issue of *Collier's*.

Bibliography

Especially helpful are the chapters on *The Jungle* in the following critical biographies of Sinclair:

Bloodworth, William A., Jr. *Upton Sinclair*. Boston: Twayne, 1971.

Harris, Leon. *Upton Sinclair: American Rebel*. New York: Thomas Y. Crowell, 1975.

Also, Harvey Swandos's article, "The World of Upton Sinclair" (*Atlantic Monthly*, Dec. 1961, pp. 96–102), contains an important discussion of *The Jungle* as an historical document.

Henry Adams (1838–1918)

Contributing Editor: Earl N. Harbert

Classroom Issues and Strategies

Explain Henry Adams's point of view as an outsider even when he writes about his own life. Note also his allusive, old-fashioned prose style, which is so different from that of (for example) Hemingway. Discuss Adams's lack of dependence on the economic rewards that his writings might bring, and his unusual authorial attitudes. Also important is an extended exploration of the meaning and usefulness of his key symbols.

In teaching Henry Adams, especially the entries included in *The Heath Anthology*, I have enjoyed the largest success when I emphasized the following five themes:

1. Although born into a tradition of elite political, social, and intellectual leadership, Henry Adams yet remained essentially an observer rather than a participant in the robust American life of the 1860–1912 period. Writing in all literary forms, his point of view is that of an outsider—even when he tells about his own life (as the third-person narration in the *Education* demonstrates).

2. A writer by choice, tradition, and careful training, Adams's economic independence allowed him always to do the work of his choice; namely, to pursue a broadly cultural and historical study of the past and present (represented in the selections from *Chartres* and the *Education*).

3. As a pioneer in intellectual history, as well as an interested student of science, Henry Adams sought to measure the European twelfth century against the American late nineteenth and early twentieth century. His method concentrated on the vital principles that characterized both eras. Thus, the medieval virgin (religion) appears first in *Chartres* and later is compared and contrasted with the modern dynamo (the force of electric power), when the conjunction becomes explicit in Chapter 25 of the *Education*. The same symbolic

progression Adams uses to suggest the path of his personal intellectual voyage to increased understanding.

4. Adams's poem defines this intellectual journey in a more personal and perhaps a more compelling form. In particular, it reveals the deference (or even skepticism) that prevents the author from accepting simplistic judgments on history, religion, and other topics that he discusses.

5. As Adams shows in the letter to James, at its best, the thought and writing of Henry Adams resist what he finds to be the narrow parochialism of American experience. Building on this belief, Adams attempts to move his readers toward some larger understanding—even at some artistic cost in didacticism and possible misinterpretation.

As a practical minimum preparation for any instructor, and as the next step for any interested student, I recommend a careful reading of the entire *The Education of Henry Adams*, edited by Ernest Samuels.

Major Themes, Historical Perspectives, and Personal Issues

1. Henry Adams's life of privilege, born into a family that had achieved three generations of elite political and intellectual leadership.
2. Henry Adams's displacement from that role in the U.S. from 1860 to 1918.
3. Henry Adams's life-long concern with finding in history (human experience) some key to understanding and useful application.
4. Henry Adams's reclusive, "anti-confessional" pose as author (versus moderns).

Significant Form, Style, or Artistic Conventions

Consider the definitions of autobiography and biography as matters of traditional literary form, modified in Henry Adams's work.

Original Audience

I raise the question of the audience for the private printings of both works, to make the contrasting attitudes of Henry Adams more comprehensible. Thus, reading becomes relative to audience.

Comparisons, Contrasts, Connections

It is fruitful to compare Adams's work to Rousseau's *Confessions*, Gosse's *Father and Son*, and St. Augustine's *Confessions*.

Bibliography

Samuels, Ernest, ed. "Introduction." In *Major Writers of America (II) The Education of Henry Adams*.

New Explorations of an "American" Self

Abraham Cahan (1860–1951)

Contributing Editor: Daniel Walden

Classroom Issues and Strategies

Students need to understand the following: (1) the Eastern European Jewish culture out of which Cahan came; (2) New York City as a fast-changing urban and technologized environment in the late nineteenth and early twentieth century; and (3) the nature of ethnicity in the context of the forces of Americanization.

To address these topics, I require I. Howe and E. Greenberg, Introduction to *Treasury of Yiddish Stories* (for the European culture), and Moses Rischin, *The Promised City: New York's Jews 1880–1920*, for the culture of New York City. For an introduction to Cahan as a realist, see Jules Chametzky, *From the Ghetto*.

I also use the following films:

1. *The Inheritance* (a documentary made by Amalgamated, 1964).
2. *The Distorted Image* (a set of slides on stereotyping by B'nai Brith, Anti-Defamation League).
3. *The Chosen* (film of Chaim Potok's novel).
4. *Hester Street* (film of Cahan's novel).
5. *The Pawnbroker* (film of Wallant's novel).

Students tend to identify with Cahan's attempts to find himself, a newcomer, a Jewish immigrant, in urban New York. They are surprised that this man, as an editor and novelist, was such a big influence in the 1900–40 era. They tend to ask about the Eastern European culture, what New York was *really* like in the 1910s, 1920s, and why and how people struggled for identity in the face of overt oppression, poverty, and discrimination.

Major Themes, Historical Perspectives, and Personal Issues

Help students understand the parallel themes of ethnicity/identity and assimilation/Americanization. In *Yekl*, Cahan begins to address these themes; in *The Rise of David Levinsky* (1917) he was able to develop character and relationships in the context of the turn-of-the-century culture.

Significant Form, Style, or Artistic Conventions

Cahan was a realist who had mastered English. His style bore the impress of his Russian literary and cultural background, as well as having come out of an Eastern European Jewish culture.

Original Audience

It is necessary to prepare a word list or glossary of those few Yiddish words that are used. A contemporary American audience has to learn to tune in the late nineteenth- and early twentieth-century Russian and Jewish cultures from which Cahan came.

Comparisons, Contrasts, Connections

The classic Russian authors, like Tolstoi, Dostoyevsky, and Turgenev, should be mentioned and briefly explained. W. D. Howells and his circle were also an influence on Cahan. Lastly, Yiddish authors like Mendele and Sholom Aleichem should be referred to. All were influences on Cahan, who absorbed their work even as he reflected the culture of New York City in the 1890–1913 era.

Questions for Reading and Discussion/
Approaches to Writing

1. (a) Explain the religio-cultural ethos of nineteenth-century Eastern European Jewry.
   (b) What was the literary culture of nineteenth-century Russia?
2. Abraham Cahan: Russian Jewish Realist.
   Abraham Cahan: Yiddishist, Reformer, Novelist.
   Abraham Cahan: Editor and Mediating Influence.
   Abraham Cahan: American Democratic Pragmatic Socialist.

Bibliography

See works listed under "Classroom Issues and Strategies."

Edith Maud Eaton (Sui Sin Far) (1865–1914)

Contributing Editor: Amy Ling

Major Themes, Historical Perspectives,
and Personal Issues

If students are to appreciate the work of Edith Eaton fully, they must be given its historical and social context, namely the reception of Chinese by dominant Americans before and during her period. Students should know that though the Chinese were never enslaved in this country, as were Africans, they were brought here in large numbers as indentured laborers or coolies. The Chinese Exclusion Act was only repealed in 1943 and naturalized citizenship for Asians was permitted in 1954, long after African-Americans and American Indians were recognized as American citizens. Initially attracted to California by the discovery of gold in the mid-nineteenth century, by the 1860s thousands of Chinese laborers were enticed here to construct the mountainous western section of the transcontinental railroad. Almost from the beginning, prejudice against them was strong. They were regarded as an alien race with peculiar customs and habits that made them unassimilable in a nation that wanted to remain white; and their hard-working, frugal ways, their willingness to work for lower wages than whites, rendered them an economic threat and thus targets of racial violence.

Into this environment, Edith Eaton came as a small child from England, living first in Hudson City, New York, and later settling in Montreal. Though her writing career began on the Montreal newspaper, *The Star*, she was to make her mark in the United States (she lived most of her adult life in Boston, Seattle, and San Francisco), writing articles and short stories using the Chinese pseudonym Sui Sin Far.

Edith Eaton's autobiographical essay and her stories, of which "In the Land of the Free" is an example, show what it was to be a Chinese woman in the white man's world. Though Eaton herself was only one-half Chinese (and one-half English), she was devoted to her mother and to the cause of counteracting the hatred and prejudice against her mother's people so pervasive during her own formative years. She took the Chinese name of a flower popular among the Chinese (Sui Sin Far means narcissus) and courageously asserted her Chinese heritage, even though this background was not evident on her face.

In "Leaves" she describes through personal anecdotes, chronologically arranged, her growing awareness of her own ethnic identity, her sensitivity to the curiosity and hostility of others, the difficulty of the Eurasian's position, and the development of her racial pride. The other theme apparent in "Leaves," and in many of her short stories, is Eaton's defense of the independent woman. The biographical fact that Eaton herself never married and the intimate details of this woman's journal entries would indicate that she is telling her own story, but she refrained from identifying herself out of a delicate sense of modesty.

"In the Land of the Free" is typical of Edith Eaton's short fiction. Her themes are of utmost importance: exposure of racial insensitivity, the human costs of bureaucratic and discriminatory laws, the humanity of the Chinese. The creation of rounded characters is a secondary concern. Lae Choo is little more than maternity personified, maternity victimized by racial prejudice. But the very portrayal of a Chinese woman in the maternal role—loving, anxious, frantic, self-sacrificing—was itself a novelty and a contribution, for the popular conception of the Chinese woman, whose numbers were few in nineteenth-century America, was that of a sing-song girl, prostitute, or inmate of an opium den. In Lae Choo, Eaton gives the reading public a naive, trusting woman whose entire life is devoted to the small child that the law of "this land of the free" manages to keep away from her for nearly one year. By the end of the story, the irony of the title becomes forcefully apparent.

Edith Eaton hoped to effect a change by means of her pen, to be the pioneer in bridging the Occident and the Orient, but the last article she published, less than a year before her death on April 7, 1914, was still a plea for the acceptance of working-class Chinese in America. She asserts that many former laundrymen become college graduates and influential people, that half the Chinese children in the Sunday School class she visited in San Francisco wore American clothes, while in eastern public schools, all the children wore American clothes. The pathetically shallow arguments she makes reflect not her thinking but that of the opposition. At the time of her death, the newspapers were full of stories about keeping Asian children out of public schools in reaction to the murder of a white woman by her Chinese "houseboy," and the Chinese Exclusion Act had been extended indefinitely.

Bibliography

Anonymous. *Marion, the Story of an Artist's Model. By Herself and the Author of Me*. New York: Watt, 1916. Biography of Sara Eaton Bosse by Winnifred Eaton. Includes anecdotes of the Eaton family life with Edith referred to as Ada.

Anonymous. *Me, a Book of Remembrance*. New York: Century, 1915. Winnifred Eaton's autobiography.

Sui Sin Far. (Pseud. of Edith Maud Eaton.) "Leaves from the Mental Portfolio of an Eurasian." *Independent* 66 (January 21, 1909): 125–32.

——. *Mrs. Spring Fragrance*. Chicago: A. C. McClurg, 1912.

Watanna, Onoto. (Pseud. of Winnifred Eaton.) *A Japanese Nightingale*. New York: Harper, 1901.

Mary Austin (1868–1934)

Contributing Editor: Vera Norwood

Classroom Issues and Strategies

Students have difficulty responding to Austin's strident individualism and her vacillation between ardent feminist and male-identified writer. The best approach is to provide contextual background that reveals that Austin was not alone in her struggles to write from both inside and outside her culture.

Once we have addressed some of the difficulties of voice in this autobiography, I have the best luck with teaching what I think Austin as a writer was best at evoking. Her strength was in describing and evaluating the interior domestic spaces of her house and the natural and built environments of the Midwest and Far West, thus raising questions about the sort of material world women valued and created. Teaching sections of the autobiography in conjunction with *The Land of Little Rain* and *Lost Borders* encourages literature students to think about various ways in which women have created appropriate spaces and changed the places they settled, both indoors as craftswomen and outdoors as gardeners and preservationists.

The main question Austin's autobiography engenders is how accurate a reflection she provides of late-nineteenth-century women's lives. Not that this is an issue with the particular selection made for the anthology, but Austin's depiction of the American Indian and Hispanic populations of the Southwest raises more questions and issues than the gender-related material. Teachers who branch out into other of her regional works will need to be prepared for these questions.

Major Themes, Historical Perspectives, and Personal Issues

Austin was a Progressive Era writer, deeply involved in supporting regional diversity, multicultural perspectives, and environmental preservation. Students understand her authorial voice better when they know something about her work in these areas. Austin belonged to a generation of creative women struggling to shift from nineteenth-century lives as private, housebound, husband-and-father dominated people, to twentieth-century roles as modern, independent individuals influencing social and political trends. Students should also know something of her private circumstances: the long separation and eventual divorce from her husband, the birth of a retarded daughter, the necessity that she write a great deal to earn her living—each played a part in the sometimes contradictory voice appearing in her work.

Significant Form, Style, or Artistic Conventions

Obviously, some familiarity with autobiographical conventions is useful. Gender is an important variable when reading any autobiography. We discuss male and female voices, stressing that women began to write after men had established the basic form and so their works often combined male traditions with female experimentation. In Austin's case, the experiment is in her use of different voices for the visionary, individualistic persona and for the traditional, good daughter.

Original Audience

Austin's audience in her time was more male than currently. Her reputation as a political activist and writer was with regionalists and environmentalists, among whom the leading lights were men. In many ways, her autobiography was written with an eye to setting herself off from the "ordinary" woman of her generation, of claiming a specialness that would put her in the male leagues while also encouraging other women to break free from gender-role proscriptions. In the process of this somewhat divisive attempt, however, she created a persona with a strong feminist character. In our time, it is that visionary woman who speaks to a much larger audience of women readers. For this audience, Austin is less interesting for what she did in the public sphere of environmentalist politics than for her scathing critique, and frustrated rejection, of the nineteenth-century gender-role model offered her by her mother.

Comparisons, Contrasts, Connections

I teach Austin with Sarah Orne Jewett and Charlotte Perkins Gilman. All three worked in approximately the same time period and struggled with the same gender-role restrictions. Jewett and Gilman are particularly useful in tempering some of the negative reactions students have to Austin's voice. Also useful are Benjamin Franklin's and Frederick Douglass's autobiographies. Teaching these with Austin provides students with a better understanding of the genre in which Austin worked.

Questions for Reading and Discussion/ Approaches to Writing

1. The main introduction I make to any autobiography is to suggest that students think about what sort of people have written their life story. Generally, such authors are engaged in an act of self-creation, which assumes that there is something unique to their life. I ask students to look at strategies the author uses to present herself as, in some way, remarkable. With autobiographies by women this becomes a particularly useful question to begin the study of how gender comes into play in issues of genre.
2. Selecting comparative/contrastive passages from the writers mentioned above and having students look for similarities/differences has been successful. With Austin, Jewett's story "The White Heron" provides a good starting point for looking at landscape values as they are impacted by gender. Also, "The Basket Maker" chapter in *The Land of Little Rain* offers an opportunity for students to analyze

how material from the autobiography matches Austin's more "fictional" work. This is a good exercise for demonstrating how much Austin created her autobiographical persona out of her earlier writing.

Bibliography

Really the best additional reading a teacher could seek is more Austin. Mary Austin was a prolific, wide-ranging writer and one should be aware of the work on which her reputation is based. I would advise reading some of the stories in *Lost Borders* and a few chapters of *Land of Little Rain* as the best preparation for teaching Austin.

Gertrude Bonnin (Zitkala-Sa) (Sioux) (1876–1938)

Contributing Editor: Kristin Herzog

Classroom Issues and Strategies

Without a knowledge of Zitkala-Sa's life and the near impossibility for an American Indian woman of her time to publish independently, students will wonder where these stories fit in. It is important to point out the extreme difficulties of a writer trying to preserve a tribal heritage and yet to communicate to a white audience.

Besides dealing with matters of biography, history, and style, I think approaching these early American Indian authors from the religious perspective (Native American spirituality versus enforced assimilation to Christian beliefs) is effective in helping students to sense the very basic dilemma of a writer, a problem of cultural and spiritual identity that goes deeper than mere issues of civil rights, important as they are.

Students easily identify with the aspect of social criticism or rebellion, but may not find the style particularly attractive because they do not know the historical and biographical background and the tastes of the literary market at this time.

Major Themes, Historical Perspectives, and Personal Issues

Zitkala-Sa is a transitional writer whose life and work are expressing deep conflicts between tradition and assimilation, literature and politics, Native American religion and Christianity. If we focus on the tension between her artistic and her political commitments, she can be seen in the middle between Susette LaFlesche, whose fiction was almost submerged by her political speaking and writing, and Leslie Marmon Silko, who is able to create a blend of traditional and modern fiction that organically incorporates a political stance.

Nor by far are all of her political activities reflected in her writings, but in her editorials for the *American Indian Magazine*, for example, she discussed controversial issues like the enfranchisement of American Indians, Indian contributions to military service during World War I, corruption in the Bureau of Indian Affairs, and allotment of tribal lands. The selections reprinted here from *American Indian Stories* are neither essays of cultural criticism nor strictly autobiographical accounts. They are an attempt at turning personal experience as well as social criticism into creative "stories."

One aspect of Zitkala-Sa's imbalanced, but path-breaking, attempt to merge cultural criticism and aesthetic form is her struggle with religion. In Parts IV and V of "School Days," she vividly describes the little girl's nightmares of the palefaces' devil and the bitterness she felt when a schoolmate died with an open Bible on her bed, listening to the "superstitious ideas" of the paleface woman taking care of her. While Charles Eastman in *Indian Boyhood* (published in 1902, two years after "School Days") uses the word "superstition" for some of his Sioux traditions, Zitkala-Sa turns the matter around: Christianity to her is superstitious.

Similarly, "Why I Am a Pagan" is an unusual statement in her time. Its sentimentality and self-consciously "poetic" language can partly be ascribed to the popular journal style of the time. There is daring in her point of view. Interestingly, she does not satirize a white preacher, but one of her own kin whom she sees as tragically duped by the Christian "superstition." Even though we learn from other sources that she and her husband denounced the Peyote religion and therefore to some extent hampered the fight for American Indian freedom of religion, the fact remains that she asserted the dignity of Indian religion and put her finger on two blindspots of Christianity that are being overcome only in our time: the disregard for nature and the disrespect for other cultures. What Christian theology is learning today from ecology and anthropology as well as from some of its own forgotten roots, Native American writers learned from their ancient tribal traditions.

Significant Form, Style, or Artistic Conventions

The selections from "The School Days of an Indian Girl" expose the blatant injustice of stripping a child of language, culture, religion, and familiar surroundings. At the same time they express the irony that the maltreated student is extremely unhappy upon returning home and finally feels the urge to return to the place of her earlier sufferings. While the style is sometimes stilted or sentimental, it is at other times direct and powerful, as, for example, in the passage on the hair cutting. In learning about American Indian customs and beliefs ("short hair was worn by mourners, and shingled hair by cowards"), we are made to experience the trauma of the child. In hearing the mother's desperate cry for help from the spirits of her departed warrior brothers, we can sense the tragic family divisions caused by forced assimilation.

Comparisons, Contrasts, Connections

The many years of literary silence in Zitkala-Sa's life seem to indicate a serious break between artistic endeavors on the one hand and relentless activism on behalf of American Indian health, education, legal representation, and voting rights on the other. However, in her few publications she actually anticipated the concerns of contemporary writers. In blending autobiography with creative narrative, elements of tribal traditions, and social criticism, she helped to pave the way for those recent writers who have focused more clearly and more comprehensively on their own traditions.

Questions for Reading and Discussion/ Approaches to Writing

1. (a) What is your knowledge of American life around 1900 in terms of what you have "absorbed" over the years? In terms of consulting recent scholarly works?
   (b) What do you suppose were the difficulties of a Native American woman writer in writing for a white audience around 1900?
2. (a) How are literary art and protest merged in Zitkala-Sa's work?
   (b) How did Zitkala-Sa pave the way for contemporary American Indian writers like Leslie Marmon Silko, Paula Gunn Allen,

or Louise Erdrich (in case contemporary American Indian women authors have been read in the class) ?

Bibliography

Allen, Paula Gunn. *The Sacred Hoop: Recovering the Feminine in American Indian Traditions*. Boston: Beacon, 1986, 82.

Dockstader, Frederick J. *Great North American Indians: Profiles in Life and Leadership*. New York: Van Nostrand, 1977, 40f.

Eastman, Charles A. *Indian Boyhood*. New York: McClure, Phillips & Co., 1902, 172, 177. Christianity and superstitions. See also Hertzberg, *The Search for an American Indian Identity*, especially 256ff. and 262.

Fisher, Alice Poindexter. "The Transformation of Tradition: A Study of Zitkala-Sa and Mourning Dove, Two Transitional Writers." Ph.D. Diss., City University of New York, 1979, 36. On the quality of the passage on hair cutting.

Fisher, Dexter. "Zitkala-Sa: The Evolution of a Writer." *American Indian Quarterly* 5 (August 1979): 229–38.

Hertzberg, Hazel W. *The Search for an American Indian Identity: Modern Pan-Indian Movements*. Syracuse: Syracuse University Press, 1971. Describes her political activities.

Littlefield, Daniel F., Jr., and James W. Parins. *A Biobibliography of Native American Writers, 1772–1924*. Metuchen, N.J.: Scarecrow Press, 1981, 17f. For a list of writings by Zitkala-Sa. See also the Supplement to this volume, 1985, 16.

Olsen, Tillie. *Silences*. New York: Delta/Seymour Lawrence, 1978. Helpful in explaining to students the many reasons for a break in creativity, especially as it pertains to women and members of minorities.

Schöler, Bo. Introduction to *Coyote Was Here*, p. 10.

Stout, Mary. "Zitkala-Sa: The Literature of Politics." In *Coyote Was Here: Essays on Contemporary Native American Literary and Political Mobilization*, edited by Bo Schöler, 74. Aarhus, Denmark: Department of English, University of Aarhus, 1984.

Young, Mary E. "Bonnin, Gertrude Simmons." *Notable American Women, 1607–1950: A Biographical Dictionary*, Vol. I.

Mary Antin (1881–1949)

Contributing Editor: Richard Tuerk

Classroom Issues and Strategies

Students are often unfamiliar with the time period treated in *The Promised Land*, especially so with aspects of the Great Migration and of immigrant settlement in America in the late nineteenth and early twentieth centuries. Especially important is conveying to them the kinds of conditions the newly arrived immigrants encountered in large eastern cities. Students are also unfamiliar with the kinds of conditions the immigrants lived in in the Old World.

I use slides made from photographs by people like Jacob Riis to try to give the students a feeling for life in the immigrant quarters. I also use books containing photographs by people like Roman Vishniak to give them a feeling for Old World Orthodox Jewish life. Frankly, I find that photographs have a stronger impact on my students than simple descriptions and statistics do.

Most of the questions I hear from students concern life in the Old World; however, most material treating Old World life has been omitted from the anthology. Other questions involve the urban environment of the newly arrived immigrant. Strangely enough, few of my students question Antin's idea that total assimilation is desirable.

Major Themes, Historical Perspectives, and Personal Issues

Antin's emphasis on Americanization and total assimilation deserves careful scrutiny. I try to discuss the values of an ethic of assimilation as well as the problems it presents. I usually contrast Antin with at least one author—usually Ludwig Lewisohn, although Leslie Marmon Silko would do as well—who questions the ethic of assimilation. Particularly apt books for contrast are Lewisohn's *Up Stream* and Silko's *Ceremony*. I also discuss the related theme of initiation in Antin's book.

The work may be treated in terms of its sociological content, that is, in terms of what it reveals about the expectations and possibilities of an immigrant girl in America around the turn of the century. It also may be treated in terms of the role of the public schools in helping (perhaps forcing) the immigrant to come to terms with American culture and society. However, the work may also be treated as a piece of literature.

Significant Form, Style, or Artistic Conventions

As I see it, *The Promised Land* is a tale of initiation, even of rebirth. Antin's being reborn as an American provides her with her principal form in terms of her contrasting Old World and New (the anthology does not contain material dealing directly with her Old World life) and in terms of her growth in the New World. The book is, among other things, a study in radical discontinuity in terms of the relations of Antin's Old World life to her New World life and of continuous growth in terms of her New World life.

Original Audience

Antin says that she is writing for all Americans, and her statement seems correct. I mention the tremendous popularity of her work and its use, either in whole or in part, in classrooms in public schools throughout America. Chapters from it became parts of textbooks used from coast to coast.

Comparisons, Contrasts, Connections

Other works of initiation are especially useful for comparison, especially those dealing with initiation into American society. Ethnic tales of initiation make instructive objects of comparison, works like Leslie Marmon Silko's *Ceremony*, Ludwig Lewisohn's *Up Stream*, O. E. Rolvaag's *Giants in the Earth*, and Richard Wright's *Black Boy*.

Even more helpful, however, is comparing Antin's book with Mark Twain's *Adventures of Huckleberry Finn*. These works are in many ways very similar yet at the same time radically different, especially in terms of their evaluations of American society. Whereas Antin desires assimilation above all, Huck learns to loathe the idea of being assimilated into American society.

Questions for Reading and Discussion/ Approaches to Writing

1. In what ways is Antin's experience in the New World unique? In what ways is it typical?

In what ways is she unique? In what ways is she typical? As you read the selection, it might help to bear in mind that she insists that she is representative of all young immigrants.

What is her attitude toward public schools?

How realistic is her evaluation of America?

2. Compare Antin's attitude toward public schools with your own attitude; what incidents in her life and in yours are responsible for the similarities and differences in those attitudes? Trace the steps by which Antin shows herself becoming Americanized.

Bibliography

Guttmann, Allen. *The Jewish Writer in America: Assimilation and the Crisis of Identity.* New York: Oxford University Press, 1971. Section 2, chapter 3. "The Rise of a Lucky Few: Mary Antin and Abraham Cahan."

Liptzin, Sol. *The Jew in American Literature.* New York: Bloch, 1966. Chapter 8. "The Promised Land."

Proefriedt, William A. "The Education of Mary Antin." *Journal of Ethnic Studies* 17.4 (1990): 81–100.

Rubin, Steven J. "Style and Meaning in Mary Antin's *The Promised Land:* A Reevaluation." *Studies in American Jewish Literature* 5 (1986): 29–34.

Tuerk, Richard. "Assimilation in Jewish-American Autobiography: Mary Antin and Ludwig Lewisohn." *A/B: Auto/Biography Studies* 3.2 (Summer 1987): 26–33.

——. "At Home in the Land of Columbus: Americanization in European-American Immigrant Autobiography." *Multicultural Autobiography: American Lives,* edited by James Robert Payne, 114–38. Knoxville: University of Tennessee Press, 1992.

——. "The Youngest of America's Children in Mary Antin's *The Promised Land.*" *Studies in American Jewish Literature* 5 (1986): 29–34.

*Modern Period
1910–1945*

Toward the Modern Age
Alienation and Literary Experimentation
The New Negro Renaissance

As with other sections in *The Heath Anthology*, the anthology itself is a good place to begin class discussion, particularly in its use of the term "modern." Attempts by the class to define this word can lead to questions about where to locate the border between the past and present—a question implied by the phrase *"Toward* the Modern Age"—and hence to questions about the uses of literary, historical, and cultural classification systems. For example, how does the adjective "modern" affect our reading of a particular text? What difference does it make to read W.E.B. Du Bois, James Weldon Johnson, and Booker T. Washington as precursors of modern African-American literature instead of reading them as descendants of and respondents to Frederick Douglass, Harriet Jacobs, or Phillis Wheatley? Or as contemporaries of Edith Wharton and Willa Cather? Groups of students could be asked to read writers collected in just these different configurations to compare the various perspectives that emerge.

These exercises suggest further experiments in classification and reclassification. In the *Instructor's Guide* entry for "A Sheaf of Political Poetry in the Modern Era," Cary Nelson asks what difference the label "political" makes in reading these poems—and by extension what difference the same label would make to other texts, or what different labels would mean to the texts in that same section. What if the poems of T. S. Eliot, Ezra Pound, or Amy Lowell were labeled as primarily "political" rather than "experimental" or "personal"? What is the effect of encountering Langston Hughes in both the section on political poetry and in the section on "The New Negro Renaissance"? Such questions also involve the instructor in the process of critical re-evaluation and reclassification, for as instructors we carry the biases and perspectives of our own academic training and reading histories. For many of us, the definition of the word "modern" in terms of literary history almost automatically suggests the term "modernism." While for many students, all of the writers in these sections will be, for others, as for most instructors, certain names will leap out, but perhaps in unusual or nontraditional places. If, as an instructor, you find it curious to see Ezra Pound and T. S. Eliot so separated in the table of contents, or Pound next to Amy Lowell and Eliot in between E. E. Cummings and F. Scott Fitzgerald, such a reaction can be brought into class discussion. These reactions are one way of situating the instructor's reading history and academic training in terms of the particular course, or providing a context in which to evaluate and understand the instructor's expertise, and also to illustrate the benefits offered by unsettling and re-examining traditional patterns of thought.

In a way, these questions of how classification systems are formed—and concomitant questions of how systems of literary and cultural evaluation are formed—return us to the use of "regionalism" as a definitive concept in multicultural pedagogy; the understanding that all classification systems, methods of reading, and historical narratives are social constructions connected to particular historical contexts serving various but equally particular social, cultural, political, and psychological purposes. While the idea of replacing the universal with the regional—or asserting the universality of being regional—may seem new, it's a move comparable to the project of modernism as traditionally understood: the effort to make "Alienation and Literary Experimentation"—terms suggestive of the marginality of the artist as social outsider—into what Eliot regarded as the mainstream of literary tradition—what we refer to today as the "canon." This paradoxical idea of the centrality of alienation often holds an added irony for many students reading these now-canonical high modernist texts for the first time in terms of their own sense of alienation from these self-consciously difficult texts.

Rather than an a *priori* assumption of the centrality of a certain definition of modernism or the deductive approach outlined earlier, an inductive approach that regards each text as regional turns student frustration and puzzlement—essential parts of the learning process, after all—into material for discussion rather than barriers to be overcome. Instead of guessing ahead of time which writers certain students will find difficult, accessible, interesting, and boring, the various reading experiences students bring into class, perhaps expressed in the form of a reading log, can lead to questions of audience and purpose. "Alienation" can begin with questions about how writers—all writers, both in the anthology and in the chairs of the class—either consciously or unconsciously invite and/or discourage various groups of readers. These questions lead to other questions about the writers' purpose and strategies— the question of cultural rhetoric.

Among these purposes and strategies are claims to universality. By beginning with the assumption that all writers are regionalists, we move beyond the idea that while certain groups of writers write for everyone, others represent a special or local case. The writers of "The New Negro Renaissance," for example, are typical, not exceptional, in their attention to the specific contours of particular cultural experiences: the place of African-Americans in U.S. society; the role of the intellectual in the African-American community; the experience of being members of a literary and cultural movement. From this perspective, T. S. Eliot and Ezra Pound, William Carlos Williams and Wallace Stevens are also regionalists, writing from particular cultural positions to particular audiences. If the traditional high modernists claim universality and cultural transcendence as part of their strategy, these claims are just that—strategies—and thus comparable with the strategies and claims for universality of Kay Boyle, Langston Hughes, Theodore Dreiser, or Edna St. Vincent Millay. Issues of race, gender, and class affect these strategies in terms of the traditional assumptions they carry about centrality, marginality, and importance: Gertrude Stein and Ezra Pound are both gendered writers; T. S. Eliot and Zora Neale Hurston are both writers who deal with issues of race, as well as what constitutes a literary tradition.

Finally, questions of canonicity raise questions of influence; how later writers and readers are affected by the poetic strategies and cultural theories of earlier writers and the implications for reading implicit in those strategies, issues that Eliot himself foregrounded as part of his artistic project. If some students bring to class assumptions about the inherent difficulty and obscurity of poetry, about the need to "interpret" poetry, or even about what constitutes poetry, the consideration of these writers as making various claims about what literature is, who should write it and read it, and what its cultural purposes are, can help students construct a genealogy of their own ideas about literature and reading and/or the ideas they have encountered in previous English classes.

Issues and Visions in Modern America

The texts in this section continue to address the questions of assimilation, confrontation, and transformation of the evolving myth of "Americanness" raised in "New Explorations of An 'American' Self," focusing particularly on the experiences of Native Americans, Asian-Americans, and Southerners. This seemingly incongruous grouping highlights important issues related to that myth: both how that myth is profoundly regional in definition within the borders of the United States (where does the "All American" live? What are the images associated with the idea of a "typical" American town?) and how various immigrants' experiences became conflated within that myth into a single archetypal immigrant's story, usually centered on the arrival of European immigrants in New York. The poetry of anonymous Chinese immigrants not only allows for an exploration of the experience and challenges faced by Asian immigrants arriving in the American West, traveling east to a new land against the traditional European myth of westward expansion, but points out again the importance of recognizing the classroom as region—whether it is located in the South, the West, the Midwest, or the East; and paying attention to and making a subject of class discussion the specific immigration histories the students bring with them as part of their identities.

In addition to the continuing exploration of cultural assimilation and resistance, the other major issue addressed in these selections is the Great Depression, the collapse of the U.S. economic system that intensified patterns of internal migration (from East to West and from South to North) that continue to this day. As with immigration, class discussion can start by investigating the images of the depression in the historical consciousnesses of the class and asking students to explore their own relevant family histories. Such explorations will inevitably raise questions of social class and work, particularly as they relate to various educational institutions (community colleges, regional public universities, research institutions), including questions about the relation of a modern college education to the demands of the marketplace. Thus, reading the work of Meridel LeSueur, Clifford Odets, or Pietro Di Donato highlights not only questions about the role of the artist and the purpose of art, but also the purpose of the college literature course for students facing an increasingly competitive and constrained economic future. Such a discussion provides an important perspective for considerations of canonicity in terms not just of creating demographically representative curricula in an abstract sense but of classes that address the concerns and ambitions of students by choosing groups of texts that in their action and interaction reflect, amplify, complicate, and clarify these concerns. Reading proletarian literature from the thirties in conjunction with T. S. Eliot, for example, broadens the implications of both types of texts and opens the paths of access to them as well.

Toward the Modern Age

Booker Taliaferro Washington (1856–1915)

Contributing Editor: William L. Andrews

Classroom Issues and Strategies

Students typically ask questions like these: Why was Washington such an accommodationist? Why did he seem so ready to accept the values of the dominant culture and political system? Why was he always so restrained and unwilling to say anything to upset the white supremacy status quo? I point out Washington's training at Hampton Institute, where he learned very early what white people wanted and how little could be accomplished without pleasing them. Also note that Washington is trying to build a source of black power in the South and cannot do so unless he makes his work seem apolitical (when it isn't).

Consider also these questions: What is the best way for a minority group to advance their own cause when faced with either outright hostility or fear and mistrust? Is Washington's tactic the most effective? What are its costs and advantages?

Major Themes, Historical Perspectives, and Personal Issues

What is Washington's relationship to Douglass, the leader whose mantle he adopted? What kind of realism is Washington advocating and how does it accord with literary realism? How does Washington fit into the tradition of the Franklinesque self-made man?

Significant Form, Style, or Artistic Conventions

What sort of slave narrative is Washington writing, in contrast to Douglass's? Compare the first two chapters of both men's autobiographies to see where they resemble each other and differ. Generally Washington poses as a man of facts, not feelings, but does he sometimes betray strong feelings?

Original Audience

Stress the willingness of turn-of-the-century readers to believe a black man who is full of optimism about progress. How might such a message be received today—with how much suspicion?

Comparisons, Contrasts, Connections

Compare to Douglass and Chesnutt, especially in their depiction of slavery. Why would Washington play down the horrors of slavery?

Bibliography

I recommend the chapter entitled "Lost in a Cause" in Robert Stepto's *From Behind the Veil*. Urbana: Illinois University Press, 1979.

W.E.B. Du Bois (1868–1963)

Contributing Editor: Frederick Woodard

Questions for Reading and Discussion/ Approaches to Writing

"The Song of the Smoke" is a poem of celebration of blackness. It was written during a period of great social and political weakness of black people. List the attributes of blackness celebrated in the poem and suggest how each attribute contributes to a positive image. Consider why Du Bois may have felt it necessary to write of blackness in such exalted terms.

Ask students to characterize the effect of verbal repetition, rhythm, and variation of line length in the poem. How do these characteristics relate to the central metaphor, "smoke"?

"The Damnation of Women" is an expression of Du Bois's concern for the right of women to choose for themselves the life worth living. What is the basis for this belief? How does this belief relate to feminism? What role, in Du Bois's estimation, does economics play in the subordination of women? What specific details indicate Du Bois's appreciation for independent thinking and action in women?

Select an edition of the volume *The Souls of Black Folk* and peruse the beginning of each chapter. Find lines of poetry and a musical score.

Consider the possible significance of these two art forms to the major theme of the book. Note that "Of the Sorrow Songs" contains comments on the music and names the songs.

The "veil" is one of Du Bois's most famous symbols. Consider possible meanings for it in "Of Our Spiritual Strivings," particularly at the beginning of the essay, where he boasts of living "above the veil."

Relate the section in "Of Our Spiritual Strivings" out of which the famous Du Bois passage on twoness comes (beginning with "After the Egyptian and the Indian, the Greek and Roman" and ending with, "Shout, O Children!/Shout, you're free!/For God has bought your liberty!") to a reading of "The Unhappy Consciousness," a chapter in Hegel's *Phenomenology of Mind*. Then develop a list of supporting evidence to justify the probable influences of the Hegelian argument on Du Bois's thinking in his essay. Additional reading in Hans-Georg Gadamer, *Hegel's Dialectic: Five Hermeneutical Studies*, translated by P. Christopher Smith (New Haven: Yale University Press, 1976) should provide excellent analysis of Hegel's ideas and method. See particularly Chapters 2 and 3.

Note throughout the essays collected here that Du Bois uses the terms Negro, black, and African-American almost interchangeably. On closer examination, you may discern a specific context that differentiates the use of each term. Develop a rationale for use of each term in a specific context.

"Of the Sorrow Songs" is considered one of Du Bois's most enduring statements on African-American folk art. Using the content of the essay, trace the evolution of the African song to a unique American folk expression.

James Weldon Johnson (1871–1938)

Contributing Editor: Arthenia J. Bates Millican

Classroom Issues and Strategies

Next to James Weldon Johnson's name and date of birth in a biosketch is the familiar catalog of his accomplishments as educator, journalist, lawyer, composer, librettist, poet, novelist, editor, social historian, literary critic, diplomat, fighter for the rights of his people and the rights of all. Yet, he is remembered today, almost exclusively, as the author of

"Lift Every Voice and Sing"; and to some degree as the author of the "Creation," the first sermon in *God's Trombones*.

One mythic error is still in vogue for the less ardent student—and that is the indictment leveled against the author who "talks black" but who was never really given to the black ethos. This accusation comes as an error of identification. Some students assume that Johnson himself is the protagonist of the novel, *The Autobiography of an Ex-colored Man*. Actually, the author's friend, "D_____," Douglas Wetmore, is model for the protagonist. Thus, one encounters the problem of coping with an author with name popularity, but who is not known despite his myriad contributions to American and African-American literary culture.

The writer can best be made accessible to students, first, by introducing *Along This Way*, his authentic life story, as well as the history of the Harlem Renaissance and the rise of Marxist ideology. In the index, the entry "Johnson, James Weldon" is a reference guide in chronological order that gives the chance to examine items of choice.

Johnson may stand in clearer relief by using an "exchange" pattern of image-making. For example, discuss W.E.B. Du Bois as a "politician" who engaged in "political" actions at times.

An indirect form of transformation of real life act to art can be traced in an evolutionary process that produced *Trombones*. First, Johnson visited a Jacksonville church during his childhood days where he saw the African shout. Second, he visited "Little Africa." Third, he listened to his father as a gospel preacher. And finally, he heard gospel preachers when he was field secretary for the NAACP. The Kansas City sermon spurred these recollections and brought on a feeling that gave him import to black soul, the African communal spirit.

Students usually respond to the following issues:

1. The failure of the "Talented Tenth" to understand the economic imperatives that would involve all Americans.
2. The failure of the Johnson legacy to maintain itself with the onset of Marxism and the rise of proletarian literature.
3. The failure of Fisk and Atlanta universities to play a significant role in building a Johnson file of note.
4. The reason so little is known about J. Rosamond, Johnson's co-editor and collaborator.
5. In a quiet way, Johnson is receiving scholarly interest. Will it be potent enough to take him into the twenty-first century?

Major Themes, Historical Perspectives, and Personal Issues

Exemplary themes of major import in the Johnson canon begin with "Lift Every Voice" and "Bards." They relate to the black presence in America via the "peculiar institution," slavery, but maintain relevance to the American Dream, "holy hope," and self-realization. Typical themes of historical significance are: freedom and authority; liberty and responsibility; the artist in America; and society and the individual. On the personal level, in terms of the author's race and his innate concerns, the theme of historical reference is stressed in order to give credence to and assess values that originated in Africa. Other themes in the "personal" category are: men's ways with God; the mystical aura of the creative imagination; the power, beauty, and "essential rhythm" of indigenous black folk poetry; justice, liberation, and peace.

Significant Form, Style, or Artistic Conventions

Johnson's reputation as a writer rests on his novel and *God's Trombones*. His idea that prose should state facts enables him to write a realistic novel. He treats themes such as namelessness, racial self-hatred, the black mother's ambiguous role, and the white patron/white liberal who appears in the modern novel by blacks.

As a poet, he went through a long evolutionary stage of development. His first poems, *Jingles and Croons*, are written in the "Dunbar" tradition of accommodation, imitation, and limitation in terms of the two emotions allowed: pathos and humor. The plantation and the minstrel stage are background sources.

When Johnson wrote "Lift Every Voice" in 1900, he had become imbued with the Victorian conventions of English verse. Rudyard Kipling, the poet laureate (the court poet), wrote many occasional poems, including "Recessional," which served as a model for the black national anthem in form and structure.

Walt Whitman, the poet who gave birth to a new American poetry, wrote in free verse. *Song of Myself* set the stage for the freedom, individual experimentation, and the new theme of egalitarianism that appear in one aspect of Johnson's poem "Brothers." He used free verse in *Trombones*.

The coming of the New Negro to New York in the post–World War I period, "thoughtwise" and "boywise," combined to form Harlem as the New Jerusalem for blacks. This city became the place for conscious black artists who revered their African past and their southern roots. *Trombones* is grounded in this tradition. It makes use of African rhythms; it employs intonations of southern folk idioms, thus enforcing the power of black speech devoid of the artificial "cant of literary dialect." Therefore, Johnson set the stage for future poets who desired to honor the oral tradition in their conscious literary works.

Original Audience

Black literature written in the nineteenth century and in the first four decades of the twentieth century was written basically for a white reading audience. At that time there were few if any student audiences on any level who studied works by blacks. In black schools, great racial personalities were presented to the students during Negro History Week. Now there is Black History Month.

Black literature in class is a phenomenon of the 1960s. Black studies programs became a part of the school curriculum in America. Therefore, the audience in class is a rather new phenomenon.

The class audiences that began as "black" or "white" at first might be one now of new minority constitution: women, handicapped people, elderly citizens, third world students, and/or others. The appeal of the black work to be valid, then, must have appeal to other ethnic groups, since the world is now a global village.

For the new class, forums, debates, formal and informal class reports by individual students may enhance interpersonal communication. For the dissemination of facts, the wonders effected by technology are countless. Students may have access to films, recordings, videotapes, and audio tapes for reviewing material introduced earlier in formal class lectures by the professor.

Comparisons, Contrasts, Connections

Fellow novelists of the Harlem Renaissance who honored the theme of "passing" (Johnson claimed authorship for *The Ex-colored Man* in 1927), such as Walter White in "Flight" (1926), Jessie Fauset in "Plum Bun" (1928), and Nella Larsen in *Passing* (1929), promoted the aesthetic indigenous to African literature: art for life's sake. The "for-life's-sake" element is now dated because these authors were intent on presenting the "better elements" in black life to squelch the ardor of the *Nigger Heaven* (1926) vogue fathered by Carl Van Vechten and adhered to even by Claude McKay in *Home to Harlem* (1928).

Stephen Henderson, author of *Understanding the New Black Poetry* (1973), has indicated that black speech, black song, black music (if one can make such distinctions) are imbued with "experiential energy." On this premise, Johnson, the poet who cultivated his black ethos, is best compared with Langston Hughes (1902–1967).

Questions for Reading and Discussion/ Approaches to Writing

1. Does Johnson's high degree of Euroamerican acculturation deflect from his African-American altruism?
2. Is he rightfully classed as a Victorian in terms of middle-class prudery and respectability?
3. Do you agree with George Kent's view that "his cosmopolitanism always extends his reach and his grasp" (*In Blackness and the Adventure of Western Culture*, 1972, p. 30)?
4. The editors of *The Conscious Voice* (1965) suggest that the poem is the rendering of experience—which also suggests "the intricacy of the poet's involvement in the world." Does Johnson use a suitable aesthetic distance from his subject matter in the poems: "Lift Every Voice" (1900); "Fifty Years" (1853–1913); and "Saint Peter Relates An Incident" (1930)? (Refer to outside sources for the latter two poems.)
5. How can one justify the author's use of the compensatory Christian ethic in "Lift Every Voice," "Bards," "Listen Lord"—a prayer—and the sermons in *Trombones*, when he himself is an agnostic? (Refer to outside sources for the latter two poems.)
6. Three reigning poets influenced Johnson's development as the second outstanding African-American poet: Rudyard Kipling, English; Walt Whitman, American; Paul Laurence Dunbar, African-American. How?
7. Racial violence in the poem "Brothers" (1916) is attended with a plea for brotherhood. What is its advantage over literary dialect?
8. How does the longevity of the oral tradition substantiate its worth in the use of black idiomatic expression in African-American literature?

Suggested paper topics:

Period and Genre: The Color-line Novel

1. Before Johnson (1912)
2. During the Awakening (1915–1920)
3. During the Harlem Renaissance (1920–1930)
4. During the 1960s in Louisiana (Ernest Gaines)

Period:

1. The Influence of the Harlem Renaissance on West African Poets
2. Influence of the African poets, like Leopold Senghor, on African-American Poets during the 1960s

Genre:

1. Poetry by "White" Black Authors
2. Protest Poetry
3. The "Coon Song" on Broadway
4. The Folk Sermon as Literary Genre

Bibliography

Copeland, George E. "James Weldon Johnson—a Bibliography." Master's thesis, School of Library Science at Pratt Institute, Brooklyn, New York, May 1951.

Davis, Thadious. "Southern Standard-Bearers in the New Negro Renaissance." In *The History of Southern Literature* 2 (1985): 291–313.

Fleming, Robert. "Contemporary Themes in Johnson's *Autobiography of an Ex-colored Man.*" *Negro American Literature Forum* IV (1970): 120–24.

Johnson, J. W. "The first and second book of American Negro Spirituals, 1925." *God's Trombones*, 1927.

Levy, Eugene. *James Weldon Johnson: Black Leader Black Voices.* 1973. The J. W. Johnson "Prefaces" offer rich critical insight about his work *The Book of American Negro Poetry*, 1922, 1931.

Mcghee, Nancy B. "The Folk Sermon." *College Language Association Journal* I (1969): 51–61.

Millican, Arthenia Bates. "James Weldon Johnson: In Quest of An Afrocentric Tradition for Black American Literature." Doctoral dissertation, LSU, 1972. Chapters 6, 7, and 10 detail facts on the form and structure of dated poems.

Edwin Arlington Robinson (1869–1935)

Contributing Editor: Nancy Carol Joyner

Classroom Issues and Strategies

Robert Stevick has said that "Robinson's poetry deserves the attention it does not contrive to attract" (Barnard, *Centenary Essays*, 66). To introduce Robinson's subtlety, read the poems out loud and more than once. Robinson once told a reader who confessed to being confused about his poetry that he should read the poems one word at a time. Robinson was very sensitive to the sound of words and complained of not liking his name because it sounded like a tin can being kicked down the stairs. He also said that poetry must be music. This musical quality is best perceived by reading his poetry aloud.

Major Themes, Historical Perspectives, and Personal Issues

Robinson is a "people poet," writing almost exclusively about individuals or individual relationships rather than on more common themes of the nineteenth century. He exhibits a curious mixture of irony and compassion toward his subjects—most of whom are failures—that allows him to be called a romantic existentialist. He is a true precursor to the modernist movement in poetry, publishing his first volume in 1896, a decade notable from the point of view of poetry in America only because of one other publication: the first, posthumous, volume of poems by Emily Dickinson. As the introduction emphasizes, many of Robinson's poems are more autobiographical than their seeming objectivity indicates immediately.

Significant Form, Style, or Artistic Conventions

Although Robinson's subject matter and philosophical stance differ markedly from that of his predecessors', his form is unremittingly traditional. He considered movies, prohibition, and free verse "a triumvirate from hell," and said that if free verse were as easy to write as it was difficult to read, he was not surprised there was so much of it. In his early work Robinson experimented with difficult French forms, like the villanelle and rondeau, but his longer work is written almost exclusively in blank verse. Robinson is one of America's greatest practitioners of the sonnet and the dramatic monologue.

Original Audience

For the first twenty years of Robinson's writing career, he had difficulty in getting published and attracting an audience. He published his first two volumes privately and the publication of the third was secretly guaranteed by friends. He did receive positive reviews from the beginning, however, and with the publication of *The Man Against the Sky* in 1916 his reputation was secure. For the rest of his life he was widely regarded as "America's foremost poet," as William Stanley Braithwaite put it. Both academics and the general public held him in high esteem, as attested by the fact of his winning three Pulitzer Prizes for poetry for volumes published in 1921, 1924, and 1927, when his *Tristram* became a national best-seller.

Comparisons, Contrasts, Connections

Critics have pointed out that Robinson is a descendant of Anne Bradstreet, and in their deceptively plain style and solitary careers they make an interesting comparison. Sometimes Robinson and Edgar Lee Masters have been confused, with people mistakenly assuming that Masters had an influence on Robinson, when the reverse must be true.

The most obvious and fruitful writer for comparison/contrast is Robert Frost, only five years younger than Robinson but nearly twenty years behind him in publication. They share a New England background, contemporaneity, and allegiance to formal writing, but they were decidedly different in life-style, in personality, and finally in their poetry, with Robinson's being the more honest. (Biographers of both poets report that Frost was extremely jealous of Robinson but the reverse was not true.)

A comparison in the presentation of women in "Aunt Imogen" and Frost's "A Servant to Servant" or "Home Burial" is instructive in showing differing attitudes the poets hold toward women. Unlike many of Frost's poems, Robinson's sympathetic portrayal of his characters seems genderless.

Questions for Reading and Discussion/
Approaches to Writing

1. Discussions of point of view, tone, and especially individual diction choices are useful in class. How does the word "alnage" work in

"The Clerks," for instance, or what meanings can be placed on "feminine paradox" in "Aunt Imogen"? Robinson is spare in his allusions, but such reticence gives greater force to them when they appear. Discuss the ironic context of "Momus," Apollo in "The Tree in Pamela's Garden," and Roland in "Mr. Flood's Party."

2. Possible paper topics are contrasts between Robinson's poems from a woman's point of view and similar poems by contemporaneous authors, such as Robert Frost and T. S. Eliot; comparisons of characters in Robinson's poems, such as Pamela and Aunt Imogen; and imagery in "Mr. Flood's Party" and "Eros Turnannos." Numerous close readings have been published on the last two poems mentioned. Reviews of criticism along with an original interpretation of either would be an accessible research topic.

Bibliography

Coxe, Louise O. *Edwin Arlington Robinson: The Life of Poetry*. New York: Pegasus, 1969.

Joyner, Nancy Carol. "Edwin Arlington Robinson." *Dictionary of Literary Biography*, Vol. 54, 366–88.

Squires, Radcliffe. "Tilbury Town Today." In *Edwin Arlington Robinson: Centenary Essays*, edited by Ellsworth Barnard, 175–84. Athens: University of Georgia Press, 1969.

Ellen Glasgow (1873–1945)

Contributing Editor: Linda Pannill

Classroom Issues and Strategies

Glasgow fails to make the New Woman convincing. The philosopher Judith Campbell takes her iconoclastic new book from a muff and presents it ("my little gift") to the lover for whom she is willing to sacrifice a career. She does not perceive his jealousy of her own job offer. In dialogue she repeats his words back to him. That Judith Campbell seems more like a southern belle than a philosopher speaks to the power over heroine and perhaps author of an old-fashioned ideal of womanhood and to the difficulty for writers of Glasgow's generation who are working to create new characters and plots.

When teaching Glasgow's work, symbolism is a good place to start. Estbridge's idealism and his ruthlessness are seen in fire images: the portrait of Savonarola over a fireplace; the "flame" of love; "burned his boats"; burning his papers; the reference to the Grand Inquisitor. Other symbols include Judith's veils, the storm, Estbridge's name (East? China?), the Christmas setting (connected with his feeling "born anew" and her initials), and the doctor's garden. Judith is compared to a cypress, presumably like the one that did not survive. The remaining tree is a tough ailanthus, common though originally from China. Estbridge feels Judith is the "temptation" to disobey society's rules, but after all he will stay in his fallen garden with his sick wife. (That the younger colleague is named Adamson reinforces the Edenic motif, a favorite of the author's.)

The burden on a woman of trying to live up to a man's ideal, a theme throughout Glasgow's work, is interesting to the students. Yet they find Glasgow herself old-fashioned in her preoccupation with romantic love and with the goodness and beauty of her heroines. Along with the dire plots and the reappearances of weak male characters, this calls for an explanation that students will seek first in the author's life. They should be encouraged to look beyond.

Major Themes, Historical Perspectives, and Personal Issues

Because of wide reading on the subject, Glasgow considered herself something of a philosopher. Like Judith Campbell, she wrote, and like her she had an affair in New York with a married man, by some accounts also a doctor. In *The Woman Within*, the author depicts a conflict in her own life between woman and artist roles, love and ambition. Neither choice seems right.

Significant Form, Style, or Artistic Conventions

Irony underlines John Estbridge's self-centeredness and Judith Campbell's self-sacrifice, traits Glasgow found typical of men and women. Judith gives up an appointment at Hartwell College, previously her heart's desire, to run off with Estbridge. He misses the appointment with Judith to accept a faculty appointment. His is the "Professional Instinct," hers the "instinct to yield." A too-obvious irony is the timing of the traffic accident that gives Estbridge the opportunity to betray Judith (or the author the opportunity to rescue her).

Original Audience

Both Raper (in *The Sunken Garden*) and Godbold point to a letter from Pearce Baily, a prominent New York neurologist, advising Glasgow on the story. "The Professional Instinct" deals, of course, with a doctor who has helped a writer in her work. Ellen Glasgow decided not to publish the short story and seems not to have finished revising.

Comparisons, Contrasts, Connections

Mary Hunter Austin and Willa Cather, like Glasgow, were long considered regional writers, though not all their work is set in the desert Southwest or Nebraska, as not all Glasgow's is set in Virginia. Recent feminist scholarship emphasizes these authors' concern with sex roles and their problematic self-concepts as women writers.

Questions for Reading and Discussion/ Approaches to Writing

1. (a) Explain the allusion to Savonarola.
   (b) Why is the point of view effective?
   (c) Consider Tilly Estbridge and Judith Campbell as foil characters.
   (d) What seems to be the target of Glasgow's satire?
   (e) To what extent is the reader prepared for the ending?
   (f) To what extent is Glasgow the literary realist she considers herself?
2. (a) Why might Glasgow have chosen not to publish the story?
   (b) To what extent are both Judith Campbell and John Estbridge autobiographical characters?
   (c) Ellen Glasgow considered herself a feminist. How is the feminism of her period (not our own) reflected in the story?
   (d) In Glasgow's version of society, what kinds of power, if any, do women have?
   (e) How might the influence of Darwinism and Social Darwinism be seen in Glasgow's depiction of the relationship between the sexes?

Bibliography

Glasgow, Ellen. *The Woman Within*. New York: Harcourt, Brace, 1954. Chapters 1, 8–9.

Wagner, Linda. *Ellen Glasgow: Beyond Convention*. Austin: University of Texas Press, 1982. Chapter 1.

Edith Wharton (1862–1937)

Contributing Editor: Elizabeth Ammons

Classroom Issues and Strategies

In my experience, students divide sharply on Wharton. Some love her work, responding particularly to the elegance and precision of her prose and the sharpness of her wit; others don't like her at all, finding it hard to "get into" her fiction because she seems so cold, the prose seems so detailed and self-conscious, and the subject matter is so elite.

Mainly I try to get the two groups talking/arguing with each other. The result usually is that each can appreciate the point of view of the other, and we can start there: with a view of Wharton in which she is both marvelously accomplished as a stylist within a particular aesthetic and—in some ways on the very same grounds—limited as a writer by class and temperament.

One issue students are very interested in is sexuality in Wharton's fiction, ranging from what birth control was available at the time and in the class she wrote about to what her own attitudes toward sex were. Another question is: Why care about all these rich privileged people in Wharton's fiction? Who cares? (One response I give to this is that the top of the pyramid gives a very good sense of what the whole culture aspires to, since those are the people that everyone envies and wishes to be—or is supposed to envy and wish to be. Wharton's fictive world tells us a lot about how the whole culture works and what it values and is supposed to value.) Finally, a question that often gets asked is "What other works by Wharton would you recommend reading?" A good sign.

Major Themes, Historical Perspectives, and Personal Issues

Major themes in Wharton's work include the effects of class on both behavior and consciousness (divorce, for example, often horrifies the established upper class as much for its offense against taste as for its violation of moral standards); the American belief in progress as actual and good (many "advances" Wharton welcomed; others she was contemptuous of); the contrast between European and American customs, morality, and sensibility; the confinement of marriage, especially for women; women's desire for and right to freedom in general, and particularly sexual and economic freedom, and the reality that, usually, the desire and right are thwarted; the preference of powerful, white, usually upper-class men for childish dependent women; the complexity and pain of relationships between women within patriarchal culture, including (and especially) rivalry and animosity among women.

Historically, Wharton was both the product and the beneficiary of a highly developed, even if recent, high-culture tradition of brilliant, educated women able to write and publish fiction for a living. Before Wharton, in France and England George Sand, Madame de Staël, Jane Austen, George Eliot, Mrs. Gaskell, and the Brontës had used fiction to examine many of the issues that engaged Wharton: marriage, the restraints of class, the repression of "respectable" women's sexual desire, the structure of patriarchal power, and the desire of middle-class white women for respectable, paid work. In the United States, in addition to popular women novelists in the nineteenth century, artistically ambitious women writers such as Elizabeth Stuart Phelps and Sarah Orne Jewett preceded Wharton. Contemporary with Wharton was a whole group of accomplished women fiction writers—Chopin, Austin, Hopkins, Glasgow, Cather, Stein. The point is that Wharton's work, historically, is rooted not only in the tradition of social and psychological realism commonly associated with Howells and James (writers she admired), but also in the realism and social criticism of women writers publishing before and contemporary with her who were concerned with many of the same issues that engaged Wharton, particularly issues centered on women's experiences and problems.

Personally, Wharton treated many of the issues of her own life in her fiction: her estrangement from and anger at her mother; her frustration with the limitations placed on women, and especially women of the upper class; her miserable marriage and the stigma against divorce, again particularly in her class but also generally; her fear of the ways in which cautiousness and selfishness can corrupt one's soul; her knowledge that female sexuality, despite society's repression of it, was a potent source of creativity.

Significant Form, Style, or Artistic Conventions

"The Valley of Childish Things" is a parable, but the other selections here are classic conventional modern short stories in terms of form and effect. Wharton can be used to show perfect mastery of conventional form. Her taut, elegant prose and expert command of dramatic structure beautifully manipulate the conventional Western short story pattern of exposition/conflict/complication/climax/resolution. Typically, the climax appears almost at the very end of a Wharton story, creating a very long, strong build-up of anticipation and then a swift, deft finish. You can practically teach the standard modern Western short story—at its best—from a Wharton story.

Original Audience

Wharton was a best-selling author at the turn of the century and into the 1920s; she was also highly acclaimed by critics. After the 1920s, she was taught less and less in schools and universities until before and following World War II she was virtually untaught. She was viewed as a disciple of Henry James and he, but not she, was taught. In the late 1960s and then on through the 1980s, Wharton has steadily and dramatically regained both an academic audience and a general readership, clearly as a result of the most recent wave in the women's movement. In other words, her work attracts attention now for the very reasons it was generally dismissed in the middle of the twentieth century: its focus on women and women's experiences and its emphasis on social context, customs, pressures, and manners as human variables rooted in time, class, gender, nationality, and culture.

Comparisons, Contrasts, Connections

Useful contrasts could include authors such as Harriet Beecher Stowe or Frances Ellen Watkins Harper, who wrote fiction for explicit and avowedly political ends; Mark Twain, who was interested in communicating an almost felt sense of a very different America, the rural Midwest and the white South; Upton Sinclair (whose politics Wharton did not like but whose right to say what he wanted she vigorously defended), who identified with the working class and the poor and wrote muckrakers; or Jack London, who celebrated much of the same white masculine power ethic that Wharton disliked. Another good contrast is Henry James;

though often cited as Wharton's mentor (he was one), James is also quite different from Wharton: He is much wordier, more intrusive and self-indulgent authorially, and inclined to Victorian notions of self-sacrifice and self-immolation.

Questions for Reading and Discussion/ Approaches to Writing

1. When I use study questions for Wharton, I use standards closely keyed to the piece at hand: e.g., for "Roman Fever": Where does the hatred between the two women come from? What is its source? What is the source of the source? For "The Other Two" I might ask: Where do Wharton's sympathies lie in this story? On what do you base your opinion?

2. In addition to standard analytical/critical papers that ask students to work out an interpretative position by arguing closely from the text (which works very well for Wharton), I have found that Wharton is a good author to use for creative-writing paper assignments, which I do in "straight" English courses on the theory that one excellent way of getting inside poetry or fiction is to try to create some yourself, even if you're not very good at it. For Wharton, I might ask students to reread "The Valley of Childish Things" and then write their own gender parable for the late twentieth century of about the same length and structural strategy. For "Roman Fever," I might ask them to write a short story about the two middle-aged women from Barbara's point of view. I spin off Wharton either formally or specifically in subject matter; also I give a rather directed assignment, since one of my goals is to get students to think more about a particular piece by Wharton, how it works or what it says. I have learned that if the creative assignment is too loose, it can let them wander so far from the Wharton text that they discover no more about it than they knew before writing.

Bibliography

See Barbara A. White, *Edith Wharton: A Study of the Short Fiction* (1991). Relatively little Wharton criticism focuses on the short stories, so often it is necessary to adapt general criticism on her. Three provocative books are: Elizabeth Ammons, *Edith Wharton's Argument with America* (1980), Cynthia Griffin Woolf, *A Feast of Words: The Triumph of Edith Wharton* (1977), and Candace Waid, *Edith Wharton's Letters from the Underworld* (1991).

Good articles can be found in Harold Bloom, ed., *Edith Wharton* (1986) and a forthcoming volume, *Critical Essays on Edith Wharton*, to be published by G. K. Hall.

Edgar Lee Masters (1869–1950)

Contributing Editor: Ronald Primeau

Classroom Issues and Strategies

Some students expect—even demand—that poetry be very "difficult" to be deemed worthwhile. When Masters is relatively simple in form and message, that throws them. To address this issue, talk about popular arts, the oral tradition, the enormous popularity of *Spoon River*, and the fact that all poetry need not be academic.

Masters provides a good chance to talk with students about what they think poetry is or ought to be and how the literary establishment can or cannot control popular opinion. Use some multimedia presentations, reading out loud. Bring in some actors from university theater.

Students are interested in events from the poet's life and factors that led him to write this kind of poetry. They wonder how any book of poems could have been *that* popular. No TV back then, they suspect.

Major Themes, Historical Perspectives, and Personal Issues

Consider what it means to live in small-town America, how it is attractive to try to sum up a lifetime on a gravestone, the importance of peer pressure and what others think. Think about Masters's life as a lawyer and how that affected his poetry.

Significant Form, Style, or Artistic Conventions

It is important to discuss basic elements of form and meter in order to see how Masters alluded to, and modified, existing conventions. It is crucial to see that he was outside developing critical norms and how that has clearly limited his inclusion in the critical canons.

Original Audience

Spoon River reached a mass audience when it was written and still sells better than most poetry. Today, however, the audience is largely academic and concerns are more in the direction of scholarship and how to teach the works rather than popularity and whether they speak to an age. Discuss with students questions of popular taste and the split between mass art and high art.

Comparisons, Contrasts, Connections

Compare with Thornton Wilder's *Our Town*. Perhaps even show a video if there's time. There are recordings of *Spoon River*—and a musical. Read Masters alongside Whitman. Talk about how he hid copies of Shelley and Goethe behind law books when people thought he was supposed to be working.

Questions for Reading and Discussion/ Approaches to Writing

1. (a) Who are these speakers?
   (b) To whom are they speaking?
   (c) What is our role as readers?
   (d) What have you underlined or written in the margin and why?
   (e) Which of these characters would you like to know better and why? What was Spoon River like as a place?
2. (a) Discuss the conflicts between standards for "high" art and "mass" art. Who sets criteria and how?
   (b) Compose your own gravestone biography and message to the world—à la *Spoon River*.
   (c) Write a portrait of your home town—à la *Spoon River*.

Bibliography

Flanagan, John T. *The Spoon River Poet and His Critics*. Metuchen, N.J.: Scarecrow, 1974. A very useful reference guide.

Primeau, Ronald. *Beyond Spoon River: The Legacy of Edgar Lee Masters*. Austin: University of Texas, 1981. Re-evaluates Master's place in the American tradition; see Chapters 1–2 for useful background on Masters.

Willa Cather (1873–1947)

Contributing Editor: Margaret Anne O'Connor

Classroom Issues and Strategies

It's hard to do justice to a novelist by looking at a single short story, but "Old Mrs. Harris" promises to be a better representative story to introduce Cather and her major concerns as a writer than any story previously anthologized. More than any other, "Old Mrs. Harris" treats the midwestern locale of her best known Nebraska novels. It is also extremely autobiographical, an emphasis that offers an instructor the advantage of introducing the life history of this important novelist as more than mere background information.

The headnote to this Cather story stresses biographical information, which should prompt questions that will stimulate classroom discussion. Philip Gerber's bare-bones chronology in his Twayne volume on Cather is an accurate outline and an excellent choice for a chronology to supply to students. Sharon O'Brien's more detailed and topic-oriented chronology (in her edition of five of Cather's book-length prose publications for the Library of America in 1986, pp. 1296–1318) would be an excellent biographical summary for instructors to have at their disposal.

Since this story is about a family and one important plot element features a young girl's impatient hunger to go to college, instructors have a natural way to involve student readers in the story through questioning students' own reasons for being in college, the depth of their own commitment to knowledge compared to that of the young woman, and a then/now discussion of options open to young women.

Cather is often considered a regional writer, but one who wrote knowledgeably of many regions in her best known works—Nebraska, New Mexico, Canada, and even Virginia in her last novel. This story presents an excellent opportunity to discuss class members' perceptions of midwesterners vs. southerners, the class structure of small town America in the 1890s, the religious, class, gender, age, and ethnic differences that all come into play in the story. Discussing any of these questions would enhance students' awareness of the complexity that underlies the calm prose style of this story.

Major Themes, Historical Perspectives, and Personal Issues

Published as a story in *Ladies' Home Journal* in the fall of 1932, the original title of "Old Mrs. Harris" was "Three Women." The story could be said to concern the life of WOMAN and the options she has, the ages of a woman as represented by "old Mrs. Harris" and the two generations that follow her, as well as the temper of the time and place—Skyline, Colorado, in the early 1890s—in relation to the generations of women described there.

Significant Form, Style, or Artistic Conventions

Point of view is very important in the story; there is no single first-person narrator or Jamesian "central consciousness" directing the story. Instead, a third-person omniscient narrator goes into the minds of key figures in the narrative to present their reactions. Students often agree with contemporary reviewers of the story that the last two paragraphs are a great departure from the established technique of the rest of the story—very "old-fashioned" and intrusive. What is the effect of this "shift"? Compare it to the ending of Sarah Orne Jewett's "The White Heron." What does each author hope to achieve in her closing commentary?

Original Audience

The themes of this story are timeless. Still, it is set in the past and said much about the need for forbearance to depression-era readers who were its first audience. One excellent point for discussion might be just how much Americans of the 1990s value the patience that Mrs. Harris and Mandy exhibit in the story. In the story, patience is more often seen in the older characters, and the impatience of youth is specifically lamented in the last paragraph.

Comparisons, Contrasts, Connections

Compare Cather to Sarah Orne Jewett. Cather knew Jewett and admired her work. She even wrote an appreciative preface to a two-volume edition of Jewett's stories in 1925. An expanded version of the preface appears in the essay "Miss Jewett" in *Not Under Forty* (1936), an essay that makes it clear that Cather saw herself as aspiring to achieve many of the strengths as a writer that she found in Jewett's work.

Questions for Reading and Discussion/ Approaches to Writing

1. (a) In your reading of the story, who is the most important character? In your reading, who is the most reliable narrator? Who is the "hero"? Who is the most sympathetically presented character?

   (b) Cather used "Three Women" as the title of this story when she published it in a magazine, but "Old Mrs. Harris" when it appeared in a collection. What is the difference in emphasis? Which title do you prefer and why?

   (c) Describe the Templeton marriage. Whose fault is it that this family's life is less than perfect? Does the story attempt to place blame on husband or wife?

   (d) How does this story treat the issue of "motherhood"?

   (e) How is the southern background of the Templeton family important to the story?

   (f) Discuss the economic and social structure of Skyline, Colorado. Who's on top? On the bottom? Why? Who is inside the structure and who is outside? Where do the Templetons fit? The Rosens?

2. One writing assignment I would suggest is in the form of a reading "quiz." Before discussing the work in class on the day it is the assigned reading, ask students to write a one-sentence summary of the story. Ask everyone to exchange papers and have students read aloud sentences that described a different central issue than the one each of them selected as at the heart of the story. These responses should lead easily into the study questions given above.

Bibliography

For the most part, the recent biographies by O'Brien, Woodress, and Lee, and book-length critical studies such as those by David Stouck and Susan Rosowski present the most sensitive readings of Cather's life and work.

One particularly fine "older" source is *Willa Cather: A Pictorial Memoir* (Lincoln: University of Nebraska Press, 1974), with photographs by Lucia Wood and text by Bernice Slote. It's an excellent brief introduction to the world of Willa Cather.

Marilyn Arnold has an extremely useful discussion of "Old Mrs. Harris" in *Willa Cather's Short Fiction*. Athens: Ohio University Press, 1984, pp. 141–52.

Susan Glaspell (1876–1948)

Contributing Editor: Arthur Waterman

Classroom Issues and Strategies

It's important to show how the details of the play "Trifles" transcend local color and address universal concerns. Students should come to see that the precise setting and time lead to a universal and timeless experience.

Ask students to envision what the play would be like if it were three acts and the background and main characters were fully presented. Point out how the very restrictions of the one-act play enhance the tensions and meaning. The play has been popular since it was first produced and has been seen recently (1987, 1988) on PBS television, which indicates that it appeals to diverse audiences.

Susan Glaspell is an interesting example of the late nineteenth-century woman writer, raised in the local color tradition, who radically altered her life and art after her marriage and moved east. She "came of age" about the same time American writing moved from regionalism to modernism and she helped found the modern movement in American drama. Once her experimental period was over, she returned to fiction and to her earlier themes—much more maturely presented. Whether her retreat back to regionalism was because her husband died or because she felt more secure in the older tradition, no one can say.

Major Themes, Historical Perspectives, and Personal Issues

1. Regional: The play conveys the brutal experience of being a farm wife in Iowa during the latter half of the nineteenth century.
2. Sexual: In this play women are pitted against men—Minnie against her husband, the two women against their husbands and the other men. The men are logical, arrogant, stupid; the women are sympathetic and drawn to empathize with Minnie and forgive her her crime.
3. Mythic: The setting—a lonely, bleak, cold landscape; the main characters are never seen on stage and assume a shadowy, almost archetypal presence; the struggle between them is echoed by the antagonisms between the two women and three men on stage; the

result is that a brutal murder is forgiven because of the more terrible tragedy beneath it.

Significant Form, Style, or Artistic Conventions

This play presents most of the qualities of local color writing: exact detail, local speech and customs, a strong sense of place. It avoids some of the excesses of that genre: idealization of character, emphasis on the unique and colorful aspects of the locale, and sentimentality. The demands of the one-act drama, its compression, single set, limited characters, tight plot, single mood—all protect the play from the excesses of its convention and enhance its virtues.

We should also note that the play carefully distinguishes between the affairs of men and the concerns of women. The men intrude on the woman's world, dirtying her towels, scoffing at her knitting and preserves. As we move into the kitchen, the men are left out and the awful details of Minnie's life are revealed to Mrs. Peters and Mrs. Hale, so that when the men return, we see how blind they are and we, the audience, accept their decision not to reveal Minnie's motive.

Original Audience

We know the play was based on an actual trial Susan Glaspell covered as a reporter in Des Moines. In this sense, the play was written for a midwestern audience to dramatize the terrible life of a farm wife, isolated and dependent on her husband for her physical and emotional needs, with the occasional tragic consequences the play depicts. But the play was written after Susan Glaspell had left the Midwest, after she had lived abroad, married, and moved to Provincetown. She had time to ponder the implications of the event and see the tragedy in larger terms, so she was able to transform a journalistic story into a universal drama.

Comparisons, Contrasts, Connections

Zone Gale's "Miss Lulu Bett" (1920) is about a Wisconsin spinster who revolts against midwestern prudishness to seek her own fulfillment. The play has many local color attributes and treats ironically some of the themes in "Trifles."

A better comparison is to be found with John M. Synge's "Riders to the Sea," a one-act tragedy about the lives of fishermen in the Aran Islands. Both plays transcend local color detail to reach mythic concerns, both use a piece of irregular sewing to reveal information, and both present an essential conflict between the men who go out to battle nature, while the women remain to nurture beauty and sustain life.

Questions for Reading and Discussion/ Approaches to Writing

1. If students have been reading someone like Bret Harte, I'd suggest they think about the advantages and disadvantages of local-color writing. Also, I would suggest they examine the one-act play form to see what can and cannot be done with it.
2. I would center on short questions about technique: How does the physical location of the characters help develop the theme? Who are more fully developed, the two women or the three men? Indicate several ways Susan Glaspell conditions the audience to accept the final decision.

Bibliography

See the primary and secondary works listed with the headnote.

Robinson Jeffers (1887–1962)

Contributing Editor: Arthur B. Coffin

Classroom Issues and Strategies

Many readers/critics feel that Jeffers's most readable poetry is in his lyric poems; others feel that his most powerful verse is in his long narrative poems, which, of course, cannot be anthologized. It is useful—perhaps necessary—therefore to provide students a sense of the larger context in which the lyrics stand and to describe the evolution of Jeffers's personal philosophy, which he called "Inhumanism." Even students who respond readily to Jeffers's reverence for a distant God made manifest in the "beauty of things" (i.e., nature)—and many of them embrace these views instantly—will ask, "Where's this guy coming from?" Consider some of the following suggestions.

One may assign individual students or groups of students narrative poems to read and report on to the class, but, with the exception of "Roan Stallion," this is long and sometimes laborious work. And it is time-consuming in the classroom. The traditional approach of lecturing to provide the necessary context is the most efficient one. (As the bibliography indicates, there is a large body of scholarly work to draw on for this purpose.)

Another possibly more appealing approach from the students' perspective is to introduce Jeffers's *Not Man Apart* (ed. David Brower, Sierra Club, San Francisco, 1965: Ballantine Books, New York, 1969), which, taking its title from a Jeffers line, is a collection of magnificent Ansel Adams photographs of the Big Sur landscape (accompanied by quotes from Jeffers), which has a central role in this poetry.

Hearing these poems is very important, and, whether or not the instructor is a competent reader of these verses, he or she might consider obtaining recordings of William Everson's superb reading of them (available from Gould Media, 44 Parkway West, Mount Vernon, NY 10552-1194; Tape #826—*The Poetry of Robinson Jeffers* by William Everson).

Students respond to Jeffers's concern for the beauty of nature and the divinity he finds there. Often they are receptive to the theme of the destructive nature of human beings, especially to human pollution of the earth. Many students are drawn to what they identify as Jeffers's isolationism, his fiercely held individualism. In addition to questions about Jeffers's religious views and his varied intellectual background, they often ask about the poet himself, biographical data which, in this instance, do not take one far from the texts.

Major Themes, Historical Perspectives, and Personal Issues

With the publication of the long narrative "Tamar" (1924), Jeffers declared his literary independence and attempted to write poetry appropriate to the times as he saw them. In "Self-Criticism in February," which reviews this effort, he wrote, "[this] is not a pastoral time, but [one] founded / On violence, pointed for more massive violence." Like T. S. Eliot and others, Jeffers searched myth and literature for a "usable past," but he employed these materials more radically than his peers, who, he thought, were fading out in effete aestheticism. Generally, Jeffers saw Euripides's vision as more akin to his own than those of Aeschylus and Sophocles; in the Roman poet Lucretius (*On the Nature of Things*, which embodies the materialism of Epicurus) Jeffers found support for his view of nature and divinity; classical mythology and tragedy helped him to structure his personal vision and his poems. American capitalism was morally bankrupt and defacing the landscape; both American politics and international affairs were threatened by "Caesarism"—ruthless leaders and timid followers. The advent of nuclear war seemed to assure the imminent destruction of human beings—but, for Jeffers, not of the world itself—which change, the poet believed, would allow the beauty of the world (the manifest God) to start over again, without the contaminating presence of mankind. His doctrine of Inhumanism—"a shifting of emphasis from man to not-man; the rejection of human solipsism and recognition of the transhuman magnificence"—encourages humans to become "uncentered" from themselves. "This manner of thought and feeling," he wrote, "is neither misanthropic nor pessimistic. . . . it has objective truth and human value."

Significant Form, Style, or Artistic Conventions

Jeffers's early verses are late-Victorian in manner, reflecting the influences of Dante Gabriel Rossetti, Algernon Swinburne, and George Moore, but prior to writing "Tamar" he decided to break with modernism, which he saw typified by Mallarmé and his followers. These modernists had forsaken content, Jeffers believed, in favor of aesthetics, which weakened their verse. His narrative poems are heavily laden with statement and action, and their lines are long and supple after classical models. "Apology for Bad Dreams" and "Self-Criticism in February" tell us nearly all there is to hear about Jeffers's poetic. Despite Jeffers's disclaimer (and the views of critics who agree with him on this point), I see him as a modernist sharing much with other modernists such as Robert Lowell, T. S. Eliot, Wallace Stevens, and Theodore Roethke, who also tried to re-order a fragmented world and to find adequate structures for the task. It may be useful to compare Jeffers's views of religion, order, fictive constructs, and reality with the more sophisticated ones of Wallace Stevens (cf. Stevens's "Sunday Morning," "The Idea of Order at Key West," "The Snow Man," and others).

Original Audience

In several places, Jeffers said that he wrote for all time, not for the moment (even though many of his lyrics of the 1940s are very topical, like carping letters to the editor that criticize world leaders indiscriminately), because he believed poetry should bespeak permanence. His work was very popular during the late 1920s and the 1930s (he appeared on the cover of *Time* magazine), but his audience left him during WWII, when his individualism and their patriotism diverged in a wood. During the 1960s and 1970s, his work was widely translated in Europe, where he gained an enthusiastic readership in the Slavic countries. On this continent, he has been adopted by members of the ecology movement, disaffected members of traditional institutional religions, and academic scholars, who together have revived his reputation. Although Jeffers has been severely slighted in the academic texts of the last decades, he is one of the few poets, I find, that the general student is most apt to have read *before* taking an American literature or poetry course.

Jeffers's disinterest in a particular audience—his writing for all time—simplifies the audience problem in class and permits a wide range of responses.

Comparisons, Contrasts, Connections

Compare Jeffers's themes to Euripides's, whose tragedies he used and "adapted" as in Jeffers's Broadway hit "Medea." He follows the Greek closely, but the differences are arresting.

Consider also Lucretius, whose version of Epicurus's materialism attracted Jeffers, who fused it with his pantheistic view of nature.

For another interesting comparison, look at Shelley, whose view of Prometheus and the poet as legislator are reflected in Jeffers. Jeffers's incest theme has been traced to Shelley.

Nietzsche's philosophy appears to have attracted but not to have held Jeffers. Nietzsche's *Thus Spake Zarathustra, Beyond Good and Evil,* and *The Birth of Tragedy* would be the main texts of interest.

Wallace Stevens's interest in the imagination, reality, and fictive constructs provides bases for comparison/contrast.

T. S. Eliot's use of mythic materials and the literary tradition to construct an authentic religious outlook suggests some interesting similarities and dissimilarities.

Eugene O'Neill was similarly preoccupied with Greek tragedy.

Theodore Roethke's mystical view of nature and of the spirit that resides in nature offers fertile possibilities for comparison/contrast.

W. B. Yeats's interest in towers, in social unrest versus change, and in the cycles of nature compare with those of Jeffers.

Ansel Adams's photographs of "Jeffers country" offer opportunities for discerning comparisons/contrasts between visual and literary texts.

Questions for Reading and Discussion/
Approaches to Writing

1. After reading the Jeffers poems included in the text (and any others of his you wish to look at), write two or three pages of response to them. In your brief paper, assume that you are a developer (real

estate or commercial, for example), or an environmentalist (perhaps a member of the Sierra Club or other similar group), or a TV evangelist, or some other role of your choice. You should imagine how you think the person you choose to be in your paper would most likely respond to Jeffers's work.

2. You have just been reading Jeffers, and your roommate or brother or sister or parent comes and says, "Reading Jeffers? What does he have to say? Should I read his poems?" Assuming that you and your interrogator are on good terms, write a compact essay summarizing what Jeffers says and include in your response to the last question why you make the recommendation you give. Saying simply "yes" or "no" or "you're too young (or old)" to the last question is to evade its point; develop a reasoned reply. Be specific.

Bibliography

For the instructor in survey courses, the handiest and most comprehensive source is Robert Brophy, *Robinson Jeffers*. Boise: Western Writers Series, 1973; James Karman, *Robinson Jeffers: Poet of California* (1987) is excellent for biographical information.

To keep abreast of Jeffers scholarship, one should consult *Robinson Jeffers Newsletter* (Occidental College, 1600 Campus Road, Los Angeles, CA 90041).

Robert Frost (1874–1963)

Contributing Editor: James Guimond

Classroom Issues and Strategies

Students generally respond well to the basic emotional or psychological experiences expressed in Frost's poems. Some of them—for example, ones who have had a philosophy course or two—may raise questions about the implications of poems like "Design." Students often have difficulty appreciating (a) the skill and subtlety with which Frost uses traditional poetic devices such as rhyme and meter; (b) the sparse pleasures he discovers in some of his rural and natural subjects; (c) the bleakness and/or ambiguity of his more "philosophical" poems. Sometimes they also have difficulty understanding that the values he presented in his poems were derived from a type of community or society that was very different from their own: one that was rural, fearful of change, distrustful of technology, proud of craftsmanship, and deeply committed to privacy and self-reliance.

Regarding the formal devices and ambiguity, there is no substitute for traditional "close reading." (Quotes from Frost's essays, "The Constant Symbol" and "The Figure a Poem Makes" can be helpful in this regard.) The sparse pleasures can be seen in poems like "The Pasture" and "The Investment," and the bleakness can be discerned in the endings of "Once by the Pacific" and "Desert Places." The social values can be seen in dramatic poems like "The Fear" and "The Ax-Helve," as well as in "Mending Wall."

When teaching the dramatic poems, it is helpful to discuss their plots and characters with students because Frost sometimes presents these elements in an oblique way.

Major Themes, Historical Perspectives, and Personal Issues

Major themes would include:

1. The limitations and isolation of the individual in either a social or natural environment, plus the related theme of how difficult it is for the self to understand existence.
2. The ambiguity of nature when it is considered as a source of wisdom.
3. Frost's sensitivity to the theme of entropy, doom, and extinction.

Frost usually deals with personal issues so covertly in his poetry that it is not very fruitful to discuss those topics in detail. If the teacher wishes to do so, however, he/she should consult Thompson's biography. For historical issues, the Cowley and O'Donnell essays in James Cox's *Robert Frost: A Collection of Critical Essays* are helpful.

Significant Form, Style, or Artistic Conventions

Special emphasis should be placed on:

1. His skill in synthesizing traditional formal devices with vernacular speech patterns and language.
2. His ability to develop metaphors.
3. How relatively "unmodern" or traditional he was in relation to some of his contemporaries.

Original Audience

I emphasize that during the 1920s, 1930s, and 1940s Frost had a strong appeal for a conservative readership who did not understand or appreciate modernism very well. Since such readers could be quite influential in academic, editing, and Pulitzer-Prize-judging circles, some of Frost's popularity should be considered in this context.

Comparisons, Contrasts, Connections

Contrasts with Wallace Stevens, William Carlos Williams, Ezra Pound, and T. S. Eliot are appropriate; and comparisons with Henry Wadsworth Longfellow, William Cullen Bryant, Edward Arlington Robinson, and the British Romantics and Georgians (e.g., Edward Thomas) can be helpful.

Questions for Reading and Discussion/
Approaches to Writing

1. (a) What would it be like to live on an isolated farm in 1900?
   (b) Find the rhymes in specific poems and discuss why Frost emphasized these words.
   (c) What are the emotional connotations of the images in certain poems?
   (d) Who is the speaker of the poem, and why is he/she speaking?
   (e) How does Frost develop a metaphor in an assigned poem?
2. (a) Comparison-contrast topics work well if they are focused on specific issues like free verse versus traditional meters.
   (b) What is Frost's persona and how does he develop it in a variety of poems?
   (c) How does Frost create conflict or tension in his poems and how does he resolve it?
   (d) How closely does Frost follow his own poetic "rules" as he states them in "The Figure a Poem Makes"?
   (e) Compare the "philosophy of life" which is expressed in a poem like "Directive," "Design," or "Desert Places" with the ideas in an essay by Ralph Waldo Emerson, such as "Nature."

Bibliography

The books by Richard Poirier and Frank Lentricchia are particularly useful, and there are good essays in the critical anthologies edited by Cox, Gerber, Bloom, and Cady and Budd.

Sherwood Anderson (1876–1941)

Contributing Editor: Martha Curry

Classroom Issues and Strategies

Teachers should avoid three erroneous approaches to Sherwood Anderson's writings: regarding him primarily as a novelist, as a regional writer, or as author of only one important book, *Winesburg, Ohio*.

Regarding the first error: even in his best novel, *Poor White*, Anderson has difficulty sustaining plot and characterization. Anderson succeeds best in the smaller narrative form of the short story. "Death in the Woods" exemplifies many of the characteristics of the masterpieces of Anderson's story-telling art: direct authorial address to the reader; a circular, not linear, narrative structure; plot subordinated to characterization; simple style and vocabulary; and images drawn from elemental aspects of nature.

Regarding the second error: Although Anderson is one of the many regional writers who chronicle the changes that took place in the Midwest at the turn of the century as a result of industrialization, primary emphasis should be placed on his role as a story-teller.

Regarding the third error: Anthologies should never amputate individual stories from the artistic whole that is *Winesburg, Ohio*. Teachers should urge students to read all of *Winesburg*, pointing out that it is Anderson's best book-length work, but they should also tell students that many of Anderson's best stories are not found in that collection.

Winesburg, Ohio and *Death in the Woods* are not collections of isolated stories but, rather, short story cycles; that is, collections of stories with common themes, imagery, and tone, and often with common setting and characters. An understanding of the short story cycle, from Homer's *Odyssey* to Chaucer's *Canterbury Tales* to Joyce's *Dubliners* will help in understanding Anderson's work.

Students are amazed how contemporary Anderson is. He speaks to their concerns regarding loneliness, fragmentation, and the search for beauty and wholeness. They also are intrigued by the artistry that a small work like a short story can achieve.

Major Themes, Historical Perspectives, and Personal Issues

After they study "Death in the Woods," urge students to read the whole of *Winesburg*. Reading the story of Ma Grimes will prepare students for

Anderson's central theme of the grotesque. Ma Grimes is one of these grotesques, someone trapped in her own inability to find the "truth" of her life and thus to grow to maturity.

Regarding historical issues: Point out to the students that for ten to twelve years, as he claims both in his *Memoirs* (edited by Paul Rosenfeld [New York: Harcourt Brace, 1942], p. 286) and in his *Writer's Book* (edited by Martha Curry [Metuchen, N.J.: Scarecrow, 1975], p. 28), Anderson tried to write this story to his satisfaction. As we know from a note attached to a holograph housed with the Sherwood Anderson Papers in the Newberry Library in Chicago, Anderson's first attempt to write this story is a short sketch called "Death in the Forest." Chapter XII of *Tar: A Midwestern Childhood* (Cleveland: Press of Case Western Reserve University, 1969, pp. 129–41), also tells the story of an old woman's death in the woods on a snowy night. A slightly expanded version of this episode, told by a first-person narrator, appeared in *American Mercury* (IX, 7–13), in September of the same year, that is, 1926. Since the 1933 title story in the collection *Death in the Woods* is practically identical with the version of the story that appeared in *American Mercury*, we can assume that Anderson worked on "Death in the Woods" from the mid-1910s, the time he was writing the *Winesburg* stories, until 1926.

When we consider this background concerning the composition of "Death in the Woods," we can see that the story itself exemplifies Anderson's usual method of story-telling. Anderson writes and rewrites his stories until he is satisfied with them, just as his narrators try again and again to tell the "real" story hidden beneath surface events. "Death in the Woods," then, is a remarkable example of Anderson's method of composition as well as a remarkably unified short story.

Significant Form, Style, or Artistic Conventions

Attention should always be drawn to the importance of the narrator in Anderson's stories. The narrator in "Death in the Woods" is actually describing the creative method that Anderson uses in writing the story. The central character is not Ma Grimes but the mature narrator who looks back on earlier experiences: the sight of an old, oppressed woman trudging from her farm into town in order to obtain the necessary food for her men and animals; the time he worked for a German farmer who hired a "bound girl"; the moonlit winter night he saw half-wild dogs almost revert to wolves in the presence of the near-death of a human.

In order for the teacher to help students comprehend "the real story I am now trying to tell," the teacher must stress the role of the mature narrator as he struggles to weld his diverse experiences and images into a whole that will bring order out of their diffuseness and beauty out of their ugliness. All of her days Ma Grimes "fed animal life." Only at the end of the story does the reader realize that the most important life Ma Grimes fed was the creative life of the narrator. Thus, the story as a whole demonstrates, as Anderson explains in its final sentence, "why I have been impelled to try to tell the simple story over again." The reader feels, as the story comes to a close, that now, after perhaps ten or twelve years, Anderson has been able to create a beautifully unified work of art.

Comparisons, Contrasts, Connections

Since much of Anderson's fiction relies heavily on his own experiences, the best background materials for teaching "Death in the Woods," to my mind, are primary, not secondary, sources, although excellent critical articles on "Death in the Woods" can easily be found by means of the standard indexes. Nonetheless, the best background information still remains Anderson's own words. Anderson's three autobiographies, *Tar*, *A Story Teller's Story*, and *Memoirs*, all available in critical texts edited by Ray Lewis White, have excellent indexes that will lead the reader to the appropriate sections.

Questions for Reading and Discussion/ Approaches to Writing

1. Before the students have read the story, point out:
   (a) The various levels of the story: story of Ma Grimes, her relationship to the men and animals in the story, her role as "feeder" of life.
   (b) The function played by the dogs, both literal and symbolic.
   (c) Growth of the narrator from a young boy to a mature artist.
   (d) The difficulty the narrator has in telling the story.
   (e) The many images in the story, both from nature and from art.
2. I have had great success in having students write a short story or character sketch about one of the "grotesques" they meet in everyday life, someone they see on the bus or subway, in the supermarket or on the street, at home or in school. They must approach this character with great respect and love, as Anderson does, and try to imagine and then tell the character's story of isolation, fear, and, ultimately, of beauty.

Bibliography

Read: *Winesburg, Ohio*, a very short book. Several other stories in Maxwell Geismar's *Sherwood Anderson: Short Stories*.

If there is time, read: Chapter XII of *Tar*. "Death in the Forest," edited by William Miller and printed as an appendix to Ray Lewis White's critical edition of *Tar*, pp. 231-36. Selections from White's critical edition of Sherwood Anderson's *Memoirs*.

Chapter I of *Representative Short Story Cycles of the Twentieth Century* by Forest L. Ingram (The Hague: Mouton) for Ingram's theory of the short story cycle.

The Chicago Renaissance in American Letters: A Critical History by Bernard Duffey (Westport, Conn.: Greenwood Press, 1954), Chapter 10, "Three Voices of the Liberation," about Francis Hackett, Harriet Monroe, and Margaret Anderson and the little magazines they founded, and Chapter 11, "The Struggle for Affirmation—Anderson, Sandburg, Lindsay."

Theodore Dreiser (1871–1945)

Contributing Editors: James M. Hutchisson and James L. W. West III

Classroom Issues and Strategies

Dreiser's style is unconventional. If students have heard of him, they've heard that he's a clumsy stylist. They also will have difficulty understanding Ida's dilemma in "Typhoon."

The instructor should explain that Dreiser was trained as a journalist whose main duty was to record the who, what, where, when, why, and how of a story. Graceful style was a small concern. In fact, some of Dreiser's verbal clumsiness was more or less deliberate. His writing possesses its particular power, its ability to move the emotions, in part because of its bluntness, its lack of grace. Try to imagine "Typhoon" told by a facile stylist, for example, by F. Scott Fitzgerald. It would lose much of its voltage.

It's a good idea to show students how thoroughly trapped and damned Ida Zobel is by an illicit pregnancy. Children of the 1990s will likely try to foist their own standards back onto her time and place. Students identify with this story because they feel much peer pressure in matters of sex. Ask them to try to argue sympathetically for Haupt-fuhrer. Can it be done? Where did Dreiser's sympathies lie?

Another good theme to discuss is Ida's being "forgiven" by the public, her almost automatic innocence before the court, and her adoption by the wealthy socialite. Dreiser is indicating some things here about the influence of the fourth estate over the administration of justice. We sympathize with Ida, of course, but her exoneration for the killing is suspect. Certainly she still feels great guilt; it is the major motivation for her suicide.

Major Themes, Historical Perspectives, and Personal Issues

Like virtually all of Dreiser's major characters, Ida Zobel in "Typhoon" is a seeker. She searches for beauty and love in a repressive, unenlightened society. She is ignorant and at the mercy of instincts and drives that she does not understand. She is naive enough to be duped by Haupt-fuhrer largely because of her obsessively sheltered upbringing. This was ever one of Dreiser's major themes—his hatred of repressiveness and its consequences. The theme fits in well with the general rebelliousness and nonconformity of American writers of his generation and the generation following it.

Significant Form, Style, or Artistic Conventions

Dreiser is best taught as a writer who held philosophically conflicting ideas in suspension simultaneously. His best writing springs from the tensions generated by these opposing ideas. On the one hand he was virtually a textbook naturalist; on the other, a mystic, romantic, and sentimental writer. He was also a left-leaning social activist, a stance which, strictly speaking, is incompatible with naturalistic beliefs.

Original Audience

The instructor should emphasize that this story was magazine fiction, written to sell. In it, Dreiser was dealing with sensational tabloid material. The story was written in 1926 in order to follow up on the great success of *An American Tragedy*, published in 1925 and also based on a real murder case. The story borrows elements from the *Tragedy*—also from *Sister Carrie* (1900) and *Jennie Gerhardt* (1911), Dreiser's first two novels.

Comparisons, Contrasts, Connections

This story is written in Dreiser's late style, a fragmented, free-association style that attempts to accomplish many of the same things that stream-of-consciousness writers like James Joyce and William Faulkner were trying to do during the 1920s. Dreiser may have known of *Ulysses*; Faulkner wasn't really on the scene yet. Dreiser *had* been reading Freud and was much interested in the workings of the subconscious mind. One can teach this story as an example of early stream-of-consciousness writing.

Questions for Reading and Discussion/ Approaches to Writing

1. Ask students to reflect on the following before class: guilt and innocence; "peer pressure"; the narrative voice—is it slanted or objective?
2. Have them read a big-city newspaper of the period on microfilm and find similarly sensational material. They might compare the style of reporting ca. 1926 with the style used today and reflect on what this says about changes in American society over the past sixty years.

   Another useful topic is a discussion of free will as it operates (or does not) in "Typhoon." Are these characters in control of their destinies?

   A good short theme can be developed on the last line of the story. How does it resonate back through the entire narrative?

Bibliography

Gerber, Philip. "Theodore Dreiser." Biographical sketch in *Dictionary of Literary Biography*, Vol. 9. Detroit: Gale, 1981.

Griffin, Joseph. *The Small Canvas: An Introduction to Dreiser's Short Stories.* Fairleigh Dickinson, 1985.

Hutchisson, James M. "The Composition and Publication of 'Another American Tragedy': Dreiser's 'Typhoon.'" *Papers of the Bibliographical Society of America* 81: 1 (1987).

Edna St. Vincent Millay (1892–1950)

Contributing Editor: John J. Patton

Classroom Issues and Strategies

Students have few problems reading Millay's poetry because the poet is forthright in expressing her emotions, ideas, and experiences. Obviously such references as those to Euclid and Endymion require explanation. Occasionally the diction needs some explication because of Millay's fondness for archaic and Latinate words.

Not much more is required than the teacher's ability to clarify some allusions and an occasional word or phrase. Any teacher of modern American literature should also have no problems with the references to city life and to issues of the times, which are generously sprinkled throughout Millay's work. As for accessibility, some benefit will come from placing Millay in the context of the poetry of the 1920s and 1930s as one of those like, for instance, Robert Frost, Archibald MacLeish, and Edward Arlington Robinson, who carried forward the more traditional verse form and techniques in the face of the experimentalism of T. S. Eliot, Ezra Pound, Wallace Stevens, and William Carlos Williams. Millay also wrote on subjects that have a long history in English verse—the natural scene, romantic love, impermanence and death, and even poetry itself and the poet. Some students may therefore possibly view her as "old-fashioned" in contrast to the more experimental poets of her time. What must be emphasized is that Millay and other technically conservative poets flourished alongside the "New Poets," the modernists, and similar poets and that they produced poetry with less emphasis on intellectualization and more on overt feeling. It is characterized by forthrightness of expression, clarity of diction, and avoidance of ambiguity and of the esoteric and erudite as a source for figurative language.

Millay is one poet in particular whose work benefits from being read aloud in order to do justice to its melodic qualities. In her own recording of some of her poems, Millay emphasizes the song-like nature of much of her verse. Teachers should play this recording for students or, of course, have them read the poems aloud themselves.

Students often raise gender issues. For example, they ask whether it makes any difference that the poet is a woman. Does gender show itself in any apparent way, allowing for those instances where the poet deliberately displays it as in the speaking voice used or the pronoun gender? How is Millay's stance as a "liberated" woman shown in her poetry if at all? Another issue is relevance. In what ways are Millay's poems relevant to today's lives? Are her concerns significant to present-day readers? Is it readily apparent that her poetry dates largely from the 1920s and 1930s?

Major Themes, Historical Perspectives, and Personal Issues

Millay's interest in heterosexual relationships is a major theme in her poetry, whether between husband and wife, as in "An Ancient Gesture," or between disaffected lovers, as in "The Spring and the Fall." Few American poets in this century have written on this subject with the combined artistry and diversity of Millay. "Love is not all" and "Oh, sleep forever in the latmian cave" are from *Fatal Interview*, a fifty-two sonnet sequence that deals with the course of a love affair from beginning to end.

Millay should not, however, be associated exclusively with this kind of poetry. Another major theme is the integrity of the individual, which Millay valued highly for herself as well as for others. "The Return" describes a man who has apparently "sold out" in order to escape into the illusory "comfort" of nature. In "Here Lies, and None to Mourn Him" Millay is describing a humankind that has fatally compromised itself by, perhaps, a reliance on technology (others see it as a comment on war).

A related theme, the integrity of the artist, is touched on in "On Thought in Harness." Millay also had a high degree of social consciousness. She spoke out against the execution in 1926 of the anarchists Sacco and Vanzetti, she wrote about the wars in Spain and China, and she devoted a volume of verse, *Make Bright the Arrows*, to concern about World War II. "Here lies, and none to mourn him" is one of an eighteen-sonnet sequence in this volume.

Significant Form, Style, or Artistic Conventions

Millay's relationship to the poetry of her time should be discussed, as well as her antecedents in verse and her achievements in the sonnet and the lyric. Her immediate contemporaries include notably E. E. Cummings, T. S. Eliot, Robert Frost, Amy Lowell, Marianne Moore, Ezra Pound, and Edward Arlington Robinson. Millay, like Frost and Robinson, was a conservative in verse form and technique, a "traditionalist." Although highly aware of the work of her contemporaries, she steered clear of all "schools," such as imagists, modernists, objectivists, etc. Some critics place her in a line of descent from such late-nineteenth-century English poets as Robert Browning and Algernon Swinburne.

A widely read person, Millay absorbed influences from sixteenth- and seventeenth-century English poets, hence her devotion to the sonnet form, in which she has no peer in all of American literature. The sonnet "His stalk the dark delphinium" is noteworthy because Millay uses tetrameter verse rather than the more common pentameter. Millay's lyrics display a wide variety of form. Students may gauge her breadth in lyric poetry by contrasting the mixed verse feet and line lengths in "Spring" and its abrupt turns of phrase with the melodic flow of "The Spring and the Fall" and its regularity of form.

Original Audience

Millay continues to appeal to a large audience, as shown by the publication in the fall of 1987 of a new edition of her sonnets. A very large audience of readers in her own time admired her frequent outspokenness, her freshness of attitude, her liberated views as a woman, and the reflection in her poetry of an intensely contemporary sensibility. She is quintessentially modern in her attitude and viewpoint even if her language is often redolent of earlier poets. Although it is true that Millay's poetry has great appeal to women readers, she must not be either presented or viewed as writing solely for women because of the evident limitations it would place on appreciation of her accomplishment.

Comparisons, Contrasts, Connections

To illustrate Millay's mastery of the sonnet, a comparison should be made with Keats as her nearest equivalent. Both display the same ease and control in the form. The sonnets of Sir Philip Sidney, for one, may be used to show Millay's historical connection with the great sonneteering tradition in English. Direct comparison with Shakespeare would be useful only to illustrate her range of achievement—181 sonnets in the new edition.

Millay's lyric poetry can be compared with that of several late-nineteenth-century English lyricists, such as Dowson, D. G. Rossetti, and Housman (Browning and Swinburne have already been mentioned).

Her relationship to older American poets is less clear. She seems to have been little interested in them. Commentators have related her work in ways to that of Emerson and Holmes and perhaps some of Whittier and Longfellow, but not at all to Whitman and Dickinson. As noted above, Millay stands apart from the experiments and innovations in verse in her own time. She should be more meaningfully compared with

Robinson, MacLeish, Frost, and Masters, among others, who, while employing conservative prosodic techniques, expressed a contemporary point of view.

Questions for Reading and Discussion/ Approaches to Writing

1. "Spring": What is suggested about life by images of the empty cup and uncarpeted flight of stairs?

   "The Return": Why is Earth not able to comfort the despairing Man?

   "Here lies, and none to mourn him": What seems to have "cut down" Man (the human race)?

   "Love is not all": Although love is not "all," would the poet easily give it up?

   "On Thought in Harness": Explain the significance of the title with reference to the poem.

   "Oh, sleep forever": Restate the last two lines in your own words.

   "His stalk the dark delphinium": Explain why "all will be easier" when the mind grows its own "iron cortex."

2. The student who selects Millay could read more of her work and then write about a major theme in the work.

   Another possibility is that a student might read further in her sonnets, read sonnets by others, e.g., Sidney, Donne, and Keats, and then write an analytical paper on differences and/or similarities in form, predominant subject matter, diction, etc.

   Another assignment would be to read other American women poets of the time (Crapsey, Teasdale, H.D., Wiley, Amy Lowell) to show any similarities based on their sex.

Bibliography

The following items are recommended because most teachers should have little trouble in gaining access to them and they provide a cross section of opinion and comment:

Dash, Joan. "Edna St. Vincent Millay." In *A Life of One's Own*, New York: Harper and Row, 1973, 116–227.

Flanner, Hildergarde. "Two Poets: Jeffers and Millay." In *After the Genteel Tradition*, edited by Malcolm Cowley, 124–33. New York: W. W. Norton, 1937.

Gassman, Janet. "Edna St. Vincent Millay: 'Nobody's Own.' " *Colby Library Quarterly* 9 (1971): 297–310.

Gray, James. *Edna St. Vincent Millay*. Minneapolis: University of Minnesota Press, 1967. Forty-six small pages provide a thoughtful overview.

Hillyer, Robert. "Of Her Essential Voice and Spirit." *New York Times Book Review* (15 April 1954): 5.

Kelmans, Patricia. "Being Born A Woman." *Colby Library Quarterly* 15 (1979): 7–18.

Salter, Mary Jo. "The Heart Is Slow to Learn." *New Criterion* (April 1922): 23–29.

Sprague, Rosemary. "Edna St. Vincent Millay." In *Imaginary Gardens: A Study of Five American Poets*. Philadelphia: Chilton, 1969. 135–82.

Walker, Cheryl. "Women on the Market: Edna St. Vincent Millay's Body Language." *Masks Outrageous and Austere*. Bloomington: University of Indiana Press, 1991. 135–164.

Wilson, Edmund. "Epilogue 1952: Edna St. Vincent Millay." In *The Shores of Light*, 744–93. New York: Farrar, Strauss, and Young, 1952.

Alienation and Literary Experimentation

Ezra Pound (1885–1972)

Contributing Editor: Betsy Erkkila

Classroom Issues and Strategies

Pound's announcement of the principles of imagism in "A Retrospect" provides an excellent introduction to the poetics of literary modernism. Like Hemingway in prose, Pound turns away from the "emotional slither" and abstract rhetoric of romantic and Victorian writers toward an emphasis on precision and concision in language and imagery. The poem "In a Station of the Metro" puts Pound's imagist theory into practice. Pound was struck by the beauty of a crowd of faces he observed in the Metro at La Concorde in Paris; he tried to represent the experience first in a thirty-line poem; then through a Kandinsky-like splash of color; finally, he says, he found the best form for the experience in the model of Japanese *haiku* poetry. The poem interweaves subjective impression with objective expression, presenting in miniature the controlling myth of Pound's work: the discovery of light amid darkness, fertility amid waste, figured in the myth of Persephone in the Underworld.

In teaching "Hugh Selwyn Mauberley" and *The Cantos* you might want to prepare a handout explicating some of the allusions in the poem. You can use Ruthven's *Guide to Personae*, Brooker's *Student's Guide to the Selected Poems of Ezra Pound*, and Kearns's *Guide to Ezra Pound's Selected Cantos*. Begin by asking students to think about the overall import of "Hugh Selwyn Mauberley." On the broadest level, the poem is a compelling critique of the modern age; more specifically, it is about the plight of the artist, and of Pound in particular, in the modern world. Look at the ways the opening section on "E.P." works formally. The poem moves not by linear progression but by the juxtaposition of images as emotional and intellectual complexes; meaning develops not through direct authorial statement but by engaging the reader in a continual process of interpretation.

Major Themes, Historical Perspectives, and Personal Issues

While Pound buries the aesthete figure of his early period in the opening section of "Hugh Selwyn Mauberley," he does not renounce the value of artistic creation as a source of personal and social renewal; he represents and asserts the enduring value of beauty and song in "Envoi," which is modeled on the poem "Go, Lovely Rose" by the seventeenth-century English poet Edmund Waller.

The postwar context of the poem should be emphasized; sections IV and V contain one of the most negative and moving chants against war in modern literature.

Significant Form, Style, or Artistic Conventions

If Pound is the first or only modern writer you are discussing, you might want to begin by discussing the relation between an increasingly complex and allusive form and content among modern writers and the increasing isolation and alienation of the artist in the modern world. Pound went abroad both physically and mentally in his early period, seeking models and masks in past literatures, including Greek (Homer), Latin (Virgil, Ovid, Catullus), Italian (Dante, Arnaut Daniel, Guido Calvalcanti), French Provençal (Bertran de Born), and Chinese (Li Po, Confucius). During the war years, as he began to turn his attention toward the contemporary world, he also turned backward toward the native tradition of Walt Whitman. This turn is evident in the raw and comic exuberance of "Salutation the Second" and in "A Pact," where Pound seeks to come to terms with Walt Whitman.

Comparisons, Contrasts, Connections

Pound's evocation of war might be compared with Eliot's *The Waste Land*, Hemingway's *A Farewell to Arms*, and "The Walls Do Not Fall" in H.D.'s *Trilogy*.

After "Hugh Selwyn Mauberley," Pound turned his main attention to his epic *Cantos*, which he worked on for the remainder of his life. In a letter to W. B. Yeats, he said he intended to write one hundred cantos, modeled on a Bach fugue: "There will be no plot, no chronicle of events, no logic of discourse, but two themes, the Descent into Hades from Homer, a Metamorphosis from Ovid, and mixed with these, medieval or modern historical characters." As Pound's comment suggests, the poem has three analogues: an Odyssean journey, modeled on Homer's *Odyssey*; an ascent through Inferno and Purgatory toward the light of Paradiso, modeled on Dante's *Divine Comedy*; and from Ovid's *Metamorphosis* a series of "magic moments" in which divine energies are revealed in the physical world.

Pound speaks in a personal voice that anticipates the confessional strain in the poems of Allen Ginsberg, Robert Lowell, and Sylvia Plath.

Questions for Reading and Discussion/
Approaches to Writing

Ask students to note how Canto XLV examines the relationship between politics and poetry. Normally, the students respond positively to this poem as a chant against the commercialization of the modern age; in fact, the poem might be compared to Ginsberg's chant against Moloch in section II of *Howl*. Ask the students if there is any problem with the term *usury*, which Pound defined as "A charge for the use of purchasing power, levied without regard to production; often without regard to the possibilities of production." Discuss the ways the charging of interest became—through Christian prohibition—associated with the Jewish people. Is Pound's chant against usury also a chant against the Jews; and insofar as it is, how does this affect our reading and evaluation of the poem?

This discussion should raise some of the same questions about the relationship between politics and poetry, fascism and modernism, that were at the center of the debate about Pound receiving the Bollingen Award for the *Pisan Cantos* in 1949. The same questions, it might be pointed out, are at the center of the reconstruction of American literature. The "Pound Problem" is a telling instance, not only of the ways poetry is political, but of what happens when the poem's politics are "out of tune" with the politics of the dominant culture. One might ask how Pound's anti-Semitism differed in kind and degree from the racism and anti-Semitism that one finds in other major American writers. And why was Pound singled out for persecution at this time?

The "pull down they vanity" section of Canto LXXXI in the *Pisan Cantos* reveals a new attitude of *humilitas* and *humanitas*; Pound speaks in a personal voice that anticipates the confessional strain in the poems of Allen Ginsberg, Robert Lowell, and Sylvia Plath. The *Cantos* are incomplete and inconclusive: They end with two fragments, Cantos CXVII and CXX, which are like the *Cantos* themselves a figure of the fragmentation and incompleteness of the modern world. Pound's final words are at once an apology and an admission of failure: "Let those I love forgive/what I have made." Ask the students if they agree with Pound's final assessment of his epic. Is there, ultimately, any value in his work?

Bibliography

See works cited in the section on "Classroom Issues and Strategies."

Amy Lowell (1874–1925)

Contributing Editor: Lillian Faderman

Classroom Issues and Strategies

I generally use Amy Lowell's work to explore two major issues: the imagist movement as it was imported into the United States and the treatment of lesbian material by a lesbian poet who felt the need to be more closeted in her writing than in her life. While the subject of

Lowell's imagism is easy to introduce, the subject of homosexuality in her life and writing has been more difficult because students are sometimes uncomfortable with the topic, and they are ignorant of the history of censorship and homophobia in the United States. The study of Lowell's life and work presents a good opportunity to open these important subjects to discussion.

Lowell's lesbianism and the ways in which it is manifested in her writing generally stimulate some of the liveliest discussions of the course. For example, some students question, as did the critics who dampened her popularity in the years immediately after her death, whether a writer who is homosexual can have anything significant to say to the heterosexual majority. My approach is to draw an analogy (or, with any luck, to have students in the class draw the analogy) to the profound impact on white readers of works by writers of color. "Differentness" becomes the theme of the discussion.

This preliminary discussion of ethnic and racial difference and its impact on writing and reading leads to a discussion of sexual difference and its parallel impact. Either members of the class or I will bring up other writers with whom most of the class may be familiar and whose work they considered no less effective because those writers were gay or lesbian (for example, Walt Whitman, Carson McCullers, Tennessee Williams, Elizabeth Bishop). The focus of the discussion then turns to the value of borrowing the spectacles of one who is different in order to glance at the world. The session is useful for all students but especially important for homosexual students whose lives are seldom recognized or affirmed in classroom discussion.

Major Themes, Historical Perspectives, and Personal Issues

In a discussion of Lowell's life and work, I introduce two kinds of history—literary and social—and I show the ways in which they mesh. I first focus on the history of the imagist movement that I began when the class read Pound and H.D.; then I explore what attention Lowell garnered for imagism in the United States, why and how she succeeded, and how she modified imagism in her work. I also look at her creation of the dramatic monologue and discuss the historical background of public literary performance.

I am equally concerned with raising the issue of self-censorship and encoding in Lowell's poetry, especially in those poems in which she does not create a literary persona but rather speaks in what appears to be her own voice. To this end I talk about the shifting notion of "standards of decency" and censorship laws. I talk at some length about Lowell's own erotic and affectional relationships with women, and the discrepancy between her brash self-presentation in public and her subdued self-presentation in her autobiographical writing, such as the 1919 series "Two Speak Together," from which many of the Lowell selections in *The Heath Anthology* are taken. Lowell's self-censorship motives are revealed to the class through a letter she wrote to D. H. Lawrence, whose patron she was, scolding him for endangering his literary reputation by trying to publish material such as the lesbian scene in his novel *The Rainbow*, which got him into trouble with the censors:

> I know there is no use in counselling you to make any concessions to public opinions in your books and, although I regret sincerely that you cut yourself off from being published by an outspokenness which the English public does not understand, I regret it not in itself . . . but simply because it keeps the world from knowing what a great novelist you are. I think you could top them all if you would be a little more reticent on this one subject [explicit sexuality]. You need not change your attitude a particle, you can simply use the india rubber in certain places, and then you can come into your own as it ought to be. . . . When one is surrounded by prejudice and blindness, it seems to me that the only thing to do is to get over in spite of it and not constantly run foul of these same prejudices which, after all, hurts oneself and the spreading of one's work, and does not do a thing to right the prejudice.

The class then explores the ways in which Lowell appears to have taken her own advice. If the beloved in the "Two Speak Together" series is Ada Russell, as Lowell admitted to John Livingston Lowes, Lowell herself may be presumed to be the speaker. I introduce the topic of encoding and its ubiquitousness in homosexual literature of earlier eras. How does Lowell disguise the fact of her gender and thus the lesbian content in these poems? How does she use her "india rubber"? What in terms of her sexual identification is hidden and what is overt in her poem about women writers, "The Sisters"?

Finally, I look with my class at the treatment of heterosexuality in Lowell's poetry. Students are often surprised when they realize that "Patterns," a poem that speaks quite explicitly about a woman's heterosexual desires, was published only a decade and a half after the end of Victorianism. Many students praise Lowell's courage in her use of this material. Others suggest that her heterosexual erotic images lack originality and mimic the stuff of cheap romance novels. (One student compared them to the clichés of Harlequin romances of our era: pink and silver women surrendering their soft and willing bodies to heavy-booted men in dashing uniforms.) In general, my students come to prefer the short lyric poems whose material seems fresher and more deeply felt than her dramatic monologues such as "Patterns," which, for decades, remained the only of Lowell's poems to be frequently anthologized.

Significant Form, Style, or Artistic Conventions

With regard to style and form, I spend most of the Lowell sessions considering her as an imagist or an "Amygist." We discuss her interest in orientalism, which predated her Pound years. If I have not already done so, I introduce the class to the haiku and tanka forms. I also bring in some examples of "imagist" poems Lowell wrote even before she learned of the existence of the imagist movement.

We also discuss Lowell's other poetic innovations, such as her polyphonic prose (prose poetry) and her interest in some of her poetry in the folk materials of non-Euro-Americans. This emphasis leads to a further consideration of how writers who are different often develop a literary interest in other forms of differentness. Finally, we discuss the dramatic monologue form and the use Lowell makes of it in "Patterns" and other poems.

Comparisons, Contrasts, Connections

Lowell's imagism should, of course, be compared to that of Pound and H.D. Her dramatic monologues should be compared to Pound's *personae* and to the Victorian British author Robert Browning's *dramatis personae*. The class will also find a comparative discussion of Lowell and Gertrude Stein interesting. Both saw themselves (and were) movers and shakers in the business of literature. Both were extremely interested in experimental literary techniques and had a coterie of young writers around them whom they helped and influenced. Both were approximately the same height and weight. Both had women lovers who served them as muses, secretaries, critics, housekeepers, and guards against an intrusive public. Astrology buffs in the class will be amused to learn that Lowell and Stein were both born in 1874, in the eastern United States, less than a week apart. On a more serious note, the ways in which Lowell encodes her lesbian material should be compared to Stein's lesbian encoding and to H.D.'s treatment of her own bisexuality in her writing.

Questions for Reading and Discussion/ Approaches to Writing

1. My study questions emphasize the form and content of her work as well as the particular challenges she faced as one who wrote poetry that was often erotic while she felt constrained to conceal the lesbian source of her eroticism. I encourage students to pay attention to how Lowell's imagist techniques are manifested in many of her long poems as well as in her shorter, more tanka-like poems. My questions also draw attention to the feminist message in Lowell's work (while I point out that, paradoxically, she rejected an affiliation with the feminist movement of her day, insisting—as did Gertrude Stein—that such concerns had little to do with her). Finally, my questions address the subject of encodement in literature and the ways in which Lowell, in particular, encodes.

2. I allow my students who wish to write on Lowell a choice of approaches. Several students who have elected to write analyses of her longer poems have been interested in exposing Lowell as a feminist writer, focusing on "Patterns" (an expression of a woman's right to sexual desire, a complaint against the ways in which women are constrained) and "The Sisters" (how women writers "think-back"—to use Virginia Woolf's phrase—through their female predecessors).

My students have also been interested in writing comparisons between Lowell and H.D., or Lowell and Pound as imagists.

Lowell's work often inspires students to ask if they can do a creative writing assignment in which they try their hand at the haiku, the tanka, and then Western imagism.

Some of the most successful assignments have been those that explore gender encoding in Lowell's short poems: for example, how do we know (or do we know?) that the speaker (who is the lover) in the "Two Speak Together" series is a woman?

Bibliography

From the years immediately following her death until the 1970s, Lowell was largely neglected by critics. Students will be interested in exploring the grounds on which she was dismissed after having been so successful during her lifetime. Therefore, the following works will be of historical interest: Clement Wood, *Amy Lowell*. New York: Harold Vinal, 1926; Hervey Allen, "Amy Lowell as a Poet," *Saturday Review of Literature*, 3:28 (February 5, 1927), 557–58; Winfield Townley Scott, "Amy Lowell Ten

Years After," *New England Quarterly*, 8 (June 1935), 320–30. The books included in the bibliography that follows the Lowell section in the text were, for the most part, influenced by the resurgence of interest in women writers that came about through the feminist movement of the 1970s. In the present climate, where a consensus is being built to reconsider neglected authors whose work was of worth, scholars are again turning their attention to Lowell, but as of this writing no major new book on Lowell has been produced.

Gertrude Stein (1874–1946)

Contributing Editor: Cynthia Secor

Classroom Issues and Strategies

Many students will have heard that Stein is "difficult" so they come to her work expecting not to understand. They expect "style" and "experimental strategies," but not content. There exists no cottage industry "explicating" her difficulty, so one does not have easy sources of data such as *Readers' Guide to Gertrude Stein* to which to refer students. In addition, her lesbianism and feminism put off some readers, if they get far enough into the text to see it.

One needs to begin by saying that these texts are the creation of an extremely well-educated woman—an American, a Jew, the child of immigrant parents, a lesbian, and a feminist—whose life experience and literary production bridge the Victorian and modern eras.

Her two enduring concerns are to portray the experience of woman and to explore what it means to present the fact or act of perception—which can be described as how we organize what we see.

How Gertrude Stein organizes what she sees and how she presents "seeing": this is probably enough metaphysics for a beginning.

When students see that the texts are about something, something very serious and important to the author, they relax and "read" the text.

The texts included here allow you to trace the evolution of Stein's style from realistic and naturalistic through abstract and cubist to simple and straightforward. You can also compare and contrast her representation over the years of women, femininity, and culturally determined depictions of women. Bridgman (p. 104) notes this preference in subject matter. Why and how she chose to depict women adds a new dimension to American literary history. My students have enjoyed "opening up" the style only to discover that it really is about "something."

Consider asking your students to write about a subject matter of their own choice in each of the styles represented in the anthology. Ask them to choose something from their own experience that they think will "fit" with that style. Have them comment on what they have learned from the exercise. Does the style determine a range of appropriate experiences? Can you truly use her style with your experience? How does the "fit" fit? When does it not? Did you learn something new about your experience by "seeing" it as Stein would have at the time she used that style? The underlying point here is that her "style" literally changes from text to text. The style is specific to the matter at hand.

Students become engaged with Stein's ideas, values, and experience as a woman. Her response to war interests them. They are interested in her ideas about democracy, race, geniuses, about why ordinary people are worth so much serious attention. They like the children's stories, when we get into what it means to write for children. Detective story buffs get into her ideas about the detecting mind.

My experience has been that once students believe she is serious, they give her serious attention and are fascinated by how she chooses to present the fabric of her life. Hers is a powerful mind and they respond to it. How she turns marginality into centrality is of interest to most of us.

Even so, their question continues to be, "Why is she so hard?"

Major Themes, Historical Perspectives, and Personal Issues

Gertrude Stein is interested in:

> what it is to be an American
> what it is to be a woman
> how people see things
> how people tell stories

She describes her own ordinary experience.

She writes about ordinary, commonplace people in such a manner that the absolute uniqueness of each is captured. This is her contribution to the American tradition of democracy and individualism.

She writes extensively about her life, and her growth into her life, as a major American writer of the twentieth century. She comments on culture, art, politics, and sexuality.

Significant Form, Style, or Artistic Conventions

Begin by showing how her work grows out of the American tradition of realism and naturalism.

Then show how she, in a typically twentieth-century fashion, becomes concerned with how we see what we see. As an American, a first-generation child of European Jewish parents, a woman, a lesbian, a feminist, and an artist, she is fully aware of marginality and centrality and ponders the process by which we organize experience and assign centrality, value, and worth. Remember that she is educated at Harvard University in philosophy and at the Johns Hopkins University in medicine.

She is fully aware that what she is has not historically been treated as fully human, fully civilized. Her literary strategies of a lifetime can be seen to be attempts to portray each life, each point of view, as fully real, absolutely present, and of equal value.

Original Audience

I focus on her willingness to continue writing serious and challenging texts without benefit of a wide contemporary audience. She says she writes for herself and strangers.

Serious writers, common readers, the audiences of her operas, and readers of her autobiographies and essays are variously able to articulate what attracts them and compels their attention. She tries very hard not to be influenced by "audiences."

Comparisons, Contrasts, Connections

Stein is so self-consciously American and so well read that it is fruitful to take her poetry and prose and set it beside such writers as Dickinson, Whitman, James, Wharton, Norris, Dreiser, and see what she does with related subject matter—her forms are radical critiques of the relation between content and form in American naturalism, romanticism, and realism.

Flaubert and Mann are interesting set beside her early prose works. Similarly Hemingway's early short stories are profitably set beside hers. One can see how she evolves a prose style in which the subject matter and the mode of narrative are about equal in weight. It helps to see that she is looking steadily at the "real" world, as she evolves her prose and poetic (and hybrid) conventions.

Cluster T. S. Eliot, Joyce, Pound, and Stein. Often these male contemporaries are on her mind as she does something different. She does not share their interest in the past. She evolves a presentation of female persons independent of patriarchal myth.

Questions for Reading and Discussion/ Approaches to Writing

1. I ask them to recall what was happening politically, socially, and artistically from 1874 to 1946. What events, achievements, personalities, movements, and concepts associated with those years have a bearing on how we perceive women, Americans, immigrants, Jews, lesbians, and geniuses? This lets us look at who "we" are, what we "see," and how it provides for us a context for understanding what Stein is doing with her writing.

2. (a) Consider *Tender Buttons*, "Preciosilla," and *Four Saints in Three Acts*. Characterize Stein's "modernist" strategies. T. S. Eliot and James Joyce add layers of meaning and mythic reference; she seems bent on stripping meaning away and living in a literal present represented as fully as possible. Is this a strategy for writing beyond patriarchy rather than shoring it up or representing fully its complexity?

   (b) Stein's impulse to describe, speculate, and pontificate places her firmly in the tradition of Emerson and others. She writes about herself as a Jew, a lesbian, a westerner, an American, an expatriate, and a bourgeois Victorian lady of limited but comfortable means. How does she expand our definition of American individualism?

   (c) How does one integrate her comparatively large body of erotic poetry into the American literary tradition? What does it mean that a major American woman writer born in 1874 writes extensively about sex, and that her partner is a woman? How does it enlarge our concept of female sexuality and of female experience?

   (d) It is useful to talk about the tradition of female biography, autobiography, letters, and memoirs, and how this differs from the male tradition. Stein both writes directly about her experience (*Everybody's Autobiography, Paris France*) and incorporates it into fiction (*The Making of Americans*, "Ada," and *Ida, A Novel*). How does she extend our understanding of this mode?

   (e) A number of Stein's works, including *Four Saints in Three Acts* and *The Mother of Us All*, have been set to music or produced for the stage. What critical language is appropriate for discussing prose and poetry that experiment with generic conventions and concepts normally applied to scene design, ballet, opera, or piano compositions?

(f) What does it mean that forty years after her death, we still do not have major editions of her letters; her notebooks; scholarly editions of her works; adequate representation in teaching anthologies; study guides that would make her obscurity as clear as we find that of T. S. Eliot, James Joyce, and Ezra Pound?

(g) What did Stein gain and lose by living in a foreign country, where the daily language was other than the language of her childhood, her art, and her domestic life? Hemingway, Wharton, and Baldwin also lived abroad. Why? What other American writers chose to live abroad for long periods of time? Why?

(h) What does it mean that over half of her work was published posthumously and that most of her serious work, when published in her lifetime, was not widely read or understood? What comparison can be made with Emily Dickinson's accomplishment, limitations, and reputation?

Bibliography

Bassoff, Bruce. "Gertrude Stein's 'Composition as Explanation.' " *Twentieth Century Literature: Gertrude Stein Issue* 24, no. 1 (Spring 1978): 76–80.

Benstock, Shari. *Women of the Left Bank: Paris, 1900–1940*. Austin: University of Texas Press, 1986. Chapter Five.

Dubnick, Randa. *The Structure of Obscurity: Gertrude Stein, Language, and Cubism*. Urbana and Chicago: University of Illinois Press, 1984. Chapters Two and Five.

Katz, Leon. "Weininger and *The Making of Americans.*" *Twentieth Century Literature: Gertrude Stein Issue* 24, no. 1 (Spring 1978): 8–26.

Kostelanetz, Richard. *The Yale Gertrude Stein*. New Haven and London: Yale University Press, 1980. Introduction.

Secor, Cynthia. "Gertrude Stein: The Complex Force of Her Femininity." In *Women, the Arts, and the 1920s in Paris and New York*, edited by Kenneth W. Wheeler and Virginia Lee Lussier, 27–35. New Brunswick: Transaction Books, 1982.

——. "*Ida*, A Great American Novel." *Twentieth Century Literature: Gertrude Stein Issue* 24, no. 1 (Spring 1978): 96–107.

Sutherland, Donald. *Gertrude Stein: A Biography of Her Work*. New Haven: Yale University Press, 1951. Chapter Four.

William Carlos Williams (1883–1963)

Contributing Editor: Theodora R. Graham

Classroom Issues and Strategies

Students' assumption that what appears simple is simplistic can be a problem with teaching Williams's poetry. Some students feel the need to sketch in the house, barn, and fields behind the wheelbarrow and white chickens. For others, lack of experience with innovative line breaks and visual effects causes initial confusion. Many do not at first listen for the voice(s). They do not pay attention to speakers and therefore miss the tonal shadings, irony, humor, and other effects, including the sometimes clinical objectivity of poems related to visual art.

I recommend that students read poems aloud from the beginning. I read a poem aloud myself in class as a "possible interpretation" and have students comment on or revise the reading. I also use transparencies of shorter poems, occasionally changing the line breaks in an "edited version" to call attention to Williams's technique of fragmentation (not breaking necessarily with a syntactic unit). In addition, I sometimes use art slides that relate to specific poems (Demuth's "I Saw the Figure 5 in Gold," "Tuberoses"; Picasso's "The Girl and the Hoop"; Sheeler's "Classic Scene").

Students often ask if Williams is usually the speaker in the poem. They wonder how autobiographical his work is and ask whether his work as a doctor really influenced the way he wrote and what he wrote about. Those interested in form ask whether a single sentence, broken up on the page, can be a legitimate poem.

Major Themes, Historical Perspectives, and Personal Issues

Williams champions the American idiom and the "local"—either the urban landscape or one's immediate environment. He pays close attention to ordinary scenes (some purely descriptive; others as compositions as in visual art), the working class and poor. Williams's work often demonstrates the artist's need to destroy or deconstruct what has become outworn and to reassemble or recreate with fresh vision and language. His own "hybrid" background is, in his view, particularly American. He uses his experience as a doctor, married man and father, son and friend, in some of the poems, fiction, and plays. In addition, he demonstrates the need to discover rather than impose order on reality.

Significant Form, Style, or Artistic Conventions

It is important to be familiar with imagist principles and the serious thrust of Williams's "no ideas but in things," as well as his sometime view of the poem as "a machine made out of words." Students should be aware of inductive process and attempt to relate this to Williams's emphasis on particulars, perhaps comparing it with Frost's statement that a poem does not begin with an idea. But whereas Frost embraced and adapted traditional forms, around 1915 Williams began experimenting in shorter poems with innovative line breaks, speaking voices, and a kind of stripped-down language (as he said of Moore, washing words with acid). Readers of Williams should also be familiar with the Armory Show (1913) and how cubist fragmentation and photography became sources for new ideas in the arts through Alfred Stieglitz's Gallery "291" and magazine *Camera Work*, through gatherings at the home/"gallery" of Walter Arensberg in New York City. Since Williams lived a short train ride from the city, he was able to frequent these shows, gatherings, and even studios, like that of Marsden Hartley, with Demuth, a good friend.

That the young Williams was at first influenced primarily by Whitman and Keats and began by writing conventional verse makes his departure from tradition all the more radical.

Original Audience

Point out through a dateline on a transparency the birth dates of Frost, Stevens, Williams, Pound, Moore, and Eliot—and include on the same sheet how old each poet was in 1912 (the date of what is sometimes referred to as the beginning of a poetic renaissance: the start of *Poetry* magazine). Audience was created by editors of little magazines (as new audiences for art were stimulated by opening of small galleries in New York), some—like Williams (see *Contact* I and II)—poets or fiction writers. *Poetry, Others,* the *Egoist, Criterion* (see *Little Magazines,* ed. F. Hoffman) and other magazines published on both sides of the Atlantic gave poets a place to present their work without considering the strictures of conventional larger-circulation magazines. The *Dial,* edited in the twenties by Marianne Moore, offered a coveted prize, which Williams was awarded.

The audience was not mainstream, not large; but it was generally sophisticated and knowledgeable about new developments in the arts and music. It could also be educated by the writers to be responsive to new work.

Now, of course, the modernists are all anthologized and acknowledged, both in their own rights and as influences for poets of following generations. That does not make them, however, easy to read. And the poems anthologized for secondary-level students often do not present their most controversial, and perhaps interesting, writing.

Comparisons, Contrasts, Connections

Students may be asked to discuss how poems begin, or to compare two or more poets' process of revision. They may be asked to compare/contrast the speakers' dilemmas in Frost's "Design" or other "dark" poems and Williams's "These." They could look as well at the forms each poet has chosen and discuss the possible reasons for what Frost would consider the "playing tennis with the net down" of Williams's verse. One could also discuss Williams's relationship to Pound and the latter's influence on early Williams, as well as Williams's negative views of Eliot's expatriation and verse.

Questions for Reading and Discussion/
Approaches to Writing

1. Students generally have a set of strategies for reading that include giving attention to speaker, setting (time of year, time of day, description, etc.), various devices, audience, etc., that they have adapted to their own use as they become more sophisticated readers. I try not to reduce each writer to a set of questions but do suggest that with Williams they read aloud and look carefully at how Williams develops a speaker, how words—used sparingly—can

"tell" more because of juxtaposition or because of their place in a visual composition.

2. Students are particularly interested in interrelations among the arts, in particular with Williams of poetry and visual art. Williams's favorite painter among the cubists was Juan Gris. Some of his work, because it includes what Williams called "the recognizable object" in a new relation to its context, can be interesting to compare with carefully selected Williams's poems (and they can see *Spring and All* for Williams's comments on Gris). Too, Williams's work in relation to that of Charles Demuth, Charles Sheeler, and Alfred Stieglitz provides stimulating possibilities. Can a linear art such as poetry come close to resembling a spatial art such as painting or photography?

Bibliography

The secondary bibliography on Williams is very long. An instructor might consult Paul Mariani's edition of the secondary sources, arranged according to periods in Williams's writing, chronologically (published by the American Library Association). And then select more recent articles from this book's lists.

James Breslin's story of *WCW* and Thomas Whitaker's shorter introduction in the Twayne series remain useful.

Specialized studies of Williams and the arts by Bram Dijkstra, Dickran Tashjian, Peter Schmidt, and Christopher MacGowan provide helpful background.

Williams's *Autobiography* and *I Want to Write a Poem* (ed. Edith Heal) offer insights, not always totally reliable, in the poet's own words.

The *William Carlos Williams Review*, published since 1975, prints articles, reviews, biographical information, unpublished letters, and other manuscripts.

Eugene O'Neill (1888–1953)

Contributing Editor: James A. Robinson

Classroom Issues and Strategies

Problems with teaching O'Neill include (1) students' lack of acquaintance with drama as a genre, which leads to problems of point of view, etc.;

(2) for *Hairy Ape,* fragmentation of the action and styles—its anti-realism—bewilders some; I often scan the final scenes in discussion in explaining the expressionism of earlier scenes; (3) difficulty with identifying tone: students don't know whether the work is tragedy, comedy, or satire; whether to identify with the hero or laugh at him.

To address these issues (1) emphasize the absence of point of view as an opportunity, not a problem, and use the central conflict to generate theme—in what ways do Yank and Mildred contrast? What do these contrasts represent (socially, sexually, psychologically)? (2) Relate the fragmentation of setting to that found (or made possible) by film as medium; compare other fragmentations to poetry (T. S. Eliot's *The Waste Land*) and fiction (Faulkner) contemporary with the play. (3) Define Yank as both hero and anti-hero (using Esther Jackson's definition in *The Broken World of Tennessee Williams*); identify targets of satire (distorted characters, for example) and ask how they relate to Yank's tragic journey toward awareness and toward death.

Consider approaching this play as an existential text (as Doris Falk does in her book on O'Neill) in which Yank is guilty of "bad faith" in his early identification with something outside of himself—steel—leaving him no place to turn when that identification collapses. Finally, consider a Freudian approach for some scenes like scene 3 with its blatant phallic and vaginal symbolism; you could also see Yank as "id" struggling toward "ego" in some ways, as animal striving to become a human individual.

Major Themes, Historical Perspectives, and Personal Issues

Personal Issues: O'Neill's relationship to women, particularly his blaming of his mother for his "fall" from innocence; O'Neill's lapsed faith in the Catholic God, leading to a philosophical search similar to Yank's; O'Neill's love of death.

Historical Issues: modern industrial capitalism as destructive of harmony (Paddy versus Yank) but O'Neill's lack of faith in social solutions (repudiation of Long).

Themes: alienation as major theme, not "belonging"—dramatized in dialogue, setting, sound effects, and character distortions, as well as in action, a quintessential modern theme.

Significant Form, Style, or Artistic Conventions

The primary question is the theatrical mode of expressionism, and why O'Neill chose a style employing distortion and fragmentation for themes of industrialism and alienation.

A related issue is how this expresses the experimental spirit of the 1920s and the questioning of American bourgeois culture spearheaded by Mencken and others—particularly the recognition of class divisions apparent in other works, like *Gatsby*.

Original Audience

The Broadway audience of the 1920s accepted O'Neill's experimentation, partially because he was promoted by influential critics; but the reviews of *Ape* were mixed. I frankly don't work much with this problem in class, though you could cite reviews from leftist journals about the criticism of capitalism in the play to ignite discussion as to whether this is a central theme.

Comparisons, Contrasts, Connections

As indicated above, the play invites comparison with *The Waste Land* (fragmentation), *The Great Gatsby* (social criticism), as well as with figures like Stephen Crane and Theodore Dreiser and Jack London (the latter influenced O'Neill, in fact), whose American naturalism emphasized the animal, instinctual behavior of man. Darwinism, the struggle toward evolution (note Yank's emergence from the sea onto land in scene 5) clearly informs the assumptions of the play.

Questions for Reading and Discussion/ Approaches to Writing

For "genre": the key is central conflict (here, Yank versus Mildred) and how this generates the themes of the play.

For expressionistic aesthetic: point out parallels to/influence of cinema, especially *The Cabinet of Dr. Caligari* and *Metropolis*.

Bibliography

Read the *Ape* chapter in Doris Falk, *Eugene O'Neill and the Tragic Tension*; "Eugene O'Neill as Social Critic," *American Quarterly* (Winter 1954; rpt. in Oscar Cargill et al., *O'Neill and His Plays*—which is also useful for O'Neill's extra-dramatic utterances, several of which are in *Ape*); the chapter on *Ape* in Timo Tuisanen, *O'Neill's Scenic Images*; the chapter on *Ape* in Travis Bogard, *Contour in Time: The Plays of EO*; and my article, "O'Neill's Distorted Dances," in *Modern Drama* 19 (1976).

Djuna Barnes (1892–1982)

Contributing Editor: Catharine R. Stimpson

Classroom Issues and Strategies

Problems with teaching Barnes are also opportunities. They include: (1) Her life and complicated childhood, e.g., a suffragist grandmother, a lecherous father; (2) her Bohemian adulthood—she lived and worked in avant-garde circles in New York and Europe and was also bisexual; (3) her comic wit and anguished vision; and (4) the range of her writing. Because she was a professional writer, with no other income for the most part, she took on a gamut of styles (journalism, plays, poems, stories, burlesques). She often parodies older forms, e.g., *Ryder*, the bildungsroman, and picaresque novel. If students don't know the original, they miss her great wit.

Her biography is still emerging, but tell the story of her life. Let students see her courage, adventurousness, and harsher characteristics, e.g., she traveled in hard-drinking circles. Critics/readers are rediscovering and recovering Barnes, seeing afresh how much she did, who she was, what her circles were, how much it mattered that she was a woman writer, how destructive that ghastly childhood was. Make the class part of the process of rediscovering and recovery, part of the adventure. Show students, too, what she was parodying, what part of literary history she was utilizing.

Help students with her dualistic vision, her sense of contradiction and irony. We are born, but born to die. The womb is a tomb. We are corrupt, but we love and desire. We descend in order to ascend.

Major Themes, Historical Perspectives, and Personal Issues

Trace the travails of a young, beautiful, really bright, ironic, bisexual woman making her way in a tough world. Culturally, look at what it means to be modern, to be avant-garde, to go for the new, vital, disorderly, outlawed, carnivalesque. Barnes knew almost everyone, so that she is a way into modern culture, e.g., she interviewed James Joyce. Historically, she is twentieth century. She lived through two world wars, in a world where God had disappeared, though she yearned for faith; in which the corrupt and vile seemed to dominate history.

Significant Form, Style, or Artistic Conventions

Barnes mastered several genres. Use her journalism to show the mass media, especially the mass newspaper. Use her short stories to show a combination of flat realism and the grotesque, the wierd; use *Ladies Almanack*, for one, to show both satire and inside jokes (Barnes was spoofing women's circles in Paris in the 1920s). Use *Nightwood* to show the modern novel, its suspicion of a straight, linear narrative; its interest in consciousness and language and clashing points of view; the darkness of vision, life as a nightwood; its wild humor; its blurring of sexual identities; its sense of history as a fall. Like a surrealist, Barnes explores the unconscious. Like a symbolist, she incarnates the invisible in a sensible thing.

Original Audience

Barnes was very conscious of writing for specific audiences. She also cared, despite her bohemianism, for the approval of male cultural authorities, especially T. S. Eliot, who endorsed *Nightwood*. Toward the end of her life, Barnes wrote very little, but certain people kept her reputation alive because they loved her, despite her bitter, often destructive, wit, and the difficulty of her work. After her death, feminist critics have helped to re-evaluate her. Another biographer, Andrew Field (1983)—who also writes about Vladimir Nabokov—likes quirky, elusive, brilliant, cosmopolitan figures.

Comparisons, Contrasts, Connections

Try teaching her stories with Sherwood Anderson, *Winesberg, Ohio* (1919), for the meticulous observation of despair; *Ladies Almanack* with Gertrude Stein, *The Autobiography of Alice B. Toklas* (1933), for Parisian adventures; *Nightwood* with *Ulysses* for the experimental modern novel; and, for very hard work, the play *Antiphon* with T. S. Eliot's *The Cocktail Party* (1950), for the use of older dramatic forms for metaphysical and psychological exploration.

Questions for Reading and Discussion/ Approaches to Writing

1. I prefer to have students keep journals rather than ask study questions because the journal picks up students' immediate reactions, no matter how hostile they are. If the class is too large, you might ask them to write out their own study questions. If a study question is a necessity, try to get at her sense of family, which is bleak but convinced of the family's necessity; or her sense of differences: how different people can be, perhaps, from "ordinary" life. Though students might not adore this, ask about futility, and, among the deluded, about failure.

2. Barnes was also a good artist. A student might write about her use of pictures, her visual skills, either through her own illustrations or through her vivid, metaphoric, visual language.

Bibliography

Silence and Power, edited by Mary Lynn Broe, Carbondale: Southern Illinois University Press, 1991, uses the lens of feminist criticism.

Douglas Messerli, *Djuna Barnes: A Bibliography* (1975), is an excellent survey of criticism up to the mid-1970s.

Elizabeth Madox Roberts (1881–1941)

Contributing Editor: Sheila Hurst Donnelly

Classroom Issues and Strategies

Discuss point of view with emphasis on the use of a central consciousness; provide information about the development and social implications of regionalism; instruct students about the use of symbolism and other figurative devices; prepare them for a complicated story structure. Such a general introduction will help readers appreciate Elizabeth Madox Roberts.

Until recently students have not been exposed to Roberts's work. Because her short stories are unavailable, my students are familiar with her best novels, *The Time of Man* and *The Great Meadow*. Some students find her complex structure and style of "symbolism working through poetic realism" difficult. Most enjoy the challenge; the characters many times face the perennial problems of youth. More experienced "city kids" have trouble empathizing with the rural mentality—social reality, sense of community—until the basics are explored: love, sex, birth, death—the equalizers.

Major Themes, Historical Perspectives, and Personal Issues

Roberts is concerned with the universal, the "Everyman" theme, as it grows out of her Pigeon River community. She is preoccupied with the intimate connection between the past and the present. This connection is often reflected in her innovative stylistic techniques. Oftentimes she bounces between past and present with little warning. Many of her works develop initiation themes through penetrating dramatization of psychological crises.

Roberts's writing was influential to early modern American literature because of her introspective and poetic style, her sense of southern rural community, her concern for the individual, and her emphasis upon the indomitable human spirit. Her works are primarily concerned with the way individuals apprehend reality. Here again innovative technique comes into play.

In contrast to the novels, her stories are highly concentrated: limited in time and space and rendered in swift, artful strokes. But, like her best novels *The Time of Man* and *The Great Meadow*, her stories derive their substance from the characters. Their points of view convey the stories, which oftentimes are variations on the initiation theme. Her best stories in this vein are "On the Mountainside," "The Scarecrow," "The Sacrifice of the Maidens," "Swing Low Sweet Chariot," and "Death at Bearwallow."

Significant Form, Style, or Artistic Conventions

A thorough discussion of regionalism is helpful in introducing Roberts and solidifying her important place and influence in southern renaissance literature. While a discussion of her admiration for Berkeleian philosophy may be a point of interest and investigation for advanced students, it is not necessary for the enjoyment of her work.

Original Audience

Roberts can be discussed against the backdrop of the Lost Generation (*The Time of Man* was published in 1926, the same year as Hemingway's

The Sun Also Rises) as well as the movement toward an agrarian revival of the 1920s and 1930s (*I'll Take My Stand: The South and the Agrarian Tradition*). Today, a discussion of her Kentucky women provokes some high-powered and thoughtful commentary on women then and now. Many of her works lend themselves well to feminist and New Historical criticism.

Comparisons, Contrasts, Connections

Comparisons can be made to Ellen Glasgow, Willa Cather, Jesse Stuart, William Faulkner, and Robert Penn Warren, to name a few. She can also be compared to the many more modern female writers such as Kate Chopin, Zora Neale Hurston, Carson McCullers, and Toni Morrison. She can be contrasted to any of the Lost Generation authors. Bases for comparison and contrast lie in personal background, fictional style, theme, region, and current meaningfulness. Mainly, fruitful comparison and contrast are gained from her novels, as her characters are more complex and profoundly developed than those in her short stories. Her works can be contrasted to more short-sighted regional stories, in that they represent "small self-contained centres of life" (Allen Tate), which root in a specific geographical region, adapt to the land, create a pattern of life, and then in turn become aesthetic, taking on universal and archetypal dimensions.

In all her works, Roberts masterfully blends poetry and realism. She, like William Faulkner, is never far from the sweat and agony of the human spirit and, like Faulkner too, she believes that humanity will not only endure, but will prevail.

Questions for Reading and Discussion/ Approaches to Writing

1. How do events in your past affect moments, decisions, relationships, etc., in your present, future?
2. What sentiments do you attach to sense stimuli: smells, places, particular events, garments, etc.—the stuff of symbolism?
3. I have had special success with two types of papers:
   (a) Position papers in which students take issue with the characters' responses to particular events. They engage in hypothetical arguments and bring to bear their individual beliefs. These papers tend to generate a more penetrating discussion of all that shapes a character while encouraging students to trust their own analytical skills.

(b) Explication of the text using a quote from the author about her work, which forces students to grapple with an understanding of the author's artistic credo in conjunction with her works. For example, Roberts would say, "Life is from within, and thus the noise outside is a wind blowing in a mirror." This riddling line can be applied to many of her stories and novels, including "Death at Bearwallow."

Comparison/contrast papers with instructor's guidance are also a favorite of mine.

Bibliography

The Southern Review, Autumn 29, no. 4 (1984) has several essays as well as personal reminiscences.

Read Campbell and Foster's study *Elizabeth Madox Roberts: American Novelist* (1956).

See the headnote for a list of secondary sources and additional explication of "Death at Bearwallow" for specific references.

H.D. (Hilda Doolittle) (1886–1961)

Contributing Editor: Susan Stanford Friedman

Classroom Issues and Strategies

Like much modernist poetry (e.g., Pound, Eliot), H.D.'s poetry is "difficult" for students. Mythological and biblical allusions are common in her poetry. Her imagist poetry is "impersonal" (like Eliot's)—that is, its relationship to human emotion is often deeply encoded. Her epic poetry is vast and complex in scope; its linguistic, religious, and psychological dimensions are sophisticated and multi-layered. Her perspective as a woman is quite different from the modernist male poets with whom she shares a great deal.

I have found students very responsive to H.D. when I have used the following strategies. Contextualize H.D.'s work in relationship to (1) modernism (students often expect a male poet to be "difficult," but resist having to work hard to read a woman poet); (2) women's poetry and feminist theory—especially feminist concepts of revision of patriarchal myths and traditions; (3) the mythological allusions (get students to relax and see that without footnotes, H.D. provides all the information they need); (4) the musical and syntactic structures of her poetic language. Her imagist poems can be read as poems about the (female) self resisting stereotypical femininity (they are not "nature" poems). I have had great success in teaching *Trilogy* as a poem about war from a pacifist perspective akin to Virginia Woolf's in *Three Guineas*.

Students are intrigued by the following: (1) Gender. They are fascinated by H.D. as a window into the problems and achievements of women's creativity. They love, for example, to read her famous "sea garden" poems (e.g., "Sea Rose") as encoded statements of female vulnerability and rejection of a suffocating femininity. (2) War and peace. Students are very interested and moved by her response to war. They are intrigued by the goddesses and matriarchal religions. (3) Initially, students are afraid of H.D.—real "poetry anxiety." They think they won't be able to understand it because it has so many allusions. But when they are given a framework for thinking about the poetry, they are very responsive.

Major Themes, Historical Perspectives, and Personal Issues

The headnote summarizes the major themes. To summarize, I think H.D. should be taught with emphasis on the following themes:

1. her attempt to understand the roots of cataclysmic violence and propose a revision of renewal and peace
2. the intersection of the historical and the personal in her stance as a woman
3. her characteristically modernist sense of quest in a shattered and war-torn world
4. her sense of the sacred, manifested in both female and male forms
5. her exploration of language—its magic (as logos), its music, its power as something women can claim to reconstitute gender and a vision of the cosmos

Significant Form, Style, or Artistic Conventions

H.D. is best taught as a modernist and a woman writer. The selections give you the opportunity to show her development from an imagist poet in the teens to an epic poet of the 1940s and 1950s. Her imagist poetry—represented here by two poems from *Sea Garden* ("Sea Rose" and "The Helmsman") and her most frequently anthologized poem "Oread" (often discussed as the "perfect" imagist poem)—was highly innovative in its form and a central influence on modern poetry.

Imagism, however, became a craft in the service of larger visions after 1917. "Helen," published in the 1920s, is characteristic of a large number of revisionist myth poems that she began writing in her post-imagist phase and that have had a strong influence on contemporary women's poetry. In writing epics (some critics prefer the term "long poem"), H.D. went against the engrained masculine conventions of the genre to forge a woman's epic form. The selections from *The Walls Do Not Fall* and *Tribute to the Angels* (the first two volumes from *Trilogy*) emphasize the poet's placement in history (literally, in London, during the nightly bombing raids of World War II) and the syncretist mythmaking of the modernist poet-prophet. These sequences can be taught in the context of religious poetry, but students should be encouraged to compare her female-centered vision with those traditions that she transforms. In teaching any of H.D.'s poetry, its strong musical quality can be emphasized. Within the *vers libre* tradition, she nonetheless established complex patterns of sound based on assonance, dissonance, occasional rhyme (including internal and off rhymes), rhythmic and syntactic patterns, and repetition.

Original Audience

H.D.'s work should always be grounded in its historical period. H.D.'s imagist verse was written in the exhilarating prewar world of the avant-garde and then during the devastating Great War. Her epic poetry was written in the forties and fifties after another great war. Her audience during these years was in effect primarily the avant-garde that was "making news" in all the arts. She was not a "popular" poet, but has often been known as a "poet's poet." Since the second wave of feminism, she has been widely read by women and men who are interested in women's writing.

Comparisons, Contrasts, Connections

1. Male modernists: Ezra Pound, T. S. Eliot, William Carlos Williams, Wallace Stevens, Robert Hughes, W. B. Yeats, and D. H. Lawrence. Like these men, she experimented with poetic language. Like them, she increasingly wrote quest poetry in which the poet figures as a central mythmaking figure creating new meanings in a world whose symbolic systems have been shattered.
2. Female modernist writers: Marianne Moore, Virginia Woolf, Gertrude Stein, and Djuna Barnes are modernist women writers with whom H.D.'s reconstructions of gender share a great deal—thematically and linguistically.

3. Fruitful comparisons can also be made with William Blake, Emily Dickinson, Dante, and Homer.

Questions for Reading and Discussion/ Approaches to Writing

Explication assignments work well with H.D.'s imagist poems. But the best papers I have received from undergraduates ask the students to examine how H.D. engages in a gender-inflected revisionist mythmaking in her poems. The students trace the conventional myth H.D. invokes and then examine thematically and linguistically how she uses and transforms the tradition.

Bibliography

Bloom, Harold, ed. *Modern Critical Views: H.D.* New York: Chelsea House, 1989. Especially essays by Morris, Friedman, Gubar, Martz, and Gelpi.

DuPlessis, Rachel Blau. *H.D.: The Career of That Struggle.* Brighton: Harvester Press, 1986.

Friedman, Susan Stanford. *Psyche Reborn: The Emergence of H.D.* Bloomington: Indiana University Press, 1981. Especially 56–59, and Chapters 7 and 8.

———. *Penelope's Web: Gender, Modernity, H.D.'s Fiction.* Cambridge: Cambridge University Press, 1990. Introduction and Chapter 1.

Friedman, Susan Stanford and Rachel Blau DuPlessis, eds. *Signets: Reading H.D.* Madison: University of Wisconsin Press, 1990. Especially essays by Morris, Pondrom, Gregory, Laity, Gubar, Gelpi, and Ostriker.

Rich, Adrienne. "When We Dead Awaken: Writing as Re-Vision." In *On Lies, Secrets, and Silences: Prose.* New York: Norton, 1979. 33–49.

Showalter, Elaine. "Feminist Criticism in the Wilderness." In *The New Feminist Criticism.* edited by Elaine Showalter. New York: Pantheon, 1985. 243–70.

A Sheaf of Political Poetry in the Modern Period

Contributing Editor: Cary Nelson

Classroom Issues and Strategies

Instructors who have followed the efforts to expand the canon in recent years will have read poems like the ones in this section before. Many students, however, may not have. My own experience is that most undergraduates find this poetry quite exciting and are eager to talk about it. The only exception may be those English majors who have been persuaded by other instructors that good poems are never political. An open debate on these issues is the best way to handle the problem. Certainly the clichés about political poetry being rapidly dated and stylistically flat and uninteresting should not survive reading this section. Among the things that students may find surprising are efforts by white poets like Boyle and Taggard to address the problem of race in America. A number of these poems will benefit from detailed close readings; they can also be grouped together in a variety of ways for more general discussions.

Major Themes, Historical Perspectives, and Personal Issues

This section offers both an opportunity to study several poets (Hughes, Rolfe, and Taggard) in detail and a chance to reflect on the wide visibility of political poetry in the modern period. Political poetry was influential not only in the 1930s but also throughout a thirty-year period beginning about 1915. After students have read through this section they may want to ask what justifies the category "political poetry." What holds this section together and differentiates it from other twentieth-century poetry? Are Langston Hughes's poems here "political" in a way some of his poems elsewhere in *The Heath Anthology*, including "The Negro Speaks of Rivers" and "The Weary Blues," are not? Are Taggard's poems political in a way, say, poems like Amy Lowell's "Venus Transiens" and "Madonna of the Evening Flowers" are not? Is Edwin Rolfe political in a way that Robert Frost and Wallace Stevens are not?

As a descriptive category, political poetry has been around for some time. Our sense of what poems belong in that category, however, continues to change. For some readers, political poetry is either poetry written about major, public historical conflicts, like wars, or poetry supporting some political cause, party, or set of beliefs. Of course, those beliefs have to be set aside, culturally and marked as "political" rather than "natural." If, on the other hand, we define politics more broadly as a concern with all of the hierarchical structures that shape social life, that empower some people and disempower others, that elevate some values and concerns and trivialize or demonize others, then clearly "politics" is a much larger subject than some of us have thought. In that sense, all modern poems dealing with race, gender, and economic equality are deeply political. One effect of studying this section and thinking about that issue may be to begin making connections with other poems in *The Heath Anthology* and making politics in this broader sense central to modern literary history. Certainly from my perspective the poems in the anthology by Muriel Rukeyser, Countee Cullen, Claude McKay, and Langston Hughes, among others, along with the section of anonymous poems by early Chinese immigrants, should be considered honorary members of this section.

As the introduction to the section suggests, one important issue here is the relevance such purportedly "topical" poems have to us many years later. As these poems suggest, the topics many political poems take up—injustice, prejudice, inequality—unfortunately have a long and continuing life. Kalar's abandoned papermill is hardly unfamiliar in the industrial workplace of the 1990s. The working environment in Olsen's "I Want You Women Up North to Know" can be found replicated throughout contemporary America. Fearing's critique of the culture of consumption, commodification, and greed in "Dirge" is, if anything, more pertinent now that it was when the poem was written. Hughes's attack on religious hypocrisy in "Goodbye Christ" speaks to problems with institutionalized religion that are unique neither to that decade nor this century.

Yet just as we need to highlight the continuing relevance of these poems, we also need to recognize the special historical conditions to which they speak. Two things instructors may want to do are to supply additional information about the poems' historical contexts and to encourage students to do further background reading on their own. Some (necessarily condensed) examples of that kind of information follow.

"Papermill" (Kalar), "Dirge" (Fearing), "In a Coffee Pot" (Hayes), "Season of Death" (Rolfe), and "Up State—Depression Summer" (Taggard): These poems all deal with the experience of the Great Depression. Kalar was a worker-poet who worked in the timber industry in Minnesota prior to the widespread unemployment of the 1930s. Rolfe grew up in New York City and worked in a number of jobs before becoming a journalist and poet; he was periodically unemployed in the depression. "Season of Death" and "In a Coffee Pot" both depict New York settings, but they are also typical of other depression-era cities. A "coffee pot," by the way is a small coffee shop. A background lecture on the economic, social, and political effects of the depression might be helpful. It is also useful to make students aware that journals, newspapers, and anthologies publishing poems like these helped make depression poetry something of a collective project. Hundreds of poems like these made the protest poetry of the depression part of a mass movement. For more detailed information on "Dirge," see Fearing's *Collected Poems* (1993).

"A Communication To Nancy Cunard" (Boyle) is based, as the note to the poem points out, on the famous Scottsboro case of the 1930s. The nine young black men (aged thirteen to twenty-one) were arrested in March of 1931 and quickly tried and convicted—without adequate representation and on the basis of unconvincing evidence. All but one were sentenced to death. The radical legal-action group International Labor Defense took up their case and helped publicize it both here and abroad. Widespread protests combined with the ILD's legal actions won a new trial in 1933, just before which Ruby Bates repudiated her rape charge. Nevertheless, an all-white jury convicted them again. That trial was then overturned, and two years later the U.S. Supreme Court ruled that defendants' rights were violated by the exclusion of blacks from juries. A 1936 trial failed again to get them released. After that, a plea bargain won freedom for four of the men, while five remained in prison. The last was released in 1950. Also see Countee Cullen's poem "Scottsboro, Too, Is Worth Its Song."

"Goodbye Christ" (Hughes) and "Stone Face" (Ridge) were both reprinted in unique broadsides that gave those poems special meaning and distinctive social uses. Hughes's poem was reprinted on hate sheets several times in the early and late 1940s as part of national right-wing smear campaigns against Hughes. Ridge's poem was published as a very large and quite striking broadside as part of the effort to free Mooney from prison. (For reproductions of both broadsides see Nelson, "Modern Poems We Have Wanted to Forget," *Cultural Studies*, 1992.) Mooney was imprisoned from 1916 to 1939. With perjured testimony, he was convicted of murder, despite the fact that he was nowhere near the scene when the bomb was planted. A federal commission later found that Mooney was indicted only because he was an effective labor organizer whom conservatives wanted to eliminate. The judge and jury publicly admitted the verdict was an error. Under the circumstances, President Woodrow Wilson made a plea for mercy, and Mooney's death sentence was commutated to life, but he remained in jail. It may be interesting to compare "Stone Face" with Boyle's "A Communication To Nancy Cunard" and with Edna St. Vincent Millay's "Justice Denied in Massachusetts," since all mount left critiques of American justice.

"First Love" and "Elegia" were both written some years after Rolfe returned home from service in the Abraham Lincoln Battalion in the Spanish Civil War. The introduction to Rolfe's *Collected Poems* (1993) includes detailed analyses of both these poems, and the notes to the poems at the back of that book are considerably expanded from what it was possible to present here. Instructors may find it interesting to compare these poems with the earlier poems Rolfe wrote while he was in Spain from 1937 to 1938. It is important to be aware that "Elegia" was written in Los Angeles in 1948, after the Hollywood blacklist was in place and the long postwar purge of the Left had begun. Its sense of mourning for an antifascist alliance politics is thus relevant not only to Spain but also to the United States.

"Proud Day" (Taggard) commemorates a concert that Marian Anderson presented on the steps of the Lincoln Memorial in Washington, D.C., after her request to present an Easter Sunday concert at Constitution Hall, the largest Washington auditorium, was turned down by the Hall's manager and by its owners, the Daughters of the American Revolution. The D.A.R. maintained a "white artists only" policy for Constitution Hall, and Marian Anderson was black; thus neither that date nor any other was acceptable to them. In protest against the D.A.R.'s action, Eleanor Roosevelt, then First Lady, resigned from the organization and helped arrange the alternative concert at the memorial. It should be noted that Washington was a rigidly segregated city during the 1930s.

Significant Form, Style, or Artistic Conventions

Among the most important things to note about this group of poems is its rhetorical, formal, and stylistic diversity. A number of the poems employ experimental modernist devices for social commentary and political advocacy, offering convincing evidence against the uninformed but common claim that political poets rejected modernism. On the other hand, there are many opportunities here to compare and contrast different styles—lyrical, reportorial, satiric, elegiac, hortatory, reflective. There are long and short poems, traditional and mixed forms. Opportunities for comparison and contrast with more canonical modern poets abound. One may also question what it was possible to accomplish in different genres by comparing these poems with some of the socially conscious prose in *The Heath Anthology*.

Original Audience

This is at once a very difficult question and an important one. Our interest, first of all, should not only be in the original audience for a poem but in all the significant audiences that are part of its reception and use. Several of these poems have immensely complex and interesting histories of dissemination in different contexts. Their "original" audience may in fact be partly accidental, an historical effect not part of the poet's intentions. But the whole history of reception and interpretation by different audiences often helps explain a poem's present status. Again, I cannot present that history for all eighteen poems, but I can give a few instructive examples.

Olsen's poem was first published in *Partisan* in 1934. *Partisan* was the magazine of the John Reed Club in Hollywood, California. It featured the work of young revolutionary writers who regularly met together to comment on one another's work. There were John Reed Clubs in a number of U.S. cities in the early 1930s. Olsen's first immediate audience was thus the growing constituency of radicalized writers and those who followed their work. It would be another matter entirely for her poem actually to reach the bourgeois "women up north" whom the poem addresses. Getting that message across would thus be a task for the readers of *Partisan*.

Langston Hughes's "Goodbye Christ" was written in the Soviet Union and first published in *The Negro Worker*, probably without Hughes's permission, in 1932. That appearance was, however, a good deal less important than its subsequent redistribution in a prolonged racist and anti-communist campaign against Hughes, which included its republication in the *Saturday Evening Post* in 1940, its quotation in a J. Edgar Hoover speech in 1947 (read by one of Hoover's deputies), and its being read into the U.S. Senate Record in 1948. See Rampersad's *The Life of Langston Hughes* (1986, 1988) for further details.

Edwin Rolfe's "Elegia," written in 1948, was rejected for publication by the journal *Masses and Mainstream,* in part because the editors objected to the religious references. It was translated into Spanish by the scholar and Spanish exile José Rubia Barcia. Barcia sent the Spanish version to the filmmaker Luis Buñuel in Mexico, who in turn gave it to the poet and Spanish exile Manuel Altolaguirre. Altolaguirre printed it as a pamphlet in Mexico City in 1949, and the poem was subsequently read aloud in groups of Spanish exiles throughout Latin America. The original English-language version was not published until 1951.

Questions for Reading and Discussion/ Approaches to Writing

With sixteen poems by nine different poets, the number of questions one might ask about this sheaf of poems is considerable. Let me offer a few examples:

1. Taggard's "Up State—Depression Summer" and Fearing's "Dirge" deal respectively with rural and urban settings and are written in very different styles. Do they share any explicit or implicit values?
2. One might argue that Kalar's "Papermill," Hayes's "In a Coffee Pot," Hughes's "Air Raid Over Harlem," and Rolfe's "Season of Death" all deal with devastated human landscapes. How do they compare with Eliot's *The Waste Land,* a poem written a decade earlier and with a different political understanding of what may be related social realities?
3. What kind of impact does Olsen's "I Want You Women Up North to Know" have on the audience addressed in the title?
4. What is the relationship between the more lyrical and more polemical language in Rolfe's "Elegia"? What role does romantic love play in his "First Love"? How does he transform the ballad stanza in "Asbestos"?
5. What role does wit play in Hughes's "Goodbye Christ" and Fearing's "Dirge"?
6. How does Ridge complicate our sense of the public use of individual suffering in "Stone Face"?
7. What different and similar kinds of cultural work might these poems do in their own time and ours?

Questions like these can serve either for class discussions or for paper topics. For term papers, however, I like to encourage students to read further in a poet's work. One interesting question not answerable without further reading is what happened to these poets after the 1940s. Some did not survive the decade; others stopped writing poetry. But Boyle, Hughes, and Rolfe continued to write powerful political poems after World War II and into the 1950s. Students could write about that later work or make it the subject of in-class reports.

Bibliography

Students interested in reading widely in depression-era political poetry face some difficulty, since much of the work is out of print. The work of several of these poets, however, is readily available. *Collected Poems* were published for both Fearing and Rolfe in 1993, and both books have critical introductions and detailed textual notes explaining historical references that may now be obscure. Boyle's *Collected Poems* (1991) remains in print. Students should be warned that Langston Hughes's most widely distributed book, his *Selected Poems* (1959), excludes his more aggressively political poems; for that work students should consult the *second* edition of *Good Morning Revolution* (1993) and *The Panther and the Lash* (1967). Although Taggard's books are all out of print, they will be available in most research libraries. The two volumes that include most of her political poems are *Calling Western Union* (1936) and *Long View* (1942). In addition to the general critical books listed in the introduction to this sheaf of poems, students or faculty interested in some of the specific historical issues addressed might consult the following: Dan Carter, *Scottsboro: A Tragedy of the American South* (1984); Richard Frost, *The Mooney Case* (1968); Robert McElvaine, *The Great Depression* (1984); Robert Rosenstone, *Crusade of the Left* (on the Americans in Spain, 1969); Hugh Thomas, *The Spanish Civil War* (1977).

E. E. Cummings (1894–1962)

Contributing Editor: Richard S. Kennedy

Classroom Issues and Strategies

Sometimes students are not aware that the *visual* presentation of a poem is part of its overall statement. In addition, they are sometimes puzzled by Cummings's unusual linguistic usage: the use of nouns as verbs, other locutions of nouns, etc. (e.g., the world is made of "roses & hello," "of so longs and ashes").

When I call students' attention to ways that words or presentations on the page actually function, this most often brings home an effect that may have been missed (e.g., in the poem "l(a" to point out the way the letter "L" and the word "one" are introduced, as the word "loneliness" and "a leaf falls" are intertwined). Sometimes I simply ask students for their individual responses and find that they really can *feel* the significance of an unusual expression.

An extreme example of Cummings's play with language is his poem in pseudosonnet form "brIght." Note some of the patterns in evidence here. The three-letter words "big," "yes," and "who" are used three times; the four-letter words "soft," "near," "calm," "holy," "deep," and "star," four times; the five-letter word "bright," six times. The lines are arranged in a numerical progression from the first line standing alone to a final five-line group. Another progression moves from "s???" to the full spelling of "star," as if a star gradually comes into being. "brIght" orthographically disappears into "?????T." as if dawn comes, isolating the morning star, and then causes it to fade. The pattern of capital letters at length spells out BRIGHT, YES, and WHO. Suggestion builds that the poem has reference to the star of Bethlehem because of the allusions to the Christmas hymn "Silent night, holy night/All is calm, all is bright."

I have sometimes begun class by asking, "How does Cummings indicate in his poems that he is a painter as well as a poet?" Another simple approach is to ask, "How does Cummings seem different from any other poet whose work you have read?" I have also asked students at some point in a discussion, "Why are these linguistic presentations that Cummings makes classified as poems?" (This last, of course, is not asked about his sonnets or rhymed stanzaic verses.)

Students vary in their responses, but most of them react deeply to his outlook on life—his valuing of love, nature, human uniqueness. Fewer students appreciate his play with form. Almost all enjoy his humor and satire. Nearly every student joins him in his antiwar stance.

Major Themes, Historical Perspectives, and Personal Issues

Cummings is, in his general outlook on life, an unabashed romantic. He affirms life wholeheartedly in all its multiplicity, but especially in whatever is simple, natural, loving, individual, unique. Above all, he emphasizes feeling and emotion rather than thought or analysis. He rejects those social forces in life that hinder the unique and individual expression of each person's essential being. He is particularly hostile to forces that promote conformity, group behavior, imitation, artificiality. He regards technology and the complexities of civilization as dehumanizing. Above all, he abominates war, which he looks upon as the ultimate negation of human values.

Although Cummings maintains the same general views throughout his life, he is more affirmatively exuberant in his early career and more lightheartedly iconoclastic. In his later career, he is more serene in his response to the basic good things of life and to the beauties of the natural world, but more harshly satiric in his denunciation of what he opposes.

Cummings's play with language, punctuation, capitalization, and his visually directive placement of words on the page are congruent with the new movement in the arts that began in the 1900s in European painting—the movement toward "break up and restructuring" that was part of the revolt against realism in modern art.

Original Audience

Cummings does not address a particular audience, although he assumes that his readers are generally educated in literature and the arts.

Comparisons, Contrasts, Connections

Cummings's work may be associated with the experiments in language and form that are found in the writings of T. S. Eliot, Ezra Pound, Gertrude Stein, and John Dos Passos. He may be contrasted with writers in the realistic or naturalistic vein, such as Theodore Dreiser, Sherwood Anderson, Edward Arlington Robinson, Robert Frost, and Ernest Hemingway.

Questions for Reading and Discussion/ Approaches to Writing

1. I have sometimes lectured on his characteristic ideas and attitudes and then asked students to point out which poems illustrate these best. Or I have lectured on his special techniques and expressive devices in order to alert the students to ways of reading and understanding his work.
2. I have sometimes asked students to compare a Cummings sonnet with a conventional one, or to compare a Cummings lyric with one by Frost.

   I have also asked students to point out the likenesses and differences between a specific Cummings work and one by Eliot or Pound.

Bibliography

Richard S. Kennedy's introduction to the typescript edition of *Tulips & Chimneys* by Cummings (Liveright, 1976) summarizes his view of life and his poetic techniques.

Norman Friedman's *E. E. Cummings: The Art of his Poetry* (Johns Hopkins, 1960), Chapters Three and Four, deal clearly with his attitudes and his poetic devices.

Richard S. Kennedy, *Dreams in the Mirror: A Biography of E. E. Cummings* (Liveright, 1980) is the definitive biography.

T. S. Eliot (1888–1965)

Contributing Editor: Sam S. Baskett

Classroom Issues and Strategies

For the uninitiated reader, Eliot's poems present a number of difficulties: erudite allusions, lines in a number of foreign languages, lack of narrative structure compounded by startling juxtapositions, a sense of aloofness from the ordinary sensory universe of day-to-day living. For the more sophisticated, Eliot's "modernism," his quest for "reality," may seem dated, even "romantic"; the vision of the waste land, stultifying and bleak; the orthodoxy of "The Dry Salvages" a retreat from the cutting edge of late twentieth-century thought and poetic expression.

To address these problems, explain the most difficult and essential passages, providing some framework and background, without attempting a line-by-line gloss of all the references and their ramifications. The poems, especially *The Waste Land*, should not be treated as puzzles to be solved, but rather, the early poems at least, as typical "modernism" which Eliot "invented" in *The Waste Land* and "Prufrock," a product of symbolism, images, and aggregation. Emphasize that this is all the expression of a personal, intense, even romantic effort by Eliot to get things "right" for himself in his search for order in his life, a validation of his existence, in a word, for "salvation." Emphasize continuing themes, continuing and changing techniques as Eliot attempts to translate, as he said of Shakespeare, his own private agony into something rich, strange, and impersonal.

Students often ask why Eliot is so intentionally, even perversely, difficult. Why the erudite allusions, the foreign languages, the indirectness? What is his attitude toward women? What of the evidence of racial prejudice? What of his aloofness from and condescension to the concerns of ordinary human existence?

Major Themes, Historical Perspectives, and Personal Issues

The symbolism of the waste land, garden, water, city, stairs, etc., as Eliot expresses the themes of time, death-rebirth, levels of love (and attitude toward women), the quest motif on psychological, metaphysical, and aesthetic levels. Dante's four levels—the literal (Eliot's use of geographic place is more basic than has been given sufficient attention), allegorical, moral, and anagogic—are interesting to trace throughout Eliot's developing canon. The relations between geographic place and vision, between the personal, individual talent and the strong sense of tradition, are also significant.

Significant Form, Style, or Artistic Conventions

Eliot's relation to romanticism, his significance in the development (with Ezra Pound) of modernism, his role as an expatriate effecting a "reconciliation with America" in "The Dry Salvages" are all important considerations. His techniques of juxtaposition, aggregation of images, symbolism, the use of multiple literary allusions, the influence of Dante are all worth attention, as is his use of "free verse" and many various poetic forms. Note also the musicality of his verse, his use of verbal repetition as well as clusters of images and symbols.

Original Audience

When Eliot's works first appeared, they seemed outrageously impenetrable to many, although he quickly became recognized as the "Pope of Russell Square." This recognition was partly through Pound's efforts, as well as Eliot's magisterial pronouncements in his criticism. Even as he challenged the literary establishment, he was in effect a literary "dictator" during much of his life, despite the shock felt by his followers when he announced in 1927 that he was "catholic, royalist and a classicist." With the religious emphasis of *Ash Wednesday* (1930) and *Four Quartets* (1943), as well as in his plays of the '30s and '40s, it seemed to many that he had become a different writer. A quarter of a century after his death, it is possible to see the continuing figure in the carpet, Eliot as a major figure in modernism, a movement superseded by subsequent developments. His eventual importance has been severely questioned by some critics (e.g., Harold Bloom).

Comparisons, Contrasts, Connections

Compare Eliot with Ezra Pound, Robert Frost, William Carlos Williams, Wallace Stevens. Pound for his influence as "the better craftsman" and for his early recognition of and plumping for Eliot; all of these poets for their combined (but differing) contribution to modernism and the search for reality as a way out of "the heart of darkness." Williams and Stevens

(Adamic poets) make interesting contrasts with their different goals and techniques: Williams criticizing Eliot's lack of immediacy, Stevens commenting that Eliot did not make the "visible a little difficult to see."

Questions for Reading and Discussion/ Approaches to Writing

1. What are the similarities and differences in Eliot's protagonists?

    What is the continuing fundamental theme in his work?

    Is "The Dry Salvages" essentially different from his early poems? How so? Are there any continuities?

    Consider the thrust of a particular poem on literal, allegorical, moral, and anagogic levels.

    What is Eliot's attitude toward women?

    What are the techniques by which Eliot's poems achieve intensity?

2. Compare and contrast the protagonists of two poems.

    Trace the quest motif through Eliot's poems.

    How do the late poems ("DS") differ from "Prufrock"? *The Waste Land*?

    Discuss Eliot's attitude toward death as expressed in the poems.

    Discuss Eliot's symbolism, the use of water as a symbol.

Bibliography

Basket, Sam S. "Eliot's London." In *Critical Essays on The Waste Land*. London: Longman Literature Guides, 1988, 73–89.

———. "Fronting the Atlantic: *Cape Cod* and 'The Dry Salvages.'" *The New England Quarterly* LVI, no. 2 (June 1983): 200–19.

Drew, Elizabeth. *T. S. Eliot: The Design of His Poetry*. New York: Charles Scribner's Sons, 1949. Especially pp. 1–30.

Gordon, Lyndall. *Eliot's Early Years*. Athens: Ohio University Press, 1977.

———. *Eliot's New Life*. Athens: Ohio University Press, 1988.

Kermode, Frank. "A Babylonish Dialect." In *T. S. Eliot*, edited by Allen Tate, 231–43. New York: Delacorte Press, 1966.

Langbaum, Robert. *The Poetry of Experience*. Chicago: University of Chicago Press, 1985.

Litz, A. Walton, ed. *Eliot in His Time*. London, 1973. Several useful, illuminating essays.

Martin, Jay, ed. *A Collection of Critical Essays on The Waste Land*. Englewood Cliffs, N.J.: Prentice Hall, Twentieth Century Interpretations, 1968. Several useful, illuminating essays.

Miller, J. Hillis. *Poets of Reality*. Cambridge: Belknap Press of Harvard University, 1965. 1–12.

Moody, A. D. *T. S. Eliot*. Cambridge: Cambridge University Press, 1979.

Williamson, George. *A Reader's Guide to T. S. Eliot*. New York: Farrar, Straus & Giroux, 1967.

F. Scott Fitzgerald (1896–1940)

Contributing Editor: John F. Callahan

Classroom Issues and Strategies

Students often tend to identify Fitzgerald with the nostalgic sensibility of his protagonist, Charlie Wales, and have a corollary tendency to view Fitzgerald as a participant in the excesses of the Jazz Age rather than as a writer who cast a critical eye on his generation's experience.

Fitzgerald's essays serve as important companions to his fiction. I fall back on the trick of photocopying one or more of the following essays: "Echoes of the Jazz Age"; "My Lost City"; "The Crack Up"; "Sleeping and Waking"; or "Pasting It Together." On the relationship between Fitzgerald and Wales, I focus on the overlay of observation and allusion that gives the story a perspective much deeper than Charlie Wales's rather superficial, self-pitying point of view.

Students are very interested in the relationship between Fitzgerald's life and his work and in his sense that the best possibilities of American history are in the past. Their questions include why relationships between men and women seem often bound up with money and social status, and whether or not Fitzgerald maintains a critical detachment from his characters' views of reality.

Major Themes, Historical Perspectives, and Personal Issues

Note the relationship hinted at in the story, between the twenties and thirties, the Boom and the Crash. Also it is important to note that although Wales is once again very well off, despite the depression, his emotional and psychological stock is precarious. Can personal and historical issues be separated? Again, this is why it is important to use or at least refer to Fitzgerald's essays and letters.

Significant Form, Style, or Artistic Conventions

How, and how successfully, does Fitzgerald's evocative, lyrical prose set up an interplay of identification with and detachment from the protagonist's nostalgic sensibility? To what extent does Fitzgerald's style mirror the story's conflict of sensibility; namely, the contrast between a spare, pared-down modern style showing Hemingway's influence, and a metaphorical, romantic style reliant on a rich, sensuous imagery?

Original Audience

I call attention to Fitzgerald's self-conscious awareness of a double identity as a popular writer of stories for the *Saturday Evening Post* and a serious novelist aspiring to the company of Conrad, Joyce, and James. I consider the relationship, the compatibility between popular and serious fiction in a democratic and vernacular culture.

The issues of freedom and responsibility, the cost of self-indulgent personal behavior seem particularly appropriate to our time.

Comparisons, Contrasts, Connections

The following stories in Volume 2 of *The Heath Anthology* might provide a useful frame of reference: Hemingway's "Hills Like White Elephants"; Porter's "Flowering Judas"; Toomer's "Blood-Burning Moon," "Seventh Street," and "Box Seat." All involve landscape, social milieu, memory, and transitional moments of experience.

Bibliography

The best sources on "Babylon Revisited" are Fitzgerald's essays listed above, a piece called "Ring," written after the death of Ring Lardner, and also Fitzgerald's letters.

Katherine Anne Porter (1890–1980)

Contributing Editor: Jane Krause DeMouy

Classroom Issues and Strategies

Porter's stories are powerful, but understanding their true content requires thought and sensitivity. They should be read for the psychological as well as the representational reality. In addition, her style is highly complex; even the best critics are not very specific in describing exactly what it is Porter does to achieve her impact. She may be difficult for undergraduates to understand, but I think some fruitful discussion can come from focusing on issues of identity. This is an issue that all students know about instinctively; it can lead to interesting discussion to note that Granny Weatherall has had the same problems with identity that many adolescents have; one question becomes whether she has ever shaken them.

Students of Porter would do well to remember the Jamesian principle that art is selection. When Porter, like other artists, chooses certain subjects, she is not only shaping an entity but saying what she considers important, so it is essential to know what she is writing about. Porter does utilize personal experience in her work, but more often than not it is her internal experience that is true, while the factual events have been heightened, dramatized, and symbolized into fiction. In her most complex stories, symbols carry multiple meanings, and the writer's memories are transformed into mythopoeic structures based on the alogical associations common to dreams, rather than precise logical sequences. Since art exists not in facts, but in myth, it is also important to note what she does to change personal knowledge into meaningful, universalized fiction.

Students respond strongly to Porter's theme of rebellion—the wish for independence and personhood.

Major Themes, Historical Perspectives, and Personal Issues

Themes include the conflict between personal freedom and belonging to conventional society; Porter's Miranda/Laura as a female American Adam; the human confusion experienced when one has to confront the passing of the traditions/myths/structures of old southern society into the chaos of a technologically speeded-up, wartorn, and jaded society; biological, cultural, and traditional constraints on women.

Miranda, for instance, has grown up seeing that women are valued for their beauty and ability to bear children; that women who want identity or power can get it only by marrying and bearing children; that land, money, and political voice (real power) belong to men; that women who want these are outcasts.

Miranda's problem is that while she has come to recognize that these practices and beliefs are inherently unjust, they are also part of her cultural imperative. She internalizes the moral "rightness" of these things even as she rejects them. This results in enormous conflict for her. Choosing her culture's values, she is biologically trapped; choosing her self, she must reject everything she has been without knowing what she might be. Being unable—or refusing—to choose results in the emotional paralysis of characters like Laura in "Flowering Judas."

Perhaps most important in approaching a study of Porter are several caveats. Readers must, first of all, be wary of false biographical accounts, and the tendency of reviewers and critics to confuse Porter's fiction with those false accounts. For specific facts, one can consult the only biography currently available, Joan Givner's *Katherine Anne Porter: A Life* (New York, rev. ed., 1991), which carefully tracks a monumental amount of detail to clarify names, dates, and events. It is a diligent compilation of research, but a book that fails to find the personality that charmed lovers, friends, and audiences to the last days of Porter's life. Thomas F. Walsh's *Katherine Anne Porter and Mexico: The Illusion of Eden* (University of Texas Press, 1992) is a thoroughly researched and insightful discussion that sheds light on both Porter's biography and work.

Significant Form, Style, or Artistic Conventions

"I shall try to tell the truth," she said in "My First Speech," (*Collected Essays*, p. 433), "but the result will be fiction." Porter felt that we really understand very little of what happens to us in the present moment, but by remembering, comparing, and waiting for the consequences, we can begin to understand the meaning of certain events. For her, that process of remembering and comparing takes place as she writes. It is a process clearly recorded in "The Jilting of Granny Weatherall," "The Grave," and "Old Mortality."

Fiction is made, she said, first of legend: those things told to her or read when she was a child. It is also made of memory: her childhood emotional experiences of certain events, as well as present memory; the adult's memory of what happened and explanation to herself of what that meant to the child. This confusion of experiences that took place in and over time is difficult to understand, but humanly true. Each person is a mesh of his or her "child," and what they understand themselves to be in the present, which may be illusory, deluded, or "true" by someone else's objective observation.

It is out of this understanding that Porter creates richly layered characters, events, and conflicts. Characters are who they *were*, who they *are*, who they *think* they were and are, as well as who they are *going to be*—given what happens to them in the story and their capacity to deal with that conflict. It is no wonder that Porter's stories have tremendous impact while being incredibly hard to decipher.

Porter is a master of the twentieth-century short story; it was her métier—so much so that she found it all but impossible to write *Ship of Fools*.

Original Audience

These stories are universal and timeless; however, the diversity of Katherine Anne Porter's experience and stories offers a wealth of teaching approaches. Her stories range from the regional focus of nineteenth-century Texas ("The Grave," "Old Mortality," and others) to the urban sophistication of twentieth-century New York and Mexico ("Theft," "That Tree," "Hacienda") and even to horrible visions of an inverted brave new world, where every man is for himself; moral standards do not exist; and the waste land is realized in loveless sex and human isolation.

Comparisons, Contrasts, Connections

Thematically, the bildungsroman experiences and the loss of innocence recorded in "The Grave" and other stories in "The Old Order" invite comparison with Hemingway's Nick Adams stories, just as do "Pale Horse, Pale Rider" and *A Farewell to Arms*. Like Faulkner, Porter has the historic memory of the southern temper, but it is a more feminine and particular vision, arising from a heightened social awareness that makes her sensitive to social mores, moral values, and the individual strengths that allow a person to survive.

Bibliography

To best understand Porter, one can do no better than to thoroughly read her essays, particularly "Portrait: Old South"; "Noon Wine: The Sources"; the "Introduction to *Flowering Judas*"; and "Three Statements About Writing."

The most comprehensive bibliography is Kathryn Hilt and Ruth M. Alvarez, *Katherine Anne Porter: An Annotated Bibliography* (Garland: New York, 1990).

Probably the best secondary source, Lodwick Hartley and George Core's *Katherine Anne Porter: A Critical Collection*, is out of print, but available in library collections.

Robert Penn Warren's *Katherine Anne Porter* for the Twentieth Century Views series (Englewood Cliffs, N.J.: Prentice Hall, 1979) also contains some of the seminal critical essays on Porter and essays that represent the critical controversy over *Ship of Fools*.

The newest collection of this kind is Harold Bloom's *Modern Critical Views: Katherine Anne Porter* (New Haven: Yale, 1987).

Thomas F. Walsh's *Katherine Anne Porter and Mexico: An Illusion of Eden,* already mentioned, provides interesting perspective on how Porter's experience with her "familiar country" reflected her psychology and informed her art. Good articles may also be found in Virginia Spencer Carr, ed., *"Flowering Judas:" A Casebook* (Rutgers University Press, 1993).

Expanded comment on the ideas in this article are in Jane DeMouy's *Katherine Anne Porter's Women: The Eye of Her Fiction* (Austin: Texas University Press, 1983); and those interested in the role of southern women will want to look at Anne Firor Scott's *The Southern Lady: From Pedestal to Politics, 1830–1930,* 1970.

In addition, a fine overview of Porter, including interviews with her contemporaries Robert Penn Warren and Eudora Welty, as well as dramatization of parts of "The Grave" and "The Circus," is available in the one-hour PBS program, "Katherine Anne Porter: The Eye of Memory," American Masterworks Series, produced by Lumiere Productions, New York, 1986.

Marianne Moore (1887–1972)

Contributing Editor: Bernard F. Engel

Classroom Issues and Strategies

The general student block against poetry often causes difficulties. With Moore, it is useful to observe that she seeks accuracy of statement, that the alleged difficulty of her work does not arise from abstruse symbolism or reference to obscure autobiographical matters, but from precision:

seeking exact presentation, she does not fall back on expected phrasings. The attentive who will slow down and read thoughtfully can understand and enjoy.

Advise students to read through once quickly to get perspective. Then they should read slowly, and aloud. I also advise them that after this first reading they should let the poem sit two or three days, then repeat the process. In class, I read through short poems a few lines at a time, pausing to ask questions; I also ask students to read passages aloud. With undergraduates, I prefer not to spend hours on any one poem. It is better that they read carefully, but without the extended analysis that is appropriate in some graduate classes.

Students need help with the rhetoric and syntax; they need to be shown how to read with care. They rarely raise (automatically) the abstruse questions of aesthetics or moral philosophy that fascinate the literary critic.

Major Themes, Historical Perspectives, and Personal Issues

Point out:

1. The fact that though there is usually a "moral" point in a Moore poem, the overall aim is aesthetic: The moral is to contribute to the delight, not to dominate it.
2. The way the poems relate to the modernism of Wallace Stevens and others.

Significant Form, Style, or Artistic Conventions

In a freshman class, I focus on the poem itself; with juniors and seniors, I bring out relationships to modernism. The rhetorical form of a poem is usually worth pointing out; metrics should be mentioned, but only in passing.

Original Audience

I mention the fact that until the 1960s Moore's work was considered too difficult for any but the most elevated critics. I also point out that her early admirers were generally male, that only in the last few years have a number of women come to appreciate her. She does not fit the stereotype of woman as emotional (in contrast to supposedly rational man). Moore, indeed, once remarked that only two or three American women have "even tried" to write poetry—meaning, one may be sure, Emily

Dickinson and herself. (In her last years, she might have added Elizabeth Bishop to her list.)

Early strong objections to her work came from Margaret Anderson of the *Little Review*, who in 1918 asserted that she wrote too intellectually; Anderson reprinted her remarks in 1953. Babette Deutsch in 1935, and again in 1952, voiced similar objections. Some recent feminist critics have also had doubts. Emily Stipes Watts in *The Poetry of American Women from 1632 to 1945* (1977) found Moore practicing a "feminine realism" that "will ultimately be unacceptable"; Watts saw male appreciation of Moore's poetry as condescension.

Comparisons, Contrasts, Connections

Moore knew and corresponded with William Carlos Williams, Ezra Pound, T. S. Eliot, and Wallace Stevens. All of them published comments on her, and she in turn wrote of them. There are obvious comparisons and contrasts in the work of these, the chief American modernists.

Questions for Reading and Discussion/ Approaches to Writing

1. I sometimes use study questions. They usually focus on the "mere rhetoric"—what the poem "says": its argument or moral, the way it expresses feeling (with Moore, often the feeling of delight).
2. "Poetry": In both versions of the poem, Moore's speaker says, "I, too, dislike it. . . ." Why would a lifelong poet say this? What does the speaker like?

   "The Pangolin": The poem starts in a seemingly casual manner—"Another armored animal"—but moves quickly into exact, patient observation of the animal's structure and behavior. Is the speaker coolly rational? Delighted? Or . . . ? What kind of grace is the ultimate subject of this poem?

   "England": The poem is about America (an example of Moore's waggish wit). Compare it to the essay by Randolph Bourne, "Trans-national America."

   "Nevertheless": How can a strawberry resemble "a hedgehog or a star-/fish"? How do apple seeds, the rubber plant, and the prickly, pear illustrate the point that "Victory won't come/to me unless I go/to it"?

   "The Mind Is an Enchanting Thing": What is the difference between "enchanted" and "enchanting"? Explain the paradox in "conscientious inconsistency" (stanza 4).

Bibliography

For students and the hurried instructor, the most convenient assistance may be found by looking up the pages on individual poems in the indexes to the books by Engel (revised edition), Nitchie, Hall, and Phillips. These books deal with all or most of Moore's poetry.

Excellent critical studies by Stapleton, Costello, and others give an overall perspective but usually deal with fewer individual poems. There is now a full-length biography by Charles Molesworth: *Marianne Moore: A Literary Life* (1990).

Louise Bogan (1897–1970)

Contributing Editor: Theodora R. Graham

Classroom Issues and Strategies

The instructor needs to explain Bogan's often distancing herself from the poem's ideas, creating what Adrienne Rich has called a "mask" or "code." Her use of the more traditional lyric form (though not in most of the poems selected for the anthology) raises questions about her relationship to the experimental verse that poets of the prior generation and those of her own were writing. Bogan seems quite accessible—except in poems like "The Sleeping Fury" and "After the Persian," which require calling students' attention to language, imagery, contrasts.

Introducing Bogan's more general literary career—and perhaps ideas from her essays, reviews, and Ruth Limmer's edited autobiography—will enrich students' understanding of the difficulties women faced as writers and the extraordinary success some achieved as editors (cf. Harriet Monroe, Marianne Moore) and reviewers.

Major Themes, Historical Perspectives, and Personal Issues

A number of Bogan's poems concern love and the woman's need to maintain her identity. She also writes, indirectly, of the poet's demons, the "sleeping fury" that must be addressed in its violence and appeased. Bogan also turns her attention to skillful observation, both of crafted objects (and indirectly to the crafted poem) and of natural things (such as the dragonfly). In "Women" she offers a critique of some women's choice of a restricted, passionless, and dull existence.

Significant Form, Style, or Artistic Conventions

A poem entitled "Rhyme" ends "But once heart's feast/You were to me." A love poem about the rhyme between a man and a woman, the poem could also be read as Bogan's tribute to rhyme itself. In "Women" and "Roman Fountain" she demonstrates a distinct ability and interest in what might have seemed in 1922 and 1935 an old-fashioned technique. (The former consists of 5 stanzas rhyming abcb; the latter, more ingenious, like the fountain it describes, rhymes aabc / aabb / abcabca.) However, other poems selected are dramatically different in formal organization and are unrhymed. Bogan's line breaks, unlike (e.g.) William Carlos Williams's, generally follow syntactic units. But in "The Sleeping Fury" and "After the Persian" she writes in long lines, form following thought. Both poems contain a kind of elegance, issuing even from the fear and violence of the former.

Bogan's scope is not grand, but her talent in crafting verse and summoning images is noteworthy.

Original Audience

Bogan—like Marianne Moore—was writing for a man's world. Neither made concessions to the popular audience to gain a greater readership. Yet their natural reserve and privacy turned them in a direction away from the more soul-baring tendencies of some of their contemporaries. "The Sleeping Fury" could be about the poet's demon-muse; but it could equally concern her breakdowns, the warring sides of her own personality. That she was poetry editor for the *New Yorker* for many years indicates that she understood a broader public's taste and chose to write a taut, lyric verse.

Comparisons, Contrasts, Connections

It is useful to compare her treatment of natural objects and personal, cloaked subjects with that of Emily Dickinson, and with later poets such as Adrienne Rich and Denise Levertov, who use the personal "I" in more self-revealing ways.

Questions for Reading and Discussion/ Approaches to Writing

1. I prefer to give students several pages of extracts from Bogan's prose, including reviews and Limmer's biographical collection.
2. Those interested in women writers might want to explore the kinds of verse other women of Bogan's generation—particularly those who reached out to a larger audience—chose to write. What were women reading from *Ladies Home Companion* and other popular magazines? How does Bogan's writing compare?

Bibliography

See Bogan's prose and Ruth Limmer's *A Journey Around My Room* extracted as autobiography from Bogan's diaries and other prose.

Ernest Hemingway (1899–1961)

Contributing Editor: Margaret Anne O'Connor

Classroom Issues and Strategies

Most students have already read something by Hemingway, and they come into class with preconceptions. They usually love him or hate him and try to pin labels rather than give his work a new reading. Also they want to concentrate on biography and biographical readings of his works, since most find his well-publicized life even more interesting than his work.

As the headnote to this story suggests, biography is important to understanding Hemingway's approach to writing, but I try to turn students' attention biographically from Hemingway the Adventurer-Philosopher to Hemingway the Writer. Since "Hills Like White Elephants" is much less often anthologized than other Hemingway stories, its newness to students might tempt them to read and reread in order to see how the story fits with other works they've read by him. I approach teaching this taut story as if it were a poem. Word choice and phraseology are keys to its success.

One possible strategy might be to ask two students, a male and a female, to read the dialogue aloud to the class as if it were a drama. Then class discussion would move toward tone of voice. Questions of the man's sincerity and the girl's sarcasm would naturally emerge. The less preparation for this exercise the better since a "flat" delivery would remind listeners that Hemingway expects his readers to "interpret."

Students are interested in the philosophy of life they discern from Hemingway's works, the code of behavior his characters follow that gives their lives dignity in the author's eyes. This story seems a self-critique of that code. Careful readers don't believe the girl at the end of the story when she says she's "fine." She's composed herself; she won't make a scene, but she's not "fine." Students want to know how Hemingway has succeeded in making us know that the man is lying to the girl—and perhaps to himself—throughout the story. There's no easy answer to this question, but a close reading of key phrases such as "the only thing that bothers us," "it's perfectly simple," or "I feel fine" will help them see how carefully constructed the story is.

Major Themes, Historical Perspectives, and Personal Issues

"Hills" is a good story to shatter the false impression that Hemingway was insensitive to women. This carefully constructed vignette has a nameless man and woman discussing their relationship against the backdrop of the mountain landscape. As in the very best of Hemingway's novels and stories, the authorial stance is ambiguous; readers must pay close attention to small details to understand the progress of the narrative. Students should be encouraged to focus on the dialogue between the man and girl in order to discern their relationship. The issue of abortion and how each speaker feels about it is central to the story. Yet abortion itself is not the main issue; it is the not-too-subtle pressure "the man" is placing on "the girl" to have the abortion that is the key issue.

Significant Form, Style, or Artistic Conventions

Hemingway's minimalist style in this 1927 story deserves consideration. If Faulkner confuses readers because he offers so many details for readers to sift through in order to understand what's going on, Hemingway confuses by offering so few.

Original Audience

The central issue in this story is the abortion the girl is being pressured to have by her male companion. The author's stance on the issue of abortion is ambiguous, but the story clearly comes out against the male pressuring the female into an abortion that she doesn't seem to want. Pro-choice and pro-life students might want to concentrate class discussion not on abortion alone, but on the issue of subtle pressure at the heart of the story.

Comparisons, Contrasts, Connections

Of many possible works of comparison, one of the most fruitful would be T. S. Eliot's *The Waste Land*. Compare this rootless couple escaping the commitment of parenthood with Eliot's set of lovers in Book II of his poem. The song of the nightingale "so rudely forced" is "Jug, Jug," which is echoed in the man's choice of a nickname for the girl.

Questions for Reading and Discussion/ Approaches to Writing

1. What's the purpose of the trip the two travelers are taking?
2. Why are the speakers only identified as "a man" and "girl"? How do these designations affect your reading of the story? What nickname does the man use for the girl?
3. How do the descriptions of the landscape relate to the conversation between the two travelers? What about the discussion of drink orders?
4. Note each sentence or paragraph that is not enclosed in quotation marks, and explain how each brief commentary affects your understanding of the characters and the lives they lead.
5. Why does the girl repeat the word "please" seven times? Anger? Hysteria? Fear? Frustration? Why does the man leave her at the table?
6. The railroad station setting is important to the progress—the plot—of the story. How does this physical setting parallel the thematic concerns of the story as well?
7. How does the title relate to the story?

Bibliography

Jeffrey Meyers offers an excellent brief reading of this story in his biography (pp. 196–97).

Wallace Stevens (1879–1955)

Contributing Editor: Linda W. Wagner-Martin

Classroom Issues and Strategies

The sheer difficulty of apprehending meaning from some of Stevens's poems turns many students away. Yet Stevens is one of the most apt voices to speak about the perfection, and the perfectibility, of the poem—the supreme fiction in the writer's, and the reader's, lives. If students can read Stevens's poems well, they will probably be able to read anything in the text.

The elusiveness of meaning is one key difficulty: Stevens's valiant attempts to avoid paraphrase, to lose himself in brilliant language, to slide into repetition and assonantal patterns without warning. His work demands complete concentration, and complete sympathy, from his readers. Most students cannot give poetry either of these tributes without some preparation.

Close reading, usually aloud, helps. The well-known Stevens language magic has to be experienced, and since the poems are difficult, asking students to work on them alone, in isolation, is not the best tactic. Beginning with the poems by Stevens might make reading T. S. Eliot, Robert Frost, and William Carlos Williams much easier, so I would make this selection central to the study of modern American poetry.

Major Themes, Historical Perspectives, and Personal Issues

The value of poetry (and all art); the accessibility of great moral, and mortal, themes through language; the impenetrability of most human relationships; the evanescence of formalized belief systems, including religion; the frustration of imperfection; and others. Stevens often builds from historical and/or philosophical knowledge, expecting "fact" to serve as counterpoint for his readers' more imaginative exploits. But this technique is not meant to lead to easy or facile explication. It is a way of contrasting the predictable and the truly valuable, the imaginary.

Significant Form, Style, or Artistic Conventions

Stevens's intricate stanza and rhyme patterns are a school of poetry in themselves, and each of his poems should be studied as a crafted object. His work fits well with that of T. S. Eliot, as does some of his aesthetic rationale: "Poetry is not personal." "The real is only the base. But it is the base." "In poetry, you must love the words, the ideas and the images and rhythms with all your capacity to love anything at all." "Poetry must be irrational." "The purpose of poetry is to make life complete in itself." "Poetry increases the feeling for reality." "In the absence of a belief in God, the mind turns to its own creations and examines them, not alone from the aesthetic point of view, but for what they reveal, for what they validate and invalidate."

Original Audience

Modernism was so specific a mood and time that students must understand the modernists' rage for control of craft, the emphasis on the formalism of the way an art object was formed, and the importance craft held for all parts of the artist's life. Once those conventions are described, and Stevens placed in this period, his own distinctions from the group of modernists will be clearer. ("Not all objects are equal. The vice of imagism was that it did not recognize this." "A change of style is a change of subject." "In the long run the truth does not matter.") Conscious of all the elements of form, Stevens yet overlays his work with a heavily philosophical intention, and the shelves of commentary on his poetry have been occasioned because that commentary is, in many cases, useful.

Comparisons, Contrasts, Connections

The T. S. Eliot of the *Four Quartets* (likenesses) or the William Carlos Williams of the short poems (differences).

William Faulkner (1897–1962)

Contributing Editor: John Lowe

Students are resistant to texts that withhold key information, to narrative that is obscure and/or convoluted, and to characters who don't seem to have "common sense." All of these "sins" appear in Faulkner's work.

He also requires a knowledge of southern and American history that many students don't possess.

Begin by emphasizing the pleasures to be gained from unraveling Faulkner's mysteries. Especially focus on his parallels to and differences from the popular myths of southern culture, as found in *Gone With the Wind, North and South,* and popular television series set in the South. Approach his works as though they were detective stories (some of them, in fact, are). Do brief presentations of relevant historical materials. Locate the text's place in Faulkner's career, drawing parallels between the character's concerns and the way those issues touched Faulkner as well. Explain how Faulkner explored and exploded stereotypes, of southerners, African-Americans, and women.

Teachers should be prepared to answer typical questions: Students want to know if he "really thought of all those things when he was writing," referring to the hidden references we uncover in symbolism, imagery, and so on. They ask if his family owned slaves and how Faulkner felt about it if they did. Some students want to know if I think Faulkner was a racist and/or a sexist.

Major Themes, Historical Perspectives, and Personal Issues

Highlight Faulkner's tremendous importance as an interpreter of history—and not just southern or American history—at a critical moment when modernism emerged as a questioning, probing tool used to redefine human nature and our relationship to nature. Issues of sex, class, and above all, race, should be explored using a battery of interdisciplinary techniques, including historical, social, anthropological, economic, political, and feminist perspectives. "Barn Burning" has been profitably analyzed by Marxist critics as a class struggle; "A Rose for Emily" offers a perfect laboratory for testing reader-response theory.

Gender formation operates centrally in both these stories, centering on the masculine in "Barn Burning," and the feminine in "Emily." Interestingly, each of these processes intersects with issues of class and community. These conjunctions could and should be profitably explored, and linked to the way Faulkner struggled with them in his own life. "Barn Burning" also relates thematically to the *bildungsroman,* and stories of rural life, while "Emily" works within the tradition of stories and novels that deal with the possibilities and restrictions of small-town life. Thematically, *A Rose for Emily* may also be considered a tragic love story in the naturalist mode (there are strong links to *Madame Bovary,* for instance), a detective story, a "thriller," and a typical O'Henry story with surprise endings. Both stories employ mythic/biblical structures in the service of these various thematics; students should be asked to identify them and demonstrate why they are effective.

Significant Form, Style, or Artistic Conventions

Faulkner needs to be understood in both the context of southern literary traditions and modernism. "Emily" interbraids a meandering, typically southern mode of narration, replete with communal bias and obfuscation, with a modernist sense of rupture, scrambled chronology, and Freudian subtext. "Barn Burning," in its employment of Jamesian point of view as confined to Sarty's consciousness, requires detailed analysis of its narrative structure, its language, and the consequent effects on the reader. Both stories attempt to present complicated psychological conditions and situations while adhering to the firm realities of dramatic plotting.

Comparisons, Contrasts, Connections

Faulkner needs to be related to the other great modernists who so influenced him, especially Joyce and Eliot, and his work should and could be profitably compared and contrasted to the similar but sometimes very different literary experiments of Hemingway, Stein, Fitzgerald, Wright, and so on. "Barn Burning" can easily be contrasted to *Huckleberry Finn,* where a young boy must abandon his father's standards in favor of more humane, just ones, or to a female *bildungsroman* such as Wharton's *Summer*. The injustices of sharecropping discussed by Faulkner could be examined alongside other treatments of rural life such as Hamlin Garland's "Under the Lion's Paw" or Richard Wright's "Long Black Song" and "The Man Who Was Almost a Man"; the latter similarly focuses on a young boy's coming of age against a rural backdrop. Twain, Morrison, and Oates could be helpful in explaining the interconnections between the *bildungsroman* and psychological fiction.

"Emily" needs to be read as part of the American gothic tradition, alongside works by Charles Brockden Brown, Poe, Hawthorne, and O'Connor. But it also belongs with the literature of madness and psychological stunting so prominent in the work of Charlotte Perkins Gilman ("The Yellow Wall-Paper"), many of the poems of Emily Dickinson, Faulkner's own novel, *As I Lay Dying*, and the poetry of Sylvia Plath.

Questions for Reading and Discussion/ Approaches to Writing

"Barn Burning"

1. How does one establish individual independence as a teenager? Do you remember any crucial moment in your own life when you realized that you had to make a choice between what your parent(s) and/or family believed and your own values?
2. Is the destruction of another person's property ever something we can justify? Explain.
3. Does it matter that this story is rendered through Sarty's consciousness? What were Faulkner's options, and how would the story be different if he had exercised them?
4. What are the key symbols in the story, and how do they serve the thematic purposes Faulkner had in mind?
5. Do the class issues the story raises have any parallels today?
6. What is the tone of the story and how is it established?

"A Rose for Emily"

1. Discuss the ways in which Faulkner uses Miss Emily's house as an appropriate setting and as a metaphor for both her and the themes established by the narrative.
2. What are the different uses of the themes of "love," "honor," and "respectability" in the story?
3. Why does Faulkner use this particular narrator? What do you know about him? Can you list his "values," and if so, are they shared by the town? Is this narrator reliable? Does the fact he is male matter?
4. Many critics have read Miss Emily as a symbol of the post–Civil-War South. Discuss the advantages and *disadvantages* of adopting this stance.
5. Those of you who have read Charles Dickens's *Great Expectations* will see a resemblance. How does Faulkner's tale echo but also differ significantly from Dickens's?
6. How does this story handle the linked themes of female oppression and empowerment? What does it say about the various kinds of male-female relationships in American society of this period?

Paper Topics

I never arbitrarily assign students a particular story to write on; instead, I urge them to choose one they particularly like. They are then to ask themselves exactly *why* they like it, which will lead them to a topic (the humor employed, a certain character or method of characterization, a fascination with the depiction of the historical period on display, and so on).

Bibliography

"Barn Burning"

Bradford, M. E. "Family and Community in Faulkner's 'Barn Burning.'" *Southern Review* 17 (1981): 332–39.

Fowler, Virginia C. "Faulkner's 'Barn Burning': Sarty's Conflict Reconsidered." *College Language Association Journal* 24 (1981): 513–21.

Franklin, Phyllis. "Sarty Snopes and 'Barn Burning.'" *Mississippi Quarterly* 21 (1968): 189–93.

Hiles, Jane. "Kinship and Heredity in Faulkner's 'Barn Burning.'" *Mississippi Quarterly* 38, 3 (1985): 329–37.

Volpe, Edmond L. "'Barn Burning': A Definition of Evil." *Faulkner: The Unappeased Imagination: A Collection of Critical Essays,* edited by O. Carey, 75–82. Troy, NY: Whitson, 1980.

"A Rose for Emily"

Allen, Dennis W. "Horror and Perverse Delight: Faulkner's 'A Rose for Emily.'" *Modern Fiction Studies* 30, 4 (1984): 685–96.

Brown, Suzanne Hunter. "Appendix A: Reframing Stories." *Short Story Theory at a Crossroad,* edited by Susan Lohafer and Jo Ellyn Clarey. Baton Rouge: Louisiana State University Press, 1989.

Inge, M. Thomas, ed. *William Faulkner: A Rose for Emily.* The Merrill Literary Casebook Series. Columbus: Charles E. Merrill, 1970.

Both stories are treated in Hans Skei's *William Faulkner: The Short Story Career: An Outline of Faulkner's Short Story Writing from 1919 to 1962.* Oslo: University Forl, 1981, and James Ferguson's *Faulkner's Short Fiction.* Knoxville: University of Tennessee Press, 1991. See also *Faulkner and the Short Story: Faulkner and Yoknapatawpha, 1990.* Ed. Ann Abadie and Doreen Fowler. Jackson: University Press of Mississippi, 1992.

Hart Crane (1899–1932)

Contributing Editor: Margaret Dickie

Classroom Issues and Strategies

I set Crane in the context of Pound and Eliot where students can see the ambitions he shared with his fellow modernists to "make it new," to write a poem including history, even to define the role of the poet as a cultural spokesman. And, in that context, I try to distinguish the larger concerns of his career that set him apart from his fellow poets; his interest in the "logic of metaphor" as making it new, his focus on American rather than world history, and his search to find his identity in his role as a poet, all indicate how he reinterpreted the modernist program to suit his own purposes. I urge students, who may have been reading Ezra Pound and T. S. Eliot through the footnotes to their poems, to abandon that approach to Crane and to concentrate instead on those elements they find most perplexing in his work: the language, the experience, and the dislocated references.

Central to any discussion of Crane is his role as a homosexual poet. Quite apart from the task of placing him in the modernist movement, students will need to understand Crane's sense of himself as a figure marginalized both by his chosen profession as a poet in a capitalist economy and by his sexual identity as a homosexual in the ideology of literary and cultural authority that made, as Thomas Yingling has suggested, "homosexuality an inadmissible center from which to write about American life" (27). I introduce Crane with "Black Tambourine" and "Chaplinesque" where he identifies the poet with the "black man" and the tramp in order to show how he felt himself marginalized; and, as part of the discussion, I try to indicate also how he was willing to appropriate such marginal figures for his own use without much regard to their own status. In this respect, "Black Tambourine" can be compared to Gertrude Stein's "Melanctha" as similar projections onto African-American subjects of each author's homosexuality and his/her unwillingness to confront it directly.

Crane's two early poems can lead into a reading of *Voyages I, III, VI* and to a consideration of how he celebrates his love for a young sailor here in language coded to disguise its homosexual subject and to boast too of the "Infinite consanguinity" that such a subject bears. The language of these highly condensed poems will open into any number of interpretations, and students need to be encouraged to follow the "transmemberment of song" as Crane plays it out not just to understand his stylistic innovations but to see them as integral to the subject of homosexuality.

Major Themes, Historical Perspectives, and Personal Issues

Major themes developed in the early lyric poems and carried through *The Bridge* and to the last poem he wrote, "The Broken Tower," include the artist as an outcast in the modern industrialized and urbanized world, Crane's need nonetheless to find ways to celebrate the modern world and to articulate an affirmative myth of America, the search to discover in the present the positive values of the American past, Crane's deepening despair over the possibilities of accomplishing such a bold program, and finally the lifelong effort to find a means of expressing his homosexuality, of masking it, of making it viable and meaningful both for himself and for his audience.

Historically, Crane is a modernist who departs widely from the movement. His effort to write a long poem belongs to the early stages of modernism when Pound was starting *The Cantos,* Eliot completing *The Waste Land,* and William Carlos Williams was producing *Spring & All* and *In the American Grain.* Although Crane's effort, *The Bridge,* is too long to be included in full in the anthology, the selected sections—"To Brooklyn Bridge" and "The River"—should serve to indicate both his Native American subjects and the range of his style from formal quatrains through Whitmanian catalogues to collage and narrative. His place in the canon has seldom been challenged even by his earlier critics who found his long poem intellectually and structurally flawed, his life-style reprehensible, and his suicide inevitable; but his achievement is of another order from Eliot's or Pound's, and it must be read on its own terms.

Personally, the central question in Crane's life was how to be a homosexual poet, a writer able to express his own identity in culturally meaningful ways. The central issue of his career was the composition of *The Bridge,* which he worked on during most of his writing life, even when the inspiration of the long poem failed him and his belief in its purpose faltered.

Significant Form, Style, or Artistic Conventions

The modernist long poem was the form Crane hoped to invent. He offered various explanations of his program chiefly to Otto Kahn, a philanthropist from whom he sought financial aid, claiming, "What I am really handling, you see, is the myth of America. Thousands of strands have had to be searched for, sorted and interwoven. . . . For each section of the entire poem has presented its own unique problem of form, not alone in relation to the materials embodied within its separate confines, but also in relation to the other parts, *in series,* of the major design of the entire poem" (*Letters* 305). The two sections in the anthology should suggest something of Crane's method of interweaving different strands as well as the variety of forms that he employed. The design of the whole poem eluded him.

To Harriet Monroe, he described his theory of the logic of metaphor as distinct from pure logic, arguing that he was "more interested in the so-called illogical impingements of the connotations of words on the consciousness (and their combinations and interplay in metaphor on this basis) than I am interested in the preservation of their logically rigid significations at the cost of limiting my subject matter and perceptions involved in the poem." I encourage students to consider this statement, puzzling out its significance, and to examine the short poems in light of it in order to see how words interact and develop in a chain of free associations.

Original Audience

Crane's original audience included editors and readers of the little magazines of the 1920s, fellow poets, and literary friends such as Malcolm Cowley, Harry and Caresse Crosby, Waldo Frank, Gorham Munson, Katherine Anne Porter, and Allen Tate. He has always been a poet's poet, and his reputation has been nourished by the tributes of poets as different as Allen Ginsberg and Robert Lowell. The rise of gay and lesbian studies has inspired renewed interest in his career. For an extremely informative reading of his homosexual themes and style, see Yingling.

Comparisons, Contrasts, Connections

Crane pitted himself against the formidable reputation of Eliot and *The Waste Land. The Bridge* would, he hoped, be an answer to what he imagined as Eliot's negative view of modern life. He allied himself with William Carlos Williams, whose *In the American Grain* influenced him as he worked on his long poem, although the selections for Williams in the anthology are not ideal for drawing a comparison here. Perhaps Williams's "Spring and All" or "To Elsie" might serve as treatments of the American landscape and people that Crane would have shared.

Questions for Reading and Discussion/ Approaches to Writing

1. If Crane identified with the "black man" and Charlie Chaplin or with the hoboes in "The River," did he have any sympathy for their plight or was he simply appropriating them as suitable images of his own difficulties?

2. Discuss *Voyages* as a love poem. How does its language work to restrain its subject? Critics have universalized its themes. Can they be particularized as references to Crane's love affair with Emil Opffer, the young sailor who inspired them? What do such phrases as "Infinite consanguinity" mean in a love poem? What is "Belle Isle"? "The imaged Word"? Why is this language so generalized?

3. Consider why Melville would have been important to Crane. In what sense is a "scattered chapter, livid hieroglyph" an apt description of Crane's own verse?

4. Discuss the image of the Brooklyn Bridge as a technological achievement and as a significant poetic symbol for Crane.

5. In what sense is breaking an important imaginative act for Crane? Look at "The Broken Tower" as Crane's final acceptance of brokenness in himself and in his world.

The New Negro Renaissance

Alain Locke (1885–1954)

Contributing Editor: Beth Helen Stickney

Classroom Issues and Strategies

While students often have difficulty knowing how to approach nonfiction prose, particularly the kind that tends toward abstraction as Locke's essay does, once we have historically contextualized "The New Negro," students are quick both to sympathize with Locke and to become involved in a number of salient debates. One particular point of interest is Locke's own educational background; students want to know what it was like for an African-American at Oxford, and they are also generally interested in learning about the milieu at Harvard in the early 1900s.

Most will begin to sense the precariousness of Locke's position as a black intellectual struggling both to make a place for himself in an Anglo-American environment and to pave the way for other African-Americans.

The centrality of art and culture in Locke's thought and political philosophy always touches off controversy. Students divide on issues of artistic freedom versus responsibility to one's race (and/or class/gender); the racial/cultural specificity of a given art form (for example, is jazz, or rap/hip-hop, as students think today, a "black" form?); and finally, the broader concern of the role that art and culture can play in any political or social agenda (again, a point that usually prompts students to draw on their own experience).

When students do draw on contemporary culture, their references are usually to popular music, and I encourage this. Because *The New Negro* anthology itself (indeed the New Negro *movement*) was so deliberately an interdisciplinary project, I try to represent as many art forms as possible. (This is where student presentations can be profitably used.) Cary Nelson's *Repression and Recovery*, in addition to giving a history of much of the "noncanonical" literature of the period, includes reproductions (some in color) of artwork from *The New Negro* and several other small African-American periodicals. Included in my bibliography are two fine art books, both with informative essays on individual artists and on African-American culture in general. Any number of musical recordings (Duke Ellington, Louis Armstrong, Bessie Smith, the spirituals) would give the opportunity to discuss Locke's distaste for the commercialized "Tin Pan Alley" jazz and his preference for the more "authentic" spirituals (though the latter were already being Westernized for the concert halls). As students begin to see that Locke's concerns are neither merely academic nor dead issues, they will sometimes bring me newspaper clippings or mention interviews in which they detect Lockean themes being raised. These, of course, I make a point of sharing with the class.

Major Themes, Historical Perspectives, and Personal Issues

Major themes Locke develops include the entrance onto the world scene of a new social type and a new psychology in the figure of the "new Negro"; the dialectical relationship between an outer reality (social, political, and cultural conditions) and inner consciousness; the centrality of Harlem as a "race capital" and the importance of the urban experience generally in promoting the cosmopolitan ideal; pan-Africanism and the importance of uniting African-Americans with oppressed and politically awakening peoples worldwide; the significance of cultural renewal in bringing about social and political progress; the "enlarging of personal experience" as inseparable from a commitment to "a common vision of the social tasks ahead"; the authenticity of "folk" culture and the dangers inherent in empty imitation of "high" culture forms; the need for a reinvigoration of democratic ideals and institutions, and the unique ability of African-Americans to address that need; the role that the "enlightened minorities" of each race must play in bringing the races together; the urgency of seeing racial interests in a "new and enlarged way" that would ultimately transcend a narrowly racialist vision.

As the only child of educated, middle-class parents, Locke was both a product and a proponent of an elite high-culture tradition. Though known for his devotion to cultural pluralism and what he came to call "critical relativism," Locke's early education would have instilled in him Victorian, specifically Arnoldian, notions of taste and cultural value; indeed, even as he supported young artists and emerging African-American cultural forms, he was often accused of elitism and Eurocentrism (charges that had also been levelled against W.E.B. Du Bois). But while he was educated in and became a vital part of the country's elite intellectual circles, he also knew racial prejudice (note his ostracism at Oxford even as a Rhodes scholar), and he actively fought racism and worked for full social, cultural, and political recognition of all African-Americans. Thus, both privileged and oppressed, he found himself in much the same vexed position as many of his black contemporaries, most notably Du Bois and James Weldon Johnson (both of whom had also spent time in Europe, traveling and studying).

As the advance guard (in Du Bois's case one might already say, in 1925, the "older" guard) of an emerging black intelligentsia, these men, and women such as Jessie Fausset (literary editor of *The Crisis,* the NAACP's journal), Angelina Grimké, and Zora Neale Hurston, initiated and helped sustain public debate on issues of assimilation, nationalism, higher education, artistic freedom, economic independence, cultural self-determination, women's rights, and race leadership. (Here, the extensively researched and well-documented *Propaganda and Aesthetics* is extremely helpful in delineating the way these debates became public through a nexus of journals and small magazines.) Historically, these writers, artists, and activists were uniquely poised so as to inherit a set of social conditions shaped by Reconstruction, the black migration northward, economic fluctuation, U.S. participation in World War I; *and* to set the terms for addressing and representing those conditions, terms that would in turn be inherited by future generations.

Personally, Locke seems to have been able to balance an active, even extravagant, social life among Manhattan's upper crust, with his commitment to education, and even serious philosophical writing. Well-respected by prominent philosophers like John Dewey and Sidney Hook, Locke was called upon both to speak at professional gatherings and to contribute to volumes on contemporary philosophy. One can only speculate on what his stature as a philosopher might have been had be exerted more sustained efforts in that area. And yet, the poet Claude McKay referred to him simply as a "charming, harmless fellow" (and at least on one occasion as the embodiment of the "Aframerican rococco," an even less flattering picture). Perhaps not without irony, Locke humbly referred to himself as the "midwife" of a generation of writers and artists who would be responsible for Harlem's renaissance.

Significant Form, Style, or Artistic Conventions

While the primary historical and cultural importance of Locke's essay certainly lies in its content rather than in its form or style, I do stress Locke's ability to appeal to an educated, and perhaps dispassionate, reader through careful control of tone and language. I also spend some time on the essay form itself as part of an American traditional of cultural criticism. This latter approach works especially well in writing-intensive courses; student-writers are likely to take their work more seriously if they are able to see their own essays as fitting into that tradition.

Original Audience

"The New Negro" makes a nice case study in audience because of its publication history. Originally written as the lead essay for a special issue of the magazine *Survey Graphic* that Locke had been called upon to edit, it later served as the introduction to a much expanded anthology based on that issue, published as *The New Negro: An Interpretation*. As the popular version of *Survey*, a professional journal devoted to social work, *Survey Graphic* was an extensively illustrated magazine designed to acquaint a general readership with social problems of the day. The anthology, published by the well-respected Albert and Charles Boni, and illustrated with fine color portraits, drawings, decorative designs, and reproductions of African artwork, is clearly designed to avoid racial polemics and to reach an educated, enlightened audience, composed of both black and white readers. (One might even say that Locke is aiming for a primarily white audience, presenting a well-reasoned defense of his cultural agenda to potential supporters.)

Comparisons, Contrasts, Connections

Locke's essay works well alongside Du Bois's "Of Our Spiritual Striv-ings" (chapter I of *The Souls of Black Folk*); Langston Hughes's "When the Negro Was in Vogue"; James Weldon Johnson's *The Autobiography of an ex-colored Man*. However, it is also important to remember that Locke was a vital member of an *American* intellectual community—be it "Anglo" or "Afro"—and therefore can be seen as addressing issues of *national* concern. An instructive connection to make in this light is with Randolph Bourne's "Transnational America." (See also Locke's 1911 essay, "The American Temperament.") Bourne's cosmopolitanism, his notion of a "trans-nationality" and a "federation of cultures," is com-patible with Locke's own vision of an American democracy based on a rigorous sense of cultural pluralism. Further, on the dialectic between artistic innovation and cultural conservation, also an issue for Locke, see T. S. Eliot's "Tradition and the Individual Talent."

Questions for Reading and Discussion/ Approaches to Writing

Students should be able to answer questions along the lines of the following:

1. What does Locke mean by the "new" negro? How does this figure differ from the "old" negro? To what extent does this figure corre-spond to an actual social type, and to what extent might it be an idealization? What might Locke's purpose be in idealizing the new negro?
2. What does Locke hope to achieve with his essay?
3. What concerns does Locke share with other writers of his day?
4. What influence do you think Locke had on the artists of the New Negro Movement? Can this influence be seen today? What issues of importance to Locke and the New Negro Movement generally are still of concern today?

Writing assignments might range from a work of original cultural criticism (that is, attack a contemporary issue/cultural problem related to those Locke dealt with, addressing a particular audience from the stu-dent's own viewpoint), to an analysis of Locke's vision of culture and democracy vis-à-vis that of another writer, say, Du Bois or Bourne (this, of course, might involve research and further reading in each author's body of work).

Bibliography

Baker, Houston A., Jr. *Modernism and the Harlem Renaissance.* Chicago: University of Chicago Press, 1987.

Dallas Museum of Art. *Black Art, Ancestral Legacy: The African Impulse in African-American Art.* New York: Harry N. Abrams, Inc., 1989.

Huggins, Nathan Irvin. *Harlem Renaissance.* New York: Oxford University Press, 1971.

Johnson, Abby Arthur and Ronald Maberry Johnson. *Propaganda and Aesthetics: The Literary Politics of African-American Magazines in the Twentieth Century.* 2nd ed. Amherst: University of Massachusetts Press, 1991.

Lewis, David Levering. *When Harlem Was in Vogue.* New York: Knopf, 1981.

Nelson, Cary. *Repression and Recovery: Modern American Poetry and the Politics of Cultural Memory, 1910–1945.* Madison: University of Wisconsin Press, 1989.

Studio Museum in Harlem. *Harlem Renaissance: Art of Black America.* New York: Harry N. Abrams, Inc., 1987.

Jean Toomer (1894–1967)

Contributing Editor: Nellie Y. McKay

Classroom Issues and Strategies

Toomer's style is difficult, especially in view of earlier African-American literature. To a large extent, Toomer abandoned the predominant naturalistic and realistic representation of the black experience to experiment with newer modernistic techniques. When they first approach these texts, students usually feel that it is well beyond their understanding—that Toomer is engaged in abstractions that are too difficult to comprehend.

Have the students explore all the possibilities for a literal meaning of the metaphors and symbols. "Blood-Burning Moon" is less difficult for them because it has a traditional story line. In "Karintha," for instance, try to get them to see that Toomer is concerned with the sexual and economic oppression of women within their own communities where they should be safe from the former at least.

These selections lend themselves to the visual imagination. Students may find it helpful to think of the "pictures" Toomer's images present as they read and try to understand, also, the written meanings these images present.

Students respond positively to the poetic qualities of the writing, and they enjoy its visual aspects. They have difficulty interpreting the underlying themes and meanings, mainly because the language is seductive and leaves them ambivalent regarding the positive and negative qualities the writer intends to portray. It is best to lead them through one section by reading aloud in class and permitting them to use a number of methods (listening to the words, visualizing the images, etc.) to try to fathom what is going on.

Major Themes, Historical Perspectives, and Personal Issues

1. The significance of black women as representatives of African-American culture. What qualities do women have that are similar to those of the entire group of African-Americans—at least as Toomer saw them?
2. The nature of the richness as well as the pain in African-American culture.
3. The symbolistic aspects of the northern and southern black experience.
4. The role of the black artist—e.g., in "Song of the Son," in which the absent son returns to preserve the almost now-lost culture of his ancestors.

Significant Form, Style, or Artistic Conventions

Toomer is writing at a crucial time in American and African-American literary history. His friends are members of the Lost Generation of writers intent on reforming American literature. His effort is to make a different kind of presentation of African-America through the art of literature. He sees the loss of some of the strongest elements of the culture in the move toward modernization and technology. For example, he captures the beauty and pathos of the experience in "Karintha"; the brutality in "Blood-Burning Moon"; and the imitation of the white culture in "Box Seat."

Original Audience

Cane was written for an intellectual audience who could grasp the nuances the author was interested in promoting. The book sold fewer than 500 copies in its first year, but had enthusiastic reviews from the most avant-garde literary critics. It continues to appeal to intellectuals, especially those who are interested in the ways in which language can be manipulated to express particular life situations.

Comparisons, Contrasts, Connections

Toomer's work can be compared to some of Sherwood Anderson's stories, and to Hart Crane's poetry. The three men knew each other and were friends during the 1920s. They read each other's work and advised each other. Their general thrust was that human beings were alienated from the basic "natural" qualities in themselves and needed to get back to more of the spiritual values that could be found in closer unity with nature.

Questions for Reading and Discussion/ Approaches to Writing

Cane was a work to celebrate the African-American experience without denying the awful pain and oppression that made the strength of the group so apparent. Paper topics that focus on the history of black America between Reconstruction and the 1920s are useful in showing what a student can learn about Jean Toomer's reasons for the perceptions he revealed in these selections.

Bibliography

The best source on these is the discussion (in chronological order in the book) in the McKay biography of Toomer's literary life and work. The attempt here is to explicate the individual selections in the total book.

Langston Hughes (1902–1967)

Contributing Editor: Charles H. Nichols

Classroom Issues and Strategies

The primary problems encountered in teaching Langston Hughes grow out of his air of improvisation and familiarity. Vital to an understanding of Hughes's poetry and prose is the idiom, the quality of black colloquial speech and the rhythms of jazz and the blues.

The best strategies for teaching the writer involve the reading aloud of the poetry and prose, the use of recordings and films, the use of the history of the "New Negro" and the Harlem Renaissance.

Major Themes, Historical Perspectives, and Personal Issues

The major themes in Langston Hughes's work grow out of his personal life, his travels, his involvement in radical and protest movements, his interest in Africa and South America as well as the Caribbean.

Significant Form, Style, or Artistic Conventions

In regard to questions of form, style, or artistic convention, the following considerations are relevant to Langston Hughes:

1. His debt to Walt Whitman, Carl Sandburg, and Paul Laurence Dunbar.
2. His enthusiasm for the language and songs of the rural folk and lower-class urban, "street" Negro. As Bontemps once wrote, "No one loved Negroes as Langston Hughes did."
3. His capacity for improvisation and original rhythms. His use of jazz, blues, be-bop, gospel, Harlem slang.

The poetry: Point out the occasion that inspired the poem "The Negro Speaks of Rivers" (cf. *The Big Sea*, pp. 54–56). "The Weary Blues," "Drum," and "Freedom Train" use the idioms of black speech with poetic effect.

Prose: Among Hughes's finest achievements are the Simple stories. Here we have the speech and idiom presented with irony, malapropisms, and humor.

Original Audience

Hughes's audience consisted of his literary friends (Countee Cullen, Carl Van Vechten, Wallace Thurman, etc.) as well as the general public.

Comparisons, Contrasts, Connections

Comparisons or contrasts might be made with Carl Sandburg, Walt Whitman, Claude McKay. The bases of such comparisons might be the language and metaphor, the degree of militancy, etc.

Bibliography

Berry, Faith. "Saunders Redding as Literary Critic of Langston Hughes." *The Langston Hughes Review* V, no. 2 (Fall 1986).

Emanuel, James A. and Theodore L. Gross. *Dark Symphony: Negro Literature in America*. New York: The Free Press, 1968. 191–221, 447–80.

Henderson, Stephen. *Understanding the New Black Poetry: Black Speech and Black Music as Poetic References*. New York: Wm. Morrow & Co., 1973.

Hughes, L. "Ten Ways to Use Poetry in Teaching." *College Language Association Bulletin*, 1951.

——. *The First Book of Rhythms* (1954).

Miller, R. Baxter, ed. *Black American Poets Between Worlds, 1940–1960*. Knoxville: University of Tennessee Press, 1986.

——. *The Art and Imagination of Langston Hughes*. Knoxville: University of Kentucky Press, 1988.

O'Daniel, Therman B. *Langston Hughes, Black Genius: A Critical Evaluation*. For the College Language Association. New York: Wm. Morrow & Co., 1971, 65 ff. p 171. p. 180.

Countee Cullen (1903–1946)

Contributing Editor: Walter C. Daniel

Classroom Issues and Strategies

Students who read Cullen need to develop a clear understanding of the temper of the Harlem Renaissance period in U.S. literary development. In addition, they may need help with the classical allusions in "Yet Do I Marvel" and in "Simon the Cyrenian Speaks." Also, students should come to understand the reference to Scottsboro as the poet's criticism of his fellow poets' neglect of what he considers a significant matter (obviously, this requires knowing about the Scottsboro incident in 1931 and following).

Significant Form, Style, or Artistic Conventions

Countee Cullen is an important figure of the African-American arts movement known as the Harlem Renaissance. Born in Louisville, Kentucky, Cullen was reared in New York City by his paternal grandmother until 1918, when he was adopted by the Reverend Frederick Asbury Cullen. This was a turning point in his life, for he was now introduced into the very center of black activism and achievement. Cullen displayed his talent early; already in high school he was writing poetry, and in his sophomore year at NYU he was awarded second prize in the nationwide Witter Bynner Poetry Contest for "The Ballad of the Brown Girl." Encompassing themes that would remain salient for the remainder of his career, Cullen's first major poem also revealed his unabashed reverence for the works of John Keats. Cullen was firmly convinced that traditional verse forms could not be bettered by more modern paradigms. It was, therefore, the task of any aspiring writer, he felt, to become conversant with and part of a received literary tradition simply because such a tradition has the virtue of longevity and universal sanction.

Cullen's first volume *Color* established him as a writer with an acute spiritual vision. Especially noteworthy in this respect is "Simon the Cyrenian Speaks," a work that eloquently makes use of Matthew 27:32 in order to suggest an analogue between blacks and Simon, the man who was compelled to bear the cross of Christ on his back. Sublimity was not Cullen's only strong point. In "Incident," the reader is brusquely catapulted into the all-too-realistic world of an impressionable eight-year-old as he experiences overt racism for the first time on a heretofore memorable ride through the history-filled streets of Baltimore.

In 1927, Cullen edited a significant anthology of black poetry, *Caroling Dusk*, and published two collections of his own, *The Ballad of the Brown Girl* and *Copper Sun*. Representative of Cullen's philosophical development in this period is the multifaceted "Heritage," a poem that summarizes his ambivalent relationship with Christian and pagan cultural constructs.

The 1930s and 1940s saw a change of direction in Cullen's work. His poetry output almost totally ceased as he turned his attention to the novel, theater, translation, teaching, and children's literature. The 1932 novel *One Way to Heaven* was Cullen's response to Carl Van Vechten's 1926 *Nigger Heaven*, a controversial and notorious work exploring the seamy underbelly of Harlem.

Cullen's best work was his poetry; he apparently knew this when he compiled his anthology, with the self-explanatory title *On These I Stand*, shortly before his death.

Original Audience

The Harlem Renaissance period between the two world wars saw the rise and definition of the "New Negro" in social, political, and literature activities of the nation.

Cullen, along with other formally educated black poets, established a new aesthetic for racial statement.

Comparisons, Contrasts, Connections

Cullen's contemporaries (the best-known ones among the writers) were Gwendolyn Bennett, Langston Hughes, and Claude McKay; contrast the poetic method of social protest by studying poems written by each of these poets.

Cullen has been criticized for taking an elitist attitude toward racial matters and of ignoring social protest. Is this criticism fair to Cullen in light of your reading of some poems written by him and, for instance, Claude McKay?

His first volume of poetry *Color* (1925) revealed an indebtedness to traditional verse forms and an abiding interest in the tenets of romanticism, characteristics markedly absent from the blues-based folk rhythms of the poetry of Langston Hughes. Cullen looked beyond his own rich heritage for authorial models and chose John Keats, firmly convinced that "To make a poet black, and bid him sing" was a "curious thing" that God had done. So curious, indeed, that the voice of the black poet had to be assimilated to and harmonized with the bearers of an alien literary tradition. In "To John Keats, Poet. At Springtime," Cullen's adulation of the nineteenth-century lyricist is most pronounced: "I know, in spite of all men say/Of Beauty, you have felt her most."

Questions for Reading and Discussion/
Approaches to Writing

1. Identify non-black authors of the 1920s and determine their common themes in contrast with those of black writers.
2. Cullen grew up in a Methodist parsonage as the adopted son of a prominent Harlem pastor. Might the use of paradox about Christian religion and its practices in some of his poetry reflect his home experience? Which works and in which references?
3. Indications of Cullen's fascination with and influence by the English romantic poets, especially John Keats.
4. Effectiveness of the metaphor of Simon, the Cyrenian to black American life at the time; whether the allusion suggests some theological implications, such as non-redemptive suffering.
5. In the poem "Yet Do I Marvel," Cullen makes an implicit comparison between black poets and the mythical figures of Tantalus and Sisyphus. Explain how this comparison functions within the world of the poem.
6. Lying behind Cullen's title choice for "From the Dark Tower" is the phrase "ivory tower." How does this fact help explain the poem as well as its dedication to Charles S. Johnson?
7. As background to discussion of "Scottsboro, Too, Is Worth Its Song," comment on the historical importance of the Scottsboro Nine case and the trial of Sacco and Vanzetti. Why are these two events paired in Cullen's poem? What was the prevailing poetic current that prevented contemporary concerns from being broached in verse? In answering this last question, compare, for instance, some of the poems written by Wallace Stevens and William Carlos Williams during this period with the poetry of Cullen. Why did Cullen not follow the modernist precepts announced by writers such as T. S. Eliot, Ezra Pound, and Amy Lowell? How does Cullen's allusion to Walt Whitman's lines "I . . . sing myself" and "I sing the body electric" function in the context of this poem?
8. Cullen chooses to set his poem "Incident" in old Baltimore. Why?
9. With reference to "Pagan Prayer," comment on the manner in which African-Americans have used Christian religion as a reposi-

tory for radical egalitarian hopes. How is Cullen's conception of the religion of the white man different from that of a contemporary Nigerian writer, such as Chinua Achebe in his novels *Things Fall Apart* and *Arrow of God*?

10. How does Cullen accommodate traditions of English poetry to themes of problems of living black in the United States?

11. How active is the poet (Cullen) in taking the position of racial spokesman in the poems? Effective?

Bibliography

Baker, Houston. *Black Literature in America*. New York: McGraw Hill, 1971, 114–58.

Bontemps, Arna. *The Harlem Renaissance Remembered*. New York: Dodd, Mead, 1972.

Daniel, Walter C. "Countee Cullen as Literary Critic." *College Language Association Journal* XIV (March 1972): 281–90.

Davis, Arthur. *From the Dark Tower: African-American Writers 1900–1960*. Howard University Press, 1974.

Wagner, Jean. *Black Poets of the United States*. Urbana-Champaign: University of Illinois Press, 1973. Part II.

Critical discussion of Cullen's poetry was inaugurated by J. Saunders Redding in *To Make a Poet Black*, 1939. More detailed attention was given to his oeuvre in a sympathetic and forthright monograph by Houston A. Baker, Jr., *A Many-colored Coat of Dreams: The Poetry of Countee Cullen*, 1974. Alan R. Shucard in *Countee Cullen*, 1984, provides a complete overview and assessment of Cullen's life and literary endeavors.

Perceptive comments about his novel are contained in Bernard W. Bell's *The African-American Novel and Its Tradition*, 1987.

An invaluable general background of the Harlem Renaissance that also includes comments about Cullen is Nathan Irvin Huggins's *Harlem Renaissance*, 1971. Equally indispensable is Margaret Perry's *A Bio-Bibliography of Countee P. Cullen 1903–1946*, 1971.

Noteworthy articles touching upon particular aspects of Cullen's poetry are:

Davis, Arthur P. "The Alien-and-Exile Theme in Countee Cullen's Racial Poems." *Phylon* 14 (1953): 390–400.

Dorsey, David F. "Countee Cullen's Use of Greek Mythology." *College Language Association Journal* 13 (1970): 68–77.

Webster, Harvey Curtis. "A Difficult Career." *Poetry* 70 (1947): 224–25.

Gwendolyn B. Bennett (1902–1981)

Contributing Editor: Walter C. Daniel

Classroom Issues and Strategies

Almost always overlooked in discussion about the Harlem Renaissance, Gwendolyn Bennett was, nevertheless, a significant part of the most important artistic movement in African-American history. Chiefly remembered for "The Ebony Flute," a regular column appearing in *Opportunity* that chronicled the creative efforts of the writers, painters, sculptors, actors, and musicians who made Harlem the center of a profound cultural flowering, Bennett was also a poet and short story writer of considerable skill. "To Usward," for instance, a poem dedicated to Jessie Fauset in honor of the publication of her novel *There Is Confusion*, celebrates the newly discovered sense of empowerment permeating the Harlem community—a community envisioned as a chorus of individual voices at once aware of a rich African cultural heritage and prepared to sing "Before the urgency of youth's behest!" because of its belief that it "claim[s] no part of racial dearth."

More typical of Bennett's lyric voice is the deeply personal "Hatred." Although the motivation for hating is nowhere explicitly revealed, the tragic history of slavery is a barely concealed presence in the poem, welling to the surface as the speaker invokes memory as the agent for understanding her hatred. Unstated, of course, is the hope that memory will also ensure that past savagery is never again repeated. Of her two stories, the most popularly anthologized piece is "Wedding Day," a work that appeared in the sole issue of *Fire!!*, a radical 1926 periodical launched by Langston Hughes, Zora Neale Hurston, and Wallace Thurman with the avowed intent "to burn up a lot of old, dead conventional Negro-white ideas of the past," to validate the folk expression "the blacker the berry, the sweeter the juice."

The tale of Paul Watson, a black American who falsely thought he could flee prejudice in the United States by living as an expatriate in France, "Wedding Day" takes on a dirge-like quality as it recounts the stoical endurance required of black people in coping with contradictory and absurd situations even in a post–World War I Europe many of them helped to liberate.

Although her work was never collected into a single volume, Bennett's poetry and prose were, nonetheless, included in major anthologies of the period such as Countee Cullen's *Caroling Dusk* (1924), Alain

Locke's *The New Negro* (1925), and William Stanley Braithwaite's *Year-book of American Poetry* (1927). Admired for her artistic work on five covers of *Opportunity* and two covers of *Crisis*, praised for her "depth and understanding" of character nuances in her short stories by the playwright Theodore Ward, she was, in the words of James Weldon Johnson, a "dynamic figure" whose keenest talent lay in composing "delicate poignant lyrics."

Questions for Reading and Discussion/ Approaches to Writing

1. Why did the author coin the neologism "usward" as part of the title of the poem "To Usward?"
2. In Chinese culture, what is the significance of ginger jars?
3. In the poem "Advice," Bennett's choice of the word *sophist* is significant. Comment on the etymology and historical circumstances surrounding the first usage of this word.
4. Discuss the importance of Alexander Dumas as a literary figure.
5. The poem "Heritage" centers on a distinct yearning for Africa. Why did the poets of this period stress such a theme?

Arna Bontemps (1902–1973)

Contributing Editor: Charles H. Nichols

Classroom Issues and Strategies

Bontemps is a lucid, sophisticated writer whose use of tone, irony, and symbol achieves subtle and interesting effects. Students need help in interpreting these kinds of figurative language.

In teaching Bontemps it is helpful to read his works aloud and to supply the background information that helps in interpretation. You may want to refer to poems not included in this anthology. "Miracles" is a poem with allusions to the life of Christ. "Let the Church Roll On" uses the familiar setting of the black church. The stark stories from *The Old South* evoke the race relations of the 1930s.

Major Themes, Historical Perspectives, and Personal Issues

The major themes in Bontemps are historical as in *100 Years of Negro Freedom* (1961) and *Black Thunder* (1936). Bontemps wrote historical novels on slave revolts and the stunning play *St. Louis Woman*.

Significant Form, Style, or Artistic Conventions

In form and style, Bontemps is deeply influenced by the folk traditions—the spirituals, blues, and jazz. Yet he is also steeped in the finest traditions of English poetry and writes with dignity and a sense of beauty.

Original Audience

Bontemps wrote several works in collaboration with Langston Hughes. He prepared important anthologies and children's books. There have always been audiences for his writing.

Comparisons, Contrasts, Connections

Bontemps might be compared with Jack Conroy or Langston Hughes, writers with whom he collaborated. The basis of each comparison might be their relative concern for historical events or the use of folklore.

Questions for Reading and Discussion/ Approaches to Writing

1. In the poem "A Black Man Talks of Reaping," the poet presents the bitterness of the black man's experience, yet achieves a universal quality. How does the metaphor of planting and reaping remove the poem from the level of polemics?

Outside reading:

2. (a) "Miracles" is essentially transcendental. Describe the theme of the poem.
   (b) What use does Bontemps make of biblical allusion and religious imagery? How does he use the religious tradition of black people?

Sterling A. Brown (1901–1989)

Contributing Editor: John Edgar Tidwell

Classroom Issues and Strategies

Two problems come immediately to mind when I consider my past experiences in teaching Brown's poetry. First the relative obscurity of Brown's place in the American literary tradition is the biggest obstacle in teaching Brown because students think his presence in the syllabus requires some big justification.

The second problem, ironically, is much more complicated. Because Brown is a black poet, students are quite willing to interpret his poetry in light of his "blackness," by which they generally mean hard luck, pain, and suffering imposed by "Jim Crow" laws. They are less willing to acknowledge Brown as a poet, one conscientiously crafting and representing experience in poetic form. Brown's fundamental assertion of a humanistic vision is rooted in the democratic principles of the U.S. Constitution. The way in which this assertion is set forth as compelling poetry sometimes escapes the vision of students, who often want to see him engaged in special pleading. They're often reluctant to see him in a tradition established by Robert Frost, E. A. Robinson, Carl Sandburg, and Edgar Lee Masters; at times, a myopia prevents them from seeing how Brown takes aesthetic forms from black folk—the blues, folk tales, work songs—and adapts them for poetic purpose. In short, it is a problem of getting students to understand how Brown is, in fact, an Americanist, whose precepts and examples sought to argue his liberation from, as he considered it, the more narrow designation black writer.

To handle the problem of Brown's relative obscurity, I begin by placing him within a thematic and structural context of black and white writers who sought the "extraordinary in ordinary life." In part, this means illustrating Brown's comment that when Sandburg said yes to his Chicago hog butchers and stacks of wheat, he was moved to celebrate the lives, lore, and language of black folk.

To establish a context of writers using black folk traditions during Brown's era, I begin with Langston Hughes, Zora Neale Hurston, James Weldon Johnson, and Waring Cuney, among others. I discuss very generally the differing ways they made use of black folk experiences to establish texts and aesthetic contexts. What this permits is a comparative approach; it asks for ways Brown's blues poems, for example, conform and depart from those of Hughes and Cuney.

Of the various presentational techniques I've used, one has been especially useful: listening to Brown reading his own poetry, which is available on several Folkways records. Brown is an exceptional reader, in part because of his background in drama and his reputation for being a raconteur.

Most questions students pose relate to the subtle way in which Brown calls into question the panoply of Jim Crow laws. In Brown's "Old Lem," for example, they ask for clarification about the nonverbal communication suggested by Old Lem's standing with bowed head, averted eyes, and open hands, in contrast to the whites with hands balled in fists and eyes in direct, confrontational stares. The history of these gestures dating from its formalization into law during the early nineteenth century is something they usually don't understand, but come to see when it is explained.

Major Themes, Historical Perspectives, and Personal Issues

How does Brown's work simultaneously refute racial stereotypes *and* affirm the humanity of black life? What is distinctive about Brown's humor? In what ways does it borrow from the vernacular tradition brought to prominence by Twain? How does the theme of the pursuit of democracy figure into Brown's aesthetic vision? How do sociological concerns coalesce with aesthetic pursuits without one overshadowing the other? What innovations in technique and craft can be discerned in Brown's poetry?

Significant Form, Style, or Artistic Conventions

I find the issues of period and school to be particularly interesting. Brown has been vociferous in refuting the term *Harlem* Renaissance. His opposition takes on two points: First, Harlem was *a*, not *the*, center of Negro creative activity during this era. To locate it in Harlem, he continues, is to afford too much credit to Carl Van Vechten and not enough to blacks themselves. Second, he often puns, if this era was the *Renaissance*, where is the *naissance*? Critics generally include him in the group of writers who came of age during the twenties. Brown questions his inclusion in the group, by preferring to be considered a "lone wolf." And he further questions the neat periodization of the New Negro Movement into the years 1922–1929. A renaissance, he contends, is much longer.

One could use Brown's denials, then, as bases for defining problems of period, school, and even aesthetic convention. For example, how does Brown's use of black idiom differ from his immediate predecessors and from writers as early as Paul Laurence Dunbar and his imitators?

Original Audience

Brown himself is his own best spokesman on the question of audience. In terms of an external audience, he confronted "the dilemma of a divided audience." On one hand, a white readership, thoroughly conditioned by racial stereotyping to expect superficial depictions of blacks, sought confirmation of their beliefs in black poetry. Bristling at any hint of a racially demeaning representation of blacks, the audience of black readers sought glorified portraits of blacks, which became stereotypes in another direction. Brown rejected both audiences and instead hypothesized one. The oral or speakerly quality of his poetry depends in part on the audience he creates within his poetry. The dynamics of speaker-listener are central to understanding the performative nature of his work. In Brown's description, poetry should communicate something. (The explanation of "communication" can be inferred from his letter to Langston Hughes, in which he said poets should not follow the elitist path of Ezra Pound and T. S. Eliot, two poets he considers no longer talking to each other, only themselves.) Communication is accomplished by using forms and structures and the language of black folk. Such use articulates a vision of the world that celebrates the dignity, humanism, and worth of a people largely misunderstood and misrepresented.

Readers of Brown's poetry today come away with a similar sense of the performative dimensions of his poetry, I think, because much of Brown's poetry holds up today. Even though today's audience may not know the character of racial discrimination in the way Brown experienced it, his poetry has a quality that transcends particular time and place. "She jes' gits hold of us dataway" the speaker in Brown's "Ma Rainey" tells us. Readers of the poem today, like those of an earlier generation, come away with the same feeling.

Questions for Reading and Discussion/ Approaches to Writing

1. The questions I assign are determined by the approach and the poems I use. My approach to the Slim Greer poems, for example, centers on the poem as tall tale. I generally ask students to consult a literary handbook for features of the tall tale and to read the

poems in light of their findings. In this same vein, I often assign actual tall tales (such as Roger Welsch's *Shingling the Fog and Other Plain Lies*) or other examples of poetry written in this tradition (such as *Fireside Tales* by Joe Allen), as a way of suggesting Brown's distinctiveness.

2. My paper topics are assigned to extend students' understanding of works we read and discuss in class by encouraging them to build upon the assigned reading a comparative critical analysis. The issues raised in the first part of this question give students a chance to range beyond class discussion.

Bibliography

For criticism on Brown, the list of works cited at the end of the headnote is extremely useful. Important additions to the list include the following titles:

Nichols, Charles H. "Sterling Brown, Poet, His Place in Afro-American Literary History." In *The Harlem Renaissance: Revaluations*, edited by Amritjit Singh, et al., 91–100. New York: Garland Publishing, Inc., 1989.

Stepto, Robert B. "Sterling A. Brown: Outsider in the Harlem Renaissance?" In *The Harlem Renaissance: Revaluations*, edited by Amritjit Singh, et al., 73–81. New York: Garland Publishing, Inc., 1989.

Tidwell, John Edgar, guest editor. "Oh, Didn't He Ramble: Sterling A. Brown (1901–1989)," special section of *Black American Literature Forum*, 23.1 (1989): 89–112.

Wagner, Jean. *Black Poets of the United States*. Urbana-Champaign: University of Illinois Press, 1973. Chapter 11, "Sterling Brown."

Zora Neale Hurston (1891–1960)

Contributing Editor: Robert Hemenway

Classroom Issues and Strategies

While there are no particular difficulties in teaching Hurston, some students find the dialect hard to understand. To address this problem, I usually read several passages aloud to help students get a "feel" for the voices. Once they've heard Hurston read aloud, they can create her characters' speech in their minds so that it is understandable.

Major Themes, Historical Perspectives, and Personal Issues

Women's issues
Race issues
Interface between oral and written literature

Significant Form, Style, or Artistic Conventions

Short story structure
Representations of an oral culture

Original Audience

Always a complex issue when postulating the audience of a black writer.

Comparisons, Contrasts, Connections

Langston Hughes
Alice Walker

Claude McKay (1889–1948)

Contributing Editor: Elvin Holt

Classroom Issues and Strategies

I suggest that teachers begin with McKay's love poems. This approach allows students to relate to McKay on a purely human level and prepares them for the discomforting racial themes that dominate some of the other poems.

Students respond to the persistent racism in American society. Some non-black students want to know why they have to read such poems. Many of them believe the poems are "for black people." Some students object to the eroticism of the love poems.

"Flame-Heart" evokes the romantic tradition of Wordsworth and Shelley, poets whose work McKay admired greatly. This finely wrought poem, which expresses the poet's deep longing for Jamaica, his beloved homeland, highlights McKay's interest in nonracial themes.

"A Red Flower," one of McKay's most striking love poems, features brilliant conceits similar to those found in the poetry of John Donne and other metaphysical poets. Identify the metaphor in the first and last stanzas of the poem.

In "Flower of Love," McKay presents another example of his passionate, yet controlled, love poetry. Like "A Red Flower," "Flower of Love" turns on an elaborate conceit, recalling the best work of Andrew Marvell. Describe the poem's central metaphor and explain the reference to the South.

"America" is one of McKay's best protest poems. Explain the poem's central theme and describe the prophecy the speaker relates in the final quatrain.

"The Lynching," a moving expression of McKay's outrage against the senseless killings of blacks that marked the early decades of this century, depicts Christ as the victim of the lynching. Is the Christ figure an effective image, considering the context?

McKay's best-known poem, "If We Must Die," urges blacks to wage war against their oppressors. Winston Churchill used McKay's poem to revive the spirit of his countrymen during World War II.

"The Harlem Dancer" focuses on a beautiful black woman performing in a nightclub. What is the central theme of the poem? Does the poet articulate a point of view with which black feminists might concur?

"Harlem Shadows" is the title poem from McKay's 1922 collection of poetry. Who or what are the "shadows" mentioned in the poem's title? What does the poem say about the plight of black Americans in general?

Major Themes, Historical Perspectives, and Personal Issues

It is essential that students get a sense of what it was like to be black in America during the early decades of this century. Students must also realize that McKay's Jamaican background made him particularly sensitive to the plight of black Americans.

Significant Form, Style, or Artistic Conventions

It is important to give students a good introduction to the Harlem Renaissance. Students need to know what the writers (blacks) were trying to accomplish. Students should note McKay's dependence upon traditional British forms such as the sonnet.

Original Audience

I help students to understand the social history that shaped McKay's work and determined his first audience. Then I try to help students see why the poems remain fresh and vital to our own time.

Comparisons, Contrasts, Connections

Since McKay was influenced by important British poets such as Wordsworth, Shelley, and Donne, it is useful to compare and contrast his work with that of English romantic and metaphysical poets. Stylistic similarities are often evident.

Bibliography

James R. Giles's *Claude McKay* is a good book for teachers. The text is well organized, and the index makes it easy to locate specific information.

Anne Spencer (1882–1975)

Contributing Editor: Evelyn H. Roberts

Classroom Issues and Strategies

Aside from black literature anthologies and general reference sources, limited critical material is available. The poet Anne Spencer can best be made accessible to students in various ways.

1. Relating Spencer's fascination with reading and studying at the Lynchburg Seminary (note, for example, her selection as the commencement speaker).
2. Presenting an overhead transparency of one of her longer poems, "At The Carnival." Most students enjoy this poem and can relate to such an experience—comparing or contrasting with their own carnival and/or county fair experiences.

3. Showing the photographs that appear in J. Lee Greene's *Time's Unfading Garden*.
4. Using selected black literature anthologies placed on library reserve for students who wish to prepare brief oral reports or short papers.

Many of Spencer's poems show dramatic compression and sharpness of image and phrase. She is no pleader of causes, choosing not to comment on the race issue in her published poetry. Yet her biography reveals a wide acquaintance with literary dignitaries, lecturers, and other prominent citizens, black and white, who would appear as public speakers and/or artists in Lynchburg, Virginia.

Students admire Spencer's commitment to maintaining a free, independent spirit, not being hampered or restrained by husband or offspring. They also admire her determination and concentration to create despite the reality that "art is long and time is fleeting." In addition, students applaud both Spencer's assertiveness as demonstrated by her work for women's suffrage and her determination to create options that allowed her to pursue her art by diverse routes (as demonstrated by her work as the first black librarian in Lynchburg).

Students are curious about Spencer's statement, published by Countee Cullen (*Caroling Dusk*, p. 47):

"But I have no civilized articulation for the things I hate. I proudly love being a Negro woman; [it's] so involved and interesting. *We* are the PROBLEM—the great national game of TABOO."

Major Themes, Historical Perspectives, and Personal Issues

Like Ralph Waldo Emerson, Henry David Thoreau, Emily Dickinson, Amy Lowell, and Angelina Grimké, Anne Spencer maintained a strong belief in individual freedom and liberty to convey ideas and uphold ideals vital for personal expression. Further, Spencer possessed strong individual preferences and exhibited objections to various standards or beliefs that may have compromised her personal ideals. See poems not included in this anthology such as "Wife-Woman" and "Neighbors."

Further, Anne Spencer sustained a life-long admiration for poets and the art of poetry. In her poem "Dunbar," she pays tribute to Chatterton, Shelley, and Keats.

Some additional similarities can be cited showing an interrelatedness in the art of the above-mentioned poets. As Emily Dickinson advanced in years, the circle of her world grew ever smaller. Dickinson became a hermit by deliberate and conscious choice. Similarly, Anne

Spencer withdrew from the community as the years passed. For Dickinson, her isolation allowed her to become prey to the then-current Emersonian doctrine of "mystical individualism." As a flower of New England transcendentalism, she became a Puritan and free thinker obsessed with the problems of good and evil, of life and death, nature and destiny of the human soul. Toward God, Emily Dickinson exhibited an Emersonian self-possession.

Moreover, Emerson's gnomic style became for Emily Dickinson epigrammatic to the point of being cryptic; a quality that Anne Spencer, Amy Lowell, and Angelina Grimké likewise display.

Finally, Anne Spencer in some of her poems—"Requiem," "Substitution," "Wife-Woman"—appears to embrace a pantheistic view that can be compared to Emerson's view in "Hamatreya" of recognizing God in nature.

Significant Form, Style, or Artistic Conventions

Though sometimes coupled with the Harlem Renaissance period, Anne Spencer follows the tradition of neo-romantic poetry, having composed some poems before the Harlem Renaissance era was clearly identified, or designated. Her poetry communicates a highly personal experience, revealing an arresting image. Her assessment of an experience may be occasionally ironic but discloses her profundity.

Anne Spencer's style reveals her individuality, an affinity for nature imagery, and the conventions of British and American romantics, as her sensibility to form and color, a rich and varied vocabulary, and a pantheistic philosophy disclose.

An admirer of Robert Browning, one of her favorite poets, who despite his use of the idiom of conversation, achieved remarkable cogent compressed lines, Anne Spencer, likewise, achieved a similar style. Economy of phrase and compression of thought result from numerous revisions of the same poem. Compare with Emily Dickinson's extensive and/or intensive revision strategy.

Original Audience

To help students imagine Spencer's original audience, they are urged to create a yesteryear time capsule list for the poem when first written or published: listing common objects, terms, phrases, scenes, situations existing then but vastly different from the present era. For example:

	BEFORE WWII	SINCE WWII
"At the Carnival" (composed about 1919)	My Limousine-Lady fig-leaf bull-necked man sausage and garlic booth quivering female-thing Gestured assignations heaven-fed Naiad bacilli of the usual Neptune	Gay little girl of the Diving blind crowd quivering female-thing call it dancing Little Diver Carnival-tank

Comparisons, Contrasts, Connections

Both Emily Dickinson and Spencer were philosophical in their observations and perspectives. Dickinson's simple yet passionate style was marked by economy and concentration. She developed sharp intense images and recognized the utility of the ellipsis of thought and verbal ambiguity. Like Anne Spencer, Dickinson read extensively and intensively.

Compare Dickinson's "Because I Could Not Stop for Death" with Spencer's "Substitution" and "Requiem."

Ralph Waldo Emerson created his own philosophy, believing that all forces are united by energetic truth. Though he lectured and composed many extended prose works, Emerson's poems, like those of Emily Dickinson and Anne Spencer, contain the core of his philosophy. He directed considerable thought to social reform and the growing issue of slavery.

Spencer, like Emerson, composed her poems in her garden. She has voiced high ethical, aesthetic, and independent positions on the topics she addresses in her poetry.

Although Anne Spencer did not vividly express her concern for social issues as did Henry David Thoreau and R. W. Emerson, her adult civic and professional life as librarian, and occasionally her poetry, addressed her concern for social and racial progress. H. D. Thoreau conveyed a genuine feeling for the unity of man and nature in *Walden*. His deep-rooted love for one place, Walden, characterized the epitome of his universe. Similarly, Anne Spencer's garden was central to her symbolic, historic, literary, religious imagery and meaning.

Countee Cullen's "Foreword" to his work *Caroling Dusk* has asserted that "Anne Spencer [writes] with a cool precision that evokes comparison with Amy Lowell and the influence of a rockbound seacoast." (p. x1)

Note: Examine Amy Lowell's "Patterns." Compare techniques and concepts as noted in Spencer's poems, e.g., "Substitution," "Lines to a Nasturtium," and "For Jim, Easter Eve."

Both Angelina Grimké and Spencer studied well their neo-romantic models. Both writers reveal great sensitivity and emotional acuity. Neither is writing for a group or class, or a race, nor do they use the language of complex reasoning and emotional compression. Rather, there is the direct attempt to present and define an emotional experience.

Bibliography

"Anne Spencer." In *Negro Poetry and Drama and The Negro in American Fiction*, edited by Sterling Brown, 65–66. With a new preface by Robert Bone. New York: Atheneum, 1937/1978.

Cullen, Countee, ed. *Caroling Dusk*. New York: Harper, 1927. 47–52.

Green, J. Lee. *Time's Unfading Garden: Anne Spencer's Life and Poetry*. Baton Rouge: Louisiana State University Press, 1977. 204. Since Anne Spencer's poems were published in nearly every major black anthology, it is essential to include Green's work, for the appendix contains the largest collection of her published poems. Spencer never arranged for a collected publication, though she constantly composed poems, and revised many of her earlier pieces through 1974, the year prior to her death. See also Chapter 7, "The Poetry: Aestheticism" and Chapter 8, "The Poetry: Controversy."

Hughes, Langston. "The Negro Artist and the Racial Mountain." *Nation* (23 June 1926): 692–94.

Locke, Alain. "The New Negro; An Interpretation." In *The American Negro: His History and Literature*, edited by Alain Locke, 3–16. New York: Arno Press and *The New York Times*, 1925/1968.

Primeau, Ronald. "Frank Horne and the Second Echelon Poets of the Harlem Renaissance." In *The Harlem Renaissance Remembered*, edited with a memoir by Arna Bontemps, 247–67. New York: Dodd, 1972.

Stetson, Erlene. "Anne Spencer." *College Language Association* XXI (March 1978): 400–09.

Nella Larsen (1891–1964)

Contributing Editor: Deborah E. McDowell

Classroom Issues and Strategies

As students become rightly more attuned to representations of gender, race, and class in literary and cultural texts, the subtleties of Nella Larsen's *Quicksand* and *Passing* create interesting problems. Such problems derive from the general tendency of readers to elevate one social category of analysis over all others, often ignoring the interactive working of each on the other: race on gender, gender on class, etc. Readers attentive to class will find the narrow class spectrum of these novels offputting, for they can seem on the surface to be mere apologies for the black middle class, showing little awareness of and bearing on the poverty that the masses of blacks suffered in 1920s Harlem.

While attention to irony, point of view, and rhetorical strategy is essential to reading any text, with Nella Larsen, it is especially so. In *Passing*, for example, understanding that Irene Redfield, from whose perspective much of the novel is told, is an unreliable narrator, is key to understanding the novel. Equally important is the function of Clare and Irene as doubles, a strategy that undermines Irene's authority as the center of racial consciousness, clarifies the points in the narrative's critique of the black middle class, and uncovers the issues of sexuality and class that an exclusive focus on race conceals.

It is useful to read Fannie Hurst's *Imitation of Life* and to show the two film adaptations of the novel.

Students respond to the heightened attention to color and clothing and atmosphere in Nella Larsen's novels and wonder if her concentration on mulatto characters indicates an unmistakable "privileging" of whiteness.

Major Themes, Historical Perspectives, and Personal Issues

It is important to provide information about 1920s Harlem and the literary and cultural confluences that shaped the Harlem Renaissance. It is critical that the movement be defined not by its "unities," but rather, by its "contraries" and be seen as the site of a class-based contestation over the terms and production of black art. The aesthetic theories, produced by such writers and intellectuals as James Weldon Johnson (Introduction to the *Book of American Negro Poetry*), Alain Locke ("The New Negro"), Langston Hughes ("The Negro Artist and the Racial Mountain"), W.E.B. Du Bois ("Criteria of Negro Art" and "The Negro in Art: How Shall He Be Portrayed?"), Jessie Fauset (reviews in *The Crisis*), and Zora Neale Hurston ("What White Publishers Won't Print") are all essential readings. None of these attempts to articulate the terms of an emerging "black art" can be divorced from a discussion of the production and consumption of the texts, especially the system of white patronage during the period, which necessarily affected and at times constrained artistic freedom.

Significant Form, Style, or Artistic Conventions

The most obvious tradition in which to situate Larsen's novels must be the novel-of-passing, which problematized questions of race. Deemphasizing "biology," the novel-of-passing provided convenient ways to explore race as a construct of history, culture, and white supremacist ideology. Equally important is the tradition of the novel of manners, as well as the romance.

Original Audience

I note the fact that the audience for Nella Larsen's writings, as for all black writers during the Harlem Renaissance, was primarily white, though a small group of black middle-class intellectuals read them as well.

Comparisons, Contrasts, Connections

Jessie Fauset's "Plum Bun & Comedy, American Style"
James Weldon Johnson's *The Autobiography of an ex-colored Man*
Charles Chesnutt's *The House Behind the Cedars*
Edith Wharton's *The House of Mirth*

Questions for Reading and Discussion/ Approaches to Writing

1. The metaphor of passing accrues several layers of meaning. What are they? How do they relate to each other?
2. Whose story is this? Clare's or Irene's?

3. What does this passage mean: "[Irene] was caught between two allegiances, different, yet the same. Herself. Her race. Race: The thing that bound and suffocated her. Whatever steps she took, or if she took none at all, something would be crushed. A person or the race. Clare, herself, or the race. Or, it might be all three."
4. It has been suggested that *Passing* uses race more as a device to sustain suspense than as a compelling social issue. What is the relation of race to subjective experience in the text?
5. What is the significance of narrative endings in Larsen? Why does *Passing* refuse to specify how Clare is killed and who is responsible?

Bibliography

Carby, Hazel. "The Quicksands of Representation." In *Reconstructing Womanhood*. New York: Oxford University Press.

Christian, Barbara. *Black Women Novelists*. Westport, CT: Greenwood Press, 1980.

Huggins, Nathan. *Harlem Renaissance*. New York: Oxford University Press.

——. *Voices of the Harlem Renaissance*.

Lewis, David Levering. *When Harlem Was in Vogue*.

McDowell, Deborah E. "The 'Nameless, Shameful Impulse': Sexuality in Nella Larsen's *Quicksand* and *Passing*." In *Studies in Black American Literature*, Volume III, edited by Joe Weixlmann and Houston A. Baker, Jr. Greenwood, FL: Penkeville Publishing, 1988.

Tate, Claudia "Nella Larsen's *Passing*: A Problem of Interpretation." *Black American Literature Forum* 14 (Winter 1980).

Wall, Cheryl. "Passing for What? Aspects of Identity in Nella Larsen's Novels." *Black American Literature Forum* 20 (Spring/Summer 1986).

Washington, Mary Helen. "The Mulatta Trap: Nella Larsen's Women of the 1920s." In *Invented Lives*. New York: Anchor/Doubleday, 1987.

Youman, Mary Mabel. "Nella Larsen's *Passing*: A Study in Irony." *College Language Association Journal* 18 (1974).

George Samuel Schuyler (1895–1977)

Contributing Editor: Michael W. Peplow

Classroom Issues and Strategies

Satire, especially the harsher Juvenalian mode, upsets students, who see it as too negative. And when satire deals with an emotional issue such as racial prejudice, it becomes even more controversial. Some students find Schuyler's satire offensive. In addition—though it has universal overtones—"Our Greatest Gift to America" is still a 1920s period piece. Some of the issues and language pose problems for modern students.

I make sure my students have a working definition of satire and, as we read the essay, I discuss the satiric devices Schuyler employs. Once we have finished reading the essay, I ask students to discuss *why* Schuyler chose satire and whether his approach was effective. The more background the students have in Juvenal, Swift, Twain, Ambrose Bierce, and H. L. Mencken (Schuyler's mentor and friend), the better the essay works in class.

I also make sure my students read some "straight" essays that address the racial situation in the 1920s. Articles from the NAACP's *Crisis* are helpful, especially those by its editor, W.E.B. Du Bois (see Daniel Walden, ed., *W.E.B. Du Bois: The Crisis Writings* [Greenwich: Fawcett, 1972]). The more exposure students have had to African-American and other minority literatures, the more they will appreciate Schuyler. I give students notes on the Harlem (or New Negro) Renaissance and read passages from Alain Locke's "The New Negro." I tell students about KKK activities and lynchings in the 1920s. I show them copies of *The Pittsburgh Courier*, a leading black newspaper for which Schuyler worked, that featured essays on race pride but included advertisements for skin lighteners and hair straighteners. For the teacher who does not have access to these materials, a valuable resource tool is *The Chronological History of the Negro in America*.

Students sometimes say the essay is too depressing, that Schuyler exaggerates and distorts the way things really were. They feel Schuyler so denigrates blacks that he must have been disgusted with his own people and secretly desired to be white himself. Finally, students say the essay is not relevant because people just aren't prejudiced any longer. Prejudice is not a comfortable thing to admit or discuss in class. It's easier to laugh a bit nervously and go on to the next essay. But questions about present-day prejudices lead to often dramatic discussions:

fraternities or athletes on campus; a racial or religious or national group (Iranians, for example); AIDS victims and welfare recipients and street people—the list goes on.

Major Themes, Historical Perspectives, and Personal Issues

The historical issues include American racism, the Harlem Renaissance vogue, the tendency of some black publications to preach race pride and at the same time publish skin lightening and hair straightening advertisements, the tendency of some black leaders to profit from American racism, and the all too prevalent belief among whites—and blacks—that "white is right." (You might remind students of an old black saying: "If you're white, you're all right. If you're brown, stick around. If you're black, get back.")

The personal issues include Schuyler's own encounters with racism in the army and during his journalistic tours, his courtship of and eventual marriage to a white woman, and his life-long belief that America's "colorphobia" was so absurd it merited scathing ridicule.

Significant Form, Style, or Artistic Conventions

1. What literary conventions does Schuyler employ in his satire?

    The purpose of satire is to mock or ridicule human follies or vices. Horatian satire tends to be light, often comic, the assumption being that humans are more foolish than sinful and that they are capable of reformation. Juvenalian satire—Schuyler's mode—is harsh and slashing, the assumption being that humans are so corrupted they are beyond reformation. In an early newspaper column Schuyler wrote that his dominant motive was malice and that his intent was "to slur, lampoon, damn, and occasionally praise anybody or anything in the known universe, not excepting the President of the Immortals." In his long career he rarely praised but did much damning, so much so that he was accused in a *Crisis* editorial in 1965 of being the incurable iconoclast who "dips his pen in his ever-handy [well] of acid."

    In "Our Greatest Gift" Schuyler creates a satiric persona much as his role model Swift did in "A Modest Proposal" and *Gulliver's Travels* (note the reference to "Brobdingnagian"). Schuyler's persona seems to be an intelligent but "plain folks" black man, literate and unafraid to speak the truth. He despises the inner circle of black intellectuals for their willingness to capitalize on racial tension and their secret belief that "white is right." He also despises redneck whites who believe a white skin makes them special. Both groups he sets out to shock; he even uses a number of current racial slurs. By the end of the essay, the persona seems to have become so disgusted with America's "colorphobia" that he sounds like the compleat misanthrope who despairs of ever converting America to rational behavior.

Another technique Schuyler the satirist employs is irony—saying or implying the opposite of what one really believes. Throughout the essay—from the words "greatest gift" in the title, through references to "this enlightened nation" and "our incomparable civilization," to the devastating final paragraph—Schuyler is savagely ironic.

A third technique Schuyler employs is exaggeration. Whether describing black poets, race leaders, or whites, Schuyler's portraits deliberately overstate. His character sketches of three "noble rednecks"—Isadore Shankersoff, Cyrus Leviticus Dumbbell, and Dorothy Dunce—are vintage Schuyler and anticipate his much more extended character sketches in *Black No More*.

2. What literary school does Schuyler belong to?

Schuyler, noted the 1965 *Crisis* editorial, was "a veteran dissenter and incurable iconoclast," one of that "select breed of moral crusaders and apparent social misfits who, as journalists, delighted in breaking the idols of the tribe." He is a direct descendant of Ambrose Bierce, the "caustic columnist" from San Francisco and author of "The Devil's Dictionary" and *The Satanic Reader*, of Brann the Iconoclast, of H. L. Mencken, the founder and editor of *The American Mercury*. He also worked side by side with important 1920s black iconoclasts: Chandler Owen and A. Philip Randolph, Theophilus Lewis and Wallace Thurman, W.E.B. Du Bois and Rudolph Fisher—each of whom was capable of idol-smashing but not on the sustained level that Schuyler was. On an even larger scale, Schuyler, as noted before, was a satirist in the tradition of Juvenal, Swift, and Twain, all of whom he studied and admired.

Original Audience

1. Schuyler's audience was primarily black—the essay appeared in a black publication that was read by the very racial leaders Schuyler lampoons in the first part of his essay. If any whites read it at the time, they would have been those who, in typical Harlem Renaissance fashion, became obsessed with exotic and primitive blacks (see Rudolph Fisher, "The Caucasian Storms Harlem," in

Huggins's *Voices from the Harlem Renaissance*; for a good example of white fascination with blacks, see Carl Van Vechten's melodramatic *Nigger Heaven*).

2. As suggested earlier, today's audience will have difficulty relating to "Our Greatest Gift." White students usually insist that the essay is dated because there are no more lynchings or overt acts of prejudice. Black students are sometimes offended by the racial epithets and the glancing attacks on black leaders. The teacher who wishes to challenge contemporary smugness can have a field day: Is white racism really dead? Do black or other leaders ever capitalize on racial tension? Is there still a "white is right" mentality in America?

Comparisons, Contrasts, Connections

There is no one author to whom Schuyler compares well, though he uses the same satiric devices that Juvenal, Swift, and Twain employ and the same iconoclastic manner that characterized Bierce, Brann, Mencken, Fisher, Lewis, and Thurman.

Questions for Reading and Discussion/ Approaches to Writing

1. (a) Schuyler attacks two groups of people in his essay. Who are they? Is he even-handed in his double attack?
   (b) What is the satire? Distinguish between Juvenalian and Horatian satire and decide which mode Schuyler preferred.
   (c) What was the Harlem Renaissance?
2. (a) Have half the class (include the more creative writers) write a satire attacking a controversial issue à la Schuyler. Use a persona, employ irony, and develop two or three exaggerated character sketches. Have the rest of the class write reasoned essays on the same issue. Have the class discuss the best essays from both groups and determine which type of approach—satire or reasoned essay—is more effective, and why.
   (b) Write a response to Schuyler's article assuming the persona of a white racist or a black nationalist in Schuyler's own time.
   (c) First discuss in class and then write an essay on the following: A Modern Response to Schuyler's "Our Greatest Gift to America."

Blues Lyrics

Contributing Editor: Steven C. Tracy

Classroom Issues and Strategies

Many students will be totally unfamiliar with the blues tradition and will therefore benefit greatly from the playing of blues recordings in class in conjunction with the selections from blues lyrics printed in the text. In fact, playing these blues selections in class will help introduce the important point that the blues is an oral, not a written, tradition. Asking the students to write down what they hear on the recordings played brings up not only the problems that scholars have deciphering texts but also the issue of how one should render an oral production on the printed page.

Students should be encouraged to respond to the voices of the lyrics. Are they voices of resignation and defeat, of hope and transcendence, of strength and pride, or of some mixture of all of these? What is it that has given the blues their staying power? And what is it that writers like Langston Hughes, Sterling Brown, Al Young, Alice Walker, Shirley Anne Williams, and Allen Ginsberg see in them that makes these writers draw on them for their own writing? Certainly comparing these blues lyrics to various blues poems will help clarify authors' differing attitudes about the blues.

Religious and sexual themes are generally the most controversial. Students question the image of women in the blues and wonder whether the blues singer is weak and self-pitying or strong and self-sufficient. The Furry Lewis lyric is often seen as being bizarre and sick: a good starting point for a discussion of the place of humor in the blues.

Major Themes, Historical Perspectives, and Personal Issues

A number of important subjects are covered in these selections, including love, hate, sex, violence, hope, superstition, religion, and protest, indicating that the blues in fact deal with a range of subjects in a variety of ways. When blues are performed, they often provoke laughter from an audience that identifies with the experience being described or that appreciates the novel way the experience is described. There are a number of humorous verses here that could be compared for the way they achieve their effects, from Bracey's hyperbole to Carter's prurience to Cox's unexpected assertiveness to the startling images of Wheatstraw and Lewis. Such a discussion would emphasize the idea that the blues, though often discussing sadness and hardships, contain a pretty fair amount of humor. Ellison includes a good discussion of this subject in *Shadow and Act*, as does Garon in *Blues and the Poetic Spirit* (pp. 77–87).

Significant Form, Style, or Artistic Conventions

An advantage to playing the songs for the students is that it allows them to hear how the various stanza structures are fit into the music. For instance, the lyrics of Childers and Wheatstraw are both sung to eight-bar musical stanzas, but the lyric patterns are different. Students can discuss the advantages of one stanza over the other. The selection from "John Henry" is a ten-bar blues ballad, presenting in narrative form the story of the folk-hero whose strength and perseverance in the face of incredible odds is a paradigm for the African-American experience (see Sterling Brown's "Strange Legacies"). The selection from Margaret Carter is from a sixteen-bar vaudeville blues especially, but present in other kinds of blues as well. The rest of the examples included come from twelve-bar blues, but certainly the examples from Jefferson, Bracey, Cox, Robert Johnson, and Holmes are sufficiently different to indicate the possibility of diverse phrasing in the blues, even within what is sometimes considered to be a rather restrictive form.

We can also see in "Got the Blues" the presence of several stock phrases—lines or parts of lines that turn up regularly in blues that are similar to but not the same as the formulaic lines discussed by Parry and Lord. Students might be encouraged to take the first line of stanza two or six and generate an individual rhyme line that completes the thought in some kind of personal manner as a way of helping them understand how tradition has an effect on the individual blues singer.

Comparisons, Contrasts, Connections

The only blues lyric quoted in its entirety here is Blind Lemon Jefferson's "Got the Blues," interesting because, rather than developing a single theme, it progresses through associative linkages and contrasts. While some early commentary argued that the blues were often incoherent, more recently texts have been discussed as nonthematic, partially thematic, or thematic, and the presence of such associative linkages and contrasts is important to see and recognize as a textual strategy rather than an example of textual incoherence. Again, students can be encouraged to discern the associations among lines and stanzas the way they might be asked to do for poetry by Ezra Pound, T. S. Eliot, or Amy Lowell.

Questions for Reading and Discussion/ Approaches to Writing

1. Have students listen to recordings by Langston Hughes, Sterling Brown, Zora Neale Hurston, Ishmael Reed, Michael Harper, Allen Ginsberg, or Jack Kerouac that have musical accompaniment (or are sung performances, in Hurston and Ginsberg) and discuss how the music affects our response to the words.
2. Have students write a blues song and discuss their rationale for choice of stanza form, themes, images, diction, and voice, establishing clearly the relation of their song to the tradition.
3. Have students survey the various methods of transcribing blues lyrics and defend one method as superior to the others.
4. Have students pick a theme developed in a blues-influenced poem by an author like Langston Hughes and search out blues lyrics that deal with a similar theme to see how the literary artist revises the traditional treatment of the theme.

Bibliography

Interviews with blues performers are included in:

Oliver, Paul. *Conversation With the Blues*. New York: Horizon Press, 1965.

Pearson, Barry Lee. *Sounds So Good to Me*. Philadelphia: University of Pennsylvania Press, 1984.

For explanations of unfamiliar words, phrases, and places in blues lyrics see:

Gold, Robert. *Jazz Talk*. New York: Da Capo Press, 1982.

Townley, Eric. *Tell Your Story*. Chigwell, Essex: Storyville, 1976.

Other valuable discussions of blues include:

Ellison, Ralph. *Shadow and Act*. New York: Random House, 1964.

Evans, David. *Big Road Blues*. Berkeley: University of California Press, 1982.

Garon, Paul. *Blues and the Poetic Spirit*. London: Eddison Press, 1975.

Harris, Sheldon. *Blues Who's Who*. New Rochelle, N.Y.: Arlington House, 1975.

Jahn, Janheinz. *A History of Neo-African Literature*. New York: Grove Press, 1968.

——. *Muntu: An Outline of the New African Culture*. London: Faber and Faber, 1961.

Jones, Leroi. *Blues People*. New York: Wm. Morrow, 1963.

Oliver, Paul. *The Blues Tradition*. New York: Oak Publications, 1970.

——. *The Meaning of the Blues*. 1960. Reprint. New York: Collier Books, 1972.

——. *Savannah Syncopators: African Retentions in the Blues*. Kibsibm Studio Vista, 1970.

——. *The Story of the Blues*. Philadelphia: Chilton Books, 1973.

Titon, Jeff Todd. *Early Downhome Blues*. Urbana: University of Illinois Press, 1978.

For discussions of the importance of the blues to African-American literature see:

Baker, Houston A., Jr. *Blues, Ideology, and Afro-American Literature*. Chicago: University of Chicago Press, 1984.

Tracy, Steven C. *Langston Hughes and the Blues*. Urbana: University of Illinois Press, 1988.

Williams, Sherley A. "The Blues Roots of Contemporary Afro-American Poetry." In *Chant of Saints*, edited by Michael Harper and Robert Stepto. Chicago: University of Chicago Press, 1979.

Discography

Bracey, Ishmon. *Complete Recordings (1928–30)*. Wolf WSE 105, n.d.

Carter, Margaret. *Pot Hound Blues*. Historical HLP-15, 1970.

Childers, Virgil. *Piedmont Blues Vol. 2*. Flyright LP 107, n.d.

Cox, Ida. *Ida Cox Vol. 2*. Fountain FB 304, n.d.

Davis, Walter. *Think You Need a Shot*. Victor 731015, n.d.

Holmes, Wright. *Country Blues Classics Vol. 3*. Blues Classics 7, n.d.

Jefferson, Blind Lemon. *Complete Recorded Works Vol. 1*. Document DOCD 5017, n.d.

Johnson, Robert. *The Complete Recordings*. Columbia C2K 46222, 1990.

Johnson, Tommy. *Complete Recorded Works (1928–29)*. Document DOCD 5001, 1990.

Lewis, Furry. *Furry Lewis 1927–29*. Document DOCD 5004, n.d.

McClennan, Tommy. *Travelin' Highway Man*. Travelin' Man CD 06, 1990.

Rainey, Ma. *Ma Rainey*. Milestone M 47021, 1974.

Tucker, Bessie. *Bessie Tucker 1928–29*. Document DOCD 5070, n.d.

Wheatstraw, Peetie. *Peetie Wheatstraw 1931–41*. Old Tramp OT 1200, n.d.

Issues and Visions in Modern America

Randolph Bourne (1886–1918)

Contributing Editor: Charles Molesworth

Classroom Issues and Strategies

Students should be asked to discuss how America might have looked to a social critic before World War I. While some of Bourne's ideas may seem "timely" to today's students, this is due in part to the rather prophetic aspects of this essay. Bourne was of course conscious of the immigration that was reshaping American society (especially in its large cities), and he was very aware of the social and political changes being brought about by modernization (such as the routinization of work, the development of the "culture industry" and mass media, urbanization, and so on). But his idealism about America was unaffected by the large-scale tragedies associated with the world wars, the rise of fascism, the atom bomb and so forth. Also, Bourne would not have been familiar with the later developments in academic forms of social science. Thus, the "theoretical" nature of Bourne's formulations may strike some as implausible. Some of the main classroom issues might be put this way: How thoroughgoing can a criticism of American society be, and does a social critic have to be "practical" in his or her suggestions? To what extent must a social critic rely on surveys or statistical studies to justify his or her conclusions?

Major Themes, Historical Perspectives, and Personal Issues

The call for a social identity that surpasses or transcends nationalistic feeling would be (paradoxically) both implausible and yet "logical" at the end of the nineteenth century, when nationalism was perhaps the main political sentiment shaping world events. Bourne's essay challenges and responds to, even at a distance, the same moods and arguments that animated romantic nationalism of the sort that had recently shaped Italy and Germany, among others, into nation-states. The American nexus for this nationalism involved many issues, but perhaps chiefly the fervent arguments about immigrants and whether or not they could be successfully assimilated into a modern nation. Could such assimilation proceed through cultural and social means, assuming a single, "uniform," biological basis for national identity was not available to all the various immigrant groups? The issue of nativism, which claimed that only people who descended from specific racial or ethnic groups could form harmonious social and political identities, was a form of racism. In response to nativism, which he thoroughly rejected, Bourne developed his cultural criticism, so that, among other things, the very idea of identity could be redefined. This means that his focus on culture as a defining sociopolitical force was very distinctive. The German tradition of *kulturkampf* (or cultural struggle) had not been taken up in America on a large scale, but Bourne and many of his contemporaries were aware of it, having studied on the continent after their college years. Other writers at this time who shared some of Bourne's concerns were Van Wyck Brooks, Waldo Frank, and Lewis Mumford.

Significant Form, Style, or Artistic Conventions

Bourne used the essay as his main form of artistic expression. In this form, which had grown very popular through the spread of magazines, such as *The New Republic*, that were devoted to developing large readerships and influencing popular opinion and political policy, Bourne tried to advance his ideas in ways that were both oppositional and hortatory. This meant that he had to combine a certain amount of social observation (with the keen eye of a journalist), a matrix of reasoned argument (while avoiding any "dry" sense of logic), and a call to ethical values (without incurring the charge of sheer moralizing). All the while he kept in mind the general reader, an educated layperson who was assumed to have an abiding and interested stake in political issues. This meant that his vocabulary could not be a technical one, yet he had to make his argument convey more than the sense of an editorial in a daily newspaper.

Comparisons, Contrasts, Connections

Other essays in the anthology can be compared to Bourne's and studied for their stylistic approach and the contents of their arguments. For example, the selections from W.E.B. Du Bois are especially instructive in this context. T. S. Eliot's "Tradition and the Individual Talent" contains a sense of personal identity and group allegiance that can also be contrasted with Bourne's. And the place of culture and cultural politics in the New Negro Renaissance is germane to these issues: see, for example, Langston Hughes's "The Negro Artist and the Racial Mountain" and George Schulyer's "The Negro-Art Hokum." Perhaps the closest parallel is with Alain Locke's "The New Negro," where the issue of social transformation through cultural renewal is paramount.

Questions for Reading and Discussion

- How are national identities usually understood, and how are they formed? Is there more than one way to "make a nation"? Does Bourne discuss these ways?
- What other writers in the American tradition are explicitly occupied with the "national character"? Selections in *The Heath Anthology* from Franklin, Jefferson, and Whitman ("Democratic Vistas") could be assembled on this topic.
- What are the specifically modern ways that Bourne defines national and personal identity?

John Dos Passos (1896–1970)

Contributing Editor: Robert C. Rosen

Classroom Issues and Strategies

The biographies of *U.S.A.* are slices of history; their broader contexts are alluded to but not spelled out. To appreciate fully the nuances of Dos Passos's language, the significance of his descriptive details, and the force of his sarcasm, a reader needs to know a lot of history.

The teacher probably needs to do some explaining, though he or she should avoid explaining the biographies to death. To appreciate "The Body of an American," students should know something about World War I, which Dos Passos saw and many of his original readers remembered. They should understand such things as the unprecedented carnage of that war (10 million killed and 20 million wounded); the particular brutality of trench warfare; the deeper causes of the war (and of U.S. entry into the war) that lay behind the noble rhetoric; and the irony of racism at home (alluded to in "The Body of an American") and repression of domestic dissent during and after a war fought, Wilson told Congress, because "the world must be made safe for democracy." "The Bitter Drink" is more difficult than "The Body of an American" because its historical sweep is greater. Perhaps assigning (or even reading aloud) a brief sample of Veblen's writing would help; it would at least give students a sense of his approach and style. (See, for example, the title excerpt "The Captain of Industry" in *The Portable Veblen*, edited by Max Lerner; the last paragraph alone might suffice.)

Major Themes, Historical Perspectives, and Personal Issues

"The Body of an American" is about the waste of war and the public and official cant that surrounds it. These issues should be of interest to students who have friends or relatives facing military service or who are themselves of draft or enlistment age. "The Bitter Drink" is about what it means to be a serious critic of society, to tell the truth and refuse to say "the essential yes." Students soon to begin careers where they may have to compromise their values should find much to discuss.

Significant Form, Style, or Artistic Conventions

Since the excerpts included in the anthology represent only about one percent of the *U.S.A.* trilogy and only one of its four narrative devices (biographies, newsreels, conventional narratives, and the camera eye), teaching these excerpts is very different from teaching *U.S.A.* Should you find time in the course to read *The 42nd Parallel* or *Nineteen Nineteen* or *The Big Money*, you might discuss with students the relationships among the four narrative devices as well as questions about the nature of fiction and the nature of written history raised by Dos Passos's mixing of real historical figures and fictional characters. If students are reading only "The Body of an American" and/or "The Bitter Drink," you might ask them what role they think such "nonfiction" biography might play in a novel. With "The Body of an American," you might also ask about the effect of Dos Passos's running the opening words together, of his juxtapositions of different kinds of language, and of his Whitmanesque listmaking. With "The Bitter Drink," you might discuss how Dos Passos goes about communicating his own attitudes while narrating the life of Veblen.

Original Audience

Though the two excerpts in the text are brief, they should suffice to suggest the radicalism of *U.S.A.* To students surprised by it, you might explain that such views were not so uncommon during the 1930s (though, for Dos Passos, they came even earlier). At the height of the depression, with no unemployment insurance and meager public relief, over one in four U.S. citizens had no job, and millions more suffered wage cuts and underemployment. People lost all their money in bank failures; families were forced out of their homes and apartments; many went hungry while milk was dumped into rivers and crops were burned to keep up prices. The economic system seemed irrational, and millions marched in protest, fought evictions, joined unions. This was the context of *U.S.A.* for its original readers.

Comparisons, Contrasts, Connections

Almost any other work of fiction from the 1930s might usefully be compared with the excerpts from *U.S.A.* Alongside "The Body of an American" you might read Dalton Trumbo's *Johnny Got His Gun* (1939) or, for contrast, the tight-lipped antiwar fiction in Hemingway's *In Our Time* (1925). For a powerful contemporary comparison, you might look at Vietnam veteran Ron Kovic's *Born on the Fourth of July* (1976).

Questions for Reading and Discussion/ Approaches to Writing

1. With "The Body of an American," you might ask students what kinds of contrasts Dos Passos sets up between the news coverage and political declarations (in smaller print) and the story of John Doe. They'll probably point to such contrasts as the nobility of the rhetoric versus the ugly actuality of war, the superficiality of the reporting versus the depth of human suffering, and the impersonality and abstractness of the public language versus the personal detail in those lists of possible facts about John Doe and in the many biographical particulars that suggest all that went into making the adult human being whose unidentifiable remains are being buried.

2. With "The Bitter Drink," you might ask what Dos Passos means by Veblen's "constitutional inability to say yes" and why Dos Passos makes this "essential yes" a refrain. Veblen's ideas are as much implied as spelled out, and you might ask students to summarize as much of them as they can infer from the biography. You might also ask them to draw connections between those ideas and Veblen's life. Dos Passos sets this life very firmly in its historical context, and students might discuss the whole sweep of history brought to life in the biography and what patterns and recurring themes they see. Students might also speculate on whether there is too much of the apology in Dos Passos's description of his hero's "woman trouble."

Michael Gold (1893–1967)

Contributing Editor: Barry Gross

Classroom Issues and Strategies

Because Gold's intentions are didactic, he says what he has to say very directly and his language is very plain. Since he does not deal with any complex or difficult concepts or ideas, his work is immediately accessible to students.

It's useful to provide some statistics for background. For instance, the population density on the Lower East Side, the mortality rate for infants, incidence of tuberculosis and other infectious diseases, etc. It would also be helpful to show pictures, tapes, movies depicting life on the Lower East Side, although there has been a tendency to sentimentalize that life, to make it something to feel nostalgia for, and, hence, it's gotten prettified.

Major Themes, Historical Perspectives, and Personal Issues

The warpings of poverty. The malign effects of unmediated capitalism. The peculiarly American mix and juxtaposition of races, groups, minorities. The nature of a slum (a slum seems to be a slum regardless of who inhabits it). The threats to the traditional patriarchal structure of family and culture that American ghetto life posed. The role of the mother. The threats to traditional Jewish culture that America posed.

Significant Form, Style, or Artistic Conventions

Note the combination of a journalistic style characterized by short sentences, monosyllabic words, a kind of reportage we think of as Hemingwayesque, and the occasional sketches of sentimentality, exhortation, lament.

Original Audience

To the extent that *Jews Without Money* is written by a member of the Communist party who called for the overthrow of capitalism, it is very important to locate it in 1930. To the extent that it is a sentimental and intellectual and artistic autobiography, it is not so important to locate it. To the extent that it's a book about being Jewish, some historical placement is necessary. (There will be students, even Jewish students, who will think that "Jews without money" is an oxymoron.)

Comparisons, Contrasts, Connections

The Bread Givers by Anzia Yezierska, *Call It Sleep* by Henry Roth, *Yekl* by Abraham Cahan, *The World of Our Fathers* by Irving Howe, *The Rise of David Levinsky* by Abraham Cahan, and *What Makes Sammy Run?* by Budd Schulberg are the most famous of many works that deal with Jewish immigrant life on the Lower East Side. It would also be useful/interesting to compare and contrast with works by and about other immigrant groups, other minorities, other slum dwellers.

Bibliography

There is much available on the Lower East Side (*World of Our Fathers, The Golden Door*, et al.); the Anti-Defamation League of B'nai B'rith (chapters in all large cities) will usually provide bibliographies, secondary materials, source materials, study guides for educational purposes.

Albert Maltz (1908–1985)

Contributing Editor: Gabriel Miller

Classroom Issues and Strategies

It is useful for the students to have some historical/social background, particularly concerning the depression, the rise of radicalism, and its various configurations (why so many writers and intellectuals were attracted to Marxism, socialism, etc.). Many of Maltz's novels are also grounded in historical events (*The Underground Stream, The Cross and the Arrow*, and *A Tale of One January*). You might provide background lectures and readings on the history of the thirties ("The Happiest Man on Earth"). For other Maltz pieces, a knowledge of radicalism, the radical literary wars, HUAC and the blacklist would be very helpful. Concerning HUAC (House Un-American Activities Committee), many students will be interested in the blacklist, fronts, and the Hollywood Ten (Maltz was part of this group).

Major Themes, Historical Perspectives, and Personal Issues

1. The depression and displacement and disenfranchisement of the individual.
2. The totalitarian environment and the individual.
3. The ideal of the democratic individual.
4. The individual alone in nature and with the self.

Significant Form, Style, or Artistic Conventions

Discuss the "proletarian novel," the relationship of art and politics, the conventions of realism. Questions of what constitutes a political or radical novel would also be stimulating and useful.

Original Audience

The audience at least in the beginning was the "initiated": radicals who were sympathetic to Maltz's ideas. However, Maltz was always reaching out to a wider audience and would come to reject the restraints of didactic art.

Comparisons, Contrasts, Connections

More well-known writers whose work can be read along with Maltz are Richard Wright, *Native Son* (emphasis on the emerging radical consciousness, questions of class); John Steinbeck; *Grapes of Wrath* (Americans on the road, communal versus individual) and *In Dubious Battle* (political novel); James Farrell, the Studs Lonigan trilogy (realism, environment, politics); also Jack London and some of Whitman's poems, particularly those emphasizing the ideal of the democratic man.

Questions for Reading and Discussion/ Approaches to Writing

1. I have never taught Maltz but I think questions regarding the effectiveness of presenting character and the characters' relationship to the overriding issues of the story would be productive.
2. Discuss how successfully Maltz integrates didactic aims with "art." Is Maltz's best work at odds with its didactic intent? How does Maltz's work effectively convey the central issues of his time?

Bibliography

Maltz's essays in *The Citizen Writer*; his *New Masses* essay "What Shall We Ask of Writers?" (1946) in which he takes the notion of didactic art to task and for which he was harshly criticized.

Lillian Hellman (1905–1984)

Contributing Editor: Vivian Patraka

Major Themes, Historical Perspectives, and Personal Issues

What is Hellman's idea of history? Who makes history and how are events in history related? Why does she connect the events of the McCarthy Era to the Vietnam War? What is her conception of the average American's understanding of history? How is this related to the "deep contempt for public intelligence" Hellman ascribes to Nixon? Why does Hellman reserve her strongest sense of betrayal for the intellectuals who did not protest the events of the McCarthy Era? What assumptions about intellectuals did Hellman have to abandon? What qualities does she ascribe to the McCarthyites and their proceedings that should have made them the "hereditary enemies" of intellectuals?

Significant Form, Style, or Artistic Conventions

What kind of credibility does an autobiographical memoir have as compared to a history or a political science book? How convincing is Hellman in establishing her point of view about the McCarthy Era? Is she less convincing because the work identifies itself as someone's opinion? Because she is angry? How does a question like "Since when do you have to agree with people to defend them from injustice?" or a statement like "Truth made you a traitor as it often does in a time of scoundrels" make Hellman's work both persuasive and memorable? Why does Hellman use the word scoundrel and what does she mean by it?

Elsewhere, Hellman has said that in a time of scoundrels, "The pious words come out because you know the pious words are good salesmanship." The idea that the language of morality, of patriotism, and of religion can be manipulated in an entrepreneurial way to capitalize on people's fears applies to more than just the fifties. Are there any examples from contemporary times of this sort of manipulation? Who benefits from it and why? Who is harmed?

Why would Hellman use the phrase "black comedy" to describe activities she considered to be harmful and evil? Why doesn't she call them a tragedy, given that many people's lives were ruined? Elsewhere she says, "One is torn between laughter and tears. It's so truly comic.

People were confessing to sins they'd never done; making up lies of meetings they'd been in when they'd been in no such meeting; asking God and the Committee's pardon for nothing but just going into a room and listening to some rather dull talk. . . . And that, to me was the saddest and the most disgusting, as well as most comic. The effect was of a certain section of the country going crazy." What would motivate people to "confess" and "name names" in this manner?

Comparisons, Contrasts, Connections

Hellman has spoken of "the right of each man to his own convictions." Where is the line between having a conviction and being subversive or dangerous and who is allowed to interpret that for us? In what direction is that line currently moving? Playwright Arthur Miller, writing about the McCarthy Era, said "With the tiniest Communist Party in the world, the United States was behaving as though on the verge of a bloody revolution." Who would profit from creating this impression? What kinds of acts can be justified once this impression is created?

Mary McCarthy (1912–1989)

Contributing Editor: Wendy Martin

Classroom Issues and Strategies

Students will be interested in discussing McCarthy's depiction of social roles and norms and will want to relate her questioning of traditional beliefs to the social changes of the twentieth century. However, while this is a fruitful course of discussion for McCarthy's work, it is important not to lose sight of the literary artistry of her work. Students should learn to be attentive to the nuances of language, the symbolism and carefully controlled diction that characterize McCarthy's prose and make her a superb literary stylist as well as a chronicler of her times.

Major Themes, Historical Perspectives, and Personal Issues

Mary McCarthy's life extended across most of the twentieth century, and her writing is as multifaceted as the rapidly changing American society in which she lived. She was concerned with issues of social justice and responsibility, and this concern manifests itself in her work in the form of repeated examinations of assumptions about gender, race, and class. For example, her novel *The Group* (1963) explores the irony, and sometimes the ugliness, in the lives of two decades of American women, dealing openly with adultery, misogyny, divorce, and insanity. The novel ridicules traditional notions of femininity and suggests new ways of conceptualizing marriage, work, and love.

Although McCarthy's work seems to be informed by a feminist sensibility, she asserted that she was not a feminist. While it is important to establish the political and social background of the leftist intellectual circles in which she moved, it is also important to recognize that McCarthy was always an independent thinker who resisted easy categorization.

Significant Form, Style, or Artistic Conventions

McCarthy's writing took a variety of forms, from early theater columns for the *Partisan Review* to incisive political essays on Vietnam and Watergate. Her best-known works are her novels and her collection of short autobiographical narratives, *Memories of a Catholic Girlhood*, from which the selection "Names" is taken. This collection is both a product of and a deviation from previous American autobiographical narratives. In revisiting her own life, McCarthy exposes the silences and boundaries in the lives of the traditional women who inhabited her childhood. McCarthy undertakes two projects simultaneously; she demystifies cultural assumptions of silent and passive femininity, while simultaneously building up her own autobiographical persona. *Memories of a Catholic Girlhood* stands as an important model for American women's autobiography in a century of dramatic social change for women.

Original Audience

McCarthy wrote for a wide audience. She was, at one point, a staff writer for the *New Yorker*. *The Group*, her best-selling novel, has sold over five million copies worldwide. In general, both her fiction and her essays are meant to appeal to progressive and open-minded women and men, and to encourage these readers to question social traditions and assumptions that arbitrarily limit their lives.

Comparisons, Contrasts, Connections

McCarthy's intellectual background could be provided through the works of her close friend, Hannah Arendt, whose book *The Life of the*

Mind McCarthy spent two years editing. Another interesting source of background material would be the literary criticism of her second husband, Edmund Wilson.

McCarthy said herself that John Dos Passos's *The 42nd Parallel,* which she read while at Vassar, was one of her most important influences. She met Dos Passos when she joined a group of radical writers living in Greenwich Village during the late thirties; other writers she met living in the Village were Sherwood Anderson, Erskine Caldwell, and Upton Sinclair. The political and intellectual debates that she participated in during this period were important formative influences for the ideas that would later appear in her writing. It would be useful to compare and contrast the work of these male radicals with McCarthy's vision.

McCarthy also stated that she had read Louisa May Alcott's *Little Women* and *Jo's Boys.* These works and the fiction of other earlier women writers, such as Edith Wharton and Willa Cather, could be used to establish the tradition of white women's literature in which she wrote, and which she transformed to fit her individual needs. In addition, a comparison and contrast could be developed between *Memories of a Catholic Girlhood* and, for example, *Report from Part One,* the autobiographical narrative of McCarthy's contemporary, Gwendolyn Brooks.

Questions for Reading and Discussion/ Approaches to Writing

1. Many of the major issues of McCarthy's writing can be touched on in a discussion of "Names." Questions for discussion could include: What is the significance of the "frontier" setting of the narrative? How does the ethnic mix of names in the convent relate to the narrator's self-perception? How does the institutional structure of the convent force the narrator to be deceptive about "becoming a woman"? Why is she renamed at the same time that the incident with the blood occurs, and why does she say that the name "Cye" becomes her "new patron saint"? Discussion of these questions should bring out McCarthy's concern with exposing the reality beneath social surfaces and with the ways that social pressures affect the construction of the self. Another topic for discussion would be McCarthy's treatment of the women in the female society of the convent. How does she portray the various girls? The nuns?

2. McCarthy's prose at first seems light and readable, but on closer inspection it turns out to be quite dense and laden with interconnected levels of meaning. Having students write on brief passages

gives them an opportunity to explore this richness of meaning. Ask students to make connections between seemingly disparate passages. For example, what does the passage at the beginning of "Names," where she describes the society of Puget Sound, have to do with the passage at the end, in which she says, "What I wanted was a fresh start . . ."? Students should be able to discover how the theme of recreated identity, treated both seriously and with irony, runs throughout "Names."

Bibliography

For a concise overview of McCarthy's life and work, see Wendy Martin, "Mary McCarthy," in *Modern American Women Writers*, edited by Elaine Showalter et. al. (1991). For biographical information, see Carol W. Gelderman, *Mary McCarthy: A Life* (1988), and Doris Grumbach, *The Company She Kept* (1967). For a study of her autobiographical writings, such as "Names," see Gordon O. Taylor, "The Word for Mirror: Mary McCarthy," in *Chapters of Experience: Studies in Twentieth-Century American Autobiography* (1983). For a more general treatment of McCarthy's artistry, see Wendy Martin, "The Satire and Moral Vision of Mary McCarthy," in *Comic Relief: Humor in Contemporary American Literature*, edited by Sarah Blacher Cohen (1978).

Clifford Odets (1906–1963)

Contributing Editor: Michael J. Mendelsohn

Classroom Issues and Strategies

If Odets occasionally seems dated, he is less so for those who put this play into its 1930s milieu. Consider having student reports or general class discussion on major concerns in the United States in the mid-1930s. With some understanding of the depression decade, it may be less difficult for students to believe that this militant young dramatist was able to present such a play to sympathetic, even enthusiastic audiences.

Major Themes, Historical Perspectives, and Personal Issues

Playwright Odets clearly believed in 1935 that through union solidarity the little man might find a way out of the despair of America's economic and social ills. For many, American society was not fulfilling its true promise; in the big novel of the thirties, *The Grapes of Wrath*, Steinbeck asserted much the same theme. With only a touch of hyperbole, Harold Clurman called *Waiting for Lefty* "the birth of the thirties."

Significant Form, Style, or Artistic Conventions

Techniques of speaking across the proscenium, a scenery-less stage, and planting actors in the audience give instructors plenty to work with. For instructors interested in theatrical links and analogues, Pirandello or Wilder would be appropriate points of departure.

Original Audience

Audience for this work is especially important. It was intended for presentation in union halls before small, typically preconvinced audiences. It is obviously strident, intended to make a militant emotional appeal. Unlike much of our theater today, it was not intended merely to entertain or inform. Politically, Odets was going through the same sort of youthful flirtation with communism that marked the careers of many of his 1930s contemporaries. Without this sort of context, the play comes off as merely a strident little piece of propaganda.

Comparisons, Contrasts, Connections

Compare with Steinbeck's *The Grapes of Wrath* (1939).

Examine Pirandello or Wilder for some comparison of theatrical techniques of crossing the proscenium and merging actors with audiences.

Questions for Reading and Discussion/ Approaches to Writing

1. What is the unifying plot for all these episodes?
2. Is this play universal, or is it too tied to place (New York) and to time (The Great Depression of the 1930s)?

3. Is the message too blatant? Is the language too strident? Is Odets more a "revolutionary" or "reformer" if you compare, for example, Steinbeck's *The Grapes of Wrath*, a product of the same decade?
4. Which scenes have the greatest impact, and why?
5. Odets has often been praised for his use of vivid, colorful language. Which speeches work well for you? Which are less successful?
6. How successful is the playwright in crossing the proscenium and breaking down the traditional separation between audience and action? Why does he use this technique?

Bibliography

Brenman-Gibson, Margaret. *Clifford Odets*. Boston: Atheneum, 1981, 299–306.

Clurman, Harold. *The Fervent Years*. New York: Hill and Wang, 1957, 138–42.

Mendelsohn, Michael. *Clifford Odets*. New York: Everett/Edwards, 1969, 21–26.

Murray, Edward. *Clifford Odets*. New York: Frederick Ungar, 1968. Chapter 1.

Weales, Gerald. *Clifford Odets*. Indianapolis: Pegasus, 1971. Chapter 3.

Meridel LeSueur (b. 1900)

Contributing Editor: Elaine Hedges

Classroom Issues and Strategies

For both LeSueur pieces, some knowledge of the Great Depression of the 1930s is helpful—the extent of unemployment, the fears about the future of American society, the disillusionment of many writers and intellectuals with the capitalist system, and especially the impact of the depression on women. Our popular images of the period are of men standing in breadlines and selling apples. LeSueur was one of the few writers to focus on women, who also lost jobs, faced starvation, and were abandoned by husbands who were forced to seek work elsewhere.

"Annunciation" is one of the rare pieces of literature to concentrate on the feelings of a pregnant woman—an especially groundbreaking subject when LeSueur wrote her story. Students might be asked if they know of or have read other stories about pregnancy and childbirth, and why these subjects have not figured importantly in our literature until recently. As female experiences, have they been considered less important than such quintessentially male experiences as hunting or warfare?

Major Themes, Historical Perspectives, and Personal Issues

As indicated above, the depression of the 1930s is the historical context for both pieces of writing. Instructors might want to ask why women have tended to be ignored in accounts of the depression.

Both pieces emerged from LeSueur's personal experience. She herself experienced unemployment and poverty during the depression. She knew, and for a time lived with, the kinds of women she describes in "Women on the Breadlines." "Annunciation" is based on her own experience—her decision during the depression to have a child as an affirmation of faith in life, despite uncertainties and fears about the future. The story shows her own personal faith, rooted in a belief in the continuity of natural and human life. That belief, often expressed through a celebration of nature's recurring cycle and of the human life cycle, can be found in her writings throughout her career.

Significant Form, Style, or Artistic Conventions

"Women on the Breadlines" is a piece of journalism. Though the emphasis is on factual observation, with details conveyed through short, simple declarative sentences, it is not "objective" reporting. (Students might be asked what "objective" writing is and whether in fact there is such a thing.) The reportorial voice doesn't keep itself distinct from the material it describes, but, rather, identifies with the women and their suffering. Is this kind of journalism—called "reportage" in LeSueur's time—similar to the personal or "new" journalism written today?

Does the style, in its directness and simplicity, effectively capture the lives and feelings of the women described? Is it, despite being journalism, in any ways a "literary" style? Note LeSueur's use of imagery: for example, a scrub woman with hands "like watersoaked branches." Can students find other examples of figurative language?

Also examine the structure of "Women on the Breadlines." It develops through a series of vignettes or portraits. Are these arranged in any particular order? Does the piece develop, as a short story might, toward a climax? What might be the difference between this kind of journalistic feature story and a literary short story?

"Annunciation" is written in a more lush, lyrical, descriptive style. Contrast this to the more clipped style of "Women on the Breadlines." How is each style appropriate to the contents and purpose of each piece?

The pear tree is, of course, the central symbol in "Annunciation." Trace the process whereby the tree takes on meaning for the narrator, in relation to her pregnancy; what meanings does the tree eventually hold for her, and how does it become a symbol of her faith in the future? Students may need to be encouraged to read carefully, to elicit the full set of meanings that the tree—and the cycles of nature—have for the narrator. Some students see only darkness and doubt and have difficulty recognizing or understanding the narrator's affirmations.

Comparisons, Contrasts, Connections

Other writings in the anthology that describe the depression can be compared and contrasted in content and style to "Women on the Breadlines."

In its use of the cycles of nature and of human life, "Annunciation" can be profitably compared to Whitman's use of such cycles. (Whitman was an important influence on LeSueur.) The story can also be compared effectively to Leslie Marmon Silko's "Lullaby."

Thomas S. Whitecloud (Chippewa) (1914–1972)

Contributing Editor: Daniel F. Littlefield, Jr.

Classroom Issues and Strategies

Present "Blue Winds Dancing" as you would any well-written essay.

The social implication of being Indian in an Anglo-dominated society gets lost for students in the larger issue of simply feeling "at odds" as a result of "gaps"—social, political, generational, etc.

Major Themes, Historical Perspectives, and Personal Issues

1. Self-identify, self-realization
2. Individual caught between two cultures, one not fully lost and the other not fully gained
3. Culture loss and acculturation

Significant Form, Style, or Artistic Conventions

Stress the essay structure (this one is neatly divided; how do the three parts interlock, structurally and thematically?).

Stress the use of rich visual imagery. Which *seem* to be drawn from Indian heritage, which not? Is there any difference in the effects of each?

Original Audience

It fits into the context of the whole scene of social disruption in the Great Depression, heightened in this case by the sense of being kicked loose, out of touch with two cultures.

For contemporary readers, it speaks to the large themes of searching out roots and self-realization.

Comparisons, Contrasts, Connections

For earlier generations of Indian writers who deal with the theme of being caught between cultures, see Copway and Apess, Eastman and Bonnin. For later writers, see Welch and Erdrich.

D'Arcy McNickle (1904–1977)

Contributing Editor: John Lloyd Purdy

Classroom Issues and Strategies

Like so much of McNickle's fiction, "Hard Riding" is a deceptively simple story. As in the verbal arts (such as story-telling), it implies and suggests more than it states. Students often accept the "joke" played upon the Agent, and then dismiss it as clever but relatively insignificant. However, McNickle will work on them even after they have done so.

In his first novel, McNickle shows the effect of an evening of story-telling on his young protagonist, Archilde, who considers himself a "modern man" (an assimilated Indian who no longer believes as his mother and her people believe) and who easily dismisses "the old stories" they tell. On the night of a feast, however, he is captured by those same stories and taken to a new level of awareness in which he becomes an "insider" and sees his people's lives in new ways. They are no longer the residue of the old bowing under the new, but the bearers of a dynamic and important culture. In short, McNickle consistently attempted a similar end for non-Native readers, using a written medium.

Since the story "Hard Riding" is presented from Mather's point of view, one can examine what his thoughts and reactions reveal about his character at the outset. For instance, does the opening simply establish "setting" or does it enlighten an important aspect of Mather's nature, as he spurs his horse on to the meeting? Also, he is, literally, a mediator: He represents the modern, the progressive, and therefore he possesses many of the same feelings and beliefs as McNickle's intended audience. Moreover, he is privy to knowledge of "Indian ways" that he shares with us, revealing what his years of experience have taught him about the people he has been sent to manage. He becomes, at least initially and momentarily, the expert, the authority.

The story obviously hinges on the thwarted efforts of that authority, so the conclusion needs careful examination, not only as it pertains to what precedes it, but also in how we, as readers, respond to Mather's failure to have his way, that is, to spur the men "below" him to accept a new way of "justice." We are never involved in the debate that takes place among the Native American characters; instead, the action is filtered through an interpreter and the Agent himself; yet we become "insiders" when we reflect upon the implications of the maneuvering; that the orders of the "dominant society" have been followed, in form but certainly not in principle. Do we applaud, condemn, or dismiss the actions of the tribe?

Major Themes, Historical Perspectives, and Personal Issues

In 1934 McNickle took a job on the staff of the Commissioner of Indian Affairs, John Collier, who reflected the New Deal ideals of the Roosevelt administration. It was Collier's belief that, as much as possible, tribes should be allowed to direct their own affairs, using traditional, rather than Euro-American, governmental frameworks. McNickle subscribed wholeheartedly to this ideal, which in turn directed his work for the remainder of his life. We can see that concept in this story. When a federal functionary attempts to impose a new way, a way he and the readers may consider wholly logical and in the best economic interests of his charges, he is not only frustrated but humiliated. However, the significance of this dramatic crisis lies not in its overt political statement, but in its demonstration of the efficacy of traditional Native economic systems and governments in contemporary times.

As McNickle well knew, the survival and renewal of Native cultures rest in the communal aspects of tribal life perpetuated through ceremonialism and literature. Community, rather than alienation and individuality, is a major thematic concern in both, and in the writings of McNickle and those who followed him. This communalism calls for sharing hardships as well as bounty (that is, the cattle), and it is maintained through the ability to reach consensus through group reasoning and discussion, a governmental form McNickle's audience may uphold as an ideal of democracy, but fail to recognize in practice in the story. The Indians whom Mather addresses work in concert and exert control over their own affairs. In a word, they are empowered by their communal presence, their group identity as "insiders." This, again, is a recurrent theme in McNickle's fiction, and his scholarly writings. (See also the "Original Audience" section below.)

Significant Form, Style, or Artistic Conventions

McNickle was fond of the juxtaposition of very divergent points of view. For instance, in his last novel, *Wind from an Enemy Sky* (1978), he often uses chapter breaks to move from his Native American to his Anglo characters. Given his subject—American Indian perspectives—and his non-tribal audience, this is an understandable technique. He forces readers to assess what they believe about American Indians, by consistently undermining those beliefs with culture "shifting" and therefore ethnographic revelation. His humane handling of cross-cultural explorations creates moments of crisis.

In "Hard Riding," this can be seen in the final passages, where the primary point of view, that of the Indian Agent, is somehow inverted, or shifted, as readers move from "listening" to Mather's narrative to trying to understand what has happened beyond it, and how he has been duped.

McNickle also makes suggestive use of descriptions as a means of shaping an audience's preparation for events. More than simply foreshadowing, this technique often works as a symbolic subtext. For instance, in the opening ride he describes the time of day, noting the "crimson flame thwarting the prismatic heavens." This may be dismissed by students bred on stark realism as merely flowery prose; however, in discussion it could also be considered as a preface to what follows. Mather is thwarted at story's end. Considering the idea of a prismatic effect, and McNickle's perspective on the religions that had subjugated Native America, one might be able to go further with the discussion. In fact, it may not be too difficult to question the use of the name "Mather" for the main character. McNickle was an avid reader in all disciplines, including colonial history, in which the Mather family and their ethnocentric beliefs figure prominently. McNickle played with language and its allusive qualities in some interesting ways.

Original Audience

McNickle's audience changed dramatically over his lifetime, which makes him, once again, a significant figure for study. Today, his books have been continuously reprinted since the mid-seventies and remain popular because they reflect what many have come to understand as a revised and therefore acceptable image of contemporary Natives and tribal issues. When this story was first written, however, history books and novels by non-Native writers still proffered as fact the popular stereotypes we have come to recognize and reject: Native Americans as either Noble Savages or savages; as the remnants of a dying race, on the brink of extinction; as the dull and sullen subhuman at a loss to deal with civilization; and so on. They also devalued Native cultural achievements, pre-Columbian populations, and the ill effects (and the morality) of European colonization. Moreover, the ideal of assimilation—the "melting pot" of America—was equally prominent. It is little wonder that McNickle's early works, although well-received by critics, were not widely popular; he presents Indians who exert a degree of control over their lives and who take pride in their tribal identities. He presents a very different American dream than his popular contemporaries, Ernest Hemingway and F. Scott Fitzgerald, do.

Comparisons, Contrasts, Connections

The anthology provides ample points of comparison and contrast. McNickle's work can be placed, in some ways, in the context of other writings from the 1930s, writings by non-Native writers; it can also be compared or contrasted with writings by Native Americans produced before 1935. For instance, Whitecloud's "Blue Winds Dancing" (published in the same year as McNickle's first novel, *The Surrounded*) possesses some of the same issues of community and commercial

America. Most profitably, however, one can compare the ways that his work anticipates later works by Native writers. There is a great deal of "resonance" to be found here.

Questions for Reading and Discussion/ Approaches to Writing

1. Is Mather's proposal a logical one? Why or why not? On what basis is that logic built?
2. Is the group's alteration of Mather's plan a logical one? Why or why not? On what basis is its logic built? (McNickle offers another "logic," the logic of communal needs and obligations over financial expediency, and the latter is proffered as a distinct and viable alternative to that of "modern, commercial America.")
3. What is the significance of the title? How does McNickle's description of Mather's riding style reflect or imply the author's evaluation of governmental policy-making?

Bibliography

The three books on McNickle and his writings are Dorothy Parker, *Singing an Indian Song: A Biography of D'Arcy McNickle* (1992); John Purdy, *Word Ways: The Novels of D'Arcy McNickle* (1990); and James Ruppert, *D'Arcy McNickle* (1988). General criticism about McNickle's works can be found in several journals, including *Studies in American Indian Literatures* and *Western American Literature*.

Robert Penn Warren (1905–1989)

Contributing Editor: Robert H. Brinkmeyer, Jr.

Classroom Issues and Strategies

Warren is a very accessible poet, with a strong sense of narrative and a nonintimidating diction, both of which students generally enjoy.

Warren's great concern with the historical vision and the meanings found in memory and the past are distinctly southern. For students with no background in southern literature, these interests may seem forced, even bizarre in their intensity. A general overview of some of the major themes of twentieth-century southern literature would help put Warren into perspective.

The poetry speaks for itself, but I do think, as I have said, that discussing Warren's "southernness" is an effective way to begin a discussion of him. One might go from there into a discussion of which poems clearly evoke a southern perspective and which don't—and then, why and why not, which are more effective, etc.

Students generally respond well to Warren's poetry, particularly to that in which the persona struggles with problems of identity and meaning. The poetry selected here is quite varied, so questions arise about continuities/discontinuities in terms of subject matter and poetic vision between the poems, and about the different stanza forms and the lines employed by the poet. Warren's depiction of the natural world— the hawk, for instance—is quite striking, and students like to discuss this aspect of his work.

Major Themes, Historical Perspectives, and Personal Issues

1. The self in the world, particularly one's relationship with nature.
2. The meaning and significance of history.
3. The limits of the creative imagination and human knowledge.
4. The quest for meaning in continuities and in the assimilation of the self with the world outside it.

Significant Form, Style, or Artistic Conventions

Topics for questions might include: the significance of narrative and the dramatic in Warren's verse; the effectiveness of a diction that frequently tends toward the colloquial; the contrast between Warren's narrative verse ("Amazing Grace in the Back Country") and his poetry of statement ("Fear and Trembling"); the role of the persona; the form of Warren's verse, including stanza and line.

Original Audience

In "Infant Boy at Midcentury," one might discuss what was happening (and had just happened) in the world at midcentury, particularly in light of and in contrast to Warren's traditional upbringing and sympathies.

Comparisons, Contrasts, Connections

Three southern poets with similar interests come to mind: John Crowe Ransom, whose verse is more formal and controlled than Warren's; Allen Tate, who explores in his poetry the tensions arising from problems of history, time, and identity; and James Dickey, whose verse is strongly narrative. In addition, look at any of the confessional poets, but particularly Robert Lowell; a comparison with them is fruitful in trying to establish whether Warren's poetry should be read as confessional.

Bibliography

Bedient, Calvin. *In The Heart's Last Kingdom: Robert Penn Warren's Major Poetry*. Chapter 2, "His Mature Manner."

Bloom, Harold. "Sunset Hawk: Warren's Poetry and Tradition." In *A Southern Renascence Man: Views of Robert Penn Warren*, edited by Walter B. Edgar.

Justus, James. *The Achievement of Robert Penn Warren*. Section 1, "Warren the Poet."

Strandberg, Victor. *The Poetic Vision of Robert Penn Warren*. "Introduction: The Critical Reckoning."

John Crowe Ransom (1888–1974)

Contributing Editor: Martha E. Cook

Classroom Issues and Strategies

Focusing on Ransom's use of language, his wit and irony, seems to be the best route to exploring his themes on a level that students will respond to. Moving from the particular to the universal works even for the poems that seem to be fairly abstract; certainly the theme of "The Equilibrists" is one that students can react to once they have discovered or uncovered it. Using the kind of close analysis practiced by the New Critics is invaluable in studying Ransom's poetry.

Reading Ransom's poetry aloud is a very good strategy, since reading aloud reveals a lot of the liveliness that students sometimes miss on the printed page and also illuminates the ironic tone.

Students seem to be interested in the themes of transience and mutability and in the dichotomy of the body and the soul. They also sometimes get involved with Ransom's work by following up allusions to myths and legends.

Major Themes, Historical Perspectives, and Personal Issues

Themes: tradition, ritual, myth; mutability; the transience of life and love; death; the dichotomy of body and soul.

Historical issues: Ransom's relationship to the Fugitive group and the little magazine, *The Fugitive;* Ransom as a New Critic; the relationship of a classical education to modernism in poetry; the 1920s and reaction to the Great War.

Personal issues: Ransom's life as a teacher and editor; his experience as a Rhodes scholar and as a soldier in the war; his strong classical education.

Significant Form, Style, or Artistic Conventions

Ransom is so closely related to the metaphysical poets whom he knew so thoroughly that exploring this aspect of his style and form is particularly useful, as is any consideration of his juxtaposition of different levels of diction and his use of surprising words or word forms. He can be seen in the context of the Southern Renaissance of the 1920s or specifically as part of the Fugitive movement, primarily in his concern with tradition and traditional values, though not in his use of southern subjects. As one of the New Critics, his critical theories are important both for their own value and as they provide an avenue into the poetry. Howard's 1988 *Yale Review* essay gives a fascinating description of Ransom's teaching methods in a prosody course.

Original Audience

A different approach to Ransom that I have found invaluable is to place him in the context of the outpouring of literature in the 1920s and to relate his experiences in the war to those of Ernest Hemingway, William Faulkner, John Dos Passos, etc., one reason I particularly wanted to include "Crocodile." The Fugitives are often seen as a group unrelated to other writers in the 1920s, but especially Ransom's European experiences can be compared to those of his contemporaries.

Comparisons, Contrasts, Connections

Ransom can be productively compared to other Fugitive poets, especially to Allen Tate in his wit and irony; to metaphysical poets, both early and modern; to the tradition of the elegy; and to other writers who explore the same subject matter, for example,"Philomela" to *The Waste Land*.

Questions for Reading and Discussion/ Approaches to Writing

1. I tell them to be sure to look up the definitions of any unfamiliar words, and I also mention particular works we have already read that might be relevant, such as other poems on death, war, love, etc. Usually Eliot would precede Ransom or immediately follow, so I might warn students to watch for parallels and contrasts.
2. Specifically, students usually do best with Ransom when they focus on his use of language. In general, I find it useful to have students draft their own ideas, using support from the particular work, before they go to outside sources for a historical context or other critics' views.

Bibliography

Howard, Maureen. "There Are Many Wonderful Owls in Gambier." *Yale Review* 77 (Summer 1988): 521–27.

Morton, Claire Clements. "Ransom's 'The Equilibrists.' " *Explicator* 41 (Summer 1983): 37–38.

Pratt, William. "In Pursuit of the Fugitives." In *The Fugitive Poets*. New York: Dutton, 1965, 13–46.

Quinlan, Kieran. *John Crowe Ransom's Secular Faith*. Baton Rouge: Louisiana State University Press, 1989.

Rubin, Louis D., Jr. "John Crowe Ransom: The Wary Fugitive." In *The Wary Fugitives: Four Poets and the South*. Baton Rouge: Louisiana State University Press, 1978, 1–63.

Tate, Allen. "Gentleman in a Dustcoat." *Sewanee Review* 76 (Summer 1968): 375–81.

Young, Thomas Daniel. "The Fugitives: Ransom, Davidson, Tate." In *The History of Southern Literature*, edited by Louis D. Rubin, Jr., and others. Baton Rouge: Louisiana State University Press, 1985, 319–32.

Allen Tate (1899–1979)

Contributing Editor: Anne Jones

Classroom Issues and Strategies

It may be difficult to get students without some personal investment in/against the Confederacy or at least the American South to respond initially at all to a poem that presumes the identification of classical heroism with Confederate soldiery. Watching a segment from Ken Burns's popular PBS series, "The Civil War," which made much of the lives of ordinary soldiers from both sides, might help to get past initial alienation; so might a discussion of the place of the American South in contemporary ideology, especially in popular culture.

Once the distances of history and regional difference are addressed—and even if they aren't—the pairing of poem and essay makes it possible to teach close reading in an especially intimate and interesting way. Students can learn techniques of analysis from Tate's reading of his own poem, and they can at the same time sharpen their own skills by resisting specific claims of his reading. The pairing offers the opportunity as well to examine, address, and discuss the history and value of the New Criticism, of which Tate was a founder and his essay is, presumably, an example. What sorts of reading does he reject and why? What sorts does he simply fail to mention? Issues of gender and femininity in particular seem oddly and obscurely present in the essay; they invite a second look at the poem for its implicit gender stakes.

Major Themes, Historical Perspectives, and Personal Issues

Tate lays out in "Narcissus as Narcissus" what he conceived to be the major themes of "Ode to the Confederate Dead": the conflict between a vanished heroic community of "active faith" and the anomie of contemporary reductionism and isolation. These themes will be familiar to students, especially those who have read T. S. Eliot and other conservative modernists. Tate represents the conflict as taking place within the consciousness of a man standing alone at a Confederate graveyard; the conflict thus is reshaped as a problem for the imagination. What can this man's (the poet's?) imagination take hold of and how? How, in fact, does the imagination work? Tate looked first to southern history and later to the Catholic church for answers. One might ask students, with Gertrude Stein, what is the question? This might encourage looking beyond Tate's own representations to other ways of framing the issues he is engaged in.

Significant Form, Style, or Artistic Conventions

Tate, of course, addresses these issues in his essay. He compares (albeit self-disparagingly) the poem's structure to that of a Greek ode; he pays particular attention to questions of rhyme and rhythm. In short, he emphasizes poetic traditions. Yet he claims that the absence of these traditions is what shapes the "modern" side of the conflict in the protagonist's mind. Is Tate's understanding of his own formal and stylistic effects, his use and rejection of convention, adequate?

Original Audience

Tate worked on the first version of "Ode" during the winter of 1925, living in New York with his wife Caroline Gordon and, for a time, in a cramped apartment, with Hart Crane. That draft (the 1937 revision is not very severe) was published in the last collaboration of the Fugitives as a group, *Fugitives, an Anthology of Verse* (1928). It won him considerable national fame, which (in the words of Radcliffe Squires) he "took with him to Europe" on a Guggenheim fellowship in 1928. The "Ode" has remained his best-known poem, though he is no longer thought of as the national figure he once was. Why not?

Comparisons, Contrasts, Connections

T. S. Eliot's themes and images, especially in "The Waste Land" and "The Love Song of J. Alfred Prufrock," are rather clear influences on Tate's perhaps even more somber poem. Eliot's "Tradition and the Individual Talent" makes an interesting pair with Tate's more self-deprecatingly named "Narcissus as Narcissus," as does Poe's "The Philosophy of Composition," to which Tate refers. Hart Crane's name appears several times in the Tate essay; Wallace Stevens's does not, though "Sunday Morning" raises similar concerns, to resolve them differently. Both poets might well be read with Tate. And of course Tate's historical connections with the Fugitives, Agrarians, and New Critics—among them John Crowe Ransom, Robert Penn Warren, and Cleanth Brooks—provide a more regional and ideological context.

Anzia Yezierska (1881?–1970)

Contributing Editor: Sally Ann Drucker

Classroom Issues and Strategies

Because Yezierska often uses a first-person narrator who speaks with a great deal of emotional intensity, readers sometimes assume that her stories are strictly autobiographical. In addition, her use of Yiddish-English dialect can obscure the fact that she crafted these stories deliberately and carefully. Readers unfamiliar with Yezierska may focus on how these stories relate to episodes in her life, rather than on her vivid characters, rich imagery, and adept use of dialect.

It can be helpful to discuss one of Yezierska's purposes in writing—to immerse the reader in the ghetto experience. (She also wished to explore her own feelings and to earn a living in the process.) In addition, although most readers come from backgrounds totally different from that of her characters, her stories can be discussed in terms of contemporary problems encountered by new immigrants, ghetto youth, working-class employees, and women.

Photos of Lower East Side tenement scenes or films such as *Hester Street* (based on *Yekl*) are useful to set up a visual context for Yezierska's writing.

Yezierska's most-taught novel is *Bread Givers*. In that book, the patriarchal father represents traditional Jewish ways. Because of the negative aspects of the father-daughter relationship, students who are not familiar with Jewish culture come away with a skewed view of it. Even in Yezierska's other works, what the heroine is giving up in order to become Americanized—family and culture—may not be readily apparent, given the heroine's economic and status gains from the process. These issues can be clarified in class discussion.

Major Themes, Historical Perspectives, and Personal Issues

The processes of acculturation and assimilation, and the positive and negative effects of these processes, are ongoing themes in Yezierska's writing. Her work is particularly interesting for its presentation of immigrant women's pursuit of the American Dream. "America and I" was originally published in 1922, right before immigration laws changed

(1924), restricting access to everyone not from northern or western Europe. This may have affected the way Yezierska ended the story (see last paragraph).

Significant Form, Style, or Artistic Conventions

Yezierska's work has been called sentimental and melodramatic. It is important to understand that in the Yiddish language tradition that she came out of, emotionality was expected, particularly for women. Her work fuses aspects of realism (attention to detail) and romanticism (characters' idealism), ultimately making it difficult to categorize.

Original Audience

Yezierska's stories were first published in magazines that had a general readership. She wrote primarily for mainstream Anglo-American audiences of the '20s, although her work was certainly seen by Jewish-Americans and other ethnic readers as well. Contemporary audiences, particularly female readers, respond especially to the immigrant waif characters as women who forged cultural and economic identities by their own strength, energy, and perseverance.

Comparisons, Contrasts, Connections

Other works on immigrant Jewish life excerpted in this volume include the folowing:

The Promised Land, by Mary Antin
Yekl, by Abraham Cahan
Jews Without Money, by Michael Gold

Other works on immigrant life excerpted in this volume include the following:

Christ in Concrete, by Pietro Di Donato
East Goes West, by Younghill Kang
The Woman Warrior, by Maxine Hong Kingston

Questions for Reading and Discussion/ Approaches to Writing

1. It can be useful to ask about conflicts described in her writing: in this story, old versus new, expectations versus reality; in other

stories, Jewish tradition versus American opportunity, parent versus child.
2. General: Oral histories—students interview members of their families, focusing on questions of cultural transitions, such as rural versus urban, one decade versus another, immigrant conflicts, etc. Papers—on working-class women in early twentieth-century literature, on the Americanization process in literature.
3. Specific: Papers comparing this story with some of Yezierska's others in *Hungry Hearts* or *Children of Loneliness*.

Bibliography

Shorter Works:

Baum, Charlotte, et. al. *The Jewish Woman in America*. New York: Dial Press, 1976. Chapters 3, 4, 5, 91–162.

Drucker, Sally Ann. "Yiddish, Yidgin & Yezierska." *Modern Jewish Studies Annual VI* (1987): 99–113.

Henriksen, Louise Levitas. "Afterword About Anzia Yezierska." In *The Open Cage: An Anzia Yezierska Collection*. New York: Persea Books, 1979, 253–62.

Kessler-Harris, Alice. "Introduction." In *The Open Cage: An Anzia Yezierska Collection*. New York: Persea Books, 1979, v–xiii.

Pratt, Norma Fain. "Culture and Radical Politics: Yiddish Women Writers, 1890–1940." *American Jewish History* 70, no. 1 (Sept. 1980): 68–90.

Yezierska, Anzia. "Mostly About Myself." In *Children of Loneliness*. New York: Funk & Wagnalls, 1923, 9–31.

Longer Works:

Dearborn, Mary V. *Love in the Promised Land: The Story of Anzia Yezierska and John Dewey*. NY: Free Press, 1988.

Henriksen, Louise. *Anzia Yezierska: A Writer's Life*. New Brunswick: Rutgers University Press, 1988.

Schoen, Carol B. *Anzia Yezierska*. Boston: Twayne, 1982.

John Steinbeck (1902–1968)

Contributing Editor: Cliff Lewis

Classroom Issues and Strategies

Students read Steinbeck as a social critic or merely as a story-teller. The task is to define Steinbeck as a writer in the mode of the twenties. One must define such terms as illusion, mythic, archetype, depth psychology, and symbol in establishing his artistic process. Secondly, one must show a student the ongoing conflict in Steinbeck's work between expectation and change, consciousness and altered circumstances.

Students love reading Steinbeck; I cite passages from his letters to indicate his artistic interests in the above ideas. I point out particular details in the works to support my interpretations. In "Flight," I have them look for description of an Indian; I explore similar conflicts and ways of perceiving in our daily lives. For a discussion of "Flight," I ask them to define the stereotypical Indian brave, stereotypical Mexican children, the role of school and education in cultural assimilation, the future of Indian culture.

I offer the view of Steinbeck as a modern artist who sees the artist's role as analogous to a psychiatrist's: to know thyself. If each work is seen as dealing with a different human drive—sexual repression, religious quest, rejection, self-hate, security and certainty of tradition, the need to belong, etc.—Steinbeck's work takes on a pattern. By all means, link such drives to similar ones readily found in students' lives.

Major Themes, Historical Perspectives, and Personal Issues

Half of Steinbeck's writings present ethnic characters whose identity is in crisis because of the conflict between cultures. For his Indians, whether in Mexico or the United States, efforts to retain the pastoral world and its values are tragically doomed. Indeed, the call of a lost Eden brings conflict with contemporary society to most Steinbeck characters. His characters cannot escape past influences: be it biological, cultural, religious, or the collective activities of migration and war. To become conscious of these hidden drives is the human quest. Evolutionary stages are represented by either unconscious memory or expressed in cultural myths as, say, the Garden of Eden. And this pressure for change, which is

particularly American, and the conflict it brings, is the underlying Steinbeck theme. Nor should the reader overlook the domestic conflict
between men and women. It may encompass the issue of power, of cultural influence as in "Flight," or of vast unused leadership to be tapped
through Ma Joad. Certainly Steinbeck's work is saturated in history: fascism and Marxism in the thirties; the loss of national ideals after World
War II. He draws upon the intellectual movements of his time in
anthropology, biology, and psychology. His historical perspective then
was termed "holistic"—defined today as ecological, with human beings
biologically and culturally connected to the universe and using human
will to blend past and future. Steinbeck's last works are autobiographical,
questioning whether he succeeded as father, husband, artist. And,
intriguingly, he questions within those novels the extent to which his
private life influenced his fiction.

Significant Form, Style, or Artistic Conventions

Steinbeck tried to find an organic means of expression for each book
that he wrote. He considered his work to be experimental. He intentionally used a documentary style for *The Grapes of Wrath*, the fabular for
The Pearl, the picaresque for *Tortilla Flat*, and so on. Generally he
belongs to the myth-symbol school of the twenties. Dreams, the unconscious, reccurring myths, symbolic characters—these qualities are characteristic of what Jung called the "visionary" style. Realism, Steinbeck
once noted, is the surface form for his interest in psychology and philosophy. To this *The Grapes of Wrath* is no exception. I'd add that his work
about Indians follows the outlines of tragedy. Finally point out that
Steinbeck's work included film scripts, plays, and political speeches and
war propaganda.

Original Audience

Steinbeck's earliest writings, whose subject was the individual psyche,
sold poorly. With his fifth book, the picaresque *Tortilla Flat*, Steinbeck
became a popular writer, and with *In Dubious Battle* and *The Grapes of
Wrath*, novels rooted in the issues of the depression, Steinbeck achieved
international fame. Before those publications, his West Coast audience
did not comprehend his direction. For most he was a "mystic" writer,
and for Edmund Wilson, Steinbeck was writing "biological" stories. It
may be this lack of comprehension that led him to insert characters into
his novels who commented on the significance of the action. The one
reviewer who saw Steinbeck's literary subject as the "unconscious,"
received a note from Steinbeck thanking him for the insightful review.

Comparisons, Contrasts, Connections

For his treatment of the mob psyche and the group, one can find similarities in Nathaniel West. Ernest Hemingway's cultural changes in Spain, the existential world of his characters, and the industrialization of William Faulkner's South parallel Steinbeck's social dynamics. In all, pastoral worlds disappear. Both Nathaniel Hawthorne and Faulkner share Steinbeck's recognition of the power of myth; Hemingway, like Steinbeck, recognizes unfulfilled religious needs. In Hemingway's style Steinbeck found a model for his own. Yet the classics are also influential: Milton on *In Dubious Battle*, the Arthurian legends on Indians and his nonconformists, *Winesburg* on the early short stories, "Everyman" on *The Wayward Bus* among others. And everywhere are the Bible and *The Golden Bough*.

Questions for Reading and Discussion/ Approaches to Writing

1. To teach "Flight," I would direct students: To define the stereotype of an Indian and to locate supporting details. To locate cultural artifacts Pepe abandons in his regression backward to a primeval state. To ask what are the duties of Pepe's peers and the consequences. To explain the significance of the landscape starting with Pepe's home. To define manhood as Pepe understood it and explain whether his concept changed. To discuss what is pursuing Pepe—an abstraction?
2. Any of the above questions will do. And what is the role of the mother? Or ask questions about illusion, the definition of myth and symbol, the use of biological or animal imagery and its purpose.

Bibliography

See pertinent sections of Jackson Benson's biography. A collection of essays I'm editing on the above issues will soon be published by Edwin Mellen Press. R. Astro's book has good material on Steinbeck and philosophy and science.

Two *Steinbeck Study Guides* edited by T. Hayashi have good general information on Steinbeck's writings. P. Lisca's updated *Wide World of John Steinbeck* remains a valuable study. For short story analysis see J. Hughes, *John Steinbeck, A Study of the Short Fiction*, 1989; J. Timmerman, *The Dramatic Landscape of Steinbeck's Short Stories*, University of Oklahoma Press, 1990.

Richard Wright (1908–1960)

Contributing Editor: John M. Reilly

Classroom Issues and Strategies

Among sympathetic readers, there is an assumption that Wright is documentary, that his works can be read as elementary sociology. If these readers are familiar with literary movements, they also assume he can be classed as a naturalistic author displaying the experience of victims. Readers of a negative disposition are inclined to class Wright as an exponent of hate, an unreasonable writer who is not sensitive to the complexities of moral experience.

For all of these readers, a useful approach is to focus on the narrative point of view, the third-person narration (or what is technically labeled free, indirect discourse or narrated monologue) that places us within the consciousness of the protagonist. This introduces a complexity of mind, an experience of identification (but not identity) that can illustrate how we and the protagonist are "inside" of statistics or documentary, how we experience life as though we had choice and cannot be victims.

I would recommend for study of "The Man Who Was Almost a Man" some consideration of how Wright revised his work to make it less and less "realistic," more and more symbolic. This approach allows for treatment of the issue of universality. Student discussion often centers around guilt and freedom. The most commonly asked questions have to do with a tendency to allegorize the underground journey. While exploring what Wright might intend by some of his choices of settings that the character enters, it is possible to suggest that they are categorical and take him into dominant institutions while exposing the workings of the social values.

Major Themes, Historical Perspectives, and Personal Issues

The focus on point of view is also helpful for drawing attention to the interest Wright has in social psychology, which dramatizes in narrative the consciousness of a character at the crossroads of social forces (race, class) and personal impulses and self-creation. Wright is dedicated to study of the production of personality and the arousal of a self-directive being. This, after all, is the substance of African-American history: how oppressed people create a world, a culture, and remake personalities the dominant group seeks to eradicate.

Significant Form, Style, or Artistic Conventions

The challenge is to describe "protest" literature as a repudiation of the dominant discourse on race without allowing readers to believe that rejection of the dominant literary styles is to become nonliterary. Wright should be seen as a major voice of African-American modernism (see the emphasis on the black self, the effort in his work to found a subjectivity). That's his literary period. His school may well be called protest. But the selection in the anthology requires attention to the language of symbolism—the charged objects and language of racial discourse.

Original Audience

The audience in the 1940s and 1950s may have been less receptive to the symbolic element, less attuned to the existentialist outlook of a black writer. The greatest distinction of audiences, however, lies in the historical experiences of white and black readers. The protagonist is, like Bigger Thomas, a Stagger Lee, a "baadd man"; and in his story he "signifies" on white culture by use of the elements of black culture. Obviously, different people will see these differently. (See Claudia Mitchel-Kernan, "Signifying," *Mother Wit from the Laughing Barrel*, ed. Alan Dundes, Prentice-Hall, 1973, pp. 310–28.)

Comparisons, Contrasts, Connections

Compare with Ralph Ellison, *Invisible Man*, for the use of perception imagery as well as the subterranean symbolism; Albert Camus, *The Stranger*, for the experience of a protagonist who finds the assumptions of normality collapsing.

Questions for Reading and Discussion/ Approaches to Writing

1. (a) What is the meaning of Dave's final remark?
   (b) Compare this work to a crime story. Who is Wright's criminal?
2. (a) Discuss the creativity of the protagonist.
   (b) Suggest why Wright chose not to indicate the name or "vital statistics" of his protagonist.

Bibliography

Bakish, Davis, "Underground in an Ambiguous Dreamworld." *Studies in Black Literature* 2 (Autumn 1971): 18–23.

Davis, Charles T. and Michel Fabre. *Richard Wright: A Primary Bibliography*. Boston: G. K. Hall, 1982. Information on revisions and evolving form of story.

Everette, Mildred. "The Death of Richard Wright's American Dream: 'The Man Who Lived Underground.' " *CLA Journal 17* (1974): 318–26.

Fabre, Michel. "From Tabloid to Myth: 'The Man Who Lived Underground.' " *The World of Richard Wright*. Jackson: University of Mississippi Press, 1985. 93–107.

Gelfant, Blanche. "Residence Underground: Recent Fictions of the Subterranean City." *Sewanee Review* 83 (1975): 406–38.

Goed, William. "On Lower Frequencies: The Buried Men in Wright and Ellison." *Modern Fiction Studies* 15 (1970): 483–501.

Hyman, Stanley Edgar. "Richard Wright Reappraised." *The Atlantic* 225 (March 1970): 127–32. Addresses critically the protest versus symbolism in Wright's work with "The Man . . ." as an example of his finest writing.

Reilly, John. "Self-Portraits by Richard Wright." *Colorado Quarterly* 20 (Summer 1971): 31–45. On revisions and the author's personal investment in "The Man . . .".

Margaret Walker (b. 1915)

Contributing Editor: Maryemma Graham

Classroom Issues and Strategies

When she won a major award (the Yale Younger Poets Award), Walker was put in the public eye, but her writing always had a public dimension to it. Students might want to explore the pressures a writer would face if he or she were called upon to speak from more than a singular perspective. Can general experience form an urgent literary message? Can the students detect any change in Walker's style from the earlier poems and those published in the 1980s?

In the language of her novel, *Jubilee*, the rhetoric is shaped in part by a need to be informative about a subject that many people had never explored or even considered. In her poems, the use of "public" forms of expression—chants, litanies, and sermons—to generate structure as well as feeling should be explored and compared/contrasted with the novel.

Major Themes, Historical Perspectives, and Personal Issues

Freedom—in all its simplicity and complexity—is clearly the main subject of Walker's work. Much of her writing is informed by the experience of the Great Depression (she was fourteen years old when the stock market collapsed), and so racial freedom and economic freedom are intermingled in her consciousness. In some ways, the promise of post–Reconstruction political freedom for African-Americans (and equally important, the nonfulfillment of that promise) stands behind her "call" to both the future and the past. The concern with hope and tradition—neither being ultimately satisfying by itself, but both being indispensable for a full consciousness of the story of her people—is a personal focus as well as a subject matter she must engage.

Significant Form, Style, or Artistic Conventions

Clearly, the poetry uses forms drawn from sermons and chants, the so-called "folk" tradition. Yet Walker was an educated, trained writer who spent years perfecting her craft. Students should be encouraged to examine precisely how the poetic structures are adapted and where they are altered in the expression of a more "modern" consciousness.

The novel should be compared to the various slave narratives, some of which are available in Volume 1 of *The Heath Anthology*, providing a useful contrast between "first-person" and "third-person" narrative frameworks. Also, the poems and the novel both can be read in the context of Booker T. Washington and W.E.B. Du Bois, who begin the "Modern Period" in Volume 2. Here especially the theme of balancing the acknowledgement of past oppression and future hope can be fruitfully unfolded.

Questions for Reading and Discussion/
Approaches to Writing

1. Does the passage from the novel read exactly like a newspaper account, or what is sometimes called "feature journalism"? If not, where does it most differ?
2. What effect is created by using specific names in the poems when the "general" context of the poem's language is so dominant?
3. Look at Langston Hughes's poetry and compare his use of rhythms and idioms to that of Walker.

Saunders Redding (1906–1988)

Contributing Editor: Eleanor Q. Tignor

Classroom Issues and Strategies

No Day of Triumph is a very teachable text that may be approached as a personal, racial, and historical document. Redding's objective but often passionate approach to relating his experiences can be used as a "lesson" in writing style, and in understanding the interconnections among the personal, racial, and social in American history and life. Comparisons with themes treated by earlier and later African-American writers can readily be made as the suggested assignments indicate.

Major Themes, Historical Perspectives, and Personal Issues

1. The black American's double consciousness—being black and being American; its effect on self-development and on relations with others, black and white.
2. The role of the family (family philosophy and patterns, goals and values) in shaping offspring—the nurturing but also sometimes the hindrances.
3. Slavery and its effects on blacks—on personal development and behavior, on family life in the next generation and generations to come.
4. Slavery and its effects on whites, especially the master/slave "relationship."
5. The tragic mulatto—caught between being black and (not) being white.
6. Intra-racial skin color consciousness and conflict.
7. The educated Negro and the "Negro burden": extraordinary responsibility "to uphold the race"; related theme—being better than whites in order to succeed.
8. The hold of religion on blacks, especially poorer blacks.
9. The black American folk past and its vestiges, especially its effects on blacks of little education.
10. The author as family member and individualist, as man of reason and humanist.

Significant Form, Style, or Artistic Conventions

1. The effects of a text that merges personal and social history.
2. Objectivity versus subjectivity in this highly personal text.
3. Passionate tone and satirical humor.
4. Precise language.
5. Influence of the thinking of W.E.B. Du Bois (see especially *The Souls of Black Folk*); anti-Booker T. Washington philosophy (see Du Bois's *The Souls of Black Folk* and Washington's *Up from Slavery*).
6. Writing as catharsis (see the rest of *No Day of Triumph* and especially *On Being Negro in America*).
7. Skill in blending exposition, dialogue, and anecdote in the creation of a highly readable text.
8. Incorporation of black folk materials (songs, tales, prayers).

Original Audience

In 1942, most black Americans and other Americans who knew and were sensitive to the conditions of slavery and the post-slavery years would have had no difficulty with Redding's thesis and tone. The history may need to be sketched in for present-day students; skin color consciousness and the history of the slave and the free black must be understood to get the impact of each of the grandmothers on Redding, the boy.

Comparisons, Contrasts, Connections

1. Du Bois's *Souls of Black Folk* (1903) should be a major comparison. See Du Bois's chapter on Booker T. Washington (III: "Of Mr. Booker T. Washington and Others," in *Souls of Black Folk*) and Washington's *Up from Slavery*.
2. For the theme of being black in America, also highly personal as well as social responses, see for comparison: Richard Wright's "The Ethics of Living Jim Crow" (in Richard Wright's *Uncle Tom's Children*); James Baldwin's "The Discovery of What It Means to Be an American" and "Nobody Knows My Name: A Letter from the South" (both essays in Baldwin's *Nobody Knows My Name*); Maya Angelou's *I Know Why the Caged Bird Sings*.
3. For facts and commentary on slavery, see Redding's *They Came in Chains*, as well as any slave narratives taught in the course.
4. For an understanding of the stereotyping of the mulatto and other black stereotypes in American literature, see Sterling A. Brown's "Negro Character as Seen by White Authors," *Journal of Negro*

Education, 2 (1933), reprinted in *Dark Symphony,* ed. James A. Emanuel and Theodore Gross (New York: The Free Press, 1968).

5. For autobiographical comparison/contrast with other black boys who became famous men, see Richard Wright's *Black Boy* and Langston Hughes's *The Big Sea* (Part I, Chapters 2–16).

Questions for Reading and Discussion/ Approaches to Writing

1. State your impressions of the Redding daily household. Support your impressions, explaining how you arrived at them.
2. State and explain the tone of Redding's opening to the chapter, prior to his introduction of Grandma Redding.
3. Contrast Grandma Redding and Grandma Conway, as they appeared to Saunders Redding, the boy.
4. Does Redding, the man, in retrospect, admire either grandmother, neither, or one more than the other? Explain.
5. Through their different manners of death and Redding's description of each death, what is implied about each of the grandmothers?
6. Who in the chapter is "troubled in mind"? Give your analysis.
7. Using Redding's style of writing as a model, write an analysis of your own "roots."

Bibliography

Baraka, Imamu Amiri. "A Reply to Saunders Redding's 'The Black Revolution in American Studies.' "*Sources for American Studies,* edited by Jefferson B. Kellogg and Robert H. Walker, 1983.

Kellogg, Jefferson B. "Redding and Baraka: Two Contrasting Views on Afro-American Studies." *Sources for American Studies,* edited by Jefferson B. Kellogg and Robert H. Walker, 1983.

Thompson, Thelma B. "Romantic Idealists and Conforming Materialists: Expressions of the American National Character." *MAWA Review* 3 (June 1988): 6–9.

Vassilowitch, John, Jr. "Ellison's Dr. Bledsoe: Two Literary Sources." *Essays in Literature* 8 (Spring 1981) 109–13.

Pietro Di Donato (1911–1992)

Contributing Editor: Helen Barolini

Classroom Issues and Strategies

The lack of perception of Italian-American authors as literary and the general lack of knowledge concerning the body of Italian-American writing is an obstacle to be overcome. In particular with Di Donato's classic work, *Christ in Concrete*, there is the question of linguistic uniqueness—a result of transposing Italian thought forms into English. This lends richness and texture to the work, but must be explained.

The Italian-American author and his/her work can be examined in terms of the general theme of the outsider and can be related to authors of other groups, bridging the narrow ethnic theme to the more general one. Students are interested in issues of workers' exploitation, what impels immigrants toward the American dream, and what the country was like fifty years ago as compared to today.

The language can be dealt with by showing how language forms thought patterns, and so viewpoints. However, beneath the uniqueness lies the same human feelings and their expression.

There is a film version of *Christ in Concrete* that could be useful to promote classroom discussion.

Major Themes, Historical Perspectives, and Personal Issues

Di Donato's *Christ in Concrete* is an achievement in giving literary form to the oral culture of the immigrant peasant transformed into urban worker. His is a prime example of the proletarian novel of the 1930s.

Significant Form, Style, or Artistic Conventions

Di Donato created an American language that accommodated the oral culture of his protagonists, a language that reflects the texture of the peasant-worker discourse. It is important to note that dignity and intelligence are not the social prerogatives of the more articulate social group.

Original Audience

Di Donato's work was written in the 1930s period of the depression, social protest, and growing interest in socialist solutions for the ills of the world and its workers. It was hailed, at its appearance, as "the epithet of the 20th Century." In some ways it continues to be extraordinarily actual, as witness the collapse of the building in Bridgeport during the summer of 1987 that duplicated the tragedy of *Christ in Concrete* with the loss of workers' lives.

Comparisons, Contrasts, Connections

Di Donato can be related to Clifford Odets, another writer of social protest, who had some influence on him. Also, compare with the lyric proletarianism of Steinbeck's *The Grapes of Wrath* and with John Fante's evocation of his mason father in *The Brotherhood of the Grape*.

It could be useful, also, to link Di Donato with the passionate outcry of James Baldwin in *Go Tell It on the Mountain* or with the working-class women of Tillie Olsen's *Yonnondio*.

Questions for Reading and Discussion/
Approaches to Writing

1. I think it is useful to have some perspective on the social conditions of the times in this country as reflected in *Christ in Concrete*.
2. Study the techniques of characterization. What makes a character live, or, on the other hand, fade? What makes a successful character?

    How do Di Donato's Italian-American working-class characters relate to all people everywhere?

Bibliography

Esposito, Michael P. "The Evolution of Di Donato's Perceptions of Italian Americans." In *The Italian Americans Through the Generations*. Proceedings of the 15th annual conference of the American Italian Historical Association. Staten Island: AIHA, 1986.

——. "The Travail of Pietro Di Donato." MELUS 7, no. 2 (Summer 1980): 47–60.

Sinicropi, Giovanni. "Christ in Concrete." *Italian Americana* 3 (1977): 175–83.

Viscusi, Robert. "The Semiology of Semen: Questioning the Father." In *The Italian Americans Through the Generations*. Proceedings of the 15th annual conference of the American Italian Historical Association. Staten Island: AIHA, 1986.

——. "De Vulgari Eloquentia: An Approach to the Language of Italian American Fiction." In *Yale Italian Studies*, 1, no. 3 (Winter 1981): 21–38. An interesting commentary on language usage.

Mourning Dove (Okanogan) (1888–1936)

Contributing Editor: Kristin Herzog

Classroom Issues and Strategies

Students tend to see these stories as folklore, not realizing their complexity and philosophical background. They cannot measure the difficulty of translating a corporate tradition into the narrative voice of an individual writer. They will wonder for what audience the stories were written.

Consider approaching Mourning Dove from the world of American Indian spirituality, especially since the sweat-house tradition is still alive in some tribes.

In order to teach the excerpts from *Coyote Stories*, a basic understanding of the trickster figure in the legends of various tribes is necessary. Though the trickster's shape can be Raven, Blue Jay, Raccoon, Crow or Spider, and though his function differs in detail, he is most frequently Coyote, the creature of playful disguises and clever self-seeking, the breaker of taboos, teller of lies, and creator of possibilities. He is the restlessly moving, ever-changing, indomitable spirit of survival. Coyote is always at the mercy of his passions and appetites; he holds no moral or social values, yet through his actions all values come into being. Trickster tales give humorous vent to those impulses that the tribes had to repress in order to maintain social order.

Major Themes, Historical Perspectives, and Personal Issues

Mourning Dove had to surmount almost incredible obstacles to become an author, and she personifies the ambivalent position of many ethnic women writers. Besides the lack of education and the ordeal of daily life in migrant labor camps, she had to contend with suspicious members of her tribe who did not see any purpose in giving away their sacred stories or who expected payment for telling them, since some ethnologists had established that custom.

She also had to deal with the two men who made her publications possible: Lucullus McWhorter and Heister Dean Guie, the former an eminent scholar and faithful friend, the latter a journalist who wanted to establish a reputation as illustrator and editor. Both badgered her continually with questions of verification for certain customs' names or spellings. Both considered themselves authorities on the selection of stories "proper" for a white audience and on the addition of notes. Guie decided to eliminate at least ten tales from the final manuscript because they dealt with subjects like incest, transvestism, and infanticide. Donald Hines has retrieved these stories from Mourning Dove's manuscripts and has restored all the tales as closely as possible to her original version.

Significant Form, Style, or Artistic Conventions

Most difficult to grasp for the white reader is probably the concept of power. Usually an individual's power derived from or was related to an animal to which he or she felt kinship. Power for the Okanogans is not identical with what we call the mind or the soul, but instead is more like the Christian concept of a guardian angel—a force that protects and leads. When a young girl or boy received power, they also received a "power song" that was their very own. Thus power is immediately related to words.

Original Audience

When the oral tradition entered the literary mainstream, it first had to take on the conventions and proprieties of white literature. Only decades later was the mainstream audience able to understand orality "in the raw." In Mourning Dove's time, the often bizarre or obscene behavior of Coyote could easily be understood as reflection on Okanogan morals. Besides, *Coyote Stories* was written first of all for children.

Comparisons, Contrasts, Connections

Compare with Zitkala-Sa in terms of "translating" tribal traditions into white western narrative form.

On the surface, of course, the story of "The Spirit Chief Names the Animal People" is simply entertaining and educational. But, like any creation myth, it expresses a complex "philosophy." The animal people's need for "names" points to the coming of humans with a new kind of speech. But there were "tribes" already inhabiting the earth together with the animal people, and they were threatened by "people-devouring monsters." In a type of "Fortunate Fall" parable, it is the Coyote, the bragging, bungling fool, who by divine mercy is given the task of conquering these monsters. His special power may at times falter, but if he dies, his life can be restored by his twin brother, Fox, or by "others of the people."

The reader trained in the Judeo-Christian tradition may want to compare this story with biblical images and concepts. The Spirit Chief is "an all-powerful Man Above"—as McWhorter's note phrases it—but he has a wife who could be compared to the Sophia of the Hebrews: she participates in the creation and is the human, commonsensical aspect of the divinity who knows what the people need.

Questions for Reading and Discussion/ Approaches to Writing

1. Compare the creation myths of various world religions or of various American Indian tribes. What do they have in common?
2. In what sense did Mourning Dove herself become a "trickster"? How do these stories compare with fairy tales and fables?

Bibliography

Allen, Paula Gunn. *The Sacred Hoop: Recovering the Feminine in American Indian Traditions.* Boston: Beacon Press, 1986. 81–84, 151.

Astrov, Margot. *American Indian Prose and Poetry.* Quoted in *Pocahontas's Daughters: Gender and Ethnicity in American Culture,* edited by Mary V. Dearborn, 28. New York: Oxford University Press, 1986.

Fisher, Alice Poindexter. "The Transformation of Tradition: A Study of Zitkala-Sa and Mourning Dove, Two Transitional Writers." Ph.D. Dissertation, City University of New York, 1979. 36. On the quality of the passage on hair cutting.

Fisher, Dexter. "Introduction." In *Cogewea, the Half-Blood: A Depiction of the Great Montana Cattle Range,* by Hum-ishu-ma, v–xxix. Lincoln: University of Nebraska Press, 1981.

Hines, Donald M. ed. *Tales of the Okanogans, Collected by Mourning Dove.* Fairfield, Washington: Ye Galleon Press, 1976. 14.

Radin, Paul. *The Trickster: A Study in American Indian Mythology*. New York: Philosophical Library, 1956; rpt. New York: Greenwood Press, 1969.

Schöler, Bo. "Introduction." In *Coyote Was Here: Essays on Contemporary Native American Literary and Political Mobilization*. Aarhus, Denmark: Department of English, University of Aarhus, 1984, 9.

Yanan, Eileen. *Coyote and the Colville*. Omak, Washington: St. Mary's Mission, 1971. 29.

John Joseph Mathews (Osage) (1894–1979)

Contributing Editor: Andrew O. Wiget

Classroom Issues and Strategies

The principal issue in *Sundown* is the notion of progress. Students frequently identify progress with material improvements in life-style or increasingly complex technology. This selection questions whether those are the true marks of civilization. To see this, however, students must realize that this selection comprises two parts, each of which portrays a different moment, widely separated in time in the life of the principal character, Chal Windzer. Chal (short for "Challenge," so named because his father wanted him to be a challenge to the new generation) is a teenager in the first section, still closely identified with some element of his traditional Osage life-style. Note, however, that he is moving rapidly toward accepting the values of Anglos, as is suggested by his distance from the group of Indians he encounters during the storm.

The second section of the story occurs over a decade later. Chal has gone off to the University of Oklahoma, where he has been exposed to prejudice, bigotry, and romance. Falling in love with a white girl, he comes to despise his Indian appearance and later tries to pass himself off as a Spanish (not Mexican) gentleman. During World War I, he serves in the Army Air Force as an aviator and develops a passion for flying, which fulfills his need for a career. He loves the excitement, the danger, the thrill of flying. After serving in the Army Air Force, he returns home where he falls back into an indolent life-style, marked by long periods of drunkenness. He is just coming out of one of these periods, referred to in the last section of this selection, when he attends the hearings at which Roan Horse speaks.

In addition to providing background plot information, I also certainly call attention to certain literary devices. For example the oil derricks symbolize both the march and retreat of "progress." I'd also remind students a little bit of the history of this period of time. Osages were exempted from the provisions of the Dawes General Allotment Act, along with the Five Civilized Tribes, because they held their land under patented title, not by treaty. The surface of their reservation land had been allotted and much of it alienated through sale, but the mineral rights were retained by the Osage tribe in common and leases were given out. In the 1920s, royalties from these leases brought the tribe up to 20 million dollars per year, divided equally, amounting to around 25 thousand dollars per capita. A county court in Oklahoma had declared the Osages incompetent to manage their estates and had appointed guardians who charged a fee to manage these estates. Between exorbitant fees and the malfeasance of these guardians, much money and land was lost to the Osages.

In 1925, Congress transferred supervision of these mineral rights from the county court alone to the county court working in conjunction with the Osage agency. The federal investigators referred to in the last section are not only members of Congress but agents of the Federal Bureau of Investigation. The so-called "Osage Oil Murders" are a historical event of great notoriety and served to establish the credibility of the FBI as a law enforcement agency. As Mathews indicates, a conspiracy evolved to murder people who owned rights to oil land so that their inheritors would receive those rights. By murdering the inheritors, the conspirators planned to channel those rights into the hands of one person, an Anglo man who had married an Osage woman. She was the last person on the hit list, which today still leaves a trail of twenty-four unsolved murders and bombings.

The Osage oil boom needs to be understood in the context of the free-for-all capitalist economy of the 1890s and the first two decades of this century, during which the excesses of the Robber Barons were finally curbed by the creation of federal regulatory agencies. From the point of view of Indians in Oklahoma, however, the real question that needs to be asked is this: What happens to a community of people who go from a subsistence economy, based on communal land, barter, and credit, to an excess of cash, in the neighborhood of 25 thousand dollars per person per year (at the value of the 1920s dollar), all within the space of one generation? How does such a change affect people's values, beliefs, and behaviors?

Students seem concerned about the ambivalence of the ending, especially about whether or not Chal is really capable of being a challenge to his generation, as his father had hoped. After reading about Chal's life of indolence, it is difficult for students to believe that he will make such a bold move, requiring such a commitment of effort, especially if that move is motivated only by observing the very brief appearance of Roan Horse. On the other hand, Chal has shown the desire to be a warrior, and he has great ambitions. Does the ending mark a real turning point in his life?

Major Themes, Historical Perspectives, and Personal Issues

I would highlight the structure of the boom town society that appears in the beginning of the selection. I would indicate the characters' attitudes toward the upcoming storm (bad for business, dangerous) and contrast that with the attitudes of some of the older Indians, such as Black Elk. In between we have younger Indians, such as Sun-On-His-Wings and Chal.

The various attitudes that each of these people takes toward the onset of the storm and toward the damage that the storm does provide a keen insight into the different sets of values that are coming together under the pressure of "progress" and assimilation in this reservation community.

Significant Form, Style, or Artistic Conventions

I would point to the oil derricks as a symbol of "progress"; I would also look at the change in Chal's character between the first section and the second section. It's especially important that students try to understand Chal's apparent indifference and his drunkenness as a response to an excess of easy money in the absence of compelling community values. The recognition of this, on Chal's part, is what moves him to respond so affirmatively to Roan Horse's brief speech.

Original Audience

This book was published in the 1930s, where it met a receptive audience of people in the middle of the depression, who understood the tremendous personal cost and human devastation that was brought about by the unchecked exploitation of natural resources and poor people. In this context, especially, American Indians were highlighted as an oppressed minority within the United States. In 1928 the Meriam Report, commissioned by the U.S. government, found that Indians had a mortality rate twice as high as the white population, an infant mortality rate three times as high as the white population, and that in spite of all this, the government had been spending only fifty cents per year on the health care of each Indian. Statistics like this shocked the nation, and Indians became the object of renewed federal attention. Under the Roosevelt administration, the U.S. government took a number of important steps to redress these failures of its trust relationship, though many of them, such as the Indian Reorganization Act (1934), which allowed tribes to form their own governments with written constitutions, were controversial. Nevertheless, Mathews's work needs to be seen as speaking to the notion that the major difficulties on Indian reservations come from what today we would call a "culture of poverty." And that these can be remedied by government treatment.

Comparisons, Contrasts, Connections

Insofar as Mathews gives us a good picture of the transition on Indian reservations, he can be compared usefully to Oskison and Bonnin. Lynn Riggs's play *The Cherokee Night* also gives a good picture of the deculturation that has been visited upon American Indians as a result of the abuses in the trust relationship that they had with the U.S. government.

Questions for Reading and Discussion/ Approaches to Writing

1. How do the oil derricks mark the changes in the life of the Osages and also in the personal history of Chal? Why is Chal impressed by Roan Horse's speech?
2. In the first section of the story a young Indian comments about Black Elk: "His body is here but his mind is back in a place where we lived many years ago." How does this observation reflect the forces that are creating the conflict in this story?
3. At the very end of the story, Chal says that he is going to go off to Harvard Law School and become an orator. What do you think is the likelihood of Chal fulfilling this stated goal? How would you support your judgment?

Bibliography

Wiget, Andrew. "Modern Fiction." In *Native American Literature*. Boston: Twayne, 1985.

Wilson, Terry. "Osage Oxonian: The Heritage of John Joseph Mathews." *Chronicles of Oklahoma* 59 (1981): 264–93.

Younghill Kang (1903–1972)

Contributing Editor: Elaine H. Kim

Classroom Issues and Strategies

Students will generally be unfamiliar with Korean history and society, both past and present. They will also have trouble with Kang's archaisms. To address these problems, provide extensive socio-historical background and place the work within United States literary context, especially the Asian-American literature context.

Teach Kang in tandem with Korean-American women writers (e.g., Ronyoung Kim, *Clay Walls*, 1987) depicting the same period. Also, consider comparing Kang to the following:

1. Contemporary Korean-American writers (e.g., T. Y. Park, *Guilt Payment*, 1983).
2. Chinese, Filipino, and Japanese portrayers of community life (e.g., Louis Chu, Bulosan, Milton Murayama).
3. "Refugee" writing (e.g., Wendy Law-Jone, *The Coffin Tree*, 1983).

Major Themes, Historical Perspectives, and Personal Issues

Consider the following possibilities:

1. Immigrant (as opposed to sojourner) view.
2. Class perspectives when facing race discrimination.
3. Portrait of early Korean-American community life, through three major characters and a narrator.

Original Audience

East Goes West was written by a non-white immigrant for an Anglo audience at a time of intense anti-Asian activity in the United States.

Comparisons, Contrasts, Connections

Compare with Carlos Bulosan, *America Is in the Heart*; Lin Yutang's work, "selling" China to western readers. Examine the class perspective of immigrants versus elite sojourners.

Bibliography

Give them one of my overview essays on Asian-American lit., e.g., from
> *American Studies International* Fall 84
> *Cultural Critique* Spring 87
> *Columbia Literary History of the U.S.* (1988)

Carved on the Walls: Poetry by Early Chinese Immigrants

Contributing Editors: Him Mark Lai, Genny Lim, Judy Yung

Classroom Issues and Strategies

Because of the exclusion of racial minorities such as Chinese Americans from our American education and their continuous stereotyping in the popular media, most people do not have the historical or literary background to understand and appreciate Chinese poetry as written by the early immigrants at the Angel Island Immigration Station.

The headnote includes background information on the history of Chinese Americans and their detention experience at Angel Island as well as explanations of the literary style and content of the Chinese poems. We have also included footnotes to explain the literary and historical allusions used in the poems. It is important that students be aware of this background material in their reading of the poems as well as their significance as part of the earliest record of Chinese American literature and history written from the perspective of Chinese immigrants in America.

As you teach these selections, consider a simulation exercise where students can experience how Chinese immigrants must have felt as unwelcome aliens arriving at Angel Island. As students read these poems, they are made aware of the impact of discriminatory laws. They also learn to appreciate a different poetic style of writing. On the other hand, most students are puzzled by the historical context of the poems and by the larger moral issues of racism.

Major Themes, Historical Perspectives, and Personal Issues

The poems express strong feelings of anger, frustration, uncertainty, hope, despair, self-pity, homesickness, and loneliness written by Chinese immigrants who were singled out for exclusion by American immigration laws on the basis of race. As such, they are important fragments of American history and literature long missing from the public record as well as strong evidence that dispels the stereotype of Chinese Americans as passive, complacent, and illiterate.

Significant Form, Style, or Artistic Conventions

Most of the poems were written in the 1910s and 1920s, when the classical style of Chinese poetry was still popular and when feelings of Chinese nationalism ran strong. Of the 135 poems that have been recovered, about half are written with four lines per poem and seven characters per line. The remainder consist of verses with six or eight lines and five or seven characters per line. The literary quality of the poems varies greatly, which is understandable considering that most immigrants at this time did not have formal schooling beyond the primary grades. Many poems violate rules of rhyme and tone required in Chinese poetry and incorrect characters and usages often appear. However, these flaws do not appear in the translation, in which we chose to sacrifice form for content.

Original Audience

The Angel Island poems were written as a means to vent and record the response of Chinese immigrants to the humiliating treatment they suffered at the Angel Island Immigration Station. They were intended for other Chinese immigrants who would follow in the footsteps of the poets. But as read now, they are an important literary record of the experience and feelings of one group of immigrants who, because of their race and a weak motherland, were unwelcome and singled out for discriminatory treatment.

Comparisons, Contrasts, Connections

The only other work published so far that would serve as a useful tool of comparison in terms of form and content is Marion Hom's *Songs of Gold Mountain: Cantonese Rhymes from San Francisco Chinatown* (Berkeley: University of California Press, 1987)—a collection of Chinese folk rhymes first published in 1911 and 1915. It would also be useful for students to read about the European immigrant experience at Ellis Island in order for them to see the different treatments of immigrants to America due to race.

Questions for Reading and Discussion/ Approaches to Writing

1. (a) What are the themes of the Angel Island poems and how do they reflect the historical circumstances for Chinese immigrants coming to the United States between 1910 and 1940?

   (b) How would you describe the nameless poets based on your reading of the Angel Island poems?

2. (a) Compare and contrast the Angel Island poems with those written by another American poet in the early twentieth century.

   (b) Show how the image of Chinese immigrants as reflected in the Angel Island poems confirms or contradicts prevailing stereotypes of Chinese Americans in the popular media.

Bibliography

Lai, Him Mark, Genny Lim, and Judy Yung. *Island: Poetry and History of Chinese Immigrants on Angel Island, 1910–1940*. Seattle: University of Washington Press, 1991.

Lowe, Felicia. "Carved in Silence." A film about the Chinese immigration experience at Angel Island, 1988, available from Felicia Lowe, 565 Alvarado St., San Francisco, CA 94114; video available from National Asian American Telecommunications Association, 346 9th Street, 2nd Floor, San Francisco, CA 94103.

Takaki, Ronald. *Strangers from a Different Shore: A History of Asian Americans*. Boston: Little, Brown and Company, 1989.

Tsai, Shih-Shan Henry. *The Chinese Experience in America*. Bloomington: Indiana University Press, 1986.

Contemporary Period
1945 to the Present

Literature of the Cold War: Orthodoxy and Resistance
New Communities, New Identities, New Energies
Postmodernity and Difference: Promises and Threats

In Ralph Ellison's *Invisible Man,* the unnamed narrator explains the method behind his circular narrative by declaring that "the end is in the beginning," and in a way the three sections on contemporary literature bring us back to issues raised by the texts about the origins of America that open *The Heath Anthology.* The introduction to the sections "Native American Oral Literatures" and "Cultures in Contact" suggest that the class consider the "creation stories" that students bring with them in order to come to some sense of that cultural construct we call "America." Such a discussion questions how such stories are produced, by what groups of people, and for what purposes. Throughout the section introductions, this approach is described as an analysis of "cultural rhetoric"—the consideration of texts not as static artifacts with self-contained meanings but as strategic examples of what Jane Tompkins calls "cultural work"—the products of dynamic processes of cultural confrontation, negotiation, assimilation, and transformation. These processes include the printing and dispersal of these texts in *The Heath Anthology,* the assignment of these texts in college classes, and the particular reading experiences of the students in the class taken as both individuals and as members of various communities. Such an approach demonstrates as well that since the study of the past involves the active creation of knowledge on the part of students and teachers, history becomes an active part of the present.

The study of contemporary culture reverses this equation as a part of the same pedagogical approach by regarding the present as part of history. The historical debates over the so-called "canon" of American literature can be illustrated for students by having them define a contemporary canon by themselves. To do this, the class will have to consider what is meant by contemporary culture, how we define what is central, what is marginal, why we might want to undertake such definitions, and what the consequences of different definitions might be. The anthology itself (as well as the class syllabus) can then be regarded as just one such example of canon-building, complete with explanations and justifications of the choices made.

In regard to the section on contemporary literature in particular, discussion can center on the classification system used to organize these texts. If a copy of the first edition is handy, the class can compare how categories have been revised from one edition to the next and why. For example, the second edition can be seen as grouping contemporary texts by decades—the fifties, the sixties (and the extension of the sixties into the seventies), and the eighties/nineties—under rubrics that highlight a particular historical interpretation of each decade: "Literature of the Cold War: Orthodoxy and Resistance"; "New Communities, New Identities, New Energies"; "Postmodernity and Difference: Promises and Threats." From another perspective, however, these titles are contemporaneous, not chronological—Joyce Carol Oates and Raymond Carver from Part I are primarily writers of the last two decades; Hisaye Yamamoto and Ralph Ellison, while included in Part II, are writers of the forties and fifties as well. All of the above suggests the complexity of cultural forces at work in contemporary society: the tension and sometimes dialectic between culture and counterculture ("Orthodoxy and Resistance"); the (re)emergence of multicultural literature following the liberation movements of the sixties ("New Communities, New Identities, New Energies"); the self-consciousness and self-reflexiveness of contemporary literature, including contemporary multicultural and countercultural literature ("Postmodernity and Difference: Promises and Threats").

Such an analysis of the textbook naturally suggests inviting the class to construct their own textbook—their own canons—and to engage in the same operation of historicizing the present and near-present past by examining the associations students have in conjunction with terms like "the fifties," "the sixties," "the seventies," and "the eighties." Where do these associations come from? How are they perpetuated through the mass media and the popular culture and for what ends? Political? Commercial? What other categories and groupings could we use to organize, read, and interpret the texts in this section? "Women Writers"? "The African-American Tradition"? "Poetic Experimentation"? This kind of pedagogical approach emphasizes multiculturalism as an activity, not an inert state of being, an activity that reads texts—all texts, not just texts by "ethnic" writers (as if it were possible for there to be "nonethnic" writers)—as complex, hybrid forms of discourse.

In a similar way, Gloria Anzaldúa developed the concept of "mestiza consciousness" primarily as a way of describing how her own complex identity as a multilingual, multinational lesbian Chicana writer taught her to "cope by developing a tolerance for contradictions, a tolerance for ambiguity" by learning how to "juggle cultures." She also implies, however, that such an experience is typical rather than exceptional, and that we are all to a more or less extent juggling cultures as well, the difference being not between the pure and the mixed in terms of cultural identity, but between the conscious recognition of the complicated interrelationship of diverse cultural backgrounds and a kind of willful innocence/ignorance of this diversity.

> The struggle is inner: Chicano, *indo*, American Indian, *Mojado, mexicano*, immigrant Latino, Anglo in power, working class Anglo, Black, Asian—our psyches resemble the borderlands and are populated by the same people. The struggle has always been inner, and is played out in the outer terrains. Awareness of our situation must come before inner changes, which in turn come before changes in society. Nothing happens in the "real" world unless it first happens in the images in our heads. (87)

Anzaldúa's reference to the outer terrains—the rhetorical space where these internal issues of cultural definition, resistance, and transformation are played out—serves well as a pedagogical coda to this instructor's guide, reminding us that the point of cultural contestation or consensus, the site of struggle and mastery, doesn't lie between the covers of any particular anthology, but takes place in what Louise Rosenblatt called the transaction between reader and text, a transaction that includes both the immediate historical context of the reader as well as that of the text. Whatever the particular selections made for any given class syllabus, the real focus of the class is that transaction—the "images in our heads" that constitute the internal terrain of American literature.

Bibliography

Anzaldúa, Gloria. *Borderlands/La Frontera: The New Mestiza*. San Francisco: Aunt Lute Books, 1987.

Ellison, Ralph. *Invisible Man*. New York: Vintage Books, 1989.

Part I   Literature of the Cold War: Orthodoxy and Resistance

Arthur Miller (b. 1915)

Contributing Editor: Robert A. Martin

Classroom Issues and Strategies

Written and first produced for the 1953 drama season in New York, *The Crucible* continues to interest students for its witchcraft theme and setting in Salem and for its more recent political association as a historical parable against the dangers of McCarthyism. While the latter issue has generally faded in the public mind, it was very much *the* issue when the play opened. The several layers of meaning—historical (witchcraft), political (McCarthyism and the activities of the House Un-American Activities Committee), and the ever-present approach to the play as stagecraft and theater—allow an instructor to open the play to a class probably not knowledgeable about any of the layers. I have found that such a class is quickly taken up to the level of the play. Miller has added a running commentary on the issues and personalities of Salem. It is important to point out that there is no character in the play "who did not play a similar—and in some cases exactly the same—role in history" (Arthur Miller in his "Note" on the historical accuracy of *The Crucible*).

The witch-hunt that occurred in Salem in 1692 resulted from a complex society at a turning point when the power of the Massachusetts theocracy was weakening. Reverend Parris was more representative of absolute church authority than Miller makes him out. Once the issues came into the open, he found that the whole "devilish" conspiracy needed wiser and more learned minds to uncover it, even if he was absolutely convinced of the reality of witchcraft. I usually begin a class by stating that at Salem on Gallows Hill in the spring of 1692, nineteen men and women were hanged; one man, Giles Corey, was pressed to death for standing mute; and two dogs were also hanged for witchcraft. The classroom then becomes a different place; the question of witchcraft, or how could those people have believed in it, brings out some interesting and fruitful ideas, discussions, viewpoints. Discussion of the play, however, should identify the McCarthyism parallels in a way that students can understand. Miller has said that the theme of the play is "the handing over of conscience to the state." The question is not entirely a remote one, as almost any major newspaper or television exposé can make the issue clear to today's students.

Major Themes, Historical Perspectives, and Personal Issues

Central to this play, in addition to Miller's theme stated above, is one of illusion versus reality. In a society that held a doctrinal belief in the power and reality of the devil to "overthrow God's kingdom," the powers of persuasion to see "specters" where there were none resulted in mass hysteria. When John Proctor, a born skeptic, challenges the illusion, he is subsequently brought down by the reality of his adultery. As the witch-hunt spread to eventually cause the arrest of prominent citizens, some form of common sense prevailed and the girls were silenced. The Salem hysteria has been investigated and researched widely, and many excellent sources are available. One recent theory proposed that the whole business was the result of ergot poisoning, a bacteria that produces hallucinations if wheat is stored for too long and is allowed to ferment. This, of course, was the theory of a modern-day scientist who also happened to be a graduate student. It was a neat and "scientific" solution to a very old question. Unfortunately, the whole theory collapsed when expert senior biologists looked at the idea closer and declared it bad science. Miller, possibly as a result of the play, was called before the House Un-American Activities Committee in 1956 on the pretense of issuing him a passport. He was convicted of contempt of Congress for refusing to answer questions about the communistic connections of others. The decision was later reversed. Miller had in effect been convicted on the same principle as John Proctor—guilt by association—and like Proctor he refused to name others.

Original Audience

In the early 1950s there was something resembling a cohesive audience for serious plays. That audience was both shocked and fearful that the theme and subject of the play would unleash still further inquiries by the forces of McCarthyism. Reviewers, reflecting the mood of the audience, had several reactions. Some praised the acting, some thought it was a play without contemporary parallels, and others avoided the play's obvious point altogether. The best way to understand the response by critics is to read their reviews in the 1953 volume of *New York Theatre Critics' Reviews*.

Bibliography

Miller has written at length on the play and on the context of the time. The following are easily available sources I have my students use in their research. The first and probably most important are Miller's comments in volume one of *Arthur Miller's Collected Plays* (Viking, 1957), pp. 38–48. All of Miller's essays are reprinted in my *The Theater Essays of Arthur Miller* (Viking, 1978), including several comments made over the next several decades. An early work on *The Crucible* was (at the time) nicely complete and informative for its comprehensive critical collection of essays on the play, the history behind it, and the context: *The Crucible: Text and Criticism* (Penguin, 1977, first published by Viking in 1971), ed. Gerald Weales. John H. Ferres edited a useful collection of essays on the play titled *Twentieth Century Interpretations of The Crucible: A Collection of Critical Essays* (Prentice-Hall, 1972). Also of interest for its judicious selection of essays and an interview with Miller in 1979 in which many references and comments on *The Crucible* occur is *Critical Essays on Arthur Miller* (G. K. Hall, 1979), ed. James J. Martine. Somewhat of broader scope, but nevertheless useful for its international Miller bibliography by Charles A. Carpenter and a fine essay by Walter Meserve on *The Crucible* is *Arthur Miller: New Perspectives* (Prentice-Hall, 1982), ed. Robert A. Martin. My essay, "Arthur Miller's *The Crucible*: Background and Sources," has proven of use to many students and scholars who seek to learn some of the connections between the play and Salem in 1692, and has been reprinted numerous times, most recently in *Essays on Modern American Drama* (University of Toronto Press, 1987), ed. Dorothy Parker, and in Martine's *Critical Essays* noted above. I recommend that my students read selectively in *Conversations with Arthur Miller* (University of Mississippi Press, 1987), ed. Matthew C. Roudane. There are fifty-two page references listed in the index for *The Crucible*. Miller's comments in conversations and interviews are frequently more enlightening than any other playwright in our history because he is articulate as well as theoretically sophisticated. Finally, a more recent account is *The Crucible: Politics, Property, and Pretense* (New York: Twayne Masterworks Series, 1993), by James J. Martine, which is one of the most complete and comprehensive studies of *The Crucible* to date. Martine is a well-known Miller scholar and his critical judgment is astute.

Tennessee Williams (1911–1983)

Contributing Editor: Thomas P. Adler

Classroom Issues and Strategies

Students may tend to respond to the heroines, especially in Williams's earlier plays up through the end of the 1940s, differently from what he intended because their value system is not the same. His sensitive, poetic misfits who escape from reality into a world of illusion/art are likely to seem too remote, too soft. The very things that Williams values about them—their grace, their gentility—nowadays may appear dispensable adjuncts of life in an age when competition and aggressiveness are valorized among both sexes. So students need to be sensitized to Williams's romantic ideals and to what he sees as the civilizing, humanizing virtues.

It helps to place Williams in context as a southern dramatist, and also as one who propounds the feminizing of American culture as a counter to a society built on masculine ideals of strength and power. Students also need to understand that Williams is a "poetic" realist, not simply in his use of a lyrical rhetoric but in his handling of imagery, both verbal and visual. If they attend carefully to his command of visual stage symbolism, they can oftentimes discover the necessary clues about Williams's attitude toward his characters.

Any discussion of "Portrait of a Madonna" will necessarily focus upon Williams's characterization of his sexually frustrated and neurotic heroine, whose upbringing in a succession of southern rectories, under the nay-saying and guilt-inducing "shadow" of the church and of the cross, has left her totally unprepared for life and prey to crazed delusions. Miss Collins becomes almost the archetypal unmarried daughter, restricted by the responsibility of caring for an aged mother, sensing the social pressure to be sexual and yet denied any morally sanctioned expression of these feelings, finally forced into madness as a result of unrealistic expectations. The image of the Madonna and Child becomes central to an understanding of the play: the Virgin and Mother whom Lucretia costumed for the Sunday School Christmas pageant; the children she visits twice a year on religious holidays with her scrapbooks of Campbell soup kids; Richard's many children; the fabricated "child" to be born of a woman virginal in body and heart, defiled only in her dreams.

Brief though it is, Williams's play is amenable to many critical approaches other than the psychological and feminist. A formalist approach might examine the way in which Williams structures his play—as he later will *Streetcar*—around a series of dichotomies: past/present; memory/fact; gentility/brutality; shadow/light; sanity/insanity; freedom/repression; virginal/defiled; harmless illusion/harmful delusion. A literary-historical approach could place the work within the tradition of southern gothicism, while a sociocultural framework could explore the way in which the myth of southern chivalry curtails Lucretia's independence, as well as the way in which utilitarian technology threatens the artistic sensibility (elevator cage as machine played off against the music on the gramophone). A generic approach might consider the possibilities for seeing the play as a tragedy, while a biographical approach might trace the relationship between Lucretia and Williams's own schizophrenic sister Rose. For some considerations of various new theoretical approaches in literary criticism together with examples of their application to a dramatic text by Williams, you might consult *Confronting Tennessee Williams's "A Streetcar Named Desire": Essays in Cultural Pluralism,* edited by Philip C. Kolin (Westport: Greenwood, 1993).

Major Themes, Historical Perspectives, and Personal Issues

Central thematic issues include the question of illusion and reality, the relationship between madness and art, and the role of the artist in society, as well as the necessity to respond compassionately and nonjudgmentally to the needs of God's sensitive yet weak creatures who are battered and misunderstood. Historically, Williams's relation to the myth of the cavalier South should be explored. Finally, Williams's close identification with his heroines needs to be seen in light of his relationship with his schizophrenic sister Rose, as he admits in his *Memoirs,* the most intensely emotional attachment in his personal life.

Significant Form, Style, or Artistic Conventions

Although "Portrait" itself is essentially a realistic, albeit somewhat poetic, play, Williams himself should be approached as an innovator of a new "plastic" theater, a practitioner, along with Arthur Miller, of what some have termed "a theatre of gauze." To handle this aspect of Williams's aesthetic, the instructor might either read or reproduce as a handout the dramatist's Production Notes to *Glass Menagerie,* along with Tom's opening narration in that play, which really differentiates Williams's practice—"truth in the pleasant disguise of illusion"—from the strict realism—"illusion that has the appearance of truth"—of others.

Original Audience

The choice of the one-act play form itself tells something about Williams's intended audience. Rather than aim at a commercial production, "Portrait" seems more appropriate for an amateur (academic or civic) theater presentation, where the interest will be largely on character and dialogue rather than production values. Thus, it appears intended for a limited audience of intense theatergoers. From the perspective of the dramatist, it serves partly as a "study" for larger work(s), in the same way a painter might do a series of studies before attempting a full canvas. And so, in a sense, the artist too is his own audience.

Comparisons, Contrasts, Connections

Lucretia Collins bears comparison with other Williams heroines in "The Lady of Larkspur Lotion," *The Glass Menagerie, A Streetcar Named Desire*, and *Summer and Smoke*. Students might also contrast the way Miss Collins escapes from the sociocultural milieu that constricts her freedom with the heroines' responses in Susan Glaspell's short play "Trifles" and William Faulkner's short story "A Rose for Emily."

Questions for Reading and Discussion/ Approaches to Writing

1. (a) Consider the dramatic function(s) of the minor characters, the Porter and the Elevator Boy, in the play.
   (b) Could "Portrait of a Madonna" have been expanded to a full-length work? To accomplish that, what else might Williams have dramatized? Would anything have been lost in the transformation?
2. (a) The director of the original production of "Portrait" had Lucretia exit clutching a doll. What, if anything, would justify such an interpolation in Williams's text, and what might be the impact on the audience?
   (b) Discuss the theater metaphor in "Portrait": the minor characters as onstage audience; the bedroom, scene of illusions, as stage; Mr. Abrams as stage manager/director, etc.
   (c) In what way does Williams's characterization of Lucretia Collins lead the audience to conclude that he considered her story "tragic"?

Bibliography

Spoto, Donald. *The Kindness of Strangers: The Life of Tennessee Williams.* Boston: Little, Brown, 1985.

Ann Petry (b. 1908)

Contributing Editor: Hilary Holladay

Classroom Issues and Strategies

So much is going on in Petry's novels and short stories that you may wonder where to begin a classroom discussion. For a discussion of "The Witness," racial conflicts, power plays between men and women, and problems within the community of Wheeling are all equally valid starting points. Petry rarely dwells exclusively on one social problem, though students particularly sensitive to one or another issue (racism, for instance) may not recognize the range of her concerns on a first reading. Therefore, asking students to discuss the connections between matters of race and gender in "The Witness" may help them grasp this story. Once they see how entwined the social issues are in "The Witness," they will be well on their way to understanding the scope of Petry's vision.

Major Themes, Historical Perspectives, and Personal Issues

Prejudice is a central concern in Petry's writing. In almost all of her works, complex relationships develop among individuals prejudiced against each other for reasons of race or gender. But her fiction contains few characters who are solely victims or solely oppressors. Never one to make snap judgments, she imbues even her most objectionable characters with humanity. The would-be rapist Boots Smith in *The Street*, for example, has been a victim of racial prejudice. While Petry does not excuse his behavior, she does acknowledge the pathos of his life. Likewise, in "The Witness," she provides the delinquent boys with a social context: They are intelligent young men, stifled by both church and school, who have no positive outlet for their myriad frustrations.

In addition to exploring the intersections of racism and sexism, Petry chronicles the ways in which people chase after the American dream only to find that it is illusory. Petry's characters typically experience a profound disillusionment in their quests for success and/or peace of mind. This disillusionment drives them toward a drastic act that has significant implications for the whole community as well as the individual protagonist. This is true of "The Witness" as well as of Petry's novels.

In their emphasis on troubled communities and individual journeys toward freedom, Petry's works contain echoes of nineteenth-century slave narratives. *The Street*'s Lutie Johnson is a prime example of an oppressed character whose life devolves into a series of desperate escapes. The endings of Petry's works, however, depart from those of prototypical slave narratives: neither Lutie Johnson nor Charles Woodruff achieves a meaningful victory merely by escaping an intolerable situation.

Significant Form, Style, or Artistic Conventions

Although Petry's writing is clear and simply stated (reflecting her journalistic background), her frequently discursive style finds its full power in novels and long stories. Since her fiction focuses on relationships and communities, she often uses multiple points of view, flashbacks, and other devices that enable her to portray whole towns as well as individuals. Throughout her career, she has skillfully employed realism and naturalism (in her novels), stream-of-consciousness (notably in *The Narrows*), and indirect discourse (in her novels and many of her stories).

Her experiments with varied techniques and voices (male and female, black and white) underscore Petry's fascination with multiple perspectives. In "Has Anybody Seen Miss Dora Dean?" and *Country Place*, she explores the complementary roles that narrators and listeners play in a story's creation. "The Witness" contains a related theme: As readers, we "witness" Woodruff's tale, just as he witnesses a crime. At the end of "The Witness," we are in a position quite similar to Woodruff's. Our personal perspective influences our understanding of his tale. Given our individual circumstances, will we repeat his tale? Or will we try to keep the story, and all its difficulties, as a troubling secret?

Comparisons, Contrasts, Connections

Petry defies easy categorization, partly because she has lived so long that she is contemporary with writers as far removed from each other in time and aesthetics as Richard Wright and Toni Morrison. But Petry can be productively compared and contrasted with authors representing several different strands of American literature.

As an African-American woman, she fits in a historical continuum including Harriet Wilson and Harriet Jacobs in the nineteenth century; Nella Larsen, Zora Neale Hurston, and Gwendolyn Brooks in the first half of the twentieth century; and Toni Morrison, Alice Walker, Gloria Naylor, and Terry McMillan (among others) today. The beginning of her career in the mid-1940s also suggests a natural grouping with

Wright as well as with Ralph Ellison and Chester Himes. As a writer preoccupied with communities and the social problems they harbor, Petry invites comparison with William Faulkner and Eudora Welty. And her fictional explorations of New England put her in the company of writers as diverse as Henry David Thoreau, Nathaniel Hawthorne, and Sarah Orne Jewett.

Questions for Reading and Discussion/ Approaches to Writing

1. Students reading "The Witness" will have several natural points of identification: their experience as teenagers, their contact with teachers/authority figures, and their perceptions of race relations and sexual politics. But because "The Witness" invites us to transcend individual perspectives, I use study questions that probe the story's intriguing ambiguities: How does this story complicate conventional perceptions of protagonist versus adversary? Identify the characteristics that prevent Charles Woodruff and Dr. Shipley, the Congregational minister, from being wholly "good" characters. Are the boys who attack Nellie entirely "evil"? Explain your opinion. How are these boys different from the students Woodruff describes as the "Willing Workers of America"? How do the boys' violent acts reflect on the town of Wheeling? How might Woodruff's relationship with his wife (encapsulated in his memories) affect his decision to leave Wheeling? How might we as readers, and potential critics, identify with Woodruff's plight at the end of the story?
2. Critical essays might address the following topics: the theme of "witnessing" in both its religious and secular senses; the double standard Woodruff endures as a black male authority figure; and the story's connections between racism and sexism (a recurring theme in Petry's work). For longer papers, students might compare "The Witness" to one of the other Wheeling stories in *Miss Muriel and Other Stories*, or compare Woodruff with *The Street*'s Lutie Johnson.

Bibliography

Petry criticism is appearing with increasing regularity in mainstream journals. Hazel Arnett Ervin's *Ann Petry: A Bio-Bibliography* (1993) provides a useful introduction to the criticism and includes interviews with Petry as well. Also see Hilary Holladay's *Ann Petry*, forthcoming from Twayne.

Carlos Bulosan (1913–1956)

Contributing Editors: Amy Ling and Oscar Campomanes

Classroom Issues and Strategies

Some readers may be repulsed by what they consider an overly negative portrayal of American society. Their reactions range from incredulity to discomfort to rejection of what they consider to be exaggeration. Other readers are quick to dismiss Bulosan on aesthetic criteria, believing *American Is in the Heart* to be autobiographical and sociological rather than "literary." The issue of genre is another problem area: His fiction seems autobiographical, his poetry prosy, his short stories read like essays and his essays like short stories.

Providing students with biographical background on Bulosan, showing that he was primarily a writer rather than a farm laborer/ factory worker, and giving them historical information on Philippine immigration will set this text into its proper context. This text is primarily a novel and at the same time, as Carey McWilliams has pointed out, "it reflects the collective life experience of thousands of Filipino immigrants who were attracted to this country by its legendary promises of a better life."

If a slide show on Philippine immigration is obtainable, it would provide useful information. The film *Manongs* from Visual Communications in California is an excellent introduction.

As students read Bulosan, they ask, "Who is this man? What group does he belong to? What are his concerns? Is the plight of the immigrant today different than it was in the 1930s and 1940s?"

Major Themes, Historical Perspectives, and Personal Issues

Bulosan's major theme is exile and return—the effect of departure from home and the necessity to return to the Philippines in order to make sense of the exile's experience in the United States because of the colonial status of the Philippines.

His second purpose is to record his own, his family's, and his friends' experiences and lives, their loneliness and alienation.

Significant Form, Style, or Artistic Conventions

Bulosan wrote with an eye to violating literary conventions, as mentioned above. As a political activist and labor organizer, he also believed that creative literary activity and social purpose cannot be separated. Some of his later stories are magic realist in style. "Silence" is certainly meant to be read as symbolic rather than literal.

Original Audience

Bulosan, at the beginning of his career, wrote for a mainstream American audience, and was placed in the position of cultural mediator, a bridge between the Philippines (which America wanted to know better during World War II) and the U.S. Late in life, he consciously cultivated a Filipino audience, sending stories back to the Philippines, most of which were rejected. In the 1970s, he was "rediscovered" by Asian-Americans delighted to have found a spokesperson as prolific and multi-faceted as he.

Comparisons, Contrasts, Connections

In his unadorned, deceptively simple prose style, he resembles Ernest Hemingway; in his social concerns, John Steinbeck's *The Grapes of Wrath.* Bulosan may be compared with Maxine Hong Kingston in that both were critically acclaimed by a wide audience but denounced by certain portions of their own community who accused them of having "sold out." With Kingston he also shares a reliance on peasant forms of story-telling as well as the seeming incoherence of their works and the question of genre.

Questions for Reading and Discussion/ Approaches to Writing

1. The students may be directed to think about whether there are distinguishing characteristics to Filipino immigrant experience setting it apart from Chinese, Japanese, Korean, or any European group.
2. Ask students to keep a journal of their random reactions to the text. On a sheet of paper, have them record quotes, phrases, or words from the text that were particularly significant to them; on the right-hand side of the sheet, they are to record their reactions. Later they write a one-page statement of their responses, setting up a dialogue between themselves and their instructor. The instructor then makes a response and dittoes up the dialogue so

that the entire class can enter into the dialogue. Finally the class writes papers on the entire classroom-wide dialogue.

Bibliography

Amerasia Journal 6:1 (1979). Special issue devoted to the writings of Carlos Bulosan.

Campomanes, Oscar and Todd Gernes. "Two Letters from America: Carlos Bulosan and the Act of Writing." MELUS (Spring 1990).

"Carlos Bulosan." 500-word biographical entry in the *Encyclopedia of the American Left*, by Oscar Campomanes (Brown University).

Evangelista, Suzanne Potter. *Carlos Bulosan and His Poetry: A Biography and an Anthology*. Seattle: University of Washington Press, 1985.

San Juan, E. "Tunnelling Out of the Belly of the Beast." In *Crisis in the Philippines*. South Hadley, Mass.: Bergin & Garvey, 1986.

Eudora Welty (b. 1909)

Contributing Editor: Jennifer L. Randisi

Classroom Issues and Strategies

Like many lyric novelists, Welty is easy to read. She therefore seems (to many students) very simple. They like her work, generally, and don't want to ruin their enjoyment by having to analyze it.

I like to begin by looking at what makes Welty seem simple (her lovely sentences, her homey metaphors, her "impulse to praise"). The difficulty here is not a lack of accessibility, but rather that Welty seems too accessible, too superficial. The challenge is to get students to read Welty seriously, critically, analytically.

Welty has said that except what's personal there's so little to tell. I'd start where she did: with the hearts of the characters she's writing about—the universal emotions they share with us. Why do we feel a certain way about the story? The situation? The character? What is evoked? How is Welty able to evoke a certain response from us? What values emerge? A strong sense of values is something Welty shares with writers like William Faulkner, Flannery O'Connor, Katherine Anne Porter,

Walker Percy, and Alice Walker. These novelists believe in certain things and the communities created in their fiction share both a value system and a sense of what words like "love" and "compassion" mean.

As with most of the southern writers, Welty's humor, her use of the grotesque, and her dialogue are often initial difficulties for students, who tend to take her too literally and thus miss the fun she's having. Welty's books often work the way folk or fairy tales do; students aren't used to this.

Major Themes, Historical Perspectives, and Personal Issues

Major themes include the problem of balancing love and separateness (the community and one's sense of self), the role and influence of family and the land ("place"), and the possibilities of art (story-telling) to inform life. Welty is also very concerned with resonances of classical mythology, legend, and folk tale, and with the intersection of history and romance.

Significant Form, Style, or Artistic Conventions

Welty clearly owes something to fellow Mississippian William Faulkner, and to the oral tradition of the South. She has a terrific ear, reproducing cadences of dialect and giving much insight into her characters by allowing her readers to hear them talk. Welty's work also owes something to the grotesque as developed in the American South.

Original Audience

Since Welty hasn't been grouped with writers critical of the South (her issues are neither political nor social in a broad sense), her work hasn't been read much differently over the years. She's been criticized for not attacking the South; that has never been her interest or her aim.

Comparisons, Contrasts, Connections

Any of the southerners writing in the twentieth century could be compared to Welty in terms of voice, violence, attitude toward the land, feelings about community, and ways of telling a story. William Faulkner, Flannery O'Connor, Katherine Anne Porter, Walker Percy—even Alice Walker—would be good to start with.

Questions for Reading and Discussion/ Approaches to Writing

1. I like to start with what students see. I think study questions (except for general questions relating to the elements of the story—point of view, character, theme) direct their reading toward what they think I want them to see rather than allowing them to see what they see.
2. I am fond of the short paper (2–3 pages) and of the directed journal. The former allows students to focus on a very specific problem or concern; the latter allows students to carry issues from one author to the next, or from one book to the next. I like assigning a formal paper from one of the journal entries.

Bibliography

Welty's essay "Place in Fiction" is very good. Welty's book of photographs, *One Time, One Place*, is a nice companion piece, as is her collection of essays, *The Eye of the Story*. Peggy Prenshaw's *Conversations with Eudora Welty* has some helpful information and I think her collection of essays (*Eudora Welty: Critical Essays*) and John F. Desmond's (*A Still Moment: Essays on the Art of Eudora Welty*) are both worthwhile reading.

My chapter on *Losing Battles* (in *A Tissue of Lies*) is also worth reading.

Lee Smith (b. 1944)

Contributing Editor: Anne Jones

Classroom Issues and Strategies

There should be little difficulty drawing students into an engagement with "Artists," since the style is accessible and the concerns familiar. The task may rather be in some sense to de-familiarize the story, to complicate what may initially seem to students its self-evident meanings. One way to do this would be to suggest that the conclusion seems to offer a clearcut "solution" to the problems of the story: The narrator rejects her grandmother's "art," accepts Mollie Crews as another kind of artist—an artist of the possible? of the body?—and thus "grows up." Her grandmother's "art" metamorphosizes into children's toys, thus capitulating, in effect, to the "art" of Mollie Crews. The story, "Artists," thus becomes a moral tale of oppositions, of illusion and reality, false art and true, and so on.

A teacher might then invite students to argue with this claim. What, if anything, feels unsatisfactory about it? What areas of the narrative are not addressed by it? Are there ways in which the story itself contests its own apparently explicit meaning and conclusion? What should we make of such contradictions? On the other hand, those who find the conclusion a satisfactory "kernel" of meaning to take away might be asked to defend their view. Are these two views of the story analogous in some ways to the two views of "art" represented in the story by the grandmother and Mollie Crews? How might such an analogy affect one's sense of the story? And how does the narrator evolve as an "artist" in the terms of the story?

Major Themes, Historical Perspectives, and Personal Issues

The title offers a major theme: Artists come in several varieties. How they vary constitutes several related themes. Social class and class mobility, for example, seem to be linked with two different forms of art; Is the grandmother's art of denial and illusion a sign of class pretension and Mollie's art—in her "studio" over Western Auto—a sign of class "authenticity"? If so, does the story reify class (and class stereotypes, such as associating sexuality with the working class) and resist mobility? Or are there other issues involved in the grandmother's aesthetic denials? The third "artist"—the narrator, Jenny—suggests another major theme: a girl's accession to womanhood. Why does she associate it with cutting her hair and kissing Scott? Is her self-described "growing up" only an acceptance of gender expectations?

Significant Form, Style, or Artistic Conventions

The narrative strategies seem most interesting here. At which points and why does Jennifer shift the tense of her narration? When, how, and why does her diction shift? A close analysis of the first paragraph will introduce most major themes to students; working as a class to unpack this paragraph could be a good exercise in teaching close analysis. Key images—like the *David* figure—can also offer students an opportunity to develop those skills.

Original Audience

"Artists" appeared first in *Redbook* and was later collected in *Cakewalk*. Thus its audience was initially popular and female. This offers the opportunity to discuss the question of high/low culture and its permutations in modernism and postmodernism. How could we "categorize" "Artists," and what are the effects of such categorizations? How does "Artists" take this as its own theme?

Comparisons, Contrasts, Connections

"Artists" can be read in several contexts: as an example of Lee Smith's work (this would require outside reading, of course); as a southern story (with Eudora Welty, Flannery O'Connor, Zora Neale Hurston, Alice Walker, and Ernest Gaines, for example, in this anthology); as a story of art and artists (with, for example, Hawthorne's "Artist of the Beautiful" and Alice Walker's "Everyday Use"); and as a contemporary story in its subjects and strategies.

Saul Bellow (b. 1915)

Contributing Editor: Allan Chavkin

Classroom Issues and Strategies

I think the best strategy is to focus on specific parts of the story by asking a series of specific questions. This particular story can be approached on two different levels, for it is both a realistic depiction of a relief worker's dedicated attempt to search for an unemployed, crippled black man in the slums of Depression Chicago in order to deliver a welfare check and a symbolic quest to discover the relationship between reality and appearances.

My approach to the story is generally conventional—asking questions and prompting class discussion on key issues. Another possible approach would be to play all or part of an excellent unabridged audio-recording of the story by Books on Tape, P. O. Box 7900, Newport Beach, CA 92658–7900, and discuss the interpretation that the Books-on-Tape reader gives to the story.

Students often respond actively to the following issues raised by "Looking for Mr. Green":

1. Money as a formative influence on the creation of identity.
2. The problem of the noncompetitive in a highly competitive society.
3. The clash between idealism and cynical "realism," between the noble idealist and the cynic.
4. The quest of a stubborn idealist in an irrational world.
5. Racism and stereotyping.

Major Themes, Historical Perspectives, and Personal Issues

Historical Issues and Themes: How does society help the downtrodden (in this story an unemployed, crippled black man) in bad economic times (e.g., the depression)? The story also examines the problems of race, class, and gender. Other issues that the class might focus upon are: the plight of the noncompetitive in a capitalistic, highly competitive society; how money influences character; the alienation of the urban black man.

Personal Issues and Themes: How does an idealistic humanist (i.e., the typical Bellow hero) reconcile noble ideas with the harsh facts of the human condition? Is man essentially a victim of his situation or is he the master of his fate? What is Bellow suggesting about the problem of human suffering and evil? The relationship of the individual to his society? The relationship of appearance to reality? The clash between the human need to order and make sense of life according to moral principles and life's amoral disorder, discontinuity, irrationality, and mystery?

Significant Form, Style, or Artistic Conventions

The story can be discussed as a bildungsroman; as a parable; as a symbolic quest; as a realistic depiction of the depression and of the alienation of the urban black man.

Comparisons, Contrasts, Connections

The story might be compared with some works by such black writers as James Baldwin, Richard Wright, and Ralph Ellison, or any other writers who have written about the depression (e.g., John Steinbeck). The story could be compared to some stories by such naturalistic writers as Theodore Dreiser and Jack London who are also concerned with the free will versus determinism theme. An interesting comparison would be with F. Scott Fitzgerald, who wrote on the formative influence of money on the self. The idea that illusion is necessary for the survival of self in a harsh, predatory world is a central theme of modern American drama

(Eugene O'Neill, Tennessee Williams, and Arthur Miller), and this story might be compared to the most important modern American plays. Bellow's depiction of women might be compared to that of other writers.

Questions for Reading and Discussion/ Approaches to Writing

1. (a) What is the purpose in the story of Grebe's supervisor Raynor? What is Bellow's attitude toward Raynor's cynical "wisdom"? Is concern for the individual anachronistic? For philosophical studies?

   (b) What is the purpose of the encounter with the Italian grocer who presents a hellish vision of the city with its chaotic masses of suffering humanity?

   (c) The old man Field offers this view of money—"Nothing is black where it shines and the only place you see black is where it ain't shining." Discuss. What do you think of the scheme for creating black millionaires? Why does Bellow include this scheme in the story?

   (d) What is the purpose of the Staika incident in the story? Raynor sees her as embodying "the destructive force" that will "submerge everybody in time," including "nations and governments." In contrast, Grebe sees her as "the life force." Who is closer to the truth?

   (e) The word "sun" and sun imagery are repeated throughout the story. Discuss.

2. (a) Discuss the theme of appearance versus reality.

   (b) Bellow ends the story with Grebe's encounter with the drunken, naked black woman, who may be another embodiment of the spirit of Staika. Why does Bellow conclude the story this way? Has Grebe failed or succeeded? Is he deceiving himself?

   (c) David Demarest comments: "Grebe's stubborn idealism is nothing less than the basic human need to construct the world according to intelligent, moral principles." Discuss.

   (d) Believing that "Looking for Mr. Green" needs to be seen "as one of the great short stories of our time," Eusebio Rodrigues argues that the Old Testament flavors it. This story is "a modern dramatization of Ecclesiastes." Discuss.

Bibliography

Chavkin, Allan. "The Problem of Suffering in the Fiction of Saul Bellow." *Comparative Literature Studies* 21 (Summer 1984): 161–74.

Demarest, David. "The Theme of Discontinuity in Saul Bellow's Fiction: 'Looking for Mr. Green' and 'A Father-to-be.' " *Studies in Short Fiction* 6 (Winter 1969): 175–86.

Fuchs, Daniel. *Saul Bellow: Vision and Revision.* Durham: Duke University Press, 1984, 287–89.

Kiernan, Robert F. *Saul Bellow.* New York: Continuum, 1988, 121–24.

Opdahl, Keith Michael. *The Novels of Saul Bellow.* University Park: The Pennsylvania State University Press, 1967, 100–03.

Rodrigues, Eusebio L. "Koheleth in Chicago: The Quest for the Real in 'Looking for Mr. Green.' " *Studies in Short Fiction* 11 (1974): 387–93.

Raymond Carver (1938–1988)

Contributing Editor: Paul Jones

Classroom Issues and Strategies

Carver has been quoted as saying that his stories could happen anywhere. That is pretty much true. Additionally, they are so contemporary that they require almost no background material or preparation for reading and understanding by an American audience. Even the issues of class (most of Carver's characters, if they have jobs, are marginally employed), although they do exist in Carver stories, are not too heavily at play in "A Small, Good Thing." However, this lack of location, class, and even time can be used to start a classroom discussion. You might ask: Where is this story set and in what year? How old are the characters? How does this affect your reading of the story? Does this lack diminish the story? Would it have been a better story if we knew it had been set in, say, Cleveland in May 1978? How would this story be read by readers outside of Carver's culture? Would it be understood differently in France or in Cameroon? The questions can draw the class toward a discussion of style in literature and to one of the major issues for Carver: What constitutes a good story?

To bring Carver himself into the classroom, I recommend the Larry McCaffery and Sinda Gregory interview found in *Raymond Carver: A Study of the Short Fiction* or in *Alive and Writing: Interviews with American Authors of the 1980s* as sources for rich Carver quotes and his own insights into the stories and the writing process. For example, Carver cites Isaac Babel's dictum, "No iron can pierce the heart with such force as a period put in just the right place," as one of his own guiding principles.

Major Themes, Historical Perspectives, and Personal Issues

In many of Carver's stories, issues of loss and of alcoholism are a part of the larger issue, which is the isolation and terror of people when a total breakdown of survival systems is at hand. The near-inarticulateness of his characters in the face of this terror and loss is significant and has been a major point of contention among his critics. Some say that Carver's characters are too ordinary, underperceptive, and despairing to experience the philosophical questions of meaning into which they have been thrust. His defenders say that Carver characters demonstrate that people living marginal, routine lives can come close to experiencing insight and epiphany under pressure of intruding mysteries, such as the death of a loved one.

Significant Form, Style, or Artistic Conventions

You would definitely want to talk about "minimalism" in fiction. The style has become so pervasive that students may just assume that this pared-down method of story-telling is simply how one writes fiction. Frederick Barthelme writes that as a minimalist "you're leaving room for the readers, at least for the ones who like to use their imaginations." John Barth counters with this definition of a minimalist aesthetic: "[its] cardinal principle is that artistic effect may be enhanced by a radical economy of artistic means, even where such parsimony compromises other values: completeness, for example, or richness or precision of statement." Carver was at first the most influential practitioner of minimalism, and then, through the rewriting of his earlier stories, a writer who repudiated the style.

Luckily, Carver's stories can be used to show both the power of the so-called minimalist approach and its limits. Have the students first read the brief (ten-page) story "The Bath," which was the earlier version of "A Small, Good Thing." "The Bath" is an excellent example of what minimalism does well and can be more terrifying and unsettling than anything by Stephen King. Contrasting and comparing "The Bath" and "A Small, Good Thing" from Carver's later, more expansive period will allow the students to participate in the intense debate about style. Carver preferred the second version, but he didn't pass judgment on those who like "The Bath" best.

Another useful approach for showing the nuances of revision at work in Carver's writing is to look at a few other versions of his stories. A particularly illustrative case is a short-short-story of under five hundred words that has been known as "Mine" (*Furious Seasons*), "Popular Mechanics" (*What We Talk About When We Talk About Love*), and "Little Things" (*Where I'm Calling From*). The last two differ only in title, but there are significant differences in "Mine." Students need not be textual critics to talk about the choices that Carver has made in the various versions of his stories.

Original Audience

Carver's stories were published in most of the important slick magazines of the seventies and eighties including *Esquire* and *The New Yorker*. All along the way his work also appeared in small literary magazines. David Bellamy called Carver "the most influential stylist since Donald Barthelme." He was writing for writers, for those who appreciated experimental literature as well as for a general, though sophisticated, reading audience.

Comparisons, Contrasts, Connections

Anton Chekhov, Franz Kafka, and Ernest Hemingway are the obvious influences on Carver's work. The seemingly simple pared-down style of writing follows straight through to Carver. You might consider teaching Carver and Hemingway and perhaps Donald Barthelme together, then entering into a discussion of the bare bones style of each.

Another way to consider Carver's style is to remember that he began writing poetry before he tried fiction and continued writing and publishing poetry throughout his career. He said (in a *Paris Review* interview with Mona Simpson), "In magazines, I always turned to poems first before I read the stories. Finally, I had to make a choice, and I came down on the side of fiction. It was the right choice for me." Carver's poetry has been compared to that of William Carlos Williams, although I see many obvious differences in their approach, sense of the line, and sense of narrative. His poetry can also be compared to that of James Wright, particularly with respect to the class of people from which the poems and stories are drawn.

Bibliography

The following collections by Carver include stories mentioned above:

"Mine." In *Furious Seasons and Other Stories*. Santa Barbara: Capra Press, 1977.

"Little Things." In *Where I'm Calling from: New and Selected Stories*. New York: Atlantic Monthly Press, 1988.

"Popular Mechanics" and "The Bath." In *What We Talk About When We Talk About Love*. New York: Vintage Books, 1982.

Critical books on Carver are as follows:

Campbell, Ewing. *Raymond Carver: A Study of the Short Fiction*. New York: Twayne, 1992.

Runyon, Randolph. *Reading Raymond Carver*. Syracuse: Syracuse University Press, 1992.

Saltzman, Arthur M. *Understanding Raymond Carver*. Columbia: University of South Carolina Press, 1988.

Carver talks about his writing and the writing of others in the following books:

Carver, Raymond. *Fires: Essays, Poems, Stories*. New York: Vintage Books, 1984.

Gentry, Marshall Bruce and William L. Stull. *Conversations with Raymond Carver*. Jackson: University Press of Mississippi, 1990.

The following book of photographs helps show the locations for several of Carver's stories:

Adelman, Bob. *Carver Country: The World of Raymond Carver*. "Introduction" by Tess Gallagher. New York: Scribner, 1990.

I find it always helpful to hear the author read his stories, which is especially true in the case of Carver, although only the following early tape is available:

Ray Carver Reads Three Short Stories. Columbia: American Audio Prose Library, 1983.

"A Small, Good Thing" can be found on tape (but not read by Carver) in the following:

Where I'm Calling From. Read by Peter Riegert. New York: Random House Audio Publishers, 1989.

Flannery O'Connor (1925–1964)

Contributing Editor: Beverly Lyon Clark*

Classroom Issues and Strategies

My students have trouble dealing with the horror that O'Connor evokes—often they want to dismiss the story out of hand, while I want to use it to raise questions. Another problem pertains to religious belief: Either students lack any such belief (which might make a kind of sense of O'Connor's violence) or else, possessing it, they latch onto O'Connor's religious explications at the expense of any other approach.

I like to start with students' gut responses—to start with where they already are and to make sure I address the affective as well as the cognitive. In particular, I break the class into groups of five and ask students to try to build consensus in answering study questions.

In general, the elusiveness of O'Connor's best stories makes them eminently teachable—pushing students to sustain ambiguity, to withhold final judgments. It also pushes me to teach better—to empower students more effectively, since I don't have all the answers at my fingertips. My responses to O'Connor are always tentative, exploratory. I start, as do most of my students, with a gut response that is negative. For O'Connor defies my humanistic values—she distances the characters and thwarts compassion. Above all, O'Connor's work raises tantalizing questions. Is she, as John Hawkes suggests, "happily on the side of the devil"? Or, on the contrary, does the diabolical Misfit function, paradoxically, as an agent of grace? We know what O'Connor wants us to believe. But should we?

Major Themes, Historical Perspectives, and Personal Issues

One important context that I need to provide for my students is background on O'Connor's Christianity. The most useful source here is O'Connor's own essays and lectures, which often explain how to read her works as she would have them read. Certainly O'Connor's pronouncements have guided much of the criticism of her work. I'll summarize some of her main points:

---

*With thanks to LynAnn Mastaj and her classmates for comments on these questions.

She states that the subject of her work is "the action of grace in territory held largely by the devil" (*Mystery and Manners* 118). She tries to portray in each story "an action that is totally unexpected, yet totally believable" (118), often an act of violence, violence being "the extreme situation that best reveals what we are essentially" (113). Through violence she wants to evoke Christian mystery, though she doesn't exclude other approaches to her fiction: she states that she could not have written "A Good Man Is Hard to Find" in any other way but "there are perhaps other ways than my own in which this story could be read" (109).

In general O'Connor explains that she is not so much a realist of the social fabric as a "realist of distances" (44), portraying both concrete everyday manners and something more, something beyond the ordinary: "It is the business of fiction to embody mystery through manners . . . (124). She admits too that her fiction might be called grotesque, though she cautions that "anything that comes out of the South is going to be called grotesque by the northern reader, unless it is grotesque, in which case it is going to be called realistic" (40). And she connects her religious concerns with being southern, for, she says, "while the South is hardly Christ-centered, it is most certainly Christ-haunted" (44).

I also find it important to address the question of racism in the story. Is the story racist? I ask. Is the grandmother racist, in her comments on cute little pickaninnies and her use of "nigger"? Does the narrator endorse the grandmother's attitude? And what do we make of her naming a cat Pitty Sing—a pseudo-Japanese name that sounds less like Japanese than like a babytalk version of "pretty thing"? Is O'Connor simply presenting characteristically racist attitudes of not particularly admirable characters? I find Alice Walker's comments helpful here, on O'Connor's respectful reluctance to enter the minds of black characters and pretend to know what they're thinking.

Comparisons, Contrasts, Connections

O'Connor is usually compared to writers who are southern or gothic or Catholic or some combination thereof: e.g., William Faulkner, Nathanael West, Graham Greene. Louise Westling (in *Sacred Groves and Ravaged Gardens: The Fiction of Eudora Welty, Carson McCullers, and Flannery O'Connor* [University of Georgia Press, 1985]) has made fruitful comparisons with Eudora Welty and Carson McCullers, though most critics seem to find it difficult to discover points of comparison with other women writers.

Questions for Reading and Discussion/ Approaches to Writing

The following questions can be given to students in advance or used to guide discussion during class:

1. What qualities of the grandmother do you like? What qualities do you dislike? How did you feel when The Misfit killed her? Why?
2. How would you characterize the other members of the family? What is the function of images like the following: the mother's "face was as broad and innocent as a cabbage and was tied around with a green head-kerchief that had two points on the top like a rabbit's ears" and the grandmother's "big black valise looked like the head of a hippopotamus"?
3. How does O'Connor foreshadow the encounter with The Misfit?
4. What does the grandmother mean by a "good man"? Whom does she consider good people? What are other possible meanings of "good"? Why does she tell The Misfit that he's a good man? Is there any sense in which he is?
5. What is the significance of the discussion of Jesus? Was he a good man?
6. What is the significance of the grandmother's saying, "Why you're one of my babies. You're one of my own children"?
7. What is the significance of The Misfit's saying, "She would of been a good woman if it had been somebody there to shoot her every minute of her life"?

There are, of course, no absolute answers to these questions; the story resists easy solutions, violates the reader's expectations.

Bibliography

Other O'Connor stories well worth reading and teaching include "The Displaced Person," "The Artificial Nigger," "Good Country People," "Everything That Rises Must Converge," "Revelation," and "Parker's Back" (all in *The Complete Stories* [Farrar, 1971]). O'Connor's essays have been collected in *Mystery and Manners* (Farrar, 1969). The fullest collection of works by O'Connor is the *Collected Works* (Library of America, 1988).

As for secondary sources, the fullest biography so far, at least until O'Connor's long-time friend Sally Fitzgerald completes hers, is Lorine M. Getz's *Flannery O'Connor: Her Life, Library and Book Reviews* (Mellen, 1980).

For discussion of O'Connor's social, religious, and intellectual milieux see Robert Coles's *Flannery O'Connor's South* (Louisiana State University Press, 1980). A fine companion piece is Barbara McKenzie's photographic essay, *Flannery O'Connor's Georgia* (University of Georgia Press, 1980).

Four collections of essays provide a good range of criticism on O'Connor:

1. *The Added Dimension: The Art and Mind of Flannery O'Connor*, edited by Melvin J. Friedman and Lewis A. Lawson (1966; rpt. Fordham University Press, 1977).
2. *Critical Essays on Flannery O'Connor*, edited by Melvin J. Friedman and Beverly Lyon Clark (Hall, 1985).
3. *Flannery O'Connor*, edited by Harold Bloom (Chelsea House, 1986).
4. *Realist of Distances: Flannery O'Connor Revisited*, edited by Karl-Heinz Westarp and Jan Nordby Gretlund (Aarhus, 1987).

The Friedman and Clark collection, for instance, includes the Walker and Hawkes essays alluded to above: John Hawkes, "Flannery O'Connor's Devil," *Sewanee Review* 70 (1962): 395–407; Alice Walker, "Beyond the Peacock: The Reconstruction of Flannery O'Connor," *In Search of Our Mothers' Gardens*. Harcourt, 1983.

Overall, criticism of O'Connor has appeared in more than forty book-length studies and hundreds of articles (including those published annually in the *Flannery O'Connor Bulletin*). Most criticism continues to be either religious or formalist. But for a discussion that situates O'Connor's work historically, in the postwar era, addressing its intersections with liberal discourse, see Thomas Hill Schaub's chapter on O'Connor in *American Fiction in the Cold War* (Wisconsin, 1991).

Joyce Carol Oates (b. 1938)

Contributing Editor: Eileen T. Bender

Classroom Issues and Strategies

In a time of instant fare—both literal and intellectual—Joyce Carol Oates is most demanding. Several of her more recent novels (she has published eighteen as of 1988) are, like the nineteenth-century work she parodies, voluminous. Oates has produced an amazing variety of excellent work in all genres: novels, short fiction, drama, critical essays, poetry, reviews of contemporary writing and ideas. She reads, edits, and teaches, currently holding a chair professorship at Princeton University. She defeats those readers who want artists to fit certain categories. Extremely well read and at home in the classroom, Oates is often deliberately elusive.

While she calls her writing "experimental," Oates's individual works are highly accessible—at least at first glance. Often, as in "Where Are You Going, Where Have You Been?" they begin in familiar territory. The central characters and the scenes are vivid and recognizable. Details (in this case, the drive-in teen culture, the sibling rivalry, the snatches of popular songs) enhance the sense of *déjà vu*. Yet by the end, dark and violent forces surface to baffle conventional expectations of both character and plot. Once again, the so-called "Dark Lady of American Letters" creates a disturbance, challenging the reader to think of both fiction and reality with new and deeper understanding.

Because of the variety of her work, Oates can be viewed as a "woman of letters." Students will be interested in a writer who is constantly engaged in public discussion (in print most frequently) of the arts: they should watch for her letters to the editor, interviews, essays, and reviews in the *New York Times*, and the popular press.

Oates's work itself can be approached at different levels of sophistication. It is always interesting to explore the many allusive patterns in her fiction. Several of her short stories are meant as explicit imitation of famous forebears (e.g., "The Dead," "Metamorphosis," "The Lady With the Pet Dog"), and those can be read in tandem to see the complexity of Oates's relationship to literary tradition.

In "Where Are You Going, Where Have You Been?" Oates makes an ordinary tale extraordinary by juxtaposing two powerful legends: the modern rock hero (the story is dedicated to activist-song writer Bob Dylan), and the ancient demon lover. Drawing together these threads, Oates is able to tell a chilling tale of a young adolescent, tantalized by glamorous surfaces, unable to resist more satanic designs. In this case, the "accessible" story needs to be peeled back, in order for Oates's intentions and the full sense of the work to be understood.

In responding to this story, students are disturbed by the violence that erupts from ordinary reality, and question its function or purpose—especially if they view literature as a kind of moral lesson or as an escape into a world elsewhere (the romantic paradigm). They will ask questions about the author herself, surprised that so academic and soft-spoken a person is capable of describing such violence in her stories. These responses provide an ideal occasion to discuss the creative process, and the difference between author and character, biography and literature, reality imagined and imaginative reality.

Major Themes, Historical Perspectives, and Personal Issues

At the center of much of Oates's work is concern about the singular power of the self, and the high cost of the struggle for autonomy. In this, she is like those contemporary "third force" psychologists she has studied and admired (chiefly Maslow and Laing) who posit a different human ideal: communion rather than mastery. Readers might focus on the patterns of selfhood and the possibilities for relationship in her work.

Oates also calls herself a "feminist" although she does not like the restrictive title of "woman writer"; rather, she prefers being described as a woman who writes. In her exploration of character and relationships, the nature of love and sexual power are frequently at issue. Again, this would be a fruitful topic for further reading and discussion, using Oates's own essays on androgyny, feminism, and the special circumstances of the "woman who writes" as starting point.

Oates is not only an avid student of literature and reader of history, psychology, and philosophy; she is a keen interpreter of the contemporary scene, concerned in her work with issues relevant to most modern readers. Besides feminist questions, her work has dealt with politics, migrant workers, medical and legal ethics, urban riots, and, most recently, boxing. Such work is immediately accessible to students. It also allows Oates to expose her own sense of the wonder and mystery of human character and personality.

Significant Form, Style, or Artistic Conventions

Interestingly, among her "imitations" and allusive fictions, Oates has tested almost every major literary school or set of conventions: naturalism, existentialism, social realism, detective stories, epic chronicle, romance. Presenting excerpts from Oates's novels would not only show her versatility, but would convey the way literature has an important and imposing influence on the modern writer.

While the story in this anthology unfolds chronologically, and appears conventional, the more surrealistic subtext imposes itself and frustrates the fairy-tale or "happy ending" quest. The subversion of one convention by another here is not only interesting in its own right, but enforces Oates's thematic design.

Original Audience

"Where Are You Going, Where Have You Been?" is of course a contemporary story; yet it also rests on a diminishing sense of recent history. It was written for an audience who had a vivid sense of the tumultuous American 1960s, with its antiwar activism, folk and rock music, and emergent "youth culture." If indeed the hippies of that time are the yuppies of today, it would be important for students to reacquaint themselves with the work Bob Dylan (the story's dedicatee) and others represented, as well as the perilous uncertainty of those times, which would have heightened the risks of adolescent passage.

Comparisons, Contrasts, Connections

While Oates has been variously compared and contrasted with Eudora Welty, William Faulkner, John Steinbeck, and even Theodore Dreiser, one of the more interesting writers with whom she might be compared is Flannery O'Connor. (Oates even wrote a moving poem about her, following O'Connor's death.) "Where Are You Going, Where Have You Been?" can best be compared with O'Connor's "A Good Man Is Hard to Find," in which gratuitous and even mindless violence bursts through and destroys the pious confidence of O'Connor's ordinary country people. Both Oates and O'Connor emphasize the reality and presence of evil. But in O'Connor's case, the imminence of evil transforms visible reality into mere illusion. For Oates, naivete (not innocence) is dangerous in a perennially fallen but vividly real world.

Questions for Reading and Discussion/ Approaches to Writing

Questions useful *before* reading the selection would concern the two "legends" that are important to the story: Dylan and Demon.

1. Why is this story dedicated to Bob Dylan?
2. Who is Arnold Friend? Do you think he is appropriately named? What is the significance of his car? His clothing? His language?
3. When and why does Connie begin to question his identity? What impact does her confusion have on her own personality? How are "personality" and "identity" displayed and defined in this story?

Additionally, students may need more background on Dylan and the '60s to understand Oates's view of the demonic aspect of those times in America.

In dealing with this story, students might be asked to put themselves in the place of Connie's sister or one of Connie's "real" friends, describing Friend or their perception of what has happened. The title should be discussed. Students can be asked to find the Dylan lyric that gives the story its title, play it for the class, and lead a discussion of the culture and politics of the 1960s; photographs of that time could be especially useful in picturing the look and style Friend tries to emulate. Students might write about the danger of "codes": their power to distort perception.

Another approach could be aesthetic: specifically, viewing the story not as realistic but surrealistic. Here, paintings of modern masters such as Magritte or Dali could illustrate the hauntingly familiar contours of the surrealistic imagination—another possible written assignment. Oates herself refers to an earlier surrealist, Bosch, in the title of an early novel, *A Garden of Earthly Delights*. That painting might generate a lively discussion of Oates's vision of evil.

Bibliography

Bender, Eileen T. *Joyce Carol Oates, Artist In Residence*. Bloomington: Indiana University Press, 1987.

Clemons, Walter. "Joyce Carol Oates: Love and Violence." *Newsweek*, 11 (Dec. 1972): 72–77.

Creighton, Joanne. *Joyce Carol Oates*. Boston: G. K. Hall, 1979.

Friedman, Ellen. *Joyce Carol Oates*. New York: Ungar, 1970.

Kazin, Alfred. *Bright Book of Life*. New York: Atlantic/Little, Brown, 1973.

Norman, Torburg. *Isolation and Contact: A Study of Character Relationships in Joyce Carol Oates's Short Stories*. Goteburg, Sweden: Gothenburg Studies in English 57, 1984.

Wagner, Linda. *Critical Essays on Joyce Carol Oates*. Boston: G. K. Hall, 1979.

John Updike (b. 1932)

Contributing Editor: George J. Searles

Classroom Issues and Strategies

It is sometimes said that Updike is too narrowly an interpreter of the WASP/yuppie environment, a realm of somewhat limited interest;

another is that his work proceeds from a too exclusively male perspective. The former concern will, of course, be more/less problematic depending on the nature of the college (more problematic at an urban community college, less so at a "prestige" school). The latter charge, however, provides the basis for fruitful discussion in any academic environment.

First, it's important to point out what Henry James once said, to the effect that we must grant an author's donnée and evaluate only in terms of what is made of it. But in Updike's case, it's also necessary to stress that his real concerns transcend his surface preoccupations. Although he's often described as a chronicler of social ills, really he's after larger game—the sheer intractability of the human predicament. Students must be shown that in Updike the particular is simply an avenue to the universal.

In addition to Updike's stories, students should be referred to the magazine articles listed in the bibliography and to the 1979 short story collection *Too Far To Go*, which reprints all the previous "Maples" stories, along with several then-new ones including "Separating." Also useful is the videotaped television special based on that collection. Another instructive exercise is to compare this story with some of Updike's early poems, particularly "Home Movies"—a little gem in its own right. Indeed, there's a direct echo of this poem near the story's conclusion: "We cannot climb back . . ./ To that calm light. The brief film ends" is rendered in "Separating" as "You cannot climb back . . . you can only fall."

Major Themes, Historical Perspectives, and Personal Issues

During the course of his long and prolific career, Updike has produced a series of interlocking short stories about Richard and Joan Maple, an upwardly mobile but unhappy couple whose ill-fated union closely parallels Updike's own first marriage to his college sweetheart, Mary Pennington. As critic Suzanne Henning Uphaus has neatly summarized it:

"The stories, written over a span of twenty-three years, follow the outward events. . . . Dick Maple, like Updike, married in the early fifties when he was twenty-one; both couples had four children, separated after twenty-one years, and finally received one of the first no-fault divorces granted in the state of Massachusetts."

This is probably the place from which to launch a classroom treatment of a story like "Separating."

Consider the protagonist's bleak assertion in Updike's *Roger's Version*: "There are so few things which, contemplated, do not like flimsy trapdoors open under the weight of our attention into the bottomless pit below" (74). Surely this has much to do with Dickie's baleful question "Why?" at the end of "Separating," and his father's perception of the boy's query as "a window thrown open on emptiness."

Significant Form, Style, or Artistic Conventions

Updike is acknowledged as a master stylist. "Separating" provides ample evidence of his skill in this area. Note, for example, the story's subtle but relentless accumulation of negative imagery. Again and again, key details reinforce Maple's inner sense of inadequacy, failure, and dread. Simultaneously, however, these images are juxtaposed with details of an ironically playful nature, thereby establishing a balance of sorts between angst and whimsy, a tone of amused negation that's perfectly suited to Updike's view of the human condition.

Original Audience

As this is a contemporary story, the "when/now" issue is not relevant. As for audience, I think that Updike sees himself writing for people more or less like himself: WASP, affluent, etc. But again, it's important when teaching Updike's work to show that the problems his characters confront are in a broad sense everyone's problems: responsibility, guilt, mortality, etc.

Comparisons, Contrasts, Connections

Updike is an exceptionally autobiographical writer. Perhaps that's the place to begin with a story like "Separating." Although this approach violates several critical tenets, it will get things rolling, and will lead ideally to discussion of the relationship between fiction and autobiography . . . how writers transmute personal experience into art. Comparisons can be drawn in this regard between Updike and Philip Roth and John Irving. Useful, too, is a consideration of the several *New Yorker* short stories by Updike's son David, collected in *Out On the Marsh* (New American Library, 1988): "Separating" from another angle.

Questions for Reading and Discussion/ Approaches to Writing

In a lower-level course (e.g., Freshman Comp, Intro to Lit) Updike's work—and especially a story like "Separating"—can generate good "personal experience" papers, as so many students today have first- or second-hand knowledge of separation and divorce.

Obviously, the story also lends itself exceptionally well to treatments of the whole "responsibility to self vs. responsibility to other" idea.

In an upper-level course, more strictly "literary" topics emerge.

Bibliography

Atlas, James. "John Updike Breaks Out of Suburbia." *The New York Times Magazine* (10 December 1978): 60–64, 68–76.

Howard, Jane. "Can a Nice Novelist Finish First?" *Life* (4 November 1966): 74–82.

Kakutani, Michiko. "Turning Sex and Guilt into an American Epic." *Saturday Review* (October 1981): 14–22.

——. "Updike's Struggle to Portray Women." *The New York Times* (5 May 1988).

"View From the Catacombs." *Time* (26 April 1968): 66–75.

Paule Marshall (b. 1929)

Contributing Editor: Dorothy L. Denniston

Classroom Issues and Strategies

One strategy for approaching Marshall's fiction is to explain the "Middle Passage" to illustrate the placement of blacks all over the world (African diaspora). It might also be helpful to discuss the notion of traditional African cyclical time, which involves recurrence and duration, as opposed to Western linear time, which suggests change and progress. The cyclic approach applies thematically (Da-duh's symbolic immortality) and structurally (the story comes full circle). Also important is the traditional African view of the world as being composed of dualities/ opposites that work together to constitute a harmonious moral order. (For a more complete explanation, see Marshall's "From the Poets in the Kitchen" in *Reena and Other Short Stories*.)

Consider also discussing the African oral tradition as a recorder of history and preserver of folk tradition. Since it is centered on the same ideas as written literatures (the ideas, beliefs, hopes, and fears of a people), its purpose is to create and maintain a group identity, to guide social action, to encourage social interaction, and simply to entertain. The oral arts are equally concerned with preserving the past to honor traditional values and to reveal their relevance to the modern world. Marshall's craftsmanship is executed in such a dynamic fashion as to elicit responses usually reserved for oral performance or theater.

Students readily respond to similarities/differences between black cultures represented throughout the diaspora. Once they recognize African cultural components as positive, they re-evaluate old attitudes and beliefs and begin to appreciate differences in cultural perspectives as they celebrate the human spirit.

Major Themes, Historical Perspectives, and Personal Issues

A major theme is the search for identity (personal and cultural). Marshall insists upon the necessity for a "journey back" through history in order to come to terms with one's past as an explanation of the present and as a guiding post for the future. For the author, in particular, the story becomes a means to begin unraveling her multicultural background (American, African-American, African-Caribbean). To be considered foremost is the theme embodied in the epigram: the quality of life itself is threatened by giving priority to materialistic values over those that nourish the human spirit.

Significant Form, Style, or Artistic Conventions

Questions of form and style include Marshall's manipulation of time and her juxtaposition of images to create opposites (landscape, physical description, culture). This suggests an artistic convention that is, at base, African as it imitates or revives in another form the African oral narrative tradition. In fact, Marshall merges Western literary tradition with that of the African to create a new, distinctive expression.

Original Audience

All audiences find Marshall accessible. It might be interesting to contrast her idyllic view of Barbados in "To Da-duh" with her later view in the story "Barbados." The audience may wish to share contemporary views of third world countries and attitudes toward Western powers.

Comparisons, Contrasts, Connections

Both Toni Morrison and Paule Marshall deal with ancestral figures (connections to the past) to underscore cyclical patterns or deviations from them. Morrison's *Song of Solomon* (1977), *Tar Baby* (1981), or *Beloved* (1988) might be effectively compared to Marshall's *Praisesong for the Widow* (1983), *Brown Girl, Brownstones* (1959), *The Chosen Place, The Timeless People* (1969), or *Daughters* (1991).

Questions for Reading and Discussion/ Approaches to Writing

Discuss the use of African and Caribbean imagery and explain why it is essential to Marshall's aesthetic.

Bibliography

Barthold, Bonnie. *Black Time: Fiction in Africa, the Caribbean and the United States*. New Haven: Yale University Press, 1981.

Christian, Barbara. *Black Women Novelists: The Development of a Tradition, 1892–1976*. Westport: Greenwood Press, 1980.

Denniston, Dorothy. "Early Short Fiction by Paule Marshall." *Callaloo* 6, no. 2 (Spring–Summer, 1983). Reprinted in *Short Story Criticism*. Detroit: Gale Research Co., 1990.

——. Forthcoming volume on the complete works of Paule Marshall to be published by the University of Tennessee Press.

Evans, Mari, ed. Section on Paule Marshall in *Black Women Writers (1950–1980): A Critical Evaluation*. Garden City, New York: Anchor, 1983.

Marshall, Paule. "Shaping the World of My Art." *New Letters* (Autumn 1973).

Review especially the following:

Marshall, Paule. "From the Poets in the Kitchen." In *Reena and Other Short Stories*, 3–12. Old Westbury, New York: The Feminist Press, 1983.

Mbiti, John S. *African Religions and Philosophies*. New York: Doubleday and Co., 1970.

John Okada (1923–1971)

Contributing Editor: King Kok Cheung

Classroom Issues and Strategies

Students need historical background concerning World War II and the internment of Japanese-Americans. Explain how people often internalize the attitudes of the dominant society even though the attitudes may seem unreasonable today.

Major Themes, Historical Perspectives, and Personal Issues

Historical context is crucial to the understanding of *No-No Boy*, since the novel explores unflinchingly the issues of Japanese American identity. Is it half Japanese and half American, or is it neither? After the bombing of Pearl Harbor, Japanese Americans in various coastal states—Washington, Oregon, California—were interned on account of their ethnicity alone. Camp authorities then administered a loyalty questionnaire that contained two disconcerting questions: "Are you willing to serve in the armed forces of the United States in combat duty wherever ordered?" and "Will you swear unqualified allegiance to the United States of America and faithfully defend the United States from any or all attacks of foreign or domestic forces, and forswear any form of allegiance or obedience to the Japanese Emperor, to any other foreign government, power, or organization?"

These questions divided the Japanese American community and aggravated generational conflict. In some cases the parents still felt attached to their country of origin, while their American-born children— *nisei*—strived for an American identity. In other cases, the parents wanted to be loyal to America, but their children were too bitter against the American government to answer yes and yes.

Significant Form, Style, or Artistic Conventions

Okada commands a style that is at once effusive and spontaneous, quiet and deep. He has a keen eye for subtle details and psychological nuances that enables him to capture the reserved yet affectionate interaction of Kenji's family.

Yet Okada seldom lingers on one key. He can change his note rapidly from subdued pathos to withering irony, as when he moves from depicting the silent grief in Kenji's household to exposing racism at the Club Oriental where Kenji feels totally comfortable because his being Japanese there does not call attention to itself. At that very moment, there is a commotion at the entrance: the Chinese owner reports that he has to prevent two "niggers" from entering the club with a Japanese. The one place where Kenji does not feel the sting of racial prejudice turns out to be just as racist as others.

Comparisons, Contrasts, Connections

Compare *No-No Boy* with Joy Kogawa's *Obasan* and Jeanne Wakatsuki Houston and James Houston's *Farewell to Manzanar*. All three describe the adverse impact of the internment on Japanese American families.

Questions for Reading and Discussion/ Approaches to Writing

1. (a) Why does Ichiro feel alienated?
   (b) Why is Ichiro rejected by the people in his own ethnic community? Who are the exceptions?
   (c) How would you characterize the interaction in Kenji's family?
2. (a) Compare the dilemmas of Ichiro and Kenji.
   (b) Who is responsible for Ichiro's suffering? Ichiro himself? His family? The Japanese American community? America at large?

Bibliography

Book-length literary works that dwell on the Japanese internment include the following:

Houston, Jeanne Wakatsuki and James O. Houston. *Farewell to Manzanar*. Boston: Houghton Mifflin, 1973.

Inouye, Daniel and Lawrence Elliot. *Journey to Washington.* Englewood Cliffs: Prentice-Hall, 1967.

Murayama, Milton. *All I Asking for Is My Body.* San Francisco: Supra, 1975.

Ota, Shelley. *Upon Their Shoulders.* New York: Exposition, 1951.

Sone, Monica. *Nisei Daughter.* Boston: Little, Brown, 1953.

For a detailed study of the relation between historical circumstances and literature see the following:

Kim, Elaine. *Asian American Literature: An Introduction to the Writings and their Social Context.* Philadelphia: Temple University Press, 1982.

A brief survey of Chinese American and Japanese American literature is:

Baker, Houston A. Jr., ed. *Three American Literatures.* New York: MLA, 1982.

See also the following:

McDonald, Dorothy Ritsuko. "After Imprisonment: Ichiro's Search for Redemption in *No-No Boy.*" MELUS 6.3 (1979): 19–26.

Sato, Gayle K. Fujita. "Momotaro's Exile: John Okada's *No-No Boy.*" In *Reading the Literatures of Asian America,* edited by Shirley Geok-lin Lim and Amy Ling, 239–58. Philadelphia: Temple University Press, 1992.

Tillie Lerner Olsen (b. 1912)

Contributing Editor: Deborah S. Rosenfelt

Classroom Issues and Strategies

Olsen's work is relatively easy to teach since it addresses themes of concern to contemporary students and since its experiments with language remain within the bounds of realism. *Tell Me a Riddle* is among the most difficult of Olsen's works and some students have trouble for two reasons: They are unfamiliar with the social and political history embedded in the novella and they are confused by the allusive, stream-of-consciousness techniques Olsen employs for the revelation of that history's centrality in the consciousness of the protagonist.

Since the knee-jerk negative reaction to "communists" is often a problem, I make sure I discuss thoroughly the historical soil out of which *Tell Me a Riddle* grows. Sometimes I show the film *Seeing Reds*. I always read students a useful passage from *A Long View from the Left: Memoirs of an American Revolutionary* (Delta, 1972, p. 8) by Al Richmond.

Showing the film version of *Tell Me a Riddle* can be a good strategy for provoking discussion. The film itself is one of the rare representations of older people's lives and one of the few in which an older woman figures as the protagonist. Reading passages from Olsen's *Silences*, especially the autobiographical ones, also proves helpful and interesting to students.

Students respond most immediately and deeply to Eva's rage and anger about the sacrifices her life has involved. They also get into painful discussions about aging and dying, and about the limited options for the elderly in American society. The questions they ask include the following: Why won't the grandmother (Eva) hold her grandchild? Please help us figure out the configuration of family relationships in the story (here it helps if students have also read the other stories in the *Tell Me a Riddle* volume). Why doesn't Eva want to see the rabbi in the hospital? Where do they go when they go to the city on the beach (the answer to that one is Venice, California, an area near Los Angeles that houses an old Jewish community lovingly documented in the book and film, *Number Our Days*). Why won't David let her go home again?

Major Themes, Historical Perspectives, and Personal Issues

Tell Me a Riddle is very rich thematically, historically, and personally. Its central themes include the confrontation with aging, illness, and death; the deprivations and struggles of poverty; the conflicts, full of love and rage, in marital relations; the family, especially motherhood, as a site of both love and nurturance and of repression; the burying of women's sense of self and the silencing of their capacities for expression over years of tending to the needs and listening to the rhythms of others; the quest for meaning in one's personal life; and the affirmation of hope for and engagement on behalf of a freer, more peaceful, more just and humane world.

The themes of *Tell Me a Riddle* are in many ways the themes of Olsen's life. Olsen's parents took part in the 1905 revolution and became Socialist party activists in the United States. Olsen herself became a communist in the years when communism as a philosophy and as a movement seemed to offer the best hope for an egalitarian society. Eva is modeled partly on Olsen's mother, who died of cancer, as does Eva.

I see Olsen as belonging to a tradition of women writers in this country associated with the American left, who unite a class consciousness and a feminist consciousness in their lives and creative work.

Significant Form, Style, or Artistic Conventions

In *Tell Me a Riddle*, Olsen is deliberately experimental, fracturing chronological sequence, using stream-of-consciousness techniques to represent the processes of human consciousness, insisting on the evocative power of each individual word. Though remaining within the bounds of realism, she draws fully on the techniques of modernist fiction to render a humanistic and socially impassioned vision rare in modernist and postmodernist writing.

Original Audience

The question of audience is, I think, less relevant to contemporary writers than to those of earlier centuries. I do speak about Olsen's political background and about her special importance for contemporary women writers and readers. It is also important that the stories of the *Tell Me a Riddle* volume were written during the McCarthy era. All of them, especially *Tell Me a Riddle*, subtly bear witness to the disappointment and despair of progressives during that era, when the radical dreams and visions of the thirties and forties were deliberately eradicated. Olsen's family was one of many to endure harassment by the FBI. *Riddle's* topical allusions to Nazi concentration camps and the dropping of the atomic bomb at Hiroshima, and David's yearning for a time of belief and belonging, contribute to the subtext of anguish and betrayal so characteristic of the literature of the period.

Comparisons, Contrasts, Connections

I find it useful to compare *Tell Me a Riddle* to other works by women authors that record the tensions of "dual life," especially those which, like *Riddle*, deploy an imagery of speech and silencing not only to delineate the protagonist's quest for personal expression but also to develop her relationship to processes of social change. Among the many works that contain some configuration of these themes and images are Agnes Smedley's novel *Daughter of Earth*, Harriet Arnow's *The Dollmaker*, Maxine Hong Kingston's *The Woman Warrior: Memoirs of a Girlhood among*

Ghosts, much of the poetry of Audre Lorde and Adrienne Rich, Alice Walker's *The Color Purple*, and Joy Kogawa's *Obasan*.

As stories of "secular humanist" Jewish family life, the work might be compared with Grace Paley's fiction or Meridel LeSueur's *The Girl*.

As part of the tradition of working-class writers, she could be compared with Rebecca Harding Davis's *Life in the Iron-Mills*, Agnes Smedley's *Daughter of Earth*, Mike Gold's *Jews Without Money*, Henry Roth's *Call It Sleep*, and Fielding Burke's *Call Home the Heart*.

As a story exploring the consciousness of one who is dying, students might want to compare *Riddle* to Tolstoi's *The Death of Ivan Ilych*.

Questions for Reading and Discussion/ Approaches to Writing

1. What is the immediate cause of the conflict in this story? Does the author take sides in this conflict? Does this conflict have a resolution? What underlying causes does it suggest?
2. Try to explain or account for the story's title. What about the subtitle?
3. Who is the "hero" of this story? Why?
4. This is a story about a woman dying of cancer. Did you find it "depressing" or "inspiring"? Why?
5. Why is Eva so angry about the appearance of the rabbi in the hospital? What does she mean by "Race, human; religion, none"?
6. What do we learn about Eva's girlhood? Why do we learn it so late in the story?
7. Discuss Jeanne's role in the story.
8. Is David the same man at the end of the story as he was at the beginning? Explain your answer.

Bibliography

Olsen's personal/critical essays, those in *Silences* and that in *Mother to Daughter, Daughter to Mother*, are very important sources of insight and information. Especially recommended: pp. 5–46 in *Silences*, "Silences in Literature" (1962), and "One Out of Twelve: Writers Who Are Women in Our Century" (1971).

Other recommended reading:

Coiner, Constance. "Literature of Resistance: The Intersection of Feminism and the Political Left in Tillie Olsen and Meridel LeSueur." In *Politics of Literature: Toward the 1990's*, edited by Lennard Davis and Bella Mirabella. New York: Columbia University Press, forthcoming.

Orr, Elaine Neil. *Tillie Olsen and a Feminist Spiritual Vision.* Jackson: University Press of Mississippi, 1987. Especially Chapters II and IV.

Rosenfelt, Deborah. "From the Thirties: Tillie Olsen and the Radical Tradition." *Feminist Studies* 7:3 (Fall 1981): 371–406.

Muriel Rukeyser (1913–1980)

Contributing Editors: Cary Nelson and Janet Kaufman

Classroom Issues and Strategies

The earliest poem here, taken from Rukeyser's second book, dates from 1938; the most recent poems, taken from her last book, date from 1976. These poems thus range across forty years of a career and forty years of American culture and American history. Though there are very strong continuities in Rukeyser's work, it would be a mistake to imagine that all these poems were written by a single consciousness in a single historical moment. Their diverse forms and rhetorical styles represent the work of a poet who sustained her core beliefs and commitments while responding to changing historical, aesthetic, and cultural opportunities and pressures. She wrote long sequence poems, documentary poems, short lyrics, and elegies. Of all the responses one might make to this selection, the simplest one—and the one most to be hoped for—is the decision to read more widely in her work. That is, in a way, almost necessitated by this particular selection, since two of the poems, "Absalom," and "*Les Tendresses Bestiales,*" are taken from longer poem sequences. Certainly the instructor should read those sequences in their entirety and give the class some sense of each poem's context. The sequences, "The Book of the Dead" and "Ajanta," are available in both her *Collected Poems* (1979) and the *Selected Poems* (1992). Readers should be warned that her earlier *Selected Poems* is not a very successful representation of her work.

Since a number of these poems combine states of consciousness and physical sensation, it is important for students not only to analyze them rhetorically but also to place themselves empathetically inside the poems and read them phenomenologically. What does it feel like to be the mother in "Absalom" who has lost her family to industrial exploitation? What does it feel like to speak in the two very different voices Rukeyser gives her? How can one elaborate on the closing lines of "Martin Luther King, Malcolm X": "bleeding of my right hand/my black voice bleeding." What is the effect of identifying with the visionary and erotic ecstasy of "Poem White Page White Page Poem"? These poems are at once gifts to the reader and demands made of us. In "Then," a poem published shortly before her death, Rukeyser wrote, "When I am dead, even then,/I will still love you, I will wait in these poems."

Major Themes, Historical Perspectives, and Personal Issues

Some of Rukeyser's major concerns are summarized in the headnote to the poems themselves. Her biography, however, is not, so we sketch it briefly here: Rukeyser was the elder child of upwardly mobile, Jewish, American-born parents. In 1944, at the very moment when the outlines of the Holocaust were becoming known, she opened the seventh poem in her sequence "Letter to the Front" with the startling lines, "To be a Jew in the twentieth century/Is to be offered a gift." Her father was a partner in a sand-and-gravel company in New York. Seeing the concrete poured for sidewalks and skyscrapers made her feel part of the city; later, somewhat like Hart Crane, she would celebrate technology. From the Ethical Cultural and Fieldston Schools in New York, she went on to study at Vassar and Columbia until her father's supposed bankruptcy prevented her from continuing. Her mother had expected her to marry and write poetry only as an avocation. Instead, Rukeyser made poetry the focus of her life, traveled, lived in New York and California, and bore and raised a son as a single mother.

Her career as an activist began when she traveled to Alabama to cover the trial of the Scottsboro boys and was arrested. In 1972 she went to Vietnam with Denise Levertov on an unofficial writers' peace mission. She taught at the California Labor School in the mid-forties and from the mid-fifties through the sixties at Sarah Lawrence. She taught children in Harlem and led writing classes for women in the seventies. Especially in her later years Rukeyser broke taboos about female sexuality. In poems like "Waiting for Icarus" and "Myth" she rewrote classical myths from a woman's perspective. Here in "Rite" she dramatizes the culture's investments in gender and in "The Poem as Mask" overturns gender dichotomy by treating it as a constructed myth. In a culture that does not recognize the sexuality of old age, Rukeyser celebrated it. She never labeled her sexuality, but in poetry and letters she celebrated her intimate relations with both women and men.

Significant Form, Style, or Artistic Conventions

"Absalom" is the ninth of twenty poems in Rukeyser's "The Book of the Dead" in her 1938 book *U.S. 1*. A number of the poems are given over to the perspective of individual figures in the Gauley Tunnel tragedy. Stylistically, the poem is unusual for shifting from journalistic reportage to interior monologue to lyrical description. It mixes public rhetoric and private speech, judges America's history and its contemporary institutions, and interrogates natural and industrial power. It is one of the most important modern poems in mixed forms and one of the major achievements of her career.

"*Les Tendresses Bestiales*" is the third of five poems in Rukeyser's "Ajanta" sequence in her 1944 book *Beast in View*. The Ajanta caves in India are a series of twenty-nine Buddhist cave-temples and monasteries cut into cliffs in the north, near Ajanta, Maharashtra. Built over several centuries beginning in the second century B.C., they were abandoned in the seventh century and rediscovered in 1819. Most of the cave walls have large-scale tempura murals depicting the lives of the Buddha, while the ceilings are decorated with flowers and animals. The compositions are rhythmic, naturalistic, and generally drawn with soft, curving lines. Rukeyser had not see the caves themselves, basing her descriptions, as in "*Les Tendresses Bestiales*," on a large portfolio of reproductions. In her sequence the caves are not only a space for collective narrative representation but also a space of the body and of the self.

Questions for Reading and Discussion/
Approaches to Writing

As with all socially conscious and progressive poetry read within a discipline that has doubts about its viability, it is important to raise both general intellectual issues and questions that lead students to read closely. Here are a few examples:

1. Compare and contrast how several white poets and several black poets deal with issues of race—perhaps Rukeyser, Genevieve Taggard, Kay Boyle, Jean Toomer, Gwendolyn Bennett, Claude McKay, and Langston Hughes.
2. Rukeyser's "Absalom" is a 1930s poem that would have been read at the time as part of the proletarian literature movement. Compare this with the 1930s poems in "A Sheaf of Political Poetry in the Modern Period."

3. Read about the classical myths behind "The Minotaur" and "The Poem as Mask: Orpheus" and discuss how Rukeyser adapts and transforms them.
4. What model of political action is put forward in "How We Did It"? What does the poem say about means and ends?
5. "Rite" manages with its economical phrasing to both describe a rite and enact one. Are they different?

Robert Hayden (1913–1980)

Contributing Editor: Robert M. Greenberg

Classroom Issues and Strategies

It's important to get students to fully appreciate Hayden's effects of sound, image, and atmosphere. For better appreciation of the poems' aural qualities, have students read such selections as "Summertime and the Living" and "Mourning Poem for the Queen of Sunday" out loud.

Discuss a condensed narrative poem such as "Tour 5" as a short story. This should permit a discussion of the evolving point of view of the travelers and the evolving psychological quality of the imagery.

Point out also Hayden's control of voice. "Mourning Poem," for example, is spoken in the idiom of the black church, as if by a chorus of mourners; and if one reads the final lines to mean that the congregation *did* suspect her of misbehaving, then the poem becomes a masterpiece of wryness and irony.

Students are interested in questions like the following:

1. Is it possible to be both an ethnic and a universal (or liberal humanist) writer? What constitutes universality? What constitutes successful treatment of ethnic material?
2. Can a writer from a minority group write for a general educated audience without giving up in resonance what is gained in breadth of audience and reference?

Major Themes, Historical Perspectives, and Personal Issues

Major themes are tension between the imagination and the tragic nature of life; the past in the present; the nurturing power of early life and ethnically colored memories.

Significant Form, Style, or Artistic Conventions

Precede discussion of form and style with a discussion of the function of a particular type of poem. For example, Hayden wrote spirit-of-place poems such as "Tour 5," which depend heavily on imagery; folk character poems such as "Mourning Poem for the Queen of Sunday," which depend on economy of characterization and humor; and early neighborhood poems such as "Summertime and the Living," which depend on realism mixed with nostalgia, fancy, or psychological symbolism.

Original Audience

It is important to realize Hayden always wrote for a general literate audience, not exclusively or even primarily for a black audience. The issue of audience for him relates to the issue of the role of a poet.

Comparisons, Contrasts, Connections

Compare Yeats as an ethnic-universal poet to Hayden.

Questions for Reading and Discussion/ Approaches to Writing

1. "Tour 5"
   (a) Discuss the human situation the poem describes. Consider its treatment of both the external and internal aspects of the experience for the travelers.
   (b) Discuss the allusive quality of the adjectives used in the first stanza to convey a festive mood and in the last three lines to convey the violence of the Civil War and the cruelty of slavery.
   (c) Discuss what makes this a poem of the first order. Conciseness, controlled intensity, human drama, eloquence, and powerful symbols are some of the qualities you might touch on.

2. "Summertime and the Living"
   (a) Discuss Hayden's use of a third-person retrospective point of view to write about childhood. (It gives him the ability to be both inside and outside the child's perspective.)
   (b) Discuss the sound of words and their connection with sense. Hayden is highly conscious of the aural dimension of language.
   (c) What is the function of the title, which is taken from a song in George and Ira Gershwin's opera *Porgie and Bess?*
3. "Mourning Poem for the Queen of Sunday"
   (a) Discuss the viewpoint of the speakers about the murdered diva. Discuss the final two lines. Are they at all ironic? Are the speakers totally surprised?
   (b) Discuss the importance of tone throughout the poem.
   (c) Discuss the poem's atmosphere and how elements other than tone contribute to the black church feeling.

Bibliography

Greenberg, Robert M. "Robert Hayden." In *American Writers: A Collection of Literary Biographies*, Supplement II, Part I, edited by A. Walton Litz, 361–83. New York: Charles Scribner's Sons, 1981. Has biographical, critical, and bibliographical material.

Hayden, Robert. *Collected Prose: Robert Hayden*, edited by Frederick Glaysher. Ann Arbor: University of Michigan Press, 1984. Has excellent interview material with Hayden about particular poems.

Theodore Roethke (1908–1963)

Contributing Editor: Janis Stout

Major Themes, Historical Perspectives, and Personal Issues

Personal Background: Roethke had extremely ambivalent feelings about his father, who was managing partner in a large greenhouse operation in Saginaw, Michigan.

Significant Form, Style, or Artistic Conventions

"Frau Bauman, Frau Schmidt, and Frau Schwartze"

The three "ancient ladies" preside over processes of growth (both vegetable and the poet's own) almost as personifications of natural forces, or even the three Fates. Their presence, like Mother Nature's, is somewhat ambiguous; there is a note of threat in their tickling of the child and in their night presence. The three women's vigor and authority should be noted, as well as their avoidance of limitation by sex-role stereotypes: clearly female (they wear skirts, they have a special association with the child), they also climb ladders and stand astride the steam-pipes providing heat in the greenhouse.

"Root Cellar"

"Root Cellar" and "Big Wind" represent the celebrated "greenhouse poems," a group characterized by close attention to details evident only to one who knows this particular world very well—as Roethke did. They are distinguished from, say, Wordworth's nature poems in that they celebrate equally the natural processes themselves and the human effort and control involved. They share Wordsworth's ability to appreciate the humble or homely elements of nature. Here, in particular, we see Roethke's wonder at the sheer life process even when manifested in forms that would ordinarily seem ugly or repellent.

"Big Wind"

We might say "Big Wind" celebrates the tenacity of human effort in the face of hostile natural forces, an effort that wrests out of chaos the beauty of the roses. However, that idea should not be pressed so far as to exclude the creative force of natural vitality. Nature and human effort join together in producing roses. The greenhouse itself, shown as a ship running before the storm, seems almost a living thing.

"The Lost Son"

"The Lost Son" illustrates three major elements in Roethke's work: surrealistic style; reflection of his own psychological disorders; and mysticism, his vision of spiritual wholeness as a merging of the individual consciousness with natural processes and life-forms.

1. "The Flight" is a poem of anxiety about death and loss of identity.
2. "The Return" associates wellness with the greenhouse world of childhood. The return spoken of is the return of light and heat—of

full heat, since the greenhouses would scarcely have been left unheated on winter nights. The plants are both an object of the poet's close observation and a representation of his life.

"Meditations of an Old Woman"

Probably the most far-reaching question that can be asked of students, but also the most difficult, is, What difference does it make that the speaker is an old woman? Old, we can understand; we think of wisdom, experience, release from the distractions of youth. But why not an old man? One tempting answer is that our society has typically seen passivity and the passive virtues (patience, for instance) as feminine.

"Elegy"

Not often anthologized, this funerary tribute approaches a fusion of comedy with high seriousness. Aunt Tilly is a wonderfully strong, assertive, independent-minded woman who both fulfills traditional roles (housewife, cook, nurse, tender of the dead) and transcends them. The comedy emerges in the last stanza when Aunt Tilly comes "bearing down" on the butcher who, knowing he has met his match, quails before her indomitability and her clarity of vision.

Bibliography

Seager, Allen. *The Glass House* (1968).

Stout, Janis P. "Theodore Roethke and the Journey of the Solitary Self." *Interpretations* 16 (1985): 86–93.

Sullivan, Rosemary. *Theodore Roethke: The Garden-Master* (1975).

Elizabeth Bishop (1911–1979)

Contributing Editor: C. K. Doreski

Classroom Issues and Strategies

Bishop's poems are highly accessible and do not present problems for most mature readers. I have found that more students come to hear the poetry of Bishop when they commit some of her work to memory. I often challenge students to find the poetry first and then discuss the theme. This encourages them to begin to find relationships among form, language, and topic.

Significant Form, Style, or Artistic Conventions

Bishop's voice communicates rather directly to beginning readers of poetry. What is difficult to convey is the depth of expression and learning evidenced in these poems. Her work shows not merely experience but wisdom, the ability to reflect upon one's life, and that makes some poems difficult for younger readers.

For younger women readers, Bishop often seems old-fashioned, fussy, or detached. This perplexed the poet in that she felt that she had lived her life as an independent woman. This "generation gap" often provides an interesting class opportunity to talk about historical, cultural, and class assumptions in literature—and how those issues affect us as readers.

Students are often quite taken by Bishop's regard for animals. With the spirit of a Darwinian naturalist, the poet is willing to accord the natural world intrinsic rights and purposes. The dream-fusion world of the Man-Moth provides many students with an opportunity to discover this avenue into Bishop's world.

Original Audience

Bishop presents a curious "generational" case in that the circumstances of her childhood (raised by her maternal grandparents and an aunt) skew some of her references in favor of an earlier time. The kitchen setting in "Sestina" (not in this anthology), for example, seems more old-fashioned than Robert Lowell's interior scenes in "91 Revere Street." Otherwise her poems may be seen as timely—or timeless.

Comparisons, Contrasts, Connections

In the British lyric tradition, Bishop, by admission and allusion, draws heavily from Herbert, Hopkins, Wordsworth, Tennyson, Keats, and Blake.

Most pertinent American contrasts are with her mentor Marianne Moore (large correspondence at the Rosenbach Museum, Philadelphia), her friends Robert Lowell (correspondence at Houghton Library, Harvard University; Vassar College Library, Poughkeepsie) and May Swenson (correspondence at Washington University Library, St. Louis).

Questions for Reading and Discussion/ Approaches to Writing

1. "The Man-Moth"
   (a) This is but one of Bishop's many dream poems. In what ways does Bishop demonstrate her interest in and reliance upon surrealism?
   (b) How does Bishop attempt to humanize her exile through a multitude of sensory impressions? Are they effective?
   (c) The final stanza addresses the reader. How does Bishop intensify her creature's humanity through his ultimate vulnerability? Are we made to feel like the man-moth?

2. "Filling Station"
   (a) As Bishop describes setting and inhabitants of this "family filling station," she deliberately builds upon the initial observation, "Oh, but it is dirty!" Why dwell upon and develop this commentary? Does it suggest a missing family member? Is this station without a feminine presence?
   (b) The scale of the poem seems deliberately diminutive. Does this intensify the feminine quality of the poem? Is this intentional?
   (c) The closing stanza returns a sense of order or at least purpose to this scene. The symmetry of the cans lulls the "high-strung automobiles" into calmness. With the final line, "Somebody loves us all," does Bishop suggest a religious or maternal caretaker for this family?

3. Describe the voice and tone in a single poem. The casual humor of Bishop's world is often missed by casual readers (obsessed with travel and loss as themes).

4. Bishop owes much to her surrealist heritage. Sleep and dream states animate the worlds of the "Man-Moth" and "Crusoe in England." Such an essay would allow students to discover a new topical frame for discussion of experience, language, and poetic form.

5. A useful technical assignment would be to discuss Bishop's reliance upon simile rather than metaphor as her chief poetic device to link her world with the reader's. It says something critical about Bishop's belief in the limits of shared knowledge, experience.

Bibliography

Primary Works

North & South, 1946 (Houghton Mifflin Poetry Award); *Poems: North & South—A Cold Spring* (Pulitzer Prize, 1956); *Questions of Travel*, 1965; *The Complete Poems*, 1969 (National Book Award); *Geography III*, 1976; *The Complete Poems, 1927–1979*, 1983; *The Collected Prose*, 1984.

Secondary Works

Candace MacMahon, *Elizabeth Bishop: A Bibliography, 1927–1979*, 1980; Lloyd Schwartz and Sybil Estess, *Elizabeth Bishop and Her Art*, 1983; Harold Bloom, *Modern Critical Views: Elizabeth Bishop*, 1985; Robert Dale Parker, *The Unbeliever: The Poetry of Elizabeth Bishop*, 1988; Thomas J. Travisano, *Elizabeth Bishop: Her Artistic Development*, 1988; Bonnie Costello, *Elizabeth Bishop: Questions of Mastery*, 1991; Lorrie Goldensohn, *Elizabeth Bishop: The Biography of a Poetry*, 1992; C. K. Doreski, *Elizabeth Bishop: The Restraints of Language*, 1993; Brett Millier, *Elizabeth Bishop: Life and the Memory of It*, 1993.

Robert Traill Spence Lowell, Jr. (1917–1977)

Contributing Editor: Linda Wagner-Martin

Classroom Issues and Strategies

Lowell's poetry is more difficult than readers expect, deceptively difficult. Since many students come to him expecting an accessible poet (after all, he's one of those "confessionals"), they sometimes resent having to mine his poems for the background and the allusive sources they contain. Attention to an explicative preparation usually helps. "New Critical" methods are very appropriate.

Major Themes, Historical Perspectives, and Personal Issues

The combination of the historical with the personal is one of Lowell's most pervasive themes. His illustrious and prominent family (the Lowells) created a burden for both his psyche and his art. The reader must know history to read Lowell. The human mind in search, moving with intuitive understanding (as opposed to a reliance on fact), sometimes succeeding, sometimes not, is Lowell's continuing theme.

Significant Form, Style, or Artistic Conventions

A range of forms must be studied—Lowell is the most formal of poets, even toward the end, with the so-called "notebooks." Studying his intense revision (hardly a word left unchanged from the original version to the final) and examining his effort to skew natural language into his highly concentrated form are both good approaches.

Original Audience

Consider the whole business of the confessional, as Lowell moved from the historical into his unique blend of the personal and the historical.

Address the issue of location. Boston, the New England area, held not only Lowell's history but the country's.

Comparisons, Contrasts, Connections

Compare Lowell's poetry to that of Randall Jarrell, Anne Sexton, Theodore Roethke, Elizabeth Bishop, and Sylvia Plath.

Bibliography

Refer to the headnote in the text for complete information.

Gwendolyn Brooks (b. 1917)

Contributing Editor: D. H. Melhem

Classroom Issues and Strategies

Brooks's work is generally accessible. Occasionally, however, and more likely in some earlier works, like *Annie Allen* and individual poems like "Riders to the Blood-red Wrath," intense linguistic and semantic compression present minor difficulties.

My book *Gwendolyn Brooks: Poetry and the Heroic Voice* can be used as a guide to her published works. As holds true for most poetry, Brooks's should be read aloud. In the process, its power (boosted by alliteration), the musicality, and the narrative are vivified and made easily accessible.

Although I have not had the opportunity to teach Brooks extensively, students seem taken with identity poems like "The Life of Lincoln West" and the didactic "Ballad of Pearl May Lee," which was Hughes's favorite. The narrative aspect seems to be especially appealing. As these are not in this anthology, you may wish to recommend them as extra reading.

Major Themes, Historical Perspectives, and Personal Issues

Themes include black pride, black identity and solidarity, black humanism, and caritas, a maternal vision. Historically, racial discrimination; the civil rights movement of the fifties; black rebellion of the sixties; a concern with complacency in the seventies; black leadership.

Significant Form, Style, or Artistic Conventions

Brooks was influenced at first by the Harlem Renaissance. Her early work featured the sonnet and the ballad, and she experimented with adaptations of conventional meter. Later development of the black arts movement in the sixties, along with conceptions of a black aesthetic, turned her toward free verse and an abandonment of the sonnet as inappropriate to the times. She retained, however, her interest in the ballad—its musicality and accessibility—and in what she called "verse journalism."

Comparisons, Contrasts, Connections

In the earlier works: Langston Hughes, Paul Laurence Dunbar, Merrill Moore, Edna St. Vincent Millay, Claude McKay, Ann Spencer.

In the later works: Amiri Baraka, Haki R. Madhubuti, and again, Hughes.

Bibliography

The most useful books on Brooks are the following:

Melhem, D. H. *Gwendolyn Brooks: Poetry and the Heroic Voice*. University Press of Kentucky, 1987.

Chronologically discusses each major work in a separate chapter; biographical introduction; biocritical, prosodic, and historical approach; discusses correspondence with first publisher.

——. *Heroism in the New Black Poetry: Introductions and Interviews.* University Press of Kentucky, 1990.

The first of six chapters that offer introductions to and interviews with six outstanding black poets who bear some relation to or affinity with Brooks presents a summary of her life and art. Includes a discussion of new work (*The Near-Johannesburg Boy,* "Winnie" in *Gottschalk and the Grande Tarantelle*), an essay, "The Black Family," a new poem, and an interview arranged for the book. This American Book Award-winning work also features Dudley Randall, Haki R. Madhubuti, Sonia Sanchez, Jayne Cortez, and Amiri Baraka.

Other books include the following:

Mootry, M. K. and G. Smith, eds. *A Life Distilled* (essays). University of Illinois Press, 1987.

Shaw, Harry. *Gwendolyn Brooks.* New York: Twayne, 1980. Presents a thematic approach.

Richard Wilbur (b. 1921)

Contributing Editor: Bernard F. Engel

Comparisons, Contrasts, Connections

1. Compare Wilbur's vigorous defense of traditional patterns, metrics, and rhyme with Charles Olson's essay "Projective Verse" or similar arguments for "open form." Early comments on Wilbur's tight artistic discipline appear in M. L. Rosenthal's *The Modern Poets* (Oxford University Press, 1960). Rosenthal admires Wilbur's technical skill but argues that his work is overly traditional. A strong defense of Wilbur as a "darker" poet, one "more complex, passionate, and original" than critics sometimes take him to be, appears in Bruce Michelson's book. A number of critical views are summarized in Engel's *Research Guide* article.
2. Donald Hill's *Richard Wilbur* (1967) has several passages discussing critics who compare Wilbur's work with that of Robert Lowell,

Howard Nemerov, and others. Useful comparison could also be made with Richard Eberhart—a poet who is equally convinced that the flesh is poetry's environment but is nevertheless more willing to move into mysticism and exclamation.

Questions for Reading and Discussion

" 'A World Without Objects Is a Sensible Emptiness' "

1. This poem expresses Wilbur's repeated conviction that "mirages" are not enough, that "all shinings" must be worked out in the world of sensory reality. Compare Ralph Waldo Emerson's insistence in "The American Scholar" on knowing "the meal in the firkin, the milk in the pan."
2. The quotation used as the title is from Meditation 65 in Thomas Traherne's *Second Century.* Asserting that one lacking someone or something to love would be better off having "no being," Traherne says: "Life without objects is a sensible emptiness, and that is a greater misery than death or nothing." Donald Hill discusses the poem in *Richard Wilbur,* pages 62 through 65.
3. In the first two stanzas, the "spirit" of the speaker is attracted to the supposed "vast returns" of a world without objects. Students might be asked what the speaker thinks such a world would be.
4. In stanzas 3 through 5, the speaker warns the spirit to beware the enticing but "accurst." Students might consider what it is that is cursed.
5. Stanzas 4 and 5 cite as examples two "shinings," the painted saints of medieval days, and "Merry-go-round rings." Ask what these objects represent.
6. After again telling his spirit to turn away from "the fine sleights of the sand," the speaker advises that the true oasis is not to be found in grand imaginings. Students might be asked to explain how and where the speaker would have his spirit look for grandeur.

"Pangloss's Song: A Comic-Opera Lyric"

1. Though this lyric was deleted from the New York production of Wilbur's "comic operetta" based on Voltaire's *Candide,* Wilbur has since published it as a separate poem.
2. Students should note how Wilbur uses humor to avoid the distasteful in this lyric. Wilbur also does not use the word "syphilis," though that obviously is the disease Pangloss suffers from. Written in 1961, the poem assumes that Columbus's men brought the disease back to Europe from the New World. Students should know

that there is now much controversy over the origin of syphilis, with people of the Caribbean maintaining that Europeans brought it to them.

3. Without attempting to impose too much philosophical freight on this *jeu d'esprit,* one might ask how it satisfies Wilbur's insistence that the idealist must be aware of sensory realities.

4. Does the poem express a celebration of love? Is it in any way a burlesque?

"In the Field"

1. In mythology, Andromeda (stanza 3) was rescued from a sea monster by Perseus; Wilbur has observed that Euripedes's lost play *Andromeda* may have told of her transformation into a constellation.

2. In stanzas 5 to 8, Wilbur's speaker recognizes that "none of that"— ancient myths about the stars—"is true." The speaker knows that the stars are in motion, with the result that constellations imagined by the ancients are now often "askew." Stanza 6 gives an example of the effects of motion: the north star is now Polaris, but 2,500 years ago Alpha Draconis (the brightest star in the constellation Dragon) was in that position. Stanza 7 observes that because of star motion the "cincture of the zodiac," the astrologer's fancied order, is now outmoded, has "nothing left to say/To us."

3. Students should note the change from the mythological view of the heavens in the first four stanzas to the dismissal of that view in stanza 5 and the discussion of scientific ideas in stanzas 6 to 10. They also should be aware of the difference between astronomy and astrology.

4. The seventh stanza apparently refers to the "Big Bang" theory, the idea that the universe began as an infinitely tiny blob of "matter" that exploded outward, producing all that our senses show us; the stars are believed to be still traveling away from the point of origin at incomprehensible speeds. Stanza 8 refers to the hypothesis of some astronomers that eventually the energy of the original "bang" may become so weak that the motion will be reversed, with all "matter" rushing back until it is once again compressed into a minute object.

5. Stanza 10 notes that astronomy has made Antares, one of the brightest stars, "only a blink of red." In stanza 11, the speaker concedes that he and his friends can still feel the power of the myths they have read about in schoolbooks, and may even for a moment let imagination seem to show them a sky emptied of all objects by

their "spent grenade" (perhaps the science that has blown away the world of myth).

6. Students might consider why the speaker in line 69 says that it would be a "mistake" to assume that flowers are an answer to the "fright" he experienced in contemplating the stars.

7. Students might also consider how the idea that the flowers give an answer, though said to be in error, nevertheless leads to the faith expressed in the last two stanzas.

8. Discussion might focus on the assertion of the last two stanzas that "the one/Unbounded thing we know" is "the heart's wish for life.

"The Mind-Reader"

1. For the foreign words and phrases in this poem, see the footnotes.

2. Students should be able to explain the contrast in lines 20 to 23.

3. What do lines 64 and 65 ("I am not/Permitted to forget") reveal about the speaker's idea of himself?

4. Students should be aware of the meaning of "vatic" (line 67), "magus" (line 74), "trumpery" (line 90). How does the speaker make his living?

5. Students should know that the archangel Michael (lines 80 to 81) is said to have led the forces of God to their triumph over the rebellious Satan.

6. Why does the speaker in line 121 ask "What more do they deserve"? What might be the "huge attention" he speculates on in line 131?

7. In the last stanza, are the speaker's "habit of concupiscence" and his "hanker" for the places of the lost presented in order to destroy any view of him as a wise adviser? Are they meant rather to support such a view of him? Consider Wilbur's insistence on the importance of the sensory.

8. Does the poem as a whole suggest that the speaker is wise? Merely a weary or cynical faker? One of the "truly lost" mentioned in line 1?

Robert Creeley (b. 1926)

Contributing Editor: Thomas R. Whitaker

Classroom Issues and Strategies

"Hart Crane"

Dedicated to a friend of Crane who became a friend of Creeley, this is the opening poem in *For Love*. Is it a negative portrait or a sympathetic study of difficulties central to Creeley's own career? Certainly it contains many leitmotifs of Creeley's poetry: stuttering, isolations, incompletion, self-conscious ineptness, the difficulty of utterance, the need for friends, the confrontations of a broken world.

"I Know a Man"

The colloquial anecdote as parable? How does the stammering lineation complicate the swift utterance? Why should the shift in speakers occur with such ambiguous punctuation—a comma splice? According to Creeley, "drive" is said not by the friend but by the speaker.

"For Love"

The closing poem in *For Love*, this is informed by the qualities attributed to Crane in the volume's opening poem. "For Love" is one of many poems to Bobbie—wife, companion, muse, and mother of children—that wrestle with the nature of love, the difficulty of utterance, and a mass of conflicting feelings: doubt, faith, despair, surprise, self-criticism, gratitude, relief. The poem is a remarkable enactment of a complex and moment-by-moment honesty.

"Words"

This poem drives yet further inward to the ambiguous point where an inarticulate self engages an imperfectly grasped language. Not the wife or muse but "words" seem now the objects of direct address, the poem's "you." Nevertheless, the poem's detailed phrases and its movement through anxious blockage toward an ambiguously blessed release strongly suggest a love poem.

"America"

Though seldom an explicitly political poet, Creeley here brings his sardonic tone and his belief in utterance as our most intimate identity to bear on the question, What has happened to the America that Walt Whitman celebrated? "The United States themselves are essentially the greatest poem," Whitman had said in his Preface to the 1855 *Leaves of Grass*. And he had often spoken of the "words" belonging to that poem, as in "One's-Self I Sing" and in the reflections on "the People" in *Democratic Vistas*.

"America" modulates those concerns into Creeley's own more quizzical language. We may read it as a dark response, a century later, to Whitman's "Long, Too Long America" in *Drum-Taps*. For Creeley's more extended response to Whitman, see his *Whitman: Selected Poems*.

Significant Form, Style, or Artistic Conventions

In "Projective Verse" Charles Olson quotes Creeley's remark that "Form is never more than an extension of content." Creeley liked, as an implicit definition of form, a Blakean aphorism that he learned from Slater Brown: "Fire delights in its form." His central statement of open poetics, involving "a content which cannot be anticipated," is "I'm Given to Write Poems" (*A Quick Graph*, pp. 61–72).

It is useful to know that, when reading his poetry aloud, Creeley always indicates line-ends by means of very brief pauses. The resultant stammer—quite unlike the effect of Williams's reading—is integral to Creeley's style, which involves a pervasive sense of wryly humorous or painful groping for the next line.

Comparisons, Contrasts, Connections

William Carlos Williams told Robert Creeley, "You have the subtlest feeling for the measure I have encountered anywhere except in the verses of Ezra Pound." For Creeley's relation to Williams, see his essays in *A Quick Graph* and Paul Mariani, "Robert Creeley," in *A Usable Past* (Amherst: University of Massachusetts Press, 1984). For his relation to Pound, see "A Note on Ezra Pound" (*A Quick Graph*), and for his sustained and mutually valuable relation to Charles Olson, see again *A Quick Graph*.

Perhaps the class would like to compare "Hart Crane" with Robert Lowell's "Words for Hart Crane" in *Life Studies*. Two views of Crane, two modes of portraiture, and two historically important styles of mid-century American verse; these plus "The Broken Tower" itself would make a fascinating unit of study.

Bibliography

Refer to headnote in the text for complete information.

Gary Snyder (b. 1930)

Contributing Editor: Thomas R. Whitaker

Questions for Reading and Discussion/ Approaches to Writing

"Riprap"

As Snyder tells us in his first volume, riprap is "a cobble of stone laid on steep, slick rock to make a trail for horses in the mountains." In *Myths & Texts* (p. 43), he calls poetry "a riprap on the slick rock of metaphysics." This poem may suggest the "objectivism" of William Carlos Williams— "No ideas but in things"—and yet it finally evokes an infinite, ever-changing system of worlds and thoughts. Such idealism, of course, also enters Williams's *Paterson*. Central to the poetics of both Williams and Snyder are strategies that enable particulars to evoke a pattern and so provide a link with the universal. What strategies can the class find here? Some poems for comparison: "Mid-August at Sourdough Mountain Lookout" and "Piute Creek" in *Riprap*, and "For Nothing" in *Turtle Island*—all concerned to relate "thing" and "mind" or "form" and "emptiness."

"Vapor Trails"

How does this poem relate aesthetic patterns, natural patterns, and the patterns of human violence? Is the poem finally a lament over such violence? Or a discovery of its beauty? Or a resignation to its naturalness? Or all or none of these? Can the class trace the shifting tone of the meditation from beginning to end?

This poem, too, has affinities with Williams's work. See, for example, such studies of symmetry and craft as "On Gay Wallpaper" and "Fine Work with Pitch and Copper." Does the ironic use of "design" at the end of "Vapor Trails" obliquely recall the concerns of Robert Frost's "Design"?

"Wave"

This poem, like others in *Regarding Wave*, links various manifestations of energy—inorganic, organic, sexual, linguistic, mental—through images and etymologies that evoke a cosmic wave, motion, or dance. Snyder's riprap, a human construction that enables a mental ascent, seems now to have yielded more fully to the perception of patterns inherent in natural process, patterns in which we dancingly participate.

Wave: wife. As that analogy develops, does the poem suggest that nature is our muse and that the energy of all sentience and all cosmic process is fundamentally sexual?

Would the class enjoy some visual analogies to "the dancing grain of things/of my mind"? If so, you might look at the photographs and calligraphy in Lao Tsu, *Tao Te Ching*, translated by Gia-Fu Feng and Jane English (New York: Random House, 1972).

"It Was When"

This reverie over moments when Snyder's son Kai might have been conceived is both a love poem to his wife Masa and a celebration of the "grace" manifest in their coming together. Its imagery, cadences, and reverence for vital processes strongly recall the poetry of D. H. Lawrence. The class might like to make comparisons with Lawrence's "Gloire de Dijon" and perhaps other poems in *Look! We Have Come Through!*

"It Was When" is a densely woven pattern of alliteration and assonance. How do those sound effects cooperate with the poem's cadences and its meanings?

You may want to consult other poems in *Regarding Wave* that continue Snyder's meditation on his marriage and Kai's birth: "The Bed in the Sky," "Kai, Today," and "Not Leaving the House."

"The Egg"

This is another poem in a rather Lawrentian mode. Among its issues: What does the "egg" hold in potential? Can the body it generates—the body of one's own son—be a kind of articulate utterance, a manifestation of organic syntax? And can that utterance express the whole process of cosmic evolution?

The epigraph comes from Robert Duncan's "The Structure of Rime I," *The Opening of the Field* (New York: New Directions, 1960,

p. 12). In the sequence begun by that poem, Duncan explores language, the psyche, the organism, and the cosmos in ways that Snyder here recapitulates from his own point of view. In "The Egg" and "snake" is, among other things, the *kundalini* of Tantric yoga, a movement of energy from the body's sexual "root" to the "third eye," an organ of transcendental vision in the forehead. How does the poem ask our attention to mediate between the concrete particulars of Kai's lively body and such evolutionary and cosmic implications?

Comparisons, Contrasts, Connections

Snyder often plays variations on the imagist mode in which Ezra Pound and William Carlos Williams did much of their earlier work. D. H. Lawrence's love poems and animal poems are also important antecedents, as are Kenneth Rexroth's meditations amid Western landscapes and his translations from Japanese poetry.

Central to the poetics of both Williams and Snyder are strategies that enable particulars to evoke a pattern and so provide a link with the universal.

Bibliography

Refer to headnote in the text for complete information.

Charles Olson (1910–1970)

Contributing Editor: Thomas R. Whitaker

Classroom Issues and Strategies

It will be most practical to approach Olson after some detailed work with poems by T. S. Eliot, Ezra Pound, and William Carlos Williams. Despite many stylistic similarities, Olson's poetic "enactment" dictates a different kind of progression and a different use of literary and other allusions. The teacher might suggest that the formalist concept of a "speaker" or "protagonist" (a character in a poetic drama outside of which the poem's maker is imagined to stand) might be replaced by the poet himself in the act of writing (a self-reflexive Charles Olson in the drama of making this poem). Although Pound's *Pisan Cantos,* Eliot's *Four Quartets,* and

Williams's *Paterson* are partially amenable to this approach, Olson commits himself to it more fully in both shorter and longer forms.

His abstract style, his refusal to commit himself to the modernist "image," may also be a difficulty. The student can be reminded that all speech, all thought, even an "image," is the result of an abstractive process. Olson characteristically works with syntax and conceptual reference that are "in process"—often fragmentary, self-revising, incremental—as he struggles to "say" what is adequate to his present (and always changing) moment. Comparisons with Robert Creeley's often abstract and stammering forward motion may be illuminating.

Those interested in Olson as a teacher and as a collaborator with other poets and artists should consult *Letters for Origin* and *Mayan Letters*, and also Martin Duberman, *Black Mountain: An Exploration in Community* (1972), which is richly informative. Duberman also quotes a comment by Merce Cunningham on Olson as a dancer, which may suggest one way of approaching Olson's poetic style: "I *enjoyed* him; . . . he was something like a light walrus" (p. 359). For Olson's own appreciation of Cunningham as a dancer, see the poem "Merce of Egypt," which is a meditation on man-the-maker that might be compared to "For Sappho, Back."

Questions for Reading and Discussion/ Approaches to Writing

"The Kingfishers"

It may be useful for the instructor to have worked through this poem with the help of a commentator, such as Sherman Paul, Thomas Merrill (cited in headnote), or Guy Davenport, "Scholia and Conjectures for Olson's 'The Kingfishers,' " *Boundary 2* 2 (1973–74): 250–62. Students can then be encouraged to approach the poem as a meditation on the need for change, and the will to change—as of 1949 but with contemporary applications. The poet sees the need to move beyond Eliot and Pound, beyond the irony and despair of *The Waste Land* and the modern inferno of *The Cantos*, without overlooking the cultural crisis to which they allude. What sources of vitality does he find amid the decay? What suggestions for personal and cultural renewal? And for a new poetic practice? Can we understand this poem on the model of elliptical diary notations by someone who is working toward a statement of position? What are the stages of its progress?

Students with an interest in the poem's philosophical implications may wish to explore Plutarch's "The E at Delphi" or G. S. Kirk, *Heraclitus: The Cosmic Fragments*. Students wondering how "feedback" may relate to social and poetic processes should turn to Norbert Wiener's

Cybernetics or *The Human Use of Human Beings.* Of great interest in that direction is also the work of Gregory Bateson: see *Steps to an Ecology of Mind* (the chapter on "Cybernetic Explanation") and *Mind and Nature: A Necessary Unity.*

"For Sappho, Back"

In some respects more traditional in form and subject than the other Olson poems included here, "For Sappho, Back" might be a useful introduction to Olson's style for students not at ease with allusive modernism. How does the poem expand the tribute to a specific woman-poet so that it becomes a meditation on woman, nature, and poetry? What specific qualities of Sappho's style does it allude to? Does Sappho become here a Muse figure or Nature Herself? D. H. Lawrence has said in *Etruscan Places* (which Olson admired) that the Etruscan priest sought an "act of pure attention" directed inward. "To him the blood was the red stream of consciousness itself." As Olson wrote to the anthropologist Ruth Benedict, "I am alone again working down to the word where it lies in the blood. I continually find myself reaching back and down in order to make sense out of now and to lead ahead." (See Clark, *Charles Olson*, p. 95.) Does this help us with "Back" in the title and the use of "blood" later? Clark suggests that, on one level, this is a personal love poem, taken by its recipient, Frances Boldereff, to be a "very accurate portrait" of herself (p. 171). Olson often chose to incorporate in such love poems allusions to his wife Constance; can we find such clues here? How, finally, do we relate the historical, personal, and archetypal concerns of this poem?

Robert von Hallberg (*Charles Olson: The Scholar's Art*, pp. 34–38) offers suggestions for stylistic analysis of the use of fragmentary and self-revising syntax in this poem.

"I, Maximus of Gloucester, to You"

Students might usefully compare this poem to Hart Crane's "To Brooklyn Bridge"; both are invocations and statements of subject at the outset of modern "personal epics." One might also consult the preface to Williams's *Paterson.* What are the social issues in each case? What dominant images are established? What relations does Olson suggest between love and form? How do images gradually accrue additional meanings as the meditation proceeds? Does it help to know that this was happening in the process of composition—and that in an earlier draft "next second," was "next/second"? (See Clark, *Charles Olson*, p. 166.)

"Maximus, to himself"

As a self-assessment, this poem might usefully be compared with Cree-ley's "For Love." Both have the air of spontaneous meditation; both deal largely in abstractions; both are sharply self-critical. To what degree is the form of each an "extension of content"? How, in each, does a seem-ingly unplanned meditation assume the form of a coherent monologue, moving through a problem toward its momentary resolution?

Bibliography

Refer to the headnote in the text for complete information. Sherman Paul, Thomas Merrill, and Robert von Hallberg will be especially useful for those looking for annotation or critical reading. Olson's essays—especially "Projective Verse" and "Human Universe"—will take the reader directly into the poet's own vantage point.

Frank O'Hara (1926–1966)

Contributing Editor: David Bergman

Classroom Issues and Strategies

Frank O'Hara's works look so effortless, spontaneous, so stitched from his daily life, that students may forget just how hard it is to make things look easy. It is important to stress the ways the poems are drawn from his life, more than a laundry list of "I do this, I do that." For example, in "The Day Lady Died," the precise and banal details of his train schedule and the presents he is bringing set the stage for the memory of Billie Holiday, a memory that seems to exist out of time. It is Holiday who breaks through the hustle and bustle of his life and has captured through her art—her voice—something nearly eternal. Although she has "stopped breathing" in reality, in his memory of her it is the audience who is dead and she is the one most alive.

O'Hara's connection to abstract expressionism is well established. It might be helpful to show the work of Mike Goldberg, Willem De Kooning, or Grace Hartigan. You might want to discuss the relationship between action painting and O'Hara's aesthetic, especially as developed in "Why I Am Not a Painter."

O'Hara studied music, and for quite a time believed he would become a composer. He worked with Ned Rorem and was a friend of Virgil Thomson. (The Rorem/O'Hara collaboration is available on CD [PHCD 116].) Invite students to read the poems aloud. One discovers a subtle music in them. O'Hara diverges from modernist poets because of his emphasis on voice rather than on image. For all of his interest in painting, it is the immediacy of O'Hara's voice that is the most striking part of his poetry.

Some teachers are afraid to address the homosexual content of his poems. I have discovered that addressing the issue as just one more subject reduces the students' discomfort. If students remain uncomfortable, the best position to state is, "We are all grown-ups here. We must be ready to confront attitudes and positions we both share and do not share."

Major Themes, Historical Perspectives, and Personal Issues

Like John Ashbery, O'Hara's friend and fellow Harvard alumnus, O'Hara is always concerned with time and mutability. These questions of time spawn several subthemes: (1) the relationship of art to time (can art take us out of time?); (2) the weakness of the body, its susceptibility to disease, death, and pain; (3) the fleetingness of emotions, particularly love; (4) the pressure of friends and the difficulties of maintaining the bonds of friendship.

Openness is a key word for O'Hara. He wants his poems and his love to be open. We can discuss open poetic forms, open relationships, openness to experience, a willingness to court vulgarity and sentimentality. But openness makes one vulnerable. O'Hara is haunted by this sense of vulnerability to outside enemies and forces. In some ways this mirrors the American psyche of the Cold War—its sense of strength, its desire to be an open society, and its fears—frequently irrational—of enemy attack.

Significant Form, Style, or Artistic Conventions

O'Hara's work is free verse, but as the footnote suggests, "Poem" echoes Shakespeare's sonnet "When in disgrace to fortune and men's eyes." It might be useful to look at how the form of the sonnet, although not copied, haunts the structure of this poem. O'Hara's line breaks look arbitrary, but they often are extremely effective.

Comparisons, Contrasts, Connections

O'Hara's work is often compared to John Ashbery's. One can see their wit, humor, and desire to incorporate things from daily life into their work. But whereas these poems are open to the reader, Ashbery's poems often are hermetic. Allen Ginsberg was also one of O'Hara's friends. The homoerotic world of "A Supermarket in California" compares with O'Hara's "Poem." O'Hara disliked Robert Lowell's poetry. Lowell's formalism and highly wrought poetic surface contrasts strongly with O'Hara's work of the same period.

Questions for Reading and Discussion/ Approaches to Writing

Students may be encouraged to try their own I-do-this-I-do-that poems and see why the details in O'Hara's add up to something much more than a list of appointments. What are the similarities and differences between poetry and the other arts? How autobiographical should a poem be? How distanced from the poet's life does a poem have to be to affect a reader? Do the names of so many of O'Hara's personal friends keep the poem from communicating to you as a reader, or does this specificity—even if you don't know who these people are exactly—make the experience seem more immediate? When does gossip become art? How does O'Hara's expression of homosexual love differ from heterosexual love? Or does it?

Denise Levertov (b. 1923)

Contributing Editor: Joan F. Hallisey

Classroom Issues and Strategies

With an adequate introduction to her life and works, Denise Levertov is not a difficult author. Levertov can best be made accessible to students when they are familiar with the poet's own prose reflections on poetry, the role of the poet, and "notes" on organic form. You might prepare an introduction to her work by making reference to her quite precise discussion of these themes in *The Poet in the World* (1973); *Light Up the Cave* (1982); and *New and Selected Essays* (1992).

Consider using tapes of Levertov reading her own poetry. The most recent cassette, "The Acolyte" (Watershed), contains a fine sampling from her earlier poetry through *Oblique Prayers*. Encourage students to listen both to her poetry readings and interviews and to incorporate information from them in class or seminar discussions and presentations or as material for research papers. When students are doing a class presentation, strongly urge them to be certain that their classmates have copies of the poems they will be discussing.

Students respond favorably to Levertov's conviction that the poet writes more than "[she] knows." They also respond positively to the fact that an American woman "engaged" poet has spoken out strongly on women's rights, peace and justice issues, race, and other questions on human rights.

Students may ask you if Levertov is discouraged in the face of so much darkness and disaster evident in the late twentieth century. This presents a good opportunity to have the students examine "Writing in the Dark" and "The May Mornings" (*Candles in Babylon*, 1982) and her essay "Poetry, Prophecy, Survival" (*New and Selected Essays*, 1992).

Major Themes, Historical Perspectives, and Personal Issues

Levertov's work is concerned with several dimensions of the human experience: love, motherhood, nature, war, the nuclear arms race, mysticism, poetry, and the role of the poet. If you are teaching a women's literature course or an upper-level course focusing on a few writers, several of these themes might be examined. In a survey course, you might concentrate on three themes that include both historical and personal issues: poetry, the role of the poet, and her interest in humanitarian politics.

Significant Form, Style, or Artistic Conventions

Levertov in "Some Notes on Organic Form" tells the reader that during the writing of a poem the various elements of the poet's being are in communion with one another and heightened. She believes that ear and eye, intellect and passion, interrelate more subtly than at other times, and she regards the poet's "checking for accuracy," for precision of language that must take place throughout the writing not as a "matter of one element supervising the others but of intuitive interaction between all the elements involved"(*The Poet in the World*, p. 9).

Like Wordsworth and Emerson, Levertov sees content and form as being in a state of dynamic interaction. She sees rhyme, echo, reiteration as serving not only to knit the elements of an experience "but also as being the means, the sole means, by which the density of texture and the returning or circling of perception can be transmuted into language, apperceived" (Ibid., p. 9).

You might point out that as an artist who is "obstinately precise" about her craft, Levertov pays close attention to etymologies as she searches for the right words, the right image, the right arrangement of the lines on the page. It will be helpful for students to be able to recognize other poetic techniques that Levertov uses in her poetry: enjambment, color, contrast, and even the pun to sustain conflict and ambiguity. Levertov will sometimes make use of the juxtaposition of key words and line breaks.

Levertov does not consider herself a member of any particular school.

Original Audience

Levertov has said, on several occasions, that she never has readers in mind when she is writing a poem. She believes that a poem has to be not merely addressed to a person or a problem *out there*; but must come from *in here*, the inner being of the poet, and it must also address something *in here*.

It is important to share Levertov's ideas with the students when you discuss audience. One might stress the universality of some themes: familial and cultural heritage, poetry, and the role of the poet/prophet in a "time of terror." There is a "timeless" kind of relevance for these themes, and they need not be confined to any one age.

Comparisons, Contrasts, Connections

There is enough evidence to suggest that a fruitful comparison might be made between several of Muriel Rukeyser's finest poems ("Akiba," "Kathe Kollwitz" [*Speed of Darkness*, 1968], "Searching/Not Searching" [*Breaking Open*, 1973]) and some of Levertov's poems on comparable themes.

Questions for Reading and Discussion/ Approaches to Writing

1. (a) What kinds of feelings do you have about the Holocaust? About nuclear war?

   (b) What do you think the role of the poet should be today? Do you think she/he should speak out about political or social issues? Why? Why not?

2. (a) Several of Levertov's poems can be used for a writing sample and subsequent discussion at the beginning of the course. Brief poems that students respond strongly to are: "The Broken Sandal" (*Relearning the Alphabet*), "Variation on a Theme from Rilke" (*Breathing the Water*), and "The Batterers" and "Eye Mask" (*Evening Train*, 1992).

   (b) One might give a short assignment to compare the themes, tone, and imagery of Levertov's "The Broken Sandal" with Adrienne Rich's "Prospective Immigrants—Please Note."

   (c) Examine several of Levertov's poems on poetry and the role of the poet in light of Ralph Waldo Emerson's call for the "true" poet in several of his essays, most notably in "The Poet," "Poetry and the Imagination," and "The American Scholar."

Bibliography

Denise Levertov's *The Poet in the World* (1973); *Light Up the Cave* (1982); and *New and Selected Essays* (1992) are essential primary source materials for a deeper understanding of the poems included in the text.

"The Sense of Pilgrimage" essay in *The Poet in the World* and "Beatrice Levertoff" in *Light Up the Cave* offer valuable background material for teaching "Illustrious Ancestors."

Levertov has acknowledged the significant influence of Rilke on her poetry and poetics throughout her career, and several of her recent "Variation on a Theme from Rilke" poems will be enriched by Edward Zlotkowski's insightful essay "Levertov and Rilke: A Sense of Aesthetics" in *Twentieth Century Literature*, Fall 1992.

Audrey Rodger's *Denise Levertov's Poetry of Engagement* will be helpful in discussing Levertov's understanding of the role of the poet and her poetry of engagement.

Sylvia Plath (1932–1963)

Contributing Editor: Linda Wagner-Martin

Classroom Issues and Strategies

Students usually begin with the fact that Plath committed suicide and then read her death as some kind of "warning" to talented, ambitious women writers. (The recent biography by Stevenson only supports this view, unfortunately.) What must be done is to get to the text, in each case, and read for nuance of meaning—humor, anger, poignance, intellectual tour de force. Running parallel with this sense of Plath as some inhuman persona is a fearful acknowledgment that women who have ambition are not quite normal. Plath receives a very gender-based reading. A good corrective is to talk about people who have tendencies toward depression, a situation that affects men as well as women.

Focus on the text and ready information about the possible biographical influence on that text. Often, however, the influences are largely literary—Medea is as close a persona for some of the late poems as Plath herself—T. S. Eliot, Wallace Stevens, W. S. Merwin, W. B. Yeats, etc. Criticism is just now starting to mine these rich areas. Some attention to the late 1950s and early 1960s is also helpful: seeing the poetry and *The Bell Jar* as the same kind of breakthrough into the expression of women's anger as Betty Friedan's or Simone de Beauvoir's is useful.

Hearing Plath read from her own late work is effective: She has an unusual, almost strident voice, and the humor and gutsiness of the 1962 poems come across well. Caedmon has one recording that has many of the late poems backed with Plath's interview with Peter Orr for the BBC, taped on October 30, 1962 (many of the poems she reads were written just that week, or shortly before). The PBS *Voices and Visions* Plath segment is also fairly accurate and effective.

As mentioned above, the fact of Plath's suicide seems primary in many students' minds. Partly because many of them have read, or know of, *The Bell Jar*, it is hard to erase the image of the tormented woman, ill at ease in her world. But once that issue is cleared, and her writing is seen as a means of keeping her alive, perhaps the study of that writing becomes more important to students: It seems to have a less than esoteric "meaning."

Major Themes, Historical Perspectives, and Personal Issues

Themes include women's place in American culture (even though Plath lived the last three years in England, thinking wrongly that she had more freedom in England to be a writer); what women can attempt; how coerced they were by social norms (i.e., to date, marry, have children, be a helpmeet, support charities); the weight society places on women—to be the only support of children, to earn livings (Plath's life, echoing her mother's very difficult one, with little money and two children for whom she wanted the best of opportunities); the need for superhuman talent, endurance, and resourcefulness in every woman's life.

Significant Form, Style, or Artistic Conventions

Versatility of form (tercet, villanelle, many shapes of organic form, syllabics), use of rhyme (and its variations, near rhyme, slant rhyme, assonance), word choice (mixed vocabularies)—Plath must be studied as an expert, compelling poet, whose influence on the contemporary poetry scene—poems written by men as well as women—has been inestimable. Without prejudicing readers, the teacher must consider what "confessional" poetry is: the use of seemingly "real" experience, experience that often is a supreme fiction rather than personal biography; a means of making art less remote from life by using what might be life experience as its text. Unfortunately, as long as only women poets or poets with abnormal psychiatric histories are considered "confessional," the term is going to be ineffective for a meaningful study of contemporary poetry.

Original Audience

Although most of Plath's best poems were written in the early 1960s, the important point to be made is that today's readers find her work immediate. Her expression of distrust of society, her anger at the positions talented women were asked to take in that society, were healthful (and rare) during the early 1960s, so she became a kind of voice of the times in the same way Ernest Hemingway expressed the mood of the 1920s. But while much of Hemingway's work seems dated to today's students (at least his ethical and moral stances toward life), Plath's writing has gained currency.

Comparisons, Contrasts, Connections

The most striking comparison can be made between the early work of Anne Sexton and Plath (Plath learned a lot from Sexton), and to a lesser extent, the poems of Theodore Roethke. W. D. Snodgrass's long poem "Heart's Needle" was an important catalyst for both Sexton and Plath, as was some of Robert Lowell's work. If earlier Plath poems are used, Wallace Stevens and T. S. Eliot are key. And, in moderation, Ted Hughes's early work can be useful—especially the animal and archaic tones and images.

Bibliography

Susan Van Dyne's essays on the manuscripts are invaluable (see *Centennial Review*, Summer 1988). See also the *Massachusetts Review* essay, collected in Wagner's *Sylvia Plath: Critical Essays* (Boston: G. K. Hall, 1984) and Van Dyne's 1993 book from the University of North Carolina Press.

Wagner's Routledge collection, *Sylvia Plath: The Critical Heritage* (1988) includes a number of helpful reviews.

Linda Bundtzen's *Plath's Incarnations* (University of Michigan Press, 1983), Steven Axelrod's 1990 *Sylvia Plath, The Wound and the Cure of Wounds*, along with the Wagner-Martin biography of Plath, are useful. See also Linda Wagner-Martin's *Plath's The Bell Jar, A Novel of the Fifties* (1992).

Anne Sexton (1928–1974)

Contributing Editor: Diana Hume George

Classroom Issues and Strategies

Anne Sexton's poetry teaches superbly. It is accessible, challenging, richly textured, and culturally resonant. Her work is equally appropriate for use in American literature, women's studies, and poetry courses. The selections in this text represent many of the diverse subjects and directions of her work.

Three problems tend to recur in teaching Sexton; all are interrelated. First, the "confessional school" context is troublesome because that subgenre in American poetry is both misnamed and easily misunderstood; Sexton has been the subject of inordinately negative commentary as the first prominent woman poet writing in this mode. Second, contemporary readers, despite the feminist movement, often have difficulty dealing with Sexton's explicitly bodily and female subject matter and imagery. Finally, readers often find her poetry depressing, especially the poems that deal with suicide, death, and mental illness.

If the course emphasizes historical context, a sympathetic and knowledgeable explanation of resistance to the confessional mode is helpful. (Ironically, if historical context is not important to presentation of the material, I suggest not mentioning it at all.) Academic and public reactions to the women's movement, even though Sexton did not deliberately style herself as a feminist poet, will help to make students understand the depth and extent of her cultural and poetic transgressions. The third problem is most troubling for teaching Sexton; teachers might emphasize the necessity for literature to confront and deal with controversial and uncomfortable themes such as suicide, mortality, madness. A discussion of the dangers of equating creativity and emotional illness might be helpful, even necessary, for some students. It's also important to demonstrate that Sexton wrote many poems of celebration, as well as of mourning.

Students often want to know how and why Sexton killed herself. They want to disapprove, yet they are often fascinated. I recommend one of two approaches. Either avoid the whole thing by not mentioning her suicide and by directing students toward the poems and away from Sexton's life; or engage the issue directly, in which case you need to allow some time to make thoughtful responses and guide a useful discussion that will illuminate more than one life and death.

Major Themes, Historical Perspectives, and Personal Issues

A balanced presentation of Sexton would include mention of her major themes, most of which are touched upon in the selection of poems here: religious quest, transformation and dismantling of myth, the meanings of gender, inheritance and legacy, the search for fathers, mother-daughter relationships, sexual anxiety, madness and suicide, issues of female identity.

Significant Form, Style, or Artistic Conventions

The problem of placement in the confessional school can be turned into an advantage by emphasizing Sexton's groundbreaking innovations in style and subject matter. Sexton's early poetry was preoccupied with form and technique; she could write in tightly constrained metrical forms, as demonstrated in *To Bedlam and Part Way Back* and *All My Pretty Ones*. She wrote in free verse during the middle and late phases of her poetic career. Most important is her gift for unique imagery, often centering on the body or the household.

Original Audience

Many of Sexton's readers have been women, and she has perhaps a special appeal for female readers because of her domestic imagery. She also found a wide readership among people who have experienced emotional illness or depression. But Sexton's appeal is wider than a specialist audience. She is exceptionally accessible, writes in deliberately colloquial style, and her diversity and range are such that she appeals to students from different backgrounds.

Comparisons, Contrasts, Connections

Among other confessionals, she can be discussed in context with Robert Lowell, Sylvia Plath, John Berryman, W. D. Snodgrass. Among women poets, she shares concerns of subject and style with Adrienne Rich, Denise Levertov, Sylvia Plath, Alicia Ostriker, and, in a different way, Maxine Kumin. It's also appropriate to mention her similarities to Emily Dickinson, another female New England poet who wrote in unconventional ways about personal subjects, religion, and mortality. Because she was a religious poet whose work is part of the questing tradition, she might be usefully compared with John Donne and George Herbert. Since many of her poems are spoken from the perspective of a child speaker, the standard literary tradition for comparative purposes can include Blake and Wordsworth, Vaughan and Traherne. Extra-literary texts that illuminate her work include selections of psychoanalytic theory, especially Freudian.

Questions for Reading and Discussion/
Approaches to Writing

1. I try to avoid giving students a predisposition to Sexton, and instead discuss difficulties and questions as they arise in discussion.
2. (a) Examine the range of Sexton's subject matter and poetic style.

    (b) Pick a theme in a Sexton poem and trace it in other poems she wrote.

    (c) In what sense is Sexton a religious poet? A heretic?

    (d) Examine several surprising, unconventional images from several Sexton poems. What makes them surprising? Successful?

    (e) If Sexton is confessional, what is it that she is confessing?

    (f) Compare one of Sexton's "Transformations" with the original version in the Brothers Grimm.

    (g) Select another poet with whom Sexton can be compared, such as a confessional poet, a feminist poet, a religious poet, and discuss similarities and differences in their perspectives.

    (h) What are some of the possible uses for poetry that speaks from the perspective of madness or of suicide?

Bibliography

Excellent articles on Sexton are most readily available in recent and forthcoming anthologies of criticism. Instructors can select articles that bear most directly on their concerns.

    Sexton: Selected Criticism, edited by Diana Hume George, University of Illinois Press, 1988, includes many previously published articles from diverse sources in addition to new criticism, as does *Anne Sexton: Telling the Tale*, edited by Steven E. Colburn, University of Michigan Press, 1988.

    Original Essays on Anne Sexton, edited by Frances Bixler, University of Central Arkansas Press, 1988, contains many new and previously unpublished selections.

    Critical Essays on Anne Sexton, edited by Linda Wagner-Martin, G. K. Hall, 1989, includes a number of reviews as well as essays and reminiscences.

    J. D. McClatchy's *Anne Sexton: The Poet and Her Critics*, Indiana University Press, 1978, is the original critical collection.

    Diane Wood Middlebrook's *Anne Sexton: A Biography* was published by Houghton Mifflin in 1991.

    Critics who specialize in Sexton or who have written major essays on her, whose works will be found in most or all of the above anthologies, include Alicia Suskin Ostriker, Diane Wood Middlebrook, Diana Hume George, Estella Lauter, Suzanne Juhasz, and Linda Wagner-Martin.

James Wright (1927–1980)

Contributing Editor: George S. Lensing

Classroom Issues and Strategies

The poems of Wright, on the surface, seem simple and accessible. Yet they also seem distinctively "poetic." Students might be asked to discuss *how* and *why* the poems are both simple and poetic. This could easily lead to a discussion of images in the poems, and examples from any of the four included here might be used. The example of the moon in "Having Lost My Sons, I Confront the Wreckage of the Moon: Christmas, 1960" might be a good illustration. Have the students identify the verbs with which the moon is introduced and discuss the cumulative effects of the moon imagery generally. Then have them identify the other images of city, frost, silos, graves, etc. How are these latter images used in contrast to the moon? Careful consideration should be given to the title. Finally, how does the phrase "the beautiful white ruins / Of America" at the end of the poem encapsulate and summarize the contrast between beauty and its opposites in the poem? This is a strategy, of course, of close reading adapted particularly to Wright's work.

Another strategy might be to consider Wright as a social poet addressing American society in the 1960s and 1970s. Ask the students what impression of America during those decades emerges from the poems. How, from the poems in the text, can you justify Wright's identity with those individuals outside middle-class American society? Who are those individuals? What do they have in common? What is the nature of their appeal to Wright?

Major Themes, Historical Perspectives, and Personal Issues

A typical theme explored in Wright's poetry is rural America versus the modern urban America of the middle class with its wealth, political power, and control over the oppressed. This theme was particularly relevant in the America of the 1960s and 1970s when Wright wrote. America was involved in the Vietnam War, and Wright sees that involvement as a kind of national illness.

Both a theme and a technique is Wright's movement inward and within the self, often through a rural or small-town setting. Images in particular lead him inwardly toward moments of sudden self-revelation: ("Flayed without hope, / I held the man for nothing in my arms" in "Saint Judas," or "I am lost in the beautiful white ruins / Of America" in "Having Lost My Sons," or "I have wasted my life" in "Lying in a Hammock at William Duffy's Farm in Pine Island, Minnesota."

Significant Form, Style, or Artistic Conventions

The "how" of a poem by Wright is intrinsic to the "what." Here, the participation of Wright in the "deep image" movement is important. "Lying in a Hammock at William Duffy's Farm in Pine Island, Minnesota" is a good example to illustrate that movement. The poet is located at the farm of a friend; he is recumbent in a hammock. His mind is not operating in the usual logical and rational way but is dream-like and given to random associations. The boundaries between human and non-human life are being erased through various kinds of personifications: the butterfly is "asleep" and "Blowing like a leaf." Cowbells "follow one another." Droppings "Blaze up." Images define the poet's free play of mind as he moves from the sight of the butterfly, to the sound of the cowbells, to the droppings of the horses, to the darkening of the evening, to the flying chicken hawk. The timing of the images and their cumulative play upon each other are crucial to this process. They are images of beauty, of metamorphosis in some cases, of things in their proper and natural locations. (The chicken hawk is "looking for home" and will undoubtedly find it.) However, the title tells us that the poet is not in his usual location, but the farm of a friend. Now he is profoundly drawn in to the images that surround him. The poem suddenly "leaps" to its conclusion: "I have wasted my life." That leaping occurs among the images that surround him and that startle him abruptly into a knowledge of himself. But the connection is not made through narrative exposition; it is left to the reader's own association and recognition of the images and their timing. The process has not been rational but almost surreal. This poem and other poems of the deep image depend upon the successful "leaps" and their effect upon the reader. How much does Wright's self-revelation, for example, become our own?

Original Audience

Poetry and poetry readings were very popular during the 1960s in America, especially on campuses where the resistance to the Vietnam War was also often centered. Wright gave many public readings at American colleges. His reputation grew steadily over the course of his career and was shortened by his death from cancer at the age of fifty-two.

Comparisons, Contrasts, Connections

An important influence upon Wright was the poet Robert Bly. (See *The Heath Anthology* headnote for Wright.) But other poets, like William Stafford, Louis Simpson, Robert Creeley, and Gary Snyder, were also writing in a similar mode; they knew and influenced each other. Wright also translated poetry by figures like Georg Trakl, Cesar Vallejo, Pablo Neruda, Juan Ramon Jimenez, and others. Their poems became important influences on his own work. An important magazine owned and edited by Bly—called the *Fifties* (during that decade), the *Sixties,* and for a brief time, the *Seventies*—published Wright's poems and translations as well as those of Bly and other figures of the deep image school.

Questions for Reading and Discussion/ Approaches to Writing

1. See the questions related to "Having Lost My Sons" in the first subsection above.
2. How is the figure of Judas, the betrayer of Christ, presented in the early sonnet "Saint Judas"? How does Judas anticipate and prefigure other outsiders in Wright's poems—especially Little Crow in "A Centenary Ode: Inscribed to Little Crow, Leader of the Sioux Rebellion in Minnesota, 1862"?
3. How is American society during the 1960s and 1970s depicted in Wright's poetry?
4. How do the various images in the poems and their "leaping" relation to one another lead to the conclusions usually expressed in the poems' last sentence?

Bibliography

See the bibliography at the end of the Wright headnote in the text.

Lawrence Ferlinghetti (b. 1919)

Contributing Editor: Helen Barolini

Classroom Issues and Strategies

Ferlinghetti's work is immediately accessible and appealing, and these qualities should be emphasized. He uses everyday language to articulate his themes. A problem could be his critique of social problems in America; conservative students may find him too sharply satiric about their image of this country. You might note that although Ferlinghetti articulates the "outsider" view of society, he also espouses hope for the future; for instance, poems like "Popular Manifest" (not in this anthology) give a sense of vision and expectation.

Tape recordings of Ferlinghetti reading can be effective.

Major Themes, Historical Perspectives, and Personal Issues

Ferlinghetti is a political activist and his poetical career spans and reflects thirty years of U.S. political history.

His personal voice brings poetry back to the people. He has done this not only as a poet, but as a publisher, editor, translator, and discoverer of new talent.

Significant Form, Style, or Artistic Conventions

Ferlinghetti has been prominently identified with the beat movement of the 1950s. It is important to consider the beat movement as an ongoing part of American bohemianism, and to contrast it, for example, with the expatriate movement of post–World War I.

The hip vocabulary can well be examined, and the beat experience of alienation can be connected with other marginals in the society.

Original Audience

The work of Ferlinghetti can be placed in the specific social context of the beat movement in the fifties—beats were the anarchists in a time of general post-war conformism.

Comparisons, Contrasts, Connections

Ferlinghetti can certainly be compared with his fellow beats, like Allen Ginsberg and Gregory Corso, and contrasted with other poets of the time—for instance, the more mannered Wallace Stevens. There is also much to compare, stylistically, with E. E. Cummings.

Questions for Reading and Discussion/ Approaches to Writing

1. With this particular poet, the most effective approach is to plunge right into the work. He elicits the questions.
2. Discuss the San Francisco Renaissance, which centered around Ferlinghetti's City Lights Bookstore.
3. What is the counterculture in America?

Bibliography

General

Charters, Samuel. *Some Poems/Poets: Studies in American Underground Poetry since 1945.* Oyez, 1971.

The Postmoderns: The New American Poetry Revised. New York: Grove, 1982.

Particular

Cherkovski, Neeli. *Ferlinghetti: A Biography.* New York: Doubleday, 1979.

Hopkins, Crale D. "The Poetry of Lawrence Ferlinghetti: A Reconsideration." *Italian Americana* 1, no. 1 (Autumn 1974): 59–76.

Kherdian, David. *Six Poets of the San Francisco Renaissance.* Fresno: Giligia Press, 1967.

Vestere, Richard. "Ferlinghetti: Rebirth of a Beat Poet." *Identity Magazine* (March 1977): 42–44.

Allen Ginsberg (b. 1926)

Contributing Editor: Linda Wagner-Martin

Classroom Issues and Strategies

Teaching Ginsberg requires addressing rampant stereotypes about the beats and the kind of art they created; i.e., the drug culture, homosexuality, Eastern belief systems, and, most important, the effects of such practices on the poem.

By showing the students what a standard formalist 1950s poem was, I have usually been able to keep them focused on the work itself. Ginsberg's long-lined, chant-like poems are so responsive to his speech rhythms that once students hear tapes, they begin to see his rationale for form. Connections with Walt Whitman's work are also useful.

Major Themes, Historical Perspectives, and Personal Issues

Ginsberg's dissatisfaction with America during the 1950s prompted his jeremiads, laments, "Howls." When his macabre humor could surface, as it does in "A Supermarket in California," he shows the balance that clear vision can create. His idealism about his country marks much of his work, which is in many ways much less "personal" than it at first seems.

Significant Form, Style, or Artistic Conventions

Consider the tradition of American poetry as voice dependent (Whitman and William Carlos Williams) rather than a text for reading. The highly allusive, ornate, "learned" poems of T. S. Eliot or Wallace Stevens have much less influence on Ginsberg's work, although he certainly knows a great deal about poetry. His poems are what he chooses to write, and he makes this choice from a plethora of models. The highly religious influence shapes much of his work (he once described himself as a Buddhist Jew with connections to Krishna, Siva, Allah, Coyote, and the Sacred Heart). Ginsberg was a personal friend of the Jewish philosopher Martin Buber. It was largely through Buber's influence that he gave up drugs.

"Howl," the first part of which appears here, is one of the most famous artifacts of the 1950s. Struggling to recover from the McCarthy trials that spelled doom for anyone charged with difference, the late

1950s was the edge of both promise and fear. The 1960s, with their recognition of the value of change and difference, were about to strike every American citizen, but "Howl" when it was first published in 1956 was still a threatening work. (A decade later, when a recording of the poet reading the work was played on radio, people responsible could have lost their jobs.) In alluding to the experiences of the beats, especially Carl Solomon, whom Ginsberg met when both were patients at the Columbia Psychiatric Institute in 1949, the poem brings into focus a quantity of events unknown to the (polite) literary world, a more advantaged world.

It also alludes to the travels of William S. Burroughs, whose first book *Junkie* (1953) was published through Solomon's efforts; Herbert E. Huncke, a con artist and junkie from New York; and Neal Cassady, a Denver hipster whose travels with Jack Kerouac were recreated in the latter's *On the Road* (1957). As a collective chronicle, the work draws on a number of people's experiences—all united in being marginal, offensive, and generally threatening to most academics and students.

Original Audience

Ginsberg's work can usefully be approached as protest as well as lament. Connections with the writings of racial minorities can help define his own Jewish rhythms.

Comparisons, Contrasts, Connections

Walt Whitman	Robert Creeley
William Carlos Williams	Langston Hughes
Theodore Roethke	Lawrence Ferlinghetti
Gary Snyder	Etheridge Knight
Denise Levertov	Pedro Pietri

Part II   New Communities, New Identities, New Energies

Lorraine Vivian Hansberry (1930–1965)

Contributing Editor: Jeanne-Marie A. Miller

Classroom Issues and Strategies

The primary problem that might be encountered is the student's lack of familiarity with black American drama. The images of blacks on the early American stage reflected their place in American life. Dramatic expression, exclusively by white authors, made of them contented, faithful slaves or servants, tragic figures of mixed blood, and comic characters. The comic figures were dominant.

Despite prejudice and racism, black playwrights were known in the American theater as early as 1823 when a play entitled *King Shotaway*, written by Mr. Brown (whose first name is uncertain) was produced by the African Grove Theater and Company. Also in the nineteenth century, William Wells Brown, a former slave, published *The Escape; or, A Leap for Freedom* (1858), and William E. Easton's play *Dessalines* was produced in Chicago (1893). From the beginning, the concern of most black playwrights has been the realistic depiction of the black experience.

During the twentieth century, growing out of the increased interest of American writers in folk material, came a renewed interest among white playwrights in blacks as source material for drama. Consider, for instance, Eugene O'Neill's *The Emperor Jones* (1920). The 1920s, the period of the Harlem Renaissance, also introduced the first serious (that is, nonmusical) dramas by black playwrights on Broadway—for example, Willis Richardson's *A Chip Woman's Fortune* (1923) and Garland Anderson's *Appearances* (1925).

One of the most popular plays on Broadway during the 1930s was *The Green Pastures* (1930), a black folk fable written by Marc Connelly, a white playwright. As the depression worsened, plays that protested against the social and economic conditions that sorely afflicted people were produced. Paul Peters and George Sklar's *Stevedore* (1934), for example, centers on a black militant hero who defends his rights as a man and a worker on the New Orleans docks.

Though blacks were gaining some experience on Broadway, in community theaters, and in drama groups in black institutions of higher learning, it was the Federal Theater Project, which grew out of the depression and provided work for unemployed theater people, that gave a major boost to blacks in theater. The post–World War II years found some white playwrights concentrating on the tense situation that existed when black soldiers, who had been in Europe fighting for democracy, returned to a segregated America. For instance, *Strange Fruit* (1945), a drama adapted from a novel by its author Lillian Smith and her sister Esther, makes a bitter commentary on racial segregation, intolerance, and injustice in this country.

Two dramas by black playwrights reached Broadway in the 1940s: white playwright Paul Green and Richard Wright's *Native Son* (1941) and Theodore Ward's *Our Lan'* (1947). The play *Native Son* is a dramatization of Wright's powerful novel about Bigger Thomas and the corrosive effects of American society on him. *Our Lan'* concerns a group of newly freed slaves who search for economic independence and security during the latter days of the Civil War and the early Reconstruction period.

Ironically, as the heightened period of the civil rights movement of the 1950s produced a plethora of plays by black writers affected by the mood of the country, white playwrights who employed black themes and characters returned to the traditional images of blacks. Consider, for instance, Berenice Sadie Brown, a black cook, in Carson McCullers's *A Member of the Wedding* (1950) and the black slave from Barbados who confesses to being a witch in Arthur Miller's *The Crucible* (1953) (the setting is the Salem witchcraft trials in 1692).

During the 1950s, Off Broadway teemed with plays by black writers: William Branch's *Medal for Willie* (1951) and *In Splendid Error* (1955); Alice Childress's *Trouble in Mind* (1955) and Loften Mitchell's *Land Beyond the River* (1957), for example. At the end of the decade, twenty-eight-year-old Lorraine Hansberry made her debut on Broadway with *A Raisin in the Sun* (1959). She was the first black woman to have a play produced on Broadway and the first black playwright and youngest playwright to win the New York Drama Critics Circle Award. The production was significant in other ways. Not only were the playwright and the cast, except for one, black, but so were the director and some of the investors. Blacks came out in large numbers to see this award-winning work that truthfully depicts a black working-class family who triumphs over the debilitating conditions of the ghetto. With *Raisin* American drama and blacks reached a new milestone. The play has been translated into over thirty languages and produced in many countries. In 1961 it became a film and in 1973 a Tony Award-winning musical.

Major Themes, Historical Perspectives, and Personal Issues

Some of the major themes of her works are as follows: the slave system and its effect on Americans; the deprivation and injustice suffered by blacks because of racism; moral choices; deferred dreams of black Americans; self-determination of African countries; ability to control one's own destiny; negative effects of voguish movements; and relationships between men and women. The major historical and personal issues that should be emphasized are slavery and the Civil War; contrasting portraits of slavery; the civil rights movement of the 1950s and 1960s, whose antecedents were in the black protest and revolt of slaves, such as Hannibal in *The Drinking Gourd*; and feminism.

Significant Form, Style, or Artistic Conventions

Hansberry followed the trend of realism. In her dramas she wished to illustrate character. As an artist she believed that all people had stature and that there were no dramatically uninteresting people. She searched for the extraordinary, the uniqueness in the ordinary. She embraced the social nature of art, and she dissected personality as it interacted with society. Her dramatic style included the use of colloquial speech, a sense of the rhythm of language, the use of symbolism, and departures from realistic speech into the lyrical.

Original Audience

Hansberry wrote for the general theater audience. The particular audience for whom *The Drinking Gourd* was written was the general television audience of 1960. The drama was commissioned by NBC for producer-director Dore Schary to initiate a series of ninety-minute television dramas commemorating the centennial of the Civil War. This drama was a pre-*Roots* work, which was to have exposed audiences to a portrait of slavery by a black writer. Since *Roots* was presented on television during the 1970s, audiences seem to be better educated about a black writer's point of view about the issue of slavery.

Comparisons, Contrasts, Connections

At the center of *The Member of the Wedding* (1950), a drama by Carson McCullers, a white writer, is a black cook who holds together the white family for whom she works. Unlike McCullers's play, in which the black cook's family is hardly ever seen, Hansberry's *A Raisin in the Sun* dramatizes the story of a black domestic and *her* family. It is a story told from inside the race. *The Drinking Gourd* treats the family relationships of a slave-owning family and their slaves.

Other dramas about slavery with which *The Drinking Gourd* may be compared and contrasted are the following by white authors: George L. Aiken's *Uncle Tom's Cabin* (1852), a dramatization of Harriet Beecher Stowe's novel; Dion Boucicault's *The Octoroon* (1859); James D. McCabe, Jr.'s *The Guerrillas* (1863); and James A. Herne's *The Reverend Griffith Davenport* (1899). The earliest extant play by a black writer is also about slavery: William Wells Brown's *The Escape* (1858).

Questions for Reading and Discussion/ Approaches to Writing

Some study questions that students might find useful are as follows:

1. (a) What is Hansberry's background?
   (b) What is her philosophy of art?
   (c) How does she move from the particular to the universal in her plays?
   (d) How does she use language in her plays?

Paper topics that have proved useful are as follows:

2. (a) The role of women in Hansberry's plays
   (b) Family relationships
   (c) Language in Hansberry's plays
   (d) Love between man and woman
   (e) Relationships between women and men

Bibliography

The introductions to *Les Blancs: The Collected Last Plays of Lorraine Hansberry*, written by Julius Lester for the 1972 edition and by Margaret B. Wilkerson for the 1983 edition, as well as the critical backgrounds by Robert Nemiroff in each of these editions.

The collection of essays and the bibliography that appear in the special issue of *Freedomways* (vol. 19, no. 4, 1979) entitled "Lorraine Hansberry: Art of Thunder, Vision of Light."

The first two chapters on Hansberry's life in Anne Cheney's book *Lorraine Hansberry*, Boston: Twayne Publishers, 1984.

A film entitled *Lorraine Hansberry: The Black Experience in the Creation of Drama*, Princeton, N.J.: Films for the Humanities, 1976.

Edward Albee (b. 1928)

Contributing Editor: Carol A. Burns

Classroom Issues and Strategies

The Zoo Story is accessible to most students even in introductory courses, and few students have difficulty in recognizing Albee's central point about the paucity of human relationships. However, teachers need to lead students to recognize how well crafted and "of a piece" the play is as well as how powerful (and equivocal) the play's final statement is.

I usually begin by encouraging students to see that while Jerry and Peter are obviously very different (not just in their life-styles but in their desire to reach and to be reached by other people), Jerry was only a short time ago as withdrawn from others as Peter (e.g., his relationships with women, his "please" and "when" letters). And, more importantly, the milieux in which Peter and Jerry live are similarly sterile. Peter's family life seems vapid. Jerry's rooming-house is a "zoo" in which all the residents are carefully separated from one another. The landlady is the one person who seeks contact with someone else and she is as psychically spent as her appearance suggests. She does not wish to establish an emotional relationship with Jerry; he is merely "the *object* of her sweaty lust" (my italics) which can easily be satisfied by a delusion. Initially, Jerry, in simply wanting to be left alone (like Peter, like most people, Albee would say), responded to the very different overtures from both the landlady and her dog by appeasement—conjure a fantasy for the lady, throw some meat to her dog—designed to gain him "solitary free passage." Jerry's "fall from physical grace" suggests his fall from spiritual grace as well, manifested in his blithe indifference to others.

A good question here for students is what Jerry learned from his encounter with the dog. Ironically, the dog was different from most people in that it tried to reach him. Indeed, Jerry finally regards the dog's attempt to bite him as an act of love for just this reason. And Jerry's feeding the dog was truly a hostile act because he was trying to prevent contact. Therefore, although Jerry gains his initial objective, "solitary free passage," he eventually understands that he has lost—"and what is gained is loss." Jerry learns that in his fallen world, the only contact that seems possible is with an animal, that it is hurtful (of course, any contact is potentially hurtful), and that it ultimately fails. Ironically, again, the dog recalls Jerry to his human nature and Jerry realizes that human relationships are now bestial (or worse). That Jerry is able to wrestle such an illumination from his innocuous tussle with his landlady's dog is testimony to his intelligence and sensitivity.

However, Peter is less willing to undergo the conversion process and he resists recognition of the truth implicit in Jerry's dog story. Having learned that in our present inhumane state, simple kindness alone no longer works, Jerry continues to use his mixture of kindness and cruelty to reach Peter because "the two, combined, together, at the same time, are the teaching emotion." Students are usually quick to see the metatheatrical nature of the play, the extent to which the director-actor Jerry leads the unknowing Peter through a preplanned scenario. The kindness and cruelty characteristic of Jerry's conversation with Peter early in the play now becomes physical as he first tickles and then shoves Peter off the bench that is an image of Peter's isolation. Cruelty then clearly takes the upper hand as Jerry physically and verbally assaults Peter. In fact, he whips Peter's feelings up to a frenzy so that he can engineer his own death at Peter's hands.

However bleak the play's final statement is, Jerry does succeed at what he so obviously set out to do, i.e., make contact with another person and convey his message to him. Peter's final understanding and the extent to which Jerry has reached him is communicated not with words alone but also with his "pitiful howl" of "OH MY GOD!" It is the howl of an animal. Peter is finally aware of people's basic animal nature, "what other people *need*." Interestingly, the zoo image carries both negative and positive connotations—people live in a zoo separated from one another by cages of their own making, but they can destroy their bars by recognizing their own basic animal nature. To become an animal is to become more fully human; as Peter says to Jerry, "You're an animal, too." This and Jerry's several repetitions of Peter's words, particularly the latter's final words, "Oh . . . my . . . God," suggest not only the men's unity but the respect Jerry now accords Peter.

Bibliography

Bennett, Robert B. "Tragic Vision in *The Zoo Story*." *Modern Drama* 20: 55–66.

Bigsby, C. W. E. *Albee*. Edinburgh: Oliver, 1969.

——, ed. *Edward Albee: A Collection of Critical Essays*. Englewood Cliffs: Prentice-Hall, 1975. See articles by Brian Way and Rose Zimbardo.

Cohn, Ruby. *Edward Albee*. Minneapolis: University of Minnesota Press, 1969.

Gabbard, Lucina P. "At the Zoo: From O'Neill to Albee." *Modern Drama* 19: 365–74. Compares *Zoo* to O'Neill's *The Hairy Ape*; provides some historical perspective on *Zoo*.

Nilan, Mary M. "Albee's *The Zoo Story*: Alienated Man and the Nature of Love." *Modern Drama* 16:55–59. Sees Jerry as incapable of genuine contact with other people.

Wallace, Robert S. "*The Zoo Story*: Albee's Attack on Fiction." *Modern Drama* 16:49–54. Sees *Zoo* as criticism of people's affinity for fiction instead of experience; deals with some metatheatrical aspects of *Zoo*.

Ralph Ellison (b. 1914)

Contributing Editor: Linda Wagner-Martin

Classroom Issues and Strategies

While readers often find an excerpt from Ellison's *Invisible Man* in anthologies, his 1944 story, "King of the Bingo Game," introduces many of his characteristic themes—issues of self-knowledge, marginalization, and postmodern angst in an evocative, surreal text. One of the last stories he wrote before starting the masterful *Invisible Man*, "King of the Bingo Game" integrates politics, history, and ritual with Ellison's grounding of African-American folklore. According to Robert G. O'Meally, it was the writer's use of black sermons, tales, games, jokes, boasts, dozens, blues, and spirituals that set his work apart from that of other mid-century African-American writers. His incorporation of folklore gave his work a richer textual base and thematically unified his aesthetic and the black community.

Useful exercises, for Ellison as well as Zora Neale Hurston, James Weldon Johnson, and even Nella Larsen, are discussions of that folklore. Because Ellison studied *American Humor* by Constance Rourke, a book from the 1930s that is still valuable, student reports on her work might be interesting; as would be those on specific secondary criticism of Ellison's unique style and sources for his writing. "King of the Bingo Game" is the kind of writing that benefits from both close reading and cultural theory applications. The same kind of student research on the more recent "magical realism" of the American South and Central American novelists would help to explain Ellison's blend of realism and absurdist, dreamlike fantasy.

Major Themes, Historical Perspectives, and Personal Issues

As in *Invisible Man,* here too the protagonist's question is, "Who am I?" and "How do I fit in this world?" Unemployed, poor, and worried about his sick wife, Ellison's "hero" still hopes he can succeed enough (he is still plagued with the remnants of the American Dream, which tells him that if he leads a good and moral life, and works hard, he will be prosperous and happy) to at least buy medicine for his wife. But the randomness of the spinning wheel closes off even that slim hope, and throughout the dreamlike stages of his realization that even if he should win, what he gains will be too little—that his battle is really with history and fate, not with any personal or individual existence—the character's behavior changes dramatically.

The changes are tied to interruptions from the myths that have brought him this far into the absurd, materialistic American modern world. Ellison sets the story in a movie theater, that place for learning about—and envisioning—the American Dream. The protagonist is hungry; the woman in front of him is eating peanuts, a symbolic southern product. He misses the South (Rocky Mountain, North Carolina, specifically) and in his nostalgia for the camaraderie he remembers having found there, the reader is shown that he has come North, made the crucial trip from the land of slavery to the land of freedom. Yet, having come North, he finds himself almost hopeless—poor, hungry, and afraid that people in this strange part of the country will think he is "crazy."

As he watches the love scene in the film, which acts as a catalyst for his worry about his wife Laura (a borrowed reference from the mainstream culture to the haunting "Laura," a popular ballad), his attention moves to the stream of white light coming from the projection room. Symbolic of both technology and the control of power (white ownership of the theater, of the film industry), the projectionists become, in the protagonist's interior monologue, those in control: "they had it all fixed. Everything was fixed." His fantasy is that the film will be shown "wrong" and will come to include a scene of sexuality. When rules don't work, it might be permissible to break them.

The last bit of foregrounding before the story proper begins—the Bingo game itself—is the protagonist's falling asleep, dreaming of narrowly escaping an oncoming train. Like a traditional hero, the protagonist should achieve something besides that escape—instead, he screams, and his neighbor gives him a drink of whiskey from his bottle. Still in the dark, ritually equated with his own blackness, he moves from seat to seat, positioning himself for the bingo drawing down front in the brightly lit arena of the stage.

The dialogue between the man running the bingo game and the protagonist is filled with ethnic references—"one of the chosen people," "boy," "all reet," coming down off the mountain, and so on. But the terror of being exposed to the eyes of the white culture, of being unable to control the button properly, and, at base, his recognition that nothing will come of even this "winning," lead him into the macabre, uncontrolled, and uncontrollable behavior that closes the story. In the midst of the audience's shouts that he get off the stage, revelling in what might be called power, he screams his plaintive, "Who am I?" His monologue in response to their rude reply is the theme for *Invisible Man*, another fiction about an essentially nameless character: "They didn't know either, he thought sadly. They didn't even know their own names, they were all poor nameless bastards. Well, he didn't need that old name; he was re-born. For as long as he pressed the button he was The-man-who-pressed-the-button-who-held-the-prize-who-was-the-King-of-Bingo." Ellison's reflection on names throughout the story, particularly the pointed reference to slaves' taking the name of their owners instead of any lineage of their own, undergirds his later exploration of the ways people are known in contemporary society.

"King of the Bingo Game" is an expression of the ultimate irony. The road North does not lead to freedom, the process of being saved does not lead to heaven, the work ethic has no reward—except jail, bereavement, and perhaps even insanity. And yet Ellison lays no blame on any explicit character, race, or people. Rather than a moral universe, his fiction takes place in a realistic one, in which people like winners—and only winners.

Major themes are alienation, in the great American tradition from the nineteenth century; separateness of black from black, as well as black from white; disenfranchisement from cultural norms and attitudes; sheer loneliness; the role of names and lack of names; cultural signals about belonging, possession, place.

Bibliography

Awkward, Michael. *Inspiriting Influences*, 1989.

Busby, Mark. *Ralph Ellison*, 1991.

Kostelanetz, Richard. *Politics in the African-American Novel*, 1991.

See headnote for additional material.

Martin Luther King, Jr. (1929–1968)

Contributing Editor: Keith D. Miller

Major Themes, Historical Perspectives, and Personal Issues

Context for "I Have a Dream"

Unfortunately, many students remain blissfully unaware of the horrific racial inequities that King decried in "I Have a Dream." In 1963, southern states featured not only separate black and white schools, churches, and neighborhoods, but also separate black and white restrooms, drinking fountains, hotels, motels, restaurants, cafes, golf courses, libraries, elevators, and cemeteries. African-Americans were also systematically denied the right to vote. In addition, southern whites could commit crimes against blacks—including murder—with little or no fear of punishment. The system of racial division was enshrined in southern custom and law. Racism also conditioned life in the North. Although segregationist practices directly violated the Fourteenth and Fifteenth Amendments of the Constitution, the federal government exerted little or no effort to enforce these amendments. Leading politicians—including John Kennedy, Robert Kennedy, and Lyndon Johnson—advocated racial equality only when pressured by King, James Farmer, John Lewis, Ella Baker, Fannie Lou Hamer, and other activists who fostered nonviolent social disruption in the pursuit of equal rights. Fortunately black students are often knowledgeable about the civil rights era and can help enlighten the rest of the class.

Content for "I Have a Dream"

"I Have a Dream" has been misconstrued and sentimentalized by some who focus only on the dream. The first half of the speech does not portray an American dream but rather catalogues an American nightmare. In the manner of Old Testament prophets, Frederick Douglass's "What to the Slave Is the Fourth of July?" oration and Vernon Johns, King excoriated a nation that espoused equality while forcing blacks onto "a lonely island of poverty in the midst of a vast ocean of material prosperity."

Context for "I've Been to the Mountaintop"

By the time of King's final speech, the heyday of the civil rights movement was over. Large riots in major cities and the divisive issue of the
Vietnam War had shattered the liberal consensus for civil rights and created an atmosphere of crisis.

Content for "I've Been to the Mountaintop"

King clearly wanted to energize his listeners on behalf of the strike. He
analyzed the Parable of the Good Samaritan, identifying the Memphis
strikers with the roadside victim and urging his listeners to act the part
of the Good Samaritan. He also arranged the strike in a historical
sequence that featured the Exodus, the cultural glory of Greece and
Rome, the Reformation, the Emancipation Proclamation, the Great
Depression, and—late in his address—the lunch counter sit-ins for civil
rights and his major crusades in Albany, Birmingham, and Selma. By
placing the struggle in Memphis in the company of epochal events and
his own greatest achievements (neglecting to mention his more recent,
unsuccessful campaign in Chicago), King elevated the strike from a
minor, local event to a significant act in the entire Western drama.

Significant Form, Style, or Artistic Conventions

African-American Folk Pulpit: "I Have a Dream"

Important in reaching King's enormous and diverse audience were the
resources of black folk preaching. These resources included call-and-
response interaction with listeners; a calm-to-storm delivery that begins
in a slow, professorial manner before swinging gradually and rhythmi-
cally to a dramatic climax; schemes of parallelism, especially anaphora
(e.g., "I have a dream that . . ."); and clusters of light and dark
metaphors. Black students can frequently inform their classmates about
these time-honored characteristics of the African-American folk pulpit
that give life to King's address.

African-American Folk Pulpit: "I've Been to the Mountaintop"

Elements of the folk pulpit that animate "Mountaintop" include call-
and-response interaction; calm-to-storm delivery; the apocalyptic tone of
much evangelistic, revivalist preaching ("The nation is sick. Trouble is in
the land"); and the updating of a prominent analogy (or typology) of
black Christians equating blacks with Old Testament Hebrews and slave-
owners with the Egyptian Pharaoh. King resuscitated the analogy by
labeling his opposition as Pharaoh and by urging solidarity among
Pharaoh's oppressed and segregated slaves. Concluding "Mountaintop,"

King boldly likened himself to Moses and foretold his own death prior to blacks'/Hebrews' entry into the Promised Land.

Familiar Symbolism: "I've Been to the Mountaintop"

As with "I Have a Dream," King defined his appeal by explaining nonviolence and by applying standard patriotic and religious symbols to his effort. His protest became an exercise of the First Amendment; an attempt to rebuild a New Memphis akin to a New Jerusalem; a later chapter in the book of Exodus; and in his last sentence, a merging of his vision with that of "The Battle Hymn of the Republic."

Original Audience

King spoke "I Have a Dream" to an immediate crowd of 250,000 followers who had rallied from around the nation in a March on Washington held in front of the Lincoln Memorial. His audience also consisted of millions across the nation and the world via radio and television.

Important in reaching King's enormous and diverse audience were the resources of black folk preaching, including call-and-response interaction with listeners.

King's audience in "Mountaintop" consisted of 2,000 or so ardent and predominantly black followers gathered to support the cause of striking garbage workers in Memphis, Tennessee.

Comparisons, Contrasts, Connections

Old Testament prophets, Frederick Douglass's "The Fourth of July" oration, John Lewis's speech preceding "I Have a Dream," and speeches by Malcolm X.

In "I Have a Dream" are the voices of Lincoln, Jefferson, Shakespeare, Amos, Isaiah, Jesus, Handel's *Messiah*, "America the Beautiful," a slave spiritual, and the black folk pulpit.

Bibliography

For a valuable analysis of King's 1963 address, see Alexandra Alvarez, "Martin Luther King's 'I Have a Dream': The Speech Event as Metaphor," *Journal of Black Studies* 18 (1988): 337–57.

I also encourage teachers to compare and contrast "I Have a Dream" with Frederick Douglass's "The Fourth of July" (*Rhetoric of Black Revolution*. Ed. Arthur Smith, Boston: Allyn and Bacon, 1970. 125–53).

Useful for such a discussion is Robert Heath, "Black Rhetoric: An Example of the Poverty of Values," *Southern Speech Communication Journal* 39 (1973): 145–60.

For background on King, see James Cone, "Martin Luther King, Jr.: Black Theology—Black Church," *Theology Today* 40 (1984): 409–20; James Cone, *Martin and Malcolm and America*, Maryknoll, NY: Orbis, 1991; Keith D. Miller, *Voice of Deliverance: The Language of Martin Luther King, Jr., and Its Sources*, New York: Free Press, 1992.

Playing records or audio-video tapes of King's speeches substantially facilitates discussion of the oral dynamics of the black pulpit that nurtured King and shaped his discourse. The PBS series "Eyes on the Prize" is especially useful. "I Have a Dream" is available from Nashboro Records and, under the title *Great March on Washington*, from Motown Records. Tapes of these and many other addresses by King are available from the Southern Christian Leadership Conference in Atlanta.

Malcolm X (1925–1965)

Contributing Editor: Keith D. Miller

Classroom Issues and Strategies

Malcolm X is one of the most controversial figures one could study. Most students, recognizing his enormous impact on recent American culture, will revel in discussions—or passionate debates—about his merits. Those who have read the popular *Autobiography of Malcolm X*—or seen the Spike Lee movie based on it—will argue that Malcolm X was foolish to be duped by Elijah Muhammed or brilliant to recognize that he had been duped; that Malcolm X reached a beautiful, universal vision at the end of his life or that he did not; that he was unforgivably sexist or that his sexism was typical of the period.

Students will invariably attempt to relate Malcolm X to the 1991 racial uprising in Los Angeles and to other issues in race relations, including those on their own campuses.

The first need is to direct the students, at the very least initially, to focus on "The Ballot or the Bullet" instead of jumping to an ultimate verdict on the *Autobiography*, on Malcolm X, or even on race relations in America.

Major Themes, Historical Perspectives, and Personal Issues

Malcolm X used the same major rhetorical strategy in "The Ballot or the Bullet" that he employed in other speeches and in the *Autobiography*. He attacked the well-established, sometimes unexamined tendency of African-Americans to identify with white America, passionately insisting that blacks identify instead with Africans, with their slave ancestors, and with each other. In that vein, he declares, "No, I'm not an American. I'm one of the twenty-two million black people who are victims of Americanism." Speaking to American blacks, he explains, "You're nothing but Africans. Nothing but Africans."

The use of "X" as a replacement for a given last name is part of this rhetorical strategy. Malcolm X urged all African-Americans to reject their last names, which were those of slave-owners, replacing them with "X" to stand for the lost African names of their ancestors. Thousands belonging to the Nation of Islam adopted this practice. Because the "X" substituted for last names, it defined members of the Nation as a single "family" of brothers and sisters, aunts and uncles. The use of "X" also bracketed the names of other African-Americans, implicitly declaring that all of them were mistakenly identifying with whites, their slave masters.

The issue of violence loomed large in Malcolm X's rhetoric. In this speech and elsewhere, he refused to repudiate violence, realizing that most of the white Americans who applauded Martin Luther King's nonviolence would not react nonviolently themselves in the face of brutality. By refusing to embrace nonviolence, Malcolm X made King look more moderate and more palatable than he would otherwise have appeared.

By the time of "The Ballot or the Bullet," race dominated America's domestic agenda. Millions watched police dogs tear into young African-American children protesting for integration in Birmingham. Presidents Kennedy and Johnson responded by proposing major civil rights legislation, which passed in the summer following "The Ballot or the Bullet."

Though many believed that such an initiative signified racial progress, Malcolm X disagreed. Not only did conservative whites fail blacks, he maintained, so did "all these white liberals" who were supposedly allies. As he explains in this speech, many white liberals belonged to the Democratic party, which was often dominated by southern segregationists. Unlike white liberals and the NAACP, Malcolm X did not want blacks to integrate white hotels. He wanted blacks to own the hotels.

Malcolm X's own bleak childhood and criminal young adulthood helped shape his radical views and gave him insight into the lives of his primary audience—hundreds of thousands of African-Americans trapped in the ghettos of America's largest cities.

Significant Form, Style, or Artistic Conventions

Malcolm X's jeremiads owe something to the appeals of Marcus Garvey, an earlier leader who instilled racial pride, and to Malcolm X's own father, a Garvey disciple. Even though Malcolm X advocated Islam instead of Christianity, his style and impact derive in part from the role of the black Protestant preacher—a revered patriarchal figure free to denounce from the pulpit whomever he saw fit.

Original Audience

Malcolm X delivered "The Ballot or the Bullet" to a predominantly African-American meeting in Cleveland of the Congress of Racial Equality (CORE), which was shifting from nonviolent protest to Malcolm X-like black nationalism. Helping provoke this shift were speeches like this one, which was received enthusiastically.

Students can compare this talk to those that Malcolm X gave to largely white listeners. See, for example, the addresses collected in *Malcolm X Speaks at Harvard* (1991), edited by Archie Epps.

Comparisons, Contrasts, Connections

Comparing the language of King and Malcolm X can be helpful. In some ways their analyses of the evils institutionalized in American life are quite similar. Though Malcolm X's blowtorch denunciations are harsher than King's, the main difference lies in King's willingness to grant whites a way around the guilt that King so skillfully evoked. In King's rhetorical world, whites—even ardent segregationists—could listen, change their ways, and learn to practice love and democracy. King claimed that his methods could actually win opponents over to his view.

During most of his career Malcolm X gave whites no such break. Instead he demanded separation from whites. He regarded integration not as a goal, but as a sentimental fiction. Toward the end of his life, he seemed more accepting of some whites, but his evolving vision was not entirely clear.

As James Cone explains, toward the end of their lives, King and Malcolm X were, in some ways, thinking alike. Both realized that, without economic muscle, masses of blacks would never prosper, no matter how much this nation espoused the theory of integration. In "I've Been to the Mountaintop," King stressed the need for economic self-help and racial solidarity. For both leaders, the divisions of economic class loomed as important as—and were inseparable from—the issue of race.

Questions for Reading and Discussion/ Approaches to Writing

Who is Malcolm X's primary audience? If it is primarily African-Americans, why did he address whites as well and the white news media? Why did he (co)author a best-seller often read by and, in some ways, aimed at whites? Why did he criticize whites in such an uncompromising fashion instead of flattering his audience as speakers usually do? Why did he define grounds of disagreement with whites instead of grounds of agreement, which orators usually seek and are taught to seek? Why did he also often criticize blacks who heard him—sometimes calling them "brainwashed"—and why did they applaud him when he did so?

If Malcolm X was sincere in rejecting nonviolence, why did he characteristically refuse to carry a gun and always, in fact, practice non-violence? If blacks were brutally oppressed, as he claimed, and if retaliation was justified, as he claimed, why did he never lead such retaliation? Since he gave fiery speeches but never organized either nonviolent or violent protests against whites, was he sincere? Or was he a "paper tiger"? Did he mean to be taken literally? If not, how did he mean to be taken?

Bibliography

Millions continue to read the *Autobiography of Malcolm X* (1965), co-authored by Alex Haley. I strongly recommend *Remembering Malcolm* (1992) by Malcolm X's assistant minister Benjamin Karim, who shows a sensitive leader inside the Muslim mosque and reveals information available nowhere else.

No thoroughly reliable, full-scale biography of Malcolm X exists. Many details about his life (especially before his public career) remain unknown. In *Malcolm* (1991), a detailed, provocative biography, Bruce Perry claimed that the *Autobiography* features blatant exaggerations and outright falsehoods. But some of Perry's own claims seem unsupportable. Joe Wood compiled *Malcolm X: In Our Own Image* (1992), which contains helpful essays by Cornel West, Arnold Rampersad, John Edgar Wideman, Patricia Hill Collins, and others. In *Martin and Malcolm and*

America (1991), James Cone usefully compares and contrasts King and Malcolm X, as do John Lucaites and Celeste Condit in "Reconstructing Equality: Culturetypal and Counter-Cultural Rhetorics in the Martyred Black Vision." *Communication Monographs* 57 (1990): 5–24.

Alice Walker (b. 1944)

Contributing Editor: Marilyn Richardson •

Major Themes, Historical Perspectives, and Personal Issues

1. The bemused black women for whom a creative, witty, and compassionate union with the universe is as natural as breathing.
2. The volcanic forces that go into the creative life and work of a heroine like the narrator. See her account of her encounter with Bessie Smith.
3. The theft of black music by white musicians who do not understand what they are performing.

Significant Form, Style, or Artistic Conventions

The narrative voice in this story is deceptively informal and uneducated. Gracie Mae Still is in fact extremely subtle and sophisticated. The reader must put aside assumptions about her speech and learn from her on her own terms.

Bibliography

"Alice Walker Reads 'nineteen fifty-five' " and an "Interview with Alice Walker" in which she discusses the story are tapes available from The American Audio Prose Library, P.O. Box 842, Columbia, MO 65205.

Grace Paley (b. 1922)

Contributing Editor: Rose Yalow Kamel

Classroom Issues and Strategies

The challenge in teaching "The Expensive Moment" lies in the fact that most students in the conservative 1990s define family values in direct contrast with the middle-aged Faith Asbury. Her character is a redefinition of that term; she is a secular humanist who is unabashedly sexual, and who has a relationship with her children that encourages them to argue, confront, and engage with her, a single parent, as an equal. Furthermore, younger students not only unfamiliar with this story's context—the aftermath of the Chinese Cultural Revolution—but ignorant about *our* government's confrontations with its youth in the 1960s and 1970s, may find it difficult to understand why Faith mourns Rachel, her friend's daughter who went underground as a result of an "expensive moment" of choice to bomb military plants and prisons housing radical activists like Rachel herself.

I would therefore (1) encourage discussion and journal writing about the delicate balance that single mothers face maintaining their own personhood amidst political and personal biases that marginalize them; (2) expose students to other Paley stories told from Faith Asbury's first-person point of view (for example, "A Conversation With My Father," "Friends," "Ruthie and Edie"), that depict this eponymous maternal narrator in her youth and middle age as receptive to change, yet consistent in advocating a green and sane world where children can live out their lives; (3) invite guest speakers familiar with the cultural context of the 1960s and 1970s; and (4) show political documentaries questioning establishment values, for example, "Letters From Vietnam," footage about the Kent State disaster juxtaposed with the Tiananmen Square massacre. As sophisticated media users, students will be better able to see the interrelatedness of national/international generational conflict.

Major Themes, Historical Perspectives, and Personal Issues

Paley's is a multicultural perspective, historically aware of the great waves of immigration that peopled the vibrant New York neighborhoods she evokes so well. Woven into the texture of her fiction are the problems of grass-roots working-class mothers who as urban, leftist Jews link playground politics with global conflict. Moreover, Paley is always aware that female sexuality is a source of literary creativity but never separates the craft of literature from the personal and political contexts in which gender conflicts arise.

Overarching is Paley's womanism, maternal and comradely rather than self-reflexive. It is that womanism that, despite the difference in their cultural backgrounds, links Faith with Xie Feng, newly arrived from mainland China to visit New York's teeming Vesey Street. Of an age, both women understand patriarchy, history, and the need to fight for a future to endure their loss of lovers, husbands, and especially, beloved children.

Significant Form, Style, or Artistic Conventions

Paley uses a stylistic collage—fragments and ellipses, a merging of past and present tense—that conveys a sense of wholeness in which setting, character, and point of view coalesce and render with absolute fidelity a small urban world. Tonal irony as well as a near-perfect ear for dialogue make Paley a writer's writer.

Structurally, Paley's stories resemble women's diary writing—fragmented, fact-focused, immersed in the transitory, seemingly disconnected aspects of daily life that define women's lives.

Original Audience

Paley's reading audience for her earlier stories about growing up as a second generation immigrant child ("The Loudest Voice," for example) was cosmopolitan, college-educated, and attuned to literary experimentation. Because the audience was not as responsive to political feminism as today's readers, Paley was considered a seamless stylist.

Comparisons, Contrasts, Connections

Some thematic comparison and contrast can be made with Tillie Olsen, whose ethnic and politically activist background is similar to Paley's. Olsen's "I Stand Here Ironing" and *Tell Me a Riddle* involve class and intergenerational conflicts; in fact, in Olsen's novella, feisty, elderly Jews, like Paley's parents, hold on to the secular humanism that they brought with them to America. But Olsen uses women's sexuality more sparingly, making it a problem of gender, rather than physical urgency for women. Furthermore, Olsen's lush, elegiac style differs from Paley's deft use of irony, humor, economy, earthiness. Another writer reminiscent of Paley in her depiction of the parent-child conflict and woman-bonding in a fluid and changing world is Amy Tan, whose novel *The Joy Luck Club* has bits of dialogue and irony similar to Paley's, though Tan's humor is more life-affirming.

Questions for Reading and Discussion/Approaches to Writing

1. (a) Keep a journal focusing on the importance of place in your life. To what extent does place influence identity?
   (b) Write a first-person narrative focusing on your memory of exploring an experience or discovering an idea markedly different from those of your parents.
2. Compare the neighborhood settings in two other Grace Paley stories, "An Interest in Life" and "The Long-Distance Runner." Discuss the way settings in these stories make the first-person narrator feel integrated or marginal in her community.
3. Keep a collection of tapes or photograph albums focusing on intergenerational ties as well as conflicts.

Bibliography

Blanche Gelfant, "Grace Paley: Fragments for a Portrait in Collage," *New England Review*, 3: 285, is a lucid analysis of Paley's narrative style.

"To Aggravate the Conscience: Grace Paley's Loud Voice" in Rose Kamel's *Aggravating the Conscience: Jewish American Literary Foremothers in the Promised Land*, New York: Peter Lang, 1989, 115–49, is an analysis of Paley's short fiction in context with her life and beliefs.

Adrienne Rich (b. 1929)

Contributing Editor: Wendy Martin

Classroom Issues and Strategies

Rich's poetry is extremely accessible and readable. However, there are a few allusions that cannot be understood and, from time to time, there will be references to events or literary works that will not be immediately recognized by students. This material or these references are glossed in the text so the student can understand the historical or literary context.

Other problems occur when there is fundamental hostility to the poet over feminism. The instructor will have to explain that feminism simply means a belief in the social, political, and economic equality of women and men. Explain, also, that Rich is not a man-hater or in any way unwilling to consider men as human beings. Rather, her priority is to establish the fundamental concerns of her women readers.

Major Themes, Historical Perspectives, and Personal Issues

It is important to read these poems out loud, to understand that Rich is simultaneously a political, polemical, and lyric poet. It is important also to establish for the poems of the '60s, the Vietnam War protests as background as well as the feminist movement of the '60s and '70s.

It is also important to emphasize that in many respects the '60s and '70s were reaction to the confinement of the '50s and the feminine mystique of that period. In addition, stress that the political background of the poems by Adrienne Rich connects the personal and the political.

Significant Form, Style, or Artistic Conventions

Rich employs free verse, dialogue, and the interweaving of several voices. She evolves from a more tightly constructed traditional rhymed poetry to a more open, loose, and flexible poetic line. The instructor must stress again that poetic subjects are chosen often for their political value and importance. It is important once again to stress that politics and art are intertwined, that they cannot be separated. Aesthetic matters affect the conditions of everyday life.

Original Audience

Adrienne Rich has written her poetry for all time. While it grows out of the political conflicts and tensions of the feminist movement and the antiwar protests of the sixties and seventies, it speaks of universal issues of relationships between men and women and between women and women that will endure for generations to come.

Comparisons, Contrasts, Connections

The feminist activists poets like Audre Lorde, June Jordan, and Carolyn Forché would be very useful to read along with Rich. Also, it might be useful to teach poets like Allen Ginsberg and Gary Snyder, who were, after all, poets of the beat movement of the late '50s and early '60s. They were poets with a vision, as is Rich.

Questions for Reading and Discussion/ Approaches to Writing

1. It might be useful to discuss the evolution of the more free and more flexible line that begins with Walt Whitman and the greater flexibility of subject matter that also begins with Whitman and Emily Dickinson and to carry this discussion on through William Carlos Williams and Allen Ginsberg to discuss the evolution of the free verse that Rich uses.
2. Any writing topic that would discuss either the evolution of flexible poetics or aesthetics—that is, a concern with people's actual lived experiences, for the way they actually talk and think.

   In addition, in the case of Rich, any paper that would link her to other women writers of the twentieth century (and the nineteenth, for that matter) would be useful. Rich is often quoted as an important cultural critic who provides the context for feminist thought in general in the twentieth century. It might also be useful to assign parts of her prose, either in collected essays or in *Of Woman Born*.

Bibliography

I would highly recommend my own book: *An American Triptych: The Lives and Work of Anne Bradstreet, Emily Dickinson, and Adrienne Rich*. I am recommending this book because it provides both a historical and an aesthetic context for the poetry of Rich. It links her to earlier traditions that have shaped her work and demonstrates effectively how American

Puritanism and American feminism are intertwined. It gives a lot of biographical material as well as historical background and literary analysis.

Bernard Malamud (1914–1986)

Contributing Editor: Evelyn Avery

Classroom Issues and Strategies

Jewish in style and character types, Bernard Malamud's fiction appeals to a broad range of students who appreciate the author's warmth, ironic humor, and memorable characters. Above all, they find his blend of the universal and the particular appealing and unique.

A writer who uses fantasy and history, who creates tragic and comic characters, who can write realistically and metaphorically, Malamud will challenge and delight students of varied backgrounds. Occasionally, "Yiddish" expressions or Jewish ritual will have to be explained, but, for the most part, meaning will be derived from context.

Since the effects of suffering are central to Malamud's fiction, students should learn that his Jews symbolize all victims and that his characters cannot be easily categorized as heroes or villains.

Major Themes, Historical Perspectives, and Personal Issues

Writing in the last third of the twentieth century, Malamud was aware of social problems: rootlessness, infidelity, abuse, divorce, and more, but he believes in love as redemptive and sacrifice as uplifting. Often, success depends on cooperation between antagonists. In "The Mourners," for example, landlord and tenant learn from each other's anguish. In "The Magic Barrel," the matchmaker worries about his "fallen" daughter, while the daughter and the rabbinic student are drawn together by their need for love and salvation.

If Malamud's readers are sometimes disappointed by ambiguous or unhappy endings, they are often reassured about the existence of decency in a corrupt world. Malamud's guarded optimism reflects several influences. He cites American authors, Nathaniel Hawthorne and Henry James, as guides to moral and spiritual struggles. Like them, Malamud holds individuals responsible for their behavior. He also admires Russian writers, Fyodor Dostoyevski and Anton Chekhov, for their vibrant portrayal of the self versus society. Although he does not mention other Jewish writers as influences, he concedes "a common fund of Jewish experience and possibly an interest in the ethical approach."

In interviews, Malamud credits his hardworking "Yiddish" parents and their Eastern European immigrant generation with providing models of morality, but he emphasizes that humanity is his subject, that he uses Jews to communicate the universal just as William Faulkner created a universe from a corner of the American South.

Despite his universality or perhaps because of it, Malamud resembles a number of American Jewish authors, including earlier twentieth century writers, such as Abraham Cahan, Anzia Yezierska, and Henry Roth, as well as post–World War II authors such as Isaac Bashevis Singer, Saul Bellow, and Philip Roth. Because Jewish fiction can reflect life's uncertainties and absurdities, it has broad appeal to contemporary readers, who applaud the attempt of ordinary people to determine their fate. Such themes, however, are evident in non-Jewish literature that Malamud recognized when he described himself, in a 1975 interview, as "an American . . . a Jew, and . . . a writer for all men."

His universality, however, is rooted in distinctive character types, settings, and details. Thus, the "schlemiel," a common type in Eastern European Yiddish literature, appears in some American Jewish fiction. Although at times a victim of bad luck, the "shlemiel" compounds his problems by choosing wrongly. Yakov Bok (in *The Fixer*), fleeing his Jewish identity, Morris Bober (in *The Assistant*), attempting to burn his store down, and Leo Finkle (in "The Magic Barrel"), insisting that his future wife be young and beautiful, learn to revise their values, reject assimilation, materialism, and conformity; and embrace sacrifice and spirituality. Trapped in depressing, even dangerous settings, in cramped, deteriorating stores, suffocating apartments, condemned buildings, in a nation, Russia, where Jews are at risk everywhere, Malamud's characters are both archetypal Jews and suffering humanity. Malamud's awareness of Jewish pain is best portrayed in *The Fixer*, a novel of extreme anti-Semitism in Tzarist Russia, which for many critics evokes the Holocaust.

Although a serious writer, Malamud uses humor to underscore the preposterous, to highlight grief, and to instruct readers. Thus Frank Alpine (in *The Assistant*) tumbles into the grocer's grave, Seymour Levin (in *A New Life*) lectures with his pants unzipped, and Yakov Bok (in *The Fixer*) rescues an anti-Semite whose gratitude will later lead to Bok's persecution. If Malamud's fiction produces sorrow, it also provokes laughter, albeit nervous laughter.

Original Audience

A best-selling, critically acclaimed author, Bernard Malamud, like Isaac Bashevis Singer and Philip Roth, earned success with the publication of his early Jewish works, *The Magic Barrel* (a collection of short stories) and *The Assistant* in the late 1950s. Although the American Jewish literary renaissance peaked in the 1960s and 1970s, writers like Malamud continue to be read and enjoyed. In fact, his reputation is steadily growing as students are introduced to his works. Moreover, the general interest in ethnicity draws readers to Jewish literature, where they discover that Bellow, Malamud, Ozick, and Singer, to name a few, speak to all sensitive, intelligent readers.

Comparisons, Contrasts, Connections

As indicated earlier, Malamud's fiction may be compared and contrasted with works by certain European, American, and Jewish authors. Like Fyodor Dostoyevski's characters, Malamud's protagonists are tormented, guilt-ridden, and paranojac. Their suffering recalls *Crime and Punishment* and *Notes from the Underground* as well as Nathaniel Hawthorne's and Henry James's psychological tales. While Malamud has been identified as an American Jewish writer, his work can be differentiated from Saul Bellow's (considered more cerebral) and from Philip Roth's (judged more satiric). Perhaps the best of his old world stories resemble those of Isaac Bashevis Singer, whose work attempts to reconcile the old world and the new.

Questions for Reading and Discussion/ Approaches to Writing

1. A variety of questions can be posed about Malamud's fiction. Is Malamud, for example, a Jewish writer or a writer who happens to be Jewish? Since "The Magic Barrel" includes a rabbinic student and a matchmaker, how universal is the story? Does the story have a happy ending? What happens? Is this tale representative of the author's works?

2. More ambitious assignments can analyze literary influences on Malamud, his style in comparison to other Jewish writers, or male-female relationships; or possibly an imaginative option such as rewriting the story's conclusion.

Bibliography

Since Malamud's death in 1986, his reputation continues to grow. With the establishment of the Bernard Malamud Society and the publication of a newsletter, Malamudian scholars are kept apprised of research and conferences. For further information contact Dr. Evelyn Avery at Towson State University, Towson, Maryland, 21204; or Dr. Lawrence Lasher, English Department, University of Maryland, Baltimore County, Baltimore, Maryland, 21228.

Hisaye Yamamoto (b. 1921)

Contributing Editor: King Kok Cheung

Classroom Issues and Strategies

It is useful to spend some time introducing Japanese American history and culture, especially the practice of "picture bride" (which sheds light on the marriage of Mr. and Mrs. Hayashi) and the style of communication among Issei and Nisei.

It would be helpful to analyze "Seventeen Syllables" in terms of a double plot: the overt one concerning Rosie and the covert one concerning Mrs. Hayashi. Students often relate to the interaction between mother and daughter and are appalled by Mr. Hayashi's callousness.

Instructors may also consider showing *Hot Summer Winds,* a film written and directed by Emiko Omori, and based on Yamamoto's "Seventeen Syllables" and "Yoneko's Earthquake." It was first broadcast in May 1991 as part of PBS's *American Playhouse* series.

Major Themes, Historical Perspectives, and Personal Issues

1. The relatively restrained interaction between Issei (first generation) and Nisei (second generation) as a result of both cultural prescription and language barrier;
2. The historical practice of "picture bride," according to which the bride and the groom had only seen each other's photos before marriage;
3. The theme of aborted creativity; and

4. The sexual and racial barriers faced by the author herself, who came of age in an internment camp during World War II.

Significant Form, Style, or Artistic Conventions

Stress the narrative strategies of the author, especially her use of naïve narrator. While Yamamoto may have been influenced by the modernist experimentation with limited point of view, she also capitalizes on the scant verbal interchange between her Japanese American characters to build suspense and tension.

Original Audience

The work has always been intended for a multicultural audience, but the reader's appreciation will undoubtedly be enhanced by knowledge of Japanese American history and culture.

Comparisons, Contrasts, Connections

1. James Joyce (*Dubliners*) for the use of naïve narrator;
2. Grace Paley for the interaction between husbands and wives, between immigrant parents and their children; and
3. Wakako Yamauchi and Amy Tan for the relationship between mothers and daughters.

Questions for Reading and Discussion/ Approaches to Writing

1. (a) How do cultural differences complicate intergenerational communication in "Seventeen Syllables"?
   (b) Are there any connections between the episodes about Rosie and those about her mother?
   (c) What effects does the author achieve by using a limited point of view?
2. (a) How does Yamamoto connect the two plots concerning Rosie and her mother in "Seventeen Syllables"?
   (b) Analyze the theme of deception in "Seventeen Syllables."
   (c) Compare the use of the daughter's point of view in Hisaye Yamamoto's "Seventeen Syllables" and Grace Paley's "The Loudest Voice."

(d) Compare the communication between parents and child in "Seventeen Syllables" and in Grace Paley's "The Loudest Voice."

(e) Contrast the story "Seventeen Syllables" and the film *Hot Summer Winds*.

Bibliography

Cheung, King-Kok. "Introduction." *Seventeen Syllables and Other Stories* by Hisaye Yamamoto. New York: Kitchen Table, 1988. xi–xxv.

——, ed. *"Seventeen Syllables"/Hisaye Yamamoto*. New Brunswick: Rutgers University Press, forthcoming in 1994.

Crow, Charles L. "The *Issei* Father in the Fiction of Hisaye Yamamoto." *Opening Up Literary Criticism: Essays on American Prose and Poetry*, edited by Leo Truchlar, 34–40. Salzburg: Verlag Wolfgang Neugebauer, 1986.

——. "A MELUS Interview: Hisaye Yamamoto." *MELUS* 14.1 (1987): 73–84.

Kim, Elaine H. *Asian American Literature: An Introduction to the Writings and Their Social Context*. Philadelphia: Temple University Press, 1982. Chapter 5.

McDonald, Dorothy Ritsuko and Katharine Newman. "Relocation and Dislocation: The Writings of Hisaye Yamamoto and Wakako Yamauchi." *MELUS* 6.3 (1980): 21–38.

Nakamura, Cayleen. *"Seventeen Syllables": A Curriculum Guide for High School Classroom Use in Conjunction with "Hot Summer Winds."* Los Angeles: Community Television of Southern California, 1991.

Yogi, Stan. "Legacies Revealed: Uncovering Buried Plots in the Stories of Hisaye Yamamoto." *Studies in American Fiction* 17.2 (1989): 169–81.

——. "Rebels and Heroines: Subversive Narratives in the Stories of Wakako Yamauchi and Hisaye Yamamoto." In *Reading the Literatures of Asian America*, edited by Shirley Geok-lin Lim and Amy Ling, 131–50. Philadelphia: Temple University Press, 1992.

Pedro Pietri (b. 1944)

Contributing Editor: Frances R. Aparicio

Classroom Issues and Strategies

As with other Nuyorican poets, the language switching and references to either Spanish or Puerto Rican culture need to be explained. Preparing a handout with a glossary and giving a small introduction to life in El Barrio (perhaps with photos, pictures, or videos) might also be helpful.

Pedro Pietri has produced two records, "Loose Joints" and "One is a Crowd" (Folkway Records). If available, they would be good for classroom use.

Some students might have a difficult time understanding the anger and the bitterness of Pietri's voice against "the system," an issue for disagreement and discussion.

Major Themes, Historical Perspectives, and Personal Issues

Pietri's poetry is political poetry in its most direct sense: a poetry of denunciation, directed to create a cultural consciousness among the members of the Puerto Rican community. Other themes are the demythification of authority figures and social institutions (government, schools, church, "the system"); alienation in contemporary urban life; a surrealistic search for the truth in the irrational and the absurd. In addition, the political status and the poverty levels for Puerto Ricans in New York can be discussed in light of Pietri's denunciation of "the system." How do students feel about the welfare system and about the Hispanic poor in this country? About the First World/Third World dichotomies within the United States?

Significant Form, Style, or Artistic Conventions

"Puerto Rican Obituary" can be read as a parody of an epic poem (the dream and the search and the epic deeds of a nation inverted), and within an antiaesthetic attitude. Again, as in Laviera, this is oral poetry to be recited and *screamed*. In *Traffic Violations*, Pietri's poetry falls within the surrealistic mode, fragmented images, search for the absurd in everyday life, irrational, surprising metaphors and imagery, humor, and sarcasm.

Original Audience

Though quite contemporary, Pietri's poetry has to be understood in terms of its original objective of addressing the masses as oral poetry. This is important in order to achieve a true understanding of his use of popular language, anger, and antiaesthetic style.

Comparisons, Contrasts, Connections

I believe that fruitful comparisons may be drawn if one looks into Allen Ginsberg and other poets of the beat generation and of the '60s (as poetry of social denouncement, protest, and harsh, antiacademic language). Also compare with contemporary African-American poets who deal with urban themes, alienation, and social injustice.

Questions for Reading and Discussion/ Approaches to Writing

1. For "Puerto Rican Obituary," questions dealing with theme: What is it denouncing? How are the "puertorriqueños" portrayed? Analyze image of *death*. Would you define it as an "epic" poem? What is the use of Spanish in the poem? Consider the poem as an example of urban literature; define the utopian space that Pietri proposes.
2. Paper topics might deal with Puerto Rican migration; use of Spanish and English (for aesthetic effect); functions of humor and irony; analyze the poems as "outlaw" literature.

Bibliography

Two general articles on Puerto Rican writers discuss Pietri's work:

Acosta-Belén, Edna. "The Literature of the Puerto Rican National Minority in the United States." *The Bilingual Review* 5:1–2 (Jan.–Aug. 1978): 107–16.

Cruz, Arnaldo. "Teaching Puerto Rican Authors: Modernization and Identity in Nuyorican Literature." *ADE Journal* published by the Modern Language Association (December 1988).

Rolando Hinojosa-Smith (b. 1929)

Contributing Editor: Juan Bruce-Novoa

Classroom Issues and Strategies

Most students know nothing about the author or the context of this selection. Useful information can be found in Hinojosa's interview included in *Chicano Authors, Inquiry by Interview* (Juan Bruce-Novoa).

I find it useful to ask students to write an accurate version of something they have experienced as a group: a short reading, a brief video, or even a planned interruption in class by an outsider. They then must consider the differences in the accounts of the same event. Sometimes I ask them to write an accurate description of an object I place in their midst; then we compare versions.

They respond to the element of different versions and observe how justice, represented in the newspaper reports, is not necessarily served. They ask if the person is guilty, raising the question of what is guilt.

Major Themes, Historical Perspectives, and Personal Issues

The major themes are the search for an accurate version of any event in the midst of the proliferation of information; the conflict between oral and written texts; the historical disregard for the Chicano community in South Texas and elsewhere; and the placement of the author in the role of cultural detective. The selection can be read as an allegory of Chicano culture within U.S. history in which Mexicans have been criminalized without a fair hearing.

Significant Form, Style, or Artistic Conventions

The basic form is that of a criminal investigation, related to the detective story. Yet it breaks with the genre in that it does not resolve the case by discovery of the culprit; instead, the frame of the story maintains its position, and—if anything—gets worse, the degradation of process reflected in the errata contained in the final segment.

Fragmentation does not bother students much now. The small units emphasize the postmodern experience of life as short sound bites.

The style is marked by shifts in voices, an attempt to capture the community in its speech patterns.

Original Audience

In the period of Chicano renewal (1965–1975) there was a need expressed then in literature to search for communal history. It was aimed at an audience that would sympathize with the victim, considering itself an abused and ignored group in a society controlled by the forces represented in the newspaper clippings that frame the story. This has changed. Now audiences are much less sympathetic to marginal peoples, and even Chicanos are not as willing to accept the old version of oppression of minority groups.

Comparisons, Contrasts, Connections

Faulkner's creation of a fictional county in several works coincides well with Hinojosa's project. The use of multiple voices to give different perspectives is quite similar.

Questions for Reading and Discussion/
Approaches to Writing

1. I ask students to consider what is history. What is news reporting? What is a fact? I often ask them to look up the etymology of fact and consider its relation to manufacture.
2. Assign the reporting of an imaginary event; give them the basic facts and characters and even an official summary statement. Then have them reconstruct the fragments as seen from one perspective. Compare the papers.

Bibliography

Refer to the headnote in the text for complete information.

Rudolfo Anaya (b. 1937)

Contributing Editor: Raymund Paredes

Classroom Issues and Strategies

Bless Me, Ultima is a *bildungsroman* and can be compared usefully to other works of this type, notably James Joyce's *A Portrait of the Artist As a Young Man*. Another important quality of *Bless Me, Ultima* is its heavy reliance on Mexican folklore, particularly such well-known legends as "La Llorona." There are many collections of Mexican and Mexican-American folklore that would give students a sense of the traditions that influence Anaya's novel. I recommend, for example, Americo Paredes's *Folktales of Mexico* (which has a very useful introduction) and *Mexican-American Folklore* by James O. West. Another important issue to consider is how Anaya tries to impart a flavor of Mexican-American culture to his work. In the excerpt from *Bless Me, Ultima*, Anaya uses Mexican names, Spanish words and phrases, and focuses on one of the strongest institutions of Mexican-American life, the Catholic church. If it is true that much of American culture and literature grow out of Protestantism, it would be worth examining how those parts of American culture that are based in Catholicism are distinctive.

Major Themes, Historical Perspectives, and Personal Issues

The protagonist of *Bless Me, Ultima* is Antonio, who is coming of age at the conclusion of World War II. Participation in the war has clearly had a dramatic impact on Antonio's older brothers, who now regard the rather isolated life of central New Mexico as dull and confining. Clearly, Antonio's community is in a state of transition and its citizens must face the inevitability of greater interaction with the world beyond their valley. Not far from Antonio's community, at White Sands, the atomic bomb is being tested. Anaya uses the bomb not only to represent the unprecedented capacity of the human race to annihilate itself but to symbolize the irresistible encroachment of modern technology not only in rural New Mexico but everywhere.

Perhaps the major question that Anaya confronts is how Mexican-Americans can retain certain key traditional values while accepting the inevitability—and desirability—of change. In dealing with this issue,

Anaya places the boy Antonio under the tutelage of the wise *curandera* (folkhealer), Ultima, who prepares her charge for the future by grounding him in the rich Spanish and Indian cultures of his past. For Ultima, tradition is not confining but liberating.

One of the striking characteristics of *Bless Me, Ultima* is its critical stance towards Catholicism, which is presented here as rigid, intimidating, and, at least to Antonio and his friends, largely unintelligible. The Catholic God is punishing while Antonio and his friends long for a nurturing deity. In attacking certain aspects of Catholicism, Anaya follows a long line of Latin American, Mexican, and Chicano writers including José Antonio Villarreal and Tomás Rivera.

Significant Form, Style, or Artistic Conventions

Bless Me, Ultima is a fairly conventional novel structurally, although Anaya does use such devices as stream of consciousness, flashbacks, and shifting narrators. As noted above, the key formal and stylistic question is how Anaya attempts to present his novel as a distinctly *Chicano* work of fiction. Again, Anaya employs Spanish words and names (a boy called Florence, for example, from the Spanish "Florencio") and focuses on important cultural events in Chicano experience. But for the most part, in terms of formal qualities and structure, *Bless Me, Ultima* is very much a contemporary American novel.

Original Audience

Bless Me, Ultima is a work that intends to explain and depict Mexican-American culture in New Mexico for a general American audience. Nevertheless, Anaya's presentation of Mexican-American culture is relatively "thick" so as to appeal to Chicano readers as well.

Comparisons, Contrasts, Connections

Bless Me, Ultima has clearly been influenced by Joyce's *A Portrait of the Artist as a Young Man*. Another interesting juxtaposition is with *Native Son*, Richard Wright's account of a young man—older than Antonio—who comes of age without much of a sense of his past and with few prospects in the harsh, urban environment of Chicago. Anaya's presentation of the Catholic Church can be fruitfully compared to that of José Antonio Villarreal in *Pocho*; Anaya's focus on Mexican-American childhood is complemented nicely by Tomás Rivera's *. . . y no sé lotragó la tierra* and Sandra Cisneros's *The House on Mango Street*.

Questions for Reading and Discussion/ Approaches to Writing

1. The excerpt from *Bless Me, Ultima* focuses on events surrounding Lent. Students can be asked to write about their experiences of this occasion or other important religious events. Comparing different sorts of religious experiences could be very useful.

2. As Anaya presents Catholicism, the Church emphasizes punishment and damnation rather than forgiveness and salvation. What is the effect on Antonio and his friends? How do they respond to church practices and rituals? Do students have any ideas about how religion might be presented to children more positively and successfully?

3. Have the students consider the *bildungsroman* as a literary form. Why is it so enduring? How would the students write one of their own lives? What would be the central experiences they would focus on?

Bibliography

See headnote in *The Heath Anthology*.

Ernest J. Gaines (b. 1933)

Contributing Editor: John F. Callahan

Classroom Issues and Strategies

The simplicity and tautness of Gaines's "The Sky Is Gray" sometimes lulls students to sleep and leads them, at first, not to look for some of the abiding, archetypal patterns in this story. Partly, this is due to the young boy's voice. Given the changes in race relations between the time in which the story was set, then written, and now, students need to read very carefully to pick up the nuances of this 1940s social milieu.

Instructor and students should read large chunks of the story out loud. Secondly, background on this milieu is very helpful; for this reason I urge that Gaines's essay "Miss Jane and I" (*Callaloo* 1, no. 3 [May 1974]) be offered as a companion to the story.

Students often ask about the actuality of segregation—they wonder whether Gaines's details are accurate. In addition, they ask whether the story's voice is consistently that of the young boy James.

Major Themes, Historical Perspectives, and Personal Issues

The story is about a young boy having to grow up earlier than he might have wished or than the adults in his family might have wished because his father is serving in World War II. The boy's mother must be father as well as mother to James. He learns about courage and dignity, about pain, and about the love and will that make pain bearable. The story also shows breaks in the color line enforced by Jim Crow laws and customs.

Significant Form, Style, or Artistic Conventions

How authentic are young James's voice and point of view? How (and why) does Gaines rely on the oral tradition of story-telling in his fiction?

Original Audience

Gaines has said over and over again that he writes especially for young people, with particular reference to the young whites and, preeminently, the young blacks of the South. That is worth exploring along with three different layers of time: (1) the story's time of the 1940s; (2) the writer's time of the mid-1960s; and (3) the reader's changing moment.

Comparisons, Contrasts, Connections

Other relevant stories in Vol. 2 of the anthology include: Faulkner's "Barn Burning"; Steinbeck's "Flight"; Wright's "The Man Who Was Almost a Man"; Ellison's "King of the Bingo Game"; and McPherson's "A Solo Song: For Doc."

Questions for Reading and Discussion/ Approaches to Writing

1. When does James become a man?
2. How does James come into his own voice?

Bibliography

See the special issue of *Callaloo* 1, no. 3 (May 1978) devoted to Gaines and his work.

Callahan, John F. "The Landscape of Voice in Ernest J. Gaines's *Blood-line*." *Callaloo* 7, no. 1 (Winter 1984): 86–112, especially pp. 86–90, 96–99.

James Baldwin (1924–1987)

Contributing Editors: Trudier Harris and John Reilly

Classroom Issues and Strategies

Problems surround Baldwin's voicing the subjectivity of characters, the great sympathy he awards to the outlook of the marginalized. Students normally meet the underclass as victims perhaps objectified by statistics and case studies. For that matter, students who are not African-American have difficulty with the black orientation arising from Baldwin's middle-class characters: the artists and other, more conventionally successful people.

The strategies flow from the principle that people do not experience their lives as victims, even if Baldwin's popular social autobiographical essay *Notes of a Native Son*—the portion where he recounts contracting the "dread, chronic disease" of anger and fury when denied service in a diner—might be useful in raising the issue of why Baldwin says every African-American has a Bigger Thomas in his head. The anger may become creative, as might the pain. A companion discussion explores the importance of blues aesthetic to Baldwin: the artful treatment of common experience by a singular singer whose call evokes a responsive confirmation from those who listen to it. In addition, an exploration of the aesthetic of popular black music would also enhance the students' understanding.

Within a literary context, the strategies should establish that fictional narrative is the only way we know the interior experience of other people. The imagination creating the narrative presents an elusive subjectivity. If a writer is self-defined as African-American, that writer will aim to inscribe the collective subjectivity under the aspect of a particular character. Of course, the point is valid for women writers and other groups also, as long as the writers have chosen deliberately to identify themselves as part of the collective body.

Major Themes, Historical Perspectives, and Personal Issues

Themes of personal importance include the significance of community identification, the communion achieved in "Sonny's Blues," for example; the conflicted feelings following success when that requires departure from the home community; the power of love to bridge difference. The chief historical issue centers on the experience of urbanization following migration from an agricultural society. The philosophical issue concerns Baldwin's use of religious imagery and outlook, his interest in redemption and the freeing of spirit. Interestingly, this philosophical/religious issue is often conveyed in the secular terms of blues, but transcendence remains the point.

Significant Form, Style, or Artistic Conventions

Baldwin's frequent use of the first-person narration and the personal essay naturally associates his writing with autobiography. His fiction should be discussed in relation to the traditions of African-American autobiography which, since the fugitive slave narratives, has presented a theme of liberation from external bondage and a freeing of subjectivity to express itself in writing. As for period, his writing should be looked at as a successor to polemical protest; thus, it is temporally founded in the 1950s and 1960s.

Original Audience

In class I ask students to search out signs that the narrative was written for one audience or the other: What knowledge is expected of the reader? What past experiences are shared by assumption? Incidentally, this makes an interesting way to overcome the resistance to the material. Without being much aware that they are experiencing African-American culture, most Americans like the style and sound of blues and jazz, share some of the ways of dress associated with those arts and their audiences, and know the speech patterns.

Comparisons, Contrasts, Connections

One can make a comparison with Herman Melville's *Benito Cereno* and Richard Wright's *Native Son*. The basis is the degree of identification with African-Americans accomplished in each. How closely does the writer approach the consciousness of the black slave and street kids?

Measure and discuss the gap between the shock felt by Delano and the communion of the brothers in Baldwin's story.

Questions for Reading and Discussion/ Approaches to Writing

Keeping in mind that James Baldwin's first experiences with "the word" occurred in evangelical churches, see if that influences his use of the "literary word."

What does Baldwin's short story tell you about the so-called ghetto that you could not learn as well from an article in a sociology journal?

College students are responsive to questions of the ethics of success. They may raise it with this story of "Sonny's Blues" by wondering why the narrator should feel guilty and even by speculating about what will happen to the characters next.

Bibliography

" 'Sonny's Blues': James Baldwin's Image of Black Community." *Negro American Literature Forum* 4, no. 2 (1970): 56–60. Rpt. in *James Baldwin: A Collection of Critical Essays*, edited by Keneth Kinnamon, 139–46. Englewood Cliffs, N.J.: Prentice-Hall, 1974. Also reprinted in *James Baldwin: A Critical Evaluation*, edited by Theman B. O'Daniel, 163–69. Washington, D.C.: Howard University Press, 1977.

James Alan McPherson (b. 1943)

Contributing Editor: John F. Callahan

Classroom Issues and Strategies

Students are unfamiliar with the railroads and the extent to which black men were a fraternity in the service jobs on the trains. There is some need to explain the argot of railroading, to familiarize students with the vocabulary and syncopated accents of the black vernacular.

Involve students with the rich variations of the oral tradition. Get them telling stories, in particular stories of how they met and came to know people of very different backgrounds because of summer jobs. It helps to read chunks of the story out loud.

Students are often interested in Youngblood's attitude toward the story-teller and the story-teller's attitude toward Doc Craft.

Major Themes, Historical Perspectives, and Personal Issues

The complexity and richness as well as the hardships of the lives lived by black traveling men; the initiative and kinship developed by the black workers; the qualities of the trickster; also the ways racism surcharges the attempts by blacks and whites to master situations and each other. Once again, the fact that the story is told by an old-timer about to quit (in 1964 or so) to Youngblood—the college student in a temporary job— about working on the road for the last twenty years or more sets up important contrasts between the past and the present, particularly the impact of technology on older ways of work and life.

Significant Form, Style, or Artistic Conventions

The relationship of oral story-telling as an initiation ritual to McPherson's craft of fiction writing, particularly his resolve to initiate readers of all races into a facet of their culture passing quickly out of sight.

Comparisons, Contrasts, Connections

See Baldwin's "Sonny's Blues"; Ellison's "King of the Bingo Game"; Walker's "Nineteen Fifty-Five"; and Silko's "Lullaby."

Questions for Reading and Discussion/ Approaches to Writing

What is the significance of the name Doc Craft?

Bibliography

Ellison, Ralph and James McPherson. "Indivisible Man." *Atlantic* (December 1970): 45–60.

McPherson, James. "On Becoming an American Writer." *Atlantic* 242, no. 6 (December 1978): 53–57.

Mari Evans

Contributing Editors: Joyce Joyce and John Reilly

Classroom Issues and Strategies

In her Afro-centric writing, Evans challenges readers to accept that she directs her words to African-Americans. Tone and references in the poetry make these uninvited readers feel excluded. In response, they may be dismissive.

This must be directly confronted with some discussion of the "special orientation" of other writers. Does Robert Frost write for the descendants of Irish and Italian immigrants in the New England cities? If not directly, then does he obliquely say something to the urban citizens, to us? In addition, the appearance of vernacular speech in writing sanctioned as poetry creates a stir of interest in the question of whether or not there is an inherently acceptable language for literature.

Major Themes, Historical Perspectives, and Personal Issues

Mari Evans puts a high value upon culture, which makes the language of a poem and the alleged commercialism of other poets cause for battle. In her belief that control of language can make a difference and that a poem is an act of resistance and social construction, this dissident poet calls for an exploration of the theory of culture. The valorization of culture must be associated with the black liberation movement, black political power, and the ideas of revolution advanced in those causes during the 1960s and 1970s.

Significant Form, Style, or Artistic Conventions

The free verse form, reflecting a belief in the native orality of poetry and the political need to "perform" poetry in the community, helps to define the meaning of Evans's remark that poems are wholes. This poetry can be related to other performative lyrics such as the blues and popular song.

Original Audience

This is a fundamental issue for Evans. She has rejected the double consciousness identified by W.E.B. Du Bois in *Souls of Black Folk* (1913) by addressing her work to a black audience. This can be studied in class, at the risk of denaturing the poetry, by talking about it as a technique of a school of poetry and by a brief discussion of the new black aesthetic developed by Larry Neal, Amiri Baraka, Hoyt Fuller, et. al.

Comparisons, Contrasts, Connections

Evans may be compared with Allen Ginsberg in order to show the similarity of avant-garde positions regarding popular American culture. This places Evans in a literary, historical context that illustrates a shared purpose among authors seeking to create a new voice. She may be compared to Gwendolyn Brooks with an eye to the creation of a character. For example, looking at "We Real Cool" and "I Am a Black Woman" could lead to a useful discussion of the uses of voice to characterize.

Questions for Reading and Discussion/
Approaches to Writing

1. Prepare annotations for the historical references in the second stanza of "I Am a Black Woman."
2. Look back at the poetry of Emily Dickinson and note the similarities and differences between Dickinson's "I Dwell in Possibility" and Evans's "conceptuality."

Bibliography

Evans's own critical writing is most illuminating. Her book *Black Women Writers* is an excellent source of statements.

June Jordan (b. 1936)

Contributing Editor: Agnes Moreland Jackson

Classroom Issues and Strategies

Students of the 1960s and early 1970s (as well as today's college-age youth) thought about and acted on nonfamilial kinships, that is, relationships between individuals *having agency*; groups, personhood in the community, space or turf—local/national/global; responsibility—private and corporate; power/powerlessness; most of the "-isms" and phobias of historical and contemporary societies worldwide. These are some of the recurring subjects in Jordan's three poems included in *The Heath Anthology* and throughout her volumes of poetry and essays. She belongs to the world (though it despises and rejects her); and her voice of discovery, pain, rage, and resolution penetrates our minds and emotions. College students, therefore, recognize her concerns while also wondering sometimes whether Jordan's societal and world portrait is "as bad" as her texts declare. Even those as wounded as she describes herself have to think deeply to make the connections, see the intricate patterns, and analyze situations to determine Jordan's accuracy or error about social and human conditions. Because the issues in her poetry reflect our everyday experiences, we can comprehend Jordan's poetry and note correspondences between and among the following: Jordan's observations and protestations; daily news about victims of violence whose lives are affected by political and economic decisions. An invitation to discuss the poems here could prompt students' own sharing of their personal experiences (of physical or emotional assault, acceptance or rejection of opportunity, and reaction to media images, health, and health services).

Moreover, *hearing* Jordan is crucial to appreciating and understanding the power of her poetry. Beyond urging my students to read all poetry aloud (and we read aloud in class), I stress the rich *orality* of poetic expression by many African-Americans (from Dunbar to Hughes and Brown, from Hayden and Walker and Brooks to Evans and Sanchez and Cortez, as well as Lorde, Knight, Reed, Clifton, and Harper), among whom Jordan is outstanding for the "being-spoken-now" qualities of her poems. Two of the "talking passages" (describing aptly the entire 114 lines) in "Poem about My Rights" are its opening and lines 45 to 49. Reading this poem aloud in a class need not be difficult in any college for at least two reasons: its personal, intimate, talking-directly-to-you quality and the generally acknowledged present-day awareness of the twenty-five percent probability that rape might become real to any woman in the U.S. Single voices (including those of male students) reading the poem in sequence diminish possible embarrassment over the sustained and repeated use of the words "rape," "penetrate," and "ejaculate" as reality and as metaphor. The poem's insistence upon the *equal status* of *all* oppressions stimulates serious discussion that includes not only homo- and bisexuality; instead, interest remains for persistent philosophical quests to engage and understand freedom and responsibility, law and justice, power and respect, and so on. Students usually agree with the linking of all oppressions, not withstanding the risk of having to reveal their own characteristics and/or prejudices. Anglo males, especially, need time and much reassurance that female peers understand the socially constructed bases of male behavior deemed to be oppressive, for Jordan denounces hurtful action, not its causes—including females complicit in maintaining patriarchal privilege to oppress.

"To Free Nelson Mandela" has the oral qualities of a ritual chant. Its repetitions enhance (1) recognition of the many years of Mandela's imprisonment and—hence—(2) the near miracle of his survival which invokes urgent and continually growing *cosmic* demands that he be freed, and (3) the power and rightness of a wife's loyalty *and work*—instead of withdrawal into seclusion (hence, no Penelope is she but a warrior who has taken up the battle). However protracted, however gross, atrocities do not dehumanize their victims, nor can horror outlast living "waters of the world" as they "turn to the softly burning/light of the moon." Ironically, almost mystically, atrocities eventually cause oppressed people, however despised, to come together in reaffirmation and in ritual, including the ceremonies of life to be lived fully before dying. (Cf. African slaves in the Western world, their understanding of self-worth, i.e., somebodiness conferred by a *believed-in* God—despite the ineffable horrors of bondage.)

Major Themes, Historical Perspectives, and Personal Issues

These three poems reveal the speakers' firm understanding that their respective experiences (or those witnessed and reported on in "To Free Nelson Mandela") validate the deduction by the speaker in "Poem about My Rights" that she and all other oppressed persons, nations, and peoples are victims because they are *viewed by their torturers* to be *wrong*. Therefore, *wrong* are the victims enumerated in lines 7 through 12 in

"To Free Nelson Mandela": the "twelve-year-old girl," "the poet," "the students," "the children." "[M]urdered Victoria Mxenge" (1.17) was *wrong* to have been a lawyer who "defended [B]lacks charged with political crimes" (*The Hollywood Reporter*, July 19, 1991), writes the reviewer of the hit musical "Sarafina," based on the horrors of and spiritual triumphs over South African apartheid. Martyred in 1985 in the midst of her daring and skillful work, "Durban human rights lawyer" (*Agence France Presse*, June 22, 1993) Mxenge was killed (by the official police, think most in the world) "the day before she was scheduled to defend 17 . . . [Black activists] on charges of treason" (Los Angeles *Times*, August 29, 1991). Her ANC-supporter spouse, Griffiths Mxenge, also a lawyer, had been murdered in 1981.

These data, only the tip of the iceberg, demonstrate again Jordan's total immersion in the lives of oppressed people of color wherever they suffer in the world. Revelations in the 1990s—most carried in newspapers around the globe—about allegedly police-perpetrated murders in South Africa during the mid-1980s were not news to Jordan, who in 1989 had published the Mandela poem among other "new" poems composed between 1985 and 1989. From line 36 through line 57 of "To Free Nelson Mandela," Jordan commemorates the beginning-to-heal black township community of Lingelihle (outside Cradock), where in 1985 (as reported in *The Guardian* of August 11, 1992) "[f]rom all over South Africa, tens of thousands of mourners converged on . . . [the township] . . . for the funeral of . . . [four Black activists]" including Matthew Goniwe, an "immensely popular leader" in a " 'backveld revolution' [that had swept] South Africa" in 1983. Less poetic than Jordan's rendering of Goniwe's transformational impact on his comrades in suffering is the following very helpful newspaper explanation of why his death was felt so deeply by so many:

> Son of a domestic servant and a seller of firewood, he had inspired the community to form a residents' association which demanded urgent reforms in the dusty, poverty-stricken township. Studious, quiet, small and bespectacled, Goniwe had raised educational standards, given self-respect to unemployed young [B]lacks and stopped much of the drinking and pot smoking. Repeatedly detained and accused of agitating, he remarked, "[Agitation] is not required when you have apartheid—the greatest agitator of all."
>
> (*The Guardian*, 8/11/92)

The journalistic furor in 1992 about events in 1985 was sparked by the publication in June 1992 of an official, top-secret message "dated June 7,

1985" that revealed senior officers in South Africa's security forces to have plotted the murders of Goniwe and three others. On March 9, 1991, the Chicago *Tribune* had carried a report of Amnesty International's having cited the death of Victoria Mxenge among other crimes against human rights.

In her 1976 essay "Declaration of an Independence I Would Just as Soon Not Have" (in the 1981 collection of essays *Civil Wars* published by Beacon Press), in which she remarks on the practical necessity of folk's uniting and working together to effect changes toward justice, Jordan writes of the "hunger and . . . famine afflicting some 800 million lives on earth" as "a fact that leaves . . . [one] nauseous, jumpy, and chronically enraged." She says also that "with all . . . [her] heart and mind . . . [she] would strive in any way . . . to eradicate the origins of . . . [the] colossal exploitation and abuse" experienced by "[t]he multimillion-fold majority of the peoples on earth [who] are neither white, nor powerful, nor exempt from terrifying syndromes of disease, hunger, poverty that defies description, and prospects for worse privation or demeaning subsistence" (115–16; 117). Jordan's rage at injustices and violations of personhood, as well as her compassion and empathy, are large and constant, as can be recognized by even a quick reading of her poetry and essays.

Although not among her most recent poems, "Moving Towards Home" is as significant as any to be related to Jordan's personal life, a life informed by her love of black people, a love that anchors her love for, and work and yearning for, freedom and justice for all oppressed people. She can relate to, can feel as, can *be* a Palestinian because the space, the room for living has become smaller and smaller geographically and in all other ways that destruction, death, bigotry, and hatred have crowded out life. "[T]o make our way home" would be to reclaim life, to reclaim "room" for "living" for ourselves and oppressed others. (In September, 1993 the Israelis and the Palestinians took their first steps toward that "way home" for both peoples.)

Significant Form, Style, or Artistic Conventions

Like many contemporary black and other poets of the U.S., Jordan uses language boldly and fully, not shying away from stereotypically or conventionally "ugly" words or ideas. Thus, she writes about what is real and what should not be: all manner of injustice, repression, oppression; diverse kinds of denial of self- and personhood. "Poem about My Rights" captures most completely the unbounded range of Jordan's subjects, as well as the rich juxtaposing and combining of free verse, linearly arranged sentences, parallelism, unpunctuated parenthetical remarks, repetition, freely (but *not* randomly) used virgules or slashes to hold or pull ideas together. Opening the poem *in medias res* gives form to Jordan's repeated thesis that self-determination is precluded by *all* oppressions and *any* oppression—occurring in any order at any age anywhere on the earth, and perpetrated by nominal friends (e.g., parents, members of one's own racial, sexual, occupational, and gender group) or recognized enemies. Jordan makes situational analogies and projections that meld all aspects of her being into one seamless *personal:* family; politics—local, national, worldwide, as well as racial and sexual; geography—general space, particular places, personified places, urban and rural spaces; history; esthetics; economics; her body and the bodies of others; sexism, racism, classism, ageism.

Comparisons, Contrasts, Connections

As is true for her contemporaries Adrienne Rich and Audre Lorde, sexuality is a crucial attribute of June Jordan's identity and her premise for self-expression and interaction with others. These distinguished, radically iconoclastic writers demand full recognition of the "difference/s." Lorde emphasizes her blackness, femaleness, lesbianism——in "butch" and "fem" roles (as I read her essays, particularly), her relatedness to all other women needing/seeking autonomy of personhood, and the ultimately fatal possession of her life by cancer. Progressively through her poetry and essays, Lorde becomes a winner, psychologically triumphant over all of these popularly acknowledged detractors from fullness of living. Rich defines herself as female, lesbian, white, southern, and a Jew. Together with emphatically engaging myriad and worldwide economic, cultural, educational, and political oppressions (as Jordan does), both Rich and Lorde, respectively as applicable, recognize and experience (as Jordan does) abuses of power—shaped usually as sexism, heterosexism, homophobia, racism, anti-Semitism, classism, and ageism—and "triggered," presumably, by the women's "differences"—however ageless and normal, immutable, and real. For Jordan add bisexuality, i.e., difference with a difference, and she stands out from the others in the triad. Possessing sexualities, Jordan experiences discrimination among the less complex or more "normal" lesbians. This experience is what seems to have clarified her view that any oppression equals all other oppressions without hierarchical or invidious distinctions. Jordan also refuses to privilege oppressors who are more "like" her than some other oppressors might be. Thus, African-Americans and lesbians who would presume to judge her bisexuality or any attribute or freely chosen, nonthreatening behavior toward others must be called what they are: tyrants ("A New Politics of Sexuality," *Technical Difficulties* 90; the entire essay is *must* reading for any who would try to comprehend Jordan fully).

Questions for Reading and Discussion/ Approaches to Writing

The following are suggestions for class enjoyment of reading/thinking aloud about Jordan's "Moving Towards Home": (1) Do students detect any slowing down, possibly an emphasis at lines 35, 37, and in lines where the persona quotes other people's voices? (2) Does it matter that readers might not/probably do not know the actual speakers? That the quoted passages might be/might not be historical? (3) Ask students to consider structure, meaning, and context by noting differences between the quoted passages and lines 47, 48, 49; (4) The importance of reading aloud and carefully can be stressed by discussing the difference between ". . . those who dare" in lines 35, 39, 41 and "those who dare" in line 46; (5) Visual interest enhances that of sound as readers notice that "speak about" in the poem's first thirty-one lines all line up/stack up, one above the next succeeding instance, that "about unspeakable events" breaks this pattern spatially as well as linguistically in the reversed order of the main words, and in the negativizing of "speak" by use of the prefix *un*. All events that the persona does "not wish to speak about" *are* spoken with chilling effect; *about* from line 53 to the end precedes *home & living room; home* envelopes *living room*.

Bibliography

Arnold Adoff's 1973 anthology *The Poetry of Black America* includes four outstanding Jordan poems, while Erlene Stetson in *Black Sister* (1981) contains only one by Jordan (a must, however, about Native Americans) but six by Lorde, seven by Jayne Cortez, and three by Sanchez.

Sonia Sanchez (b. 1934)

Contributing Editors: Joyce Joyce and John Reilly

Classroom Issues and Strategies

There is a widespread feeling that protest and politics are either inappropriate to literature or, if acceptable at certain times, the time for it has now passed.

The whole course should be founded upon an acceptance of the fact that there are no *a priori* definitions for literature. Poetry is what the poet writes or the audience claims as poetry. The real issues are whether or not the poet sets out a plausible poetics (one neither too solipsistic nor so undiscriminating as to dissolve meaning) and whether or not the practice of the poet has the local excitement and disciplined language to make it aesthetically satisfying. Upon these premises, the study of Sonia Sanchez can proceed with attention to her idea of revolutionary poetry associated with nation building, as it was discussed in the 1960s and 1970s.

Operating on the assumption that there is some common tradition underlying work of poets who declare ethnicity (African-American) as their common identity, useful discussion is possible about ways Sanchez differs from Michael Harper and Jay Wright. What differences in aesthetic and practice account for the relative complexity of Harper and Wright when contrasted with Sanchez? But, then, what allows us to consider them all black poets? Surely not merely the selection of subject matter?

Major Themes, Historical Perspectives, and Personal Issues

The historical and political are boldly set out in Sanchez's poetry. The personal may be overlooked by the hasty reader, but the poetry develops a persona with a highly subjective voice conveying the impression of a real human being feeling her way to positions, struggling to make her expressive declarative writing conform to her intuitions and interior self. This tension once observed makes all the themes arranged around the black aesthetic and black politics also accessible.

Significant Form, Style, or Artistic Conventions

The "eye" devices (lowercase letters, speed writing, fluid lines) along with the free form of verse and vernacular word choice are avant-garde devices seen in the work of many other poets. The point here is to see them associated with an aesthetic that privileges the oral and musical. For Sanchez it would be valuable to point to the frequency with which African-American poets allude to jazz performers, even making their lines sound like a musical instrument, just as, historically, musical instruments imitated the sounds of voice in early jazz and blues. This would make the vigor of the poem on the Righteous Brothers understandable, for music is a talisman of African-American culture. It would also set up a useful contrast between poetry written for print and poetry written to simulate the ephemerality of performed music or song.

Original Audience

For Sanchez these questions have great importance, for she has undergone important changes that have brought the spiritual and personal more forward in her verse. Dating her poems in connection with political events is very important. One might, for example, talk about an avowedly nationalist poetry written for a struggle to assert values believed to be a source of community solidarity. There are many parallels to suggest, including the writing of Irish authors in English, Jewish-American writers adapting the sounds of Yiddish to an exploration of traditional values in English, etc. Following the nationalist period of her work we see a shift of focus. One must ask students if the elements centered in the newer poems were not already present before. The appropriate answer (yes) will permit assertion of the developing nature of a writer's corpus, something worth presenting in all courses.

Comparisons, Contrasts, Connections

"Just Don't Never Give Up on Love" could be contrasted with confessional verse such as Plath's "Daddy" to distinguish the ways feeling can be distanced. Similarly the feminist voices of Adrienne Rich and Marge Piercy can introduce subtle distinctions when contrasted with the same Sanchez narrative/poem. What, we might ask, is the basis of distinction: formal or attitudinal?

Questions for Reading and Discussion/ Approaches to Writing

1. Recalling the use made of the mask by Paul Laurence Dunbar, consider what differences have occurred to change the meaning of that image in the 88 years until Sanchez published "Masks."
2. A society may be culturally diverse; yet, that does not mean that cultures are similarly powerful or influential. Discuss the way that Sonia Sanchez and other revolutionary black poets see the relationship between their culture and that of the dominant white society.

Bibliography

Palmer, Roderick. "The Poetry of Three Revolutionists: Don L. Lee, Sonia Sanchez, and Nikki Giovanni." *CLA Journal*, xv (Sept. 1971): 25–36. Reprinted in *Modern Black Poets*, edited by Donald Gibson, 135–46. Englewood Cliffs, N.J.: Prentice-Hall, 1973.

Etheridge Knight (1931–1991)

Contributing Editor: Patricia Liggins-Hill

Classroom Issues and Strategies

Students often lack the knowledge of the new black aesthetic, the black oral tradition, and contemporary black poetry, in general. I lecture on major twentieth-century black poets and literary movements. In addition, I provide supplementary research articles, primarily from *BALF* (*Black American Literature Forum*) and *CLA* (*College Language Association*).

Since Knight has read his poems on various college campuses throughout the country, I use tapes of his poetry readings. I also read his poetry aloud and invite students to do likewise, since his punctuation guides the reader easily through the oral poems.

Students, black and white, identify with the intense pain, loneliness, frustration, and deep sense of isolation Knight expresses in his prison poetry. They often compare their own sense of isolation, frustration, and depression as college students with his institutional experience.

Students often ask the following questions:

1. Why haven't they been previously exposed to this significant poet and to the new black aesthetic?
2. How did Knight learn to write poetry so well in prison with only an eighth-grade education?
3. What is the poet doing now? Is he still on drugs?
4. What is the difference between written and transcribed oral poetry?

Major Themes, Historical Perspectives, and Personal Issues

Knight's major themes are (1) liberation and (2) the black heritage. Since slavery has been a crucial reality in black history, much of Knight's poetry focuses on a modern kind of enslavement, imprisonment; his work searches for and discovers ways in which a person can be free while incarcerated. His poems are both personal and communal. As he searches for his own identity and meaning in life, he explores the past black American life experience from both its southern and its African heritage.

Knight's poetry should be taught within the historical context of the civil rights and black revolutionary movements of the 1960s and 1970s. The social backdrop of his and other new black poets' cries against racism were the assassinations of Malcolm X, Martin Luther King, Jr., John and Robert Kennedy, also the burning of ghettos, the bombings of black schools in the South, the violent confrontations between white police and black people, and the strong sense of awareness of poverty in black communities.

What the teacher should emphasize is that—while Knight shares with Baraka, Madhubuti, Major, and the other new black poets the bond of black cultural identity (the bond of the oppressed, the bond formed by black art, etc.)—he, unlike them, has emerged after serving an eight-year prison term for robbery from a second consciousness of community. This community of criminals is what Franz Fanon calls "the lumpenproletariat," "the wretched of the earth." Ironically, Knight's major contribution to the new aesthetic is derived from this second sense of consciousness which favorably reinforces his strong collective mentality and identification as a black artist. He brings his prison consciousness, in which the individual is institutionally destroyed and the self becomes merely one number among many, to the verbal structure of his transcribed oral verse.

Significant Form, Style, or Artistic Conventions

Consider the following questions:

1. What is the new black aesthetic and what are Knight's major contributions to the arts movement?
2. What are the black oral devices in Knight's poetry and what are his major contributions to the black oral tradition?
3. What are the universal elements in Knight's poetry?
4. In the "Idea of Ancestry" and "The Violent Space," how does Knight fuse various elements of "time and space" not only to denote his own imprisonment but also to connote the present social conditions of black people in general?
5. How does Knight develop his black communal art forms in his later poems "Blues for a Mississippi Black Boy" and "Ilu, the Talking Drum"?
6. What are the major influences on Knight's poetry? (Discuss the influences of Walt Whitman, Langston Hughes, and Sterling Brown.)

7. How does Knight's earlier poetry differ from his later poems? (Discuss in terms of the poet's voice, tone, and techniques, e.g., oral devices, imagery.)

Original Audience

Knight addresses black people in particular, and a mixed audience in general. He uses a variety of communal art forms and techniques such as blues idioms, jazz and African pulse structures, as well as clusters of communal images that link the poet and his experience directly to his reader/audience. For the latter, the teacher should use examples of images from "The Idea of Ancestry" and "The Bones of My Father" (if this poem is available).

Comparisons, Contrasts, Connections

Langston Hughes, Sterling Brown, and Walt Whitman are the major influences on Knight's poetry. Knight's "The Idea of Ancestry" flows in a Whitmanesque style and his "Blues for a Mississippi Black Boy" stems from the transcribed oral, blues poetic tradition of Hughes and Brown. He has indicated these influences in "An Interview with Etheridge Knight" by Patricia L. Hill (*San Francisco Review of Books* 3, no. 9 [1978]: 10).

Questions for Reading and Discussion/ Approaches to Writing

1. (a) How does Knight's poetry differ in content, form, and style from that of the earlier oral poets Hughes and Brown? How is his poetry similar to theirs?
   (b) How does Knight's poetry differ in content, form, and style from that of Baraka, Madhubuti, and the other major new black aesthetic poets? How is his poetry similar to theirs?
2. (a) The Western "Art for Art's Sake" Aesthetic Principle versus the New Black Aesthetic.
   (b) The Importance of Knight's Prison "Lumpenproletariat" Consciousness to the New Black Aesthetic.
   (c) The Major Poetic Influences on Knight's Poetry.
   (d) The Written and Oral Poetry Elements in Knight's Poetry.
   (e) Whitman's versus Knight's Vision of America.
   (f) Knight's Open and Closed Forms of Poetry.

Bibliography

Nketia, J. H. Kwalena. *The Music of Africa*. New York: W. W. Norton, 1974.

Ishmael Reed (b. 1938)

Contributing Editor: Michael Boccia

Classroom Issues and Strategies

Ishmael Reed frequently offends readers, who feel that they and the institutions they hold sacred (the church, American history, schools, etc.) are attacked and ridiculed by him. His humorous exaggerations and sharp barbs are misunderstood partly because satire and irony are so often misunderstood. In addition, most students are ignorant of the many contributions to American culture made by blacks and other minorities. Black and minority contributions in every field are highlighted in Reed's work. Reed often lists his historical, mythical, or literary sources in the text itself and has his own version of history, politics, literature, and culture.

Pointing out that Reed is a jokester and a humorous writer often makes his work more palatable to students. Once they begin to laugh at Reed's humor, they can take a more objective look at his condemnations of society. Of course, students refuse to accept his version of history, politics, and religion. Most commonly, students want to know if Reed's version of the "truth" is really true. They challenge his veracity whenever he challenges their beliefs. This permits me to send them off to check on Reed's statements, which proves rewarding and enlightening for them.

Of course, Reed does not want readers to accept a single viewpoint; he wishes our view of reality to be multi-faceted. In Reed's Neo-HooDoo Church, many "truths" are accepted. In fact, one source that is extremely helpful in understanding Reed's viewpoint is the "Neo-HooDoo Manifesto" (*Los Angeles Free Press* [18–24 Sept. 1969]: 42).

Major Themes, Historical Perspectives, and Personal Issues

Reed covers the gamut of issues, writing about politics, social issues, racism, history, and just about everything else. Most of his satire is aimed at the status quo, and thus he often offends readers. It is important to remind students that he is writing satire, but that there is truth to his comic attacks on the establishment. Closely related to his allusions to black artists and history are his themes. He views the counterculture as the vital force in life and hopefully predicts that the joyous side of life will triumph over the repressive side.

His radical beliefs appear as themes in his work. Knowledge of the cultures (popular, American, African, etc.) Reed draws upon is very helpful. Knowing about black history and literature is very valuable and can best be seen through Reed's eyes by reading his own commentary. *Shrovetide in Old New Orleans* is especially helpful in this area.

Reed's vision of history cries out for the recognition of minority contribution to Western civilization. Estaban (the black slave who led Cortez to the Grand Canyon), Squanto (the Native American who fed the Pilgrims), Sacajawea (the Native American woman who helped Lewis and Clark) and many other minority contributors are referred to in Reed's work, and because students are often ignorant of these contributions, some small survey of minority history is very useful.

Significant Form, Style, or Artistic Conventions

Reed's originality is rooted in his experimental forms, so introducing the traditional art forms that Reed distorts often helps readers understand his experiments. A survey of the forms of novels, journalism, television and radio programs, movies, newsreels, popular dances, and music will help students understand the fractured forms Reed offers.

The symbols Reed selects also reflect the eclectic nature of his art, in that the symbols and their meanings include but transcend traditional significance. Reed will blend symbols from ancient Egypt with rock and roll, or offer the flip side of history by revealing what went on behind the veil of history as popularly reported. In all cases one will find much stimulation in the juxtaposition of Reed's symbols and contexts.

Original Audience

The students are often angry at Reed's satire of their culture. The provocation that they feel is precisely the point of Reed's slashing wit.

He wants to provoke them into thinking about their culture in new ways. Pointing this out to students often alleviates their anger.

Comparisons, Contrasts, Connections

Introducing students to Swift's "A Modest Proposal" is an effective way to clarify how Reed's satire functions. Few readers think that eating babies is a serious proposal by Swift, and once satire is perceived as an exaggeration meant to stir controversy and thought, students are willing to listen to Reed's propositions.

Placing Reed in literary context is difficult because he writes in numerous genres and borrows from many nonliterary art forms. No doubt his innovations place him with writers like James Joyce and William Blake, and his satire places him among the most controversial writers of any literary period.

Certainly his use of allusion and motif is reminiscent of T. S. Eliot or James Joyce, but Reed likes to cite black writers as his models. Reed feels that the minorities have been slighted and a review of some of the black writers he cites as inspiration is often helpful to students.

Questions for Reading and Discussion/ Approaches to Writing

Students respond well to hunting down the literary, historical, and topical references in the poetry. I often ask them to select a single motif, such as Egyptian myth, and track it through a poem after researching the area.

Bibliography

I strongly recommend reading Reed on Reed: *Shrovetide in Old New Orleans*, especially "The Old Music," "Self Interview," "Remembering Josephine Baker," and "Harlem Renaissance."

For a detailed discussion of his literary and critical stances, see John O'Brien, "Ishmael Reed Interview," *The New Fiction, Interviews with Innovative American Writers*, edited by David Bellamy, 130–41. Urbana: University of Illinois Press, 1974.

For a view of the Dionysian/Appollonian struggle as portrayed by Reed, see Sam Keen, "Manifesto for a Dionysian Theology," *Transcendence*, edited by Herbert W. Richardson. Boston: Beacon Press, 1969: 31–52.

For a general overview, see Henry Gates, "Ishmael Reed," *The Dictionary of Literary Biography* 33.

Half of *The Review of Contemporary Fiction* 4.2 (1984) is devoted to Reed.

Toni Cade Bambara (b. 1939)

Contributing Editor: Sue Houchins

Classroom Issues and Strategies

Some students may have difficulty with the rhythm of the demotic language in this selection. There are a few examples of what poet Edward Braithwaite calls "nation language," author Marlene Nourbese Philip calls "cultural speech or demotic," critic Houston Baker may term "the vernacular," and some may call "dialect"—or worse yet—"slang"—for example, the term "jones," which means habit or addiction, or even the "My Man" of the title, which bears the double valence of a greeting between men and the designation for a woman's conjugal or cohabital partner. However, some students have more trouble with Bambara's representation of the conversational cadence of Miss Hazel's speech. The first four or five lines of the short story are a case in point. It might be helpful, therefore, for you to read a paragraph or so aloud and then to request a student to read a portion so that your class can develop an ear for this language that Bambara maintains is central to an African-American aesthetic.

In addition, students are finding it increasingly difficult to appreciate the political issues, motivations, and strategies of the sixties and seventies. Therefore, you might want to read from or to place on reserve some of the essays of Eldridge Cleaver, Claude Brown, Stokely Carmichael, or, better yet, assign passages of Alice Walker's *Meridian*. Further, you might ask whether Miss Hazel is truly apolitical and whether the narrative's critique of "the Movement" is necessarily an indictment or a repudiation of it.

Major Themes, Historical Perspectives, and Personal Issues

This short story begs us to read and to problematize issues of gender, race, age, and class; and to locate the intersection of these discourses. For example, Task, Elo, and Joe Lee's (mis)reading of their mother's allegedly indecorous behavior with old blind Bovanne and her unseemly dress mark the discursive space where gender and age collide—would Hazel's appearance and conduct be so egregious had she been younger?—and where the social construction of woman as mother denies her sexual agency—doesn't her children's reaction to Hazel's dancing withhold from her the status of either subject or object of desire? Thus, she must deny the erotic content of her dance: "Wasn't about tits." But if it wasn't about breasts as sensual/sensuous organs, was it about breasts as sources of nurture, and can the two functions be separated? The piece asks that we reconsider *the body/bodies*—female and male, young and old—and our culture's complex readings of them—raced, sexed, aged—as they interact with each other, thereby constructing social meaning—mother/daughter ("puttin a hand on my shoulder like she hasn't done since she left home and the hand landin light and not sure it suppposed to be there"); mother/son and father/son ("Task run a hand over his left ear like his father for the world and his father before that"); woman/man (not just "sex starved [old folks]," nor just old men seeking and mature women dispensing "Mama comfort," but also "vibrations" upon drum skins and a mutual "hummin" reminiscent of an encounter with the sacred, "like you in church again"). In the light of these constructions of the body/these touchings, how do we understand the ritual bathing described at the end of the story? And how do we understand the title of the short story?

Also, Miss Hazel's body, specifically her hair, is one textual site where race and gender are problematized. Though Bambara, as a member of the Black Arts Movement, is one of many African-American authors of that era seeking to define and exemplify a black aesthetic (see Addison Gayle, *The Black Aesthetic*), her fiction avoids a simplistic essentialism both through the tropes of Hazel's wig and cornrows as well as by Elo's self-censorship, her uncompleted assertion that the generation gap is a white phenomenon.

Bambara, who has always identified herself first as a social and political activist/community organizer, is acutely aware of the contradictions in some so-called grass roots movements that depend[ed] on the uncredited and unrewarded labor of women (see Walker, *Meridian*, Paula Giddings, *When and Where We Enter*, or Bambara, *The Salt Eaters*) and that give only lip service to respecting and empowering the disenfranchised poor, elderly, and disabled.

Significant Form, Style, or Artistic Conventions

The Eleanor Traylor introduction to this short story stresses the importance of black speech in and the orality of Bambara's work. Pay particular attention, therefore, to the cadence/rhythm and tone of this very conversational piece, an episode, related to the reader as if she and Miss Hazel were talking over a cup of herb tea, embedded, as are all good oral narratives, with pieces of other conversations among the related incident's participants. Appreciate as well Hazel's irony and wit.

Original Audience

Toni Cade Bambara, writing in the late sixties and early seventies, is speaking to a new generation of African-Americans who are avidly reading reprinted works by black authors of the nineteenth and early twentieth centuries and who are equally eager for each new book off the press. Teachers in newly formed black studies departments are beginning to educate students and their professorial colleagues to the value of black texts and the strategies for reading them. So Bambara can write in her highly original, but still culturally situated, voice and expect a wide and racially diverse audience for whom she need not translate her idiom.

Comparisons, Contrasts, Connections

In the foregoing discussion, I have already suggested Alice Walker as an author with whom one might compare Bambara; in addition to *Meridian*, there are short stories in *In Love and Trouble* that treat some of the same themes. Paule Marshall's *Brown Girl, Brownstones* examines, among other things, mother-daughter conflict, but among Caribbean immigrants in Brooklyn. And both for the complex and subtle exploration of the issues of race, gender, and sexuality as well as for the lyrical linguistic cadence representing black speech, compare Bambara with Toni Morrison.

Questions for Reading and Discussion/ Approaches to Writing

I have already suggested some questions in the preceding discussion of major themes; for example, one might ask students about the significance of the title, or about the "meaning" of the ritual bathing at the end of the story. Also, because the persona of Miss Hazel requires students of traditional college age to step into the skin of a more mature adult and to empathize with their antagonist across the gender gap, you might ask them about what they learned from this experience.

Bibliography

Refer to the headnote in the text for complete information.

Amiri Baraka (LeRoi Jones) (b. 1934)

Contributing Editor: Marcellette Williams

Classroom Issues and Strategies

The typical problems in teaching Baraka's poetry have to do with what has been called his "unevenness"—perhaps more accurately attributable to the tension inherent in balancing Baraka's role as poet and his role as activist—and the strident tone of some of his poems—also related to his political activism.

Both problems are probably best addressed directly by inviting the students to describe or characterize their impressions of the impetus for the poems as they read them (stressing "their reading" is critical and complements what current reading theory regards as the essential role of the reader in any reading paradigm), then asking them to substantiate textually those impressions. Such a strategy finesses the temptation to engage in a definitive debate of the politics of the time as the genesis and raison d'être of Baraka's poetry. Further, such a strategy allows students to explore the aesthetics as well as the politics of his poetry and understand better the inter/inner-(con)textuality of the two.

Because the "sound" of Baraka's poetry is essential to texturing or fleshing out its meaning, readings aloud should contribute to discussions as well as to the introduction to his work.

Students respond almost always to the intimacy of Baraka's poems; sometimes they are offended by that intimacy, and this posture often leads to discussions of poetic necessity. Students also raise the question of the paradox of Baraka's clear aesthetic debts and his vehemence in trying to tear down that very Western ideal.

Major Themes, Historical Perspectives, and Personal Issues

It is important to emphasize the themes of death and despair in the early poems, moral and social corruption with its concomitant decrying of Western values and ethics, the struggle against self-hatred, a growing ethnic awareness, and the beneficent view of and creative energy occasioned by "black magic."

The issues to focus on historically involve the racial tenor of the decades represented by his poetic output as well as the poetic aesthetics of imagism, projectivism, and Dadaism—all of which influenced Baraka to some extent.

From the perspective of personal issues, his bohemian acquaintances of the fifties (Charles Olson and Allen Ginsberg, for example), his marriage to Hettie Cohen, his visit to Cuba, his name change, the death of Malcolm X, and his Obie for *The Dutchman* are all important considerations.

Significant Form, Style, or Artistic Conventions

It is appropriate to refer to the question of "school," here again in the context of the poet's use of sound and images as the articulation of form and meaning. I would further encourage the students to pay careful attention to Baraka's use of repetition—at the lexical, syntactic, semantic, and phonological levels. What is its effect? Does it inform? If so, how? Are there aspects of the poems one might regard as transformations? If so, what might they be? What effect might they have? How might they function in the poem?

Baraka's consideration of the significance of "roots" appears to evolve in his poetry. How might you characterize it?

Original Audience

A consideration of progenitors and progeny provides a convenient point of departure for a discussion of audience for Baraka's work. Students interested in imagism and projectivism, for example, will certainly value Baraka's efforts as an effective use of those aesthetic doctrines toward the shaping of poetry of revolution appropriate for the time.

Baraka's influence is apparent in the poetry of Sonia Sanchez and Ntozake Shange. What aspects of this influence, if any, might contribute to considerations of audience with regard to time and poetry?

Comparisons, Contrasts, Connections

In considering Baraka's conscious use of language for poetic effect, comparisons with William Carlos Williams (for the use of the vernacular and the idiom) and with Ezra Pound (for its communicative focus) are appropriate. Sometimes in discussions of Baraka's early poems, the criticism compares them in tone and theme—moral decay and social disillusionment—with T. S. Eliot's *The Waste Land*.

Questions for Reading and Discussion/ Approaches to Writing

1. Frank Smith discusses the "behind the eyeball" information a reader brings to text. Louise Rosenblatt discusses the expectations and experiences a reader brings to "transact" or negotiate meaning with text. Given these considerations of the reader, prediscussion questions might be designed to elicit from the reader whatever information or preconceptions he/she has about the author and/or his work. If the students are totally unfamiliar with Baraka, then questions eliciting experiential responses to the broad issues of theme or technique would be appropriate—"What, if anything, do the terms social fragmentation and/or moral decay mean to you?" "What would you imagine as a poetic attack on society? Or a poetic ethnic response to a dead or dying society?"

2. Writing assignments and topics for the students are derived from the assumption that as readers their participation is essential to meaning. Topics are not generally prescribed but, rather, derived from the questions about and interest in the author and his (Baraka's) work. These assignments sometimes take the form of poetic responses, critical essays, or "dialogues" with Baraka.

Bibliography

Brown, Lloyd W. "Baraka as Poet." In Lloyd W. Brown's *Amiri Baraka*. Boston: Twayne Publishers, 1980, 104–35, Chapter 5.

Harris, William J. "The Transformed Poem." In *The Poetry and Poetics of Amiri Baraka: The Jazz Aesthetic*. Columbia: University of Missouri Press, 1985, 91–121.

Lacey, Henry. "Die Schwartze Bohemien: 'The Terrible Disorder of a Young Man' " and "Imamu." In *To Raise, Destroy, and Create*. Troy, New York: The Whitstone Publishing Company, 1981, 1–42, 93–162.

Sollors, Werner. "Who Substitutes for the Dead Lecturer?: Poetry of the Early 1960s." In *Amiri Baraka/LeRoi Jones: The Quest for a Populist Modernism.* New York: Columbia University Press, 1978, 83–95.

Lucille Clifton (b. 1936)

Contributing Editor: James A. Miller

Classroom Issues and Strategies

Clifton's poetry is generally very accessible, so accessible that careless readers may overlook the way she often achieves her poetic effects. Her poetry is best read aloud and students should be encouraged to read and hear her poems first, then to explore issues of language, form, and theme.

Major Themes, Historical Perspectives, and Personal Issues

Clifton is deeply concerned with the ways in which the weight of racial memory and history extends into the present, with family and community history, and with the possibilities of transcendence and reconciliation. A deeply spiritual vein shapes much of her poetry, which conveys a sense of wonder and mystery as well as optimism and resilience.

Significant Form, Style, or Artistic Conventions

Clifton's poems seem guided by the dictates of her own experience and consciousness rather than by any *a priori* sense of form or poetic conventions. Her primary commitment is to economical, everyday language, and to the rhythmic and musical qualities of the language that shapes her poems.

Original Audience

Clifton's first collection of poems, *Good Times,* was published during the heyday of the Black Arts Movement and her early work in particular owes important debts to the mood and outlook of that period, particularly in her celebration of the ordinary life of African-Americans.

Comparisons, Contrasts, Connections

Clifton can fruitfully be compared with other African-American women poets who emerged out of the same historical moment—Mari Evans, June Jordan, and Sonia Sanchez, for example—but she can also be read in conjunction with Amiri Baraka and Etheridge Knight. Her poems can also be compared with those of her predecessors like Langston Hughes, Sterling A. Brown, Margaret Walker, Robert Hayden, and Gwendolyn Brooks. And intriguing relationships can also be established between her works and the poems of Emily Dickinson and Walt Whitman.

Questions for Reading and Discussion/ Approaches to Writing

1. Discuss the domestic images in "The Thirty Eighth Year" and "I Am Accused of Tending to the Past." How do images of nurturing function in these poems? What is the relationship of these images to the consciousness which shapes the poems?
2. Discuss the function of history in Clifton's poems. What, for example, is the poet seeking "at the cemetery, walnut grove plantation, south carolina, 1989"? Is there any relationship between this poem and "Reply"?
3. Discuss the relationship between "I" and "Them" in "in white america." Trace the development of the poem through the final stanza and comment upon the resolution the poem achieves.

Bibliography

Evans, Mari, ed., *Black Women Writers 1950–1980: A Critical Evaluation*, 1984, 137–161.

Harris, Trudier and Thadious Davis, eds., *Dictionary of Literary Biography: Afro-American Poets Since 1955*, 1985, 55–60.

Marge Piercy (b. 1936)

Contributing Editor: Estella Lauter

Classroom Issues and Strategies

I have taught Piercy's poems in a Women in Literature course offered for credit in general education and in a course on American Women Poets. Most students find her very direct and accessible, but some are unnerved by her openness in expressing her feelings and describing her experience while others are daunted by her high expectations of herself and other human beings. Students generally profit from small group discussions where they can share related experiences and discuss the pressures Piercy's poems exert on them.

If I had enough time to use one of her novels in relationship to the poems, it would be wonderful to contrast their highly researched, intricate plots with the structures of the poems. Her own voice in the poems is direct; it's fascinating to see how she suspends it in the novels for various narrative purposes.

Major Themes, Historical Perspectives, and Personal Issues

Piercy's poems raise important issues related to feminism, ecology, imperialism, civil rights, religious heritage, love, and effective relationships. Often one issue leads to another. Like Thoreau, she works at living ethically and peacefully in an environment ravaged by greed, anxiety, and fear.

Significant Form, Style, or Artistic Conventions

In her own brief introduction to *Circles on the Water* (1985), Piercy writes that she intends "to be of use" for readers rather than for other poets, to "give utterance to energy, experience, insight, words flowing from many lives." Although the voice is always hers, the experiences sometimes belong to others. Line length and rhythm follow from the material. She writes political and/or didactic poetry as necessary, out of a belief that poets belong to a social context and speak for constituencies; but the primary purpose of poetry from her point of view is to align the psyche, to heal the alienation of thought and feeling, and to "weld mind back into body seamlessly." Walt Whitman is one of her models. Although she does not name Denise Levertov as an influence, she must have profited from Levertov's articulation in the sixties of an organic theory of poetry.

Original Audience

I talk about Piercy's ability to speak for women, to open up subjects that haven't been understood. I've heard her read three times to audiences with varying degrees of sophistication, and I've spoken with her at length about her political concerns. So I share these experiences with the students. (Others could speak from her forthright essays in *Parti-colored Blocks* or from her essay in *Contemporary Authors*.) I always tell the story of her first reading of the poems about her mother that appear in *My Mother's Body*. It was at a National Women's Studies Conference, and she told the audience that she had brought the poems not knowing whether or not she would be able to share them. Their warm response allowed her to do so. She talked about the pain of writing poems that address issues too difficult for others to hear. This always turns out to be an encouraging story for students who write without an audience.

Comparisons, Contrasts, Connections

Piercy shares many concerns with Denise Levertov, Adrienne Rich, and Audre Lorde. All four are political poets who share a deep concern for women and who value the capacity to care, but they have very different styles, voices, attitudes, feelings, blind spots, and so on. Levertov refuses to identify herself as a feminist, for example, as the others do. Rich never speaks about her relationship with her mother and rarely deals with her biological sister, whereas Lorde is relatively open about both, Piercy has a long sequence on her mother, and Levertov has a sequence on her sister. Levertov, Rich, and Piercy handle their Jewish heritage differently; Piercy's celebration of her feminist and Jewish sources is more like Lorde's response to her African heritage. And so on. This kind of comparison helps students to understand and respect differences among women.

Questions for Reading and Discussion/ Approaches to Writing

1. I prefer to give students several poems on the same general subject and ask them to work out the differences and similarities in point

of view in discussion. This seems to give more room for them to experience the poems.

2. In Piercy's case, several topics keyed to her poem cycles work exceptionally well: the value of marriage ("The Chuppah"); mother-daughter relationships ("What Remains"); the lunar calendar ("The Lunar Cycle"); the tarot cards ("Laying Down the Tower"); the power of religion ("The Ram's Horn").

Bibliography

The most useful materials to date are Piercy's own essays in *Parti-colored Blocks* and *Contemporary Authors*, but a few articles have appeared and a bibliography of her writings has been compiled by Elaine Tuttle Hansen and William J. Scheick in Catherine Rainwater and W. J. Scheick, eds., *Contemporary American Women Writers: Narratives Strategies* (Lexington: University Press of Kentucky, 1985).

See also:

Contoski, Victor. "Marge Piercy: A Vision of the Peaceable Kingdom." *Modern Poetry Studies* 8 (1977): 205–16.

Wynne, Edith J. "Imagery of Association in the Poetry of Marge Piercy." *Publications of the Missouri Philological Association* 10 (1985): 57–63.

N. Scott Momaday (Kiowa) (b. 1934)

Contributing Editor: Kenneth M. Roemer

Classroom Issues and Strategies

In several areas, teachers of *Rainy Mountain* are in agreement. For example, whether an instructor uses excerpts or the entire book (the University of New Mexico paperback is the best classroom edition), acquainting students with a few of Momaday's other works can help them to establish important thematic, generic, and cultural contexts for reading *Rainy Mountain*. Especially relevant are the two sermons delivered by the Kiowa Priest of the Sun in Momaday's novel *House Made of Dawn* (1968), the intense Oklahoma landscape descriptions (for example, Book 3, Section 4) in *Ancient Child* (1989), and Momaday's essay "The Man Made of Words" (available in Geary Hobson's anthology *The*

Remembered Earth [1979]), which outlines the major phases of composition of *Rainy Mountain* and sets forth Momaday's theory of language. The excellent interviews in Charles Woodard's *Ancestral Voice*, especially in the "Center Holds" and "Wordwalker" sections, and Kay Bonetti's fine recorded interview *N. Scott Momaday*, available from American Audio Prose Library, also offer significant insights into Momaday's concepts of identity and language.

Beyond recommending an acquaintance with *House Made of Dawn* and "Man Made of Words," there is little agreement among teachers of *Rainy Mountain* about how much "background" information students "need to know" in order to "understand" Momaday's book. This apparent confusion can become the focus for classroom discussions of an important question: How can works frequently omitted from literary canons and characterized by unfamiliar subject matter and unusual forms of expression be made accessible and meaningful to "typical" college students? One approach to this question is to ask students to complete their first readings and initial discussions of the excerpts from *Rainy Mountain* before they have received any background information; students should even be discouraged from reading the headnote. The initial discussion can center on questions about what type of writing the excerpts represent (e.g., should they be in a poetry section?) and about what types of information (if any) they think they need to understand the excerpts.

Major Themes, Historical Perspectives, and Personal Issues

The forms and themes of *Rainy Mountain* suggest numerous other classroom strategies, many of which are described in detail in Part Two of *Approaches to Teaching Rainy Mountain* and in my *College English* essay on teaching survey courses (37 [1976]: 619–24).

The importance of landscape in Momaday's book also suggests a way to bridge discussions of nineteenth-century classic American literature and *Rainy Mountain*. As J. Frank Papovich has argued in "Landscape, Tradition and Identity" in *Perspectives on Contemporary Literature* (12 [1986]: 13–19), students should be made aware that there are alternatives to the concept of the American landscape articulated in the myth of the isolated male hero escaping from domesticity and society to confront the challenges of the wilderness. By contrast, Momaday's nature is a place teeming with intricate networks of animal, human, and cosmic life connected by mutual survival relationships, story-telling traditions that embrace social gatherings at his grandmother's house as well as the growth of a babe into the Sun's wife, and an imagination that can transform an Oklahoma cricket into a being worthy of kinship with the moon.

Significant Form, Style, or Artistic Conventions

Autobiography, epic, sonnet, prose-poem, history, folk tale, vision, creation hymn, lyrical prose, a collection of quintessential novels—these are a few of the labels critics, scholars, and N. Scott Momaday have used to describe *The Way to Rainy Mountain*.

Comparisons, Contrasts, Connections

I recommend comparisons between Momaday's written excerpts and parallel Kiowa oral narratives or pictorial histories (e.g., comparing the buffalo story in XVI to the narrative in Boyd, Vol. 2 [70–73] or comparing the descriptions in XVII of how women were treated to Mooney's accounts drawn from Kiowa calendar histories [280, 281, 294]).

Within the context of American literature courses, various comparative studies can be made between *Rainy Mountain* and other more familiar works. Instructors interested in narrative structure can compare Momaday's discontinuous and multivoiced text to poetic works by Edgar Lee Masters, T. S. Eliot, and Ezra Pound and to prose works by Sherwood Anderson and William Faulkner.

Momaday's treatment of identity formation can be compared to other authors' attempts to define personae who—because of their ethnic heritage, gender, or class status—had to integrate creatively the apparently unrelated elements of their mainstream and nonmainstream backgrounds and experiences.

Questions for Reading and Discussion/ Approaches to Writing

One participatory approach to the identity issue is to require students to select a significant landscape in their own backgrounds and to use this selection as the basis for composing three-voice sections modeled on the structure of *Rainy Mountain*.

Bibliography

Roemer, Kenneth M. *Approaches to Teaching Momaday's The Way to Rainy Mountain*. New York: MLA, 1989.

Leslie Marmon Silko (Laguna) (b. 1948)

Contributing Editor: Norma C. Wilson

Classroom Issues and Strategies

When I first began to read Silko's poetry and fiction, I attempted to use the critical methods I had used in my prior study of European and American literature. I sought primary sources of the traditional stories that appeared in her work. But I soon found that very little of the traditional literature of the Lagunas had been recorded in writing. I realized that I needed to know more of the background—cultural and historical—of Silko's writing.

In the spring of 1977, I arranged to meet with Silko at the University of New Mexico. She explained to me that her writing had evolved from an outlook she had developed as a result of hearing the old stories and songs all her life. She also led me to a number of helpful written sources, including Bertha P. Dutton and Miriam A. Marmon's *The Laguna Calendar* (Albuquerque: University of New Mexico Press, 1936) and the transcript of an interview with Mrs. Walter K. Marmon in the Special Collections Department of the Zimmerman Library, U.N.M. Another source I've found helpful is Leslie A. White, "The Acoma Indians" (*Forty-seventh Annual Report of the Bureau of American Ethnology*, Washington, D.C.: U.S. Government Printing Office, 1932).

One can use the videotape, *Running on the Edge of the Rainbow*, produced by Larry Evers at the University of Arizona, Tucson. I often begin looking at Silko's writing by using a transparency of her poem "Prayer to the Pacific." Students frequently come to think in new ways about their relationships to nature and about the exploitation of Native American people and the natural earth. They ask such questions as, "Did the government really do that to the Navajos?"

Major Themes, Historical Perspectives, and Personal Issues

In teaching "Lullaby," the idea of harmony is essential—the Navajo woman is balanced because she is aware of her relation to the natural world, that she is a part of it and that is the most important relationship. This allows her to nurture as the earth nurtures. One should emphasize forced changes in the Navajo way of life that have resulted from the encroachment of industry and the government on Navajo land. Today the struggle centering on Big Mountain would be a good focus. Of course, alcoholism and the splitting up of Indian families would be other important issues to focus on.

Significant Form, Style, or Artistic Conventions

It is important to note that Silko's fiction is a blending of traditional with modern elements. And just as "Lullaby" ends with a song, many of Silko's other works are also a blend of prose and poetry.

Original Audience

"Lullaby" seems to be a story from out of the 1950s. We talk about the U.S. government's relocation policy during that decade. Relocation was an attempt to remove Indians from reservations and relocate them in urban environments. We also discuss the long history of the U.S. government removing Indian children from their families and culture. Recently this kind of removal has been somewhat reversed by the Indian Child Welfare Act, which gives tribes authority over the placement of the children enrolled in these tribes.

Comparisons, Contrasts, Connections

One might compare and contrast Silko's work with that of Simon J. Ortiz. One might also consider comparing and contrasting it with the work of James Wright, Gary Snyder, and Louise Erdrich.

Questions for Reading and Discussion/ Approaches to Writing

One might ask the students to look up specific places mentioned in the story on a map—Cebolleta Creek, Long Mesa, Cañoncito, etc.

1. Discuss the importance of the oral tradition in Silko's writing.
2. Discuss the structure of Silko's fiction. Is it linear or cyclic?
3. What is the image of woman in Silko's fiction? Compare or contrast this with the images of women in the broader context of American society and culture.
4. What criticisms of American society are implicit in Silko's fiction?
5. What Navajo cultural values are evident in the story "Lullaby"?

Bibliography

Allen, Paula Gunn. "Special Problems in Teaching Leslie Marmon Silko's *Ceremony*." *American Indian Quarterly* (Fall 1990): 379–86.

Fisher, Dexter. "Stories and Their Tellers—A Conversation with Leslie Marmon Silko." In *The Third Woman: Minority Women Writers of the United States*. Boston: Houghton Mifflin, 1980.

Silko, L. M. "An Old-Time Indian Attack Conducted in Two Parts." In *The Remembered Earth*, edited by Geary Hobson. Albuquerque: University of New Mexico Press, 1979.

James Welch (Blackfeet-Gros Ventre) (b. 1940)

Contributing Editor: Linda Wagner-Martin

Classroom Issues and Strategies

Welch's fiction is immediately accessible. Students find it powerful. They shirk from its relentlessly depressing impact, but Welch has written *Winter in the Blood*, *The Death of Jim Loney*, and much of his poetry to create that impact. His writing is protest literature, so skillfully achieved that it seems apolitical.

Sometimes hostile to the completely new, students today seem to be willing to rely on canon choices. Once Welch is placed for them, they respond with empathy to his fiction.

The general setting of the culture, the hardships generations of Native Americans have learned to live with, the socioeconomic issues make deciphering characters' attitudes easier. The strengths of the Indian culture need to be described as well, because students in many parts of the country are unfamiliar with customs, imagery, and attitudes that are necessary in reading this excerpt.

Welch's precision and control must be discussed. Students must see how they are in his power throughout this excerpt. Further, they must want to read not only this novel, but the others as well.

Major Themes, Historical Perspectives, and Personal Issues

It is also good to emphasize the choice of art as profession. For Welch, giving voice to frustration has created memorable fiction and poetry. His most recent novels, *Fools Crow* and *Indian Lawyer*, do much more than depict the alienation of the contemporary Native American man—but to do so, he draws on nineteenth-century history as the basis of his plot in *Fools* and a different stratum of culture for *Lawyer*.

Significant Form, Style, or Artistic Conventions

Questions of realism and how realistic writing is achieved: characterization, language, situation, emphasis on dialogue rather than interior monologue.

Questions of appropriateness: What is believable about the fiction, and how has Welch created that intensity that is so believable? Why is a plot like this more germane to the lives Welch describes than an adventurous, action-filled narrative would have been?

Original Audience

The issue of political literature (which will occur often in selections from the contemporary section) will need attention. How can Welch create a sympathetic hero without portraying the poverty and disillusion of a culture? How can he achieve this accuracy without maligning Native Americans?

Comparisons, Contrasts, Connections

Ernest Hemingway and Richard Wright are obvious choices for comparison, but the differences are important as well. Wright relied in many cases on dialect, with language spelled as words might have been pronounced, and Hemingway used carefully stylized language in his quantities of dialogue, so that identifying characters by place or education was sometimes difficult. Welch creates a dialect that is carefully mannered, as if the insecure speaker had modeled his language, like his life, on the middle-class TV image of a person and a family.

Bibliography

Refer to the headnote in the text for complete information.

Tomás Rivera (1935–1984)

Contributing Editor: Ramón Saldívar

Classroom Issues and Strategies

Rivera's novel is written in nonsequential chronology, with a multiplicity of characters, without an easily identifiable continuous narrator, and without a strictly causal narrative logic. While each of the selections is coherent within itself, students will need to be prepared for the apparent lack of continuity from one section of the work to the next.

I begin with a careful discussion of the first selection, "The Lost Year," to show that there is, at least in sketchy form, the beginnings of a narrative identity present. As in other modernist and postmodernist writings, in William Faulkner's *As I Lay Dying* and *Go Down, Moses*, for example, or in Juan Rulfo's *Pedro Páramo*, the narrative is not expository, attempting to give us historical depiction. It offers instead complex subjective impressions and psychological portraiture. Students should be asked to read the first selection looking for ways in which the narrative does cohere. Ask: Who speaks? Where is the speaker? What does the speaker learn about him/herself here, even if only minimally? As students proceed to the following selections, it is appropriate to ask what this unconventional narrative form has to do with the themes of the work.

Rivera's work is openly critical of and in opposition to mainstream American culture. What does it accomplish by being oppositional? What does it share with other "marginal" literatures, such as African-American, feminist, gay and lesbian, or third world writings? Instead of attempting to locate Rivera within American or modernist writings, it might be useful to think of Rivera's place within the group of other non-canonic, antitraditional, engaged writings.

Students are sometimes misled by the apparent simplicity of the first selection: They might need to be carefully alerted to the question of identity being posed there. Also, the historical context of racial violence and political struggle may need to be constructed for students: They may want to see these stories as exclusively about the plight of *individuals* when in reality Rivera is using individual characters as *types* for a whole community.

Major Themes, Historical Perspectives, and Personal Issues

General Themes: The coming to maturity of a young child, as he begins to get a glimmer of the profound mystery of the adult world. The child, apparently a boy, raises in the second selection the traditional *lehresjahre* themes, having to do with the disillusionment of childhood dreams.

Specific Themes: This coming to maturity and the posing of universal existential questions (Who am I? Where do I belong?) take place within the specific historical and social context of the working-class life and political struggle of the Mexican-American migrant farmworker of the late 1940s and 1950s in Texas.

Universal themes are thus localized to a very high degree. What does this localizing of universal themes accomplish in the novel? Also, the question of personal identity is in each of the three selections increasingly tied to the identity of the community (*la raza*). The stories thus also thematize the relationship between private history and public history.

Significant Form, Style, or Artistic Conventions

Questions of style are intimately involved with questions of substance in these selections. Rivera claims to have been influenced by his reading in James Joyce, Marcel Proust, William Faulkner, and the great Latin American novelists. Rivera also acknowledged that he had been profoundly influenced by the work of the great Mexican-American anthropologist and folklorist Américo Paredes, whose ethnographic work realistically pictured turn-of-the-century life in the Southwest. Why does this work about the "local" theme of life in the American Southwest offer itself in the form of high modernism? Would not a more straightforward social realism have been more appropriate for the themes it presents?

Original Audience

The work was originally written in Spanish, using the colloquial, everyday cadences of working-class Spanish-speaking people. Bilingual instructors should review the original text and try to point out to students that the English translations are but approximations of a decidedly *oral* rhythm. Written at the height of the Chicano political movement and in the midst of an often bitter labor struggle, at times Rivera's work bristles with anger and outrage. The turmoil of the late 1960s and early 1970s plays a large role in the tone of the work.

Comparisons, Contrasts, Connections

Rivera claimed to have been influenced by many modern authors, Faulkner chief among them. A useful discussion of the relationships between form and theme might arise by comparing Rivera's work with Faulkner's *As I Lay Dying* or *Absalom, Absalom!* What does narrative experimentation have to do with social realism? Why does an author choose nontraditional narrative techniques? What does one gain by setting aside causally motivated character action?

Questions for Reading and Discussion/ Approaches to Writing

1. Many of the questions posed by this study guide might be fruitfully addressed to students before they read Rivera's work. Especially useful are those questions that ask students to think about the relationship between form/content and that take into account the historical/political circumstances of the period during which these stories were written.
2. Students might consider in the piece entitled "And the Earth Did Not Devour Him": Why does the earth not devour him? What does the narrator learn and why does this knowledge seem so momentous? Concerning the last selection, "When We Arrive," students might discuss the journey motif: Where are these migrant workers going? What will they find at the end of the road?

Bibliography

Ramón Saldívar, *Chicano Narrative* (Madison: University of Wisconsin Press, 1990), pp. 74–90, includes a discussion of the selections. *International Studies in Honor of Tomás Rivera*, edited by Julian Olivares (Houston: Arte Público Press, 1985) is an excellent collection of essays on *And the Earth Did Not Devour Him*.

Nicholasa Mohr (b. 1938)

Contributing Editor: Frances R. Aparicio

Classroom Issues and Strategies

Mohr's writings are quite accessible for the college-age student population. There is no bilingualism, her English is quite simple and direct, and her stories in general do not create difficulties in reading or comprehension.

Major Themes, Historical Perspectives, and Personal Issues

1. The universal theme of "growing up" (bildungsroman), and in her case in particular, growing up female in El Barrio.
2. The theme of the family; views of the Hispanic family and the expectations it holds of its members, in contrast to its American counterpart.
3. Sexual roles in Latino culture; traditional versus free vocations (for men).
4. Mother/daughter relationships; tensions, generational differences.
5. Women's issues such as career versus family, the economic survival of welfare mothers, dependency and independence issues.
6. Outside views of the barrio "ghetto" in relation to the voices of those who have lived in the inner cities.

Significant Form, Style, or Artistic Conventions

The autobiographical form is quite predominant in Mohr's writings, as is James Clifford's concept of "ethnobiography," in which the self is seen in conjunction with his/her ethnic community. And Mohr employs traditional story-telling, simple, direct, accessible, chronological use of time, and a logical structure.

Very dynamic discussions emerge when students are asked to evaluate Mohr's transparent, realist style as good literature or not. This discussion should include observations on how many U.S. Latino and Latina writers have opted for a less academic and so-called "sophisticated" style that would allow for wider audiences outside the academic world.

Original Audience

It is important to read many of Mohr's works as literature for young adolescents. This explains and justifies the simplicity and directness of her style.

Comparisons, Contrasts, Connections

Fruitful comparisons could be made if we look at other Latina women who also write on "growing up female and Hispanic in the United States": Sandra Cisneros's *The House on Mango Street* (Houston: Arte Público Press, 1983); *Cuentos by Latinas*, eds. Alma Gómez, Cherríe Moraga, and Mariana Romo-Carmona (New York: Kitchen Table Women of Color Press, 1983); and Helena Maria Viramontes's *The Moths and Other Stories* (Houston: Arte Público Press, 1985). Viramontes's stories promise fruitful comparisons with Mohr's *Rituals of Survival*.

In addition, Mohr has been contrasted to Piri Thomas's *Down These Mean Streets*, another autobiographical book in which El Barrio is presented in terms of drugs, gangs, and violence. I would propose a comparison to Eduard Rivera's *Family Installments* as yet another example of ethnobiography.

Finally, interesting contrasts and parallelisms may be drawn from looking at North American women writers such as Ann Beattie and the Canadian Margaret Atwood; while class and race perspectives might differ, female and feminist issues could be explored as common themes.

Questions for Reading and Discussion/
Approaches to Writing

1. Study questions: Specific questions on text, characters, plot, endings, issues raised. More major themes could also be explored such as: How do we define epic characters, history, and great literature? Where would Mohr's characters fit within the traditional paradigms?
2. Writing assignment: Students may write their own autobiography; experiment with first- and third-person narratives; contrast female students' writings with male students'.

   Paper topics: (a) Discuss the role of women within family and society in Mohr's stories; (b) discuss Mohr as a feminine or feminist writer; (c) analyze the Hispanic cultural background to her stories *vis-à-vis* the universal themes.

Bibliography

Not much has been written on Nicholasa Mohr's work per se. The following are good introductory articles, and the Rivero article is particularly good for the study of bildungsroman in Latina women's writings:

Acosta-Belén, Edna. "The Literature of the Puerto Rican National Minority in the United States." *The Bilingual Review* 5:1–2 (Jan.–Aug. 1978): 107–16.

Cruz, Arnaldo. "Teaching Puerto Rican Authors: Modernization and Identity in Nuyorican Literature." *ADE Journal* (December 1988).

Mohr, Nicholasa. "On Being Authentic." *The Americas Review* 14:3–4 (Fall-Winter 1986): 106–09.

——."Puerto Rican Writers in the United States, Puerto Rican Writers in Puerto Rico: A Separation Beyond Language." *The Americas Review* 15:2 (Summer 1987): 87–92.

Rivero, Eliana. "*The House on Mango Street*: Tales of Growing Up Female and Hispanic." Tucson: Southwest Institute for Research on Women, The University of Arizona, Working Paper 22, 1986.

Michael S. Harper (b. 1938)

Contributing Editor: Herman Beavers

Classroom Issues and Strategies

Harper's poems often prove difficult because he is so deft at merging personal and national history within the space of one metaphor. One must be aware, then, of Harper's propensity toward veiled references to historical events. One can think here of a series of poems like "History as Apple Tree." The result, in a series like this, is that the reader cannot follow the large number of historical references Harper makes—in this case, to the history of Rhode Island and its founder, Roger Williams. The poems can be seen as obscure or enigmatic, when, in fact, they are designed to highlight a mode of African-American performance. In the same manner that one finds jazz musicians "quoting" another song within the space of a solo, Harper's use of history is often designed to suggest the simultaneity of events, the fact that one cannot escape the presence of the past.

Harper's interviews are often helpful, particularly those interviews where he discusses his poetic technique. Harper is a story-teller, a performer. He is adept at the conveyance of nuance in the poems. A valuable strategy is teaching Harper's poems in conjunction with a brief introduction to modern jazz. Team teaching with a jazz historian or an ethnomusicologist while focusing on Harper's strategies of composition is a way to ground the student in Harper's use of jazz as a structuring technique in his poems. Moreover, it allows for dialogue between literary and musical worlds. Since Harper's poems are often about both music and the context out of which the music springs, such a dialogue is important for students to see. As far as history is concerned, pointing the student toward, for example, a history of the Civil War or a biography of John Brown will often illuminate Harper's propensity to "name drop" in his poems. What becomes clear is that Harper is not being dense, but rather he sees his poetic project as one of "putting the reader to work."

You might introduce Harper by showing the film *Birth of a Nation* in order to flesh out Harper's revisionary stance toward myth. Using the film as a kind of counter-milieu, one can point out that Harper's poetry is designed to create a renewed, more vital American mythos. Also, a class where the students can hear John Coltrane's *A Love Supreme* album will prove invaluable to understanding Harper's jazz poems.

Students often protest the inaccessibility of the poems: e.g., "I don't understand this poem at all!" There are often questions regarding Harper's use of the word "modality." Also they do not understand Harper's use of repetition, which is designed to evoke the chant, or the poem as song.

Major Themes, Historical Perspectives, and Personal Issues

Harper is very concerned in his poems with the "American tradition of forgetfulness." In his poetry, one finds him creating situations where the contradictions between oral and written versions of history are brought into focus. Because Harper thinks of poetry as a discourse of song, the poems utilize improvisation to convey their themes. The intent of this is to highlight the complexity of American identity.

Harper's personal issues are, further, not necessarily distinguishable from the historical in his poems. If one were to point to a set of events that spur Harper's poetic voice, it would be the deaths of two of his children shortly after birth. Harper's poems on the subject express not only the personal grief of his wife and himself, but also the loss of cultural possibility the children represent. As a black man in a country so hostile to those who are black, Harper's grief is conflated into rage at the waste of human potential, a result of American forms of amnesia.

In short, the historical and the personal often function in layered fashion. Thus, Harper may use his personal grief as the springboard for illuminating a history of atrocities; the source of grief is different, but the grief is no less real.

Significant Form, Style, or Artistic Conventions

While Harper does not write in "forms" (at least of the classical sort), his work is informed by jazz composition and also several examples of African-American modernism. Clearly, Sterling Brown, Ralph Ellison, and Robert Hayden have each had an impact on Harper's poetry, not only formally, but also in terms of the questions Harper takes up in his poems. I would also cite W. H. Auden and W. B. Yeats as influences.

Formally and stylistically, Harper's poetry derives from jazz improvisation. For example, in one of his poems on the jazz saxophonist John Coltrane, Harper works out a poem that doubles as a prayer-chant in Coltrane's memory. What this suggests is that Harper does not favor symmetricality for the mere sake of symmetricality; thus, he eschews forms like the sonnet or the villanelle. One does find Harper, however, using prosody to usher the reader into a rhythmic mode that captures the nature of poetry as song as opposed to written discourse.

Original Audience

Harper's poems have indeed been widely read. However, his work has undergone a shift in audience. When he came on the scene in the late sixties, the black arts movement produced a large amount of poetry, largely because of poetry's supposed immediacy of impact. For that reason, I believe Harper's work was read by a number of people who expected militancy, anger, and a very narrow subject matter. However, one can see that his work has a different stylistic quality than that of many of his contemporaries who claimed to be writing for a narrower audience. Harper's poetry is more oriented toward inclusiveness, thus his poems utilize American history as a poetic site rather than just relying on a reified notion of racial identity that is crystallized into myth. Thus, after the sixties, Harper's audience became more clearly located in the poetry establishment. Though he still writes about musicians and artists, his readership is more specialized, more focused on poetry than twenty years ago.

Comparisons, Contrasts, Connections

Compare Harper with Brown, Ellison, Auden, and Yeats, as well as James Wright, Philip Levine, and Seamus Heaney. Hayden, Wright, and Yeats can, in their respective fashions, be considered remembrancers. That is, their work (to paraphrase Yeats) suggests that "memories are old identities." Hence, they often explore the vagaries of the past. A fruitful comparison might, for example, be made between Harper's and Hayden's poems on Vietnam. Brown and Harper are both interested in acts of heroism in African-American culture and lore. Ellison and Harper share an inclusive vision of America that eschews racial separatism in favor of a more dualistic sense of American identity.

Questions for Reading and Discussion/ Approaches to Writing

The letter-essay is extremely effective. Here the student writes a letter to Harper, a figure who appears in one of his poems, the instructor in the class, a classmate, etc., and engages the poems through their own personal response to the poems. The exercise allows students to feel more comfortable posing questions as part of their inquiry and also provides an opportunity to reflect on the poem's impact on their lives both experientially and exegetically.

Bibliography

See the interview with Harper in John O'Brien's *Interviews with Black Writers*. Also see his interview in *Ploughshares*, Fall 1981.

Read Robert B. Stepto's essay on Harper's work in the anthology *Chant of Saints* (Urbana: University of Illinois Press, 1979) and his essay on Harper's poems in *The Hollins Critic* (1976).

Michael G. Cooke has a chapter on Harper in his book *Afro-American Literature in the Twentieth Century* (New Haven: Yale University Press, 1985).

The most recent retrospective on Harper's work can be found in *Callaloo* 13, no. 4 (Fall 1991): 780–800.

Michael Herr (b. 1940)

Contributing Editor: Raymund Paredes

Classroom Issues and Strategies

It's probably necessary and certainly a good idea to provide some sort of historical context for the consideration of Herr's work. This can be done by assigning supplementary reading or lecturing on the history of the Vietnam War. As a Vietnam War veteran myself, I relate my own personal experiences of the war to students to compare with Herr's. If you, or any older students, have direct experience with the Vietnam era, this is a useful approach. There are many good films about Vietnam (both feature and documentary) that could complement Herr's book.

Students respond very strongly to the graphic depiction of the inhumanity and insanity of the war. They want to know more about the causes of the Vietnam War and the political climate of the United States at the time.

Major Themes, Historical Perspectives, and Personal Issues

The major themes in the excerpted passage are the dehumanizing and brutalizing influences of war, particularly the way war renders soldiers incapable of functioning in "normal" social circumstances; the relationship between the writer's style and presentation of the war and the drug culture of the 1960s and 1970s; and the author's view that the war was fundamentally immoral, even more so than other wars. Key here is Herr's use of the Spanish phrase "la vida loca" (the crazy life). On a personal level, Herr emphasizes his troubling, even macabre, attraction to the war, its combination of bloodshed, madness, camaraderie, and heroism.

Significant Form, Style, or Artistic Conventions

Dispatches is an extraordinary work stylistically, a brilliant execution of the speaking styles of young American soldiers: fast paced, full of slang, very much shaped by popular culture (films, television, rock and roll music) and the drug culture. Herr is also adept at capturing the officialese of the U.S. military establishment. Many of the formal and stylistic qualities of *Dispatches* connect Herr to postmodernism.

Original Audience

Dispatches is a very contemporary book in terms of its values, its point of view, a book about young people written by a young person.

Comparisons, Contrasts, Connections

Herr's work can be compared to that of other writers about the Vietnam War and with the so-called "new journalists" such as Tom Wolfe. The second connection is especially interesting. Students might note how Herr uses literary/fictional techniques—figurative language, characterization, narrative development—in what is ostensibly, as indicated by the title, a work of journalism. Students might look at other treatments of the Vietnam War—both fictional and journalistic—to compare points of view about the war, its impact on the humanity of the soldiers, etc.

Questions for Reading and Discussion/ Approaches to Writing

1. What is the author's attitude toward the war? What are the effects of the war on human behavior? From your knowledge, is Herr's position on the war widely shared?
2. How would you describe Herr's style? In what ways is Herr's style compatible (or not) with its subject? From what sources does Herr draw his images, his metaphors? How does this compare with the practices of other writers? In what sense is the notion of "la vida loca" symbolic of both the literary situation and the temper of the times?

Bibliography

Other books on Vietnam are very useful. I recommend: Stanley Karnow's *Vietnam*, Neil Sheehan's *A Bright Shining Lie*, Wallace Terry's *Bloods*, and Philip Caputo's *A Rumor of War*.

Norman Mailer (b. 1923)

Contributing Editor: Barry H. Leeds

Classroom Issues and Strategies

To begin with, any approach to teaching Norman Mailer's work must take into consideration his flamboyant and controversial public image, which often obscures critical responses to the works. Amazingly, many college students will not recognize Mailer's name at first; but those who do will very probably be armored in negative preconceptions, often based on incomplete or erroneous information.

The selections from *The Armies of the Night* presented in the anthology provide an opportunity to deal effectively with this issue: Mailer is ultimately shown, not as an unconscionable egotist presenting himself as his own hero, but as a rather self-deprecating narrator/protagonist. For example, crossing the line of MP's in his act of civil disobedience, he describes himself as a somewhat ridiculous figure:

"It was his dark pinstripe suit, his vest . . . the barrel chest, the early paunch—he must have looked like a banker himself, a banker, gone ape!" (pp. 150–151, Signet edition).

Again, before being arrested, Mailer feels, almost unwillingly, that "a deep modesty was on its way to him . . . as well as fear, yes now he saw it, fear of the consequences of this weekend in Washington" (Signet, p. 93).

This emerging new sense of self leads to a crucial realization: "No, the only revolutionary truth was a gun in the hills, and that would not be his, he would be too old by then, and too incompetent, yes, too incompetent said the new modesty, and too showboat, too lacking in essential judgment . . ." (Signet, p. 94).

Yet despite the constant interplay here (as in his life and work as a whole) between the performer and the thoughtful commentator, what looms far larger is Mailer's evocative capacity to strike to the heart of an issue of national significance in his prose. Consider the forceful and moving conclusion to *The Armies of the Night*, entitled "The Metaphor Delivered" (Signet, p. 320).

The unusual point of view used here, which was to become a hallmark of Mailer's nonfiction of the 1970s, provides interesting possibilities for a discussion of point of view and genre.

Major Themes, Historical Perspectives, and Personal Issues

The historical themes are obvious from the nature of *The Armies of the Night* and its relationship to the Vietnam War. Mailer's preoccupation with existential choice, personal courage, and integrity are evident in the passages selected.

Significant Form, Style, or Artistic Conventions

As I have explained in my headnote, Mailer's development from a derivative and naturalistic vision in *The Naked and the Dead* (1948) to a unique and highly existential one in later works such as *An American Dream* (1965) is evident in *The Armies of the Night*. The concept of the "nonfiction novel" and the unusual third-person participant/narrator point of view are important in any discussion of *Armies* and Mailer's subsequent work.

Original Audience

It is interesting and important to discuss the significance (or perceived insignificance) of those events recounted in *The Armies of the Night* to today's students. Further, my footnotes will to some degree ameliorate unfamiliarity with particular people or events.

Comparisons, Contrasts, Connections

Parallels can be drawn to Ernest Hemingway's *Green Hills of Africa* (1935), Tom Wolfe's *The Electric Kool-Aid Acid Test* (1968) and even *The Education of Henry Adams* (1907). Further, Mailer's early work, notably *The Naked and the Dead* (1948) was influenced profoundly by James T. Farrell, John Dos Passos, and John Steinbeck.

Questions for Reading and Discussion/ Approaches to Writing

1. Do you find Mailer's use of himself as a third-person participant effective or confusing? This book, which won both a Pulitzer Prize and the National Book Award, has often been cited, along with Tom Wolfe's *The Electric Kool-Aid Acid Test* (1968) as an example of the "new journalism." But a similar point of view was used by Henry Adams in *The Education of Henry Adams* as early as 1907, and

the concept of a "nonfiction novel" dates back at least as far as Ernest Hemingway's *Green Hills of Africa* (1935). Does this relatively unusual form attract or repel you?

2. Mailer writes (Signet, p. 63): "The American corporation executive . . . was perfectly capable of burning unseen women and children in the Vietnamese jungles, yet felt a large displeasure and fairly final disapproval at the generous use of obscenity in literature and public." Do you agree with Mailer that depersonalized governmental violence is more obscene than the use of four-letter words?

3. Consider Mailer's final statements in "The Metaphor Delivered." Do you feel that Mailer, despite his antiwar civil disobedience, is a patriot? Do the U.S. Marshals who think him a traitor love their country more? Were you emotionally moved by this conclusion?

4. These events took place more than twenty years ago. Do they seem to have any bearing on your life, and on the America you live in today, or do they seem like ancient history? Are the participants (e.g., Robert Lowell, Dwight MacDonald) familiar or alien to you?

5. Can you envision any future national situation in which similar demonstrations might occur? Are there any that you might find justifiable?

Bibliography

"The Armies of the Night," in *The Structured Vision of Norman Mailer* by Barry H. Leeds (NYU Press, 1969) seems to help render the book more accessible to my students. Chapter 8. Also:

Lennon, J. Michael, ed. *Critical Essays on Norman Mailer*. Boston: G. K. Hall, 1986.

Manso, Peter. *Mailer: His Life and Times*. New York: Simon and Schuster, 1985.

Carolyn Forché (b. 1950)

Contributing Editor: Constance Coiner

Classroom Issues and Strategies

Because two of the three poems included in this anthology appear in the section of *The Country Between Us* (*TCBU*) titled "In Salvador, 1978–80," students will need some introduction to the situation in El Salvador at the time when Forché went there as a journalist/poet/human rights investigator. My students have been curious about the U.S. role in El Salvador's twelve-year civil war that ended with a United Nation (U.N.)-brokered peace accord on January 1, 1992. In "A Lesson in Commitment" (*TriQuarterly* [Winter 1986]: 30–38) Forché recounts the events that led to her going to El Salvador—an interesting, even amusing story that students will welcome. Forché's "El Salvador: An Aide Mémoire" (*The American Poetry Review* [July/August 1981]: 3–7), which both prefaces and theoretically frames the "El Salvador" poems, is essential to students' understanding "The Colonel" and "Because One Is Always Forgotten."

Findings of the U.N.-sponsored "truth commission," which investigated some of the worst human rights abuses of the twelve-year civil war, appear, for example, in *The New York Times*—"U.N. Report Urges Sweeping Changes in Salvador Army" (March 16, 1993, A1 and A12) and "How U.S. Actions Helped Hide Salvador Human Rights Abuses" (March 21, 1993, Section 1, pages 1 and 10). Consider also "The Military Web of Corruption," *The Nation* (October 23, 1982, 391–93), by Forché and Leonel Gomez. Students could also profit from renting on their own or your showing clips from *Romero*, a 1989 film directed by John Duigan and featuring Raul Julia as Monsignor Oscar Romero, the Archbishop of San Salvador to whom Forché dedicated the eight "El Salvador poems." (Romero was murdered by a death squad in 1980 while saying mass at a hospital for the terminally ill.)

Students and teachers who want more background on El Salvador's history and the country's political and economic conditions can consult the following: *El Salvador: Another Vietnam* (1981), a fifty-minute documentary produced and directed by Glenn Silber and Tete Vasconcellos; Robert Armstrong and Janet Shenk's *El Salvador: The Face of Revolution* (Boston: South End Press, 1982); *A Decade of War: El Salvador Confronts the Future*, eds. Anjli Sundaram and George Gelber (New York: Monthly Review Press, 1991); and the North American Congress on Latin

America (NACLA), an independent organization founded to analyze and report on Latin America and U.S. foreign policy toward Latin America. NACLA (475 Riverside Drive, Room 454, New York, NY 10115; 212-870-3146) publishes a journal and has a library open to the public.

I strongly recommend addressing the controversy in the U.S. concerning "political poetry," perhaps at the beginning and then at the end of your discussion of Forché's poems. Forché herself addresses this controversy briefly in "El Salvador: An Aide Mémoire." Forché's poetry and her views point to differences between formalist and "cultural studies" approaches to literature, differences that can also be usefully discussed in relation to other writers assigned in your course.

An audiocassette of Forché reading from *TCBU* is available from Watershed Tapes, P. O. Box 50145, Washington, D.C. 20004. Students respond favorably to hearing Forché read the poems. I also ask for volunteers to read the poems aloud. They have done so effectively, especially if given a few days to prepare.

"The Colonel"

Forché invented the term "documentary poem" for "The Colonel." This alternative form works partly because she sparingly employs traditional poetic forms as touchstones within it and partly because its seeming "artlessness" elicits belief from her readers.

In the journalistic way that it sets the scene, "The Colonel" takes little poetic license, inviting readers to trust that it has not caricatured the truth. Its simple, declarative sentences do not resemble poetic lines. Even visually, with its justified right-hand margin, the piece resembles a newspaper report more than a poem. In the twentieth century, the lyric has become by far the dominant poetic form, but because Forché wants her readers to experience what she witnessed in El Salvador from 1978 to 1980, she consciously resists lyricizing the experience. Before turning to Forché's poems, I define and provide examples of well-known lyrical poems so students can better understand how she subverts traditional lyrical poetry.

Forché first draws us into "The Colonel" by conversing with us about the rumors that have crept north of brutal Latin American military dictatorships: "WHAT YOU HAVE HEARD is true." Forché extends that sense of familiarity for her reader by creating in the first lines a scene that, except for the pistol on the cushion, could occur in any North American home: The wife serves coffee, the daughter files her nails, the son goes out for the evening; there are daily papers, pet dogs, a TV turned on even at meal time. The minutiae of ordinary domestic life draw us into the scene, as if we're entering the room with Forché; we feel as if *we're* having dinner with the colonel.

"The moon swung bare on its black cord over the house" is one of two figures foregrounded in the poem, and Forché deliberately draws attention to its artfulness. Although the image is ominous, suggestive generally of the gothic and particularly of a swinging interrogation lamp or of someone hanging naked from a rope, it is too decorative for its place between a pistol and a cop show, thus announcing itself as art.

The following lines portray the colonel's house as a fortress: "Broken bottles were embedded in the walls around the house to scoop the kneecaps from a man's legs or cut his hands to lace. On the windows there were gratings like those in liquor stores." The outside of this fortress, constructed to mutilate anyone who tries to get inside, stands in stark contrast to the several images of "civilization" and affluence inside, such as "dinner, rack of lamb, good wine, a gold bell [that] was on the table for calling the maid."

Until the parrot says hello from the terrace, triggering the colonel's anger and the action of the poem—that is, his spilling human ears on the table—the poem is a string of the verbs "to be." As passive as her verbs, the poet can only catalog nouns, unable to exercise control or take action. In fact, her friend warns her with his eyes: "say nothing." And so, many readers identify with the poet rather than feel manipulated by her; like us, she is frightened, wary. (Students may be surprised to learn that Forché did not invent the Colonel's displaying severed ears as a startling, violent metaphor. The incident actually occurred, she has reported.)

Note the contrast between the single stylized line, "the moon swung bare on its black cord over the house," and the numerous declarative, weak-verb sentences

> There were daily papers . . .
> On the television was a cop show. It was in English.
> Broken bottles were embedded in the walls . . .
> On the windows there were gratings like those in liquor
> stores.

This contrast between the stylized line and the weak-verb sentences suggests the range of possible responses to situations such as dinner with the colonel as well as the range of possible responses to *reading* about dinner with the colonel: Will the poet run away from this experience by lyricizing it? Will the poet remain impotent, unable to invent strong verbs—in other words, be unable to take action? Do more appropriate responses exist? Forché thus puts her readers in her place, in that room with the colonel, in a state of nascent political and moral awareness. The form itself suggests that we must make choices and take positions, not only as we read "The Colonel" but also as we respond to military dictatorships and to our government's support of them.

With the poem's second foregrounded figure, a simile describing the ears as "dried peach halves," the poet at once manipulates the mundane and is confined by it. She knows we have all seen dried fruit and so she could not more vividly describe those severed ears, but she apologizes for the limits of her inherited poetic and for the limits of language itself, acknowledging simply: "There is no other way to say this." However, she also defends poetic language here. Because "there is no other way to say this," she must rely on a poetic device, a simile, to communicate with us.

The colonel shakes one of the ears in the faces of his guests. A human ear is an unusual—an even extraordinary—metonymy, as Forché well knows. It stands for the Salvadoran people, for those who have been mutilated and murdered as well as for those who continue to resist the military dictatorship. It might be helpful to students to think of the colonel's actions as a perverse magic show. He is able to make a severed ear come "alive" by dropping it into a glass of water, just as the death squads are able to make Salvadorans disappear. The sweeping gesture ("He swept the ears to the floor with his arm and held the last of his wine in the air") is theatrical and sends the ears down to the floor while the colonel elevates his glass of wine. The glass of wine carries us back to the "good wine" at dinner and the other markers of the affluent life maintained within the colonel's fortress at the expense of the extreme poverty outside. The glass of wine, then, is a metonymy for all the trappings of "civilization" we have seen in the colonel's fortress and for the power of the military over ordinary Salvadorans. And as the ears of ordinary Salvadorans go down to the floor, that wine glass, that metonymy for the affluence of the few, is hoisted triumphantly above them.

With this theatrical action come the colonel's climactic words: "Something for your poetry, no?" Most immediately, "Something" refers to the grand theatrical show the colonel has put on for his guests' "entertainment." But the colonel's ironic sneer also mocks Forché's position as a North American poet, drawing attention to the belief held by many North Americans that poetry has certain "proper" subjects, and that mutilation—and by extension politics—are not among them. Since the eighteenth century, mainstream North America has lost touch with the sense of literature as political catalyst. Nineteenth-century romanticism and some twentieth-century poetry promoted by New Criticism has been especially individualized, introspective, and self-referential. In "A Lesson in Commitment," Forché recalls how Leonel Gomez Vides tried to persuade her to come to El Salvador, asking her, "do you want to write poetry about yourself for the rest of your life?" Forché, who came to understand Gomez Vides's point, believes that the "twentieth century human condition demands a poetry of witness" ("El Salvador: An Aide Mémoire").

Now look at the poem's final lines: "Some of the ears on the floor caught this scrap of his voice. Some of the / ears on the floor were pressed to the ground." Some of the ears seem to be alive, even though the colonel didn't believe for a minute during his mock magic show that he was actually bringing a dead ear back to life. Some of the ears seem to be listening and feeling for vibrations, for sounds and motion of resistance to the colonel's fortress. This poem, especially these concluding lines, implicitly questions the reader: Is *your* ear pressed to the ground? Are *you* listening? Have *you* "HEARD" (to return to the poem's opening words, written for emphasis in uppercase)? Are you responding to and involving yourself in resistance to the brutality of this colonel and others like him?

"Because One Is Always Forgotten"

This poem makes an excellent pedagogical companion piece to "The Colonel." As in her documentary poem, Forché writes in calculated relation to bourgeois forms, calling attention to the limits of inherited poetic forms and at the same time insisting that poetry can be used for political as well as aesthetic purposes. The obverse of "The Colonel," which appears artless, this elegy is the most highly structured piece in *TCBU*. Before turning to "Because One Is Always Forgotten," I define the elegy and provide examples of well-known elegies.

Forché wrote "Because One Is Always Forgotten" in memory of José Rudolfo Viera, who was Salvador's Deputy of Agrarian Reform under President Napoleon Duarte. (If teachers have read aloud excerpts from "A Lesson in Commitment" or made copies available, students will recall that Leonel Gomez Vides visited Forché in San Diego, urging her to come to El Salvador; Gomez Vides was Viera's assistant Deputy for Agrarian Reform.) Viera discovered that money that had been designated for agrarian reform (that is, an attempt to divide some of the largest landholdings so that most of the country's wealth would no longer reside in the hands of a few families) was being pocketed by members of Duarte's administration and men high up in the military. Some of that money was coming from the Carter administration in the U.S., from U.S. taxpayers, and going not toward agrarian reform but to support the expensive tastes of a few. Think for a moment of words from "The Colonel"—rack of lamb, good wine, a gold bell for calling the maid. Think for a moment, too, of Forché's words in "El Salvador: An Aide Mémoire": "I was taken to the homes of landowners, with their pools set like aquamarines in the clipped grass, to the afternoon games of canasta over quaint local pupusas and tea, where parrots hung by their feet among the bougainvillea and nearly everything was imported, if only from Miami or New Orleans."

Viera, who reported the corruption on news televised in San Salvador, was murdered by "the White Glove," a right wing death squad. Viera was shot along with two North Americans, Michael Hammer and Mark Pearlman, who were in El Salvador as consultants for agrarian reform. At the time of the murders, the three men were having a meal in the Sheraton Hotel dining room in San Salvador. No one was arrested, much less brought to trial, for the murder of the three men. Some North American newspapers reported the deaths of Michael Hammer and Mark Pearlman, but because Viera's death was not included in those reports, Forché felt the need to memorialize Viera.

"Because One Is Always Forgotten" tightly compresses rhythm and images, suggesting that traditional forms necessarily strain or snap under the weight of political imprisonment, murder, mutilation. After the second line, the lines start "losing" beats, as if atrocities in Salvador defy even one more word or beat. Forché undercuts the stylization that would comfort us, that would provide the consolation and closure that elegies have traditionally provided.

She also uses "heart," a word common in poetry, in a way that is the opposite of what we expect.

> I could take my heart, he said, and give it to a *campesino*
> and he would cut it up and give it back:
>
> you can't eat heart in those four dark
> chambers where a man can be kept years.

"You can't eat heart" is a spondee—all unaccented syllables have been removed. A spondee represents language at its most compressed, its most structured, because English is more naturally a combination of accented and unaccented syllables. "You can't eat heart" also announces the limitations of poetic language. You can't *eat* it. It cannot, literally, sustain human life. In other words, an elegy, however necessary, is not a sufficient response to events such as those in El Salvador.

Students may volunteer that "those four dark chambers" refer to the left and right ventricles and the left and right auricles of the heart. But unless they have read "The Visitor," one of Forché's "El Salvador" poems not included in *The Heath Anthology*, they won't know that "dark chambers" also refers to "la oscura" (the dark place), a prison within a prison that inspired "The Visitor." Forché describes "la oscura"—where men were kept in boxes, one meter by one meter, with barred openings the size of a book—in her introduction to "The Visitor" on the Watershed audiocassette; she also describes "la oscura" in "El Salvador: An Aide Mémoire."

Now look at the following lines from the fourth stanza:

> A boy soldier in the bone-hot sun works his knife
> to peel the face from a dead man

The second line of this stanza stops abruptly; again, it is as if the atrocities in Salvador defy even one more word or beat. "To peel the face from a dead man" is no more an invented metaphor than "The "Colonel" 's severed ears; in Salvador Forché actually saw human faces hanging from tree branches. Too often we have been taught to expect hearts and flowers from poetry, sometimes used sentimentally, but such sentimentality is turned on its head here. "Flowering with such faces" uses conventional poetic language in an extraordinary way.

Ask students what they make of the last, paradoxical stanza: "The heart is the toughest part of the body / Tenderness is in the hands." This stanza asks readers to examine something we have long accepted, the cliché of the tender heart, implying that we should probe some of our other assumptions as well.

Hands can *do* something; they can take action. *TCBU* includes many other references to hands, suggesting a wide range of possibilities for their use. Hands can "peel the face from a dead man / and hang it from the branch of a tree." The colonel uses his hands to spill human ears on the table and to shake one of the ears mockingly at his guests. Hands can be the White Glove (the name for a notorious Salvadoran death squad). But hands can also be tender; hands can connect people (the poet and Victoria in "As Children Together" hold "each other's coat sleeves"); hands can communicate (Forché tells Victoria to write to her). Rather than provide consolation and closure, as would a traditional elegy, "Because One Is Always Forgotten," like "The Colonel" and other poems in *TCBU*, asks readers to consider choices about their hands, their actions, their lives.

"As Children Together"

This poem is included in the section of *TCBU* titled "Reunion." Addressed to Forché's girlhood friend, Victoria, this poem gives us a sense of the poet's working-class roots. Although Forché continues to identify strongly with the class of her origin and with other oppressed groups, even as a youngster she "always believed . . . that there might be a way to get out" of Detroit. Victoria, ashamed of the "tins of surplus flour," the "relief checks," and other trappings of poverty, was also eager to escape: "I am going to have it," Victoria asserted, while believing that granting sexual favors to men was her only conduit.

The first stanza represents the girls' lives and futures as boxed in, closed off: the snow is "pinned"; the lights are "cubed"; they wait for Victoria's father to "whittle his soap cakes away, finish the whiskey," and for Victoria's mother to turn off the lights. Confined by "tight black dresses"—which, in this context, arguably represent a class marker—they nevertheless attempt to move away from the limitations of class, "holding each other's coat sleeves" for support. They slide "down the roads . . . *past* / crystal swamps and the death / face of each dark house, / *over* the golden ice / of tobacco spit" (my emphasis). They try to move away from their diminished options—the "*quiet* of ponds," "the *blind* white hills," "a *scant* snow" (my emphasis). But, sliding on ice, their movement is literally as well as metaphorically precarious.

Like "The Colonel" and "Because One Is Always Forgotten," this is a documentary poem, if less apparently so. The poet reports to Victoria and to us the poet's memory of their life together as children, the little she has heard about Victoria since their childhood, and one major event in the poet's life since their childhood ("I have been to Paris / since we parted"). In this stanza we hear the voice of the reporter, as we do in the other two poems. Although the poet doesn't know Victoria's current state, she reports what "They say."

If what "they say" is true, and if Victoria reads this poem, the poet has two simple messages for her childhood friend: "write to me" and "I have been to Paris / since we parted." On first reading, many students may think that the poet is bragging about the contrast between her own adult life and what she believes that of Victoria to be (the poet has been to Paris, while Victoria did not even get as far as Montreal, the city of her childhood dreams). However, by taking the last line in the context of the entire poem, we see the implications, not of going to Paris, but how the poet got there: *not* by relying on the men of this poem as her vehicle. "Write to me" suggests that the poet wants to share with Victoria her experiences of—and perhaps her strategies for—getting out.

Victoria has not escaped the cycle of poverty and battered men. In the second-to-last stanza the poet reports a rumor that Victoria lives in a trailer near Detroit with her children and with her husband, who "returned from the Far East broken / cursing holy blood at the table" and whose whittling of soap cakes associates him with Victoria's whiskey-drinking father, who appears in the first stanza.

At first glance, "As Children Together" seems far removed from Salvador's civil war. In the context of *TCBU*, however, "As Children

Together" links "the Far East" (Vietnam) to El Salvador. Young men from Forché's working-class neighborhood were drafted by or enlisted in the military when many of the more privileged of their generation managed student deferments or, after the draft lottery was established, other alternatives to military service. In "A Lesson in Commitment," Forché reports that her interest in Vietnam was fueled partly by her first husband's fighting in Vietnam and his suffering "from what they now call Post-Vietnam Syndrome." The Vietnam War, as well as her opposition to it, schooled Forché for "another Vietnam" in El Salvador.

"As Children Together" provides a good opportunity to discuss the range of meanings for the deliberately ambiguous title of *The Country Between Us*. "Between" can mean something that separates and distances people, but "between" can also mean that which we share, that which connects us. The "country" is El Salvador, but it is also the United States. "Us" can be people on opposing sides of a civil war, people polarized by their opinions about political issues, or people sharing a common opposition to oppression. "Us" can be people inhabiting two nations (Salvador and the U.S.). "Us" can also refer to two individuals, such as the poet and Victoria, who may be at once separated by geography and recent experience but connected by common roots and class origin. The poet's saying to Victoria "write to me" suggests a desire for "between" as separation to become the "between" of reunion and connection.

Major Themes, Historical Perspectives, and Personal Issues

1. U.S. imperialism.
2. The difference between poetry that calls attention chiefly to form, and poetry like Forché's that is formally interesting as well as socially and politically engaged.
3. The difference between poetry that is individualized and self-referential and poetry like Forché's that addresses social and political issues and engenders human empathy.
4. *TCBU* has renewed the controversy about the relation of art to politics, about "suitable" subjects for poetry. This peculiarly American debate assumes that only certain poems are political, stigmatizing "political" poems and failing to acknowledge the ideological constitution of all literary texts. The opposition to "political" poetry, as Forché herself has observed, extends beyond explicitly polemical work to any "impassioned voices of witness," to any who leave the "safety of self-contemplation to imagine and address the larger world" ("A Lesson in Commitment").

5. Forché's poetry resonates with a sense of international kinship. "For us to comprehend El Salvador," Forché has written, "for there to be moral revulsion, we must be convinced that Salvadorans— and indeed the whole population of Latin America—are people like ourselves, contemporary with ourselves, and occupying the same reality" ("Grasping the Gruesome," *Esquire*, September 1983). Forché's poetry moves us with a forceful sense of "the other" rare in contemporary American verse.
6. The merging of personal and political.

Significant Form, Style, or Artistic Conventions

In the twentieth century, the lyric has become the preponderant poetic form, but in *TCBU* Forché is a story-teller, her poetry predominantly narrative. Because she wants her readers to experience what she witnessed in El Salvador from 1978 to 1980, she consciously resists lyricizing experiences. Forché has said that "the twentieth-century human condition demands a poetry of witness" ("El Salvador: An Aide Mémoire").

To show how Forché departs from the lyric, teachers should define the lyric and provide well-known examples. To show how Forché departs from the elegy in "Because One Is Always Forgotten," teachers should define the elegy and provide well-known examples. For "The Colonel" teachers should define and provide other examples of "metonymy."

Original Audience

The particular audience for Forché's poetry is the American people. Monsignor Romero (again, the Archbishop of San Salvador who was assassinated by a right wing death squad while praying at mass) urged Forché to return to the U.S. and "tell the American people what is happening" ("El Salvador: An Aide Mémoire"). Poets do not often so purposefully address such a wide audience.

Students should discuss whether—and, if so, in what ways— Forché's poems effectively address the wide popular audience she seeks, one that would include more people than the "already converted." Do the three poems under consideration avoid or fall into off-putting didacticism? Students, of course, will have their own responses, but I would argue that Forché has consciously adopted strategies throughout *TCBU* that invite the reader into the poems. One of those strategies is to acknowledge her own ignorance rather than point to the reader's; another is to place herself or someone else in the poem as an object of ridicule or admonition rather than the reader. For example, the colonel sneers at the poet; the poet does not upbraid her reader. And in "Because One Is Always Forgotten," a hungry *campesino* would reject Viera's heart, admonishing: "you can't eat heart."

Comparisons, Contrasts, Connections

Denise Levertov, Muriel Rukeyser, Adrienne Rich, Pablo Neruda—these are anti-imperialist, politically engaged writers whose lives and literary texts promote a global as well as a private kinship.

The private anguish of Sylvia Plath's, Anne Sexton's and Robert Lowell's confessional poetry provides a provocative contrast to the public issues of human rights violations, U.S. foreign policy, war and class oppression addressed in "The Colonel," "Because One Is Always Forgotten," and "As Children Together."

Questions for Reading and Discussion

"The Colonel":

1. How does the capitalization of the first four words function in the poem?
2. Can anyone identify the traditional poetic forms that Forché sparingly employs as "aesthetic centerpieces" in this "artless," "journalistic," documentary poem? (I'm thinking here of "the moon swung bare on its black cord over the house" and the simile describing the ears as "dried peach halves").
3. Why is the television "cop show" in English, the commercial in Spanish?
4. Why the proliferation of to-be verbs (is, was, were)?
5. What are the women in this poem doing?
6. What might the colonel have in mind when he says, "Something for your poetry, no?"
7. What are the implied and explicit cultural and political relationships between Salvador and the U.S.?

"Because One Is Always Forgotten":

1. In the first line, what does "it" refer to?
2. What are the relationships between "heart" and other body parts?
3. Who is "you" in the third stanza?
4. Identify similarities/differences (including formal ones) between this poem and "The Colonel."

5. This poem concludes the section of *TCBU* titled "In Salvador, 1978–80." Why might have Forché chosen "hands" as the last word of this section?

"As Children Together":

1. What are some of the similarities/differences between Victoria and the poet as children? What might be some similarities/differences between them as adults?
2. What is the significance of "Paris" in the last line?
3. What are some of the difficulties of remaining in touch with one's community, cultural group, or class of origin after being separated from them by emigration, formal education, or class mobility?
4. What's the difference between the poet's saying, "I always believed this, / Victoria, that there might / be a way to get out" and Victoria's asserting, "I am going to have it"?
5. Identify similarities/differences (including formal ones) between this poem and "The Colonel" and "Because One Is Always Forgotten."

Approaches to Writing

Students in my undergraduate courses write one-page (double-spaced, typed) "response" essays to each assigned text, which they turn in before I have said anything about the writer or text(s). In these essays, students reflect on why they have responded to the text(s) as they have, including some identification of their own subject position (gender, race, national origin, class origin, political views, and so on), but they must also refer specifically to the text. In the case of these three poems, students could choose to focus the response essay on just one poem or they could write about a recurring theme, image, and strategy, briefly citing all three poems.

A few students have elected to write creative responses, trying their hand at imitating the form of one of the assigned poems.

Bibliography

Forché, Carolyn. "El Salvador: An Aide Mémoire." *American Poetry Review* (July/August 1981): 3–7.

——. "A Lesson in Commitment." *TriQuarterly* (Winter 1986): 30–38.

Greer, Michael. "Politicizing the Modern: Carolyn Forché in El Salvador and America." *The Centennial Review* (Spring 1986): 160–80.

Kufeld, Adam. *El Salvador: Photographs by Adam Kufeld*. "Introduction" by Arnoldo Ramos and poetry by Manlio Argueta.

Mann, John. "Carolyn Forché: Poetry and Survival." *American Poetry* 3.3 (Spring 1986): 51–69.

Mattison, Harry et. al., eds. *El Salvador: Work of Thirty Photographers*. Text by Carolyn Forché. New York: Writers and Readers Publishing Cooperative, 1983.

Useful interviews include David Montenegro's in *American Poetry Review* 17.6 (November/December 1988): 35–40; Constance Coiner's in *The Jacaranda Review* (Winter 1988): 47–68; and Kim Addonizio and John High's in *Five Fingers Review* 3 (1985): 116–31.

Gish Jen (b. 1955)

Contributing Editor: Bonnie TuSmith

Classroom Issues and Strategies

The father's patriarchal and feudal attitudes can easily arouse feminist ire. While such attitudes need to be acknowledged and discussed, it is important to point out the narrator's viewpoint toward her father. The narrator pulls no punches in pointing out Ralph Chang's sexist and domineering ways. Such information does not, however, trigger brooding resentment or a desire for vengeance. In addressing this issue in the classroom, the instructor can combine feminist and cultural theories to promote a richer understanding of difference.

Major Themes, Historical Perspectives, and Personal Issues

A key theme found in Jen's work is the Asian immigrant's coming to terms with American society. For people who come from cultures that are significantly different from the hegemonic European one, the process of acculturation can be awkward and even destructive. Like the father's western suit, Asians who take on what they consider typically American culture often find that this does not fit well. The mother's statement "But this here is the U—S—of—A!" reveals the dis-ease with which non-white, non-Europeans attempt to assimilate into European

American society. Historically excluded from the "good life," Americans of Asian descent necessarily exhibit ambivalence toward symbols of American success, such as the town country club that is about to be sued by a waiting black family.

Significant Form, Style, or Artistic Conventions

The two-part structure of the story offers us a view of the father's feudal lord behavior in two different settings. In the first, treating his employees like servants—even if done magnanimously—simply does not work. In the second, the same arrogant impulse stands him in good stead when confronting racism. The structure gives us a clear picture of Ralph Chang's background and personality and enables us to consider the appropriateness of social behavior based on class and cultural differences.

The use of an observer/child narrator who is older and more reserved than the talkative younger sister Mona lends credibility to the narration and situates the story in a comfortable, firsthand point of view. The narrator's English fluency and assumption of her American birthright render her voice easily accessible to a white audience. In this story, at least, there are no barriers based on language.

Original Audience

Since the author is fairly new on the literary scene, her audience is comprised of contemporary readers as young as adolescents and older who are interested in multicultural literature.

Comparisons, Contrasts, Connections

Jen's stories are easily anthologized and can be compared to numerous American short stories—immigrant, classic, and ethnic—that explore issues of Americanization and the tensions which exist among various American cultures.

Questions for Reading and Discussion/
Approaches to Writing

In teaching ethnic literature I use the approach of moving from the familiar—what Euro-American students already know about and have in common with all human beings as well as what they know about literature—to the unfamiliar. This strategy helps students and instructors get past their fear of what seems foreign or the "exotic other." Thus, questions such as the following might be helpful:

1. Describe the dynamics of this nuclear family. What is the relationship of each family member to the others, and how does this reflect or challenge your notions of family?
2. Identify the source of humor in this story. How does humor contribute to the tone, mood, and overall message of the work?
3. How does the two-part narrative structure of the story enable meaningful comparison/contrast between the father's own society and the rest of American society? Is there ironic contrast between the two sections?
4. Does the dialogue seem realistic? How does the writer use dialogue to convey the racist, sexist, and classist attitudes of the characters?

Aurora Levins Morales (b. 1954)

Contributing Editor: Frances R. Aparicio

Classroom Issues and Strategies

Since Levins Morales's major book is authored in collaboration with her mother, Rosario Morales, it would be appropriate to present her work in this context. Instructors could familiarize themselves with *Getting Home Alive* and make a selection of texts in which the dialogue—as well as the differences—between mother and daughter is exemplified.

Major Themes, Historical Perspectives, and Personal Issues

Major themes in Aurora Levins Morales's work: identity as a female minority in the U.S.; feminism; multiple identity (Puerto Rican, Jewish, North American), also inherited versus self-defined identities; concept of *immigrant*; Jewish culture and traditions; mother/daughter relationships; importance of language, reading, words, and writing; remembering and memory as a vehicle to surpass sense of fragmentation and exile/displacement; images of spaces and cities; "internationalist" politics.

Significant Form, Style, or Artistic Conventions

Heterogeneous forms and texts constitute Levins Morales's writings. *Getting Home Alive* is a collage of poems, short stories, lyrical prose pieces, essays, and dialogues. Note the importance of eclectic style: She is lyrical, subdued at times, sensorial, and quite visual in her imagery. She does not belong to any major literary movement; her writings cannot be easily categorized into one style or another, though they definitely respond to the preoccupations of other U.S. women of color.

Comparisons, Contrasts, Connections

Fruitful comparisons can be drawn to the works of other women of color, such as Cherríe Moraga, *Loving in the War Years* in *Cuentos: Stories by Latinas*, eds. Gómez, Moraga, Romo-Carmona (New York: Kitchen Table Press, 1983). Levins Morales has been particularly influenced by Alice Walker. In addition, I believe comparisons and contrasts with mainstream U.S. feminist writers would also prove valuable.

Questions for Reading and Discussion/ Approaches to Writing

1. Study questions would deal with textual analysis and with clarifying references to Spanish words, places in Puerto Rico or El Barrio, and other allusions that might not be clear to students.
2. (a) Have students do their own version of "Child of the Americas" in order to look into their own inheritance and cross-cultural identities.

   (b) Paper topics might include the importance of multiple identity and "internationalist" politics; comparison and contrast of mother's and daughter's experiences, points of view, language, and style; meaning of language, reading, and writing for Levins Morales; an analysis of images of space, borders, urban centers, mobility, exile, displacement; contrast to Nuyorican writers from El Barrio: How would Levins Morales diverge from this movement, and why should she still be considered as representative of Puerto Rican writers in the United States?

Bibliography

Benmayor, Rina. "Crossing Borders: The Politics of Multiple Identity." *Centro de Estudios Puertorriqueños Bulletin* 2:3 (Spring, 1988): 71–77.

Rojas, Lourdes. "Latinas at the Crossroads: An Affirmation of Life in Rosario Morales and Aurora Levins Morales's *Getting Home Alive*." In *Breaking Boundaries: Latina Writing and Critical Reading*, edited by A. Horno-Delgado, E. Ortega, N. Scott, and N. Saporta-Sternbach. 166–77. Amherst: University of Massachusetts Press, 1989.

Part III   Postmodernity and Difference: Promises and Threats

David Henry Hwang (b. 1957)

Contributing Editor: James S. Moy

Classroom Strategies and Issues

Because *M. Butterfly* draws attention to the issue of western stereotyping of Asia, a discussion of the representational construction of "Asianness" in America can provide a useful platform for an inquiry into Hwang's development as a playwright. Begin by defining some of the stereotypes of Asianness, both male and female. Discussions of the "dragon lady," Charlie Chan, Fu Manchu, and the Asian houseboy stereotypes will prove useful. Film clips showing these constructions usually generate lively discussion. Some fruitful avenues of conversation might examine the tension between these stereotypical representations and the realities of late twentieth-century Asian life in America. And, indeed, to what extent do such stereotypes figure into the conduct of American international policy today?

Major Themes, Historical Perspectives, and Personal Issues

Hwang attacks western stereotypes by refiguring the well-known Madama Butterfly theme. Using Brechtian devices that place the viewer in a position to critically evaluate the representations in his play, Hwang hopes to break the century-old butterfly myth of Asian submissiveness to western dominance.

A theatrical tour de force, *M. Butterfly* is a powerful indictment of white America's stereotyping of Asia. Still, the play leaves open the issue of just what images of Asianness are appropriate. Indeed, with a transvestite as the most important Asian figure, the play proves problematic in addressing this question.

Original Audience

M. Butterfly was originally intended for the Anglo-dominant culture audience that patronizes the Broadway theatre of New York City.

Comparisons, Contrasts, Connections

Comparisons with other works by Hwang (especially *F. O. B.*, *The Dance and the Railroad*, and *The Sound of a Voice*) will lead to a deeper understanding of how his representations of Asianness interact with Anglo expectations of racial representation. In addition, comparison with plays by Frank Chin and Philip Kan Gotanda will provide insight into other Asians who have addressed some of the same issues.

Bibliography

Leong, Russell, ed. *Moving the Image: Independent Asian Pacific American Media Arts.* Los Angeles: UCLA Asian American Studies Centre, 1991.

Moy, James S. *Marginal Sights: Staging the Chinese in America.* Iowa City: University of Iowa Press, 1993.

Toni Morrison (b. 1931)

Contributing Editor: Sue Houchins

Classroom Issues and Strategies

For the last twenty years I have taught at a women's college where ninety-five percent of the population is what we call "the traditional age," seventeen through twenty-two years old. These students always express dismay at three violent episodes, all of them in this selection: Eva's maternal infanticide, Sula's digital immolation, and Chicken Little's accidental death. I have as yet found no way to soften, prior to their reading the text, students' outrage. However, their discomfort is allayed by our discussion of the text and of Morrison's exploration in this book and in *Beloved* of the figure of the mother who believes she "owns her offspring" (and, therefore, who reasons she has the right to exercise the ultimate decision over her children) and our conclusion that Morrison is not advocating abuse of authority.

Some of you might also encounter the argument that Morrison engages in a vilification/feminist castration of African-American men. I suppose some might point to Boyboy in this selection as an example of the denigration of the black man; however, I would suggest that the narrator, if not Eva, shows some compassion toward this figure who was dragged west by his employer and who despite his posturing was "defeat[ed]" by life. Further, the passages on manlove delight in black men, celebrate their sexuality, and rejoice in their verbal skills. I contend that the allegations against Morrison arise from an erroneous assumption that to write about gender is to ignore race, or, in the words of some theorists, the discourse of race and the discourse of gender are mutually exclusive. Critics such as Dorine Kondo and Mae Henderson would argue that they are not, that few have learned to read and hear race and gender together. I hope the following will suggest some strategies for doing so.

Major Themes, Historical Perspectives, and Personal Issues

This selection from Morrison's *Sula* constitutes some of the most hotly contested passages in African-American women's fiction today. As you are undoubtedly aware, a number of critics—among them Barbara Smith in "Toward a Black Feminist Critical Theory"—suggest that, embedded within these chapters that celebrate "manlove" and heterosexuality, there is a lesbian "disloyal" subtext (see Teresa de Lauretis, "Sexual Indifference and Lesbian Representation," in *Performing Feminisms: Feminist Critical Theory and Theatre* edited by Sue Ellen Case for a discussion of this term). Whether you choose to explore in your classroom this homosexual reading is up to you; however, these chapters demand that you discuss the following issues of race, gender, and sexuality: (1) the social construction of race through the figure of Tarbaby and the trope of Carpenter's Road, named after Boyboy's employer, which defines and delimits the town; (2) the social construction of gender and its problematizing through Eva's "test[ing] and argu[ing]" with her gentlemen callers while at the same time epousing a philosophy of a wife's duty to be the obedient helpmeet, Eva's matriarchal dominion over the house she crafted, through Hannah's sexual agency and the danger she represents to married couples, through the sexual autonomy exercised by the three generations of women in Eva's household; (3) the social construction of heterosexuality in the discourse on "manlove"; (4) the social construction of motherhood and its problematizing through the story of saving the infant Plum, the myth of Eva's sacrificed leg, the killing of her only son, and Hannah's remark about loving but not liking Sula.

The "theme" of mother-daughter relationships is sometimes expanded to include the bond of female friendship, such as the one depicted between Nel and Sula. Traditionally feminist critics read the girls' intimacy through a Chodorowian paradigm that, to summarize too simplistically, posits that female friendships reproduce the experiences of being mothered and of mothering and, therefore, are in some ways symbiotic and, thus, are related to pre-Oedipal stages in psychic development (see Nancy Chodorow, *Reproducing Motherhood*). Such readings hint at strategies for deploying *subtle* Freudian interpretations of parts of this selection: for example, to explain the digital mutilation, the hole-digging episodes, the death of Chicken Little, and Eva's amputation. The inquiry into the development of our cultural understanding of childhood is obviously related to the tropes of adolescent female friendships and a female's development into sexual maturity. Some examples are girlhood (remember the book ends with Nel recalling and lamenting, "We was girls together") and the enigmatic deweys appropriated by Eva and transformed by her in the community's imagination.

In addition, these passages introduce a number of themes that are reiterated in succeeding novels: scapegoating (of Boyboy by Eva, of Hannah by the townswomen, National Suicide Day as a variation on scapegoating, Pilate in *Song of Solomon*, or Sethe as the outcast in *Beloved*); flying (read Chicken Little's death against Eva's fall later in *Sula*, the death of Macon Dead I, Pilate, and Robert Smith in *Song of Solomon*, or the myth of Solomon's flight in the same novel— the folktale of the "flying African" recounted many times in slave narratives—see Virginia Hamilton's *When People Could Fly*, a children's book); symbolic naming—for example, Shadrack, or Nel, whose name reverses the letters in the heart of her mother's name, Helene; the house, as in *Beloved* or other geographical sites—such as the Bottom in *Sula* or "Not Doctor Street" in *Song of Solomon*—as characters in the text.

Significant Form, Style, or Artistic Conventions

You might find it fruitful to place Morrison's work within the tradition of magical realism. Like her Latin American colleagues, her work is almost epic in scope, chronicling as it does the history of a people over five decades, for it begins *in medias res* and then looks back to the ante-bellum period when the first blacks settled in the area that was to be known as Medallion. This small Ohio town and the three generations of the Peace matriarchy that inhabit the house at 7 Carpenter's Road write in microcosm the struggle of the African-American down from the bottom, thus critiquing the myth of the American dream, the legend of "up from slavery." In addition, faithful to the dictates of the genre, Morrison paints the small town landscape, portrays almost every African-American character, represents linguist and cultural idiosyncrasies with an almost surreal/super-real clarity; and yet at the core of this descriptive fidelity is the incongruent, the illogical, the intuitive, the magical.

Original Audience

I believe that all of Morrison's novels have been written for a culturally diverse audience. While each work is situated within the black American community (U.S. or Caribbean), focuses almost exclusively on African-American characters, and draws upon black folk traditions and folktales, her books seem to appeal to a wide spectrum of readers as evidenced by the selection of *Sula* by the Book-of-the-Month-Club, of *Beloved* for the 1988 Pulitzer Prize, and the award of the Nobel Prize in Literature to Morrison in 1993.

Comparisons, Contrasts, Connections

Houses, such as Eva's on Carpenter's Road or Baby Suggs and Sethe's on Bluestone Road (*Beloved*), figure importantly, albeit ambiguously throughout the history of black women's writing. So you might compare and contrast Eva's imprisonment but relative power with the plight of Linda Brent in *Incidents in the Life of a Slave Girl* or of the protagonist in *Our Nig*, or compare her to Silla in Paule Marshall's *Brown Girl, Brownstones*. Marshall's first novel is also excellent for comparing the treatment of a girl's achievement of psychic and sexual maturity. *Meridian* by Alice Walker may serve as another example of a text that examines an adolescent's growing to sexuality, gender-political issues between black men and women, troubled mother-daughter relations, and the female hero as outcast. Michelle Cliff's *Abeng* treats many of the same themes—especially the episode of hunting the wild pig and the killing of

Miss Mattie's prize bull—in the life of a Jamaican girl and even recounts the myth of the flying African. Richard Perry's *Montgomery's Children* deliberately draws upon the same themes and folk motifs as *Sula* and *Song of Solomon*. Look at Gloria Naylor's *Women of Brewster Place* for a portrait of mother-son relations.

Questions for Reading and Discussion/ Approaches to Writing

Study and discussion questions: Ask students to research the biblical derivation of the appropriate characters' names and to ascribe significance to the choice of appellation. For example, what radical theology is suggested when the character of Eve, temptress and sinner, is termed "creator and sovereign"? Or what is the significance of Hannah's namesake, the mother of Samson? It might be helpful to assign some students the task of contextualizing the novel by researching significant events in African-American political, intellectual, and social history from 1919 (the beginning of *Sula*) until the end of the selection. Also, you can ask for a reading of a troubling passage (that is, the killing of Chicken Little, Nel and Sula digging holes in the field) or troubling characters (Shadrack, Tarbaby, the deweys).

Bibliography

The works cited at the end of Morrison's headnote in the anthology are most helpful.

Maxine Hong Kingston (b. 1940)

Contributing Editor: Amy Ling

Classroom Issues and Strategies

The primary question for any initial reading of Kingston's *The Woman Warrior* has to do with genre or form. Is this text nonfiction? (It won the National Book Critics Circle Award for the best book of nonfiction published in 1976.) Since the word "memoirs" is in the title, is it autobiography? Or is it a piece of imaginative fiction, which seems most apparent in the "White Tigers" chapter included in this anthology? *The Woman*

Warrior, of course, is all of the above, sequentially and simultaneously, a collage of genres.

As Kingston does not maintain a unity of genre, neither does she maintain a unity of diction. "White Tigers" begins with a colloquial tone, a woman speaking informally about her Chinese-American female upbringing. It then goes into a conditional tense and a story-telling mode—"The call *would* come from a bird that flew over our roof"—into a narration filled with magical details, described at times in a matter-of-fact manner, at other times in an elevated, poetic style. Then, without warning, the language and the subject matter lapse abruptly from the fanciful to the everyday in the sudden, disruptive line, "My American life has been such a disappointment." In diction and language also, *The Woman Warrior* is dialogic.

In terms of content, "White Tigers" has been called, by David Li, a critic from the People's Republic of China, "a version of the Kung Fu movie interspliced with a Western." Feminists, however, admire the anger and power of the female avenger whose patient and lengthy training enables her to slice off the head of the misogynist baron in one stroke. Chinese-Americans appreciate Hong Kingston's skill not only in beautifully elaborating on a popular ancient Chinese ballad, "The Magnolia Lay," but in making its traditional Chinese heroine relevant to a contemporary Chinese-American girl's life.

Major Themes, Historical Perspectives, and Personal Issues

Since her mother's talking-story was one of the major forces of her childhood and since she herself is now talking-story in writing this book, stories, factual and fictional, are an inherent part of Kingston's autobiography. Finding one's voice in order to talk-story, a metaphor for knowing oneself in order to attain the fullness of one's power, becomes one of the book's major themes.

As the second chapter of a five-chapter book, "White Tigers" is best understood in the context and thematic structure of the entire work. The book's first chapter, "No Name Woman," tells the story of the paternal aunt who bears a child out of wedlock and is harried by the villagers and by her family into drowning herself; the family now punishes this taboo-breaker by never speaking of her, by denying her her name. The author, however, breaks the family silence by writing about this rebel whom she calls "my forebear." "No Name Woman" presents the cautionary tale of woman as victim; "White Tigers," however, provides the model to emulate. This pattern, woman as victim then victor, is repeated through-out the text.

In like manner, Kingston inverts historical misogynist Chinese practices, such as footbinding and female infanticide, by claiming that perhaps women's feet were bound because women were so strong. Victory over handicaps, over racial and sexual devaluation is Kingston's purpose.

Significant Form, Style, or Artistic Conventions

One of the distinctive accomplishments of *The Woman Warrior* is that it crosses boundaries between genres, dictions, styles, between fact and fiction, as it crosses the boundaries between cultures, Chinese and American. In the collage of style and form, in the amalgam of language and content, in the combination of Chinese myth, family history, and American individualism and rebelliousness, Kingston defines herself as a Chinese-American woman.

Original Audience

The Woman Warrior is decidedly a product of the sixties, of the civil rights and women's liberation movements. It directly addresses Chinese-Americans, whom it seeks to bring into its exploration of identity, but, as an immigrant story for a nation of immigrants, it is obviously intended as well for a mainstream audience.

Comparisons, Contrasts, Connections

Like other women and ethnic writers such as Leslie Marmon Silko, Toni Morrison, and Adrienne Rich who appropriated and revisioned myths for their own uses, so Kingston appropriated the tale of the legendary Fa Mulan for her own purposes. The original ballad of the Chinese woman warrior is recorded in a fifth-century ballad of sixty-two lines; Kingston elaborates considerably on this ballad. Her most significant addition, however, is the woman warrior's marriage and childbearing while still in armor disguised as a man. In the original ballad, Mulan performs these roles sequentially; in Kingston's version, simultaneously. With this change, Kingston crosses gender barriers and separate spheres, creating a heroine who is at once a feared warrior and a tender mother.

Questions for Reading and Discussion/ Approaches to Writing

1. Which aspects of Kingston's childhood experience is true of all immigrants in the United States? What is particular to Chinese-Americans?
2. Of what use is the fabulous story of the woman warrior to the daily life of the narrator?
3. Has Kingston in her life inverted the woman as victim into woman as victor? Research and explain.

Bibliography

Blinde, Patricia Lin. "The Icicle in the Desert: Perspective and Form in the Works of Two Chinese American Women Writers." *MELUS* 6.3 (1979): 51–71.

Cheung, King-Kok. " 'Don't Tell': Imposed Silences in *The Color Purple* and *The Woman Warrior*." *PMLA* 103 (1988): 162–74.

Chua, Chen Lok. "Two Versions of the American Dream: The Golden Mountain in Lin Yutang and Maxine Hong Kingston." *MELUS* 8.4 (1981): 61–70.

Juhasz, Suzanne. "Towards a Theory of Form in Feminist Autobiography: Kate Millet's *Fear of Flying* and *Sitar*; Maxine Hong Kingston's *The Woman Warrior*." *International Journal of Women's Studies* 2.1 (January-February 1979): 62–75.

Kingston, Maxine Hong. "Cultural Misreadings by American Reviewers." In *Asian and Western Writers in Dialogue: New Cultural Identities*, edited by Guy Amirthanayagam, 55–65. London: Macmillan, 1982.

Li, David Leiwei. "The Naming of a Chinese American 'I': Cross-Cultural Sign/nifications in *The Woman Warrior*." *Criticism* 30.4 (Winter 1988): 506.

Ling, Amy. "Thematic Threads in Maxine Hong Kingston's *The Woman Warrior*." *Tamkang Review* 14 (1983–1984): 5–15.

Rabine, Leslie W. "No Paradise Lost: Social Gender and Symbolic Gender in the Writings of Maxine Hong Kingston." *Signs* 12.3 (1987): 471–92.

Louise Erdrich (Chippewa) (b. 1954)

Contributing Editor: Andrew O. Wiget

Classroom Issues and Strategies

One problem in teaching *Love Medicine* is the intensity of religious experience, which many students in today's secular society may have difficulty relating to. Another is the surrealistic imagery that Marie Lazarre uses in describing her relationship with Sister Leopolda. And yet a third is understanding the historical and cultural context of reservation life at this period of time in the 1930s.

In terms of the historical and cultural context, I would point out to students that Indian reservations in the 1930s were notorious for their poverty, their high mortality rate, their chronic unemployment, and the destruction of the fabric of Native American social and cultural forms. One of the principal policies of the United States government was to transform Native Americans into carbon copies of Anglo-Americans, and one of the principal ways that they hoped to accomplish this, ever since the Grant administration in the 1870s, was through religion.

During the 1870s, the Native American communities were allocated among the various major Christian sects, and missionary activity was understood to be an agent of social and cultural transformation. The objective was to get rid of the Indian while saving the man. Culture was imagined as a number of practices and behaviors and customs, which—if they could be changed—would eliminate all the historic obstacles to the Indians' participation in Anglo-American culture. Of course, if they were eliminated, so would the Indian nest be eliminated. Religion then is hardly a simple spiritual force, but an agent of the interests of the Euro-American majority. Such an understanding, I think, should help students appreciate the intensity with which Marie and Sister Leopolda enter their confrontation.

A fine introduction to this story would be to spend a good deal of time focusing on the first paragraph, trying to understand the tone of the narrator and also the structure of her vision of herself, which she repeats later in the story. I would use the imagery and the tone as a way of developing the narrator's sense of herself, and I would try to account for her intense antagonism to the "black robe women on the hill."

Most students are puzzled by the intensity of the antagonism, and they have real questions as to whether or not Marie or Leopolda or both are crazy. Students tend to think that they're crazy because of the surrealistic imagery and because of the intensity of the emotion, which strikes most of them as excessive. Students need to realize that religion, especially when it is the lens through which other issues are magnified, can become the focus of such intense feelings, and that when one's feelings are so intense, they frequently compel the creation of surrealistic imagery as the only means to adequately shape what one sees.

Major Themes, Historical Perspectives, and Personal Issues

I think that there are two major themes that could be addressed in this story. The first is to understand religion, as described in the previous question, as a field upon which two different sets of interests contest their right to define the terms by which people will understand themselves and others. For all the black comedy in this story, the battle that Leopolda fights with the Dark One over the soul of Marie Lazarre is understood by both Leopolda and Marie as a very real battle. Leopolda represents a set of values, and so does the Dark One. Marie is understood as struggling to choose between the values of the Dark One and the values of Sister Leopolda, and these values are cultural as well as spiritual, for it is precisely the Indian character of Marie—her pride, her resistance to change, her imagination—that Leopolda identifies with the Dark One.

A second theme is to view the formation of identity in bicultural environments as an enriching, rather than an impoverishing, experience. Too often in bicultural situations, Indian protagonists are represented as being helpless, suspended in their inability to make a decision between two sets of values offered to them. The John Joseph Mathews novel *Sundown* is an example. In this story, however, Marie Lazarre chooses, and she chooses to identify herself as an Indian over and against the black robe sisters precisely by turning their own naiveté against them. The "veils of faith" that she refers to early in this story not only prevent the sisters from seeing the truth, but they also obscure their faith from shining forth, like the Reverend Mr. Hooper's veil in Hawthorne's story "The Minister's Black Veil."

Significant Form, Style, or Artistic Conventions

This story succeeds principally as a study of characterization. I would ask students to pay special attention to matters of tone and point of view. Since this story is told in the first person, I would ask them, on the basis of what they have read, to form an opinion of Marie Lazarre and, secondly, to develop some sense of her judgment of Sister Leopolda. I would ask them to look especially at the imagery and the language that Marie uses to describe her encounters with Leopolda and to describe herself, as the basis for their opinions.

Original Audience

The audience for whom this story is written is contemporary, but differs from the students we meet in university settings by perhaps being older and therefore more familiar with a traditional religiosity. Students who are not Catholic may need to know something about Catholicism, especially the role of nuns, and the historic role of missionaries in relationship to Indian communities. Other explicitly Catholic references, such as to the stigmata, are explained by their context in the story.

Comparisons, Contrasts, Connections

This story can be usefully contrasted with some of Flannery O'Connor's stories, which focus on the discovery of real faith, especially from a Catholic perspective. The emphasis on surrealistic imagery provides interesting connections with poems like those of Adrienne Rich; since this is a retrospective narrative, one might usefully compare this probing of a formative event from the narrator's past with Rich's poem "Diving into the Wreck." Insofar as this offers us a sensitive and imaginative teenage minority narrator, the story invites comparisons with the work of Toni Morrison and Alice Walker. In Native American terms, useful comparisons would be to Gertrude Bonnin's "Why I Am a Pagan," as well as John Oskison's "The Problem of Old Harjo."

Questions for Reading and Discussion/ Approaches to Writing

1. I've never used questions ahead of time for this particular story, though if I did, I think they would be addressed to issues of characterization and tone.
2. An interesting assignment, because this story is told from Marie's point of view, is to retell the encounter between Marie and Sister Leopolda from Sister Leopolda's perspective. This would require students to formulate characterizations of Leopolda and of Marie, which would be useful touchstones for evaluating their comprehension of the issues on which the conflict in this story rests.

Bibliography

Erdrich, Louise. "Whatever Is Really Yours: An Interview with Louise Erdrich." *Survival This Way: An Interview with American Indian Poets.* Tucson: University of Arizona, 1987, 73–86.

Wiget, Andrew. "Singing the Indian Blues: Louise Erdrich and the Love that Hurts So Good." *Puerto del Sol* 21.2 (1986): 166–75

Amy Tan (b. 1952)

Contributing Editor: Amy Ling

Classroom Issues and Strategies

Amy Tan's work is greatly indebted to and inspired by that of Maxine Hong Kingston, particularly to Kingston's first book, *The Woman Warrior*. Thus, it would be useful to read these two authors back-to-back as well as to compare Tan with other bicultural women writers who found their voices in the wake of the civil rights and women's liberation movements.

Major Themes, Historical Perspectives, and Personal Issues

Thematically, *The Joy Luck Club* and *The Woman Warrior* share three foci: the mother/daughter relationship, story-telling, and finding one's own voice or identity. The mother/daughter tension, universally caused by generational conflicts, is here intensified by cultural differences. In Tan's novels, the mothers have immigrated from China to the United States for the express purpose of providing their daughters with greater opportunities. To their surprise and dismay, the daughters have grown up American and thus "foreign" and incomprehensible. Through story-telling, each of the four mothers and daughters attempts to make herself comprehensible to her other half. "The Red Candle" is one such attempt and a fine short story in its own right. Though set in China, where women had few rights and almost no autonomy, it nonetheless provides a feminist exemplum, showing how a clever girl uses the very customs meant to constrain her to achieve her liberation.

Significant Form, Style, or Artistic Conventions

The Chinese tile game of mahjong is not only the means of creating joy, diversion from the terrors and horrors of war, but it also structures the narrative. Each side of the four-sided table is named a wind after one of the four cardinal points—East Wind, North Wind, and so on—and each player successively opens the game, so the mother and daughter pairs successively tell their stories, and the "directional winds" play a significant part in several stories. In "The Red Candle" the heroine uses the wind, her own breath, to change her situation.

Questions for Reading and Discussion/ Approaches to Writing

1. What similarities/differences do you find between the two foremost Chinese-American writers, Maxine Hong Kingston and Amy Tan?
2. How can you account for the tremendous interest in Amy Tan's novel *The Joy Luck Club* that kept it on the *New York Times* best-seller list for nine months?
3. Some Asian-American readers accuse Tan of catering to the majority culture's taste for the exotic. Do you agree or disagree?

Bibliography

There are no separate works on Amy Tan, but several newspaper articles and interviews were published in prominent national papers in 1990. Biographical facts and a discussion of her work in relation to Maxine Hong Kingston's may be found in my book, *Between Worlds: Women Writers of Chinese Ancestry*. New York: Pergamon Press, 1991.

Audre Lorde (1934–1992)

Contributing Editor: Claudia Tate

Classroom Issues and Strategies

Students need to be taught to empathize with the racial, sexual, and class characteristics of the persona inscribed in Lorde's works. Such empathy will enable them to understand the basis of Lorde's value formation.

Students immediately respond to Lorde's courage to confront a problem, no matter what its difficulty, and to her deliberate inscription of the anguish that problem has caused her. Both the confrontation and the acknowledged pain serve as her vehicle for resolving the problem.

It is difficult to secure the entire corpus of her published work. Most libraries have only those works published after 1982. Many of those published prior to this date are out of print.

To address this issue, I have made special orders for texts that are still in print and asked the library to place them on reserve. In other cases, I have selected specific works from these early texts and photocopied them for class use.

Major Themes, Historical Perspectives, and Personal Issues

Lorde's work focuses on lyricizing large historical and social issues in the voice of a black woman. This vantage point provides stringent social commentary on white male, middle-class, heterosexual privilege inherent in the dominant culture, on the one hand, and on the disadvantage accorded to those who diverge from this so-called standard. In addition, students should be aware that there have historically been racial and class biases between white and black feminists concerning issues that centralize racial equality, like enfranchisement, work, and sexuality.

Significant Form, Style, or Artistic Conventions

Students studying Lorde's poetry should familiarize themselves with the aesthetic and rhetorical demands of the lyrical mode. In addition, they should be prepared for the high degree of intimacy inscribed in Lorde's work.

Comparisons, Contrasts, Connections

Although Lorde is known primarily as a poet, she also wrote a substantial amount of prose. Her most prominent prose includes *The Cancer Journals* (1980), the record of her struggle with breast cancer; *Zami: A New Spelling of My Name* (1982), an autobiography; and *Sister Outsider* (1984), a collection of essays and speeches. Students should be encouraged to explore Lorde's prose in order to see how genre mediates the expression of her most salient themes. Comparisons can also be drawn with the work of Adrienne Rich, June Jordan, and Ntozake Shange in order to stress the intimacy of the woman-centered problematic that informs and structures Lorde's work.

Bibliography

Over the last decade Lorde has attracted considerable scholarly interest. See the headnote for a listing of recent criticism. Also see the selections in *Some of Us Are Brave*, eds. Barbara Smith et. al.; *Sturdy Black Bridges*, eds. Gloria Hull et. al.; *Color, Sex, and Poetry*, edited by Gloria Hull; and *Wild Women in the Whirlwind*, edited by Joanne M. Braxton.

Judith Ortiz Cofer (b. 1952)

Contributing Editor: Juan Bruce-Novoa

Classroom Issues and Strategies

Ortiz Cofer is quite clear and accessible, although students have questions about who she is and why she uses Spanish.

I present the students something from my own cultural background, with allusions to Mexican history and culture. Then I ask them to jot down what has been said. We compare the results, finding that those who do not share the background will choose different elements out of the material than those who come from a background similar to my own. We discuss the function of ethnic identification through shared allusions about the drawing of the ethnic circle around some readers, while excluding others, even when the latter can understand the words.

Students respond to the theme of the abandoned female, which often results in discussions of the single-parent family.

Major Themes, Historical Perspectives, and Personal Issues

The theme of male absence and women who wait is perhaps the major one touched on here. Also, there is the historical theme of Puerto Ricans and other minorities in the military as a way of life that both gives them mobility yet divides their families.

The colonization of Puerto Rico by the U.S. and the division of its population into island and mainland groups are reflected in the division of the family. The bilingual child is another result of the confluence of these two nations, reflected in the preoccupation with which language authority will accept from would-be participants.

Significant Form, Style, or Artistic Conventions

This is confessional poetry, but with a twist. The author walks a fine line between writing for her own group and writing for the general audience. Thus she introduces Spanish and some culture items from the island, but recontextualizes them into English and U.S. culture. The style becomes an intercultural hybrid.

Original Audience

There is the Puerto Rican audience that will bring to the poems a specific knowledge of cultural elements that they share with the poet. This audience will place the poem in a wider catalog of cultural references. The non-Puerto Rican audience must draw only from the information given, and will perhaps apply the situations to universal myths or archetypes.

Comparisons, Contrasts, Connections

You can compare her well to many other women writers, especially in the sense of women alone in a male world. For example, "Claims" can be read with Lorna Dee Cervantes's "Beneath the Shadow of the Freeway."

Questions for Reading and Discussion/ Approaches to Writing

1. I ask them to consider what is the function of ethnic writing. How does it work for insiders as compared to outsiders? They should try to determine at what point ethnic writing becomes incomprehensible to outsiders, and what it means to open it to readers beyond the ethnic circle.
2. Write on the theme of the distant patriarch in U.S. contemporary life.
3. Write on the pros and cons of foreign language in literature. The "God" of "Latin Women Pray" can be taken as a metaphor for the U.S. reading public.

Bibliography

Refer to the headnote in the text for specific information. Consult also Acosta-Belen, Edna. "The Literature of the Puerto Rican National Minority in the United States." *The Bilingual Review* 5:1–2 (Jan.–Aug. 1978): 107–16.

Bernice Zamora (b. 1938)

Contributing Editor: Juanita Luna Lawhn

Classroom Issues and Strategies

To make Zamora more accessible, translate Spanish phrases, refer students to outside reading that explains the religious beliefs of the Penitents, and encourage students to read poets—such as Robinson Jeffers, Gullivec, Shakespeare, and Hesse—whose works serve as the intertextual basis for some of Zamora's poetry.

I recommend that Zamora's work be viewed from a feminist perspective, giving special attention to the serpent motif that is present throughout her work and relating the serpent motif to the symbolism associated with goddesses.

I would also recommend that her work be studied from a third world perspective. From this perspective, the student can take into consideration race, class, and gender.

Major Themes, Historical Perspectives, and Personal Issues

The major themes that the writer develops are freedom, justice, love, hate, violence, death, assimilation, and isolation. Some of the issues that the writer develops are the entrapment of women in a man's world, socially and politically; the violence that permeates communities that are deprived economically and educationally; the violence that women as well as men suffer because of the double standards in social values and mores.

Significant Form, Style, or Artistic Conventions

I recommend Bruce-Novoa's article, "Bernice Zamora y Lorna Dee Cervantes: Una estetica feminista."

Original Audience

When I speak of Zamora's work, I give a brief background of the Chicano literary movement. I indicate that Zamora's work was published and distributed by a Chicano publishing company and its audience was an ethnic audience, especially one that was well versed in American literature. I also indicate that she was one of the first major Chicana poets who published her work in book form. While her work is not limited to a feminist audience, it does lend itself to be read by one who is a feminist in the U.S. as well as by third world women. Because of the present trends to include minority writers in American literature anthologies, her audience has been expanded to reach a cross section of U.S. society.

Comparisons, Contrasts, Connections

Since Bernice Zamora is presented as one of the representatives of the Chicana poet, it would be wise to recommend readings by other Chicana poets. The following is a representative list of works by Chicana poets:

Cervantes, Lorna Dee. *Emplumada*. Pittsburgh: University of Pittsburgh Press, 1981.

Cisneros, Sandra. *My Wicked Wicked Ways*. Bloomington, Indiana: Third Woman Press, 1987.

Corpi, Lucha. *Palabras de Mediodia/Noon Words*. Trans. Catherine Rodriguez-Nieto. Berkeley: El Fuego de Aztlan Publications, 1980.

Moraga, Cherríe. *Loving in the War Years: Lo que nunca paso por los labios*. Boston: Southend Press Collective, 1983.

Villanueva, Alma. *Bloodroot*. Austin: Place of Herons Press, 1977.

I recommend that her work be compared and contrasted with the work of Adrienne Rich, Marge Piercy, and Judith Ortiz Cofer.

Questions for Reading and Discussion/ Approaches to Writing

1. (a) Define *Aztlan*.
   (b) Define *Nahault*.

    (c) Define *community*.

    (d) Define *ritual*.

    (e) What is the universal symbolism of the serpent?

2. (a) Discuss several feminist issues that Zamora confronts with her poetry (the entrapment of women in a man's world, the issue of double standards in society, the exclusion of women from sacred rituals in a community, the exclusion of women in arts, and the function of women in society as objects to be utilized by men to serve their own needs).

    (b) Trace the serpent leitmotif in Zamora's work.

    (c) According to Zamora's poetry, what is the artist's role in society?

    (d) Trace the androgynous images in Zamora's poetry.

Bibliography

Eger, Ernestina N. *A Bibliography of Criticism of Contemporary Chicano Literature*. Berkeley: University of California Chicano Studies Library Publication, 1982.

Lawhn, Juanita. "Victorian Attitudes Affecting the Mexican Woman Writing in *La Prensa* during the Early 1900s and the Chicana of the 1980s." In *Missions in Conflict*, edited by Renate Von Bardeleben, Dietrich Briesemeister, and Juan Bruce-Novoa. Tübingen, W. Germany, Gunter Narr Verlag, 1986.

Penitentes of New Mexico, edited by Carlos E. Cortez. New York: Arno Press, 1974.

Jay Wright (b. 1935)

Contributing Editor: Phillip M. Richards

Classroom Issues and Strategies

Often the central dramatic action of the poem is the contemplation of past events or the attempt to recover a community's experience. One might ask students, what is the purpose of these historical quests? Jay Wright's poems often dramatize a persona's attempt to discover his continuity with past ancestors and events. The poetry attempts to recapture historical experience as a means of establishing the poetic persona's personal identity.

Major Themes, Historical Perspectives, and Personal Issues

The crucial themes in Wright are the poet's quest to establish himself as a member and artist-spokesman for his tribe (African-Americans, Africans, and Hispanics). The poet seeks to establish this sense of kinship by dramatizing the historical and psychological continuities that link him with his ancestors. Wright's books, then, are quests for identity by means of historical understanding.

Significant Form, Style, or Artistic Conventions

Wright's poetry is closely allied to the Black Mountain school as it is exemplified by the work of Charles Olson.

Original Audience

The bulk of Wright's published poetry was written during the 1960s and 1970s during a period of interest in the African roots of the African-American experience. Some of the work of *The Homecoming Singer* (Wright's first book) shows the influence of the beat movement. Significantly, he alludes to early poems by Amiri Baraka, which were influenced by the same beat ethos.

Comparisons, Contrasts, Connections

Wright's attempts to link himself with an African past reflect a central theme in twentieth-century black poetry. Wright's efforts in this connection recall poems on Africa by Langston Hughes and Countee Cullen. One might compare the primitivism of Hughes's and Cullen's early poetry with Wright's attempts to give cultural specificity to African ritual. Wright's historical themes also link him to the historical poetry of Robert Hayden as well as to that of Michael Harper.

T. S. Eliot is a hidden influence in much of Wright's work. The early poems in *The Homecoming Singer* feature a youthful, male, self-mocking persona much like that of "Portrait of a Lady" or "The Love Song of J. Alfred Prufrock." Wright's ritualistic poems that meditate upon history and its meaning owe something to *Four Quartets*.

Bibliography

The best introductions to Wright appear in *Callaloo* 6 (Fall 1983), which includes good essays by Stepto and Barrax, and a highly theoretical essay by Kutzinski.

Jay Wright's own statement on his poetic craft, "Desire's Design, Vision's Resonance" in *Callaloo* 10 (Winter 1987): 13–28, is also extremely useful.

Vera Kutzinski's chapter on Wright in her book, *Against the American Grain: Myth and History in William Carlos Williams, Jay Wright, and Nicolas Guillen*, is the most comprehensive critical statement on Wright's poetry.

Garrett Hongo (b. 1951)

Contributing Editor: Amy Ling

Classroom Issues and Strategies

Explain that Hongo's themes and craft are evident even in the small selection we have in this text. The title poem of his first book, *Yellow Light*, emphasizes the centrality of the Asian perspective by ascribing a positive, fertile quality to the color commonly designating Asian skin and formerly meaning "cowardly." By focusing his sights on ordinary people in the midst of their daily rounds, as in "Yellow Light," "Off from Swing Shift," and "And Your Soul Shall Dance," by describing their surroundings in precise detail, by suggesting their dreams, Hongo depicts both the specificities of the Japanese-American experience and its universality. "And Your Soul Shall Dance" is a tribute to playwright and fiction writer Wakako Yamauchi.

Major Themes, Historical Perspectives, and Personal Issues

The work of any Asian-American writer is best understood in the context of the black civil rights and the women's liberation movements of the 1960s and 1970s. These movements by African-Americans and women led Asian-Americans to join in the push for change. Asian-Americans as a group had endured racial discrimination in the U.S. for over a century, from the harassment of Chinese in the California gold mines to the internment of thousands of Japanese-Americans during World War II. Furthermore, the last three wars the United States has engaged in have been fought in Asia, a fact that further consolidated a sense of community among the hitherto disparate Asian groups in this country

Significant Form, Style, or Artistic Conventions

In Hongo's volume *Yellow Light*, we no longer find a dependence on language and rhythm borrowed from African-American culture nor strident screams of bitterness and anger characteristic of polemic Asian-American poetry, the dominant mode and tone of the 1970s. Hongo is at home in his skin, positive about his background and the people around him, confident in his own voice, concerned as much with his craft as with his message.

Hongo's poems paint portraits of the people around him, and he invests his people with dignity and bathes them in love. Pride in an Asian-American heritage shines through in the catalogue of foods in "Who Among You Knows the Essence of Garlic?" Hongo's eye has the precision of seventeenth-century Flemish still-life painters, but his art is dynamic and evokes the sounds, smells, and tastes of the foods he describes.

He has combined the consciousness of the late twentieth-century ethnic nationalist with the early twentieth-century imagist's concern for the most precise, the most resonant image, and added to this combination his own largeness of spirit.

Comparisons, Contrasts, Connections

The examples of Lawson Inada and Frank Chin excited Garrett Hongo, who was encouraged by their work to do his own.

Frank Chin displayed his artistic and verbal talent, making his claim for a place in American history and expressing his deep ambivalence about Chinese-Americans in his plays. "Chickencoop Chinaman" was a dazzling display of verbal pyrotechnics but underlying the surface razzle-dazzle is a passionate throbbing of anger and pain for the emasculation of Chinese men in the United States.

Lawson Fusao Inada was another visible and vocal model for younger Asian-American writers. His book of poetry *Before the War* provided a range of models and styles from lyrical musings, to sublimated anger from a Japanese-American perspective, to colloquial outbursts inspired by black jazz and rhythms.

Hongo acknowledges other models and mentors as well: Bert Meyers, Donald Hall, C. K. Williams, Charles Wright, and Philip Levine.

Bibliography

Hongo, Garrett, Alan Chong Lau, and Lawson Fusao Inada. *The Buddha Bandits Down Highway 99*. Mountainview, Cal.: Buddhahead Press, 1978.

——. *River of Heaven*. New York: Alfred A. Knopf, 1988.

Kodama-Nishimoto, Michi and Warren Nishimoto. "Interview with Writer Garrett Hongo: Oral History and Literature." *Oral History Recorder* (Summer 1986): 2–4.

Tato Laviera (b. 1951)

Contributing Editor: Frances R. Aparicio

Classroom Issues and Strategies

Give handouts or glossaries that explain local references and Spanish words; also it might be helpful to try to translate Spanish phrases and words, in order to show the unique value of bilingualism within Laviera's poetry, and the fact that most of it is untranslatable.

It would be wonderful to recite Laviera's poems aloud and to introduce them to the students as such, as oral poetry. One might also relate his poetry to the tradition of rapping in New York City. Again, students need to clarify references to Puerto Rico and El Barrio with which they might be unfamiliar. They respond to issues of bilingual education, social criticism, and language (Spanish in the United States). Discussions on how Anglo monolingual students feel when reading Hispanic bilingual poetry such as Tato Laviera's and Hernández Cruz's texts can lead to fruitful observations on patterns of exclusion and marginalization in the United States via language and linguistic policies.

Major Themes, Historical Perspectives, and Personal Issues

Major themes are tension between Puerto Rican and Nuyorican societies and identity; language and bilingualism as ethnic identity markers; life in El Barrio; music and popular culture; denouncement of social institutions such as schools, Puerto Rican and U.S. governments, the Catholic church, etc.; major context of the history of Puerto Rican immigration to the U.S. and Operation Bootstrap in the 1940s and 1950s; presence of African-Caribbean and African-American cultures.

Significant Form, Style, or Artistic Conventions

Laviera's poetry best exemplifies the new genre of bilingual poetry in the United States. Discuss historical context of bilingual literature in other countries, aesthetic innovation within contemporary literature, political stance, use of oral speech and traditions versus written, academic, and intellectual poetry; relate to Mexican-American poets, and to African-American poets of the 1960s and discuss the common space between the black poets and Laviera's work regarding the reaffirmation of the African heritage for both communities. How do they differ and what do they have in common?

Original Audience

This is poetry meant to be sung and recited. Originally addressed to the Puerto Rican community in New York and presented in the Nuyorican Café, it is poetry for the masses.

Comparisons, Contrasts, Connections

There is a good basis for comparison with Alurista, the Mexican-American poet who was the first to publish bilingual poetry in this country. (See *Floricanto en Aztlán*.)

Questions for Reading and Discussion/ Approaches to Writing

Study questions for Laviera would try to help students contextualize his poetry both historically and aesthetically. For example:

1. How would you describe El Barrio in New York? How does Laviera present it in his poems?
2. After reading Laviera's poems, how would you define poetry? What kind of language is appropriate for poetry? Would Laviera's work fit into your definition?

A good and challenging writing assignment is to ask students to write their own bilingual poem (using any other language they may know). Discuss problems and effects.

Paper topics would include textual analysis of one poem; a discussion of the functions of language and bilingualism, and its problems; language and ethnic identity; the functions of humor and irony.

Bibliography

Juan Flores, John Attinasi, and Pedro Pedraza, Jr., "La Carreta Made a U-Turn: Puerto Rican Language and Culture in the United States," *Daedalus* 110:2 (Spring, 1981): 193–217; Wolfgang Binder, "Celebrating Life: The AmeRícan Poet Tato Laviera," Introduction to *AmeRícan* by Tato Laviera, 1985, 5–10; Juan Flores, "Keys to Tato Laviera," Introduction to *Enclave* by Tato Laviera, 1985, 5–7; Frances Aparicio, "La vida es un spanglish disparatero: Bilingualism in Nuyorican Poetry," *European Perspectives on Hispanic Literature of the United States*, ed. Genvieve Fabre, 1988, 147–60.

Helena María Viramontes (b. 1954)

Contributing Editor: Juan Bruce-Novoa

Classroom Issues and Strategies

The story touches on so many social issues that class discussion is almost assured. Some students, however, may express a sense of overkill: too many social and political ills too rapidly referenced to produce a profound impression. The class may also divide over the issues, some finding that they are so often covered by the media that they hardly need repetition, while others like the story because it seems like a familiar exposé on subjects they consider everyday reality.

You may find yourself in a discussion more of the headnote and its advocacy of the rights of undocumented aliens than of the story itself. I would try to focus on close textual reading to prevent the discussion from drifting away from the text and into arguments over social and political policies. Yet, some explanation of U.S. immigration policies and the political issues in Central America may be necessary (see "Historical Perspectives").

Major Themes, Historical Perspectives, and Personal Issues

Viramontes has published few stories and the headnote provides ample information on her themes and the personal connection with them. Historically, however, students may need more help. The Latino characters are undocumented aliens, and as such they can be detained by Immigration and Naturalization agents. After a hearing, they can be repatriated to their country of origin. However, in the recent past the process for Central Americans has more often than not tended to allow delay of their return, especially for those who claim political asylum. For Mexican aliens, the process is usually more automatic, although their return to the U.S. is also quite usual. The headnote suggests that the female refugee comes from El Salvador, which may provoke some confusion, since in the story her son is accused of collaborating with "Contras," a right wing terrorist group supported by the U.S. in the 1980s to undermine the Sandinista regime in Nicaragua. This could lead to ambiguous interpretations (just who has killed the woman's son, the Nicaraguan left or the Salvadorean right?) that can be used to lend the story interesting ambiguity to undermine simplistic political positions of right and wrong.

Significant Form, Style, or Artistic Conventions

Narrative perspective varies, moving from one character to another. While the technique may disorient some students, most will have encountered it in previous studies. It is important for them to note how Viramontes changes diction levels to achieve characterization. The use of interior monologue, especially in Section II, is noteworthy but not difficult to comprehend. The dashes of the "Rashamon" technique—the viewing of the same event from different perspectives at different times—adds to the text's fragmented feel.

Original Audience

Viramontes addresses a contemporary U.S. audience with topics relatively well known to most readers.

Comparisons, Contrasts, Connections

Comparisons can be made with Rolando Hinojosa's selection, which also utilizes the fragmented narrative while the subtlety of Hinojosa's social commentary can be contrasted with Viramontes's blatant approach. One might also place Viramontes in the tradition of such writers as Harriet

Beecher Stowe, Frances Ellen Watkins Harper, or Upton Sinclair, writers who did not shy away from explicit advocacy of political positions, even at the risk of melodramatic excess. While the headnote refers to García Márquez and Isabel Allende, there is little of the Latin American Magical Realism associated with those authors; the connection would be to their political positions, not to their style.

Questions for Reading and Discussion/ Approaches to Writing

1. The basic assignment here is to establish how the story is being narrated: From whose perspective is something seen? Then I ask students to characterize the different perspectives by picking specific words, turns of phrases, motifs, and so on.
2. I ask students to identify the specific Latino content of the story. Then I ask them to consider if the experiences apply to other immigrant groups, or the human condition in general.
3. This story lends itself to creative writing assignments. Have students pick a recent news event and narrate it from the objective perspective of a reporter and then from at least two others; for example, a witness of and a participant in the event.

Bibliography

Almost no criticism has been published on Viramontes. See the headnote for sources.

Pat Mora (b. 1942)

Contributing Editor: Juan Bruce-Novoa

Classroom Issues and Strategies

The ethnic background of the students will greatly determine the nature of class discussion. How sympathetic they are to Mora's position will vary. Students may be first-generation immigrants who themselves are adapting to English and U.S. culture, or second- or third-generation residents whose relatives are the living reminders of the process. Others may see it as an experience their ancestors went through years ago, while some will never have asked themselves if their ancestors ever spoke anything but English. You may find yourself in the middle of a heated discussion of English as the official national language or the threat to American culture that the use of other languages represents for many people. I prefer to guide the discussion toward the universal quality of the experience of acculturation the poems express.

Major Themes, Historical Perspectives, and Personal Issues

The Mora selections feature the theme of English language acquisition as a painful experience of conflict and suffering for native Spanish speakers. In each poem, school is at least partially the setting for the conflict. Her perspective characterizes the experience as one of gain and loss, emphasizing the latter as the loss of cultural authenticity, while the value of the gain is left in doubt. This position is common among proponents of bilingual education and ethnic pluralism, and can be found among the majority of writers from the Chicano communities. It reflects a turn away from the historical paradigm of U.S. culture as English-based that in turn made the learning of English a necessary rite of passage. However, it should be noted that each poem includes a touch of ambivalence: The characters are attracted to English-based culture, producing a desire whose satisfaction they seek.

For the personal connection, see the headnote.

Significant Form, Style, or Artistic Conventions

Mora's form and style are direct and should present few problems for students. The most notable feature is the use of Spanish words, but she does so on the most basic level that requires only dictionary translating for understanding. One should note, however, that the girl's name, "Esperanza," in "Border Town," means hope—an obvious pun.

Original Audience

Mora tends to publish in small presses specializing in distribution to a Latino readership. Hence, her poetry can count on a mostly sympathetic audience, one that probably will not find the smattering of Spanish hinders comprehension.

Comparisons, Contrasts, Connections

Mora can be placed in the context of Bernice Zamora and Lorna Dee Cervantes, among Chicana writers included here, as well as Judith Ortiz Cofer. For a similar depiction of the situation faced by Chicanos in Texas schools, see Tomás Rivera's *And the Earth Did Not Part*; for the ambivalent attitude of desire and fear, see Richard Rodriguez's *Hunger of Memory*; for a contrasting view on the question of English language acquisition, see Linda Chavez's *Out of the Barrio*.

Questions for Reading and Discussion/ Approaches to Writing

1. Students can be asked to locate the verses in each poem in which the dilemma of attraction and repulsion are conveyed. Ask them to consider the pros and cons of acculturation, especially as it relates to education.
2. Have students write about their own experience and, specifically, about whether education has demanded of them anything similar to what Mora describes. They could consider the question of private versus public codes of discourse and if education can serve both.

Bibliography

No major criticism has been published on Mora.

Víctor Hernández Cruz (b. 1949)

Contributing Editor: Frances R. Aparicio

Classroom Issues and Strategies

Cruz's poetry may seem hermetic at times, and partly this is due to the use of imagery, words, and references that originate in Hispanic culture or mythology. Also, his poetry demands a reader who is familiar with both English and Spanish since he frequently plays with both languages.

I would advise students to read carefully and aid them by preparing a glossary or handout that would clarify the difficult references. (The problem is that not all English teachers have access to the meaning of local references to Puerto Rican towns, Indian gods, mythological figures.)

I would emphasize the importance of the concrete poetry movement in relation to Cruz's work. The importance of the collage text, the use of space, the page, the graphics, and the significance of *play* as integral elements in the reading of a poem, could be clearly explained by a visual presentation of concrete poems from Brazil, Europe, and the United States.

Major Themes, Historical Perspectives, and Personal Issues

Urban life; meaning of language as an identity construct; importance of the cultural and historical past and how it flows into the present; importance of music and drugs as a basis for the poet's images; Hispanic culture and identity: how is it reaffirmed through literary creation?

Significant Form, Style, or Artistic Conventions

Focus on the importance of collage or hybrid texts; influence of concrete poetry; linguistic mixtures and lucid bilingualism; concept of metaliterary texts; contemporary American poetry: free verse, fragmentation, minimalism, surrealism.

Comparisons, Contrasts, Connections

Compare and contrast with Allen Ginsberg and other poets of the beat generation (use of imagery based on drugs, music of the '60s, influence of surrealism and irreverent language); an additional comparison to E. E. Cummings, as well as to the concrete poets, would be helpful in terms of use of space, punctuation, and the page as signifiers. Contrast with poets like Pedro Pietri and Tato Laviera, in which the elements of popular culture are central to the understanding of their works (Cruz is much more introspective and abstract, and does not fit totally into the paradigm of Nuyorican aesthetics).

Questions for Reading and Discussion/ Approaches to Writing

Study questions will focus mostly on the assigned text and would require students to identify major theme, use of language and imagery, and aesthetic effect of each poem.

Paper topics would focus on major themes. For example:

1. Discuss how "Speech changing within space," the epigraph to *By Lingual Wholes*, encapsulates Víctor Hernández Cruz's poetics.
2. Would you agree that English is transformed or affected by Spanish in Cruz's works? If so, how is this achieved?
3. Discuss the presence of Hispanic culture within contemporary, urban life in the United States as it is reflected in Cruz's literature; that is, how he tropicalizes the U.S. cultural identity.
4. Analyze Cruz's texts as an example of urban literature: How do his point of view, attitudes, imagery, and rhythms create a sense of life in American cities?
5. Write on Cruz's use of music and drugs as basis for his poetic imagery.

Bibliography

Acosta-Belén, Edna. "The Literature of the Puerto Rican National Minority in the United States." *Bilingual Review*, Vol. 5, no. 1 and 2. Jan.-Aug. 1978: 107–16.

Aparicio, Frances. "Salsa, Maracas and Baile: Latin Popular Music in the Poetry of Víctor Hernández Cruz." *MELUS* 16:1 (Spring 1989–1990): 43–58.

Cruz, Arnaldo. "Teaching Puerto Rican Authors: Modernization and Identity in Nuyorican Literature." *ADE Bulletin*. MLA, Dec. 1988: 45–51.

Cruz, Víctor Hernández. "Mountains in the North: Hispanic Writing in the USA." *The Americas Review*, 14: 3–4 Fall/Winter 1986: 110–14.

John Ashbery (b. 1927)

Contributing Editor: David Bergman

Classroom Issues and Strategies

Students should be encouraged to explore the connections between seemingly unrelated passages. These connections are probably best found if the student is encouraged to move freely through the poem at first, finding whatever connection he or she can spot. Richard Howard convincingly argues that each Ashbery poem contains an emblem for its entire meaning. If allowed time, students usually find such emblems. Second, drawing connections between Ashbery's method and such graphic methods as collage and assemblage often helps. Students, of course, should be reminded to read the notes.

I have found it useful to present Ashbery in relation to the visual arts, in particular the shifting perspective of comic strips, the surprising juxtapositions of collage and assemblage, the vitality of abstract impressionism, and the metaphysical imagery of de Chirico.

Major Themes, Historical Perspectives, and Personal Issues

The selection highlights three major themes or questions running through Ashbery's work: (1) the problem of subjective identity—Whose consciousness informs the poem? (2) the relationship between language and subjectivity—Whose language do I speak or does the language have a mind of its own? (3) the connection between subjectivity, language, and place—What does it mean to be an American poet?

Significant Form, Style, or Artistic Conventions

Ashbery has long been interested in French art, especially dada and surrealism. Such interests have merged with an equally strong concern for poetic form and structure, as evinced by the sestina of "Farm Implements" and the 4 x 4 structure (four stanzas each of four lines) of "Paradoxes and Oxymorons," a structure he uses through *Shadow Train*, the volume from which the poem was taken. Ashbery's combination of surrealism and formalism typifies a certain strain of postmodernism.

Original Audience

Obviously Ashbery is writing for a highly sophisticated contemporary audience. The decade he spent in France provided him with an international perspective.

Comparisons, Contrasts, Connections

Frank O'Hara, Kenneth Koch, and James Schuyler are or were close friends of Ashbery; together they formed the nucleus of what is sometimes dubbed the New York School of Poetry. The dream-like imagery bears some resemblance to John Berryman and Allen Ginsberg. Walt Whitman provides a particularly vital touchstone to an American tradition.

Questions for Reading and Discussion/ Approaches to Writing

How do comic strips (and other forms of popular art) inform both the content and the style of Ashbery's poems? Who is speaking in an Ashbery poem? What is American about John Ashbery?

Bibliography

Altieri, Charles. "John Ashbery." In *Self and Sensibility in Contemporary American Poetry*. New York: Cambridge University Press.

Berger, Charles. "Vision in the Form of a Task." Lehman, 163–208.

Bergman, David. "Introduction: John Ashbery." In *Reported Sightings: Art Chronicles 1957–87*. New York: Knopf, 1989, xi–xxiii.

——. "Choosing Our Fathers: Gender and Identity in Whitman, Ashbery and Richard Howard." *American Literary History* 1 (1989): 383–403.

Lehman, David, ed. *Beyond Amazement: New Essays on John Ashbery*. Ithaca: Cornell University Press, 1980.

John Barth (b. 1930)

Contributing Editor: Julius Rowan Raper

Classroom Issues and Strategies

To call an author "a writers' writer" is often the kiss of death. Yet Barth in "Lost in the Funhouse" and in other works goes out of his way to draw to himself this label that sets him apart from more popular "men's writers" (or "businessmen's writers") like Ernest Hemingway or "women's writers" like Willa Cather. By foregrounding the writerly nature of his work, Barth, perhaps more than any American author before him, prevents his readers from ignoring the style and form of his work while they pursue the content. Rather than focus on the relatively accessible content about Ambrose, Peter, Magda, and the three adults, as a teacher I want students to speculate about Barth's reasons for so intrusively and self-consciously focusing on the writing process.

Major Themes, Historical Perspectives, and Personal Issues

At least three large explanations for the self-consciousness of Barth's works come to mind. In *Chimera* he will have the Genie report that in the U.S. in our time "the only readers of artful fiction [are] critics, other writers, and unwilling students who, left to themselves, [prefer] music and pictures to words." In short, a serious writer has to recognize that his only willing readers *are* other writers; that he or she is, in fact, a writers' writer.

A second explanation is that, for postmodern writers, especially for Barth, the traditional modes of fiction have been used up—in Barth's favorite term, exhausted. This is especially true of the *bildungsroman,* the story of the development of an individual, and even more so if that individual happens to be an artist. In our century, James Joyce had his Stephen Dedalus, D. H. Lawrence his Paul Morel, Sherwood Anderson his George Willard, Thomas Wolfe his Eugene Gant, Ernest Hemingway his Nick Adams, William Faulkner his Quentin Compson, and so on. " 'Is anything more tiresome, in fiction, than the problems of sensitive adolescents?' " indeed! Even this self-negating idea has to appear in quotation marks because it has been uttered before. Rather than ignore this remark, which could easily alienate already unwilling students (one of the three groups remaining among readers of artful fictions), I would note the curious detail that Barth has his own seemingly autobiographical portrait of an artist in the character named Ambrose Mensch (meaning roughly "Immortal Man"), who appears here and in other stories of the collection and figures as well as a major figure in the later megafiction, *LETTERS: a Novel.* Why would Barth devote such energy to an apparently exhausted fictional form? He obviously believes that problems of adolescents are important and that such stories can be told in a new way that "replenishes" (another key term for Barth) an entire mode of fiction. That new way must include "metafiction," an important postmodern device that allows novelists to write the criticism of their own fiction while creating the fiction itself. The reasons metafiction has become important in our time are another large topic that could lead the class to fruitful discussions.

A third explanation for the self-consciousness here is at once more personal and more cultural. The narrator of Ambrose's story is a writer trapped inside his story, unable to come to its end. He is a blocked writer. In a number of works, Barth fictionalizes the writer's block he apparently suffered after the two gigantic novels of the early 1960s. Self-consciousness and writer's block may belong to a single vicious circle; each may lead to the other. Barth takes writer's block as his theme so often that one suspects it represents more than a personal event—no matter how engrossing such "autobiographic" episodes may be to readers primarily interested in "real life." At this other level, the blocked writer provides an appropriate motive for producing the metafictional passages with which Barth frames his fictions, the seeming digressions that allow him to create an audience for his generally non-realistic stories.

Significant Form, Style, or Artistic Conventions

In giving up the conventional mimesis of realism, Barth, however, elects the contrary powers of what, in *Chimera*, he terms the Principle of Metaphoric Means, "the investiture by the writer of as many of the elements and aspects of his fiction as possible with emblematic as well as dramatic value" (*Chimera* 203). This device leads to an additional motive for Barth's frequent dramatizations of the blocked writer. Such writers may be metaphors for something important in our culture. Students in class discussion may want to explore possible referents for the metaphor by asking themselves what aspects of American or Western culture appeared especially "blocked" in 1968, a year that, it turns out, may stand roughly as the midpoint of the Cold War. What is there about contemporary culture that it has lost its ability to move forward in the progressive fashion that the Enlightenment, Positivism, and modern scientific thinking once promised?

Students may then move to the possibility that every individual is a potential writer, that each of us lives out a script that someone else will write for us if we do not write it ourselves, that many women and men seem caught, like the narrator of this story, in scripts they do not want and whose end they cannot find. The next step would be to explore the degree to which the devices Barth employs, including metafiction, parody, Metaphoric Means, and (elsewhere) myth and fantasy, could be used to frame the stories of blocked lives, to liberate one from such narratives, and to write more promising life scripts. In short, can Barth's postmodern approach free up blocked lives or replenish a stymied, possibly exhausted culture? If not, might the attempt to do so still comprise a tragic gesture with a touch of the heroic in it? Students could then weigh the elements of parody, satire, and muted tragedy in Barth's story.

Consideration of Metaphoric Means as a global device leads to a careful reconsideration of every aspect of the story, including seeming authorial mistakes. If in the postexistential world we are all writers, then not only must we watch how we dot our i's and cross our t's, but how we drop our apostrophes. For example, the narrator mentions "Peter and Ambrose's father" but speaks of "Ambrose's and Peter's mother." Is this a simple slip, or a telling one? Students may want to pay special attention to parallel usages in the story or explore the later adventures of Ambrose, Peter, Magda, their parents, and/or Uncle Carl in *LETTERS*.

Original Audience

It may appear that Barth's audience is made up of other writers, critics, and writing teachers. If we are, however, to write our way out of the (doomed?) scripts we inherited from our culture, then every thinking person may have something to learn from Barth. The risks Barth takes indicate he arrived on the literary scene when the success of T. S. Eliot and James Joyce in having critics prepare an audience for their difficult texts inspired him to trust that time would provide readers for his works. By 1968, however, like other metafictionists to come, he was covering himself by providing guidelines, sometimes ironic ones, for critics still working within the modernist aesthetic.

Comparisons, Contrasts, Connections

The most useful comparisons for Barth are to the international fiction-ists whom he cites as inspirations: Jorge Luis Borges, Vladimir Nabokov, and Italo Calvino; and to the experimental writers who are his fellow postmodernists: Robert Coover, Thomas Pynchon, Raymond Federman, Cynthia Ozick, John Hawkes, Donald Barthelme, Lawrence Durrell, John Fowles, and others. The most obvious contrasts are to traditional flat realists like Cather and Hemingway, naturalists like Theodore Dreiser, engaged novelists like John Dos Passos and John Steinbeck, and representative modernists like Faulkner and Joyce, especially as the latter two use the mythic method that Barth in *Chimera* and elsewhere stands on its head. Less obvious contrasts would be to the two contemporary trends that retreat from the more audacious experiments of the postmodernists: the minimalists like Raymond Carver, Bobbie Ann Mason, and Ann Beattie; and the Magical Realists, who make minimal use of the fantasy devices that Barth, like Coover, Fowles, Durrell, and Pynchon, employs with such relish. Another sort of contrast can be made—in an age that commodifies not only space and time but also gender, class, and race—to Toni Morrison, Adrienne Rich, Alice Walker,

James Baldwin, E. L. Doctorow, Allen Ginsberg, among others. While for many of his contemporaries the message has become the *merchandise*, Barth persists in focusing on the challenges and powers of the fictional medium itself.

Questions for Reading and Discussion/ Approaches to Writing

1. "Lost in the Funhouse" cries out for student papers of two types. First, one might want students to try a reader-response approach, to let them work out their anger against the intrusive metafictional commentary, to identify the causes of their anger, and perhaps discover reasons for Barth's choosing this device. Next, students could employ a traditional close-reading approach to take up the following questions:

2. What are the indications in the story that Barth has taught creative writing courses? Is this story good pedagogy, or a parody thereof?

3. Why doesn't the narrator complete many of his sentences? How does this fit with Barth's interest in the literature of exhaustion? How does Barth attempt here to replenish the exhausted story of sensitive adolescents?

4. What is the temporal setting of the paragraph in which the narrator says, "I'll never be an author"? What is the author's problem here and how does Ambrose's problem mirror it?

5. What happened to Ambrose in the toolshed when he was ten? How did it influence his later life? Is the lyre important?

6. What does Ambrose see under the boardwalk? How does it affect him?

7. What is odd about Ambrose's invitation to Magda to accompany him through the funhouse? How can you explain it?

8. What metaphors for a life, or the world of fiction, can you develop as effectively as Barth does the funhouse?

9. How do the "head" and "eye" getting in the way affect the self-consciousness theme dramatized in the technique of the story? Is there a "human tragedy" in this problem?

10. Is Barth in danger here of turning the medium into the merchandise as well as into his message? What subject other than fiction itself would writers be in so expert a position to offer their readers? On what topic did Homer, Dante, Petrarch, Shakespeare, Milton, Goethe, Lawrence, and others purport to be experts? On what authority did they write of these subjects? Why might writers of Barth's period lack the confidence of earlier ones in exploring parallel realms of knowledge?

Bibliography

Key works appear in the headnote to Barth. Of these, the books by Morrell, Harris, Stark, and Waldmeir provide good points of entry. Weixlmann's annotated bibliography is a guide to more specific issues. Of course, there is Barth's own commentary in the works from 1968 onwards, especially in *The Friday Book*.

Donald Barthelme (1931–1989)

Contributing Editors: Linda Wagner-Martin and Charles Molesworth

Classroom Issues and Strategies

The brevity and irony of Barthelme's work are sometimes surprising to students. Again, the high modernist quality—every word crafted for its purpose, but caught in a web of style and form that makes the whole seem artlessly natural—must be explained. Students may have read less contemporary fiction than modern and what contemporary fiction they have read may well be limited to the genres of romance, science fiction, and mystery. As with any period of art, the determining craft and language practices need explication.

In the case of such a short selection, ask students to write about the work at the beginning of the class—and again at the end, once discussion has finished—something simple like "What were your reactions to this work?" Then ask them to compare their two answers with the hope of showing them that reading must be an active process, that they must form opinions. And in this author's case, getting his readers to respond is his first priority.

Major Themes, Historical Perspectives, and Personal Issues

People's inability to learn to live in their culture, and the omnipresent romantic attitudes that society continues to inscribe, whatever the subject being considered, are the main subjects of Barthelme's fiction. At base is the belief that people will endure, will eventually figure it out. Barthelme's fiction is, finally, positive—even optimistic—but first readings may not give that impression.

Significant Form, Style, or Artistic Conventions

Discuss the way humor is achieved, the interplay between irony and humor, the effects of terse and unsentimental language—students must be given ways of understanding why this story has the effect it does.

Contemporary fiction—whether minimalist or highly contrived parodic or allusive and truly postmodern—needs much more attention in the classroom. Connections must be made between writing students already understand, such as Ernest Hemingway's, and more recent work, so that they see the continuum of artistry that grows from one generation to the next.

Original Audience

Anticonservative in many ways, Barthelme's fiction taunts the current society and its attitudes at every turn. The teacher will have to be subtle in not claiming that "we all" think the way Barthelme does, or the legions of all-American conservatives will be on his/her doorstep; but the fiction itself can do a great deal to start students examining their own social attitudes.

Comparisons, Contrasts, Connections

Barthelme is given as a kind of example of metafiction, which flourished in the 1970s and 1980s. Interesting approaches can be created by contrasting this fiction with much of that by writers of minority cultural groups—James Welch, Alice Walker—to see how such fiction differs.

Bibliography

Refer to the headnote in the text for complete information and add *The Teachings of Don B.*, ed. Kim Herzinger, 1993. Also, see *The Ironist Saved from Drowning: The Fiction of Donald Barthelme* (University of Missouri, 1983), by Charles Molesworth, where this story is discussed in detail.

Thomas Pynchon (b. 1937?)

Contributing Editor: Richard Pearce

Classroom Issues and Strategies

Problems in teaching Pynchon are contradictory. On the one hand, students feel that the story is superficial and limited to the stereotype of the sixties they know from television. On the other hand, even by the end of this short section, they begin to feel overloaded—too much coincidence, too much happening.

To address these problems, emphasize the comedy. Deal with the problem of coincidence and overloading head on. List all the events and coincidences; discuss them. Work with elements of popular culture: radio, television, rock music, advertising, technology. Relate all the plots to the vague sense that someone or some organization may be plotting. Ask what we know about Pierce Inverarity. Relate to the post–World War II development of the suburbs, automobiles and superhighways, plastics, electronics, and the military-industrial complex. Focus on two goals: (1) understanding the decentered novel—too much going on for us to grasp, to understand what's important, to distinguish the good guys from the bad guys (and later radicals from reactionaries); and (2) recognizing that everything is connected. End with questions about this paradox: Is it positive—the ultimate democratic novel, where there are no hierarchies, where people from all classes and many subcultures will become interconnected, and where a woman can take on the role of hero (and Oedipus)? Is it negative—a writer running out of control, the ultimate paranoic nightmare, a random world where there is no connection and no meaning?

A specific strategy that worked very well this year was to divide the class into groups to investigate a common problem, not to solve it but to work through the novel systematically and come in with a list of "facts." The most successful project was the hardest: What do we know about the Tristero? The students came up with not only many facts, but a firsthand understanding of Oedipa's quest, how it felt, the desire to connect effects to their causes, the value of connecting with one another, the nature of plotting, the difficulty of understanding history, the momentum of capitalism, and the contradictions of democracy.

Major Themes, Historical Perspectives, and Personal Issues

Focus on the modern problems of (1) ordinary people being controlled by big business, the media, government, and (2) having access to so much information that we can't grasp connection or meaning.

Significant Form, Style, or Artistic Conventions

See the discussion of postmodernism in the headnote. Have students identify as many styles and allusions as possible—from pop (the Shadow, Baby Igor) to Papa (Oedipus). See how they relate, or don't relate.

Original Audience

By understanding the complex context of the sixties, we can understand the novel's pertinence today.

Bibliography

See the chapters on *Lot 49* in Joseph Slade's *Thomas Pynchon* (New York: Warner, 1974); Tony Tanner's *Thomas Pynchon* (London and New York: Methuen, 1982); and Alan Wilde's *Middle Grounds: Studies in Contemporary American Fiction* (Philadelphia: University of Pennsylvania Press, 1987).

See also my brief introduction to *Critical Essays on Thomas Pynchon* (Boston: G. K. Hall, 1981), which was reprinted in *American Writers: A Collection of Literary Biographies* III, Part 2, ed. A. Walton Litz (New York: Scribner's, 1981).

Among the most important critical works is the chapter on Pynchon in Tony Tanner's *City of Words: American Fiction 1950–1970* (New York: Harper and Row, 1971), reprinted in *Twentieth Century Views of Thomas Pynchon*, ed. Edward Mendelson (Englewood Cliffs, N.J.: Prentice-Hall, 1978).

One of the most intelligent discussions of *The Crying of Lot 49* is the chapter in Thomas H. Schaub's *Pynchon: The Voice of Ambiguity* (Urbana: University of Illinois Press, 1981), reprinted in *Critical Essays on Thomas Pynchon*, ed. Richard Pearce (Boston: G. K. Hall, 1981).

Setting *Lot 49* in the context of this anthology is Wendy Steiner's essay in *Reconstructing American Literary History*, ed. Sacvan Bercovitch (Cambridge, Massachusetts: Harvard University Press, 1986).

For important recent studies, see: John Dugdal, *Thomas Pynchon's Allusive Parables of Power*, 1990, and Patrick O'Donnell, ed., *New Essays on the Crying of Lot 49*.

John Edgar Wideman (b. 1941)

Contributing Editor: James W. Coleman

Classroom Issues and Strategies

I usually start by discussing the students' typical responses to Wideman with them. Students, like most readers generally, want to read linear narratives that purport to relate directly to their lives, or that they can visualize in a clear real-world context, and the aspects of Wideman's works that challenge their notions about narratives and their approaches to reading put them off. I ask them to examine their very traditional assumptions about narratives, about how narratives should relate to them, and about how they should read and judge fiction. Another question that I eventually ask is whether Wideman might have a purpose (beyond the desire to be a difficult writer) for writing as he does. And what is one of the first things about Wideman's fiction that they should see before they try to determine his meaning and relate to his work in their usual fashion?

They should see that Wideman disrupts their normal narrative approach because as he questions and tests the process in which he engages as the writer, he wants readers to question what they do too. If students will think about it, they will see that words written on a page cannot replicate the concreteness, complexity, and convolution of their experience. The language of a narrative may pretend and appear to do so, but it cannot. This is one of the first things that Wideman reminds them of and that they must accept when they approach Wideman's work. This does not mean that they should no longer read narratives that give them what they expect. But might there be a place for Wideman's kind of writing, too?

Wideman shows students this, not to abdicate a social, political, and real-life responsibility in his fiction, but to indicate the difficulty of the writer's task and the truth of what narratives are and what they do. Some students, perhaps many, however, will not be convinced by this. But some will appreciate Wideman, and one can also generate a pretty good discussion based on the students' pure emotional response to fiction such as Wideman's that requires them to work so hard.

Major Themes, Historical Perspectives, and Personal Issues

Wideman indeed portrays clear historical perspectives and intense personal issues; however, in the context of his postmodern approach, he also questions the ability of writing to do fully and successfully what he wants it to do. In the selection in *The Heath Anthology*, "Valaida," the Jewish experience of the Holocaust and the African-American historical experience of racism intersect, and Wideman also foregrounds the life and history of a black entertainer, Valaida Snow, whom few of us know. In a historical perspective, racism and oppression are pervasive themes in Wideman's work.

If we move beyond "Valaida" to examine Wideman's work since 1981, we see him focusing very directly on himself personally, on his family, and especially on the tragedies and tribulations of specific family members. Wideman's fiction often takes as a theme the very thing that he struggles with as a writer—the quest to be a black writer who writes about the black community and its experience and makes a difference through his writing. Wideman sometimes makes himself (or a surrogate writer figure) a character in his fiction, and shows himself as a character undergoing the struggle that he undergoes as a writer in real life. He writes intimately about people in his family and about a community of black people in this process.

The tragic stories of Wideman's brother and son have also become major aspects of his work since 1981. Starting in *Hiding Place* (1981) and *Damballah* (1981) and reaching a focus in the semifictional *Brothers and Keepers* (1984), Wideman deals with his relationship to his younger brother Robby, jailed for life for robbery and murder. And in *Philadelphia Fire* (1990) and some of the stories in *The Stories of John Edgar Wideman* (1992), he talks to his son, also locked away for murder.

Significant Form, Style, or Artistic Conventions

As I have been saying, Wideman will seem very unconventional to many student readers. He uses modernist techniques and creates dense modernist fictional forms in his early work, but the majority of his work since 1981 utilizes postmodernist approaches and techniques. However, this later work also draws increasingly on black cultural forms, on religious rituals and practices, black folk stories, and black street ways, for example. "Valaida" is a story that combines a postmodernist approach with the traditional African-American themes of racism and oppression.

Original Audience

Wideman has always enjoyed high praise from critics, intellectuals, and some academics, but he has never had a wide general audience. Few undergraduates have heard of Wideman, and fewer have read anything by him. Yet Wideman's books continue to win awards, and critics continue to praise him. Perhaps Wideman's work draws acclaim from critics, intellectuals, and academics for the same reason (its complexity and ingenuity) that it denies access to more general readers.

Comparisons, Contrasts, Connections

On the one hand, Wideman provides a contrast to other black writers who do not make the writing itself an explicit theme, and this is the large majority of them, I think. This would include so difficult and complex a writer as Toni Morrison, who manages to keep her focus on the theme of black struggle without foregrounding the problems and difficulties of writing the narrative itself. But on the other hand, there are black writers such as Charles Johnson who share concerns about writing similar to Wideman's, and Wideman's thematic concern with racism and the black cultural tradition connects him strongly to the black literary tradition generally. I would also point out that Wideman's work separates itself from the radical textuality, the complete focus on language and the workings of the narrative, of such white writers as Raymond Federman and Ronald Sukenick. And the reality of Wideman's narratives is not the same detached reality of a writer such as Thomas Pynchon.

Questions for Reading and Discussion/ Approaches to Writing

The following study questions may be helpful for "Valaida": How do the story's style and form force you to approach it? What is the connection of the italicized section at the beginning to the rest of the story? What is the relationship between the story Mr. Cohen tells Mrs. Clara and the beginning section? What is Mr. Cohen trying to do by telling Mrs. Clara the story? How do style, form, and theme coalesce in the story? Students might start to approach writing about "Valaida" by looking at this convergence of style, form, and theme and the resulting tension between postmodernist treatment and social and political intention.

Bibliography

Although Wideman published his first book in 1967 and has published ten books since then, one still finds relatively few works about him. The most comprehensive source is James W. Coleman's *Blackness and Modernism: The Literary Career of John Edgar Wideman* (1989), which has an interview with Wideman as an appendix. Other helpful interviews are John O'Brien's in *Interviews with Black Writers* (1973) and Wilfred Samuel's "Going Home: A Conversation with John Edgar Wideman," *Callallo* 6 (February 1983): 40–59. Good analyses of Wideman's works also appear in Bernard W. Bell's *The Afro-American Novel and Its Tradition* (1987); Michael G. Cooke's *Afro-American Literature in the Twentieth Century: The Achievement of Intimacy* (1981); and Trudier Harris's *Exorcising Blackness: Historical and Literary Lynching and Burning Rituals* (1984). Kermit Frazier's "The Novels of John Wideman," *Black World*, v. 24, 8 (1975): 18–35 is one of the very first pieces on Wideman and is still useful.

Gary Soto (b. 1952)

Contributing Editor: Raymund Paredes

Classroom Issues and Strategies

As a Chicano working-class poet, Soto sometimes uses figurative language that might be unfamiliar to and difficult for some readers. Occasionally, he uses a Spanish word or phrase. As a poet with a strong sense of kinship with people who are poor, neglected, and oppressed, Soto tries to create poetry out of ordinary working-class experience and images. All this is very different from typically bourgeois American poetry.

It is useful to connect Soto's work to contemporary events in Mexican-American experience. Reading a bit about Cesar Chavez and the California farm worker struggle places some of Soto's sympathies in context. General reading in Chicano (or Mexican-American) history would also be useful. It is also useful to consider Soto among other contemporary poets whose sensibilities were shaped by the post-1960s struggles to improve the circumstances of minority groups and the poor.

Urge students to try to see the world from the point of view of one of Soto's working-class Chicanos, perhaps a farm worker. From this perspective, one sees things very differently than from the point of view generally presented in American writing. For the tired, underpaid farm worker, nature is neither kind nor beautiful, as, for example, Thoreau would have us believe. Soto writes about the choking dust in the fields, the danger to the workers' very existence that the sun represents. Imagine a life without many creature comforts, imagine feelings of hunger, imagine the pain of knowing that for the affluent and comfortable, your life counts for very little.

Students are generally moved by Soto's vivid and honest presentation of personal experiences, his sympathy for the poor, and the accessibility of his work. They generally wish to know more about Mexican-American and Mexican cultures, more about the plight of farm workers and the urban poor.

Major Themes, Historical Perspectives, and Personal Issues

Despite Soto's distinctiveness, he is very much a contemporary American poet. Like many of his peers, he writes largely in an autobiographical or confessional mode. As an intensively introspective poet, he seeks to maintain his connection to his Mexican heritage as it exists on both sides of the border. His work often focuses on the loss of a father at an early age, on the difficulties of adolescence (especially romantic feelings), and the urgency of family intimacy. On a broader level, Soto speaks passionately on behalf of tolerance and mutual respect while he denounces middle- and upper-class complacency and indifference to the poor.

Significant Form, Style, or Artistic Conventions

Again, Soto is very much a contemporary American poet, writing autobiographically in free verse and using images that are drawn from ordinary experience and popular culture. His sympathies for the poor are very typical of contemporary writers from ethnic or underprivileged backgrounds. It is also important to note that some of Soto's poetry has been influenced by the "magical realism" of modern Latin American writing, especially Gabriel García-Márquez.

Original Audience

Although Soto is a Chicano poet in that his Mexican-American heritage is a key aspect of his literary sensibility, he nevertheless aims for a wider audience. He clearly wants a broad American audience to feel sympathies for his poetic characters and their circumstances. The product of a contemporary sensibility, Soto's poetry is topical and vital.

Comparisons, Contrasts, Connections

Again, as an autobiographical poet, Soto can be compared with such figures as Robert Lowell, John Berryman, and Sylvia Plath. His working-class sensibility is reminiscent of James Wright and Philip Levine (who was Soto's teacher at California State University, Fresno). His celebration of certain Chicano values and denunciation of bigotry is comparable to that of other Chicano poets such as Lorna Dee Cervantes.

Questions for Reading and Discussion/ Approaches to Writing

1. Students might be asked to look for clues in his work as to ethnic background, economic status, and geographical setting.

   Furthermore, they might be asked to consider certain formal qualities of his work: Where do Soto's images and symbols come from? Does Soto attempt to make his work accessible to ordinary readers?
2. Soto's work is fruitfully compared to other autobiographical poets (Lowell, Berryman, Plath) and to working-class poets such as Wright and Levine.

   Soto's book *The Tale of Sunlight* (particularly its final section) might be studied for its elements of "magical realism."

   Soto, of course, can be studied in connection to other Chicano poets such as Lorna Dee Cervantes and Umar Salinas.

Bibliography

Probably the most useful general source of information on Soto (complete with various references) is the article on Soto in *The Dictionary of Literary Biography*, volume 82, "Chicano Writers" (1989).

Joy Harjo (Creek) (b. 1951)

Contributing Editor: C. B. Clark

Classroom Issues and Strategies

It's important to make certain that students read the biographical notes and footnotes provided in the text. Consider also using audiotapes of Harjo reading and discussing her own work.

Major Themes, Historical Perspectives, and Personal Issues

Imperialism, colonialism, dependency, nostalgia for the old ways, reverence for grandparents and elders, resentment of conditions of the present, plight of reservation and urban Indians, natural world, sense of hopelessness, power of the trickster, idea that the feminine is synonymous with heritage, deadly compromise, symbol of all that has been lost (such as the land), tension between the desire to retrieve the past and the inevitability of change, the arrogance of white people, problems of half-breeds (or mixed-bloods).

Significant Form, Style, or Artistic Conventions

Harjo uses free verse. She is aware of classic European form, but chooses not to use it. She does try oral chant, as in "She Had Some Horses." She is not in any school, except American Indian.

Original Audience

Ask the question: Is there any audience outside American Indians? The second audience is the student and the third is the general reader.

Questions for Reading and Discussion/ Approaches to Writing

1. Who are the Creeks? What is their origin? What impact did removal have on the Five Civilized Tribes? Where are the Creeks today? How are they organized? What was the role of the Christian missionary? What is traditional Creek religion? What is a Stomp

Ground? Does Harjo travel much and is that reflected in her poetry?

2. Hand out a reading list, containing ethnographic, historical, and contemporary works on the Creeks. Hand out a theme list, containing such items as removal, acculturation, identity. Hand out a subject list containing topics such as removal, alcoholism, and jails. Ask the students to write an essay on each of the lists. Require some library research for the essays, which will provide background for the poetry.

Bibliography

There are no separate works on Harjo. Bits on her can be found in critical pieces on her work, in collections, in autobiographical pieces, and through interviews.

Published works that deal in part with her include Joseph Bruchac's *Survival This Way* and Andrew O. Wiget's *Native American Literature*, part of the Twayne series, as well as *World Literature Today*, Spring, 1992.

Roberta Hill Whiteman (Oneida) (b. 1947)

Contributing Editor: Andrew O. Wiget

Major Themes, Historical Perspectives, and Personal Issues

The most important consideration in Whiteman's poetry is her unification of both the personal and historical sense of loss. In poems like "In the Longhouse, Oneida Museum," "Dream of Rebirth," and "Scraps Worthy of Wind" she has internalized the loss and alienation that have come from the Oneida experience of removal. This historic consciousness is echoed by her own personal loss in the death of parents and the loss of loved ones. It is a sense of loss that creates tremendous longing, a longing edged with anger, that's reflected in poems like "Underground Water" and "Scraps Worthy of Wind."

Significant Form, Style, or Artistic Conventions

As the headnote to this section indicates, Whiteman owes a lot to Richard Hugo, and so her poetry falls squarely within the mainstream of contemporary American poetry. Thus, it should not present any unusual difficulties in terms of form or imagery or rhetorical strategy for the reader. Whiteman is very much a classic poet, if contemporary poetry can be said to have produced "classical" poets, and pays a good deal of attention to form. Call the reader's attention to her use of line breaks and the tremendous balance of stresses in her lines. Also, she moves very keenly between abstract language of great rhetorical power and very concrete immediate images that haunt the mind. A reference probably lost on students in "Lines for Marking Time," for instance, is the comparison of the inside of an operating radio of the old-fashioned tube design to "a shimmering city." I would also ask students to formulate their sense of the tone of these poems.

Comparisons, Contrasts, Connections

Whiteman compares favorably to a number of contemporary poets for whom the loss of contact with their ethnic, occupational, or cultural past has been one of the defining factors in the formation of their identity. She would work very well with others from different traditions such as Judith Ortiz Cofer, Cathy Song, and Janice Mirikitani, as well as other poets for whom the burden of memory has been a dominant theme. Her "Underground Water" is usefully compared to Adrienne Rich's "Diving into the Wreck." Historically, one could read Roberta Hill Whiteman's poetry as a response to the deculturation of American Indians reflected in other writings in the anthology by Native Americans, including John Joseph Mathews, John Milton Oskison, and Gertrude Bonnin.

Questions for Reading and Discussion/
Approaches to Writing

1. What about these poems reveals them to have been written by an Indian author? How would you describe the writer's attitude toward the past? What seems to be this writer's overriding concern?
2. Find a line or image from these poems that you think best represents the interest or personal vision of this author, and use it to explore her poetry.

Bibliography

"Massaging the Earth: An Interview with Roberta Hill Whiteman." In *Survival This Way: Interviews with Native American Poets*, edited by Joseph Bruchac, 329–35. Tuscon: University of Arizona, 1987.

Wiget, Andrew. "Review of *Star Quilt*." *American Indian Culture and Research Journal* 8 (1985): 92–96.

Wendy Rose (Hopi) (b. 1948)

Contributing Editor: C. B. Clark

Classroom Issues and Strategies

Background knowledge about Indian culture and history will help students pick up on comments about imperialism, removals, atrocities, resentments, etc.

Major Themes, Historical Perspectives, and Personal Issues

Themes are colonialism, imperialism, dependency, nostalgia for the old ways, reverence for grandparents, resentment for conditions of the present, plight of reservation and urban Indians, sense of hopelessness, the power of the trickster, feminism as synonymous with heritage, deadly compromise, symbolism of all that has been lost (such as land), tension between the desire to retrieve the past and the inevitability of change, arrogance of white people, problems of half-breeds (or mixed-bloods).

Significant Form, Style, or Artistic Conventions

Rose uses free verse. She is aware of classical European form but chooses not to use it. In addition, she is less an oral poet using chants and more of a lyric poet. She is not in any school, except American Indian.

Original Audience

I ask this question: Is there an audience outside American Indians? A second audience, of course, would be the students in class. A third audience would be the general reader.

Questions for Reading and Discussion/
Approaches to Writing

1. What are major themes of Hopi religion? Who are the Hopi? Where do they live? Why do they live atop mesas? Where do the Hopi claim to come from? How did they get to where they are today? What contemporary problems do they face? What is the Hopi relationship to the outside world? Who are some Hopi leaders today? How do the Hopi view the world?

2. Hand out a reading list on the Hopi, containing ethnographic, historical, and contemporary works. Hand out a theme list, containing topics like manifest destiny or acculturation. Hand out a subject list, with subjects like alcoholism, jails, and kachinas. Then, ask students to write an essay using Rose's works in reference to any of these topics.

Bibliography

No single biographical or critical work exists on Rose. Information must be gleaned from critical pieces, collections, and book reviews. Additionally, information can come from autobiographical statements preceding selections printed in anthologies of American Indian works.

Rose is included in Joseph Bruchac's *Survival This Way*, Swann and Krupat's *I Tell You Now*, and Andrew Wiget's *Native American Literature*.

Cathy Song (b. 1955)

Contributing Editor: Shirley Lim

Classroom Issues and Strategies

Offer entry points to students by discussing Hawaiian immigrant history and cultural embedding of Asian-Japanese images and themes.

Use posters of Utumara woodcuts and Georgia O'Keeffe paintings to make imagistic style come alive for students; also discuss narratives of picture brides.

Students are interested in issues of family/kinship networks. They question how Song's networks are different from their own, looking for specific cultural markers.

Major Themes, Historical Perspectives, and Personal Issues

Asian immigrants into Hawaii, plantation culture; picture-bride customs; Asian emphasis on filial pieties, family ties; the poet's painterly interests in themes and style—these are among Song's themes.

Significant Form, Style, or Artistic Conventions

Consider: imagistic conventions forming part of modernist, Williams's school of thought; the influence of aesthetics drawn from visual arts, also part of Williams's convention; Song's style of compression, density, natural rhythms of everyday speech.

Original Audience

Her poetry is in every way contemporary; her audience is intimately drawn into the observations.

Comparisons, Contrasts, Connections

Good comparisons would be with William Carlos Williams and early Adrienne Rich.

Questions for Reading and Discussion/ Approaches to Writing

1. Have students write down some of their own family history.
2. Discuss mother-daughter relationships.
3. What are the most fundamental elements of modern American poetry?

Bibliography

I recommend my own review in *MELUS* (Fall 1983).

Rita Dove (b. 1952)

Contributing Editor: Hilary Holladay

Classroom Issues and Strategies

In my experience, students like Dove's poems, even though they don't fully understand them. I found that dividing the class into small groups (and providing them with several discussion questions) works well with her poems. This gives students a chance to raise issues they might not air otherwise—and accommodates poems that seem to be more about asking questions than answering them. Walking from group to group, I am able to address specific concerns without usurping control of a free-flowing discussion.

Major Themes, Historical Perspectives, and Personal Issues

In her poems, Dove often distills the experiences of oppressed groups: women, blacks, and working-class Americans, among others. She does not strike a victim's pose, however. Whether she is dealing with contemporary scenes or historical events, she speaks with the calm confidence of one who knows she will be listened to.

As an African-American woman who has spent virtually her entire adult life affiliated with one university or another, she represents an intriguing mix of "outsider" and "insider" perspectives. The academic life seems to have provided her with a forum quite compatible with her interest in the intersections of the personal, the political, and the intellectual. As an American who believes strongly in the value of traveling to other countries and learning other languages, Dove brings an international perspective to many of her poems as well.

Significant Form, Style, or Artistic Conventions

Although Dove has published a novel and a collection of short fiction, she seems most at home in poetry. She writes primarily in free verse, in both first- and third-person. Although the prose poem published here is a departure from her usual style, it is characteristic of Dove's interest in obliquely stated narratives. *Thomas and Beulah*, a narrative sequence, is hardly straightforward in its development; in that Pulitzer Prize-winning collection, Dove provides the pieces with which we can envision (and continually re-envision) the evolving puzzle of two interwoven lives.

Comparisons, Contrasts, Connections

Dove can be grouped with other African-American poets, women poets, and poets exemplary for their use of imagery. Because of her German and Scandinavian influences, her poems would also work well in a comparative literature course.

Questions for Reading and Discussion/ Approaches to Writing

1. Study questions for the Dove poems selected here might focus on voice and perspective, characterization, and rhetorical strategies. For example, how would you describe the speaker in each of these poems? What is the speaker's perspective on the events described in each poem? How does the mood differ from poem to poem? How does "Kentucky, 1833" blend the historical with the personal? What are the paradoxes at work in this poem? How is the poem's form significant? How would you paraphrase "Ö"? Can you think of other words, in English or other languages, that change "the whole neighborhood"? Explain your selections. What do you think the speaker in "Arrow" means by "the language of fathers"? What is the significance of the enjambment and the three-line stanzas in "The Oriental Ballerina"?

2. Students writing about Dove's poems should read all (or at least a couple) of her poetry collections so they will have a sense of the breadth of her concerns. Their papers could address family relationships, narrative perspective, or her enigmatic image patterns. They could also explore her international themes or compare one or more of her poems about family life with those of another woman poet—such as Sylvia Plath, Adrienne Rich, or Lucille Clifton. An alternative assignment: Write a letter to Dove and present her with a possible interpretation of one of her poems. Then pose several questions that would help you develop your interpretation and perhaps help you better understand her other poems as well. This latter assignment worked well in an advanced composition class, because it enabled students to develop their skills in writing query letters as well as analyzing poetry.

Janice Mirikitani (b. 1942)

Contributing Editor: Shirley Lim

Classroom Issues and Strategies

Students need to learn about the internment of Japanese-American citizens during World War II. You might consider reading historical extracts of laws passed against Japanese-Americans during internment or passages from books describing camp life. If possible, show students paintings and photographs of internment experience. Students tend to resist issues of racism in mainstream white American culture; counter this tendency by discussing the long history of persecution of Asians on the West Coast.

Deal with the strong aural/oral quality of Mirikitani's writing—the strong protest voice.

Students often raise questions about the poet's anger: How personally does the reader take this? How successfully has the poet expressed her anger and transformed it into memorable poetry? What kinds of historical materials does the poet mine? Why are these materials useful and significant?

Major Themes, Historical Perspectives, and Personal Issues

Themes are the historical documentation of legislation against Asians in the United States; internment during World War II; Mirikitani's own experience in Lake Tule during World War II; economic and psychological sufferings of Japanese-Americans during that period; position of Asian-American women historically and politically.

Significant Form, Style, or Artistic Conventions

Consider the issue of protest and oral poetry; traditions of such poetry in black literature in the 1960s and 1970s; influence of "black is beautiful" movement on Mirikitani.

Original Audience

Consider the didactic and sociopolitical nature of the writing: a divided audience; her own people and an audience to be persuaded and accused of past prejudices. Much of her poetry was written in the 1970s at the peak of social protests against white hegemony.

Comparisons, Contrasts, Connections

Compare her poems with Sonia Sanchez and Don L. Lee, for example, on sociopolitical and minority concerns.

Questions for Reading and Discussion/ Approaches to Writing

1. Personal accounts or observations of racism at work in their own society.
2. How they themselves perceive Asian-Americans; their stereotypes of Asian-American women.

Bibliography

Refer to Mini Okubo's books on camp life, the movie of the Houstons' book on Manzanar, and newspaper accounts of the recent debate and settlement of repayments to Japanese-Americans for injustice done to them by the U.S. government during their internment period.

Lorna Dee Cervantes (b. 1954)

Contributing Editor: Juan Bruce-Novoa

Classroom Issues and Strategies

Students may object to the strident tone of "Poem for the Young White Man." Even Chicanos can get turned off by it. The feminism has the same effect on the men. Why is she so hostile toward males, they ask. Some now say that she is passé, radicalism being a thing of the sixties. I prepare the students with information on feminist issues, especially on the single-parent families, wife abuse, and child abuse. I also prepare them by talking about racial and ethnic strife as a form of warfare, seen as genocide by minority groups.

I use Bernice Zamora's poetry as an introduction. Her alienation from the male rituals in "Penitents" produces the all-female family in "Beneath . . . ." The sense of living in one's own land, but under other's rules (Zamora's "On Living in Aztlán"), explains the bitterness of "Poem for the Young White Man." And both of the poets eventually find a solution in their relation to nature through animal imagery; yet just like Zamora in "Pico Blanco," Cervantes maintains an uneasy relationship with the machoworld with which women still contend.

Major Themes, Historical Perspectives, and Personal Issues

The historical theme of the disappearance of the nuclear family in the United States is primary here. There is also the effect of urban renewal on ethnic and poor communities whose neighborhoods were often the targets for projects that dislodged people from an area. In "Crow" there is the theme of finding a link in nature to counter urban alienation.

On the personal level, Cervantes's family history is reflected auto-biographically in "Beneath . . . ."

Significant Form, Style, or Artistic Conventions

Cervantes uses the form of the narrative poem, with a few key metaphors. Her confessional mode is reminiscent of Robert Lowell's. Her style is conversational, direct, unpretentious, but there is a constant sharp edge to her verses, a menacing warning against overstepping one's welcome.

Original Audience

Although her audience was and is generally "third worldist" and Chicano, these poems show a range of different target audiences. "Beneath . . ." is a feminist poem, appealing greatly to women. When it was first published, there was little discussion of the issue of female heads of households in Chicano circles because few wanted to admit to the problem in the Chicano community. Now the discussion is much more common.

"Poem for . . ." had great appeal in the closing days of the radical movement, but has since faded to a smaller audience of older Chicanos who have heard the radical poetry to the point of exhaustion. However, mainstream liberals like "Poem for . . ." because it speaks as they assume all minorities should speak, harshly, bitterly, and violently. Young Chicanos are once again picking up the strident tone, faced as they are with the economic decline that has exacerbated social problems, especially in urban schools.

Comparisons, Contrasts, Connections

I compare her to Margaret Atwood in their sense of women being submerged and needing to surface by finding their own traditions. They both have a capacity for stringent statement when pushed by violent circumstances. Both have strong links to nature, in which their ancestors cultivated, not only food, but their culture. Comparisons with Bernice Zamora are suggested above.

Carlos Castaneda's theory of the enemy is significant for Cervantes. It explains how the "Young White Man" is tempting the author into violence.

Questions for Reading and Discussion/ Approaches to Writing

1. Students are asked to consider the significance of mainstream construction projects on local communities; from here they are asked to ponder the cycle of change and its victims.
2. Write on the links between "Beneath . . ." and "Poem for . . . ."
3. Write on Cervantes's view of the world as a threat to existence and what she offers as a response.

Bibliography

The best article is my "Bernice Zamora and Lorna Dee Cervantes," *Revista Iberoamericana* 51, 132–33 (July–Dec. 1985): 565–73. See also Cordelia Candelaria's *Chicano Poetry* and Martin Sonchez's *Contemporary Chicana Poetry*.

Bharati Mukherjee (b. 1940)

Contributing Editor: Roshni Rustomji-Kerns

Classroom Issues and Strategies

It is important to read and discuss Mukherjee's "A Wife's Story" as an integral part of twentieth-century American literature and not as an "exotic" short story by a foreign writer. As the essay accompanying "A Wife's Story" points out, Mukherjee identifies herself very strongly as an American writer writing about twentieth-century Americans. Although most of her stories are about South Asian-Americans (South Asia in the contemporary geopolitical arena usually consists of Bangladesh, India, Pakistan, Sri Lanka, and the Maldive Islands), she sees herself as being primarily influenced by, as well as being part of, the tradition of Euro-American writers. In a brief interview published in the November, 1993 issue of *San Francisco Focus* in which she discusses her novel, *The Holder of the World* (published in 1993 after the publication of the second edition of *The Heath Anthology*), she says, "I think of myself as an American writer . . . I want to focus on the making of the American mind." But instead of an exploration of the making of the American mind, *The Holder of the World* is a reflection and an echoing of the existing, dominant American attitudes and concepts about the American colonial period and the "exotic" India of the past with self-indulgent emperors and rajas, wealthy merchants and self-sacrificing women.

In order to avoid the trap of reading "A Wife's Story" as being from a "marginal" group, I have found it best to first discuss the crafting of the story as a literary work in the tradition of English/American literature, and then move on to the aspects of the story that deal with specific concepts and cultures.

Keeping in mind Mukherjee's own comments on racism, multiculturalism, and literary influences, it is interesting to discuss how she uses, or does not use, her ideas on these subjects in "A Wife's Story." A classroom discussion on the students' views regarding these concepts helps them understand the importance of these concepts in American literature.

Questions for Reading and Discussion/ Approaches to Writing

I have found the following assignments/approaches helpful:

1. Discuss the story as a literary work.
2. Read stories and poems by other American writers who deal with the American expatriate/immigrant experience and compare/contrast "A Wife's Story" with the other readings. The bibliography that follows includes some collections of immigrant/expatriate writings.
3. Gain some knowledge of the history of Asian-Americans, especially within the context of the different patterns of immigration in the U.S.
4. I have sometimes asked students to interview expatriates or immigrants from South Asia on the campus or in their community and see how Mukherjee's story and her distinctive literary style differ from, expand upon, imitate, or use the style and subject matter of the oral history/interviews conducted by the students. This is often a suitable time to discuss, compare, and contrast the styles and techniques of oral and written literature.
5. I have sometimes invited South Asian women from the community to speak to us of their experiences in the United States with an emphasis on how they would communicate their experiences to a larger audience. For example, we ask the guest speakers about the kind of stories they would like to write for a book or for a TV show that deals with South Asian-Americans.
6. Interestingly, after having read the works of South Asian-American writers, many students have explored the immigrant histories of their own families and have then written stories, poems, essays, and screen/TV scripts based on their projects.

Further discussions of the story, especially on specific issues related to Mukherjee's major themes and the literary influences that emerge out of her root culture, may be based on the statements made in the following parts of this Instructor's Guide essay.

Major Themes, Historical Perspectives, and Personal Issues

Mukherjee's earlier works dealt mainly with encounters between cultures that take place when her South Asian-American protagonists who live in Canada or the U.S. return as visitors to their home in India

(*Tiger's Daughter*, and *Days and Nights in Calcutta*). Her later, and maybe more important works, deal with these encounters as they take place in America. The protagonists in her later works are not all from South Asia, but nearly all of them are people who have arrived in America during this century.

Her 1993 novel, *The Holder of the World*, takes place in the United States as well as in India. It also takes place across historical time. The framework of the novel takes place in contemporary United States and India. The central story takes place in seventeenth-century America and India. The Euro-American women protagonists of this work have lovers who are from other cultures or countries.

A significant number of her stories and novels present the encounters between cultures in the context of encounters between women and men either of different root cultures or from the same root culture. Some of these very personal encounters have the poignancy of underlying affection, some of them range from gentle humor to an attempt at broad satire, some are marred by stereotypical characters and events, while others reveal the dangerous, violent side of such encounters.

"A Wife's Story" is an excellent example of encounters between cultures presented in a narrative of encounters between women and men. It is a fascinating story because it presents the surprise of role reversal and because of the sense of a dramatic presentation that permeates the story. It is the wife, not the husband, who has come to America and who is knowledgeable about this new home. Panna is the guide and often the protector for her husband who is visiting her. And her story is constantly dramatic. It begins with her in a theatre and every episode that follows is carefully situated in a stage-like setting with set actors.

The story also contains echoes of the memory and nostalgia for the past that play a significant role in the writings of many South Asian-Americans. This memory and nostalgia for the landscape of places and people of the writers' childhood is often juxtaposed with the excitement and challenge of their new life and the unfamiliar landscape of the people and places of the U.S. It is interesting to explore how Mukherjee uses these two strands in this story, bringing one or the other—memory or the excitement of novelty—into the foreground to present her characters and to build the circular, winding pattern of her story.

Significant Form, Style, or Artistic Conventions

Much as Mukherjee seems to insist that she belongs to the Euro-American traditions of American literature and as easily as she is able to be fit into that tradition, there are aspects of her work that are derived mainly from her cultural roots in India. She has spoken of the important influences in her life of the images and ideas of her childhood in India and the sounds and sights of the great traditions of Indian mythology and literature. Her awareness of these influences enriches her stories and novels. For example, she can give the impression of a larger work even in a short story such as "A Wife's Story," which carefully meanders from one place to another and in which stories live within other stories. This technique of winding stories and embedding stories within stories dominates the Sanskrit epics, the *Mahabharata* and the *Ramayana*, and much of Indian literature.

Her ability to let us hear her characters speak to us not only about themselves but as narrators of others' experiences is a reflection of the oral traditions of Indian literature. In "A Wife's Story," we can hear Panna telling us not only the many stories of her life in India and in New York but also the stories of the people she introduces to us.

Bharati Mukherjee is an enthusiastic and extremely knowledgeable collector of Indian miniatures. Keeping in mind this interest in miniatures, we see that Mukherjee can also paint small-scale yet detailed episodes and characters.

Mukherjee's careful manipulation of moods and emotional tones in her stories may be influenced by classical Indian literature, art, and music. In Indian classical art, the universally recognizable essence of an emotion or a mood often dominates the work of art. In "A Wife's Story," Mukherjee portrays Panna through her emotions and moods that move from anger and outrage to perplexity and frustration, to humor and affection, and in the end to the joy of self-discovery of her body and her sense of freedom. Even the memory of old customs, and the excitement of new discoveries for both Panna and her husband are presented in terms of emotions and moods.

Comparisons, Contrasts, Connections

These are dealt with in other parts of this essay.

Bibliography

Collections that contain South Asian-American writings:

A Meeting of Streams: South Asian Canadian Literature. Toronto: South Asia Review, 1985.

Katrak, Ketu H. and R. Radhakrishna, eds. *The Massachusetts Review. Desh-Videsh: South Asian Expatriate Writing and Art* (Winter 1988–1989): 29.4.

Making Waves: An Anthology of Writings by and about Asian American Women by Asian Women United of California, 1989.

Mukherjee, Bharati and Ranu Vanikar, eds. *The Literary Review: Writers of the Indian Commonwealth* (Summer 1986): 29.4.

Our Feet Walk the Sky: Women of the South Asian Diaspora by Women of South Asian Descent Collective, 1993.

Rustomji, Roshni, ed. *Journal of South Asian Literature: South Asian Women Writers. The Immigrant Experience* (Winter–Spring 1986): 21.2.

South Asians in America:

Agarwal, Priya. *Passage from India: Post-1965 Immigrants and Their Children,* 1991.

Fisher, Maxine P. *The Indians of New York City,* 1980.

Jensen, Joan M. *Passage from India: Asian Indian Immigrants in North America,* 1988.

Saran, Parmatma. *The Asian Indian Experience in the United States,* 1985.

Singh, Jane. *South Asians in America: An Annotated Selected Bibliography,* 1988.

Takaki, Ronald. *Strangers from a Different Shore: A History of Asian Americans,* 1989.

——. *A Different Mirror: A History of Multicultural America,* 1993.

Anthologies of cross-cultural and multicultural writings:

Brown, Wesley and Amy Ling, eds. *Imagining America: Stories from the Promised Land,* 1991.

Divakaruni, Chitra B. *Multitude: Cross Cultural Readings for Writers,* 1993.

Hongo, Garrett. *The Open Boat: Poems from Asian America,* 1993.

Verburg, Carol J. *Ourselves among Others: Cross Cultural Readings for Writers,* 1991.

Watanabe, Sylvia and Carol Bruchac. *Home to Stay: Asian American Women's Fiction,* 1990.

Sandra Cisneros (b. 1954)

Contributing Editor: Lora Romero

Classroom Issues and Strategies

Students generally find reading Cisneros a delightful experience. The brevity and humor of her stories help make them accessible even to those unfamiliar with the Mexican-American culture in which much of her writing is set. In fact, one of my colleagues taught Cisneros very successfully to students in Galway, Ireland.

One potential source of discomfort for students is Cisneros's manifestly feminist sensibility. Some students may accuse her (as they would accuse virtually any other feminist writer) of "man-bashing." When this issue comes up, I point out that, ironically, defining feminism in that way makes men the center of attention. Then I encourage students to talk about what they think feminism means and/or should mean. Sometimes students with more sophisticated definitions of feminism can convince their peers that feminism does not reduce to man-hating; in any case, giving the students a forum for talking through the issue is usually productive since it is one about which they will probably have strong (if unexamined and unarticulated) opinions.

The feminism of women of color, however, is complicated by ethnic identification. Some students will be assuming that ethnic authors should offer only "positive" images of minorities—which means, in effect, talking about sexism in minority communities is off-limits. I encourage students to interrogate their assumptions about ethnic authors' "duties." At the same time, I acknowledge that being both a woman of color and a feminist can be a difficult task since one of the stereotypes of Latino men (and non-white men generally) is that "they treat their women badly." Then I try to turn students' attention back to the text to see if they can find evidence that some tension between ethnic and gender identity is shaping the narrative.

Major Themes, Historical Perspectives, and Personal Issues

Students may bring to Cisneros's work a conception of immigrant culture that is based on the model of European immigration to the United States. That model is not entirely appropriate; in fact, Chicanos have a saying: "We didn't come to the United States. It came to us." Before the Mexican-American War (1846–48), most of what is now the southwestern United States (including Texas and California) was part of Mexico. After the war, many erstwhile Mexicans automatically became U.S. citizens when it annexed the land where Mexicans had lived since the sixteenth century. Reminding students that national boundaries are often arbitrarily imposed should help deepen their understanding of national culture. In addition, most students will have only linear and unidirectional models of "assimilation" for understanding ethnic cultures, but the culture of Latinos living in the U.S. has been shaped by a very different historical experience. Anthropologists and historians have argued that the southwestern United States is really part of a much older, regional culture that includes Northern Mexico, and that this regional culture is constantly being reinvigorated by a continuous flow of population back and forth over the border.

One important theme in Cisneros's work is the heterogeneity of the Mexican-American community (as it is expressed through differences of class, gender, education, language use, politics, and so on). Cisneros is, typically, more interested in detailing the dynamics of her own community rather than representing conflicts between Anglo-Americans and Mexican-Americans. Conflicts between Anglo and Latino cultures are, of course, present in Cisneros's writing, but they often take the form of encounters between relatively assimilated Latinos and relatively unassimilated ones.

The shape of such encounters undoubtedly reflects personal issues in the sense that Cisneros, as an educated, middle-class intellectual, seems simultaneously committed to identifying with her Mexican-American characters and to never losing sight of her difference from them. Often in her stories, there is a narrator or character who seems to represent Cisneros herself: a Chicana artist who has done something to scandalize her community, who exists (as it were) on the border between Mexican-American and Anglo-American cultures, and who has an uneasy relation to both.

Significant Form, Style, or Artistic Conventions

Cisneros's stories typically move in the direction of reconciliation of the Chicana intellectual with the Mexican-American community, but not all of her stories achieve that resolution. Cisneros's work thus provides fertile grounds for discussion of the politics of narrative closure. For this reason, it would be helpful if, before reading Cisneros, students had some sense of the conventions of the short story. Cisneros writes in a modernist narrative mode with both North American and Latin

American precursors. Her stories do not typically center on a single consciousness or point of view; they are often populated by voices rather than characters; if there is an identifiable narrator, she is usually ironized.

In a more advanced class where you can assume some familiarity with modernist narrative, you could use Cisneros as a test case for differentiating between modernism and postmodernism. In addition to formal considerations, some topics crucial to such a discussion would include Cisneros's feminism, her ethnic identification, and her attitude toward mass culture.

Comparisons, Contrasts, Connections

To encourage students to think about how ethnic feminist writers negotiate between their gender and their ethnic identifications, it would be worthwhile to compare Cisneros to writers like Toni Morrison, Maxine Hong Kingston, Louise Erdrich, and Helena María Viramontes. On the other hand, reading Cisneros in the context of contemporary Latin American women writers (for example, Claire Lipesector, Isabel Allende, Carolina María de Jesus) would put pressure on received categories of national/cultural identity. Including even one Latin American writer at the end of a course on what is called "*American* Literature" can be a useful way of getting students to think about the ethnocentrism of the term and the politics of cultural study more generally.

For contrast as much as comparison, Cisneros might also be placed in the context of nonfiction writings by lesbian Chicana writers like Gloria Anzaldúa and Cherríe Moraga. The comparison/contrast helps bring attention to the specifically heterosexual nature of Cisneros's feminism: How does the fact that Cisneros is heterosexual (and hence unable to declare herself simply "independent" of men) shape her articulation of feminism and illuminate the particular erotic dilemmas faced by her female characters? In order to highlight the question of class, pairing Cisneros with Tomás Rivera works well because—although Cisneros has certain stylistic affinities with Rivera—his work is more obviously compatible with the version of Chicano identity constructed by the Chicano movement.

Questions for Reading and Discussion/
Approaches to Writing

"Little Miracles, Kept Promises" appears to be a compilation of voices with no authorial intervention; as students are reading, encourage them to think about Cisneros's agency by noticing what kinds of voices she includes and which she excludes, if some voices seem to speak with more authority than others, and which voices (if any) represent the authorial perspective.

Bibliography

Cisneros's *House on Mango Street* has already generated a number of critical responses, including: Ellen McCracken, "Sandra Cisneros' *The House on Mango Street:* Community-Oriented Introspection and the Demystification of Patriarchal Violence" in Asunción Horno-Delgado et. al. (eds.), *Breaking Boundaries: Latina Writings and Critical Readings* (1989); Julián Olivares, "Sandra Cisneros' 'The House on Mango Street' and the Poetics of Space" in María Hererra-Sobek and Helena María Viramontes (eds.), *Chicana Creativity and Criticism: Charting New Frontiers in American Literature* (1988); and Ramón Saldívar, *Chicano Narrative: The Dialectics of Difference* (1990). One study of *Woman Hollering Creek* in the context of inter-American feminism is Sonia Saldívar-Hull's "Feminism on the Border: From Gender Politics to Geopolitics" in Héctor Calderón and José David Saldívar (eds.), *Criticism in the Borderlands: Studies in Chicano Literature, Culture, and Ideology* (1991).

Simon Ortiz (Acoma Pueblo) (b. 1941)

Contributing Editor: Andrew O. Wiget

Classroom Issues and Strategies

The principal problem with Ortiz's poetry from a student perspective is that it is so intensely political and that it takes a political view of past events. Students can be reactionary and feel that what is past is past, and that there has been too much of a tendency to cast aspersions upon America's reputation in recent years. This jingoism is often accompanied by a belief that poetry should not be political, but rather should concern itself with eternal truths. These are not problems that are associated with Ortiz's poetry exclusively, of course, but are part of the naive vision of poetry that teachers of literature struggle to overcome.

I think it's very important to begin this poem with a reflection upon the historical experiences of Native Americans. Begin with the historical epigraph describing the Sand Creek Massacre of Black Kettle's band which gives this poem sequence its name. That particular massacre is very well documented and students should spend some time trying to understand the forces that came together to create that massacre: Colonial Chivington's own political ambitions; his ability to mobilize the fears and anxieties of the frontier Colorado communities; his success at taking advantage of the militarization of the frontier during the Civil War; the remoteness of Chivington's forces from federal supervision; and the nonresistance of the Indians.

A second important issue to be discussed is how we all use key events in the past to give us a sense of what our history is, emphasizing that the historical memory of people is selective and formed for very contemporary reasons.

I think that there are certain key lines in the poetry that are worth looking at in some detail. In addition, I ask students to look at the relationships between the epigraphs and the poems, how each speaks to the other. Finally, I ask students how these poems as a group, framed as they are by the boldfaced short poems about America, and prefaced by the historical statement concerning the Sand Creek Massacre, all work together to create a unified statement.

The poems move between some very concrete historical references (on the one hand) such as those to Cotton Mather, Kit Carson, and Saigon, and (on the other hand) to some highly surrealistic imagery and abstract language. Students frequently have difficulty bringing the two together, and it's helpful to explore some of Ortiz's more provocative statements as a way of creating the matrix of values from which the poetry emerges.

Major Themes, Historical Perspectives, and Personal Issues

The major theme of Ortiz's poem sequence is that Euro-Americans were as much victims of their own ambitions and blindness as were Native Americans, and that the recognition by Euro-Americans that they have victimized themselves is the first step toward the beginning of a healing of America that will be based on a common appreciation of our shared responsibility for her future.

Significant Form, Style, or Artistic Conventions

Certainly the principal formal question will be the juxtaposition of the epigraphs, with their blunt ideological focus, and the poems, with their convoluted syntax and high rhetoric. It would be important to remind students, I think, that Ortiz's cycle of poems about the American historical experience is only one example in a long history of poetry about the American historical experience that stretches back through Hart Crane's *The Bridge* and Walt Whitman's *Leaves of Grass* to early national poems such as Joel Barlow's *The Columbiad*.

Original Audience

I don't think the original audience for this poetry is significantly different from the student audience, except perhaps in their political orientation (the students may be more conservative). These poems were written at the end of the seventies and represent in some sense a considered reflection upon the traumatization of the American psyche by the domestic turmoil of the 1960s, the loss of confidence evoked by Watergate, and crisis of conscience provoked by the Vietnam War. Many of the younger students who will be reading these poems for the first time remember none of those events.

Comparisons, Contrasts, Connections

Certainly I think Whitman, whom Ortiz does admire greatly, can be invoked. Ortiz tries to cultivate a prophetic voice and a historical vision similar to Whitman's. I think he may also be effectively contrasted with many writers for whom a historical criticism of America's past terminates in an attitude of despair. Ortiz has transformed anger into hope through compassion.

Questions for Reading and Discussion/
Approaches to Writing

I would look at the first poem and ask students what is meant by the juxtaposition of the lines "No waste lands, / No forgiveness," Or have students look at the third poem, which may be an even more provocative example, and ask them why Ortiz believes he should have stolen the sweater from the Salvation Army store, and why, in the end, he didn't.

Bibliography

Ortiz, Simon. "The Story Never Ends: An Interview with Simon Ortiz." In Joseph Bruchoc, *Survival This Way: Interviews with American Indian Poets*. Tucson: University of Arizona, 1987, 211–30.

——. "Sending a Voice: The Emergence of Contemporary Native American Poetry." *College English* 46 (1984): 598–609.

Wiget, Andrew. "Contemporary Poetry." *Native American Literature.* Boston: Twayne, 1985.

——. *Simon Ortiz.* Boise State University Western Writers Series, Number 74. Boise: Boise State University, 1986.

Afterword: Classroom Issues in Teaching a New Canon

Paul Lauter
General Editor
The Heath Anthology of American Literature

I want to sketch what I perceive to be the main areas of pedagogical concern raised by the changes, registered in *The Heath Anthology*, of what we teach in "American literature." I do not pretend to have solutions to all the problems I'll mention, but experience tells me—and some of my citations illustrate—that there are many practicing teachers, like those who have contributed to this instructors' guide, whose approaches to these problems will be helpful. My sketch is an effort to provide a theoretical framework, based on a good deal of listening to and reading about what teachers are actually doing, and thus to encourage them (you) to contribute to this discussion.

i

Let's begin at beginnings. I have usually started the second term of my American literature survey course with Rebecca Harding Davis's "Life in the Iron Mills." It has seemed to me a peculiarly appropriate starting point for a number of reasons: its subjects, crucial to this period of American history, are industrialization and class conflict, both of which it dramatizes in vivid and pedagogically useful ways; its narrative strategy, involving a challenge to presumptively middle-class readers, raises a whole set of questions about audience, narrator, and their relationships; one of its subtexts involves the connections of gender, class, and art, including the "trespass vision" (to use Tillie Olsen's phrase) displayed by Davis herself; its realism links it, on one hand, to earlier women writers like Caroline Kirkland and Alice Cary and, on the other, to later male and female realists like Mary Wilkins Freeman, Stephen Crane, and William Dean Howells; if its subject in some sense evokes Marx and Engels, its Evangelical outlook places it squarely in its particular moment, that of Stowe and Garrison, one might say. Finally, the story of its resurrection offers a kind of paradigm for the opening of the canon that has marked the study of American literature these past twenty years.

How could one invent a better starting point, a touchstone for much of the term?

And yet, in fact, I've not found the story all that successful, at least with my privileged, largely upper-middle-class students. They may argue about the ideological positions the story sets out, but the arguments have seemed to me intellectualized, abstracted not just from their lives but even from the story itself, which has always deeply moved me. Worse still, they seldom evoke the story in what they talk about later in the term, which defeats one major purpose of starting with it. This time, therefore, I devised an initial reading assignment that included not only "Life in the Iron Mills" but also Paul Laurence Dunbar's "Mr. Cornelius Johnson, Office Seeker" and John Milton Oskison's "The Problem of Old Harjo." I then asked the students to write about the differences implied in starting with one or another of these texts. The writing assignment did not strike me as particularly effective, but we were able in class to talk about the social and political contexts in which these stories carried out their cultural work. We also discussed the relationships of those contexts, the authors' subject positions, and the narrative styles they adopted. It seemed to me that the students could quickly grasp the connections between the masks and indirections Dunbar deploys and the emplacement of *de jure* segregation in the 1890s. Likewise they could account for the combination of ironic humor, mute appeal, and quiet anger that marks both Oskison's narrative and his character, Harjo, in the context of federal Indian policy at the turn of the twentieth century. Moreover, these discussions have been echoing, so far, through the term, as we consider other marginalized writers of the time, and especially the problem of audience, and the cultural work of texts.

As I've thought about this practical question of starting points, it occurred to me that while Davis's story is profoundly interesting to me, rather little in it receives an echo from the works we study later in the term. Moreover, its combination of later nineteenth- and early twentieth-century political issues with mid-nineteenth-century religious sentiments is peculiarly difficult for our postmodern students to accommodate: for them, both the problems of the working class and a practicing Christianity are as remote as Aldebaran. Have I been trying to foist on them my own cultural bias, including my involvement in first republishing "Life in the Iron Mills," onto my students? Furthermore, can they take hold of the stories by Dunbar and Oskison precisely because they, too, are involved with learning how to talk about racial matters in a culture deeply conflicted about them—which is, I think, the real content of what is denigrated as "political correctness"? Whatever the answers in my particular case, these considerations seem to me to illustrate a pedagogical question seldom given sufficient attention: starting points and sequences.

Most of us are familiar with the well-worn tactic of focusing on a text's opening lines: "Robert Cohn was once middle-weight boxing champion of Princeton," to cite one notorious example; or, to mention two other favorites: "For Godsake hold your tongue, and let me love" and "It is a truth universally acknowledged, that a single man in possession of a good fortune, must be in want of a wife." If, as I have been proposing, our course syllabus is to be read as a text, we need to be more conscious of what is invested in its initial moments. To begin with Columbus, as the Quincentennial made obvious, says something different from beginning with the Zuni "Talk Concerning the First Beginning." These considerations were dramatized for me this year by Eric Sundquist's choice for the opening chapter of his new book, *To Wake the Nations*. He begins with a section devoted to Nat Turner's "Confessions"—*not*, I need hastily to say, William Styron's unfortunate novel, but the text taken down by the real Turner's attorney of record, William Gray. Sundquist makes this text into a fascinating prototype of African-American creative production: Turner's problem is to maintain control over his text and thus to reach beyond Gray to an audience largely divided not only by race but by literacy. And this, despite the fact that the "Confession" will, in the first instance, be used to convict Turner of insurrection and murder and will, moreover, become Gray's property to publish, copyright, and exploit. In Sundquist's book, Nat Turner's "Confessions" becomes a lens through which we reenvision works by later black and white writers, like Herman Melville and Frederick Douglass. The point of Sundquist's strategy becomes most apparent when we set his book beside F. O. Matthiessen's *American Renaissance*, a defining text for its time. Matthiessen, as you will remember, begins with Emerson, and particularly with issues of consciousness and eloquence, as refracted from Emerson's journal and *Nature*. It is from this angle of vision that Matthiessen projects the structure he calls "American Renaissance," so influential in defining the field of American literature for half a century—influential as much for what it places beyond or on the periphery of our vision as for what it brings into sharp focus.

It is not only the initial text or figure that signifies, of course. So, importantly, do first-day exercises; indeed, I strongly believe that initial day's use of the classroom and the time can model the character of the entire term. In my American literature survey, I like to use three poems, which I reproduce and hand out, since none of them are in Volume 2 of *The Heath Anthology*: Edwin Markham's "The Man with the Hoe," Joe Hill's "The Preacher and the Slave," and Frances Ellen Watkins Harper's "Aunt Chloe's Politics." These provide some wonderful opportunities for students to talk about how language reveals position and politics.

The Man with the Hoe
Edwin Markham (1852–1940)

Bowed by the weight of centuries he leans
Upon his hoe and gazes on the ground,
The emptiness of ages in his face,
And on his back the burden of the world.
Who made him dead to rapture and despair,
A thing that grieves not and that never hopes,
Stolid and stunned, a brother to the ox?
Who loosened and let down this brutal jaw?
Whose was the hand that slanted back this brow?
Whose breath blew out the light within the brain?

Is this the Thing the Lord God made and gave
To have dominion over sea and land;
To trace the stars and search the heavens for power:
To feel the passion of Eternity?
Is this the dream He dreamed who shaped the suns
And marked their ways upon the ancient deep?
Down all the caverns of Hell to their last gulf
There is no shape more terrible than this—
More tongued with censure of the world's blind greed—
More filled with signs and portents for the soul—
More packt with danger to the universe.

What gulfs between him and the seraphim!
Slave of the wheel of labor, what to him
Are Plato and the swing of Pleiades?
What the long reaches of the peaks of song,
The rift of dawn, the reddening of the rose?
Through this dread shape the suffering ages look;
Time's tragedy is in that aching stoop;
Through this dread shape humanity betrayed,
Plundered, profaned, and disinherited,
Cries protest to the Judges of the World,
A protest that is also prophecy.

O masters, lords and rulers in all lands,
Is this the handiwork you give to God,
This monstrous thing distorted and soul-quenched?

How will you ever straighten up this shape;
Touch it again with immortality;
Give back the upward looking and the light;
Rebuild in it the music and the dream;
Make right the immemorial infamies,
Perfidious wrongs, immedicable woes?

O masters, lords and rulers in all lands,
How will the Future reckon with this Man?
How answer his brute question in that hour
When whirlwinds of rebellion shake all shores?
How will it be with kingdoms and with kings—
With those who shaped him to the thing he is—
When this dumb terror shall rise to judge the world
After the silence of the centuries?

                                        1899

Markham's poem is filled with university-learned references to Plato and
the Pleiades, and with phrases like "immemorial infamies" and "immedicable woes." In its apprehension at the rising of the masses, and in its
appeal to "masters and rulers in all lands," the poem epitomizes the
middle-class anxieties we will encounter later among many modernists.
By contrast, Joe Hill's poem is best sung—as it might have been among
his Wobbly comrades:

The Preacher and the Slave
Joe Hill (1882–1915)

1. Long-haired preachers come out ev'ry night,
   Try to tell you what's wrong and what's right,
   But when asked about something to eat,
   They will answer with voices so sweet:

   CHORUS:
   You will eat (you will eat), bye and bye (bye and bye),
   In that glorious land in the sky (way up high).
   Work and pray (work and pray), live on hay (live on hay),
   You'll get pie in the sky when you die (that's a lie!).

2. And the starvation army they play,
   And they sing and they clap and they pray,
   Till they get all your coin on the drum—
   Then they tell you when you're on the bum:

3. If you fight hard for children and wife—
 Try to get something good in this life—
 You're a sinner and bad man, they tell;
 When you die you will sure go to Hell.

4. Working men of all countries, unite!
 Side by side we for freedom will fight.
 When the world and its wealth we have gained,
 To the grafters we'll sing this refrain:

LAST CHORUS:
You will eat (you will eat), bye and bye, (bye and bye),
When you've learned how to cook and to fry (way up high).
Chop some wood (chop some wood)—twill do you good (do you
 good)
And you'll eat in the sweet bye and bye (that's no lie!).

c. 1910

Harper's "Aunt Chloe" evokes yet a different style of performance—and perform is very likely what Harper did—as well as a
practical politics focused on votes for women and public schooling:

Aunt Chloe's Politics
Frances Ellen Watkins Harper (1825–1911)

Of course, I don't know very much
 About these politics,
But I think that some who run 'em,
 Do mighty ugly tricks.

I've seen 'em honey-fugle round,
 And talk so awful sweet,
That you'd think them full of kindness,
 As an egg is full of meat.

Now I don't believe in looking
 Honest people in the face,
And saying when you're doing wrong,
 That "I haven't sold my race."

When we want to school our children,
 If the money isn't there,
Whether black or white have took it,
 The loss we all must share.

And this buying up each other
  Is something worse than mean,

Though I thinks a heap of voting,
  I go for voting clean.

1872

These texts bring into the classroom varieties of verse and of rhetoric, take a small step toward demystifying poetry (which most of my even well-educated students fear), free up some humor and play, and provide a basis for a small initial lesson in comparative study, which I believe is central to the new canonical enterprise, and to which I will return below.

ii

My second large set of issues is more abstract and somewhat more theoretical: what is a course listed under "English" (or "Literature" or "Humanities," and the like) really "about"?[1] When I was in college and graduate school in the 1950s, and for a good many years thereafter, that seemed reasonably obvious: we studied "primary texts"—poems, novels, plays, in the main—and particularly their structures, their uses of literary devices like metaphor and symbol, their forms as discrete works of art—in short, aesthetics. To be sure, underlying the kinds of formal inquiry I learned was a set of values that privileged what was called "literature" as an intellectual and finally moral stay against the chaos of the modern world.[2] But in classroom practice, the New Criticism focused on the careful explication of structure and form *within* discrete literary texts. What we expected our students to learn, most of all, was close reading, some conception of how literary works were artistically constructed, and a sense of what constituted the differences in writers' styles.

By contrast, the structures that interest many teachers of the new canons are those that produce and reproduce literary value or significance and cultural meaning.[3] This move does *not*, I want to emphasize, imply discarding the skills of close reading. Rather it involves the application of those (and other) skills to reading a variety of what we now call "texts," including a syllabus or anthology, the classroom itself, the history of literary study, and even differences in authority among those differently situated in a university. This shift seems to me at least as critical to the fierce debate between literary traditionalists and canon revisers as the issue of the content of a canon. From the point of view of traditionalists, this change of focus turns the "literature" classroom into some form of "sociological" study and may even deny students the pleasure of appreciating the artistry and the insights of classic works. From the perspective of revisionists, the new emphasis not only helps students to grasp the dynamics by which cultural formations—like a canon, a syllabus, a discipline, a university, what is demarcated and valued as "literature" or "American"—are historically constructed, but it also enables them to experience the fun of becoming players (rather than merely consumers) in this significant cultural work.

In both kinds of classrooms, we claim that we wish students to leave with new knowledge. But what constitutes that knowledge, and how is it arrived at? The conception that, it seems to me, undergirds the traditional literature class is of knowledge as a kind of object, a pearl of precious price that one extracts from more or less resistant texts through more or less heroic intellectual efforts. Once grasped, this knowledge becomes a form of capital; it can be exchanged for other goods or deployed to the advantage of its possessor. The value of such pearls of knowledge is, however, frequently derided in the world of commodity exchanges, the marketplaces of capitalism—particularly in America. Therefore, the significance of possessing literary knowledge has often been portrayed by intellectuals as a mark of distinction, separating them from ordinary people.

In many of today's humanities classrooms, by contrast, knowledge emerges not as a precious object but as an intellectual construction, situated in a particular historical moment and erected within a specific cultural space. It will not outlast all wind and weather; indeed, it may bend and twist over time, be broken into fragments and shards, and be put to uses and into new structures very different from those that provoked its creation. Many people, very differently situated, contribute to this process of construction, not just the learned. Indeed, "you don't have to be a weatherman to know which way the wind blows."

Knowledge as a pearl is, I was taught, arrived at by close reading and deep diving. One examines the object itself with care, penetrating through the intensity of one's wit the surface that have oft been viewed but ne'er so skillfully displayed. Now I do not want to be heard as denigrating this process of "diving into the wreck"; it is daring and inspiring. Still, to this end, a group is largely an unprofitable drag on an individual critic's ingenuity, although the group may provide intellectual mirrors to reflect the brilliance of critical performance.

By contrast, I think that knowledge conceived as a construction emerges precisely from a group effort, within which diverse individuals can play a variety of roles. Because the process of constructing knowledge takes place so differently in differently constituted classrooms,[4] the process is facilitated by heterogeneity within a group, which, by providing a multiplicity of perspectives, can help keep in view the very constructedness of the conceptions arrived at. In the group, students best learn that knowledge is produced by producing it (as distinct from simply consuming it). This may seem a truism, but it foregrounds a fundamental pedagogical conception: that process and product, how and what, are by no means separable. Indeed, as Jules Henry pointed out long ago, the critical learnings of the schoolhouse are precisely those produced by the process.[5]

If you pursue the direction in which I'm headed, you quickly bump into two widely held ideas in American education; I'd describe them this way: "knowledge is a utilitarian product" and "knowledge is valuable to the extent that an individual can appropriate it for his or her own use." The connection between these ideas is, to my mind, one of the basic, unexamined cultural learnings generated by American schools. As generation after generation of educational reformers has discovered, challenging, much less breaking, the link between knowledge as utilitarian product and as an object of individual appropriation turns out to be enormously difficult. Indeed, I can think of few projects more Utopian, particularly in this historical moment, than calling into question the devotion to individualistic methodologies and instrumental goals that marks education in this country. Yet it does seem to me that some such countervailing project inevitably lurks in the variety of pedagogies now emerging from efforts to teach previously noncanonical texts. For establishing any new canon implies a degree of shifting cultural power among groups, not individuals, as well as redefining what constitutes desirable social goals as well as knowledge. Such a revisionary project will not leave unexamined the individualistic, instrumental assumptions upon which everything from raising hands to grading practices are based.

I have one further remark about the character of knowledge in the different classroom universes I have been constructing. While in the past we did pay a certain lip service to remaining open to ever-renewed readings of a text, a certain tendency toward closure—ruled over by the professor or the hegemonic textbook—prevailed. The forms of knowledge produced through a new-canonical pedagogy will be less stable, probably more contentious, less subject to professorial closure than traditional ideas of what constitutes learning. Gloria Anzaldúa's formulation is helpful (if conflicted) here:

> These numerous possibilities leave *la mestiza* floundering
> in uncharted seas. In perceiving conflicting information
> and points of view, she is subjected to a swamping of her
> psychological borders. She has discovered that she can't

> hold concepts or ideas in rigid boundaries. The borders
> and walls that are supposed to keep the undesirable
> ideas out are entrenched habits and patterns of behav-
> ior; these habits and patterns are the enemy within.
> Rigidity means death. Only by remaining flexible is she
> able to stretch the psyche horizontally and vertically. . . .
> The new *mestiza* copes by developing a tolerance for con-
> tradictions, a tolerance for ambiguity.[6]

I want to chart the implications carefully, because nothing in today's colleges seems to have enraged traditionalists more than the idea of the contingency of knowledge. I am not arguing that "everything is relative" and we should pack up our brains because "there is no truth" but only politics, opinion, and self-interest. If *no* account of a text, an event, an observation is absolute, in the sense of exhausting its possible meanings and power, *some* accounts are, in fact, better than others. They are more useful in a particular situation, they explain more, open more, engage readers more fully. Perhaps they are simply more elegant as intellectual structures. Those, for example, who deny the Holocaust deny the overwhelming weight of evidence, observation, and logic. If *no* syllabus perfectly and perpetually represents antebellum American literary production and its relation to slavery, *some* syllabi will be more effective toward that end than others; but even these will change as students, conditions, and the functions of an institution or a course change. The practical problem is this: how can teachers, disciplined to devote attention to the traditions of culture and the norms of profession, enable students to question traditions and disciplines without leading them out onto the slippery slope of a relativist discourse that ends in an intellectual swamp where half-baked "opinions" crowd out scholarship and intelligence?

One last reflection on the question of what a course may and may not be about concerns its boundaries. Is the end of the syllabus, the final exam, the grade report the operative boundary? Or does the course lead out of the classroom and, one way or another, down the corridor and into the streets? To be sure, no one really argues that the learning involved in a course ends with the term—we all *claim* to be teaching beyond the ending. But in practice, I want to suggest, forms of organization can effectively lead to closure or to continuation. Nor would I argue that anyone has the formula to insure extension of the cultural work of a class beyond its ending, but it seems to me important here—as in connection with the other rather abstract considerations I have grouped in this section—to be conscious of the choices we make that are often hidden by our assumptions concerning what a course is about.

iii

My third broad category concerns the classroom as a place. I want to argue that it is seldom, if ever, a neutral, unconflicted site of learning, or a safe and homey environment supportive of any and all revelations. Rather, it is a *public* space, and therefore subject to a variety of *political* interactions that are features of public spaces. Far from being insulated from differential power relationships, a classroom is constituted by them. Educational reformers of the 1960s were obsessed, I think it is fair to say, precisely with the need to reduce discrepancies of power in the classroom, and we consecrated endless energy to techniques devoted to that goal. It soon became clear, however, that changing seating arrangements, validating all student responses to texts, democratizing classroom procedures, or otherwise attempting to transfer more authority from teacher to learner ran hard against how institutions structure power and, often, student expectations as well. Initially, educational reformers understood the problem as student "resistance" to our efforts to "liberate" them, a kind of "false consciousness" that simply needed to be overcome.

In time, however, it came to seem that the "false consciousness," if it existed, might reside more in the heads of instructors who tried to ignore the quite uneven relationships of power inherent in any situation in which one party organizes and judges and the others are expected to respond and be judged. A teacher could, for example, devise a variety of grading procedures, such as contracts or group processes, but it remained clear—certainly to students—that the *power* to determine procedure and therefore final product (grade) necessarily remained with the instructor, as surely as fines do with a traffic court judge. Furthermore, by deploying a professional discourse over which their training had given them some command, instructors could, without necessarily being aware of it, magnify power differences between themselves and their students. Even if one could virtually eliminate the structural causes of power differences, students fearful of being swept away into uncharted seas would seek authority within texts themselves.[7]

It does not demean the classroom to think of it politically, indeed as a colonizing site. Teachers and students have significant interest in turning the texts under consideration into cultural capital. Texts are, as it were, mined for their uses within the classroom and in other cultural situations in which they can be made to "pay off." Teachers have both personal and professional interests in colonizing students as acolytes, as enrollees in other courses, or simply as numbers that demonstrate their own value to the collegiate or departmental enterprise. Likewise, students have a serious interest in the transcript, letter-file, and network value of particular professors with whom they choose to study.

Finally, the academic norms that pervade almost all classrooms are by no means culturally neutral. For example, most of us tell students that silence in the classroom will not "hurt their grade," for in liberal style we wish to respect the rights of the student who prefers not to speak. Implicit here, however, is the assumption that speech in the classroom is *ipso facto* a preferred form of behavior, and most of us are more likely to tolerate expressive silliness than silence. Similarly, we assume that classrooms are, at any time, appropriate sites for discussion of any and all texts. But some Native American storytellers—and, I suspect, religious fundamentalists as well—would claim that certain stories should not be told or talked about at certain times of year, or in inappropriate settings. They would wish to sustain a line, rendered invisible in most Western classrooms, between secular and sacred textual functions. I raise this consideration not because I believe in jettisoning the secular commitment of American education, which at least theoretically mark our discipline, but to illustrate the particularity rather than the neutrality of such norms.

To say that power is always already operating in the classroom is *not*, however, to say that power is all that functions there. First of all, a variety of other forms of "social affiliation" with which we are all familiar deeply shape the classroom space: pleasure, eroticism, friendship, display.[8] To concentrate on the dynamics of power can easily lead to missing the play and the possible enhancement of such forces.

More important, while differences in power cannot, in my judgment, be expunged, *responsibility* can more fully and systematically be distributed. The goal here, as Teresa McKenna has framed it, is to create a learning community in which all participants are responsible for what is learned. Toward that end, instructors can open course elements often perceived as foreclosed. For example, in his MLA presidential address, Houston Baker discusses what political activists will recognize as a brief *agenda debate:* an undergraduate student wished to introduce into his seminar discussion of what an African-American writer like Phillis Wheatley "means to the black community per se" rather than concentrating solely on what the instructor wished to consider, like neo-Classical conventions and Wheatley's subversion of them. As activists also know, such agenda debates are generally awkward modes of carrying out a struggle over political and intellectual priorities. Providing a standard for self-criticism, Baker enables us to recognize that by putting the student down, he foreclosed the opportunity of eliciting "a response from the undergraduate that helped us understand the connections among Phillis Wheatley, the seminar room, male critical power, the white university geographies of Locust Walk, and the surrounding world of black West Philadelphians."9

Not only are such opportunities missed, but students withdraw and, in Anne Bower's words, "continue to think of literature as selected and arranged and therefore owned by others."10 Bower proposes one alternative:

> So long as the instructor does the bulk of structuring, discussing, and devising assignments, students—be they reluctant readers or literature lovers—take the role of consumers. Since I'm trying to introduce the concept that American Literature is something *we* create, I need a classroom methodology in which the students "do" American literature. . . . What if I were to let the students participate in choosing our selections? Choices wouldn't range entirely free of course. We have to order our textbooks well ahead of each quarter. So I decided to order an anthology containing a good range of material from which students could select our readings. . . . My authority would be exerted in choosing the two novels we could read, and I would also allow myself to choose a few of our shorter selections, working to pick underrepresented genres or populations. . . . Students would be offered instruction, in the classroom and through conferences, on how to select a text and how to present it.

In such a classroom, students finally select more than half of what is read; they can use the anthology or go outside of it. Moreover, students have a variety of responsibilities in addition to choosing texts: devising assignments and homework, leading discussion, developing ideas about how they will produce additional texts (that is, writing). As Bower suggests, this approach not only demands that students assume an unusual classroom responsibility, but it also foregrounds the constructed nature of "American literature."

Another area in which responsibility can be distributed involves context. History, for example, is usually deemed to be the instructor's responsibility, students being accounted as historically ignorant. But Sue Danielson offers a strategy for involving students even in that deeply important form of classroom work. Her upper-division American literature course was titled "Domestic Strains," and "took for its central inquiry the debate surrounding the 'woman question' as presented in several nineteenth-century texts." By focusing on a *theme* rather than on a sequence of texts or even a group of authors, Danielson was able to engage students in the specific social discourses within which "literary" works were being created. She devised three key departures from usual practice:

> First, through a series of student reports on primary source materials, I focused our attention on the "private," female sphere in which marriage, divorce, and sexuality are privileged over the "public," male sphere of business. Second, I subordinated canonical works, in this case *The Blithedale Romance* and *The Bostonians*, to the reading of historically neglected fiction: *Mary Lyndon: or, Revelations of a Life*, published in 1854 by Mary Gove Nichols, *Incidents in the Life of a Slave Girl*, finally published in 1860 by Harriet Jacobs . . . and *Iola LeRoy*, published in 1894 by the most widely read black woman writer of the last century, Frances Harper. Finally, I invited continuous discussions of literary "valuation," asking students to use a reading journal to reflect on the assumptions underlying the ways in which they had traditionally categorized "good" and "bad" literature.[11]

Danielson's strategy introduces a key issue: thematically-organized courses are in many departments looked upon as suspicious—or worse, as intrusions from American Studies. They are said to introduce "nonliterary" historical or sociological concerns, into literary work. If they are encouraged, as in institutions influenced by Chicago's Aristotelianism, they tend to involve "great themes," supposed to transcend mere history, like "the hero" or "peace and war" or "dimensions of time." Or they mark out in a kind of empty gesture a more or less traditional clump of writers, as in the American Renaissance or Modernism. It seems to me that the resistance to organizing courses around historically specific themes—like the one proposed by Danielson, or the antebellum debate over slavery and race, or later fictions of industry and work—represents one of the ways in which earlier formalist paradigms persist in pedagogical practice. For the historical divisions that structure most departmental offerings and many courses within those frameworks, seldom have any substantial influence on how texts are studied, much less understood in relation to social and cultural movements. And while texts themselves may be examined from "new historicist" perspectives, in practice these often—ironically, most often when they are well done—seem to defeat the objective of distributing responsibility to students for historicizing and contextualizing what they are reading.

These examples are meant to suggest that a classroom is not a given, preformed space. On the contrary, it can be shaped toward a freer, more open, safer—or perhaps more creatively dangerous—environment than it often is. But it would be disingenuous to imagine that all change—or even any—will be welcomed by all students. In a sense, to the extent that teachers place the distribution of responsibility higher on the classroom agenda, the focus of the course shifts from the material to the people. An old dilemma reemerges: do we teach subjects or students? The terrain here is fraught with danger, for as humanities faculty, subject matter is our professional bread and butter, not experiments in student development. Moreover, subject matter offers relatively stable ground amidst the quicksands of process. For all that, the departures from convention I have summarized here suggest how urgently reconstructed canons drive us toward reconstructed classrooms.

One further reflection on the very definition of a classroom: Alexander Astin reports in his new book *What Counts in College?* that student intellectual development is fostered most by peer interactions, especially those that take place in informal discussions of classroom material. If Astin's findings are accurate, and I think they are, then one of our major problems is reconceptualizing the boundaries of what constitutes a "classroom," that is to say where learning takes place. The kind of question that then comes to the foreground is not so much what can we encourage students to do, as individuals or collectively, to bring information and ideas *into* class, but what can we do in class to encourage students in groups to carry the discussion outward. That will sound absolutely visionary to those on commuter campuses, where studies suggest that students spend less than two minutes and fifteen seconds—or something equally absurd—on campus after their last classes. The new interactive computer technologies will be of some help here, as might, also, the old-fashioned carpool.

As to carpools, I have little to say, since I drove a 1974 Duster until recently. And I have only a little more to contribute regarding computerization, except to note some paradoxes. These are, I should acknowledge, based upon limited concrete experience: my coteacher of the Trinity College American Studies junior seminar and I are using a system in which students work anonymously in computerized writing groups. They put drafts of their papers into a "sharing" file; the other students in their group read and make anonymous comments; then they revise and place draft, comments, and final version in a "drop" file to which only the instructors have access. It is a slightly complicated and cumbersome system, time-consuming for everyone. It surely is for students, as the length and detail of some of their comments indicate. Reading them, I began to feel both cheered and—to approach my first paradox—increasingly superfluous. The students' comments dealt not only with issues, but with organization, grammar, punctuation; one even urged, nay demanded, that the recipient of the comments visit the Writing Center! What remained for me to say or do, apart from the clerical task of insuring that papers and comments *had* been turned in and to badger the delinquents?

Logically pursued, this process could, perhaps should, lead to my disappearance, like the State under true socialism. My simile isn't altogether far-fetched, since the process in a sense involves replacing individualism and hierarchy—the Party speaks for the people, the Central Committee for the Party, the General Secretary for the Central Committee—with a largely democratic and collective project. To be sure, work in institutions seldom pursues thoroughly logical agendas, or even those that grow from a strong burden of evidence, so I don't anticipate that my occupation will soon be gone. But I would recollect here Astin's finding about the power of learning from peers, and therefore taking the discussion out from the walls of the traditional classroom. Here we approach a second paradox: the isolation of the single person before the single keyboard and the single screen seems to enable construction of a kind of community most traditional classrooms discourage. Is the classroom as usually constituted in late twentieth-century American schools *dis*abling? Or, perhaps it would be more accurate to say, how is it disabling?

To consider that paradox and such questions, I wish to turn to a fourth general category, the people in the classroom—students and teachers—and the work we do there.

iv

We bring with us into the classroom a variety of personal identities, but classroom dynamics impose certain normative behaviors. Departing from anticipated roles can, in fact, prove risky on either side of the desk. It is therefore not surprising that classrooms, at least in the way in which they exact loyalty to certain institutional expectations, are among the more conservative locales on campus: my own teachers probably would not recognize the syllabi I construct as "American Literature," but for better and for worse, they would find rather familiar my instructional methods, that is, the roles I play in the classroom.

The role of the instructor is often dichotomized: he performs in the classroom or facilitates interactions, exercises power, or fosters democracy. On the one hand, the instructor is pictured standing by the blackboard or alongside the lectern, determining the content and flow of work; on the other, she is seated with the other classroom participants in an interactive circle where all are, at least potentially, equal in the conversation. In my observation, such dichotomies, while reflecting certain truths, often misrepresent what actually takes place in practice. The individualistic, performative instructor can model for students usefully authoritative (and not necessarily authoritarian) approaches to the presentation of ideas; similarly, the forms of democratic participation exemplified by the circle often require careful direction by an instructor who knows where she is headed, if not all the pathways thereto. In thus questioning the usual dichotomy, I wish to shift attention toward other fundamental, and to me more significant, elements of what the people in classrooms do; these concern leadership, the student "mix," and the related problems of "subject position" and vulnerability as matters for classroom discussion.

Phyllis Palmer has commented, regarding leadership, that sharing it "requires understanding what tasks a group needs to function successfully and, then, recognizing that anyone in the group takes leadership by fulfilling a need when it arises."[12] Palmer's formulation leads, I think, to conceptualizing classroom tasks somewhat differently; instead of focusing on what needs to be "covered" in a given hour, one might wish to break down the work into discrete parts—in the sense both of units and of dramatic elements. This is difficult, or course, but probably less so than trying each day to generate discussion from the standing start, as one might call it, represented by invariable teacher-initiated talk. Given such a goal, it hardly matters how one defines "parts," so long as they aren't trivial or makework. In fact, however, the format this strategy suggests opens some significant avenues. For example, if you are studying Native American texts, as will now almost invariably be the case in a current nineteenth- and twentieth-century American literature course, one might appoint two or three students as the specialists in changing federal Indian policies of the period. The idea is not to have them "report" at the beginning of a class, but rather to enable them to enter the discussion with their special knowledge when it seems appropriate. As we all know, most students love the opportunity to show what they know; one thus "seeds" the classroom in the process of dividing and sharing tasks. Similar forms of specialization can usefully be devised for all of the previously marginalized cultures that constitute what we have been calling the "new canon": what are the immigration policies that affect Asian-American writers and characters and therefore texts clear through the first half of the twentieth century? How do marital property acts and issues of contraception and domestic violence help shape women's lives and work? What is happening to midwestern farms and farmers, or to Maine seaports, that so shape the worlds of Garland's and Jewett's people? Similarly, one can identify critical points in upcoming readings and have students focus on each of them; I am thinking not only of allusive and symbolic details, but also of characters or events a few students can give special thought to. The point, however, is not somehow to create instant specialists, in any literal sense, out of undergraduate students, but rather to divide and share tasks, and thus leadership. In fact, in the course of a term, one might well find individuals and groups of students building considerable specialized knowledge about the "specialized" areas you have identified.

That process is facilitated when the classroom is significantly heterogeneous, for it cannot be denied that many—though not all—undergraduates display particularist concerns for their own origins. The research being conducted by Frances Maher and Mary Kay Tetrault has produced striking evidence that the single most significant determinant of how a text gets discussed is the mix of people in the classroom. These findings anchor a set of problems: If the course includes multicultural or otherwise noncanonical texts, students will often hide unfamiliarity and nervousness behind reluctance to engage—or will retreat into forms of exoticizing texts, instructors, or both. If a course is required, moreover, students often wish to get through it without being deeply involved or taking on the additional responsibilities toward which I have been pointing. We have other vulnerabilities, too, not only those imposed by the limits of our own knowledge, especially in fields that are rapidly changing and enormously expanding by career pressures and departmental norms. Moreover, a multicultural environment or even a multicultural course can produce serious anxiety in a white teacher. Such problems can block intellectual development, becoming walls behind which people retreat into the apparent safety of rejection. In short, both student resistances and vulnerabilities *and* our own can stand in the way of reshaping classrooms.

On the other hand, these mutual vulnerabilities can also offer a basis for extending the sense of community within a classroom—provided that they can be brought to the surface and talked through. A starting place, Teresa McKenna has suggested, may be provided by discussing students' and instructor's subject positions. While these may seem far afield from the designated subject matter, they may be critical to the process of reconstructing the classroom environment. The objective, I think, is not to eliminate its tensions and political dimensions, but to widen the ground upon which the differing people in the classroom can honestly stand in common. Commonality does, after all, build trust, without which any effort to redistribute responsibility and redesign the operations of power will necessarily come to naught. It may seem counterintuitive to talk of widening common ground by focusing on different subject positions, but what is involved is shifting part of the definition of classroom identity from the dichotomy "instructor/student" to the shared category of "subject position." That is something we all have, with the strengths and limits each entails. For everyone in the classroom to become aware of both strengths and limits in *all* others is, I think, to build a basis for commonality and trust.

v

I have suggested elsewhere that to include previously marginalized cultures in what is called "American literature" is to transform that academic specialty into a "comparative discipline."[13] I want to make a similar claim regarding pedagogies for a new canon. What is implied? First of all, I think we have a good deal to learn from the traditions of comparative literary study; in my own case, I have been significantly influenced by the training of Ann Fitzgerald as a medievalist. In that trade, one is concerned not only with textuality—language, iconography, forms of presentation—but with historical function or cultural work, audience, and the interactions of art forms. Similarly, in teaching the literatures of America, one needs to utilize equivalent categories within the specific matrix defined by—as well as into and out of—North American history and geography.

I want to underline two components of such comparative study. First, one needs to look at both distinction and similarity. One set of texts I like to use deals with immigrant experience: Mary Antin's *The Promised Land*, Abraham Cahan's *Yekl*, and Sui-Sin Far's "In the Land of the Free." The markers of identity Mary Antin is all too anxious to abandon—language, clothing, name—are precisely those that the Chinese parents in Sui-Sin Far's story maintain as valued connections to the old world. But why? What accounts for the difference? Here some of the "specialized" knowledge I talked about before can be helpful, especially an understanding of the provisions and impact of the Chinese Exclusion Act (would an immigrant from Europe need papers for a child?), and of radically different patterns of immigration and remigration (Eastern European Jews and Chinese stand at opposite ends of the remigration spectrum). Which text, then, provides a model for the "immigrant experience"? Clearly, the answer to that depends upon whose immigrant experience you mean.

These texts also raise my second point: one of the limitations of older forms of comparative literature was that differentials of power were seldom part of the discussion. Yet they are never absent from cultural comparisons. We need only recollect that back when graduate schools required two foreign languages for the doctorate, those languages at the most elite institutions had to be French and German, *not* Spanish. Moreover, where I grew up, one had a choice as to beginning French or Spanish in junior high school; guess which one I and my middle-class friends chose. Indeed, there was no choice involved, for Spanish was a declassé language, spoken by "them." Difference, as we have learned, involves hierarchy. To use another example from "immigrant" literature, Juan Flores points to the conditions that shaped some of the distinctive qualities of Puerto Rican texts:

> The most important difference, which has conditioned the entire migration and settlement, is the abiding colonial relationship between Puerto Rico and the United States. Puerto Ricans came here as foreign nationals, a fact that American citizenship and accomodationist ideology tend to obscure; but they also arrived as subject people. The testimonial and journalistic literature of the early period illustrate that Puerto Ricans entering this country, even those most blinded by illusions of success and fortune, tended to be aware of this discrepant, disadvantageous status.
>
> For that reason, concern for the home country and attachment to national cultural traditions remained highly active, as did the sense of particular social vulnerability in the United States.[14]

Flores's underlying point, though obviously not his details, will help us understand the concrete operations in cultural domains of the differentials of power to which are given names like "colonial," "race," "feminine." What, in short, the practice of comparative study helps focus are the conditions of power distinctions as experienced and expressed in literary texts.

These pages really constitute "notes in progress" toward a more comprehensive understanding of the pedagogies appropriate to teaching the range of works included in *The Heath Anthology of American Literature*. We thought they might be helpful, provocative, and interesting to users of this instructor's guide. And I thought, personally, that some of you might wish to carry on the dialogue these "notes" invite, perhaps in the pages of the *Heath Newsletter*. As I suggested in the beginning, these are not meant as anything like definitive answers to the problems implicit in the vast expansion of the category "American literature." But I hope they will prove useful as we continue to pursue the critical collective enterprise of transforming what we do in our classrooms.

Notes

1. It will be apparent in what follows that I am always on the edge of constructing intellectual binaries and thus overdetermining the kinds of responses I mean to elicit. I follow this path with some deliberation. I think it is helpful to dramatize real distinctions, even if one must then back off and confess that one's good guy/bad guy dramatic confrontation seldom accounts fully for the complex, intractable facts of actual classroom experience. Still, I think readers may find the contrasts useful, if only as signposts indicating that, finally, South Central and Hollywood lie in *different* directions from downtown LA.
2. See, for example, Allen Tate, "The Man of Letters in the Modern World," *The Man of Letters in the Modern World* (New York: Meridian Books, 1955), pp. 20–22.
3. See, for example, Marcia S. Curtis and Anne J. Herrington, "Diversity in Required Writing Courses," *Promoting Diversity in College Classrooms*, Maurianne Adams, ed. (San Francisco: Jossey-Bass, 1992), p. 76: "It is perhaps worth emphasizing here that it was our primary intention, not to use pedagogy to further any single political agenda, but, quite the contrary, to understand the politics of curriculum development and canon formation in order to further pedagogical goals."
4. See, for example, Frances Maher, "Toward a Richer Theory of Feminist Pedagogy," *Journal of Education* 169 (1987): 91–99.
5. "Golden Rules Days." *Culture Against Man.*
6. *Borderlands/La Frontera* (San Francisco: Spinsters/Aunt Lute, 1987), p. 79.
7. See, for example, Peter Caccavari, "Making the World Safe for Democracy and the Classroom Safe for Slavery: Teaching America to Americans," *The Canon in the Classroom*, John Alberti, ed. (Westport: Garland, forthcoming): "The text is 'directing' and 'enforcing' the students. The act of reading is intimately tied to their understanding of the act of learning. To counteract this tendency, I thought that I would make discussion and not lecture the method of teaching and learning in the course. What I did not realize was that not only did my technique not liberate the students, but it created an authority vacuum which they then supplied with 'the text.'"
8. See Homi K. Bhabha, "Conference Presentation," *Critical Fictions: The Politics of Imaginative Writing*, Philomena Mariani, ed. (Seattle: Bay Press, 1991), p. 65.
9. "Local Pedagogy, or How I Redeemed My Spring Semester," *PMLA* 108 (May 1993): 403.
10. Anne L. Bower, "Sharing Responsibility for American Lit.: 'A Spectacular and Dangerous World of Choice,'" *The Canon in the Classroom*, op. cit., mspp. 3, 5.
11. Sue Danielson, "Domestic Strains: The Woman Question, Free Love, and Nineteenth-Century American Fiction," *The Canon in the Classroom*, op. cit., mspp. 9–10.
12. "To Deconstruct Race, Deconstruct Whiteness," *American Quarterly* 45 (June 1993): 284. Palmer is drawing on Nancy Schneidewind's

developmental theory of the women's studies classroom, one particularly appropriate to upper-division classes.

13. "The Literatures of America—A Comparative Discipline," *Canons and Contexts* (New York: Oxford, 1991). pp. 48–96.
14. Juan Flores, "Puerto Rican Literature in the United States: Stages and Perspectives," *Redefining American Literary History*, A. LaVonne Brown Ruoff and Jerry W. Ward, Jr., eds. (New York: Modern Language Association, 1990), p. 213.

Index of Authors

Trapped in a Vice

CRITICAL ISSUES IN CRIME AND SOCIETY

Raymond J. Michalowski Jr., Series Editor

Critical Issues in Crime and Society is oriented toward critical analysis of contemporary problems in crime and justice. The series is open to a broad range of topics including specific types of crime, wrongful behavior by economically or politically powerful actors, controversies over justice system practices, and issues related to the intersection of identity, crime, and justice. It is committed to offering thoughtful works that will be accessible to scholars and professional criminologists, general readers, and students.

For a list of titles in the series, see the last page of the book.

Trapped in a Vice

THE CONSEQUENCES OF CONFINEMENT FOR YOUNG PEOPLE

ALEXANDRA COX

RUTGERS UNIVERSITY PRESS

New Brunswick, Camden, and Newark, New Jersey, and London

Library of Congress Cataloging-in-Publication Data

Names: Cox, Alexandra, 1978– author.
Title: Trapped in a vice : the consequences of confinement for young people /
  Alexandra Cox.
Description: New Brunswick : Rutgers University Press, [2017] | Series: Critical issues
  in crime and society | Includes bibliographical references and index.
Identifiers: LCCN 2017007405 (print) | LCCN 2017023691 (ebook) |
  ISBN 9780813570488 (Web PDF) | ISBN 9780813575650 (epub) |
  ISBN 9780813594187 (mobi) | ISBN 9780813570471 (cloth : alk. paper) |
  ISBN 9780813570464 (pbk. : alk. paper)
Subjects: LCSH: Juvenile detention—United States. | Juvenile delinquency—United
  States. | Juvenile justice, Administration of—United States.
Classification: LCC HV9104 (ebook) | LCC HV9104 .C625 2017 (print) | DDC
  364.360973—dc23
LC record available at https://lccn.loc.gov/2017007405

A British Cataloging-in-Publication record for this book is available from the British
  Library.

Jamaal May, "There Are Birds Here" from *Hum*. Copyright © 2013 by Jamaal May.
Reprinted with permission of The Permissions Company, Inc.,
on behalf of Alice James Books, www.alicejamesbooks.org.

♾ The paper used in this publication meets the requirements of the
American National Standard for Information Sciences—Permanence
of Paper for Printed Library Materials, ANSI Z39.48–1992.

www.rutgersuniversitypress.org

Manufactured in the United States of America

For everyone I've seen in the pens and through to the other side of them: your spirit keeps me fighting and your humor reminds me that we're in it together for the long haul.

Contents

There Are Birds Here

by Jamaal May

For Detroit

There are birds here,
so many birds here
is what I was trying to say
when they said those birds were metaphors
for what is trapped
between buildings
and buildings. No.
The birds are here
to root around for bread
the girl's hands tear
and toss like confetti. No,
I don't mean the bread is torn like cotton,
I said confetti, and no
not the confetti
a tank can make of a building.
I mean the confetti
a boy can't stop smiling about
and no his smile isn't much
like a skeleton at all. And no
his neighborhood is not like a war zone.
I am trying to say
his neighborhood
is as tattered and feathered
as anything else,
as shadow pierced by sun
and light parted
by shadow-dance as anything else,
but they won't stop saying
how lovely the ruins,
how ruined the lovely
children must be in that birdless city.

Trapped in a Vice

Introduction

"It was strange wanting to be a witness in a place no one
cares about."
—Reginald Dwayne Betts, *A Question of Freedom*

IN 2003, WHEN I was twenty-five years old, I took a job as a
caseworker at a public defender's office in Harlem. I had never lived in New
York City, and I had no experience doing social work nor any knowledge
of the New York City court system. Before I got the job, I had worked for a
few years in criminal justice policy reform, so I understood a bit about the
behemoth system I would be taking on. I knew the work would be emotionally challenging, but I wasn't prepared for the ethical and political questions it
would force me to confront.

One of my many duties at this job was to go regularly to Rikers Island to
meet with our clients. Anyone from New York City who is sixteen years or
older and accused of a crime goes to Rikers Island to be held in detention if
they have bail set or if they are remanded to custody by a judge. The island has
around 10,000 inmates housed in ten smaller jails, with approximately 9,000
staff members. Just north of LaGuardia Airport, the island's soundscape mixes
planes taking off and landing with buses transporting family members and
staff and the massive physical plant machinery that it takes to manage what is
effectively a small city.

To see my clients, I had to possess what is called a "corrections pass." This
allowed me to bypass the lengthy lines of visitors waiting to see their loved
ones, drop off clothing, pay bail, or pick up property. After checking in with
a front-desk sergeant at the main intake building, I would wait for a white
school bus reserved for official visitors and corrections officers to take us to
one of the jails on the island.

One day, I arrived at Rikers during a shift change. I waited outside the
intake building with a large crowd of corrections officers. In my first days at
Rikers, I assumed that the officers and I would have some camaraderie; we all
worked in the same system, after all. A number of my clients even had family
members who worked as corrections officers. However, I soon realized that

my brown legal accordion file tipped the officers off that I was connected
to defense attorneys, the individuals their jobs had taught them to detest.
My external marks of privilege—my clothing and my mannerisms—and the
fact that they were overwhelmingly Black and Latina/o while I was white—
perhaps also added to their perception that I was yet another white bourgeois
lawyer-type coming to see the overwhelmingly black and brown clients under
their care. The guards demonstrated no camaraderie with anyone associated
with the defense; their body language—the rolling of eyes, their decision to
steer clear of us on the buses that led out to the facilities, and their brusque
manner when we would try to engage in conversation with them made it
clear that any association by guards with defense attorneys was to be avoided.
I knew I was viewed with contempt.

The officers were not wrong: my office existed to challenge the law
enforcement apparatus that employed them. Yet the paradox of Rikers was
such that, in the minds of many of the men and women, boys and girls incarcerated on the island, we all represented the neglectful, abusive, and violent
state. The guards enforced order, sometimes brutally, while the public defenders pressured clients to plead guilty in the limited time they spent with them.
To the people behind bars, we were all the same representatives of a dirty and
corrupt criminal "injustice" system: my clients called the corrections officers
"police" and often conflated the roles of public defenders and district attorneys. "The system" became, for so many individuals who faced it over and over
again, simply a process that screwed them over. "The system" felt particularly
heavy and oppressive for my teenaged clients who were locked in solitary
confinement for upward of eighty days because they spat at an officer or
for the people who were forced to plead guilty to double digits because the
alternative—losing at trial—could be so much worse.

As I stood in that parking lot alone while the guards made small talk with
each other, I grappled with the question about whether state actors could ever
play a positive role in the lives of people accused of crimes. I thought that the
guards' contempt for me was misplaced, unfair: I was going to Rikers Island to
listen to people, to help them. But there is a long history of privileged white
folks "saving" people of color from a system that was unmistakably akin to
slavery, and thus largely intractable. Perhaps the officers' attitude was, if you
can't beat it, join it?

I attended graduate school in England, where my questions about the state
and its role in people's lives were challenged even further. Despite its strong
safety net and expansive social state, I witnessed similar dynamics of social
exclusion in English prisons—particularly for poor people of color—to what
existed in the United States. The same questions about social neglect emerged:
how can the state buffer citizens from the crises that force them into the hands
of the criminal justice system? And what if the crises that force people into

the criminal justice system are actually a consequence of an inadequate social safety net and social welfare supports? Again, my questions focused on the role of the state in helping its citizens rather than oppressing them. In time, a more refined set of questions emerged: how is it possible to escape the punitive state? How are helping agencies implicated in punishment?

Pursuing answers to those questions led me to write this book. I sought to examine the role that the state plays in young people's lives, and in turn, how young people perceive the state's role in ostensibly helping them. I was particularly interested in the political and philosophical puzzle that young people in trouble with the law presented: as citizens-in-waiting who were brought into an inherently paternalistic juvenile justice system, what were some of the ways that they could exercise agency and self-determination?

I argue that the approach the state and its agents take with young people accused of crimes is harmful, illiberal, and racist. The system exerts a viselike grip over the lives of young people once they enter its grasp. Shaped by the forces of racism, classism, and sexism, the system demands responsibility of teenagers in the absence of social structures and supports that would allow them to meet those demands. As a result, they often falter.

One of these young people was Jacob, whom I met when he was just fourteen years old and incarcerated at the Hooper Secure Center in the Hudson Valley.[1] When Jacob was ready to leave Hooper, he gathered up his belongings, which included his GED certificate (high school equivalency), his books, and a check for the money he had earned while he worked at the facility's kitchen. He got into a state van, and a staff member from the facility drove him just a short way to the local Amtrak station, where he boarded a train to New York City. He looked out at the Hudson River, wearing his own clothes for the first time in several years. Leaning back in the plush upholstered seat of the train car, he turned his gaze toward the commuters going from Albany to New York City and wondered if anyone knew that he had just been released from a juvenile facility.

Jacob got a job within a few weeks of his release, enrolled in college a few months later, and even secured a lease on a car. He gave speeches to younger kids who had been in the system, was interviewed by reporters, and went to a conference; he became a "poster child." Yet just a few years later, Jacob was serving a two-year sentence in an adult prison. Now he's starting over again.

Many researchers have written about why individuals like Jacob struggle to live a life free of crime. Some have focused on the roadblocks that those from America's impoverished urban core face as they reckon with the stigma and burdens of a criminal conviction and the structural disadvantages of poverty and racism. This has helped us to understand the mechanisms structuring our high incarceration and recidivism rates, yet the whole story remains untold.

This book focuses on the neglect of young people like Jacob by the very institutions and individuals responsible for helping him get and stay out of the criminal justice system. It focuses on the moments when youth in the criminal justice system don't conform to our expectations of how they should behave, only to disappear into homeless shelters, psychiatric hospitals, and adult prisons, as they cross the threshold from the juvenile to the adult system. It focuses on the institutions and actors who discard the young once their actions began to reflect the complex constellation of systemic and personal abandonment that have defined their entire lives. But it is also about the heavy hand of the state—for instance, the ways that Jacob first entered the system when he was fourteen, living in foster care, and desperate for money, and how he fell into the hands of the police, jail, and a lengthy sentence filled with behavioral change programming.

Impoverished young people in trouble with the law, like Jacob, are uniquely situated at the crossroads of multiple interlocking systems of social welfare and punishment. Because of their poverty, their often-troubled family existences, and their risk-taking, teenagers encounter the disciplinary power of poverty management in unique and important ways.

This book is about a generation of young people who have grown up in extreme poverty. The story begins in 2008, shortly after the global financial collapse. Many of these young people were born in or around 1996, when the federal government enacted welfare reforms that replaced Aid to Families With Dependent Children with Temporary Assistance for Needy Families, which placed caps on the amount of welfare assistance that individuals could receive in their lifetimes and imposed strict requirements on individuals to find work. The individuals who have most suffered under these and a number of other social welfare programs are the most impoverished Americans, especially single parents and their children. State-based general assistance programs, which provide a safety net for the poorest of the poor, especially single men and individuals without children who do not qualify for other government assistance programs—like Jacob—have been cut significantly in the past decade.[2] New York's general assistance levels have fallen in real terms by about $100 a month per recipient.[3] In a recent study of the prevalence of extreme poverty (living on the equivalent of $2 a day), researchers found that this form of poverty has risen "sharply" between 1996 and 2011.[4] So too has social inequality, or the rising gap between rich and poor, and the increasing barriers for individuals seeking social mobility. Households with children living on no income are the most deeply affected by the welfare policy changes.

Almost every teenager I interviewed for this book lived in a household where his or her parents were unemployed or had very low-income service-sector jobs. Some of their parents participated in training programs mandated by welfare centers, such as those for home health aids, but their engagement in those programs provided them with no income.

Young people seem to struggle the most under the burdens of social inequality. These forms of inequality play a significant role in determining their life outcomes.[5] Young people faced higher rates of unemployment than adults after the world financial collapse.[6] Yet job training and employment opportunities are scarce. For example, only 7 percent of the 200,000 "disconnected" sixteen- to twenty-four-year-olds in New York City were served by existing educational and job training programs in 2008, and there were an estimated 12,000 program slots available to serve this group.[7]

These teenagers and their families frequently interacted with state actors and agencies charged with helping poor people—welfare centers, social security offices, Medicaid offices, corrections officers and cops, public hospitals, jails, family court, and child welfare offices. Government officials treat them in a manner that has been termed neoliberal *paternalism*. This form of governance "emphasizes self-mastery, wage work, and uses of state authority to cultivate market relations."[8] It is both paternalistic in that individuals facing government interventions see them as heavy-handed and focused on facilitating their change toward waged workers, better parents, more effective students, and so on, and neoliberal in that it emphasizes their role in the market as individuals capable of self-direction and sufficiency.

This book is one of a number of recent studies about young people's experiences in the juvenile justice system. These studies have provided us with a rich and troubling story about the deeply negative effects of punishment and incarceration in young people's lives. The studies, which have taken place in all parts of the United States, from Rhode Island to California, have revealed that much of what young people experience in custody and in the system more broadly across the country are very similar to what I have observed in New York; many young people struggle to manage the dual philosophies of care and control that exist in the juvenile justice system; the young people often "fake it to make it" through treatment, and they face harsh material and structural obstacles upon release from custody that prevent them from stopping offending.[9] It is clear that our current system of punishment does not work; many, many young people—at rates as high as 90 percent of boys in New York—enter the adult system after spending time inside of a juvenile prison.[10] Involvement in the juvenile justice system actually harms individuals more than it helps them.

This book situates the story of Jacob and similar young people in the context of this contemporary political economy and a juvenile justice system that is undergoing rapid change and that is raising new questions about help and hurt in the lives of young people. The setting is New York State, the birthplace of the first juvenile prison in the country and now the site of a serious experiment in closing juvenile prisons and system reform. The experiments that are being conducted in New York today (and elsewhere around the country) seek to provide more therapeutic and less punitive interventions in the lives of young people accused of crimes than have ever existed. Juvenile facilities have closed across the United States, unprecedented numbers of young people are being shifted to community-based alternatives to incarceration, and there are historically low numbers of youth crime. However, much of what we see happening today has happened at several other points in U.S. history, and much of the logic that undergirds it—that is, that system involvement may actually make young people more likely to commit crime—has been happening since the late nineteenth century, even if it is undergirded by new evidence today. While facilities close, new therapeutic interventions have been expanded that include a deeper penetration into the lives of children and their families.

The juvenile justice system is a palimpsest: the system we have today bears many traces of its predecessors. The first juvenile prison was established in New York in 1825, and the first separate court for young people was created in Chicago in 1899. The founders of the nation's juvenile justice system believed that children should be treated differently from adults and thus served in a separate system. But not every child was considered worth saving. Black children weren't worth saving. Nor were Native American or Mexican children. Children who were considered to be "imbeciles" or mentally or physically deficient were banished to facilities for life. Thus, the original form of the juvenile justice system was one that was fundamentally exclusionary in that its practices were focused on keeping out those young people deemed to be unworthy in our society.[11]

Today, we still exclude youth from our vision of who should be saved, but in less visibile ways. Juvenile facilities are no longer racially segregated. Young people are no longer held for life in mental hospitals and asylums. But police officers in this country disproportionately arrest high numbers of youth of color. The vast majority of young people who enter the criminal justice system are impoverished, and their families have encountered various social welfare institutions—from public assistance, social security disability, public housing, to health care. Young people accused of violent crimes in New York and across the country face lengthy sentences.

The current system, and system actors, exclude and abandon young people but does so through engagement with them as liberal citizens. By "liberal" I am referring to the values of civil and social rights and freedoms in citizenship. American liberals have been committed to notions of "freedom," even if those opportunities are facilitated by law and policy, as in the case of efforts to achieve racial justice in the country in the 1960s.[12] In today's juvenile justice system, the individuals left behind in this quest to promote liberal citizenship are those kids who are not virtuous enough in their demonstration of citizenship. After leaving juvenile facilities and jails, violating probation, or failing their community-based alternative to incarceration programs, getting sanctioned by public assistance and finding themselves homeless and riding on the subway instead of living in homeless shelters, or running out of psychotropic medication and declining into a delusional panic, these young people end up in adult jails, prisons, and other institutions of social exclusion when they do not meet the expectations set for liberal citizenship by the individuals who have managed them. Yet it is the liberal state itself that creates the very standards for failure.

In previous systems, overtly racist and segregationist practices and policies reigned. What is different today is that many of the individuals in charge of the juvenile justice system will disavow racism and actively participate in a federal initiative to reduce racial disproportionality within the system. At Rikers Island, the system is also no longer staffed overwhelmingly by white people; more than half of the staff in New York's juvenile prisons are black. A Latina woman led the charge to close to thirty of New York's facilities. The former commissioner of the New York City Department of Probation, who went on to lead New York City's criminal justice reform efforts, led efforts to overhaul the District of Columbia juvenile justice system and has publicly declared that large juvenile training schools should be shut down. A recent book calling for the abolition of juvenile prisons has hit the newsstands in force, and its author has made the progressive public speaking circuit.[13] Hundreds of private foundations and liberal-minded groups have direct access to policymakers and legislators and are actively involved in promoting what many would consider to be a movement away from incarceration—including more alternatives to incarceration, more therapeutic interventions, more job programs and greater access to education. Young people may in fact be forced to work in a social structural system that "exists at least in part because it meets the needs of economic and political interests that favor social order and social control over poor communities, immigrants, and people of color."[14]

Yet so many teenagers like Jacob find themselves in the adult justice system because the process of governing young people charged with crimes inevitably results in a class of the "ungovernable"—those who cannot and will not meet the standards and expectations set out for liberal citizenship by the individuals who run juvenile justice systems and the ancillary social welfare sector. Once they are deemed ungovernable, this class of individuals effectively disappears, only to turn up in other systems of social control and punishment beyond the juvenile justice system. We don't necessarily have statistics to track this group; once young people exit the juvenile justice system and enter adulthood, they are branded with a different state identification number to track them through a new system. No longer desirable "poster children" in need of saving, they've aged out of foster care, too old to mentor, with the debts, children, failed relationships, health and mental health problems, and the crises of an adult. They "fail," but in more important respects, they fail to submit to a system aimed at their submission by revealing the parts of themselves that are sometimes ugly or discomfiting to those in charge.[15]

When I was working at the public defender's office in New York, I had a client who was a poster child and then decided not to be one. I met Nina in 2004 when she was sixteen years old. Brilliant, fiercely mature and sophisticated for her age, Nina was incredibly resourceful. She had been taking care of herself for two years after her parents abandoned her for their drug addictions. She had worked her way up a small local crack-selling network, a girl among men, but one who was a formidable competitor in that game.

My job was to get Nina into school; she had been arrested and charged with selling drugs, and although the judge had kept her out of jail, the only way we could help her get out from under the case was to make sure she was back in school. Nina needed a parent's signature to reenroll, and nearly a year later, with both of her parents on the streets and then incarcerated, we still had no way to get it. Yet we found a solution—a GED/college program miraculously accepted an opinion written by a lawyer from a community-based youth program that Nina met all of the criteria for being an emancipated minor. In short order, Nina ascended from drug dealer to college student.

Nina became a poster child. She was asked by the organization's director to speak at our annual fundraiser and charmed everyone she met, with a narrative that confirmed the idea that if only we give teenagers a chance to grow out of crime and a few strong resources, they will thrive. I quickly learned, however, that the poster child narrative forces us to ignore the long-lasting damage wrought on individuals by poverty, racism, and systemic neglect. Like many teenagers, particularly those whose early childhoods were marred by neglect, Nina struggles with deep emotional pain and depression, and although her successes have been enormous, they wouldn't be legible or obvious to many.

The poster child is a liberal's fantasy: the young person who has left the streets for college or for a middle-class job with social mobility. By leaving "the ghetto," they leave all of their troubles behind, for it was really just their position in the ghetto that made them commit crimes. This story, of course, denies individuals access to the complexity of human existence; it ignores the scars of racism and structural disadvantage in individual's lives, of one's racial identity and social history and its importance in shaping one's orientation to oneself and one's community, and to some extent it participates in the very narratives about the American Dream that so many liberals would disavow as mythology.

This book is about individuals like Nina who lead complex and unique lives; it is an imperfect attempt to situate those lives in a broader historical and political context to talk about the ways that the system affected them. Books like this necessarily elide the complexity of people's lives, their motivations, and their agency. In my time outside of academia, I continue to work with public defenders to present individuals' life stories to judges and prosecutors. I am reminded daily that it is impossible to draw sweeping conclusions about why people commit crimes and what led them down the paths they traveled. In presenting the claims I do, I attempt to convey the damage that is done when we treat individuals in trouble with the law as objects that can be poked and prodded according to the whims of a system that refuses to recognize their individuality.[16]

THEORETICAL ORIENTATION

The philosophical orientations and governing ideologies about youth crime have great consequences for the everyday lives of individuals charged with crimes. They steer individual actors' decisions about where to intervene in teenagers lives, and most important for this book, where not to intervene. I focus on the present-day ideologies about the governance of youth crime, using New York as a case study. Governing authorities force youth to express responsibility for their offending actions and for their future compliance with the law, but they do not actually facilitate the attainment of that responsibility, or more important, that ability to get out and stay out of the system. Those youth who are unable to live up to the expectations set out for them by governing agencies are abandoned. I argue that this process of responsibility-making is marked by assumptions about appropriate expressions of gender, race, and class.

This book examines four elements of the punitive philosophy that are used against impoverished and "risky" youth: ungovernability and worthiness, responsibility, and redeemability.

Young people in trouble with the law—especially young people of color—are deemed to be ungovernable and thus in need of court interventions. The book charts the efforts of adults in the criminal justice system to manage young people whom they consider to be unmanageable. Interventions that rely on the idea that the young people who are inherently bad and ungovernable (that this is an assumed part of their culture) fail to recognize the effects of a bad and pathological social structure on individual's lives.

New York, like many other states across the country, has faced significant reductions in government support for welfare since 1996, when federal welfare reform occurred. The federal welfare reforms were partially facilitated by the strong embrace by political actors of the concept of individual responsibility in the marketplace. This idea, stemming from neoliberal political philosophies that prioritize the role of the free market, a reduced social state, and individual responsibility and accountability, was popularized in the United States during the Reagan era and embraced by politicians of all stripes.[17]

In response to the retrenchment of welfare supports, state actors in places like New York have effectively been forced to promote notions of individual responsibility for those individuals who are under the control of the state. Put more simply, for young people about to leave a juvenile facility, it is in the state's best interest to encourage them to pull themselves up by their bootstraps and find work and education because the state itself does not have the resources to provide such services to them. At first, Jacob succeeded in realizing this goal; he was able to find at least moderately stable forms of employment and education on his own.

Many of the interventions aimed at young people charged with crimes in New York and elsewhere are guided by state actors' desires for the realization of redemptive narratives in the lives of young people who have violated the law. In recent years, many states, including New York, have publicly embraced what they call more rehabilitative and therapeutic strategies with young people, turning away from a lengthy period, during the 1990s and early 2000s, of harsh law-and-order approaches to them, which often involved the imposition of lengthy sentences, the introduction of adult-level penalties, and the use of get-tough interventions, such as boot camps and "scared straight" programming.

Punitive ideologies have shifted away from these law-and-order approaches toward the use of more treatment and the expansion of social control interventions in young people's lives in their communities (as opposed to in prison). Although these are not necessarily experienced as less punitive by the young people who encounter them (and thus the palimpsest: new strategies always bear the traces of old ones), the ideologies undergirding these approaches frame young people as inherently redeemable. The redemptive pathway is as follows: young people engage in offending behavior, often seen to be caused by their troubled pasts; they are then provided rehabilitative services by the state and into the light of "success," generally marked by engagement in higher education and employment.

At first Jacob displayed all of the signs of effective redemption—he spoke about "seeing the light" while in residential care, deciding to change himself and his life, and then making determined efforts to do so once he was released. His story was compelling to people in the system and even those on the outside—he, like Nina, overcame the obstacle of a criminal conviction and, on his own, made a life for himself despite it. Jacob reflected what for many system actors was an ideal: the realization that if the government stepped back and watched him from a distance, then individuals like him who had been governed would engage in a process of self-government.

The theoretical orientation of the research was inspired by and builds on the work of Michel Foucault, a French social theorist who was among the first to express cynicism about this process of self-government. Foucault was interested in the relationship between individual's experiences or perceptions of self-regulation and control and the forms of control exercised by governing authorities that were aimed at those individuals. He argued that an individual's expression of self-control may actually be a product of the forms of regulation and control exerted by governing authorities.[18] The imprint of the government's role in these forms of self-control may not be immediately visible to others. Foucault's followers further developed this notion of what he termed "governmentality," which is rooted in the idea that governments stimulate the cultivation of subjectivities in the service of particular aims. This has been used to study everything from hospitals and schools to ideas about child-rearing.[19] Criminologists and social theorists have subsequently extended Foucault's ideas to their analyses of what happens in criminal and juvenile justice systems, arguing that the management of risky youth requires a process of enlisting youth in the process of their own self-government.[20]

I argue that people's redemption has been elevated by contemporary state actors, policymakers, and advocates as a means by which young people can accomplish virtue in their lives as formerly bad kids. In particular, telling one's redemption story in the prison and later to the public becomes a way that youth can demonstrate their worthiness to those who have ostensibly helped them. These stories become compelling ways for advocates of intervention to feel secure that interventions are still necessary and important, and they also become new moments of governmentality in that young people are actively recruited in the telling of such redemption stories. Yet these stories are often fragile, and I argue that this has consequences for the actual process of change and development.

Jacob's own redemption story began to fall apart after a few years. He reconnected with some old friends on the streets. He accumulated debt. He stopped going to school. Then a family crisis happened, he was robbed, and everything fell apart. He began to despair, but he didn't know how to cope with his despair; while he was at the juvenile facility, he didn't receive any mental health treatment to address his serious depression and his history of suicide attempts, and he didn't get any help in learning how to build relationships with others. Upon his release, he moved into public housing projects, got a low-wage job, and had no ability to receive state assistance because he was ineligible for welfare support.

After his family crisis, Jacob fell off the grid. He told his foster care agency that he didn't want their help anymore. His philosophy of self-control that he displayed so well in his juvenile facility migrated from his involvement in education and work to his involvement in the underground and illicit gun economy. He fell outside of the world of governance and into the realm of the ungovernable.

In recent years, some criminologists have analyzed the lives of young people caught in the trap that Jacob is caught in, as well as some of the contradictions in strategies of governance that he faces—under the control of the system, but not receiving any help from it, ostensibly engaged in a process of self-governance but also participating in offending.[21] Here I use the term "ungovernable" to represent this position that young people are in. This is where they become resistant to what is expected of them and thus unable to fit into the strategies for their social control. Thus, they are abandoned by the system and left to fend for themselves.

I argue that our focus on the effects of the juvenile justice system alone, and the possibility for reform within that system, is myopic. The juvenile justice system is just one piece of a broader social welfare apparatus that is driven by interlocking structures and philosophies of punishment, oppression, and exclusion for youth. These systems both drive and reproduce the pernicious consequences of control of young people deemed to be risky in ways that are deeply illiberal in the sense that they actually inhibit the expression of liberal subjecthood; they are deeply harmful in that they perpetuate social harm and violence, both against and by young people; and they are racist, in that these systems are aimed almost exclusively at black, Latina/o, Asian, and Native American youth and uphold systems of control that are only acceptable in colonial terms—they are dominating, paternalistic, and oppressive but almost exclusively for those youth, not the primarily privileged white youth who themselves engage in risky and dangerous behavior. The young people taught me these lessons—none of them saw the juvenile justice system alone as the cause of their frustration and anger at racism and harms inherent in "the system." I learned from them what was resonant for me on Rikers Island: all state agents and actors are representative of the same forces of marginalization, labeling, and control that they encounter daily and in deeply alienating ways, much like a colonial force. Thus, juvenile justice system reforms that seek to integrate alternatives to incarceration, including social work and therapeutic assistance, in the homes of young people and their families, ankle-monitoring programs, and antiviolence initiatives that are focused on bolstering policing and safety monitoring and strategies, for example, all simply perpetuate the paradoxes of state involvement in young people's lives—they are both deeply penetrating but also punitive and alienating. Young people are trapped in a vice—a system that pushes out as much as it pulls in.

CHAPTER 1

Reproducing Reforms

It seems to me that there has been a lot of nonsense written lately about the change in the training school from
custody to treatment. If we ever had a philosophy of pure
custody, we moved out of it a long time ago, even before
we discarded the uniforms, the strict discipline and the
"yes sir," "yes ma'am" relationships that had persisted as
anachronisms along with the celluloid collars on the shirts
we gave boys with their parole suit . . . what we are trying
to do is now moving out in so many different directions
that it may well seem confusing and uncoordinated.
—Willard Johnson, Director of the New York
State Department of Social Welfare, 1964[1]

NEW YORK'S JUVENILE JUSTICE system was born nearly 200
years ago. It has always been paternalistic in its orientation but seemingly
protectionist in its presentation. Reformers in New York have always arguably been benevolently motivated by their aim to protect and provide for the
state's most vulnerable citizens who have passed through the system. This is a
uniquely northern American phenomenon, in that northern states have always
sought to distinguish themselves as models of liberal, rational, and democratic
governance.

A young person arrested in Rochester, New York, today can walk through
the very same gates of the juvenile facility that one of his or her family members could have walked through five generations earlier. In 1902, the State
Industrial School was built on a sprawling campus in a rural area outside of
Rochester. Today, it is simply referred to as "Industry," or the Industry Residential Center. In 1902, young people did agricultural or industrial trade work
on the campus; today, they receive therapy and go to school. The facility has
recently initiated an agricultural initiative aimed at training kids in aquaponics (indoor fish and plant growth). Despite these new innovations, the focus
on young people's character has remained: according to a staff psychologist
at Industry who was interviewed about the aquaponics initiative, "It's not so
much about growing food as building character. . . . They learn about working

13

hard and making sacrifices, and they feel better about themselves. They recognize they can accomplish more in life and school."[2] One hundred and sixty-six years separate the lives of the first young person to enter the facility and the ones who enter today, but arguably little in the rhetoric and approach to reforming children has changed.

For 160 years, the same questions and debates have circulated through juvenile justice reform: should teenagers who commit crimes be treated like adults? Should juvenile facilities be big or small? Should juvenile institutions focus on education or vocational training, treatment, or punishment? Should young people be treated in their home communities or in institutions? Willard Johnson, quoted at the beginning of this chapter, was right: the history of juvenile justice reform often seems confusing and uncoordinated. As I've reviewed the archives of New York's juvenile justice system, or interviewed staff members, former system commissioners, and reformers, I've been struck by the consistency of these questions, the familiarity of the concerns, and even the similarity of the rhetoric.[3] Often, the only people who aren't repeating the same questions are teenagers themselves.

There is a term that has been used to describe the young people who have been enmeshed in America's juvenile justice systems: "other people's children."[4] State agents are arguably always trying to find new ways to regulate the behavior of other people's children within a liberal democracy. To strike the right balance—one that recognizes and respects individual freedoms but asserts the right to control a category of people without rights—is a difficult task: it would be illiberal to punish those children too harshly, for they are, after all, children; but there is pressure on the state to prevent those children from offending again.

A question that preoccupies reformers and administrators in New York and other states across the country is both simple—how do we get young people out of adult prisons and jails?—and one that carries great consequences. It happens to have been the first question asked by the individuals who sought to address risk-taking behavior by young people.

A SITE OF EXPERIMENTATION

Until the middle part of the nineteenth century, teenagers and young people who committed crimes were housed in adult institutions. Concerned that teenagers would become corrupted by their time in adult institutions, middle-class reformers in New York founded the first correctional institution to separate young people from adults in 1825. Called the House of Refuge, it was a juvenile detention center and prison for vagrant and delinquent youth.[5] The Western House of Refuge was founded in Rochester, the northern part of the state, in 1849.[6] The creation of these separate institutions for the care and control of young people sprang from the sense that young people were more malleable and thus susceptible to reform in a way that adults were not.[7]

Once open, the Refuges detained children adjudicated as delinquents and those engaged in "protocriminal" behavior. This included children who "wandered about the streets, neither in school or at work and who obviously lacked a 'good' home and family."[8] The reformers embraced the philosophy that there were deviant "types," and when children arrived in the institution, they would be classed according to the degree of their moral depravity, from good, to bad, to "wicked."[9] Boys and girls were assigned tasks that were aligned with expected behavior for their gender: boys were employed in buildings and grounds work, and girls were taught domestic tasks.[10]

Critics like the French scholar Alexis de Tocqueville, who visited the New York City House of Refuge in 1831, argued that these institutions caused more harm than good.[11] Others argued that the asylums were not sufficiently rehabilitative for young people and focused too much on a single model of care, rather than individualized and case-by-case approaches to delinquency. These created what they called "reformatories," institutions aimed at educating children in developing forms of self-discipline, industriousness, and deference, a more individualized model of care than the one practiced by the Houses of Refuge.[12]

The young people who initially populated the country's juvenile justice system were Irish, German, Polish, Italian, and Russian children whose families arrived in New York during a surge of immigration in the mid to late nineteenth and early twentieth centuries. Their families formed the backbone of the new American working class, and although they were white, they presented a challenge to middle-class white people already living in the United States. The prospect of new immigrants wielding growing influence on the nation's laws and norms sparked xenophobic anxieties.[13] Within this context, the boundaries of acceptable behavior for new white migrants were enforced by the white middle- and upper-class native-born residents of New York City through the uses of reformatories.[14]

The group of middle-class white reformers organized themselves around the goal of "saving" impoverished immigrant children from what they perceived to be the potentially criminogenic threats of poverty. These "child savers," a largely wealthy group of individuals, pushed for the passage of laws and the establishment of institutions that resulted in the moral regulation and control of poor children. For example, they promoted child labor laws as a means of both eliminating the threat that low wage, largely child-dominated sweatshop labor posed to mass production.[15] They invested their time and their money in the establishment of large orphanages and asylums for neglected and delinquent youth and played a role in marking out what kinds of youthful behavior could be considered to be worth punishing or saving.

Over the early part of the twentieth century, a number of reformatories were built by the state across the rural parts of upstate New York.[16] Charles

Loring Brace, a white middle-class educated man from Connecticut who founded the Children's Aid Society, sought to take immigrant children out of their homes in the cities and place them with rural, farming families. Brace and others theorized that rural life offered both physiological and developmental benefits to urban children. As a result, the state's rural landscape is still full of prisons, residential juvenile facilities, and residential children's facilities. Many of those facilities were built in the nineteenth century; the ones that were built more recently still bear the traces of their predecessors.

Large as these reformatories were, they drew from small facilities scattered across a residential campus, each run by a set of "parents." Through this cottage system, the state agencies sought to decentralize the forms of control that existed in previous institutions.[17] The cottage-based residential treatment systems were intended to resemble an ideal-typical rural, agrarian family life that could offer moral guidance and sanctuary for urban children who were considered to be ravaged by rapid urbanization and development.[18]

This was the first time where reformers focused on the size of facilities for young people charged with crimes; yet since then, ideas about facility size, including the ratio of staff to children, the layout of facility units, and the relationship of units to larger institutions, have dominated juvenile justice reform conversations. Reformers have argued that facilities should be as small as possible, allowing children to participate in treatment and facilitating their emancipation from care. The discussion today bears the traces of the past; notions about the intimacy of home and family life, and its benefits in particular in the care of children, have been consistent in discussions about what works for young people in trouble with the law. This doesn't always mean keeping children in their homes but does operate under the assumption that a homelike structure is best for children.

The project of removing children from their homes and placing them in rural areas or upstate cities has also been a critical thread through the history of reform. Continuing in the project of expansion of the state's facilities to rural areas, the New York State legislature passed laws at the turn of the twentieth century authorizing the use of lands in far upstate New York, near Rochester, and closer to New York City, in the Hudson Valley, for the building of a state training school for boys who were charged as juvenile delinquents, shifting boys away from the Houses of Refuge, where they had previously been placed.[19]

The New York State Training School for girls was founded in Hudson, New York, in 1904. The school identified the girls as "pupils" and expected them to engage in traditionally feminine disciplines such as sewing and dressmaking, cooking, and cleaning. According to one early report from the Training School, the girls were there to learn the "common decencies of life."[20]

These new institutions considered only some groups of young people reformable. Black children, for example, were often placed in separate institutions or units from white children, often with adults, in part because their "rehabilitative potential was doubted."[21] They often faced longer terms in custody.

Child welfare and custodial institutions for poor African American children were deeply underfunded in the early part of the twentieth century in New York.[22] Although the population of African American people in New York City rose substantially in the latter part of the nineteenth and early twentieth centuries, there were few social services available for African American children, particularly for those who were considered to be abused and neglected by their families. Child welfare services remained segregated by race, with the vast majority of beds available for white children.[23] In 1939, there were only four voluntary agencies in New York City that even accepted African American children.[24] To find a placement for these young people, the only place judges felt they could send them was into the juvenile justice system, which had beds available for them.[25] Although the segregation of child welfare services was not allowed by law, the state's interpretation of the landmark case *Plessy v. Ferguson*, which allowed facilities to be "separate but equal," allowed these practices to persist.[26]

The first institutions in New York were built in the context of fears about unruly immigrant children and black children who arguably posed an existential threat to the ruling classes that sought to build a thriving industrial center in New York City. Sociologists of childhood have pointed to the ways that adolescence has always been constructed as a time of storm and stress and that periods of social change have often coincided with heightened concerns about youth crime and risk.[27] As some prominent scholars of childhood argue, "risk anxiety is primarily expressed as fear for children—worries about their safety and well-being—but also as fear of children, of what children might do if they are not kept within the boundaries of acceptable childish conduct."[28] Although crime rates among young people have fluctuated since the inception of the juvenile justice system, it is arguable that many of the same concerns about youth crime have persisted from the very beginning.

In the years following World War II, there was a significant uptick in arrests of young people and a subsequent growth in the number of juvenile facilities in the state.[29] Among the causes were concerns about black radicalization, the emerging influence of the Black Muslims, and the rise of youth gangs.[30] By the mid-1950s, the New York State Department of Social Welfare responded by expanding their institutions, establishing joint local and state financial responsibility for children who were sent to training schools and private facilities.[31]

During the 1950s and 1960s, the state repurposed a former sanatorium in Otisville, New York, a former stable for carriage horses from New York City in the Delaware River watershed, and created juvenile facilities near the upstate communities of Hudson and Troy. The number of state institutions expanded from four to eleven, and by 1964, there were more than 6,000 young people in care; by contrast, there were only 539 youth admitted into custody in 2013.[32] During the 1950s and 1960s, the state agency also expanded its community-based operations, focusing on programs to provide casework and support to young people based in the community.[33]

During the early to middle part of the twentieth century, New York State used a wide range of interventions with young people charged with crimes. Staff in juvenile institutions began using psychotherapy, milieu therapy, and other behavioral interventions.[34] Those involved in institutional care felt that psychiatry and psychology would make the institutions more rehabilitative.[35] Yet although some said that these interventions signaled a change in approach from custodial care to treatment-based care, others, like Willard Johnson, the former state director of social welfare, noted that there was never a "philosophy of pure custody" used in New York's system; he pointed out that the first psychiatrist and psychologist were introduced into New York's institutions in the 1930s and that social workers had long been a part of institutions.[36] It is thus clear that the debates about whether juvenile facilities should be punitive or therapeutic are age-old.

A System under Scrutiny

> The juvenile justice system of New York City has slipped into confusion and despair, caught in a crisis so severe that judges and jailers alike often say they are harming more children than they are helping.
>
> —*New York Times*, 1970[37]

> New York State's juvenile justice system is an expensive, dismal failure that does great harm to children and families without making our neighborhoods safer.
>
> —*New York Daily News*, 2008[38]

New York's journalists have long investigated the conditions of its juvenile justice system and, with striking consistency, have conveyed the idea that the system does more harm than good to young people. Thirty-eight years separate the opinions expressed above by the *New York Times* and the *New York Daily News*, yet they essentially say the same thing.

Over the course of the twentieth century, numerous studies pointed to the ineffectiveness of juvenile institutions at ending offending by young people.[39]

By the 1960s, a number of critical studies of New York's and other states' treatment of young people in prisons and juvenile facilities, produced by advocacy organizations and academics, began to challenge the models of "rehabilitation" that were used in juvenile facilities.[40] Organizations like the New York City Legal Aid Society, the city's primary indigent criminal defense organization, and the Citizen's Committee for Children published critiques of the state system. They advocated strongly for community-based interventions over institutions and were supported by the federal government in their efforts.[41]

In a report published in 1960, the Citizen's Committee for Children first made the pitch for community over custody, and then repeated that pitch again in 1969:

> We believe that many children who are now institutionalized could be helped in the community. However, a small number of children are best treated or protected away from home and the community. (1960)[42]

> We believe that New York State must be brave and imaginative enough to help children while they live within or very close to their own communities. We may use foster homes, day centers, small residences, community mental health services, or other means. (1969)[43]

The notion that "community" is better than "custody" is one that seems, at first, anti-paternalistic—reformers want the state to stop removing children from their families. But this critique was also arguably rooted in assumptions about the dysfunctional working-class family in need of interventions.[44]

The reformers arguing for a shift from custody to community in the 1960s drew from labeling theory in making their claims. They also drew from the idea of "radical noninterventionism" in the lives of young people charged with crimes.[45] The idea that the very interventions aimed at young people could actually cause them to offend resonated with reformers, who asked, through their critiques, whether it was in fact possible that the very sanctioning of criminal behavior by young people might cause them to internalize the identity of a deviant and reenact it. Did institutionalization itself act as a "labeling" force, regardless of whether it was therapeutic?

In 1960, system leaders in New York created a program for fifteen- to seventeen-year-olds charged with crimes called the "Division for Youth" (DFY) as an alternative to the large training school model. They also began to run experimental treatment programs in residential care.[46] In the years after the establishment of DFY, system leaders, in part informed by the labeling research, helped to close some facilities. As a result, the population of young people in the training schools dropped dramatically, smaller facilities with innovative forms of care emerged, and there was a rise in alternative-to-incarceration programs.[47] Abraham Novick, who was the superintendent of the New York State

Training School for Girls in Hudson, wrote in a white paper on the subject in 1963: "Commitment to or placement in an institution should be looked up on as a last resort. Last resort is not to be defined as a process of identifying the impossible child for shipment to Siberia, but the considered decision of responsible people that a relatively controlled environment is required for rehabilitation and eventual adjustment."[48] Novick recommended that the youth who remained in facilities should be provided with a range of rehabilitative services rooted in "sociological" approaches, which included group-oriented treatment and vocational training, while those who remained for what he called "psychological" reasons would receive individualized treatment.[49]

The facility landscape created in the 1950s had begun to unravel. The subsequent nationwide decline of the so-called rehabilitative ideal in the 1970s, which involved challenges by academics, policymakers, and advocates to indeterminate sentencing laws and the "correctional" model of imprisonment, transformed approaches toward young people charged with crimes.[50] This movement was bolstered by empirical evaluations of treatment programs that demonstrated that few programs "worked" to rehabilitate offenders.[51] The "nothing works" movement in part led to a period of deinstitutionalization and diversion in both the adult and juvenile justice systems in the early 1970s.[52] In 1970, 10 percent of young people charged with crimes in New York were placed in community-based settings; by 1976, that number had risen to 46 percent.[53]

In the 1960s, emboldened by the legacy of litigation successes in the civil rights movement, a new group of lawyers began to challenge what they saw as the overly paternalistic nature of juvenile courts and their effects. Gerald Gault, a fifteen-year-old teenager who was placed into confinement for a seven-year sentence after his adjudication for making a lewd phone call, raised questions about his treatment by the courts. His case made its way to the U.S. Supreme Court. The court's majority decided, in its *In re Gault* decision in 1967, to provide some of the people procedural safeguards that existed in the adult court system to young people like Gault who were processed in the juvenile court system.[54]

A burgeoning children's rights movement was emerging, one primarily led by white middle-class advocates who felt that the child-saving efforts of their predecessors had gone too far. This also meant that there was greater attention to the uses (and abuses) of placement, leading to efforts to reduce the placement of status offenders, such as runaways and truant youth.

In the 1970s, lawyers raised critical challenges to racial segregation in the child welfare and juvenile justice systems. Some of these agencies were forcibly desegregated after a lawsuit was filed in 1973 on behalf of a young woman, Shirley Wilder, who was placed in the Hudson Training School for Girls after her parents allegedly abused her and no other social services placements could be found for her.[55]

However, the procedural protections that were added in the juvenile courts did not necessarily eliminate the broader philosophies and orientations embedded since the founding of separate courts for young people at the turn of the nineteenth century. Institutionalization was still reserved for those deemed the most "risky" in the state—by the 1970s, those were poor, largely male, youth of color.

The system remained a palimpsest. Despite reforms that strengthened children's rights and recognized the harmful role that system involvement may play in young people's lives, the foundational and paternalistic approaches to treating "other people's children" arguably remained at the core. For all that liberal reforms had chipped away at the rights that young people received, they had not in fact altered the population who faced the deep end sanctions in institutions.[56] The number of young people in custody may have gone down, and their access to civil rights may have been enhanced, yet those in custody arguably still faced people who saw them as manageable only when they were institutionalized.

In 1975, in keeping with the wave of political sentiment against the institutionalization of children and in favor of community-based alternatives, New York State governor Hugh Carey appointed a new reform-minded director of the state's Division for Youth. The new director, Peter Edelman, was working at the University of Massachusetts. Massachusetts came to national attention after the director of that state's system, Jerome Miller, famously closed the state's large juvenile training schools.[57] Convinced that there were too many training schools in New York, Edelman reduced the state's reliance on them as a form of secure placement. He also identified a number of other problems in the system, including poor mental health services, weak educational programs, inadequate aftercare supervision, and too few small placement settings.[58] During his time in the agency, Edelman shifted care away from large institutions and toward smaller ones. As the juvenile facilities began to close, there was a significant amount of pushback to the reforms from the staff working in the facilities.[59]

Two incidents galvanized Edelman's opponents. In early 1977, youth residents at the Austin McCormack facility near Ithaca set the facility on fire; staff members reportedly sat and watched as the facility burned down.[60] In June 1977, a thirteen-year-old boy from Buffalo named David Smith was murdered at the Industry Residential Center, located just outside of Rochester. In both instances, state lawmakers and the media blamed the putative "softening" of the system.[61]

In the early 1970s, there was substantial legislative and public attention to serious youth crime in New York, especially robbery and gang violence.[62] The Juvenile Offender law, which allows adolescents as young as thirteen to be charged as adults, was enacted in 1978 in New York in response to a highly publicized criminal case involving a fifteen-year-old named Willie

Bosket, who was charged with robbing and killing two subway passengers in New York City.[63] Because Bosket was fifteen years old, he was charged in the city's Family Court, and received a maximum sentence of five years in a juvenile facility. The relatively lenient sentence created significant public furor.[64] Correctional interest groups began to question the legitimacy of the state's juvenile justice administration, which prompted investigations of serious juvenile crime.[65] Although violent crimes by young people were actually on the decline during this period, cases like Willie Bosket's stoked public fears.[66]

During the summer after the Bosket murders, Governor Hugh Carey faced a tough reelection battle, complete with accusations that he was soft on crime. In response, Carey threw his support behind a proposed Juvenile Offender law, which would require that thirteen-, fourteen-, and fifteen-year-olds charged with certain violent felonies be automatically prosecuted in adult court, and behind a provision that would allow a panel of psychiatrists, a district attorney, and a judge to determine a young person's eligibility for release.[67] The Juvenile Offender law forced a significant uptick in the number of youth in care.

The passage of the Juvenile Offender law reflects the connections between politics and punishment in the United States. The treatment of young people who offend is dependent not only on individual caretakers but also on political cycles: the commissioners of the state's juvenile justice are political appointees. Although many individuals working in the system are civil servants who work their way up through the programs, the commissioners often come from outside of the system, thus enacting programs of reform which reflect their ideological orientations, not necessarily their experience in the system

The 1980s were a relatively quiet time for reform in New York's system. The system's commissioners focused on building up the state's programming for young people charged under the Juvenile Offender law. The facility's commissioners continued existing treatment programs, such as Guided Group Interaction, but also initiated programs like Aggression Replacement Training.[68]

During the 1990s, there was a well-documented surge in youth arrests, similar to the period of panic about youth crime in the 1950s. There were several high-profile cases of white teenagers who engaged in school shootings, teenage gang violence, and teenagers involved in murdering their peers. Many states passed laws heightening penalties toward teenagers.[69] In her account of juvenile justice in the 1990s, Elaine Brown points to the ways that the white teenagers engaged in school shootings were described as alienated victims, while the teenagers of color who committed homicides were characterized as evil murderers.[70] During the 1990s, the system was brimming with young people of color, especially during the years when Republican Governor George Pataki led the state and when law-and-order politics were ascendant.

Unlike other states, which amped up their penalties against young people, New York did not adjust its already quite harsh laws allowing teenagers to be automatically arrested and convicted as adults, even though there were some calls to do so. The juvenile facilities continued to function as they had, significantly expanding a cognitive change treatment model, Aggression Replacement Training, into their programming.[71]

The state also started a military boot camp program in the early 1990s. Despite some claims about a hardening of the system toward a more "correctional" model, however, it appears that the 1990s were a time when treatment programming continued to be tinkered with in the facilities as it had throughout the twentieth century. The major difference was that the system appeared to be under relatively little scrutiny by outside reformers, and each juvenile facility had some autonomy and little supervision from above from the state commissioners. There was also a relatively inactive litigation and juvenile justice reform movement at the time. There is little documentation of any critical reports or investigations of the system issued during the 1990s.

THE CONTEMPORARY LANDSCAPE OF JUVENILE JUSTICE

In the spring of 2015, New York's governor, Andrew Cuomo, proposed to raise the age of responsibility from sixteen to eighteen years. Although many advocates had called for the age to be raised at other points in New York's history, this was seemingly the first time a state governor was behind such a policy change, and he received support from law enforcement for his efforts.[72] This is representative of a larger shift occurring across the United States—bipartisan support for criminal justice system reforms is gaining traction, and "nonviolent" teenagers, who the bill would affect, seemed to be low-hanging fruit in reforms aimed at saving money for the states, in that their diversion to less costly systems of care than prisons would be a political move that posed seemingly little threat.

Those who supported raising the age argued that the adult prison system where teenagers are placed is overly harsh and punitive. Community-based organizations in New York City sent busloads of teenagers to Albany to lobby in support of Cuomo's proposal to raise the age. Many of the teenagers who came out in support of the bill were clients of alternative to incarceration organizations or had been incarcerated at Rikers Island (a jail for adults but where teenagers as young as sixteen can be sent). Some of these teenagers were featured in news stories, campaign literature, and even in a video put out by Governor Cuomo's office.

At the time, I was teaching a college course inside of Hooper, a maximum secure juvenile facility for young men. The young men in my class were all charged with violent crimes. More than 90 percent of young men in the facility were convicted as adults under the state's Juvenile Offender law—the so-called Willie Bosket law. The young men had heard about the governor's proposal and were excited about how it might affect them. Unfortunately, the only way it would affect them was that more young people would be joining their facility because the governor had proposed that all young people currently held in adult prisons be transferred to the state's juvenile facilities. None would have their sentences changed, nor would they cease being charged as adults. The bill would only affect those sixteen- to eighteen-year-olds charged with nonviolent crimes. The kids affected by the Willie Bosket law—those charged with serious, violent felonies, 90 percent of whom are children of color—would remain a class of individuals carved out under the law as undeserving of the mercy granted to their peers charged with nonviolent crimes.

Several years earlier, in 2008, I began doing my research inside of the facility during another period of reform—one that was aimed at enhancing the provision of treatment inside of juvenile facilities and lessening the forms of "strict discipline" that existed there. The reforms were also aimed at improving conditions of confinement. When he was fourteen years old, Jacob was sent to Hooper. Like many juvenile facilities in New York, it is located in a rural area a few hours from New York City, where most of the young people inside, including Jacob, came from. At the time, Hooper and a number of other facilities across the state were in turmoil—fighting between residents was commonplace, as were their arrests for fighting and assaults on staff; staff members were regularly calling out sick, and stories about the turmoil in the system were a regular feature in the public media.

Jacob arrived in the system shortly after Democratic Governor Eliot Spitzer appointed a longtime child advocate, Gladys Carrión, to the position of commissioner of the state's system, with the charge that she shift it from a punitive to a rehabilitative system. In November 2006, just two months before Spitzer took office, a boy named Darryl Thompson died after he was physically restrained by staff at the Tryon boys' facility.[73] Even under the previous governor, Republican George Pataki, the state's juvenile justice reform movement had picked up steam. There were a number of advocates who were involved in campaigns to stop the building of a juvenile placement facility in the Delaware River valley, as well as campaigns against the building of new juvenile detention facilities in New York City.[74] The New York Civil Liberties Union conducted an investigation into conditions of confinement in two girls' facilities, making serious allegations against the state for the overuse of force and neglectful mental health care.[75] Other state organizations investigated conditions of confinement and called for greater oversight of the state system.[76]

Carrión, who was a former child advocate and director of the nonprofit social services organization United Way, immediately embarked on a project of closing the state's juvenile facilities and cleaning house. Reformers had criticized the system as a product of the 1990s-style "lock 'em up" mentality and said that the facilities resembled prisons. The state's boot camp facility, built in the early 1990s, was still open. The directors of the facilities were appointed through an archaic political patronage-based system, and there were rumors of a cloistered culture of staff violence against youth. Carrión closed down facilities and made those that remained more humane. Meanwhile, at Hooper, a lot of staff members were unhappy at this change in direction, and kids like Jacob knew it.

Many staff members at Hooper considered Jacob to be a model resident. It helped that he was white, which allowed him to gain some favor with white staff members, and that he had mastered the art of deference to staff. Jacob and a group of other young men were hand-selected by the facility administrators at Hooper to participate in my research study; I quickly learned that this same group was frequently chosen to meet with outsiders coming in the facility. The young residents knew that a lot of changes were happening in New York's system, in part because the staff that watched over them would often grumble about the reforms and the new commissioner, Carrión, during their shifts. The teenaged residents were also, to some extent, aware that the system was under scrutiny and that changes aimed at making their lives in the facilities better were taking place—they no longer had to hold their hands behind their backs when they walked from one place to the other, they were given greater access to ombudsmen who could hear their concerns, and the rules had been changed about the kinds of incidents that might precipitate a physical restraint against them. But for the most part, few residents or staff members were actually informed by facility or system administrators about the broader agenda of the reforms, and in fact, the changes were quite minor. Residents in the facilities that closed were simply moved to another facility. Some residents experienced shorter stays in confinement than in the past, but they had no point of comparison to the previous sentencing practices because it was often their first time in the system. Yet to the outside world, the changes were deemed profound and transformative, attracting the attention of national media and the federal government.

In Washington, DC, members of the Department of Justice learned about allegations of abuse and neglect in New York's facilities and sent some of their lawyers to the state's juvenile facilities to investigate these allegations. After their investigation, in 2009, the Department of Justice published a scathing report about New York's system and forced substantial changes to their restraint policies and mental health policies, hiring monitors to inspect the progress of change.[77]

In New York City, Mayor Bloomberg hired a new cadre of liberal advocates to work in his administration to steer changes in the city's juvenile justice system, many of whom came from the same advocacy community that had pressed for reforms. Within a matter of years, the city's most notorious juvenile detention facility, Spofford, which had long been critiqued for its deplorable conditions of confinement, was closed by his administration. The mayor appointed a probation commissioner, Vincent Schiraldi, who had progressive bona fides and had overseen a dramatic transformation of DC's juvenile justice system, closing its notoriously bad juvenile facility, Oak Hill, and opening a smaller facility focused on education and youth development. Schiraldi pushed for juvenile probation reform in the city and supported the mayor's new focus on jobs for young men who were involved in the criminal justice system. By 2012, liberal advocates and city and state bureaucrats, who in the past had been on opposite sides of the political fence, were celebrating some of the most dramatic system transformations they felt could be possible: a major initiative, called "Close to Home," which involved the closure of most of the state's juvenile facilities and the development of a network of community-based care in New York City. Community triumphed over institutions in the debate over what was best for kids in trouble with the law.[78]

It is no surprise that the reforms reached their fullest force after the 2008 global financial catastrophe. In New York, as in many other states, criminal justice expenditures have been identified as a key driver of state expenses, and many states have looked to criminal justice reforms as the answer to this crisis. At the height of the New York reforms, it was estimated that it cost approximately $268,000 a year to house a young person in Office of Children and Family Services (OCFS) custody.[79] Those costs were disproportionately borne by the government of New York City, which sent the vast majority of young people into state custody. In a study of the recidivism rates of young people who were in OCFS custody in New York, which tracked a large group of young people leaving custody until age 28, not only were the vast majority of boys and girls rearrested, but 71 percent of the boys ended up spending time in an adult jail or prison.[80] In an earlier study often cited by those making a case for reform, 80 percent of young people discharged from OCFS custody from 1991 to 1995 were rearrested within six years.[81] Citing recidivism rates in making the case for reform is not new: sociologist Alexander Liazos has pointed to times as early as the mid-nineteenth century when reformers pointed to the high rates of return to custody of young people who were institutionalized.[82]

The attention to the conditions of confinement in New York paralleled a broader critique of institutional care in states across the country. A number of states, from Ohio to California, to Connecticut, Texas, and New York, significantly reduced the size of their juvenile facility populations since 2004.[83] New York closed down thirty-one facilities and reduced its juvenile facility population by more than 3,000 young people since Carrión was appointed.[84]

Carrión forced staff members to reduce their reliance on physical restraints and promoted the use of new therapeutic interventions, including a "trauma-informed" program of organizational change called the Sanctuary Model. The Sanctuary Model is "designed to facilitate the development of structures, processes, and behaviors on the part of staff, clients and the community-as-a-whole that can counteract the biological, affective, cognitive, social, and existential wounds suffered by the victims of traumatic experience and extended exposure to adversity."[85] Over the course of the research period, this model was implemented in facilities across the state. State administrators also introduced Dialectical Behavior Therapy into the facilities and a new behavioral change and treatment model (called the New York Model) that was developed in conjunction with administrators from a Missouri-based juvenile facility.

In Missouri, system administrators downsized their training schools in favor of small "homelike" facilities, where neither the young people nor staff members wear uniforms; the young people decorate their rooms and are involved in community governance of their facilities. The Missouri Model received national media attention and is frequently cited by liberal advocates as a model system. New York City in fact paid for some advocates and bureaucrats to travel to Missouri to tour its facilities. This reform shift in favor of small facilities over big ones is reminiscent of the Progressive Era efforts at emphasizing cottage-based facilities and family-style care over the large reformatory model. The George Junior Republic, a Progressive Era facility built in upstate New York, emphasized its family-like atmosphere, lack of uniforms, and youth governance after it was established in 1895.[86]

The Missouri Model appealed to New York administrators because it arguably offered a safe and humane alternative to the large-scale congregate care facilities that played such an abysmal role in young people's lives. For the New York reformers, the smaller facilities and more human and gentle approach to children embodied their commitment to the dignity and fairness that young people should expect in custody.

OCFS's plans to close facilities triggered an outpouring of responses from both progressive reformers in support of the changes and juvenile facility staff opposed to the downsizing process.[87] This coincided with growing dissent among some staff members about Carrión and her ideas about systemic reform. The death of a staff member in a community-based facility at the hands of two young men who had recently been released from custody became another lightning rod for criticism of the system, sparking a conservative Republican legislator from upstate New York to begin an investigation of the reforms.[88]

Staff members' resistance to reforms was rooted in their perception that facilities were more violent as a result of these changes, that the commissioner was out of sync with the "true" nature of the young offenders inside the facilities, and that staff members were unable to have their concerns heard.[89] In response, Carrión described the "culture of violence" that existed among staff members in the residential facilities. Media sources around the state opined about the relationship between staff "cultures" of resistance and the levels of brutality that existed in the facilities.[90] At a statewide juvenile justice advisory group meeting, Carrión said, "quite frankly, in some of my facilities, I am convinced that I cannot change the culture. It is too embedded, it is a toxic environment."[91]

In New York, an emphasis on strengths-based and positive youth justice, as well as identifying youth needs, has become de rigueur among reformers. Young people are considered by this group to be a special class of offenders who have unique developmental needs that can only be supported through age-appropriate therapeutic interventions.[92] There has been a recent effort by policymakers and advocates in the state to embrace "evidence-based practices."[93] A statewide juvenile justice task force argued that the state should "broaden the evidence-based field by supporting and conducting evaluations of new, innovative programs that apply the principles of best practice," arguing for the expanded funding of programs like Functional Family Therapy, a short-term treatment program that focuses on addressing risk and protective factors in young people charged with crimes, working with them and their families.[94]

Perhaps one of the most significant new reform efforts in juvenile justice systems across the country has been the introduction by state and local governments of risk assessment instruments. These tools are used by workers in the juvenile justice system to assess young people's risk of failing to appear for their next court date, their risk of reoffending, and also their so-called criminogenic risks and needs—essentially the individual, social, and familial factors, from their school attendance to their family circumstances, that put them in a category of individuals who have a higher likelihood of failing to appear for court or reoffending.

Risk assessment instruments have been embraced by liberal reformers as part of a broader effort to make juvenile justice systems more value-neutral and objective and to eliminate what was perceived by many to be a gaping problem in these systems—racial bias by police, probation officers, judges, and prosecutors—who were using their own discretion to make decisions about whether a young person should be detained.

Efforts to analyze young people's riskiness have emerged out of developmental psychology. Psychologists in particular have argued that young people charged with crimes possess characteristics that have compromised their positive development.[95] Risk factors may include mental health problems, a lack of stable relationships and community ties, and dysfunctional family backgrounds.[96] The criminologist David Farrington defines risk factors as "prior factors that increase the risk of occurrence of the onset, frequency, persistence, or duration of offending."[97] These factors have been roughly broken down into several areas: individual (both physiological and psychological), family, school, peer, community and neighborhood, and situational factors.[98] The individually based factors may include low resting heart rate, hyperactivity, parental criminality, truancy, and the presence of delinquent peers.[99] Macro-level factors include poverty and community disorganization.[100] Related to these notions that offending behaviors emerge out of the conditions of poverty are the ideas of Ross and Fabiano, the early advocates of social cognition efforts aimed at offenders, who argue that poverty and an attendant lack of stimulation can cause cognitive delays.[101]

The Risk Factor Prevention Paradigm area of research and policy has influenced policy and practices in youth justice around the world.[102] It focuses on interrupting the development of criminal careers. The criminologist John Muncie argues that "the 'criminal career' approach suggests that offending is part of an extended continuum of anti-social behavior that first arises in childhood, persists into adulthood and is then reproduced in successive generations."[103] Although there is some consideration of neighborhood contexts in the research, it has been argued that it is most focused on "proximate, individual factors" as opposed to "social and structural influences."[104]

Early childhood intervention programs such as Headstart are guided by the notion that investments in these interventions can prevent later engagement in offending.[105] Multisystemic Family Therapy and Functional Family therapy, the "evidence-based" practices that were recently introduced in New York, are connected to ideas about the risks that families are said to present to a young person's offending.[106] These programs were an attempt to be more meaningfully impactful in the lives of young people and their families struggling under conditions of poverty; they were aimed at doing preventative, holistic work that could make an immediate impact on the lives of these young people, assisting them in navigating a world where they would face triggering circumstances and difficulties daily.

The Risk Factor Prevention Paradigm approach has been criticized on methodological, theoretical, and ethical grounds.[107] Government interventions that prioritize risk factors arguably focus on only the negative qualities of young people to more fully control and classify them.[108] It has been said that these strategies fail to take into account the broader social constructions of risk. The risky young people enmeshed in the youth justice system thus contrast with children who take risks in "a quest for excitement or 'kicks.'"[109]

Risk factor approaches are aimed at moving juvenile justice systems to a more objective, neutral examination of children. Yet risk assessments are arguably also part of a movement toward "racial liberalism," which roots racism in racial prejudice as opposed to identifying the ways that racism becomes embedded in social structures and institutions.[110] Racial liberalism sees solutions to racially discriminatory practices in the apparent elimination of discretion by criminal justice system actors. Thus, by asking that system workers fill out forms about individuals accused of crimes, the results of which get tallied and used to determine someone's eligibility for detention and interventions, individual bias is allegedly eliminated from the process of justice. Yet risk factor approaches, as criminologist Peter Kelly argues, "recod[ed] institutionally structured relations of class, gender, ethnicity, (dis)ability and geography as complex, but quantifiable, factors which place youth at-risk."[111] Risk has, in effect, become a proxy for race.[112]

The failure of racial liberals to realize that bias can exist in the very questions that are asked about individuals, and in how they are framed, may be a result of the arguably misguided belief that individual racial bias, rather than socially structured and historically grounded racism, has shaped the disproportionate numbers of youth of color in the juvenile justice system.

Risk instruments are used as part in the juvenile justice system to decrease the numbers of young people in detention; the Annie E. Casey foundation's Juvenile Detention Alternatives Initiative relies on risk instruments to reduce the numbers of youth in detention. The Vera Institute of Justice was hired to develop such an instrument for use in courts across the state and has touted its effects in reducing detention numbers.[113] Despite these efforts, the numbers of youth of color in detention has actually risen according to their numbers in the population.[114]

The use of these risk technologies fits into the criminologist Kelly Hannah-Moffat inquiries about how "risk technologies [are] reshaped to fit with an ongoing normative 'post-welfare' commitment to therapeutic interventions."[115] Custody is reserved for the so-called bad kids; welfarist interventions are saved for the good ones. The focus is on separating the deserving from the undeserving: those young people who are said to "need" to be institutionalized are separated from those that pose the lowest risk. Anthony Bottoms describes this as the split in the punitive imagination between the dangerous and "the rest."[116]

Almost none of the groups involved in advocating for change in the juvenile justice system have invoked broader claims about economic redistribution as a solution to the overpolicing and incarceration of poor youth.[117] Almost all reformers have focused on developing solutions to the central need to discipline youth—to address their offending behaviors in ways that are seemingly less punitive. Yet they start with the principle or premise that offending behavior is the problem, not the adult actors who might be engaged in creating and re-creating reforms that have only led to the same result: the overincarceration and policing of young people of color.

Since its inception, New York's juvenile justice system has been deeply shaped by the state's liberal elite. Although it has taken distinct and different turns since the country's inception, American liberalism has been fundamentally oriented around the notion that all power should not be vested in the state and that liberty "must have resources of its own inaccessible to the state."[118] American liberals have been committed to notions of "freedom," even if those opportunities are strongly facilitated by law and policy, as in the case of efforts to achieve racial justice in the country in the 1960s.[119]

Yet New York is also unique in its approach to policymaking. Its democratic process is more restricted than other states. Political scientist Vanessa Barker notes that New York's government actors have long relied on expertise in their criminal justice policymaking in the face of "depressed democratization," which exists because the state has a high centralization of power and low civic engagement. She argues that "because the state does not pursue democracy for its own sake, the state must show itself to be useful to maintain legitimacy . . . the state prides itself on its expertise and scientific engagement with social problems and is therefore less likely to pursue strictly punitive responses, considered crass and unscientific."[120]

We see evidence of this in juvenile justice policymaking: the opinions of experts about what is right for children have long predominated in juvenile justice policymaking. Evidence-based practices play a role in boosting the legitimacy of state policymakers who are actually seeking to change practices in favor of lightening the state's financial burden as opposed to fundamentally redistributing wealth and resources.

Although there was a period during the 1970s when the Juvenile Offender law was passed when the government moved toward a more punitive approach to a small class of young people, the interventions aimed at young offenders over the course of the state's history have been dominated by an ethos of liberal paternalism, which the sociologist Loic Wacquant describes as "liberal and permissive at the top, with regard to corporations and the upper class, and paternalist and authoritarian at the bottom, towards those who find themselves caught between the restructuring of employment and the ebbing of social protection or its conversion into an instrument of surveillance and discipline."[121]

New York's long-standing system of liberal-paternalist interventionism in children's lives has foundations in its early child-saving institutions. The uses of paternalism have been justified on the grounds of a person's ability to make rational choices. The philosopher Geoffrey Scarre argues that paternalism is guided by the notion that children do not have systems of purpose that adults have that justify their rights, and thus, "it does not infringe their rights to intervene in their behalf when their irrationality threatens their well-being."[122] Today, juvenile justice reform is guided by the notion that the state's poorest children need a tight hand to be guided into adulthood. Some scholars claim that the current punishment of young people has a neoliberal orientation, and thus a focus on responsibilization, the "adulteration" of penalties, and a preoccupation with risk.[123] However, New York's approach to youth justice has always been invested in child protection, moral support, guidance, and "care," which are strongly connected to liberal New Yorkers' interest in "saving" poor children.

There are some unintended consequences of this strain of liberal-paternalism. Some of the historic patterns of segregation and discriminatory approaches to the offending of young people of color continue to play a role in their disproportionate involvement in the system as well as their perceptions of the fairness of "the system." The ways that child saving was historically oriented toward deserving children in the state, and the emphasis of current reforms—with their elevation of "low-risk" young people as deserving of community-based interventions—illustrates the trends in policymaking.

What if those seemingly pressing questions—the tilt toward punishment or reform, large or small, community or institution—are irrelevant? What if the very questions themselves, or the binaries they represent, obscure a greater project of governing young people that needs to be fundamentally challenged? What if these persistent and pressing questions have actually promoted the perennial state of reform we are in?

CHAPTER 2

Ungovernability and Worth

MICHAEL WAS SIXTEEN WHEN I met him. He had never been arrested, but most of his friends had. Growing up in the Bronx as a black teenager in the late 2000s, Michael had faced the near-constant indignity of being stopped by the police for the color of his skin, his gender, and the color of the clothes he was wearing.[1] The adults in his life had identified him as "bad"—he had bounced around different schools, pushed in and out of different classrooms by teachers who didn't like him. His parents became frustrated and angry with him about school. Yet it seemed that many of Michael's problems at school were like those of other teenagers: he was a bit of a class clown, he swore in front of his teachers, and he was sometimes late to class. His teachers told him that he had an "attitude problem." They told him he was lazy and that he didn't listen. Yet Michael was bored, his schoolwork was unstimulating, and he spent a lot of time sleeping.

Michael's teachers continuously evaluated him. One of Michael's teachers was asked to rate a range of his behavior in a school-based risk assessment. Some of the indicators on the assessment included "Picks nose, skin or other parts of body," to "Apathetic or unmotivated," to "Talks too much," to "Whining." Michael scored poorly, for example, in the "Behaves irresponsibly," "Secretive, keeps things to self," and "Sleeps in class" categories.

Michael wasn't the only teenager deemed to be ungovernable and worthless. It was close to my first day on the job at the public defender's office when one of my teenaged clients described himself to me as "bad." Over the past ten years, I have heard teenagers in trouble with the law use this word over and over and over again: "I was a bad kid," "I was bad in school," "I was bad, real bad." It took some time before I fully understood the symbolism of these expressions of badness: these words weren't necessarily reflective of young people's actual behavior; they were the ways that they had been described by their parents, their teachers, juvenile facility staff and corrections officers, psychologists, social workers, and judges. These were other people's words, other people's condemnations.

These designations are calcified through the records and forms that are linked to young people, from the Individualized Education Programs required for Special Education students, to psychiatric assessments, to child welfare reports. The records inform decision-making during a criminal court case. Through the various records and assessments, many of these young people (and their parents) are characterized as being out of control. Other scholars have identified some of the ways in which these attributions of irresponsibility and dangerousness are associated more often with African American teenagers, through the public media, and by their disproportionate presence in custody, pointing to some of the racialized dimensions of these experiences.[2] These characterizations may impact on the development of young people's institutional identities, and their sense of self-efficacy and control.

Michael, like so many other teenagers I met, was suspended from school multiple times. In New York City, the school suspension process nets a substantial number of young people each year, pushing them into what some have called the "school to prison pipeline." The school system there has more police officers than the police forces of many U.S. cities' police departments, reflecting a national trend toward the incorporation of crime control practices into the educational environment.[3] Suspensions and "pushouts" have escalated since the passage of the federal education reform No Child Left Behind in 2001, a reform that linked school funding to school achievement and has forced many young people who do not meet educational standards to be suspended and pushed out to alternative schools.[4] It is possible that unmanageable teenagers are those who are actually ungovernable—as in not able to meet the criteria for being acceptable students within the government-defined ideas of acceptability—in the era of high-stakes testing.

Michael was a talented dancer when he was a teenager, well known on the streets for his skills. He is a tall, handsome young man and a stylish dresser. When I first met him, he said that he wanted to model and aspired to go to college. Like many teenagers, he balanced the demands of girls, friends, and family in a way that often dissatisfied the adults in his life—they thought he wasn't focused enough on his schoolwork and his future. Michael is a people-pleaser: he is friends with teenagers from different and sometimes opposing gangs and cliques in his neighborhood and with different generations of people. He knew many other people in his neighborhood, in part because his great aunt was a powerful presence there. Her apartment became a convening spot for Michael's many cousins and family members. Michael said that his great aunt was probably the only person who thought he "was going to be something and still does."

Yet Michael and many of his friends had no access to fulfilling jobs. They grew up in an era when transformations in the global economy that occurred in the 1960s had a significant impact on their lives. These changes resulted in a significant loss in the manufacturing jobs that in many cases had drawn their grandparents and relatives to live in New York from the American South,

Puerto Rico, and the Dominican Republic, among other places.[5] They lived in a world where they and their parents found it nearly impossible to find a job with a living wage, let alone a fulfilling one.[6] The primary jobs available to Michael were either low-paying positions at places like McDonald's, where some of his friends worked, or the city's Summer Youth Employment Program, a lottery-based system that provided minimum wage work over the summer. Kids like Michael turned to play as an alternative to employment. The scholar Robin D. G. Kelley argues that dance, art, sports, and music have offered many young people of color from cities like New York "more immediate opportunities for entrepreneurship and greater freedom from unfulfilling wage labor" in the context of this recently transforming global economy.[7]

It was no surprise that Michael couldn't find many places to hang out with his friends besides his great aunt's house. Youth programs in New York City faced severe funding cuts in the late 1990s under Mayor Rudolph Giuliani—between 1994 and 1997, the New York City Youth Bureau lost nearly half of its annual budget.[8] By the time Michael was a teenager, when Mayor Michael Bloomberg was in office, afterschool programs also faced significant cuts. After the federal education program No Child Left Behind was implemented, New York City schools, under pressure to bring children up to grade level in reading and math, cut arts, music, and other enrichment programs.[9] Thus, Michael and other young people had few opportunities to engage in programming in their schools or their neighborhoods that would enable them to cultivate their aspirations and skills.

Adult judgments about the worth and virtue of teenagers also influenced the choices that they made about the kinds of interventions they used with them. Teachers, school administrators, child welfare and foster care workers and other government agents had assessed the worth and virtue of many young people I met as "good" or "bad" teenagers before they even entered the juvenile justice system. One teenager, Marcus, said he had been described as having a "bad attitude" when he was in school and that he was placed on a unit for the "bad" kids when he was in detention. Other young people used the identical expression, "bad attitude," to describe their behavior in school. Some would more overtly speak about the way they had been misunderstood, like Khalil, who spoke about his early experiences in school in this way: "They said I was a real angry child—an aggressive child—cause I always wanted to fight." Khalil was psychiatrically hospitalized and placed into a school for children with mental health problems. He spoke about what he called the "anger management" classes he took there, where he was taught "how to count to ten, and stuff that I didn't need to know." He was later arrested and placed in a secure residential center. I did not see these assessments as straightforward examples of labeling theory in action—or the idea that a negative attribution or label can alter an individual's self-concept and potentially lead to deviant behavior.[10] Although the young people would use the words "bad" to describe themselves, when pressed, they knew these were other people's labels, not their own. Furthermore, these adult assessments of young people did not necessarily turn young people to crime. Instead, they created clearer pathways or conduits for young people's entry into the criminal justice system: they became the evidence on which claims about their worthiness for staying in or out of the system lay, particularly when a teenager ultimately had to face a judge.[11]

These assessments of worth also seemed to be particular to the generation of teenagers that I met—all born during the early and mid-1990s in New York into impoverished, mainly African American, Puerto Rican, and Dominican families, and primarily young men. They were born in New York City at the height of the War on Drugs and at the beginning of a policing and welfare revolution that would have deep and largely negative impacts on their lives and well-being—most importantly for their opportunity to access institutions that could foster their growth and development, not prevent them. In the early 1990s, New York City Mayor Rudolph Giuliani supported the New York City Police Department (NYPD) in implementing the "broken windows" policing strategy, which was aimed at arresting individuals for low-level misdemeanor offenses and addressing crimes that were seen to impact on the quality of life of New York City residents, such as graffiti on the subways and turnstile jumping.[12] This was a generation that would ultimately become criminalized in ways that were distinct from other periods in U.S. history; in this new era, their criminalization was linked to their ability to demonstrate deference and self-control as opposed to being explicitly linked to their identity as young people of color. It was arguably an expression of a new era of "colorblind racism" in that these demands for deference were not overtly racialized or identified as racialized projects to control children of color.[13] Instead, young people of color like Michael found that in their schools and everyday lives, they were asked to submit to regimes of control that demanded their "self-control" in language that was race-neutral. Governability for these young people arguably meant participation in the white behavioral status quo.

The 1990s also marked the beginning of an unprecedented crime drop in New York City, falling 72 percent from 1988 to 2008.[14] Yet the early lives of Michael and his peers were still marked by living in high crime and highly policed communities. Even though homicide rates dropped during the 1990s, some communities, including Harlem and the Bronx, continued to have consistently high gun-related homicide rates. Individuals in these communities also saw countless numbers of their fathers, brothers, sisters and mothers sent to prison: at a think tank convened by individuals incarcerated at Green Haven prison in upstate New York in the 1990s, the inmate researchers found that 75 percent of the people incarcerated in prison in New York came from just seven neighborhoods in New York City.[15] Michael and his friends all knew someone who had been sent "upstate," the term for prisons located outside of New York City. Michael's own father had spent time in jail.[16]

While their older cousins, siblings, parents, aunts, and uncles were being arrested at high rates during their very early childhoods, Michael and his friends lived at home with parents who faced a new and harsh reality: life-altering welfare reforms which resulted in significant cuts to cash benefits, and mandated that their parents actively seek work to obtain food stamps and other benefits. Although the federal welfare reforms of 1996 reduced the total number of people dependent on welfare, they had numerous untold consequences: for children whose parents weren't working or couldn't work, the welfare reforms forced them into deeper poverty. By the early 2000s, Michael's mother became homeless, and he went to live with his father. The families of young people like Michael also faced scrutiny by child welfare workers convinced that Michael and his friends were "crack babies," a now-discounted phenomenon, but a term used countless times by the teachers, foster care, and child welfare workers I met. The science discounting the existence of crack babies had clearly not found its way to the corridors of the welfare offices and the schools; teachers and workers were convinced that what they saw as sky-rocketing instances of hyperactivity among children were the results of drug use during pregnancy, not necessarily the effects of living in poverty, attending impoverished schools, being exposed to community-level violence, or even the inclination of school social workers and psychologists to overdiagnose children of color with such disorders.[17]

When Michael was sixteen, just as he had begun to hone his skills as a dancer and an athlete, a SWAT team shoved down his family's apartment door in the early hours of the morning, arresting Michael and his father and charging them with selling drugs. Michael spent the night in jail with his father but was released after the police realized they had arrested him by mistake. As a result of his father's arrest, the child welfare authorities got involved with the family, seeking to remove Michael's younger siblings. Just a few weeks later, Michael was stopped by police as he walking from his house to his great aunt's house. The police claimed that they saw him with a gun, but when they arrested him, they couldn't find one. Regardless, Michael was charged with gun possession.

Michael's sweet demeanor and personality, his athletic and creative talents, were never taken into account by the judge whom he had to face. From Michael's point of view, the judge saw him as a young black man from a predominantly black neighborhood, ultimately ungovernable, despite the fact that he was just sixteen years old and had never been arrested before. He said of his judge, "I think that he sees me as like a bad person or something." Michael was remanded to Rikers Island, an adult jail where teenagers can go as soon as they turn sixteen in New York.

When young people like Michael first enter the criminal justice system, they believe that their worth is a barometer that judges use in determining their eligibility for freedom. Others speculated that judges and prosecutors were jaded from seeing so many young people from the same neighborhoods, committing the same crimes. In many respects, these teenagers' experiences of being labeled as "bad" kids at an early age initiated their experiences of feeling stigmatized throughout the time of their involvement in the multiple and overlapping institutions of social control. Some young people spoke about how judges, probation officers, police, and other system agents assumed that they were incorrigible and bad. The teenagers felt that judges were particularly harsh toward those who fit into their expectations of criminality.

Michael saw the judge's perceptions of him as an indictment of his identity. Other young people were similarly influenced by their perception of what court actors thought of them, or at least their interpretation of their actions. They didn't need to have read the latest policy reports or newspaper articles illuminating the ways that racism exists in the criminal justice system, or detailing the high rates of incarceration among young black males, or exposing the school to prison pipeline—they lived these things. They also lived in a world where it cost as little as $50 to buy a gun on the street and where friends would ask friends—especially those without a criminal record, like Michael or a girlfriend—to hold onto the guns for them. Michael had a lot of friends who had guns, and he wasn't about to turn them in, despite pressure to do so from his prosecutor, because, as he told me, "snitches get stitches." Michael was also arrested shortly after the black American football player Plaxico Burress was sentenced to two years in prison after accidentally discharging a gun in a Manhattan nightclub; prosecutors and judges across New York saw Burress's sentence as an effective "message" to all individuals possessing a gun in New York: there would be no mercy at sentencing in gun cases.[18]

Time and time again, I spoke with young people whose experiences in schools, in mental health and child welfare institutions, and with the police and punitive authorities left them despairing for their chances of getting out of the system. The people they spoke about had the power to identify them as unworthy, and they had little power to control that characterization.

For Michael and other young men of color living in poverty in New York City and upstate urban communities like Poughkeepsie, Syracuse, and Troy, their gender and their race marked them as suspicious to the police and other state authorities—they inhabited the role of "criminalblackman."[19] Although not always accorded the same suspicion as their male counterparts, girls of color—especially those who engaged in violent offending—found themselves similarly pushed to the deep end of the system after they were arrested. The intersections of race, class, and gender in this group of young people's lives, and in the assessments of their worth by state actors, were profound. Legal scholar Kimberlé Crenshaw argues that we must always consider the ways that race, class, and gender identities intersect to create unique forms of oppression and privilege, and that we cannot untangle one category of identify from the other. Attributions of ungovernability and worthiness were in themselves linked to young people's race, gender, and class identities and shaped the ways that young people were responded to by state actors.

The white teenagers I met in the juvenile justice system were overwhelmingly from deeply impoverished and rural or suburban backgrounds. I met just five white teenagers inside of juvenile facilities during the course of my research. With one exception, all were from poor rural communities in upstate New York or the impoverished suburbs of Long Island, and all spent time in the child welfare and mental health systems before entering the juvenile justice system.[20] Few white teenagers enter custody, and when they do, they are often there because their custodial sentence is seen as a last resort by judges and other officials who have sent them to all other forms of placement—therapeutic foster homes, hospitals, and private residential treatment. Although the facility staff members were no less likely to describe the white youth as "bad," they more often saw white youth as troubled, rather than troublesome. Being troubled did not necessarily exempt the young person from being considered ungovernable or worthless, however.

The mental health unit at Hooper juvenile facility had disproportionately high numbers of white youth compared with the rest of the facility during the time I was there. One of those young people, who was from a rural town and whose parents were both incarcerated, had spent time in countless other mental health and juvenile facilities across the state. The staff at Hooper felt that he should not be there and that he should be at a facility designated for mentally ill or even developmentally disabled youth. But the state agencies responsible for those young people systematically rejected him: they said he had exhibited too much violence, too much impulsivity, and he had no family supports. It is arguable that his whiteness allowed him access to the privileges of such assessments, but his poverty and his "badness" made him unworthy of such help.

Girls have a complex relationship with such designations of worth. We know that in many respects poor women—and especially women of color—were the touchstone of the welfare reforms of the 1990s. They were both the enemy and the aim of such interventions.[21] Their children, the teenagers I interviewed, were born and raised into a world where their mothers were scrutinized and stigmatized by state agencies. During the 1990s, unprecedented numbers of children were removed from their drug-using mothers and placed into foster care, often with grandparents but sometimes with their father or even strangers. If the kids were older when a neglect charge was filed against their parents, they were placed into group homes. This was true for a number of the young people I met while doing the research and for countless numbers of my teenage clients. As the children of mothers who were seen as unworthy of assistance from the state, the young women grew up with complex ideas about what life should be like as young women in the world that was tied to their mothers' ability to parent them.

Genevieve was sixteen, Michael's age, when I met her. She was a serious, strong-minded, and commanding young woman. In a way, my interactions with her were highly marked by how she saw me—another white lady entering her life and asking her a lot of questions, like so many social workers and state officials before me. Yet in her responses, I learned a great deal about the frustrations of young people faced with an onslaught of individuals fascinated by their dysfunction.[22]

Genevieve's father went to prison when she was young; she vividly remembered the night that he was arrested, asking him, "Daddy, where are you going?" Her mother raised her and her two older siblings. She knew her father was incarcerated but didn't know where he was locked up. This was in part because of her dislocated childhood; she had gone in and out of foster homes, finally landing in a group home when she was fourteen. Like many young people, Genevieve was removed from her home after child welfare authorities were notified when she and her siblings stopped attending school regularly. This educational neglect accusation prompted further investigation into her family's life, and she and her siblings were taken away from their mom, separated, and placed into different homes.[23] Like many parents who have had their children taken away from them, Genevieve's mother was caught in a punishing trap—living in a homeless shelter for single women with no income, yet obligated to prove that she could find a home large enough for Genevieve and her two siblings. The only way her mother could get her children back was if she could find a job that paid enough for her to put a deposit down on an apartment large enough for her family and have adequate cash in the bank to pay the monthly rent. No shelter for families would accept her without her family.

Genevieve spent a lot of time in psychiatric hospitals. While she was at the group home, she was arrested for punching another girl in the face.[24] The judge in her case initially sent her to a psychiatric hospital to be assessed. She remembers being the only black person in the courthouse—her group home was located in a predominantly white community. After leaving the psychiatric hospital, she was sentenced to placement by her judge to Marshall, a girls' secure juvenile facility in upstate New York.

When I met her at Marshall, Genevieve was a self-described bad kid. She said "I'm a bitch" and "I'm stubborn." When I asked her how she came to think these things about herself, she, like so many others, said, "They tell me I'm stubborn and I'm a brat." The "they" encompassed all of the state officials and mental health treatment professionals she had encountered throughout her life. While at Marshall, Genevieve was put on an Egregious Behavior Protocol, a cognitive behavioral therapy intervention originally used in children's psychiatric hospitals, twelve times in a period of a few short months. Like many teenagers, Genevieve said that she "didn't care" about this in a way that signaled that she cared quite a bit.

These young people knew what it was like to be designated as unworthy of mercy before they even entered the criminal justice system. As the children of parents who had themselves been punished, either through incarceration or the child and social welfare system, they were intimately familiar with the dark pall the system cast over their lives. When they arrived at school, many of these young people were deemed too difficult to handle, too obstreperous or oppositional to their mainly white middle-class teachers, and engaged in too risky behavior in the street—or at least in enough incivilities to deem them intervenable by the state. Yet could it have been that it was the individuals making the accusations against them who shaped the boundaries of their worthiness of mercy and assistance? Or that the punishing conditions of life in the world where more money was spent to incarcerate their father than on a single year of public benefits and public education might actually shape their decisions to, in Michael's case, skip school, or in Genevieve's case, punch another girl in her foster care placement? What happened when they entered the criminal justice system itself?

Approaches to juvenile justice have evolved over time toward a greater acceptance that adolescents have diminished responsibility for criminal offending. Advocates have instead embraced developmental approaches, which seek to accept that offenders are still developing into adulthood. Many judges, advocates, and others will talk about treating children as children. However, the actions of these individuals, including teachers, police, judges, prosecutors, and system representatives sometimes convey assessments and condemnations of children's moral worth. They also still emphasize the accountability and responsibility of young people for their behaviors.[25] This is revealed in young people's use of the word "bad" to describe themselves and their feeling of condemnation by those actors; young people's words strongly convey the meanings that have been transmitted to them throughout their lives about their worth.

The actions of the adults in the juvenile justice system charged with designing and implementing interventions against young people often contradict their spoken philosophy of caring for children. It was these ironies that I pointed to when I described the ways that ostensibly liberal reforms often conceal the potential experiences of oppression that young people feel in a system aimed at their growth and development yet ultimately more concerned with care expressed as a form of control.

The actions of the adult system actors often demarcate the differences between themselves (virtuous individuals who possess the moral worth to treat, punish, and condemn youth who have violated the law) and the youth themselves—the bad kids (predominantly black and Latina/o teenagers) who are in need of interventions to facilitate their change. As such, many of the adults I observed projected a kind of moral indignation about the young people's actions, albeit in ways that were tempered by references to young people's youth and arguably inoculated those actors against critique.[26]

The actions by adult actors toward children in the juvenile justice and criminal justice system nationally and in New York involve assessments of children's risk of rearrest and reoffending through the use of actuarial tools that assess the riskiness of young people, their participation and progress in school, and their parents' employment and relative ability to care for them. Their assessments of young people's demeanor and behavior treat teenagers and their parents as deeply responsible for the routes that led them into the system.

Young people themselves can see and feel this. In fact, they've become quite accustomed to it from an early age, as children of parents on welfare who have been scrutinized by the child welfare, social security, and other poverty program authorities. Parents would sometimes say to me that the information they had to share in an intake assessment for their child in probation, an alternative to incarceration program, or residential treatment, was the same information they had shared at a welfare center or a foster care office. They would express a kind of resignation about needing to give up such personal, intimate information about themselves, yet through this they also taught me that the institutions of social welfare and punishment were often indistinguishable in their minds.

Under present-day welfare and poverty management regimes, individuals are assessed through their ability to exercise rational choices that are generally directed toward participation in the capitalist marketplace. Young people who are idle and who rob people instead of bag groceries, who play around in the hallways of school rather than sit silently in the classroom and raise their hands, or whose parents choose to sit at home and watch television rather than apply for a job at McDonald's can be deemed unworthy by those authorities. They are, as the sociologist Zygmunt Bauman puts it, "flawed consumers" who must ultimately face social exclusion for their failure to participate effectively in the capitalist marketplace.[27]

WORTH IN THE COURTS

In the initial stages of young people's involvement in the system, assessments about their worth are made by judges, who determine whether they will let them out into the community into a program or on probation. Michael wasn't so lucky at first; the judge in his case sent him directly to jail, without giving him a chance to stay out in the community and prove himself. When young people are adjudicated as juvenile delinquents, like Genevieve was, they are given risk assessments by probation officers; these risk assessments are used to guide a judge's decision making about whether to detain a young person. Teenagers are considered "high risk" if the offense they are charged of is relatively severe, if they have a prior offense history, if they have a history of going AWOL, and if they have poor school attendance.[28]

The apparatus of alternatives to detention and incarceration, which includes a network of community-based agencies, probation and parole offices, drug treatment programs, social workers, caseworkers, and advocates, is one legacy of the prison decarceration movement of the 1970s and 1980s which took place in New York and in other states across the country. As prisons, juvenile facilities, and mental hospitals closed and community-based alternatives to those institutions opened, some have argued that there may have in fact been a greater numbers of individuals who came under control of community-based agencies of social control, simply by virtue of living in communities where there was such a proliferation of control.[29] Most recently, local authorities, including probation agencies in New York, have begun to use new technologies, such as electronic monitoring of young people charged with crimes; these new technologies signal a new era of social control that raise considerable questions about the ubiquity of such forms of control in people's everyday lives.[30] These sites of control may also force more individuals into places where their worthiness for citizenship is assessed.

In New York City in particular, it is common for judges and other court actors to create highly structured service plans for young people charged with crimes, both pre- and postconviction or adjudication. In each case, there are a range of individuals who are involved in a case, including defense attorneys, prosecutors, alternative-to-incarceration program representatives, probation officers, and judges. These individuals are all involved in determining the supervisory arrangements for young people if they have been released from detention as well as their fate if they fail to do well in an alternative-to-incarceration program. The consequences they face in failing to meet a highly structured set of rules are serious, as illustrated in this New York judge's admonition to a young person charged as a Juvenile Offender in his courtroom:

> you are getting this break, but I promise you that if you slip up on this case, I guarantee you I will sentence you to the maximum that I can. And you're very young to be doing three and a third to ten years, but that's exactly what I'll do. So if you really learned your lesson, learning that lesson is going to include one hundred percent compliance with the terms of this agreement. You are not going to cut school. You are not going to be using any drugs. I am going to have you tested to see that you're drug free. There will be a curfew in place every day of the week. Your life is going to change quite a bit from this day forward so that you can walk

freely out this door. If you slip up, I am going to send you away for the maximum. Okay? If you don't slip up, you may get out of this without being a felon.[31]

The court governs a young person's process of putative self-determination by mandating programs of self-improvement. If a teenager exercises her potential for self-improvement, then she avoids the lengthy sentences that are at the judges' disposal. One judge who presided over the cases of a number of young people spoke about his desire to create a courtroom "where the atmosphere is such that the presiding judge would be able to recognize and respond to the salvageable youth."[32]

Young people are arguably uniquely salvageable or capable of worth because they are still malleable. The court interventions are particularly tailored for individuals who aren't yet adults, but in the process of becoming them in ways that are central to their role as social citizens.[33] For example, in New York, young people charged as adults who have mitigation in their offense are eligible to receive "Youthful Offender" treatment, which allows them to have a clean record after they have completed their sentences.

For those young people in New York who are given a chance to stay out of detention or to do an alternative-to-incarceration program, they participate in a number of different programs based in the community. In New York City, there are a relatively high number of nonprofit alternative-to-incarceration programs specifically oriented toward young people. In upstate communities, there are far fewer, particularly for young people charged as adults; there, probation is often the key agency providing services or contracting them out. A significant number of teenagers in New York are given an opportunity to participate in a community-based alternative-to-incarceration program, either while their case is pending (instead of waiting in detention) or as an alternative-to-incarceration: in 2006, for example, only 13 percent of juvenile delinquents statewide were sentenced to placement, and 32 percent received a sentence of probation.[34] For the teenagers charged as "Juvenile Offenders" in New York City in 2008, approximately half were remanded to custody after they were arraigned, and more than 60 percent were ultimately kept out of custody upon conviction.[35]

Slam, like Michael, grew up in a heavily policed and predominantly black neighborhood. Both of his parents spent time in and out of prison, and he was raised by his grandparents. Unlike Michael, who was relatively new to the criminal justice system, Slam had been arrested several times and had been in and out of detention. When I asked him about his experience with the police, he said that police assume "most black people [like him] do bad things." Slam's words reveal his recognition of the salience of the "criminalblackman" status that he inhabited in the minds of the police. After being arrested as an adult at age fifteen for possessing a gun, Slam spent some time in detention, and then a judge gave him a chance to participate in a program. Slam was obligated to attend the program in person at least a few times a week, receive regular drug tests, get counseling and treatment, and have curfew monitoring. Workers from the alternative programs report on a young person's progress at their court dates. If young people fail to meet these requirements in the pre-pleading period or during probation, they will face a period of detention, they will have their probation revoked and could be sentenced to custody or placed in a residential drug treatment program.

The workers at Slam's program frequently found him to be "noncompli-ant": he failed to go to school and meet his curfew. After repeated mistakes in the program, he was ultimately sentenced to time in residential custody. A psychiatrist evaluated him for court after he had failed in the program and noted that he should develop "measures to address his noncompliant behavior, some impulsivity, poor judgment, and his poor ability to cope with stressors." The only evidence of his "noncompliance" provided was his problem with school attendance and meeting his curfew. This report, along with Slam's fail-ures in his program, were used as the basis for the judge's decision to send him to placement. His personal limitations and failings in the program, and in the mind of the psychiatrist, are perhaps seen as indicative of his capacity for self-control, compliance, and deference to authority.

After violating his probation, Slam was sentenced to placement in a small juvenile facility in rural upstate New York, in the middle of predominately white hunting, fishing, and farming country. The facility, where there were a number of layoffs during the time I spent there, offered some of the best jobs in the area. A number of local residents had staked their claims on the hope that hydrofracking might expand to the region, part of the Marcellus Shale, but so far none of their hopes had come true as Governor Cuomo held off on allowing fracking to occur. Life at the facility was tense as staff members wor-ried about job loss and security. The residents complained to me that the staff members took out their anger on them, often in a racialized way. They felt that staff targeted black and Latino kids for harsher punishment than the white kids and were stricter with them about small behavioral rules, like keeping their shirts tucked into their pants.

Before going there, Slam was evaluated by a probation officer, who noted that "the probationer felt there was nothing more to say on behalf of himself because he felt the Judge has already made up her mind to put him in place-ment." Not only was Slam deemed to be unworthy of a second chance, he had accepted his designation and punishment in a defeatist way.

The other young people I met in custody spoke about their experiences of being deemed unworthy for any kind of mercy—even if just an expres-sion of humanity or recognition by their judges and lawyers—after making their own worst mistake. I regularly met with a small group of young men at Hooper secure residential center, a facility reserved for teenagers charged with serious and violent felonies under New York's Juvenile Offender law, which allowed them to receive adult convictions and adult time. That group was made up entirely of black and Latino teenagers. They were all born during the 1990s and were just a little older than Michael, Genevieve, and Slam.

Tony, a bookish, self-contained young man who often kept to himself and who had aspirations to go to college and become a lawyer, had been sentenced to fifteen years to life for a homicide. He said that he knew that a judge might simply look at which neighborhood he came from and his race (black), and make a simple assessment about his worthiness for mercy; he knew that by receiving the maximum possible sentence he could have received that mercy was not extended to him. It wasn't until years later when I learned the charges against him—he had killed a member of his family—that his comments came into relief. This was a young man who, although he committed a heinous act, knew that he was only seen as a cold and calculating sociopath, not as an individual whose act may in fact be suggestive of a complex life history that may deserve further and deeper consideration and investigation. The tabloid newspaper accounts of his case corroborated this characterization.

Smitty, another young black man in the group at Hooper, came from an impoverished upstate rust-belt town. He said he thought that all a judge did was look at his rap sheet, the reputation of his neighborhood, and his race, then made a simple and negative determination about his fate. The young men reasoned that the judges in their cases might have become jaded because they saw so many young black men appear before them, in case after case, from the same neighborhoods.[36]

COMMUNITY-BASED ASSESSMENTS OF WORTH

Almost all of the young people I interviewed were charged as adults. In New York City, the vast majority of younger teenagers charged as Juvenile Offenders—80 percent in 2008—were charged with robbery. Close to 80 percent of sixteen- and seventeen-year-olds in New York are arrested and charged with robbery.[37] Assessments of a young person's worthiness for treatment and help, as opposed to punishment, were vexed—these were young people charged with serious crimes, but there was also a recognition that many of the robberies they engaged in were done in groups, with other teenagers, and thus may be indicative of the kinds of risky, peer-driven behavior in which many teenagers engage.

Billy had this experience of being analyzed and assessed for his worthiness and salvageability after he was charged with committing a robbery. After he was arrested, the judge sent him to detention for some time, but eventually released him so he could participate in an alternative-to-incarceration program. He described this as a time while the judge "like wait and observe and see like my behavior," and that "basically he [the judge] put the ball in my hand trying to see if I could hold it and not give it back." The judges, alternative-to-incarceration program workers, and probation officers envisioned a young person who would be buffered from the allure of a deviant lifestyle by the intense array of supervisory tactics that were created for them. The court actors sought to help young people become more responsible by requiring them to call in for curfew, attend school, and pass drug tests. The implicit understanding of these adults seemed to be that the more services a young person was engaged in, and thus the more points of contact and surveillance by the system, the more likely they were to stay out of trouble. Yet the expectations set by the adult actors and the various contact points that these actors laid out for these teenagers were actually out of step with how they could achieve the expectations.

Malcolm, also sixteen years old, was released from court and allowed to participate in a community-based program after he was arrested for a robbery. After Malcolm failed to go to school, call in for curfew, or engage in services at his alternative-to-incarceration program, his caseworker reported that Malcolm was making the "wrong choices" and that he needed to be reminded by the judge of the "consequences he is facing if he continues to make wrong choices." In response to repeated frustrations voiced by the court advocate and by Malcolm's guardian about Malcolm's behavior, the judge sent him to jail to try to "wake him up." The reform process that is envisioned here is one in which Malcolm's full participation in services is the only possible way to measure his change and in which the deprivation that jail time inflicts is seen as a kind of antidote to his resistance to change. The expression used in the courts for this term of temporary detention is "therapeutic tune-up," although the law requires judges to have a legal reason for incarcerating someone.

One way that the differences in worth between young people and adults was arguably symbolized was through the adults' assiduous record-keeping about young people's behaviors. Staff in alternative-to-incarceration programs monitored young people's school attendance, the times they arrived and left school, when they were at home, their alcohol and drug consumption (through frequent drug testing), their friendships and associations, and their participation in mental health and doctor's appointments.[38] Prosecutors and police were known to monitor the Facebook and Twitter pages of young people they deemed to be suspicious, and a New York City Police Department unit called the Juvenile Robbery Intervention Program started checking in on young people who had open robbery cases, including going to their schools to find out if they were attending them.

The interventions used with young people charged with crimes assume that change occurs in these young people's lives as a result of the interventions.

Yet it remains an empirical question as to whether "change" occurs at all. In her book about juvenile drug courts, sociologist Leslie Paik has argued that notions of "accountability" used in these courts do not necessarily translate into a reduction in drug use but more often fit in with drug court staff members' notions of "responsible" citizenship.[39]

Ironically, Slam's repeated failures to participate in school and follow the rules of the judge, not his reoffending, pushed the judge to sentence him to time in a juvenile facility in upstate New York. The psychiatrist who evaluated Slam noted that ". . . it appears that to some degree, the respondent's most problematic recent behavior is related to school attendance and open disregard of the Court's directives." The judge felt that Slam was unworthy of a continuing chance to stay at home because he couldn't exercise the requisite self-control and responsibility set by the court.

When young people couldn't successfully demonstrate their ability to participate in community-based programs and parole—when they engaged in both the "bad" or unworthy behavior that would mark them as unsuccessful program participants—judges would sentence them to time inside of juvenile facilities or prisons. It was there that their badness transformed in a way that would have serious consequences for their sense of self-worth and ultimately their chance to be recognized as citizens on the outside of custody.

INSIDE JAIL AND RESIDENTIAL FACILITIES

Michael spent several months on Rikers Island, including in solitary confinement, before his family bailed him out. Teenage boys are sent to a facility on Rikers called the Robert N. Davoren Center (RNDC); girls are sent to a facility known informally as Rosie's, or formally as the Rose M. Singer Center. You didn't have to travel far in New York City to hear about the reputation of RNDC. It was notorious for its violence, both inmate-on-inmate and guard-on-inmate. In late 2009, the rate of serious injuries against young people was four times higher than any of the adult facilities on Rikers.[40]

On nearly every visit I made to see my young male clients at Rikers Island, they cried as they talked about their desire to be released; sometimes I asked them if they wanted to be placed in protective custody (PC), but PC offered no respite from the horrific conditions of confinement in an outdated jail that was never warm or cool enough and whose staff relied on a famous "program" that involved deputizing teenage inmates to manage their peers.[41] The practice of deputization of young people by staff was practiced openly in the institutions, and seen as partially essential for the maintenance of order, as young people far outnumber staff.[42] In October 2008, an eighteen-year-old, Christopher Robinson, was beaten to death by guards on the island. Almost everyone who had a family member or friend at Rikers knew about Christopher Robinson. Less than a year after Robinson's death, Michael was remanded to the island by his judge. Michael described his emotions after he entered the facility:

A: When you were in jail, did you feel unsafe?

M: Yeah.

A: Did you feel like those parts of yourself that you just talked about, do you feel like you had to hide some of them?

M: I had to change my whole mentality.

A: What did you become?

M: I had to be the way the judge looks at me. Inside there.[43]

Expressions of "badness" in custody may be one means of securing respect among their peers and protecting their self-esteem, as suggested in the work of other scholars who have studied these forms of badness among impoverished young men.[44] However, Michael's self-awareness about his performance of badness also suggests his attempts to manage his fear and anxiety about his personal safety and his loss of control upon entering custody may not be a straightforward expression of his culture but rather an example of his adjustment to the structural conditions that are created by warehousing thousands of young people deemed unworthy of social uplift and support. He had to become bad because that was the expectation by both the guards and the other inmates.

Michael found that being bad in custody enabled him to survive inside custody but also, in some ways, to fulfill the role of badness that had been established for him and his peers on Rikers Island. Many of the teenagers at RNDC were fulfilling the expectations of those who oppressed them, even if they did not do it consciously. At a meeting I attended for advocates to speak to corrections officials about conditions of confinement, Martin Horn, the now-former commissioner of the New York City jails, spoke about what he described as the adolescent culture of brutality and gang violence. His consistent message throughout his tenure, in response to data that suggested that there were higher rates of assault in the teenage jails, was that teenagers were inherently worse than adults and that "disputes among adolescents develop and escalate more rapidly than among adults."[45] Among the solutions he proposed included the addition of more surveillance cameras and higher levels of staff as well as the ability to do lockdowns. He also recognized publicly that idleness contributed to conflict and proposed adding more cultural and educational programming to the jails. In the process, the commissioner repeated an oft-cited idea about teenagers: that they are greater risk-takers, more hotheaded, and quicker to anger than adults.

Yet in the meeting I attended and in a number of other contexts, Commissioner Horn tended to absolve adults of any responsibility for the forms of violence that occur behind bars as a result of the conditions of confinement, including the staff practices of violence and containment. He also failed to acknowledge the fact that 90 percent of inmates at Rikers Island were black and Latina/o, and that they were controlled by corrections officers who were overwhelmingly black and Latina/o themselves.[46] Implicit in his discussion about "bad kids," then, was an acknowledgment by him and his audience members alike that these were "other people's children." Although the white commissioner never made it explicit, everyone he spoke to in the largely white policy audiences knew that he was talking about the need to control black and Latina/o teenagers, and he was asking his largely black and Latina/o staff to do it.

Michael had some protection while he was in Rikers because he had a family member who worked there who was watching out for him.[47] But it didn't make the experience any less scary for him. He described what he saw as the "big bad wolf act" that young people engaged in:

A: What did people do to put on the big bad wolf act, like what ways do they act?

M: They try to take what you have, like take your phone calls, take your stuff, fight you for it, lots of things.

A: Like predators kind of?

M: Yeah.

A: Did you feel like that was mandatory for survival there?

M: Mmhmm [indicating yes].

A: What happens to the guys who don't participate in that?

M: They just get picked on, all they stuff tooken, and get bullied.

Like many young people in detention at Rikers Island, Michael never received a visit from his lawyer, nor did he learn when his case would be resolved. He did not even know when he was going to be bailed out by his family, who promised him they would:

M: I was just like, I was thinking like, my life is over, so, I might as well just get my GED [General Equivalency Diploma], and I was just honestly like when I was in there I was thinking like I'll probably get out of here in the next three and a half years, life is over for me, me, I'll probably be like twenty-two, twenty-one so I'm just might as well just be a BA.[48]

A: What's a BA?

M: Bad ass.

A: . . . yeah.

M: I couldn't think of nothing I could do, like to get myself out of the situation, to keep going, so. I didn't finish high school or nothing.

A: Yeah, I can understand that. It's like, what else can you do?

M: I'd gave up.

Michael links his decision to become a "bad ass" to his loss of hope. His decision is thus a choice to both "give up," take the plea offered to him in his case (of three and a half years in state prison) and also an assumption of a new self-representation, one that is marked for survival. He acknowledges that this identification with badness is a performance; however; becoming a "bad ass" is a choice to become a jail archetype. Michael expressed resignation about the status that he saw as so linked up with incarceration—one that was the antithesis of what he saw he might become on the outside, a college-educated, artistic, and athletic young man. A mutually reinforcing process of fear and predation occurred in the institutions where eliminating one's fears was seen to be accomplished by inspiring fear in others. Unworthiness thus correlates with a transformation in one's self-identification that can have powerful and violent consequences.

Like Michael, other young people performed badness in confinement. They connected these performances to the maintenance of their safety, to the preservation of respect, and to the acquisition of privileges and relief from some of the pains of confinement. The words used by young people to describe these performances—"masquerading" and "fronting"—suggest the self-awareness that is involved in these performances. Described by young people as "being bad," these performances were most frequently enacted by young men and were forms of self-representation that were respected (or at least feared) by peers. In many respects, these young men were displaying what has been called a form of hegemonic masculinity—dominance, power, and control over others through strength, the defense of respect, and one's hardness.[49] What I found was that these young men engaged in forms of "being bad" that were both resistant to and arguably in line with the expectations of institutional staff and the individuals like Commissioner Martin Horn who ruled over those staff. "Being bad" was thus a response to being designated as bad and ungovernable; it was a symptom rather than a cause of the violence the young people experienced.[50] It was an embodied response to being identified as bad.

A number of the teenagers I met whom police and other court actors considered to be aficionados of the jail life were in fact a great deal more cynical about the hardening potential of jail than they were assumed to be. At each court appearance, the prosecutor in Billy's case would routinely allude to Billy's involvement in gang culture and his "hoodlum"-like behavior to continue to plead for his incarceration over his release to a community-based program. The prosecutor invoked stereotypes about gangs and gang life, their hardness and capacity for violence, as well as their "out-of-control" natures, in part to justify the continued need for Billy's containment and incarceration.

Yet Billy was of course a far more complex human being than the prosecutor made him out to be; although Billy was indeed engaged in the street life, his feelings about that life were deeply ambivalent. He wanted to leave the street life, and occasionally, he did. He wanted to be in a school that challenged him and valued his intelligence, but his special education classification of "Emotionally Disturbed" forced him to be rejected from three separate schools over the course of six months. While he was in detention, Billy describes it as a place that "you don't want to be." He said, "It's a horrible place. It somewhere where you don't want to be. You don't have no say so. Somebody control, like you control yourself, like, you got other people telling you what to do so basically you're being controlled by somebody higher when people, the COs [corrections officers] in the facility. You sleeping there, somebody go into your cell, you gotta wait to get fed, like fed when it's time to get fed, you gotta ask to use the bathroom." Billy was concerned about his ability to exercise self-control and to express a form of self-actualization. He spoke about how "it basically make you feel like you're a caged animal. There's no lesson to be learned from being there. It's just, the only lesson, it is a lesson—just don't come back." Michael also felt that "jail is for animals, like wild animals, like tigers or something." Yet when Billy eventually left jail, he continued to struggle; he was under no illusion that the horrific experiences inside would actually deter him from being sucked into the life of the streets again.

Contrary to some assumptions that time in jail is a "rite of passage" or source of pride for some young men from impoverished urban communities, and thus a place they may "want" to go, it was for many of these young people a time when their sense of humanity, dignity, and self-control was challenged—a place where they absolutely did not want to go.[51] The teenagers were fearful as they faced a loss of control over their autonomy and safety. Like Billy explained, jail is rife with degradations.[52] It was a deeply alienating place for young people.

Some teenagers charged as adults got to escape the fate of Rikers Island and its brutality. They were instead sent to one of the many juvenile detention and residential juvenile facilities that exist across New York State. At the time I did my research, there were about twenty state facilities and quite a few privately operated, publicly contracted residential facilities located across the state. The latter included some pastoral, open campuses that looked much like private boarding schools; they didn't have barbed wire fences or any of the typical trappings of criminal justice institutions. They often had young people who were sent there from both the juvenile justice system and the child welfare system. The juvenile facilities, on the other hand, were generally surrounded by barbed wire fences, the staff wore uniforms and had keys and walkie-talkies, and the young people were confined to locked units. These facilities ranged from the secure centers—where teenagers charged as adults went until their twenty-first birthday—to limited and nonsecure facilities, locked facilities that were for teenagers adjudicated as delinquents.

Tory got lucky. Even though he had an adult court case, his judge allowed him to be sentenced to custody through his delinquency case, sending him to a privately operated facility in Westchester County. The sprawling campus had well-groomed athletic fields, small residential cottages, and large brick buildings that held the school and staff offices. In theory, this was a better placement than a secure facility because Tory would have the opportunity to do home visits, which he couldn't do while in "secure," and the facility at least felt and looked a little less sinister than a secure juvenile facility.

For the most part, young people's discussions about being bad in jail and prison contrasted with those about their experiences in residential centers. Billy's mother in fact spoke about how she would prefer her other son Marcus, who had spent time in a residential facility, to go back there rather than spend his time at Rikers when he was arrested shortly after his release from the facility. Although the residential facilities were not devoid of violence—in fact, there had been several high-profile incidents involving fights between residents and staff assaults—they tended to be environments marked more deeply by boredom and fatigue than the chaotic environments young people described at Rikers and in detention. Nonetheless, these were environments where "being bad" and assessments of worth continued to be salient.

Assessment and record keeping also defined the day in the residential facilities, and became yet another way for adults to judge the worthiness of the young people under their care. Staff members kept copious log books of young people's movements in and out of their units, their participation in groups and school, and in particular any behavior that was considered to be manipulative, deviant, or otherwise "bad." Bad behavior was marked through further record keeping—the deployment of "levels" that were essentially bad behavior slips. Staff would also engage in a weekly meeting with young people to give them a "Resident Behavior Assessment."

Some young people spoke about the ways that being "bad," defiant, or resistant in residential facilities helped them achieve recognition from staff and other young people within institutions. Being "bad" helped them to maintain a reputation among their peers and staff, allowing them more attention and resources. Tory described this as "juice," or a kind of power:

T: . . . in [name of detention center] and all these other secure facilities, you gotta be bad to get what you want.

A: Really?

T: Be bad, staff will go to look at you and they'll like, if you bad staff will always be nice to you . . . you always gotta most likely be talking with every staff. If everybody know you for being bad—like here they got a crisis center. If you always bad you just go to crisis every day. Once you start being good, crisis won't know you because you used to come there so they just going to be nice to you, buy you soda, give you privileges with them. If you was never bad, you just quiet, not a lot of people will recognize, not a lot of staff will recognize you, acknowledge you and you can't really get what you want.

The crisis center, which was a kind of seclusion area, was also, paradoxically, a place for young people to get attention.

A: So it's kind of about getting your name out there—being heard, being seen?
T: Like with the staff they call you, up here, they say it's "juice." If you have juice with staff. So if I like, if I can ask the staff, tonight on the phone, get on the cell phone, and the staff say yeah, but you haven't lot of juice with that staff.
A: Oh, I got that.
T: . . . the staff isn't going to, if you just always sitting there and quiet watching TV you don't pay nobody no fine, staff don't look at that, they look at you why else, they try to calm you down.
A: I got that. So juice is kind of like a certain kind of power?
T: Yeah, but you can only have it with staff, like.
A: You can have it with other residents?
T: No, residents, you just gotta have respect for them.

For some young people, being acknowledged satisfied a critical need to be "seen" or heard. This quest for acknowledgment and recognition relates to that described by criminologist Monica Barry, who argues that young people may often "act out" to accumulate some symbolic power.[53] However, this negative form of attention speaks to the difficulty young people might face in being acknowledged by institutional staff, and thus the need to "be bad" to achieve that recognition, which may ultimately perpetuate their enmeshment in the system.[54] Bad behavior by residents would provoke staff to write furiously in their logbooks, whip out "level" or disciplinary slips, and prepare themselves for a physical restraint.

Bell was also identified as ungovernable by staff in the residential facility where she was incarcerated. Accused of a violent felony that landed her in adult criminal court, Bell was sentenced to time as a Juvenile Offender at Marshall girls' facility. When I met her, Bell was seventeen years old. Her presence in a room was undeniable—even though she was only five and a half feet tall, she felt like the tallest girl in the room and she had a palpable physicality, moving around a lot, sometimes sitting close to the other girls, sometimes moving closer to me. She would sing and dance and sometimes pout—everyone always knew when she was in the room. When she was just four years old, she was "taken away" from her mother after she tried to jump off the fire escape of her building. She did this after she was sexually abused by someone in her mother's home. After that, she was placed in foster care. She was subsequently molested in one of her foster homes and said she continued to be molested, including by staff at a juvenile detention facility, throughout her childhood and early adolescence. When she was fourteen years old, Bell ran away from her foster home and became a sex worker. She continued prostituting for several years until she was incarcerated after getting into a fight with her boyfriend.

Bell was placed on the "secure" unit, reserved for girls convicted as adults. This was a small unit—typically there are only a handful of girls in the state convicted and sentenced to time in custody as adults each year. In 2008, there were just twelve girls admitted to secure custody.[55] The rest of the facility had units filled with girls adjudicated as juvenile delinquents (called the "limited secure" side) and the revocators' unit. Bell and her cohort on the secure side wore maroon sweat suits to distinguish themselves from the girls on the "limited secure" side, who wore blue sweat suits. Otherwise, their experiences in custody were relatively similar—the facility was surrounded by a high, barbed-wire fence, the girls' movements were tightly controlled, and they each had individual rooms on their units that staff members could lock at any time.

When Bell first arrived at Marshall, she was given her uniform and a pair of shoes with white shoelaces. These shoelaces symbolized the behavioral stage that she would be on—called "Orientation."[56] To advance to the next stage, Bell would need to follow a set of rules and requirements laid out for her within a facility rulebook given to her on the first day. After arriving at the facility, Bell was assigned to a facility line staff member who was considered her "mentor." In her case, she was assigned to a middle-aged white man. Bell pointed to the irony of the racial and cultural differences between herself and her "mentor"; she said that they inhabited "different worlds."

After arriving in the facility, Bell was required to become familiar with the basic rules there. The basic rules required deference to staff authority, compliance with rules and procedures, "work[ing] out problems" through treatment programs, exercising "self-respect" and respect for others, honesty, cleanliness, and being quiet.[57] If a young person violated a major rule in the facility, such as possessing contraband or assaulting another resident or staff member, they would have to appear before a disciplinary committee where they could participate in an administrative hearing where they were provided with a legal representative. The hearings themselves looked and felt a lot like a school suspension hearing. During my time in the facility, some people, including Bell, were even arrested.[58] If they committed a facility-based infraction, young people like Bell who had received an adult-level sentence can lose the opportunity to leave after two-thirds of their sentence has been completed, the minimum amount of time they serve out of their sentence in New York.

Bell struggled to conform to the behavioral rules. She was constantly in trouble in the residential facility, often fighting with residents and staff, both verbally and physically. While she was in the facility, she was placed on "Egregious Behavior Protocol." Under this protocol, a young person is required to write and reflect on the "chains" and "links" that lead to their "egregious behavior," and then apologize to the other members of their residential unit. The process is meant to be aimed at "repairing harm."[59]

One can almost think of two Bells: one of them is the fantasy of a Bell changed by system interventions that is harbored by adults in the system and codified in the system's manuals and behavioral treatment guides. This Bell (I'll call her "Compliant Bell") is someone who receives an intervention, say an Egregious Behavior Protocol, and responds to that intervention by immediately taking responsibility for her deviant actions, apologizing to her peers and staff members, and internalizing that sense of responsibility such that at the next opportunity she has for violating the facility rules. She thinks twice about engaging in her actions because she has recognized that there are negative consequences for them—not only could she lose the ability to get out when her sentence ends and lose privileges, she could also receive the condemnation of her peers. The other Bell (I'll call her "Noncompliant Bell") is the human being behind the fantasy. She was the Bell who, despite multiple inducements from staff to comply with facility rules, continued to violate them. After numerous episodes of defiance of staff rules, Bell was ultimately arrested for assaulting a staff member in the facility, and she was sent to a local jail. Because Bell was older than sixteen when she was arrested in the facility, she would no longer be eligible to stay in a juvenile detention facility; she was sent to the local county jail.

Bell linked some of her physicality and defiant behavior in the facility to her despair, frustration, and voicelessness there. She said that "kids are fragile" and that a lot of staff in the facility could not recognize this. She said even at the age of four, "I was so angry." Referring to the abuse she suffered as a child, she said, "I spent all my life grieving it." Her defiance of the facility rules was neither rational (a "choice") nor fully conditioned by her past and her environment; instead, her resistance to the rules was a more complex, integrated, and embodied psychosocial response. This was a response to both the negative evaluations of her worth (as a young and black female former sex worker with no known family who had violated the law by engaging in violence) and her marginalized status both in the facility and the outside world. Bell knew that as a black teenager who violated the rules in a facility with a number of white staff and teachers, she also posed an existential threat to those individuals: she was their racist nightmare of an angry black girl who needed to be kept under control, yet she continued to defy the rules despite those perceptions.[60] Bell's despair contributed to her frustration, and she "acted out" in defiance of facility rules. She ultimately related her behavior in the facility to the expression of this anger and grief.

For many staff members at Marshall, Bell was one of the more intransigent and difficult young people in the facility. She was what mainstream psychologists might describe as prototypically "oppositional"; she had also been charged with a violent felony, which was an external brand of deviance and difficulty, particularly as a young black woman.[61] According to the residential facility staff I talked to, Bell made no "progress" in treatment. She was one of a number of young people who talked about "faking" her way through the program requirements. The distinctions between Bell's identity as a defiant young woman in the public stage of the program and a reflective and analytical person in the back stages shows some of the ways in which the demands of the facility for her to conform to a particular kind of "institutional self" created frustrations and tensions for her.[62]

Girls in the justice system are often considered to be more "difficult" to work with than young men.[63] The director of the girls facility, who described the young women in her facility as "my girls," also said that "they are a very very tough bunch," and that they are "really damaged kids" who engage in a huge amount of physical aggression. Bell was emblematic of this kind of "difficult" girl, as were many others in the facility. This notion of girls as difficult and damaged constructs them as uniquely out of control: unlike their male counterparts, their behavior is perhaps seen as less reflective of their "criminal" behavior (their "badness") and more reflective of their vulnerabilities, their personal weaknesses, and their ostensibly inherent inability to exercise self-discipline and appropriate femininity.

Other efforts by young people to get "juice" with staff and other residents involved using surveillance cameras. When some teenagers arrived at the residential facilities, they "wiled" or acted out in front of the video cameras. They did this not only because they knew that staff members would review the footage of the cameras and make assumptions about their character, but also because they knew that staff would discuss their misbehavior in front of other young people. Thus, "acting out" in front of a video camera became a means of establishing a reputation for toughness in front of one's peers and attention from staff members.

The sociologist Jack Katz suggests that being by being bad, individuals are capable of "manifest[ing] the transcendent superiority of their being" and demonstrating the "dominance of their will."[64] Arguably, for the young people in the residential facilities the performance of "being bad" is paradoxical: it demonstrates dominance but also vulnerability and anxiety. Thus, it is indeed a kind of demonstration of will, but a kind of will that is highly circumscribed; in a future chapter, I discuss the ways that adults in the system spelled out the proper exercise of the will for young people.

Part of the vulnerability and anxiety that young people experienced arguably grew out of their acceptance that the facilities themselves would do nothing to improve their chances at getting a job or building a better life for themselves once they got out. The teenagers were also under no illusion that the people in charge of them would see them as any more worthy of assistance once they got out. They knew that many of the staff in the facilities simply saw them as "criminals." One staff member described to me how he saw a clear difference between "criminals" and "adolescents," suggesting that many of the young people under his care were just "criminals" who engaged in acts so heinous as to be irredeemable, as opposed to an "adolescent," who just engages in dumb behavior that may ultimately diminish over time. His words echo those of system administrators, who characterized the differences between youth as "sociological" and "psychological," often in ways that reflected racialized assumptions about who was deserving of individualized care and intervention and who was in need of an approach focused on socialization to middle-class white norms of behavior.

The implicit (and sometimes explicit) assumption among some of the young people was that every intervention in their lives, however benevolently framed, ultimately leads to confinement. They knew, in other words, that they lacked worth in the eyes of the authorities they so often encountered. In 2009, African American and Latina/o people in New York City were stopped and frisked nine times more often than white people.[65] "Getting hassled" by the police on an everyday basis, particularly in the context of the rise of more aggressive policing strategies, inevitably impacts on the "collective consciousness" of those individuals, and in particular, people of color, who face the most scrutiny by the police and the system.[66] By the time they ended up in residential care, teenagers felt a sense of resignation about how the system saw them—as deserving of confinement.

GOVERNING THE UNGOVERNABLE

Before Michael even entered the criminal justice system, he was scrutinized and assessed at every level, and a determination had been made by adults that he was a bad kid. The same was true for many young people—they'd bounced around from school to school, from foster home to group home, to hospitals and mental health facilities—they were intimately familiar with "being bad" by the time they made it into the system marked most explicitly by its association with "badness"—the courts. These assessments of a young person's worth that were made by individuals working for state and local government agencies were arguably guided by racialized assumptions about how riskiness and badness can be expressed. It could be argued further that these assumptions were also colonial in nature, in the sense that they were expressive of a desire to make governable the ungovernable; the poor, largely youth of color who had been deemed to pose a threat to perceptions of order and stability. Identifying these young men and women as ungovernable but also unworthy of mercy, of treatment, and in need of punitive forms of detention and placement upheld the continuing reliance on incarceration as a form of social control of the poor.

Badness is a lack of deference. It is about resisting the boundaries of appropriate comportment. When a young person violated the law, their badness was fully realized. Many of the young people I met did indeed engage in acts of harm and violence—as the largest percentage of the young people I interviewed were teenagers accused as adults, they had been engaged in robberies involving guns, attempted murder, murder, and crimes involving sexual violence. Thus, in many respects they were "bad." Yet I would like to suggest that their experience in the criminal justice system itself played a role in actually perpetuating and enhancing their construction as individuals unworthy of state support, mercy, or social uplift. By engaging in serious offending, or even more minor acts, such as the assault that Genevieve committed, young people resisted the boundaries set by the constraints of surveillance and policing. They became the individuals for whom "being wild" or a badass is seen to be one's fate, part of one's inherent character or a "risk factor," as opposed to actually having been partially caused by the experience of colonialism and domination.

Michael's family ultimately bailed him out from Rikers Island. His judge accepted a plea offer that would allow him to earn Youthful Offender treatment—no conviction on his record—if he successfully completed a term of probation. A police officer that Michael's family knew came to court to advocate for him, and his lawyer enlisted me to write a presentencing report about him to ask for his release. After he was bailed out, he made improvements at school and made it onto a basketball team. He got the sense that there might be a greater chance of receiving probation. He also felt more confident and happier about his life more generally, and thus he felt optimistic as he reconnected with friends, found some adult mentors, and gained some confidence.

Michael's ability to enter college was shaped in part by his opportunity to stay out of prison and by his access to some—albeit limited—networks and opportunities provided by the adults in his life. Had he gone to prison, Michael would not have been able to finish high school at home or been given access to the resources and knowledge about college provided by a high school guidance counselor. He also would not have been able to continue to dance and perform in the way that he enjoyed.

After Michael was released from jail, he continued to stay connected to me, his lawyer, and other adults in his family. He's now working on producing his own music album.

So was Michael ultimately found to be worthy? Perhaps yes, but in many respects, his self-representation and his life outcomes will have been indelibly shaped by his experience in jail.

CHAPTER 3

Racialized Repression

BARRIERS TO THE EMANCIPATION OF YOUNG PEOPLE AT THE EDGES OF THE SYSTEM

It's easy to get in trouble, but it's so hard to get out.
—Angela, mother of Billy and Marcus

ANGELA NEVER GOT TO see what happened to her two sons, who were enmeshed in the criminal justice system starting when they were both fourteen years old. She died after a short battle with cancer while Marcus was incarcerated. He was brought to the funeral in shackles, guarded by officers from the New York State Department of Corrections.

Marcus was sixteen in 2009 when he was released from a residential facility in upstate New York, where he spent two years after being sentenced as an adult. Since he was considered an adult in the terms of the criminal justice system (although he had not reached the age of "adulthood" in the sense that he was able to live independently and make decisions about his financial and personal opportunities), he was expected to report to a meeting with a parole officer alone, without his parents. The City of New York also required that Marcus reenroll in a high school because he had not yet reached the age at which he could legally leave school. However, his parole officer was unable to provide him with information about how to reenroll in school. His mother Angela thus attempted to decipher the notoriously labyrinthine public high school bureaucracy, without access to the Internet or to anyone to tell her where to go. After a lengthy period of time, Marcus and his mother found a school for him to attend.[1]

The police aggressively monitored the block where Marcus lived, concerned about emerging gang rivalries. A number of the young people that Marcus had grown up with were police-identified gang members. Spending time with these friends, he was arrested several times soon after he was released from custody. The first time he was arrested he was with a group of his friends on the sidewalk when the police asked them to move off the sidewalk.[2] When they refused, they were arrested for disorderly conduct. Marcus was subsequently arrested for a misdemeanor offense—possessing a razor blade. Marcus soon stopped attending school.

When Marcus's parole officer learned about his arrests, he asked Marcus to report to his office. Marcus's father, who had spent a number of years in prison and who had been on parole, knew that these arrests would likely trigger a parole violation and that his son would be placed in custody. Knowing this, he wanted to be present with his son in the parole meeting so that he could advocate for him and ask the officer to allow his son an opportunity to participate in a program rather than go to jail; his father asked me to attend the parole meeting as well. Marcus's parents located a General Equivalency Diploma (GED) course for Marcus to attend and got him to take an admissions test, anticipating that the officer might ask what Marcus was doing to stay out of trouble.

Marcus and his father went to the parole office to have a conversation about some of the difficulties he had faced in getting back into school and resettling into the community. We entered through a large metal-mesh enclosure that resembles a cage. Immediately, we were faced with signs detailing various prohibitions: no hats, no cell phones, no do-rags, no gum, and no food. We sat down on a row of benches facing a bulletproof glass window, where Marcus was expected to check in. The vast majority of the room was filled with black and Latino men. In New York City, just 5 percent of parolees are white.[3]

When Marcus was summoned by his parole officer, and his father and I accompanied him into the office. The officer began speaking with Marcus and his father while he administered an oral drug test to another client who was still sitting in the office. Marcus began to explain to his officer that he had been unfairly arrested. The officer interrupted him, saying that he could easily establish not only that Marcus had violated parole, but that Marcus was someone who had engaged in continued criminal activity and that he could say to a parole judge, "He's just a plain criminal."

The parole officer said that he was willing to wait some time to see whether the cases resolved themselves in court—all parole officers are able to exercise such discretion. He then said to Marcus's father and to me, "If you hadn't have come in, I would have taken him into custody." Marcus's father said that he did not want his son to go to jail, because "he'll become a monster" there. The officer indicated that he did not want to send Marcus to jail either, but that his "hands were tied" if Marcus was ultimately found guilty and that his decision to exercise discretion in that moment was a small act of mercy.

Like the client who was there before him, Marcus was required to take a drug test. Several weeks later, Marcus's drug test came back positive for marijuana, and his father preemptively found a residential drug treatment program for him to enter, which the officer expressed some willingness to consider. In response to the choice between entering a residential drug treatment program for at least a year or going to jail, Marcus decided to run away from home. I received a voicemail message from the officer shortly afterward, informing me that he had decided to file a violation and bring Marcus into custody:

> I gave Marcus a break, as per your suggestion, and Marcus did not enter Carter House as instructed. He had a bed available yesterday, and his father had until 11 o'clock today in order to bring him to Carter House, and he refuses to enter Carter House.[4] So, uh, I told the father to encourage him, cause if he does not enter today, a warrant will be issued for his arrest . . . so he's in violation now, and in all possibilities, or all probabilities, I will be taking him into custody, tomorrow, Wednesday, when he reports. I'm sorry it didn't work out, you need to talk to him, his cell phone is disconnected, but maybe you can talk to his father again. I have no idea what you could do. I know he's a young guy, I thought maybe you could help, obviously . . . uh . . . this gentleman doesn't want any help.

The officer, like a number of other criminal justice agents I interviewed, framed Marcus's continued violation of the terms of his parole as his inability to effectively engage with the help he was offered. Marcus and other teenagers were characterized as individuals who lacked the requisite self-efficacy and agency to lift themselves out of their personal predicaments.

Marcus was found at home early one morning by a warrant squad several months later. Marcus spent the next year in Rikers Island, during which time his charges were "bumped up" to a felony, and the prosecutor's initial offer of time served was upgraded to an offer of several years in custody. During his time in jail, Marcus was repeatedly placed into solitary confinement after engaging in fights. During his time at Rikers, Marcus felt defeated and hopeless, which contrasted sharply with the characterizations of him by the prosecutor in his criminal case as an active gang member who had a proclivity for violence. He called his mother in tears, speaking about his frustrations about the case, his life prospects, and the inevitability of prison time. Marcus eventually pleaded guilty to the offense he was arrested for and received an indeterminate sentence of two to four years in a state prison.

Although it placed him at a more serious risk of being incarcerated, Marcus's choice to go on the run from the courts and parole was arguably driven by fear, and a sense that he had little control over his case. While on the run, he called his mother one night, crying and saying that he did not know if he could trust his parole officer's promise that he might be able to do a program, nor could he even cope with the choice of entering a drug treatment program, facing the possibility of being away from home for another year. His mother Angela told me that she was worried that Marcus was experiencing a "mental breakdown." Marcus's choice, in effect, was to withdraw from his world and to become more deeply alienated from opportunities to build social supports, enhance his personal skills, and ultimately build a sustainable life for himself.

He finally got out of prison when he was twenty-two years old, having spent a few months on the streets since age fourteen.

This chapter examines the systems and people outside of the custodial institutions that act as barriers to young people's growth and development. Developed in communities across the United States to respond to risk-taking by young people while they have an open case or after they have been released from custody, these systems and institutions are repressive structures that inhibit young people's potential rather than facilitating it, even though they are actually set up to support young people. In that sense, they resemble colonial practices because they involve oppressive and dominating practices by one group over another that they perceive to be inferior.[5] In the present day, colonial models are complex, especially given that many of the workers in criminal justice and social welfare bureaucracies are now largely people of color; thus, parole and probation officers, foster care workers, and other agents of the state, who are themselves predominantly black and Latina/o, are exercising these forms of social control over members of their own race and ethnicity, as opposed to a clear white–black oppressive structure.[6]

THE CRIMINAL CONVICTION, POVERTY, AND MARGINALITY

When she was seventeen years old, Shayla was arrested for selling drugs in front of public housing projects in her neighborhood. After she was arrested, she received a notice banning her from trespassing on the grounds of those projects, where her mother lived. Although she lived nearby in a private apartment with her grandmother, Shayla couldn't even walk through the grounds of the buildings to get to the nearby subway stop.

New York City's public housing projects receive federal subsidies. As such, they are subject to a set of federal rules enacted just three years before Shayla was born, in 1988. Emerging at the height of the War on Drugs, these rules were gradually expanded over the course of the 1990s until eventually President Bill Clinton gave them a name when he signed the strongest version of the law into action: the "One Strike" policy. Individuals who engaged in criminal activity on public housing grounds, or public housing tenants who engaged in criminal activity, would be banned or evicted from public housing, no questions asked. Even someone believed to be using drugs or alcohol or who had a history of drug or alcohol abuse could be barred from applying for public housing.[7]

Shayla was banned from the projects even though she had received the equivalent of a second chance—Youthful Offender treatment, an opportunity given to young people in New York up to age nineteen that allows one misdemeanor and one felony to be removed from their record. It is the equivalent of a second chance, in recognition that young people are less culpable for their crimes than adults. But in the minds of the New York City Housing Authority policymakers, Shayla was allowed no such chance.

In theory, Youthful Offender treatment also allows young people the opportunity to apply for jobs without having to check a box denoting their criminal conviction. Yet many of the young people that I met overwhelmingly perceived that they would not get a job as a result of their criminal case, regardless of whether they had a conviction or not—even those with a juvenile delinquency adjudication, which does not appear on a criminal record, or Youthful Offender treatment, felt that a potential employer might somehow find out about their time in the system. In some cases, this dissuaded them from even applying for a job. Their perceptions were linked to the realities of the waged labor market: employers do actually discriminate against individuals with criminal convictions.[8] Just under half of the participants I interviewed expressed fears about applying for jobs with a criminal conviction and being denied a job because of that conviction.[9] These fears were particularly pronounced in the wake of the financial crisis of 2008.[10] This news was often discussed by residential facility staff, who themselves faced layoffs, and served to affect young people's perceptions about their job opportunities.

Once he was released from Rikers Island, Michael desperately wanted to get a job. Michael felt pressure to work to support his own needs and those of his family, particularly because his own father had lost his job as a result of his arrest. As a lover of fashion and style, Michael hoped to work at a clothing retailer. Yet he found that a substantial number of job applications at local retailers where he wanted to work—including at Foot Locker, his primary choice—had a section that asked whether he had ever been arrested.[11] Discouraged by the question, Michael was pessimistic about his chances at obtaining the job whether he left the answer to the question blank or answered it truthfully.

Almost all of the young people I met wanted to go to college and dreamed of embarking on a range of careers. Jacob, for example, actively researched colleges while he was incarcerated and recited off a list of names that included Harvard, Princeton, and Yale. Jacob and Jamal also both spoke about their desire to attend a criminal justice college because they were both interested in pursuing a career in law enforcement. Yet a number of the young people expressed concerns about realizing these career aspirations because of their criminal convictions. Tony wanted to become a lawyer, and Jacob wanted to become police officer, but both of them knew that their time in the system would create barriers to realizing these goals.

If Shayla had applied to college, she may have again faced a felony conviction box. Even though Shayla had the ability to check "no" on that box because of her Youthful Offender status, many other young people I met did not have that luxury. Even those with Youthful Offender treatment often checked the box, assuming that they were obligated to—they had been processed through the criminal court, after all. The full weight of their Youthful Offender adjudication may have been explained to them, but they never fully understood it.

These teenagers were born into a world where the collateral consequences of a conviction were everywhere. Many young people, including my own students and colleagues, believe that a criminal conviction alone will block someone from going to college or receiving financial aid. In 1996, Congress passed an amendment to the Higher Education Act that denied individuals with a drug conviction from receiving financial aid, but that provision has long since been revised; it now more narrowly denies people from receiving aid if they get a felony conviction while they are in college. Yet this distinction is poorly understood on the ground. While he was incarcerated on Rikers Island, Michael spoke with resignation about his future prospects to go to college, saying, "I wanted to go to college," but "I'm in here, because of the felony."

It was also during the 1990s that the State University of New York (SUNY) decided to add a felony conviction box on their application. After applicants check the box, they receive a letter from SUNY demanding an array of paperwork related to their conviction, including their rap sheet, which costs $65 to obtain from the state, detailed inmate administrative records, and psychological treatment histories. They then usually face a felony review committee that assesses their fitness to join the campus. Unsurprisingly, a substantial number of people who check the felony conviction box and receive the letter demanding the supplemental information do not proceed with their application; this is a process that has been termed "denial of admission through attrition."[12] In August 2016, the SUNY Board of Trustees decided to eliminate the felony conviction box from the application.[13]

The process of applying for college itself, including the federal student financial aid forms, can often be intimidating for young people who have been enmeshed in the system for much of their adolescence. Three years out of custody and living at home with his mother in Brooklyn and unemployed, Andrew never started college in his community despite possessing his GED and some college credits that he obtained while in custody. Upon his release, his parole officer made him participate in drug treatment and anger management classes before he could even begin to apply to college. These mandated programs and the burdens of supporting his mother, along with Andrew's confusion about the processes of applying to college, have prevented him from even applying for college again, even though he wants to go.

A criminal conviction in New York is also accompanied by an array of fines and fees that can create burdensome debt for individuals.[14] Shayla faced mandatory surcharges in the courts as a result of her conviction, as well as fees associated with the programs she was eventually sentenced to. Jesse was convicted of a misdemeanor sex offense—"forcible touching"—when he was eighteen years old. After he was released from Rikers Island, he was homeless and unemployed. Yet his conviction, which resulted in ten years of probation supervision, also required that he pay for a sex offender treatment class. If he would not pay for his classes, he would violate the terms of his probation. At the time, he wasn't working and thus was unable to pay.

The barriers to accessing housing, employment and education that Shayla and the other young people faced are just a few of what have been called the "collateral consequences" of a conviction.[15] Many of these consequences were enacted into state and federal laws and regulations around the time they were born, as part of a national project of politicians in the 1990s who were tough on individuals accused of crimes—who created laws that subjected them to numerous civil penalties outside of a criminal conviction that treated their convictions as representative of the ways that they had violated the expectations of citizenship. Their parents were considered to be individuals whose relationship to the state, as dependents on welfare, public housing, and public education, was considered provisional by governing authorities. People who committed drug offenses faced particularly harsh consequences as a result of their arrests, but other people who were convicted of crime faced restrictions on their civic life. The people who faced the harshest restrictions were those who received any kind of state assistance, from housing to welfare. Federal lawmakers who created these penalties were of the belief that if people violated the law, they must face penalties that would communicate to them that their assistance on the state would be put in jeopardy if they violated the laws of that state.

For a number of the young people I met, their initial criminal conviction had compounding effects. New York has particularly punitive laws with respect to multiple felony convictions; under the "Mandatory Persistent" statute, individuals can face serious prison time if they have a second or third conviction. In the six years I have known him, Billy has been arrested several times and has been and out of detention, including Rikers Island. Tory was sixteen when he faced his first adult-level conviction; after getting out of a residential facility, he was arrested not long afterward and charged with attempted murder. Now twenty-two, he is doing a twelve-year sentence in an adult prison in upstate New York.

In other words, a conviction is not just a conviction, nor is an arrest just an arrest. After an arrest, these teenagers face barriers in social systems beyond the criminal justice system. These barriers prevent them from realizing their desire to work and to go to school, and they expose them to more time in detention and prison. A young person's arrest can set into motion an array of punitive responses that play a deep role in shaping their lives.

Yet so many of the teenagers I met had desires to go to school and to work. Not only were there explicit prohibitions on their ability to reach these goals, but there were also ways that the adults they worked with at various points in the system would press them to lower their expectations about their desires.

A number of scholars have studied the career aspirations of poor and working-class youth. Paul Willis, in his 1977 study of working-class boys, found that the young men felt the attainment of "qualifications" was "a deflection or displacement of direct activity," and they rejected the middle-class concept of job "choice," instead accepting the inevitability of their entrenchment in working-class vocations.[16] Allistar MacLeod also found that young people from a low-income housing development in an American city had "depressed aspirations" that affected their social mobility.[17] The work of these scholars has been highly influential in understanding the choices made by working-class and impoverished young people about the labor markets. Yet, as indicated earlier, the aspirations of the young people in this research were wide-ranging, and not necessarily uniformly "low." More recently, the sociologist Jennifer Silva examined the difficulties working-class young people face in realizing their career aspirations in a depressed contemporary job market and identified the ways that they identified their route to success through willful self-change.[18] Although a number of the young people I met were aware of the realities and challenges of the waged labor market, many of them still aspired to jobs or to educational pathways that departed from those understandings (see Table 3.1).

For the young people who would not have a criminal conviction on their record, their family court adjudication still loomed large in their perception of what they might be able to do with their lives. This was compounded by the fact that they were often confused about their rights with respect to their convictions, and system actors often added to this this confusion. For example, a number of young people given Youthful Offender status were often given the wrong advice about what this adjudication meant. Possession of a Youthful Offender adjudication means they could complete a job application and say they had not been convicted of a criminal offense. I observed at least one staff member at a residential facility encourage young people to reveal their criminal conviction in job interviews or on a college application, telling those young people with Youthful Offender status to be "honest" about their convictions. Although this represented a misunderstanding of the law by the staff, it also reflected staff members' understandings that these were young people who should and would be forever marked by their convictions. Peter, a Youth Counselor at Hooper, suggested to the young men that it was important for an employer to know about a young person's conviction in making their judgment about hiring them. Peter, like other staff members in residential facilities, alternative-to-incarceration programs, parole, and probation, may have played a role in "framing" young people's expectations about their potential in the labor market, but in a broader sense, in their life's work.[19]

TABLE 3-1
Desired Career Paths

Criminal justice careers
Christina: Youth development aide (in an Office of Children and Family Services facility) Jacob: police officer Jamal: police officer
White-collar professions
Tony: lawyer Nina: accountant Maya: veterinarian
Creative work
Newz: celebrity photographer Izzy: architect Genevieve: magazine editor Michael: model, professional basketball player
Blue-collar work
Marcus: Sanitation worker Billy: Bicycle repairman Bell: House cleaner
Other working-class professions:
Olivia: Amtrak (train) conductor Eddie: Barber Jenelle: Home health aide

CONFRONTING LOW EXPECTATIONS OF CHANGE

A number of the young people confronted system actors who had little faith in their ability to change, which played a role in dampening their expectations of themselves. The irony of such expectations was that they existed in a system that exerted strong expectations over them for positive change.

Young people's interpretations of these perceptions sometimes related directly to their decisions to "give up" in the context of a criminal case. Malcolm said of the judge and his alternative-to-incarceration program staff that "they just want me locked up." He described the unfairness of his court process, his feelings of defeat, and his desire to do time in custody rather than complete a program. Slam similarly communicated his feelings of defeat and frustration, which were recognized during an official probation interview. Billy said his teachers expected the worst of him, which had an impact on his motivation to go to school and to work hard, even though his court case demanded that he participate in school fully. A young woman in confinement spoke angrily about how the staff "think we're animals" and that she could do little to defeat that presumption.

A number of young participants expressed ambivalence about changing in the face of what they felt was a lack of recognition about their potential for growth and change. Some young people in custody frequently spoke about their feelings that staff expected them to return to custody, and this was often both overtly communicated to them, but also felt by the young people through staff members' body language and other cues.

Young people were sometimes frustrated that they could not meet institutional expectations of change. At a focus group at the girls' residential facility, some of the girls said that the "staff bash us so much," saying things like "you need to work on this." One of the girls said that she felt like saying to the staff that "you're not seeing that I'm trying." The girls felt that their progress in treatment—if there was any—was rarely acknowledged (or "seen"), despite their feelings that they had actually changed. This emotion had particular salience when it came to feelings about the structural impediments posed by their racialized identity, and the young men would talk about their feeling that "all we have in our mind is that we're the minority and we're not gonna make it." Newz similarly described his resistance to his implicit fate that "you black, you a man, you are one of two things: you might end up dead before you turn 21 or you going to be in jail." Yet while Newz and these other young people speak with a measure of defeat, they also speak about defeating the presumption of their failure.

The young people who were in the community spoke frequently about the expectation of failure they confronted in school and from the police. Police, for the most part, were seen as inherently lacking the ability to exercise understanding or empathy, particularly with respect to young people of color. Slam noted, for example, that police assume "most black people do bad things." When I asked Slam whether he believed, in fact, that "most black people do bad things," he said "yes." His emotion is complicated, particularly in the context of a conversation with me, a white woman from a different class position of whom he may have felt some distrust. Yet it reveals a degree of resignation about and perhaps an internalization of the functional and symbolic equivalence of "blackness" and "risk" that permeate popular culture and policing strategies. Slam may indeed feel forever "marked," but his resignation also reflects similar emotions expressed by those living under conditions that resemble colonialism: that there is little room for resistance to these constructions of blackness and criminality, and they are thus assimilated into one's way of constructing identity.[20]

Some participants recognized that if the police were to assume the worst about them, it would be better to avoid the indignities, humiliations, and potential pains of contact with individuals who not only use physical force against them, but who also simply see them as archetypes against whom they are incapable of exercising mercy and discretion. The young people also often spoke about how their words could be "twisted" by the police, and used against them, and that they could be manipulated by the police into "snitching" on their peers.[21] They felt the police would "railroad" them, which they define as the practice by which the police rapidly and summarily pursue convictions without understanding or attempting to verify the broader truths and contexts of their situation.[22] Being railroaded means that there is no opportunity to refute the assumption that one has done wrong and always will.

Some teenagers felt that it was impossible to comply with the requirements of their case. Billy, while in detention after being arrested for robbery, spoke about his pessimism about getting probation instead of time in custody, after hearing in court that the prosecutor was only offering him three to nine years in custody. Speaking in a sullen and dejected manner soon after he had been placed into detention, Billy indicated to the judge that he had been told by someone in detention that only 21 out of 1,652 people received probation for robbery offenses.[23] The judge in his case had said to him "don't let that scare you," which made Billy more sanguine about the outcome. Ironically, after finally receiving probation, Billy met with the judge and his lawyer in his case in private and revealed his fears that no one would check on him or look out for his best interests anymore. This spoke to some of the contradictions inherent in his experience: while he hated the indeterminate nature of the punishment, he appreciated the support and care he received from the individuals who were most involved in helping him fight his case and find a better outcome for his life.

Shayla similarly wanted a probation sentence for her felony offense, and eventually received it. However, while on probation, she was frustrated about her officer's ability to help her and low expectations of her. Shayla asked her probation officer how many of her clients had succeeded, and the officer told her that about 1 out of 100 people did. Shayla felt that her officer conveyed a general sense that she would fail on probation and be sent to prison. Izzy said that judges and criminal justice agents (including staff in facilities) hear so many more "failure stories than success stories" and he felt that they would base their judgment on those stories.

Michael, the young man who was charged with gun possession and who waited for months on Rikers Island for an outcome in his case, relied on his father to plead with his attorney to try to get him into an alternative-to-incarceration program. Michael's attorney said to them "in the ten years I've been doing this, I've only seen one or two people successfully complete a program." Failure in these contexts literally means incarceration, but it also seems to convey a broader assessment about young people's essential deficiencies as human beings that they cannot and will not meet the expectations of responsibility and compliance meted out by the courts.

Adults like Peter, the counselor in Hooper boy's facility, would frequently attempt to moderate what they perceived to be young people's too-lofty expectations. Some staff at the girls' facility, for example, spoke about how the girls had "unrealistic" expectations of their futures and that these expectations needed to be brought under control so that the girls would not be set up for failure. A teacher in the girls' facility spoke about how it is too hard to "try to get them to learn" and that it would in fact make more sense to teach the girls skills that were more "real," as opposed to English, math, and science. This accords with researchers' findings that poor kids of color are often given "dumbed down" curricula and face lower expectations for their success in schools.[24]

Similarly, in the boys facilities, some staff emphasized the need for the state to train young men in skills, such as automobile maintenance or carpentry, which they said would enable them to receive a job, arguing that the disproportionate emphasis of the reforms on treatment, as opposed to education and training, were hampering the young men's potential. The jobs and skills that a number of staff felt were aligned with what was "realistic" for the young men were largely service industry positions. Peter, a youth counselor, encouraged Jamal to apply for a job working at a delivery and package service at the airport rather than trying to go back to school. Slam spoke about his aspiration to work in a pet store after he had been told by a residential facility staff member that this would be a good position for him. The staff members who told me about their desires to get these young men in trade-based employment echoed some of the same claims made by those who established training schools for juvenile delinquents in the early part of the twentieth century. The assumptions of these individuals were that working-class kids need to be prepared to do working-class jobs; then, the kids were largely Italian American and Irish immigrants; today they are black and Latina/o teenagers.[25]

Peter and other staff members spoke about how it would be better for the young men to be in adult prisons, which offered more vocational training programs. Some of the residential facilities provided young people with the opportunity to receive vocational training, but the programs differed by facility and were often dependent on the availability of appropriate teaching staff. At Hooper, there was a horticulture class, training in maintenance work, a career class, and a print shop. The McClary facility did not have any vocational training programs, although some staff members would enlist the young people to help take care of the plants surrounding the facility. The Marshall girls' facility had a career and financial management class, training in office skills, and in the culinary arts. At the facility where Slam served his time, there was an automobile maintenance shop and the wood shop. A staff member who gave me a tour of the facility vocally lamented the lack of support the central administration of the state agency had provided the facility to properly sustain its vocational program, instead focusing its resources on therapeutic interventions.

The teenagers recognized the limits and realities of the labor market and their position as working-class kids within that market, but they also saw the ways that the adults in charge of their lives sought to limit their opportunities. The young men's group that I met with at Hooper spoke to me about their realizations about the barriers that were being erected around them. Eddie, one of the older boys in the facility, was serving a fifteen-year to life sentence for which he would be transferred to an adult prison on his twenty-first birthday, which was imminent. He had received his GED while he was inside the facility and was on an "Honors"-level behavioral change stage. So too was Aaron, who was serving a fifteen-year to life sentence. Jacob, the young white man serving time for a robbery case, was the youngest member of the group and was going to be released soon. Panama, who was also on the Honors stage, was getting ready to be released as well. Before arriving at the facility, Panama had been arrested multiple times and had violated his probation. It was unclear to him whether he had received Youthful Offender status, but no one at the facility had helped him to clarify that status.

All four of the young men had spent quite a lot of the time in the education program in the facility. The facility, like many across the country, did not offer the young people the opportunity to receive a high school diploma, only a GED. Also, every residential unit attended school as a group; the classrooms were not divided by grade level, reading ability, or other abilities. Thus, it was often quite possible that each classroom had young people with a wide range of abilities in it, from a fifth-grade reading level to a high school graduate. The curriculum was recycled each year, so young men with multiple-year sentences would be taught the same materials year after year. In 1994, in another moment of 1990s-era "zero tolerance" for people with criminal convictions, the federal government prohibited the use of Pell Grants for people who were incarcerated and in college programs, which existed in prisons across the country. Thus, even if they had received their GED, teenagers in New York's juvenile facilities were not able to access college courses for free unless they were lucky enough to land in the one facility that had started a full-time pilot college program that was being financed by a private donor.

Teachers in the state facilities are recruited through a state civil service system, and although they are certified, they are not always placed in classrooms to teach in their subject matter expertise. There are no full-time special education teachers in each classroom; there is generally just one special education teacher per facility. Substitute teachers were often hired on the basis of personal connections, not because they possessed any qualifications or expertise. The classes themselves are plagued by frequent interruptions. During my time in the facility, I spent a number of hours observing classroom sessions;

very few of those hours were devoted to instruction time. Instead, classes often took a long time to start and were interrupted by alarms or facility-wide emergencies, and treatment team meetings.[26]

In the classes themselves, the teachers often struggled to maintain the interest level of students. A number of the young men fell asleep in class, talked to each other while the teacher spoke, and sometimes even got into fights. Youth Division Aides (YDAs), or guards, were required to sit in every classroom, but the YDAs were frequently disengaged themselves; I observed some of them falling asleep during class. Additionally, a number of young people decided that they did not want to go to school, but some facilities, unable to force them to go, developed incentives-based systems to try to get them to go; for example, they would get more time on the television or access to Play Stations.

Contrary to the assumption of some staff members that these were just inherently "bad kids," it became clear to me that their disengagement in school and lack of motivation to do well there was in part caused by the facility staff and the structure of the facility education programs. During my interviews with the young people, they told me that they did not pay attention in their classes because the classes did not stimulate them or hold their interest. Besides the curriculum being recycled every year, almost all of the teachers in the facilities were white, the textbooks and course books were completely outdated, the classroom technologies were limited, and the materials were often clearly irrelevant to the lives of the young people. Whereas in a traditional high school the teachers might have access to ongoing professional continuing education and keep apprised of the latest ideas and technologies, the juvenile facilities are isolated from present-day discussions about pedagogy and curricular development. In fact, a number of teachers would tell me that working at the facilities was often a last resort for them; some were retired and looking for extra work; others had looked for other jobs in education but could not find them due to the very tight educational job market. A number of the teachers I met were motivated by their desire to help young people but were provided few financial incentives and support to do the work that they wanted to do; they thus relied on the resources that were in the facility or sometimes paid out of their own pockets for extra ones.

As a teenager who had spent quite a lot of time at the facility, Eddie had extensive firsthand knowledge about how the teachers and staff approached the young men there. He said that the "maximum expectation" by teachers and staff of students in the residential facilities is to get their GED and how "that's poor," because it is essentially just a ninth-grade education. He noted that it was difficult for an individual with a higher-level degree, such as a master's degree, to find a job in the context of the current economy, so it would be even more difficult for someone who only had a GED. He said "to me, there's no hope for your future." In a context in which residential facility staff members have a great deal of influence over these expectations, both in their ability to facilitate connections for young people and to provide counsel to them, their moderation of young people's expectations may play a role in shaping their sense of what is achievable.

All of the young men in the group that I spoke with acknowledged what was happening in the world outside of the facility: layoffs in many industries and limited job prospects for many. But they resisted the notion that there was any hope that lay in the educational programs in the facilities to help them make their way past that barrier. They thus held onto the idea that they were capable of doing work that was meaningful but critiqued the system for preventing them from achieving their goals.

"THE SYSTEM": PEOPLE-CHANGING INSTITUTIONS IN YOUNG PEOPLE'S LIVES

For a number of the participants, the word "system" meant much more than the system of punishment in which I encountered them. Their relationship to the criminal justice system was often peripheral to their many other concerns about governance. Their use of the word "system" represented the interpenetration of government agencies into their lives and which they felt structured and determined where they could go when they left confinement. "The system" was the force that repressed them—it served as the source of their frustrations as well as their inability to grow up and proceed with their lives.

Sam was at the facility for the second time after he had violated parole. Like many of the other young men in the facility, he came from a heavily policed neighborhood in New York City with poor, failing schools. He was an eager participant in our focus groups despite attempts by staff members to bar him from attending; they told me that he had been engaging in "negative" behavior on the units. Peter, the youth counselor, related Sam's influence with the other boys on his unit to that of a dog attracting fleas.

Sam defined the word "system" as anything that had to do with "not staying home," which included "cops, detectives, captains, generals, juvenile system, everything that has to do with being incarcerated" as well as foster care.[27] Participants would also call corrections officers or guards "police." For so many of the young people, it didn't matter what adult system actor they were dealing with—all of these people, whether they were a child welfare worker or a police officer—represented a negative form of social control in their lives.[28] These individuals were largely focused on policing and repression, and ultimately on removing the young person's freedom.

The fluidity between systems was arguably the strongest between the child welfare and juvenile justice systems. Skippy was a white kid from a poor family in suburban Westchester County. Skippy's parents drank and used drugs for most of his childhood. He was placed into foster care with a relative who physically abused him. He was then returned to his mother's house and was arrested for multiple delinquency cases until he was finally arrested for a more serious attempted murder case—he stabbed his mother's boyfriend. In his delinquency case, he was seen by the same judge who saw him after he was removed from his mother; Skippy said that the judge had known him "my whole life." The judge initially placed him in a private residential facility. He left that facility and then was placed into McClary, the lowest security-level facility in the state. It was rare for me to see a young person charged with such a serious offense, and to have such a serious history of child welfare involvement, in such a low-security-level setting. Both Skippy and I felt that this may have been a reflection of his whiteness.

In court, a young person's involvement in the mental health and child welfare systems, as well as their educational status, is frequently discussed by court actors, and in fact plays a significant part in decision-making about their placement and the outcome of their cases. Delinquency cases may also flow out of neglect cases if young people fail to participate in mandatory services or because they are facing more scrutiny by the state as a result of their involvement in the neglect case.

A number of the participants who were incarcerated, and a disproportionate number of the girls from upstate New York, were there because they had failed in previous mental health and child welfare placements. In a recent study of a sample of young people in New York State Office of Children and Family Services custody, researchers found that 65 percent of girls and 46 percent of boys had received child welfare services before they came into custody. Forty-eight percent of girls and 24 percent of boys had received foster care services before they were placed into custody. A higher percentage of girls were also noted as having a "significant" mental health problem upon entry into custody, and girls in the juvenile justice system have disproportionately experienced sexual abuse and violence.[29] A large-scale national survey of young people also found that girls had more significant histories of abuse than boys.[30]

Girls' pathways into the child welfare and juvenile justice systems have been found to be different from that of boys, with interventions in their lives more often being framed as a form of care, protection and treatment.[31] Girls are more likely to be perceived and treated as "troublesome" if they resist the boundaries of their care or treatment; this is perhaps borne out in the various ways that girls in trouble with the law are often described in the courts, in community-based programs, and in residential care as somehow more "difficult" than boys to work with.[32] Also, girls are said to more often report a history of abuse and mental or emotional problems than boys, but this does not necessarily indicate their disproportionate experience of such problems and could more likely reflect the ways that discourses of abuse and mental health problems are gendered.[33] The girls described their experiences as ones of an almost systemic purgatory, and these experiences are evidenced by a recent piece of research done on children in New York City's foster care system on their sometimes-dramatic lengths of stay in care.[34] Researchers have also found strong links between a history of maltreatment and a young person's involvement in delinquency, as well as a history of experience in the child welfare system with their later incarceration.[35]

I met a young woman named Maya both inside the facility and after she got out, and as I saw her confront the demands of the foster care and juvenile justice system, Sam's words about "the system" were realized for me. At a certain point in time for Maya, almost all of the adults in her life were in some way connected to controlling her body, her movements, and even what she felt was her mind.

One of the most striking aspects of the repressive therapeutic and behavioral change practices inside of the facilities were their failure to acknowledge the ways that the teenagers like Maya and Sam were complex beings who were not simply "bad," but who also had desires, despair, hope, anxiety, and fear. They gossiped and fought and cried but also encountered rules and practices that treated such engagement as toxic and problematic, rather than as a normal part of human interaction.

The girls in the group whom I met with at the Marshall facility felt that the staff expected the worst of them; one of them said that the staff members would often tell them that they thought they would reoffend soon after they were released. The girls said that staff members would almost expect them to violate rules and would shake their heads with an "I told you so" attitude after the girls messed up. The girls spoke about how the staff members in their facility were frustrated because they were not getting proper "respect" from the girls but that they did not acknowledge that asking fifteen- and sixteen-year-old girls for "respect" might be an impossible task—or a fantasy. Unlike the staff, the girls understood that pushing boundaries was in fact an inherent part of adolescence. One of the girls wondered why the staff members complained about the residents so much because, after all, they had families to go home to. The girls I spoke with expressed frustration that "everybody is trying to control us."

Maya and Genevieve were in the same focus group, and after they spent some time catching up and gossiping during one of my group sessions, Genevieve told her that the girls on her unit thought that Maya was the prettiest girl in the facility. Maya demurred, as she was quiet and reserved, and didn't like the attention. Maya told me she liked to play basketball, and she also wanted to be a veterinarian. When she was little, she loved to make things, and told me about doing crafts and making a teddy bear for her grandmother. She had eight siblings and split her time in her childhood between her grandmother and her mother. Yet like so many other teenagers, Maya got into a lot of trouble as a child. When I asked her why, she said "I was being bad" and "I didn't listen." She said that she had "started being bad" after child welfare authorities removed her siblings and her from their mother. She said that she was first suspended from school when she was ten years old; as a young black girl, she was surprisingly not alone in this experience—black girls actually face higher rates of suspension and expulsion than boys.[36] She first went into the foster care system when she was eleven years old; by the time I met her, she had been in ten foster homes.

When Maya was fourteen years old, she received a twelve-month sentence in family court. When I asked her about her experience in court, and she said, "I didn't understand one word they said." She remembered hearing something about AWOL and that her probation was violated. She said that her lawyers didn't come to see her in detention, and she didn't really remember anything about them. Maya's alienation from the court process and from her attorneys was not unusual; it represented her distance from a system that she was both a part of but also controlled within. So many of the teenagers felt that they couldn't understand the process, their attorneys, or the judges. They felt a great social distance from the people who ran the court, and they were perplexed by the proceedings and afraid to ask questions about them. The young people occupy a social space—"the system"—that is controlled by agents who have more social power than they do.

Maya did well enough during her time in the juvenile facility to qualify for a few privileges, including a trip to a local community college, although she begrudged the facility staff for requiring the girls to wear their uniforms on the trip, identifying them as coming from an institution.

Maya's release from the facility was delayed because the state Office of Children and Family Services (OCFS), which was responsible for her care as both a juvenile delinquent and as a neglected child, could not identify a foster home for her. Shortly before she was adjudicated and sent to the facility, she was removed from her mother's home and placed into foster care. Foster care placements are notoriously difficult to find for teenagers. Maya grew increasingly frustrated and agitated as she waited for a placement because no one in her facility would give her a definite date when she would be leaving. Maya was getting into trouble as a result of her frustrations and told me, "I'm tired of this place." During this waiting period, she complained that every resident who was "doing the program" is "faking it." She called the program at the facility "day care," a claim that I heard a lot of young people make. It was often intended to mean that they felt the program was a joke—that they were simply being treated as infants, rather than engaged and stimulated.

When I asked Maya what she was most looking forward to when she got out, she talked about "seeing my family." I asked what she was least looking forward to, and she said "going back to school." When I asked her why she felt that way about school, she talked about how she had "been away for so long" and that she hadn't been in a "regular" school in a while.

Maya was finally released from Marshall, and by the middle of the summer, she was in a foster home in Queens. She wanted to find a summer job. No one, from her foster mother to the agency that represented her, helped her with this. The apartment where she was staying was run by a West Indian woman who had a few teenagers under her care.

Ms. Roberts, the foster mother, must have assumed that I worked for the state, as she immediately reported to me how poorly Maya was adjusting to her home and to her rules. Instead of asking me who I was, she immediately began telling me that Maya was "doing bad" and that she had not come home one night and had missed her curfew. Ms. Roberts said that she was required to report Maya's behavior to the foster care agency because she would ultimately be blamed if Maya got rearrested or into more trouble. Ms. Roberts was preoccupied with getting "blamed" for Maya's absence; she said she wanted to call the police because at least they might document her efforts to help Maya. She was even worried that she could be arrested if she was accused of neglecting Maya.

Foster parents in New York City get paid on average about $750 a month for their teenaged foster children and also receive clothing subsidies for the children. Ms. Roberts had several other teenaged foster children in her home. She didn't have a full time job, and thus the foster children were her primary source of income. She told me "I get paid by the day," and so she thought that if Maya didn't get home by midnight, "I won't get paid."

Ms. Roberts spoke at length about Maya's need to obey the rules. She repeated the word "rules" throughout our conversations, saying that when she was a child, she "followed the rules," never sleeping in, and working hard enough to travel to the United States to work. She implied that Maya was a child who had never learned to follow rules, and "that is how she ended up upstate—she wasn't following the rules."[37] She showed me signs that she had posted outside of the door that Maya shared with her other foster child indicating their curfew time.

After Maya missed a number of her appointments and other obligations, such as her curfew, her social worker said to me, "She's really lazy, too. You can lead a horse to water, but you can't make it drink." The worker refused to refer Maya to any summer programs until she attended therapy and made her curfew, saying, "I don't reward bad behavior." No one set up any programs or activities for Maya that summer. At times, the teenagers' boredom that I often witnessed was representative of the ways that the individuals from the state who are responsible for their lives and well-being neglect to see them as adolescents and see them instead as wards of the state.

Maya hadn't been given any information about when she would return to her biological mother, and she yearned to be with people who knew her well.

As she spoke in front of Maya, who remained silent during the conversation, she said, "She's been in care since she was eleven years old" and then implied that she was a child who knew no boundaries and who was getting herself into trouble during the day. When I asked Ms. Roberts if she knew when Maya would be off of aftercare—the equivalent of parole for young people in the juvenile delinquency system—she said she did not know. I was surprised that the person who had such important responsibility for Maya would not know when this supervisory arrangement would be over.

After she got out of the Marshall girls' facility, Maya was unable to cash a stipend that she received through foster care because she lacked photographic identification. Her foster care agency had lost all of her vital documents, which she needed to obtain her identification card. The agency was responsible for obtaining new documents but failed to do so for the entire summer. Maya's social worker arranged for her to go to a number of appointments with a therapist but did not organize any other activities. She said that Maya should be responsible for getting her own photo identification. Maya would often skip her appointments with her therapist. Of therapy, she said, "I don't know when I'm going to outgrow therapy, but they're going to give—I don't know, just, I never asked for therapy a day in my life, they gave it to me, they felt I needed it . . . I swear they know how we feel and stuff. So I don't." Maya felt that the government actors in her life—the lawyers, foster care workers, after-care workers, and her foster mother—thought, but did not know, how she felt. It was clear that Maya recognized and reiterated that she was being governed, not cared for. She was being repressed, not recognized.

When it came time for Maya to re-enroll in school, the Board of Education told her that her classification of "Emotional Disturbance" in the Special Education criteria barred her from attendance at the school to which she was assigned. Billy too was rejected from numerous schools because of his "Emotional Disturbance" classification. Jenelle had taken the requisite number of classes to obtain a high school diploma while she was in the juvenile facility, but her high school at home didn't recognize the credits she had received at her juvenile facility, even though there was a recently enacted statewide law mandating such recognition. After Maya was rejected by the school she was assigned to, she was expected to go to the Board of Education in person to find a new school.

After a number of months, Maya ran away from her foster home. I have searched for Maya for the intervening years since then—on Facebook, through public databases, and Ms. Roberts, but she has vanished. Perhaps some would take this as a good sign—she hasn't turned up on Rikers Island or in any official arrest databases, thus she is a "success" in official understandings of teenage well-being in the criminal justice system; she hasn't recidivated. But, to me, there remain broader questions about whether Maya was given the opportunity to be a teenager and to grow up.

Maya was not alone in experiencing adults who were "ungiving" in terms of information about public benefits or assistance in regard to opportunities to enhance their well-being and grow up. The various forms of community supervision that young people encountered were more directly focused on monitoring, as opposed to offering guidance, referrals, and support, or "care."[38] These forms of governance were thus ones that were putatively aimed at ensuring the welfare and development of young people but neglected to ensure either.

FRUSTRATION BORNE OUT OF INDETERMINACY

One of the most striking experiences of following young people as they go through adolescence is to witness the significant process of change that takes place between early and late adolescence. For so many of the young people I met in 2008, and then see again today, I am struck that what often gets neglected in our understandings of the impact of criminal cases on their lives is that these cases are happening to young people as they are undergoing the tremendous changes that accompany adolescence. Thus, young people like Maya, Skippy, and Shayla are not only negotiating their legal cases, but their identity, friendships, sexuality, independence, and autonomy. These issues were particularly complex for those teenagers whose relationships to their families had been disrupted not only by incarceration, but also by the child welfare system—the meanings of independence were fraught for them, as well as their ideas about who and where they could find protection and care from.

In the context of juvenile justice systems, many scholars have written about young people's abilities to "age out" of crime. They extensively studied the processes of maturation that contribute to the relationship between age and crime.[39] Some have argued that there is a relationship between the development of maturity of judgment and the exercise of responsibility, temperance, and perspective, all of which may play a role in decision-making that leads to offending.[40] But what is perhaps less studied is the texture and complexity of that maturation process as it takes place within the institutional settings that comprise the juvenile justice system. The indeterminacy of the court cases was another piece of the repressive structure that young people faced: not only was the court process a difficult one for them, it often lasted many years and included a sprawling array of obligations and pressures.

The court interventions sometimes lasted for months or even years. Only one of the young people I met with had their case fully resolved during the year that I followed them, even though I met a number of them long after they had been sentenced.[41] If teenagers were sentenced to custody, they sometimes faced lengthy periods of parole or probation after those sentences. Teenagers who are charged with less serious crimes find themselves moving in and out of juvenile justice, child welfare, and mental health institutions for long periods of time.[42] The structure of the court system also creates and sustains the indeterminacy of the sentences. Depending on their age, young people can face either short, determinate jail sentences or a sprawling ever-expanding form of surveillance by the state. For young people charged in family court with less serious offenses such as drug sales, minor theft, and assault, they may actually receive a longer period of supervision in family court than if they were charged as adults. One participant, Luis, spent three years in custody in OCFS for a cocaine-related charge that he received as a juvenile delinquent in family court. After he returned home at age seventeen and was arrested and sentenced on a similar charge, he did a 30-day jail sentence as an adult charged with a misdemeanor in criminal court.

Billy and Malcolm continued to attend their alternative-to-incarceration programs well over a year after their initial arrest. Tory faced five years of probation after spending eighteen months at a residential facility. Others confronted up to a lifetime of parole after they completed their adult-level sentence, as in the case of two participants who had received sentences of fifteen years to life. For others who experienced the uncertainty of the child welfare system, in which they did not know when or if they would be reunited with their birth families, returning to group homes or foster homes after custody was experienced as a continuation of custody. The group homes often prevented young people from going off property, and some foster homes had strict rules about curfews.

The legal cases also tend to last for long periods of time because of the intricacies of legal process, but also because of the frequency with which young people violated the terms of their probation sentences, returning to the original courtroom where they were sentenced. Billy, for example, spent more than two years in court for a robbery case that he was arrested for when he was fourteen years old. He has been arrested several times since his first arrest and has spent time in a juvenile and an adult detention center. He has graduated from two alternative-to-incarceration programs, which he reported to at least twice a week. He had a curfew for over two years, and was expected by his judge to be with an adult family member at all times when he left his home. At one point, his probation officer discovered marijuana in his home and required him to go to a long-term residential drug treatment program (see Table 3.2 for descriptions of the participants' pathways through the system).

This sense of indeterminacy provoked a range of emotions among the teenagers, from desperation and deep pessimism to rage.[43] Maya spoke about the various court interventions she had to engage in before she violated her probation and was sent to the residential facility by saying, "I had so much, it

TABLE 3-2
Examples, Lengths of Time Spent in Custody and the Community

Name	Comments	Name	Comments
Ellen	Spent time in a residential mental health treatment facility before she was sent into custody.	Khalil	Spent time in detention, then went into custody, violated his aftercare and went back into detention pending the outcome of his violation hearing. Was sent back to residential facility.
Maya	Spent time on probation, then violated probation and was sentenced to time in the facility. She stayed longer in the facility than she was supposed to while her foster care placement was made.	Skippy	Was placed in a residential facility and got into trouble in the facility then "bumped up" to a more secure facility.
Christina	Spent time in multiple residential mental health placements prior to being sent to custody. Was placed into a residential treatment program after she was released from custody.	Oliver	Spent time in a residential treatment facility, got into trouble there, and was sent to a secure facility.
Genevieve	Was in a residential treatment center and a psychiatric hospital before she was placed into custody. She went back to the residential treatment center after released from custody.	Jose	Spent time in detention, residential facility, and is now in adult correctional facility. Was given an indefinite sentence of five to ten years for assault and robbery.
		Jamal	Spent time in detention and then in a residential facility.
Gina	Was in foster care before being placed in custody. Received an extension of placement in custody due to the seriousnessw of her offense. Was eventually released from custody in November 2010.	Izzy	Spent time in detention and in a residential facility. Was given a sentence of one and one-third to four years for robbery.
		Jacob	Spent time in a group home, then in detention, then in a residential facility. Had a sentence of one and one-third to four years for robbery.
Bell	Spent time in secure detention before she was sentenced to custody.	Tony	Spent time in detention, then in a residential facility, now in an adult prison. Serving an indefinite sentence of fifteen years to life for murder.
Jenelle	Had an indefinite sentence of one to three years in custody.		
Victoria	In detention then sentenced to the secure facility for an indefinite sentence of one to three years.	Jamy	Spent time in detention then a residential facility.
Don'te	Spent time in one secure facility, then got an extension of placement and was moved to another secure facility.	Sam	Spent time in detention, then the residential facility, then violated parole and was arrested again and was sent back to the residential facility. Now in adult prison finishing a three- to ten-year indefinite sentence.

(continued)

TABLE 3-2

Examples, Lengths of Time Spent in Custody and the Community (Continued)

Name	Comments	Name	Comments
Panama	Spent approximately five years in a residential facility.	*Shayla*	Spent time on Rikers Island, then in programs; five years probation plus programs.
Eddie	Spent time in detention and a residential facility, and is now in adult prison finishing an indefinite sentence of fifteen years to life.	*Billy*	Under court supervision for close to two years; completed two alternative to incarceration programs; spent time in Rikers Island and juvenile detention center; now on five years of probation.
Tory	Spent time in an alternative to detention program, then was placed in detention after he was rearrested, then he was placed in a private residential treatment program for 12 months, and was released to a community based program after release. Now on Rikers Island after being rearrested three times since his release from the residential program.	*Michael*	Rikers Island, then received five years of probation.
		Marcus	Spent time in detention, then residential facility on a one and one-third to three-year sentence, then Rikers Island (for a year awaiting outcome of new case), served two years of a two- to four-year sentence in adult prison.
Malcolm	Spent time in detention, then at a program, then received conditional discharge.	*Newz*	Spent time in detention, then in residential facility, and now in adult prison, serving a three- to nine-year sentence.
Slam	Spent time in a Functional Family Therapy and a Multisystemic Therapy program with his family. Was arrested again and spent time in detention, then was sentenced to 12 months of probation, which was revoked, and then he was sentenced to 12 months in custody. He was released from custody and given a six-month extension of placement, to be served at a community based alternative to incarceration program. Since being released from custody, he has been rearrested twice and has spent time on Rikers Island.	*Antonio*	Spent time in residential facility (three years), then three months in Rikers Island.
		Nina	Spent time on Rikers Island, received five years probation.

tortures me." Many court actors might argue that these pains and frustrations are an integral part of young people's need to integrate these new responsibilities into their lives where they were once absent, but it is arguable that this experience of "torture," or perhaps, to a lesser extent, deep frustration, affects young people's ability to fulfill their potential in the sense that they struggle to locate a focus for the expression of their sense of self-efficacy and their process of growth.

The teenagers felt powerless in the face of the indeterminacy of the custodial terms and were often ambivalent and frustrated about what it actually meant to change. In the courts, judges had the ultimate power over when and how they sufficiently met the court's terms of participation in an alternative-to-incarceration program, which often meant that they would stay in the programs for months, or even years.

There were many years where Shayla struggled to find such freedom from her court case. She had already faced a great challenge, as a young person, to establish her identity as a gay black woman. When she was younger, she worried about a large birthmark on her face, her skin color (she felt it was too dark), and her hair. She wanted to wear boys clothes and always felt more like one of the boys, but her family didn't approve of this—they wanted her to wear "girlie girlie" clothes—and she was teased at school. She did well in school when she was younger, and she was considered one of the smartest students in her class, but her grades began to slip, and she was ultimately kicked out of school for bringing marijuana to school. By the time I met her, she had left her high school and was trying to enroll in a GED program.

After she was arrested and charged with selling drugs on the grounds of the public housing project from which she was ultimately banned, Shayla was sentenced to five years' probation and mandatory participation in an alternative-to-incarceration program, which referred to intensive outpatient drug treatment for her marijuana use. She said, "I'm tired of traveling back and forth and all that" to the program and that "it makes it harder when you stressed out like that, it makes you want to relapse." Shayla wanted to go to college, but then she felt like she would "have to worry about" not meeting the expectations of the program she was in and "have to worry about my probation officer." She said to me, "Honestly, I don't want to do any more programs. Like, I'm grouped out. Like, I don't want to sit in a chair, I don't want to talk no more, I don't want to do that. I just want to move forward, and keep going. I want to be done with . . . and that's it."

Shayla used terms from the drug treatment program ("relapse," and later in the interview, "sobriety"), perhaps subconsciously recognizing that she might have to use this language to justify her desire to get out of the program.[44] Although she was an occasional marijuana user, she had been constructed as an addict for the purposes of the court intervention and thus had to prove her distance from that identity to get out of the program. She threatened to "relapse"—even though she knew she probably would have never used that terminology before, particularly about marijuana use—because she hated the program and wanted to give up on it. For Shayla, there were limited opportunities in her life, postconviction, to express and exercise responsibility, in part because of her adolescence, and in part because of her position in the courts. So her talk about "relapse" may have been one way of gaining a sense of power or control over her circumstances. Young people may develop unique strategies "aimed at gaining some control over their environment so that they could access individual freedom, autonomy and esponsibility."[45]

Shayla had to identify as a drug addict to stay out of prison. For many teenagers, marijuana use was a way of coping with the extreme anxiety associated with their lives, particularly in the absence of their access to mainstream mental health routes to overcome anxiety. Shayla said that "for a person like me to see a person that grew up in a urban neighborhood, and they smoke weed, and they get arrested, and they have to stop smoking, and like, that could be really hard on them . . . It could change their attitude, their aspect, their outlook on life and could really shut them down as a person." She said that the court forced her, through the imposition of the programs and controls, to "stop being the person you was before" without recognizing that by imposing behavioral standards and controls without being attuned to where they were coming from, it would create problems in their lives. She said that "for them to throw you back in the same environment where you came from, before you got arrested, and before you had to make these life altering decisions, it's, it's difficult." She found that one of the biggest challenges came when trying to navigate her life as a teenager, "because you want to hang out with the same people, and you want to go to the same parties, and you want to see the same girls, and you want to do the same things you did before. But you gotta, you gotta wonder, well if they're smoking weed over there, I can't go, because it might tempt me if they are doing this over there. I can't go, I can't do this." Shayla's response to this dilemma was to simply stay at home and close herself off from the world: "So you shut yourself down, and you become antisocial, and you live in a box for the rest of your life and you don't want to do nothing."

Shayla's words could be interpreted as a kind of denial of her marijuana addiction and her lack of responsibility in avoiding her deviant peers. However, she is frustrated that the court interventions fail to recognize her life context: she said, "You have to stop being the person you was before," despite living in the same place. She described wanting to "move forward, and keep going," fulfilling her potential in the ways that she desires. After she was first arrested, Shayla also expressed a similar frustration that her capacity for change wasn't recognized, saying "only my teachers from my school know what a good kid I am." She said that they know about "my initiative, my passion . . . how much I value my education." The program made her feel stuck. In response, she argues, it is possible to "shut yourself down" and withdraw. Shayla perceptibly recognized that the courts may never see her for who she is. At a meeting I had with Shayla on Rikers Island, she conveyed the complexity of her emotions about being accepted into the program to me. The following is an extract from my field notes about that meeting:

> I told her [her lawyer] that had spoken with [the alternative-to-incarceration program], and that they were willing to accept her—S responded emotionally (I think she even cried), and her demeanor seemed to express that this was more than just about being in a program—it was about getting out, seeing her grandmother, and so on. I almost thought that being accepted might also represent being seen as a good person, as someone with potential. S also spoke about how much she wanted to go home, and how she was feeling about being "violated" by the judge.

Shayla was never able to confer legitimacy on the alternative-to-incarceration program because she primarily perceived it as a means to an end—freedom from incarceration. She located her aspirations and hopes outside of the program itself, in college. Shayla engaged in a form of "creative compliance" in which her participation in the program is on the surface one of compliance, but she is actually seeking out sources of change for herself that exist beyond that program.[46] Thus, her process of change and growth is in part frustrated by her feelings that she is unable to exercise her abilities to express those capacities for change but is instead fixed into her identity as a marijuana addict, unable and incapable of change until she has done her time in the program.

Like Shayla, Malcolm, a black teenager from the Bronx, was also sentenced to an alternative to incarceration program after he was arrested and charged with a felony as an adult. Malcolm was a taciturn, wary kid who came from a very large family. His mother suffered from an addiction, and he had bounced around from family member to family member, eventually ending up with an uncle who lived as a woman. His uncle would frequently come to court for Malcolm, and Malcolm, who always tried to wear the latest fashions and convey a cool demeanor, seemed pained and embarrassed each time his uncle stood up to the court bar to speak on his behalf or to tell the judge what Malcolm was doing wrong at home.

Malcolm felt that the outcome of his case was preordained and that his acquisition of knowledge about the case was "not going to change nothing," because the judge was "gonna do whatever he wanna do." I interviewed him one day in his alternative to incarceration program, which was located in his neighborhood. Located in a small neighborhood storefront that had been converted into a program space, kids would sit around and do their homework, gossip with each other and program staff, and play video games after school. Malcolm was frustrated by his counselor there, who he thought was too hard on him, and was always threatening to report him. He said, "I don't have no freedom now. I still gonna keep on going back and forth to court. Don't know when I'm going to be locked up. In here, I could get locked up. I don't have no freedom." He felt that the case was interminable—that it "could be going on every day." Dejected and frustrated, Malcolm wondered what the point was of continuing on with the program and his court appearances, because he felt that "right now, I see it is going to be me getting locked up and then coming home. That is the way it's going to end." He said, "I'm trying to do better in school. I'm trying hard—ain't nothing changing . . . it been like that for eight months." Looking back after his first arrest, he felt like "well if I'd just got arrested before and got locked up right there, I wouldn't be going through none of this." I asked him if it would have felt better to have just been locked up; he said, "It don't feel better, like it's not gonna ever feel better to get locked up, but that's how they making it seem."

Malcolm later spoke about how the indeterminacy of the program "affects everything" and that his frustration over this led to his feeling that he may just want the certainty of jail instead. He said, ". . . still having no freedom at all it just makes you wanna do something like, makes you wanna go past your curfew, whatever." Malcolm felt the program had set him up to fail and that jail was in some ways a more straightforward path to freedom. Like Shayla, he described the direct relationship between the frustrations of the program and his desire to break its rules. Just a few years later, he was arrested and charged with robbery in the second degree and sentenced to four years in state prison.

These feelings of frustration with the indeterminacy, and perhaps the all-encompassing nature of the programs sometimes led some teenagers to resist the terms of the program, seek out forms of what the political scientist Cathy Cohen describes as "lived opposition" and "intentional deviance."[47] Approximately five months after he had been arrested and charged with robbery, Billy called me and asked if I could find out a way that he could actually get back in to detention (he had spent some time there, but was released by the judge), because the frustration of being out and not knowing when his case would end was "driving him crazy." His feelings were compounded by the fact that his parents could not afford to pay for him to get the clothes he wanted for school. He expressed a desire to be in jail, where the clothes he wore and how he looked wouldn't matter. He also said that he felt like going out and robbing someone so that he could either get the money he needed to pay for the clothes or face the almost-certainty of a prison sentence. Cathy Cohen argues that some counter-normative practices and acts of deviant resistance like the ones that Billy describes cannot be understood simply as acts of deviance or of politicized resistance:

> these acts, decisions, or behaviors are more often attempts to create greater autonomy over one's life, to pursue desire, or to make the best of very limited life options. Thus, instead of attempting to increase one's power

over someone, people living with limited resources may use the restricted agency available to them to create autonomous spaces absent the continuous stream of power from outside authorities or normative structures.[48]

Billy's urgent desire to gain some sense of control and certainty, and his willingness to put himself at risk of a substantial prison sentence, speak to the complicated nature of deviance he describes. His ability to exercise agency is deeply frustrated, yet he also expresses an extraordinary desire to engage in the only form of action he feels he has available to him, which is violent. The responses of the teenagers to the sprawling nature of their court cases points in part to the contradictions present in interventions that are aimed at protection and control but are experienced as sprawling and constricting. It is notable that the ways in which individuals like Billy seek to resist these interventions are through further deviance. Young people's intimate knowledge with the repressive forms of governance they face is potentially a force behind their resistance to those forms of governance. This intentional deviance is a way of combatting the forces, albeit one that results in their continued enmeshment in the system.

EXPERIENCES OF VOICELESSNESS AND POWERLESSNESS

Teenagers' responses to these interventions relate in part to their feelings of powerlessness in their legal case and their inability to determine the outcomes in their case. They would often describe feeling hopeless about the indeterminacy of the interventions and paranoia about the legal actors in their case. A number of them felt that the legal actors involved in their interventions expected them to fail. These perceptions ultimately play a role in guiding the choices that young people make about complying with the interventions as well as their motivation for a greater opportunity for social inclusion.[49]

Young people expressed frustrations with both their voicelessness and their feeling that they were not heard even when they had voice. Terrell came to the McClary residential facility after he absconded from an earlier placement in a residential treatment program. He was arrested on a warrant and returned to court, where he was sent back from custody. He was frustrated with his experience in court because his lawyer told him that he would not have to do any time in custody. He said he would have more readily accepted his placement if his attorney had been forthcoming about its possibility: "I just think that the lawyers really need to listen to [kids] more." Izzy, who spent nearly three years in custody for a robbery he committed at age fifteen, said that "they [lawyers] probably don't even care" what young people think, and that he ultimately "didn't feel like the choice was in my hands" when it came to the outcome of his case. These emotions are in part engendered by the structure of the legal case: it is often to a young person's detriment to speak in court, because their pleas of innocence, attempts to explain themselves, or their expressions of change may actually hurt their legal defense. Thus, many defense attorneys, and even judges, will stop young people from speaking in court, except at moments when their speech may be safe, for example, during an allocution at a guilty plea, or when young people can describe their compliance with treatment.[50] Dialogue has little room in this context, except for very narrowly circumscribed—and potentially scripted—moments.[51] Other scholars have found that the expression of voice and participation are key to individuals' judgments of fairness in the court context.[52]

Young people often felt that while the court was a setting in which their lives, motivations, failures, and progress were debated openly and at length, they could not play a role or offer any account of their own self or narrative of events in that setting. Malcolm, for example, said "I think it's not right because it's about me . . . and I don't get a chance to say something." Similarly, Shayla was frustrated about not being able to speak for herself, especially when the stakes were so high: for example, she failed a drug test in her alternative-to-incarceration program and got into a fight with another participant, and was potentially going to be remanded to custody, but was unable to speak during the court hearing which was called in response to these incidents. She said of her court appearance:

> usually when you get up there like, you can't say anything. I'm getting to the point now that, if she [her lawyer] doesn't say what I want her to say, I'm just going to like cut her off and start talking myself, like listen here, Judge, like I appreciate everything [the program] has done for me, it's been a whole six months I've been there, like I learned so many things, but I want to start school and I don't want to stress myself out.

Izzy noted that "we can't even speak in the courtroom" and that there was a "zip on our mouth." José said that his lawyer "didn't listen" to him. I asked a group of young men at Hooper whether they were told explicitly that they could not speak or they just felt that way—they said that they just "got the vibe" that they shouldn't speak. Malcolm similarly recognized that speaking wasn't going to help him get a better outcome in court:"when I first started, I was like, I could say whatever I want, but then again I don't know if this would be a good thing." Panama said that his lawyer "seemed like he was scared of the DA" in his case, and that he wondered, "why aren't you defending me?" He also said that his lawyer never came to visit him while he was in detention, a common experience for the participants.

In part in response to the criticism that young people are often tokenized rather than called on for their meaningful participation in reforms, system-involved youth perspectives have been solicited more frequently in recent years. It is not uncommon to see system-involved young people headlining juvenile justice reform events, speaking at lobbying days, and helping to design reforms. State and nationwide commissions and panels almost always involve system-involved youth; in fact, each state has a juvenile justice advisory group responsible for distributing federal monies to local agencies. These groups are required to have a formerly system-involved youth member. This movement toward inclusion and voice was started by individuals who were incarcerated, who recognized that those who have been in the system should become a part of developing solutions about it. However, it was unclear whether this form of youth participation—in a reform context—actually elevated and expanded youth participation in the court, alternative to incarceration, and residential facility context. The dangers of tokenism reside in the risk that the participants already have a "credibility deficit" in the minds of the listeners, thus making the listening process objectifying as opposed to meaningful.[53]

Young people and their families also expressed paranoia about the court process, which seem to be related to their feelings of powerlessness and voicelessness in that process. Angela, the mother of Billy and Marcus, frequently spoke about how she felt that her son's attorney and the prosecutor were "working together," which she felt resulted in her son's harsh punishment. Other young people and their parents frequently described their concerns about all court actors "working together" and were attuned to the conversations that took place between them. George's mother, Rose, said of her son's attorney, "It looked like to me he was right down with the DA, the judge, and all of them," and that that her son had been "railroaded" by all of them. The participants often located their concerns about their public defenders around their pay structure, with one young participant noting that "they get paid to just look at your files—it doesn't matter if they win or not." Victoria said that her lawyer in her case "wasn't paid," so "I knew he wasn't going to go all out." She said that "he did try to get me less time," however. She said that "he never really told me anything," but he did talk a little bit to her mom. Others expressed the sentiment that because the lawyers are not paid for each case, they do not feel the incentive to win, so they are therefore not invested in keeping young people out of jail. Rose said, "That why I call them appointed lawyers. Point you right to jail."

The participants' fears about being excluded from court cases were often highlighted during court hearings, when defense attorneys would engage in collegial conversations with prosecutors or would speak at the bench with judges or law secretaries. In her research about the juvenile courts, sociologist Alexes Harris has argued that the juvenile court reforms of the 1960s resulted in a redistribution of power in the juvenile courts, granting prosecutors more power, and making judicial decision-making processes reliant on "therapeutic" aims more tenuous.[54] This has also potentially created the need for defense

attorneys to appeal to the enhanced power of prosecutors. Although the collegial nature of the process was, for some attorneys, a critical part of obtaining
a negotiated settlement that was, they felt, in the young person's best interests,
the young people interpreted these conversations with much more suspicion.
Other researchers have found that young people lack trust in their defense
attorneys if they are paid by the state.[55]

Social-psychological and psychiatric discourses are often in tension in the
juvenile court context, in which a substantial number of the young people
who face a judge have been diagnosed with a mental illness. Thus, their displays of paranoia may be also "read" as indicative of signs of delusion, and thus
a mental disorder, which could arguably serve to further alienate them from
these figures of authority.

Governmental actors are often perceived by young people as an undiffer-
entiated mass, whether they are legally endowed with the young people's trust
and care, as in the case of their defense attorneys, or in opposition to them,
as in the case of the prosecutors—many of them represent "the system" that
represses them. Yet criminal defense is intended to act as a "shield" for people
from the abuses of the state.[56] There are some well-documented reasons for
some of the obstacles facing defense attorneys in achieving this goal, including
a lack of funding, adequate training, and supervision. There are, of course, a
number of public defenders who are able to provide representation that is perceived by young people as supportive and vigorous. However, the prevalence
of the perception by the young people that all court actors were in some way
functioning together revealed some of the potential sources for young people's
subsequent decisions to withhold information from their attorneys or lie to
them or to experience them as oppositional to their interests.

It was common for teenagers to deploy information strategically with
their attorneys. They often presented a narrative about their lives and cases
that reflected their understanding of their attorneys as actors endowed with
the power to represent a version of themselves, and not always faithfully. This
happened in part because of a lack of understanding about the confidentiality of the lawyer–client relationship, but also because of their sense that their
attorneys were colluding with the prosecution; young people may also struggle to fully comprehend the concepts of confidentiality and client loyalty.[57]
This meant that a young person like Michael, who was charged with gun
possession as an adult, may present his attorney with a narrative of the facts
of his case that would be a kind of "truth" he felt would be best equipped to
exonerate him. He said that a group of boys from his neighborhood, whose
names he did not know, asked him to hold on to their gun for a little while.
His attorney did not believe this version of events, but Michael was also fearful
about revealing the identities of the individuals whose gun he held, for fear
of retaliation.

The young people, seeing that staff in juvenile facilities had a low assessment of their moral worth and value, would often also express concern that the "system" more broadly was rigged as a "set up" for their failure in life. Newz, an African American teenager who was a seasoned "Honors" stage resident who had achieved some of his own juice in his facility by acting not in a "bad" way but in a deferential and polite manner to staff, spoke about the younger people who first entered the system by saying, "A lot of people think they can beat the system, but they can't." He continued, "Nobody can beat it—it is set up for you to fail." He had learned that he could not try to make the program revolve around him by being bad because "you will fail." Thus, he had made a decision to succumb to the program, to become institutionalized. His decision connected to Michael's decision to become a "badass"—giving up meant, for each of them, succumbing to what the adults in charge expected them to be, either unruly fighters in jail or hyper-compliant yes-men.

Sam, another older teenager from New York City who had been to Hooper twice after he violated parole when he was first released, felt "set up" when he was released from custody for the first time and was obligated by parole to return to a neighborhood where he knew he would be unsafe. I realized that in part what he meant was that his parole officer had a low estimation of his worth on the street. Although he made a request to his parole officer to live elsewhere, his officer told him "you're gonna be alright," indicating that Sam's safety would not be compromised if he stayed in his neighborhood, and the officer refused to allow him to move. Sam was frustrated by his officer's inability to recognize the danger that he felt he was in. Sam subsequently reconnected with his former gang to obtain protection and was then involved in a homicide, for which he was rearrested and sent back to custody. Young people like Sam speculated about the possible ways that judges, prosecutors, and defense attorneys made money by pushing for incarceration; Tony, from Hooper, made a more concrete claim: he said that people in "the system" would rather the young men be locked up than give them a job. As we met in early 2009, shortly after the global financial crisis, Tony was well aware of and referenced the dire unemployment figures.[58]

Sam similarly claimed that the state may actually think that it is better to "contain us" rather than to "keep us out there causing havoc" because "that's one less person to pay for." I also often heard young people, both in my research and my work at the public defenders' office, refer to the idea that system actors—including public defenders—were being paid to send people to jail and prison. Conspiracies about the system and its insidious intentions have long framed conversations about criminal justice system interventions and government interventions among poor people of color, particularly because the system has long been marked by its relationship to enslavement, brutality, and harm against African Americans, Native Americans, and other people of color.[59] During the time I was doing my research, a prominent case was published in the news about Pennsylvania judges who were in fact taking money from private juvenile residential programs in exchange for the placement of kids in their centers.

The phrase "set up" spoke in part to the undercurrents of paranoia that have framed conversations about criminal justice system interventions and government interventions among black people.[60] It may also represent or be symptomatic of a recognition of the colonial relationship between the state—represented largely by white power-holders—and the people controlled by that state—largely black and brown—described earlier. A deep sense of cynicism and injustice about the criminal justice system has long existed among black people, whose relationship to the system has been marked by its connection to slavery, brutality, and harm. Feelings and expressions of insecurity and paranoia in the face of these interventions reflect the sediment of racially unjust forms of punitive governance aimed at the communities the young people come from. Distrust of defense attorneys, judges, and prosecutors flows directly out of a longstanding history of racialized repression on the part of state actors toward people of color.

The implicit (and sometimes explicit) assumption among some of the participants was that every intervention in their lives, however benevolently framed, ultimately leads to confinement. Police stop-and-frisk practices have tripled in New York City since 2003. In 2009, African Americans and Latinas/os were stopped and frisked nine times more often than whites.[61] "Getting hassled" by the police on an everyday basis, particularly in the context of the rise of more aggressive policing strategies, may influence the "collective consciousness" of those individuals—and in particular, people of color—who face the most scrutiny.[62] The sociologist Pierre Bourdieu argues that "history" is the foundation of habitus or dispositions, in the sense that unconscious processes and habits may be created by objective structures.[63]

The young people also recognized that they were treated as unable to comprehend or contribute fully to their legal case. Indeed, researchers have found that many juvenile defense attorneys often advocate for what they perceive to be their client's best interests, as opposed to their expressed interests, which may have an impact on young people's sense of alienation from the process but also reflects the strains of paternalism that may motivate such advocacy.[64] The participants also experienced court procedures and discourses that were difficult for them to comprehend. Maya, for example, said, "Half the time you don't really know what they be talking about." This confusion perhaps contributed to the alienation that young people felt from the court actors.

It has been argued that the construction of children in public is often one of "moral incompetence" and that this position may deter young people from "engaging with or seeking advice from adults."[65] The young people often expressed that they could not depend on the help of others to earn their freedom from the court processes. Izzy and Terrell indicated that they were unable to be recognized as key actors in their court cases. Both ultimately decided that their attorneys were not working in their best interests, and they thus shut themselves off to building a relationship with them. Izzy never felt or expected to trust his attorney; he spoke about him in the same tone he spoke about other court actors, as someone who was functionally involved in seeing him be incarcerated and who was indifferent about his future. In the interview selection that follows, Izzy does not distinguish between the judge and the lawyer when he discusses his experience in court:

A: What was going through your mind [at the moment you got sentenced]?

I: I'm doing good in [detention], I'm thinking I'm coming out in a couple of months. When I go up, it's a totally different story. Like I didn't know nothing about the court system, so I was told lies from the bench.

A: And what had you been told about going upstate to OCFS?

I: Oh, if you do good where you at, you go before the parole board, which I knew nothing about, they will let you go home in a couple of months.

A: And was that what your lawyer told you?

I: Yeah, that what's my lawyer told me.

A: . . . So he said OK, you'll be sentenced, and there's a good chance you could get home?

I: He said don't worry about it, you'll be home in a couple of months. I could do a couple of months up top.

Izzy ultimately spent a year and a half in an OCFS facility. These reflections about his attorney and the judge, made after being released from custody, demonstrate his alienation from those court actors, and his sense about the unfairness of the process. Izzy ultimately resigned himself to a period of custody, not demanding more of his attorney, not filing for an appeal in his case, nor investigating the case any further. When he learned that he was to spend much more time in custody than his lawyer suggested, he said he felt like he "can't really do anything" about it. He felt defeated and simply ready to do his time and come home. He said, "I was just so, you know, it is what it is."

The young people often felt that they had no control over the outcome of their cases. Some felt that their future incarceration was inevitable. At the very least, they felt they would be enmeshed in a system of coercion, whether it was prison or foster care. Tory felt that he did not have a "choice" in court and that even though he felt that he had a personal capacity to change, he wasn't able to prove it: "I just wish that it was my choice about whether I could leave [my residential program] early or not, 'cause my lawyer . . . feels I might make a mistake and go back to jail. I don't feel I'll make a mistake because I know I've been through here and I don't want to be back in jail, but, I don't know . . . see you feel like you want a chance to prove yourself, right?" Tory felt that there are particular dimensions of his personal processes of change that cannot be articulated in a simple way—or at least the way that is demanded by the courts, which focuses on how few incidents he has been engaged in, how many treatment modules he has done, and how well he has done in school. Over the course of his time in residential treatment, he spoke about his changed perspectives on friendship and family, his feelings about maturity and being someone who his peers looked up to, and even his abilities to articulate some quite complex emotions. However, these dimensions could not necessarily be captured in a treatment report, or even, he felt, in his lawyer's words to the judge.

Some of the young people expressed more ambivalent responses to this feeling of powerlessness, in part because they were proud and confident as they progressed well through their programs. This was enhanced by the public assessments of change that occurred in the courtroom, with judges openly congratulating young people who were doing well in programs or even asking an entire courtroom to applaud for a young person who had done "well" in a program. Billy captured the ambivalence that accompanied this powerlessness when he said, "I don't have no say so, except maybe to do well here [in the program]." He knew that he could grasp some sense of power through his active participation in his program, which involved group work and individual therapy, in addition to meeting regular reporting goals for the court (such as curfew, program attendance, and drug testing), which tended to be the more active markers of his progress in a court appearance. But he also acknowledged that he could ultimately end up in prison, regardless of whether he did well in the program itself.

RECOGNITION AND RESPECT

Some might understand these young people's actions of avoidance or dismissal of the agents of authority in their lives as a form of "condemning the condemners," or a strategy of neutralizing their delinquency.[66] Yet this strategy may also reflect their feelings of alienation from "the system." The young people could be responding to the humiliation engendered by their "social invisibility," or the lack of "individual identification" they experience between themselves and the figures of authority in their lives.[67] The philosopher Axel Honneth describes recognition as the notion that the other person possesses "social validity," and as such, one can "do justice" to them.[68] It is arguable that the young people believe that many system actors lack this "social validity" because these actors do not sufficiently recognize them. Thus, systems of liberal paternalism, which prioritize the care and protection of young people, and the need to facilitate their responsibilities and their agency through intervention, actually neglect to recognize these young people as agents. Young people's feelings about being misunderstood may play a role in inhibiting their growth.

Young people's frustrations about their experiences in the system and their feelings about its lack of fairness are not uncommon experiences, particularly for marginalized youth of color. Researchers have found that young people, and especially young people of color, tend to view the police less favorably than adults.[69] In their study of young people from New York City, the researchers Jeffrey Fagan and Tom Tyler found that cynicism about legal authorities increased among young people over time after their repeated interactions with those authorities, whom they viewed as harsh and unfair.[70]

Several social psychologists have explored the relevance of procedural justice for young people in the context of research on individual's attitudes toward the police.[71] This early literature found that procedural fairness mattered to young people and that even very young children may be able to make moral assessments about certain procedurally unfair circumstances.[72]

Class, race/ethnic, gender, and sexual inequality and injustice pervade the lives of many of the young people whom I interviewed and certainly may influence their deeply held beliefs about fairness in a broader sense. Thus, young people's assessments of fairness and justice may also connect to their experiences of poverty and disadvantage. Lind and Tyler's "group-value" theory of procedural justice demonstrates that an individual's investment in the fairness of authority is deeply connected to a feeling of inclusion in society.[73] This theory notes the importance of the "feelings that one is viewed by authorities as a full-fledged member of society."[74]

The diffuse, expansive, and indefinite nature of the interventions that the young people face play a role in limiting their sense of freedom. It shows that some of these interventions neglect to recognize the role that structural impediments play in frustrating young people's opportunities for exercising their choices, as well as the subjective domains of experience which may help them to grow, such as their opportunities to express their "voice" and their interests in their legal cases.

CHAPTER 4

The Responsibility Trap

DAVID BROOKS KNEW WHAT it was like to be considered unworthy. Before he became a Youth Division Aide (YDA) in a juvenile facility, he was a young black man growing up in one of the most impoverished and violent neighborhoods in Rochester. After attending college on a football scholarship, David took a job as a YDA, working with kids who came from the same neighborhood where he had grown up. By the time I met him at Hooper, he had worked for the state for more than twenty years. He was married, had children, and had built himself a comfortable, middle-class life.

For people in some parts of upstate New York, state jobs like the one that Brooks has are the only vehicle to a middle-class life. After manufacturing jobs declined in the years following World War II, state jobs increased during the 1960s as New York's Governor Nelson Rockefeller expanded the state's public administrations and authorities; state colleges; universities; and other public programs.[1] Line staff members at juvenile facilities like Brooks often made well above the median income for their counties, particularly if they worked overtime. One juvenile facility line staff member told me, "When I was growing up, anyone's parent who worked for the state was like a God."

Brooks was invested in his job. He believed the teenagers under his charge could improve. He had worked in the system long enough to see behavioral and treatment approaches come and go, depending on the political climate or what was en vogue among the commissioners in Albany. Instead he offered the kids a kind of tough love approach.

Brooks began working in the system in 1990, a unique moment in the history of juvenile and criminal justice. The Democratic governor, Mario Cuomo, was firmly committed to the war on crime and would lead the largest prison building project in the state's history.[2] Leonard Dunston served as commissioner of the state juvenile justice agency. A black man appointed by Democratic governor Cuomo, Dunston began his career as a street outreach worker. This experience led him to commit the agency to providing positive opportunities for development. He enhanced aftercare programming, enlisting the support of people like Eddie Ellis, a formerly incarcerated former member of the Black Panther party, to create a cultural enrichment program for young men of color coming out of facilities.³ But Brooks also arrived in the facilities at the beginning of a peak in youth crime in New York and in the country. The symbolic representation of those crimes was the Central Park jogger case, which happened in April 1989: five young men of color were accused of brutally attacking and raping a white woman in Central Park. Four of those young men were sent to juvenile facilities in New York. By 1995, a Republican governor, George Pataki, was elected in New York, and he appointed a new commissioner for the state's juvenile justice system, John Johnson, who came from a correctional background.

The year that Brooks started working in the system, admissions to the residential facilities increased substantially—by more than 20 percent from the previous year. The majority of the young people coming in were black and Latino and male. Young people coming in for drug-related offenses increased by more than a 500 percent and more than 125 percent for firearms-related offenses. There were close to 2,500 young people who entered care in the system in 1990.⁴ By the time I met Brooks in 2011, there were just ninety-nine kids admitted to custody that year.⁵

The group of young people in the facilities I studied were born during the 1990s. Significant political and economic changes happened during this time, which would have consequences for the lives of the young people and the staff in the juvenile facilities.

Life in juvenile facilities cannot be understood without examining the broader political climate staff and young people exist in. Juvenile and criminal justice systems are the sites of state-level projects of crime control, and their practices reflect state-level ideologies about crime and offending. Criminologist David Garland analyzed the history of the criminal justice system in the twentieth century and identified a clear shift in state ideologies in places like England and the United States away from the idea that the state is fully responsible for preventing and controlling crime toward the idea that individuals and communities should take on these responsibilities. The new ideology focused on people charged with crimes owning up to their engagement in those crimes. This has been called a "responsibilization" strategy.⁶ Garland argues that responsibilization is not simply about government relinquishing its authority but rather is a form of governing-at-a-distance, which actually extends the ability of the state to influence the lives of individuals.

Responsibilization practices are linked to neoliberal political and economic policies, emphasizing individual freedom in the marketplace. Under neoliberal policies, "each individual is held responsible and accountable for his or her own actions and well-being."⁷ To accomplish this, neoliberal policies have focused on limiting state spending on social welfare; privatizing previously public entities, such as prisons; and asserting the prominence of the free marketplace as a source of individual and societal success. Although there are no private prisons in New York, the state's juvenile justice agency increased their reliance on a federal program that would allow the state to use federal funds to support the placement of young people in privately operated not-for-profit agencies; this process began in the 1970s, and today New York City relies almost entirely on this program to fund the placement of young people.

Yet the history of neoliberalism in this country has not been solely about shrinking the role of the state in individuals' lives: political scientists have found that the governance of the poor has taken a peculiar turn—the state has reduced social welfare benefits while amping up social control—it is both paternalistic and neoliberal.[8] Some have argued that the state, in offering what it says is a form of protection, actually engages in domination by imposing rigorous standards of behavior and respectability, punishing work regimes, and harsh punitive consequences for noncompliance with state agencies.[9] In the youth justice context, the shape that this has taken has been what one scholar terms "repressive welfarism."[10]

These transformations in the global economy were significant for life within the juvenile facilities because the impoverished children of color made up the great influx of children committed to these facilities in the 1990s. Within the context of the management of the poor, the term "personal responsibility" achieved an elevated status in social life and discourse during this time. During the height of welfare reform, we saw this in the language used by politicians and welfare workers alike. Mothers dependent on welfare were seen as being "irresponsible" and their personal problems and sufferings not as symptoms of poverty, of racism, or even of state policy but of their individual failures.[11] This extended to their children: in the context of the juvenile justice system, the language and rhetoric used by policymakers and lawmakers focused on young people being held accountable for their actions, on owning up to the personal failings that led them to the system: arresting and punishing people was a direct way of ensuring such accountability.[12] By 2008, the police weren't arresting as many young people as they did in the 1990s in New York, but the idea that young people could and should be held accountable for their actions and take responsibility for them was a clear ideology expressed by many—not all—adult actors in the courts and the juvenile facilities, including by Brooks.

Many criminologists have recently claimed that the philosophy of neoliberalism can be seen at every level of the criminal justice system. I would argue that in the juvenile prisons, the approach embraced toward young people is not purely neoliberal but rather rooted in the idea that young people should be guided into an acceptance of the responsibility for their actions. Staff members like Brooks embody the complexity of this approach, which includes an older and more enduring idea that has existed for so long in the lives of young people charged with crimes: that the young person needs a strong—and even

sometimes caring—hand to support them in achieving change and in expressing self-controlled and motivated actions. It is not quite neoliberal as much as
it is part of an age-old concern with the management and submission of the
working poor; what previous scholars have less seriously addressed, however,
are the ways that the system itself has become more recently oriented around
the submission of primarily poor children of color, yet one where the staff
members themselves in the facilities are also increasingly people of color.[13]

The transformation of the global economy changed the lives of facility
staff members like Brooks. The rhetoric of responsibility resonated with those
who had managed, like Brooks, to find stable employment in a stagnant rural
economy. They believed that they had worked hard and pulled themselves up
by their bootstraps, despite significant obstacles. Facility staff, many of whom
had grown up in impoverished upstate communities or had moved up to the
area in search of a better life, sought out this state job in an effort to gain some
social mobility in the context of an economy with limited opportunities for
individuals from working class backgrounds with limited education. The New
York State Office of Children and Family Services (OCFS) was willing to hire
someone with just a high school equivalency and offer them a pay rate that
exceeded that of many jobs in rural New York. To obtain and keep a job like
the one that Brooks had on its surface seemed like a triumph of personal will
and responsibility—a success in the face of limited opportunities.

People like Brooks also felt emboldened to talk to young people about
pulling up their bootstraps and embracing a sense of personal responsibility because they had faced similar economic and structural challenges—and
seemingly overcome them. Brooks felt that he knew and understood the teenagers in the facilities because "I was one of them." As he held his fingers just a
few inches apart, he said that as a teenager he was "this close to being locked
up." He recognized the young people's misbehavior and felt he knew what
worked to control it and change it because he had been raised in the same way
as they had. He felt that "these kids respond to fear" and that he was able to get
them to follow his program standards because he conveyed to them the need
to "listen to you because you can kick my ass." He felt strongly that "respect is
driven by fear." This came from experience: when he was in the eighth grade,
he was suspended from school. His football coach scared him, and because he
didn't want to fail that coach, he worked hard to go back to school so that he
could stay on the team.

Brooks felt like his background—and those of other staff members like
him—was an advantage in his work with the kids. "I think they look at it as
these guys are real," and that "they know I went to college," and "a lot of times
they are surprised" by me. Brooks felt that the kids were "raised and bred to
have people fear them," but "that's just the street mentality" that they come
from. He felt that they've "got a wall so thick, it is hard to get their trust."

Throughout his twenty-one years working in the facilities, Brooks, like many of his peers, felt he had become an expert in what worked for the kids under his care. His approach treaded the line between compassion and toughness. This style, shared with his coworkers from similar backgrounds, emerged out of their personal history and experience working in the facility, not necessarily what he had been trained to do.

YDAs like Brooks are tasked with running a facility unit. They usually work with one other YDA, and they have eight-hour shifts, but, during the time I was doing the research, they often worked sixteen consecutive hours at the facility as a result of mandatory overtime. They are technically responsible for movement and control, but because they are the staff members who spend the most time with young people, they end up doing much more with them than simply watching them, punishing them, and making sure they move smoothly through the facility. They talk them down from a crisis, play cards with them, suggest books for them to read, help them with their homework, talk to them about girlfriends, boyfriends, college, and religion. One YDA described his role as a "de facto counselor," "role model," and "house parent." Another YDA said, "I'm the psychologist, bartender, and cab driver" for the young people. Brooks had honed his tough love approach over the years; he knew that building strong relationships with the young people enabled him to do his job daily. He believed in balance: it was important to be hard on the young people when they "acted out," and it was also "very important that we have conversations with the kids when they are not having problems."

THE BEHAVIORAL CHANGE SYSTEM

One of the expectations of staff members like Brooks at the facilities was that they monitor the residents' behavior and decide whether they would be ready to ascend a stage in a behavioral change system. System administrators developed these stages to provide incentives for good behavior and consequences for bad behavior. The treatment program in OCFS, as in other juvenile correctional institutions, is a tightly guided system of change. The behavioral change system is an amalgamation of various cognitive change curricula and forms of behavioral modification that are used in juvenile facilities and correctional facilities across the world.[14] The program has many stated aims, including reducing offending, encouraging prosocial behaviors, and shaping young people into responsible and productive wage earners. The institutions involved a mixed emphasis on obedience and punishment, reeducation, development, and treatment.[15]

Depending on the level of residential care (nonsecure, limited secure, secure), residents advanced to a new stage in the behavioral change system after an administrative review process. In secure facilities, it has taken over six months for teenagers to earn their first stage in this a behavioral change system.[16] This system is premised on the notion that young people will "modify" their behavior in response to various consequences or rewards that it produces.[17] However, even with the possibility of shifting behaviors to adapt to the program, it's still impossible for many teenagers to advance to the highest stages.

In the residential child-care context, there is a healthy debate about the generalizability of such incentives and earned privileges systems.[18] This debate focuses on the idea that young people's motivation to succeed inside facilities—and thus their behavioral adjustment to such regimes—may not be sustainable outside of the facilities, where parents rarely impose similar token economies at home and where behavioral change is not contingent on the threat of coercion and incarceration. This debate wasn't happening much on the facility floors.

Upon entering a facility, teenage residents are given a manual in which they learn about the stage expectations and rules they need to follow. The basic rules require deference to staff authority, compliance with rules and procedures, "work[ing] out problems" through treatment programs, exercising "self-respect" and respect for others, honesty, cleanliness, and being quiet.[19] Major rule infractions could result in a meeting of a disciplinary committee or the arrest of the young person. Residents who violated facility rules were entitled to a quasi-administrative hearing. If they commit a facility-based infraction, teenagers charged as adults (Juvenile Offenders) can lose the opportunity to leave after two-thirds of their sentence have been completed, the minimum amount of time they serve when they first arrive at the facility. Staff members like Brooks were expected to police the facility rules, and they had the power to write disciplinary slips, called "levels," if a resident violated the rules.

Teenagers in the juvenile facilities wore different color shoelaces that symbolized the place they were on the behavioral change system—white shoelaces represented the "Orientation" stage, identified as the "Reluctant Learner" stage in staff training manuals, and green shoelaces represented the "Honors," or highest stage (see Table 4-1). When residents were in the orientation stage, staff were expected to teach them that they "will be watched very closely by staff," according to their training manual. In their own manual, residents are taught that if they follow the staff directives, "it will also improve the way you control yourself."[20] In the next stage (Adjustment, described as an "Enthusiastic Learner"), a resident is expected to work without direction, demonstrate improvements in programs, and to show "other evidence that you are accepting your placement and understand why you have been placed here."[21] In the third stage (Transition, a "Cautious Performer"), residents are expected to take more initiative in their deference to the rules of the program, using the "skills" that they have obtained in the facility (such as "anger control" and "problem-solving") and show that "you are able to say that you feel sorry for your crimes and take responsibility for your negative behaviors,

TABLE 4-1
"The Stage System"

Orientation	Adjustment	Transition	Honors
Reluctant Learner (White)★	Enthusiastic Learner (Blue)	Cautious performer (Yellow)	Competent and Committed performer (Green)
Watched closely by staff.	Demonstrates acceptance of placement.	More initiative in deference in program, demonstration of skills and responsibility for actions.	Leader to peers and cooperation with program expectations.

★Color denotes the color of shoelaces which corresponds to each stage in the system.
SOURCE: This chart has been developed from information in the OCFS resident's manual.

without blaming others."[22] In the highest level stage (Honors, a "Competent and Committed Performer"), a resident should be encouraging his or her peers to "be positive and to make good choices" by showing "improved self-esteem by cooperating with staff and program expectations."[23] The use of the word "performer" in the staff manual, of course, indicates the way that young people are "performing" well in the program.

While Brooks was not shy about administering level slips to young people, and he, like all staff members, filled out the various forms and paperwork required in the behavioral change system, he was less interested in getting the kids to follow the facility rules than in getting them to do their schoolwork. Brooks felt strongly that educational success was their route out of their lives in the criminal justice system. While Brooks was certainly not alone in his interest in emphasizing schoolwork over behavioral change, many staff simply enforced the behavioral change rules because they were required to but also because they knew that obedience would help them do their work more easily.

The principles behind the behavioral stage system that was used in the facilities—and used in juvenile facilities across the country—stem from the idea that, through these interventions, individuals will be prepared to make more rational choices about the world around them, particularly about committing crimes. The young person's evolution toward these choices closely follows models of moral development developed by the psychologist Jean Piaget.[24]

Developmental psychologists have advanced theories of learning about children's purported malleability that clearly resonated with juvenile justice administrators intent on creating interventions that could facilitate changes in "bad" teenagers.[25] Psychological theories were first introduced into juvenile facilities in the United States in the early part of the twentieth century.[26] Jean

Piaget, an influential theorist of children's moral development, argued that "development is a journey away from disorder and failure to discriminate between self and world, toward order and discrimination, a 'transition from chaos to cosmos.'"[27] Piaget was interested in "assimilation, accommodation, [and] adaptation," and although he was influenced by psychoanalytic theories, his focus was seemingly on the processes and elaboration of cognition.[28] Piaget argued that the moral development of young people involved their acceptance and understanding of social rules. Thus, if juvenile justice interventions could help rule-defying teenagers to understand social rules, they may get set back on the path of appropriate development (because the assumption is and was that by committing crimes, they are inappropriately developed).

The psychologist Lawrence Kohlberg, a follower of Jean Piaget, argued in his "cognitive developmental" theory that moral behaviors are related to the development of skills of rational reasoning.[29] Kohlberg and others appeal to the notion that individuals are endowed with the "capacity for rational thought."[30] These theories have contributed to the perspective that cognitive skills can be enhanced and developed within individuals, ultimately leading to self-mastery.[31] These perspectives have arguably become influential in interventions used in juvenile facilities. Cognitive behavioralists believed that "crime was the outcome of insufficiently or unevenly developed rational or cognitive capacities" in individuals, and thus developed interventions which sought to address those capacities.[32] Kohlberg and others argued that young people who engaged in delinquency had failed to advance from "preconventional" (or "rule-obeying") to "conventional" thinking (or "rule-maintaining") stage.[33] These stages map closely onto the shoelace stages used in the residential facilities.

Also influential in the thinking about interventions in the lives of young people charged with crimes is the criminologists Michael Gottfredson and Travis Hirschi's self-control theory. These scholars argued that low self-control is the primary reason for individuals' engagement with crime. For Gottfredson and Hirschi, low self-control stems from poor family socialization and disciplinary practices.[34] Self-control or "personal control" has long been a preoccupation of those involved in studying the causes of juvenile delinquency.[35]

Cognitive behavioral therapies like those used in OCFS, now dominant in juvenile justice interventions, were introduced in the 1980s into Canadian and American prisons in part because they appealed to the desire of prison administrators to introduce programs that were affordable and could be easily taught to front-line correctional staff and thus lessened the system's dependence on outsiders for program provision.[36] For many years, those outsiders who arrived in prisons represented left-leaning social welfare organizations, activist groups, and other organizations who were committed to prison reform. These individuals were deemed to be problematic and incendiary following the famous disturbance in Attica prison in 1971, in which the prison was taken over by the people incarcerated there and the state's governor at the time, Nelson Rockefeller, ordered the National Guard to open fire on the facility, killing numerous guards and incarcerated people.[37] Cognitive behavioralism also arrived in prisons and juvenile facilities in the context of a widespread rejection of traditional correctional methods that were aimed at addressing individual pathologies and the underlying causes of crime.[38] These methods were seen by correctional administrators to be too time-consuming and incapable of producing tangible results.

Myriad evaluations of cognitive behavioral programs in the juvenile justice context have pointed to the ability of such programs to reduce recidivism.[39] These studies have largely relied on the use of questionnaires and surveys that analyze the extent to which young people engage in "cognitive distortions" and randomized controlled trials of the impact of the interventions on subsequent delinquency. What they haven't studied, however, are how these programs have influenced young people's senses of themselves, their identities, and their life trajectories.

The primary aim of cognitive behavioral interventions, to prevent reoffending, constructs an offender's will or agency in offending as a malleable quality.[40] However, these strategies cannot be untangled from the long-standing history of concern by adults working in the juvenile justice system and other child-saving institutions with the preservation of childhood vulnerability.[41] In other words, it is necessary to look at these interventions as ones that embrace a paradox: they seek to stimulate young people to become active in their own process of responsibility taking but in a way that actually involves submission to the regime and the people who were its representatives. A number of adults in the system—regardless of their own racial identity—also embrace a desire for young people, and particularly young people of color, to act deferentially toward them. For them, the ideal resident is the one who is ideally compliant.

Every Wednesday in the facilities, school shuts down for the afternoon, and a few of the residents have a meeting with their youth counselor, a teacher, and occasionally a YDA like Brooks. These Treatment Team meetings happen about once a month for each resident. The rest of the residents who are not meeting with their counselors usually sit on their units, with no planned activities. The youth counselors are expected to fill out a form called a "Resident Behavior Assessment" at this meeting. The resident's progression on the stage system is based on this assessment. They are also sometimes also given "Behavior Improvement Plans" at the meeting (see Figure 4-1). Staff members also reviewed the number of level slips that a young person had received during the meeting.

The number of forms that track a resident's progress through treatment is often bewildering for staff members and residents alike. In addition to the

Resident Behavior Assessment form, the counselor has to fill out a Resident Progress Report (see Figure 4-2). There is a different progress report for each stage that the resident is on. Paperwork constitutes a substantial part of the working day of staff at the facilities. Counselors and aides sit at desks on the units that look out over the main common area and the young people's rooms, writing in enormous log books in which they register movements, unusual incidents, and young people's participation in the "program" of everyday life. Staff members have the books with them almost everywhere they go. Young people were as conscious of the forms as staff were; level slips could also be given out for positive forms of behavior, and some young people put these slips in their parole files or what they called their "portfolios," which were binders of positive information that they maintained throughout their time in the facilities. The residents also know that any incident required a stream of paperwork that was extremely burdensome for staff members to fill out.

For both residents and staff members, the behavioral change system can feel scripted in that they must follow a tight set of rules and expectations that are laid out for them, rather than organically responding to the demands and expectations of the facility programing.[42] The programs are largely aimed at encouraging residents to embrace the principles of the program, rather than discovering an internal motivation to be successful in the program.[43] Staff members like Brooks recognized that much of their daily life was spent enforcing the rules of a program rather than having the time to build relationships and seek to understand young people and why they were in the facilities.

Slam was considered by the staff in his facility to be a difficult resident. After he failed to complete the requirements of his community-based alternative to incarceration program, his judge sentenced him to time in a facility located in a rural part of the state. According to a staff member at the juvenile facility who filled out a Resident Progress Report about him, Slam engaged in multiple incidents and rule violations, which are the markers of resistance to change in the institutional setting, at least in terms of his ability to be released and to receive a higher level stage. Yet he complied or exceeded with all of the expectations listed in the report, except for the expectation to "describe acceptable methods for controlling impulsive behavior and use them with staff direction." In this case, Slam's initial delinquency offense was less important in the context of the juvenile facility than his continuing misbehaviors after he was arrested, both while he was in the program in the community and at the program.

While doing an alternative-to-incarceration program in his community, he lived with his grandparents, who had adopted him after his mother abandoned him as a child, choosing to maintain her drug addiction. While in residential care, Slam started receiving letters from his incarcerated father for the first time in his life, learning that his father was going to be released within months and wanted to see him. The letters from his father were affixed to the wall of his room. However, when Slam's abilities to make choices and solve problems were evaluated by facility staff, they did not take his father's incarceration and imminent release into consideration, even though they may have played a role in shaping his behavior in the facility.

There are expectations of residents to behave in a particular way inside of the facility, and the "skills" they learn are supposed to have some bearing on the resident's life on the outside. The residents are expected by the system to be engaged in this process. Yet staff members like Brooks knew that even though they were expected to fill out these forms, and, as a result of filling them out, were somewhat invested in their utility as a tool, for the most part, they relied on their own strategies for change that existed outside of the paper-based systems.

Brooks, like a number of other staff members, was skeptical that the behavioral change system fully worked to change individual behavior. He understood that some of the actions and behaviors that were expected of the young people may have felt foreign or unrecognizable to them. Brooks would encourage the kids to "fake it to make it" through the behavioral change program, because he felt he had had to do some faking of his own in his life. When the kids asked him how he got out of his neighborhood and to college, and he told them that "I faked it until it became a habit." When the kids questioned him about the inauthenticity of faking it, he would reply, "Guess what? We all fake it . . . faking it ain't that bad."

Brooks, like many staff members I talked to who had worked in the system for a long time, felt that the new commissioner of OCFS, Gladys Carrión, had introduced reforms that "made it difficult" to keep up norms of behavior and standards of consistency. Like many others, he complained about the introduction of more ombudsmen, who were responsible for oversight, to the system. During the time I was doing research, ombudsmen would come regularly to the facilities, and young people were encouraged to call the ombudsman's office with complaints and grievances about facility life. Brooks said that a teenager told him that the ombudsman told him, "I don't have to do nothing." He said he responded to the young person by saying, "Do you think the ombudsman's kid does nothing?"

The staff members' critiques of the oversight process may have been somewhat predictable; no one likes having outsiders looking in. There have been strong cases made for external oversight of prisons and juvenile justice systems, and it is arguable that the introduction of the ombudsman to the facilities was an important step in providing a level of accountability that had not previously existed in the facilities.[44] However, one of the issues that the staff began to identify was that the ombudsman were not truly independent;

OCFS-4642 (Rev 9/2004)

NEW YORK STATE
OFFICE OF CHILDREN AND FAMILY SERVICES
BEHAVIOR IMPROVEMENT PLAN

RESIDENT NAME	Date of BIP
FACILITY PROGRAM	RESIDENTIAL UNIT/COTTAGE

RESIDENT'S CURRENT STAGE	☐ ORIENTATION ☐ ADJUSTMENT	☐ TRANSITION ☐ HONORS	DURATION OF BIP

Reason for Plan:

What resident assets can be utilized?

Goal (What needs to be achieved or corrected?)

What does the resident need to do to achieve the goal?

How will the plan's success be determined and by whom?

What will staff do?

WERE PRIVILEGES LOST? ☐ YES ☐ NO	PRIVILEGES LOST?	BEGIN LOP	FOR HOW LONG?

STAFF DEVELOPING PLAN

_____ / /
Signature   Title   Date

YDC OR ABOVE APPROVING PLAN

_____ / /
Signature   Title   Date

RESIDENT

_____ / /
Signature   Date

PLAN COMPLETION REVIEW	Plan Completed? ☐ YES ☐ NO

_____ / /
Signature   Title   Date

Attach Activity Report
cc: Original to Resident; Youth Development Log

FIGURE 4-1. Behavior Improvement Plan

```
(Rev. 4/2006)                                                                    Page 1
                              NEW YORK STATE
                    OFFICE OF CHILDREN AND FAMILY SERVICES
                       RESIDENT PROGRESS REPORT
                               MENTOR
                           Orientation Stage
```

	DATES	/ /	/ /

Rate the following resident responsibilities by checking either "Complies or "Exceeds" or "Needs Improvement".

DEFINITIONS:

Complies or exceeds expectations: An established pattern of behavior that meets or exceeds performance expectations (90-100% compliance).

Needs improvement: An irregular pattern of compliance with performance expectations; or established pattern of non-compliance. (Less than 90% compliance).

WITH CONSTANT STAFF DIRECTION, YOU ARE EXPECTED TO:

Complies or Exceeds	Needs Improvement		Treatment Team Focus Items
SET 1		**Self Discipline**	
01 ☐	☐	Obey laws and comply with facility rules with staff direction.	01 ☐
02 ☐	☐	Describe non-violent alternatives for resolving conflicts and use them with staff direction.	02 ☐
03 ☐	☐	Describe acceptable methods for controlling impulsive behavior and use them with staff direction.	03 ☐
04 ☐	☐	Acknowledge rule violations, but minimizes its importance.	04 ☐
05 ☐	☐	Describe the problem solving steps and use them with staff direction.	05 ☐
ET 2		**Interpersonal Relationships**	
06 ☐	☐	Tell the truth.	06 ☐
07 ☐	☐	Seek clarification from staff about program expectations.	07 ☐
08 ☐	☐	Avoid peers who engage in anti-social behaviors.	08 ☐
09 ☐	☐	Avoid taking a negative leadership role.	09 ☐
10 ☐	☐	Describe the importance of establishing positive interpersonal relationships.	10 ☐

CURRENT TREATMENT TEAM FOCUS ITEMS: _____

_____

_____

_____

Mentor Meeting Dates: Week 1: _____   Week 2: _____

Staff Signature: _____   Review Date: _____

Residents Signature: _____   Review Date: _____

Distribution: Youth Development Log

FIGURE 4-2. Resident Progress Report

they were in fact employed by OCFS, and their oversight of the agencies, and thus their ability to hold staff accountable, presented some degree of conflict in the facilities.

LOSING CONTROL

It was nearly impossible to go to a facility without hearing staff members talk about how the facilities had descended into violence since the new commissioner had arrived. During the time that I was doing my research, the state relied heavily on overtime, as many staff members were calling out sick and missing work, in part, they said, as a result of some of the reforms that were happening.[45] Brooks's work partner, Barton, explained that so many staff members were on overtime in his facility because they were "injured like crazy," an explanation I heard from other staff; their supervisors would tell me that they felt that staff were engaging in foot dragging and malingering, not coming into work because they simply disliked the way the reforms were making the facility operate.

Barton noted that the job was "tough" on the kids of staff who worked at facilities. Barton's father had been a YDA at the very same facility. His father had missed a number of his sports games growing up. He too was a black man—more than 50 percent of the staff in the facilities was black.

On a typical day in the facility, as the twelve young people he supervised start preparing for their mealtime, Brooks started barking at them to get ready. The young people lined up, shouting out their room numbers as they did. He told the residents that if weren't on their doors in fifteen seconds, then he would start escalating the punishments against them. As the young people quickly fell into line in response to his commands, Brooks yelled at them, "We set the pace, you don't!" He explained that as a young person ascended the behavioral stage system, he would no longer need to ask for permission to move freely about the unit. When we arrived in the cafeteria, the young people ate in silence in observance of a facility-wide rule that they refrain from speaking to each other during meals.

Brooks spoke about how one of his goals in leading his unit was to let the "house take care of themselves," and that ideally it was important to "get the kids to regulate themselves." Brooks felt that young people's self-regulation or self-control would make their lives, as well as those of staff, easier. Brooks felt that it was important to instill in the young people the idea that "you're not going to make it unless you're doing good program." He felt that the behavioral change rules would ultimately provide benefits to this group of young people who "don't know how to follow directions" and that the program was intended to instill this sense in them.

Brooks felt that "we fail if a piece of the puzzle is missing." He gave the example of how there were four members of the gang the Crips on the unit at one point, and though it took them a little while to figure out that the Crips were there, once the problem was known, they could manage it.

Barton and Brooks said that they believed in developing "consistency in the program" and that if they achieved this, their program worked well. Brooks also said that the program was also very school-oriented, and they were focused on "challenging them educationally." He said to me that as a young white woman, "You had people telling you you would do well," but these kids did not have that (and nor did he, as he was growing up). He felt that the emphasis on school "doesn't leave time for other bullshit."

But Brooks was also known for being serious and tough, focused on control and discipline. He said that "when a kid comes here, he knows he is coming to our house." He spoke about how "we make our own schedule here." He said that he and Barton had decided that if the young people on the unit didn't do their homework, "gym won't happen." He talked about how it was important that the staff members were "on the same page" with each other and how that didn't always happen, especially in terms of getting teachers on board with their ideas about how the program should be run. He said, for example, that he didn't personally mind if a young person's pants were not pulled up, but if another staff member on duty with him cared about this, they needed to enforce it together. He said it was important to recognize that the kids weren't just dealing with one staff member, they were dealing with the entire staff. He spoke about how the unit is "almost like family." He said that in some parts of the facility, there was a "prison mentality" among the young people and staff, which he rejected; he felt strongly that the mentality made life in the units break down.

MAINTAINING CONTROL

Brooks believed that the kids needed to feel "you're in control" of the units to feel safe themselves; "We force the kids to adjust" to the unit, which "becomes an expectation." He said that a young person usually enters his unit and is then in counseling for two to three days because he is "not conforming with the program" in the rest of the facility and that "he's gonna realize that he's not in control." He said that most kids realize this. He gave an example of a kid who was in the counseling room and said that he was ready to talk to the staff, but Brooks said to the kid, "We don't conform to you," and the kid would have to stay in the room a while longer until he got "things straight." He said he tells the kids, "We're going to control you, you don't have control." On the wall of one of the units where Barton and Brooks worked, there were some caricatures of staff members that a young resident had drawn—Brooks's caricature had a picture of him saying a version of "Shut your trap."

Some other staff members felt that they needed to regain "control" from the young people, seeking out what they felt was a need for more "safety" in their environments. Many staff members felt that control had been yielded to young people in the new facilities; this was a particularly prominent sentiment expressed by white male staff members. A middle-aged white male administrator at one facility argued that the young people, who he said were already "maladjusted and manipulative," had become more so in the new environment. This staff member said that the new policies had "empowered" the young people, and this was "tantamount to putting a gun in their pocket and holding us hostage." This narrative about a transfer in control was central to some staff members' comments, often directly to young people, that more overt forms of control would make the environment safer. Staff members frequently expressed feelings of responsibility for the safety and rehabilitation of young people inside, but ultimately a kind of resignation about what might happen to them after they were released from the facilities. Their perception was that the teenagers in the facilities came from environments that lacked structure, and thus that the facilities themselves needed to impose a kind of order or "structure" over those young people's lives; this perception was largely derived from stereotypes and assumptions rather than a meaningful sense of the lived realities of the young people. It was many years in the making—the idea that a juvenile facility could offer young people who committed crimes a sense of daily structure was built into the founding philosophy of the juvenile justice system. Yet the young people themselves had a wide range of experiences as children—structurelessness was not, however, always the defining feature of their childhood existence.

The notion of "structure" was also reinforced situationally in the residential facilities: staff instantly separated young people at the start of a fight, and the teenagers were required to keep their hands behind their back whenever they walked through the facility (although this requirement was eliminated soon after the reforms began). The architecture of their common living areas emphasized the separation of young people through the arrangement of chairs in a row facing the front of the room, where the main security staff sat, and where there was a television, rather than in circles or in a way that might be conducive to conversation between residents.

Brooks felt that OCFS had taken a "cookie-cutter" approach to dealing with the kids in their reforms and that they're "selling woof tickets" to them—or providing them with empty promises of success in their future lives. "If you open up a crack for these kids," he said, "they manipulate" the situation easily. He, like a number of other staff, felt that the agency was focusing on becoming kinder and nicer toward children without an attendant emphasis on structure and control. He felt that the kids "will exploit" those staff who are "nice."

One of the approaches attempted during the 1990s by facility administrators, when Brooks first began working in the agency, was to develop interventions based on a young person's supposed risks of reoffending. Contemporary court interventions with young people in the United States and elsewhere in the world are often justified with reference to a range of empirical research that has been done on young people's "developmental" pathways to antisocial behavior, rooted in the notion that there are certain risk factors, like exposure to physical and sexual abuse, interrupted school histories, and neglect, that have prevented children from meeting a series of developmental milestones that most allegedly normal young people have achieved.[46] The court interventions are intended to provide a fix for those problems, primarily by using cognitive behavioral interventions aimed at adjusting young people's decision-making and impulse control capacities—those arguably focused on responsibility taking and responsibility making behaviors.

Starting in the 1990s, when Brooks had just begun working in the system, the agency developed and implemented a treatment model derived from research in Canada that was responsive to the risks of reoffending and the "criminogenic needs" of young people.[47] The interventions that staff used in the facilities include various kinds of cognitive behavioral programming, including Dialectical Behavior Therapy (DBT), Multisystemic Therapy, Moral Reconation Therapy, Aggression Replacement Therapy (ART), Structured Learning Techniques (SLT), Moral Reasoning, and Adolescent Portable Therapy.[48] ART was introduced into the facilities by Leonard Dunston, the commissioner who led the agency from the 1980s until the 1990s, and the program was expanded nationally after it was first introduced in New York.[49] ART involves teaching youth how to build social skills, to control their anger, and to develop their moral reasoning. Thus, it is consistent with the model of development proposed by the early developmental psychologists like Piaget.

When I asked Brooks and his partner Barton what kinds of interventions they used on their unit, they said, "We make it up as we go along." Brooks said that "ART is ridiculous, I'm going to tell you straight. It's bullshit." He suggested that the ART model didn't mimic the real-world provocations that young people would face on the street. Brooks felt that he should teach the kids that "you've gotta prepare yourself for angry situations." He shared that if the kids told Barton to "suck his dick, he goes crazy," suggesting that many individuals get angry and cannot simply control their anger—that these provocations are a part of everyday life. Instead of implementing ART, Brooks and Barton would use informal techniques with the young people to teach them about managing their frustration. They would try to teach the kids that "you don't always have to respond to something." When I asked them if they felt that this was a kind of anger management tool, they said yes.

Some staff members felt that straightforward behavioral techniques were best equipped to manage the young people—that they should be yelled at if they made a mistake or restrained if they were being obstreperous. For example, a teacher, when speaking about his frustrations with a new disciplinary model in the system said, "If a dog comes and pees on the floor, you don't talk nicely to him." Another staff member discussed how he had employed the same techniques of sanction and reward with a young person that he had used with his dog, referencing his dog's electric collar.

Of course not all staff members embraced this strongly behaviorist orientation to young people, and, much like in any school or external child-serving institution, the facility staff members represented a range of personal and political ideologies, particularly about young people's pathways to crime and offending, that were often in conflict with each other.

One of the interventions that was being expanded in the facilities during the reforms in New York was DBT, "the application of a wide assortment of cognitive-behavioral strategies combined with a philosophical emphasis on dialectics."[50]

Late in 2011, when DBT was being rolled out at Hooper, Brooks said that "whenever I hear acronyms, I get nervous," because "it's the next bullshit" program that they bring in, and "you may say that that they have mental health issues" but they don't, because "they're criminal thinkers." He explained his opinion that even though the young people under his care were called teenagers, and sometimes children, they actually lived lives much like adults— "these are adults," he said, and they are having sex, paying bills, and taking on the responsibilities of adulthood, but in a "less developed" mind. Instead of focusing on their feelings, he said, you've "gotta train them not to eat your ass." A white staff psychologist who had worked at the agency for a number of years similarly felt that the treatment models that were being used weren't appropriate for the population of young people in the facility: he said the new interventions are a "square peg, round hole" problem—there is nothing really to "object to" in interventions like DBT, but that making it a success in the "correctional environment" is not something that was "intended." He said that they need to modify these programs to the "secure environment," noting that they had only been used in environments where young people weren't under lock and key. Countless times, staff members would say that therapeutic interventions were inappropriate for a locked facility environment; their sentiments revealed an age-old tension between care and control: they were expected to be jailors while also providing treatment, a role tension they struggled to manage in their lives.

Brooks's words about "criminal thinkers" didn't come out of nowhere or simply reflect his personal philosophy about offending. In fact, he had been asked by agency administrators for years to use an approach with the young people that was rooted in the assumption that they engaged in critical thinking errors that led to their offending. These ideas were firmly ensconced in juvenile residential facility curricula, which included courses called "Thinking Errors" that were still in place in many facilities that also used DBT. Although DBT has a strong evidence base, the staff members' interpretations of it suggest that they had not been fully immersed or even fully understood how the intervention could be efficacious in young people's lives.

The discipline of psychoanalysis, which formed the backbone of early interventions used in juvenile facilities, played a pivotal role in the development of ideas about adolescent criminality and criminal thinking. Psychoanalytic theories about the relationship between the mother and the child became the locus of concerns about child and adolescent adjustment.[51] The American post-Freudian tradition of ego psychology, manifested in the work of Anna Freud and Erik Erikson (among others), focused in particular on notions of self-mastery, ego growth and defense, and adaptation.[52] Ego psychology theories influenced the practices of those aimed at treating delinquency, such as Edward Glover, who founded the Institute for the Study and Treatment of Delinquency in England, and August Aichhorn, a disciple of Anna Freud's.[53] Psychoanalysis also played a role in juvenile justice practices and group treatment for adolescents aimed at halting "neutralizations." Neutralizations are said to be "excuses and justifications that deviants use to rationalize their behaviors."[54] These neutralization-halting practices, popular in juvenile facilities, which involve the prevention of youth engaging in "thinking errors" or cognitive distortions, are partially rooted in psychoanalytic theories about defense mechanisms located in the realm of the subconscious.[55]

Many of the treatment modalities used in the facilities encouraged the development of rational thinking in young people, and the elimination of cognitive distortions, "faulty beliefs" or "thinking errors." Following is a sample of language from one of these intervention manuals that existed in New York's facilities:

> You are capable and worthy of positive changes in your life but you are the only one who can make them happen.
>
> What would be a more responsible and rational way of thinking?
>
> I can clear up my beliefs.
>
> Many young people cling to the false belief that life is always fair to everybody else.

The emphasis of the program modules is on engendering change in young people by helping them to eliminate their feelings of victimhood.

The "thinking errors" curricula were influenced by theories which relate the neutralization of one's deviant actions to the development of delinquency.[56] Neutralizations could include inconsistencies, denial of fear, or failure to plan ahead.[57] The sociologist David Matza famously argued that the focus of the juvenile justice system on identifying the source of young people's involvement in crime to their family backgrounds and the environments in which they grew compounds the problem of neutralization, and thus, delinquency. Young people become aware of the discourses used to define their delinquency and draw on them in explaining their actions. However, by doing so they can be seen to be offering explanations for their behaviors, rather than taking responsibility for their actions.[58]

As black men working in a facility filled with young men of color, Barton and Brooks felt it was impossible to evade discussions about the racism that existed in their lives and the lives of the young people under their care. The official curriculum about neutralizations suggested that a young person's critique of racist criminal justice practices might be evidence of their evasion of responsibility for their actions; a number of white staff throughout the facility embraced this ideology. One white male facility director refused some books that I offered to donate, including *Race, Crime and the Law*, by Randall Kennedy (he had never read the book), because he said that young people needed to focus on taking personal responsibility for their actions and that the title of this book might suggest that they could blame racism instead. A white male judge, while speaking to a group of young men at Hooper, echoed this sentiment when he told them, "You have the keys to your jail cell in your control." These notions that "getting out" of treatment are connected to an individual's focus entirely on themselves is one that has increasing purchase in contemporary prisons, which have highly individualized forms of punishment and treatment.[59]

Other efforts to engender ideas about "personal responsibility" were evident in a number of staff members' use of the expression "You come here alone, you leave here alone," which was propounded by a number of staff members in institutions, often in an effort to discourage young people from engaging in conflict or seeking out the approval of their peers. It helped that the program of treatment interventions and behavioral modification constructed the ideal participant as wholly responsible for his or her actions.[60]

But as a black male who had grown up in a predominantly black and heavily policed neighborhood, Brooks knew that the young people's relationships to racism and responsibility were complicated. He understood that the young people were naturally suspicious of the white YDAs because "kids know the cops are white," and they saw the YDAs' power as closely resembling that of the police. He felt that it was important to "break race down" for the kids in the facility and that "we talk about it." He spoke about how "being yourself" is important; implicit in this idea was that staff needed to present their genuine, unencumbered and authentic experiences of racism to the young people. Barton said that the kids would often tell him about racist staff members, but he said that he tries to tell the young people that "this is life"—the racism expressed by the staff members toward them would be their reality. He said, "Sometimes you've gotta eat it" adding that "anything is a teachable situation." He had distributed an article about how poor African American people have bad dental health because they lack insurance, and then he set up a group discussion on his unit about this article. Brooks's sociological approach to this issue contrasted somewhat with his focus on young people's need to follow the rules of the program but perhaps represented the balance that he felt must be struck between recognizing the structural forces behind young people's experiences and their need to combat those forces in their personal choices and lives. He felt that it was important to teach young people about "pushing back" against the assumption that they would fail; he avoided using the words "fight back" because he felt that fighting had such negative connotations in their lives.

Barton and Brooks would frequently tell the kids on their unit to "shut the fuck up." Laughing, Brooks said that this expression would probably not be looked upon favorably by those in power, but that it was one which worked well on the unit, and was about teaching the young people to stay quiet in appropriate moments, avoid conflict when it was unnecessary, and realize when it was best actually to stay quiet to avoid further trouble.

Brooks and Barton said that they ran groups almost every day on their unit, rather than the youth counselors who were technically tasked with such a job. During their groups, Barton and Brooks talked about family life and parenting with the young people. Brooks felt strongly that "they are all our sons." They would tell the kids things like "we're trying to save your life, son," along with "shut the fuck up," testing the boundaries of toughness and love.

Responsibilization Practices

The requirement for teenagers to take responsibility for their advancement or progress in treatment is common to programs aimed at reducing offending.[61] The central premise behind these programs is that the denial of responsibility represents an externalization of blame, and thus the displacement of the processes of change to sources beyond one's control.[62] Thus, the objectives of treatment—that young people will move from having externally related goals to internally related ones—is related to these models. There is an implicit link that is made between these "excuses" or processes of externalizing blame and a continuing inclination to offend.[63] Yet criminologists Shadd Maruna and Ruth Mann, drawing from extensive research on the processes of responsibility-taking in sex offender treatment, have argued that the relationship between excuse-making and recidivism may not be so straightforward because excuse-making itself is a normative reaction to shame, blame, and stigma.[64] In his research on long-term offenders who desist from crime, Maruna has found that there may be processes through which desistance from crime occurs because of some forms of self-deception, in which one reconstructs one's identity as a nonoffender.[65]

Young people noted the ironies of the thinking errors curriculum in their lives. Newz, who spent four years in two residential facilities and went through multiple cycles of treatment programming, said that it was nearly impossible not to engage in a thinking error, as defined by those who designed the curriculum for the programs: he said that eating too many cookies, for example, could be representative of a thinking error.

The range of therapeutic offerings was not consistently implemented across the facilities, and some staff engaged in a kind of "mix-and-match"–style approach to the therapies, some abandoning previously used interventions in favor of the latest "silver bullet," the words of one staff counselor, who brought me into his office to show me a discarded pile of books on Moral Reconation Therapy, which he had been asked to implement, albeit briefly. According to an assessment of the treatment interventions in OCFS conducted by outside evaluators:

> our conversations in several of the facilities revealed that some of the staff were confused about the distinctions—or similarities—between the various therapies and, more importantly, how they were linked to an overall agency philosophy regarding the treatment of committed youth. Staff and youth in one facility knew the acronyms of the different approaches (some of which were listed on a bulletin board) but had difficulty explaining what they stood for or entailed.[66]

I observed staff members experiencing the same confusion in all of the facilities that I visited.

Starting around 2008, OCFS introduced new treatment modalities and implemented a new system of care, called the Sanctuary Model, which was aimed at recognizing the trauma that young people had experienced before confinement. The roll out of these new programs was different in each facility, and yet rumors about their implementation dominated facility life—the changes were rapid and constant. Brooks felt that "I'm starting to think that the agency doesn't care anymore" and that they're just motivated by saving money. Agency administrators and key reformers across the state would often repeat the same claim in public forums and in the media: it cost more than $200,000 to incarcerate each child in New York's juvenile facilities. Brooks said, "You can't tell me that you're spending as much as you are" when the school program was as inadequate as it was.

Staff members like Brooks and Barton had the power to enforce compliance with the rules through the use of physical restraints. Physical restraints were used to control young people who were seen to be posing a threat to themselves or to the safety of others in the facility. The staff in OCFS facilities were trained to do prone restraints, which involved holding a young person face down on the floor while holding his or her hands together and then handcuffing the hands and legs together—this is also known as a "hog-tie" restraint.[67] Staff can also confine young people in their rooms if they deem them to be defiant, or they can request that a young person be escorted to a room confinement area if he or she has resisted staff directives. He or she stays in that area until it is determined that he or she is ready to be released.

Shortly before I began doing research, the rules governing the use of restraints changed, narrowing the criteria for triggering such restraints. This happened in part in response to concerns that restraints were being used too often as a tool for treatment and were resulting in high levels of physical harm to both residents and staff. During that time, each facility started keeping track of the number of restraints that happened in them, and there were regular statewide meetings of facility administrators and administrators in Albany, who would review the restraint reports. Facilities were pressured from the administrators in Albany to lower their use of restraints. The decision to place limits on the use of restraints was highly controversial among staff members who had long relied on the belief that restraints could be used as a means of securing compliance in treatment. They would often talk about this decision as one that was key in removing their "tools" for control. In the staff language, there is also a conflation of "rehabilitative assumptions with managerial prerogatives"; their reference to Skinnerian-style behavior control also ultimately provides them with an easy route to controlling the young people under their care.[68]

Brooks said that if a kid said to him, "I'm going to punch you in the face," he would "knock him down." He said that he does this because everyone on the unit is watching; if he restrains the young person, the other kids will see this, see where he stands, and presumably be deterred from misbehaving. He felt that there were some units on the facility where staff members had lost control over the young people and that "kids are refusing to do program unless they get up with their friends." He said that the kids there were "ganged up" there and that the facility had allowed them to be. He felt that there was no response from the central office about the gang problems and violence they were facing. Of the central agency administration, he noted, "They think they pay us to take an ass whupping." He said that if staff members get hit by the kids, they are discouraged by facility administrators from reporting it.

Other staff members spoke about restraints in the context of their own experiences with physical punishment. Mumford started working at OCFS as a YDA in 1988, shortly before Brooks. He had always worked at a secure facility, where young people charged as Juvenile Offenders were sent; many of those young people would go on to prison. Mumford, a black man, said he had learned that it was important to let the kids know that "there are consequences." "When they go up to the big house [prison]," he said, "it is not up for debate." When I first met Mumford, he was sitting on a unit eating some fruit, and he was making exaggerated faces as he put the fruit in his mouth, making the kids on the unit laugh at him. He wore a button on his uniform with the number 10 on it and told me he wore it every day to remind himself that his standard with the kids was a "10"—that he would give his best to them every day. Yet, like Brooks, Mumford embraced the idea that the kids must be physically disciplined: "When you let the kids dictate the program without consequences," he told me, "and no one is held accountable," there are problems. He said that "whipping" kids is a "deterrent." When he was a child, his father would beat him if he did something wrong. His mother would say to him, "Wait until your father comes home," and he said that he would hide under the couch and "piss in bed" in fear of his father. Interestingly, he implied that this was a strategy that worked to impose discipline in his life, even as he described the extreme fear he felt of his own father. He felt that "a little physicality" worked with this group of kids.

Ramirez was another frontline staff member who had grown up experiencing physical discipline in his own family. In his fifties, he had relocated to upstate New York from the Bronx, where he had grown up. He had also worked for the agency for many years. He felt that under the new system, "I just think they took too much away" from the staff, and how "I grew up and used to get the belt." He said that because he was from the Bronx, "I see some of the stuff that they gotta go back to" such as gangs, and "some of the things we put up with now you never heard of" in previous eras. "There are good kids here, but they get lost," he said. Ramirez, like many staff members I spoke to who had worked at the agency for some time, spoke wistfully about the agency's past: he said "I used to love these kids," that "they would take care of me," and that there was "no disrespect" from them. "I used to take care of them," he said, and "I used to read these kids." He, like Brooks and many other staff members, felt that things would fall apart for the kids when they returned home: he said that when the facility sends them home, "it's like sending an alcoholic to a bar to work." Barton similarly felt that the young people were simply returning to environments where they would regress: "a lot of them go back to the neighborhoods they are from, and their survival techniques set in." He felt that "you first have to train the young people that you can't punch someone in the mouth." Brooks similarly felt that there were "very few success stories" after the young people had left the facility. Like other staff members who felt the young people returned to structureless environments when they returned home, he said, "You take a lion from the jungle and "he'll conform," and you put them back "out there" and "they've gotta survive." Barton added that until the kid "feels safe" and "until he doesn't feel he will be victimized," he will not be able to take on the program.

Around 2013, a member of the State Commission on Corrections, an oversight agency that had access to video surveillance footage from the facilities, illegally released footage of young people assaulting a staff member, and those videos had circulated throughout the news media. Many staff felt vindicated by the videos—that they showed how difficult they felt their jobs were. Brooks, like many staff members, felt that they had been portrayed as brutish and harsh. He said, "We have been so villainized in the media" and "I don't think anyone understands who we are dealing with," referring to the young people under their care. "I don't blame Carrión," he said. "She's just another commissioner who doesn't know."

The approach that Barton and Brooks took to the young people—the idea that they were their collective responsibility—clashed somewhat with the official, on-paper ideas about individual responsibility that circumscribed the young people's behavior in the facility. Under the models of development embraced officially by the agency and promulgated through the paperwork, a young person who never moves beyond the white shoelace stage—perhaps because he or she talks back to staff too much or gets in too many fights—is considered to be unchanged or underdeveloped. Rather than perhaps what some have termed an African worldview, which might value collective responsibility for problems and issues, the value-orientation in the facilities is centered around individual responsibility, or what has been identified as a more middle-class, white, and Western orientation to responsibility.[69]

In fact, it was on Brooks's unit where I witnessed the only group work I saw during my entire research experience. The group discussion was focused on drug and alcohol. Young people were expected to write and present a personal biography, which included an account of their dependency on drugs and alcohol. One young person started arranging chairs in a circle in the middle of the unit, which typically had the chairs facing forward, toward the television. Everyone sat down in the circle, including me, Barton, and Brooks. After everyone sat down in a circle, the resident who had been pulling the chairs into a circle started asking a series of scripted questions to the resident who had done his biography. He asked questions about the resident's drug use history, which included how often he used, what triggered him, who used in his family, and so on. The questions and answers were somewhat formulaic; each resident read from a piece of paper in front of them.

After the questions and answers, Brooks initiated a discussion about the residents' responses to the questions. Brooks felt it was important to note that tobacco was a substance and said that it was important that the resident had put tobacco down on his form about his drug use history. Another part of the discussion was about marijuana use and dependency and whether there were differences between heavy use and addiction. One resident talked about how he used heavily but that he didn't think he was addicted. There was one other resident in the room who said that he had a marijuana addiction problem.

After the discussion, Brooks asked the residents to go around the room and gave feedback to the resident about his presentation. Most of his responses were monosyllabic and brief. Brooks said that we then had time for another presentation, and so another resident went to his room and got a piece of paper out to read from. This resident seemed a bit older, and it turned out that he had been on the unit for longer and was about to be released from the facility. His piece was about responsibility, more generally, and about some of the things he had learned in the facility, like about humility, learning how to "shut the fuck up," and recognizing where he had gone wrong. Some of the things he said sounded a bit like platitudes about personal responsibility—simply regurgitations of facility-based language—but some of them were quite specific to his situation, making it clear that he wasn't just repeating back what was expected of him. He also spoke about the need to ask for help.

After the resident spoke, he got quite a lot of positive feedback from Brooks and Barton. They talked about how far he had come, and Brooks said that it was a shame he was leaving so soon because he felt that he needed more time with the resident to really feel like he was making progress with him. Brooks said that there was another resident in the facility who was charged with murder, but he was a "good guy"; yet the crime, which took place in just fifteen seconds, meant that his life was essentially over.

The group discussion that followed included a complex mix of meanings and messages; on the one hand, the young people were expected to engage in scripted programs of change; on the other hand, their own processes of and struggles with change were recognized by the staff members who knew them for so long and so well.

Shortly after the group meeting that day, one of the residents on the unit came up to his door and gestured toward Barton, asking to speak with him. He was unable to get out of his room because the residents were locked down in their room during the shift change that was happening in the facility.

Barton went into the resident's room and spoke with him for a little while. He came out and said that the resident was feeling paranoid that he might be jumped by other residents (he had remained in his room during the entire group session). Barton and Brooks explained that the resident was going to be released in a month but had nowhere to go and he was "unraveling." Apparently, he had come to the facility from foster care, and he had stolen from his foster parents, which is why he was arrested. He had exhausted a number of his foster care placements, and the state had not found any other placements for him. The staff explained that the counselor had been searching for placements, but there wasn't anywhere or anyone who would take the teenager.

The shift change began, and two new staff members showed up. The four staff members began talking about the teenager. All of the staff seemed to agree about their concern about the kid, and the fact that he was unraveling. They also spoke about their feelings of helplessness in the matter; technically, the resident's community placement was the responsibility of his youth counselor, who wasn't really doing any work to ensure that this placement would happen. The YDAs had no responsibility for aftercare placements and in fact were discouraged from helping young people with them. One of the YDAs who had just arrived spoke with me about how she thought that there must be good mental health placements in the city, and she thought that he might have a diagnosable mental illness, but she did not know for sure. In fact, although the line staff members spent the most amount of time with the young people, it was only the counselors or the mental health staff, who saw the young people more infrequently, who knew whether they had a mental health diagnosis. The YDAs felt frustrated that nothing was happening for this young person who was going to get out, so several of them had taken it upon themselves to try to research placement options for the boy. While we talked, he paced back and forth in his room. We would all occasionally glance back at him.

Brooks loved to read, and he would often bring books from home for the kids on his unit to read. He recognized that "these kids love to read" while they were in detention and in the facilities because it kept them occupied in the face of extreme boredom, helped them to feel a sense of escape, and gave them access to worlds behind the bars. In particular, they loved the Harry Potter books, the Hunger Games series, and other fantasies or books by Walter Dean Myers, a young adult author whose books captured the lives of young African American teenagers. Brooks and other staff would often talk to the young people about the books they were reading at home with their own children. I observed Brooks and several other staff members engaged in reading clubs on their units.

Brooks and Barton kept in contact with a lot of the kids after they left confinement, which a number of other staff members told me they did too. Officially, the agency barred staff from staying in contact with young people to protect the young people from the possibility of sexually predatory behavior. But the young people themselves would frequently call back to the facility, and the staff members felt conflicted about following the official rule. "When they get in trouble, they call us," Brooks said, "What would we be if we turned our back on them?" He continued, "To do this job correctly, you better be invested" in the young people.

Brooks felt that the central administration of OCFS "haven't drawn the link between education and recidivism." His assumption was that if a strong academic curriculum was brought into the facility, then kids are "thinking more," and they also know more about the "consequences of their behavior." He said that as soon as the kids started caring about their grades, the staff members feel like "we got them." For example, they noticed that there was a gap in the schedule between 9:30 and 11 AM when no educational services were happening. They created a study time during that gap.

THE PEOPLE–PRACTICE RELATIONSHIP

There were a number of facility staff and administrators who engaged in small acts of resistance against the broader structures of the program to try to facilitate better outcomes for young people. Criminologists have identified a gap between theory and practice that exists in present-day criminal justice programming where staff members exercise their discretion to try to meet the immediate needs of the people they are working with. This gap is where the work takes place that arguably reveals some of the flaws in the architecture of the behavioral change model. It was revealed to me when I would observe staff members affectionately hugging a young person who had made parole or releasing the shackles from them, temporarily, while they were in court. It was also revealed to me in the complex interactions between facility and state administrators, facility staff, young people, and their families, when those administrators would come to recognize that it was often the power of their discretion that could be exercised to bypass a state requirement that stood in the way of a young person's success. In short, these moments of discretion confirm that the staff and administrators are not automatons of a binding system; they are human beings responding to a restrictive and powerful state apparatus. The small moments mattered in conveying that.

The people and practices in facility life are like overlapping tectonic plates. The practices, envisioned by theorists and academics, translated by administrators, are intended to address the perplexing puzzle of youth misbehavior. The people—line staff—are expected to implement these practices. Yet facilities are living, breathing organisms—the people in them do not always react and respond to the practices in the way intended by their creators. As the people meet the practices, like tectonic plates, the seams are not always aligned.

While there is no single story or even clear typology of a frontline staff member, David Brooks conveys the complexity of the people–practice relationship. For many outsiders seeking to reform facilities, Brooks's and others' appreciation of tough talk and physical restraints were antithetical to their view of the appropriate treatment of children; yet throughout my time in the juvenile facilities, I witnessed staff members like Brooks embrace this perspective while also expressing extraordinary warmth toward young people. These seemingly contradictory positions may have reflected their somewhat complex relationship to their jobs. As individuals who were expected to focus their day on getting young people to follow the rules of the facility, with the broader goal of translating that rule-following into conformity in the community, yet who saw that rule conformity was more about performance than actual change, the staff would often grow frustrated and fall back on ideas and beliefs that felt familiar to them—those they knew from childhood and from their own socialization processes. Their engagement with the treatment programming, and thus their uses of it in the context of facility life, thus reflected their ambiguous relationships to conformity, defiance, violence, and trauma.

The staff perspectives on treatment programming may have also reflected their ground-level responses to what they saw as the limits of treatment programs that, in their minds, embraced an irrelevant and inaccurate view of

young people's capacities for change. Recent critics have challenged the theoretical underpinnings of the rational problem solving model, drawing from
recent advances in cognitive science to point out that "when making judge-
ments individuals do not necessarily go through a process of sustained reflection and logical analysis but often rely on the immediate perception of situations and more intuitive processes."[70]

The services provided to residents are linked to the assessment that young
people are administered at intake, despite research indicating that none of the
risk assessment tools used had prescriptive validity or reliability.[71] There have
also been no systematic evaluations of the quality or effectiveness of facility-
based programs, although some of the models themselves are ostensibly "evidence based."[72] In recent years, the state has made efforts to used cognitive
behavioral approaches that are more strongly evidence based, but the question
remains as to whether those programs, even as they are refined, will raise similar challenges for young people and staff.

The criminologist David Garland suggests that the recent trend in harsher
penal sanctions in places like the United States is partly driven by the idea
of people who offended as "rational opportunists or career criminals whose
conduct is variously deterred or dis-inhibited by the manipulation of incentives."[74] The construction of the rational offender who is governed through a
system of punitive interventions has played a role in the development of interventions aimed at reducing offending. Cognitive behavioral therapies embody
these concerns.

CHAPTER 5

Change from the Inside

The walls of the institution cut the child off from real life, force him into fantasy experiences so that it becomes difficult for him to correct his wishful thinking with reality.
—August Aichhorn, *Wayward Youth*

WHEN VEHICLES ENTER HOOPER secure center, they must drive into a chain link enclosure, the entrance and exit of which are controlled by an officer watching a video monitor. Drivers wait in the enclosure until they get approval to enter from the staff inside the control booth. The facility has a preapproved gate list for each day, which allows for a relatively easy entrance for those on the list. As I drove up to the facility one day, I saw four state police SUVs pull out of the enclosure, one of which was the canine unit.

After I entered the facility through the pedestrian walkway, which included a similar chain link enclosure, I learned that the state troopers had just finished searching the facility. The search had lasted for two hours. During that time, a transport van from a New York City detention facility, with one recently sentenced teenager and the staff member tasked with escorting him, had been sitting inside of the chain link vehicle enclosure while the search was conducted. The glass for the passenger seats of the van is encased in steel mesh, so the teenager could not see out of the van. I entered the facility at the same time as the staff member who had transported the teenager. He was a middle-aged black man. As he signed in, he wearily told the staff inside of the control booth that he had been sitting in the van for two hours outside the facility waiting for the search to clear. After a three-hour drive from New York City to the facility, the young person and staff member had to sit in the chain link enclosure together, waiting for the facility to be "cleared."

The police conducted a search of the facility after a staff member reported a smell of marijuana on one of the units. The report of the smell triggered a call into the state police, who arrived to conduct a full facility search in which they upended beds, spilled food, ruffled through papers, and shook out books, looking for the offending substance. The search left young people and staff frustrated and upset.

In the facility, there is a classroom used by students in a specialized educational program that has windows facing out into the chain link enclosure. During the searches, the young people and staff who were in that classroom saw the detention van sitting in the enclosure—the kids recognized it as the van that many of them had come to the facility in from New York City. They talked about how unfair it was that the young person who was about to start his first day in the facility had spent much of it sitting in the van, unable to look outside of it.

In many ways, the teenager in the van represents young people's experiences of change from the inside—"the inside" represents their views on change from inside of locked juvenile facilities, but it also represents the internal processes that they undergo while they are inside of these controlled spaces. Often, we see and read about young people's experiences inside of juvenile facilities and in the system as those filled with abuse and exploitation—through representations like photographs or documentaries of teenagers in confinement and stories about the violence and punishment in the facilities.[1] If we view the van from the outside, we might perceive the unfairness and randomness of a system where security trumps dignity and where eliminating drug use in the facility, and holding individuals responsible, becomes prioritized over ensuring that the immediate needs of the individuals—the youth and the staff—in the van are met. We would see a young person exit the van in shackles, a small figure overwhelmed by the apparatus of incarceration.

Yet, if we enter that van, we might experience a different story. We might see one where the divide between system and youth is not as clear—where the young person and the staff member have shared interests and pains; where the young person copes with the ambivalence of his position, free from the facility, yet confined; and where the full confusion of confinement is represented by the design of the van itself, an enclosed space where the person inside has no ability to see or understand where he is being transported or what is happening to him. This, in many ways, is the experience of confinement for so many young people.

Facility life does not tend toward extremes of violence and chaos. Rather, it is filled with boredom, introspection, confusion, and alienation, among other emotions. These emotions help us to understand the harms of incarceration in young people's lives; for if a facility does not tend toward abuse and violence yet remains profoundly stifling for so many inside, is it actually allowing them to grow, develop, and build their characters?

In many ways, what is most crucial is young people's route into the facility. We know already from the experiences of Michael, Maya, and others that teenagers enmeshed in the criminal justice system are considered to be "bad," ungovernable and discardable. So many of the teenagers who enter juvenile facilities across the country are trapped in a moment of alienation and despair before they enter those facilities—they are stuck in their lives, deemed unworthy, ungovernable, and unmanageable, immersed in systems of control that are beyond their control. For so many of the young people, the crime they committed, or their probation violation or parole violation, did not hold as much significance for them as the experiences they were having before they were arrested. Their arrest may have been one of many cases they had, or a short moment in their rapidly unfolding teenage years, or even the product of being the enemy of their local police precinct. Even for those charged with significant and serious crimes—rape, homicide, or a serious and violent robbery—their lives before committing that crime, and surrounding that crime itself, were often full of profound and difficult concerns and questions. Their sentence to a juvenile facility loomed large in their lives—they were being sent to a place that communicated to them that they were flawed, wrong, and in need of change in their lives. Their experience in the facility thus represented a kind of deep freeze in their lives, in that they were removed from their homes and their lives to deal with themselves. The structure of the juvenile court system and its goal—to intervene in children's "best interests"—also communicates to them that their crimes are symbolic of broader flaws in their characters, their moralities, and their sensibilities. And yet, the adult ideas about what was bad and wrong with them often differed profoundly from their own ideas about what might have been going wrong or have been difficult in their lives.

As with many teenagers, the group of teenagers entering the facility had responsibilities, families, and lives that presented them with complex challenges. Many of them were also trapped in educational, legal, and social service systems with little power to advocate for themselves and limited choices to extract themselves from their homes, lives, families, and systems they often found to be oppressive and alienating. As the British criminologist Jo Phoenix argues, the group of young people who are in juvenile justice systems are often overpoliced and underprotected: "young people are held to account (i.e., punished) for their actions when many of those actions are shaped by conditions over which, because they are still children in the legal sense and at times developmental sense, they are utterly unable to change or affect."[2] It is arguable that this precarious position of being overpoliced and underprotected resulted in young people's despair and alienation both before and during their time in confinement. When they entered the juvenile facilities with those emotions and were forced to encounter adult-constructed and managed interventions that often disregarded those emotions, they developed strategies to cope that were unique to their age and to their experience.

ON THE STREETS: LIFE BEFORE CONFINEMENT

Olivia knew what it was like to feel underprotected. She remembers the day she first met Damien, an adult charged with protecting her, but who

instead exploited her. She was twelve years old, living with her elderly grandparents, and had recently started taking care of them after her grandfather had
fallen ill. She would go shopping, cook for them, and take care of their everyday needs. She said, "I used to clean for them. They used to make sure that
everything, everything was all right, laundry and all that. And, basically I just
made sure they had what they needed." When her grandmother started getting
sick, "basically what I did was just like, okay, I don't know how long I'm going
to have my grandparents, so let me just do what I gotta do. So I could survive."

That is when Damien offered her a solution. She remembers what she was
wearing when she first met him: "I had on some black tight jeans with a pair
of black flats and a white shirt with a little top, and I had a bra on, and I had
it stuffed with socks, and I had my hair swooped to the side, coming down."
Olivia was born a boy, so the socks helped give her the appearance of a girl.
"When I was younger," she said, "I wanted to be a woman, like a girl, not even
a girl, I wanted to be a woman, cause I never felt young, I never really had a
childhood, so I felt like, I had my titties, I was twelve years old with my fake
little titties." Damien picked Olivia up that day, even though she put up some
resistance to him: "I told him like I don't need no ride, I'm fine. But the thing
was I was only twelve years old, so the thing was I was feeling grown. I was
always feeling grown so like it was just crazy. . . . I used to do it on my own
so I was really waiting for somebody to come through, but him the way he
approached me at the moment I didn't really like want to you now like to get
in like I wasn't feeling it, so I crushed him off but when he came back (laughing), it was over." She was drawn to his light brown, watery, cartoonish eyes.
Damien let her be who she wanted to be—he called her his "baby boy" and
paid to get her hair done like a girl, but let her dress like a boy.[3]

Just a couple of weeks after that, Damien asked her, "Are you going to let
me be your pimp?" She was shocked. She said, "When he asked me that, the
first thing that came to my mind was, you need somebody to love you." So she
agreed to work for him. She would pretend she was leaving for school in the
morning, but Damien would pick her up instead.

Damien and Olivia started traveling around the country so that Olivia
could act as an escort. It was not the first time that Olivia had sex with older
men; when she was ten, she had sex with a man in his late twenties. Olivia's
therapists called this act "rape," but she denied this label. She said that her first
lover "changed my life," and that "I thought I didn't want nobody else but him."

When she was out doing work for Damien, Olivia would tell her grandparents that she was visiting her father. Olivia's grandparents never found out
what she did. She felt an enormous amount of guilt. Olivia led a shadowy
existence, with no adults really caring for her. Even Damien withheld money
from her, so she lived under an illusion of survival: he would pay for her to
get her hair done and for her to buy presents for her family members, but he

never actually paid her for her work. I asked her how the transactions worked, and she said:

O: well . . . Shew, that was the worst part of all. That was the scariest part, because when you think you that you being slick, and that you gonna get a certain amount more, and that you can hide what he think he getting, and it's one of his regulars, and he call them to check and see if you made it behind your back, and you go to him, and he know what you supposed to have and you hiding it, it's hard. It's just crazy.

A: So you're supposed to give everything?

O: You're supposed to give him everything . . .

A: And his job is to give you food money, and stuff like that?

O: He gave, with me, what he gave me really, he didn't really, honestly he didn't really give me nothing, cause I was really, you could say, staying with him, cause I used to like go, like I told you I used to take care of my grandparents in the day and I used to go out at night. When I was out at night, doing what I did, I used to stay with him, and the next morning, I would get up and go take care of them. So it was like the only thing that he provided me with what I didn't really need because I had on my own, he provided me with shelter, that's it really. And whatever clothes I felt that I needed, whatever shoes I felt I needed, he bought 'em for me, and he gave me the money. If I needed money he woulda gave it to me. But when I would go out and do what I do, and give him the money, he wouldn't give me nothing else. Cause at the end of the day, I would be sleeping right next to him.

A: And that was your reward? That was your compensation.

O: That wasn't my reward for it, but that was his way of rewarding me.

This was the context in which Olivia arrived in OCFS custody after she was arrested and adjudicated as a delinquent when she was fifteen years old. She had been in and out of family court, mainly for prostitution charges. She was initially placed in a private residential program but was then modified to a state juvenile residential facility.

Olivia's placement in confinement involved not only an immediate severing of ties from her pimp and from the lifestyle she was living, but also separation from her family and the uncertainty of an indefinite period of placement. Although Olivia recognized the limits of living a life where she was being sexually exploited, she had not left that life willingly. She still loved the man who exploited her. Before she entered the facility, in fact, she didn't think she would be long for this world:

In terms of my future, I was thinking [long pause]. I was thinking I wasn't going to be here. And it's not only because, you know, not only because

I didn't think my grandparents was gonna be here but I don't think I was going to be here either because, I was just, you know doing things that was risking my life. It was like when it came down to the future it was just like, whatever tomorrow's just another day, that's how I used to think about it so when it came down to my future like, I would think like okay, okay, whatever, I'm gonna be dead. So, I'm just gonna do what I gotta do to survive for today, and tomorrow's another day so, come tomorrow, it's just that it be tomorrow. (Starts crying) So, that's how was, and that's how it took me a long time to him, start finally planning for the future. I never thought about a future. I never ever thought about a future. And I'm not even going to sit here and lie to you. I never ever thought now okay, I'm going to go to college and never thought, I merely get a high school diploma. I never ever thought about that. Because I didn't think I was gonna make it.

Olivia's alienation was profound; her despair was palpable. And yet her sentence forced her to interrupt that sense of herself; it required that she confront her past and contemplate an alternative path than the one she had originally chosen.

Entering the Facility

For so many young people like Olivia, entering a residential facility prompts questions about whether the process will make their lives better. They wonder how a system so analogous to all of the other systems they have encountered in their lives could actually help them to grow and change. Many of them wonder why they couldn't be trusted with the freedom to change their lives without being sent to an institution. Finally, they wonder how their experience would go—how would they ultimately get and stay out?

A number of young people experienced feelings of ambivalence about their freedom as they entered the facility. Some, like Olivia, who knew that their lives on the outside were not making them happy or healthy, could see that the facility offered them an escape from that life, but it was an escape that they knew might involve its own pain and deprivations. Other young people, especially young men, found that the facility offered a respite from their near-constant exposure to police violence and the violence of their peers; they would continue to be in a place where they were policed, but they were also escaping their near-constant exposure to violence, and the stress of engagement with violence, on the streets.

A number of the teenagers entered the facility with feelings of loss and regret. The most well-documented form of loss for young people entering juvenile facilities is their separation from one's family, yet for many of the young people I met, like Olivia, their relationships to their families were complex, ambiguous, and sometimes very negative. Many were in foster care before they arrived in placement; some had parents who were incarcerated; others still had parents who were neglectful or absent. Even those with parents who were present and supportive had a complicated relationship to the loss that accompanied their sentence. All too often, stories about loss and separation do not recognize that children involved in the justice system often face angry, fearful, and frustrated parents after they have committed crimes. They have parents who want them to leave home because they feel they will change when they are punished or want them to leave home so they will be safer than when they live in their communities. Thus, their sentence and their departure from home is not a straightforward process of sadness and separation; it is one tinged with regret, pain, and suffering as well.

Many young people also struggle with feelings of guilt and regret, or denial and disassociation, that often accompanies the experience of engaging in crimes that harm others, but there is little opportunity in their time before entering custody to address those feelings, particularly through the formality of the adjudicatory process. The sentencing process itself, which involves a formal requirement that they allocute to their guilt and the facts of their crime, or in which they are found guilty by a jury, cannot possibly capture the complicated emotional landscape that accompanies a finding or admission of guilt.

Teenagers who enter juvenile residential facilities find themselves forced to acknowledge that they are not only physically contained, but they are enclosed within a system of behavioral control that deeply shapes their everyday lives. This kind of programming distinguishes juvenile prisons from adult ones: young people's daily lives are highly structured by the routines and rhythms of the program that include their required school attendance, their participation in treatment programming, and the unique approaches to their bodies and minds that have much to do with their youth. The young people and staff call this way of approaching daily life in the facilities "doing program."

Doing program allows teenagers to acquire considerable privileges, including more time on the phone, more money to spend in commissary, better jobs, and access to more personal items, such as music players. Ultimately, doing program bought residents more space from staff members, allowing for more time to talk to peers, spend time alone, or experience less intense disciplinary standards.

Sociologists of prison life have studied the way that this process is one that requires people in prison to make particular kinds of adaptations to the pains and deprivations of imprisonment.[4] When confronted with these pains and deprivations, they argue, individuals develop unique strategies for responding to these conditions. In juvenile facilities, young people's adaptations to confinement are unique to their age and the structure of everyday programming and life.

Most teenagers who entered the facility viewed "the program" with a great deal of skepticism when they first entered confinement. Most residents quickly saw that the program wasn't individual or group treatment; rather it constituted the entire experience of daily life—every bodily movement, yes or no, and choice was the program. The structure of this program, from the expectation that residents make their beds neatly, to their polite behavior toward staff, was reinforced at every moment of the day. Even when young people had downtime, they were watched by staff, and any unusual movements they made were logged into the large ledger books that staff members kept in front of them.

The teenage residents in the facility were often skeptical that the programming would actually help to change them, and thus they struggled with the idea of authentic engagement with the program. They experienced these daily rituals and interventions in their lives as punitive rather than helpful, disciplining rather than rehabilitative.[5] They knew, then, that their recruitment into this system of control was fraught: if they did the program, then they were implicitly consenting to a system of punishment that they had totally submitted to, rather than one that they were active participants in.[6]

Some teenagers spoke about a journey that they had undergone in which they had "realized" about why and how program should be done. Tory was sent to a private residential facility where, he said, "At first I wasn't really doing good." For him, that meant "not making group and, schools slips, there's a lot of stuff." It meant that he wasn't actively participating in the behavioral programming and everyday expectations of the facility. But he realized that "I'm going to be here for a long time," so he decided he "might as well do good." Although he knew that if he did well in the program, he would be able to go on home visits, it didn't really click with him at first. Then he realized that the people who went home, called "A men," got to go home, stay up later, and have more freedoms inside. He said there was "no point in . . . not bein' 'A' man, without goin' home twice a month to just wiling out and not making my group." But he realized that becoming an 'A man,' or doing good, would require hard work:

> Me, I have to work for hard for it. Other people might not have to, like. Other people might, just by the way they act they get a two,[7] because that's how they is, but me, I have to change what I, like what I do everyday. I can't do, if I wanna make my group, I gotta get good points so I can get my group, be good, clean up, like you gotta step up, like let's say is you do your chore? You could step up and you'll get a three cause you really like, let's say the school when you do a chore like, you don't get no slips, and you just have a regular day, and you get a two, but you like you go to school, you get a good slip, then you do other people's chores, and your chair, you don't game play, play act, right? You'll get a three.

Tory decided to "do good" in part after going to court for an update on his progress and discovering that his sentence was going to last considerably longer than he first expected. Thus, rather than spending his time avoiding in-facility responsibilities, he started taking simple steps, such as doing chores or going above and beyond his normal responsibilities. "Stepping up" for him meant taking responsibility, but in a motivated way, such as "stepping up" and being a father to a child. "Being good" is, for Tory, about meeting expectations. He also distinguishes himself from those for whom being "A man" is easy, or perhaps, an act. He does not deride those people but suggests that being "A man" is harder work for him. Yet Tory's preoccupation with obtaining points suggests that his compliance with the program, and his decision to "adapt" to it, is not a straightforward recognition of the benefits it will afford him in terms of his personal change but rather a way of relieving the pressures of confinement.

Newz was facing a sentence of up to nearly a decade in custody, and he entered his placement uncertain about how he would do his time. He was arrested when he was fourteen years old. Like many young people, he had already spent some time in residential treatment facilities, so he knew a little bit about institutions that were focused on behavioral management and control. When he arrived, he felt like he knew what was ahead of him. "I tried to make Hooper revolve around me," he said. He felt partially empowered to do this because he is physically big and strong—he intimidated a lot of the residents and staff members. The fact that he is black was significant in his characterization by the newspapers who wrote about his case, describing him as a "thug"—so rarely is the term "thug" applied to young white men. It was clear that facility staff similarly felt that Newz represented thugishness.

At one point in time, Newz was two points shy of making a higher stage in the behavioral change program, which meant that he had to wait twenty-five months to even be considered for another stage. He said that he then decided to go "off the wall" because "I said, you know what? Forget it, I'm not trying no more." However, another resident helped him realize that his esteem with staff would decline precipitously if he chose to resist in this way, and this would have larger consequences. But he later realized that his efforts at making the facility revolve around him wouldn't work: "I was new, so I messed up." He realized that that staff would think that "It's going to look like he don't want to change, he's an asshole, he's like that and so it happened and I realized right before my eyes it was going to happen. So I said you know what? I can't do this. I'm not going to let that come true. So I started getting my act together. I eventually got my adjustment stage." Newz had to accept that life inside was about "adapting." He realized that he "didn't really adapt to" the previous residential treatment facility he was in.

Newz struggled with the idea of complying with treatment, resisting it, or performing it. In some ways, he had little to lose: he had a long sentence ahead of him, and he didn't have much to go home to. Newz spent the first four years of his life living with his mother, a prostitute, in the room where she took clients and was then sent to live with his father, who sold drugs. He had also recently been reunited with his birth family, whom he was separated from after being placed in foster care as a result of his mother's neglect, and he felt he needed to demonstrate to his younger siblings that he could be a role model—maybe by becoming a successful resident, he could do this. He said he didn't want to be like his mother. Newz equated messing up the program with an abandonment of his siblings, like his mother had.

Knowing few other routes to performing well in the program, he started imitating a new resident who he thought "did perfect program." He said, "I used him as competition." He decided that he was "gonna be a Mr. Robot. I gonna do everything perfect. I so I started living my program off of robots." After he started doing what he did, he said that the staff in the facility "left me alone." By the time he reached the highest behavioral stage level, where he wore green shoelaces, he felt that he had earned respect from residents and staff "because of my laces."

As Newz observed the other resident—the Mr. Robot—he noticed that the resident was showing a strong level of submission to staff authority. Newz noticed that he was "raising his hand, and for not necessary things," like asking his teacher, "can I get a pencil? Or when he know he can get it he still, 'can I get it? can I do this?' And 'can I do that?'" Thus, when Newz became more attuned to what the program involved, he realized that it was, quite simply, about "behav[ing]," and then, the higher he ascended in the behavioral change system, "leadership." At first, he said, his decision to engage in the program was a "performance," but then, he felt it "became real."

After he had done the program for quite a while, Newz realized that his performance may have been less real than he initially thought, but rather that it straddled the line between realness and performance. He recognized that for him to get through his time in the system, he had to fake his way through it to reach authentic engagement. He decided that if he could change himself, then he could do better on the outside, when he was released.

A: What do you think about the robot thing now?
N: You know, if you do it long enough it becomes you.
A: Yeah.
N: I was told that as well. See some sometimes you gotta fake the funk, know what I'm sayin'? And, it happened.

Newz's notion of change was arguably tied to the experiences of his childhood, although he admitted that he had never shared them with staff at the residential facility, even during the stage in his sex offender treatment when he was required to tell his life story as part of the process of "reform," but also to move toward release from the treatment program.[8]

Like Olivia, Newz had to develop survival skills at an early age. He remembered leaving his house as early as age four to go and buy food from the local corner store. He said he pulled on a pair of his father's pants to go outside. The four-year-old Newz, struggling to hold up oversized pants that represented adulthood, knew from an early age that survival in a context where he was receiving few forms of support might require some form of imitation. Newz never had a chance to talk about his early childhood experiences with any staff members in the facility; his family secrets stayed with those of us on his defense team who had learned about them through our own investigations.

When I first learned that Newz had reached the Honors stage, I was slightly surprised. In particular, I was surprised to learn that he had made it past the Transition stage, the third stage (a "Cautious Performer" in the staff handbook), in which residents are expected to take more initiative in their deference to the rules of the program, using the skills that they have obtained in the facility (such as anger control and problem-solving) and show that "you are able to say that you feel sorry for your crimes and take responsibility for your negative behaviors, without blaming others." This was surprising to me because as long as I had known him, Newz was resistant to speaking about the crimes he had committed. Even at his plea, when he was expected to describe what he had done, he spoke elliptically about the crimes. As his legal team, we did not see his sex offense as indicative of psychopathy but reflective of the deep and embedded forces, particularly from his childhood, that led him both to offend but also to struggle to make sense of his own actions and gain insight into them; thus, we felt his silence about his crime reflected his inability to make sense of his actions and his lack of insight into them, not necessarily his denial of them, as the court might suggest. An Honors stage resident, who wore green shoelaces, was described as a "Competent and Committed Performer" in the staff manual. According to the resident manual, a resident should be encouraging his peers to "be positive and to make good choices," showing "improved self-esteem by cooperating with staff and program expectations."

Newz distinguished his process of imitating the other resident from what he called "institutionalization." The term "institutionalized" was used by young people and staff to refer to the young people who were actively resistant to the regime and thus not "doing program." Young people and staff perceived institutionalized people as undisciplined and unaware. They were seen as dependent on confinement and lacking a critical engagement with it. Other residents had described Newz as "institutionalized," which he did not like. When I asked him why he did not like it, he said that it was because, "in a way, I am." Newz said that as someone who is institutionalized "you forget that you are in jail. So it's like, when you're a robot, you are constantly think-ing about being in jail."

Billy spent time in a juvenile detention facility and on Rikers Island, where institutionalization also mattered. While he was in the detention facility, he saw that the kids he was locked up with "just had the attitude that they didn't care, they didn't have a positive attitude as I had." He felt that while he was in deten-tion, he maintained his positive attitude by "not getting institutionalized. Think-ing about being incarcerated they whole life. Thinking about other things, like going to school, trying doing right while you were still in there, to prove to somebody that you can like do something with yourself as you don't gotta be in here and act like a knucklehead." For Billy, being institutionalized was about resisting the regime—being a knucklehead. He said that he felt a lot of kids thought that it was their destiny to be incarcerated. He said that they just give up, they "just say I ain't going home, like, I don't even care, just get in fights. When they have the 'I don't care attitude,' they basically just keep fighting."

For Billy, being "institutionalized" represents a resignation that one is and will always be incarcerated. It is about losing hope and believing that one is bound into "the system" for life. Billy argues that the "institutionalized" person is at greater risk of staying in jail because the judge will look at his record while he is in jail and decide that "this could be a very dangerous person to let out to the streets."[9] Billy implicitly recognizes that there is a dynamic relationship between one's in-facility identity and the imputation of delinquency. He says that institutionalized people feel like "I don't care, I was already here, I'm back again, it's nothing to them. It's like a process, something they used to bein.'"

Those who openly resisted the system felt that succumbing to it repre-sented submission to a power structure that was racist, oppressive, and funda-mentally pointless. José said that when many residents came into the system, they were "hostile" to the idea of it, because they had lost faith in the ability of the system to help people. They may also have been frustrated by the feel-ings of alienation engendered by the court process, the experience of being arrested, and generalized feelings of injustice and alienation that the experi-ence brought about. José and many other young people believed that the system was oriented around profit, and it was thus easy for system administra-tors to sacrifice the rights of the residents. Other teenagers spoke about the interconnections between prison and slavery, and the long legacy of racialized humiliations that the processes of imprisonment are simply a continuation of. Stax said he had initially resisted the program because he felt that it lacked legitimacy in his mind, but then he made a deliberate choice to "fake it" so he could receive more privileges in his daily life. Maya, in a moment of frus-tration and resignation about the facility she was in, said that everybody who is "doing the program" was "faking it." She also expressed frustration that "everybody is trying to control us." Elena also felt that "nothing is real" inside and that authentic relationships, respect, and connection weren't possible.

Panama, an older resident at Hooper who was on the Transition stage, which was a stage right below Honors, said that some of the younger residents would say to the Honors and Transition group members that "the system got y'all," and "you've changed." Panama argued that this kind of accusation did not bother him because he was at least closer to going home than those who accused him of succumbing to the system. Newz similarly spoke about the young people who "fight" the program as individuals who aren't able to get "out," saying, "I don't know about you, but I want to stay out." Panama and Newz, although literally speaking about being released from the facility, also argued that the process of institutionalization means someone's identity becomes entrapped in the cycle of incarceration, and reliant on it.

Eddie, another resident at Hooper who, like Newz, was on the "Honors" stage of the resident behavior system, also struggled against the idea of being institutionalized. Eddie was someone who appeared to be "doing the program" but also resisting it. At times, he was considered a "model" resident by staff and administrators: he was on the student council and was involved in planning a social event that took place in the summer of 2009 and involved a number of girls coming to the facility. He was often introduced to visitors who came to the facility, including administrators from the central office.[10] He participated in a college-level course, which was reserved for the best-behaved residents. He was serving a sentence of fifteen years to life, and he had not only been at the institution for a long time but also had status and respect as a "lifer" among both staff and the young people. Yet, in a twist of irony, the staff also acknowledged him to be an in-facility leader of a gang.

Eddie felt that his period of incarceration had "made me the way I am." He said he had become "disciplined, respectful," and he had "loyalty." He said that these qualities came from the facility and the "program" that he had engaged in there. He had been affected in small ways about how to act and behave through living there and through the program. He felt he had learned "responsibilities" and how to be a "man" from the place. Eddie suggested that his sense of responsibility was cultivated from the facility, partly through the experience (and thus the interactions with his peers, the opportunities for leadership, both licit and illicit, among them), but also, like Newz, by observing, mimicking, and modeling himself after the behavior of staff.

As someone facing a lengthy sentence, Eddie was going to be transferred to the adult Department of Corrections when he turned twenty-one. As he got close to the time of his transfer, Eddie got involved in a fight on his unit. The residents there were asked to "lock down" in their rooms, but the electronically activated locking system broke down. During that period, he got

out of his room and physically assaulted a staff member; he subsequently transferred to an adult prison ahead of his twenty-first birthday.[11]

Although his actions could be straightforwardly read as evidence of the
continued presence of his "criminal" mindset, the context of the incident is
also important: according to the staff members, Eddie was designated by the
young people in his unit as a leader and was sent out to attack a staff member who was unpopular and threatening. This suggests a more complicated
dynamic at play than a simple regression into criminality and thus institutionalization. Eddie enacted the role that was clearly marked out for him within
the institution and was even endorsed by staff: he was a gang leader and a
"leader" in the behavioral change system, a model of autonomy, and also ultimately capable of making "choices," albeit resistant ones.

When Eddie arrived at the adult prison after the incident, he said that he
had been well prepared from his previous facility to take care of himself and
that he would make his bed and fold his clothes every day, even though he
wasn't required to, as he had been at Hooper. I asked him whether he felt he
was "institutionalized," and he said that he wasn't, because, he indicated, he
had some of the requisite self-possession and self-knowledge that might distinguish him from someone who was institutionalized. Khalil, another young
man who had spent time at McClary, similarly spoke about how it took him
a while to become "unprogrammed" upon his release from the facility. He
said that he had been "programmed" to follow the routines and structures of
everyday life ingrained in him, such as the time he went to the shower and
waking up early.

Eddie struggled throughout his time with who he was and how incarceration had shaped him. In a conversation at the residential center, he spoke
about how "we got that jail talk in us," describing some of the difficulties he
thought he might face in shedding the dispositions of institutional life once he
would be released, and thus pointing to his recognition that the "jail" identity
is also something that is not easily abandoned.

Eddie spoke only elusively with me about the violent incident that he had
been involved in. However, he lamented the fact that he had been "kicked to
the wind" by the staff and administrators who had previously supported him,
in part because he had so explicitly deviated from his performance of comportment and upright behavior that had earned him his Honors stage status.
He pointed to the ironies by which his identity as a gang leader was tacitly
acknowledged, but his explicit acts of violence were uniformly condemned
and became the cause for his excommunication from Hooper.

Both Eddie and Newz described some of the tensions inherent in the
notion of "institutionalization": the term can symbolize both a resistance and
a submission to "the program." This reveals the anxieties young people faced
in trying to maintain their sense of control over their own process of change

while "doing program" in confinement. Eddie and Newz felt they had the ability to recognize the ways that the expression of self-mastery and discipline may also help them to keep a kind of psychological distance from their environment or exercise control over it. Thus, for them, "doing good program" was not simply about submitting to it.

The expression "fake it 'til you make it" was used by staff and young people throughout the system to describe the performance of treatment.[12] From a therapeutic perspective, those individuals who perform treatment could be understood to lack "readiness" for that treatment and thus have poorer long-term outcomes.[13] However, alternative interpretations suggest that faking it can help to move individuals toward change. Faking it or "passing" has also been encouraged in drug-treatment programs because there is an assumption that people may reconstruct their selves through this process.[14] Some researchers argue that the structures of juvenile correctional programs, in which progress in treatment is tied to rules, reinforce these processes of manipulation.[15] However, undergirding some research is the assumption that there may be potential for young people to authentically engage in treatment. This could be considered a process of developing "blind faith" about the powers of treatment and ultimately submitting to its supposed effectiveness.[16]

Faking it could also be a form of "censoriousness," by using the language and discourse of treatment to subvert it, a way of "taking on" the system, "beating it" before it beats them, and reducing lengths of confinement.[17] Young people often invoked the language of "faking it" in an effort to distance themselves from the institution, to point to the hypocrisy or idiocy of treatment, and to express a sense of autonomy. It could be a means of what the criminologist Ben Crewe calls "frontstage compliance and performed commitment" to "accelerate progression through the system," while maintaining a stance of resistance toward it in the backstage by being a "player."[18]

It is of course nearly impossible to discern the degree to which "faking it" is actually happening, in the same way in which "change" is not clearly demonstrable.[19] Once performances are repeated, they can become "naturalized" and may even become "sedimented" in a way in which they become central to a person's habitus—or their dispositions, routines, and modes of being.[20]

Yet in the residential juvenile facility landscape, "fake it to make it" was an expression that reflected a more self-aware and reflexive state of being as opposed to full and complete submission to the project of governance. When I asked a group of older adolescent boys at Hooper what kinds of behaviors would be necessary in moving from adjustment to the transition stage, they said, "You have to be active." Movement through the stage system could not be done in a passive manner but instead required a serious level of engagement with the program; this also meant that the engagement had to be highly visible, or sometimes enacted in an exaggerated manner.[21] The color of a resident's shoelaces, which symbolized this progression, was the outward expression of this level of participation.

However, it became difficult to distinguish between performances that resisted the dominant treatment discourses and the actions of those that may have submitted to them. As Ben Crewe argues, "It is almost impossible to gauge from the 'public transcript' whether an appeal to the dominant value system represents a prudent and strategic performance of ideological concord or genuine ethical incorporation."[22]

FALLING BACK

One strategy for a more reflexive engagement with treatment was what young people described as "falling back."[23] This expression conveys the full complexity of "doing program," as it is simultaneously defined as "doing program" and not participating in aspects of program life. In this sense, it represents the tightrope-like quality of program participation. Falling back, in slang, means to lay low, or chill out.[24] Young people defined this expression as "mellow[ing] out" and "straighten[ing] up." Residents who "fall back" are those who "want" to change and who decide to pull themselves back from the "negativity" of the institutional environment.[25]

For a number of young people, falling back was about finding a small place in their confined lives where they could carve out a sense of freedom through the process of internal change that wasn't imposed on them from above. It was a place where they could grapple with themselves without being forced to be understood in terms of their "criminal" identities.

Some young people spoke about a degree of sincerity in their process of change, and one that was related to a personal insight or turning point in their lives. Olivia said that when she was initially placed in treatment, she wasn't interested in "participating." But then, she said, "This past year, I really started caring" because "I felt like I had to change." She located this source of change in a therapeutic alliance that she had built with a psychologist in a previous, private placement, which she was ultimately kicked out of.

Olivia felt that she could truly change when she had let go of her feelings of love for her pimp, Damien. These feelings about Damien, she later revealed, were deeply intertwined with emotions about her family members; the pimp played a father-like and protective role in her life, which had been missing for her. Olivia was in confinement because of an assault charge, not for prostitution. Her time inside forced her to understand more deeply the life she had on the outside: "Everything that I was out there is draining now. The memories is coming back, so everything is just like slowly brushing off. Everything is just slowly brushing off. So it's taking time to go away, but it effects me too because it depresses me."

Olivia had to find strategies for coping with her depression on the inside. She didn't find them in the treatment groups. She said, "The groups to me is like . . . sometimes they can be very pointless because, especially to me because I know personally, I feel as if I know what and what not to do, and I feel as if I know right from wrong, and I feel like I know what to do if a cop stop you and I feel as if . . . like all that stuff is like, it's jus . . . it's late to me, like, I already know this stuff. But some of the groups, I can actually benefit from, like, so it's jus. . . ." Olivia recognized that the groups were limited in what they could give her. She found that they were helpful in some instances, "like I didn't care about the future but now like, to think, like OK, I want that to be something in my head, like when I get out 'what am I gon do? Am I gon hit that person and get back in here again? Or am I gon walk way?' So I like the groups like that." She found that the groups assisted her in ignoring other teenagers who annoyed her—a common occurrence in a facility that generally only had a handful of young people at once. The facility would often reach a boiling point of tension if there were just a few internal conflicts between the teenagers. Olivia felt that she learned from the groups that "all you gotta do is learn how to ignore. If you can ignore somebody, if you can ignore negativity, you will be the best person that you can ever be. You can be the best."

Yet even in Olivia's words about the treatment groups there was a persistent idea that she was seeking a way to be invested in her future outside of the facility, which cognitive behavioral strategies to walk away, or ignore, could not ultimately address. Many of the ways that Olivia described her process of change were about more deeply educational, relational, and spiritual dimensions of her life, which people and programs at the facility couldn't provide. Olivia felt the counselors were not that helpful to her—that they provided "support, but not comfort." She felt that "some people so used to the American Dream, quote on quote, that they just can't handle the real life." Olivia was elusive here, but she was referring to the primarily white and middle-class counselors who worked in the facility and whose own lives and trajectories may not have allowed them to see or understand her life. She told me that she wanted to write a book about her life, and it would be titled *Hood Start: Not the American Dream.*

Olivia found solace in writing poetry and engaging in school, and in dreaming about going to college, something she had not thought about before entering the facility. Ironically, going to school was not really considered "doing program" in the facilities, even though school took up most of the days. In fact, the story of juvenile facility life told in the public media and in reports about facilities, the story of juvenile facilities often neglects to recognize that these are in fact, primarily, schools.[26]

Olivia also found comfort in relationships—in helping other residents understand that their lives could be less difficult. She said that she would tell other residents, "You can make it. And you can make it, and you can trust me, you can make it. You can be at the bottom, like . . . it's so easy, it's so simple, like all you gotta do is put your mind to it and you can make it, like I told you, I did not believe that I was gonna make it this far. I did not even imagine turning sixteen years old. I thought I was going to be gone before I turned fourteen. So, I feel good. I feel more than good. I'm happy that I made it this far."

While she was at McClary, Olivia met and fell in love with another resident. In many ways, their relationship was the most normal one she had ever had. They flirted with each other, wrote letters to each other, and finally confessed their love to each other. Being in the relationship with the other resident allowed Olivia to realize that Damien was actually abusive and harmful toward her. But, she realized, "I don't hold a grudge because in a way I feel as if I learned a huge lesson from him, so I don't really want to hold a grudge against him even though I really like, I despise him, hate him." She said that if she saw him on the street he would probably stop the car and ask her to get in, but "once he realizes that . . . [I'm] not the same little boy that I was before, he might get a little aggressive, probably get out, probably try to chase me . . . probably try to block me in a corner." Damien had a history of hitting Olivia, and she knew that he was capable of doing it again. But Olivia felt that she could resist the temptation of him if she saw him again: she said, "I don't want that those gold teeth in his mouth, I don't want that look, that look, that sincere look in his eyes to manipulate me, I don't want that pretty skin to manipulate me, I refuse to let that happen." She thought about what she would have done differently on the first night she met him to refuse his demands.

Olivia felt that since she had been locked up, she began to identify the differences between her "needs and her wants." She said:

> This past year since I've been locked up, I realize that everything I've been doing, everything I used to do was just like I ain't gonna say it was pointless, because I used to always get something from it . . . it was something that was just adding on to comfort and pleasure. I didn't need it. I wanted it. And that's the thing, I think I told you before I used to confuse my needs and wants. And I used to mix them up. And when I used to mix what I needed and what I wanted, I had a problem. So, since I've been locked up I realized that, you know what, what I need and want don't have nothing in common.

When she did this, it helped her to realize that she had been manipulated by Damien—that she had been made to think she was on the path to making a lot of money and to finding material comfort, but it was quite the opposite. While she was inside, she decided that she instead wanted to be a train conductor—a job that would allow her to go on different kinds of journeys from the ones that Damien had taken her on.

Other young people like Olivia spent much of their time inside engaged in a deep process of introspection while they were in the facilities. Victoria, who was facing a sentence of one to three years for a robbery case, said that she realized while she was in the residential center that she put her mom through a lot while she had been away from home. She said that when she was at home, "I was easily influenced," and now "I learned to just focus on me." I asked her what she learned in the facility, and she said that she "came to myself" and "I found myself." She said that she started writing in a journal and that when she looks back at her journal notes from when she first got there, "it's like I'm reading about a different person." Victoria talked about how she kept to herself, bonding with a few staff members, drawing and writing in her room, but mainly tried to avoid other young people as she worked on "changing."

José spoke about how "when I first came in to [the system], I followed the rules, but I didn't understand them." He said that he "didn't care" and that he "faked it at first." His change came when he got sentenced and was "sent up here"; within about a year, he started "improving himself" and learned how to be more "humble." José frequently spoke about the process of change as being important to him in his in-facility identity. He held a coveted job in the kitchen and was allowed to participate in a social event with girls from the outside because of his infraction-free record. He often spoke about how younger residents hadn't yet learned how to change and that "kids have to be willing to change and learn." He frequently contrasted his choices to change with those of the younger residents, saying, "Maturity is a state of mind, not of physical being." José, elusive about his past but clear that he had "made mistakes" and gotten caught up with the "wrong crowd," thought it was important to point out that he came from a close-knit, intact family. He spoke frequently about how he had disappointed his family and how he desired to change so that he could fulfill his potential as someone who had had more privileges than those around him.

For the residents, "falling back" meant not participating in open and active resistance to the regime, at least in the form that was made emblematic by the more younger residents who were said to embrace a "street" culture. It also meant becoming more thoughtful, pensive, and quieter and, paradoxically, taking the time into one's own hands. In this sense, it became a form of resistance to the institution, but not one that was easily discernable by staff members. In this state, young people can say that they've taken more control over their time, but it also involved engaging with the power structure, thus facilitating its reproduction and acknowledging its legitimacy.[27]

Residents who "fall back" tend to be highly literate and intelligent about the institutional terrain and what "doing program" involves. Olivia, for example, was smart enough to know that if she said to staff members that she had learned a few good lessons from group treatment, she would be respected by the adult staff members who administered that form of treatment. Olivia also knew that if she opened up just enough about her past, staff members would feel that she was sufficiently engaged in the program. Newz and Eddie knew how to "show leadership" in Hooper, which was a larger facility of older boys and where the demonstration of leadership involved a more clear display of self-control and seriousness.

For many of the boys, becoming literate in the institutional landscape involved the cultivation of listening and observation skills, competency in mimicry, craft in the use of "street" and institutional language, and the capacity to take risks in jeopardizing an official status to maintain status with one's peers. It involved the use of "hidden transcripts," code words, and secret languages, as well as dominant institutional discourses, frameworks, and ideas.[28] In other words, it was a kind of balancing act: these individuals constantly negotiate different forms of "authenticity," and seek out forms of self-expression that may be respected within the competing worlds that exist in the institution.

It was arguably the girl's facility where it was the most difficult to "fall back" in some ways because the girls were almost expected to be difficult, and thus their efforts at time alone and introspection could be read as evidence of mental illness or difficulty. Thus, for the girls, "faking it" actually didn't represent a status that would garner them that many privileges.

Obstacles to Falling Back

One of the primary barriers to young people's process of change, falling back, and discovering space for themselves was the pervasive inactivity in the facilities. While active engagement with the program was seen as a necessary part of progress, a large part of young people's time in the facilities was spent "doing" very little. The young people faced intense boredom. This generally occurred in the afternoon and evening hours after school, during school vacation times (or on days when there were teacher trainings or school was not in session), and on weekends. During school "vacation," when the teachers did not work in the facilities, there were almost never any activities planned for the young people. When nothing was planned, young people sat on their units and watched television, played video games or cards, read, or worked on their homework. Although some staff in the facilities made efforts to combat this boredom, including the initiation of reading groups, crocheting, and recreational competitions, these activities were rare.

Almost all of the activities in the facilities centered around school, group treatment, and time in the gymnasium. During the summertime, some facilities offered arts and other activities that extended beyond the traditional school curriculum, but during the school year, these activities were rare. Logistical and security concerns predominated in the facility; it was hard to find the appropriate number of staff to supervise outdoor recreational activities, or even enough space. Staff members also experienced this boredom and were given few incentives or resources to change the situation.

In fact, when I first gained access to the facilities, I anticipated that I would focus my research on treatment programming and group work. I spent nearly three years doing research inside of the facilities, from morning until late at night. I remember observing only a few treatment groups happen during the entire time I was in the facilities. When I asked staff members why there were not more groups, I was told that they happened less and less since the reforms had been introduced into the facilities because the staff felt that they were too focused on security and control there.[29] Even individual therapy was rare—it almost never occurred inside of the boy's secure facility, and only sometimes occurred in the girl's facility. During my time doing research in the system, there was only one psychologist devoted to the entire network of juvenile facilities across the state. When I asked Gina, for example, if therapy had helped her address her needs during her time in confinement, she said, laughing, "What therapy? I've never seen that before."

A number of the young people spoke about their feelings of being "cooped up" and how those feelings contributed to a sense of listlessness, boredom, depression, and fighting. The young men at Hooper said that they had "too much free time" and that they needed to expend energy and be "more productive." They said that this experience of boredom and being "cooped up" might exacerbate the negative experience of a bad phone call or their difficulty in thinking about home. A number of the young people spoke about the ways that the boredom had an impact on the levels of fighting in the facility. One young man at McClary, for example, said that sitting around all the time "just frustrates a lot of people and that's how we clash." Slam said that the boredom made him "angry."

In speaking about her boredom, one young woman said, "It makes me depressed." She wished for structure and fun "at the same time," noting her desire, like many others, for there to be a balance struck between stimulating, pleasurable activities and a clear and coherent system of rules and guidelines.

Staff members also openly acknowledged the negative impact of boredom on facility life. One facility director said that "the less you do with kids, the more aggravating they're going to be." The boredom of staff members was also visible; some Youth Division Aides fell asleep during the classroom and study hours (they were expected to sit in the classrooms at all times), which had a visible impact on young people's motivation.

The idleness experienced by the young people and conveyed through the staff played a role in shaping the emotional climate of the facility. While active engagement was an expectation of treatment, the realities of facility life meant that young people often lacked the energy and motivation that might make that engagement more active and creative. The irony of this boredom was that it was experienced in a context in which the weight of the behavioral change "program" was quite deeply felt.

Doing Me

The participants who were in residential care overwhelmingly expressed a form of agency that was solipsistic. This is a sense of agency that is grounded in the notion that only the self can possess the tools to effect change in one's future. The expression "you come here alone, you leave here alone" best embodied this form of agency: it circulated throughout residential institutions and was used by both young people and staff in a mantra-like way. However, the repetition of this term belied the experiences of young people within the institutions, as they would often find that survival rested on their ability to mimic others, develop relationships and bonds with others, and to sustain their connections with those on the outside world.

The notion of "freedom coming from within" can be found in some narratives and literature written by people who have been in prison and is one that is arguably a source of ontological security and grounding for people experiencing incarceration, and a source of relief from some of the feelings of loss of control that imprisonment evokes.[30] A number of the young people felt that time in custody was their sole responsibility and that it was entirely "on them" to do that time; this may be distinct from this notion of freedom from within. After leaving jail, Izzy's girlfriend spoke reflectively about how some people made the "choice" to go to jail and stay in the jail "life" and become dependent on it, saying, "Yeah, they get used to it. After a while you get used to it. And once you get used to it, it's over for you." She spoke about how there would be no one in the institution to help, and thus it was necessary to rely on oneself to emerge through that time, and not "get used to it."

Young people would reflect these notions of individualized progress in their descriptions of treatment. Newz said that while he was in the residential facility, "I've been in control 100 percent of the time" and "every decision I made was on my own." Olivia similarly spoke about her realization that the only way she could do her time in residential custody was to "do me."

Elena arrived at Marshall girls' facility after bouncing around in foster care for a number of years. She was frustrated with her experience in the child welfare system and uncertain about where she would live and with whom she would live as she was awaiting the possibility of being released. She felt that her status in foster care had prevented her from being released, and she felt voiceless in the court process: "I feel like if I had spoken, I would have gone home."

Elena was on the student council at Marshall girls' facility and was considered a "model" resident. She initially conveyed a well-developed position about where she stood in her program. She suggested that each person should exercise "responsibility" in her program and do it to her best degree and that no one should not let other people interfere with that process. Elena spoke about how each person's program was her "responsibility" and that this could only be accomplished successfully alone. She embraced the official, institutional language of "choice" and spoke at length about how important it was to stick to the program. Elena spoke about the need for residents to recognize the benefits they would reap if they did program: "If you want help [in this facility], you're gonna get help." Elena also said that she wanted help "a long time ago" (e.g., at the beginning of her stay there); she said that at first she did not get it, but now that she "does the program," she has the help she needs.

However, Elena later revealed that she had been physically restrained a number of times, suggesting that she had not always clearly occupied the role of model resident in the minds of staff. She said that the way she had learned to survive confinement was to remember that she was there alone. Another young woman, who Elena said was in confinement despite being wrongfully convicted, had given her the advice "you come in here alone, you leave alone." In the context of her discussion about the frustrations about her pathway to confinement (as well as about the pains of imprisonment), Elena's words about being "alone" in the program are arguably distinct from her putative embrace of the formalized treatment ideology of individualism and choice. They are a form of individualism that is more resigned and less active than the treatment program envisions. Elena feels alienated and alone, and despite official efforts to provide her with "help" in finding a foster care placement, she rejected the idea that the system was aimed at helping her. She expressed some resignation and sadness, saying "anything that happens in here, it's not real," speaking elusively about relationships, friendship, and also about the lessons imparted by the program, which, she argued, had no relevance in the "real world." Elena's narrative reveals some of the complicated ways in which official discourses of change can become assimilated in young people's language, and thus "faked," but also lose their traction as young people grapple with the nature of individualism these narratives require.

In the "program," Elena was sometimes constructed by staff members as recalcitrant, at times as mentally ill or dependent, and other times as a model resident. The paperwork and the color of the shoelaces that marked her institutional identity reflected those ambiguities. For Elena, seeking groundedness was a complicated and difficult task, and one that was accompanied by a form of resignation. Elena's early use of the language of responsibility in our conversation (and our first meeting) may have been an effort to "shore up" some of her more ambiguous feelings about self-responsibility, and reflected her strategies at emotion management as she prepared to leave the facility.[31]

This sense by Elena and others that their time was "on me" was not straightforward and may have been more likely a stronger reflection of their assimilation and incorporation of official treatment language—the need to "do program"—in combination with their desire to find a way to cope through confinement. This idea of doing their time alone was also often belied by their actions: they formed strong friendships that continued after their time in custody. During focus groups, the participants would chat, gossip, and "par-lay" (or chat or network). Eddie said that another resident, Sam, had provided him with the name of his private defense attorney to help him with his legal appeal. Newz spoke about the other resident who had helped him learn how to "do program," noting "that's my man right there. He's the reason why I am a success." Ellen, seeing that Christina was often distressed when she witnessed physical restraints, hugged and comforted her, speaking about her desire to support Christina through her time. At the girls' facility, staff members pub-lished a newsletter with articles and poems by the young people; Ellen proudly displayed some work she had written, and Elena spoke about a poem written by another girl that had inspired her.

The sense of support and friendship continued after confinement. Jacob, Izzy, Maya, Jamal, and the others who were released from custody continue to seek informal support and friendship from a network of young people they met in custody. Other participants communicate with their friends from cus-tody through social networking sites like Facebook and MySpace, and they call their teachers and former staff members to seek advice from them and tell them how they were doing.

SELF-DISCIPLINE

The facilities were full of contradictions—despite acknowledging the importance of relationships and support, some young people would also speak about the need for hard discipline. In particular, many of the young men expressed a desire for control to be imposed on them externally by institu-tional actors or through situational controls because they felt that their efforts to exercise self-control were insufficient. This desire was expressed in response to what they felt were the "temptations" of returning to "the street." Staff and residents alike would characterize "the street" as a place where self-control was difficult, if not impossible, to achieve.

Skippy was one of the young people who felt that he could only achieve a sense of self-control—not even change, just self-control—if other people imposed those forms of control over him. Skippy went to the McClary facility when he was fifteen years old. He was white and from Westchester County; he came to McClary from a residential treatment facility. He had walked out of the previous facility several times and gotten into a number of fights there. Thus, his sentence was modified so he could go to a more secure setting. Reflecting on his time at the previous facility, he said it was "really easy." He even admitted to feeling the allure of being in a more secure setting so he could toughen himself up; he was a committed street fighter and felt that his time in the secure juvenile facility could help make him physically stronger and a better fighter. He said that if he stayed long enough in the facility "I might be big and huge." He had heard through the grapevine that kids got physically restrained at the secure facilities if they got into trouble. He said, "I thought that's what I needed."

Skippy was taught by his father that "if you have a problem, fight." His dad had been in and out of jail, and both of his parents suffered from addiction problems. His life at home was chaotic, and he frequently fought with his mother and her boyfriend. He fought at school and in the street and was constantly getting into trouble. He was in and out of foster care.

Skippy felt that his time in the facility wasn't teaching him anything. Like a lot of young people, he noticed that the kids who did poorly in the facility were the ones who got the most individual attention from staff: "it seems like only the kids who are doing bad see the counselors." Yet Skippy found that he struggled with his anger: "It scares me sometimes, I feel I can't control it." He said that "I get mad for a split second. . . . I think I'm bipolar or something." He would find that "I'll be in the meanest rage, then I start laughing." Skippy's father had been diagnosed with bipolar disorder, so he was concerned that he might have inherited it.

Even though McClary was more secure than the previous facility he was in, he felt that it wasn't strict or structured enough. He felt that "this place doesn't really show discipline" and that there should be more "outcomes" for misbehavior, just like he had experienced at home, at the hands of his father, who would physically discipline him if he did "stupid things" like get poor grades. He felt that he should have been in an even more secure setting, "I still feel like I should've been in a secure setting," because "I would've learned a lot more" there. He even felt that being in a boot camp would have really changed him.

Skippy, who participated in local fight clubs with his friends before he went into custody, asked his aftercare worker if he could have an ankle bracelet because "I'm worried about fighting."[32] He grappled with the idea of resisting his inclination to fight once he got home. He said that "if I want to live where I am my whole life I have to stay the same" and that "I have so many enemies" at home. But he also found fighting exciting and appealing; it was an escape for him.[33] Other young people were concerned that when confronted with the demands of street codes of retaliatory violence they wouldn't be able to resort to the "problem-solving steps" and anger management techniques they had been provided in treatment programs at the facility and would instead participate in the violence.

Skippy also felt that the only way he could control himself was by being controlled by others. Shortly before he was set to be released, he left the facility with his counselor to go and visit the high school he was supposed to be attending after he was released. He felt apprehensive and ambivalent about the experience: "I feel like I'm going to get into trouble when I'm not always being watched, especially when I get out of here because when I went to the school there was no one there and I felt like really free, all I had was shackles on my feet and my hands were free and stuff to walk around, and I felt like, I don't know, like I didn't belong on the outside. . . . I couldn't wait to go back." Skippy had been inside of residential facilities for so long that "I'm used to being told what to do and stuff." He still wanted to go home, "but it's just like kinda like nervous." He felt nervous about fighting, about joining his old friends, but also about drinking and smoking pot, which he had been doing heavily before he was arrested, but also which he knew his parents did.

Other young people spoke about a desire to exercise a form of self-control that has been described as "diachronic" self-control, or "self-binding," in which people impose restrictions on themselves.[34] For example, Shayla wanted to spend time with her friends but feared that she would want to smoke marijuana and start selling drugs again so that she could obtain the material goods she coveted, like sneakers and hats. She thus stayed inside her grandmother's house and also avoided certain street corners where her friends socialized to prevent herself from engaging in these activities. Because she was also banned from the public housing projects nearby, where she had been arrested, she was not legally allowed to go and see her friends who lived there. Billy also decided to stay inside his home, although his decision to stay at home was in part motivated by his desire to avoid the constant scrutiny of the police. Billy later asked me if he could be placed back into detention to prevent himself from robbing someone again.[35] Nearly eight years after I met him, Billy remains inside his home nearly all day every day; he still hasn't completed high school, and he now has two small children. When I saw him recently, he told me, "I'm staying out of trouble," which meant he hadn't been arrested; yet he hasn't held a job, hasn't applied for public benefits, and hasn't obtained his high school equivalency. He has also, at the young age of twenty-two, faced significant stress-related health problems that have remained unaddressed. These forms of self-control that Billy and others engaged in were also external in the sense that young people felt that being indoors might also insulate them from the temptations they felt before they were placed into custody and offer them sanctuary from those temptations. In other words, they were places where a form of passive self-control could be exercised.

Within the residential facilities, a number of young people like Skippy spoke about their desire for "structure" and "discipline" to be imposed by staff members. Many staff members vented to me that the facilities had become more out of control and chaotic since the new commissioner, Gladys Carrión, had arrived and had been implementing rule changes about restraints. Over and over again, staff members would complain that there had been a loss of "structure" in the facilities since her arrival; in particular, they felt that they had been stripped of their "tools" for exercising control. It was always made clear to me by staff members that the word "tool" was a euphemism for a physical restraint. Some program staff in the facilities suggested that "structure" and "accountability"—and in particular, the power of the physical restraint as a tool of accountability—were necessary because young people came from environments that were so devoid of these qualities.[36]

Additionally, congruencies existed between notions of structure on the street and within the facilities. When I asked the group of older adolescent boys at Hooper what "structure" meant to them, Eddie and Sam offered that it was about how "everybody knows their place," and that they know their "position," so that "if you're a nobody, be a nobody." Thus, "structure" is about people knowing their place in a hierarchy and sticking to it. The young men at Hooper suggested that Jacob was a good example of this kind of individual: he stuck to himself, recognized the hierarchies of age and street allegiances, and yet was also a model of self-discipline. Tony offered an example of a young person in the facility who violated this "structure": a resident on his unit complained that he did not have enough sugar on his breakfast cereal; after he started complaining, everyone had to go back to their wing, and that resident faced "no consequences." Sam said that if you get out of this "structure," "there are consequences." The participants at Hooper all said that this resident "structure" made their lives better in the facility. José reflected these sentiments when he said that that kids should be treated like dogs, because a dog clearly knows "who his master is."

Some young people bemoaned the recent shift in programmatic policies, which they felt "loosened" the forms of control that staff could extend over them, and discussed their desire for what they called a more "hands-on" approach involving physical restraints. In fact, the term "looser" was used often by young people and staff to describe the evolution of the facility's program since systemic reforms had happened: a staff member who allowed young people to "do loose program" would allow that young person to be undisciplined, some felt. Newz, who was placed in the facilities before the reforms occurred, spoke about how young people learned to "respect authority" in the old system when staff literally "slam[med]" them against walls. Other young men said that the environments were "calmer" when the staff used a more "hands-on" approach. It is arguable that young people also desired an approach that was more explicit and direct in its expression of control; under the new system, control was exercised in less overt but perhaps no less powerful ways.

Yet there were congruencies between these notions of discipline and the ways that young people described the violence in their lives outside of the facilities; the "old" form of overt control was, in some sense, familiar to them. Not only had these young people disproportionately been exposed to forms of parental discipline that mirrored that of staff discipline, they also spoke about the parallels between the violence of the streets and that of staff.[37] José, for example, spoke about how he felt that "to control this environment, you need

'hostility' from staff" and that "we're from the street" and so "we respect who-
ever" can instill that respect in a way that mirrors that expressed by individuals
on the street. He said that "we just don't like authority," referring to the young
people in the residential facility. He attributed this antipathy toward authority
that young people in the institutions possessed to "the streets," and he said that
this process occurred through "socialization." When I asked José what he felt
"authority" meant on the streets, he said that it was about who gets the most
money, like the "gangbangers." He said that on the streets, people look at the
police as just "snitches, cops, and pigs" and that they lack the authority and
respect of the gangbangers. He was of the belief that younger teenagers "want
to explore" and doing crimes meets "emotional needs."

José's anthropological analysis of the young men in the facility, among
which he implicitly included himself, reflected a confidence born out of his
five years in custody. He spoke derisively about those peers who hadn't come
under "control" as he had. However, José's analysis of authority also revealed
his assessment of the relationship between authority in institutions inside and
outside of the residential facilities and the role that those authorities play in
the production of compliance, but not necessarily change. José recognizes
that his compliance with facility programs—and his demonstration of self-
control—did not necessarily translate into personal change as much as it represented deference or even submission to authority.

But the institutions may have also been places where young people felt
"out of control" and thus in search of a place where they could gain some
sense of control. Young people's desire for externally imposed control stemmed
in part from their feelings about losing self-control once they entered institutions but also from their desire for a sense of security and consistency within
the institutional environments. These desires may also find their fruition in
young people's attachments to those individuals who are the sources of their
subjection, such as the residential facility guards.

Struggling with the Demonstration of Change: Moving On and Out

Because the residential juvenile facility is intended to be an incubator of
change, young people knew that they would be expected to demonstrate that
change; however, if their process of change was not itself related to their crime
but was softer and more internal, how to define that change to people in the
system became murkier.

A number of young people had adult convictions and would face a parole
board that would determine their readiness for release. In New York, a young
person's completion of treatment programs and attainment of educational success means very little in the minds of parole, who overwhelmingly focus their
decision-making around the individual's crime and his or her alleged level

of dangerousness. The irony is that for many of the young people charged as adults who were sent to juvenile facilities, their entire time "doing program" actually meant little in the minds of the parole board. Almost all of the participants had been "hit" with more time after their first parole appearance. Many of the residents obsessed about their parole board hearings, and they frequently asked me and other adults about the best strategies for what to say and do in a parole hearing or for letters of support for the board.

For young people adjudicated as delinquents, the judges in their cases had the authority to extend their placement until their eighteenth birthday. Staff in the juvenile facilities could recommend that a young person's placement be extended. Thus, their progress in treatment did matter toward their ultimate ability to get out and stay out.

Tony, the young man who had a sentence of fifteen years to life for homicide that he received when he was fifteen years old, often worried out loud about his future beyond bars and his eligibility for parole. Tony frequently asked about his ability to pursue careers that he had aspired to, such as being an attorney, with a felony homicide conviction. He also expressed some fears about where and how he would live on the outside. Thus, he recognized the serious obstacles he would face in building a life for himself after his imprisonment. On the inside, Tony was engaged in college-level coursework and actively participated in religious services offered at the facility. He enjoyed writing, reading, and reflection and would often pepper me with questions about college, graduate school, and opportunities outside of imprisonment. He expressed an interest in "helping his community" and asked about how he might be able to do this. He spoke about his desire to act as a leader, even if younger residents who resisted the program would thwart his efforts. He said, "I feel a responsibility to help others" and that when he first came to the facility, he was immature, and there were people there who helped him. He said that there was a resident who returned to the facility on a parole violation who saw Tony resisting the program and encouraged him to follow the program.

Tony wondered why the parole board would not be able to understand that he had grown up since he had first entered custody when he was fifteen years old. He asked, "How can you show this change?" He continued, "you mature a lot" after you are fifteen years old. Tony, like many others, struggled against the assumption that he had done wrong and would continue to do so and that despite his feelings about his internal, authentic processes of self-transformation, the parole board will ultimately decide to release him based on a cursory examination of his facility records. Tony struggles to express his humanity, his potential, and his similarity with so many others who have grown up and matured past their teenage troubles.

Tony is now in a maximum security prison in upstate New York. He entered custody there in 2009 and will have his first parole hearing in 2019.

By the time he reaches parole, he will have spent the primary years of his young adulthood behind bars. Like many people with lengthy sentences, he has received just a handful of visits from family. He has never had the opportunity to continue college, which he started in his juvenile facility. He has never received individual therapy to address the violence he experienced in his childhood. He's grown physically large after years of lifting weights on the prison yard, but he has experienced limited emotional growth since I met him six years ago.

THE CONTOURS OF CHANGE

Recidivism rates become the measure of success in a world of criminal and juvenile justice that is dependent on federal and state funding to steer programming and rehabilitative resources. Will young people reoffend if they take a series of cognitive behavioral interventions? Will their demonstration of personal responsibility lead them to accept fault for what they have done in the past and thus avoid doing the same in the future? Will the "structure" of facility life, coupled with the threat of physical punishment, ingrain a fear of consequences in their lives?

Young people are deeply distanced from these questions about reoffending. Few teenagers behind bars are exclusively focused on how they will stop offending but are instead concerned with the broader dilemmas of living a precarious life as a young adult: how can they stay safe and free from incarceration and policy custody when they get home? How can they gain access to college and a career? How can they find love and friendship, support and certainty? These young people rarely ask whether the system can give them these things, with the exception of the few staff members who go above and beyond with them and who they stay in touch with them. They rarely explicitly identify a program, module, or intervention as the source of their hope. Instead, they grapple, in multiple dimensions, with how they can stay sane, free, and seek a place of reflection in a place that is, paradoxically, highly controlled but also deeply alienating, unchallenging, and unstimulating.

Olivia left McClary and drifted to the wind. I searched far and wide for her—on social media, through her family—but I never found her. Olivia was one of a few teenagers, including Maya, whom I have never found again, despite the ease of access that social media allows for. Olivia's disappearance is not necessarily a sign of her repeat offending—although it could be—but a mix of complex and difficult things. She could well not want to be found. The only sign that she was still alive was a moment last year when she turned up in the New York city courts database as a defendant charged with a minor crime.

Skippy, now twenty-one, is in jail. Sadly, as with a number of other young people in this book, the only way that I can locate him is through the publicly available Internet search for jail and prison inmates.

The time eventually came for Newz to be released from prison, where he was sent from the residential juvenile facility on his twenty-first birthday. He had few options about where to live upon his release. His adopted parents' home was located near a school, a zone that registered sex offenders were banned from. Newz reached out to a few of us that he knew and asked for help; he learned in the prison that unless he could find a place to live, with a fixed address, he would stay there indefinitely. A team of us scrambled together to find any place that he could go, from a program in Albany, to ones in New York City, where he was from. He was systematically rejected from every program, until finally we learned that the main men's shelter in New York City would take him in.

Newz walked out of prison and into the city's largest adult men's shelter. I knew it well for its inhospitable conditions and its reputation for violence; a number of my adult male clients chose to sleep on the subway instead of spending the night in the shelter. Later transferred to a smaller men's shelter, Newz struggled. The first time I saw him after he got out, he boasted that he had purchased a pair of expensive boots with money that his adopted parents had given him. He spoke proudly of the boots to me and a social worker who worked at my old office; after he left, we both talked about how struck we were by the incongruity of his existence: he had just told us that he couldn't find a job, had been rejected from a number of programs he had applied to, and that the money that he had earned as a kitchen worker in the juvenile facility was running dry. Soon afterward, we lost touch with Newz; according to the New York State Division of Parole, he went AWOL from his supervision. He eventually turned up in the supervision of the New York City Department of Corrections; he has been charged with failing to register as a sex offender, and thus with a violation of parole. He remains in jail pending his parole revocation hearing.

On the outside, José spoke little about his family, but rather about spending time outside of confinement enjoying his new found freedoms. Although he was required by parole to engage in anger management and drug treatment courses, José suggested a kind of ambivalence about the parole requirements. After he told me that all parole does is check in with him and sometimes come to his house, I asked if it would be helpful if parole was more supportive; José said no, because he usually goes back to his old ways if people are breathing down his neck. He said that he liked things the way they were right now, just being able to "chill" without anybody getting in his way.

José implied that he had not gone back to offending but that he also did not want to engage in the model forms of responsibility laid out by the courts and "the system" in a broader sense. He uses the word "chill" to suggest his interest in relaxing, being left alone, and enjoying a relative sense of autonomy. Yet this lifestyle of "chilling" was also being sustained by income from his previous "old ways."Thus, there is a tension in José's newfound sense of being in the world.[38]

Residential juvenile facilities are in their very mission focused on facilitating change in young people. The apparatus of programs, rules, levels, and punishment was developed with the idea that the young people who enter the facilities must change their lives and their behaviors to successfully reenter the world.Yet young people's relationships to these official notions of change reveal that their relationships to the institution are often as much about identifying and carving out a sense of ownership about their own process of change that is separate and apart from institutional norms about change. For those young people who embrace official ideas about discipline, like those who argue that they must be restrained or physically punished, their alignment with institutional ideas about behavioral control are in fact ones that may symbolize a submission to their domination and control. However, it is clear from hundreds of years of collective research knowledge that physical punishment, isolation, and separation are not conducive to human growth.

The conditions of human growth must also be attuned to broader social-structural forces that relate to such growth. The world outside of prisons, detention facilities, and custodial institutions that young people charged with crimes face are ones that are racialized social systems. These are systems that are defined by the sociologist Eduardo Bonilla Silva as those in which "economic, political, social, and ideological levels are partially structured by the placement of actors in racial categories or races."[39] These systems actually deepen the damage done by repressive social structures to the primarily black and brown and impoverished white young people by upholding a myth of progress and individual change that is just that, a myth.[40] The interventions used in the juvenile justice system today focus on facilitating internal self-control within young people. As such, they are shaped by racial hierarchies and strategies of domination that insist on and demand that self-control be exercised as a form of deference and submission. Any restructuring of this model or challenge to the hierarchical structure poses a threat to the racialized social system. "Threats" are represented through behavior that is deemed to be bad or "ungovernable."Thus, there are few social incentives that exist in the juvenile justice system that provide young people with the conditions to move beyond their roles as deferential, submissive figures. State agents therefore absolve themselves of the responsibility of eliminating the many structural barriers that exist in these young people's lives. The preservation of a racialized social system actually depends on these barriers existing, for they help to maintain a race and class hierarchy that the juvenile justice system depends on for its very functioning.

Even though there have been contemporary nods to the sanctity of youth "voice," self-help and representation in the present-day system and an acknowledgment of the disproportionate representation of youth of color, there are processes and systems in place at the front and back ends of the system—through policing, parole and probation practices, institutional arrangements, and ideologies of "help"—that actually preserve existing systems of racial domination and repression and result in the continuing need for a juvenile justice apparatus. These processes and systems were arguably set into motion with the establishment of the first separate juvenile institution in New York in 1825, when the impoverished children of immigrants to the country were served in a way that demanded their submission to the legal authorities who "helped" them.[41]

So many of the young people who enter custody are grappling with ideas about change; they want to be able to imagine better lives for themselves. Many of the young people saw the institutional focus on making them rule-compliant as something that didn't serve their interest in building a better life for themselves; thus, although a number of young people found a way to follow the rules and thus make their everyday lives a little easier, they also focused on growing with the limited resources that they had available to them to grow—time with friends, writing in a journal, reading, or talking to a sympathetic staff member. In short, the program itself did not play a significant role in facilitating change for young people; for them, change came "from the inside," not from inside the facilities.

Conclusion

OUR JUVENILE JUSTICE SYSTEMS inhibit young people's growth and development, treat the largely black and brown teenagers as discardable and worthless, and create more harm than they provide help. When I tell people that this is what I have found in my research, they ask me, "Well, what would you do?" This is the wrong question. The focus of so many liberal reformers for so many years on "doing" has had often-fatal consequences for young people. Although I am preternaturally opposed to inaction, I believe that "doing" has all to often involved attempts to fix other people's children—to intervene, help, and change the individual, or even in some cases, the system. This has left us in an almost perennial state of "reform" but without any opportunity to seriously consider why we spend so much time attempting to fix a young person who has, in some cases, committed a single bad act over the course of just a few minutes. So, in short, I would ask instead: why do we keep on doing this the wrong way?

For a moment in the 1970s, the concept of radical noninterventionism, or just "leaving them the hell alone," was floated in leftist academic circles.[1] This was rooted in the idea that the very arrest and reform of teenagers was the cure that harmed. Radical noninterventionism recognized that most young people will grow out of crime, and the more we fiddled with young people's lives, the worse off they would be.

Radical noninterventionism is rooted in the idea that we should just stop messing around with these kids and let them be. Instead, we should develop resources for their communities and fundamentally redistribute wealth, especially in a place like New York (one of the richest states in the country) so that the wealthiest are adequately taxed and there is enough funding for early childhood services, better schools, and more social supports. This is indeed a version of what I want.

But I also think a fundamentally moral question remains unaddressed by the issue of radical noninterventionism.

Today, among juvenile justice reformers, there is a popular belief, among large foundations to current and former system commissioners, that we should close juvenile prisons entirely. Indeed, some may say that my book is irrelevant because the facilities that I studied in 2008 are rapidly closing and changing—that under New York's "Close to Home" initiative, the vast majority of young people are no longer even being sent upstate. That facilities are out of favor, and the ones that remain look and feel nicer than the ones I researched.

But I have spent time in the bowels of the New York State Archives, reading the memos, letters, and reports of former system commissioners, advocacy groups, and wardens, dating back to the nineteenth century, and their words haunt me. Not only could the words from 1850 and 1950 be substituted for those of reformers today—the call to do something new for kids; to make smaller, nicer facilities; to focus on rehabilitation instead of punishment—but the kids inside have remained exactly the same. They've been shuttled around different facilities—some small, some big, operated by agencies with different names, that look a little different or feel a little different, that are located within a few miles of home or hundreds of miles from home. Some kids who were once locked up are now on electronic monitoring or are at home and see a social worker instead of a juvenile facility counselor. But they are the same.

These kids are the ungovernable. They challenge our notions of normativity, of safety and security. They are the children who we deem to be incapable of change and incapable of being changed, in ways that are deeply tinged by the sociopolitical dynamics of the time. Today, our notions of governability are deeply racialized; the children who are deemed to be worthy of being saved and who are exempted from deep-end facilities are growing in number, but there remain a category of children, primarily black and brown and male, who are understood to be incapable of change in their own homes and in need of removal from them. These ungovernable children are then forced to be governed through behavioral change interventions that demand total submission to state authority.

The facilities that I was in in 2008 now have a different behavioral change system—the differently colored shoelaces have been discarded for a new model of behavioral advancement; some of the forms that staff had to fill out have been replaced by forms with different names; the Marshall girls facility closed and has reopened elsewhere. All of these changes have been made in the name of reform—they have been done to make the facilities look and feel better and nicer. Yet, as some have argued, are they in fact representative of a trend of "carceral humanism" or "carceral welfare"?[2] In this case, punitive practices are essentially re-packaged to look nicer, to be more welfarist in their orientation, and to express a more seemingly compassionate approach. Yet they remain tied to the carceral state—they are still a form of punishment. At Marshall, the girls can now paint their rooms, and they seem to engage in more treatment practices; there are also arguably changes that have been made in response to the Department of Justice investigation into the system that do a much better job of protecting children in crisis. Yet if the facilities are more broadly "nicer," does this actually mean that young people's lives will change for the better?

I believe that my work suggests this is not possible. At the heart of the residential facility are children who are undergoing a process of change in their lives—that of adolescence and young adulthood—which is obscured, stultified, and hindered by the state's focus on the child's crime and their moral worth.

The criminalized child is the crucible of this story. Criminalized children become the children unto whom work must be done to fix them, even though their own relationship to being fixed, their own internal struggles about the acts they have committed, their own sense of worth, and their very relationship to the adults who criminalize them is so seldom understood by them. In fact, in all of the thousands of pages of archival documents, the hundreds of interviews, the hours of fieldwork, I have rarely heard any adult exhibit empathy for this group of children but rather a resounding sympathy coupled often with a kind of condemnation.

The reader might ask how it is possible to be both sympathetic and condemning. I think this is possible when a young person is understood to be ungovernable. The paradox of ungovernable children is that they are always the children who are seen to be in need of fixing—the children whom we should help, feel sorry for, change, or address. But, as a class of individuals who are other people's children, they are also seen as unwieldy, scary, capable of harm, inherently bad—they are also, perennially, unfixable or ungovernable. What I am suggesting is that the hidden spectre of juvenile justice reforms is the unfixable and ungovernable child. The child is always the problem, not the confounding system that they enter, not the confusing and ever-changing treatment practices, not the boredom behind bars, not the unreasonable expectations of conformity and compliance, not even their adolescent struggles to make sense of their identity and their relationships to themselves. The criminalized child is the problem. If they comply fully with the system intended to change them, they are a sociopath; if they don't comply, they are resistant. If they reoffend, which the vast majority of children do who go through juvenile justice systems across the country, then they are in need of further governance. If they reoffend as adults, like Jacob, then they are not the problem of the juvenile justice systems and therefore are more easily abandoned.

Young people's experiences of being criminalized are intimately connected to the ways that the adults in their lives assessed their governability and their moral worth. These assessments have consequences not only for their routes into the criminal justice system, but also for their aspirations and their social mobility. Teenagers who are considered ungovernable in their communities are often sent to institutions, including foster and group homes, hospitals and mental health treatment facilities, juvenile facilities, and prisons, to be governed, but often, while there, they are found to be ungovernable. This perpetual state of ungovernability and unworthiness had deep and negative impacts on young people.

Michael's ability to behave in ways that were considered respectable by his teachers, or his mother's ability to demonstrate her fitness for work while living in the homeless shelter, became the evidence on which their worth and value as social citizens were assessed by agents of the state. The assessments of them raised considerable questions about the relationship between young people and the state actors they encountered throughout their lives: what impact did these condemnations of their families and themselves have on young people? What motivated these assessments of worth? The young people I met found their own aspirations shaped and twisted by these negative assessments of their worthiness. These young people struggled to engage in behavior that was considered virtuous by those who had the power to deem it so, and they were thus considered to be worthless and bad. So, if they, like many teenagers, were only partially "bad," what happened when they engaged in an explicit form of badness—violating the law?

A "bad" kid is one who is seen by adults as ungovernable, unable to appreciate and respond to the demands and commands of his or her schoolteachers and the police who monitor his or her community. This construction of ungovernability seriously hampers a young person's navigation of the broader systems they must encounter to thrive. So once they encounter schools that turn them away, housing institutions that prevent them from living there because of a conviction, employers who deny them work, and parole and probation officers who presume they will fail, they often give up, withdraw, or turn back to offending. This is not because of their inherently criminal natures, or the "culture" of offending they come from, but it grows out of the very ideas about their worth that are produced and reproduced.

In much juvenile justice rhetoric, it has become common practice to point to the conservative commentators of the 1990s who propagated racist, classist, and sexist beliefs about young offenders that resulted in zero tolerance policies toward them. Liberal reformers condemn these perspectives and argue for a welfarist approach to young people, one rooted in the idea that young people can be saved from a life of crime through treatment and interventions. Yet in many ways, this perspective entrenches an oversimplified idea of the young offender as a troubled young person who can change if only given the right forms of treatment and support systems. What this idea of the young person doesn't include is the notion that it is the very pathological social systems they have encountered, coupled with the institutional racism, sexism, and classism, that have arguably contributed to their criminalization process. These social systems have caused the "young offender" to emerge. When those same social processes and systems inform the very treatments that young people are given—for example, the cognitive behavioral therapies that are informed by the idea that the "responsible" subject who has fully accepted his or her fault in offending, or the family therapy that assumes it is the pathological (primarily black and brown) family that has erred in raising their children; or the risk-informed technologies, which identify previous arrests as a source of risk without acknowledging that black and brown young people are arrested more often than white children—these processes and systems are simply reembedded in the juvenile justice system. It is no surprise, then, that children continue to be rearrested, to get into trouble in institutions, and to be restrained by staff members who find them to be intractable and ungovernable.

There are individuals and institutions in today's juvenile justice system who believe that some children are worth saving and some are not. Some believe that there's nothing to be done once a teenager who has been given help commits another crime, relapses, or goes on the run. Today's juvenile justice system is arguably deeply liberal in its dependence on state intervention and reform to force positive change in young people's lives, but strangely illiberal in its effects. These effects are often cruel and unusual, as the practices of lengthy sentencing, solitary confinement, educational neglect, physical restraints, and limited due process rights are reserved for the poorest, most seriously mentally ill, and most marginalized members of the system.[3]

We must craft political solutions for serious youth offending that actually transform existing social structural inequalities and relationships rather than preserving them. These political solutions include a fundamental transformation of the social welfare safety net for young people in peril: they must be provided with adequate access to safe housing through young adulthood, including and especially young people who are in the foster care system; they must be provided with expanded access to outpatient and inpatient mental health services, especially those that do not discriminate against children who have been accused of, adjudicated for, or convicted of a crime; they must have access to schools that love and nourish them instead of reject them; they must have real and meaningful access to employment, particularly during the summer months when they are not in school.

We must cultivate notions of growth and change for young people— and ultimately freedom from injury, despair, and the grips and seductions of violence, which are themselves arguably produced by racism and structural violence. We should not treat the intervention into the crime as the cure or reforms to the police and punitive state as the solution, but instead we should boost the potential of the state to enact social good through the infusion and redistribution of resources to individuals whose growth depends on those resources. That growth involves life-sustaining food, shelter, and medical care; unfettered access to nourishing relationships with friends and family; the highest quality education; and the ability to realize a collective dignity.

We also cannot overlook the day-to-day lives of the individuals who inhabit these systems. We must not be seduced into the idea that abuse and violence must be physical and brutal to rise to our attention and that therapy is the antithesis of punishment. Juvenile facilities can have a deep and negative impact on the lives of the people who inhabit them—staff and young people—without ever including violence. Behavioral change regimes can be boring, confusing, and demanding in and of themselves, and this can have serious effects on an individual's capacity to grow and change.

I critique the cognitive behavioral programming in the facilities fully aware and respectful of the systematic and thorough research that has been done about these programs and the effects they have on subsequent reoffending. Other scholars will argue that the evidence is robust: cognitive behavioral programming and multisystemic family therapies have a greater impact on subsequent reoffending than any other approach. I don't dispute these findings, which have important consequences for our understandings of the harms that young people's offending can do in our communities. What I dispute are the ways that young people's lives—and their ability to live those lives—are conceptualized in the approach those programs take to them. Simply understanding those young people as vessels for the application of management and control strategies, rather than human beings with complex lives in the pursuit of dignity is, in my mind, a fundamentally inhuman approach to them. These programs also inherently exclude a structural analysis about what leads certain groups of young people to be arrested; the groups of individuals who are studied are those who are sentenced to juvenile facilities, residential treatment centers, and community-based alternative-to-incarceration programs, not the young people who I went to high school with at an elite private boarding school but who similarly challenged authority, violated the law, and made errors in their thinking patterns. What I would argue is that our question to find ever more effective tools for behavioral management in juvenile facilities comes at the cost of decency, mercy, and respect.

Often, at the facility level, the most simple changes are the ones that can potentially have the most transformative effects on the lives of young people and staff. These are arguably the changes that are rooted in and responsive to the dignity of the individuals within them: like all teenagers, young people inside juvenile facilities seek nourishment and growth in multiple dimensions of existence: their minds, their bodies, and in their spiritual lives. When facilities focus exclusively on behavioral change programs, as many of them do, without an attendant focus on athletics, education, the arts, and the spiritual and emotional lives of young people, they ignore the multiple and varied ways that young people's suffering and their strengths can be addressed and nourished. During my time in New York's facilities, the athletic fields surrounding the facilities often remained sometimes hauntingly empty; although basketball games were common, and the young people would occasionally play some intramural sports, I was always struck by how seldom they engaged in athletic activities in the way that is common to their peers in high schools across the country. The same goes for artistic and creative activities; although high schools across the country see these activities as an essential component of adolescent development both within and beyond the classroom, almost no state juvenile facilities in the country include funding for such enrichment activities. If they do exist, they are conducted by volunteers or outside organizations. Young people who enter juvenile facilities do not stop being teenagers, and yet they are treated as if the act or acts that they have committed constitute the entire content of their character. This is a dangerous approach to individual growth and change; it misrecognizes the inner lives of young people, their needs, and their dignity. This book attempts to convey the harms that can be done when the bad child, rather than the extraordinary and promising child, becomes the center of our interventions.

METHODOLOGICAL APPENDIX

THE RESEARCH STUDY TOOK place between 2007 and 2011. The New York State Office of Children and Family Services (OCFS), which runs the state's secure residential facilities for young people charged with crimes, generously allowed me inside of their facilities to interview youth and staff over an extended period of time.[1] The sociologist Loic Wacquant detailed the need to analyze of the dynamics of everyday life in American correctional institutions in the context of what has been termed "mass imprisonment" and noted that few researchers had found their way into prisons in recent years.[2] Wacquant argues that it is important to scrutinize the daily life of these institutions to develop theories about the mechanisms that help to support, reproduce, and sustain mass imprisonment.

Thirty-nine teenagers participated in the first stage of my research, which took place for a year and a half, starting at the end of 2008. In 2010, I initiated a study about staff, interviewing more than seventy frontline staff members and administrators from across the state. In addition to analyzing young people's and staff's experiences in the state's juvenile facilities, I also talked to young people about their perspectives on court, detention, and alternative to incarceration programs. I was a participant observer in more than twenty meetings with system administrators, policymakers, and reformers about the processes of reform I described earlier. After I left the field, I continued to stay in touch with the young people, and I continue to visit juvenile facilities and prisons across the state, where I engage in teaching, sentencing, parole, and reentry advocacy work.

I used a mix of research methods. I conducted focus groups and individual interviews, did extensive observational field work, and taught a group of young people in a research methods course, using participatory action research methods to gather data. The research sites in the first study included residential treatment facilities, jails, courts, alternative-to-incarceration programs, and group homes, as well as the young people's homes, street corners, and the social networking sites they frequented.[3] I spent time with the teenagers on the phone, in their homes, at restaurants, hospitals, welfare offices, funeral homes, shelters, and many other places. I did not live in the young people's communities, nor did I spend the night in their homes. I built relationships focused on respect but also founded on a clear sense of boundaries—as a young white woman from a privileged background in a doctoral program, I could not become a seamless part of my participants' lives. I was there to learn, and inasmuch as I could, reciprocate that learning with my knowledge of the law and the system that these individuals had been so alienated from.

The research involved the development of sustained relationships with the participants, as well as attention to the contexts that they existed in and the broader political landscape that impacted on their experiences in the courts and in custody. The research also involved interviews with the young people's family members and friends, residential facility and community-based program workers, and government officials involved in the juvenile justice system.

The specific aims of the research were to:

- Understand how young people express agency in the context of the contemporary youth justice system.
- Identify some of the ways in which they believe they can get out and stay out of the system.
- Examine what role the state plays and can play in either inhibiting or facilitating young people's exit from the system.

ETHNOGRAPHIC AND PHENOMENOLOGICAL APPROACHES

My approach was strongly rooted in the interpretivist tradition of qualitative research and driven by the goal of achieving a contextual understanding of the lives of participants.[4] Ethnographic approaches also seek to understand the meanings of action within a social world.[5] Ethnography holds the potential to create a "dialogic" encounter between the observer and participant.[6] Such methods help to understand how young people relate to their experiences of punishment, and the meanings they give to their experiences within this context.[7]

Ethnographies of residential facilities can aid in developing thicker understandings of the ways in which "institutional selves" are expressed and negotiated.[8] Criminologist Ben Crewe argues that observational fieldwork in a prison can help to access the "hidden transcripts" that may illuminate some of the dynamics of prison life that relate to the study of individual agency in the face of coercive power.[9]

Ethnographies of coercive contexts are naturally limited by the researcher's ability to gain unfettered access to the research site. Not only was I not incarcerated myself, I was unable to spend all day and night inside of the facilities as a true participant observer. There are also ethical complexities involved in choosing to participate in a context in which one is a clear outsider.[10]

Although motivated by the aim of painting a detailed portrait of institutional landscapes and experiences, this was not an immersive ethnography.

My aim was to understand "how members accomplish, manage and reproduce a sense of social structure."[11] This approach was concerned with how human consciousness and perceptions are constitutive of the objects and structures that they exist in.[12] Approaches to understanding processes of growth are difficult because it is often hard to disentangle performances from lived truths and experiences, and, in turn, these may be complicated by emotions. "Emotion work" is central to the "human capacity for, if not the actual habit of, reflecting on and shaping inner feelings."[13] This approach was used to analyze young people's negotiation of identity and "change" in the continuum of punishment. It allowed for a closer examination of the role that emotion played in young people's struggles to grow up and out of the institutions of punishment they encountered.

SITE SELECTION

I chose two sites for my research: residential juvenile facilities operated by the OCFS, a statewide agency also responsible for the administration of the child welfare system, and the "community" in which the young people lived while court involved if they were not in institutional care. Notwithstanding my attempts to capture the breadth and depth of their experiences, this research design could not accommodate for the fact that young people frequently moved in and out of a vast range of institutions. I traveled to the residential facilities on a regular basis. I would typically spend between four and six hours in each facility on each visit.

I chose one secure facility that confines young people charged as so-called Juvenile Offenders (thirteen- to fifteen-year-olds charged as adults) until they turn twenty-one years old.[14] Juvenile delinquents (seven- to fifteen-year-olds adjudicated in family court) reside in limited secure and nonsecure facilities, and they are sent to these facilities based on an assessment of their risk and readiness for release at intake. Young people charged with delinquencies but who are assessed as having the lowest level of risk reside in "nonsecure" facilities, which are locked but generally do not have razor-wire fences outside them.

The girls' facility, Marshall, was in a rural area outside of a small city in the northern, formerly industrialized part of the state. Marshall's campus included the girls' secure and limited secure facilities, the girls' intake facility for the state, and a boys' facility. The girls' facility consisted of six living units that had anywhere from nine to sixteen girls on them.

Both the girls' and the boys' facilities were brought under federal receivership after the U.S. Department of Justice found that the facilities had inadequate mental health treatment and that staff overused physical restraints.

The boys' secure facility, Hooper, is in a rural but more affluent part of the state than Marshall, closer to New York City. It has a budgeted capacity of 180 beds and had a smaller self-contained facility adjacent to it that served as a substance abuse treatment unit. There are ten units in the main building consisting of fifteen beds each, with one mental health unit, as well as a unit called the Modified Services Program, which was used for boys from across the state who had committed a serious infraction of facility rules. The substance abuse program (in the adjacent facility to the main building) was for boys who are designated at intake as having a drug or alcohol dependency. It was widely regarded by residents and staff as a place that was more orderly, "easier" for staff to work in, and generally a more relaxed environment.

Both facilities at Hooper are surrounded by concertina wire, a sally port that visitors must go through up on exit and entry, and every unit is secured by a lock that is controlled in a central security unit (but can also be accessed by keys provided to the staff). The movements of the residents are tightly controlled. Each residential unit goes to meals, gym and school at separate times (and some units actually have a classroom attached to them, so the teacher comes directly to the unit to teach). Residents are required to walk in a line to and from each activity, often counting their room numbers out loud as they passed by a control point, and were required to hold their hands behind their backs whenever they walked through the facility.

McClary residential center was selected because of its status as a model program in the minds of state administrators and national advocates. It was perceived to be a facility that best embraced the therapeutic direction that the state's administrators were moving toward. It is a non-secure facility, thus representative of the least restrictive kind of setting in the state.[15] McClary has a budgeted capacity for twenty-two residents and comprises two living units. One of them is a mental health unit. There is a separate building for a gymnasium. There is also an outdoor swimming pool and other recreational facilities.

McClary serves a number of young people who identify as transgender girls and who are openly gay males. The staff members were required to call the young people by their preferred names and genders per an LGBT nondiscrimination policy. Young people who were considered to be more vulnerable, either because of a serious mental health disorder or because of their histories of foster care placements, were also placed in this facility.

I also visited four other residential facilities: a boys' secure facility and a limited secure facility, both about two hours north of New York City, a boys' non-secure facility in the Catskill mountains, and a limited-secure and secure boys' facility near Rochester, a larger city in the northern part of the state.

The second research site was in the community. I obtained access to the participants in this setting through my previous employer, a public defender's office based in New York City. I had worked there as a sentencing mitigation specialist. A mitigation specialist compiles family histories, social histories, medical and mental health records, school records, and other documents to complete a dossier on the client that would aid in his or her defense or at sentencing. My job required that I made referrals for clients to community-based programs and services and advocated for them in schools, welfare offices, and mental health settings.

I attended and observed court appearances, visited with participants in the court holding cells and attorney visit areas, and at Rikers Island, juvenile detention facilities, and adult prisons. I also went to a police precinct, a parole office, the probation department, and alternative to incarceration programs.

I engaged in participant observation in several committees of a statewide juvenile justice coalition, adopting a backseat role in these group meetings. I attended other meetings and conferences over the course of the year, including one held at the Rikers Island adolescent facility with the commissioner of corrections, as well as multiple police–community meetings in the participants' neighborhoods, city council hearings on the subject of juvenile justice, and multiple conferences and research presentations on juvenile justice reform in New York.

Sampling

The sampling strategies in this research were dictated in part by the nature of the sample (vulnerable, transient, and "hard to reach"), by theoretical and analytical considerations, and by practical constraints presented by the research settings. The final sample size was thirty-nine young people between the ages of fifteen and twenty-one, with twelve girls and twenty-seven boys.

I engaged in theoretical and snowball sampling for the facility staff and other institutional actors and family members. During the first research stage, I conducted interviews with thirty-eight staff members and engaged in informal conversation with a number of others. The second research study, focused on staff, involved more than forty site visits to facilities and interviews with more than seventy-five staff members from the beginning of 2011 until the fall of 2012.

The Community Sampling Process

The community sample was constructed primarily on the basis of existing relationships that I had with young people and their attorneys. Attorneys at the public defender's office referred clients to me, and I would then ask the clients if they were interested in volunteering for my research, seeking informed consent.

To deepen the observations and perspectives, I conducted interviews with nine family members of the participants. I spent hundreds of hours with the family of Billy and Marcus. I met the family early in the research and built a strong rapport with them. I helped the boys' sister apply for college, I tutored

Juvenile Delinquents in New York State in 2006 (25,000+ total)

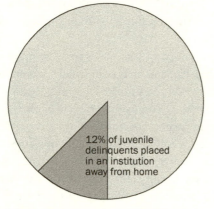

12% of juvenile delinquents placed in an institution away from home

There were more than 25,000 young people referred to court as juvenile delinquents in New York State in 2006 (the past year for which data were available), and 12 percent of those cases resulted in a young person being placed in an institution away from home.

SOURCE: *KWIC, 2010—Office of Court Administration Data set*

Young people (16–18 years) arrested in New York State in 2008.

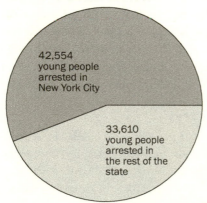

42,554 young people arrested in New York City

33,610 young people arrested in the rest of the state

42,554 young people between the ages of 16 and 18 were arrested in New York City in 2008, and 33,610 young people arrested in the rest of the state in 2008.

SOURCE: *New York Division of Criminal Justice Services*

Young people admitted to custody in OCFS (1,632 total)

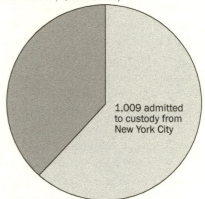

1,009 admitted to custody from New York City

There were a total of 1,632 young people admitted to custody in OCFS in 2008; 1,009 of those admissions were from New York City.

SOURCE: *Office of Children and Family Services (OCFS), 2008 Annual Report*

Young people (13–15 years) arrested as Juvenile Offenders

1,808 young people were arrested as Juvenile Offenders (13–15 year olds charged with serious offenses as adults) in New York City in 2009.

SOURCE: *Gewirtz, 2010*[16]

Young people (18 years and under) on probation

7,187 young people (18 and under) were on probation in New York City in 2008.

SOURCE: *Cannon et al., 2010*[17]

their younger sister, helped the mother with some issues concerning her hous-ing, and assisted the family in navigating the justice system, which they were often embroiled in. The boys' father had spent a substantial amount of time in prison since he was a teenager, and I interviewed him about his experiences. I regularly spoke on the phone with the family, and they would call me when their sons were arrested (which happened at least six times during the course of the research) and ask me to come to the police station or court. I continue to speak and meet with the family.

Ethical Reflections

My methods were rooted in principles of deep listening, drew from strong feedback and supervision, and were consistently focused on and respectful of young people's confidentiality. A number of the participants had suffered from abuse and trauma, disproportionate levels of violence, and histories of mental illness, psychiatric hospitalizations and experience in the child welfare system. It was clear that these experiences, which would have exposed this group of young people to a wide variety of risk assessments, psychological evaluations, surveys, and requests for participation in other kinds of research, may lead them to feel wary that they were being exploited, concerned that the research would be used for purposes other than those that were stated (for example, a child welfare intervention), or distrustful of my motives. Another concern was that the research experience might further traumatize the young people by encouraging them to discuss their personal histories and experiences, and perhaps compound the distress they were already feeling.

I was also attuned to the ways that my identity as a white woman, with its connotations of racial, class, and professional privilege, might affect the research dynamics. My concerns with young people's relationships to (primar-ily white) authority figures, and my sense (and experience) that these relation-ships may be tinged with distrust, also led me to believe that I might also be perceived with similar levels of distrust by them.

This research captured the voices of the young people by exercising a commitment to making their voices the centerpiece of the research. Alderson argues that the principles of respect and justice dictate in part that children as research subjects be respected as "sensitive dignified human beings."[18] Hollway and Jefferson express the need to pursue honesty, sympathy, and respect in the research context to mitigate dependence or avoidance on the part of both the researched and the researcher.[19]

Preventing Exploitation in the Research Process

Some accounts of young people's experiences of punishment can repeat the pattern of their systematic exclusion from discourses about their rights by decontextualizing their words and forgetting to recognize the ways that they can be part of the project to construct legitimate knowledge. Young people's participation in research or policy endeavors can become tokenistic. These concerns have been raised and developed in the area of critical pedagogies and action-oriented research more generally.[20] These scholars have argued that the practice of engaging with and prioritizing the voice of the marginalized "other" is itself a resistant act, disrupting "exclusionary tendencies," potentially promoting transformations of structures.[21] Some potentially deeply upsetting moments for both me but especially for the participants (arrests, running away from home, loss, and death), for example, became interesting information for my work. Although I made note of these experiences, I also felt a strong ethical obligation not simply to make note of them, but also to treat them with the kind of humanity and urgency that were demanded of them, thinking sensitively and carefully about my role if I was asked for help or if I was not.[22]

Power imbalances in the research process can be minimized by being sensitive to the ways in which participants express their perspectives and feelings about their life worlds.[23] Pierre Bourdieu advocates that sociologists do not simply try to "cancel the social distance" between interviewer and interviewee (in cases where that social distance exists) but to attempt to show that she is "mentally capably of putting herself in their place."[24]

One of the themes to emerge in the research was young people's consistent frustration with their lack of "voice" in the criminal court process. By recording their voice through the interview process and also responding to their stated frustrations (often with a simple acknowledgment of them), I played a role in the disruption of their narratives, and potentially shifted (in a small way) some of the power relations that they commented on. The participants also had the power to control what they did and did not share with me, as I had the power to decide what I focused on in my analysis. This also relates to the process of "framing" that has particular salience in the criminal justice context: how young people are understood, by whom, and at what point, plays a role in deciding how and where they may end up along the carceral continuum. I was potentially perceived as possessing that power to shape their outcomes.[25]

The interviews were driven by the sense that individuals may offer a different public portrayal of themselves than in private. They became a window into young people's constructions of their identity. However, it was sometimes difficult to fully engage young people in this process. In contrast to my experience as a social worker, where my role in the context of a criminal case had an explicit emphasis on helping young people get out from under their legal cases, my role as a researcher with more ambiguous aims made these interviews more challenging. A number of the young people, especially the young men, were often reticent to talk to me during the interviews and potentially distrusted my motives. This was an unexpected challenge, and so I adopted an interview approach that began by asking them how they were doing, what was happening in their lives, and responding accordingly. This approach attempted to convey that the establishment of a relationship between us was critical to the research's success. I also engaged in the practice, following Henry Stack Sullivan's school of psychological engagement, of ending each encounter by acknowledging and affirming what we had discussed, highlighting key moments, and conveying appreciation and my own insight building process.[26] Sullivan argues that individuals seek a feeling of "personal security" in interpersonal situations that relates to their need to "avoid, alleviate, or escape from anxiety."[27] Sullivan's philosophy is that this process is deeply humanizing; it helps to remind people that they are not alone and that they are acknowledged and understood.

KNOWLEDGE OF THE FIELD

My knowledge of the criminal justice system in New York deeply informed this research process. My background knowledge of the social institutions, politicians, and key landmarks (parks where kids play basketball, stores where they shopped, physical structures, and so on) also aided me in establishing a rapport and conveying my knowledge of the street. My connection to the public defender's office in Harlem also allowed me access to a great deal of information about neighborhood-based incidents, trends, and so on that were useful in helping me to construct a broader picture of the research terrain.

I attempted to mitigate the effects of exploitation by establishing other forms of reciprocity with the participants than that described above. There were times when I felt that I had built a strong rapport with participants inside of the facilities, but I could not locate them once they had been released. As I realized the challenges in finding time as well as in building the trust and rapport with the participants, facilitating access to various opportunities became one way of maintaining contact with them. It also acted as a form of social capital, which it became alarmingly clear they were missing, particularly as I received a number of unsolicited appeals for help finding jobs, programs, and help with college applications.[28]

My role in young people's lives sometimes played an integral part in helping me to understand the very processes of liberal governance and abandonment that this book is about. I saw this when one of my participants, Izzy, asked me for help with a legal case. He had just been released from a juvenile facility and was trying hard to find a job and get back on his feet when he was arrested for riding his bicycle the wrong way down the street. Even though the charge was minor, it was a huge setback for Izzy because it could have implications for parole. It also added to his mounting distrust of the police and what he termed "the system," which represented every government agency with which he had come into contact, including police, parole, and welfare. Izzy's experience shaped my analysis of the governance of young people, but

I also knew he wanted help in addressing the situation. Thus, I asked one of my friends who is a private defense attorney if he might represent him, which he did for free; it is highly unusual for people to be represented by counsel in minor cases like these. My friend discovered that the police had charged Izzy under an incorrect statute. As a result of my friend's intervention, Izzy was exonerated of this charge.

IDENTITY AND REFLEXIVITY

My identity as a former social worker (and the knowledge that accompanied it) also sometimes caused me to be understood in that way, as opposed to being understood as a researcher. My ethnicity and my gender, as well as my style of dress, also caused some participants and their families to think of me as a "helping" agent, and so they sometimes asked me for advice or help without knowing my background. For example, I arrived at the apartment of the grandmother of one of my participants who was incarcerated at Rikers Island, and she proceeded to take me on a tour of the apartment, showing me where her granddaughter kept her clothes, where and how she slept, where she did her school work, and so on. I sensed the grandmother believed I was there to do a home assessment, rather than simply being there to interview her. For others, particularly the sample from the community who had been introduced to me by the attorneys as a former social worker, it was more difficult to disentangle my researcher identity from that of a social worker, and so I was sometimes described by parents as a social worker, or someone "helping" their family or by one participant as her "advocate." It was often difficult to disentangle my helping role from my researcher role.

The research took place in contexts that were symbolically and literally "masculine," as well as being segregated by gender. The residential facilities in particular were places where sexism was, in a sense, condoned by staff: I would often walk through the hallways of the facility and get stared at, commented on, and called names by the young men, and staff members at the facilities did not stop the young men from engaging in these practices, some staff members staring at me themselves. The working environments were also ones where homophobia and sexism were openly practiced and became a key way of making jokes, building rapport, and bonding.

The participants themselves had frequently experienced strong forms of paternalism and masculine domination. Thus, my role as a woman who was embedded in these gender hierarchies became central to my forms of engagement, providing both limitations and advantages to the research. My gender may have also affected the tones of my conversations and the implicit "dangers" that staff in the residential facilities sometimes felt I was engaged in, warning me about the (sexual and financial) motives of the young men (and sometimes the young women) with whom I spoke and suggesting my potential to be exploited and manipulated because of my status as a white woman.

The sociologist Howard Becker recognized that those interested in the study of deviance may chose to conduct their research through the lens of the subordinate member of an institution in an effort to break through the "refractory" nature of those institutions and challenge the "hierarchy of credibility" that exists within established orders.[29] He argued that it is important for researchers to militate against the potential question of bias that their sympathies may raise. I initially chose to focus almost exclusively on young people's perspectives, but I discovered over the course of this process that other institutional actors, including those in power, would help to deepen my understanding of the field.

The relationships that I established with staff members in the residential institutions presented challenges with respect to the questions of politics and power and whose "side" I was on. My appreciative approach to the staff perspectives also raised some internal dilemmas as I began to develop sympathies for them and the difficulties of their jobs.

One way I built trust with staff was through a "sponsor" at one of the facilities who vouched for my authenticity with other staff and my interest in hearing and recording their perspectives. The relationships I established in this institution also allowed me access to some key "backstage" conversations and pieces of confidential and candid information that were critical in my assessment of the psychosocial landscape of the institution.[30]

When I interacted with staff, I often expressed a kind of naiveté about institutional life, conveying a wish to appreciate staff perspectives, which I developed in response to what I observed to be some staff members' forms of defensiveness in response to feeling that their expertise had been underappreciated by the new commissioner.

A Psychosocial Approach

I adopted what has been termed a psychosocial approach in the research and the analysis of the data. Simon Clarke argues that it is a "position whereby the researcher is aware of the unconscious and emotional dynamics that fuel the social construction of realities."[31] Ian Craib writes about the inextricable relationship between narrative accounts of one's life and the experiences from early childhood that structure our relationships and how the disorganized features of the subconscious are in fact distinctly opposed to the coherence of narrative thinking.[32] He argues: "It is best to regard narratives as defences: they enable us to survive in the world unless they become too comprehensive and inclusive, when they cease to be able to contain the disruptive flow of our internal world."[33] This approach also challenges the notion that the field data simply speaks the truth of an individual's experience and thus calls for an analysis that is reflexive and acknowledges the research as an emotionally informed process.

Psychoanalytic approaches may be useful in reading adolescents' accounts of their lives, which are often influenced by child development narratives and frameworks which may be too neat for analysis.

It is arguable that the focus on the subconscious complements the sociological approaches that are aimed at understanding the reproduction of social structure. Individual actions are both socially structured and play a role in structuring social landscapes. Yet there are ways in which the subconscious and emotions must be confronted in analyzing the reproduction of socially structured experiences, such as marginalization and alienation. Feelings of persecution, defensiveness, and anxiety, for example, which emerge in contexts of interaction with criminal justice authorities, are complex and layered emotions that are both deeply personal but also reflect historical and socially structured processes.

By employing an ethnographic approach that is structured by a psychosocial analysis, this research unearthed and revealed the texture of young people's experience. Thus, it is not able to make broadly generalizable conclusions about the likelihood of reoffending and the overall "success" of interventions but is rather aimed at making sense of young people's stories and understanding how they have been shaped and what they signify in the larger context of youth offending and youth justice.

ACKNOWLEDGMENTS

THIS BOOK OWES ITS life to the people who gave me access to their lives. The experience of facing a criminal charge is one of the most despairing, stigmatizing, and challenging experiences in one's life. By spending time with teenagers inside of the jails and juvenile facilities, I have come just a tiny bit closer to experiencing the dignity, despair, and vulnerability they have, and I am eternally grateful to every young person I spoke to, and their parents and loved ones, for opening up their lives to me. To the facility staff members, probation and parole officers, lawyers, judges, and caseworkers who spent hours talking to me and teaching me about the system, I thank you wholeheartedly. Many of the individuals who work in the system are so close to the heart of problems and the solutions in the system, yet are so frequently misunderstood as being either overtly oppressive or bleeding hearts; I have found so many of the individuals who work in the system to be full of compassion, a deep and nuanced analysis of the challenges that young people face, and a full-hearted understanding of the struggles of adolescence. I am also grateful to those, including Leonard Dunston, Peter Edelman, Ned Loughran, and Jim Purcell, who provided me with a historical perspective on the system.

Nina is the inspiration for this project and the person who keeps me honest, who reminds me that an extraordinary life comes out of struggle and that the struggle is not over when one graduates from school or gets a job, even after facing countless obstacles. She has also taught me that tokenizing young people can cause great harm in their lives and that we must listen deeply, be patient, and respect their dignity and despair before, during, and after their time in the system.

To my former clients who keep on calling and keep the work going, especially Champagne, Colesvintong, and Philip. You've got this.

Elsie Chandler has been my analytical and emotional guide and the true and fierce warrior whom I seek to emulate for the rest of my life. You taught me to recognize the power of acting as a lightning rod in a system that hates children. You changed my life and you saved my life.

Dwayne Betts is the intellectual interlocutor sine qua none. Dwayne, thank you for keeping me sharp and for being a friend in literature and in law.

I have become the thinker that I am through the extraordinary intellectual mentorship and partnership of several key scholars (although there are countless others I am sure I have neglected to include on this list). For consistent and deep support and challenging me to develop my work seriously, I especially thank Ben Crewe, Loraine Gelsthorpe, Shadd Maruna, Osagie Obasogie, Shaun Ossei-Owusu, Fergus McNeill, Josh Page, Tony Platt, and Jo Phoenix. So many additional thanks to Kofi Boakye, Avi Brisman, Johnna Christian, Léon Digard, Jonathan Jacobs, Issa Kohler-Haussman, Naomi Murakawa, Jeff Lane, Alison Liebling, Mikaela Luttrell-Rowland, Robert Perkinson, Jothie Rajah, Randy Meyers, Michelle Phelps, Judah Schept, Michael Scholssman, Gilly Sharpe, Justice Tankebe, Robert Werth, and Alex Vitale.

For my teachers, the warrior advocates: Daniel Abrahamson, Nancy Ginsburg, Jonathan Gradess, Tanya Greene, Tracy Huling, Rick Jones, Leonard Noisette, Alan Rosenthal, Benay Rubenstein, KJ Rhee, and Deborah Small. For the many colleagues who have provided support and collaboration: Christine Bella, Joyce Burrell, Peggy Cooper-Davis, Hon. Michael Corriero, Khalil Cumberbatch, Michelle Deitch, Mishi Faruquee, Libby Fischer, Felipe Franco, Bill Gettman, Craig Gilmore, Jennifer Gonnerman, Cory Greene, Chino Hardin, Anthony Hough, Russ Immarigeon, Dionna King, Jim LeCain, Matt Knecht, Jennifer March-Joly, Laura McCargar, Zachary Norris, Gabrielle Prisco, Anna Roberts, Tim Roche, Liz Ryan, Nancy Smith, Wilfredo Sta. Ana, Josie Whittlesey, and Jason Ziedenberg.

To the wonderful women who paved the path for research in this field: Laura Abrams, Jamie Fader, Michelle Inderbitzin, and Anne Nurse.

For the wonderful faith, patience, and support of Peter Mickulas at Rutgers University Press, my anonymous peer reviewers, and Brandon Proia for his able editing assistance. Erica Mateo provided invaluable research assistance in the institutions and beyond and is an incomparable and brilliant thinker. I owe Martin Stolar my sanity and my hope.

I am grateful to the Gates Cambridge Trust and to the Open Society Foundations Soros Justice Advocacy Fellowship program for so generously supporting this work. Thank you also to the members of the Yale Law School Justice Collaboratory.

I have been so incredibly fortunate to have colleagues at SUNY New Paltz who are unparalleled in their ability to provide support, mentorship, humor, and friendship. Thank you all so immensely for making my new home so great and for creating the conditions for me to thrive. For my incredible students: you have taught me that we must listen deeply to you, witness you, and be compassionate to you because you are the people who will do the work that we require.

To my brothers and sisters from other mothers: David, Desiree, Renee, Quinnie, and Brian. I love you and do my most vigorous work in the world because of you. To all the other wonderful friends, for keeping me on my toes and making me laugh: Nico, Will, Alli, Cy, Ve, Nic, Lindsay, Meredith, Ari, Michael, Jennifer, Thomas, Brooke, Jess, Bear, Sonia, Gabe, Kyle, Marc, Rob W., Andrew, Cormac, Wafle, Rob G., and Anna. To my family for providing me with love and unparalleled support in this now twenty-year journey; to Sam, for giving me a copy of *The Corner* in 1997 and to recognizing the work. And to S, for love.

Notes

INTRODUCTION

1. All of the names I use in this book are pseudonyms. To further protect the confidentiality of my participants, I have also changed some details of the participants' lives that would not affect the significance of the analysis, such as where they are from or the length of their sentences.
2. L. Schott and C. Cho, "General Assistance Programs: Safety Net Weakening Despite Increased Need," (Center on Budget and Policy Priorities, 2011).
3. Ibid.
4. H. L. Schaefer and Kathryn Edin, "Rising Extreme Poverty in the United States and the Response of Federal Means-Tested Transfer Programs," in *National Poverty Center Working Paper Series* (National Poverty Center, 2013).
5. Andy Furlong and Fred Cartmel, *Young People and Social Change: New Perspectives* (Berkshire: Open University Press, 2007); Jennifer Silva, *Coming Up Short: Working-Class Adulthood in an Age of Uncertainty* (New York: Oxford University Press, 2013).
6. Catherine Rampell, "Teenage Jobless Rate Reaches Record High," *New York Times,* September 4, 2009. Andrew Sum et al., "The Continued Collapse of the Nation's Teen Job Market and the Dismal Outlook for the 2008 Summer Labor Market for Teens: Does Anybody Care?" (Boston: Center for Labor Market Studies, Northeastern University, 2008).
7. L. Treschan and C. Molnar, "Out of Focus: A Snapshot of Public Funding to Reconnect Youth to Education and Employment" (New York: Community Service Society, 2008).
8. J. Soss, R. Fording, and S. Schram, *Disciplining the Poor: Neoliberal Paternalism and the Persistent Power of Race* (Chicago: The University of Chicago Press, 2011).
9. Michelle Inderbitzen, "Lessons from a Juvenile Training School: Survival and Growth," *Journal of Adolescent Research* 21, no. 1 (2006); "Inside a Maximum Security Training School," *Punishment and Society* 9, no. 3 (2007); Anne Nurse, *Locked Up, Locked Out: Young Men in the Juvenile Justice System* (Nashville, TN: Vanderbilt University Press, 2010); Laura Abrams and Ben Anderson-Nathe, *Compassionate Confinement: A Year in the Life of Unit C* (New Brunswick, NJ: Rutgers University Press, 2013).
10. Rebecca Colman et al., "Long-Term Conseqences of Delinquency: Child Maltreatment and Crime in Early Adulthood" (Rensselear, NY: New York State Office of Children and Family Services 2009).
11. D. Tanenhaus, "The Evolution of Juvenile Courts in the Early Twentieth Century: Beyond the Myth of Immaculate Construction," in M. Rosenheim, F. Zimring, D. Tanenhaus, & B. Dohrn (eds.), *A Century of Juvenile Justice* (Chicago: University of Chicago Press, 2002); A. Platt, *The Child Savers: The Invention of Delinquency* (Chicago: University of Chicago Press, 1969/1977); G. Ward, *The Black Child-Savers:*

Racial Democracy and Juvenile Justice (Chicago: University of Chicago Press, 2012); M. Chavez-Garcia, "Intelligence Testing at Whittier School, 1890–1920," *Pacific Historical Review*, 72, no. 2 (2007) .

12. W. Chafe, *The Achievement of American Liberalism: The New Deal and Its Legacies* (New York: Columbia University Press, 2003).

13. Nell Bernstein, *Burning Down the House: The End of Juvenile Prison* (New York: New Press, 2014).

14. Jeffrey Butts, "Critical Diversion," *Criminology & Public Policy* 15, no. 3 (2016).

15. See also D. Maynard, "Person-Descriptions in Plea Bargaining," *Semiotica* 42, no. 2/4 (1982).

16. In his book about black and Latino boys living in Oakland, California, Rios points to the need to write scholarly texts that do not simply perpetuate ideas about "the urban poor as creatures in need of pity and external salvation." V. Rios, *Punished: Policing the Lives of Black and Latino Boys* (New York: NYU Press, 2011).

17. David Harvey, *A Brief History of Neoliberalism* (Oxford: Oxford University Press, 2005).

18. Foucault and some of his followers claim that notions of "life" and "self" are enmeshed in relationships of power. See Michel Foucault, *The History of Sexuality: An Introduction, Volume 1* (New York: Vintage Books, 1978); Michel Foucault, *The Care of the Self: The History of Sexuality, Volume 3* (London: Penguin Books, 1986); Michel Foucault, "The Ethic of Care for the Self as a Practice of Freedom: An Interview with Michel Foucault on January 20, 1984," in J. Bernauer and D. Rasmussen (eds.), *The Final Foucault* (Cambridge, MA: MIT Press, 1994); Paul Rabinow and Nikolas Rose. "Biopower Today," *BioSocieties* 1 (2006). They term this phenomenon "biopower," which relates to the attempts of those in power to "intervene upon the vital characteristics of human existence" (Rabinow and Rose, pp. 196–7). Foucault argued that the very fact that we believe we are autonomous agents is a product of discourse and power. Power, he argues, produces subjectivities.

19. D. Garland, Governmentality and the Problem of Crime: Foucault, Criminology, Sociology. *Theoretical Criminology* 1, no. 2 (1997); N. Rose, *Governing the Soul: The Shaping of the Private Self* (London: Routledge, 1989).

20. P. Gray, "The Politics of Risk and Young Offenders' Experiences of Social Exclusion and Restorative Justice," *British Journal of Criminology* 45 (2005); H. Kemshall, "Risks, Rights and Justice: Understanding and Responding to Youth Risk," *Youth Justice* 8, no. 1 (2008); J. Muncie, "Governing Young People: Coherence and Contradiction in Contemporary Youth Justice," *Critical Social Policy* 26, no. 4 (2006; Lynne Haney, *Offending Women: Power, Punishment, and the Regulation of Desire* (Berkeley: University of California Press, 2010).

21. R. Myers, "The Biographical and Psychic Consequences of 'Welfare Inaction' for Young Women in Trouble with the Law," *Youth Justice* 13, no. 3 (2013): 218–233; J. Phoenix and L. Kelly, "'You Have to Do It for Yourself': Responsibilization in Youth Justice and Young People's Situated Knowledge of Youth Justice Practices," *British Journal of Criminology* 53 (2013).

Chapter 1. Reproducing Reforms

1. This quote comes from documents obtained from the New York State Archives. W. Johnson. "The Training School in Transition: A New Search for Values," presented at the Third Annual Conference of New York State Training Schools, September 21, 1964, p. 6.

2. Justin Murphy, "Incarcerated Kids Tend High Tech Garden," *Democrat and Chronicle,* February 25, 2014.

3. I'm not the first person to be struck by the repetitive character of reforms. See, for example, A. Liazos, "Class Oppression: The Functions of Juvenile Justice," *The*

Insurgent Sociologist 1 (Fall 1974); Thomas Bernard, *The Cycle of Juvenile Justice* (New York: Oxford University Press, 1992); D. J. Rothman, *Conscience and Convenience: The Asylum and Its Alternatives in Progressive America* (Boston: Little, Brown and Company, 1980).

4. See, e.g., J. Pickett and T. Chiricos, "Controlling Other People's Children: Racialized Views of Delinquency and Whites' Punitive Attitudes toward Juvenile Offenders," *Criminology* 50, no. 3 (2012).

5. J. M. Hawes, *Children in Urban Society: Juvenile Delinquency in Nineteenth Century America* (New York: Oxford University Press, 1971); S. L. Singer, *Recriminalizing Delinquency: Violent Crime and Juvenile Justice* (New York: Cambridge University Press, 1996).

6. Robert S. Pickett, *House of Refuge: Origins of Juvenile Reform in New York State, 1815–1857* (Syracuse, NY: Syracuse University Press, 1969).

7. Barry Feld, *Bad Kids: Race and the Transformation of the Juvenile Court* (New York: Oxford University Press, 1999), 51.

8. Ibid. Hawes, *Children in Urban Society,* 33.

9. Rothman, *Conscience and Convenience,* 5; Hawes, *Children in Urban Society,* 48.

10. Ibid.

11. G. de Beaumont and A. de Tocqueville, *On the Penitentiary System in the United States and Its Application in France* (Carbondale: Southern Illinois University Press, 1833/1964). Hawes, *Children in Urban Society*; Pickett, *House of Refuge*; Edmund F. McGarrell, *Juvenile Correctional Reform: Two Decades of Policy and Procedural Change* (Albany: State University of New York, 1988).

12. S. Schlossman, *Love and the American Delinquent: The Theory and Practice of "Progressive" Juvenile Justice, 1825–1920* (Chicago: The University of Chicago Press, 1977). Rothman, *Conscience and Convenience.*

13. Matthew Jacobson, *Whiteness of a Different Color: European Immigrants and the Alchemy of Race* (Cambridge, MA: Harvard University Press, 1998).

14. Schlossman, *Love and the American Delinquent*; Liazos, "Class Oppression."

15. Anthony Platt, *The Child Savers: The Invention of Delinquency* (Chicago: The University of Chicago Press, 1969/1977).

16. McGarrell, *Juvenile Correctional Reform*; Pickett, *House of Refuge.*

17. Pickett, *House of Refuge*; Platt, *The Child Savers.*

18. Platt, *The Child Savers.*

19. New York State L. 1902, Ch. 527, An act authorizing the selection of lands for the new site of the state industrial school; New York State L. 1904, Ch. 718, An act authorizing the selection of lands as a site for the New york state training school for boys, and establishing the said school.

20. R. Immarigeon, "The New York State Training School for Girls: An Annotated Bibliography of Annual Reports, 1904–1928" (Hudson, NY: Prison Public Memory Project, 2013), 2.

21. Geoff Ward, *The Black Child-Savers: Racial Democracy and Juvenile Justice* (Chicago: The University of Chicago Press, 2012).

22. G. Markowitz and D. Rosner, *Children, Race and Power: Kenneth and Mamie Clark's Northside Center* (London: University of Virginia Press, 1996). Nina Bernstein, *The Lost Children of Wilder: The Epic Struggle to Change Foster Care* (New York: Vintage Books, 2001).

23. New York's House of Refuge had a "colored" section. M. Soler, D. Schoenberg, and M. Schindler, "Juvenile Justice: Lessons for a New Era," *Georgetown Journal on Poverty Law & Policy* XVI, Symposium Issue (2009), 529.

24. Justine Wise Polier, *Juvenile Justice in Double Jeopardy: The Distanced Community and Vengeful Retribution* (Hillsdale, NJ: Lawrence Erlbaum Associates, 1989).

25. Ibid; Markowitz and Rosner, *Children, Race and Power.*

26. Scholars have pointed to the connections between the practices of slavery, in which families were forcibly torn apart and children taken away from their parents, and child welfare interventions, which are disproportionately experienced by families of color; see Dorothy Roberts, *Shattered Bonds: The Color of Child Welfare* (New York: Basic Books, 2002). They have also demonstrated the ways in which child welfare interventions are subjectively experienced in similarly punitive and repressive ways as those practices established during slavery.

27. Furlong and Cartmel, *Young People and Social Change: New Perspectives* (New York: Open University Press, 1997).

28. Elizabeth S. Scott and T. Grisso, "The Evolution of Adolescence: A Developmental Perspective on Juvenile Justice Reform," *The Journal of Criminal Law and Criminology* 88, no. 1 (1998): 691.

29. Jason Barnosky, "The Violent Years: Responses to Juvenile Crime in the 1950s," *Polity* 38, no. 3 (2006). Joseph H. Kane, Director, Annex of Boys' Training Schools, Goshen, New York, "Social Welfare Institutions Serving Delinquent Children," Presented at the New York State Council of Probation Administrators, Poughkeepsie, NY, April 22, 1964; The Training School System of the New York State Department of Social Welfare as an Organization, Andrew Kreiger, Graduate School of Public Affairs, Theories of Administrative Organization, Prof. Norris Schaefer, Fall 1965.

30. The Training School System of the New York State Department of Social Welfare as an Organization, Andrew Kreiger, Graduate School of Public Affairs, Theories of Administrative Organization, Prof. Norris Schaefer, Fall 1965.

31. Johnson, "The Training School in Transition." Today New York's reliance on joint state and local responsibility for the payment of institutional care created a financial panic in Albany in the wake of the Great Recession of 2008, ushering in major reforms geared toward reducing the financial burden on the state.

32. Johnson, "The Training School in Transition," 3.

33. Ibid.

34. Milton Luger, "Innovations in the Treatment of Juvenile Offenders," *The Annals of the American Academy of Political and Social Science* 381, no. 1 (1969); McGarrell, *Juvenile Correctional Reform.*

35. Rothman, *Conscience and Convenience,* 268.

36. Johnson, "The Training School in Transition," 6.

37. Lesley Oelsner, "Juvenile Justice: A City Crisis." *New York Times,* April 4, 1973.

38. Erroll Louis. "Broken Juvenile Justice System Wastes Millions of Dollars and Fails Our Kids." *Daily News,* February 10 2008.

39. See, e.g., Sheldon Glueck and Eleanor Glueck, *One Thousand Juvenile Delinquents: Their Treatment by Court and Clinic* (Cambridge, MA: Harvard University Press, 1934). Rothman, *Conscience and Convenience,* 286–7.

40. Howard Polsky, *Cottage Six: The Social System of Delinquent Boys in Residential Treatment* (New York: Russell Sage Foundation, 1962); McGarrell, *Juvenile Correctional Reform.*

41. The President's Commission on Law Enforcement and the Administration of Justice in 1967 issued a report titled "Juvenile Delinquency and Youth Crime," which included deinstitutionalization as among its recommendations. Liazos, "Class Oppression."

42. Alfred Kahn, "When Children Must Be Committed: Proposals for a Diversified System of Facilities," (New York: Citizen's Committee for Children, 1960).

43. Citizen's Committee for Children report, 1969.

44. Alexandra Cox, "Fresh Air Funds and Functional Families: The Enduring Politics of Race, Family and Place in Juvenile Justice Reform," *Theoretical Criminology* 19, no. 4 (2015): 554–70.

45. E. Schur, *Radical Non-Intervention* (Englewood Cliffs, NJ: Prentice-Hall, 1973).

46. McGarrell, *Juvenile Correctional Reform*.

47. Ibid; personal communication, Leonard Dunston, former commissioner of the state's system.

48. A. Novick, "Diversification and Integration of Rehabilitation Services for the Juvenile Delinquent," paper presented at the National Institute on Crime and Delinquency, Sessions of the National Association of Training Schools and Juvenile Agencies, Miami Beach, Florida, June 10, 1963, p. 2.

49. Ibid, 6–7.

50. David Garland, *The Culture of Control* (Oxford: Oxford University Press, 2001); Feld, *Bad Kids*.

51. Andrew von Hirsch and L. Maher, "Should Penal Rehabilitationism Be Revived?," in Andrew von Hirsch and Andrew Ashworth (eds.), *Principled Sentencing: Readings on Theory and Policy* (Oxford: Hart Publishing, 2004).

52. William McCord and José Sanchez, "The Treatment of Deviant Children: A Twenty-Five Year Follow-up Study," *Crime and Delinquency* 29, no. 2 (1983); Andrew Rutherford, *Growing Out of Crime* (Middlesex: Penguin, 1986).

53. McGarrell, *Juvenile Correctional Reform*, 115.

54. Feld, *Bad Kids*; K. Majd and Patricia Puritz, "The Cost of Justice: How Low-Income Youth Continue to Pay the Price of Failing Indigent Defense Systems," *Georgetown Journal on Poverty Law & Policy* XVI, Symposium Issue (2009).

55. Bernstein, *The Lost Children of Wilder*.

56. Naomi Murakawa powerfully argues that liberal reforms in criminal justice systems have actually "reinforce[d] and raise[d] African American vulnerability to premature death" by focusing on system functioning rather than racial justice. N. Murakawa, *The First Civil Right: How Liberals Built Prison America* (New York: Oxford University Press, 2014), 154.

57. Jerome Miller, *Last One Over the Wall* (Columbus: Ohio State University Press, 1991).

58. Testimony of Peter Edelman, Director, New York State Division of Youth, before Committee on Child Care, New York State Assembly, January 16, 1976. Personal communication, Peter Edelman.

59. This pushback also existed in Massachusetts during their deinstitutionalization and reform process, and was likely known by New York administrators, some of whom had come from Massachusetts Miller, *Last One Over the Wall*.

60. Singer, *Recriminalizing Delinquency*, 184.

61. Personal communication, Peter Edelman. It should be noted that none of the facility-based reforms that Edelman enacted were undone during the period of legislative change.

62. McGarrell, *Juvenile Correctional Reform*; Vanessa Barker, *The Politics of Imprisonment: How the Democratic Process Shapes the Way America Punishes Offenders* (New York: Oxford University Press, 2009). Singer, *Recriminalizing Delinquency*.

63. Singer, *Recriminalizing Delinquency*; E. J. Dionne, "Only Politicians Have Found Easy Answers to Youth Crime," *New York Times*, July 9, 1978. Fox Butterfield, *All God's Children: The Bosket Family and the American Tradition of Violence* (New York: HarperCollins, 1996).

64. In New York, the Family Court has jurisdiction over delinquency and child welfare cares, as well as family dispute matters, such as divorce. To read an account of Bosket's life that contextualizes the violence in which Bosket participated, see Fox Butterfield's (1996) *All God's Children*.

65. McGarrell, *Juvenile Correctional Reform*.

66. "Crimes, Punishment," *New York Times*, December 19, 1978. J. Treaster, "State Delinquent Center: No Punishment or Reform," *New York Times*, March 2, 1976.

67. Singer, *Recriminalizing Delinquency*; Butterfield, *All God's Children*; Dionne, "Only Politicians Have Found Easy Answers to Youth Crime." Barker (*The Politics of Imprisonment*) argues that although the Juvenile Offender law was indeed a harsh development, there were diversion programs for lower level, nonviolent offenders, as well as noncustodial sanctions (albeit in the adult court context) also passed at this time. She found that New York generally has low levels of imprisonment but harsh approaches to more "dangerous" offenders.

68. Personal communication, Leonard Dunston, former commissioner of the Division for Youth, and Pat Sullivan, former director of the Brookwood secure facility.

69. Elaine Brown, *The Condemnation of Little B* (Boston: Beacon Press, 2002).

70. Ibid., 42–3.

71. This model was first used at one facility in the 1980s, introduced by former commissioner Leonard Dunston (personal communication, Leonard Dunston). See also Bruce Frederick, "Factors Contributing to Recidivism among Youth Placed with the New York State Division for Youth," (Albany: Office of Justice Systems Analysis, New York State Division of Criminal Justice Services, 1999).

72. The only other record I have found of a previous statewide campaign to raise the age of criminal responsibility occurred in the 1930s, and law enforcement widely opposed this effort at the time. See Rothman, *Conscience and Convenience*.

73. C. Feldman, "State Facilities Use of Force Is Scrutinized after a Death," *New York Times*, March 4 2007; M. Anich and J. Subik, "Groups Call for Tryon Investigation," *Leader-Herald* 2006. A staff member at the same facility also died around that time after young people threw a chair at him, although his exact cause of death was not attributed to the chair incident but to a heart attack.

74. Dana Kaplan, "Challenging Incarceration in the Empire State: Community Resistance in Urban, Rural and Suburban New York to Carceral Geographies" (master's thesis, CUNY, 2012).

75. Mie Lewis, "Custody and Control: Conditions of Confinement in New York's Juvenile Prisons for Girls" (New York: Human Rights Watch American Civil Liberties Union, 2006), www.aclu.org/other/custody-and-control-conditions-confinement -new-yorks-juvenile-prisons-girls.

76. See, e.g., Citizen's Committee for Children, "Inside Out: Youth Experiences inside New York's Juvenile Placement System" (New York: Citizen's Committee for Children of New York, 2009), www.cccnewyork.org/data-and-reports/publications /ccc-report-inside-out-youth-experiences-inside-new-yorks-juvenile-placement -system).

77. Loretta King, "Investigation of the Lansing Residential Center, Louis Gossett, Jr. Residential Center, Tryon Residential Center, and Tryon Girls Center" (Washington, DC: U.S. Department of Justice, 2009).

78. For context about Bloomberg's focus on reforms leading up to Close to Home, see A. Cannon, R. Aborn, and John Bennett, "Guide to Juvenile Justice in New York City" (New York: Citizens Crime Commission of New York City, 2010); S. Goldsmith, "Bloomberg Wants Control of City's Expensive, Ineffectual Juvenile Justice System," *New York Daily News,* December 21, 2010.

79. V. Schiraldi, "Testimony to the New York City Council Committees on Juvenile Justice and General Welfare" (testimony at *New York City Council Meeting,* New York City, January 26, 2011).

80. Colman, Rebecca, Do Han Kim, Susan Mitchell-Herzfeld, and Therese A. Shady. "Long-Term Consequences of Delinquency: Child Maltreatment and Crime in Early Adulthood." Rensselear, NY: New York State Office of Children and Family Services, 2009, 7.

81. This includes young people charged as Juvenile Offenders (JOs), Juvenile Delinquents (JDs), and Persons in Need of Supervision (PINS). Frederick, "Factors

Contributing to Recidivism among Youth Placed with the New York State Division for Youth." The same is true for young people across the United States: the sociologist Bruce Western has noted that imprisonment has become a "modal life event" for young African American men with little education; B. Western, *Punishment and Inequality in America* (New York: Russell Sage Foundation, 2006).

82. Liazos, "Class Oppression: The Functions of Juvenile Justice."
83. S. Hockenberry, Melissa Sickmund, and A. Sladky, "Juvenile Residential Facility Census, 2008: Selected Findings" (Washington, DC: Office of Juvenile Justice and Delinquency Prevention, 2011).
84. National Juvenile Justice Network and Texas Public Policy Foundation, "The Comeback States: Reducing Youth Incarceration in the United States" (Washington, DC: National Juvenile Justice Network, 2013).
85. S. Bloom, "The Sanctuary Model of Organizational Change for Children's Residential Treatment," *Therapeutic Community: The International Journal for Therapeutic and Supportive Organizations* 26, no. 1 (2005).
86. Rothman, *Conscience and Convenience*, 265–6.
87. M. Anich, "Tryon Employees Receive Pink Slips," *Leader-Herald,* June 4, 2009; Kerry McAvoy, "Union Blasts State over Tryon Cuts," *Leader Herald,* November 15 2008. S. Ference, "OCFS Wants to Close Underutilized Youth Facilities," *News 10 Now,* March 27, 2008.
88. An investigation about the number of worker's compensation claims related to assaults in the facilities since the reforms were initiated in 2007 was also published; see Lancman (2010) as well as a report on an alleged incident of staff malfeasance involving a social event at a residential facility (New York State Commission of Correction, 2010). Both of these reports garnered a significant amount of media attention. Lancman, Rory. "Employee Safety in the NYS Juvenile Justice System." Albany: New York State Assembly Member Rory Lancman's office, 2010. New York State Commission of Correction. "In the Matter of a Resident Social Event at the Goshen Secure Center." Albany: New York State Commission of Correction, 2010.
89. R. Mangus, "Senator Maziarz Calls Meetings with Nys OCFS 'Very Disappointing'," (2009); R. Karlin, "Youth Facility Staff Fear for Their Safety," *Times Union* 2008. R. Mangus, "Influence & Publicity Concern for NYS OCFS Commissioner Carrion" (2009); "NYS OCFS: "A Culture of Brutality" at Tryon" (2009).
90. David King, "'Culture of Violence' Plagues New York's Juvenile Prisons," *Gotham Gazette,* January 11, 2010; "Juvenile Injustice," *New York Times,* January 5, 2010.
91. Juvenile Justice Advisory Group Meeting, September 30, 2009.
92. American Bar Association, "Adolescence, Brain Development and Legal Culpability" (Washington, DC: American Bar Association, 2004); Coalition for Juvenile Justice, "What Are the Implications of Adolescent Brain Development for Juvenile Justice" (Washington, DC: Coalition for Juvenile Justice, 2006).
93. There is some ambiguity about the way that this term is used and what it refers to. Generally speaking, the "evidence-based" practices that have been introduced are those that have been used to some effect in other jurisdictions, such as Multisystemic Family Therapy and Functional Family Therapy. Edward Borges, "Statement from New York State Office of Children and Family Services Commissioner Gladys Carrión" (Office of Children and Family Services, August 24, 2009).
94. Task Force on Transforming Juvenile Justice, "Charting a New Course: A Blueprint for Transforming Juvenile Justice in New York State" (New York: Vera Institute of Justice, 2009), 40.
95. He Len Chung, Michelle Little, and Laurence Steinberg, "The Transition to Adulthood for Adolescents in the Juvenile Justice System: A Developmental Perspective," in D. Wayne Osgood et al. (eds.), *On Your Own without a Net: The Transition to Adulthood for Vulnerable Populations* (Chicago: University of Chicago Press, 2005).

96. David P. Farrington, "Childhood Risk Factors and Risk Focused Prevention," in Mike Maguire, R. Morgan, and Robert Reiner (eds.), *Oxford Handbook of Criminology* (Oxford: Oxford University Press, 2007); J. David Hawkins, Todd Herren Kohl, David P. Farrington, et al., "Predictors of Youth Violence," *Juvenile Justice Bulletin* (U.S. Department of Justice, April 2000), www.crim.cam.ac.uk/people/academic _research/david_farrington/predviol.pdf. Researchers have also identified "protective" factors that have been said to play a role in "mitigating the effects of risk exposure"; ibid, 7.

97. Farrington, "Developmental Criminology and Risk-Focused Prevention," 664.

98. Hawkins et al., "Predictors of Youth Violence."

99. Ibid.

100. Ibid. Another area of "risk" for young people is the "risk" of violence that they face in their everyday lives. Rates of violence against young people are extremely high in the United States (Howard N. Snyder and Melissa Sickmund, "Juvenile Offenders and Victims: 2006 National Report" [Washington, DC: U.S. Department of Justice, Office of Justice Programs, Office of Juveinle Justice and Delinquency Prevention, 2006]), and the lives of young people in New York City and other urban areas are often infused with the presence of violence, at the hands of families and strangers (Margaret Hughes, "Turning Points in the Lives of Young Inner-City Men Forgoing Destructive Criminal Behaviors: A Qualitative Study," *Social Work Research* 22 [1998]). The "fear of crime" that is so often spoken about in the popular media doesn't often address the "fear of crime" in the very neighborhoods that provoke that fear.

101. Robert Ross, E. Fabiano, and C. Ewles, "Reasoning and Rehabilitation," *International Journal of Offender Therapy and Comparative Criminology* 32, no. 1 (1988). Tony Ward and Claire Nee, "Surfaces and Depths: Evaluating the Theoretical Assumptions of Cognitive Skills Programmes," *Psychology, Crime & Law* 15, no. 2–3 (2009).

102. K. Haines and S. Case, "The Rhetoric and Reality of the 'Risk Factor Prevention Paradigm' Approach to Preventing and Reducing Youth Offending," *Youth Justice* 8, no. 1 (2008).

103. John Muncie, *Youth and Crime* (London: Sage, 2004), 25.

104. Haines and Case, "The Rhetoric and Reality of the 'Risk Factor Prevention Paradigm'," 11.

105. David P. Farrington, "Understanding and Preventing Youth Crime" (Layerthorpe: Joseph Rowntree Roundation, 1996). Charles Hamilton Houston Institute for Race and Justice, "No More Children Left behind Bars: A Briefing on Youth Gang Violence and Juvenile Crime Prevention" (Boston: Harvard Law School, 2008); Edward P. Mulvey, Laurence Steinberg, Jeffrey Fagan, et al., "Theory and Research on Desistance from Antisocial Activity among Serious Adolescent Offenders," *Youth Violence and Juvenile Justice* 2, no. 3 (2004): 213.

106. Deborah Greene, "Functional Family Therapy (FFT) in New York State" (Albany: New York State Office of Mental Health, 2003); Thomas L. Sexton and James F. Alexander, "Functional Family Therapy" (Washington, DC: Office of Juvenile Justice and Delinquency Prevention, 2000); C. Borduin B. J. Mann, L. T. Cone, et al., "Multisystemic Treatment of Serious Juvenile Offenders: Long-Term Prevention of Criminality and Violence," *Journal of Consulting and Clinical Psychology* 63, no. 4 (1995).

107. Derrick Armstrong, "A Risky Business? Research, Policy, Governmentality and Youth Offending," *Youth Justice* 4, no. 2 (2004); K. Haines and S. Case, "The Rhetoric and Reality of the 'Risk Factor Prevention Paradigm'."

108. K. Haines and S. Case, "The Rhetoric and Reality of the 'Risk Factor Prevention Paradigm'."

109. Furlong and Cartmel, *Young People and Social Change*, 105.

110. Murakawa, *The First Civil Right*, 212; E. Bonilla-Silva, *Racism without Racists: Color-blind Racism and the Persistence of Racial Inequality in the United States* (Lanham, MD: Rowman and Littlefield, 2003).

111. Peter Kelly, "The Dangerousness of Youth-at-Risk: The Possibilities of Surveillance and Intervention in Uncertain Times," *Journal of Adolescence* 23 (2000): 469.

112. Bernard E. Harcourt, "Risk As a Proxy for Race: The Dangers of Risk Assessment," *Criminology and Public Policy, Forthcoming* 27 no. 4 (2015). See also Monahan, John, and Jennifer L. Skeem. "Risk Assessment in Criminal Sentencing." *Annual Review of Clinical Psychology* 12 (2016).

113. J. Fratello, Annie Salsich, and S. Mogulescu, "Juvenile Detention Reform in New York City: Measuring Risk through Research" (New York: Vera Institute of Justice, 2011).

114. Eli Hager, "Our Prisons in Black and White," *The Marshall Project*, November 18, 2015.

115. K. Hannah-Moffat, "Criminogenic Needs and the Transformative Risk Subject: Hybridizations of Risk/Need in Penality," *Punishment and Society* 7, no. 1 (2005): 31.

116. A. E. Bottoms, "An Introduction to 'The Coming Crisis'," in A. E. Bottoms and R. H. Preston (eds.), *The Coming Crisis* (Edinburgh: Scottish Academic Press, 1980), 7.

117. See also the history of liberal public interest organizations in the 1980s and 1990s, which spoke primarily about quality-of-life issues as opposed to redistribution with respect to poverty issues. J. Soss, R. C. Fording, and F. S. Schram, *Disciplining the Poor: Neoliberal Paternalism and the Persistent Power of Race* (Chicago: University of Chicago Press, 2011).

118. A. Schlesinger, "Liberalism in America: A Note for Europeans," in *The Politics of Hope*, ed. A. Schlesinger (Boston: Riverside Press, 1956): 91.

119. William Chafe, *The Achievement of American Liberalism: The New Deal and Its Legacies* (New York: Columbia University Press, 2003).

120. Barker, *The Politics of Imprisonment*, 45.

121. Loic Wacquant, *Punishing the Poor: The Neoliberal Government of Social Insecurity* (Durham, NC: Duke University Press, 2009).

122. Geoffrey Scarre, "Children and Paternalism," *Philosophy* 55 (1980): 123–4.

123. John Muncie, "Youth Justice: Globalization and Multi-Modal Governance," in Tim Newburn and Richard Sparks (eds.), *Criminal Justice and Political Cultures: National and International Dimensions of Crime Control* (Cullumpton, England: Willan, 2004); Vikki Bell, "Governing Childhood: Neo-Liberalism and the Law," *Economy and Society* 22, no. 3 (1993).

CHAPTER 2.   UNGOVERNABILITY AND WORTH

1. In the last quarter of 2008, when I met Michael, close to 50 percent of the more than 540,000 total police stops in New York City were of young people aged fourteen to twenty-four (Source: NYCLU Stop and Frisk data). In a recent study by the Vera Institute of Justice, of thirteen- to twenty-one-year-olds in New York City, 44 percent of study participants reported being stopped by the police nine or more times. J. Fratello, A. Rengifo, and Jennifer Trone, "Coming of Age with Stop and Frisk: Experiences, Self-Perceptions, and Public Safety Implications" (New York: Vera Institute of Justice, 2013). Yet this kind of behavioral profiling arguably starts at a much younger age: in a recently released study from the U.S. Department of Education, researchers found that the vast majority of preschoolers who are suspended from school are African American. Cory Turner, "Why Preschool Suspensions Still Happen (and How to Stop Them)" [radio broadcast], *All Things Considered*, June 20, 2016. Available at www.npr.org/sections/ed/2016/06/20/482472535/why-preschool-suspensions-still-happen-and-how-to-stop-them.

2. G. Bridges and S. Steen, "Racial Disparities in Official Assessments of Juvenile Offenders: Attributional Stereotypes as Mediating Mechanisms," *American Sociological Review* 63 (1998); Loic Wacquant, "Race as Civic Felony," *International Social Science Journal* 57, no. 183 (2005).

3. Children's Defense Fund, "America's Cradle to Prison Pipeline" (2007); E. Mukherjee, "Criminalizing the Classroom: The Over-Policing of New York City Public Schools," (New York: New York Civil Liberties Union, 2007); P. J. Hirschfield, "Preparing for Prison?: The Criminalization of School Discipline in the USA," *Theoretical Criminology* 12 (2008). A recent national survey of young people in custody found that 61 percent of the youth surveyed said that they were suspended or expelled in the year before entering custody. Andrea J. Sedlak and Karla S. McPherson, "Youth's Needs and Services: Findings from the Survey of Youth in Residential Placement," *OJJDP Juvenile Justice Bulletin*, April (2010).

4. Advancement Project, "Test, Punish, and Push Out: How "Zero Tolerance' and High-Stakes Testing Funnel Youth into the School-to-Prison Pipeline" (2010).

5. Some have characterized this moment of high employment in manufacturing as an ideal for black people involved in this kind of work, yet those individuals still faced significant employment discrimination and degrading work conditions. See Michael B. Katz, Mark J. Stern, and Jamie J. Fader, "The New African American Inequality," *Journal of American History* 92, no. 1 (2005).

6. Lucia Trimbur, *Come Out Swinging: The Changing World of Boxing in Gleason's Gym* (Princeton: Princeton University Press, 2013); Robin D. G. Kelley, *Yo' Mama's Disfunktional!* (Boston: Beacon Press, 1997); L. Wacquant, *Punishing the Poor: The Neoliberal Government of Social Insecurity* (Durham, NC: Duke University Press, 2009).

7. Kelley, *Yo' Mama's Disfunktional!*, 57.

8. Kim McGillicuddy, "Cityview: NYC's Young and Restless," *City Limits*, May 1, 1997.

9. D. Herszenhorn, "Basic Skills Forcing Cuts in Art Classes," *New York Times,* July 23, 2003; Office of the Comptroller City of New York, "State of the Arts: A Plan to Boost Arts Education in New York City Schools" (2014).

10. Howard Becker, *Outsiders: Studies in the Sociology of Deviance* (London: Free Press, 1966); J. Bernburg and M. D. Krohn, "Labeling, Life Chances, and Adult Crime: The Direct and Indirect Effects of Official Intervention in Adolescence on Crime in Early Adulthood," *Criminology* 41, no. 4 (2003).

11. My perspective contrasts somewhat with that of Victor Rios in his ethnography about young people growing up in Oakland, California, and facing criminalization. Rios argues that there is a kind of "labeling hype" that occurs with young people who are first criminalized; he says that once young people are initially criminalized, they get "caught in a spiral of punitive responses" that places them "at risk for being granted additional, more serious labels." This, he argues, results in the boys' decisions to engage in deviance. Rios, *Punished: Policing the Lives of Black and Latino Boys* (New York: NYU Press, 2011), 45.

12. J. Q. Wilson and G. L. Kelling, "Broken Windows," *Atlantic Monthly* (March 1982); James Austin and Michael Jacobson, "How New York City Reduced Mass Incarceration: A Model for Change?" (New York: Vera Institute of Justice & Brennan Center for Justice, 2013).

13. Bonilla-Silva, *Racism without Racists: Colorblind Racism and the Persistence of Racial Inequality in the United States.*

14. Austin and Jacobson, "How New York City Reduced Mass Incarceration."

15. Francis X. Clines, "Ex-Inmates Urge Return to Areas of Crime to Help," *The New York Times* 1992; Juan Rivera, "A Non-Traditional Approach to a Curriculum for Prisoners in New York State," *Journal of Prisoners on Prisons* 4, no. 1 (1992).

16. See also Todd Clear, Imprisoning Communities: How Mass Incarceration Makes Disadvantaged Neighborhoods Worse (New York: Oxford University Press, 2007).

17. D. Frank and M. Augustyn, "Growth, Development, and Behavior in Early Childhood Following Prenatal Cocaine Exposure: A Systematic Review," *JAMA* 285, no. 12 (2001); United States Department of Justice, "Defending Childhood: Protect Heal Thrive." In a twenty-four-year study, Hallam Hurt from the Children's Hospital of Philadelphia found that poverty is more influential on child outcomes than prenatal cocaine exposure. Hallam Hurt, "Poverty Is Worse for Children Than Gestational Cocaine Exposure," *Spotlight on Poverty and Opportunity* (May 19, 2014).

18. Even though there is little evidence to suggest that deterrence-based 'messaging' policies like this one actually work or even get transmitted to the individuals most affected by these laws, it was clear in the New York city legal community that everyone arrested with a gun would be sentenced to a minimum of two years in state prison.

19. Michelle Alexander, *The New Jim Crow: Mass Incarceration in the Age of Colorblindness* (New York: The New Press, 2010), citing legal scholar Kathryn Russell.

20. In 2008, 11 percent of youth in Office of Children and Family Services (OCFS) custody were white (white youth comprised 17 percent of my sample); "Youth in Care: 2008 Annual Report" (Rensselaer, NY: Office of Children and Family Services, 2009).

21. Soss, Fording, and Schram, *Disciplining the Poor*; Nancy Fraser and Linda Gordon, "A Genealogy of Dependency: Tracing a Keyword of the U.S. Welfare State," *Signs* 19, no. 2 (1994).

22. See also Kelley, *Yo' Mama's Disfunktional!*

23. Legal scholar Dorothy Roberts has compared the contemporary child welfare system to that of the impact of slave masters forcefully separating family members from each other. Roberts, *Shattered Bonds: The Color of Child Welfare.*

24. Genevieve told me this was her charge. It is possible that she had different charges than this.

25. This conception of young people may have also evolved through the shifting legal terrain of the juvenile courts in the past forty years, in which judges in juvenile and criminal courts rely more fully on formal reasoning and decision-making (based on the offense), as opposed to substantive decision-making (based on extra-legal, consequentialist concerns). Alexes Harris, "Diverting and Abdicating Judicial Discretion: Cultural, Political, and Procedural Dynamics in California Juvenile Justice," *Law & Society Review* 41, no. 2 (2007).

26. In his article about the origins of moral panics, Jock Young describes Alfred Cohen's concept of "moral indignation," which is defined as "concerned with punitiveness (whether in terms of penal law or informal fury) about the behavior of groups who do not directly harm one's interest" (9). Jock Young, "Moral Panic: Its Origins in Resistance, Ressentiment and the Translation of Fantasy into Reality," *British Journal of Criminology* 49 (2009).

27. Zygmunt Bauman, "Social Uses of Law and Order," in David Garland and Richard Sparks (eds.), *Criminology and Social Theory* (Oxford: Oxford University Press, 2000). See also Henry Giroux, *Youth in a Suspect Society: Democracy or Disposability* (New York: Palgrave MacMillan, 2009).

28. These detention risk assessment instruments are now used across New York State. They were rolling out across the state during my fieldwork period. They have been promoted as a tool in reducing the numbers of young people in detention. Yet although their use has resulted in the reduction of young people in detention, the numbers of black youth in detention has risen in jurisdictions where these risk assessments are used. As some have argued, risk is an easy proxy for race: Harcourt, "Risk as a Proxy for Race."

29 Stanley Cohen, Visions of Social Control: Crime, Punishment and Classification (Cambridge: Polity Press, 1985).

30 Erin Murphy, "Paradigms of Restraint," *Duke Law Journal* 57 (2008).

31. Aaron Kupchik, "Youthfulness, Responsibility and Punishment," *Punishment and Society* 6, no. 2 (2004).

32. Michael A. Corriero, "Youth Parts: Constructive Response to the Challenge of Youth Crime," *New York Law Journal* (1990). Wheeler et al. discovered in their research in the juvenile courts that a judge's ostensibly paternalistic outlook and his or her knowledge of the research literature on juvenile delinquency did not necessarily lead to a more lenient approach to sentencing. Stanton Wheeler et al., "Agents of Delinquency Control," in Stanton Wheeler (ed.), *Controlling Delinquents* (New York: John Wiley and Sons, 1968).

33. Young adults have long been constructed as existing in the stage of "becoming." Nick Lee, *Childhood and Society: Growing Up in an Age of Uncertainty* (Buckingham, England: Open University Press, 2001).

34. Vera Institute of Justice, "2nd Subcommittee Meeting: Re-Entry and Community-Based Alternatives to Residential Placement Subcommittee Members" (New York: Vera Institute of Justice, 2009); Ruben Austria, "Investing in Community-Based Alternatives to Incarceration for Court-Involved Youth in New York" (New York: Community Connections for Youth, 2008). Cannon, Aborn, and Bennett, "Guide to Juvenile Justice in New York City."

35. M. Gerwitz, "Annual Report on the Adult Court Case Processing of Juvenile Offenders in New York City, January through December 2008" (New York City Criminal Justice Agency, 2009).

36. When I meet new clients, I often tell them that my job is to tell a story about them that goes beyond the papers—the criminal complaint and indictment—that represent them in court. It recognizes the ways that individuals experience the feeling of being reduced and judged by teachers, police officers, judges, lawyers, and probation officers.

37. Public Safety Commission on Youth, and Justice, "Final Report of the Governor's Commission on Youth, Public Safety and Justice: Recommendations for Juvenile Justice Reform in New York State," (2015).

38. Jonathan Simon has argued that drug testing has become one way of governing individuals in the context of the War on Drugs and the War on Crime. Jonathan Simon, *Governing through Crime: How the War on Crime Transformed American Democracy and Created a Culture of Fear* (New York: Oxford University Press, 2007).

39. Leslie Paik, *Discretionary Justice: Looking Inside a Juvenile Drug Court* (New Brunswick, NJ: Rutgers University Press, 2011).

40. Board of Correction, New York City Board of Correction Meeting (January 8, 2009).

41. Graham Rayman, "Rikers Island Fight Club: The Knockout Punch," *Village Voice* (April 15, 2009); G. Rayman, "Rikers Violence: Out of Control," *Village Voice* (May 9, 2012); John Eligon, "Correction Officers Accused of Letting Inmates Run Rikers Island Jail," *New York Times* (January 22, 2009).

42. Geoffrey Gray, "The Lords of Rikers," *New York Magazine* (January 30, 2011).

43. In the interview excerpts, I am represented by the letter "A."

44. Elijah Anderson, *Code of the Street: Decency, Violence, and the Moral Life of the Inner City* (New York: W.W. Norton & Company, 1999); J. Fagan and D. Wilkinson, "Guns, Youth Violence, and Social Identity in Inner Cities," *Crime and Justice* 24 (1998).

45. Board of Correction Meeting Minutes, January 8, 2009.

46. E. Yaroshevsky, "Rethinking Rikers: Moving from a Correctional to a Therapeutic Model for Youth," (New York: Cardozo Law, 2014).

47. Michael, like many other young people in New York City who were detained at Rikers Island, had family members who were guards, which meant that they were able to be on a unit which was considered to be safer than others. Jamal had a family member who worked there who gave him some tips for survival and provided him with some protection.

48. Individuals incarcerated in state juvenile facilities and prisons and local jails have the opportunity to take the exam for this diploma but not to earn enough credits to have an actual high school diploma. For some, like Michael, there is a stigma attached to having this form of qualification instead of a "real" high school diploma.

49. See also C. Cesaroni and Shahid Alvi, "Masculinity and Resistance in Adolescent Carceral Settings," *Canadian Journal of Criminology and Criminal Justice* 52, no. 3 (2010). Y. Jewkes, "Men behind Bars: 'Doing' Masculinity as an Adaptation to Imprisonment," *Men and Masculinities* 8, no. 1 (2005); Robert L. Clark, "Punks, Snitches, and Real Men: Negotiations of Masculinity and Rehabilitation among Prison Inmates," *Theory in Action* 3, no. 3 (2010).

50. See also N. Scheper-Hughes, "Dangerous and Endangered Youth: Social Structures and Determinants of Violence," *Annals of the New York Academy of Sciences* 1036 (2004). Scheper-Hughes argues that interpersonal violence is often a symptom of structural and symbolic violence.

51. D. Huizinga and Kimberly Henry, "The Effect of Arrest and Justice System Sanctions on Subsequent Behavior: Findings from Longitudinal and Other Studies," in A. M. Liberman (ed.), *The Long View of Crime: A Synthesis of Longitudinal Research* (New York: Springer, 2008).

52. Crewe, *The Prisoner Society: Power, Adaptation, and Social Life in an English Prison*; Erving Goffman, *Asylums: Essays on the Social Situation of Mental Patients and Other Inmates* (New York: Anchor Books, 1961).

53. Monica Barry, *Youth Offending in Transition: The Search for Social Recognition* (Abingdon, England: Routledge, 2006).

54. Anderson describes the quest for "juice" on inner-city streets by young men as a means of gaining a share of respect and a maintenance of honor; it is often gained by showing that one is not "someone to be 'messed with' or dissed." Anderson, *Code of the Street*, p. 73. The application of "street" terms to the institutional context is an interesting example of the ways that these terms take on complex new meaning in residential life.

55. OCFS, "2008 Annual Report: Youth Placed in Custody" (Rensselaer, NY: Office of Children and Family Services, Division of Juvenile Justice and Opportunities for Youth, 2008).
. OCFS, "Resident Manual: Secure Facilities" (Rensselaer, NY: New York State Office of Children and Family Services, 2008).

56. According to the Prison Public Memory Project, at the Hudson Girls' Facility in Hudson, NY, girls were once expected to wear different-colored hair ribbons that indicated their achievement of various behavioral change expectations.

57. New York State Office of Children and Family Services, "Resident Manual: Secure Facilities."

58. During my fieldwork, several young people, including Bell and Newz, were arrested after committing offenses in the facilities. Facility staff had the discretion about whether to call the police during an incident, and the discretion to facilitate an arrest was highly politicized and varied by facility. For example, after Eddie assaulted a staff member, he received an administrative transfer to an adult prison, but he was not arrested.

59. Citizen's Committee for Children, "Inside Out: Youth Experiences inside New York's Juvenile Placement System."

60. See, e.g., b. hooks, *Ain't I a Woman: Black Women and Feminism* (Boston: South End Press, 1981).

61. See, e.g., Nikki Jones, *Between Good and Ghetto: African American Girls and Inner City Violence.* New Brunswick, NJ: Rutgers University Press, 2010).

62. J. A. Holstein and J. F. Gubrium, *The Self We Live By: Narrative Identity in a Postmodern World* (New York: Oxford University Press, 2000).

63. Gilly Sharpe, "The Trouble with Girls Today: Professional Perspectives on Young Women's Offending," *Youth Justice* 9, no. 3 (2009). Meda Chesney-Lind, "Challenging Girls' Invisibility in Juvenile Court," *The Annals of the American Academy of Political and Social Science* 564, no. 1 (1999).

64. Jack Katz, *Seductions of Crime: Moral and Sensual Attractions in Doing Evil* (New York: Basic Books, 1988).

65. Delores Jones-Brown, Jaspreet Gill, and Jennifer Trone, *Stop, Question and Frisk Policing Practices in New York City: A Primer* (New York: John Jay College of Criminal Justice, 2010).

66. Rod Brunson and Jody Miller, "Young Black Men and Urban Policing in the United States," *British Journal of Criminology* 46, no. 4 (2006); Rod Brunson, ""Police Don't Like Black People": African-American Young Men's Accumulated Police Experiences," *Criminology and Public Policy* 6, no. 1 (2007).

CHAPTER 3. RACIALIZED REPRESSION

1. For many years, New York's public high schools refused to recognize the credits that young people obtained in custody, saying that the schools that existed in custodial institutions were not officially accredited by the state's Department of Education. This meant that many young people who were in custody were funneled into General Equivalency Diploma programs or "alternative," non–degree-granting high schools. In early 2011, the Eastern District Court approved a settlement between a group of advocates and the state's Department of Education that mandated that New York's schools accept these students into their schools, and an office was created to facilitate this entry process. However, for students and families lacking the social capital or information necessary to locate the number for this office, this process did not work as smoothly as anticipated for many.

2. There is a New York law that prevents unlawful assembly on a sidewalk (New York Pub. L. 240.10).

3. New York State Division of Parole, 2009 data.

4. Carter House is a pseudonym for the drug treatment program.

5. Becky Tatum, "The Colonial Model As a Theoretical Explanation of Crime and Delinquency," in *African American Perspectives On: Crime, Causation, Criminal Justice Administration, and Crime Prevention* (Woburn, MA: Butterworth-Heinemann, 1994).

6. Celeste Watkins-Hayes, *The New Welfare Bureaucrats: Entanglements of Race, Class, and Policy Reform* (Chicago: University of Chicago Press, 2009).

7. Human Rights Watch, "No Second Chance: People with Criminal Records Denied Access to Public Housing" (Human Rights Watch, 2004).

8. R. Apel and G. Sweeten, "The Impact of Incarceration on Employment during the Transition to Adulthood," *Social Problems* 57, no. 3 (2010); D. Pager, *Marked: Race, Crime, and Finding Work in an Era of Mass Incarceration* (Chicago: University of Chicago Press, 2007).

9. New York State prevents private and public employers from discriminating against individuals with a criminal conviction, unless the job has a direct relationship to the crime of conviction (Legal Action Center, n.d.). However, in practice, many employers will not employ individuals if they know that they have a criminal conviction (see also Pager, *Marked*). Legal Action Center. "Overview of State Laws That Ban

Discrimination by Employers." http://www.lac.org/toolkits/standards/Fourteen _State_Laws.pdf.

10. Young people faced higher rates of unemployment than adults after the world financial collapse. Catherine Rampell, "Teenage Jobless Rate Reaches Record High." *New York Times*, September 5, 2009; Andrew Sum, Daniel McLaughlin, Ishwar Khatiwada, and Sheila Palma, "The Continued Collapse of the Nation's Teen Job Market and the Dismal Outlook for the 2008 Summer Labor Market for Teens: Does Anybody Care?" (Boston: Center for Labor Market Studies, Northeastern University, 2008). Yet job training and employment opportunities are scarce. For example, only 7 percent of the 200,000 "disconnected" sixteen- to twenty-four-year-olds in New York City were served by existing educational and job training programs, and there are an estimated 12,000 program slots available to serve this group (see L. Treschan and C. Molnar, "Out of Focus: A Snapshot of Public Funding to Reconnect Youth to Education and Employment." New York: Community Service Society, 2008.)

11. It is illegal for employers to ask whether someone has been arrested in New York and elsewhere (although employers can ask applicants if they have ever been *convicted* of a crime). However, in practice this happens frequently, and many individuals are often unaware of their legal right to refuse the question or express doubts that a potential employer will judge them fairly if they refuse to answer the question.

12. Center for Community Alternatives, "Boxed Out: Criminal History Screening and College Application Attrition" (Syracuse, NY: Center for Community Alternatives, 2015).

13. This change happened after years of organizing efforts by a number of statewide groups, including Education from the Inside Out and the Center for Community Alternatives. I served on a SUNY-appointed central committee that spent more than a year investigating the issue before we put forward a proposal to the Board of Trustees to eliminate the felony conviction box.

14. Alexes Harris, Heather Evans, and Katherine Beckett, "Drawing Blood from Stones: Legal Debt and Social Inequality in the Contemporary United States," *American Journal of Sociology* 115, no. 6 (2010). A. Rosenthal and M. Weissman, "Sentencing for Dollars: The Financial Consequences of a Criminal Conviction" (Syracuse, NY: Center for Community Alternatives, 2007).

15. Christopher Uggen, Jeff Manza, and Melissa Thompson, "Citizenship, Democracy, and the Civic Reintegration of Criminal Offenders," *Annals of the American Academy of Political and Social Science* 605, no. 1 (2006); Margaret Love, Jenny Roberts, and Cecelia Klingele, *Collateral Consequences of Criminal Convictions: Law, Policy and Practice* (Washington, DC: Thomson West, 2013).

16. P. Willis, *Learning to Labour: How Working Class Kids Get Working Class Jobs* (Aldershot, England: Gower, 1977/1988), 94–9.

17. J. MacLeod, *Ain't No Makin' It: Aspirations and Attainment in a Low-Income Neighborhood*, 3rd ed. (Boulder: Westview Press, 1995/2009), 4.

18. Silva, *Coming Up Short*.

19. See also Keith Hawkins, "Order, Rationality and Silence: Some Reflections on Criminal Justice Decision-Making," in L. Gelsthorpe and Nicola Padfield (eds.), *Exercising Discretion: Decision-Making in the Criminal Justice System and Beyond* (Cullompton, England: Willan, 2003).

20. F. Fanon, *Black Skin White Masks* (New York: Grove Press, 1967).

21. "Snitching" has been defined as the practice by which people who offend "give information to the police in exchange for material reward or reduced punishment"; R. Rosenfeld, B. Jacobs, and R. Wright, "Snitching and the Code of the Street," *British Journal of Criminology* 43, no. 2 (2003).

22. The Oxford English Dictionary defines this version of "railroad" to mean "To send to prison, convict, or punish (a person) with summary speed, esp. on false evidence

or without a fair trial."The OED traces its use back to the late nineteenth century, when it was used to describe the sentence of the Irish boxer Joe Coburn after shooting a police officer.

23. It was unclear where Billy received this number from or whether it was in fact accurate.

24. Nancy Lopez, *Hopeful Girls, Troubled Boys* (New York: Routledge, 2003).

25. Liazos, "Class Oppression: The Functions of Juvenile Justice."

26. In a recent report by the U.S. Departments of Education and Justice, the agencies identified some serious limitations to the provision of educational instruction in secure juvenile facilities that reflect this study's findings. U.S. Department of Education and U.S. Department of Justice, "Guiding Principles for Providing High-Quality in Juvenile Justice Secure Care Settings" (2014).

27. Herzfeld describes the way that the phrase "the system" is used to "reify bureaucracy" and how it "becomes an impersonal force on which all manner of individual and collective misfortunes may be blamed"; Michael Herzfeld, *The Social Production of Indifference* (New York: Berg, 1992), 144–5.

28. "The system" is akin to the ways in which researchers have described the experiences of welfare recipients and the weight the law exerts over their lives: "the law surrounds them as rules, as threats, and as commands; it is there as police officers, caseworkers, lawyers, and fraud control investigators; it is there in constructing their status as dependents of the state"; John Gilliom, *Overseers of the Poor: Surveillance, Resistance, and the Limits of Privacy* (London: University of Chicago Press, 2001), 11. See also Austin Sarat, "'. . . The Law Is All Over': Power, Resistance and the Legal Consciousness of the Welfare Poor," *Yale Journal of Law & the Humanities* 2 (1990).

29. Colman et al., "Long-Term Consequences of Delinquency"; Malika Saada Saar et al., "The Sexual Abuse to Prison Pipeline: The Girls' Story" (Washington, DC: Center for Poverty and Inequality, 2015).

30. Sedlak and McPherson, "Youth's Needs and Services."

31. Teresa O'Neill, "Girls in Trouble in the Welfare and Criminal Justice System," in Gwynedd Lloyd (ed.), *'Problem' Girls: Understanding and Supporting Troubled and Troublesome Girls and Young Women* (London: Routledge Falmer, 2005).

32. Ibid; M. Baines and C. Adler, "When She Was Bad She Was Horrid," in M. Baines and C. Adler (eds.), *. . . And When She Was Bad? Working with Young Women in Juvenile Justice and Related Areas* (Hobart, Australia: National Clearinghouse for Youth Studies, 1996). Sharpe; "The Trouble with Girls Today: Professional Perspectives on Young Women's Offending."

33. Sedlak and McPherson, "Youth's Needs and Services."

34. Children's Rights, "The Long Road Home: A Study of Children Stranded in New York City Foster Care" (2009).

35. T. Thornberry, T. Ireland, and C. Smith, "The Importance of Timing: The Varying Impact of Childhood and Adolescent Maltreatment on Multiple Problem Outcomes," *Development and Psychopathology* 13, no. 04 (2001); Melissa Jonson-Reid and Richard P. Barth, "From Placement to Prison: The Path to Adolescent Incarceration from Child Welfare Supervised Foster or Group Care," *Children and Youth Services Review* 22, no. 7 (2000). C. Cruickshank and Monica Barry, "Nothing Has Convinced Me to Stop" (Glasgow: Who Cares? Scotland, 2008); G. R. Cusick, Mark E. Courtney, Judy Havlicek, and Nathan Hess, "Crime during the Transition to Adulthood: How Youth Fare as They Leave Out-of-Home Care" (*grant report, U.S Department of Justice*) (2010).

36. A recent report by the African American Policy Forum at Columbia University pointed to the ways that young girls of color are disproportionately disciplined and suspended in public schools. Federal data confirms this. Kimberlé Williams

Crenshaw, Priscilla Ocen, and Jyoti Nanda, "Black Girls Matter: Pushed Out, Over-policed and Underprotected" (African American Policy Form, 2015).

37. Ms. Roberts's reference to "upstate" is about the juvenile facility. "Upstate" is often shorthand for prisons and other custodial institutions.

38. See also Monica Barry, "The Mentor/Monitor Debate in Criminal Justice: 'What Works' for Offenders," *British Journal of Social Work* 30 (2000).

39. John H. Laub and Robert J. Sampson, "Understanding Desistance from Crime," in Michael Tonry (ed.), *Crime and Justice* (Chicago: University of Chicago Press, 2001).

40. Laurence Steinberg and Elizabeth Cauffman, "Maturity of Judgment in Adolescence: Psychosocial Factors in Adolescent Decision Making," *Law and Human Behavior* 20, no. 3 (1996).

41. Those whose cases had finished continued to stay on some form of court supervision, such as parole, probation, or conditional release. The participant who had finished her case was Nina, who I have known for five years, since she was first arrested. She was recently released early from her five-year probation term, a very unusual practice.

42. This is not unique to New York, nor to the United States. See Smith for a brief discussion of an analogous situation of "over-intervention" in England and Wales, which is partly confused by the long-standing confusion of justice and welfare considerations. D. Smith, "Out of Care 30 Years On," *Criminology & Criminal Justice* 10, no. 2 (2010): 119–35.

43. See also I. Durnescu, "Pains of Probation: Effective Practice and Human Rights," *International Journal of Offender Therapy and Comparative Criminology* (2010); J. Petersilia, "When Probation Becomes More Dreaded Than Prison," *Federal Probation* 54, no. 1 (1990); Léon Digard, "When Legitimacy Is Denied: Offender Perceptions of the Prison Recall System," *Probation Journal* 57, no. 1 (2010).

44. Earlier in the year, before her program involvement and when we spoke about her marijuana use, she did not use those terms.

45. Elizabeth Such and R. Walker, "Young Citizens or Policy Objects? Children in the 'Rights and Responsibilities' Debate," *Journal of Social Policy* 34, no. 1 (2005): 52.

46. D. McBarnet, "When Compliance Is Not the Solution but the Problem: From Changes in Law to Changes in Attitude," in *Taxing Democracy: Understanding Tax Avoidance and Evasion*, ed. V. Braithwaite (Aldershot, England: Ashgate, 2003).

47. Cathy Cohen, "Deviance as Resistance: A New Research Agenda for the Study of Black Politics," *Du Bois Review* 1, no. 1 (2004): 27.

48. Ibid, 40.

49. See also S. Farrall, A. E. Bottoms, and Joanna Shapland, "Social Structures and Desistance from Crime," *European Journal of Criminology* 7, no. 6 (2010).

50. See also Rose Peralta to Children's Rights Litigation, July 16, 2013, http://apps .americanbar.org/litigation/committees/childrights/content/articles/spring2013–0413-say-what-translating-courtroom-colloquies-for-youth.html.

51. A young person's ability to speak in court is also bounded by the need for their attorneys to protect them (as they would with adults) from exposing information which may be detrimental to their legal case. From a criminal defense perspective, there is thus an often problematic way that the voices of young people who have been in the criminal justice system are used in reform strategies, as these voices can often later be used against them in job searches, applications to college, and even in later criminal justice matters.

52. John Thibaut and Laurens Walker, *Procedural Justice: A Psychological Analysis* (Hillsdale, New Jersey 1975); M. R. Fondacaro et al., "Identity Orientation, Voice, and Judgments of Procedural Justice During Late Adolescence," *Journal of Youth and Adolescence* 35, no. 6 (2006).

53. Fricker, Miranda. *Epistemic Injustice: Power and the Ethics of Knowing.* New York: Oxford University Press, 2007.
54. Harris, "Diverting and Abdicating Judicial Discretion."
55. Majd and Puritz, "The Cost of Justice"; K. Henning, "Loyalty, Paternalism, and Rights"; *Notre Dame Law Review* 81 (2005).
56. Majd and Puritz, "The Cost of Justice."
57. Henning, "Loyalty, Paternalism, and Rights."
58. Wacquant, *Punishing the Poor*; Graham Rayman, "Rikers Violence: Out of Control," *The Village Voice* May 9, 2012; Fagan and Wilkinson, "Guns, Youth Violence, and Social Identity in Inner Cities."
59. Gary Alan Fine and Patricia A. Turner, *Whispers on the Color Line: Rumor and Race in America* (Berkeley: University of California Press, 2001); John. L. Jackson, *Racial Paranoia: The Unintended Consequences of Political Correctness* (New York: Basic Civitas, 2008).
60. Fine and Turner, *Whispers on the Color Line*; Jackson, *Racial Paranoia.*
61. Jones-Brown, Gill, and Trone, "Stop, Question and Frisk Policing Practices in New York City."
62. Brunson and Miller, "Young Black Men and Urban Policing in the United States"; Brunson, "'Police Don't Like Black People'."
63. Richard L. Jenkins, *Pierre Bourdieu* (Abingdon, England: Routledge, 2002).
64. Majd and Puritz, "The Cost of Justice"; Henning, "Loyalty, Paternalism, and Rights." The debate around best versus expressed interests is long and complicated and has included considerations about the relevant role of parents in the legal defense of their children. This has also raised interesting questions about whether the attorney is involved in protecting the child from the state or from his or her parents (Henning, 2005: 253–4).
65. Such and Walker, "Young Citizens or Policy Objects?" 51.
66. G. M. Sykes and David Matza, "Techniques of Neutralization: A Theory of Delinquency," *American Sociological Review* 22, no. 6 (1957); Shadd Maruna and Heith Copes, "Excuses, Excuses: What Have We Learned from Five Decades of Neutralization Research," in Michael Tonry (ed.), *Crime and Justice: A Review of Research* (Chicago: University of Chicago Press, 2005).
67. A. Honneth, "Invisibility: On the Epistemology of 'Recognition'," *Proceedings of the Aristotelian Society* 75 (2001): 115.
68. Ibid, 115–18.
69. Yolander G. Hurst and James Frank, "How Kids View Cops: The Nature of Juvenile Attitudes toward the Police," *Journal of Criminal Justice* 28 (2000); Brunson and Miller, "Young Black Men and Urban Policing in the United States"; Brunson, "'Police Don't Like Black People'."
70. J. Fagan and T. Tyler, "Legal Socialization of Children and Adolescents," *Social Justice Research* 18, no. 3 (2005).
71. Peggy S. Sullivan, Roger G. Dunham, and Geoffrey P. Alpert, "Attitude Structures of Different Ethnic and Age Groups Concerning Police," *The Journal of Criminal Law and Criminology* 78, no. 1 (1987); Tom R. Tyler, "What Is Procedural Justice: Criteria Used by Citizens to Assess the Fairness of Legal Procedures," *Law and Society Review* 22, no. 1 (1988); Laura J. Gold, John M. Darley, James L. Hilton, and Mark P. Zanna, "Children's Perceptions of Procedural Justice," *Child Development* 55, no. 5 (1984).
72. Gold et al., "Children's Perceptions of Procedural Justice."
73. T. R. Tyler and E. A. Lind, "Procedural Justice," in J. Sanders and V. L. Hamilton (eds.), *Handbook of Justice Research in Law* (New York: Kluwer Academic/Plenum Publishers, 2001); E. A. Lind and T. R. Tyler *The Social Psychology of Procedural Justice* (New York: Plenum Press, 1988).
74. Tyler and Lind, "Procedural Justice," 75.

CHAPTER 4. THE RESPONSIBILITY TRAP

1. Paul Castellani, *From Snake Pits to Cash Cows: Politics and Public Institutions in New York* (Albany: State University of New York Press, 2005).
2. Murakawa, *The First Civil Right: How Liberals Built Prison America*. Rebecca Hill, "'The Common Enemy Is the Boss and the Inmate': Police and Prison Guard Unions in New York in the 1970s–1980s," *Labor: Studies in Working-Class History of the Americas* 8, no. 3 (2011).
3. Personal communication, Leonard Dunston.
4. New York State Division for Youth, "Youth in Care: Annual Reports 1989 and 1990" (Rensselaer, NY: New York State Division for Youth, 1991).
5. "2012 Annual Report," (Rensselaer, NY: New York State Office of Children and Family Services, Division of Juvenile Justice and Opportunities for Youth, 2012).
6. David Garland, "The Limits of the Sovereign State," *The British Journal of Criminology* 36, no. 4 (1996); Pat O'Malley, "Risk, Power and Crime Prevention," *Economy and Society* 21, no. 3 (1992). Nikolas Rose, "Government and Control," *British Journal of Criminology* 40 (2000); John Muncie, "Governing Young People: Coherence and Contradiction in Contemporary Youth Justice," *Critical Social Policy* 26, no. 4 (2006).
7. Harvey, *A Brief History of Neoliberalism*.
8. Soss, Fording, and Schram, *Disciplining the Poor*.
9. Wendy Brown, *States of Injury: Power and Freedom in Late Modernity* (Princeton: Princeton University Press, 1995); Frances Fox Piven and Richard A. Cloward, *Regulating the Poor: The Functions of Public Welfare* (New York: Random House, 1971/1993).
10. Jo Phoenix, "Beyond Risk Assessment: The Return of Repressive Welfarism?" in Fergus McNeill and Monica Barry (eds.), *Youth Offending and Youth Justice* (London: Jessica Kingsley Publishers, 2009).
11. Dorothy Roberts, "Welfare and the Problem of Black Citizenship," *The Yale Law Journal* 105, no. 6 (1996). Jacquelin Scarborough, "Welfare Mothers' Reflections on Personal Responsibility," *Journal of Social Issues* 57, no. 2 (2001).
12. Wacquant, *Punishing the Poor*.
13. See Liazos, "Class Oppression: The Functions of Juvenile Justice"; Wacquant, *Punishing the Poor*. Liazos, writing about juvenile justice interventions in the 1970s, said, "All of the programs through the years have aimed at control and discipline of the poorer classes; they have tried to resocialize the boys and girls of the poor, working class, and minority groups so they would accept the place capitalism (in its various forms) chose for them" (1974, 2). In New York State, more than 51 percent of line staff members are African American. African Americans represent 30.9 percent of the total Office of Children and Family Services workforce, indicating that they represent a greater proportion of the frontline staff. African Americans also represent a significantly higher proportion of the corrections officer workforce than whites in the United States, as well as the less prestigious justice jobs in general (see Geoff Ward, "Race and the Justice Workforce: A System Perspective," in R. Peterson, L. Krivo, and J. Hagan (eds.), *The Many Colors of Crime: Inequalities of Race, Ethnicity, and Crime in America* (New York: New York University Press, 2006), 78. On the basis of my interviews with leading figures in the voluntary sector, there is also strong evidence to support the idea that the frontline workers inside of privately run and publicly contracted private agencies are also overwhelmingly people of color (perhaps even more so than in the public sector).
14. See, for example, A. E. Bottoms, "Theoretical Reflections on the Evaluation of a Penal Policy Initiative," in Lucia Zedner and Andrew Ashworth (eds.), *The Criminological Foundations of Penal Policy: Essays in Honour of Roger Hood* (Oxford: Oxford University Press, 2003); Mary Bosworth and Alison Liebling, "Incentives in Prison

Regimes: A Review of the Literature" (Cambridge: Institute of Criminology, 1995); Laura Abrams, Kyoungho Kim, and Ben Anderson-Nathe, "Paradoxes of Treatment in Juvenile Corrections," *Child & Youth Care Forum* 34, no. 1 (2005).

15. This list is drawn from the classical typologies of juvenile correctional organizations that Street et al. (1966) created. David Street, Robert D. Vinter, and Charles Perrow, *Organization for Treatment: A Comparative Study of Institutions for Delinquents* (New York: The Free Press, 1966).

16. I obtained this information from facility staff members.

17. Abrams, Kim, and Anderson-Nathe, "Paradoxes of Treatment in Juvenile Corrections."

18. P. Tompkins-Rosenblatt and K. VanderVen, "Perspectives on Point and Level Systems in Residential Care: A Responsive Dialogue," *Residential Treatment for Children & Youth* 22, no. 3 (2005). A. Kazdin, "The Token Economy: A Decade Later," *Journal of Applied Behavior Analysis* 15, no. 3 (1982).

19. New York State Office of Children and Family Services, "Resident Manual: Secure Facilities."

20. "Youth Development System: Staff Manual" (Rensselaer, NY: New York State Office of Children and Family Services, 1997). These directions are taken from a resident manual from a secure center.

21. "Resident Manual: Secure Facilities," 36.

22. Ibid.

23. Ibid, 37.

24. Merry Ann Morash, "Cognitive Developmental Theory," *Criminology* 19, no. 3 (1981).

25. James, Jenks, and Prout, *Theorizing Childhood*.

26. Liazos, "Class Oppression."

27. Jean Piaget, *The Construction of Reality in the Child* (New York: Basic Books, 1955), xiii.

28. Cathy Urwin, "Developmental Psychology and Psychoanalysis: Splitting the Difference," in M. Richards and P. Light (eds.), *Children of Social Worlds* (Cambridge: Polity Press, 1986).

29. Lawrence Kohlberg, "Moral Stages and Moralization: The Cognitive Developmental Approach," in Thomas Lichona (ed.), *Moral Development and Behavior: Theory, Research, and Social Issues* (New York: Holt, Rinehart and Winston, 1976); Richard A. Shweder, Manamohan Mahapatra, and Joan G. Miller, "Culture and Moral Development," in Jerome Kagan (ed.), *The Emergence of Morality in Young Children* (Chicago: The University of Chicago Press, 1987).

30. "Culture and Moral Development," 2–7.

31. Antonio Viego, *Dead Subjects: Toward a Politics of Loss in Latino Studies* (Durham, NC: Duke University Press, 2007); Alan France, "Towards a Sociological Understanding of Youth and Their Risk-Taking," *Journal of Youth Studies* 3, no. 3 (2000).

32. S. Duguid, *Can Prisons Work? The Prisoner as Object and Subject in Modern Corrections* (Buffalo: University of Toronto Press, 2000), 83. Ward and Nee, "Surfaces and Depths: Evaluating the Theoretical Assumptions of Cognitive Skills Programmes." According to Duguid, a historian of the cognitive behavioral movement in prisons, "few in corrections had any illusions or, indeed, desires for their charges to reach the final, principled stages of development, stages in which decisions about actions in the world are based on the individual's understanding of the principles behind the rules" (2000: 186).

33. June L. Tapp and Lawrence Kohlberg, "Developing Senses of Law and Legal Justice," *Journal of Social Issues* 27, no. 2 (1971); Morash, "Cognitive Developmental Theory." Kohlberg's stages of moral development are pre-conventional, conventional, and post-conventional.

34. M. R. Gottfredson and Travis Hirschi, *A General Theory of Crime* (Stanford: Stanford University Press, 1990). It is worth noting, however, that Gottfredson and Hirschi argue that social institutions cannot usually make up for the deficiencies caused in the home. The influence of this model of "individual positivism" arguably coincided with the decline of sociologies of deviance and the rise in influence of more conservative criminological theories on policy and public discourse (Jock Young, "Cannibalism and Bulimia: Patterns of Social Control in Late Modernity," *Theoretical Criminology* 3, no. 4 (1999): 384–407; Garland, David. *The Culture of Control* [Oxford: Oxford University Press, 2001]). The influence of this theory could also be connected to strategies aimed at engendering self-responsibility in welfare recipients.

35. See, e.g., A. Reiss, "Delinquency As the Failure of Personal and Social Controls," *American Sociological Review* 16, no. 2 (1951).

36. Duguid, *Can Prisons Work?*

37. Loic Wacquant, "The Curious Eclipse of Prison Ethnography in the Age of Mass Incarceration," *Ethnography* 3, no. 4 (2002).

38. Morash, "Cognitive Developmental Theory."

39. M. Lipsey and David Wilson, "Effective Intervention for Serious Juvenile Offenders," in Rolf Loeber and David P. Farrington (eds.), *Serious and Violent Juvenile Offenders: Risk Factors and Successful Interventions* (Thousand Oaks, CA: Sage, 1998); D. A. Andrews et al., "Does Correctional Treatment Work? A Clinically Relevant and Psychologically Informed Meta-Analysis," *Criminology* 28 (1990); Mark W. Lipsey, Gabrielle L. Chapman, and Nana A. Landenberger, "Cognitive-Behavioral Programs for Offenders," *The Annals of the American Academy of Political and Social Science* 578, no. 1 (2001); Anna J. Bogestad, Ryan J. Kettler, and Michael P. Hagan, "Evaluation of a Cognitive Intervention Program for Juvenile Offenders," *International Journal of Offender Therapy and Comparative Criminology* 54, no. 4 (2010).

40. Duguid, *Can Prisons Work?*; Ross, Fabiano, and Ewles, "Reasoning and Rehabilitation."

41. Platt, *The Child Savers.*

42. C. Banks, *Alaska Native Juveniles in Detention: A Qualitative Study of Treatment and Resistance* (Lewiston, NY: The Edwin Mellen Press, 2008).

43. Ward and Nee, "Surfaces and Depths: Evaluating the Theoretical Assumptions of Cognitive Skills Programmes," 169.

44. M. Deitch and M. Mushlin, "Opening Up a Closed World: A Sourcebook on Prison Oversight," *Pace Law Review* 30, no. 5 (2010).

45. G. Paniza, "Examining Spending at the Office of Children and Family Services" (Albany: Independent Democratic Conference, 2011).

46. Haines and Case, "The Rhetoric and Reality of the 'Risk Factor Prevention Paradigm' Approach to Preventing and Reducing Youth Offending"; France, "Towards a Sociological Understanding of Youth and Their Risk-Taking"; Beth Blue Swadener and Sally Lubeck, "The Social Construction of Children and Families "at Risk": An Introduction," in Beth Blue Swadener and Sally Lubeck (eds.), *Children and Families "at Promise": Deconstructing the Discourse of Risk,* (Albany: State University of New York, 1995); Paniza, "Examining Spending at the Office of Children and Family Services."

47. D. A. Andrews, J. Bonta, and J. Stephen Wormith, "The Recent Past and Near Future of Risk and/or Need Assessment," *Crime and Delinquency* 52, no. 1 (2006). New York State Office of Children and Family Services, "Prescriptive Programming Intake Home Visit and Youth Risk Assessment Manual," (Rensselaer: New York State Office of Children and Family Services, 1998).

48. Abrams notes that most programs for juvenile offenders "blend" their approaches to treatment, involving a range of strategies that range from punitive to therapeutic;

Laura Abrams, "Listening to Juvenile Offenders: Can Residential Treatment Prevent Recidivism," *Child and Adolescent Social Work Journal* 23, no. 1 (2006).

49. Personal communication, Leonard Dunston.

50. Eric Trupin et al., "Effectiveness of a Dialectical Behavior Therapy Program for Incarcerated Female Juvenile Offenders," *Child and Adolescent Mental Health* 7, no. 3 (2002): 122. Trupin was hired by OCFS to act as a consultant in the implementation of evidence-based practices.

51. Nikolas Rose, *Governing the Soul: The Shaping of the Private Self* (London: Routledge, 1989).

52. A. Elliot, *Psychoanalytic Theory: An Introduction* (Durham, NC: Duke University Press, 2002). Viego argues that in ego psychology "adaptation and autonomy become the measure of mental health"; Antonio Viego, *Dead Subjects: Toward a Politics of Loss in Latino Studies* (Durham, NC: Duke University Press, 2007), 8.

53. Edward Glover, "Delinquency Work in Britain: A Survey of Current Trends," *The Journal of Criminal Law, Criminology, and Police Science* 46, no. 2 (1955); August Aichhorn, *Wayward Youth* (New York: Meridian, 1925/1955).

54. Maruna and Copes, "Excuses, Excuses," 2; Sykes and Matza, "Techniques of Neutralization."

55. It has been argued that more current readings of neutralization theory interpret such thoughts and processes to be made deliberately and consciously. Maruna and Copes, "Excuses, Excuses."

56. Sykes and Matza, "Techniques of Neutralization: A Theory of Delinquency." Maruna and Copes, "Excuses, Excuses."

57. Banks, *Alaska Native Juveniles in Detention: A Qualitative Study of Treatment and Resistance.*

58. David Matza, *Delinquency and Drift* (New York: John Wiley and Sons, 1964). See also Maruna and Copes, "Excuses, Excuses"; J. McKendy, "'I'm Very Careful About That': Narrative and Agency of Men in Prison," *Discourse & Society* 17, no. 4 (2006).

59. Crewe, *The Prisoner Society: Power, Adaptation, and Social Life in an English Prison.*

60. The notion of "personal responsibility" is said to be consistent with the "ethos of individual autonomy" associated with philosophies of advanced liberalism and how they relate to inducements to self-government. Rose, "Government and Control."

61. B. Thomas-Peter, "The Modern Context of Psychology in Corrections: Influences, Limitations and Values of 'What Works'," in Graham Towl (ed.), *Psychological Research in Prisons* (Oxford: Blackwell Publishing, 2006); Crewe, *The Prisoner Society*; Kathryn J. Fox, "Reproducing Criminal Types: Cognitive Treatment for Violent Offenders in Prison," *The Sociological Quarterly* 40, no. 3 (1999).

62. Shadd Maruna and Ruth Mann, "A Fundamental Attribution Error? Rethinking Cognitive Distortions," *Legal and Criminological Psychology* 11 (2006).

63. Ibid.

64. Ibid.

65. Shadd Maruna, *Making Good: How Ex-Convicts Reform and Rebuild Their Lives* (Washington, DC: American Psychological Association, 2001).

66. Task Force on Transforming Juvenile Justice, "Charting a New Course: A Blueprint for Transforming Juvenile Justice in New York State," 91.

67. M. Masi and D. Boyd, "Behavior Support and Management: Coordinated Standards for Children's Systems of Care" (Rensselaer, NY: Council on Children and Families, 2007).

68. A. Reich, *Hidden Truth: Young Men Navigating Lives in and out of Juvenile Prison* (Berkeley: University of California Press, 2010), 128. Steckley and Kendrick have pointed to the complexities of staff and adolescent understandings of the uses and necessity of restraints in an English residential care context which are partly related to prevailing concerns about childhood vulnerabilities and demands for safety in

institutional care. L. Steckley and A. Kendrick, "Physical Restraint in Residential Childcare: The Experiences of Young People and Residential Workers," *Childhood* 15, no. 4 (2008).

69. Kobi Kambon, "The Africentric Paradigm and African-American Psychological Liberation," in D. Azibo (ed.), *African Psychology in Historical Perspective and Related Commentary* (Trenton, NJ: Africa World Press, 1996).

70. Ward and Nee, "Surfaces and Depths: Evaluating the Theoretical Assumptions of Cognitive Skills Programmes," 172.

71. Bruce Frederick et al., "Validity of Commonly-Cited Risk and Protective Factors for Assessing Release Readiness among Incarcerated Delinquents," presented at the *American Society of Criminology Annual Conference* (Chicago, 2002).

72. Concerns were recently raised by various state and federal watchdog organizations that the use of "scoring" related too closely to a residents' ability to be released and to the quality of treatment, and that young people with mental health problems may struggle in this system. King, "Investigation of the Lansing Residential Center, Louis Gossett, Jr. Residential Center, Tryon Residential Center, and Tryon Girls Center"; Citizen's Committee for Children, "Inside Out"; Task Force on Transforming Juvenile Justice, "Charting a New Course." Thus, readiness for release, rather than being based on a points system, is now decided by a young person's community-based workers, who work with them throughout their time in the system, as well as with input from the young person and their family. Citizen's Committee for Children, "Inside Out," 42. An evaluation of a Multi-systemic Therapy program in use for young people released from facilities in their communities was conducted by OCFS and researchers found that the model did not work well with the OCFS population. Susan Mitchell-Herzfeld et al., "Effects of Multisystemic Therapy (MST) on Recidivism among Juvenile Delinquents in New York State" (Rensselaer, NY: Office of Children and Family Services, 2008). At the time of the research, the agency was in the process of introducing a new family-focused model that is an attempt to remedy some of the limitations of the program identified through the evaluation.

73. Garland, *The Culture of Control*, 130.

CHAPTER 5. CHANGE FROM THE INSIDE

1. See, e.g., Bernstein, *Burning Down the House: The End of Juvenile Prison*. Richard Mendel, "Maltreatment of Youth in U.S. Juvenile Correctional Facilities: An Update" (Baltimore, MD: Annie E. Casey Foundation, 2015). Steve Liss, Marian Wright Edelman, and Cecilia Balli, *No Place for Children: Voices from Juvenile Detention* (Austin: University of Texas Press, 2005).

2. Jo Phoenix, "Against Youth Justice and Youth Governance, for Youth Penality," *British Journal of Criminology* (2015): 13.

3. I have assigned the female gender pronoun to Olivia. Although a discussion later in the chapter will reveal the fluidity of her conceptions of gender identity, her decision to use a feminine-identified name informed my choice for this chapter.

4. G. M. Sykes, *The Society of Captives: A Study of a Maximum-Security Prison* (Princeton: Princeton University Press, 1958/2007); J. Irwin, *The Felon* (Englewood Cliffs, NJ: Prentice Hall, 1970); James Jacobs, *Stateville: The Penitentiary in Mass Society* (Chicago: University of Chicago Press, 1977); Goffman, *Asylums*.

5. See also Anna Gradin Franzén, "Responsibilization and Discipline: Subject Positioning at a Youth Detention Home," *Journal of Contemporary Ethnography* 44, no. 3 (2014).

6. In a therapeutic community-oriented drug-treatment program studied by Paik, residents similarly used the term "doing the program" to describe what she terms

"efforts at institutional self-construction" Leslie Paik, "Are You Truly a Recovering Dope Fiend? Local Interpretive Practices at a Therapeutic Community Drug Treatment Program," *Symbolic Interaction* 29, no. 2 (2006): 216.

7. "Two" refers to the points-based incentives and earned privileges system.

8. I worked with Newz's attorney on the case that led him to confinement. While working on the case, I had interviewed him at length about his past and had access to this history through records and interviews with family members. My knowledge of Newz's past inevitably influenced my analysis of his interpretations of change.

9. The detention facilities, like the one that Billy was in, send regular reports about young people's behavior to the judge.

10. There were large numbers of outside visitors to the residential facilities during the field-work period, including a state legislator, the president of John Jay College, judges, and advocates, in part because the scrutiny that the Office of Children and Family Services was facing in the public media and because the field-work process coincided with an investigation of the system by a statewide task force on juvenile justice.

11. The state has the authority to transfer a resident to the Department of Corrections as soon as they turn eighteen years old. Eddie's behavior could in part be related to Erving Goffman's notion of "playing it cool," by supporting the "counter-mores" with his fellow residents and "conceal[ing] from them how tractably he acts when alone with the staff." Goffman, *Asylums*, 64–5. This is also related to Feld's notion of "doing time" or simply waiting until one's time is up; Barry Feld, *Neutralizing Inmate Violence: Juvenile Offenders in Institutions* (Cambridge, MA: Ballinger, 1977). "Playing it cool," in other words, is a form of "falling back," by making one's institutional life easier and trying to escape some of the harms that come from both fully engaging in the potential dangers of resistance and those of complete assimilation.

12. Other researchers have found that young people engage in this practice of "fake it to make it" inside custody. See, for example: Abrams, Kim, and Anderson-Nathe, "Paradoxes of Treatment in Juvenile Corrections"; Abrams, "Listening to Juvenile Offenders"; Laura Abrams and Jemel Aguilar, "Negative Trends, Possible Selves, and Behavior Change: A Qualitative Study of Juvenile Offenders in Residential Treatment," *Qualitative Social Work* 4, no. 2 (2005); Michelle Inderbitzen, "Guardians of the State's Problem Children," *The Prison Journal* 86, no. 4 (2006); J. Fader, *Falling Back* (New Brunswick, NJ: Rutgers University Press, 2013).

13. Andrew Day et al., "The Process of Change in Offender Rehabilitation Programs," *Psychology, Crime & Law* 12, no. 5 (2006).

14. In her study of a drug treatment program, Paik found that the official sanctioning of a form of "faking it" "hinders the ability to determine if a peer is faking the new self in an effort to adopt it. In short, because 'act as if' is an official part of the self-construction process, members believe that it is necessary to peel away the layers of pretending to assess how a client is really doing in the self- construction process." Paik, "Are You Truly a Recovering Dope Fiend?" 215.

15. Abrams, Kim, and Anderson-Nathe, "Paradoxes of Treatment in Juvenile Corrections."

16. J. Mullins, "Spirituality and the Twelve Steps," *International Journal of Applied Psychoanalytic Studies* 7, no. 2 (2010); Fox, "Reproducing Criminal Types: Cognitive Treatment for Violent Offenders in Prison."

17. T. Mathiesen, *The Defences of the Weak: A Sociological Study of a Norwegian Correctional Institution* (London: Tavistock, 1965); Ben Crewe, "Power, Adaptation and Resistance in a Late-Modern Men's Prison," *British Journal of Criminology* 47, no. 2 (2007); Bosworth and Liebling, "Incentives in Prison Regimes"; C. Bartollas, "Survival Problems of Adolescent Prisoners," in Robert Johnson and Hans Toch (eds.), *The Pains of Imprisonment* (Beverly Hills, CA: Sage, 1982).

18. Crewe, *The Prisoner Society: Power, Adaptation, and Social Life in an English Prison* (Oxford: Oxford University Press, 2009), 207.

19. See Shadd Maruna et al., "Pygmalion in the Reintegration Process: Desistance from Crime through the Looking Glass," *Psychology, Crime & Law* 10, no. 3 (2004).

20. Judith Butler, *Gender Trouble* (New York: Routledge, 1990), xv; Judith Butler, *Excitable Speech: The Politics of Performance* (New York: Routledge, 1997), 153.

21. See also Crewe, "Power, Adaptation and Resistance in a Late-Modern Men's Prison."

22. Ibid., 257.

23. This idea of falling back is slightly different from that described by Jamie Fader in her book *Falling Back*. There, the expression is used to explain the avoidance of reoffending.

24. See also Alice Goffman, "On the Run: Wanted Men in a Philadelphia Ghetto," *American Sociological Review* 74 (2009).

25. Bartollas similarly describes young people in training schools who "play it cool" by "simply 'doing time'," . . . by keeping "his emotions under control and to do whatever was necessary to shorten the institutional stay." Bartollas, "Survival Problems of Adolescent Prisoners," 176.

26. Although see the work of David Domenici and the Center for Educational Excellence in Alternative Settings.

27. See also Willis, *Learning to Labour*.

28. Jim Scott, *Domination and the Arts of Resistance: Hidden Transcripts* (New Haven: Yale University Press, 1990).

29. This was what staff told me; I did not independently confirm this observation with the facility administrators.

30. See, e.g. Nathan McCall, *Makes Me Wanna Holler: A Young Black Man in America* (New York Vintage Books, 1994).

31. See, e.g., McKendy, "'I'm Very Careful about That'."

32. Aftercare workers are assigned to all young people adjudicated as juvenile delinquents. The workers meet with the young person before they are released from custody and serve a supervisory role once they are released from custody.

33. Criminologists who study crime and the emotions have argued that we have often neglected to understand psychosocial dimensions of engagement with crime, and to acknowledge that crime allows individuals, especially teenagers, to engage in a quest for excitement and kicks. See, e.g., Jeff Ferrell, Keith Hayward, and Jock Young, *Cultural Criminology: An Invitation* (Thousand Oaks, CA: Sage, 2008); David Gadd and T. Jefferson, *Psychosocial Criminology* (London: Sage, 2007); Katz, *Seductions of Crime*.

34. A.E. Bottoms and Joanna Shapland, "Steps Towards Desistance among Male Young Adult Recidivists," in *Escape Routes: Contemporary Perspectives on Life after Punishment*, ed. Shadd Maruna and M. Hough (London: Routledge, 2010). Jeanette Kennett and Michael Smith, "Synchronic Self-Control Is Always Non-Actional," *Analysis* 57, no. 2 (1997). Jeanette Kennett, *Agency and Responsibility: A Common-Sense Moral Psychology* (Oxford: Clarendon Press, 2001).

35. Billy was arrested at least four times and stopped at least twenty times during the course of the fieldwork period. He was identified by the police as a gang member, and he said he could not travel more than one city block with his friends without being stopped by the police. Thus, one part of his desire to return to detention was about avoiding the constant indignities of being stopped by the police.

36. Adam Reich, in his book about a juvenile facility in Rhode Island, made a similar finding. Reich, *Hidden Truth*, 134.

37. See also Colman et al., "Long-Term Conseqences of Delinquency"; D. Shelton, "Health Status of Young Offenders and Their Families," *Journal of Nursing Scholarship*,

Second Quarter (2000). A number of staff members also spoke to me about their exposure to physical forms of discipline in their childhood, often implying that these forms of discipline had helped them to become more *self*-disciplined.

38. According to the New York State Division of Parole, José was discharged from Parole in February 2011. There is no record of him having any violations. However, I have not spoken to him since March 2009 and thus do not know if he has been rearrested.

39. Bonilla-Silva, *Racism without Racists*, 37.

40. Bonilla-Silva, *Racism without Racists*; Becky Tatum, "Toward a Neocolonial Model of Adolescent Crime and Violence," *Journal of Contemporary Criminal Justice* 16, no. 2 (2000).

41. Schlossman, *Love and the American Delinquent: The Theory and Practice of "Progressive" Juvenile Justice, 1825–1920.*

CONCLUSION

1. Schur, *Radical Non-Intervention.*

2. James Kilgore, "Repackaging Mass Incarceration," in *Counterpunch* (2014); Judah Schept, *Progressive Punishment: Job Loss, Jail Groth, and the Neoliberal Logic of Carceral Expansion* (New York: NYU Press, 2015).

3. See also the work of Ben Crewe, who calls the treatment and punitive approaches in British prisons neo-paternalist. Ben Crewe, *The Prisoner Society.*

METHODOLOGICAL APPENDIX

1. As far as I know, the only other researcher who has conducted extensive qualitative research inside New York's system was Rose Giallombardo. See, e.g., Rose Giallombardo, *The Social World of Imprisoned Girls: A Comparative Study of Institutions for Juvenile Delinquents* (Huntington, NY: Robert E. Krieger Publishing Company, 1981).

2. L. Wacquant, The Curious Eclipse of Prison Ethnography in the Age of Mass Incarceration. *Ethnography*, 3, no. 4 (2002): 371–97. Wacquant neglects to recognize the rich history of ethnographic research on women's prisons, however.

3. None of these spaces are entirely free of the presence of government, as was demonstrated during the course of the research when I learned that young people's social networking experiences (e.g., Twitter, MySpace, and Facebook) were being monitored by the police and was admissible in court.

4. Jennifer Mason, *Qualitative Researching* (Thousand Oaks, CA: Sage, 2002).

5. A. E. Bottoms, "The Relationship between Theory and Empirical Observations in Criminology," in *Doing Research on Crime and Justice* (Oxford: Oxford University Press, 2007). M. Hollis, *The Philosophy of Social Science: An Introduction* (New York: Cambridge University Press, 1994).

6. M. Burawoy, "Introduction," in M. Burawoy et al. (eds.), *Ethnography Unbound: Power and Resistance in the Modern Metropolis* (Berkeley: University of California Press, 1991); Alison Liebling, "Whose Side Are We On? Theory, Practice and Allegiances in Prisons Research," *British Journal of Criminology* 41 (2001): 475.

7. Chris Jenks, "Zeitgeist Research on Childhood," in Pia Christensen and Allison James (eds.), *Research with Children: Perspectives and Practices* (London: Routledge Falmer, 2000).

8. J. F. Gubrium and J. A. Holstein, *Institutional Selves: Troubled Identities in a Postmodern World* (New York: Oxford University Press, 2001), 16.

9. Crewe, "Power, Adaptation and Resistance in a Late-Modern Men's Prison," 259. Scott, *Domination and the Arts of Resistance: Hidden Transcripts*. Crewe, "Power,

Adaptation and Resistance in a Late-Modern Men's Prison," 259. Although the residential facilities and detention centers that I conducted research in are not technically considered to be "prisons," the literature on ethnographic methods in prisons has some relevance here in considering the complexity of analyzing secure institutional life.

10. I. Jarvie, "The Problem of Ethical Integrity in Participant Observation," in R. Burgess (ed.), *Field Research: A Sourcebook and Field Manual* (London: Routledge, 1982).

11. J. A. Holstein and J. F. Gubrium, "Phenomenology, Ethnomethodology and Interpretive Practice," in Norman Denzin and Yvonna Lincoln (eds.), *Handbook of Qualitative Research* (Thousand Oaks, CA: Sage, 1994), 264.

12. Anthony Giddens, *The Constitution of Society* (Berkeley: University of California Press, 1984). Pierre Bourdieu, "Symbolic Power," in D. Gleeson (ed.), *Identity and Structure: Issues in the Sociology of Education* (Driffield: Nafferton Books, 1977).

13. Hochschild, A. "Emotion Work, Feeling Rules, and Social Structure," *The American Journal of Sociology* 85, no. 3 (1979): 557.

14. Young people are also sent to these facilities if they have been adjudicated with serious felonies as juvenile delinquents or if they have received serious disciplinary charges while they were in custody in a lower-level facility.

15. Before selecting my research site, I spoke with Mark Steward, who helped to establish a national "model" in juvenile justice practices, based in Missouri. Solomon Moore, "Missouri System Treats Juvenile Offenders with a Lighter Hand," *New York Times*, March 26, 2009. Steward consults with state governments on their juvenile prison systems, and he had been hired by the commissioner of OCFS, Gladys Carrión, to examine New York's system. Steward told me that McClary was a facility that most resembled the "Missouri Model."

16. Gewirtz, M. "Annual Report on the Adult Court Case Processing of Juvenile Offenders in New York City, January through December 2009." New York: Criminal Justice Agency, 2010.

17. Cannon, A., R. Aborn, and John Bennett. "Guide to Juvenile Justice in New York City." New York: Citizens Crime Commission of New York City, 2010.

18. Priscilla Alderson, "Ethics," in Sandy Fraser et al. (eds.), *Doing Research with Children and Young People* (London: Sage, 2004), 98.

19. W. Hollway and T. Jefferson, *Doing Qualitative Research Differently* (London: Sage, 2000), 99.

20. Michelle Fine et al., "Youth Research/Participatory Methods for Reform," in D. Theissen and A. Cook-Sather (eds.), *International Handbook of Student Experience in Elementary and Secondary School* (Dordrecht: Springer, 2007).

21. Maggie O'Neill and R. Harindranath, "Theorising Narratives of Exile and Belonging: The Importance of Biography and Ethno-Mimesis in "Understanding" Asylum," *Qualitative Sociology Review* II, no. 1 (2006): 44.

22. See also N. Scheper-Hughes, "The Primacy of the Ethical: Propositions for a Militant Anthropology," *Current Anthropology* 36, no. 3 (1995).

23. McCarry, "Conducting Social Research with Young People: Ethical Considerations." A. McRobbie, "The Politics of Feminist Research: Between Talk, Text and Action," *Feminist Review* 12 (1982). L. Gelsthorpe and Gilly Sharpe, "Criminological Research: Typologies Versus Hierarchies," *Criminal Justice Matters* 62, no. Winter 2005/06 (2005).

24. Pierre Bourdieu, "Understanding," *Theory, Culture & Society* 13, no. 2 (1996): 22.

25. Hawkins, "Order, Rationality and Silence."

26. Harry Stack Sullivan, *The Psychiatric Interview: A Guide for Therapists and Other Interviewers, by the Founder of the Interpersonal Theory of Psychiatry* (New York: W. W. Norton & Company, 1970/1954).

27. Ibid, 122.

28. In addition to assisting a participant with his math homework, I traveled with a participant to her interview for a place in an alternative-to-incarceration program, introduced a participant to a friend who was an architect and took us on a tour of her firm, I worked with a participant to find a basketball league to play with, and I took others to visit animal shelters.

29. Becker, "Whose Side Are We On?," 242.

30. See also Anna Souhami, *Transforming Youth Justice: Occupational Identity and Cultural Change* (Cullumpton, England: Willan, 2007).

31. Simon Clarke, "Thinking Psychosocially about Difference: Ethnicity, Community and Emotion," in Shelley Day Sclater et al. (eds.), *Emotion: New Psychosocial Perspectives* (London: Palgrave Macmillan, 2009), 112.

32. I. Craib, "The Unhealthy Underside of Narratives," in C. Horrocks et al. (eds.), *Narrative, Memory and Health* (Huddersfield, England: University of Huddersfield Press, 2003).

33. Ibid, 7.

Index

ABOUT THE AUTHOR

ALEXANDRA COX is a lecturer in sociology at the University of Essex in England and was previously an assistant professor of sociology at SUNY New Paltz. She was a Gates Scholar at the University of Cambridge, a Soros Justice Advocacy Fellow, and a Research Scholar in Law at Yale University Law School's Justice Collaboratory. She has also worked as a sentencing mitigation specialist in New York State and at the Neighborhood Defender Service of Harlem and Drug Policy Alliance. She has served on the boards of the New York State Defenders Association and Drama Club (which provides theater programming for teenagers in prison).

Susan L. Miller, *Victims as Offenders: The Paradox of Women's Violence in Relationships*

Torin Monahan, *Surveillance in the Time of Insecurity*

Torin Monahan and Rodolfo D. Torres, eds., *Schools under Surveillance: Cultures of Control in Public Education*

Ana Muñiz, *Police, Power, and the Production of Racial Boundaries*

Leslie Paik, *Discretionary Justice: Looking Inside a Juvenile Drug Court*

Anthony M. Platt, *The Child Savers: The Invention of Delinquency*, 40th anniversary edition with an introduction and critical commentaries compiled by Miroslava Chávez-García

Lois Presser, *Why We Harm*

Joshua M. Price, *Prison and Social Death*

Diana Rickard, *Sex Offenders, Stigma, and Social Control*

Jeffrey Ian Ross, ed., *The Globalization of Supermax Prisons*

Dawn L. Rothe and Christopher W. Mullins, eds., *State Crime, Current Perspectives*

Jodi Schorb, *Reading Prisoners: Literature, Literacy, and the Transformation of American Punishment, 1700-1845*

Susan F. Sharp, *Hidden Victims: The Effects of the Death Penalty on Families of the Accused*

Susan F. Sharp, *Mean Lives, Mean Laws: Oklahoma's Women Prisoners*

Robert H. Tillman and Michael L. Indergaard, *Pump and Dump: The Rancid Rules of the New Economy*

Mariana Valverde, *Law and Order: Images, Meanings, Myths*

Michael Welch, *Crimes of Power and States of Impunity: The U.S. Response to Terror*

Michael Welch, *Scapegoats of September 11th: Hate Crimes and State Crimes in the War on Terror*

Saundra D. Westervelt and Kimberly J. Cook, *Life after Death Row: Exonerees' Search for Community and Identity*